ANCIENT CHRISTIANITY

The Development of Its Institutions and Practices

ANGELO DI BERARDINO

iccspress.com

Copyright © 2021 by ICCS Press

First published in 2021 by ICCS Press, Inc., 616 Prospect Street, New Haven, CT 06511. www.iccspress.com

First issued as an ICCS Press paperback, 2023.

All rights reserved. No part of this book may be reproduced in any form or by any electronic or mechanical means, including information storage and retrieval systems, without written permission from ICCS Press, except for the use of brief quotations in a book review.

Cover Design: Gina Peterson, Speers Design Associates, LLC.

Cover Image: Alamy.com

Library of Congress Cataloging-in-Publication Data

Di Berardino, Angelo
Ancient Christianity: the development of its institutions and practices / Angelo Di Berardino.
Includes bibliographical references and index.
ISBN: 978-1-62428-015-3 (Cloth); 978-1-62428-018-4 (HC); 978-1-62428-029-0 (PB).
1. Church history—Primitive and early church, ca. 30-600.

Library of Congress Control Number: 2021938229

Printed in the United States of America on acid-free paper.

To Thomas Oden,
Great Mind and Great Heart

CONTENTS

Foreword	ix
Introduction	xi
1. PROBLEMS, METHODOLOGY AND SOURCES	1
Problems and Methodology	1
Sources	8
Dissemination and Application of the Texts	16
Summary	21
2. SPACE AND TIME IN ANCIENT CHRISTIANITY	25
The Roman Empire up to the 6th Century	26
The Christian Space	31
Number of Christians	58
Conclusion	66
3. CHRISTIAN INITIATION AND ITS RITES	72
Initiations and Initiation	72
Christian Initiation and the Term Christian	76
The Preliminary Phase (Catechumenate)	81
Christian Education	95
The Crucial Phase: The Baptismal Rites	100
Validity of Baptism	110
Baptism-Confirmation-Eucharist	112
4. ECCLESIAL MINISTRIES	125
People of God: *ordo* and *plebs*	128
Progression (cursus) Through the Ministerial Ranks	131
The Ministry and the Priesthood	133
Selection and Requirements of the Clergy	141
Legal Conditions for Joining the Clergy	155
Rites and Symbols for the Transmission of Authority	157
Conclusion	163

5. MINISTERIAL HIERARCHY OF THE EARLY CHURCH   170
   Major Orders   170
   Minor Orders and Other Functionaries   186
   Other Minor Ministries   192

6. AUTHORITY, ORGANIZATION AND ECCLESIAL COMMUNION   214
   Authority in the Church   214
   Authority as Service   221
   The Ecclesial Community and Signs of its Koinonia   224
   Patterns of *Koinonia* in the Early Christian Centuries   232
   Institutional Forms of Authority   238
   The Church's Territorial Structures   249
   Conclusion   261

7. MONASTICISMS AND CHRISTIAN MONASTICISM   269
   The Origins of Monasticism   273
   Eastern Monasticism   280
   Western Monasticism   290
   Monastic Rules   294
   Monasticism and Institutions   298

8. VIRGINITY, WIDOWHOOD AND ABSTINENCE (CELIBACY)   306
   Virginity   306
   Widows and Deaconesses   316
   Ecclesiastical Celibacy   320

9. THE SINNER, PENANCE, EXCOMMUNICATION AND ANOINTING OF THE SICK   335
   Ecclesial Penance in the First Three Centuries   335
   The Evolution of Penance in the Fourth to Sixth Centuries   342
   Anointing of the Sick   361

10. MARRIAGE AND FAMILY   369
    The Christian Vision of Marriage in the Ancient Context   369
    The Christian Experience of Marriage   378
    Christian Marriage and Civil Legislation   380
    Celebration of Marriage   393

11. THE LITURGY: ORIGIN AND DEVELOPMENT   410
    The Christian Liturgy   411
    Liturgical Books   432
    Christian Assemblies   433
    Liturgical Furnishings   453

Communal Prayer and Gestures	455
Eucharistic Prayers and Anaphoras	460
Conclusion	462

12. THE ORIGINS OF THE CALENDAR AND CHRISTIAN FEASTS — 472
- Some General Elements — 473
- The Basis of the Calendar — 475
- Ancient Calendars — 477
- Sunday and Easter — 485
- Other Christian Feasts — 492
- Christian Feasts and Late Antique Society — 500
- Pilgrimages — 506
- Conclusion — 509

13. DEATH AND BURIAL OF CHRISTIANS AND THE CULT OF MARTYRS AND SAINTS — 517
- Burying the Dead — 520
- Christian Cemeteries — 532
- The Cult of the Martyrs, Saints, and Relics — 536

14. ECONOMIC AND SOCIAL CONSIDERATIONS — 547
- A Christian Perspective — 552
- Scriptural Understanding of Rich and Poor — 554
- Labor — 561
- Private Property — 564
- Usury — 568
- Slavery and Christianity — 570
- Church Finances — 575
- Concluding Thoughts — 594

15. CHARITABLE AND SOCIAL WORK — 613
- Almsgiving — 615
- Organized Charity and Forms of Assistance — 621
- Some Organized Forms of Assistance — 631
- Welfare Institutions — 637
- Clergy Support — 640

Index — 653
Bibliography — 661

FOREWORD

Fr. Angelo has served almost four decades at the Institutum Patristicum Augustinianum in Rome where he lectured countless students from around the world who are now leaders in the church at large. As a teacher and as President of the Institute Fr. Angelo has dedicated his life to reading, writing and researching the fathers of the early church. That dedication has resulted in expanding the "temporal bandwidth" of his students and his many readers as well. And now he is willing to share the wisdom he has gained over a lifetime with all of us.

The present volume is a summation of his lectures over the past thirty five years exploring the depth of the Christian *experience*—more so than its *theology*, although there is plenty of theology to go around as well. The chapters in this volume are taken from the classroom and adapted to book form. You will hear the lecturer's voice on any number of occasions. We have chosen to let Fr. Angelo's voice as teacher be heard in this English translation of the Italian. As such, the reader gets the rare opportunity to sit at the feet of one of patristic studies' giants in the field and learn what life was like for Christians after the time of Christ and the Apostles, as well as for Fr. Angelo's students. This makes the book unique in the field of patristics and in the broader literature regarding the early church. It delves into the life of the average Christian and tells us what we can truly know—and also what we can't but perhaps thought we knew.

As a master of the historical method, Fr Di Berardino takes a magnifying glass to the sometimes scant sources the historian has at his or her disposal. He recognizes that many of the statements that start out with "the early church did _____" or "the early church taught _____" often assume facts not in evidence. In his meticulous study, Fr. Angelo recognizes that there were regional differences in practice, exacerbated by the different eras in which some practices developed that must be taken into account when pronouncing about what the early church did or taught—or what it didn't do or teach. The pages in this volume are the readers guide into some of these intricacies, letting us know what we can say with certainty as well as where we should be more circumspect.

Here we also have a window into an era in many ways different than our own, even as the reader will also notice some things that are universal to the human condition. What was it like to get married back then? How did they handle funerals? How were pastors paid? What was it like to be a monk and how did they live together? How did the church handle its finances? How did Christians care for the poor? Questions such as these and many more are answered in the pages which follow. We invite the reader to join Fr. Angelo on this journey back through time to reacquaint us with our forbearers in the faith.

Fr. Di Berardino has dedicated this book to our mutual friend and colleague Thomas C. Oden. Tom was the main reason why we and our colleagues in the Institute for Classical Christian Studies (ICCS) became involved in the study of the early church. The ICCS has provided a generous grant in order to bring this volume to print in English. Our partnership with Tom, with Howard and Roberta Ahmanson, and the wonderful colleagues at Fieldstead Inc., have made this a labor of love to celebrate the life of Thomas Oden and the career and work of our friend and colleague Fr. Angelo Di Berardino.

Joel C. Elowsky
President, ICCS
Dean of Advanced Studies and Professor of Historical Theology
Concordia Seminary, St. Louis, MO

Michael Glerup
Executive Director, Center for Early African Christianity
Publisher, ICCS Press
New Haven, CT

INTRODUCTION

The title of this volume could be: "The Life of Christians in the First Centuries."[1] Such a title, or something like it, was common a century ago. Many works had such titles as: *Daily Life of the Greeks*; *Life of the Romans*; *Daily Life in Antiquity*, etc. Another possible title could be: *Christian Antiquities*. This would recall a glorious precedent that was very successful, known as *The Antiquities of the Christian Church* (1708–1722), published in nine small volumes by the Anglican curate Joseph Bingham. The work was translated into Latin (*Origines Ecclesiasticae*, 1724–1729) and has been reprinted several times in English and Latin. Its purpose, in imitation of the treatments of Greek, Roman, and Jewish antiquities, was to offer an overview of the antiquities—or institutions—of the ancient Church. This work still remains fundamental. Unfortunately, it is not easy to find the citations of ancient works, since they were made according to editions of that time. The *Encyclopedia of Ancient Christianity*, edited by me and translated into various languages, works along the same lines but with a broader vision.

Moreover, today the term "antiquities" still refers to the study of some particular disciplines regarding ancient history, especially studies of public and sacred institutions. The ancients already carried out some antiquarian studies. Those who come to mind especially are Varro with his monumental work *Antiquitates Rerum Humanarum et Divinarum* (*Antiquities of Human and Divine Things*), and Josephus Flavius with his *Antiquitates Iudaicae* (Ἰουδαϊκὴ ἀρχαιολογία; *Antiquities of the Jews*), which tells the history of the Jewish people.

In 1958 Jean Gaudemet used a title of a more general character (*L'Église dans l'empire romain (IVᵉ-Vᵉ siècles)*. This is a magisterial work that was part of a vast project only partially completed for antiquity by Charles Munier (1979). I was formed with these volumes and numerous writings of Gaudemet and by the friendly relationships I had with him.

We have chosen the title *Ancient Christianity: The Development of Its Institutions and Practices*. I do not enter into the discussion about using the term "Church" or "Christianity." The first term seems more ecclesiastical, the second is more general and open to historical research. For me, in this context, the terms are largely interchangeable. The use of the title *Institutiones* (*Institutions*) also has a glorious history. Some famous ancient works are the *Institutiones* of Gaius which come from the second half of the second century. It is a manual of Roman law. Even more well-known are the *Institutiones* of Justinian, a work intended for students of Roman law. Up to a few decades ago use of the term "institutions" was common, especially in texts written in Latin which referred to institutions of philosophy, institutions of history, etc.

But it is more useful to know the content of this work. The purpose is historically to retrace the first five centuries in order to see how the ecclesiastical institutions arose, developed, and were consolidated into their full maturity. It is a task fraught with difficulty because of the scarcity and fragmentary nature of the information preserved, which comes from different geographical regions and from people who have different traditions behind them. So, the problem arises of how to place the data in their chronological and geographical context, and especially how to use them to offer a more or less unified, not impressionistic, framework. Often authors cite a few texts and generalize them, offering a homogeneous but false vision. Christianity, from its beginnings and through its whole history, has always been multi-faceted.

We know about the well-developed fundamental ecclesiastical institutions. None of them, as they are structured today, however, goes back to the beginnings of Christianity. We use the same terms, which in the course of time became more precise and technical. The danger is that we might interpret an ancient text with the modern meaning of the words. The texts are either of a normative character, or of a hortatory or moral character. The normative texts prescribe what needs to be done, but not what concrete people really do; the hortatory texts reprove and criticize the conduct of Christians, laity and clerics, highlighting some of the negative aspects of Christian life not lived in conformity with the Christian faith. Such information must not be generalized in space and time, otherwise one falsifies the historical reality, which is very complex and lively.

I would like to provide two obvious clear examples of how generalizations end up happening: penance and the selection of bishops. For penance, one starts with the New Testament, then makes wide use of Hermas and Tertullian to arrive at Cyprian. The development seems linear and homogeneous. But initially the proposals were much more varied and local practices differed from each other; only in the fourth century does one come to a certain homogeneity. The modalities for selecting and ordaining bishops are also not linear. The local realities are complex in the sense that many elements play a specific role: local or regional traditions are a factor—e.g. the prior bishop suggests or selects the name of his successor, like Augustine did with Heraclius. One must also consider doctrinal conflicts, local or general canonical norms, imperial politics, the role of the people receiving their bishop who intervene with acclamations. There is also the candidate's notoriety, his charisma, his wealth as well as factors such as corruption, notable local figures, the interests of dominant local groups, the will of the metropolitan who becomes ever more forceful and dominant, etc.

The phrase "ancient Church" – "ancient Christianity" – refers to a time-span that varies according to geographical context, insofar as it is placed between two other expressions: (1) the "Original Church," (and one usually also speaks of the "Original Christianity" or the "church at the beginning") and (2) the "medieval Church," or "medieval Christianity." The expression "medieval Church" does not work well for Eastern Christian communities, however.

In our case we must start with the New Testament and proceed to the end of the sixth century. For the West, we end with Gregory the Great († 604). For other regions one must account for varying situations of development and organization of the Christian communities. At any rate, one normally focuses on the period up to the ecumenical Council of Chalcedon in 451, with some explorations into the later period. By that point all the institutions had been established. The later changes are few with only developments and clarifications to be noted.

The catechumenate fades away with the proliferation of infant baptism. Penance undergoes a radical transformation. The geographical organization of the ecclesiastical provinces, first the metropolitans and then the patriarchs, is fully established. On the other hand, the parish system is still developing.

THE APPROACH OF THE VOLUME

The present volume is divided into fifteen chapters of varying lengths. The first two chapters are more introductory in character. The second offers a historical and geographical survey of the spread of Christianity in the first centuries. The first chapter is very important. It offers some methodological reflections, the fruit of my long experience of study, of teaching, and of editing numerous works. At various points, I repeat that one must reject the method of generalizing and idealizing. I insist on local and regional diversity. Sometimes the sources do not describe the practice that was followed, but the one that should be followed. In particular, the canons of local, provincial, or general councils intend to correct deviations and impose a different practice that conforms better to the theology that is being elaborated.

In ancient Christianity, there exists no central authority that summarizes the various traditions and opinions and makes decisions for all the churches—let alone the greater part of them. From this arises the importance of communication between churches, especially between the more important ones, and the spread of synodal meetings with different levels of geographic participation. There is no code of canon law, nor a liturgical manual. There are no uniform or widespread prescriptions about the sacraments, for instance. The texts of the canonical-liturgical literature are composed by individuals or circulate anonymously. Many texts are attributed to two authors: Clement and Hippolytus. As the practice develops, such texts come to be rewritten or readapted to different geographical contexts. When they are no longer useful, they disappear. Many of them have been rediscovered only in recent times.

These types of works as well as conciliar canons must be known in order to be applied in the life of the local church. Yet their dissemination was rather limited. When Augustine was ordained bishop (395/396) he did not know the canons of the council of Nicaea (325). The lively argument between the Roman see and the bishops of the African provinces in the case of Apiarius is emblematic of the lack of circulation of written texts. The oral tradition of the individual churches or geographic areas is fundamental, but often that tradition was not put down in writing and we do not know it. The oral tradition, the *consuetudo*, developmental by its very nature, becomes normative. For many of these traditions, we have no evidence because they have not been handed on in written form. Augustine wrote a letter to the Catholic layman Januarius in answer to his questions about differing Christian practices in different churches. He distinguishes sacraments found in the New Testament and in the universal tradition and practice from other local observances. Augustine observes:

> First of all, then, I want you to hold onto what is the principal point of this discussion, that our Lord Jesus Christ, as he himself says in the Gospel, has made us subject to his yoke and burden, which are light. For this reason, he placed on the society of his new people the obligation of sacraments, very few in number, very easy in their observance, and most excellent in what they signify. They are, for example, baptism. . ... But we are given to understand that those practices we observe which are not in Scripture, but from tradition, and which are observed throughout the whole world, are maintained as taught and established either by the apostles themselves or by plenary councils, which have an authority in the church most conducive to salvation.[2]

He adduces many examples of divergences among churches.

Tertullian offers hints about the practice of the rite of baptism, about the norms for receiving the Eucharist, about fasts, about rites of prayer, about the frequent use of the sign of the cross, etc. A complex of elements is being elaborated for those who want to become Christian, according to the expression of the African writer: *fiunt, non nascuntur christiani* (Christians are made, not born).[3] In such a process of conversion, the leaders as well as the whole local community are involved in forming a new identity by belonging to a new people. This topic is treated in the third chapter: *disciplina qua fiunt Christiani* (that rule by which men become Christians).[4] The fourth, fifth and sixth chapters present the birth and development of ministers in the church including their selection, their formation, their conduct of life and their role. Other ministerial offices are created too so that with the increase of its members and its geographical spread, the community of believers may be served and fulfill the churches' reason for existing.

The differentiation of the manner of living out one's Christian dedication also generates a gradation of personal involvement and of new lifestyles concerning late antique society. Various ascetic forms arise such as different forms of monasticism, remaining in the virgin state or widowhood, celibacy, etc. These are the topics of the seventh and eighth chapters. Such forms of life are a characteristic of late antique society and will remain so for the following centuries as well.

Divine pardon belongs to the central nucleus of the Gospel. Announcing this message is the mission of the disciples and then of the church: ". . . that repentance and forgiveness of sins is to be proclaimed in his (Christ's) name to all nations, beginning from Jerusalem."[5] In the second century, the debate arose as to whether one can grant pardon to a baptized (and thus already pardoned) person when they have sinned? There were disagreements, and so a penitential doctrine for the readmission of sinners developed, which is what we deal with in chapter nine. "I heard, Lord, from some teachers that there is no other penance but that of when we descended into the waters (of baptism) and received the remission of our past sins."[6]

The tenth chapter presents the Christian teaching on marriage and the family. This arises from a reflection on Scripture, but with notable and determinative influences from Roman law, from philosophical theories of the time, especially Platonic and Stoic, and from the ancient way and mode of doing things. In contrast with ancient conceptions of marriage and family, Christianity condemns divorce, abortion, and infanticide. It affirms the equality of man and woman, but does not draw all the practical consequences from this.

The liturgy permeates many aspects of the Christian life, its institutions and its organization. We are speaking here of the whole sacramental life of the Christian communities. The liturgy is a rite and manifests itself as a rite, but one that is founded on theology. Thus, it underlies every sacrament and sacramental act. The way of praying and reciting communal and personal prayers constitutes the heart of the liturgy. The richness of the liturgy grows in time and space. We include space because of the birth of numerous so-called liturgical families already in antiquity covered in chapter eleven. Connected to the liturgy is the elaboration of the Christian calendar with the consequent development of the Christian feasts that take the place of the political and social organization of public pagan time. The twelfth chapter explores this further.

The last three chapters deal with the death and burial of Christians, the cemeteries where they were buried, and with the beneficent and administrative concerns that arose around ecclesiastical goods and property. Care for the poor, almsgiving, assistance to the needy are all at the center of the preaching and activity of the churches. At the same time the goods and properties of some churches grow, sometimes in a disproportionate way. Church construction changes the urban panorama of the cities as well as small villages and the countryside. The articulation and organization of public time, monasticism in its various forms, Christian values that spread, construction of religious buildings, and the clerics of different ranks and hierarchical and social conditions bring about a radical transformation of all the regions that surround the Mediterranean. If a citizen of the Empire of the third century were to traverse those regions in the middle of the fifth century, he would feel like a stranger away from home —as happened to the seven sleepers of Ephesus. He would no longer find the habitual forms of life of the middle of the third century. Different problems were being debated. People dressed differently. He would find himself living in a society that was very different in its values too.

SUMMARY

To be able to survive, every social or religious movement must create structures and norms of life and organization that enable its survival so that it may accomplish what it has set out to do. The numerical development and geographic expansion of Christianity forced Christian communities to be very creative. The church, separated from its Jewish matrix and its original environment and influenced by new conditions of life according to the regions into which it was expanding, slowly and progressively developed many institutions. These were affected by and sometimes inspired by the social environment in which they arose, and hence their diversity in different regions. The present volume intends to offer a panorama of their birth and development in both their variety and complexity.

---

1. I would like to give special thanks to: Michael Glerup, Joel Elowsky, Jeanette Mary Magdalene, Gilda Rorro Baldassarri, Liam Kidney, Jeffrey Lee, Vittorino Grossi, and to all who worked on the English translation (Stephen Gregg, Brian O'Sullivan, Kolawole Chabi, Robert Guessetto, Daniel Doyle, Martin Murphy, Jenny Paschall; Jonathan Arrington).
2. Augustine, *Ep* 54.1.1.
3. Tertullian, *Apologeticum* 18.4.
4. Tertullian, *De praescriptione* 19.
5. *Lk* 24:47; cf. 15:22; *Mk* 16:16; *Jn* 20:21–23
6. Hermas, *Shepherd*, Mandate 4.3.1.

CHAPTER 1
PROBLEMS, METHODOLOGY AND SOURCES

PROBLEMS AND METHODOLOGY

MANY ASPECTS OF ANCIENT CHRISTIANITY ARE ONLY ATTESTED BY FRAGMENTARY information. We have no witnesses that fill the gaps. The reconstruction of the life and institutions of ancient Christianity must be done with the proper use of available sources. These sources are fragmentary, reminding me of the beginning of the book of Job where a messenger announces a misfortune to Job: "I alone have escaped to tell you." He hears the same thing from another messenger: "I alone have escaped to tell you." And then he hears the same message a third and a fourth time with nothing further added.[1] In the same way, every fragment we find attesting to some aspect of early Christian life can be considered unique and precious, but we have no other witnesses to tell other stories and events.

Here is a typical example: After Demetrius protested the invitation Origen, still a layman, had received from Theoctistus and Alexander of Jerusalem to preach at Caesarea, the two justified their invitation in a letter to Demetrius:

> He (Demetrius) has stated in his letter that no one has ever heard of or seen a laymen preaching in the presence of bishops. I don't know how he can say what is plainly untrue. For whenever persons able to instruct the brethren are found, they are exhorted by the holy bishops to preach to the people. And so, in Laranda, Euelpis was exhorted to preach by Neon; and in Iconium, the same thing happened to Paulinus who was asked by Celsus to preach, as was the case in Synnada

when Theodorus was asked to preach by Atticus—all blessed brothers of ours. And this probably also happened in other places we don't even know about.[2]

The phrase "Ancient Christianity" refers to a period that varies according to context and the various geographical areas where Christians were present. The study of the fathers normally covers a period that extends to the eighth century, with the study of institutions extending to the end of the sixth century. In the Western church the period ends with Gregory the Great († 604). For other regions, various situations must be considered, but it usually extends to the ecumenical council of Chalcedon of 451, and occasionally later.

The first point to consider when reading the texts is whether they are normative in nature, or exhortations that have something to do with moral character. Those that are normative should be read as though one was looking into a mirror and seeing what needs to be done in one's life; but the text tells nothing about what real people were really doing at the time. Texts dealing with exhortation of moral character have the same function. Sometimes they reproach and criticize the conduct of Christians—both lay people and clerics. And so we must distinguish between ethics that were preached and the ethics people actually followed in their daily lives. The reality is that most of the behavior exhibited in ancient Christianity did not conform to what was being preached. Daily life could be so terrible that it sometimes surpasses our fantasy of reconstruction. Many texts were written and preserved because they were intended to edify the readers, not to chronicle what really happened. Eusebius of Caesarea begins his *Ecclesiastical History*—which is our main source of information for the first three centuries—by declaring that the purpose of his account was to preserve the memory of the activities of the great Christian figures. He often recorded negative elements in the life of the church in order to provide an opportunity later on to highlight when these negative elements were overcome.

The use of sources involves a delicate process, especially since those we have for the first three centuries are scarce and often insufficient in the detail they offer. We need to use whatever fragmentary evidence we have available. But since this evidence comes from different geographical backgrounds and from people with a different tradition or who have different ideas, how we can use these sources?

Every author who reconstructs the discipline of ancient Christianity uses the texts of the fathers or the canons of the Councils of the fourth and fifth centuries. They attempt to reconstruct institutions based on written laws. And yet, this is a fundamental error, because laws were made to correct and impose certain behaviors. But this begs the question: when they were promulgated were they actually observed? Actual practice is often very different from what is legislated, and there is a tendency to present an ideal image that never existed, where everything works and every piece is in place. It was not so, due to the lack of uniform and widespread laws. Laws were local and were not known or applied elsewhere.

Today we are aware that those sources must be used with great caution and with extreme prudence for two reasons, linked to the geographical distribution of those texts and their reception by the Christian communities of the different geographical areas. Just because we find concrete prescriptions of a council does not mean that they were known or that they were applied elsewhere. For example, who knew the texts of the Council of Elvira in the West, and when did they come to know them? In the East they were totally ignored or were never known. The African Councils, so useful in reconstructing many aspects of Christian life, were only partially translated into Greek in the sixth century.[3] In the West, they began circulating around this same time. The numerous canons of the local Greek councils of the fourth century were completely ignored in the West; only later were they translated.

Sometimes particular information has been generalized to give an almost homogeneous picture. Today we realize that this method distorts the reality of different churches since there were many local variations. An example is the following: In the reconstruction of the history of penance, one starts from the New Testament and then makes extensive use of Hermas, and then Tertullian up to Cyprian; the same procedure is also used for the East. Everything is clear and the development seems linear. Contrary to this scenario, the proposals and local practices between the various communities were actually quite different. Only slowly does homogeneity develop. Both rigorist and laxist groups perdure throughout Late Antiquity.

The way in which bishops were chosen and ordained is another example of a non-linear development. Local realities were complex in the sense that many elements played specific roles. There were local or regional traditions—for example, the elder suggests or chooses[4] his successor. Other factors in choosing and ordaining bishops include doctrinal conflicts, local or general canonical norms, imperial politics as well as local social situations. We dare not neglect the role of the people who either approve or disapprove the candidacy. In addition there is the individual candidate's promotion of himself, his charisma, and his wealth. Corruption, knowing who's who in the local church community, the interests of the local dominant groups, the will of the metropolitan, who becomes increasingly influential—all of these can end up being factors in choosing and ordaining bishops.[5]

Because of the significant diversity in the first three centuries, many speak of "Christianities." But then we must ask: If only some people or groups have different opinions, is it really another Christianity? How great must the differences be to constitute another Christianity? Do Jesus' disciples preach different Christianities? Is Paul's position, which rejects so many Jewish prescriptions, a different Christianity from that of Peter, James, and John? Can the same be said for the institutions?

It would seem that we must also reject the method of generalizations and idealizing that occurs when talking about institutions. Should we consider what some sources say was the practice that was followed? Or do these sources simply express a desire that these practices be followed? Are the prescriptions of some texts widely used by scholars—something that also takes place in the present volume—such as the *Apostolic Tradition* and the *Didascalia*, descriptive of practices followed or do these texts want to impose these practices? It would seem that sources of this kind should be read as though they are a mirror that partially reflects a tradition received. In addition the authors want to correct existing aberrations from that tradition and impose acceptable behavior. These texts then end up being disseminated or reworked in later texts for different contexts and different experiences which indicates that the difficulties the first authors experience were still around.

In ancient Christianity, there was no central authority that summarized the different traditions and opinions or made decisions for all the churches, or for even most of them. There was no code of canon law, no comprehensive liturgical manual, no widespread prescriptions for the sacraments and penance that all had to observe. Nor did there exist a homogeneous set of canons or rules written in the first five centuries. In other words, there was no one organized system of laws for the government of the church. In some specific activities the churches were inspired by Roman or local laws. Examples include how they organized councils, conducted criminal trials, discerned hierarchical relations; sometimes they utilized local or Roman terminology.

When the Christian religion was recognized as a *corpus christianorum* (a body of Christians), the emperors who regulated pagan religious life also intervened in church affairs and religious strife. Religion had always been a governmental matter. From the fifth century onward, in the West, the church became increasingly detached from the civil authorities. In the Byzantine East the opposite happened as the emperor became increasingly involved in the legislation of the church. Byzantine canonists constructed collections of ecclesiastical and civil laws (*nomocanon*). Churches in other countries created their own traditions as well.

In the late patristic period, diverse documents were collected or earlier texts were reworked. In each collection, as in the case of the Theodosian Code, the discordance of the texts requires not only an interpretation but also an examination of the applicability of the rules reported. Here are two examples: first, in the Byzantine collection, even the current one, the canons of the Council of Serdica are included. One of the canons states that a deposed bishop may appeal to the bishop of Rome. Naturally, this canon has no effect in the Eastern world in the light of the deliberation of the Ecumenical Council of Chalcedon in 451 which states: "Litigious clerics shall be punished according to canonical penalties if they despise their bishop and resort to the secular tribunal. . . . When a cleric has a disagreement with a bishop let him wait till the synod sits, and if a bishop has a disagreement with his metropolitan let him take the case to Constantinople."[6] This canon shows the importance the imperial episcopal see acquired between the end of the fourth century and the first half of the fifth. The Serdica canon of 343 is totally ignored.

The Coptic church, which does not have a code of canon law but only collections of ancient texts, raises the question of the applicability of these texts for today. It seems that the situation described by Meinardus regarding the Coptic church today also applies to antiquity, with some revisions.[7] He writes that in theory all the canons—even the canonical letters of the fathers—are applicable, except those that impose penalties; but since there are discrepancies between them, even theologians disagree. Moreover, the application also depends on the existence of an Arabic translation; and finally, the "twelve [20] canons of Nicaea are accepted, even if they are not well known."[8] The canons of Constantinople and Ephesus are accepted, but little known. The canons of some synods are accepted—particularly Ancyra, Neocaesarea, Laodicea—while those of other synods are not applied at all—such as Gangra, Serdica, or Carthage. The same goes for the canonical texts of some fathers. The situation is therefore very uncertain and confusing in today's Coptic Church. One might think that the situation in the fourth and fifth centuries would be similar, perhaps even worse.

And yet, the difficulty is more problematic for us than for them, because they were based on an oral tradition and followed the customs of individual churches or geographical areas. To better understand this fluid situation, here are a couple of examples. The first is taken from the Council of Nicaea and the other from Augustine of Hippo. The Council of Nicaea of 325 (can. 9) says that "ecclesiastical law does not recognize" priests who have received ordination "against the provisions of the canons" (*hoc ecclesiasticus ordo non recipit*). But to what canons, what law are they referring? There is no written prescription, unless there are some anonymous texts they are referring to that we don't know anything about. In reality, tradition and practice have the force of canons. In addition, we know that regional episcopal assemblies met according to emerging needs, where decisions were made or traditions of the various churches were exchanged. This exchange was necessary in order to consolidate the norms indispensable to the life of the communities.

The second example is taken from the life of Augustine. In 426 he appointed his successor but did not want to violate the canons of the Council of Nicaea:

> I do not wish that to be done in regard to him which was done in my own case. What was done many of you know—in fact, all of you know, except those who were not born yet at that time or had not attained to the years of understanding. When my father and bishop, the aged Valerius, of blessed memory, was still living, I was ordained bishop and occupied the episcopal see along with him, which I did not know to have been forbidden by the Council of Nicaea. And he was

equally ignorant of the prohibition. I do not wish to have my son here exposed to the same censure as was incurred in my own case.[9]

Canon eight of the Nicene Council states, among other things: "The presence of two bishops in the same city is to be avoided." Augustine had at least three bishops who ordained him—so he observed the fourth canon of Nicaea, although the African church usually required even more ordaining bishops. This proves that he himself was very attentive to ecclesiastical norms. And yet he tells us he was unaware of the prohibition of canon 8 of Nicaea. Nonetheless, the norm was important and had to be known both because it was the most important council of the fourth century and because there were so many great episcopal sees in which two bishops—today we would call them auxiliaries—would have assisted in pastoral and disciplinary activity.

Since there was no written normative tradition, it was only when the bishops met in councils that solutions were offered to the various cases concerning ecclesiastical life. What other reason than this could be at the heart of the decision of the Council of Nicaea to hold episcopal assemblies twice a year within an ecclesiastical province: one before Easter and the other in the fall (Can. 5)? The recourse to previous norms or canons is appealed to several times in other canons of Nicaea: canon 10 (ordinations); canon 13 (the viaticum for the dying); canon 15 (wandering clergy); canon 16 (priests who desert their church for another). Canon 18 states: "Neither canons nor custom allow those who may not themselves consecrate the Eucharist to distribute the body of Christ to those who can consecrate it." The term "canon" therefore included unwritten rules handed down orally but which were also meant to be observed.

Therefore, established custom (*consuetudo*) was important, especially in the first centuries, when there was no written law and the symbols of faith were quite vague. Instead, there were doctrinal, liturgical, and local disciplinary traditions. Indeed, each church had its own traditions. We have no testimony for many of them because they have not been handed down in writing. What Tertullian writes is enlightening. After having spoken of a practice concerning the rite of baptism, along with the norms for the reception of the Eucharist, fasting, rites of prayer and the frequent use of the sign of the cross—he adds: *Harum et aliarum eiusmodi disciplinarum si legem expostules scripturarum, nullam invenies* (of these and of other norms of the same kind, if you look for the norms of the Scriptures you won't find anything).[10] Therefore, established custom comes into play, which by its very nature is evolutionary, along with *disciplina* (church practice). This topic is the subject of two of his works, namely *De virginibus velandis* (*On the Veiling of Virgins*) and *De corona* (*On the Crown*).[11]

In other words, a whole set of norms and practices that were formed as early as the beginning of the third century have no biblical foundation but nonetheless have been elaborated by individual Christian communities and sometimes have passed from one community to another through contamination. Augustine also observes:

> ... as to those other things which we hold on the authority, not of Scripture, but of tradition, and which are observed throughout the whole world, it may be understood that they are held as approved and instituted either by the apostles themselves, or by plenary Councils,[12] whose authority in the Church is most useful, e.g. the annual commemoration by special solemnities of the Lord's passion, resurrection, and ascension, and of the descent of the Holy Spirit from heaven, and whatever else is similarly observed by the whole Church wherever it has been established.[13]

He adds: "There are other things, however, which are different in different places and countries: e.g., some fast on Saturday, others do not; some partake daily of the body and blood of Christ, others receive it on stated days: in some places no day passes without the sacrifice being offered; in others it is only on Saturday and the Lord's day, or it may be only on the Lord's day."[14] Augustine shows himself well informed about the great variety of situations, which he personally respects.

How should a Christian behave when traveling? He gave the following rule of conduct, inspired by Ambrose of Milan: "In regard to these and all other variable observances which may be met anywhere, one is at liberty to comply with them or not as he chooses; and there is no better rule for the wise and serious Christian in this matter, than to conform to the practice which he finds prevailing in the Church to which it may be his lot to come."[15]

> For it pains me to say that I often have perceived much anxiety caused to weak brothers by the contentious pertinacity or superstitious vacillation of some who raise undue questions in matters of this kind—for which there can be no final decision arrived at by the authority of Holy Scripture or the tradition of the universal Church, although one would hope good manners might prevail. They raise these questions from some perverse notion of their own, or from attachment to the custom followed in their own country, or even from a preference for something they've witnessed abroad, supposing that wisdom is increased in proportion to the distance to which one travels from home. And then they agitate these questions with such vigor that they think all is wrong except what they do themselves.[16]

How much wisdom in these observations of a wise shepherd! The entire letter is very useful in order to understand the way of applying rules in Late Antiquity.

SOURCES

Sources can be of any kind, including written texts as well as archaeological finds. The structure of a building of worship or a baptistery informs us how they celebrated the liturgy, how they administered baptism or how the hierarchy of the clergy was organized. Inscriptions provide much information. Preaching, particularly mystagogy, offers some insight on the sacraments. Augustine's quoted text, *Letter* 213, is of fundamental importance on how texts were disseminated and applied. It seems to me that more information is derived from the letters of the fathers, less from their speculative treaties. And finally, and above all, there are those works that are of the canonical-liturgical genre of which I will speak extensively later.

Jerome writes the following about the Christian and pagan ethics of marriage: "The laws of the Caesars are one thing, those of Christ are another; one thing is taught by Papinianus, another by Paul."[17] Augustine expresses the same idea in relation to prostitution, "which the earthly city considers lawful depravity,"[18] while the same earthly *civitas* punishes rape. What are these Christian laws (*leges*)? That there is a corpus of ecclesiastical laws seems almost self-evident since they concern disciplinary and social issues, as well as ethical concerns. The conviction is reinforced by the comparison between the very fine Roman jurist, Papinianus and the charismatic preacher Paul, the Apostle of the Gentiles. In fact, at the time of Jerome, there was no code of canon law. Indeed, we can affirm that there was no consistently established collection of ecclesiastical laws. The code of canon law in the modern sense as a body of homogeneous laws never existed in Christian antiquity, not even after Jerome. It was only born at the beginning of the 20th century and was elaborated only in the world of the Latin Church. In 1917 the first code of canon law was published (2414 canons) and then radically revised in 1983 (1752 canons). For the Eastern Catholic churches, after partial elaboration, a Code was published in 1990. The other Byzantine churches, on the other hand, did not yet have a code but only a corpus of non-homogeneous texts elaborated at different times and moments according to the list formulated by the second canon of the Council in Trullo in 692, with some later additions. Between the end of the fourth and the beginning of the fifth century some liturgical and canonical texts circulated, such as the *Apostolic Tradition*, the *Apostolic Constitutions*, and other texts, as well as collections such as the *Collectio Veronensis*. There are also collections of canons from various councils such as the *Syntagma antiochenum*,[19] which was later expanded, constituting a large collection. In Rome there is a collection that included the canons of Nicaea and Serdica. This collection was used in the dispute over Apiarius in 419 in Carthage by the Roman delegates.

The church developed its institutions slowly and progressively during the first centuries once it was detached from its Jewish matrix and its original environment, influenced as well by its expansion into different regions of the world. These institutions were affected and sometimes inspired by the social environment in which they were created, hence their diversity in the various regions.

This need is expressly highlighted in one of the oldest documents, the *Ecclesiastical Canons of the Apostles* (composed around 300).[20] The anonymous author put the various prescriptions in the mouths of the individual apostles, without resorting to a fictional genre, as happens with other apocryphal texts. He writes:

> Jesus tells the apostles, Before assigning the provinces to each of you, you must assign various ranks so that each one may take his place accordingly. Appoint the order of the bishops, the position of the presbyters, the position of priests, the function of assistant to the deacon, the prudent persons for readers, the appropriate conduct for widows and all that is necessary to found and consolidate the Church, so that everyone, knowing the image of heavenly things, may be careful to keep themselves pure from guilt, knowing that on the great day of judgment they must account for what they have not practiced after listening to it (Book 1).

The text reinforces the validity and the obligation of the various prescriptions, not only with the command of Jesus and their apostolic origin, but also with the final judgment of God on their behavior. All the members of the community, in their role, must remain faithful to these prescriptions that come from Jesus and the Apostles.

The text quoted above, which offers us an image of a large community with various articulations, demonstrates an advanced level of development of the ecclesiastical organization. The set of rules, which in the beginning is reduced to the essential, grew according to how needs developed, and was transmitted orally in the various communities. The first witnesses to an organizational structure come from the *Pastoral Letters*. The author of the *Letter to Titus* writes:

> I left you behind in Crete for this reason, so that you should put in order what remained to be done, and should appoint elders in every town, as I directed you: someone who is blameless, married only once, whose children are believers, not accused of debauchery and not rebellious. For a bishop, as God's steward, must be blameless; he must not be arrogant or quick-tempered or addicted to wine or violent or greedy for gain; but he must be hospitable, a lover of goodness, prudent, upright, devout, and self-controlled. He must have a firm grasp of the word that is trustworthy in accordance with the teaching, so that he may be able both to preach with sound doctrine and to refute those who contradict it." (*Tit* 1:5-9 NRSVCE).

This text is of enormous importance because it lays the foundations for the creation of responsible leaders and their qualities in individual communities. The First *Letter to Timothy* also provides numerous indications of an organizational nature and also rules of procedure in the case of accusations against priests. The Old Testament inspires these rules.

The norms deduced from the texts of the New Testament or from the oral tradition were not enough for more complex communities. Perhaps civil assemblies provided them with elements for how to function as a community. The local church—"the house of God, which is the Church of the living God" (*1 Tim* 3:15)—took as its model for its internal organization the Greek-Roman *domus* (household) in its complex articulation. The other element they utilized was the organization of the synagogue communities of the diaspora.

Thus, each community—or communities within a specific region—created its own unique disciplinary, organizational and liturgical heritage. In other words, it created its own tradition which it continually enriched under the practical pressures and influences of various prior practices which were transmitted orally. So, for example, based on references from Tertullian and above all from Cyprian we can know the traditions of the African church of the third century. But we cannot reconstruct how these traditions were originally constituted or how they expanded and changed during the fourth century. This process of readjustment already begins with the oldest of our documents, the *Didache*, which is itself moreover already a "collection of different traditions that were brought together at a certain time by an anonymous author which it is impossible to identify."[21] The *Didache* sometimes will be quoted verbatim in subsequent documents. The process of continuous adaptation and rewriting can be seen in the precise and systematic comparison of each passage from the *Canons of Hippolytus*, written in the first half of the fourth century, with the *Apostolic Tradition* attributed to Hippolytus, from the beginning of the third century—a comparison made by Bradshaw.[22]

The *Apostolic Tradition*, widely utilized until the fourth century, became obsolete and then disappeared in its original Greek version, of which only a few fragments are preserved. Recently the translation into Ethiopic by Alessandro Bausi has been published. A recent discovery of an Ethiopian manuscript, which derives from a Greek original (about the fifth century) contains both the *Apostolic Tradition*, in an independent version and one similar to the fragments of Verona, as well as another text *On the Charisms*.[23] The edition of this manuscript questions much of what scholars have written in recent decades. Today the *Apostolic Tradition* is widely used by liturgists and historians; however, the reader of a similar text, as it is presented today in the reconstruction of Botte, must never forget that it is a hypothetical reconstruction, even if it has solid foundations. The translation of Bausi presents us with the Ethiopian text, which is important because it coincides with the Latin text. I often quote this text, but we must keep in mind that the original is not preserved and therefore should be seen in a comparative way with the different traditions.[24]

A set of texts which are referred to as the *Pseudo-Clementines* because they are related to the figure of Clement, the successor of Peter in Rome, have passages of a liturgical and institutional nature. The current wording is considered to be from the fourth century, but the text basically dates back to the first half of the third century. The *Pseudo-Clementines* offer elements concerning ordination, the duties of the bishop, his power, the authority of Clement as the successor of Peter and the importance of the Roman church, priests and deacons, catechists, and works of charity. In the community the bishop is the central figure.

With time, the concern for fidelity to tradition, despite the need for updating along with the lack of a homogeneous canon law, led Christians to gather together different documents or to combine them without necessarily a concern for how they were put together. On the one hand, there was the desire to preserve the ancient practices; on the other the need to adapt to the changing social, political and religious conditions of Christians. This sometimes conditioned the authors to limit themselves to less radical interventions. The weight of tradition and the antiquity the text were strongly binding on the person working with the documents. Thus, a text handed down as apostolic was transformed, but was still put back into circulation under the aegis of apostolicity.[25]

The Greek-speaking church from which these translations into other languages originated had, since the beginning of the fourth century, all the canonical legislation of conciliar origin and a well-organized liturgy, so that the oldest documents were marginalized and sometimes even condemned. In the following centuries, however, the other Eastern churches, lacking a well-structured and complete canonical corpus, continued to rely on them and pass them on to subsequent generations. This process of revisiting a text in later periods was a consequence of the disappearance of the original version. In all this literature, both in the oldest anonymous literature and in the subsequent Council collections, there was an implacable principle that the later product, considered better, eclipsed the previous one, considered no longer usable.

A work of this kind could not be created by a single author but rather reflects an existing practice and common teaching. It is a collection of traditions with possible suggestions for correction and practice. Since these traditions were not the result of the legislative activity of a Council with authority, the practical norms are traced back to the authority of the apostles, both collectively and individually, and are considered to be transmitted by the work of Hippolytus and above all of Clement. In canonical-liturgical literature, these two names often recur and are associated with different writings in different languages, even in translations. Their role is not dissimilar. The author of this literature is unknown, even though the literature itself is so important for the life of Christian communities, perhaps with the exception of the *Apostolic Constitutions* which today are attributed to a certain Julian. A large body of canonical-liturgical literature is attributed to apostolic origin, but there are many texts that are transmitted under the name of Clement who is an apostolic personage, or under the name of Hippolytus.[26]

During the fourth century the Council assemblies in both the East and the West began to issue normative documents, the canons, which acquired authority not based on an alleged apostolic origin, but by virtue of the authority of the Council itself. Only in the West, in addition to the conciliar decisions, would there be papal legislation—the pontifical decrees or decretals.[27] Conciliar decisions and decrees would become the sources of canon law along with imperial legislation. The latter is particularly useful and important for the Byzantine East. Council legislation can have a local character, at various levels, or a universal character, that is, coming from the ecumenical councils. Papal decrees are linked to the person and prestige of the pope who issued such laws, such as Damasus, Leo the Great or Gregory the Great. The concept of "ecumenical council" is theological, not historical, i.e. it is the reception by the church as such. It does not depend on the number of participants or imperial participation.

Another characteristic of this literary genre is that of discrediting competing texts under penalty of punishment for the readers.[28] These procedures, like other similar ones, were used to confirm the authority and credibility of one's work, crediting its apostolic origin to the detriment of other works of the same kind. To this end, recourse was also made to threats, to blessings,[29] to prohibitions against reading false apostolic writings[30] and to secrecy—all typical procedures of religious pseudepigraphy. The apostolicity to which these texts so insistently refer is intended to ensure and establish their authority in order to give the prescriptions the force of law, but also in the sense that they are in an ideal line of continuity with the recent or far past. Indeed, in the succession of documents, there is an increase in the insistence on their apostolic origin through the use of various literary procedures. The apostles enjoy the highest authority in the ancient church; no one would have dared to say that any of their commands—even ones that are hard to accept—were dated and the fruit of times past and another context. The reader and the listener were almost always persuaded by the weight of apostolic authority because they often heard that the apostles derived their authority directly from Christ. To our eyes, the various compilers may seem like forgers, but they do not consider themselves as such before their conscience, nor are they considered as such by others.[31] From the fifth century onwards pseudo-Apostolic canonical and liturgical works were no longer written because they could not easily have proved their antiquity and also because bishops and synods were now the arbiters of what was or was not authentic and authoritative.

In the absence of anything else, the already mentioned pseudo-epigraphic texts met the concrete needs and functions of the organizational and geographical development of Christian communities in the first four centuries. They fill a void and encourage, through their diffusion, an organizational and functional uniformity. Once another type of law arose, those texts were either incorporated into canonical collections or were destined to be forgotten.

There was no longer any need to draw up other similar documents. It was quite a different situation in those geographical areas where the Council's legislation was not affirmed or disseminated. For example, Coptic Egypt and Ethiopia are instances where some of the legislation was translated at a later date and adapted to their respective needs; indeed, where new legislation from councils was lacking, new documents were created. Although this literature was written in Greek originally, it was also translated into Latin and therefore also influenced the western church.

The oldest texts, before Constantine, are the *Didache*, the *Apostolic Tradition*, the *Didascalia* and the *Ecclesiastical Canons of the Apostles*. The *Apostolic Constitutions* is the most famous work, composed around 380. It is a compilation of pseudo-epigraphic texts. It takes up and re-elaborates previous documents, in particular the *Didascalia* (1-6), the *Didache* (7.1-32), the *Apostolic Tradition* (8.3-45) including the final addition of the *Apostolic Canons*. But it also includes other texts and material such as the *First Letter of Clement*, the *Pseudo-Clementines*, apocryphal texts, liturgical formularies, as well as incorporating the liturgical practices of its own time and environment along with biblical quotations. Chapters 33-38 of the seventh book contain five prayers which seem to be an adaptation of Jewish prayers. The beginning of the eighth book could be based on the treatise on the charisms of Pseudo Hippolytus. The compiler presents the work as if it were by Clement (8.46.13; 8.47.85). He did not limit himself to simply juxtaposing existing texts but edited them with omissions, interpolation, and additions. In this way all the different ecclesiastical institutions are treated and every subdivision of its content can only be in summary, because the various themes also return elsewhere: Christian conduct, the hierarchy, the reconciliation of penitents, Christian initiation, ordinations, the liturgical year, widows, orphans, martyrs, schisms, charisms, ethics and the Eucharist. Some topics such as martyrdom were no longer part of the daily Christian life of the church but were dealt with because they were part of earlier documents. Sometimes the compiler did not succeed in amalgamating well the diversity of the sources because he had not been able to eliminate certain contradictions left here and there. For instance, the apostle James is sometimes portrayed as still alive [2.55.2; 6.12ff; 8.4.1], but in other places as already dead [5.8.1; 7.46.2].

The compilation of the *Apostolic Constitutions* can be placed in Syria, preferably Antioch, around the year 380. Its author, according to some, could be a certain Arian named Julian, also author of the Arian *Commentary on Job*[32] and the interpolator of the *Letters* of Ignatius of Antioch.[33] The Council Quinisextus (Trullo) of 691/692 repudiates the *Apostolic Constitutions* as infested with heresy, although it accepts the final part, that is, the *85 Apostolic Canons*.[34]

The extensive canon 50 presents an explanation of the triple immersion in baptism, which varies in length and content in the different redactions. The *Apostolic Canons* became an integral part of Byzantine Canon Law. Already during the fifth century they were translated into all ancient languages, including Latin, together with the *Apostolic Constitutions*. Dionysius Exiguus translated into Latin only the first 50 canons for the first edition of his collection, the *Dionysiana*.[35] But he observed that many did not accept them, although it seemed to him that popes had utilized them.[36] Some canons were in complete contrast with the traditions of the Latin Church: the rebaptism of heretics (canons 46 and 47) and the reordination of the heretical clergy (can. 68). For example the list of biblical books does not mention Revelations and Judith and includes the two letters of Clement and the Constitutions themselves (can. 85). However, although the early 6th century *Decretum Gelasianum* (*De libris recipiendis et non recipiendis*)[37] relegates the *Apostolic Canons* to the status of apocrypha, those translated by Dionysius were included in later canonical collections and continued to be used, even by Popes such as John VIII (†882) and Leo IX (†1054)[38]; 17 more of them were included in the Decretals of Gratian.

The *Epitome*, also called the *Constitutions through Hippolytus*, depends on the *Apostolic Constitutions*; it is a reworking and reduction of Book VIII. The compiler of the *Epitome* in some cases prefers to refer directly to the source (*Apostolic Tradition*), avoiding the intermediary (*Apostolic Constitutions*) altogether. There is also the *Octateuch* of Clement. The name was given by de Lagarde to a Syriac collection in eight books (thus *Octateuch*) which in many respects is a Syriac translation, revision and adaptation of earlier documents, particularly the *Apostolic Constitutions*. It has come down to us in four remarkably different recensions: Syriac, Arabic and Coptic Bohairic (composed only in 1804).

We have no such composition in the West. Only the extant conciliar texts and the pontifical decrees are valid. These are grouped in canonical collections: Decretals (*epistolae decretales*), which are pontifical answers in the form of a letter to precise questions addressed to the Apostolic see in matters of discipline or law. The answers then took on more of a general character and some were grouped into collections. The term "decretal" can also indicate all pontifical letters in the collections. The first preserved decretal or decree dates back to the time of Damasus, the *Epistula ad Gallos* (the answer of a Roman synod). It is a small manual of discipline intended for a missionary church in response to a question. According to recent research by Duval, it was written by Jerome in Rome on behalf of the Apostolic See. The decrees are indebted to the technical legal language of the imperial constitutions. The first collections of decrees were created during the fifth century and called *epistolae decretales* or *canones urbicani* and with these names are inserted in some canonical collections.[39] Like any good administration, a church must have an archive. The important archive in Rome was called the *scrinium* and was known to Jerome.[40] The African Councils often mention the use of this archive.

The *Ancient Statutes of the Church* (*Statuta ecclesiae antiqua*)—the only Western text—is composed of three parts: an examination of the candidate for the episcopal order and a profession of faith, then 89 canons, and finally canons 90-102, which concern the ritual of ordination, virgins, marriage and widows. The anonymous author[41] uses earlier councils and the *Apostolic Constitutions*.[42]

Although this canonical literature was written almost entirely in Greek in the early centuries, part of it was also translated into Latin and therefore also influenced the western church. From the fourth century onward, private individuals generally took care to preserve all legislation by compiling collections, the success and dissemination of which depended on the importance of the collection, which circulated anonymously. Thus, norms born in a precise historical and disciplinary context, for example, in a local council, acquired more universal value and were applied to other similar situations.

The first substantial collection was formed during the fourth century, called the *Syntagma antiochenum* (*Syntagma canonum*, *Corpus canonum orientale*). The Council of Chalcedon of 451 uses this collection several times, using the term *biblios* (book) or similar expressions and citing its canons. This collection utilized a continuous numbering system for the diverse canons it included: can. 1-20 (Nicaea); 21-45 (Ancyra); 46-59 (Neocaesarea: initially there were 14 canons, later can. 13 was divided into two);[43] 60-79 (Gangra); 80-104 (Antioch). We do not possess such a collection, nor does the Council specify whether it speaks of a specific collection or of any one collection, since each collection (as was the fate of works of this kind for practical use) was destined to be continuously increased and updated. However, other collections with Ancyra's canons 4 and 5 were circulating in a single text. Besides, the main churches at least had to have a canonical collection available for the use of bishops and council meetings; the collection of Antioch is the best known.

Alexandria must also have had its own collection where the acts of Ephesus of 431 were added. The Antiochene corpus had been slowly built, perhaps initially by putting together the councils of Ancyra and Neocaesarea—two cities of Pontus—and the collection is called *Pontica*. The 343 council of Gangra (also a Pontic city) was added to it. This autonomous collection circulated in Antioch to which were added the 25 canons of the Council of Antioch (341, *in Encaeniis*) around 360 or 378. In 379 under Bishop Meletius the canons of Nicaea were placed at the beginning out of respect for their authority,[44] and thus marked the acceptance of the Council of Nicaea and the triumph of Orthodoxy. Subsequently, the 60 disciplinary canons of the Council of Laodicea were appended, although we can't say when because they are missing in the Latin translation called *Prisca*.

In 410, during the synod of the metropolitan Isaac of Seleucia-Ctesiphon in Mesopotamia, the bishops of Persia adopted the Antiochene collection which already included the Council of Constantinople (381), and later added the canons of Chalcedon (451). The Antiochene collection, a private collection, has a chronological ordering, except for its placement of the Council of Nicaea at the beginning. At a later time, the four canons of the Ecumenical

Council of Constantinople (381) and the two of 382 were added as well as the one canon from the Constantinopolitan Council of 394, called the seventh canon.[45] During the fifth century this collection was compiled with the 28 canons of the Council of Chalcedon (451). However, there may have been differences in the various redactions. At an unknown date sometime during the fifth century the *Apostolic Canons* were added which were already included in the copy translated into Latin by Dionysius Exiguus. In the course of the sixth century the Greek collection grew even more with the insertion of the canons of the Council of Serdica (Sofia of 343), of Carthage (419) and of the eight canons of the Ecumenical Council of Ephesus (431) which had not published canons in the strict sense but were extracted from the texts.[46]

The now lost *corpus antiochenum*, which already included the canons of Constantinople (381), was translated into Latin in the fifth century. Two versions were made: one called *Isidoriana* (or *Hispana*) and the other Prisca (or *Itala*). It was also first translated into Syriac at the beginning of the fifth century and a second time in 500/501. It was included in the *Synodicon* of the Syriac church. This new version reported the acclamation of the Council of Ephesus (431) on the Nicene Creed and the canons of the Council of Chalcedon (451).[47] This collection is also important for the reconstruction of the original Greek text.

The collections, always made by private individuals, increased in number in the West.[48] The *Collectio Avellana* is worth mentioning. The name comes from the monastery of S. Croce di Fonte Avellana (Pesaro) where the manuscript was found. It is now referred to as *Vat. lat.* 4961. It does not contain conciliar canons but has letters from emperors, bishops and other documents numbering in total 244, the majority of which were previously unknown. These come from the period 367 to 553. It was therefore compiled after 553 by an unknown author.

DISSEMINATION AND APPLICATION OF THE TEXTS

We are accustomed to reconstructing the institutions of the ancient church using this literature and the conciliar canons, both ecumenical and local. The local canons pose other problems in that we do not know the history of their reception or whether they had binding force. For example, the canons of the Eastern Greek Councils, except those of Nicaea, were completely unknown in the West in the fourth century. The Western canons in turn have never been known in the East, except for the so-called Council of Carthage of 419. Very often we make generalizations and just assume. But what texts did the fathers actually know? If they were going to use them, they had to know them. The basis of their knowledge was the dissemination of those texts, at least the most important ones. It is not easy to reconstruct the dissemination of these texts because each text has its own peculiar history.

When does the *Didache* come to be known in the West? The *Apostolic Tradition*, as already mentioned, had wide dissemination through the texts dependent on it. How did the Latin translation spread in the West?[49] The anonymous works of the *Collectio Veronensis*[50] are the first Latin collection known to us, but of which we do not know the original Greek. It is represented by the manuscript of the Capitular Library of Verona LV (53). The manuscript contains, among other things, a third part of the *Didascalia*, half of the *Ecclesiastical Canons of the Apostles* and part of the *Apostolic Tradition*, which is why it is called the *Collectio tripartita* (Collection in three parts). The *Sententiae* of Isidore of Seville in the eighth century were written on the palimpsest of an original document from the sixth-century that was erased. This translation dates back to the end of the fourth century, as it uses the *Vetus Latina*.[51] The translator does not have a mastery of Greek and Latin, so he tries to make the Greek text as faithful as possible, sometimes transcribing the Greek term. The Latin translator did not make the collection himself but used a Greek copy. It does not seem to have been disseminated because only one palimpsest manuscript is known; in the eighth century the parchment was reused, because its content was considered useless.

On the basis of the *Syntagma Antiochenum*, in the first half of the fifth century a collection of oriental councils translated into Latin with continuous numbering was composed in Rome, or in Italy: Nicaea (325) (not only the canons, but also other texts); Ancyra (314); Neocaesarea (314/319); Antioch (341 ca); Gangra (343); Laodicea (364); Constantinople (381); and Serdica (343), the latter with the false indication of *incipit concilium Nicaenum XX episcoporum quae in graeco non habentur*; then the canons of the council for the case of Apiarius of Africa of 419 and the letters exchanged for that occasion. Composed around 425 this is the first true western collection. This collection was taken up by the *Versio Hispana*. Dionysius Exiguus, when using the collection, corrects the eastern canons on the basis of the Greek text. The collection, both in its original version and in the revision of Dionysius, was widespread in the Latin West.

In Italy, in the second half of the fifth century, before Dionysius Exiguus, another collection was made in a new and unfortunate translation from the Greek.[52] It was widely disseminated as can be seen from the number of manuscripts that attest to it. It was called *Versio Prisca* by its first publisher and *Itala* for the area in which it was disseminated.[53] This collection contains the councils of: Ancyra; Neocaesarea; Gangra; Antioch; (no Laodicea); Carthage 419 (with documents concerning Apiarius); Constantinople (381); Chalcedon (451); Nicaea and Serdica (in continuous numbering in the *Collectio Teatina* [or *Ingilrami*], the best of the group, and under the same title as Nicaea). Perhaps the canons of Nicaea and Serdica were not included in the original version.[54] Paschasinus of Lilibeo in the Council of Chalcedon (451), quoting can. 6 of the Council of Nicaea, uses this version of the *Ingilrami*.[55] Subsequently, as can be deduced from some manuscripts, other documents were added to this collection including pontifical decrees from Siricius to the Roman Council of 499 (with a letter from Jerome and two imperial letters).

To this canonical documentation, which then had a great influence on Western canon law, we add the Latin version of the canons of the Council of Serdica (now Sofia) in the autumn of 343. The Latin text differs in several respects from the Greek version which is part of Byzantine canon law. The canons of Serdica, up to Dionysius Exiguus, were considered by the Roman Church as if they came from the Council of Nicaea, as can be seen in the discussion of the case of the presbyter Apiarius of Sicca Veneria in 419 in Carthage.

Starting from the fourth century, the African canonical legislation was plentiful thanks to the decisions of the Councils of Carthage of 345/348 and 390. However, it is not certain whether all the texts attributed to African Councils were drawn up in Africa. There is "the great difficulty in attributing to a particular African council canons that are simply called emanating from a *sinodus apud Carthaginem africanarum provinciarum*, as for example, in the second version of the canonical collection elaborated by Dionysius Exiguus in Rome at the beginning of the sixth century, which involves 138 African canons. It happens that decisions dating back to a completely different geographical region are attributed to the canonical activity of the African bishops."[56]

Several collections in this province came to light under the rule of Aurelius, Primate of Carthage (391-430). In particular, the *Epitome* of the Council of Hippo in 393, composed in 397 by the bishops of Byzacena, offers a substantial summary of African canon law of the time.[57] All the provinces of the region observed its provisions and the plenary councils—reunited by the solicitude of Aurelius of Carthage and presided over by himself—reconfirmed them. The case of Apiarius, which set African bishops against Roman claims about appeals to Rome, was a good reason for the formation of large collections of previous decisions, justifying the point of view of the Council of Carthage in May 419. To prove that their canons conformed to those of Nicaea, the Africans composed a brief collection of 40 (33) canons, more commonly referred to as the *Canones in questione Apiarii* (Canons on the Question of Apiarius). On the same occasion, they transmitted to Rome extensive extracts from the Acts of their Councils (from 393 to 418). During the fifth century the *Registri Ecclesiae Carthaginensis Excerpta*,[58] published by Justel under the title *Codex canonum ecclesiae africanae*, were drawn up utilizing the set of earlier texts. Dionysius Exiguus inserted the collection in the second edition of his canonical collection. After this golden age the African church, devastated by the invasion of vandals, substantially interrupted its activity in canonical matters. Only two compilations collect the legislation of the time: *The Epitome of the deacon Ferrandus* (523/546) and the *Concordia canonum* of Cresconius.[59]

A well-known case—that of Apiarius which has already been mentioned several times—sheds light on the dissemination and notoriety of the most important canons and therefore on their application. Apiarius, priest of the church of Sicca Veneria (El Kef, Tunisia), was excommunicated—perhaps unfairly—by his Bishop Urbanus in a local synod of 418 for serious unspecified faults.[60] At the beginning of 418 Apiarius appealed to Zosimus (417-26 December 418) against the African practice that prohibited the appeal to Italian churches. Zosimus welcomed his case, sending a delegation to Carthage led by Faustinus, bishop of Potenza Picena, in the summer of 418. His requests were drafted and justified by a *Commonitorium* in which he gave instructions on the case of Apiarius and clarified some disciplinary points relating to judicial procedures in matters of faith. On May 26, 419 a long synodal letter was written for Pope Boniface in which the events were narrated and it was explained that during the meeting the bishops had asked the Roman delegates "to exhibit what was required of us from the ecclesiastical archive (*acta ecclesiastica*); instead they proceeded without any written testimony." That is to say, the African bishops strongly insisted that they quote the sources from the ecclesiastical archives. Instead, the delegates presented a text of instructions (*commonitorium*) which was read. In that text Zosimus requests they observe certain prescriptions. "In the dossier there are four points which we have been ordered by them to provide for: 1) on the appeals of the bishops to the bishop of the Roman Church; 2) the bishops should not go by sea to the imperial court if it is not appropriate; 3) the cases of the priests and deacons are to be dealt with by the neighboring bishops; 4) excommunicate, or call bishop Urbanus to Rome if he has not corrected what was proper."[61]

In a council (the date is unknown), Apiarius, having asked for forgiveness, was readmitted to communion. His bishop also corrected himself for his sins. But with written permission, Apiarius could exercise his priestly ministry wherever he wanted.[62] On the question of the appeal to Rome, the African bishops responded to Zosimus with determination, affirming that they were acting precisely in compliance with the decisions of Nicaea, finding no need to seek confirmation in the statements of the Roman bishop. Perhaps Zosimus did not have a chance to read the firm response of the Africans.[63] Zosimus' successor, Boniface, in April 419, sent a new delegation to Carthage to inform the delegates of the events that had occurred in Rome, and to confirm the mandate received from his predecessor.

On 25 May 419 a plenary council with 217 bishops was held. Also present were Augustine, Possidius and Alipius. The council requested the reading of the *commonitorium* of Zosimus. During the reading of the text, Alipius noted that the African bishops had promised to observe what was established at Nicaea. But since their text did not contain the canon cited as coming from the Council of Nicaea, they required that a delegation be sent to Alexandria, Constantinople, and Antioch in order to have a copy of the original text of the Nicene canons.[64]

The Roman Church based its claims about receiving appeals on the basis of a canon of the Council of Nicaea which actually was from one of the canons of the Council of Serdica in 343 (canon 7). The African bishops were disconcerted because this canon was not found in their collection of Nicene canons reported by Cecilianus who had participated in the Nicene

Council.[65] Also, on the appeals of priests and deacons to address neighboring bishops—as it is written in the *Commonitorium*—we read that there are "things that absolutely cannot be found in the Council of Nicaea." Augustine adds: "This too we want to respect, subject to more careful reading of the acts of the Nicene Council." They unanimously affirmed, "Everything that has been established in the Nicene Council meets with our full approval."[66]

The answers of Cyril of Alexandria and Atticus of Constantinople are preserved. "These letters—from the two bishops—with the texts of the Nicene Council, were sent to Boniface, the holy bishop of the Roman Church, through the appointed presbyter Innocent and the subdeacon of the Church of Carthage, Marcellus."[67]

In the sessions held on May 25 and 30 of the Council of Carthage (419) the African bishops drew up a group of disciplinary canons which were sent to Rome. This small collection is preserved in some later collections. In November, they wrote a complete collection to defend their positions consisting of the Nicene canons, the letters of Cyril and Atticus and the Acts of the Council. "Because of its size, this collection immediately underwent changes and mutilations, passing into the *Hispana*. Later, in 424 according to Munier, a third collection was compiled to defend the rights of African churches against Roman claims; it passed into the *Collectio Frisingensis*, where the editor tried to soften statements against papal authority. This collection was used by Dionysius Exiguus."[68]

Why were there all these serious controversies? The Roman church had a collection of canons that combined those of Nicaea (325) with those of Serdica (343). She considered them all from Nicaea. The African church possessed the collection of the canons of Nicaea, but did not know those of the Council of Serdica in which its Bishop Gratus had participated. Didn't he bring a copy with him, as Cecilianus did in 325? Certainly. In fact, he himself mentions it in the Council of 345-348, but he does not mention a text, as he uses the phrase "from memory."[69]

The Roman church, although having received all the answers of Atticus and Cyril, surely knew the authentic canons of Nicaea and yet the confusion continued. In fact, in the Theatine collection[70] composed around 525,[71] the canons of the two councils are combined using a single numbering system, ending with the expression: *explicit concilium nicaenum* (here ends the council of Nicaea). The combination of the two councils is also found in other later collections.

Did the Roman chancellery not update its archive, even though it had already received the authentic text of Nicaea in the autumn of 419? A few decades later Leo the Great, writing to Theodosius II, cites canon four of Serdica as if it were from Nicaea.[72] Galla Placidia also writes to Theodosius citing canon seven of Serdica again as if it were Nicene.[73]

The continuous numbering and combining of the canons of Nicaea and Serdica stems from the fact that the documents are arranged in chronological order, which is a guarantee of authenticity. On the other hand, the organization of the Roman archives in the first half of the fourth century is not well known; they will be better arranged towards the end of the fourth and fifth centuries.[74] In 494 Gelasius (492-496), in the problematic situation at the end of the fifth century, sent a very interesting letter/program to the bishops of southern Italy. Its beginning is enlightening: "We are forced by a necessary questioning of some questions—and thus accede to the role of moderator proper to the apostolic See—to resume the decrees of the canons of the fathers and to reconsider the prescriptions of our prelates and predecessors so that we can resolve, as far as possible and on the basis of careful reflection, what the current need of the Churches requires to address."[75] Gelasius is faithful to the previous prescriptions and at the same time, according to the needs of new situations, tries to adapt the rules.

SUMMARY

We conclude by emphasizing strongly the importance of the living oral tradition in every ecclesiastical arena, recognizing the great individual churches and the concrete practice, practiced and lived, which one learns through exercise and experience. All of these determine the institutional organization and the liturgy. We are not able to reconstruct the birth and development of the great variety of existing traditions in the first three centuries. However, and this is another point, the great churches were proud in maintaining their own tradition. That tradition, by imitation, spreads elsewhere. There is a move towards greater unity in larger geographical areas. The pontifical decretals addressed to the Italian, Spanish, Gallican and other bishops disseminated Roman customs. In the liturgy and in canonical practice it is preferred to follow the tradition received or to import practices that have worked elsewhere. The greater dissemination of written texts, more and more precise and detailed, does not mean that the prescriptions were applied; on the contrary, they are a mirror of ignorance or neglect. Moreover, their application also depends on a competent authority to make itself heard.

The almost total scarcity of manuscripts in the early Middle Ages among the eastern non-Greek churches is an important argument for enhancing their oral tradition, which in these areas was very traditional and venerable. This oral tradition reduces the excessive importance often placed on older written canonical-liturgical documentation.

---

1. Job 1.
2. Eusebius, *HE* 6.19.17-18.
3. Christian Hannick, "La fortuna dei canoni africani nell'Oriente greco," in *Africa/Ifrīqiya: Il Maghreb nella storia religiosa di Cristianesimo e Islam*, ed. C. Alzati (Città del Vaticano: Libreria Editrice Vaticana, 2016), 227-38.
4. So Augustine did when he had chosen his successor, Heraclius.

5. *Episcopal Election in Late Antiquity*, ed. by Johan Leemans and Peter Van Nuffelen (Berlin: De Gruyter, 2011). Many scholars have collaborated on this precious volume demonstrated by the variety of essays on different concrete situations.
6. Can. 9; see can. 17
7. Cf. O. F.A. Meinardus, *Two Thousand Years of Coptic Christianity* (Cairo: American University in Cairo Press, 2002), 51-52.
8. Ibid.
9. Augustine, *Ep.* 213.4.
10. *De corona* 4. On *consuetudo*: see *De virginibus velandis*, SC 424. Cf. Valentin Morel, "'Disciplina,' Le mot et l'idée représentée par lui dans les œuvres de Tertullien," *Revue Hist. Ecclésiastique* 40-41 (1944): 243-65 ; Eadem, "Le développement de la "disciplina" sous l'action de du Saint-Esprit chez Tertullien," *RHE* 35 (1939): 5-46.
11. F. de Pauw, "La justification des traditions non écrites chez Tertullien," *Ephemerides Theologicae Lovanienses* 19 (1942): 5-46.
12. Augustine speaks of the "plenary councils," referring to those in Africa, of which many texts are not preserved. For example, we do not have the decisions of a council held at the time of Bishop Agrippinus at Carthage in the early third century (around 220) or of another held at the time of Donatianus (between 238 and 346).
13. Augustine, *Ep.* 54.1.
14. Augustine, *Ep.* 54.2.
15. Augustine, *Ep.* 54.2; see *Ep.* 36.32.
16. Augustine, *Ep.* 54.3.
17. *Aliae sunt leges Caesarum, aliae Christi: aliud Papinianus, aliud Paulus noster praecipit* (*Ep.* 67.3 *Ad Oceanum*: PL 22:691). Sometimes Augustine uses the expression: cf. *sermo* 169.4: PL 38:918; *sermo* 297.7: PL 38:1362; *Contra Cresc.* 43.454.
18. *quam terrena civitas licitam turpitudinem fecit. Civ. Dei* 14.18: "Lust requires for its consummation darkness and secrecy; and this not only when unlawful intercourse is desired, but even such fornication as the earthly city has legalized. Where there is no fear of punishment, these permitted pleasures still shrink from the public eye. Even where provision is made for this lust, secrecy also is provided; and while lust found it easy to remove the prohibitions of law, shamelessness found it impossible to lay aside the veil of retirement." NPNF 2 1:275.
19. Initially it included canons of provincial councils: Ancyra (314), Neocaesarea (314/319), Antioch (341), Gangra (343) and Laodicea (343/381). At Antioch under the Bishop Meletius the twenty canons of Nicaea were added at the beginning and then those of Chalcedon. We know this through quotations recorded in the Council of Chalcedon.
20. See A. di Berardino, ed., *Encyclopedia of Ancient Christianity* (hereafter, *EAC*) (Downers Grove, IL: InterVarsity Press, 2014), 1:766.
21. W. Rordorf and A. Tuilier, SC 248:21.
22. *The Canons of Hippolytus*, P.F. Bradshaw, ed., English translation by Carol Bebawi (Bramcote, Notts: Grove, 1987).
23. Alessandro Bausi, "La nuova versione etiopica della Traditio apostolica: Edizione e traduzione preliminare," in *Christianity in Egypt. Literary Production and Intellectual Trends. Studies in Honor of Tito Orlandi*, ed. Paola Buzi (Rome: Institutum Patristicum Augustinianum, 2011), 19-69.
24. *The Apostolic Tradition: A Commentary*, by P. Bradshaw, M. E. Johnson, and L. E. Phillips, ed. by H. W. Attridge (Minneapolis: Fortress Press, 2002).
25. Cf. M. Metzger, *Les constitutions apostoliques*, SC 320:43.
26. *Apostolic Constitutions*, the *Pseudo-Clementines, Octateuch of Clement, Apocalypse of Peter* (see S. Grébaut, "Littérature éthiopienne pseudo-clémentine," *Revue des l'Orient chrétien* (1910): 208-214; *Apostolic Tradition, Canons of Hippolytus*; the *Epitome* (*Constitutiones per Hippolytum*). Cf. A. Di Berardino, "Letteratura canonica e liturgica," in *Dizionario di letteratura patristica*, ed. by A. Di Berardino, M. Simonetti, and G. Fedalto (Milan: San Paolo, 2007), 222-49.
27. Di Berardino A. (ed.), *I concili della chiesa antica*, vol. II, *Decretali pontificie e canoni di Serdica*, in collaboration with T. Sardella and C. Dell'Osso (Rome: Institutum Patristicum Augustinianum, 2007); D. Moreau, "Non impar conciliorum extat auctoritas. L'origine de l'introduction des lettres pontificales dans le droit canonique," in *L'étude des correspondances dans le monde romain de l'Antiquité classique à l'Antiquité tardive: permanences et mutations*, ed. by J. Desmulliez, Chr. Hoët-Van Cauwenberg, J.-Chr. Jolivet (Villeneuve-d'Ascq: Conseil Scientifique, Université Charles-de-Gaulle-Lille 3, 2010), 487-506.
28. Cf. *Const. Apost.* 6.16; 8.47.60.

29. See *Const. Apost.* 5.7.31; 8.48.2.
30. See *Const. Apost.* 6.16; 8.47.60.
31. Metzger, SC 230:44-46.
32. CPG 2075.
33. CPG 1026.
34. *Const. Apost.* 8.47; can. 2.
35. PL 67:141-48.
36. PL 67:142.
37. Concerning those books which should and should not be received.
38. Hefele-Leclercq, *Histoire des conciles*, 1.2.1206.
39. Di Berardino A. (ed.), *I concili della chiesa antica*, vol. II, *Decretali, concili romani e canoni di Serdica*, with T. Sardella and C. Dell'Osso (Rome: Institutum Patristicum Augustinianum, 2007).
40. Jerome. *Apologia adversus libros Rufini* 3.20. P. Blaudeau, *Le siège de Rome et l'Orient (448-536): étude géoecclésiologique* (Rome: École fran-caise de Rome, 2012), 84, note 295.
41. Munier suggests Gennadius of Marseille (476/485).
42. *EAC* 3:630-31.
43. Peter L'Huillier, *The Church of the Ancient Councils* (Crestwood, NY: St. Vladimir's Seminary Press, 1996), 209.
44. Cf. F. Maassen, *Geschichte der Quellen und Literatur des kanonischen Rechts im Abendlande* (Gratz: Akademische Druckerei und Verlagsanstalt, 1870) (reprinted, Graz 1956), 13; 112-26; 924-38.
45. E. Honigmann, "Le concile de Constantinople de 394 et les auteurs du Syntagma des XIV titres," *Subsidia Hagiographica* 35 (Bruxelles 1961): 1-83, see esp. 77.
46. L'Huillier, *Church*, 153ff and 213.
47. Cf. A. Vööbus, *The Synodicon in the West Syrian Tradition*, I, CSCO 367 (Louvain: Corpus SCO, 1975); CSCO 368, 1975; W. Selb, *Orientalisches Kirchenrecht*, 2 vols. (Vienna: Österreichische Akademie der Wissenschaften, 1981).
48. Otto Guenther, *Epistulae Imperatorum Pontificum Aliorum inde ab A. CCCLXVII usque ad A. DLIII datae Avellana quae dicitur Collectio*, CSEL 26; Rita Lizzi Testa, "La Collectio Avellana e le collezioni canoniche romane e italiche del V-VI secolo: un progetto di ricerca," *Cristianesimo nella storia* 35 (214): 77-236.
49. A. Nicolotti, "Che cos'è la Traditio Apostolica di Ippolito," *Riv. Storia del Cristianesimo* 2 (2005): 219-37.
50. Partial text palimpsest of 99 sheets published by E. Hauler, *Didascaliae apostolorum fragmenta Veronensia latina* (Lipsiae: Teubner, 1900), and later by E. Tidner, *Didascaliae apostolorum, Canonum ecclesiasticorum, Traditionis apostolicae uersiones latinae* (Berlin: Akademie-Verlag, 1963).
51. Funk II: 8-11.
52. *Ecclesiae Occidentalis Monumenta Iuris Antiquissima* (EOMIA) ed. C.H. Turner. I, 148-152; 244-248; II,150-151.
53. PL 56:747-817.
54. Cf. PL 56:818-22.
55. Maassen, n. 19; *Dictionnaire Droit Canonique* 4:1142.
56. M.-Y. Perrin, "Non solo Agostino. I "Padri africani" nella vicenda dottrinale e nella elaborazione canonistica della 'Chiesa latina,'" in *Africa/Ifrīqiya. Il Maghreb nella storia religiosa di Cristianesimo e Islam*, ed. C. Alzati (Città del Vaticano: Libreria Editrice Vaticana, 2016), 95-123, esp. 106.
57. Ch. Munier, "Les conciles africains (A. 345-525) "revisités," in *I Concili della cristianità occidentale secoli III-V* (Rome: Institutum Patristicum Augustinianum, 2002), 147-65.
58. CCL 149.173-247.
59. K. Zechiel-Eckes, *Die Concordia canonum des Cresconius. Studien und Edition* (Frankfurt am Main: Peter Lang, 1992), two volumes; cf. M.-Y. Perrin, *La Concordia canonum de Cresconius. Un reexamen*, in print *The Collectio Avellana and its revivals* ed. by R. Lizzi Testa (Newcastle upon Tyne, UK: Cambridge Scholars Publishing, 2019).
60. C. Pietri, *Roma Christiana. Recherches sur l'Église de Rome, son organisation, sa politique, son idéologie de Miltiade à Sixte II* (Rome: Ecole Francaise de Rome, 1976), 1250-75; PCBE 1:82-83; 2:750-52; J. Merdinger, *Rome and the African Church in the Time of Augustine* (New Haven/London: Yale University Press, 1997), 111-35; 182-99; *EAC* 1:167.
61. A. di Berardino, ed., *I concili africani*, 2nd. ed., 143.
62. Ibid, 141.
63. Ibid, 143.
64. Ibid, 115-17.

65. A. Di Berardino, ed., *I concili africani*, 2nd. ed., 119: the Nicene statutes "which were reported by your predecessor (that is to say Aurelius) of blessed memory the Bishop Cecilianus, who took part in it". "There remain only the copies of the Acts of the Council of Nicaea shown here, which we still keep and which were fixed by the fathers, who also sign the synod of our predecessors and who established with exemplary clarity the formalities to be followed for each ecclesiastical grade from the major to the last." 113.
66. Ibid, 119.
67. Ibid, 145.
68. *EAC* 1:564; CPL 1765; EOMIA I.2.3, 566-595; *Concilia Africae, Concilium Carthag.*, CCL 149.90-148. W. Telfer, "The Codex Verona LX (58)," *Harvard Theological Revue* 36 (1943): 169-246; F.L. Cross, "History and Fiction in the African Canons," *JTS* 69 (1961): 227-47; C. Munier, "Tradition littéraire des conciles africains," *Rech August* 10 (1975): 3-32 ; Ibid, "La tradition littéraire des dossiers africains," *Revue Droit Canonique* 29 (1979): 41-52.
69. A. Di Berardino, ed., *I concili africani*, 2nd. ed., 35.
70. The collection of Chieti, or *Ingilrami*. The manuscript is now in the Vatican Library, *Vatican. Regin.* 1997.
71. Kéry, Lotte, *Canonical Collections of the Early Middle Ages (ca. 400-1140): A Bibliographical Guide to the Manuscripts and Literature* (Washington, D.C.: Catholic University of America Press, 1999), 24f.
72. Leo the Great, *Ep.* 44,3: PL 54:826.
73. See the letters of Leo, *Ep.* 56.1; PL 54:861.
74. D. Moreau, "Non impar conciliorum extat auctoritas. L'origine de l'introduction des lettres pontificales dans le droit canonique," in *L'étude des correspondances dans le monde romain de l'Antiquité classique à l'Antiquité tardive: permanences et mutations*, eds. J. Desmulliez, Chr. Hoët-Van Cauwenberg, J.-Chr. Jolivet (Villeneuve-d'Ascq: Conseil Scientifique, Université Charles-de-Gaulle-Lille 3), 487-506 ; Ph. Blaudeau, *Le siège de Rome et l'Orient (448-536): étude géo-ecclésiologique* (Rome: École française de Rome, 2012), 84-6.
75. Gelasius, the letter *Necessaria rerum*, 14 (Ep. 9.14: PL 59:52). A. Di Berardino (ed.), *I concili della chiesa antica*, II.1, 211.

CHAPTER 2
SPACE AND TIME IN ANCIENT CHRISTIANITY

THE COORDINATES OF SPACE AND TIME PERMIT US TO MAKE AN ADEQUATE RECONSTRUCTION of the birth, development, and the spread of the organization, as well as the positive and negative developments of Christianity in the early centuries of its history. The sources used must be placed in their historical and geographical context. This process is an act of interpretation. An affirmation made in the second century has one significance; the same affirmation made at the end of the fourth century has another. For example, what does a Christian in the year 120 mean when he uses the terms bishop and presbyter, and what does one of the faithful understand by the same terms at the beginning of the fifth century? The terms are the same, but the mental perception is very different.

The difficulty is accentuated for us today in that many words that we use are the same as those used by the Christians of the first century, but their meaning has changed. Words remain like the stones of a Roman building. Their meaning shifts over time. An example of a word that underwent changes in meaning in Latin is *misericordia*. For Cicero, it is an illness (*aegretudo*).[1] In Christian circles, it assumes the meaning of good works: alms, a legacy for the soul after death, compassion, pity, pardon, clemency, etc. It takes on added meaning and resonance, and this also happens in the pagan world and Roman law of the fourth century.[2]

The documents are fixed, but their interpretation changes according to the interest of the reader, their level of education, and the methodologies used. A document responds or does not respond to the questions put to it. It is important to ask the right questions to get the correct answers. If the questions are changed, we will have other answers from the documents. The questions change because of a change of interest, the sensibility of the people, and the time in which one is living. For us, often the interpretation is more important than the document itself. We move on to the interpretations, especially to the new interpretations. We follow fashion. We think that the latest book is better than the preceding one, even about the same subject.

The challenge is to try to take on the same point of view, the mentality and the sensibility of the ancient authors, be they Christian or pagan. The use of modern categories or present-day values leads us astray. For us today, the normal place of study is in the library. The literary mentality is almost innate in us. A document has to be written. One always looks for a previously written text such as in an archaeological excavation, as happens with the synoptic question. In the ancient world of the Roman Empire, there was a great deal of illiteracy. Libraries were found in the large cities but very few could read. Then again, what was understood by "being able to read"? To give an account of something, or read books? Recounting was important—orality. The people gathered and someone told a story. When I was young, very few from my hometown in Italy could read. I do not recall people reading books. The circulation of the written material is essential for the spread of ideas, but in the ancient Roman world, the instrument for the spread of Christianity was the circulation of people.

THE ROMAN EMPIRE UP TO THE 6TH CENTURY

Foundation and expansion

The Roman Empire is substantially born with Augustus Octavianus who was born in 63 BCE: Gaius Octavius. He was adopted by his great-uncle Julius Caesar in his will, and from 44 his official name became Gaius Julius Caesar (Octavianus). From 37 BCE he was known as *Imperator Caesar Divi Filius*—the imperator meant he had triumphed, not in the later meaning of *imperator*, but that of its earlier meaning as victorious commander. But his contemporaries called him Caesar. In 27 BCE, the senate conferred on him the title of Augustus (from *augere*, to lead). Subsequently, emperors would be called Caesar, and then Augustus. From 27 BCE, his official name was *Imperator Caesar D. f. Augustus* (son of Julius Caesar). At different times he was given various judiciaries. Suetonius wrote: "He received offices and honors before the usual (legal) age. Some were created especially for him and they were attributed in perpetuity."[3] The Emperor is also called Augustus (also *Caesar Augustus*); then, the two terms were separated: Augustus, who holds power, Caesar the one designated as successor. Luke notes: "In those days a decree went out from Caesar Augustus that all the world should be registered. This was the first registration when Quirinius was governor of Syria (*Lk* 2:1)." It would seem the terminology of Luke reflects the standard usage of a few decades later.

The Emperor had the following powers. 1) *Tribunicia potestas*: the first prerogative of the tribunes of the pleb was to convene the Plebian Council (annually). It consisted of the right of veto in the Senate and to propose laws for the people. 2) *Imperium proconsolare maius et infinitum*: it was the maximum amount of power, held by the consuls, and embraced both military and civil areas which would remain united until Diocletian. *Imperium* meant he was proconsular because he was in the place of the consul; *maius* because he was superior to the other consuls; *infinitum* both spatially and temporally because he was not limited to just one province and there was no time limit for his reign. Then there was the honorary title of *imperator* which was the title of a victorious general. With the *lex de Imperio* (law of the empire), he had the power to issue constitutions. 3) *Cura legum et morum*: this is the power of control over morality in public life. Based on this, Augustus proposed his law on marriage which severely punished adultery and put a heavy tax on celibacy (the tax was in effect until the time of Constantine who then abolished it). 4) *Pontifex maximus*: he was the head of the college of priests and therefore of the official worship of the *res publica* (the state). He regulated the calendar (*fasti*), etc. The emperors carried the title until 379 (Theodosius); Gratian, who already had the title, abandoned it.

Besides the imperial authority, we find there was the power of the Senate (*diarchy*) which was very important in the first century, although it experienced a progressive decline due to its struggle with the imperial power. In the fourth century, the Senate saw an increase in its constituents which also led to its discrediting as an institution. There were two senates under Constantine: one in Rome and the other in Constantinople. The latter was founded as the senate of the eastern empire. The transformation of the imperial power took place slowly, however. The emperor moved from *princeps* (first citizen) to becoming *dominus* (lord).

When Augustus died in 14 CE he was succeeded by Tiberius (14-37); then Caligula (37-41); Claudius (41-54); Nero (54-68); Galba, Otho, Vitellius (69); Vespasian (69-79); Titus (79-81); Domitian (81-96); Nerva (96-98); Trajan (98-117); Hadrian (117-138), etc. Augustus continued his politics of expansion of the Roman Empire, especially towards the East with the annexation of other territories, among them Egypt, and also founded colonies of Roman citizens, especially in Asia Minor. The defeat of the Roman Legions at Teutoburg (lower Saxony) in 9 CE stopped Roman expansion in Northern Europe. A natural border was created in the North which consisted of the Rhine River to the West and the Danube River running east all the way to the Black Sea in the Balkan Peninsula.

The expansion continued for the whole of the first century. The conquest of Britain, which had already been initiated at the time of Julius Caesar, reached the border with Scotland where Hadrian constructed a wall. There was also an expansion in West Africa (Algeria and Morocco). Trajan (†117) conquered other lands: Dacia (Romania) and many territories in the East as far as the empire could reach. Some territories beyond the rivers Euphrates and

Tigris were abandoned by his successor Hadrian, such as Armenia and the southern part of Mesopotamia.

To control this vast territory, from Scotland to Mesopotamia, was demanding. The Romans, according to the Greek geographer Strabo, applied themselves to make these great projects a reality. He greatly admired their construction enterprises, writing: "The Romans took great care in three things especially which were overlooked by the Greeks: opening roads, building aqueducts, and providing underground sewers."[4] The roads made history in that without them, there was no communication, no transfer of armies, no circulation of people, of ideas, culture, or freight.[5] The administrative efficiency of a great empire depends on the speed and security of communications. It is no accident that the deterioration of the roads in late antiquity was commensurate with the decline of the efficiency of the administration. Marcus Aurelius fought many wars in the Balkans—a portent of the threat of invasion from peoples who settled along the borders of the Empire. Also, the spread of plague which originated in the East foreshadowed difficult times ahead. In the third century, the emperors succeeded in defending the borders. But often there was military anarchy and the emperors didn't live very long. With the arrival of Diocletian in 285, the Empire was stabilized. With Constantine and his sons, there was a substantial period of tranquility with wars waged with those beyond the borders of the empire. In the fourth century, two defeats are of significance: that of Julian by the Sassanids in 363 and, in particular, that of Valens on August 9, 378 at Adrianople (modern Edirne, Turkey) by Fritigern of the Visigoths. The latter was a result of a series of errors by the Roman leaders. The Goths, defeated by Theodosius in 382, were allowed to organize themselves as *foederati* in Lower Moesia (Bulgaria) and were financed by the Romans. The battle of Adrianople was the beginning of the dissolution of the Imperial territories. In 395, Alaric was elected leader of the Visigoths. Theodosius died on January 15 of the same year.

Following the death of Theodosius, the Empire became divided into two parts. The eastern part, with its capital at Constantinople, was given to Arcadius († 408), the western part to Honorius († 423). The Empire was considered one, but in reality, each part was somewhat independent because of territorial, cultural, and political differences.

Upon the death of Alaric in 410, his successor, his brother-in-law Athaulf, went to southern Gaul. The successors of Athaulf expanded into Gaul and Spain. The Visigoth kingdom was born with King Theodoric I (419-451), and his son Euric († 484 in Arles). Because of pressure from Clovis, the Visigoth population in Gaul migrated to Spain between 496 and 507. From the beginning of the fifth century, in a few decades, many of the regions of the Western Empire were lost forever. In 407, the military garrisons began to be withdrawn from Britain. In Gaul in the fifth century, many Roman-Barbarian kingdoms were formed: that of the Franks to the north, that of the Visigoths to the southwest, and that of the

Burgundians to the east. The Franks eventually succeeded and Gaul took the name "Francia." The Germanic provinces such as *Noricum* (Austria) and *Pannonia* (Hungary) were lost in the same period. The vandals occupied Africa in 430. The conventional view is that the western Roman Empire ended in 476 at the hands of Odoacer, king of the Heruli. In 493, the Ostrogoth kingdom of Theodoric the Great once again brought about the unity of Italy which lasted until 535 when the devastating Graeco-Gothic war broke out triggered by Justinian (535-553). This war had terrible consequences for Italy. Every region was devastated, the consequences of which lasted for centuries. In 568, the Lombards arrived, conquering a large part of the peninsula and breaking up any political unity and interdependence the regions might have had.

The eastern part of the empire (the *pars Orientis*) endured much longer. In August of 636, the Byzantine army suffered a terrible defeat in the battle of Yarmuk, in present-day Jordan, at the hands of the Arab Muslims. The Muslims, led by Khalid ibn al-Walid, were united in fighting the infidels. They won a crushing victory which opened the way for the conquest of the eastern provinces and put an end to the Roman rule of the Middle East. Within a few decades, the lands bordering the southern part of the Mediterranean Sea (*Mare nostrum;* lit. "our sea") were lost.

Administration

Emperor Augustus reformed the provincial and fiscal administration and divided the Empire into: 1) *provinciae pacatae* (provinces in peace; senatorial) entrusted to a proconsul, a governor chosen from the senatorial class. Italy was not one province but had been subdivided into eleven regions. The city of Rome itself was divided into 14 administrative regions (*regiones*). 2) *Non pacatae* (provinces not in peace; *Caesaris;* imperial) provinces were those where the army stationed its legions. They were entrusted to a legate (*legatus Augusti*), also a governor from the senatorial class (ex-consuls and ex magistrates). 3) There were also special cases that might call for a prefect (*praefectus*), e.g., Pilate (inscription found in Caesarea.) Egypt is also another case in point. As an imperial province, Egypt was always entrusted to a prefect (*praefectus*) who came from the class of knights (*equites*).

The proconsul, the legate, and the prefect had judiciary, administrative and fiscal powers. For example, we read in the book of Acts: "But when Gallio was proconsul of Achaia, the Jews made a united attack on Paul and brought him before the tribunal (*Acts* 18:12)." At the time of Jesus' birth, Quirinius was described by Luke as the "governor of Syria." He was a legate (*legatus*). The legate also had legions.

This subdivision of provinces and borders varied at times but continued at least until Diocletian, who multiplied the provinces from about fifty to over a hundred. Diocletian separated the civil from the military powers by initiating a large expansion of the bureaucracy (the provincial *officia*). Lactantius writes: "The provinces were divided into minute portions, and there were many governors and a multitude of inferior officers overburdening each territory, as well as most of the cities."[6] The civil power[7] was responsible for the administration of justice and the execution of the fiscal policy of the central government; the dux was responsible for the military. With the reform, the distinction between senatorial and imperial provinces disappeared except in the Asian province and Africa Proconsularis, whose governance was entrusted to a member of the senatorial class. The separation of the two powers, civil and military, did not come about at the same time in all the provinces. In addition, the provinces were grouped into twelve dioceses which were headed by a vicar (*vicarius*), who was in turn subject to the praetorian prefect. The Diocletian reform affected the entire apparatus of the administration and imperial court, establishing new offices (*scrinia*) with specialized personnel. Also, during the fourth century, further adjustments had to be made to this administrative structure. At the beginning of the fifth century, the *Notitia dignitatum* provides us with information about both the civil and military offices and administrations that were found throughout the empire.

The Roman Empire from the early centuries was substantially a grouping of cities (*civitates*), all under the purview of the emperor and with considerably varied legal status. They were like small states. This subdivision no longer existed in the fourth century. In the traditional Greek system, with the electoral procedure, the members of the *boulè* (Council of 500) changed. Therefore, the government was not considered stable or reliable, according to the contemptuous judgment of Cicero: "Those ignorant men, rough and oblivious to everything, sat in the theatre, then started useless wars, then put seditious men in charge, then exiled the most worthy of citizens from the city."[8] In other words, unprepared and seditious people were called to govern, who began useless wars and exiled the best citizens. That means the members of the local curia (boulè) were devoid of prestige (*auctoritas*). In these eastern cities, the Romans required that the members of the curia (*curiales*) must be sufficiently wealthy to be part of the city curia. Therefore, a sort of timocratic government developed in the sense that the rights and the duties of the governors were determined by wealth. The Romans did not try to Romanize the local institutions in spite of setting up colonies. It was convenient for Roman power that the local government was in the hands of those with economic power because it assured peace and the loyalty of the provinces. The provincial aristocrats sought equestrian and senatorial careers, ensuring fidelity to Rome. The Acts of the Apostles reflect this new situation when they speak of the local notables who made decisions concerning Paul. The case was different in Corinth, which was a Roman colony and seat of the governor, or in other colonies that were still predominantly Latin (e.g., Philippi).

As is evident, this whole situation evolved over time. The fourth century was very different from the first century, with power much more centralized and cities having the same statutes and system of governance.

THE CHRISTIAN SPACE

Christian Mission and Geography

Christianity in the early centuries spread mostly in areas within the Roman Empire, but also outside its confines. For the study of Christian missionary activity and religious conversion in the Greek-Roman world, it is worth paying attention to the ancient geography for a better geographical overview of the fathers of the Church.

Here we are speaking of Christianity in general in all its forms, without distinction, including anyone who professes some relationship with Jesus Christ. Until the granting of religious liberty, those who declared themselves Christian in the civil court and refused to carry out pagan religious rituals were condemned as Christians. For the Roman civil authorities, it was sufficient that they declared themselves Christians. They were not interested in their particular creed, be it heretical or orthodox. If, when asked, "Are you Christian?" and the reply was in the affirmative, the suspect was condemned. It was considered more than enough to reply, "I am a Christian" (*christianus sum*).[9] The question of martyrdom was not just about some Christians of a particular social class. It applied to everyone: men and women, free and slaves, young and old. Also, it was not just the leaders of the community who were persecuted. Persecution concerned every Christian who practiced the "true religion," independent of their role in the community. In the *Acts* of the Scilitan martyrs, the pagan proconsul Saturninus affirmed that "we [Romans] are also religious and our religion is simple."[10] For the Christians, the affirmation of faith was not so much about simplicity as it was about truth. As an example, one of the martyrs of Lyon, Attalus, was referred to as "the witness to the truth in our midst."[11]

The Christian religion was typically missionary oriented in contrast to the polytheistic religions. In the ancient word, religion was above all about worship, not about orthodoxy or a rule of life to be followed. Cicero says that religion "is the worship of the gods," so it is about how to adore and worship them. The pagan leaves his religion in the temple,[12] so ancient religion was not concerned with the meaning of human existence, neither does it have a doctrine or an orthodoxy. The addition of new cults does not lead to the abandonment of the preceding ones but is rather considered an enrichment and addition to the faith. In this context, missionary activity, strictly speaking, does not make sense, as it does not have a truth to defend: truth pertains to the area of philosophy and not religion.

In the eastern regions, the Christian mission benefited from the presence of Jews and of synagogues both within the Empire and outside. Christianity arrived later in the places where there were no Jews, while in territories like Mesopotamia and India it arrived rather early, precisely because it was able to benefit from the Jewish network. Furthermore, initially it was easier to address the Jews than the pagans.

Since Christ commanded that Christianity be spread as far as the ends of the earth (*Mt* 28:19), it has from its birth and throughout its long history been strictly linked to geography. The study of any history has to take into account physical and ancient human geography to understand the circulation of the missionaries, ideas, texts, and liturgical traditions. The missionaries had to have knowledge of the spoken languages, the overland roads, the rivers, the sea routes. They needed to be aware of possible journeys for communication between the various churches after their foundation.

After Paul says he turned his attention to the Gentiles, he still continued his preaching among the synagogues. And in the synagogues there were also proselytes (*Acts* 13:43). The Jewish diaspora is an urban phenomenon, and hence it is in the cities that conversions take place. Therefore, Christianity is at least in certain areas an urban phenomenon. The Jews of the diaspora tended to have urban activities: production and commerce rather than agriculture and sheep-farming.

However, the Christian mission was not homogenous. Not all had the same message. There are sometimes notable differences in the success of the mission. Jesus preached in a rural context and villages. He also preached predominantly to Jews, who were the first to believe. Neither was the mission to the Gentiles univocal. There was not just one single theological position regarding the Gentiles. But above all, it was not only Paul who preached to the Gentiles but other missionaries as well.

The first missionaries in Rome, the capital of the Empire—as for most of the other cities—were unknown. Already in the first generation after the death of Jesus, however, they had created small communities of Christians in the various cities. And we have little idea when and how the first Christian community began in Alexandria in Egypt, in Antioch, in Damascus, etc. The origin of African Christianity is emblematic. In the Roman province of Africa Proconsularis, the first testimony comes from the year 180. That year on July 17, six Christians from an unknown locality, Scili (Scilli),[13] were tried at Carthage in the council chamber (*secretarium*[14]) of the proconsul Saturninus who himself had only recently been inaugurated. The village was so small it was not even identified. In the face of their persistence in the faith, the herald (*praecox*) publicly announced to the people gathered outside the *secretarium* the condemnation of the six to death, together with other believers, twelve in all.[15] The existence of the Latin translation of the Pauline letters in books that the proconsul had demanded the Christians hand over points to the existence of a very old community that already used Latin instead of Greek. Furthermore, the use of books points to a characteristic of the Christian communities: they did not only share a common worship but they had books on which they based their thought and conduct. In a way, difficult for us to understand, these books contributed to the creation of a Christian identity both in the content of their convictions and their way of living.

In the second half of the second century Abercius of Hierapolis (different than the Hierapolis where Papias lived) traveled to Rome and to the distant city of Nisibis in Mesopotamia receiving hospitality from the Christian communities. The inscription says: "He (the shepherd) sent me to Rome to behold the palace and see a queen with golden clothes and golden shoes. I saw there a people bearing a shining seal. I also visited the plain of Syria and all its cities and, beyond the Euphrates, Nisibis. And wherever I went I found fellow brothers and sisters in the faith (*confreres*)."[16]

In his travels to far off places, Abercius carried the Letters of Paul. At the time of their death, as we just saw, the Scilitan martyrs possessed some of the founding texts of Christianity and viewed them as their most prized possessions. In Carthage, from 197 onwards, the writings of Tertullian presented a vast and lively community with different currents of thought. The Christian presence had already spread widely by this time.[17]

Since these itinerant missionaries[18] were numerous, the literature of the first and second centuries has much to say about generosity towards them, precautions to take, and especially of the hospitality of individuals and communities as such.

It is clear that the incredible road system created by the Romans enormously facilitated the movement of the missionaries and relations between the churches, even between those far apart.[19] It consisted of a network that was well thought out and technically unified with enormous financial and human investment. It was also protected by the police which rendered travel safer and easier. A fourth century governor of an Arabian border province, crossed by caravans, was praised by the local population for guaranteeing "peace and safety to travelers passing through our regions and for the people."[20]

Christianity spread especially in the cities situated along the great land arteries and in the port cities. The *pax romana* which prevailed within the confines of the empire permitted the movement of people. An inscription from some decades before Paul's arrival in Anatolia captures the climate of peace, of tranquility, order, and progress in the western part of Asia Minor. It comes from the Greek city of Halicarnassus (Bodrum) in Caria, in the province of Asia. The inscription offers effusive praise to the emperor Augustus, a savior sent by the gods and a god also himself.[21] "Savior of all humanity, your provident care has not only satisfied but has surpassed the hopes of all. Both earth and sea are in peace. The cities redound with the gifts of concord, riches, and respect for the law, and the culmination and synthesis of all the good things bring the right hope and the present satisfaction."[22]

The *pax romana* favored the spread of Christianity as well as the other eastern religions, as they could all move around in an immense area without frontiers as though it were the territory of one city. At the beginning of the fifth century upon his return to his Gallic homeland, Rutilius Namatianus exclaimed: "You (Rome) have made one homeland for many peoples. It was very fortunate for barbarian peoples to be annexed to your dominion. While you offered the losers to participate in your right, you have made a city out of what was previously the world."[23]

All missionaries did not head in the same direction. In fact, they traveled to many different regions. For their mission in lands far away from their usual horizons they needed to have an idea of the geography of the time, of the connecting roads, of the peoples and of the cities they were going to evangelize. Jerusalem was a privileged place of observation and information as pilgrims came there from many regions. The Acts of the Apostles offers a geographical cross-section of people present in Jerusalem: "Now there were staying in Jerusalem God-fearing Jews from every nation under heaven (...) There were Parthians, Medes, and Elamites; residents of Mesopotamia, Judea and Cappadocia, Pontus and Asia, Phrygia and Pamphylia, Egypt and the parts of Libya near Cyrene; visitors from Rome (both Jews and converts to Judaism); Cretans and Arabs—we hear them declaring the wonders of God in our tongues!" (*Acts* 2:5-11).

These missionaries, however, did not have maps in any modern sense. In the ancient world when maps were designed they were not drawn according to the physical and human configuration of the earth's surface—as is done today for geographical maps—but according to the traveler's perspective, that is, according to his perception of his place in relation to his geography and the world around him. The maps described but did not present the physical geography; rather they presented the roads to be traveled. Furthermore, the representation and the cartographic perception were much different from ours in that we are used to geographical maps and the representation of the physical territory. The perception of the geographical space of the ancients followed the ethnographic criterion concerning the people who lived in the territories both near and far. Such peoples are described according to their customs and their way of living such as food, clothing, funeral rites, houses, and their language.[24] With the building of roads punctuated by milestones (*caput viae*) which signaled the distance from the city of reference , the Romans provided a sense of the distance from one place to another with great precision. Outside of this special concept of the Romans, the sense of distance was also given in the time taken to travel. The writers speak of a two, three, four day walk. A voyage by sea, on the other hand, was calculated differently with the understanding that sea travel was very dangerous since most ships were of a relatively small size. The measuring of geographical space and distances in general was quite relative because the speed, depending on the instruments used and the mode of travel chosen, could vary enormously.

The old saying that "all roads lead to Rome" is true at the end of the first century CE and in the successive centuries. This was because the Romans were very careful about the construction, maintenance and improvements of communications with the capital, from which all the provincial administrators left, and to which arrived the many delegations of the citizenry. In the second century, all the different Christian schools of thought and their protagonists came to Rome. It seemed a message was not effective or had no value if it did not somehow make it to Rome. Just as all roads led to Rome as a point of reference, so too all those who had a doctrine to defend came to Rome.

Christianity's Expansion

Below is a very brief geographical panorama of the spread of Christianity in the first five centuries.

In the first centuries, Christianity spread mainly within the Roman Empire but also outside its borders, in particular beyond the frontiers of its eastern provinces: in Armenia, Southern Mesopotamia, Adiabene, and even in southwestern India. The missionaries initially addressed both Jews and gentiles, but very soon almost exclusively the pagans alone. This phenomenon did not happen in the same way and at the same time in all places.

In the second generation of Christians, Christian communities were already composed of Gentiles. Perhaps it is significant that the recipients of the *First Letter of Peter*, which was closely linked to the deutero-Pauline Letters written in Rome after the 80s, was addressed in the very first verse: "To God's elect, exiles scattered throughout the provinces of Pontus, Galatia, Cappadocia, Asia, and Bithynia." There was a very rapid and effective initial missionary expansion. Soon after this, commitment to itinerant missionaries seems to have disappeared because it is no longer documented. In the second century, the missionary zeal accompanied by broad outreach seemed to lessen. The preference became more towards working in the local environment.

In many Roman provinces in the first three centuries, Christianity was an urban reality limited to large and smaller cities, but it was not the case everywhere. In some regions, it reached small towns and villages. Not only in Phrygia, Pontus and Bithynia, but one also imagines in northwest Africa where there were bishops in unknown locations and, therefore, of little importance.

Trying to understand the spread of Christianity in spatial terms presents numerous problems. What should one put on a map: only the episcopal sees, or all the places where one could show there was a Christian presence, even it was only minimal? In this regard, we meet with many inconsistencies. Here is but one example: we could put 150 episcopal sees on a map (their number was somewhat higher) in Roman Africa at the beginning of the fourth century, but there is no definitive Christian archaeological or epigraphic evidence. It is simply incredible that in a territory with a strong Christian presence, there is only a whisper of archaeological evidence before Constantine. Some evidence comes from far away Caesarea of Mauritania, today Cherchel (Algeria). Two inscriptions carry the name of a *clarissimus* ("a highly regarded man" cf. Severianus) and a presbyter.[25] The Letters of Cyprian and his councils are a precious source of information for the first half of the third century. But we do not have literary sources, and we know of no missionaries or bishops who traveled, for instance, to Dacia Traiana (now central Romania). Although there are no literary sources, there is archaeological evidence which, together with Christian symbols, proves the existence of Christians in the Dacia already before Constantine. Gnostic gems have also been found at Porolissum (Moigrad, Transylvania), three with the Abrasax inscription at Romula/Malva[26] and at Orlea,[27] on the Danube a little above the Iron Gate where Trajan had a spectacular bridge built during the war with Decebalus, remembered still with an inscription on the site of the *Tabula Traiana*.

In the west, for centuries Christianity was limited to the areas of the Roman Empire even after the empire itself had ceased to exist. The mission to the Angles and the Germans of the interior began much later. In the fourth century, Christianity had already reached Ethiopia and was pushing further east into Yemen and India. In Asia, in the fourth century, it had spread to Armenia, a land that linked the Persian Empire with the Roman Empire. In the Roman Empire, the city of Rome (*urbs*) was the political and ideal center. It was known as "the capital of the world."[28] In the first and second centuries everyone refers to Rome as the capital and many went there to visit and to settle. Rome as the center of everything breaks down in the fourth century. The mental geography, especially of the Mediterranean people, had been extended towards the east, towards Asiatic horizons, beginning with Alexander the Great. Commercial relations opened up vast horizons for the movement of goods and people and with them their ideas and religions. The *Res gestae divi Augusti*, which all could read in many cities as they were publicly displayed, offered a very impressive vast mental and geographic horizon of territories and peoples.

We know that at the beginning of the fourth century there are areas of the Roman Empire where the Christian presence is very strong, whereas in other areas the population is exclusively pagan. There are a number of examples of this. According to the testimony of Eusebius, a city of Phrygia was set on fire by Diocletian because the whole population declared itself Christian: "All the inhabitants of this city, in fact, without distinction declared themselves Christians, including the imperial commissioner (or curator), the magistrates with all the curia along with the entire population."[29] Lactantius too recalls the episode of a fire in a town of Phrygia without giving the name.[30] This city according to the hypothesis of Ramsey,[31] could be Eumeneia (today Işikli, on the lake of the same name), in Phrygia Pacatiana, because the archaeological excavations have shown that there was a fire there at that time.

In Palestine, Eusebius names only three Christian villages: Aniata, Ietheira and Cariatha. The last was a village of Idumea (Arabia) near Madaba. All were inhabited by Christians.[32] In the middle of the fourth century, we find Christian communities also in the villages in the interior of the Libyan Pentapolis, sometimes with a bishop. In 411 Synesius of Cyrene, in his letter 66 (67) addressed to Theophilus of Alexandria relates his experience of being bishop of Cyrenaica. He had gone to the villages of Palaebiscus and Hydrax, near the Libyan desert, where he was sent by Bishop Theophilus to resolve a dispute and where there was now a young bishop (Paul).

The population of Phrygia already in the third century was largely Christian, composed of both Catholics and Montanists. For example, at the beginning of the fourth century there could be a village which was majority Christian and the one beside it pagan (e.g., Orcistus and Nacoleia; Eumeneia[33] had a Christian majority). In Eumeneia and the surrounding area, many Christian inscriptions dated to the third century were found with the names of two bishops.[34] In Phrygia, inscriptions by Christian soldiers who would have certainly fought elsewhere were found. The most mobile soldiers were the members of the *comitatus*, the army which accompanied the emperor. Among these there is an interesting case study by Drew-Bear[35] concerning a Christian soldier who fought at the time of Diocletian, and who was buried in the vicinity of the ancient city of Cotiaeum (today Kütahya, Turkey). Aurelius Gaius began his service in Moesia on the Danube. He then changed to a different legion and fought in Scythia and Pannonia, making a career in the legions and becoming a member of the *comitatus*.[36] In that same area, the Christian presence was uneven and sometimes radically different. The presence of Christians did not necessarily mean there was an organized community. A few decades later, Julian the emperor attests that the inhabitants of Nisibis (Nusaybin, in Mesopotamia) were all Christians.[37] And yet his successor Jovian gave Nisibis to the Sassanid Empire in 363. Its population, which had been Roman, was replaced with 12,000 Persians. Thus the city changed its ethnic and religious identity. The deacon Ephrem along with the Christian community there was forced to emigrate and move to Edessa. To show his regret and nostalgia, he composed the *Carmina Nisibena* (the Nisibene Hymns).

PALESTINE, ARABIA

Christianity, which was born in Palestine and immediately went beyond its confines, has little presence in the region in the first three centuries. The presence of the "holy" places of the New Testament did not favor an immediate and widespread diffusion. If the first Christians were almost exclusively of Jewish origin, from the second half of the second century, they were mainly of Gentile origin.

At the time of Diocletian, according to Eusebius of Caesarea—an authoritative witness—numerous Christians witnessed to their faith by martyrdom; but in Palestine, few buildings were erected to honor them. In 2005, a place of Christian cult was discovered in Palestine,[38] at Kefar Othnay near Tel Megiddo. The house was used by soldiers as a place of prayer. In the house, dated to before the persecution (around 230), the Christian symbol of the fish and three inscriptions in Greek were found in the 54 square meter mosaic. One commemorates a centurion who had contributed to the construction,[39] while another honors three women[40] along with a fourth who had donated the altar table in memory of Jesus Christ, with the inscription in Greek: "Akeptous, one who loves God, offered the table as a memorial to God Jesus Christ." Some decades later, after 325, an intense desire to visit the "holy" places developed. Only in the sixth century, do we hear the expression the "holy land."[41] Monasticism began in Palestine early in the fourth century with Hilarion of Thavata (in the region of Gaza), with Epiphanius in Eleutheropolis (in the vicinity of Beit Guvrin) and with Chariton in the Judean Desert.

EGYPT, NUBIA, ETHIOPIA

When did Christianity arrive in Alexandria and Egypt? Eusebius of Caesarea writes that it is said that Mark, the Evangelist, went to Egypt.[42] There are no records before this 4th century reference. The Bishop Annianus (62-84) would have succeeded Mark in Alexandria. However, at the end of the second century and the beginning of the third, important personalities appear in Alexandria, such as Pantaenus, Clement, Bishop Demetrius (189-233), and the great Origen with his *Didaskaleion*. Clement testifies to the existence of a strong Christian community in Alexandria, a community of high social standing and education (see especially the *Paedagogus*). The same could not be said of the extensive Egyptian hinterland. The Christianization of the countryside is not well documented. A *libelli*, issued during the persecution of Decius (249-251), testifies to a robust pagan presence; some of these might have been Christians who had performed an act of worship or perhaps they had bought the *libelli*. Alexander, bishop of Alexandria (312-328), and Athanasius affirm that a synod of one hundred bishops had met before 325 to judge Arius. A. Martin identified only fifty-seven episcopal sees for Egypt and twenty-six for Libya and the Pentapolis at that time.[43]

The Council of Chalcedon (451) condemned Dioscorus, the bishop of Alexandria, for heresy. In 457, Timothy II Aelurus, an anti-Chalcedonian, was elected while his successor Timothy III Salophakiolos was elected on the other side. From this point until the Arab conquest Egypt was more or less divided—in particular Alexandria which frequently had two patriarchs. The first, the minority, was Chalcedonian and loyal to the empire. The second, the majority, was anti-Chalcedonian consisting of most of the Coptic population which experienced persecution under Cyrus of Phasis (†642).

In Libya, particularly in Greek-speaking Cyrenaica, from the third century the churches were closely connected to those of Alexandria whose Bishop Dionysius sent letters to two bishops of Libya: one to Ammonius of Berenice against Sabellius, and another to Basilides bishop of the ecclesial community (*paroikon*) of the Pentapolis who underwent exile twice, once at the time of Decius (250) and a second time under Valerian (258).[44] Arianism also received substantial support in Libya, although Arius himself was not from Libya. Several Libyan bishops were present at the Council of Nicaea which confirmed the traditional dependence of the Libyan churches on the bishop of Alexandria (Can. 6).

Synesius of Cyrene († 413), bishop of Ptolemais, is the best-known personage of the Pentapolis. Two of his letters (especially letters 67 and 76 to Theophilus of Alexandria) contain matters relating to the Barbarian incursions into the territory of Cyrenaica, which are of great importance for the civil history. We also gain insight concerning its religious state of affairs in the first decade of the fifth century from the events recorded in these letters concerning the diocese of Erythron of the Cyrenaica.

There were most likely Christians present in Nubia before the conversion of the country by the Presbyter Julianus and Bishop Theodore of Philae in the sixth century.[45] In nearby Ethiopia from the beginning of the fourth century evangelization is linked to a precise moment, recorded both in the inscriptions and in the coins (signed with the symbol of the cross) as well as in the literary sources. A detailed and precise description comes to us from Rufinus.[46] Around 303, among others, Meropius and two boys, Frumentius and Edesius, landed in the port of Adulis (?) to secure a fresh supply of water for their ship. They were taken prisoner, however, growing up in the king's household. Frumentius later went to Alexandria about 330/340, and Athanasius ordained him bishop, and had him return to Ethiopia where Christianity then spread quite easily.

Syria, Mesopotamia, Adiabene

The term *Syria* included a vast region including Cilicia. Christianity spread in Syria very early starting with the first Christian missions to Tyre (*Acts* 21:4-7), Ptolemais (*Acts* 21:7), Damascus (*Acts* 9:2-22), Sidon (*Acts* 27:3) and Antioch (*Acts* 11:19ff), to name a few. The Antioch community was especially open to missions both towards the East (with ties to Edessa) and the West. The two great bishops of the second century, Ignatius and Theophilus, express two different aspects of how they viewed Christianity. Ignatius expresses a high spirituality of martyrdom along with a profound sense of Christian community, while Theophilus is known for his openness towards Hellenistic culture. A prominent figure in the third century was Paul of Samosata who combined a civil career with an ecclesiastical career and was an exponent of an archaic Christology expressed in monarchical terms. In a synod of 268/269, he was condemned by 70 or 80 bishops.

The prestige of the church of Antioch is confirmed by the Council of Nicaea (325), which recognized it as having a pre-eminence together with Alexandria and Rome (can. 5). In 431, the Church of Cyprus obtained autonomy, and at Chalcedon, the Palestinian churches were made independent from Antioch. The limestone massif in the vicinity of Antioch, was filled with many churches though a few tribes remained pagan. Likewise, in some areas such as Berea and Apamea, Judeo-Christian forms tied to the Aramaic tradition spread. During the reign of Emperor Julian (361-363), strong reactions against Christians were registered in different cities such as at Arethusa, Emesa and Damascus. At Nicaea, there were 23 Syrian bishops, some of whom came from beyond the border; in the whole of the *diocesis Orientis*, there were about eighty bishops, while at the Council of Chalcedon in 451 there were one hundred and twenty.

Monasticism developed widely in Syria, as in other oriental regions. The principal source for our knowledge about Syrian monasticism up to about 444 is the *Ecclesiastical History* of Theodoret of Cyrrhus who mentions the monasteries he knew. This was during the period of the birth of the cenobitic form. Syria also was the meeting place between the Greek and Semitic Christian traditions.

Cilicia, Isauria, Cyprus. Cilicia (with Isauria) is closely connected with Syria both geographically and culturally. Ignatius speaks of Christians in Cilicia. Dionysius of Alexandria speaks of Helenus the bishop of Tarsus.[47] At Nicaea, there were nine bishops and one *chorepiscopos* (country bishop). The metropolitan see of Isauria was Seleucia which is today known as Silifke. From this province, there were ten bishops and five *chorepiskopoi* at the Council of Nicaea (a sign of ecclesiastical organization). The city of Seleucia, five kilometers from the sea, was famous for its Shrine dedicated to Thecla, the saint of Iconium.

Cyprus was the homeland of Barnabas, of the tribe of Levi (*Acts* 4:36), who was born on the island, as was also Mnason (*Acts* 21:16). The first bishop would have been Heraclides. At the time of Diocletian, some Palestine Christians were exiled to Cyprus. At the Council of Nicaea, there were three Cypriot bishops present. The ecclesiastical metropolis was Salamis (*Constantia*), a prestigious see on account of Epiphanius. From the Council of Ephesus (431) onward, Salamis was recognized as autocephalous.

Mesopotamia a Greek term indicating the territories between the two great rivers of the Euphrates and the Tigris. Today it corresponds to the territory of Iraq and is part of Turkey. There were many Jewish communities in Mesopotamia.[48] Ancient traditions date the first spread of Christianity in Mesopotamia to Thaddeus-Addai, Mari, Thomas, and Bartholomew.

Addai, one of the seventy-two disciples, would have arrived in Edessa soon after the Ascension of Jesus. According to Lavenant, "Syriac Christianity recruited its first followers in the Jewish community of Adiabene, which were numerous at the time of this kingdom, whose dynasty from very ancient times after the conversion of its sovereigns to Judaism maintained close relations with Palestine."[49] The late second century inscription of Abercius of Hierapolis attests that the author went to Mesopotamia where he met some of the brothers. During this same time period, in the *Book of the Laws of Countries*, Bardaisan certifies a Christian presence at Edessa, at Hatra and in other eastern regions including Gilan[50] and Galatias, Parthia, Media, Persia and even among the Qušan.[51] Ephrem the Syrian (or, of Nisibis; †373) was an important leader in the church at the time. The official border between the Sassanid Empire and that of Rome was quite permeable for the Christians who moved from one zone to another; above all, they were united by a common language and a common culture.

Adiabene corresponds to the heart of the Assyrian empire, extending to the east of the Tigris River. Pliny speaks of Armenian Adiabene, previously called Assyria.[52] Adiabene, conquered by Trajan, was abandoned by Hadrian who also retreated from Armenia. Tatian, an Assyrian, was a disciple of Justin in Rome around the middle of the second century. He then returned to his own country where he composed the *Diatessaron*, which is one of the earliest harmonies of the four Gospels. The greater part of Adiabene was Christian by the middle of the fourth century. The center of Adiabene was the city of Arbela (today, Erbil, Iraq). We do not know when it received its first bishop.

An Aramaic church outside of the Roman Empire developed in the Persian kingdom, a fertile area for religious syncretism. When the Sassanids invaded the Roman Empire, they deported Christians from the Middle East. Then two communities were created, one Greek-speaking and the other speaking the local language, each with its own bishop. Because of this the Council of Seleucia-Ctesiphon of 410 established that in the same city there should be only one bishop.

Armenia and Georgia

Armenia and Georgia are two regions which remained outside the Roman Empire even though occasionally Roman armies came there. However, both regions felt the empire's influence because of travel and commerce. Christianity spread in Armenia through the work of Gregory the Illuminator (†about 332) at the beginning of the fourth century. The court and its king Tiridates III (Trdat III; Latin: Tiridates) converted. At the beginning of the fifth century, a monk named Maštot created the Armenian alphabet. The spread of Christianity in Georgia came about, at the beginning of the fourth century, through the work of a woman, Saint Nino.

Asia Minor

The term Asia is fluid. In the first century, the territory of Asia Minor was divided into provinces. The province Asia embraces the western part with the cities of Smyrna and Ephesus, the capital. Evangelization came through the work of Paul and John. Paul initially worked in Galatia in the western part of the province of Asia. In certain areas, Christianity spread very rapidly, especially in Phrygia. In Bithynia and Pontus at the time when Pliny was governor, he noted that Christianity was very widespread: "Not only the city but also the villages and the countryside are rife with the contagion of this superstition."[53] Only later do the Christians reach other regions such as Cappadocia. However, the First Letter of Peter, written in Rome, is addressed "to the faithful scattered in Pontus, Galatia, Cappadocia, Asia and Bithynia" (*1 Pet* 1:1). This sentence shows that Christianity had spread, at least in the cities, in this province by the 80s of the first century. The great Christian missionaries created a small community in important cities and then left for other destinations. That community then became a center for missionary efforts in its territory. The letter of the Apocalypse to the seven churches of Ephesus, Smyrna, Pergamum, Thyatira, Sardis, Philadelphia, and Laodicea ad Lycum is important: All the cities are in proconsular Asia. The number seven is symbolic: the Christian communities would have been more, and the letter is addressed to the whole province. The Pauline letters demonstrate the existence of communities at Colossae, Laodicea, and Hierapolis; the letters of Ignatius (ca. 110) mention the communities of Tralles and Magnesia.

The sources from the second and third centuries continue to give us information on the spread of Christianity, even in secondary cities. The Christians of Smyrna wrote to the Christians of Philomelium (southeast Phrygia) upon the death of Polycarp. Some martyrs of Galatia are remembered in the second century.[54] Tertullian speaks of persecution, where he lived in Carthage.[55] The *Apocalypse* and the letters of Ignatius also mention heresies. Another problem for the Christians of Asia was their relationship with the Jews who had significant communities in some cities (e.g., Smyrna, Aphrodisias, Apamea, Sardis, Antioch of Pisidia, Iconium). The persecution of Diocletian produced numerous martyrs: many of these were venerated at the shrines built after their death. The principal shrines were: Euphemia at Chalcedon, Theodore of Amasea at Euchaita,[56] John at Ephesus, Philip at Hierapolis (Phrygia), and Tecla at Seleucia (Isauria). During the fourth century, Christianity continued to spread more widely. There were about 150 bishops from the whole of Anatolia at the Council of Nicaea in 325, some of them from very small communities. Religious diversity was still very prominent in the whole area. Phrygia was the land of the Montanists; the Novatians were widespread in Bithynia, Paphlagonia, Phrygia, and Lydia. The majority of the population was still pagan, however, practicing different cults, with some areas having a strong Christian presence (Nicomedia, Orcistus, Eumeneia, Laodicea, villages of Phrygia, territories between Isauria and Lycaonia, etc.).[57]

The decree of Maximin Daia of 312 sums up the pagan sensibility of the ruling classes of the small centers.[58] By the end of the fourth century almost all of the pagan temples had been closed and the pagan cult connected with them survived in a greatly reduced form. The testimony of the emperor Julian is noteworthy when in 362 while crossing Asia Minor, he noticed the painful state of the pagan cult and temples.[59] A few decades later, Gregory of Nyssa affirmed that in Cappadocia paganism was just a memory[60] but that was an exaggeration. Many pagan forms continued to survive also in the following century.

GREECE

Greece is a term I use to indicate territories which have different names in the Roman period: Macedonia, Achaia, Epirus, and Crete. The apostle Paul was the first to preach the gospel in Greece; we know about his mission from his letters and the *Acts of the Apostles*. Philippi, a Roman colony in Macedonia, became the first Greek city to welcome Christianity. According to the *Acts of the Apostles*, the missionary activity of Paul and his helpers continued in Thessalonica (*Acts* 17:1), at Berea (*Acts* 17:10), at Athens (*Acts* 17:17) and Corinth (*Acts* 18:1). In the *Letter to the Romans* (15:19), Paul writes: "so that from Jerusalem and as far round as Illyricum, I have fully proclaimed the good news of Christ." At Corinth, because of the refusal of the Jews, he declared: "From now on, I will go to the Gentiles." (*Acts* 18:6). The city of Thessalonica (founded in 313/314 BCE) is the most important city of Macedonia for political as well as commercial reasons; it even became a colony of the Roman Empire. Before entering Constantinople, Theodosius resided there. Thessalonica was where the famous decree known as the *cunctos populus* of February 27, 380 emanated.[61] It advanced Christianity from being the favored religion of the Empire to the official religion of the Empire.

Melito of Sardis reminds the emperor Antoninus Pius (138-161) that when Hadrian governed with him, he had written to the cities of Thessalonica, Athens, and Larissa and all the Greeks so that they would not take measures against the Christians.[62] Dionysius from Corinth wrote to the Christians of Sparta to exhort them to peace and unity.[63] Eusebius refers to Origen who was sent to Achaia to resolve some questions,[64] something which is referred to also by Jerome.[65]

The *Letter to Titus* tells of the work of Titus in Crete (*Tit* 1:5-9). He was the first bishop of the island.[66] At Bouthroton,[67] a city populated by veteran Romans from the time of Augustus the Decian martyr Terenus († 251) is mentioned. A bishop from the island of Lemnos took part in the Council of Nicaea in 325.

Those registered for the Council of Nicaea in 325 indicate there was a sparse participation of bishops from the civil diocese of Macedonia: just six bishops—two from Macedonia (Thessalonica and Stobi [Budius]), two from Achaia (Athens [Pistus] and Eubea, two from Thessaly (Thebes in the Phiotides and Larissa). The bishops of the Pauline foundations of Philippi, Berea, and Corinth, were not represented. But there was representation by the bishops of five new churches: Thebes, Euboea, Hephaestias (island of Lemnos), Stobi, and Nicopolis. There was a greater participation of bishops at the Council of Serdica (Sofia) in 342/343. Origen, according to Eusebius,[68] went to Athens, where he finished his *Commentary on Ezekiel* and began the one on the *Canticle of Canticles*. Origen himself testifies that "the Church of God which is in Athens loves order and peace; therefore, it wants to acquire the grace of the Almighty God; look at the assembly of Athenian citizens on the other hand: how loud they are, how disordered! It does not bear comparison with the Church of God in that city."[69]

Nicopolis (present day, ruins to the north of Préveza in Greece, south of Igoumenitza) is in Epirus, and it was founded near Actium, as a colony by Octavian in memory of his victory over Anthony and Cleopatra. The *Letter to Titus* affirms that Paul thought of spending the winter at Nicopolis (3:12). According to Eusebius, Origen had been in Nicopolis,[70] perhaps during his journey to Rome, where he had found the Greek translation of the Hebrew Bible by the Jewish Translator Theodotion. Eusebius points to the presence of bishops from Epirus at the Council of Nicaea, together with Thracian, Macedonian, and Achaean bishops,[71] but we do not know any of their names.

The *Letter to Titus* supposes the evangelization of the island of Crete by Paul (1:5), where he left Titus to continue his mission; moreover, the Christian community was obstructed by the Judaizers.[72] In the letter of the Cretan episcopate addressed to Emperor Leo I regarding the killing of Peter of Alexandria (454), eight suffragans dioceses supported the metropolitan of Gortyna.[73] The Cretan church venerates a group of "ten holy" martyrs under Decius.[74] The bishop Paul exhumed their remains at the time of Constantine.

Thrace

Thrace (civil diocese) was the region north of Macedonia, between the Danube, the river *Oescus* (Iskar) and the Black Sea (Bulgaria, Greece, and Turkey) and was inhabited by various tribes. Among these, the Greek culture spread first and then the Latin. In late antiquity, three entities are indicated by the term Thrace: a) the traditional Thracian territory; b) the province Thrace; c) the diocese Thrace (or *Thraciae*), which includes six provinces. Today they belong to different nationalities, but mainly to Bulgaria. Byzantium (Constantinople) was in Thrace. In various localities, we know the names of martyrs.

Scythia (today Romania on the Black Sea) would have been evangelized by the apostle Andrew.[75] Commercial contracts with the Orient and the presence of soldiers were probably the main carriers of Christianity to the lower Danube. The Diocletian persecution, according to martyrological and archaeological sources, made many martyrs in the cities there. The first known bishop of Tomis was Evangelicus. An inscription names a bishop martyr, not identified, maybe from the time of Licinius; there was a bishop whose name we do not know at Nicaea.[76] At the time of the emperor Zeno, in 480, Tomis (Constanța) was the metropolitan see and the seat of civil government, but the churches "were constantly upset by the incursions of the Barbarians."[77]

Dacia Traiana (the greater part of Romania) did not form part of the Roman Empire from the time of Aurelianus. The Roman citizens and the name were transferred to the south side of the river Danube. Constantine created the diocese of Dacia with five provinces, and two of them are called *Dacia Mediterranea* (southwest Bulgaria; capital Serdica [today Sofia]), Dacia Ripensis with its capital Ratiaria (near present-day Archar, Bulgaria) on the river Danube. The other diocese is made up of Moesia, Serbia, and other nationalities. Already from the third century starting from Macedonia and Thrace in the south Christianity began to spread. Thanks to numerous epigraphical and written sources, we know of the existence of various Christian centers and their ecclesiastical organization (bishops, priests, deacons). Significantly, an ecclesiastical council was held at Serdica in 342/43.

Following the Council of Nicaea, the Arian heresy spread in the Balkan peninsula after Arius and some of his followers were exiled there. The fact that two Illyrian Arian bishops, Valens of Mursa[78] and Ursacius of Singidunum[79] participated in the Council of Tyre in 335, can be explained by the presence of exiled Arians in the area. In 335/336 Athanasius crossed Illyria on his journey into exile in Trier and met the Nicene bishops there. In 343 he was a guest of Gaudentius of Nish (Niš, Serbia) while on his way to Aquileia. He ended up spending Easter of 345 there in Nish. In numerous areas of Moesia various buildings for Christian worship existed, although they were often in ruin: basilicas, cruciform churches, etc. The remains of over eighty churches can be found in present-day Bulgaria which includes Lower Moesia and Thrace. Moesia was a province where Latin was the principal language of the liturgy of the Christians, in contrast to Thrace where the Greek language was dominant along with the local language of the Thracians.

Gothia

Among the bishops at the Council of Nicaea (325) was a bishop named Theophilus from Gothia, which some say is an area of Tauric Chersonese, and others understand it to be Danubian Gothia. This term recurs regularly among Christian authors of the fourth and fifth centuries. Therefore, among the Goths there were Christians captured during the raids; some were killed. But missionaries also worked among the Goths. Wulfila (311-383) was one such evangelist who was ordained bishop by the Arian Eusebius of Nicomedia. Because of this, they became Arian Christians and they remained so even when they occupied and evangelized kingdoms within the Empire (in Aquitaine, Spain, Italy). Wulfila translated the Bible into Gothic. The Ostrogoths although quite tolerant always remained Arian, while the Visigoths in Spain converted to Catholicism under king Recared (586-601).

According to an ancient tradition, the apostle Andrew went to the Crimea and also spent time among the Scythians.[80] Clement of Rome was exiled to work in a stone quarry in the Crimea at the time of Trajan where he was killed by drowning in the sea. His "remains" were brought back to Rome by Saint Cyril before 869. Pope Martin was exiled to the Crimea by the Byzantine Emperor Constans II (†668) where he died of starvation in 655. The deposed emperor Justinian II († 711) was likewise exiled in the Crimea. Christian archaeological evidence from the end of the third century and the beginning of the fourth testifies to the first Christian presence. There are also coins which bear the sign of the cross.[81] The first Christian inscription goes back to 304.

Pannonia

The term *Pannonia* indicates three distinct realities: a) the Pannonian plain in the strict sense; b) the Pannonian province; c) the *diocesis Pannoniarum* in late antiquity. In this section, we will speak of both the province and the civil diocese. A great part of Pannonia corresponds to modern day Hungary. *Illyricum* (or Illyria) represents a vast geographic area. In very ancient times the term indicated the regions close to Epirus and Macedonia. In the Roman era it embraced the area from Istria to southern Albania with the eastern limits extending to the rivers Morava (central Serbia) and Vardar.[82]

Many of the Christian names in the oldest inscriptions are of Greek origin, showing that the missionaries came from the south, while from the middle of the fourth century the bishops were mostly Latins. The martyr Victorinus (†304?), bishop of Poetovio (Ptuj),[83] was of eastern origin but wrote in Latin; he has given us useful information on Christianity in Pannonia. Christianity was quite varied, also due to the presence of different heretical tendencies. Another episcopal see was that of Siscia (Savia province), whose Bishop Quirinius[84] was killed at Savaria (Szombathely), then capital of the province of Pannonia Prima. Martin, the future bishop of Tours, was born in Savaria (more probably in 316 than 336). A third see was Cibalae[85] whose Bishop Eusebius had been dead for some time, perhaps killed during the persecution of Valerian (257/259).

After the Council of Nicaea (325), the Balkan peninsula had many Arian bishops because Arius and some of his followers (two bishops, priests, and deacons) were exiled to an unknown place (perhaps Pannonia) in *Illyricum*. In the fourth century, the city of Sirmium was often the residence of emperors and where they held many conciliar meetings.[86] At Aquincum (Budapest), there are numerous testimonies to a Christian presence during the post-Constantinian period, in particular, a *basilica coemeterialis*. At Scarbantia (Sopron, Hungary) are kept the remains of Bishop Quirinus of Siscia (Sisak) who died in 308. At Sopianae (Pécs, Hungary), there is a Christian cemetery and other evidence of a Christian presence; Christian remains are at Ulpianum.[87]

DALMATIA

The term *Dalmatia* derives from one of the many Illyrian tribes[88] who lived on the Adriatic coast in the area of Salona. Therefore, it was closely connected in its historical context with Illyricum. The Pauline Letters mention the evangelization of Illyria: "So that from Jerusalem and as far round as Illyricum, I have fully preached the Gospel of Christ" (*Rom* 15:19). They also mention Dalmatia (*2 Tim* 4:10). We know nothing further and have to wait until the third century to find out more about Christianity in the area. The first bishop of Salona was Domnius, who came from Nisibis. He was martyred on April 10, 304, together with four soldiers and the presbyter Asterius. His nephew Primus (†325) succeeded him. He is buried at Manastirine, the first necropolis just outside the city. His sarcophagus is still preserved. The Bishop Maximus participated in the Council of Serdica (343). At the beginning of the fifth century, Hesychius was a well-known bishop who had received correspondence from Pope Zozimus. The inscriptions of late antiquity help us to know the history of the city and the region. They speak about its civil, military, and ecclesiastical organization.

NORICUM AND RHAETIA

Noricum and *Rhaetia* (and *Vindilicia*) were two Roman provinces created in the first century CE. They took in a vast territory which stretched from Slovenia to France below the river Danube,[89] constituting the northern limit of the Empire. The territory included Austria (west of Vienna which belonged to Pannonia), Slovenia, southern Germany, Switzerland and parts of Italy. The Christian religion in central and northern Noricum only spread in the fourth century. It spread from the south principally due to the work of the Christian communities of the Upper Adriatic—including Aquileia and Pannonia—made up of mainly merchants and soldiers. In the previous period, there is only scarce evidence of a Christian presence. Victorinus of Potovio's writings indicate there was a vibrant community there. The *Passio Floriani*, records the death of Florian, who died near the river Enns in Lorch (*castrum Lauriacense* in Austria). It mentions the governor Aquilinus who triggered persecution with the arrest of forty Christians. Among them was Florianus, the *princeps officii* (chief official) who resided in Cetium (St. Pölten). The essential nucleus of the *Passio* is considered historically valid.[90] At that time, Noricum was under the emperor Galerius. Orthodox bishops participated in the Council of Serdica (343) according to the testimony of Athanasius,[91] but the number and the sees are not indicated. The queen of the Marcomanni, Fritigil, convinced her husband to approach St. Ambrose for the conversion of his people. The construction and reconstruction of buildings for worship, even on the heights, indicates the spread of Christianity at the beginning of the fifth century into the hinterlands.

Rhaetia or *Raetia* (as it appears in the inscriptions) embraced territories which today would include Bavaria, Swabia, Switzerland, Austria, the province of Belluno and Trentino-Alto Adige. When did Christianity begin to spread in Raetia? From which direction did it come? We need to take into account two elements. *Raetia Prima* (eastern Switzerland) and *Raetia Secunda* (the northern Alpine foothills) were part of the diocese of *Italia Annonaria*, and thus have close links with the north of Italy. *Raetia Secunda* also has close links with the Gallic provinces. The oldest known episcopal sees are found in the Gallic provinces of Augusta Raurica,[92] Genava (Geneva) and Octodurum.[93]

Vindelicia was the territory inhabited by the *Vindelici*. It is the region between the Danube on the north, and the *limes germanicus* of Hadrian, i.e., the border which separated the empire from other territories up to 260 CE. The main city was *Augusta Vindelicorum* (Augsburg) which Tacitus referred to as the most splendid colonial province of Raetia.[94] At Augusta Vindelicorum there is the tradition of the martyr Afra, originally from Cyprus, who died in 304.

ITALY

The emperor Augustus reorganized the administration of this vast territory into eleven regions since Italy was not considered a province (*provincia*)—even if the term sometimes was used in late antiquity in connection with Italy. Augustus and his successors favored Italy over the provinces (*provinciae*). The division of Italy into regions was not to be understood in the sense that they were like provinces because they did not have governors of senatorial or equestrian rank. The great reform came with Diocletian who subdivided all of Italy into provinces, joining some of them to already existing provinces—Sicily, *Alpes Cottiae*, the two *Raetiae* and Sardinia and Corsica—creating the *diocesis italiciana*. Furthermore, he suppressed fiscal privileges that were enjoyed by the inhabitants of Italy. Some of these privileges had already been abolished in the third century.

The Church of Rome. We do not know who the first missionaries were qwho came to Rome, but they would have been of Jewish origin. If in 56 CE Paul affirmed that "for many years," he wished to go to Rome (*Rom* 15:23), this means that the Christians were there for some decades, most likely evangelized by Jews (*Rom* 2; 4:1ff). About twenty years after the death of Jesus, there was a substantial community in Rome. Rome was the city to which many people immigrated from the Orient. Tacitus (†c.117) writes in his *Annales* 15.44 that Nero condemned "a great multitude" (*multitudo ingens*) of Christians to be killed. Suetonius also speaks of the persecution of the Christians in his *Lives of Caesars*, *Nero* 16.2. In both authors, there already appears a clear distinction between Jews and Christians. The *Letter to the Romans*, written around the year 56 at Corinth, announces the visit of Paul to the Roman community before going to Spain. Two-thirds of the names mentioned by Paul are Greek (along with a few Latin names) indicating they were Christian immigrants. Moreover, because of the relative size of the number of Christians, Paul never uses "church" to indicate the totality of the community, but rather names different entities. The Christian community was mixed, composed of converted Jews and pagans. The Christians of Rome must have known of the triumphal celebrations in Rome over the destruction of Jerusalem and of the fact that the Arch of Titus and the Colosseum were built with the spoils of the Temple.

The *Letter to the Hebrews* is of Roman origin and contains a greeting from Italy in 13:24. The strong Jewish community also remained for some time afterward, as can be deduced from the *Letter of Clement to the Corinthians* and the *Shepherd* of Hermas. The latter, who wrote around the years 140/150, testifies to recent persecutions in which many testified but many also apostatized.[95] Justin died together with others about 165. The persecution in Rome—except that of Nero—was not general but sporadic and based on specific denunciations. As far as we can tell it was continuous, which made the life of the Christians very precarious at least until the time of the emperor Decius (†251). The advice and suggestions concerning the organization and community leadership which the *Letter of Clement* addresses to the Corinthians, provide valuable hints for in interpreting the situation of the Roman community. In the second century, Irenaeus affirmed that "the two most glorious apostles Peter and Paul founded and established at Rome this very great and very ancient church known by all."[96]

In the second century Rome is a city of Christian immigrants or visitors who were more or less educated. Justin and his companion martyrs were not alone; there were many others. Among these were Hegesippus, Polycarp, Tatian, Rhodon, Marcion, Valentine, Cerdo, etc. The *Shepherd* of Hermas presents a lively community, young and growing, albeit with organizational problems. It was composed of people who had difficulty being faithful to their baptismal commitments. Justin's *Apologies* address the imperial authorities in order to explain the situation of the Christians and highlight their strict morality. Minucius Felix collects and contrasts the pagan mentality with that of the Christians and also includes the pagan allegations. In the second half of the second-century lists of the Roman episcopal succession circulated.[97] In the meantime, for whatever reason the prestige and the authority of the Roman Church grew; no other community could be compared with it. In the fourth and fifth centuries, the doctrine of the Roman primacy over all the other churches was affirmed. The "turning point" came with Damasus (366-384) and his successors. The title *Sedes Apostolica* from the fifth century on became distinctive of the Roman see. Pope Siricius (384-399) applied the Pauline expression *sollicitudo omnium ecclesiarum* (helper of the entire church, *2 Cor* 11:28) to the ministry of the bishop of Rome. The history of this attribution in the succeeding period proved complex and tortuous both for those who claimed it and those who refused to acknowledge the claim.

Christianity in Italy

Outside of the Roman Church, information on the rest of Italy and the islands is scarce. On his later journey, Paul met Christians at Puteoli (Pozzuoli) with whom he spent a week (*Acts* 28:13-14). Luke does not mention Christians in other places. Jerome's martyrology lists martyrs at Puteoli. Evidence of a Christian presence at Pompei and Herculaneum is not clear and scholars continue to debate the point. Testimony about the presence of Christians or martyrs in any particular place does not prove the existence of an organized community. For the first three centuries, such testimonies are sometimes connected to the Roman Church. Archaeological information can be useful but is insufficient. The sources of late antiquity and the early medieval period tend to paint a prestigious past for the respective episcopal sees. Councils also took place in Rome. The first important Council was celebrated at the time of Pope Cornelius in 252 in which, according to Eusebius, sixty bishops participated.[98] The number seems excessive since we can speak with certainty of only sixteen episcopal sees at the end of the third century. There are different reasons offered for either their presence or absence. Harnack thinks that in the middle of the third century, there were about a hundred episcopal sees.[99] In the course of the fourth and fifth centuries, different episcopal assemblies took place in Rome with the participation of Italian bishops and others who might be passing through.[100]

The Roman see played a vital role in the spread of Christianity in central and southern Italy, which followed the consular routes, as demonstrated by the existence of martyrs in the areas around Rome where Christian communities had formed. Several towns in the region of Lazio boasted of martyrs. Capua had many martyrs as well. There were less in other cities in the south and the north. Just as with the civil administration, so also with the ecclesiastical, the south was tied to Rome (*Italia suburbicaria*). This was also because of the prestige of the see, the only one that could boast of traditions that went back to Peter and Paul. The dioceses were more numerous in central Italy and Campania, less so in the other southern areas, and even lesser still in the north (*Italia annonaria*). There were very few episcopal sees at the beginning of the fourth century. Beginning with Constantine's peace in 311/313, there was a notable increase of episcopal sees—55 new sees. And in the fifth century there were many more—up to 155.

Sicily was situated along the routes between Rome, Africa, and the East; the Sicilian ports received passengers from various parts of the empire. In Syracuse, archaeology shows the existence of Christian catacombs dating from the third century. The city is rich in Christian inscriptions, some of which are dated before Constantine. In 250, a letter was sent from the Roman Church to Sicily concerning the question of the *lapsi* because of the persecution of Decius; it may have been sent to the community of Syracuse.[101] According to tradition, the martyrdom of Lucius transpired at the time of Diocletian. At the request of the emperor Constantine, the Bishop Chrestus and the deacon Florentius participated in the Council of Arles in 314—a sign of the importance of the see.[102] In Catania there were some martyrs, such as Agatha who was arrested at Palermo and transferred to Catania during the persecution of Decius († 250). There was also Euplus, martyred at the time of Diocletian. An inscription remembers a Christian child, Iulia Florentina, who died at the time of Constantine near the city.[103] The child was buried "before the gates of Christian martyrs."[104] This confirms that there were Christians killed in Catania.

It would seem that Sardinia, together with Corsica, constituted a single Roman province until the time of Diocletian when they were divided into two and aggregated to the Italian diocese. It supplied grain to Rome until the Vandal occupation.[105] We know the names of some Sardinian martyrs: Gavinus, Lussorius, Simplicius, Saturnus, Antiochus, and Ephisius. The first bishop we have a record of was Quintasius of Carales (Cagliari) who was present at the Council of Arles in 314. There were probably only two episcopal sees at the time of the Council of Serdica (343).

The archaeological sources before the end of the fifth century are as scarce for early Christian Corsica as are also historical sources up to Gregory the Great.[106] Around 490, Gennadius of Marseilles speaks of the bishops of Corsica under the supposition that there were more than one.[107]

AFRICA

The term *Africa* in antiquity had a plurality of meanings. The Romans at first designated it as the territory which previously was under the dominion of Carthage. In a later period, the term Africa referred only to *Africa Proconsularis* (also called *Zeugitana*). With further conquests, Roman domination extended from the Great Sirte as far as the shores of the Atlantic; the eastern border was Cyrenaica, which was Greek-speaking. Africa itself corresponded roughly to the Arabic Maghreb. Under Roman domination, this vast territory—the civil diocese of Africa from the time of Diocletian excluded the most western part—became

Romanized in a gradual process which first affected the eastern part of the region, then the internal areas. The Romanization occurred in language, in institutions and in religion. Proceeding westward and inland, the Romanization was much less evident. Towards the beginning of the fourth century (297) Diocletian subdivided Africa into provinces under the control of the vicar resident in Carthage, who was the representative of the prefect at the praetorian of Italy.

The first Christian witness of Proconsular Africa comes from the martyrs of Scilli (Scili), a locality not yet identified who were condemned at Carthage in 180 by the proconsul. Their names were Latin but some were typically African. The fact that they had the Letters of Paul in Latin, and that they were from a marginal locality leads to the supposition that Christianity had spread not only to the cities but also the villages. Some decades later, the Christian community of the capital was numerous and welcomed people from all social classes, even if those from the upper classes were few. Through Cyprian we know more about the ecclesiastical geography of Africa in general and of Proconsular Africa in particular, in that the whole area constituted only one ecclesiastical province, as Cyprian says: "Our province is of very wide extent, for it has Numidia and Mauritania annexed to it."[108]

It is not known when Christianity reached Africa and whether it was from Rome or the East—or even from other directions because the first Christian texts are in both Greek and Latin. It is not out of the question that Christians arrived in the first century, perhaps due to the extensive commerce of its ports. The writings of Tertullian and the *Passion of Perpetua and Felicity* describe a strong and vibrant community at Carthage, which already had a history behind it at the beginning of the third century.[109] Around the year 220, a Council of about 70 bishops from Proconsular Africa and Numidia—not all African bishops were present—gathered together with Agrippinus. In 256, 87 were present at a council. It is calculated that in this period there were about 150 episcopal sees. The Acts of the Council of 256 have been preserved. In the preamble, they note "there were many bishops present from the provinces of Africa, Numidia and Mauritania [the three civil provinces], along with presbyters and deacons."[110] There were a great number of martyrs in the years 303/305. At the beginning of the fifth century, Christianization is very advanced also among the Berber tribes resident inside the Roman Empire. There remained, however, pockets of strong pagan resistance (e.g., Madauros).

The ecclesiastical organization mirrored that of the civil, with the exception of Hippo, Thagaste, Calama, Madauros and Theveste[111] which, though being part of Proconsular Africa, belonged to the ecclesiastical province of Numidia where the primate was the bishop who was oldest by ordination, not a bishop from any specific city. This was the case also in other African provinces where the primate was the oldest bishop, but Proconsular Africa was different in that the honor fell to the bishop of Carthage who enjoyed a certain primacy (not like the bishop of Alexandria or Antioch).

Because of this division, for civil matters Augustine had to refer to the proconsul resident in Carthage or to his delegate resident in Hippo. For ecclesiastical matters, on the other hand, he referred to the ecclesiastical primate of Numidia whose principal city was Constantina which was ancient Cirta before the time of emperor Constantine. In the General Councils of Carthage, Augustine participated as a representative of Numidia. The ecclesiastical province of Tripolitania was the smallest of the region with only five episcopal sees. The Council of Carthage of 397 says that in "Tripoli there were only five bishops.[112] In the North African provinces there is abundant Christian archaeological evidence of all types beginning from the fourth century: inscriptions, buildings of worship, mosaics, all later than the third century. The spread of the cult of the martyrs and the construction of numerous churches which very soon also have tombs inside them are concrete evidence of the spread of Christianity.

Ecclesiastical Africa, with the primate at Carthage, embraced a vast territory with the respective provinces coinciding with the civil ones (except for Numidia, as we have seen). Each had its own historical heritage and pride. It stretched from the Great Sirte to the border of present-day Morocco (the western border of *Caesariana*). The province *Tingitana* was annexed to Spain. Nevertheless, the limits of the provinces were fluid and uncertain at various times and also in connection with the history of the region. The plenary Councils met at Carthage, to which the distant bishops normally just sent delegates, when it was possible, because of the distance and the difficulties of communication. By the beginning of the fifth century at the time of Saint Augustine, there were about six hundred sees located in the urban centers, but also in rural villages (*casae*) because of the extension of the territories of some city centers. There were also churches in some of the large estates.

Hispania

Hispania's name is of Punic origin. It was slowly conquered by the Romans beginning from the third century BCE starting from the east coast. It integrated quite well into the Roman world. The Apostle Paul had expressed the desire to go to Spain (*Rom.* 15:24 and 28). There is no certainty whether that journey ever took place as there is no reliable evidence, even if many patristic references confirm it happened.[113] Scholars differ, however, as to whether Christianity came there from Africa or Rome. The close relationships and culture it shared with Italy, the Orient, and Africa suggest a plurality of influences and origins which also differ concerning the individual Iberian province. In *Epistle* 67 (254 CE) Cyprian certifies the existence of bishops at Mérida, Astorga-León, and Saragossa, as he also lets us know the consequences of the persecution of Decius and the relations *Hispania* had with the Roman Church. Fructuosus, with two deacons, Augurius and Eulogius, were killed on January 21, 259 in the Amphitheatre of Tarragona. During the persecution of Diocletian, we find numerous martyrs in different Iberian cities: Saragossa,[114] Calahorra[115] (which was the homeland of Prudentius), Gerona,[116] Cordova,[117] Mérida[118] and Alcalá de Heranes.[119] The historical value of their passions is uneven, as some were composed much later.

The Council of Elvira (309)—if it ever happened—with its eighty canons certainly was well structured in that it would put together later texts. However, there are also canons regarding the problems of the beginning of the fourth century. During the fourth century the Iberian Peninsula remained removed from the great theological debates; however, they did have a great protagonist, Hosius of Cordoba, who did influence the conciliar and religious decisions of the first half of the century. He was a councilor of Constantine for ecclesiastical affairs. Gregory of Elvira (†about 392) was the most important theologian of the Iberian Peninsula. His work, *De fide*, shows the existence of theological debate in Spain, for which he does not want to be defined an *academicus disputator*[120] but only wanted to show the simple truth of the faith against the Arians. Some of his *Tractates* have been preserved with a collection of his sermons. Only the orthodox writings of Potamius of Lisbon (who died long before 383/384) are preserved.

The spread of Christianity in the Iberian Peninsula, even towards the end of the fourth century, is uneven. We do not know the name of any martyr in the area of Galicia. The letter of Himerius of Tarragon to Pope Damasus provides a glimpse into Spanish Christianity. The questions to the bishop of Rome concern the re-baptism of those who converted from Arianism, the date of the celebration of Baptism (Easter or Pentecost), the apostates (Christians who returned to the worship of idols), the marriage of one betrothed to another, monks and nuns who were not faithful to their commitment to chastity and clerical celibacy. The questions also asked about the requirements to accede to orders and the comportment of the clerics especially as it related to their age, whether they could remarry, what to do with penitents, bigamists, and women who lived with ecclesiastics. They also dealt with the consecration of the monks. In the second half of the fourth century, the doctrines of Priscillian spread. He was an educated lay convert who preached a rigid ascetic doctrine in opposition to the worldly clergy.

Pacianus of Barcelona (†391) is remembered for his sermons and his treatise *An Exhortation to Repentance* (*Paraenesis ad poenitentiam*). Also significant is Egeria the great pilgrim—possibly of Galician origin—who wrote a travel diary of her trip to the East (*Itinerarium Egeriae*). Christian poetry flourished. We can single out the presbyter Juvencus with his biblical poetry inspired by the New Testament. He lived at the time of Constantine and so his poem ends with a eulogy to the Emperor. There is also another great poet Prudentius (†405) of Calagurris[121] author of numerous works, in particular the *Cathemerinon liber,* a collection of poems/prayers for the different hours of the day and for some solemnities. He is also known for the *Peristephanon*, a collection of fourteen poems on the Christian martyrs, and many other compositions.

At the end of the fourth century the Church of the Iberian Peninsula was still without a solid hierarchical structure in individual provinces and as a whole. No see was preeminent over the others. When the communities had problems, they sought solutions outside the peninsula, both at the imperial and ecclesiastical levels. At the beginning of the fifth century the invaders arrived; the Arian vandals passed through to Africa (429). The Iberian Peninsula was subdivided between the various peoples who plundered it for about a century because many of them, whether Arians or pagans, were opposed to the Christian population.

GALLIA

Gallia included a vast territory inhabited by the Gauls, a term which includes a mixture of Celtic populations from the territory west of the Rhine, between the English Channel, the Atlantic Ocean, the Rhine, the Western Alps and the Mediterranean, corresponding today to Belgium, West Germany, Luxemburg, France and Western Switzerland. Julius Caesar divided Gaul into three areas: Belgian Gaul, Aquitania, and Celtic Gaul (*Gallia Lugdenensis*).[122] On December 31, 406 waves of invaders began to arrive,[123] including the Visigoths from Italy. Then came the Franks, Burgundians and Celts who came at different times from Wales, installing themselves in Armorica, the Breton peninsula in Gaul, at the mouth of the Loire.

Christians certainly arrived in Gaul at the beginning of the second century. In the cities of Lyons, the capital, and Vienne, there were already Christian communities of Greek culture in the second half of the second century when a pogrom against them broke out. Of the 47 martyrs, some died by torture, others were condemned *ad bestias*, while still others were decapitated because they were Roman citizens. After the persecution, Irenaeus was elected bishop of Lyons. In the third century, there were several bishops in southern Gaul. Later legends record numerous apostolic foundations, not demonstrable, or some missionaries sent by Clement of Rome. According to later traditions, there were numerous martyrs, but we can only be sure of a few, such as Saturninus of Toulouse, maybe Paul of Narbonne, Victor of Marseilles, Sinforianus of Autun, and Dionysius of Paris.

The evangelization of Gaul grew in the second half of the third century and after Constantine. The Council of Arles (314) offers us a first picture of the episcopal sees. There were sixteen sees represented, but certainly there were more. The framework established at Arles was expanded by the councils of Valence (374), Nîmes (394 or 396), Riez (439) and the so-called Council of Cologne (346).[124] Before 346, thirty-four Gallican bishops supported

Athanasius. In the middle of the fourth century, Gaul had over forty episcopal sees along with new cities. The areas with the most sees were those of the central southern part of Gaul, in particular in *Viennensis, Narbonensis*, and *Lugdunensis*. The Councils, in general, were held in Arles (314 and 356), Béziers (356), Valence (374), and, in connection with the problems of the episcopate in Gaul, at Turin (398). In northeastern Gaul, Tongeren in Belgium had one bishop who was named Servatius, later bishop of Maastricht, Bavais.[125] For many cities the tradition mentions only martyrs. The growth in episcopal sees is just one sign of evangelization because it is difficult to evaluate the depth of that growth in the minds and hearts of the people and less still in the Gallic countryside.

Before the end of the fourth century, there were about seventy episcopal sees, among which there was no truly institutional preeminence. Some dioceses had very extensive territories, especially in the north; that of Poitiers was an entire region (three current districts). The system of organization of the ecclesiastical provinces under one metropolitan in Gaul arose late.

Germania

The term *Germania* indicated both the German territory under Roman rule and free Germany (*Germania libera*). Around 84 CE there were two imperial provinces in the conquered territories which essentially were defending the borders: a) *Germania Inferior* or *Secunda* (with the capital Cologne) with territory between the Rhine and the province of *Gallia Belgica*, that is, the valley of the Meuse, along with the territories of Southern Holland, Belgium of Luxemburg, France and West Germany, whose principal center was *Colonia Agrippinensis*. b) *Germania Superior* or *Prima* which bordered Southern Gaul and *Raetia* to the Southeast, comprising the Middle Rhine and present day Western Switzerland, France (Jura and Alsace), and the Southwestern part of Germany. Its major cities were Koblenz and Mainz (the capital) along with Vesontio (Besançon), Argentorate (Strasbourg) and Augusta Raurica.[126]

Irenaeus, who wrote in Lyon on the border with Germany, affirmed that the Christians were also to be found among the German population.[127] The archaeological evidence is not reliable and the literary sources say nothing very precise. At Xanten[128] there is the memory of the martyr Victor, and two other people; not far from Xanten, at Birten (*Oppidum Bertunensium*), Mallosus is remembered. For *Germania Superior*, we have no evidence of a substantial Christian presence. In the supposed Council of Cologne of 346, bishops from Mainz, Speyer and Worms attended.[129] For Mainz, the names of other bishops are known; many inscriptions from the 4th to 5th centuries, however, attest to the Christian presence in *Germania Superior*.

In *Germania Inferior* the first known bishop was Maternus of Cologne—who was third in the episcopal list. He was present at the Council of Rome in 313, and together with his deacon at that of Arles in 314. Bishop Euphrates was present at the Council of Serdica in 342/343, also Servatius of Tongern. The conversion of the German peoples began in the fifth century, favored by the Franks. Another evangelization begins only in the 7th century with the work of the Irish and Scottish missionaries.

BRITANNIA AND HIBERNIA

The Celts inhabited the northern part of Britain, sometimes known as Caledonia, a territory that was not well defined. The emperor Hadrian built a wall to separate the Roman territory from the peoples further north. The emperor Antoninus Pius built another 150 km further north, but it was abandoned almost immediately.

The Christian origins of Britain are still unclear, and certainly the legends which circulated in the Middle Ages shouldn't be given much credence. The martyrdom of Alban is said to have occurred at the time of the persecution of Diocletian, which suggests the existence of Christians in Britain. 314 is the year of the first secure evidence of the presence of a conspicuous Christian community on the island because among the signatories at the anti-Donatist Council of Arles (314) are three British bishops as well as a priest and a deacon. At the time of the Council of Rimini in 359, the number of episcopal sees would have been greater. In 395 British bishops[130] sought the help of Victricius of Rouen (*Rotomagus*) to resolve disagreements among the Britons (*intra Britannias*).[131] The retreat of the Roman army from Britain did not destroy the connection between its churches and those of Gaul, as is seen from the case of the Pelagians.

Pelagius was a Briton, even if it is difficult to establish how much his ideas had spread among the peoples of the island. The 12th chapter of the *Vita Germani* says that British bishops went to Gaul to seek their help. At a synod, it was decided that Lupus of Troyes and Germanus of Auxerre would be their delegates.[132] Prosper of Aquitaine affirms that it was Palladius, a deacon of the Roman Church and a councilor to Pope Celestine in 429 who gave Germanus, bishop of *Antissiodorum* (Auxerre), authority so that he could combat the Pelagians in Britain—especially Bishop Agricola.[133] After the departure of the Roman military, the kingdom of *Dumnonia* in Southwest Britain—which included Cornwall, Devon and Summerset—remained out of reach of the pagan Anglo Saxons and so the Christians were at peace. Literary sources regarding the spread of Christianity in Britain are very scarce. The numerous archaeological finds, in different areas, nevertheless, give us valid clues.

In 597 Pope Gregory I, having noted the very serious departure of the island from the faith sent a group of monks from the monastery of Sant'Andrea al Celio to Britain to convert the pagan tribe of the Anglo Saxons. Among them were Augustine and Laurence. The real evangelization and conversion began from then on. The conversion work of the monks started at Kent where the Romans possibly landed some centuries before. Their pagan king Ethelbert—who was later converted by Augustine—had certainly married the Frankish Christian princess Berta before 588. She was the daughter of the Merovingian king of Paris Charibert I.

The mission in Ireland (*Hibernia*) came in the fifth century through the work of Palladius, from Rome, but above all, Patrick who was ordained bishop by Germanus and sent to Ireland to continue and amplify his mission in 432. According to Prosper of Aquitaine, already in 431 Pope Celestine I had ordained the Roman deacon Palladius as bishop and sent him to Ireland principally to counteract the Pelagians.[134] The sending of a bishop suggests there was already a sizeable Christian community there. Even though Prosper speaks of the evangelization of the pagan inhabitants, Palladius in fact spent very little time in Hibernia. On his way to Ireland, he passed by Auxerre where he met Germanus. Having completed his mission in Ireland, he left for Rome and during the journey may have died either in Britain or perhaps Ireland. Patrick was then ordained bishop by Germanus and sent to Ireland to continue and expand his mission. The fact that he went personally to those peoples suggest that Palladius had some connection with Germanus and could be of Gallic origin because the name of the *Palladii* was very widespread. Southern Ireland must have been the location of his work where he also founded three churches.

The principal area of Patrick's work was the north of Ireland where, according to tradition, he founded his church at Armagh where he was eventually buried. According to another tradition, he was buried at Downpatrick. Later sources tell us that, already in Patrick's time, several episcopal sees had been constituted. Through the influence of Gallic asceticism a lively and original Irish monasticism developed.

NUMBER OF CHRISTIANS

We do not know the number of Christians at the end of the first century. According to some statistics, there were only a few thousand, but we do not have reliable numbers at the beginning of the fourth century either. All the statistics made in publications are only plausible hypotheses due to the impossibility of having reliable data, especially for the first and second centuries. The demographic statistics for antiquity rely on large margins of approximation.

Rome was the ancient city that had access to most information and instruments for calculating the number of its inhabitants—although scholars also provide very divergent numbers. According to the recent studies of Lo Cascio, "If the number of adult males included in the *plebs frumentaria* (people receiving a monthly ration of grain) in the early decades of the principality is correct, the free population of the city could not have been more than six hundred thousand."[135] Those would have been the free people, but the number of slaves would have included as many—perhaps even more. The Roman population remained substantially stable in the succeeding centuries, undergoing a decrease at the time of the great plagues at the end of the second century. The same figure was expected for the fifth century with a large reduction of the population caused by the arrival of Alaric (408-410) and the devastation he caused. We should add to this figure those who were free but not citizens (the *peregrini*) present in Rome for various reasons. There is a paucity of information about the other cities.

Concerning the Christians, I would like to cite a text of the pagan Celsus, who wrote about 180 CE. He speaks of the various Christian sects and adds: "At the beginning they were few and all in agreement. Having grown in numbers, and scattered here and there, they continue to split up and separate and each wants to have their faction [...] And once again separated from each other because of their increased number they continue to criticize one another."[136] The cited text seems to anticipate what later Christian authors would say beginning with Tertullian.

Statistical research can use quantitative or qualitative methods which are normal today in the social sciences and other contexts. Both wish to explain a phenomenon. The quantitative method studies a social phenomenon with statistics, using mathematical models, theories, and/or hypotheses concerning the object studied. That is, it tries to explain a phenomenon through the collection of numerical data which are analyzed based on mathematical models. Such a method explains its results in numerical terms. In our case, the subject is the number of Christians. But for antiquity, we do not have a register of data recording the number of members, baptisms, conversions so it is necessary to revert to interpretative models and making hypotheses and projections. The intention is to explain the result in a numerical form of percentages and statistics which are then used to interpret a wider phenomenon. Then there is a generalization in terms of the time and space selected.

The qualitative method arose as a reaction to the positivism of the reliability of historical data, regarding especially the behavior of people and the reasons which guide that conduct: the why and the how of making certain decisions. In our case, we are considering the why and how of the decisions Christians made which affected how they lived. This method, as is clear, cannot be generalized but can be used only for single cases or small communities. In both methods, the results obtained offer only indications but are not precise.

There is also the problem of method and the use of the sources. Scholars use a collection of testimonies but always in a partial way and often in an arbitrary manner. These serve to make generalizations which can only be hypothetical or give us a local vision but cannot be applied to other geographical areas. The statistics which are used today are not reliable; the figures are random. And if there is an ideological position behind what the statistician is doing, it complicates the results even further.

Those who wish to provide numbers have developed methods of calculation. A few years ago, several American scholars—in disagreement among themselves—treated the subject in the periodical *Journal of Early Christian Studies*[137] concerning the studies of Rodney Stark. This scholar has continued to study the subject in subsequent publications. The problem is that we do not have reliable statistics on the number of Christians or the percentage of the population that was Christian in the decades following the year 50 CE Since modern sensibility requires numbers, many put forward approximate calculations. A plethora of scholars discuss the numbers concerning a particular time. Many of the numbers presented are very uncertain and are unreliable because the sources do not allow it. Rodney Stark, the American scholar who has most studied the subject, offers a progressive table based on projections: for example for the year 150 he calculates there were about 39,000 Christians; for the year 250, about 1.12 million; for the year 312, about 9 million, equal to 15% of the population.[138] When the emperor Maximin was forced to suspend the persecution in the winter of 312/313, he was happy to satisfy the requests of the cities against the Christians because the Christians were continuing to grow. The reason for the persecution, he noted, was because nearly all of the people were turning to this error.[139] I'm not sure how reliable the figures are, if only because the calculations of the population of the Roman Empire itself are very approximate. The concept of the number of Christians cannot be arrived at absolutely since it is relative to the inhabitants of the place of reference.

As I have already mentioned, at the beginning of the fourth century there were some very Christianized towns or regions, but others were still thoroughly pagan. According to Filoramo, in 311 when the emperor Maximin entered Nicomedia, the capital of Bithynia and the oriental empire, he found that the majority of the population were Christian.[140] I haven't been able to find confirmation of that.

In *Phrygia Salutaris,* the Galatian border city of Orcistus,[141] is thirty miles from Pessinus (Galatia). Four roads have their beginning there.[142] Between 324 and 326 the city asked Constantine to return their status as an independent city from Nacoleia (today Seyitgazi). The emperor accepted their request because the population was Christian. Subsequently in another document of 331, in response to a complaint of the people of Orcistus, Constantine wrote: "We concede to you, in respect of your request and demand, that from now on you will not have to pay the usual sum which you paid in the past for the (pagan) cult" of the city of Nacoleia.[143] Even though Orcistus was no longer dependent on Nacoleia, it was forced to continue to pay the contributions for the official cult expenditure *(pecunia pro cultis)*: the traditional *sacra publica*, which were costly for the maintenance of the temples, the sacrifices, and the personnel. It seems that the population of Nacoleia, the biggest city of the region, was pagan, although there were probably also Christians there and it practiced the pagan cult, while Orcistus was Christian, although there were certainly still pagans there. Two neighboring localities but religiously different. It was predictable that the inhabitants of Nacoleia would oppose the recognition of Orcistus as autonomous ('free') and would still demand their contributions.

In the text, the reason for the opposition is not explained although it could have been for reasons of prestige, financial, or religious. This topic is relevant because religious affiliation, advanced by the people of Orcistus, weighed heavily in the request in that the imperial chancellery repeats it as one of the reasons for granting city status to it. If the request came from the local people, it arose from their agreement and conviction that the emperor would be more favorable to granting it if they put forward a religious reason. They knew of the emperor's new religiosity and of his tendency to favor the Christians. Already in the third century the population of Phrygia was largely Christian—of both Catholic and Montanist profession. Some decades later, the emperor Julian attested that the residents of Nisibis[144] were all Christians.[145]

In the West, Proconsular Africa was situated in an area that was quite Christianized. All the urban centers with city status had a bishop. After the Donatist split, there were two bishops—one Catholic and the other Donatist—in the same city. I say it seemed Christianized, but in reality, the presence of a bishop does not mean that the population was Christian. A century later, there were towns with a long history of Christian presence in which the majority of the population were still pagan. Proconsular Africa was dotted with many episcopal sees. Not all the sees were of the same importance.

Episcopal sees were also to be found in faraway Caesarean Mauritania, present-day Northwest Algeria, for example, in the town of Altava, which is today Ouled Mimoum, thirty kilometers east of Tlemcen in Northern Algeria. It was a military fortress inhabited already in the third century by soldiers of the cavalry and the infantry of the *cohors II Sandorum*. In 309, a *basilica dominica* (a house of the Lord) was built, attested to by an inscription.[146] There was a bishop also in the military center of Lambaesis, the headquarters of the *Legio III Augusta*. The governor of Numidia also lived there and this was the place where the Christians of the province were also brought to be judged.

Another model or interpretative scheme has been used by some to understand the geographic spread of Christian presence in the early centuries. This model has mainly been applied to Egypt. It is derived from the spread of the use of the codex for the Christian texts, both biblical and from various Christian authors. Moving from the use of the book in a scroll-shaped form (*volumen*) to that of the codex was considered a cultural change of strong social and religious impact. This change, however, had begun in Rome already from the first century and then spread to the provinces. And so it is of pagan rather than Christian origin.[147] Neither can it be assumed that the phenomenon had the support of the central Christian authorities but was a result of economic and cultural reasons.[148] Initially, the scroll remained alongside the codex, but between the third and fourth centuries, the codex almost completely replaced the scroll. There were many reasons for the spread of the codex.[149] The codex is more easily browsed through and usable. We note that the Christians preferred the codex form for their sacred writings: "It is a form that was always adopted despite the different types [of texts] due to the diverse ways the book could be used: lined copies were sometimes used in documentary and informal writings destined for private reading, copies that were more accurate were employed for liturgical offices, while deluxe copies might be produced for particular ceremonies or as a show of opulence."[150]

Christian teaching, which in the early decades was predominantly oral, had more and more need of written texts in that it became based largely on biblical texts which acquired additional commentary and were necessary for preaching and instruction for those desiring baptism. Furthermore, a widespread Christian movement in the empire aspiring to a certain unity of doctrine and lived experience needed epistolary exchanges and written texts. "This double impulse towards uniformity and organizational structure is one of the most distinctive characteristics of Christianity."[151]

Can the spread of the use of the codex made with papyrus in Egypt help us understand the presence of Christians there? Based on the existence of papyrus of the second century, there is the conviction that before the episcopacy of Demetrius of Alexandria (189-233), Christianity was fairly widespread both in the cities and in the countryside in such a way that it was possible to put in place an organization. Roger Bagnall contests this conclusion based on two principal arguments: first, the difficulty of dating the papyrus texts, and second, the uncertainty about whether papyri with biblical passages from the Old Testament should all be considered Christian and not Jewish. He has recently made calculations for Egypt, an area he knows well, and of which the extent of the Christian presence before bishop Demetrius is vague. He assumes that at the beginning of Demetrius' episcopate, the Christians were less than 20,000, while the population of the whole Empire was about 55 million. Most scholars today accept this figure as the total number of inhabitants of the Roman Empire. Bagnall, while referring to the Stark model, keeps in mind the diffusion of Christian texts, biblical and non-biblical, in Egypt. He insists that probably none of the numbers are correct, but their level of approximation is not much compromised by any change in the presuppositions on which the model is based.[152] He thinks that around the year 150, there were about 4000 Christians; about the year 200, there were 22,000, of which about 5000 were in Alexandria. At the end of the episcopate of Heraclas (247) the figure of 117,000 was reached.[153] That figure should not mislead us as it is very approximate and hypothetical. Furthermore, we do not know the distribution of the population in the different districts or the percentage of Christians.

Bagnall is criticized by E. Wipszycka both for the scarcity of documentation and for the assumption that the small communities did not need a bishop.[154] The distance from the principal city of the various districts (*nomoi*) required the multiplication of the episcopal sees concerning the size of the Christian community. In 202, Septimius Severus granted municipal status to the capital villages of the districts. According to widespread opinion, this new administrative situation would have multiplied the number of episcopal sees at the time of Bishop Demetrius in the Egyptian countryside, or *chora* (territory in Egypt outside of the city proper). The recent study of Wipszycka rejects this opinion.[155] The Polish scholar maintains that the creation of new episcopal sees was due to the ambitious personality of Demetrius who wanted to create a network of bishops subject to himself.

Another model which could help us concerns the number of martyrs in a territory and the time of the martyrdom, once the reliable testimony of Christians killed for their faith begins. The older the testimonies are, the more we can suppose that the presence of Christians and the way they lived influenced the spread of the "Christian Philosophy." Let's take an example —a criterion which could be applied to the whole Roman Empire—that of the Iberian Peninsula. Here the spread of Christianity is not very extensive at the beginning of the fourth century. The two great persecutions—that of Decius/Valerian and that of Diocletian—made martyrs in various cities in Spain. Where do the martyrs come from? Excluding Gerona/Barcelona and Saragossa, the other cities had only a few martyrs. The case of Saragossa is a particular case in point: the names of 18 martyrs are known.[156] However, we should keep in mind that the Iberian Peninsula, in the period of the tetrarchy, beginning in 293 was dependent on Constantius Chlorus who, according to tradition, did not persecute the people. Furthermore, the number of martyrs was dependent also on the attitude and convictions of the individual governors and the people in his office (*officia*).

Woman: Concerning the composition of the Christian communities—and indirectly what this composition was made up of—we can take into consideration the female and the male presence. However, the women in that society left fewer traces for us. The free men were involved in the social, political, and religious life much more than the women. It was more difficult for the women to embrace Christianity, which demanded from the men certain behaviors not compatible with the political and social requirements and conventions, while the women in some ways enjoyed more liberty. For them, it was easier to practice the Christian religion. We have some sources and clues which lead us to think that—even if it is impossible to quantify—the female component was quite a bit more than that of the male. I recall that Pliny tortured two *ministrae* in some city in Bithynia. Who were they and what function did they have in the community? And why two women? Pliny, who was pagan, interpreted their function in pagan terms.

The *Acts of Paul and Thecla* was written in the second half of the second century. Even if the work was rejected by some bishops, it was still widely read and it gave great prominence to women. When Paul was in Iconium, "many women and virgins went to Paul" (chap. 7); "all the women and young people go to him and are instructed by him" (chap. 9). The mother of Thecla is dismayed that her daughter is in love with the teaching of Paul who is "a seducer of the young and the virgins" (chap. 11) and "deprives the young and the virgins of their husbands" (chap. 12); the people shouted "(Paul) has corrupted all of our wives." There was a request to the governor to burn Thecla "because the women who allowed themselves to be instructed by this man are taken by fear" (chap. 20). Thecla "teaches the word of God" to Queen Tryphaena (chap. 39). In the city of Myra, Thecla is sent by Paul to Iconium with the task of teaching the word of God (chap. 41), which she does (chap. 42). Then Thecla goes to Seleucia of Isauria, "where she illuminated many with the word of God" (chap. 43). We know that the *Acts of Thecla* is a novel, but a novel which mirrors the mentality and the practice at the time. Its author wished to promote the prestige of Paul and an exaggerated asceticism, but it lets us see at the same time the interest of the women in the Christian religion and their commitment to converting and instructing pagans. The narrator's perspective, even if according to the sources he is a priest, is that of women who refuse the over-intrusiveness of men.

Tertullian addresses the problem of women of the higher classes and the rich who, so as not to marry Christians of inferior social status, join themselves to pagans, "husbands, slaves of the devil." He observes that the phenomenon occurs among "the more distinguished women," because "it is difficult to find a rich man in the house of God; and if one does find one, it is unlikely that he is for marriage." [157] This affirmation mirrors the situation of the Christian community of Carthage, where the women of the higher classes were in a clear majority over the men. The same situation existed elsewhere.

In Rome, according to the accusations by the author of the *Philosophoumena/Elenchos* (*Against the Heresies*), Callistus permitted the Christian women of high standing to unite with men of inferior condition outside of the Roman juridical norms. These women had to be part of the Senatorial class.[158]

Christian women of the high social classes had pagan husbands, and the cases were not infrequent, but we do not know of Christian husbands who had pagan wives. Pagan husbands, while marrying rich Christian women, were quite prepared to cover up their religion. The wife of a powerful person is not denounced lightly or with impunity. These Christian women or sympathizers became a guarantee and protection of coreligionists. For example, there is Marcia, the "God-fearing concubine" of the emperor Commodus who worked for the liberation of Callistus and others from the mines.[159]

The pagan author Cassius Dio writes; "It is said (in pagan circles) that she (Marcia) took a great interest in the Christians and she put at their service all the power she enjoyed with Commodus."[160] This was one of the resources Christians had at their disposal to avoid persecution and to win people of high social standing. Florinus, to whom Irenaeus wrote, was an important figure in the time of Polycarp, "illustrious in the imperial court."[161] At the beginning of the third century, Hippolytus refers to the case of a governor of Syria who set free a band of Christians headed by their bishop to please his Christian wife.[162] On the other hand, according to Tertullian, the governor of Cappadocia, Claudius Lucius Herminianus, deeply hurt because his wife was Christian, unleashed persecution on the Christians.[163] When he was dying of a terrible disease, he wanted to make sure the Christians did not find out. Thus, two personages of high standing reacted differently to the Christianity of their respective wives. But the reaction of the Syrian governor was the most frequent. The success with members of high society, those who applied the laws, therefore, greatly benefitted Christianity.

One of the accusations which the pagans leveled at the Christians was that in their assemblies the women dominated. Porphyry presents the Christian communities as under the domination of women.[164] He also refers to the concern of someone who went to Apollo to find out, "Which god he should propitiate in order to recall his wife from Christianity." Apollo replied: "You will probably find it easier to write lasting characters on the water, or lightly fly like a bird through the air than to call to reason a wife plagued by impiety. Let her remain as she pleases when she insists on those empty deceptions and cries her empty wailings, mourning her dead god who was condemned by right-minded judges and perished ignominiously by a violent death, the worst of the spectacles."

For this reason Jerome admonishes: "We must be vigilant so that the matrons and the females are not, as Porphyry would like, our Senate, and that they do not dominate in the churches. Let us be careful that it is not the duty of the females to judge the priestly rank."[165] The so-called Council of Elvira (309)[166] noted the existence of an abundance of Christian girls (*copia puellarum*) who, because of the shortage of boys, married pagans with the consequent danger to their faith. "Because of the abundance of girls, do not give Christian virgins as wives to the pagans, so as their young age does not lead them to adultery of the soul."[167] A few years later, the Council of Arles (314) faced the same problem and the same danger in a much larger geographical situation. It established the following: "Regarding the Christian girls who marry pagans, it is decided that, for some time, they should be kept away from communion."[168] Why make such a decision? I suppose there still existed the *copia puellarum* and the scarcity of boys (*paucitas puerorum*). A small penalty of abstention from communion was imposed. It is not to be excluded that the women were baptized earlier than the men who more easily put off baptism until an advanced age. The Hispanic epitome of the Council of Elvira, somewhat later, reworks the canon and grants to the parents the possibility of giving their daughters in marriage to pagans, when perhaps already these pagans were a small minority and true followers of the pagan religion.

The problem signaled by Tertullian of the difficulty for Christian women of the higher social classes to find a husband of their religion also continued at the beginning of the fourth century. Could such scarcity of Christian boys be a reality in only some communities, or was this a more general phenomenon in other social classes? I'm inclined to consider it a general phenomenon only of the superior classes. This vision was the reason for the proliferation of mixed marriages between Christians and non-Christians (pagans). According to the Roman legal system, marriage between different classes was not permitted (*iustum matrimonium*)—in particular of the senatorial class (*clarissimi*) with those of the lower classes (*humiliores*). In classical law, the religious problem in marriage did not exist. They were only concerned with the legal question. This situation became a problem for the legislator only in the fourth century concerning marriages with the Jews (not with the pagans).[169] At this time, the link that was established with idol worshippers (*sacerdotes idolorum*)[170] referred to the upper classes or maybe also the middle classes but not those of the *humiliores*. The other alternative was to renounce marriage and remain virgins, whether in their own families or as members of a group. But, as we saw above, there was also the option that the author of the *Elenchos* wrote about where Bishop Callistus permitted the concubinage (*concubinatus*) of some Christian matrons.[171]

CONCLUSION

I'm not able to offer statistics concerning the proportion of men and women, at least for now, without venturing into the area of pure conjecture. It may be useful to keep in mind the minutes drawn up at Cirta (Numidia) in 303 which offer us some indication. The clear majority of clothing seized was for women: "Eighty-two women's tunics, thirty-eight veils, sixteen men's tunics, thirteen pairs of men's shoes, forty-seven women's shoes."[172] The following year at Carthage, on February 12, 304 in the court of the proconsul Anulinus the trial began of 49 Christians brought from the town of Abitinae.[173] There were 31 men, 18 women and one baby boy. They were gathered to celebrate the Eucharistic liturgy in the house of the reader Emeritus—four readers were arrested—with the priest Saturninus presiding. He had four children, among them a baby boy. The bishop of the city, Fundanus, had betrayed them when he handed over the Scriptures. One of those arrested was Dativus, a courageous martyr who was a member of the local curia. There was also the martyr Victoria who had joined them from Carthage who was from a noble family. During the trial, Fortunatianus, the brother of Victoria, accused Dativus of having organized the meetings and of having brought his sister from Carthage to Abitinae while her father was away, together with two other girls, Secunda and Restituta. Victoria, opposing her brother, shouted out that she had gone spontaneously. The three courageous girls, wanting to practice their Christian faith freely, had abandoned their families in Carthage and had taken refuge in the small colony. In this large group of martyrs, the men were in the majority.[174]

At Cirta, the majority of the people helped were women. Currently, it is the common opinion among scholars that women constituted the majority in Christian communities.

---

1. *Tusculanae* 4.8.18 (see 3.10.21): *misericordia est aegritudo ex miseria alterius iniuria laborantis (nemo enim parricidae aut proditoris supplicio misericordi commovetur)* (Mercy is a sadness derived from the misery of one who suffers because of the wrong of another (in fact no one is touched in the heart by the torment of a murderer or a traitor).
2. M. Amerise, "L'idea di misericordia tra paganesimo tardoantico e cristianesimo: il caso di Giuliano l'Apostata" *Salesianum* 64 (2002): 221-29; B. Zacchelli, "Sulla formazione di 'misericors/Misericordia," *Paideia* 60 (2005): 371-80; S. Adamiak, "Asking for Human Mercy: Augustine's Intercession with the Men in Power" in *Scrinium Augustini: The World of Augustine's Letters*, ed. P. Nehring (Turnhout: Brepols, 2017), 19-40.
3. *Augustus* 26.
4. Strabo, *Geography* 5.3.8.
5. R. Lawrence, *The Roads of Roman Italy: Mobility and Cultural Change* (London: Routledge, 1999); H. Barow, *Roads and Bridges of the Roman Empire* (Stuttgart; London: Ed. Menges, 2013); *The Impact of Mobility and Migration in the Roman Empire: Proceedings of the Twelfth Workshop of the International Network Impact of Empire*, ed. E. Lo Cascio, et al. (Leiden: Brill, 2017).
6. Lactantius, *On the Deaths of the Persecutors* ANF 7:7.4.
7. Referred to as *praeses, iudex*, and other names.
8. *Cum in theatre imperiti homines rerum omnium rudes ignarique, tum bella inutilia suscipiebant, tum seditiosos nomine rei publicae praeficiebant, tum optime meritos cives e civitate eiciebant (Pro Flacco* 7.16; see 22.55).
9. N. Brenner, "Christianus sum: The Early Christian Martyrs and Christ," in *Eulogia: Mélanges offerts à Antoon R. Bastiaensen à l'occasion de son soixante-cinquième anniversaire* (Turnhout: Brepols, 1991), 11-20; C. Moss, *The Other Christs: Imitating Jesus in Ancient Christian Ideologies of Martyrdom* (New York: Oxford University Press, 2010).
10. *Passio Scil.* 3.
11. Eusebius, *HE* 5.1.43.
12. Lactantius, *Inst.* 5.20.
13. F. Ruggiero, *Atti dei martiri scilitani: introduzione, testo, traduzione, testimonianze e commento* (Rome: Accademia nazionale dei Lincei, 1991), 48f. A. Smarius, "Roman Persecution of Christians: The Scillitan Martyrs," *Ancient History Magazine* 2 (2016): 47-51.
14. A court room of the praetorium closed to the public.
15. The number is questioned, because at the beginning of the *Acta* only six Christians are named; the other names were either omitted at the beginning or they belonged to another trial and were inserted here in the redaction of the text.
16. J. Quasten, *Patrology* (Utrecht: Spectrum, 1950), 172.
17. See Tertullian *Apology* 1,7; *Ad Scapulam* 2.10.
18. The Apocryphal Acts of the Apostles speak about the itinerant missionaries, who converted the pagans to Christianity.
19. See P. Siniscalco, "Le vie di commercio e la diffusione del cristianesimo," in *Mondo classico e cristianesimo* (Rome: Istituto della Enciclopedia italiana, 1982), 17-28.
20. W. Dittenberger, *Sylloge Inscriptionum Graecarum* (Hildesheim: Olms, 1982), 685.
21. S.R.F. Price, "Gods and Emperors: The Greek Language of the Roman Imperial Cult," *The Journal of Hellenic Studies* 104 (1984): 79-95.
22. *Supplementum Epigraphicum Graecum* IV, 201, in D. Magie, *Roman Rule in Asia Minor, to the End of the Third Century after Christ* (Princeton: Princeton University Press, 1950), 490. For other exaltations of the prosperous peace of Augustus, see S.R.F. Price, *Rituals and Power. The Roman Imperial Cult in Asia Minor* (Cambridge: Cambridge University Press, 1984), 54ff.
23. *Fecisti patriam diversis gentibus unam; Profuit iniustis te dominante capi; Dunque offers victis proprii consortia iuris. Urbem fecisti, quod prius orbis erat (De reditu* 1. 63-65).

24. Ch. Jacob, *L'empire des cartes. Approche théorique de la cartographie à travers l'histoire* (Paris: Albin Michel, 1992).
25. *Corpus Inscriptionum Latinarum* (= CIL) 8:9585-9586; E. Dehl, *Inscriptiones Latinae Christianae Veteres* (=ICLV) 1583, 1179.
26. Today it is the village of Reşca, of the municipality of Dobrosloveni in Romania.
27. In the county/district of Olt, Romania.
28. *caput orbis terrarium* (Titus Livius, *A urbe condita* 1.16).
29. Eusebius, *HE* 8.11.1.
30. Lactantius, *Div. Inst.* 5.11.
31. W. M. Ramsey, *Cities and Bishoprics of Phrygia*, (Oxford: The Clarendon Press, 1895), 507-8; see. A Chastagnol, "L'inscription constantienne d'Orcitus," *MEFRA* 93 (1981): 381-416, here 410.
32. Eusebius, *Onomaticon* 112,14.
33. In Phrygia, northeast of Hierapolis.
34. *Dictionnaire d'archéologie chrétienne et de liturgie* (=DACL) 5:734-744; S. Mitchell, *Anatolia: The Rise of the Church* (Oxford: Clarendon Press, 1993), 242-46; Th. Drew-Bear, *Nouvelles inscriptions de Phrygie* (Zutphen: Terra Pub. Co., 1978), 53-114: there is also an inscription by a presbyter from 257/258. S. Destephen, "La Christianisation de l'Asie Mineure jusqu' à Constantin: le témoignage de l'épigraphie," in *Le problème de la christianisation du monde antique*, H. Inglebert, S. Destephen and B. Dumézil (Paris: Picard, 2010), 159-194, here 181ff.
35. T. Drew-Bear, "Les voyages d'Aurélius Gaius, soldat de Dioclétien," in *La géographie administrative et politique d'Alexandre à Mahomet* (Leiden: Brill, 1981), 93-141.
36. M. Colombo, "Correzioni testuali ed esegetiche all'epigrafe di Aurelius Gaius (regione di Kotiaeum in Phrygia)," *ZPE* 174 (2010): 118-26.
37. Julian, *Ep.* 9; Sozomen, *HE* 5.3,5.
38. Yotam Tepper and Leah Di Segni, *A Christian Prayer Hall of the Third Century CE at Kefar 'othnay (legio): Excavations at the Megiddo Prison 2005* (Jerusalem: The Israel Antiquities Authority, 2006); Edward Adams, "The Ancient Church at Megiddo: The Discovery and an Assessment of its Significance," *Expository Times* 120 (2008): 62-9.
39. "Gaianus, also called Porphyrius, centurion, our brother, has made the pavement at his own expense as an act of liberality. Brutius has carried out the work."
40. A third Greek inscription says: "remember Primilla and Cyriaca and Dorothea, and moreover also Chreste."
41. Cyril of Scythopolis, *Vita Sabae* 57.
42. Eusebius, *HE* 2.16.1.
43. Annick Martin, "Encadrement ecclésiastique, organisation des communautés locales et développement du christianisme en Égypte au IIIe et IVe siècles," in *Les Pères de l'Église et les ministères. Évolutions, idéal et réalités*, ed. Pascal Delage (La Rochelle: Association Histoire et Culture, 2008), 323–40.
44. Eusebius, *HE* 7.26.1 and 3.
45. See the accounts of John of Ephesus (*HE* 4.6-9; 49-53) and John of Biclaro (Spain, cf. T. Mommsen, *Chronica minora*, *Monumenta Germaniae Historica* (=MGH) AA 11: 212).
46. Eusebius, *HE* 1.9-10.
47. Eusebius, *HE* 6.46.3.
48. J. Neusner, *A History of Jews in Babylonia* (Leiden: E.J. Brill, 1965-1970).
49. *EAC* 1:780.
50. A region on the southern shore of the Caspian Sea.
51. On the northern shore of the Caspian Sea, today Dagestan. Par. 46, *Patrologia Syr.* 2:606f.
52. *Hist. nat.* 5.66; 6.25, 28, 41, 44, 114; more precise information can be found in Tacitus, *Annales* 12.
53. Pliny, *Ep.* 10.96.
54. *Dictionnaire d'historie et de géographie Ecclésiastiques* (=DHGE) 19:717ff.
55. Tertullian, *Ad Scapulam* 3.4.
56. Beyozü (province of Çorum, district of Mecitozu), in Pontus.
57. See S. Mitchell, *Anatolia*, II (Oxford: Oxford University Press, 1993), 57ff.
58. Eusebius, *De mart. Pal.* 9,2; see *Enciclopedia Cattolica* 1:1986ff; A. D. Lee, *Pagans and Christians in Late Antiquity: A Sourcebook* (London: Routledge, 2000),77ff.
59. Julian, *Ep.* 79; Sozomen, *HE* 5,4,1-2.
60. Gregory of Nyssa, *Sermo cath.* 18.3.
61. *Codex Theod.* 16,1.2 = *Codex Iust.* 1.1.1.

62. Eusebius, *HE* 4.26.10.
63. Eusebius, *HE* 4.23.2.
64. Eusebius, *HE* 6.23.4.
65. Jerome, *De viris inl.* 54.3.
66. *Apostolic Const.* 7.46.
67. In Latin Buthrotum; today Butrinti or Butrint, in Epirus, now in Albania.
68. Eusebius, *HE* 6.32.2.
69. Origen, *Contra Celsum* 3.30.
70. Eusebius, *HE* 6,16,2
71. *Vita Constantini*, 3.7.
72. Confirmed by *Acts* 2:11; see Philo, *Legatio ad Gaium* 282.
73. Mansi, 7:621ff.
74. F. de' Cavalieri, *Scritti agiografici* (Città del Vaticano: Biblioteca apostolica vaticana, 1962), 367-400.
75. Eusebius, *HE* 3.1.1.
76. Eusebius, *Vita Const.* 3.7.
77. *Codex Iust.* 1.3,35; see Sozomen, *HE* 6.21; Theodoret of Cyrrhus, *HE* 4.35.
78. Essek, not far from the confluence of the Drava and the Danube.
79. At the confluence of the Sava and the Danube which is today Belgrade.
80. See Origen, *In Gen. Comm.* 3; Eusebius, *HE* 3,1.
81. See DACL 2.2640.
82. Latin *Axius*; the Republic of North Macedonia and Kosovo, crossing Scupi [a few kilometers from what is today Skopje, in Macedonia])
83. Ptuj in eastern Slovenia, a city annexed to Noricum by Diocletian; cf. Jerome, *De vir.* 74.
84. *Acta Sanctorum*, Jun. 1.372ff.
85. In Pannonia Secunda; modern-day Vinkovci.
86. *EAC* 3:601.
87. It was later called Ulpiana, in Moesia Superior; today it is Gračanica in Kosovo.
88. *Dalmatae [delmatae]*.
89. Danuvius, or Ister, in ancient Greek Istros.
90. ASS, Mai 1:466-72.
91. Athanasius, *Apol. C. Arianos* 1 and 31: PG 25:249 and 312.
92. August and the village of Kaiseraugust; afterward, the see passed to Basilea.
93. Martigny—afterward the episcopal see passed to Sion (*Sedunum*) or Sitten in German.
94. *splendidissima Raetiae provinciae colonia.* Tacitus, *Germania* 41.
95. Hermas, *Shepherd, Simil.* 9.19.
96. Irenaeus, *Adv. haer.* 3.3.2.
97. Irenaeus, *Adv. haer.* 3.3.3; Eusebius, *HE* 4.22.3; Tertullian, *De praescr.* 32.2.
98. Eusebius, *HE* 6.43.2.
99. A. von Harnack, *Die Mission und Ausbreitung des Christentums in den ersten drei Jahrhunderten* (Leipzig: Hinrichs'sche Buchhandlung, 1906), 807.
100. See *EAC* 3:428-31.
101. Cyprian, *Ep.* 30.5.2.
102. Eusebius, *HE* 10.5.21ff.
103. CIL 10:7172; F. P, Rizzo, *Gli albori della Sicilia Cristiana* (Bari: Edipuglia, 2005), 37ff.
104. *pro foribus mart(yrum) chr(istian)orum.*
105. Salvian, *De guber.* 12; PL 53:121.
106. See *EAC* 1:615ff.
107. PL 58:1116ff.
108. Cyprian, *Ep.* 48.3.2.
109. See Tertullian, *Ad Scapulam* 3; *Apology* 37.
110. PL 3:1052A. *episcopi plurimi ex provincia Africa, Numidia, Mauritania cum presbyteris et diaconibus.*
111. Proconsular Numidia; "Numidia of Hippo."
112. *Tripoli episcopi sunt quinque tantummodo;* Mansi 3:741.

113. Jerome, *Ep.* 65.12; *Ep.*, 71.1, Id. *Ep.* 120.9; Theodoret of Cyrrhus, *Interpr. Epist. II ad Tim.*, 4.17.
114. Colonia Caesar Augusta.
115. *Calagurris*.
116. In Catalan Girona; Latin: *Gerunda*.
117. *Corduba*.
118. *Emerita Augusta*.
119. *Complutum*.
120. *Praef.* 100.1.23.
121. Calahorra, on the Ebro River.
122. Julius Caesar, *The Gallic Wars* 1.1.
123. See Cyprian, *Ep.* 68.
124. Munier, CCL 148:14, 41, 51, 71.
125. Bagacum, 60 km to the east of Lille.
126. An archaeological site 20 km east of Basel.
127. Irenaeus, *Adv. haer.* 1.10.2. SC 264:159.
128. *Colonia Ulpia Traiana*; in the Middle Ages: *Ad Sanctos*.
129. *Concilia Galliae* 314-506: CCL 148:27-9.
130. The text reads: *consacerdotes mei salutares antisites evocarunt*.
131. Vitricius, *De laude sanctorum* 1, PL 20:443-44.
132. SC 112:144.
133. Prosper, *Chronicon*, MGH AA 9:472.
134. Prosper, *Chronicon*, MGH AAA 9:473.
135. E. Lo Cascio, "La popolazione," in *Roma imperiale. Una metropoli antica*, ed. E. Lo Cascio (Rome: Carocci, 2000), 41. See W. Scheidel, "Roman Population Size: The Logic of the Debate," in *People, Land and Politics: Demographic Developments and the Transformation of Roman Italy 300 BC-AD 14*, eds. L. de Ligt, S. J. Northwood (Leiden: Brill, 2008), 17-70.
136. Origen, *Contra Celsum* 3.10-12.
137. E. Klutz, "The Rhetoric of Science in the Rise of Christianity: A Response to Rodney Stark's Sociological Account of Christianization," *JECS* 6 (1998): 162-84; K. Hopkins, *Christian Number and its Implications*, 185-226; E. A. Castelli, *Gender Theory and the Rise of Christianity: A Response to Rodney Stark*, 227-257; R. Stark, *On the Contrary*, 259-67.
138. R. Stark, *The Cities of God* (San Francisco: Harper Collins, 2006).
139. R. Lane Fox, *Pagans and Christians* (New York: Knopf, 1986), 698.
140. G. Filoramo, *La croce e il potere. I cristiani da martiri a persecutori* (Bari/Rome: Laterza, 2011), 86. He cites Eusebius, *HE* 9.7.9, where he speaks of something else.
141. Ortaköy, previously called Alikel Yayla.
142. D. Feissel, "L'adnotatio de Constantin sur le droit de cité d'Orcistus en Phrygie," *Antiquité Tardive* 7 (1999): 255-67.
143. A. Chastagnol, "L'inscription constantienne d'Orcistus," *MEFRA* 93 (1981): 381-416 (= Aspects de l'antiquité tardive, Roma 1994, 104ff; A. Chastagnol, "Les realia d'une cité d'après l'inscription constantinienne d'Orkistos," *Ktèma* 6 (1981): 373-379A. C. Johnson et al., *Ancient Roman Statutes: A Translation with Introduction, Commentary, Glossary* (Austin: University of Texas Press, 1961), rep. Clark, NJ, 2003, doc. 304, 240.
144. Nusaybin, in Mesopotamia.
145. Julian, *Ep.*9: Sozomen *HE* 5.3.5.
146. C. Gebbia, "Ancora Altava," in *L'Africa romana*, ed. by M. Akerraz, P. Ruggeri, A. Siraj, C. Vismara (Rome: Carocci, 2006), 495-505; M.A. Ruiu, "La Cohors II Sardorum ad Altava (Ouled-Mimoun, Algeria)," in *L'Africa romana* (Rome: Carocci, 2004), Vol. 1:1415-32; J. Marcillet Jaubert, *Les inscriptions d'Altava*, (Aix-en-Provence 1968), C. Lepelley, *Les cités de l'Afrique romaine au Bas-Empire* (Paris: Études augustiniennes, 1981), vol. 2.522-34.
147. S. Ammirati, "Per una storia del libro latino antico. Osservazioni paleografiche, bibliologiche e codicologiche sui manoscritti latini di argomento legale dalle origini alla tarda antichità," *The Journal of Juristic Papyrology* 11 (2010): 55-110.
148. E. Wipszycka, "Books, literacy, and Christian Communities on two recent books by Roger Bagnall," *The Journal of Juristic Papyrology* 11 (2010): 249-226, see esp. 262.

149. G. Cavallo, "Libri, lettura e biblioteche nella tarda antichità. Un panorama e qualche riflessione," *Antiquité Tardive* 18 (2010): 9-19, see esp. 11.
150. Ibid, 11.
151. R. S. Bagnall, *Early Christian Books in Egypt* (Princeton: Princeton University Press, 2009), 2.
152. Ibid, 190.
153. Ibid, 20.
154. E. Wipszycka, "Books, literacy," in *The Journal of Juristic Papyrology* 11 (2010): 254-55. Now we also see E. Wipszycka, *The Alexandrian Church: People and Institution* (Warsaw: Journal of Juristic Papyrology, 2015), 64-6.
155. E. Wipszycka, *The Alexandrian Church*, 69.
156. Z. García Villada, *Historia eclesiásitica de España*, I (Madrid: Compañía Ibero-americana de Publicaciones, 1929), 252-300; A. Fábrega Grau, *Pasionario Hispánico*, I (Madrid: C.S.I.C., 1953), 59-174; C. Garcá Rodríduez, *El culto de los Santos en Esapaña romana y visigoda* (Madrid; C.S.I.C., 1966), 219-334.
157. Tertullian, *Ad uxor.* 2.8.2.
158. S. Mazzarino, *Trattato di storia romana* (Bologna: Patron, 1976), 299 and 316.
159. Ps. Hippolytus, *Philosophoumena (Adv. omnes haer.)* 9.12, ed. Marcovich, 355-56; Michael Flexsenhar III, "Marcia, Commodus' 'Christian' Concubine and CIL X 5918," *Tyche* 31 (2016): 135-48.
160. *Roman History* 77.4.
161. Eusebius, *HE* 5.20.5.
162. Hippolytus, *Comm. Dan.* 4.18.
163. Tertullian, *Ad Scap.* 3.4.
164. See Jerome, *Comm. in Jes.* 3.2.
165. Jerome, *Comm. In Ies.* 3.2.
166. It seems to me that this mirrors the situation at the beginning of the fourth century and not of a later period.
167. Can. 15: *Propter copiam puellarum gentilibus minime in matrimonium dandae sunt virgines Christianae, ne aetas in flore tumens in adulterio animae resolvatur.*
168. Can. 12: *De puellis fidelibus quae gentilibus iunguntur, placuit ut aliquanto tempore a communione separentur.*
169. CTh. 16.8.6; 3.7.2 = 9.7.5.
170. See Jerome, *Ep. Ad Nepotianum.*
171. The concept of concubinage is different to ours. It was the union of a man and a woman characterized by stability and by the lack of the will to consider themselves husband and wife. It was recognized by Roman law. Because of the existence of prohibitions of certain matrimonial unions, concubinage became widespread. The children were considered to be born out of wedlock. D. Gemmiti, *Il concubinato nel diritto romano e giustinianeo. Con appendice sul diritto bizantino* (Napoli: LER, 1993).
172. In Optatus, *De schismate*, ed. Ziwsa, CSEL 26:1893, 186f. A.P. Schiavo, *I Am A Christian: Authentic Accounts of Christian Martyrdom and Persecution* (Merchantville, NJ: ARX Pub, 2018), 129ff.; F. Dolbeau, "La 'Passion' des martyrs d'Abitina: remarques sur l'établissement du texte," *Analecta Bollandiana* 121 (2003): 273-96.
173. Present-day Chouhoud al-Bâânear Medjez el-Bab in Tunisia.
174. C. Osiek, M.Y. MacDonald, *A Women's Place: House Churches in Earliest Christianity* (Minneapolis: Fortress Press, 2006), 303-4.

CHAPTER 3
CHRISTIAN INITIATION AND ITS RITES

INITIATIONS AND INITIATION

THE SECOND CENTURY PAGAN SATIRICAL WRITER LUCIAN OF SAMOSATA WRITES THAT THE Christians "worship" the man who was crucified in Palestine, who introduced into the world this new 'telete', that is, initiation.[1] Therefore, to a pagan writer of that period, Christianity appears as a mystery religion. And Lucian shows that he has a certain knowledge of Christian life and customs, that is, of their public and observable conduct of living. He also refers to their meetings, but he does not give the slightest description of them, perhaps because they were not known by him and were surrounded by a certain confidentiality. His intention does not seem to be the mockery of Christians, however, but rather to speak of the immoderate love for the glory of the Christian pilgrimage (Proteus). The term initiation (*telete*) is never used by Christians of the second and third centuries to indicate initiation into Christianity. Apologists employ it for pagan cults. To Lucian's eyes, Christianity appears as one of the many abundant mystery religions of that century—and it does not look that way only to him. We can ask ourselves why?[2] The post-Vatican II Council climate led to the reuse in the Catholic and Protestant spheres of certain terms concerning ancient Christian initiation. Vocabulary has also been used to try to recover some aspects of ancient baptismal practice, both in official ecclesial sectors and in groups born and raised in recent decades. The changes that have taken place since the second part of the last century have placed the problem of the Christianization of European and American countries at the center of baptismal reflection and practice.

The term initiation has different meanings today, covering a semantic area ranging from the technical reference to the rituals for admission to the ancient mysteries of the Hellenistic-Roman period, to the knowledge of occult and secretive societies, to the rituals for admission to a group or association (e.g. Freemasonry) or to any initiation into specific knowledge. Mircea Eliade, the scholar who has most dealt with this subject, offers the following definition: initiation belongs to the existential condition. "The novice emerges from the tests to which he is subjected as a completely different being: he becomes an 'other.'"[3] This definition supposes a whole conception of initiation which is the fruit of numerous studies.[4] It intends to express some of initiation's essential and always present characteristics. In a more particular field, that of religious ethnology, initiation includes ceremonies, ritual practices, and teachings through which young men and women have access to the status of adults, which makes them suitable for war and marriage. In the broadest and most metaphorical sense, it indicates the initial training, the basic instruction in science, arts and trades. The transition from the first technical and restricted meaning, that is, the ancient one, to the metaphorical sense that is now widely used, takes place through the activities associated with the professions of the medieval period (such as the alchemist, blacksmith, bricklayer, and others) which were jealously guarded secrets of the master. He would gradually communicate his knowledge and experience to his disciple, who was introduced only slowly into the realm of knowledge necessary for those trades.

The term "initiation" is from the Latin *initiatio*,[5] which in turn implies the concept of origin, in the sense of removal from a certain condition or state in order to move on to an entirely new state which marks a new beginning. It erases one's previous existence in favor of a different and new existence. It is much more than a simple change in condition. It is symbolically signified by the categories of death and resurrection. Initiation plays a very important role in religions, even if not all religions have initiatory rites of the same intensity. In fact, through initiation one enters the true world of divinity and the knowledge of truth, which are fully revealed only to the initiate. In the case where a gradual initiation is required, the revelation occurs progressively and in relation to the degree of belonging. This happens, for example, in certain mystery religions that admit different degrees of initiates, as in the case of the religion of Mithra.

Since initiation is a fundamental aspect of religion, it is essential to clarify its nature and function in different religions. The extreme difficulty of such a study should be noted here. In some cases, it is almost impossible to get to know certain aspects of a particular ancient religion. There are further difficulties with other ancient religions due to the scarcity and poor condition of some sources. In addition, there is the epistemological problem of the sciences of religion. It is assumed, according to the epistemological model, that in order to understand any religious fact, it is necessary to tune in to the same wavelength as the believer. For this reason, it is stated that one can understand the religious truth and experience only if one has personally experienced it. The average believer is normally reticent to talk about or discuss his personal and intimate religious beliefs. While it is true that only members of a religion can provide the right information, it is also true that from within you only have a partial or skewed view of your religion. Often the scholar, in addition to having no personal experience of initiation, works on the texts and data in his possession, which are often insufficient. There is also a lack of living examples of people who practice those mystery religions of the Roman period.

In Christianity itself, initiation has profoundly changed, with only a few ancient symbols and rites surviving. The difficulty is accentuated when dealing with initiation rites, at least in some religions, where there is an intense level of secrecy: the secrecy concerns both the rites themselves and the esoteric knowledge transmitted during the performance of the rites. The investigation in this case finds an objective limit. We have only fragments of rites, ceremonies and doctrines taught, which are subject to different interpretations.[6] Secrecy has a number of different levels and aspects. It may refer to membership in a secret society, that is to say, a religious or secretive association. Or it may refer to a public entity where the general requirements are known, that is, the condition of initiation, while a strict secrecy enshrouds the more esoteric religious truth—a secret jealously guarded by the followers. These are the only ones who have the privilege and the possibility of knowing what that secret is. But then they are under obligation not to reveal it to others.

Finally, the secret could be an ineffable truth, an inexplicable mystery that may be known in part by non-followers, but only the followers are in a position to be able to understand it. The initiates are placed at a higher level of understanding because they are, through initiation, at another level of being. Bleeker observes that initiation into a hidden truth can have two meanings. First of all, it can consist in the privilege of being able to participate in the expression of certain truths in worship. This means that initiation introduces a person into the right to perform certain dramatic acts of a mysterious nature. This happens in some ancient religions as well as in certain aspects of Christianity.[7] Secrecy is about cultic practice. In other cases, however, it is the same esoteric truth that is revealed to those who have passed through prescribed initiation rites. Although everyone, at least in many mystery religions, could be initiated and become a member, in practice there may have been limitations of various kinds—restrictions resulting from the age, sexual condition or morality of the person. The ancient mystery religions were open to people of both sexes, except for the cult of Mithra which was reserved for military and male personnel, although individuals who had committed certain crimes could be excluded.

Initiation comprises several themes: The first and most important theme is that of symbolic death followed by resurrection. This death can be a type of descent into hell (*descensus ad inferos*) from where one rises, or a return to birth (*regressus ad uterum*) from where one is born again. The novice must be symbolically buried for rebirth or resurrection. Rebirth consists in the passage from the condition of natural man to the cultural man in the new condition of existence. One dies not only to one's own past, but also to one's previous way of doing things; just as one is reborn into a new way of doing things in a new community, that of the saved and the enlightened ones. With neophytes, the community also regenerates and renews itself, because these new births in its bosom allow its survival. For this reason, even those who have already been initiated participate in the initiations in what can be a quite festive atmosphere.

Another very important theme which also favored the spread of mystery cults in the Roman Empire is that of salvation. Cumont notes that the primary purpose of eastern and mystery religions is the recovery of the original purity and the achievement of salvation through initiation and participation in the mysteries.[8] The salvation of the faithful is associated with that of the god who rises again. However, we must not forget what is meant by salvation in the Greco-Roman period. It embraces all present and future human life in its entirety, both spiritual and physical. In a moral sense it presupposes either a past fault—whether earthly or something that happened even before birth—or a present fault the person currently has.[9]

Even Christian baptism is sometimes presented from this perspective of the total liberation of man. In the background is an anthropology which conceives of man as a psycho-physical totality. The sinner is the prey or victim of the devil. Just as sin concerns the whole of man, so too does the illness and the consequent liberation. To be cured, the sick person must be cured in both body and soul. Baptism, conceived above all as liberation from sin, is also liberation from disease because demons are driven out of the body of the baptized. The moral aspect cannot be separated from that of the body. Therefore, the new existence, the regeneration, concerns in some way the whole person. Christian baptism also provides effective protection, especially against the devil who corrupts people and leads them to evil and thus to unhappiness. In the *Acts of Thomas*, a woman asks for baptism after being freed so as not to fall back into her previous condition: "Apostle of the Most High, give me the seal of my Lord, so that that enemy does not return to me again."[10] When Perpetua was nearing her martyrdom, she received baptism but made no specific request beyond baptismal grace: "In those very first days we received baptism, and the Holy Spirit made me understand that from that moment on there was no other grace to implore from the baptismal water."[11]

Other important themes concern purification through certain specific practices, the light, the illumination of the neophyte, and vision.[12] The neophyte is enlightened through initiation, so he passes from a condition of darkness to that of light. He is able to understand what was previously precluded, that is, to acquire another type of knowledge other than ordinary.

It is an inner vision that is only available to the initiate. Christian baptism enables another type of vision. The term "illumination" (*photismos*) is synonymous with "seal," i.e. baptism. The baptized person is referred to as "enlightened."[13] In the eastern world the baptistery is called *photisterion*, as it is the place of enlightenment. In the Passion of St. Cecilia, it is said that the groom Valerian approaches Cecilia. She tells him not to touch her because her angel would become furious. Valerian asks to see the angel and is sent by Cecilia to the Bishop Urbanus who baptizes him. Only then is Valerian able to see the angel.[14] The so-called discipline of the arcane or secrecy (*disciplina arcani*) of early Christianity is not meant to indicate—as is commonly written—that absolute secrecy was to be maintained, but rather that in order to understand the mysteries, i.e. the sacraments, one must experience them. Only then can one understand and explain them. But no one could have such an experience by their own initiative. They must be enabled, made capable of having the experience—almost as if it were an ontological change taking place in the person—as a gift from God which could open them up to experiential understanding.

CHRISTIAN INITIATION AND THE TERM CHRISTIAN

The word "Christian" was used for the disciples of Jesus for the first time in Antioch (*Acts* 11:26). We do not know, however, whether it was used by the pagans, the Roman authorities, or by the disciples themselves. The first hypothesis seems more likely because the name did not spread immediately. This would seem to indicate it was used as an accusation from outside and therefore was meant in a derogatory sense. Already in 64 CE when many Christians were being persecuted and killed in Rome and elsewhere, Nero and the Roman authorities explicitly distinguished this new group from the Jews and other religious groups, as shown by Tacitus[15] and the letter of Pliny to Trajan in 111.[16] Recently it has been noted that the term, attested for the first time in the 40-50s, must refer to a certain *Chrestos*, named by Suetonius, and would actually correspond to the righteous man in the book of Wisdom 2:12-20 who is put to the test and condemned by the wicked, but one day would be glorified. The disciples of Jesus then appropriated the title to spread the good news in a cosmopolitan city like Antioch.[17]

However, over time "Christian" replaced other terms previously used in the New Testament such as "elected," "saints," "disciples," and became the standard name to refer to followers of Christ. Some fathers derive it from "Christ," understood as a proper name, because Christians are the followers, disciples, of Christ the master par excellence. Rarely do they hesitate to explain its etymological meaning: Christ means *anointed*; in this sense Christians—the anointed—are participants in the priesthood of Christ.

In the fourth century, catechumens also tended to be called "Christians," since they too were already followers of Christ and could profess themselves as his disciples, while the term "faithful" (*fidelis*) was reserved exclusively for the baptized. Only the faithful can participate in the Eucharist and in the whole life of the church. To be counted among the faithful, a period of trial and preparation is necessary, culminating in the rites of the Easter vigil in which the sacraments of Christian initiation are received, and in the mystagogical catechesis provided the following week.

Among many of today's Christians the term "initiation" is used to indicate the entire path of conversion that must be completed before baptism. It is meant to be a time of progressive preparation and can also be used to indicate the unity of the three sacraments: baptism, confirmation and the Eucharist. These sacraments are conferred and received together. For the fathers, on the other hand, the term only indicated the moment in which the final rites were performed. The Christian truths would be revealed during the Easter vigil to the newly baptized and meant something quite different than how it is currently used. To express the period of preparation in patristic language we should rather speak of the "catechumenate" and of "catechumens." Justin[18] and Tertullian[19] found similarities with the pagan mysteries, which they attributed to the work of the demons.

The term "initiation" is already found in Tertullian.[20] The Alexandrians, Clement and Origen, use the Greek terminology of initiation: *mysterion, teleté, myeo, mystagogeo*. But given the link between these terminologies and the mystery religions, the fathers normally avoid them and try to distinguish Christian rites from pagan mysteries. In the catechesis of the fourth and fifth centuries the vocabulary of initiation that developed was used, at least by Ambrose and John Chrysostom, in the sacramental sense. This term is not found in Augustine's preaching or in his anti-Donatist writings, but in other works the verb *initiare* appears used in the sacramental sense.[21]

The fathers of the first centuries were reluctant to use traditional initiatory terminology for Christian initiation because this belonged to the language of the mystery religions such as of Eleusis or Mithra. Indeed, there was plenty of controversy about this. When there were possible ritual similarities, they were denied or explained away as diabolical imitation of the Christian rites.[22] In the course of the fourth century, on the other hand, initiatory terminology began to be used—a sign that the times and religious background had changed. In fact, ancient Christianity structured initiation[23] according to the various needs that arose because of the difficulties that emerged from changes at the heart of church and society.

There are considerable similarities between Christian initiation and that of the mystery religions which has led some to advance the hypothesis that Christianity had accepted some of their rites. This then creates a problem concerning the relationship between Christian sacraments and pagan mysteries. Concerning the first issue (the second will be taken up again later), it is undeniable that ancient Christianity presented itself as a religion of initiation.

Initiation, however, is a fundamental and natural element of any religion that intends to radically and existentially modify the convert with a complex set of teachings and rites.[24] A person who is about to be initiated into Christianity must begin a new way of living and thinking in order to create in oneself a new person while destroying the old.

Therefore, some structural similarities between the Christian religion and the mystery religions may be explained based on these grounds. Other similarities derive from a common origin or simply from belonging to a religious *koine* (community.) Still other similarities might indicate that there is ultimately some type of indebtedness. However, recent research has overcome old polemics in this regard and is rather oriented towards tracing the origin of many Christian rites in the Jewish environment, as indicated by the studies of Nock, Ligier, Talley, etc.[25] But this orientation is also undergoing a profound revision, as will be seen from the later chapter on liturgy.

Ancient Christian initiation aims at the universal nature of man and, for this reason, requires various times of duration, ways to accomplish the initiation, and conditions to be fulfilled. The path that the catechumen must take tends to create a maturity of existential faith, which is why we speak of a spiritual rebirth. This is why the newly baptized is called *neophytus* (Gr. νεόφυτος), that is, generated or newly sprouted. Another term is *neophysatos*, which has the idea of being recently enlightened. It was used because baptism was seen as an inner enlightenment, which allows one not only to see but to understand hidden things. Initiation was, in fact, serious and demanding, because it involved the annihilation of the old way of thinking and living, the deconstruction of the previous personality in order to build a new one.

At the very beginning of *De baptismo* (1.3), Tertullian writes that "we are little fish born in the water in conformity with Jesus Christ, our Fish, and only by remaining in the water can we be saved."[26] The conception of baptism as a spiritual rebirth already became current towards the end of the first century.[27] It was widely used by apologists during the second century and then in the theology of the third century as well. The primary biblical passage utilized was John 3:5: "Very truly, I tell you, no one can enter the kingdom of God without being born of water and the Spirit." This passage is frequently brought to mind—indeed it is the most quoted passage from the Gospel of John.[28] Sometimes, though less often, there is also the other concept of baptism as illumination.

As Augustine says:

> Hope in him, you whole assembly of the new offspring, you, a people being born, which the Lord has made. Strive to be brought forth in health, not fatally aborted. Look, mother Church is in labor. See, she is groaning in travail to give birth to you, to bring you forth into the light of faith. Do not wound her maternal womb with your impatience, and thus constrict the passage

to your delivery. You, a people now being created, praise your God. Praise him, you that are now being created, praise your Lord. Because you are being suckled, praise him; because you are being nourished, praise him; because you are being reared, advance in wisdom and age. He too accepted this slow business of coming to birth in time.[29]

In the second century, however, Pauline baptismal theology is completely absent: baptism understood as assimilation to the death and resurrection of Christ, a doctrine set out in Romans 6:4ff. In this regard, Benoît observes: "One must come to this conclusion: Paulinism, at least in its original form, played no role in the development of baptismal theology at this time."[30] It was evident during the third century, however, as Origen brought it back into widespread circulation. Moreover, the Pauline notion of the new man is also very widespread, a notion that can also be derived from other concepts such as "new creation," "renewal," and "restoration."[31] This doctrine, only sketched out in the *Letter to the Romans* in chapter 6, is formulated in the context of baptismal theology. It is developed in the *Letter to the Colossians*, always in the baptismal context, especially in chapter 3 where we read, "You have clothed yourselves with the new self which is being renewed in knowledge according to the image of its creator."[32]

Believing is much more than pure knowing, and catechesis is much more than solely communicating a doctrine. The *traditio fidei*, the transmission of Christian truths, involves the entire life and is not only an intellectual fact in that it tends to bring the initiate into the very mystery of God, made accessible to human existence through the Son of God, the Incarnate Word. The initiation process involves three phases: (1) the preliminary phase; (2) the liminal phase (Latin *limen*) where one is at the threshold; and (3) the post-liminal phase which is the new reality reached once one has crossed the threshold (*limen*) and entered inside.

The most important of the three was the liminal, because then rebirth, regeneration, passage, enlightenment are all accomplished, and a new beginning, a new creation is begun. The place, time, rites and ceremonies emphasize that moment and constitute a strong experience for the initiation process, one which is also emotionally charged in a highly engaging way.

Each of the phases involves modalities, times and components which vary in the individual local churches, while coinciding in substance. Tertullian writes: "Men are made, not born, Christians."[33] Describing the various stages of initiation, let us retrace the spiritual journey that a convert of the second to fourth century makes to become a Christian, that is, the personal adventure to which he is subjected. The journey is not only a private matter. It is simultaneously personal and ecclesial because the whole local community is in some way involved in the new birth, especially in the greatest of the church's solemnities, that is, the vigil of Easter. Even if some people are more directly involved in it, their involvement is only in the name of the community. It is the community that welcomes the regenerated; it is the Church as mother that generates and welcomes the newborn and educates her in the faith. The catechumenate is not perceived as an institution but as a community experience.

To understand all ancient Christian initiation, it is important to keep ecclesiology in mind, and more precisely the Church conceived as a fruitful mother who is attentive to the education of her children. The motherhood of the Church is fully manifested in baptism. For the fathers, symbolism is a form of language. Usually for the ancients the image is not a mere abstract representation of reality, but the form of reality itself; the symbol participates in the essence of reality.[34] With this clarification we can understand the wide use that the fathers make of images. In real terms they present the Church with the image of a woman, a bride and a mother,[35] an image which was already widely used in the New Testament.[36]

Delahaye points out that this image is used by writers of the first three centuries in works written to Christian communities such as homilies and catechetical and exegetical works.[37]

> The *Ecclesia* is constituted from two peoples: that of the Jews invited to recognize the fulfillment of the promises made to Israel, and that of the Gentiles also called, without distinction of race, language or nation, to share in the same fruits of salvation. But to have access to the Kingdom of God, both must be reborn to a new life, passing through the death of baptism, which introduces them to eternal life. The specific maternal function of the Church is to birth them into this new life and to sustain them until the moment of definitive mastery. During these first centuries, when baptism and martyrdom follow one another in short succession, or even become combined, soteriological and eschatological perspectives characterize the teaching presented to the catechumens during their initiation. The Church is presented as the Mother who gives her life 'freeing them' from the slavery of sin and the world.[38]

Augustine would later say: "It is not generation that creates Christians, but regeneration."[39] This is how all previous tradition thought about this. Justin writes:

> Then they are brought by us where there is water and are regenerated in the same way we were ourselves regenerated. For, in the name of God the Father and Lord of the universe, and of our Savior Jesus Christ and of the Holy Spirit, they then receive the washing with water. For Christ also said, 'Except you be born again, you shall not enter into the kingdom of heaven.' Now, that it is impossible for those who have once been born to enter into their mothers' wombs, is manifest to all.... Since at our birth we were born without our own knowledge or choice, by our parents coming together, and were brought up in bad habits and wicked training. In order that we may not remain the children of necessity and of ignorance, but may become the children of choice and knowledge, and may obtain in the water the remission of sins formerly committed,

there is pronounced over him who chooses to be born again, and has repented of his sins, the name of God the Father and Lord of the universe.... And this washing is called illumination, because those who learn these things are illuminated in their understandings.[40]

THE PRELIMINARY PHASE (CATECHUMENATE)

An adequate period of preparation for baptism was an institution that slowly took hold. It was only fully developed in the third century, reached its peak in the fourth and then began to decline due to the spread of the baptism of children. Various factors led to the need for such preparation and influenced its development: numerous heresies, the desire to break with the pagan world, the weakening of initial enthusiasm, the apostasies in times of persecution and even in times of tranquility, and the difficulties of living as Christians in a hostile society. In ancient Christianity, the terms used were "catechumen" and "catechesis" rather than "catechumenate," which is a term we do not find until the much later period of the Renaissance.[41]

In the early days we see cases of baptism occurring immediately after a short period of instruction often in the form of proclamation (*kerygma*); this is especially the case for converts from Judaism. The baptism of pagans, on the other hand, required more time and more education. In fact, previous religious formation influenced admission to baptism. However, in the apostolic and post-apostolic period we find a variety of practices that are indeed well reflected in the *Acts of the Apostles*.[42] There is no clear distinction between proclamation (*kerygma*) and education (*catechesis*).

The *Acts of the Apostles* and early Christian literature in general reflect both the instruction given to the Jews and that to the pagans, while later catechesis—what we know of it—concerns almost exclusively pagans. Moreover, Irenaeus notes both the range and the ease of the transmission of catechesis, which must have had a predominantly Christological character in its address to the Jews: "For the instruction of the former [Jews] was an easy task because they could put forward proofs from the Scriptures, and because they, who were in the habit of hearing Moses and the prophets, also readily received the First-begotten of the dead, and the Prince of the life of God."[43] The whole of paragraph 24 sets out in detail the truths that need to be communicated, showing that more time and more catechesis is needed for those who come from paganism. This same theme is taken up almost *ad litteram* by an anonymous text of the fourth century, which Groppo[44] has put back into circulation. In this text, the anonymous author discusses precisely the differences between catechesis addressed to the Jews and that addressed to the pagans. The latter had to be much broader and more clearly articulated.

The first catechesis, as described in Ps. Clementine, aims to give "the first elements of the doctrine of truth."[45] In any case, however, the indispensable condition for all is faith. Catechesis, instruction much broader than a simple proclamation of the faith, takes place primarily after baptism. Conduct before baptism is the litmus test for admission to baptism. This requires people who know the candidate and their behavior (the sponsors) who serve as the guarantors of the person's character.

From this early embryonic instruction, a better articulated pre-baptismal catechesis developed more fully for baptismal candidates who were called by the technical term "catechumens" (those who are educated). In ancient times baptism is administered not after the catechumen has given enough guarantees of having lead an irreproachable life, but precisely for having the ability to lead such a life. But by the middle of the second century we see that the preparation becomes more demanding and such an evangelizing work presupposes an extended period of time. Many texts of this period, especially of apocryphal origin, hint at such a pre-baptismal catechetical activity which takes place in the privacy of the home, which is why it is referred to as domestic-missions.[46] The pseudo-Clementine texts indicate the need for a time for education.[47] The *Recognitiones*, in particular, mentions an instruction of three months before starting the immediate period before baptism.[48] However, the one giving the instruction is not to be overly rigid. Indeed, prominence is given to baptismal grace: "If, therefore, you wish to be clothed with the Divine Spirit, first you must hurry to put off your base presumption, which is an unclean spirit and a foul garment. And there is no way you can do this unless you are first baptized in good works. And thus, being pure in body and in soul, you shall enjoy the future eternal kingdom."[49]

In the absence of information, we cannot specify the practice of education at this time: the people, the precise time, the places and the various Christian communities. One has the clear impression that much is left to private initiative. Indeed, every Christian felt obliged to communicate their faith to others. The apologist Aristides of Athens, who wrote in the years 124-126, recalls the evangelizing work of the apostles. In particular he refers to Paul and his mission in Greece, adding, "If one or other of them have bondmen and bondwomen or children, through love towards them they persuade them to become Christians, and when they have done so, they call them brothers without distinction."[50] Justin mentions this initiative. Certainly, he speaks first for himself when he writes, "And I said: I am about to relate passages of Scripture to you, though I am not anxious to present a merely artistic arrangement of arguments. For I have no ability to do this, but this grace alone was given me from God, that I might understand His Scriptures. And of this grace I pray all of you to become partakers, without payment and without holding back, lest otherwise I should be found guilty in the judgment, which God the Maker of the universe will bring about, through Jesus Christ my Lord."[51] These apologists express the sense of gratuitousness and liberality that springs from having received from God gratuitously, and therefore not only the sense of thanksgiving but above all the sense of communicating the Gospel to others. However, they insist that it is not only a personal fact, but the attitude of the Christian community which feels the need to transmit its faith: "It is our task, therefore, to afford to all an opportunity of inspecting our life and teachings, lest, on account of those who are accustomed to be ignorant of our affairs, we should incur the penalty due to them for mental blindness. And it is your business, when you hear us, to be found, as reason demands, good judges."[52] It should be noted that Justin frequently uses "we" to express an idea or issue that is representative of the whole community.

A few decades later Irenaeus expressed the same sentiments that animated Christians:

Wherefore, also, those who are in truth his disciples, receiving grace from him, do in his name perform [miracles], so as to promote the welfare of other men, according to the gift which each one has received from him. For some do certainly and truly drive out devils, so that those who have thus been cleansed from evil spirits frequently both believe [in Christ], and join themselves to the Church… It is not possible to name the number of the gifts which the Church, [scattered] throughout the whole world, has received from God, in the name of Jesus Christ, who was crucified under Pontius Pilate, and which she exerts day by day for the benefit of the Gentiles, neither practicing deception upon any, nor taking any reward from them. For as she has received freely from God, freely also does she minister [to others].[53]

These inner attitudes are reflected in the practice of bringing everyone together, without distinction of culture or social class, and therefore the popular spread of Christianity even in the humblest environments. Tatian, a disciple of the intellectual Justin, certainly expresses the practice of the church in the second half of the second century when he observes:

But with us there is no desire of inordinate pride, nor do we indulge in a variety of opinions. For having renounced the popular and earthly, and obeying the commands of God, and following the law of the Father of immortality, we reject everything which rests upon human opinion. Not only do the rich among us pursue our philosophy, but the poor enjoy free instruction. For the things which come from God surpass the reward of worldly gifts. Thus, we admit all who desire to hear, even old women and the young. In short, persons of every age are treated by us with respect while every kind of licentiousness is kept at a distance.[54]

The pre-baptismal period was absolutely necessary, because, as Clement of Alexandria observes, "Just as one cannot believe without catechesis, so one cannot even understand without gnosis."[55] Some councils of the fourth century specify that if baptism was administered out of necessity without enough preparation, after healing the baptized must learn the faith.[56] In addition, the practice already exists in the third century that those who were baptized out of necessity—the so-called *clinici*—cannot be ordained, although there are exceptions. The second canon of the Council of Nicaea specifies that those who have been catechized only for a short time cannot access the episcopate or the presbyterate because, "the catechumen, in fact, needs time and a longer trial after baptism."[57] The one being catechized needs time in his preparation for learning and the improvement of conduct. In the course of the third century we see that the Church was deeply concerned about running a serious, not to say severe, catechumenate in every case. We all know the famous text of the Apostolic Tradition attributed to Hippolytus which speaks of the catechumens: there is a first scrutiny, when the concrete life of the aspirant to catechesis, including his social activities and his dispositions, are carefully examined. It is a detailed and precise examination to ensure that there are no external impediments to embracing the Christian life which could nullify one's good aspirations and thus frustrate the period of preparation. They required precise guarantees not only from the candidate himself, but also from additional individuals. Only then was the aspirant admitted among those who can hear the word.

This period of education is not so much about intellectual knowledge and learning formulas, but rather about a system of faith and life. The catechumen confesses faith and practices it in life with words, gestures and ethical behavior. If on the one hand the authors of the second century call Christianity a "philosophy," or "true philosophy," on the other hand they realize that the Christian community is still composed mostly of poor people who, if they do not have a culture and cannot express their faith in eloquent speeches, express it nevertheless with their conduct.[58] For this reason there is an awareness of a diversity of charisms in the Church: all are called to confess their faith and to bear public and private witness to it, but some instead have the gift of teaching. Justin notes, "that every day some are becoming disciples unto the name of his Christ, and are leaving the way of error, who also receive gifts, each as they are worthy of them, being enlightened by the name of this Christ. For one receives the spirit of understanding, another of counsel, another of might, another of healing, another of foreknowledge, another of teaching, another of the fear of God."[59] This openness to all prevents Christianity from falling into intellectualism. Justin defines baptism as "a bath of repentance and the knowledge of God, the bath which has been made on behalf of the iniquity of the peoples of God."[60]

Now knowledge presupposes a period of teaching and learning. Therefore, in these authors there is a lively sense of being someone's disciples. First of all one is a disciple of Christ. The distinction is not made on the level of knowledge, but on that of life, because Christ became incarnate: "Christ served, even as far as the cross, for the various and many-formed races of humanity, purchasing them by blood and the mystery of the cross."[61] If knowledge is needed, penance is just as necessary. Ultimately this constitutes the essential structure of the catechumenate.

Origen distinguishes between desiring and being able to be a Christian. At the beginning, upon entrance to the catechumenate, the will is required and examined. Then, at the end and before the final step, the actual capacity to be a Christian is determined:

> And if they are not to be blamed for so doing, let us see whether Christians do not exhort multitudes to the practice of virtue to a greater and better degree than they. Philosophers who converse in public do not pick and choose their hearers, but he who wishes to hear stands and listens. The Christians, however—having previously, so far as possible, tested the souls of those who wish to become their hearers, and having previously instructed them in private—introduce them then into the community and not before, but only after they appear to have sufficiently evidenced their desire towards a virtuous life. One class is formed privately of those who are beginners, and are receiving admission, but who have not yet obtained the mark of complete purification. Another class is formed of those who have manifested to the best of their ability their intention to desire no other things than what are approved by Christians. Among these there are certain persons appointed to make inquiries regarding the lives and behavior of those who join them, in order that they may prevent those who commit acts of infamy from coming into their public assembly. At the same time, those of a different character are received wholeheartedly, in order that they may be made better daily. And this is their method of procedure, both with those who are sinners and especially with those who lead dissolute lives whom they exclude from their community, although, according to Celsus, they resemble those who in the market-places perform the most shameful tricks.[62]

> We, however, keeping both these things in view, at first invite all people to be healed, and exhort those who are sinners to come to the consideration of the doctrines which teach people not to sin. Those who are devoid of understanding are exhorted to accept doctrines which beget wisdom. Those who are children in thought are challenged to rise to manhood, and those who are simply unfortunate are exhorted to good fortune, or—the more appropriate term to use—to blessedness. And when those who have been turned towards virtue have made progress, and have shown that they have been purified by the word, and have led as far as they can a better life, then and not before do we invite them to participation in our mysteries.[63]

We have no precise evidence from the second century of a well-structured catechumenate, but only from the beginning of the third century. Yet, institutions are not created abruptly at a time when there are no centralized structures but are instead the result of experience and necessity. Since ancient Christianity, in some respects but not all, seeks to remain faithful to tradition during this period, it allows us to affirm that the catechumenate arose during the second century.

By the middle of the second century the elements of the catechumenate can already be seen concretely in a passage of Justin himself: "As many as are persuaded and believe that what we teach and say is true, and undertake to be able to live accordingly, are instructed to pray and to entreat God with fasting for the remission of their sins that are past, we praying and fasting with them. Then they are brought by us where there is water and are regenerated in the same way we were ourselves regenerated"[64] There is an unspecified period of instruction. There must also be teachers, whether they have an official mandate or not, and there are ritual and cultic practices. Again, for Rome the testimony of Hermas in his *Shepherd*, before Justin, is useful. It offers clues when it speaks of certain requirements for baptism. Some aspirants—hearers of the word of God—are afraid of the demands of baptism: "They are those who have heard the word and want to be baptized in the name of the Lord. Then, when they remember the purity of the truth, they change their mind and run again to their evil passions."[65]

Above all, the aim is to avoid *dipsuchias* (Gk), double-mindedness. Irenaeus writes:

> Now, since man is a living being compounded of soul and flesh, he must exist by both of these. And, whereas from both of them offences come, purity of the flesh is abstinence from all shameful things and from all unrighteous deeds. Purity of the soul is the keeping faith towards God whole, neither adding nor subtracting from it. For godliness becomes obscured and darkened by the soiling and staining of the flesh, and becomes broken and polluted, not being whole, if falsehood enters into the soul. But it will be preserved in its beauty and modesty when truth is constant in the soul and purity in the flesh.[66]

Justin († ca. 165), as noted above, also spoke of similar instruction and prayer along with fasting.[67] Here they offer only preliminary instruction and ask for faith and consequent Christian conduct. But at the beginning of the third century the catechumenate, now understood as a novitiate for all, was well structured everywhere and became a precise and articulated institution in Rome, Carthage, Alexandria and Syria. It is an institution of the church that prepares candidates with doctrinal, moral and sacramental instruction as well as with a series of ascetical rites and practices.

Tertullian († after 220) writes about the pre-baptismal period:

> Whatever, then, our poor ability has attempted to suggest with reference to laying hold of repentance once for all, and perpetually retaining it, does indeed bear upon all who are given up to the Lord, as being all competitors for salvation in earning the favor of God. But it is chiefly urgent in the case of those young novices (*novitioli*) who are only just beginning to bedew their ears with divine discourses, and who, as pups still in early infancy (*catuli infantiae*), and with eyes not yet perfect, creep about uncertainly and say indeed that they

renounce their former deed, and assume (the profession of) repentance, but neglect to complete it.[68]

The change and the reasons for it are clearly expressed by Tertullian: "That baptismal washing is a sealing of faith, which faith is begun and is commended by the faith of repentance. We are not washed in order that we may cease sinning, but because we have ceased, since in heart we have been bathed already. For the first baptism of a learner is this, a perfect fear. From that time on, in so far as you understand the Lord, faith is sound as the conscience has once for all embraced repentance."[69] The passages cited on the one hand reflect the uncertain and often tiring journey of the catechumen, and on the other hand the seriousness with which the Church considered the pre-baptismal period, implementing for this purpose a whole series of practices, which we could define as institutions, so that he "can stop sinning."

In his homilies preached in an assembly where catechumens were also present, Origen addresses them by expressing this need for a serious and effective conversion before baptism. "You who desire to receive the sacred baptism and obtain the grace of the Spirit, must first, by listening to the word of God, cut off the innate vices and pacify the barbaric and ferocious customs."[70] He elsewhere notes:

> We are baptized in the true water, the water of salvation. Come therefore, catechumens, do penance, so that you may receive baptism for the remission of sins. The one who ceases to sin receives baptism 'for the remission of sins.' But he who comes to the cleansing of baptism stubborn in sin, finds no remission of sins at all. That is why I beseech you not to approach baptism without caution and careful reflection, but instead to show at first 'fruits worthy of repentance' (*Lk* 3:8). Therefore, observe for some time an exemplary conduct, keep yourselves clean from all filthiness and vice.[71]

The need for vigilance on the part of those responsible is based on the text of Matthew's Gospel (7:6): "Do not give what is holy to dogs; and do not throw your pearls before swine, or they will trample them under foot and turn and maul you." This passage is frequently quoted precisely in reference to the catechumenal period to express the need for attention and prudence in catechesis, and for discernment of aspiring catechumens and those to be admitted to baptism.[72]

The organization of the preparation period occurs prior to the first textual witnesses we have from the various local churches. It developed and spread during the third century. In the fourth century there were secondary changes in the organization of the catechumenate along with marginal differences among the various churches. In the meantime, it had become a whole patrimony of rituals and symbols that were extremely significant in the context in which they were lived. After the catechumenate had disappeared, these rituals and symbols remained in the baptismal liturgy concentrated in a short space of time, as a reminder of the previous period, but without the emotional impact they had when they were first begun. In fact, the conversion of entire tribes or peoples and the widespread and generalized practice of baptizing children as soon as possible (*quam primum*) in favor of the now common doctrine of original sin in the West, no longer allowed a thorough and selective formation, according to the practice of the third and fourth centuries.

As preparation for the reception of the three sacraments—baptism, confirmation, Eucharist—the catechumenate itself begins when the candidate gives his name (*nomendatio*) to the person in charge. This might be a deacon, a presbyter or the bishop himself. The candidate must provide his name in order to be enrolled in the list of catechumens, also referred to as *audientes* (*auditors* in Latin.) Before official entry into the catechumenate, candidates must undergo an examination of their life and profession of faith.

> Those who are newly brought forward to hear the Word shall first be brought before the teachers at the house, before all the people enter. Then they will be questioned concerning the reason that they have come forward to the faith. Those who bring them will bear witness concerning them as to whether they are able to hear [the Word of God]. They shall be questioned concerning their life and occupation, marriage status, and whether they are slave or free. If they are the slaves of any of the faithful, and if their masters permit them, they may hear the Word. If their masters do not bear witness that they are good, let them be rejected. If their masters are pagans, teach them to please their masters, so that there will be no blasphemy. If a man has a wife, or a woman has a husband, let them be taught to be content, the husband with his wife, and the wife with her husband. If there is a man who does not live with a woman, let him be taught not to fornicate, but either to take a wife according to the law, or to remain as he is. If there is someone who has a demon, such a person shall not hear the Word of the teacher until purified. They will inquire concerning the works and occupations of those are who are brought forward for instruction.[73]

Having a different profession of faith prevents baptism. Baptism is also not accessible to those involved in pagan worship and public games, or manufacturers and traders of idols as well as more generally those who practice professions related to the pagan religion. If they do not promise to change their lives, they will not be accepted into the catechumenal group. On the other hand, some professions, such as military service, which before Constantine was considered illegal by some, were later allowed. In fact, there were actually many Christian soldiers who spread the gospel. A careful investigation into the reasons people request baptism is required. There may be people, in fact, who registered among the catechumens only out of curiosity, interest or something else. That is why the faithful who know the person must vouch for him or her, that is, to be the guarantors of their seriousness as their godparents. The figure of the godfather or godmother was born at the end of the second century.[74] The Church admits no one without a public and private guarantee along with a serious investigation into their background and the prerequisite preparation[75] in order for the person to be able to "access, enter and be sealed in the faith" (*accedere, ingredi, obsignare*).[76]

A system of guarantees was pursued. More than just the reliance on an individual, the church enacted an entire procedure designed to ensure that baptism would be administered with all due care. This practice and procedure will become a fundamental institution of the church that will undergo further transformation later on, taking on different forms depending on the place. Initially, the term for the person who served as the guarantor, *patrinus* (godfather), is not referred to in the ancient documents. In fact, the term is not found until the seventh century.[77] The godfather is the person or persons who serve on behalf of the community as the guarantor of the faith and conduct of the person who wants to be baptized. The *patrinus*, in other words, is the sponsor who, according to the classical meaning of the term (*sponsores*), offers a guarantee of good faith on behalf of the person. Pseudo Hippolytus does not use the specific term but rather speaks more generically: "Those who have brought them (the candidates) should testify if they are able to listen [to the word]. . . . If those who have introduced them testify that they have behaved properly, then they should be allowed to listen to the Gospel."[78] This account concerns a past practice that was common at the time.[79]

There is a well-known text by Tertullian, often cited, which speaks of the godparents (*sponsores*) of children. He is against the baptism of infants. One of the reasons is that godparents might not keep their promises, especially if they, as sponsors, died or the baptized person grew up with bad tendencies: "For why is it necessary—if (baptism itself) is not so necessary—that the sponsors likewise should be thrust into danger? On the one hand, they may fail to fulfill their promises if they die, or they may be disappointed by the subsequent development of an evil disposition in those for whom they stood."[80] Normally translators equate *sponsores* with the modern term "godparents."[81] After careful analysis of the text, Dujarier rejects this interpretation. He thinks that Tertullian considers baptism as a *sponsio* (engagement) between God and man with each side providing guarantees for his own part. The text therefore does not concern children, but young people; it is these same young people who would commit themselves in the first person—they, in other words, would be the human *sponsores*.[82] Frankly, this interpretation seems a bit forced. For this reason, it seems preferable to remain with the traditional approach.[83]

In any case, the figure of the godfather in ancient times should not be seen through the lens of later practice. Rather, it can be considered as a system of guarantees required by the community to administer baptism. For this reason, sponsors can be one or more persons who offer a guarantee for the candidate, thus having to publicly testify to their fitness. In many cases they may be friends or acquaintances of theirs, or those who have introduced them to Christianity or have followed them during their period of formation.

The preparation period, which lasts two or three years, can also be shortened: "Catechumens will hear the word for three years. Yet if someone is earnest and perseveres well in the matter, it is not the time that is judged, but the conduct."[84] Around 200 CE, at the end of a list of catechumens, Clement of Alexandria mentions an extended period of instruction that lasts at least three years.[85] The preparation of the listeners of the word is in the context of the inculturation of the faith: their own Greek-Hellenistic culture must serve for the instruction of the catechumens.[86] However, the duration of the preparation varied according to the different churches. For example, Augustine and his companions enrolled at the beginning of Lent in Milan in 387 and therefore only participated in the preparation for a short time.

After Constantine, the practice of deferring baptism to old age spread in order to delay the beginning of a life totally committed in the Christian sense. Ambrose and Augustine were for many years only catechumens. Some even postponed baptism until they were dying, as evidenced by numerous funerary inscriptions of neophytes. *Clinici* were those who were baptized at the time of death or during a serious illness. The latter, if healed, were looked upon with a certain distrust by the community and could not be admitted to the priesthood. Since they did not perform all the prescribed ceremonies and because they received baptism out of fear, they were deemed to have little inner commitment or conviction. Not only that, but the rules and practices were made to be observed and also violated at the same time. The Council of Nicaea of 325 states: "Forasmuch as, either from necessity, or through the urgency of individuals, many things have been done contrary to the ecclesiastical canon, so that men just converted from heathenism to the faith, and who have been instructed but a little while, are straightway brought to the spiritual laver, and as soon as they have been baptized, are advanced to the episcopate or the presbyterate, it has seemed right to us that for the time being no such thing shall be done. For to the catechumen himself there is need of time and of a longer trial after baptism" (Canon 2). Unfortunately, even after that the norm was not observed.

Augustine notes, "It is not enough to be conceived, it is necessary to be born to reach eternal life."[87] "One wishes not so much to become a Christian as to pretend to be one."[88] Elsewhere he says that in cases of invasion by barbarians or common dangers the catechumens in fear for their lives crowded the churches to receive baptism.[89] The fathers therefore urged that baptism not be delayed too long, while the councils cared for the seriously ill, allowing even a simple believer to administer the sacrament to them. Usually, once healed, the laying on of hands by the bishop was required to give the gift of the Holy Spirit.

We know that in the second half of the fourth century, the official entry into the catechumenate involved a ceremony with particular rites: exorcism, laying on of hands, the sign of the cross on the forehead, blessing and conferral of salt, etc., combined with prayers and a discourse to mark the occasion. The rituals, which vary from place to place, all have a precise symbolic meaning. The catechumenal period is marked by ritual and ascetic practices and by the instruction of a "doctor" who is, in the fourth century, either a priest or a deacon.

It is necessary to distinguish the official figure of the *doctor* from those who in private devote themselves to teaching or to carrying out missionary activity.[90] In the third century when Christianity was rapidly expanding, there must have been, especially in large communities, a fair number of *doctores* to meet the demands of Christian education, especially since it was primarily adults who received baptism. For this reason, it is legitimate to think of the existence of schools specifically charged with training, even if they are far from that of Alexandria in terms of organization and prestige. Eusebius, who mentions the *didaskaleion* of this city, makes it clear that it was an established institution when Origen took charge of it.[91]

In many texts we find *doctores* named.[92] The office is not a position so much as a function within the community. The *Apostolic Tradition* instructs: "Those who are newly brought forward to hear the Word shall first be brought before the teacher before being allowed to join the people. . . . When the teacher finishes his instruction, the catechumens should pray by themselves, separate from the faithful. . . . After the prayer, the teacher shall lay hands upon the catechumens, pray, and dismiss them. Whether he is one of the laypeople or of the clergy, let him do so."[93] Cyprian calls them teaching presbyters (*presbyteri doctores*) or teachers of the hearers/catechumens (*doctores audientium*). They are priests who also have at their disposal readers (*lectores*).[94] The *Letter of Clement to James* (8) says that catechists must above all be educated, adapt themselves to the condition of their hearers, be of impeccable conduct and experience, and clear in speech.[95]

Education in the Christian faith is a loving and generous work, to which every perfect believer is called to contribute:

> ... according to the apostle, so that receiving the pure and genuine seed of his doctrine, they may co-operate with him, helping in preaching for the salvation of others. And those who are still imperfect and beginning their lessons, are born to salvation, and shaped, as by mothers, by those who are more perfect, until they are brought forth and regenerated unto the greatness and beauty of virtue. These in turn, making progress and having become a church, assist in laboring for the birth and nurture of other children, accomplishing in the receptacle of the soul, as in a womb, the blameless will of the Word.[96]

Candidates for baptism have a special status within the Christian community, which is divided into *catechumeni* and *fideles*. Although catechumens are not yet considered among the faithful, they are not pagans either.⁹⁷ The apocryphal writings in general, and the Pseudo-Clementines in particular, make it clear that they are already Christians in some way, inasmuch as they have heard the good news and concretely manifest their conversion. At certain times they participate in the liturgical and charitable life of the community: they pray together—even though they have different places and do not exchange the kiss of peace—and they listen to the homilies.⁹⁸ Commodian expresses the same thought when he uses military language. The catechumen is a *tiro*, a new recruit, who is formed to become a soldier of Christ (*miles Christi*). The community prays for them and they receive the laying on of hands each time, then they are dismissed (*dimissio*), not being able to attend the Eucharistic liturgy, which is reserved for the faithful (*fideles*), that is, the baptized of all ages.

In addition, catechumens have many duties as baptized. They must no longer commit certain sins. Some councils of the beginning of the fourth century enacted legislation aimed at regulating their conduct including punishment for certain kinds of sin.⁹⁹

The length of the catechumenate period varies according to time and place. While the *Apostolic Tradition* speaks of a period of three years, in Alexandria Clement seems to call for a period of four years, if the context of the passage is baptismal.¹⁰⁰ The *Pseudo-Clementines*, on the other hand, make several references to three months.¹⁰¹ Canon 42 of the Council of Elvira indicates two years if the report about them is good (*si bonae fuerint conversationis*). However, it is normally stated that the duration is secondary with respect to the good conduct of the candidate. After this period of doctrinal and moral formation, of greater or lesser duration, the catechumens are allowed access to the second phase, that is, to the immediate preparation for baptism, a few weeks before Easter. From the second half of the fourth century, the Lenten period was fixed for this preparation. The candidate formally applied for admission and after careful examination passed into the class of the chosen (*electi*) who were considered competent in the faith (*competentes*). In the East they were referred to as the enlightened ones (*photizomenoi*). Lent thus becomes a robust time of intense and rigorous preparation through instruction, various ascetic and liturgical practices, so briefly expressed by Leo the Great: "According to the apostolic rule the elect must be examined and instructed with frequent sermons."¹⁰² Even the *electi* are excluded from the actual Eucharistic celebration, but with a different rite after the hearers (*audientes*).

A basic element inspires the preparation: the ability to live according to the needs of the Gospel was considered the fruit of personal commitment and the gift of God who transforms a person inwardly. For this reason, in addition to personal prayer, it is necessary that the entire community be involved in the spiritual birth of new members and the completion of the casting out of sin. In the 4th century, someone thought it was better to administer baptism first and then to give education. But Augustine responds with the practice of the church and the need for prior penance.

From all this we can make a few general observations. Through a series of institutions, there is an attempt to structure a new personality, a new self. This entails an abandonment or a decisive break not only with the previous life, but also in some way with the previous community, in order to create a new solidarity and integration into a new people with a new history of a universal character. On the one hand it is a solidarity with Israel and its history, on the other a distinction from it as a third race (*tertium genus*). They are a new people, the new Israel of the end times. These are descriptors that tend to highlight this new solidarity, this new belonging, this new collective ego. In addition, a new public and private code of conduct must be assumed along with a new language. In other words, everything is geared toward changing the self, creating a new self and not so much about bringing about a change in others, even if this aspect is a natural consequence of the desire to share one's newness with others.

As the minority, Christians of the third century are in a state of insecurity. They favor internal cohesion and are very concerned with the choice and formation of new members. Emphasis is placed on human discernment, on the discernment of those in charge of the community, but also on divine choices. Everything tends to heighten the awareness of belonging, which accentuates the aspect of exclusion both of strangers and of Christians themselves who do not have the same creed or the same practice.

In an age where there is a longing for salvation,[103] Christians accentuate salvific exclusivism. Therefore, they argue that there is no salvation outside the one Catholic Church. The insistence on salvation in the church on the one hand stimulates the faithful to missionary activity, while on the other it awakens in others the need to convert. This involves a more careful selection of candidates and gives greater importance to baptism both as a point of arrival for the previous life and as a point of reference for the next.

Baptism is an initial act that confers a new "status" of belonging to Christ. It is administered in the name of Christ because it is the baptism instituted by him. If on the one hand it is a birth into a new community, on the other hand it is the rebirth of the individual. All the institutions put in place and all the consequent rituals have the specific fundamental aim, from the negative point of view, of destroying evil, and from the positive point of view, of bringing about a new birth.

In the context of Christianity there is no difference in initiation between men and women. And yet, this does happen in other groups such as the cult of Mithra. Christians, however, view all, without distinction, as spiritual brothers, fellow members (*spiritu fratres, religione conservi*). Since initiation is something public, it belongs to the community which wants to mold through the catechumenate the new members according to its faith and its code of conduct. Practice and doctrine are closely linked.

There is a beautiful text by Cyprian from *Ad Donatum* which summarizes what has been discussed. This is a work that narrates his experience of Christian conversion, chronicling an important, albeit difficult, moment in the call to change one's life. He attributes his conversion to the grace of God. In chapter four, he writes: "I received the spirit from heaven and through a second birth I became a new man. In fact we say that we no longer sin because of faith."

Exorcisms, according to the cited *Apostolic Tradition*, must be carried out every day during the immediate preparation for baptism. In fourth century Rome they take place on three consecutive Sundays and are called *scrutinia* (scrutiny). The ceremony is quite complex. According to the ancient conception, evil and Satan penetrate everything including human beings. It is therefore necessary to free the human person from it both in body and in soul. It is necessary to detoxify him from the evil presence. Positively, there is a profound sense of redemption in that people do not free themselves from the evil that is in them. Rather, it is the action of God that acts in man through the work of the church, the whole church. In the period immediately preceding baptism, exorcism is daily and follows the instruction given during Lent to all the faithful. Augustine observes:

> What we are doing for you by invoking the name of your redeemer, you must complete by a thorough scrutiny and repentance of your hearts. We block the wiles of the ancient and obstinate enemy with prayers to God and with stern rebukes. You must stand up to him with your earnest prayers and contrition of heart, in order to be snatched from the power of darkness and transferred into the kingdom of his glory. This is now your task, and this your toil. We heap curses on him, appropriate to his vile wickedness. It is for you, rather, to join glorious battle with him by turning away from him and devoutly renouncing him. He has to be crushed, bound, shut out, this enemy of God and of you, and above all of himself. His fury, you see, is shown up as being impudent against God, abominable against you, and ruinous against himself. Let him breathe out slaughter all round, let him set his traps and snares, let him sharpen his multiple and deceitful tongues. Empty out all his poisons from your hearts by calling on the name of the savior.[104]

He adds: "So amid all these gangs of people vexing and troubling you, put on sackcloth, and humble your soul with fasting. Humility is rewarded with what pride has been denied. And you indeed, while you were being scrutinized, and that persuader of flight and desertion was being properly rebuked by the terrifying omnipotence of the Trinity, were not actually clothed in sackcloth, but yet your feet were symbolically standing on it."[105] Augustine himself reminds the newly baptized of the experience:

In this loaf of bread (Eucharist), you are given clearly to understand how much you should love unity. I mean, was that loaf made from one grain? Weren't there many grains of wheat? But before they came into the loaf, they were all separate; they were joined together by means of water after a certain amount of pounding and crushing. Unless wheat is ground, after all, and moistened with water, it cannot possibly get into this shape which is called bread. In the same way you too were being ground and pounded, as it were, by the humiliation of fasting and the sacrament of exorcism. Then came baptism, and you were, in a manner of speaking, moistened with water in order to be shaped into bread. But it is not yet bread without fire to bake it. So, what does fire represent? That is the chrism, the anointing. Oil, the fire-feeder, you see, is the sacrament of the Holy Spirit."[106]

Fasting is a fundamental component. It is not so much penitential and ascetic as spiritual, involving interior purification and therefore readiness to accept grace. The New Testament period always connected fasting with baptism.

On the Friday and Saturday mornings before Easter there is the last meeting, particularly solemn, before baptism. The final exorcisms and image filled rites, which vary in different churches, take place. The whole ceremony is focused on the solemn act of renouncing Satan, which is also the first solemn act of the baptismal liturgy. In some churches it can also take place immediately on the evening before baptism, as in Milan and Jerusalem.

CHRISTIAN EDUCATION

On the day of Pentecost, after the descent of the Holy Spirit, Peter addressed a speech to the crowd that had gathered, briefly setting out the Christian message and exhorting them to conversion: "Then those who accepted his word were baptized and that day about three thousand people joined them. They were diligent in listening to the teaching of the apostles and in fraternal union, in the breaking of bread and in prayers" (*Acts* 2:41-42). This "teaching of the apostles," which became better organized in form and content over the decades, concerns both the preparation for baptism and the post-baptismal period. There are qualified people in charge of teaching: the apostles and immediately together with them the teachers—the doctors—and then the bishops and others. From the beginning, a body of doctrines was formed for the purpose of teaching. The doctrines needed to be accepted for entrance into the church and they constituted the essential teaching to be handed down: "I make known to you, brothers, the gospel which I have proclaimed to you and which you have received, in which you remain firm and from which you also receive salvation if you keep it in the form in which I have proclaimed it to you" (*1 Cor* 15:1-2).[107]

When Augustine was preaching to the catechumens, he noted:

The first steps of my ministry, and of your conception, in which with heavenly grace you began to be generated in the womb of faith, needs to be aided by the word. In this way my sermon may contribute to your welfare and salvation, and your conception to my encouragement and consolation. We clergy instruct you with sermons; it is up to you to make progress in your conduct. We scatter the seed of the word; it is up to you to produce the harvest of faith. Let us all run the course in the footsteps of the Lord according to the vocation with which we have been called by him; none of us must look back.[108]

This doctrinal framework confers a fundamental and essential unity on Christianity, despite the differences in detail found both in the New Testament writings and in later theological development. The original announcement is progressively expanded and better structured in an educational system, i.e. in catechesis (= oral instruction). This is always, in ancient times, connected to baptism both as a preparation and as an immediate complement. The primitive scheme is Christological and goes from the ministry of the Baptist to the resurrection of Christ, with recourse to the testimonies of the Old Testament, particularly the Psalms and some Old Testament figures assumed as types (*typoi*), as a symbolic foreshadowing of "he who must come."

For example, Bishop Theophilus of Antioch of the second half of the second century wrote to a certain Autolycus a work that had an abundance of catechetical content for a pagan. He exhorts him in this way: "Try to meet more often with me, so that, having listened to me loud and clear you may learn the truth."[109] Autolycus, a pagan, must first understand the biblical and Jewish derivation of Christian monotheism. To be able to understand, however, the purification of the heart and the rejection of evil are necessary because "you have blurred the eyes of your soul by your sins and evil actions."[110] He adds: "But if you want, you can be healed. Entrust yourself to the doctor and he will open the eyes of your soul and heart to you. Who is the doctor? It is God! He heals and gives life through the Word and wisdom."[111] The *Demonstration of the Apostolic Preaching* of Irenaeus of Lyon, from the end of the second century, is a handbook of catechesis given to the catechumens.

Moreover, we know from both the canonical texts and other writings of the first and second centuries that moral, doctrinal and liturgical teaching were also imparted. A further step is taken during the second and third centuries, when catechesis was structured as a history of salvation, with the typological interpretation of the books of Genesis and Exodus.[112] It is presented as a complete teaching, essential and sufficient for both doctrinal and moral teaching. The sacraments are explained during the rites and in the days following baptism, at least in the fourth century, in mystagogical catechesis. This structure and content reach the most complete articulation in the post-Constantine period and then decline together with the catechumenate for the same reasons described above.

Catechesis is closely linked to the liturgy, and the concluding part focuses on the explanation of the symbol of faith which, in the West, was the Apostles Creed, along with the Lord's Prayer, the sacraments of baptism, confirmation (including the gift of the Spirit), and the Eucharist. Faith and prayer are explained but also expected to be lived out. Catechesis embraces two aspects: one pedagogical, which tends to arouse the desire to know those things that the faithful already knew. The other is content, that is, the essential elements of the faith, which the catechumens understand more profoundly by participation. This comes through, additionally, in the instruction given to them, as well as that given to all the faithful, which is also substantially nourished by Scripture.

The basis of catechesis is biblical. In some churches it may consist in the systematic exposition of some books, in others of selected passages, but in general it embraces the whole history of salvation, as Augustine writes "[Starting] from the beginning God created heaven and earth (*Gen* 1:1) up to our days."[113] The same thing happened in Jerusalem, according to Egeria, as they teach, "going through the whole of Scripture and giving first its literal meaning, then its spiritual one,"[114] in order to demonstrate that the Old Testament finds its fulfillment in Christ and in the Church. Thus, the catechumens of pagan origin, embracing the new religion, learn a new history, the Jewish and Christian one, which also becomes their history not so much for the occurrence of events as for their meaning. "The convert, in abandoning paganism, was compelled to enlarge his historical horizon: he was likely to think for the first time in terms of universal history."[115]

The explanation of the symbol, that is, of the formula of faith that constitutes the identity of the religious physiognomy of the Christian, the *quid credendum* (what is believed), considered as a synthesis of the whole of Scripture, represents the culmination of doctrinal formation. It is defined as *traditio symboli* (the creed that is handed on), somewhat of a gesture by which the church hands over, as a torch, its faith to the catechumen and the catechumen gives it back (*redditio*) by reciting it by heart before the community and the local bishop as a profession of faith. The symbol of faith, the so-called creed, which is then used exclusively in the baptismal liturgy, in the Latin world is the Apostles Creed and not the Nicene Creed. Only later did the profession of faith enter the Eucharistic celebration in the East between the end of the fifth and the beginning of the sixth century, in the West on different dates, in Rome only in the eleventh century. The explanation of the *Our Father*—the *traditio orationis dominicae* (the prayer handed down by our Lord) as well as the *quid orandum* (what is to be prayed)—can be done at various times. In Africa, for example, it is immediately after the explanation of the creed, while in Milan at the time of Ambrose, it comes after baptism. Here it is thought that only those who are baptized can recite it and invoke God as Father.

The *redditio*, the public recitation of the creed, and possibly that of the *Our Father*, comes at the conclusion of the catechumenate, followed by baptism. During the baptismal rite and in the following days the instruction is completed, with the so-called mystagogical catechesis. The term "mystagogy"[116] refers to what is done and said during the rites of passage and the celebration of the divine mysteries (the sacraments), in the lived context of the moment. The sacraments are received and explained in the conviction that their understanding can only be achieved while living them, as Cyril of Jerusalem expresses it, "You have been constituted in the condition of understanding the mysteries."[117] In other words, the sacraments are conceived as rites of initiation, but in the sense that the very life of the Christian is revealed through Scripture.[118]

Already in the third century and even more so in the fourth, the use of secrecy to surround certain Christian doctrines and rites during catechumenal instruction spread. This practice is called, with modern and improper terminology, the discipline of the arcane or secret (*disciplina arcani*).[119] Augustine, speaking to the newly baptized, says: "But about the sacrament of the sacred altar, which they have seen today, they have as yet heard nothing. Today they are owed a sermon on this subject. That is why this sermon has to be short, both because of the hard work it is for me, and because of their edification."[120] The bishops sometimes allude, even in a vague way, to the Christian celebrations reserved for the faithful, in particular the Eucharistic prayer. They speak of the ritual connected with it and of the meaning of the Eucharist. The information they offer is fragmented and not developed in an organic way. They also invite the faithful not to talk of the "mysteries" with outsiders. Rather it is in the post-baptismal instructions where they explain the Eucharist extensively. In the published works they speak much of the Eucharist and its meaning. Such works could, of course, be read by anyone, pagans as well as Christians.

Is it possible to keep the secret regarding the Christian sacraments? People, even those who are unbaptized, know how a baptistery is made and the baptismal rites. They know how the altar is made. They know the gifts that are offered. They know that the faithful and the bishop pray, and the faithful consume those gifts after prayer. In an ancient city, there was no privacy. From the sociological perspective, it is impossible that catechumens and others did not know about Christian rites. There were so many baptized people who had left the church over time or even became pagans. Moreover, there is no oath of secrecy, as in the case of the mystery religions. Those who so wish can also find out by reading the publications and the catecheses available in circulation.

The key to interpreting and understanding the so-called discipline of the arcane, in my opinion, is found in Ambrose himself. In many passages he insists on mystery and silence. To understand the mysteries, that is, the sacraments, the experience of them is necessary. After that experience one can then receive an explanation of the sacraments and be led to a deeper understanding of them. But for such an experience, one is wholly dependent upon an indispensable gift of God, which on an ontological level both enables and makes capable an experiential understanding. Ambrose calls this gift an opening (*apertio; aperitio.*) He says:

> So, what did we do on Saturday? The opening (the Ephphatha.) These mysteries of opening were celebrated when the bishop touched your ears and nostrils. What is the meaning of this? In the Gospel, our Lord Jesus Christ, when a deaf and dumb person was presented to him, touched his ears and mouth, his ears because he was deaf, his mouth because he was dumb. And he said: Ephphatha. . . . The bishop touched your ears, so that your ears might open to the bishop's word and exhortation. But you ask me, 'Why the nostrils?'[121] There, because he was dumb, he touched his mouth, so that, since he could not speak of the celestial mysteries, he might receive the voice of Christ.... that you may receive a sweet savor of eternal godliness, and that you may say, 'For we are a sweet savor of Christ unto God,' as the holy Apostle said; and there may be in you the full fragrance of faith and devotion.[122]

Therefore, for the understanding of the mysteries of baptism and the Eucharist, it is necessary to receive first the opening of the nostrils and eyes (*apertio narium et oculorum*). R. Étaix has published a sermon on the rite of the Ephphatha. The rite as it is observed is little known. It was written perhaps a few decades after Ambrose's preaching. The anonymous author repeats the same concept: "The hands of the priest are applied in order that your ears, which once the enemy has blocked, might be opened by the operation of the celestial mystery."[123] Therefore, the opening of the ears (*apertio aurium*) was necessary in order to hear and understand the contents of the mysteries.

Ambrose's thought is still more explicit in his third sermon: "You went, you washed, you came to the altar, you began to see that which you had not previously seen. That means by the Lord's font and by the preaching of the Lord's passion then were your eyes opened. You who before seemed to be blinded in heart, you began to see the light of the sacraments."[124] Already by the second century baptism came to be called "illumination," because it enabled the newly baptized to see the mysteries of God. In the east, the baptistery was called *photisterion*, i.e. the place of illumination, where one is born again of water and the Holy Spirit, in as much as one dies with Christ and rises with Christ, receiving light and life. That illumination was received which enabled one to comprehend the mystery of Christ and the Christian mysteries.

There is an Augustinian reticence—a rhetorical figure called *aposiopesis*, the leaving of a thought incomplete usually by a sudden breaking off—when more or less explicitly mentioning the Eucharist. Augustine very often uses the syntagma: *Norunt fideles* (the faithful know) or similar expressions.[125] In a discourse recently discovered by Dolbeau and preached in 404, Augustine says: "The faithful know in which moment of the canon the martyrs are remembered during the celebration of the sacrament, when our hopes and prayers are lifted up to God. The faithful know this, the catechumens should hasten that they be able to know it."[126] The faithful know, the others do not know and do not understand. Augustine explains: "The faithful understand what I mean: they too recognize Christ in the breaking of the bread: not any bread whatsoever but the bread receiving the blessing of Christ becomes the body of Christ. While he broke bread the two recognized him and, filled with joy, they ran to their fellow disciples, but they found them already up to date about everything."[127]

Here the faithful (*fideles*), in as much as they have a personal and direct experience, are able to understand the Eucharist and what comes during its very reception. Underlying this is the conception according to which only the faithful, in so far as they are illuminated and have an experience of it, can grasp what is said to them concerning the sacraments. This is because with their baptism they received a greater spiritual capacity for comprehension: experience and understanding go together. For the catechumens the door of understanding is closed,[128] or rather it is necessary to enter the second curtain (Ambrose). Even the catechumens, and others, if they wish, know all the details of the Eucharistic celebration, but only he who is believing, baptized, and illumined knows how to understand and rightly value the mystery of Christ's presence. The *fideles* (faithful), in as much as they are baptized, know something that they understand better than those who are not among the faithful.[129]

While in Africa the secret concerns only the Eucharist, in other churches, for example in Jerusalem, it surrounds all three sacraments of initiation (baptism, confirmation and Eucharist) and also the creed and the *Our Father*. The explanation of these is reserved both for the period in which the rites take place and for the post-baptismal period. For this reason, the normal preaching of bishops in church does not address the sacramental theme except in veiled language which only the baptized can understand.

THE CRUCIAL PHASE: THE BAPTISMAL RITES

Recent research has highlighted the breadth of the spectrum of baptismal rites in the ancient church, not only in marginal aspects but also in fundamental areas. The liturgical conformity of the various traditions in vast geographical areas does not yet exist. That occurs from the fourth century onwards under the impulse of mutual influences. More and more the rituals and interpretative differences of these rites become evident, especially among the Syro-Palestinian and other churches. These differences date back to the different primitive original liturgical traditions of the apostolic church. A primitive liturgical uniformity was postulated because the knowledge of the 4th century was projected on the 2nd century, thus offering a distorted reconstruction of the facts. Instead, the liturgy did not start from a simple and substantially uniform rite in the various churches, but from a diversity of rites, typical of the various communities in which Christianity was articulated and spread in the first decades. Since there was no ritual, no written normative text, a range of rites was immediately created in which the liturgical life of the church was expressed. Therefore, uniformity should not be sought at the beginning of the development process but only at the end.

Christian baptism in the form of immersion, or ablution more generally, goes back to Christ in the sense that it is administered by his mandate and is distinct from other types of baptism in use especially among the Jews. Regardless of who baptizes, it is always Christ who baptizes: "He will baptize you in the Holy Spirit and fire" (*Mt* 3:11). Baptism is defined by Paul as "cleansing with the washing of water by the word" (*Eph* 5:26). In the letter to Titus it is called "the water of rebirth and renewal by the Holy Spirit" (3:5). Already in the New Testament there is a rich theology of baptism: it is rebirth, regeneration, purification of the Spirit, seal of faith, union with Christ in death and resurrection, the being made children of God, forgiveness of sins and the condition for entering the kingdom of God.

Mark and Matthew begin their Gospel with the baptism of John and end with Christ's command to baptize everyone; and this is what Peter did in his first public act. To the Jews who asked him what they should do, he replied: "Repent, and be baptized every one of you in the name of Jesus Christ so that your sins may be forgiven; and you will receive the gift of the Holy Spirit" (*Acts* 2:38). Perhaps one might think that the *Acts of the Apostles*, having been drawn up a few decades later than the facts they recount, do not reflect the original practice of the church, which in the meantime could have modified the rite of the baptism of Jewish converts. In reality Paul attests that he too had been baptized. Therefore in 33/34 CE baptism is already a Christian rite, considered necessary for admission to the church[130] with a completely different meaning from the rite of purification used for proselytes. Légasse[131] has shown that there is no evidence of the existence of a Jewish baptism for the proselytes in the first half of the first century CE, but only for the second half. Christian baptism is not of a ritual character—in which case it would be repeatable—but once received, it cannot be repeated because it is a sign of the forgiveness of sins and of new birth in Christ. From the beginning it was perceived as a necessary means of salvation, even if the baptism of water did not seem absolute and necessary as an external rite. There is baptism of blood and baptism of desire. The experience of the first Christians was that many believers were killed before they had been baptized with water. This rapidly spread a conviction concerning baptism by blood. As Cyprian of Carthage says: "They are baptized in their most glorious blood."[132] Tertullian speaks of it on several occasions as a *lavacrum sanguinis* (washing of blood).[133] Commenting on Cyprian's thinking on this subject, Augustine writes:

> That the place of baptism is sometimes supplied by martyrdom is supported by an argument by no means trivial, which the blessed Cyprian adduces from the thief, to whom, though he was

not baptized, it was yet said, 'Today shall you be with me in Paradise' (*Lk* 23:43). On considering which, again and again, I find that not only martyrdom for the sake of Christ may supply what was wanting of baptism, but also faith and conversion of heart, if recourse may not be had to the celebration of the mystery of baptism for want of time. For neither was that thief crucified for the name of Christ, but as the reward of his own deeds; nor did he suffer because he believed, but he believed while suffering. It was shown, therefore, in the case of that thief, how great is the power, even without the visible sacrament of baptism, of what the apostle says, 'With the heart man believes unto righteousness, and with the mouth confession is made unto salvation' (*Rom* 10:10). But the lack [of baptism] is supplied invisibly only when the administration of baptism is prevented, not by contempt for religion, but by the necessity of the moment.[134]

In the New Testament period we do not encounter liturgical details regarding the baptismal rite. After a brief preparation, according to what has been said above, a preliminary profession of faith is required, which varies according to the churches. For converts from Judaism this profession is above all Christological, while for those from paganism it also includes the mention of God the Father. However, in any case, it must be somehow Trinitarian as is well attested in the second century. It also seems that the profession is articulated in answers that the person being baptized gives to the questions of the baptizer during the baptismal rite which, in general, is thought to occur by immersion in living water (flowing) in total nakedness.[135] Ancient sources say that before the central act of the rite, the catechumens lay their clothes aside and remain naked, both men and women. The undressing, an essential moment, and the dressing are acts rich in profound theological and spiritual symbolism.

Nudity—also required in relation to anointings—is part of the ritual and is distinct from ascetic nudity. It takes place within an engaging and dramatic ceremony.[136] The baptisms conducted in the fourth century are normally for adults, not children. Jesus is also represented naked in the mosaic of the Arian baptistery in Ravenna, built by Theodoric († 526). The few pictorial representations that present naked women are only stylizations, or depict adolescents. More frequent is the male representation "of a small figure immersed in water, to whom a larger male character imposes his hands on his head."[137] A sketch on stone in Aquileia[138]—where the candidate looks like a child—represents the scene of a baptism, but the literary testimonies are numerous and of different origins. It is not possible that this use was introduced later; this would be inconceivable. That is the common opinion.

The ancient sensibility is different from ours. Ancient art is rich in images and naked characters which express a heroic body in their depiction of nudity. In early Christian art there are representations of naked children (*putti*), but also biblical figures such as Adam, Eve,

Daniel, and Jonah. Pagan statues are condemned by Christians not because they are naked but because they represented divinities.

A terminological observation can be useful to us. According to a testimony of Chrysostom, in fact, shortly before the central act of the rite, the baptized are "naked," even though they have some clothing on. They are supposed to still have clothing during the gesture of immersion.[139] This interpretation is confirmed by Theodore of Mopsuestia.[140] A decent person is "naked" when he does not wear socially convenient clothes, like Peter in the boat. He is said to be naked, but is still wearing something (*Jn* 21:7). The language of nudity used by the fathers rather expresses the total stripping of the old man to be reborn in Christ in the realization of a radical change in the way of being and living expressed by wearing the white robe. A new birth is realized in baptism as in the nakedness at the first birth.

The tractate *On the Singleness of Clergy* (*De singularitate clericorum*) states, "Certainly it is honorable to celebrate such meetings with women (in church), in which there is no difference of nature, in which it is lawful that all be equal without any difference, so that in the same baptism no one is ashamed of nudity, where the innocence of Adam and Eve is renewed and the tunic is not taken away but rather received."[141] John of Jerusalem states: "You have stripped your tunic.... You were naked, imitating in this too the naked Christ on the cross.... You were naked at the sight of all and had no shame."[142] Since the fifth century there is evidence of the existence of various arrangements to ensure a certain privacy in the baptismal room, into which few people could enter. In the East, deaconesses were used for certain rites, for example for the anointing of the baptized.

John Moschus reports a curious episode of the presbyter Conon who finds it difficult to anoint women in baptism.[143] Some texts such as the *On the Singleness of Clergy*, the *Didascalia*, and the *Apostolic Constitutions* reflect embarrassment within the communities. Ritual nudity is not sexual promiscuity because modesty is guarded in different ways: alternating the times of baptism and the use of architectural devices.[144] Augustine distinguishes in the baptistery "the area for women."[145] Spiritual formation generates a new vision of the body. After the long, tiring and exhausting preparation through fasting, an atmosphere of collective prayer and an intense participation in the imminent spiritual rebirth, "the ritual process itself offered the means to appropriately articulate, control and sublimate individual emotions and passions"[146] in a place "where everything is innocence, everything is piety, everything is grace, everything is sanctification."[147]

Given the circumstances of the place and time, baptism can also be administered by pouring water on the head and not only by immersion. The *Didache*, a document from the Syrian countryside of the second half of the first century, describes the rite as follows: "And concerning baptism, baptize this way: Having first said all these things, baptize in the name of the Father, and of the Son, and of the Holy Spirit, in living water. But if you have not living water, baptize into other water; and if you cannot in cold, in warm. But if you have not either, pour water three times upon the head in the name of Father and Son and Holy Spirit. But before the baptism let the baptizer fast, as well as the baptized and whichever others can. You shall order the baptized to fast one or two days before."[148] The text cited also specifies the formula that accompanies the gesture. It is Trinitarian, but we do not know the exact course of the rite, so that it may not have been a true liturgical formula. The *Didache* makes no mention of any other rituals. In some texts we speak of baptism in the name of Jesus: but this meant nothing more than that we receive the baptism that goes back to him and which consecrates us to him. In western baptisteries of which numerous examples remain, the baptized enters the pool up to the waist, while the minister pours water on his head. In the churches of Syria, the formula is impersonal: NN is baptized in the name of the Father and of the Son and of the Holy Spirit.[149]

Several New Testament texts also show the existence of the gesture of the imposition of hands (*Acts* 8:14-17; 19:5-6), linked to the descent of the Holy Spirit on the neophyte. We have no certain testimony of other rites, such as renunciation of Satan, exorcism or anointing with oil, nor about the times and places or the ministers. The anointings are evident by the end of the second century when the liturgy is now the prerogative of the bishop. "Without the bishop it is not lawful to baptize or celebrate an agape feast" writes Ignatius of Antioch to the Smyrnaeans at the beginning of the second century.[150] The most remarkable and precise testimony on the baptismal rite at the beginning of the third century is offered to us by the *Apostolic Tradition* attributed to Hippolytus, which refers to previous traditions and reflects the liturgy of an urban community, unlike the archaic *Didache*. Other documents rich in information are, mainly, the *De baptismo* by Tertullian, the *Acts of Thomas* (2nd/3rd c.), and the *Didascalia* (200-250 CE). The author, a bishop, is inspired by the *Didache*, the *Shepherd* of Hermas, and the *Gospel of Peter*.

Based on these texts, and in particular of those of the fourth century, we can somewhat reconstruct the baptismal rite, which must normally take place during the Easter vigil with the bishop presiding. Various anointings take place, varying in number according to the sources and with different explanations. At least one is connected with the conferral of the Spirit. After the blessing of the water, the renunciation of Satan is performed by the one to be baptized indicating the rejection of the pagan gods. Then the exorcisms are carried out to express that Christ has dominion over all things. The renunciation of Satan, the exorcisms and the confession of faith, given the different religious context, are not practiced in the ancient Syro-Palestinian churches. The bishop anoints the catechumen on the forehead with a sign in the shape of a cross using scented oil (*myron*) as a mark of Christ's soldier and as protection against Satan.

Baptism, in the normal rite, involves a triple immersion: each to an answer of the candidate to the minister who asks questions about the Trinitarian faith. This is how the *Apostolic Tradition* describes the central rite:

> At the hour in which the cock crows, they shall first pray over the water. When they come to the water, the water shall be pure and flowing, that is, the water of a spring or a flowing body of water. Then they shall take off all their clothes. The children shall be baptized first. All of the children who can answer for themselves, let them answer. If there are any children who cannot answer for themselves, let their parents answer for them, or someone else from their family. After this, the men will be baptized. Finally, the women, after they have unbound their hair, and removed their jewelry. No one shall take any foreign object with themselves down into the water. At the time determined for baptism, the bishop shall give thanks over some oil, which he puts in a vessel. It is called the Oil of Thanksgiving. He shall take some more oil and exorcise it. It is called the Oil of Exorcism. A deacon shall hold the Oil of Exorcism and stand on the left. Another deacon shall hold the Oil of Thanksgiving and stand on the right. When the elder takes hold of each of them who are to receive baptism, he shall tell each of them to renounce, saying, 'I renounce you Satan, all your service, and all your works.' After he has said this, he shall anoint each with the Oil of Exorcism, saying, 'Let every evil spirit depart from you.' Then, after these things, the bishop passes each of them in the nude to the elder who stands at the water. They shall stand in the water naked. A deacon, likewise, will go down with them into the water. When each of them to be baptized has gone down into the water, the one baptizing shall lay hands on each of them, asking, 'Do you believe in God the Father Almighty?' And the one being baptized shall answer, 'I believe.' He shall then baptize each of them once, laying his hand upon each of their heads. Then he shall ask, 'Do you believe in Jesus Christ, the Son of God, who was born of the Holy Spirit and the Virgin Mary, who was crucified under Pontius Pilate, and died, and rose on the third day living from the dead, and ascended into heaven, and sat down at the right hand of the Father, the one coming to judge the living and the dead?' When each has answered, 'I believe,' he shall baptize a second time. Then he shall ask, 'Do you believe in the Holy Spirit and the Holy Church and the resurrection of the flesh?' Then each being baptized shall answer, 'I believe.' And thus, let him baptize the third time. Afterward, when they have come up out of the water, they shall be anointed by the elder with the Oil of Thanksgiving, saying, 'I anoint you with holy oil in the name of Jesus Christ.' Then, drying themselves, they shall dress and afterwards gather in the church. The bishop will then lay his hand upon them, invoking, saying, 'Lord God,... After this he pours the oil into his hand, and laying his hand on each of their heads, says 'I anoint you... Then, after sealing each of them on the forehead, he shall give them the kiss of peace and say 'The Lord be with you' .... From then on they will pray together with all the people. Prior to this they may not pray with the faithful until they have completed all. [151]

The liturgical use of the blessing of baptismal water is not based on Scripture but soon became established everywhere.[152] The use of blessed water outside of baptism is rather late. Because of the similarity with Jewish, pagan or syncretistic rituals, Tertullian was against its practice.[153] The whole ceremony ends with the kiss of peace from the whole community.

In the fourth century these rites tend to expand in number, length and time, even for the greater number of candidates, so in some churches certain rites are brought forward to Friday. Riley[154] has offered a detailed, precise and documented study, with numerous synoptic tables, for the churches of Jerusalem, Antioch, Mopsuestia and Milan. A simple glance at the various tables is enough to show the variety, complexity and diversity of the rites even in substantial unity. The differences would be even greater if we took into consideration other communities.

The baptized person wears the white robe for a whole week after baptism. The most solemn and dramatic rite is undoubtedly the renunciation of Satan (*pompa diaboli*). Before baptism, each candidate must make the gesture, personally and publicly, which marks the transition from one way of living and thinking to another, from one society to another. In Mopsuestia, it takes place as follows: the candidate, dressed only in sackcloth kneels down with his hands outstretched and his eyes raised to the sky. "You stand barefooted on sackcloth while your outer garment is taken off from you and your hands are stretched towards God in the posture of one who prays. First you genuflect while the rest of your body is erect, and then you say: 'I renounce Satan and all his angels, and all his works, and all his service, and all his deception, and all his worldly glamour; and I engage myself and believe, and am baptized in the name of the Father, and of the Son, and of the Holy Spirit.' While you are genuflecting, and the rest of your body is erect, and your look is directed towards heaven, and your hands are outstretched in the posture of one who prays, the priest, clad in linen robes that are clean and shining, signs you on your forehead with the holy Chrism and says: 'So-and-so is signed in the name of the Father, and of the Son and of the Holy Spirit.' And your godfather who is standing behind you spreads an *orarium* of linen on the crown of your head, raises you and makes you stand up erect."[155] The bishop then comments on this text throughout the homily that follows. After the anointing, the newly baptized is now a soldier of Christ equipped to fight against all evil under Christ's leadership. In fact, in ancient times it is customary to conceive of Christian life as a continuous battle for Christ against the powers of Satan.

The preaching of the fathers on the occasion of baptism and through the following week helps us to reconstruct the rites of the various churches, such as Cyril for Jerusalem († 387), Ambrose for Milan († 397), John Chrysostom for Antioch († 407), Theodore for Mopsuestia († 428),[156] Chromatius for Aquileia († 407),[157] Gaudentius for Brescia († 410), Augustine († 430) and Quodvultdeus († 450) for Africa.

Augustine wrote a great deal about baptism,[158] but no specific work on the baptismal liturgy has been preserved. There are many sermons addressed to neophytes with numerous references to rites, but he wrote no specific works like Ambrose did. Baptism can be celebrated at any time, but especially at Easter: "The sacrament of baptism, therefore, is beyond all doubt to be distinguished from Easter. Baptism, you see, can be received on any day. Easter may lawfully be kept only on one particular day. Baptism is given so that life may be imparted anew. Easter is celebrated to keep the memory of our religion fresh in our minds. But the fact that far and away the greater number of those seeking baptism converge on this day only means that the greater joy of the feast attracts them, not that a richer grace of salvation is to be had then."[159] Lent offers a long period of preparation: "The solemn season has arrived, which should remind us to humble our souls and chastise our bodies with prayer and fasting more earnestly and intensely than at other periods of the year."[160] On Holy Thursday, those to be baptized finish fasting and take a bath.[161] On Easter day Augustine reminds the neophytes of the journey they have made "Unless wheat is ground, after all, and moistened with water, it can't possibly get into this shape which is called bread. In the same way you too were being ground and pounded, as it were, by the humiliation of fasting and the sacrament of exorcism. Then came baptism, and you were, in a manner of speaking, moistened with water in order to be shaped into bread. But it's not yet bread without fire to bake it. So, what does fire represent? That's the chrism, the anointing. Oil, the fire-feeder, you see, is the sacrament of the Holy Spirit."[162] "Now call yourselves also to mind: you didn't exist, and you were created, you were carried to the Lord's threshing floor, you were threshed by the labor of oxen, that is, of the preachers of the gospel. When, as catechumens, you were being held back, you were being stored in the barn. You handed in your names; then you began to be ground by fasts and exorcisms. Afterward you came to the water, and you were moistened into dough, and made into one lump. With the application of the heat of the Holy Spirit you were baked and made into the Lord's loaf of bread."[163]

On the vigil of Easter the church is well illuminated "This holy celebration, brothers and sisters, which has removed night from the night, putting darkness to flight with all these lights, and making our faith bright and cheerful as if it were the daytime of our hearts, is taking place, as you know, in memory of the resurrection of our Lord Jesus Christ."[164] The whole community gathered with the catechumens spending the night in prayer, with bible readings and sermons given by the bishop. The catechumens, individually, recite by heart the symbol of faith:

> You have given back what you are to believe, you have heard how you are to pray. You would be unable to call upon one in whom you had not believed, as the apostle says: 'How shall they call upon one in whom they have not believed?' (*Rom* 10:14). That is why you first learned the creed, which contains the short and grand rule of your faith: short in the number of its words, grand in the content of its statements. But the prayer which you have received today, to be retained and

given back in a week's time, was given over, as you heard when the gospel was read, by the Lord himself to his disciples, and from them has come down to us.[165]

Even children of seven/eight years of age would undergo this: "This is why when they are baptized, they already render the Symbol and answer questions for themselves."[166]

In Hippo, baptism is administered at dawn. The catechumens in the baptistery renounce Satan, they lay their robes aside and enter the water sanctified by prayer. Baptism can also heal the body during the rite.[167] Or a newly baptized woman, touching the womb of a woman suffering from cancer, heals her "with the sign of Christ."[168] This is followed by the chrism with the oil blessed by the bishop.[169] Then "the sevenfold Spirit is invoked upon the baptized."[170] Augustine speaks of the elements and rites of baptism, but at different times. He does not distinguish between baptism and confirmation. After baptism, the newly baptized person is clothed: "O Lord, hear us. Make us, because you have made us. Make us good, because you have made us enlightened people. These here dressed in white (*isti albati*), these enlightened ones, are hearing your word through me, because being enlightened by your grace they are standing in your presence."[171] "By these shining white garments (*vestes nitidae*), as by a visible word, there is inscribed in your memories at this fresh beginning of your new life, a seedling of light. When you change them, be careful not to change what they stand for, brilliant with the light of faith and truth. Don't let it be soiled with any filth of perverse behavior, in order that you may not be found naked on that day and may pass without any difficulty from the glory of faith to the glory of sight. But when, in today's solemn ceremony, you move out of this chancel, where in your spiritual infancy you were being set apart from the others, and are mixed in with God's people, stick to the good ones!"[172] What is the meaning of baptism? Here is Augustine's summary:

> You that have been born again to new life, which is why you are called 'infants'; you who above all are seeing this only now, listen to what it all means, as I had promised you ... Now when you were baptized, or rather just before you were baptized, I spoke to you on Saturday about the sacrament of the font into which you were to be plunged. And I told you, what I don't think you have forgotten, that baptism had, or has, the same value as being buried with Christ, as the apostle says: 'For we have been buried with Christ through baptism into death, so that just as he has risen from the dead, so we too may walk in newness of life' (*Rom* 6:4).[173]

The newly baptized (*infantes*), now "spiritually reborn by God the Father and Mother Church,"[174] return to the basilica where the whole community is waiting and rejoices in, "an exultation deriving from the bonds of the new fraternity." [175] Then they participate for the first time in the Eucharist at which point for the first time they hear the words of the introduction to the Eucharistic prayer and recite: "the Lord's prayer that you have received and rendered. And then it's said: Peace be with you, and the Christians exchange a holy kiss."[176] After the Octave of Easter[177] they come out of their area in the church enclosure dressed in white (*in albis*) and mingle with the faithful: "With today's solemn rite your exit from these barriers is accomplished, which as spiritual children separate you from the other faithful."[178]

We conclude with an observation that clearly shows the new Christian mentality in relation to the Jewish tradition. The Gospels often speak of the Levitical purity of the Jews as a typical element of their way of life that is all encompassing in their contacts with the Gentiles, in food, and in any number of activities. The body of the deceased is impure, and it contracts impurities; sexual relations and menstruation create impurities. The Jews are concerned with this in any number of observances, even after the destruction of the Temple.

For Christians, baptism is of such radical importance that it purifies forever because the neophyte is reborn; the baptism spiritualizes every aspect of one's life. Therefore, as Clement of Alexandria observes, baptism makes all previous purifying ritual practices obsolete: "But the providence of God as revealed by the Lord does not order now, as it did in ancient times, that after sexual intercourse a man should wash. For there is no need for the Lord to make believers do this after intercourse since by one Baptism he has washed them clean for every such occasion, as also he has comprehended in one Baptism the many washings of Moses."[179] This is the vision of the great majority of Christians. Roughly of the same period the *Didascalia* insists on not following the Jewish traditions of purification because one is pure with baptism:

> And again, let them tell us, in what days or in what hours they keep themselves from prayer and from receiving the Eucharist, or from reading the Scriptures—let them tell us whether they are void of the Holy Spirit. For through baptism they receive the Holy Spirit who is ever with those that work righteousness, and does not depart from them by reason of natural issues and the intercourse of marriage but is ever and always with those who possess him ... For if you think, O woman, that in the seven days of your flux you are void of the Holy Spirit, if you die in those days, you will depart empty and without hope. But if the Holy Spirit is always in you, do not keep yourself from prayer and from the Scriptures and from the Eucharist without a (true) impediment. For consider and see, that prayer is also heard through the Holy Spirit, and the Eucharist through the Holy Spirit is accepted and sanctified, and the Scriptures are the words of the Holy Spirit and are holy. For if the Holy Spirit is in you, why do you keep yourself from approaching the works of the Holy Spirit?[180]

Those most connected with Judaism—the Jewish Christians—were not so radical. They, indeed, try to preserve some Jewish traditions. The numerous purifications of the Pseudo-Clementines testify to this.[181]

VALIDITY OF BAPTISM

In the middle of the third century, a bitter dispute arose over the validity of the baptism administered by heretics outside the catholic church. It is a problem still existing today with some Orthodox churches. The debate is related to the context in which the doctrine of the validity of ordination to ministry is formulated. The two disputes are closely linked. Traditional practice in Africa did not normally administer baptism to those who, although baptized in some sect, asked to enter the catholic church. Cyprian held that what heretics did was not baptism.[182] Previously it had been a matter of debate in the African church and there was bound to be a certain diversity.[183] Practice in the African Church changed around 222 according to the decisions of a council held under Agrippinus, with the participation of bishops of Africa Proconsularis and Numidia.[184] But not everyone participated. Cyprian tries not to bring up the ancient tradition which did not allow for rebaptism, but is reminded by Firmilian of Caesarea (in Cappadocia) that the Africans, unlike the Christians of Asia, have abandoned the previous practice.[185] Moreover, Cyprian himself was forced to recognize the ancient practice which is defended as ancient even by the contemporary anonymous author of *De rebaptismate*.

The controversy apparently became critical when some members of the Novatian church wanted to return to the catholic church. They had the Trinitarian faith but were rigorous in their penitential discipline.[186] The controversy was very old, from at least the time of Marcion.[187] In Africa, however, not everyone was convinced of the practice of rebaptism. The bishop of Mauretania, the most distant province, followed Roman practice; but disagreements also existed in Numidia and even in Africa Proconsularis.[188] Some dissident bishops did not participate in the Council of Carthage on September 1, 256. The objections have been preserved in the treatise *De rebaptismate*, which defends a theory different from Cyprian although, ironically, the work was placed under the aegis of Cyprian. This work of an anonymous bishop, according to Paul Mattei, was composed in the course of 256[189] at the height of the debate in North Africa to refute the theological positions of Cyprian, who was a tenacious defender of rebaptism. Cyprian replied with two letters, 74 and 75. The anonymous author instead distinguishes two types of baptism: the one with water and the one that takes place through the imposition of the hands of the bishop: "Heretics already baptized with water in the name of Jesus Christ must be baptized only in the Holy Spirit and in Jesus, the only name that has been given under heaven in which we are necessarily saved and death does not really frighten."[190] Therefore, those who had been baptized outside the catholic church, have received only the first rite. When they enter the church, only the second is necessary with the imposition of the hands of the bishop, and it is not necessary to repeat the whole rite.

The East was also divided. Firmilian of Caesarea speaks of councils held in the central provinces of Asia Minor that support the practice of rebaptism.[191] Dionysius of Alexandria knows that the doctrine of rebaptism in Africa was recently introduced and he was aware, as well, of several synods "at Iconium, at Synnada and in many other places."[192] Dionysius did not rebaptize[193] and broke communion with the bishops of Asia Minor.[194]

The debate on the validity of baptism administered outside the catholic church is, in some way, universal and the voices of distant communities cross: Carthage (Cyprian), Rome (Stephen), Caesarea of Cappadocia (Firmilian) and Alexandria (Dionysius). It is the most universal mid-third century debate; others are more regional, especially the Christological ones.

The problem of rebaptism continued throughout Christian antiquity. The problem resurfaced not only in the discussion with the Donatists, but also between Catholics. In the West, Pope Siricius,[195] echoing a long Roman tradition, writes to Himerius of Tarragona: "We associate these (i.e. the Arians) with the communion of Catholics, together with the Novatians and other heretics, as was established in the Synod, solely through the sole invocation of the sevenfold Spirit and with the imposition of the hand of the bishop, observed throughout the East and the West"(2.3). He writes these things because in Spain, at the end of the fourth century, some people were rebaptizing. Pope Pelagius (556-61) also wrote to Gaudentius, Bishop of Volterra (*Ep.* 21), in the case of the conversion of the Arians. The pope recommends the practice observed elsewhere: if they were baptized only in the name of Christ and with only one immersion, then baptism is required in the name of the Trinity, with three immersions; if in the name of the Trinity, then only reconciliation is required. Not only the church, but also the civil legislation prohibits rebaptism with numerous laws preserved in the Theodosian Code.[196]

The solution to the problem is very important because it concerns the conception of the Church and its ministry, the ordained ministers, the validity of their ordination and the validity and lawfulness of the administration of the sacraments. If baptism administered outside the "true Church" is not valid, neither are ordinations valid. Then all ministry done by these ministers is invalid. The apostolic succession is interrupted.

The current research has also reached a firm consensus on the baptism of children. Although there are no explicit texts on the subject in the New Testament writings, it is believed to have existed since the apostolic period, when the whole family was sometimes baptized. However, we have explicit testimonies only in the following centuries. Tertullian is against infant baptism.[197] Cyprian confirms the practice of the baptism of children.[198]

However, there is no special rite of baptism developed for children. For that reason, the rite practiced for adults was used with appropriate adaptations. A special rite was created only recently, after the Second Vatican Council. We know of the presence of the godparents in every type of baptismal rite. Their function was to be the guarantor of the life and conduct of the candidate at the time of admission among the catechumens, to follow and help them during the period of preparation and to testify at the end to their dignity, thereby rendering them worthy to receive baptism. Therefore, it was part of the preparatory period and not of the time after baptism. For the children, the function of godparent was carried out by the parents and for the slaves by their masters.

BAPTISM-CONFIRMATION-EUCHARIST

These three sacraments, in ancient Christianity, were closely linked, since immediately after the baptismal rites[199] (baptism and confirmation) the Eucharist was received for the first time.[200] The baptismal liturgy normally ended with the celebration of the Eucharist, except in the case of the baptism of *clinici* who were baptized out of necessity in the case of serious illness, or of small children, to whom communion is deferred. According to common practice, baptism cannot be repeated; and those who sin seriously were given the possibility of penance. The Eucharist, on the other hand, was frequently repeated in the life of the community. In the fourth century, in the East, the Eucharist was celebrated normally three times a week; in the West, generally every day.

Baptism for the forgiveness of sins and spiritual rebirth, and confirmation which imparts the gift of the Holy Spirit, are closely linked both in theological reflection and in catechetical preaching. Since they are conferred by the same minister, the local bishop, during the same liturgy, it is difficult to determine the specific rites that relate to confirmation. When Christianity spread to the countryside and ceased to be an exclusively urban phenomenon, rural parishes were created far from the cities where the bishop resided. It was in the city that the cathedral and the baptismal font were located. For practical and disciplinary reasons, in the West baptism in these rural parishes could be administered by priests, while confirmation was reserved for the bishop. In the East the one who administered baptism administered confirmation, but with oil (the *myron*) blessed by the bishop. Yet, we are now in a period in which the rites have grown in significance, with a full appreciation of the distinction between the two sacraments. The same cannot be said for the first three centuries.

Historical research, which began in England after World War II and then spread to the continent, has generated considerable clarification regarding confirmation, although neither definitive nor complete. We offer a summary here.[201] In the New Testament, we find the sentence "baptism in the Spirit." Initially, the rite of baptism itself conferred the Holy Spirit

(*Acts* 2:38). The outpouring of the Holy Spirit on the newly baptized is essential in the "new way," but we do not know much about the rite connected with it. That is why it is also called baptism in the Spirit. In the case of the centurion Cornelius it happens before baptism (*Acts* 10:44-48; 11:15-17); but this is an exceptional case. Generally, the outpouring of the Spirit occurs after baptism and by the imposition of the hands of the apostles and is considered a necessary rite to complete the baptism itself. "Now when the apostles at Jerusalem heard that Samaria had received the word of God, they sent to them Peter and John, who came down and prayed for them that they might receive the Holy Spirit; for it had not yet fallen on any of them, but they had only been baptized in the name of the Lord Jesus. Then they laid their hands on them and they received the Holy Spirit" (*Acts* 8:14-17; cf. also 19:1-6). In fact, in order to be full members of the new community, both immersion (ablution) in water and the laying on of hands are necessary. Soon we see that the rite forms a unity, without intervals, while distinguishing the various elements. Furthermore, everything is covered under the one name of baptism. Synonyms we encounter are: baptismal bath, ablution, rebirth or new birth, illumination, and *sphragis* (seal).

The ancient authors are unanimous in stating that in baptism the gift of the Holy Spirit is obtained: "There can be no baptism without the Spirit."[202] However, it is extremely difficult to specify the specific ritual because the rites had evolved, been enriched, and differentiated —even radically—in the various regions. Cyprian himself writes in another letter "Those who are baptized in the church (outside the normal rite) present themselves to its leaders and through our prayer and the laying on of hands obtain the Holy Spirit and the Lord gives them the seal of perfection."[203] Prayer and the imposition of hands (or hand) constituted the rite of the Carthaginian church—and therefore of the whole of North Africa—for the conferral of the Spirit, that is, confirmation.[204] Cyprian also adds a *signatio*, a sign of the cross on the forehead of the candidate. The same happens in Rome, according to the testimony of Pope Cornelius, while chapter 21 of the *Apostolic Tradition* speaks of a double anointing and two types of oil. Both are blessed by the bishop. Before baptism a presbyter asks the catechumen to renounce Satan and anoints him with "the oil of exorcism," saying "Let every spirit depart from you." After the baptism with water the priest anoints with the "oil of thanksgiving" the neophyte saying, "I anoint you with holy oil in the name of Jesus Christ." The rite of the laying on of hands by the bishop follows, pronouncing a prayer. Then he pours on his head "the holy oil," imposing his hand again and saying, "I anoint you with the holy oil in the Lord Almighty Father and in Jesus Christ and in the Holy Spirit." Then he anoints him on the forehead. The rite takes place as a whole, preserving a unity, as Origen also affirms, "We are baptized with visible water and with visible chrism according to the tradition of the church."[205]

For Latin Africa, Tertullian wrote a treatise on baptism in which he also makes references to ritual aspects. He affirms that in the baptism with water the Holy Spirit is not actually given: "Not that the Holy Spirit is given to us in the water, but that in the water we are made clean by the action of the angel, and made ready for the Holy Spirit."[206] Both Tertullian[207] and Cyprian[208] admit a post-baptismal anointing, the laying on of hands with the recitation of an epiclesis and the *signatio* of the baptized. Hippolytus, the author of the *Commentary on Daniel*, talks about a post-baptismal anointing with pneumatological significance. These elements coincide with the *Apostolic Tradition*, whose geographical origin and time have been discussed previously.

Ambrose of Milan, who baptized Augustine in 387, spoke extensively (albeit often with allusions) of the baptismal rite in his two works *De mysteriis* and *De sacramentis* which were dedicated to post-baptismal catechesis.[209] First of all, there is the ritual of *aperitio - apertionis mysterium*—the ritual of ephphatha which calls for the one being baptized to "open your ears well and enjoy the good smell of eternal life." The baptizing person touches the ears and nostrils (not the mouth) of the person being baptized, repeating the word ephphatha each time in order to make her able to understand the Word and profess the faith, and then the candidate enters the baptismal font. Ambrose writes:

> After this the Holy of holies was opened to you, you entered the sanctuary of regeneration. Recall what you were asked and remember what you answered. You renounced the devil and his works, the world with its luxury and pleasures. Your words are kept not in the tombs of the dead, but in the book of the living. There you saw the Levite, you saw the priest, you saw the high priest [i.e. the bishop]. Do not consider the bodily forms, but the grace of the ministrations. You spoke in the presence of the angels. . . . There is no place for deception nor for denial. He is an angel who proclaims the kingdom of Christ and eternal life. He is to be esteemed by you not according to his appearance, but according to his office. Consider what he has given over, reflect on his experience, recognize his position. Having entered, therefore, that you might discern your adversary whom you were to renounce as it were to his face, you then turn to the east. For he who renounces the devil turns to Christ, and beholds Him face to face. What did you see? Water, certainly, but not water alone. You saw the Levites (deacons) ministering there, and the bishop asking questions and hallowing.[210]

The catechumens, having entered the baptistery, lay their clothes aside and are anointed with oil by a presbyter or a deacon: "You have been anointed as an athlete of Christ, as if to contend in the contest of this world."[211] The anointing is done all over the body, similar to what is done for the athletes in the stadium. While the bishop is on the edge of the baptismal font, the candidates, accompanied by a deacon or presbyter, one at a time, descend into the holy water: "You came to the font, you descended into it, you turned your gaze to the high priest."[212] Next come the questions and answers of the profession of faith accompanied by the three immersions in water, "so that the triple confession erases the numerous sins of your past life."[213] The bishop himself anoints the head with perfumed oil (*myrum*),[214] "for eternal life."[215] This is followed by the washing of the feet—a typical rite of the church in Milan and Gaul—and the covering with white robes to indicate the "robes of innocence."[216] Then follows the spiritual seal (*sequitur spirituale signaculum*),[217] "because after the baptismal font there is nothing left but to reach perfection, when, at the invocation of the bishop, the Holy Spirit is infused, 'Spirit of wisdom' and intellect, Spirit of counsel and strength."[218] Now the neophytes return to the church to participate in the Eucharistic Synaxis for the first time. For Ambrose the essential rite consists in the prayer of invocation of the Spirit on the baptized and presumably in the imposition of hands as well. There is no mention here of anointings. We find the same ritual in Gaul and Spain.

By combining the two rites of anointing with the chrism (perfumed oil; the *myron*) and the *consignatio* (cross on the forehead) in a single act, the chrismation now slowly replaces the imposition of hands. It becomes the only essential rite, which moreover is reserved to the bishop in the West. Confirmation (Lat. *confirmare*)[219] as it began to be called in Gaul from the fifth century thus acquired its own autonomy. It continued to be administered together with baptism, but as a practice in gradual decline.

In the Eastern churches there is more variety. While in fourth century Jerusalem we find a rite similar to the western rite in the Antiochene church and in the Syriac-speaking areas, as well as in Cappadocia and in Pontus, there is no specific post-baptismal rite to which is attached the gift of the Spirit and comparable to the confirmation of the Latin rite. The third mystagogical catechesis, attributed to Cyril of Jerusalem, is dedicated to the anointing of the baptized with *myron* "After you ascended from the font of the holy waters, there was the anointing with chrism, the replica of that with which Christ was anointed, that is, of the Holy Spirit. . . . You have been anointed with *myron* and have become a companion and partner of Christ."[220] Just as the invocation that is pronounced over the bread transforms it into the body of Christ, so the oil, after an epiclesis, is transformed, becoming a gift of Christ. "Beware of supposing that this ointment is mere ointment. Just as after the invocation of the Holy Spirit the Eucharistic bread is no longer ordinary bread, but the Body of Christ, so this holy oil, in conjunction with the invocation, is no longer simple and common oil, but becomes the gracious gift of Christ and the Holy Spirit, producing the advent of His deity."[221] He then notes that the anointing happens on the forehead, ears and then on the chest. With this anointing the candidates finally become worthy of the name Christian.[222] The sacramental effects highlighted here by Cyril always remain connected in Eastern theology to the anointing with *myron*. It is precisely what we in the West will call confirmation.

The *Apostolic Tradition* (3rd century) and the *Apostolic Constitutions* (end of 4th century) testify to an anointing of the forehead and of the whole body of the baptized, "as priests and kings have been anointed, as a sign of spiritual baptism."[223] Then there is the anointing with *myron*.

Theodore of Mopsuestia attests to the same practice, where the first anointing is defined as "the beginning of the sacrament." The bishop changed his clothing by wearing a delicate and shining linen robe to indicate the novelty of the new life of the baptized, marking him on the forehead with the oil of anointing to invoke the Trinity:

> In fact, it is from there that the priest draws you near to the calling towards which you must look, and in consequence of which you ought to live above all things according to the will [of God]. The sign with which you are signed means that you have been stamped as a lamb of Christ and as a soldier of the heavenly King. Indeed, immediately when we possess a lamb we stamp it with a stamp which shows to which master it belongs. . . . A soldier who has enlisted for military service, and been found worthy of this service of the State because of his stature and the structure of his body, is first stamped on his hand with a stamp which shows to which king he will henceforth offer his service; in this same way you also, who have been chosen for the Kingdom of Heaven, and after examination been appointed a soldier to the heavenly King, are first stamped on your forehead, that part of your head which is higher than the rest of your body, which is placed above all your body and above your face, and with which we usually draw near to one another and look at one another when we speak. You are stamped at that place so that you may be seen to possess great confidence.[224]

Therefore, although we find that the texts always speak of the gift of the Spirit in baptism, modern scholars find it difficult to specify the concrete rites. In a few texts the gift of the Spirit is linked to the same baptism, in others to a pre-baptismal anointing (or anointings) with *myron*. There is no post-baptismal rite. However, we are not faced with a liturgical deviation but with a practice that is linked to an original tradition of the apostolic times. Later, the rite of Jerusalem also spread to Antioch (5th century) and other eastern regions at different times which we are not able to specify, but the two sacraments will always remain linked in the East. Only a few liturgical practices will be different.

If the gift of the Spirit follows baptism, then the reflection tends to emphasize that the role of the Spirit is that of complementing, of perfecting, and of confirming the baptized. If instead it precedes baptism, its function is to make the candidate capable of pronouncing an act of supernatural faith and of receiving the sacrament of regeneration, as in the case of Cornelius of *Acts* 10 and 11.[225] However, once the new rite is adopted, the pre-baptismal anointing loses its meaning and lays more emphasis on exorcism. The post-baptismal anointing takes on the theological meaning the pre-baptismal anointing had.

A particularity in some communities of the Quartodecimans, following the tradition of John the Baptist, is the washing of the feet (*pedilavium*). It replaces baptism by immersion according to the statement of John 3:10. In the Syriac setting this rite disappears, but the memory is still preserved in the fourth century.[226] Normally baptism by immersion is practiced. For Irenaeus, Jesus washing the feet of his disciples purified their whole body.[227]

The rite of the washing of the feet becomes connected with baptism. In Aquileia, it is placed in a position immediately before baptism.[228] In the other liturgies, however, it is found after baptism. Elvira's collection of canons dictates: "Neither bishops nor clerics wash the feet of the baptized." Ambrose in Milan explains that it can be considered a simple rite of hospitality. It purifies the "neophyte from original sin, unlike the baptismal washing which is entrusted with the purification of personal sins.[229]

According to Augustine, however, the washing of the feet has nothing to do with the sacrament of baptismal regeneration but is simply an example of the supreme humility left by the Lord to his disciples.[230] "So the Lord's action in washing their feet was not like a sacrament of cleansing, but an example of humility, as he made clear when he told them, You do not know at present what I am doing, but you will know later."[231] The combined influence of Augustine and the monastic tradition, which in the washing of the feet saw exclusively an act of hospitality and humility,[232] will condition the interpretation of the washing of the postbaptismal feet in the Gallican and Celtic areas in the early Middle Ages.[233]

* * *

Appendix

A VERY BEAUTIFUL INSCRIPTION, perhaps written at the initiative of Sixtus III (432 - 440), can be found in the restored Lateran baptistery. The inscription, entitled *ad fontem*, is engraved in the epistyle of the columns and summarizes the theology of baptism in Rome (Diehl 1513):

> Here is born from life-giving seed a people, consecrated to another city/ whom the Spirit brings forth from the fertile waters./ To plunge [*mergere*] in the holy purifying flood the sinner//whom the wave receives as old but gives forth as new. / None reborn is different from those it makes one, / One font [*fons*], one Spirit, one faith, / Mother church as a virgin brought forth those who are born, whom she conceived by the divine breath and brought into being in the flowing water. /The person who wants to be innocent is here made clean by washing/ whether from the guilt of the first parent or one's own. / Here is the font of life which bathes the whole world, / its ultimate source the side of Christ wounded./ Reborn in this font for the kingdom of heaven,/ the

blessed life does not receive those born only once. / Be not afraid of the number or kind of your sins, / for the one born in this river will be holy.[234]

---

1. *De morte peregrini*, 11; *Lucian: With an English Translation*, ed. M.D. Macleod (Cambridge: Harvard, 1967), 191.
2. Cf. F.J. Dölger, I *Ichthys; Das Fischsymbol in frühchristlicher* (Oberhausen: Peter W. Metzler, 1999), Vol. 2:516.
3. *Encyclopedia of Religion* 7:225.
4. See the fundamental study by Eliade, *Birth and Rebirth: The Religious Meanings of Human Culture* (New York: Harper, 1958).
5. The term translates the Greek terms of *teletai* and *mysteria*, which indicated some unofficial and secret cults which required special initiation rites to be admitted. For the evolution of the term see A. Brelich, *Paides e Parthenoi* (Rome: Editori Riuniti University Press, 1969, rep. 1981), 15.
6. C.J. Bleeker, "Some introductory remarks on the significance of initiation," in C.J. Bleeker, ed., *Initiation: Contribution to Theme of the Study-Conference of the Intern. Association for History of Religion held at Strasbourg Sept. 17th to 22nd 1964* (Leiden: E.J. Brill, 1965), 17-18.
7. Ibid, 18.
8. F. Cumont, *Oriental Religions in Roman Paganism* (New York: Dover Publications, 1956). See index: soteriology, salvation, savior.
9. *Pagani e Cristiani alla Ricerca della Salvezza (secoli I-III): XXXIV Incontro di Studiosi dell'Antichità Cristiana* (Rome: Institutum Patristicum Augustinianum, 2006).
10. *Acts of Thomas* 49.
11. *Passio Perpetuae* 3.5.
12. Justin, *1 Apology* 65.1. Apuleius speaks of the necessity of purifications before initiations: *Metamorphosis* 11.23.
13. Cf. Clement of Alexandria, *Paedagogus* 1.6.
14. *Passio S. Caeciliae* 8.
15. Tacitus, *Annals* 15.44.
16. Pliny, *Ep.* 10.96.
17. C. Faivre, A. Faivre, "Chrèstianoi / Christianoi: ce que "chrétiens" en ses débuts voulait dire," *Revue Hist. Ecc.* 103 (2008): 771-805.
18. Justin, *I Apology* 54.6; 66.4.
19. Tertullian, *De praesc. haeret.* 40.1-4; *De baptismo* 5.
20. Justin, *I Apology* 7.7.
21. Augustine, *Confess.* 1.11.17; *De civ. Dei* 15.26.1.
22. P.-M. Gy, "La notion chrétienne d'initiation. Jalons pour une enquête," *La Maison-Dieu* 132 (1977): 33-54; M. M. Metzger, "Katechumenat" *Reallexikon Antike und Chr.* 20 (2003): 509-10.
23. I prefer the modern use of the term to that of "catechumenate" because it is more inclusive.
24. Cf. M. Eliade, *Birth and Rebirth*, 9-15.
25. A.D. Nock, *Christianisme et Hellénisme* (Paris: Éditions du Cerf, 1973); L. Ligier, "De la cène de Jésus à l'anaphore de l'Eglise," *La Maison-Dieu* 87 (1966): 7-15; Th. Talley, "De la "berakah" à l'eucharistie : une question à réexaminer," *La Maison-Dieu* 125 (1976): 11-39; C. Giraudo, *La struttura letteraria della preghiera eucaristica* (Rome: Biblical Institute Press, 1989); P. Bradshaw, "Jewish Influence on Early Christian Liturgy: A Reappraisal," in *Liturgies in East and West: Ecumenical Relevance of Early Liturgical Development*, Hans-Jürgen Feulner, ed. (Vienna: Lit Verlag, 2013), 47-59 ; Maxwell E. Johnson, "Issues in Eucharistic Praying in East and West," *Essays in Liturgical and Theological Analysis* (Collegeville MN: Liturgical Press, 2011).
26. On the symbolism of water, see *EAC* 3:935-36.
27. Cf. J. Ysabaert, *Greek Baptismal Terminology* (Nijmegen: Dekker & Van de Vegt, 1962), 149.
28. Cf. I. de La Potterie, *La vita secondo lo Spirito condizione del cristiano* (Rome: Editrice, 1967), 35-43; C. Nardi, *Il Battesimo in Clemente Alessandrino. Interpretazione di Eclogae propheticae 1-26* (Rome: Institutum Patristicum Augustinianum, 1984), 64ff.
29. Augustine, *Sermon* 216.7.

30. A. Benoît, *Le Baptême chrétien au second siècle. La théologie des Pères* (Paris: Presses Universitaires de France, 1953), 227.
31. Cf. Ysabaert, *Greek Baptismal*, 130ff.
32. Col. 3 :10. Cf. B. Rey, "L'homme nouveau d'après S. Paul," *Revue Sciences Philosophiques et Théol.* 48 (1964): 603-29; 49 (1965), 161-95. Rey, 161ff, writes that this doctrine reaches its maximum depth in the second chapter of the *Letter to the Ephesians*.
33. Tertullian, *Apology* 18.
34. Cf.M.-L. Thérel, *Les symboles de l'"Ecclesia" dans la création iconographique de l'art chrétien du IIIe au VIe siècle* (Roma: Edizioni di storia e letteratura, 1973), 4-5; Cf. s.v. *eikon:* Theol. WNT 2:378-96; J. Plumpe, *Mater Ecclesia. An Inquiry into the Concept of the Church as Mother in Early Christianity* (Washington: Catholic University of America Press, 1943); cf. especially the work of Delahaye in the following endnote. See: F. Bergamelli, "Il linguaggio simbolico delle immagini nella catechesi missionaria di Teofilo di Antiochia," *Salesianum* 41 (1979): 257-97; P. Marone, "La metafora dell'Ecclesia Mater nella letteratura antidonatista," *Annales Theologici* 24 (2010): 129-39; *Les Pères et la naissance de l'ecclésiologie*, ed. Marie-Anne Vannier (Paris: Les Éditions du Cerf), 2009.
35. Cf. Y. Congar, introduction to K. Delahaye, *Ecclesia Mater chez les Pères de trois premiers siècles* (Paris: Éditions du Cerf, 1964), 10.
36. Cf. *Rom* 7:2-4; *Eph* 5:25-27, *Rev* 12:4-7.
37. K. Delahaye, *Ecclesia Mater chez les Pères*, 73-74.
38. Ibid, 73-74.
39. "*Christianos non facit generatio, sed regeneration.*" Augustine, *De pecc. meritis et remis*. 3.9: PL 44:196.
40. Justin, *I Apology* 61.
41. *EAC* 1:457ff.
42. Cf. *Acts* 2:14-41; 8:26-39; chapters 10 and 11; 13:16-42; 16:30-33; etc.
43. Irenaeus, *Adv. haer.* 4.24.1.
44. G. Groppo, "L'evoluzione del catecumenato nella Chiesa antica dal punto di vista pastorale," *Salesianum* 41 (1979): 235-255, here 250.
45. Ps. Clementines, *Hom. Clem.* 1.13.
46. A. Turck, "Aux origines du catéchumenat," *Revue Sciences PhT* 48 (1964): 20-31, especially 25ff.; *Persuasion and Dissuasion in Early Christianity, Ancient Judaism, and Hellenism*, ed. P. W. van der Horst (Leuven: Peeters, 2003), 161ff.
47. Ps. Clementines, *Hom. Clem.* 3.73; 11.35; 13.9.
48. Ps. Clementines, *Recogn.* 3.67.
49. Ps. Clementines, *Hom. Clem.* 8.23.
50. Aristides, *Apology* 15.2.
51. Justin, *Dialogue* 58.1.
52. Justin, *I Apology* 4.2.
53. Irenaeus, *Adv. haer.* 2.32.4.
54. Tatian, *Oratio* 32; cf. Justin, *II Apology* 10.8.
55. Clement of Alexandria, *Eclogae proph.* 28.3.
56. Laodicea, can. 47.
57. A. Di Berardino, ed., *I concili della chiesa antica*, vol. I, *I concili greci*, 19.
58. Cf. Athenagoras, *Embassy* 11.4.
59. Justin, *Dialogue* 39.1.
60. Justin, *Dialogue* 14.1 and 19.
61. Justin, *Dialogue* 134.4.
62. Origen, *Contra Celsum* 3.51.
63. Origen, *Contra Celsum* 3.59.
64. Justin, *I Apology* 61.2.
65. Hermas, *Shepherd, Vision* 3.7.3.
66. Irenaeus, *Demonstration on the Apostolic Preaching* 2.
67. Justin, *I Apology* 61.1.
68. Tertullian, *On Penance* 6.1-2. ANF 3:661.
69. Tertullian, *On Penance* 6.16-17.

70. Origen, *Hom. in Lev.* 6.2; cf. 6.5.
71. Origen, *Hom. in Luc.* 21.4.
72. Cf. Origen, already quoted, in *Contra Celsum* 3.51.
73. From the early third century document, the so-called *Apostolic Tradition* (ch. 16), whose author goes by the name of Hippolytus. Cf. Tertullian, *De idol.* 12.
74. M. Dujarier, *Le parrainage des adultes aux trois premiers siècles de l'Église; recherche historique sur l'évolution des garanties et des étapes catéchuménales avant 313* (Paris: Éditions du Cerf, 1962), 37-39.
75. Cf. Origen, *Hom. in Lucam* 21.
76. Tertullian, *De idol.* 12; 24.3.
77. Cf. *Sacramentarium Gregorianum*: PL 78:90C; *Ordo Rom.* XI, c.12, Andrieu II, 420 (VII century); *Ordo Rom.* XV, c.118, Andrieu III, 20; Fredegarius, lib.2, c. 58 (Cf. J.F. Niermeyer, *Mediae latinitatis lexicon minus* (Leiden: Brill, 1976), 775.)
78. *Apost. Trad.* chap.16 and 20.
79. Cf. M. Dujarier, *Le parrainage*.
80. Tertullian, *De baptismo* 18.4.
81. Cf., P.A. Gramaglia, *Tertulliano, Il battesimo* (Rome: Edizioni Paoline, 1979), 162.
82. M. Dujarier, *Le parrainage*, 236.
83. The corresponding Greek term of sponsor is *anadokos* (Dionysius the Areopagite: *Ecc. Hier.* 2.2.7; PG 3:396C).
84. *Apostolic Tradition* 17.
85. Clement of Alexandria, *Stromata* 2.96.1-2; cf. 6.130.1; *Pedagogue* 1.36.2.
86. Clement of Alexandria, *Stromata* 6.19.4.
87. Augustine, *Ad Simplic.* 1.2.29.
88. Augustine, *De cat. rud.* 5.9.
89. Augustine, *De urbis excidio*; PL 40:722.
90. Cf. J. Lécuyer, "Aspects missionnaires de l'initiation chrétienne selon les Pères de l'église," *Nouvelle Rev. Sc. des Missions* (1959): 1-13; E. Glenn Hinson, *The Evangelization of the Roman Empire* (Macon, GA: Mercer University, Press), 1981.
91. Cf. M. Simonetti, "Origene catecheta," in *Valori attuali della catechesi patristica*, ed. S. Felici (Rome: LAS, 1979), 93-102.
92. Cf. A. Lemaire, *Les ministères aux origines de l'église* (Paris: Éditions du Cerf, 1971).
93. *Apostolic Tradition*, Chaps.15, 18 and 19.
94. Cyprian, *Ep.*29.2.2: CSEL 3:548. Cf. V. Saxer, *Vie liturgique et quotidienne à Carthage vers le milieu du IIIe siècle* (Vatican City: Pontificio Istituto di archeologia Cristiana, 1969), 79; 82-83. For Commodianus cf. G. Groppo, "Catechesi ufficiale e letteratura apocrifa nella cristologia di Commodiano," *Cristologia e catechesi patristica*, ed. S. Felici (Rome: LAS, 1981), 98-99.
95. PG 2:48-49; cf. Ps. Clementines, *Hom.* 3.71; 8.6 (preachers must exhibit worthy behavior).
96. Methodius of Olympus, *Symposium* 3.8.
97. Tertullian, *De praescr.* 41.2; *Apostolic Tradition* 18; 21; 26-28; 41. etc.
98. In his homilies Origen mentions the catechumens who were listening to his preaching, for example *In Jer.* 3.3; *In Ezech.* 6.5; *In Luc.* 21 and 22; *Comm.in Jo.* 5.8; *In Lev.* 6.2.
99. Council of Elvira, canons 45; 62; 62; 73; Council of Neocesarea, can. 5; Nicea, can. 14. Cf. M. Dujarier, "Sur le statut du catéchumène dans l'église," *Maison-Dieu* 152 (1982): 143-73.
100. Clement of Alexandria, *Strom* 2.95.3.
101. Ps. Clementines, *Hom.* 11.35; *Rec.* 3.67; 3.72; 6.15.
102. Leo the Great, *Ep.* 16.6; PL 54:702.
103. Cf. E.R Dodds, *Pagan and Christian in an Age of Anxiety* (Cambridge: Cambridge University Press, 1965); U. Bianchi-M.J. Vermaseren, ed., *La soteriologia dei culti orientali nell'Impero romano* (Leiden: E.J. Brill, 1982); *Pagani e cristiani alla ricerca della salvezza (secoli I-III): XXXIV Incontro di Studiosi dell'Antichità Cristiana, Roma, 5-7 maggio 2005* (Rome: Institutum Patristicum Augustinianum, 2006).
104. Augustine, *Sermon* 216.6. (*Sermons* III/6. Trans. By Edmund Hill (New Rochelle, NY: New City Press, 1993), 171.)
105. Augustine, *Sermon* 216.10. (*Sermons* III/6: 173.)
106. Augustine, *Sermon* 227.1.
107. Cf. also *Galatians* 1:6-7; 2:2-9.

108. Augustine, *Sermon* 216.1.
109. Theophilus of Antioch, *Letter to Autolycus* 2.38.
110. Theophilus of Antioch, *Letter to Autolycus* 1.2.
111. Theophilus of Antioch, *Letter to Autolycus* 1.7.
112. Cf. M. Simonetti, *Profilo storico dell'esegesi patristica* (Rome: Institutum Patristicum Augustinianum, 1981).
113. Augustine, *De catechizandis rud.* 3.5.
114. Egeria, *Itinerarium* 46.
115. A. Momigliano, *The Conflict between Paganism and Christianity in the Fourth Century* (Oxford: Clarendon Press, 1963), 85.
116. The term *mystagogy* (from the verb *mystagogein*) means initiation to the mysteries and, metaphorically, the mysteries themselves (baptism and eucharist) and also the celebration of rites.
117. Cyril of Jerusalem, *Catechesis* 1.1.
118. Cf. M. Jourjon, "Catéchèse et liturgie chez les Pères," *La Maison-Dieu* 140 (1979): 41-49.
119. The discipline of the arcane, an improper and deviant expression. In particular it refers to the rites of Christian initiation, to the Eucharist, to the symbol of faith and to the prayer of *Our Father*. There is a degree of confidentiality; the non-baptized, even catechumens, do not participate in these rites. A. Di Berardino, "Augustine on the Eucharist," *Caritas Veritatis* 2 (2017): 25-59.
120. Augustine, *Sermon* 228.3.
121. Ambrose observes that since women were also baptized then the bishop instead of the mouth, touched their nostrils.
122. Ambrose, *De sacramentis* 1.2-3.
123. *applicatus es manibus sacerdotis, ut aures tuas quas tibi olim inimicus obstruxerat, operatio caelestis mysterii aperiret*: R. Etaix, "Catéchèse inédite sur Ephpheta" *REAug* 42 (1996): 66.
124. Ambrose, *De sacramentis* 3.14-15.
125. Augustine, *Sermon* 4.10; 4.28 and 31; *Sermon* 5.7; *Sermon 374 augmentatum*, 19; 56.6 and 10; *Sermon* 57.7.7; etc.
126. Augustine, *Sermon Dolbeau* 26.12.
127. Augustine, *Sermon* 234.2.
128. Augustine, *Sermon* 232.7.
129. Augustine, *Sermon* 235.3.
130. Cf. *Rom* 6:3; *Acts* 9:19; 22:6.
131. S. Légasse, "Baptême juif des prosélytes et baptême chrétien," *Bulletin de littérature ecclésiastique* 77 (1976): 3-40.
132. Cyprian, *Ep.* 73.22.2.
133. Tertullian, *De baptismo* 16.1.
134. Augustine, *De bapt. c. donat.* 4.22.30.
135. Complete nudity was a sign of an external and internal stripping of all that is old to give space to the new birth without any impediment. "No one shall take any foreign object with themselves down into the water" (*Apostolic Tradition* 21).
136. *EAC* 2:940-42.
137. *EAC* 1:323.
138. H. Leclercq, DACL 12:1804.
139. Chrysostom, *Catechesis* 1.2.
140. Theodore of Mopsuestia, *Catechesis* 2.4; 2.2 and 3.
141. PL 4:847. L. Guy, "'Naked' Baptism in the Early Church: The Rhetoric and the Reality," *The Journal of Religious History* 27 (2003): 133-42.
142. John of Jerusalem, *Catechesis myst.* 3.2 and 3.8.
143. John Moschus, *Spiritual Meadow* 3; PG 87:2852-56.
144. Cf. A. Ferrua, ""Nudus nudum Christum sequi." Sulla nudità battesimale," *Super fundamentum Apostolorum, Studi in onore di J. Ortas*, ed. A. Amato and G. Maffei (Rome: LAS 1997), 205-16.
145. Augustine, *De civ. Dei* 22.8.4.
146. V. Saxer, *Les rites de l'initiation chrétienne du IIe au VIe siècle* (Spoleto: Centro italiano di studi sullálto Medioevo, 1988), 39.
147. Ambrose, *De sacramentis* 1.10.
148. *Didache* 7.

149. Cf. Theodore, *Hom. cath.* 14.16; John Chrysostom, *Catech. bapt.* 2.26.
150. Ignatius, *To the Smyrnaeans* 8.2.
151. *Apostolic Tradition* 21. It is similar in the Ethiopian translation published by Alessandro Bausi, "La "nuova" versione etiopica della Traditio apostolica: edizione e traduzione preliminare," in P. Buzi and A. Camplani, eds, *Christianity in Egypt: Literary Production and Intellectual Trends, Studies in Honor of Tito Orlandi* (Rome: Institutum Patristicum Augustinianum, 2011), 19–69, 45.
152. Tertullian, *De baptismo* 4; Clement of Alexandria, *Exc. Theod.* 82; Cyprian, *Ep.* 70.1; Ambrose, *De sacramentis* 1.5; John Chrysostom, *Catech. bapt.* 2.10.
153. Tertullian, *De baptismo* 5.
154. H.M. Riley, *Christian Initiation. A Comparative Study on the Interpretation of the Baptismal Liturgy in the Mystagogical Writings of Cyril of Jerusalem, John Chrysostom, Theodore of Mopsuestia and Ambrose of Milan* (Washington: Catholic University of America Press, 1974).
155. Theodore of Mopsuestia, *Homily 2 on Baptism*, in *Commentary of Theodore of Mopsuestia on the Lord's Prayer and on the Sacraments of Baptism and Eucharist*, trans. by A. Mingana (Cambridge: W. Heffer & sons, 1933); R. Tonneau, R. Devreesee, "Les homélies de Théodore de Mopsuèste," *Studi e Testi* 145 (1949): 367.
156. Saliba, Saliba, "Baptism in the Homilies of Theodore of Mopsuestia and Jacob of Serugh," *Parole de l'Orient* 40 (2015): 331-59.
157. F. Placida, *Aspetti catechistico-liturgici dell'opera di Cromazio di Aquileia* (Soveria Mannelli: Rubbettino, 2005).
158. J. W. Harmless, *Augustine and the Catechumenate* (Collegeville, MN: Liturgical Press, 1995); V. Grossi, *La catechesi battesimale agli inizi del V secolo: le fonti agostiniane* (Rome: Institutum Patristicum Augustinianum, 1993); W. Harmless, "Baptism," *Augustine through the Ages*, Gen. Ed. Allan D. Fitzgerald (Grand Rapids: Eerdmans, 1999), 84-91.
159. Augustine, *Sermon* 210.2.
160. Augustine, *Sermon* 210.1.1.
161. Augustine, *Ep.* 54.7.10.
162. Augustine, *Sermon* 227.1.
163. Augustine, *Sermon* 229.1.
164. Augustine, *Sermon* 223G.1.
165. Augustine, *Sermon* 59.1.
166. Augustine, *The Soul and its Origin* 1.10.12.
167. Augustine, *civit. Dei* 22.8.6.
168. Augustine, *civit. Dei* 22.8.4.
169. Augustine, *Contra litt. Pet.* 2.104 and 237.
170. Augustine, *Sermon* 229M.2.
171. Augustine, *Sermon* 120.3.
172. Augustine, *Sermon* 260C.7.
173. Augustine, *Sermon* 229A.1.
174. Augustine, *Sermon* 260C.1.
175. Augustine, *Sermon* 227.1.
176. Augustine, *Sermon* 227.1.
177. Augustine refers to it as *sacramentum octavarum vestrarum*.
178. Augustine, *Sermon* 260C.7.
179. Clement of Alexandra, *Stromata* 3.12.82.
180. *Didascalia Apostolorum* 26.6.21-22. Ch. E. Fonrobert, *Menstrual Purity: Rabbinic and Christian Reconstructions of Biblical Gender* (Stanford, CA: Stanford University Press, 2002), 172-81.
181. B. S. Boustan, A. Y Reed, "Parting Ways over Blood and Water? Beyond 'Judaism' and 'Christianity' in the Roman Near East," in *La croisée des chemins revisitée: quand l'"Eglise" et la "Synagogue" se sont-elles distinguées?: actes du colloque de Tours 18-19 Juin 2010*. eds S.C. Mimoumi and B. Pouderon (Paris: Les éditions du Cerf, 2012), 227-59.
182. Firmilian, in Cyprian, *Ep.* 75.7.1. L. Decousu, *La perte de l'Esprit Saint et son recouvrement dans l'Église ancienne : la réconciliation des hérétiques et des pénitents en Occident du IIIe siècle jusqu'à Grégoire le Grand* (Leiden; Boston, MA: Brill, 2015).
183. Cf. Tertullian, *De baptismo* 15.2. He denies the validity of the baptism given by heretics (*De pudicitia* 19.5).

184. Cf. *Epp.* 70.1 and 2; /1.4.1; 73.3.1; 75.193. Augustine states that 70 bishops took part in it (*De unico bapt.* 13.22; elsewhere he is uncertain: *Contra Cresc.* 3.3.3). Some assume that the number 70 was symbolic; cf. G.W. Clarke, *The Letters of St. Cyprian* (New York: Newman Press, 1989), vol. 4:196.
185. Cyprian, *Ep.* 75.19.3. Cf. Clarke, *Letters*, 4:196-199.
186. Cf. Cyprian, *Ep.* 69.7; 70.2.1. Cyprian, in rejecting the baptism of heretics, speaks of the Novatians, who do not forgive sins. Therefore, it must concern them.
187. Cyprian, *Ep.* 73.4-5.
188. Cf. Cyprian, *Ep.* 70.
189. *EAC* 3:382-3.
190. Cyprian, *De rebaptismate* 12.
191. In Cyprian, *Ep.* 75.7.5; Eusebius, *HE* 7.5.5; 7.7.5.
192. Eusebius, *HE* 7.7.5.
193. P. Pietras, "Il fomdamento ecclesiologico della posizione di Dionigi di Alessandria nella controversia battesimale," in *Recherches et tradition: mélanges patristiques offerts à Henri Crouzel* (Paris: Beauchesne, 1992), 199-210.
194. Eusebius, *HE* 7.5.4.
195. Can. 1, in: *I caconi dei concili della chiesa antica*, ed. A. Di Berardino, II, *I concili latini*, 64. For the fourth century, see M. Labrousse, "La baptême des hérétiques d'après Cyprien, Optat et Augustin: influences et divergences," *REAug* 42 (1996): 223-42.
196. P. G. Caron, "'Ne sanctum baptisma iteretur' (CTh.16.6; CI.1.6)," *Atti Accademia Rom. Costantiniana* 6 (1986): 107-80.
197. Tertulian, *De baptismo* 18.
198. Cyprian, *Ep.* 64.
199. L. Decousu, "La confirmation dans l'histoire: Évolution ou fracture?" *Ecclesia Orans* 25 (2008): 61-96; 129-160; Ibid, "Imposition des mains et onction: recherches sur l'adjonction de rites additionnels dans les liturgies baptismales primitives. Première partie: L'imposition des mains," *Ecclesia Orans* 34 (2017): 11-46; "Deuxième partie: L'onction," *Ecclesia Orans* 34 (2017): 369-420.
200. M. Maccarrone, "L'unità del battesimo e della cresima nelle testimonianze della liturgia romana dal III al XVI secolo," *Lateranum* 51 (1985): 88-152.
201. Paul de Clerck, "La dissociation du baptême et de la confirmation au haut Moyen," *La Maison-Dieu* 168 (1986): 47-75; A. Elberti, *La confermazione nella tradizione della Chiesa latina* (Milan: San Paolo, 2003).
202. Cyprian, *Ep.* 70.1.
203. Ibid, *Ep.* 73.9.
204. See also Tertullian, *De baptismo* 8.
205. Origen, *Comm. in Rom.* 5.8.
206. Tertullian, *De baptismo* 6.
207. Ibid, *De baptismo* 7-8; *De resurrectione car.* 8.
208. Cyprian, *Ep.* 70.2; 73.9; 74.5.
209. Ambrose, *De sacramentis* perhaps reflects an unelaborated preaching. F. Braschi, "Luoghi e riti per la celebrazione del battesimo in epoca ambrosiana: un'ipotesi di ricostruzione," *Studia Ambrosiana* 1 (2007): 131-46.
210. Ambrose, *De mysteriis* 2.5- 3.8.
211. Ambrose, *De sacramentis* 1.2.4.
212. Ambrose, *De sacramentis* 2.6.16.
213. Ambrose, *De sacramentis* 2.7.20.
214. Transliteration from the Greek *myron*.
215. Ambrose, *De sacramentis* 3.11; *De mysteriis* 6.29-30.
216. Ambrose, *De mysteriis* 7.34.
217. The term in Tertullian designates baptism (*De spect.* 4,24; *De pudic.* 9), in Cyprian instead the gift of the Holy Spirit (*Ep.* 73.9).
218. Ambrose, *De sacramentis* 3.2.8.
219. L. Decousu, "L'utilisation technique des termes "confirmatio" et "confirmare"" en Occident, du 5e siècle jusqu'à l'époque carolingienne," *Revue de droit canonique* 60 (2010): 31-70.
220. Cyril of Jerusalem, *Mystagogical Catechesis* 3.1-2.
221. Cyril of Jerusalem, *Mystagogical Catechesis* 3.3.

222. Cyril of Jerusalem, *Mystagogical Catechesis* 3.5.
223. *Apostolic Const.* 3.16.3 and 4.
224. Theodore of Mopsuestia, *Baptismal Homily* 13.17, translation by A. Mingana.
225. Cf. *1 Cor* 12:3.
226. Aphrahat, *Dem.* 12: *De Paschate*: Cyrillona, *Hymn on the Washing of the Feet*, etc.
227. Irenaeus, *Adv. haer.* 4.22.1.
228. Chromatius, *Sermon* 25.
229. Ambrose, *De mysteriis* 6.32; *In psalm.* 48.8-9.
230. Augustine, *Ep.* 55.18.33; *De sancta virg.* 32.32.
231. Augustine, *Tract. in psalmum* 92.3.
232. John Cassian, *Institutiones* 4.19.2; *Regula Benedicti* 53.13-15, etc.
233. *Nuovo Dizionario Patristico e di antichità cristiane* 3:2757-58, with bibliography.
234. Diehl 1513; *Inscriptiones Christianae urbis Romae*, II, nr. 67, 100, nrr. 2, 3, 134; *Liber pontificalis*, 234. English translation: E. Ferguson, *Baptism in the Early Church: History, Theology, and Liturgy in the First Five Centuries* (Grand Rapids, MI: Eerdmans, 2009), 769.

CHAPTER 4
ECCLESIAL MINISTRIES

The Origin of the Ministries

WHAT WAS THE INITIAL EXPERIENCE OF JESUS' DISCIPLES IMMEDIATELY AFTER HIS ARREST and death? They fled, scattered, and felt lost, and even feared ending up like their master. The discovery of the empty tomb changed their lives, especially because of the post-resurrection appearances of the Risen One. The *Acts of the Apostles* tells us that they gathered together to pray. They also went to the temple in Jerusalem. They broke bread together. Somehow, many of them led a communal life. Did they all stay in Jerusalem, as Luke insinuates (since he includes only the appearances in Jerusalem), or did they also go to Galilee? Were they first in Jerusalem and then went to Galilee? According to Matthew and John, they were in both places. Did they then return back again to Jerusalem? A matter of utmost importance is implied in all of this: the elaboration of the memory of Jesus. Once the group of the Twelve is reconstituted, what do they do? They become aware that they must continue the mission of Jesus: to bear witness (Luke), to preach and baptize (Matthew), to forgive sins (John). How long did they stay together to process the memory of Jesus? Luke's reconstruction in his Gospel and Acts seems linear. They did not remain together long before they then split up to go to their respective mission camps.

The time after the Jewish Passover was a time for processing and taking in the memory of Jesus, of the things said and done by him. They needed to interpret his person and his actions in the light of the Jewish Scriptures, and to reformulate his conversations in the light of new situations.[1] Among the issues at hand was the interpretation of the death of the Just One, rejected, persecuted and unjustly put to death. They must also answer another question: what are they to do now? We can start from this experience and from the subsequent reflections that the followers elaborated into a set of fundamental ideas about the redeeming death of Christ, the Savior and Messiah, the forgiveness of sins, the necessity of baptism, the Eucharistic supper, the resurrection of the flesh, eternal life, the gift of the Holy Spirit, etc. According to John's Gospel, in his speech at the Last Supper Jesus promises that the Father will send the Paraclete to complete and perfect his teaching: "The Comforter, the Holy Spirit whom the Father will send in my name, he will teach you all things and remind you of all that I have told you" (*Jn* 14:26). Note that in the middle of the second century the Gospels are still referred to as the "memoirs of the apostles."[2]

The disciples of Jesus—Peter, James, John and others—become aware of being a new people, of forming a new covenant. In other words, the idea of forming an *ecclesia* grafted onto the long Jewish tradition is slowly coming to birth. From the common experience lived together in Palestine, rich in faith and hope, his followers leave for their mission to different regions. For them, the task of "remembering" is now joined by that of "testifying." The last words of Jesus before ascending to heaven were: "You will have power from the Holy Spirit who will descend upon you, and you will be my witnesses in Jerusalem, throughout Judaea and Samaria, and to the ends of the earth" (*Acts* 1:8).

The testimony of Paul is important as well. Three years after his conversion he went to Jerusalem to meet Peter because that city is the best place for the elaboration of the memory of Jesus since the tragic final events took place there. He wrote: "Then after three years I went up to Jerusalem to visit Cephas and remained with him fifteen days. But I saw none of the other apostles except James the Lord's brother. In what I am writing to you, before God, I do not lie!" (*Gal* 1:18-20). Paul already knows Jesus and has heard about him from other disciples. Why was he visiting Peter? On the one hand Paul wants to affirm his independence from the church in Jerusalem; on the other hand, he goes to the city to learn more about the memory of Jesus. Paul recognizes in the "pillars" of the community an authority and a guarantee of teaching. Peter especially became his point of reference, but also John and James, the brother of the Lord.

Where did the other apostles and disciples go if they did not remain in Jerusalem? Their mission in Palestine was only a relative success since not that many Jews adopted their new teachings. On the other hand, Paul had greater success among the gentiles outside of Israel. Ironically Paul, who had been an observant Jew and as he states a ferocious persecutor of Christians, now has been transformed into a zealous defender of the new faith. "You have certainly heard of my conduct as a Jew, how I had persecuted and devastated the Church of God" (*Gal* 1:13).

Paul completed another important trip to Jerusalem fourteen years later around the year

51. "Then after fourteen years I went up again to Jerusalem with Barnabas, taking Titus along with me. I went up by revelation; and I laid before them (but privately before those who were of repute) the gospel which I preach among the Gentiles, lest somehow, I should be running or had run in vain" (*Gal* 2:1-2). Paul feels the need to confront them because there are radical differences between him and the Apostles at Jerusalem. But they eventually show appreciation for each other and, in fact, shake hands as a sign of harmony. We are at the point of complete elaboration of the oral memory in so far as we are not aware that they put their ideas together in writing. At the same time, they have to face a wide-open sea of new situations. The *Acts of the Apostles* (15:1-29) reflect this situation of uncertainty and difficulty. In fact, "Paul and Barnabas had no small dissension and debate with those" (15:2) who were teaching the necessity to observe the mosaic proscriptions. Thus, there only exists one initial common source among many people who had different perspectives and emphases. Some were more faithful to the Jewish tradition while others were more open to new ideas. Many streams of thought were initiated but the Apostles tried to mediate the differences and arrive at a common ground. There was a diversity in communion expressed in the gesture of reconciliation.

Already at the time of the first Christian generation some remain more distant from the common position on fundamental points. The New Testament texts reflect this fluid situation. It is not easy to establish the borders. The polemics of following generations demonstrate an increasing number of groups who follow their own way and break with the original community.

The primitive Christian community was based on the radical newness brought by Jesus, and at the same time was also shaken by the refusal of the Jews to believe this. With many trials they arrived at a common conviction of being the new people of God, the new Israel, the people of the New Covenant[3] and consequently inheritors of the divine promises.[4] Paul introduces the distinction between Israel according to the flesh and Israel according to the spirit.[5] Those who believe in Christ constitute the true Israel,[6] God's Israel,[7] namely the church.[8] Consequently, on the one hand they are the spiritual inheritors of the Hebrew people and the recipients of the divine promises in full continuity with the works of God; yet on the other hand they represent a new reality both because of its components that largely come from paganism and because they are a new people born from a new covenant.[9]

Christians from the second century on find themselves in this current of ideas. They are the new people of Israel. As Trypho questioned, *"Are you Israel?"*[10] The Scriptures are the property of the church and it is the church's right to interpret them.[11] There was no turning back.

The followers of Jesus constitute a new reality—the "church of God." All the gospels, even the apocryphal texts, deal with the vocation of the apostles who must carry out a mission even as they constitute a restricted circle. Thus, they themselves express their understanding of this circle both by the use of the term "the Twelve" and by the death of Judas when they elect Matthias to reinstate the number which they perceive as an institution. The expression "Church of God" (or of Christ) expresses a local or universal community.[12] John's *Revelation* includes the church from the heavenly Jerusalem and at the same time speaks of the individual churches (the letters to the seven churches). The *Didache* includes a prayer that views the church in a universal and eschatological perspective: "So may Your Church be gathered together from the ends of the earth into Your kingdom" (9:4). "Remember, Lord, Your Church to deliver it from all evil and to perfect it in Your love; and gather it together from the four winds—even the Church which has been sanctified—into Your kingdom which You have prepared for it; for Yours is the power and the glory for ever and ever" (10:4). Certain specific people are the foundation of this church—the apostles are but one example. Paul, however, notes that human authorities do not replace Christ, who is the true foundation.

The Pauline and Johannine language is also found at the beginning of *1 Clement* in the preamble "The church of God that is a pilgrim in Rome to the church of God that is a pilgrim in Corinth, to those called who have been sanctified in the will of God through the Lord Jesus Christ."

PEOPLE OF GOD: *ORDO* AND *PLEBS*

In addition to the term *ecclesia*, the expression *populus/plebs Dei* (or *Christi*) also emerges in the Latin world. This "people of God" includes the entire Christian community. It is the Christian people in general, all the faithful (*fideles*), all Christians. When Cyprian wrote to communities, he addressed all Christians, including the clergy, with the sole word *plebs*.[13] He sometimes also used the term brothers (*fraternitas*)[14] or people (*populus*).[15] Later, in the Council of Carthage (411) the term *plebs* becomes synonymous with *dio(e)cesis*. In the following text from Lacantius, "plebem" indicates the whole Christian community in general when he writes: "That He may gather for himself a divine people" (*ut divinam sibi plebem congregaret*).[16] However, in addition to this general meaning (as was demonstrated by Loi)[17] the term *plebs* also possesses a more technical and narrower meaning. It refers to the local community with respect to its bishop, or the laity with respect to the clergy (*ordo*). This last meaning, deriving from the Roman social use, implies stratifications and distinctions within the same community as we see, for instance, with Cyprian's letters: "Cyprian to the presbyters and deacons, as well as to all the people."[18] The *ordo* is made up of the bishop, presbyters and deacons, while the *plebs* is made up of everyone else, including the minor clergy. Later, the meaning of the term *plebs* will tend to narrow even more, indicating a rural diocese, parish or country church.

In the first meaning, for example, concerning the rural diocese Augustine speaks of bishops who have abandoned their communities.[19]

The English term "clergy" derives from the Latin *clerus,* which in turn has its roots in the Greek κλῆρος. In classical Greek and the *Septuagint* the term means "lot, or that which is assigned by lot, a portion or share of something."[20] Philo adds a religious nuance: God is the *clerus* (portion) of the faithful and of the Levite, and at the same time the believer is the *clerus* (portion) of God. In Jerusalem, Matthias is chosen by the primitive community to replace Judas by the drawing of lots (*Acts* 1:26). In the New Testament the term indicates not only the drawing of lots but also the portion assigned, which often has an eschatological meaning.[21] In the ancient Christian community those who have a ministry of leadership are referred to by the collective term *clerus* to distinguish them from *laicus* (lit. belonging to the people, common). This terminology was already in use at the beginning of the third century both in the East and in the West[22] and becomes the norm.[23]

The term *clericatus* (the clerical office) and the adjective *clericus* (clerical) derive from *clerus. Clericus* is sometimes also used as a noun to indicate members of the clergy.[24] According to the Theodosian Code it was customary at least since 313 CE to designate ministers of the Christian religion with the term clerics "*qui divino culti ministeria impendunt.*"[25] The imperial authorities, however, had to specify who the members of the clergy were when they granted or revoked privileges under the law. One enters the clergy by ordination or by another rite of installation, since "clerics are all those who have been ordained into the various ranks of the ecclesiastical ministry."[26]

The clergy are distinguished from the laity not because they are in a higher position, but because they exercise a sacred function at the service of the people. An entire ecclesiology lies behind this distinction. Augustine explains the term clergy by having it derive from the episode of choosing Matthias by lot: "I think that those who have been ordained within the ranks of the ecclesiastical hierarchy are called clergy and clerics because Matthias, whom we read to have been the first person ordained by the apostles, was chosen by lot. To sum up: to inherit something as your lot is the result of a will or testament, and so the two Testaments are called 'lots', the name of the effect being transferred to the cause."[27] This explanation did not endure, however, whereas the explanation proposed by Jerome, which we also found in Philo, was quite enduring in later theology and spirituality: "Clerics are called as such either because they are the Lord's portion, or because the Lord is their portion" (*Ep.* 52.5). "In a secular tradition, impressive for its unity, the idea of being the portion of the Lord and possessing him as a portion has remained at the heart of the clerical condition."[28]

Not only is there a distinction at the socio-political level of the Roman administration between the people (*populus*) and the ranks of officials (*ordines: ordo senatorius, ordo equestris, ordo decurionum*) but also in the various colleges (*collegia*) which were professional or religious associations made up of the leaders of the group (*ordo*) and the common members (*plebs*). It seems highly plausible that the Christian community before the time of Constantine borrowed these distinctions and terminology because the church too is configured socially as an association.[29]

Even in the church (*ecclesia*), which is made up of people called by God, a distinction was introduced between the *ordo* and the *plebs,* i.e., between the clergy (*clerus, proedria*) who carry out a type of overseeing office and the *plebs*, which make up all the baptized who have not been given this type of authoritative role. The *plebs* are also referred to as the laity, lay people, the faithful, or other such terms. Tertullian, so important for Latin terminology, presents us with some difficulties because we must keep in mind when he wrote his various works, i.e., whether the writings come from the Catholic or Montanist period of his career. In the *Prescription Against Heretics*, he attributes to heretics a confusion of roles: "Nowhere can you get a faster promotion than in the camp of the rebels, where your mere presence is considered worthy service. So today one man is their bishop, tomorrow someone else. Today's deacon is tomorrow's reader. Today he is a presbyter who tomorrow is a layman. For they impose priestly functions even upon laymen" (41.6-8).

Thus, for Tertullian there is a lot of confusion among the heretics. But which heretics? This would imply that there is harmony and discipline among those who are not heretics. Before he was a Montanist he wrote that "after celebrating the liturgy, the people were discharged."[30] But during his Montanist period, he wrote that the distinction between clergy and laity was made by the church: "The distinction between the priestly order and the laity (*plebs*) was established by the authority of the Church. The priestly office is sanctified through the joint assembly of the Orders. And so, where there is no joint assembly of the ecclesiastical Order, you offer, and baptize, and are priest, alone for yourself. But where three are, there is the church, although they be laity."[31]

He also specifically includes the readers among the ordained ministries, although he does not mention any other ministries. Therefore, for him there is no ontological distinction between *ordo* and *plebs*. The distinction is only for good order within the community, that is, for the peace (*pax*) of the community. This term "pax" is not only meant to indicate harmony among the members, but something that goes far beyond, insofar as it is a gift from God and a sign of his presence in the community. Ordination does not create a "class" of distinct and superior Christians. The ordained and non-ordained are not meant to be in competition with one another, but are to exist together in peace, which only God can give.

Cyprian distinguishes the two categories by referring to clergy and people (*clerus et plebs*).[32] He too, following Tertullian, notes that the *ordo* indicates the structured body of those responsible for exercising a ministry in the communities around and together with the bishop. But this *ordo* is made up of a bishop (*episcopus*), presbyters (*presbyteri*), deacons (*diaconi*), and what are referred to as the minor orders. It is a whole that works together—it is the *ordo*—distinguished clearly from the *plebs* ontologically. The bishop is not only the center of the local community in communion with the other bishops and responsible with them for the whole church, but he also represents Christ in his community, especially during the celebration of the Eucharist insofar as the bishop (*episcopus*) represents Christ as he truly discharges the office of Christ (*vice Christi vere fungens*).[33]

The figure of the bishop, then, becomes established and increasingly important. Ambrose observes: "What bishop has ever commanded such a thing of his presbyter before the people?"[34] Clergy and *ordo* become, in this respect, synonymous, even if the term *ordo* could also be applied to the different ministries taken individually, or to groups of Christians organized by a special way of life, such as the order of bishops, order of presbyters, order of widows, order of virgins, etc.[35]

Augustine has a varied but precise terminology. He uses the following terms: clergy (*clerus*, sing. and *clerici*, pl); the office of the clergy (*militia clericatus*); overseers (*praepositi*) and oversight (*praepositura*) of the church (*ecclesiae*); ordained into the ranks of the ministry of the church (*ordinati in ecclesiasticis ministerii gradibus*). In line with the tradition, he distinguishes the presbyter from the bishop: "Because of the different titles of ecclesiastical dignity now introduced into the custom of the Church, the episcopate is of a greater degree than the presbyterate."[36] When indicating the bishop, he also uses other terms such as overseer (*praepositus*), rector (*rector*), protector (*custos*), and shepherd (*pastor*).[37] He has the episcopal authority (*episcopalis auctoritas*). He administers the sacraments of initiation, presides over liturgical assemblies, teaches, instructs the faithful, corrects them with penitential discipline and preserves the doctrine of the faith against his enemies. He administers the goods of the church, exercises the episcopal judgement (*iudicium*). The presbyter also has his role in that he is "a man who administers the sacraments and the Word of God to the people."[38] Deacons assist the bishop, instruct catechumens and collaborate in the administration of the Eucharist, like the martyr Lawrence who "was minister of the sacred blood of Christ."[39] Augustine also speaks of the subdeacons, whom he sometimes omits in his discussions of the higher orders.[40] He mentions the lectors several times. He speaks of their ordination as *ordinatus sum*, that is, he himself laid his hands on them for ordination. And, of course, he speaks of other ordinations as well.[41]

PROGRESSION (CURSUS) THROUGH THE MINISTERIAL RANKS

The Council of Serdica of 343, perhaps inspired by the public sphere's approach to careers, forbade access to the episcopate before passing through the other orders. These legal requirements were not widely disseminated or even applied initially. However, by action of the

Roman church, a norm was imposed and clarified because intervals of time (*interstitia*) were being established between the reception of one order and the next in order that the man of the church (*homo ecclesiasticus*) might exercise for a period of time the ministry he had received as preparation for the higher one. The church insisted that these ministries be practiced for a certain period of more or less duration, as preparation for the higher ranks and as proof of conduct through the individual ranks.[42] In the Roman West, the rules became more elaborate with popes Siricius (384-399) and Zosimus (417-418). But there were often instances of people who were ordained as bishop without sufficient preparation.[43] Except in exceptional cases, the clergy were self-taught in religious matters, although some provision developed to help them address the secular and religious culture in which they lived.[44]

The ecclesiastical rule regarding clergy ranking was also developed to prevent lay people from having immediate access to ordinations, especially of higher orders. It does not mean, however, that this was strictly observed everywhere both because the rule was not very well known and because the local traditions and needs of the moment often prevailed. There were, in fact, many exceptions to the rule. A few examples should suffice. For instance, even though he was not yet baptized, Ambrose was acclaimed bishop in Milan in 374. In a few days he received all the sacraments and even episcopal ordination. Augustine informs us of another case in his diocese. He had a twenty year old lector ordained a bishop for the village of Fussala:

> . . . without first having any experience in clerical orders. . . . The soul of the young man, who had suddenly ascended to the office of bishop without any merit for previous efforts, became frightened. But after seeing that both the faithful and the clerics were subject to him—and recognizing the situation for what it was—he became swelled up with the arrogance of despotism and, instead of teaching through the power of the Word he resorted to compelling everything by commands. He was pleased to be feared when he saw that he could not make himself loved.[45]

This was a very painful case for Augustine.

The rule of following a sequence in the reception of different ministries, although not entirely unknown in the third century, develops particularly during the fourth. Thus, a progression (*cursus*) is created which becomes a progressive ascent from the lower to the higher ranks, seen more and more as an *honor*, a dignity (*dignitas*) in the strong sense of the Roman legal language. "In the church there are rankings (bishop and presbyter)" writes St. Jerome.[46] The legislation the Roman bishops tried to impose was a system that required permanence in a specific ministry as well as demanding a certain amount of time (*interstitia*) at each position. Leo the Great († 461) summed up the situation of his time: "The tradition handed down to us in respect to all sacred orders must be observed in every detail. According to this, for a lengthy period, he who is to be ordained a presbyter or a deacon must advance through all the degrees of the clerical order so as to learn, in this season, what he himself must later teach."[47] The order of the episcopate, on the other hand, is not the result of a progression (*cursus*), but of a choice by the community.

This is not just an argument over terminology. From the time of Constantine onwards, an ever-widening split or separation was created between the *plebs* and the *ordo*, which was taking on the external attitudes and forms of the civil authorities. Bishops, for example, assume the *insignia* of state dignitaries, such as the *pallium* or the sandals. New elements that distinguish the clergy were also being created. Special vestments were introduced not only for conducting the liturgy but the clergy also tended to distinguish themselves from the laity in their clothing in everyday life. Ambrose, however, exhorts the clergy to wear clothes of ordinary quality without showy colors.[48] There was no special clothing yet at this time. A few decades later Pope Celestine (428) wrote to the bishops of the Southern provinces of Gaul that they should not be distinguished from others by their dress, but by their doctrine: "We must distinguish ourselves from the people and from all others by our doctrine not by our dress, by our conduct not by our way of dressing, by the purity of our mind not by our way of living. In fact, if we begin to look for novelties, we will tread upon the rules transmitted to us by the fathers and we will make room for useless superstitions."[49]

This trend was evidently already underway at that time, and we all know the sociological importance that the uniform assumes for the person who wears it. It determines his identity and distinguishes him from others.[50] The terminology becomes more precise, thanks to a whole movement of thought on the priesthood that began in the second century and developed in the following period, even if we have no evidence that before 200 a priestly vocabulary was used to refer to the various ministers. One should in fact be acutely aware that the New Testament carefully avoids priestly and cultic terminology for clergy. When we do encounter numerous ministries in the New Testament, different in name and office according to places and times, ministers are never called priests; rather the writers use exclusively non-cultic terms such as bishop, presbyter, leader (*hegumen*), or deacon.

THE MINISTRY AND THE PRIESTHOOD

The Jewish or pagan priest is chosen from a family or caste and connected to a place of worship. He is the mediator between the divine and the human. The Christian minister, in contrast, is chosen from among all the faithful and has the function of watching over (*episcopé*) the people of God, teaching, and administering the sacraments. The ministry has no sacred character because all the people are holy and there is no distinction in that sense within it. For Christians there is no sacred time—there is liturgical time of course—and there is no sacred place (*Mt* 18:20; *1 Pet* 2:4-6) and no sacred persons. All are holy, chosen and summoned to the same *ecclesia*; every restriction is abolished (*Acts* 10 and 11; *1 Cor* 10:23-31; *1 Pet* 1; *Rom* 12:1f). There are, however, some who are appointed to be "stewards of the mysteries of God" (*1 Cor* 4:1; cf. *2 Cor* 2:14). There is a ministerial structure based on service and a relationship with the entire community that has some serving as leaders and guides. This structure had no precedent, and consequently the top-down scheme—with the clergy at the top which was common among Jews and pagans—is excluded; on the other hand a democratic scheme is also excluded.

The *Letter to the Hebrews*, so exploited for priestly theology, uses the priestly theme and the respective vocabulary only for Christ, who is the only and definitive priest. In Peter's first epistle all the baptized constitute the priestly people who offer to God pleasing spiritual oblations and proclaim the wonderful works of God (*1 Pet* 2:5-9). Paul presents himself as one to whom grace has been given "by God to be a minister (*leitourgon*) of Christ Jesus to the Gentiles in the priestly service (*hierorgounta*) of the gospel of God, so that the offering of the Gentiles may be acceptable, sanctified by the Holy Spirit" (*Rom* 15:16). He feels vested with the priesthood for his preaching and the offering to God he is making of the converted pagans. Paul considers his missionary activity to be a public work (*leiturgia* or *munus*). He considers himself a priest due to his evangelical preaching and his sacrificial offering (oblation) of the pagans who, through conversion (faith and baptism), unite their death with Christ. A new priesthood thus is also celebrated in the preaching of the Gospel which calls for faith and solidarity with the mystery of Christ. In addition, Paul presents himself and his work in various ways, including that of "a skillful architect" (*1 Cor* 3:10) who lays the foundations of a building which others will continue. The image is the foundation of Pauline ecclesiology: the church as a building under construction is constantly expanding both in the sense of local community and for the increase in number both in the organizational sense and in the geographical sense as an expansion of territory.[51]

Already in the *Didache* (13:3) new ministers are compared to the priests of the Old Covenant and the Eucharist is called a sacrifice (chap. 14). This comparison takes the form of parallelism in *1 Clement* (chapters 40-44). Jesus is referred to as high priest (36.1; 61.3; 64.1), and the new ministers also perform cultic functions as part of their pastoral office, although they are not called priests. Something like this is also insinuated by Ignatius of Antioch, who refers to Jesus as high priest in the context of the Eucharist and the altar.[52] Justin mentions the presidency of the celebration of the Eucharist,[53] which he considers the fulfillment of Malachi's prophecy about the pure sacrifice.[54] Irenaeus applies the technical term *sacerdos* to Jesus, while all Christians are *sacerdotes*.[55] There is a confrontation of sorts between the ministers of the New Covenant and the priests of the Old Covenant. In these authors we begin to perceive a current of thought that tends towards a rapprochement between the two even if an identification will never be accomplished.

The Christians of the first two centuries are aware that they offer a "pure sacrifice" of which the prophet Malachi spoke (*Mal* 1:11) while celebrating the Eucharist, but they do not use priestly terminology to indicate the officiants of this sacrifice.[56] This happens, even though the very concept of sacrifice implies that of a priest, since the two concepts are related.[57] It is the whole community, the church, which offers the sacrifice as a "priestly people."[58] Baptized Christians are indeed members of a "royal priesthood" (*1 Pet* 2:9), but the ministers themselves are never called priests.[59] The priestly vocabulary, however, will be increasingly employed and more often will be used in the context of the Old Testament typologically to speak of the "priesthood of the New Covenant."

Even in the following centuries the term priest continued to be applied to all Christians, as witnessed by Augustine and Prosper of Aquitaine.[60] In addition, they make extensive use of priestly terminology by applying it to Christ, the high priest. This terminology, as applied to ministers, began to spread in the West with Tertullian.[61] He is the first author to use priestly terminology to indicate both ministers and their functions[62] and with some discretion applies this terminology to presbyters.[63] The allegorical and typological exegesis of the Old Testament no doubt influenced this terminological elaboration.

Since Tertullian usually wrote for specific situations, there is no organic treatment of this topic in his writings, so it is necessary to gather together his various statements. Indeed, Christ is the high priest of the Father (*summus sacerdos Patris*).[64] In the *Apology* that is addressed to the pagans he speaks of the Christian assemblies and affirms that: "They (the leaders) have obtained this office not with money, but with their witness."[65] Here he uses terminology that everyone, not just the Christians, can understand when he speaks of "the approved elders [who] preside over us."[66] The leaders are older, reputable people. The *Apology* refers to presbyters and, perhaps, bishops. On the other hand, in the treatise *On Baptism*, written for Christians, Tertullian is more explicit, since he affirms that the administration of baptism is primarily a matter for bishops: "The supreme right of administering Baptism belongs to the high priest, which is the bishop[67]: after him, it belongs next to the presbyters and deacons, yet not without commission from the bishop, on account of the Church's dignity. For when this is secure, peace is secure. Except for that, even laymen have the right: . . . unless perhaps you are prepared to allege that our Lord's disciples were already bishops or presbyters or deacons: that is, as the word ought not to be hidden by any man, so likewise baptism, which is no less declared to be 'of God,' can be administered by all."[68] Here the triple partition of the *clerus* is made explicit, as is its relation to the laity. The same is true in the *De fuga* (*On Fleeing in Persecution*), where he criticizes the authorities (*auctoritates*) who do not set a good example and do not guard the flock well, being the first to flee at the first sign of danger. The authorities he is referring to are the bishops, presbyters and deacons. Also indicative of the *clerus* as a whole, these leaders do not behave like true shepherds.[69]

Therefore, on the one hand, there is the order of the church (*ordo ecclesiae*), consisting of the authorities (*auctoritates*), and, on the other hand, the laity. The authorities are also called leaders (*duces*), shepherds (*pastores*), overseers (*praepositi*), elders (*maiores*), etc. There are also lectors and there is the order of widows (*ordo viduarum*). All these personnel constitute the ecclesiastical order (*ordo ecclesiasticus*), but the clergy (*clerus*) in particular is composed of those who oversee the flock (*praepositi*) as ministers. The highest authority belongs to the bishop, who presides over the community, teaches, corrects, excludes sinners from the community, and also has the power to forgive by a public act; he prescribes fasting.[70] "We take also, in congregations before daybreak, and from the hand of none but the presidents, the sacrament of the Eucharist, which the Lord both commanded to be eaten at meal-times, and enjoined to be taken by all alike."[71] Those who preside may be the local bishop or the presbyters. Access to the order is by ordination—for which he does not offer liturgical details—and by designation and choice.[72] The heretics have no discipline in their election of ministers, according to the previously quoted text of Tertullian.[73] For Tertullian the episcopate has an apostolic origin and its uninterrupted succession is a guarantee of the truth of the teaching of the church.

The early third century account of the *Passion of Perpetua* mentions by name the bishop, teaching presbyter, deacons, baptized lay people and catechumens. The position of Cyprian is more complex. He affirms that the presbyter celebrates the Eucharist and is "united to the bishop in priestly dignity,"[74] but never explicitly calls the presbyter a priest (*sacerdos*), although he very often uses *sacerdos* to indicate the bishop. In the prayer for the ordination of a bishop in the *Apostolic Tradition*, we read:

> Grant, Father who knows the heart, to your servant whom you chose for the episcopate, that he will feed your holy flock, that he will wear your high priesthood without reproach, serving night and day, incessantly making your face favorable, and offering the gifts of your holy church; in the spirit of high priesthood having the power to forgive sins according to your command; to assign lots according to your command; to loose any bond according to the authority which you gave to the apostles; to please you in mildness and a pure heart, offering to you a sweet aroma, through your Son Jesus Christ, through whom to you be glory, power, and honor, Father and Son, with the Holy Spirit, in the Holy Church, now and throughout the ages of the ages.[75]

The bishop is explicitly called a priest, while this is only inferred with the presbyters.

Origen also uses both the term "priest" and the cultic terminology several times.[76] The bishop is the priest (*sacerdos*) par excellence while the presbyter is a lower ranking priest (*sacerdos inferioris ordinis*).[77] Therefore, at the beginning of the third century the priestly vocabulary was being widely applied, especially to the bishop.[78] Priest (*sacerdos*) becomes synonymous with bishop (*episcopus*), with the Greek term like many others only transliterated into Latin. At this time only rarely is the term applied to presbyters—at times directly, but mostly indirectly, it is understood that presbyters too enjoy the priesthood (*hierosyne*) even if only of a secondary order. This use became more frequent at the end of the fourth century, especially in the East, with the Cappadocians,[79] as well as with John Chrysostom, Theodore of Mopsuestia and the *Apostolic Constitutions*. Perhaps this assimilation of terminology applied both to the bishop and to the presbyters a century later is partly due to the new situation in the church. By growing the number of Christian communities and extending into the countryside, presbyters celebrate the Eucharist, teach and lead the people, and therefore perform almost all the functions that once belonged to the bishop. For this reason, some people are also led to think, like Jerome, that the distinction between presbyters and bishops was only of a disciplinary and not a structural nature. This conception is also found in the *Canons of Hippolytus*, an Egyptian composition perhaps from the middle of the fourth century. The author extols the importance of presbyters: "The presbyter is the same as the bishop (*episkopos*) in everything except for the seat (*cathedra*) and ordination" (can. 2). From the fifth century in the East with Theodoret of Cyr and then with Ps-Dionysius the Areopagite, the term priest (*hiereus*) explicitly indicates the presbyter, while the bishop is the archpriest (*archiereus*).

In the West, the evolution of the term is slower. In the fourth century both in Milan, Africa and Rome, as elsewhere, the term *sacerdos* (and *sacerdotium*) retains the meaning of the third century and indicates mainly and normally the bishop and his office, and not the presbyter. Often, however, it has a collective meaning, and can indicate both. In the course of the fourth and fifth centuries, in addition to the terms of *episcopus* and presbyter which we use here in a more technical sense, that of *sacerdos* is used abundantly, but normally it is still reserved only for the bishop. On the contrary, in some circles, *sacerdos* (priest) is preferred to the terms *episcopus* and presbyter. Ambrose, for example, uses *sacerdos* more frequently than *episcopus*. When Rufinus of Aquileia translates the ecclesiastical history of Eusebius of Caesarea, several times he renders the Greek word *episcopos* with the Latin *sacerdos* and translates *episcopé* with *sacerdotium*. However, in the Latin texts we can deduce whether *sacerdos* should be translated with bishop or with presbyter only from the context.

Ambrose explicitly, though rarely, speaks of the priesthood of presbyters; and only once, without ambiguity, does he call them *sacerdotes*.[80] Jerome, who lives in the East, does not frequently use the terms *sacerdos* and *sacerdotium*, which, in some cases clearly indicate the bishops[81] while in other cases indicates the priests,[82] while in still others there is uncertainty.[83] For Roman usage we have the testimony of Pope Siricius (384-399) and Innocent I (402-417). In his letter to Himerius of Tarragona, Siricius uses the term *sacerdos* several times to indicate priests.[84] In the letter to Decentius of Gubbio, Pope Innocent I uses the term *sacerdos* with different meanings. In some cases it seems to indicate only the bishops,[85] in others, and more frequently, it indicates all those who participate in the hierarchical priesthood, and then ultimately the celebrant of the Eucharist.[86] The *sacerdotes* are divided into *episcopi*, who are also called *pontifices*, and presbyters. Speaking of the one who can confer the sacrament of confirmation, he writes: "In fact, presbyters, although they are *sacerdotes*, do not have the high rank of the pontificate. That it is reserved only for the pontiffs to 'confirm' or transmit the Holy Spirit, the Paraclete, is demonstrated not only by the custom of the Church, but also by that passage from the *Acts of the Apostles* (ch. 3), which states that Peter and John were sent to transmit the Holy Spirit to those who had already been baptized. In fact, presbyters, when they baptize both in the absence of the bishop and in his presence, can anoint the baptized with a chrism. But only with oil that had been consecrated by the bishop; they cannot, on the other hand, mark the forehead with the same chrism, which is the duty of the bishops alone when they transmit the Spirit of the Paraclete."[87] Even the *Constitutum Silvestri*, which dates to about 501, prescribes that no presbyter can make the chrism. That very prohibition implies that some presbyter is doing it.[88]

The letter of Pope Innocent has several interesting aspects, including the discussion of the term presbyter, which in his usage has now taken on a more precise and narrower meaning, demonstrating the limits of his reading of the text of James.[89] Discussing the anointing of the sick, he reports the passage from James' letter (5:14-15) where he speaks of presbyters needing to be called for the sick.

In the biblical text the term is used in a more general sense, while Innocent understands it in a more restricted sense, indicating precisely the presbyters, as did his interlocutor Decentius. Based on this meaning, which was common at that time, Decentius and others thought that the anointing of the sick was reserved only for presbyters and excluded the bishops from the practice. Even further, it seems that presbyters used the James passage to claim certain rights for themselves or they might have used it for polemical reasons.[90] In any case, to circumvent the difficulty Pope Innocent states that if presbyters are allowed to anoint the sick, all the more so, should the bishops be allowed to do so even though they are often busy; nevertheless, they can do so if they please. One may also infer, keeping in mind other texts, that presbyters did indeed use the text of James to defend some of their rights. Thus, at the end of the fifth century John the Deacon can say that: "every pontiff is a presbyter; not every presbyter can be called pontiff."[91]

Augustine's thought is more complex and is conditioned by the ongoing controversies with the Donatists. To save the validity of the sacraments, and therefore of the priesthood itself, he perhaps insists more than the other fathers on the one priesthood of Christ, who is the only mediator. For this reason, he is very discreet in the use of the term *sacerdos*, which he also explicitly applies to presbyters. Commenting on the phrase from *Revelation*, "They shall be priests of God and of Christ, and they shall reign with him a thousand years" (*Rev* 20:6), Augustine adds:

> ... and this refers not to the bishops alone, and presbyters, who are now specially called priests in the Church; but as we call all believers Christians on account of the mystical chrism, so we call everyone priests because they are members of the one Priest. Of them the Apostle Peter says, "A holy people, a royal priesthood (*1 Pet* 2:9)." Certainly he implied, though in a passing and incidental way, that Christ is God, saying priests of God and Christ, that is, of the Father and the Son, though it was in His servant-form and as Son of man that Christ was made a Priest forever after the order of Melchizedek.[92]

Consequently, for Augustine both bishops and presbyters are properly and truly priests (*sacerdotes*). His fundamental concern is to unite the priesthood of Christians to that of Christ. For this reason, he prefers the ancient terminology, not so much sacral as specific to the individual offices: bishop, presbyter, deacon.[93] The term priest (*sacerdos*) or co-priest (*consacerdos*) is used more frequently in the epistolary headings to his colleagues in the episcopate, while the term presbyter is addressed with the term co-presbyter (*compresbyter*)[94] or simply *presbyter*.[95] Pope Siricius speaks of the highest overseers (*summi antistites*).[96] Augustine calls Simplicianus "the overseer of the church of Milan (*Ecclesiae Mediolanensis antistis*).[97] The bishops of the Council of Arles (314) address Sylvester as *papa*.

However, in the course of the fifth century the term *sacerdos* also applies explicitly, and increasingly frequently, to presbyters, although sometimes they are defined as priests according to order/rank (*sacerdotes secundi ordinis*).[98] In the following period *presbyter* continued to be used, but was increasingly replaced with *sacerdos*, which by the twelfth century became the ordinary title of the presbyter to distinguish him from the bishop. However, in the prayers of ordination and in the celebrations of the mass, the vocabulary of the priesthood for the bishop is still used. Moreover, the liturgical texts have greater stability and continuity, and are less subject to change.

At the end of the fourth and the beginning of the fifth century, referring to the bishop with the specific name of pontiff (*pontifex*) also began to gain traction. *Pontifex*, along with the derivatives of *pontificatus* and *pontificium*, clearly distinguished him from the *presbyter*. In the West, it had strong pagan resonances since it indicated a very precise traditional Roman institution.[99] In order to indicate the most important ministry in the communities, Christians normally used the titles of bishop (*episcopus*), pope (*papa*), overseer (*antistes*), priest (*sacerdos*), leader (*praesul*), etc. The first author to apply the title *pontifex maximus* to a Christian bishop is Tertullian.[100] Cyprian is called the pontiff of Christ and of God (*Christi et Dei pontifex*) or pontiff of God (*Dei pontifex*) by his biographer.[101] Donatist bishop Marculus is called the highest pontiff (*summus pontifex*)[102] in a text written around 360. Around 370, the use of pontiff among Christian writers became more common.[103] For the first time in 380 the title of pontiff was used by the imperial authority, Theodosius, but only for Pope Damasus.[104] Peter of Alexandria on the other hand is referred to as bishop (*episcopus*). Moreover, Theodosius uses the term *pontificium* to indicate the episcopate,[105] a term also used in ecclesiastical circles.[106] The emperor Arcadius uses the phrase "pontiff of God" (*pontifex Dei*).[107]

During this period the term *pontiff* became common among Christians to indicate a bishop. The two terms became synonymous, as in Jerome's usage when he speaks of "a pontiff and bishop, who must be above reproach."[108] Jerome in fact makes extensive use of the term.[109] He frequently uses the expression "pontiff of Christ" (*pontifex Christi*)[110] and other phrases such as "pontiff of the church" (*Ecclesiae pontifices*),[111] "Roman pontiff" (*Romanus pontifex*),[112] "pontiff of the city of Rome" (*Romanae urbis pontifex*),[113] "pontiff of the city of Alexandria" (*Alexandrinae urbis pontifex*),[114] and "pontiff of the churches" (*ecclesiarum pontifices*).[115] Paulinus of Nola calls Augustine "the highest pontiff of Christ" (*summus Christi pontifex*).[116] Arnobius writes "the pontiff of the church of Alexandria" (*Ecclesiae Alexandrinae pontifex*).[117] Cassian says "the pontiff of the city of Alexandria" (*Alexandrinae urbi pontifex*).[118] Fulgentius refers to him as "Augustine the renowned pontiff" (*Pontifex inclitus Augustinus*).[119] Augustine does not normally use this term himself, but in one case he calls Ambrose "the great pontiff" (*pontifex magnus*).[120] Also, the adjective *pontificalis* is used as a synonym of episcopal,[121] as well as the term *pontificatus*.[122] By the end of the fourth century, the term *pontifex* is in common use to indicate a bishop, even in papal letters. In inscriptions, the popes from Boniface onwards are called *Pontifices*[123] as are also the bishops.[124] An anonymous medieval writer notes, "The pontiffs are called shepherds of the flock, as well as fathers who are concerned for the care of the people and the country."[125]

The highest pontiff (*summus pontifex*) is first of all Christ.[126] The term is also used to indicate a more important bishop such as a metropolitan.[127] The same can be said of overseer (*antistes*), a term used to indicate pagan priests initially, and then used to designate Christian bishops. Already in the third century the appellative *papa* (*pappas*) was being used, and becomes more widespread in the fourth century both in Latin and Greek, especially with Jerome.[128] Within the episcopate itself there is also a tendency to coin new titles, such as chief priest (*princeps sacerdotum*), or high priest (*summus sacerdos*) or other similar titles that would indicate a distinction of authority.

The use of the term co-presbyter (*compresbyter*) by bishops is not only a gesture of deference for the priesthood[129] but expresses the profound conviction of the unity of the priesthood and of action on the part of both bishops and priests. Moreover, *compresbyter* has found quite common usage since the third century, especially in Africa and with Cyprian,[130] and by this time is considered part of the Christian language.

Already in the seventh century, however, the term priest (*sacerdos*) applied almost exclusively to presbyters and became synonymous with presbyters. Also, in this case the semantic evolution is indicative of a new vision of the ministry, of a change in mentality which began in the second century, and culminated in the Middle Ages when the ministry is seen almost exclusively as a priesthood that leads worship.

Works begin to appear on the particular duties of the clergy such as *On the Priesthood* by John Chrysostom (381-385) and the *Duties of the Clergy* by Ambrose. A series of legislative measures increasingly separated the clergy from the community. There was the ban on lodging at hotels[131] at the end of the fourth century, likewise, legislation included ecclesiastical celibacy, or, if married, cultic continence, the gradual introduction of the external sign of tonsure, the prohibition of exercising certain professions, absence of voluntary mutilations, and other requirements. Other aspects, such as imperial exemptions from various taxes, different privileges (e.g. those of the forum), not being able to dispose of goods at will, making a will in favor of the church, are also of considerable social importance. These elements not only distinguished the cleric from the layman, but, as has been said, tended to constitute a group separate from the community of the faithful so that a two-fold division unfolds. On the one hand there are the baptized; on the other hand, there is the clergy which has a rigid hierarchy of offices, dignity and places within it. A bishop also determines how much each member of his clergy is to receive from the contributions of the faithful according to the office of each.[132] In this context a distinction will be introduced between the power of order (*potestas ordinis*), an authority deriving from ordination, that is, from the sacrament of order, and the power of jurisdiction (*potestas iuridictionis*), the actual exercise of that power, resulting in two divisible aspects of the priestly ministry within a hierarchy. These two institutions are, however, concepts that come after the patristic period. To seek them from the fathers, as more than one scholar has done, makes no sense because the fathers understood a bishop to exist only within a real community.

SELECTION AND REQUIREMENTS OF THE CLERGY

According to the traditional understanding of the clergy, the exercise of pastoral ministry in its broadest sense requires a "vocation," a call from outside. One needs to be "called" to avoid the ministry becoming just one profession among many, or an avenue to greater social visibility or mobility. It is not a personal choice at one's complete discretion—even if the intention is noble—to be available for the people of God. But what does this vocation consist of? Who is the one who issues the call? Who is called? What qualities are required, if there are any? Should the call be answered? To some of these questions we intend to offer some indications born from reflection on the texts of the fathers and from the experience of the first Christian communities whose experience has been enriched over time and space.

The first indications come from the word of Jesus, who invests some of his disciples with special positions, choosing them from among the other disciples with the call, "Follow me" (*Mk* 1:16ff; *Lk* 5:27ff; etc.). He entrusted them with a mission: "Go into all the world" (*Mk* 16:15; *Mt* 28:19; etc.) to proclaim "the kingdom of God" (*Lk* 9:60; *Mt* 28:19-20), to baptize those who will accept their teaching, and to make other disciples. Jesus calls only a few to cooperate closely with him in proclaiming the kingdom. In addition, Jesus had also given them rules of conduct in the exercise of service (*diakonia*), expressed synthetically in the washing of the feet. As Jesus assumed the role of the servant, so too must the disciples. For "he that will be great among you shall be your servant" (*Mt* 20:26). Those who lead must look to Peter's love for Christ as the foundation for feeding the sheep, as Augustine writes: "Therefore, let there be a commitment of love to feed the flock of the Lord."[133] This is the true *diakonia*, a term that comes from *diakoneo*, which in the New Testament normally indicates table service (*Mt* 8:15; *Jn* 12:2). In the first community of Jerusalem, table service was entrusted to seven chosen persons so the apostles could devote themselves to the "diakonia of the Word" (*Acts* 6:2). The term in the *First Letter to Timothy* indicates the service proper to deacons (*1 Tim* 3:10). Paul's collection that he takes up is also a *diakonia* for the community of Jerusalem (*Rom* 15:25; *2 Cor* 8:19). Therefore, the community is served in different ways, both with the word and the sacraments. There are different ways of *diakonia*.

In the words of Augustine:

Let it be the office of love to feed the Lord's flock, if it was the signal of fear to deny the Shepherd. Those whose purpose in feeding the flock of Christ is so that they may have them as their own, and not as Christ's, are convicted of loving themselves and not Christ, from the desire either of boasting, or wielding power, or acquiring gain, and not from the love of obeying, serving, and pleasing God. Against such, therefore, there stands as a wakeful sentinel this thrice inculcated utterance of Christ, of whom the apostle complains that they seek their own, not the things that are Jesus Christ's (*Phil* 2:21). For what else do the words, 'Do you love me? Feed my sheep,' mean other than 'If you love me, think not of feeding yourself, but feed my sheep as mine, and not as your own; seek my glory in them, and not your own; my dominion, and not yours; my gain, and not yours.'[134]

The office of leadership of the Christian community is an office of love (*officium caritatis*).¹³⁵ Augustine writes elsewhere: "Because we are not bishops for ourselves, but for those to whom we offer the ministry of the word and of the sacrament of the Lord. And for this reason, adapting ourselves to the needs of those whom we must govern without scandalizing them, we must be or not be what we are, not for our own sake, but for the good of others"¹³⁶

The author of the *First Letter to Timothy* considers it a noble commitment to aspire to the episcopate as one who is appointed to watch over the people of God. It is the same for *diakonia*, but one must have the right qualities because it is a great responsibility (*1 Tim* 3). Both the bishop/presbyter and the deacon must be aware that their choice has a salvific value for others. They must preserve "the mystery of faith in a pure conscience" (*1 Tim* 3:9). They renew and continue the experience of Peter who says to the cripple who sat at the door of the Temple in Jerusalem: "I have neither silver nor gold, but what I have I give you: in the name of Jesus Christ, the Nazarene, walk!" (*Acts* 3:6). They continue practicing "the customs of the Lord,"¹³⁷ walking "in the truth traced out by the Lord, who was a deacon, that is, a servant of all."¹³⁸

Chapter three of the *First Letter to Timothy* establishes some fundamental qualifications to which the fathers of the Church will refer. Some of those qualifications will be transformed into canons articulated in the conciliar legislation of the fourth and fifth centuries. However, those later reflections will focus on the bishop, who is the priest (*sacerdos*) and the center of the community. He has the primary responsibility for the church's mission. He is entrusted with the ministries of communion in his community and with other communities, community leadership, preaching and administration of the sacraments. One of the earliest reflections on this can be found in *1 Clement*, written before the end of the first century.¹³⁹ In Corinth there were rivalries.¹⁴⁰ There was a destructive struggle for power similar to what might happen in the political arena of a Roman or Greek city. According to this letter there was a college of elders—as was the practice—that guided the community. Some of those elders were dismissed, despite their holiness of life, and it is not clear what the reason for their dismissal was. The Roman intervention called for harmony and respect for the elders (*presbyteroi*) who were constituted in authority with the purpose of oversight (*episcopē*), a task received from the apostles, but ultimately from God himself through Jesus Christ. The proposed schema for their authority is as follows: God sends Jesus Christ, who in turn sends the apostles, who, "preaching throughout the villages and cities, appointed the first fruits of their labors, having first proved them by the Spirit, to be bishops and deacons of those who would afterwards believe."¹⁴¹ The apostles, knowing that contentions would arise over the episcopal office, established bishops and ordered them to do the same, according to what was prefigured in the Old Testament. Ministers cannot be dismissed but must be replaced only after their death. Succession is an apostolic norm. The author of *1 Clement* uses the terms bishops, presbyters and deacons. They are referred to as "eminent men." It seems the bishops and presbyters are used interchangeably. "For our sin will not be small if we eject from the episcopate those who have blamelessly and piously fulfilled its duties."[142] The ministerial terminology is still fluid: it speaks of bishops, presbyters, guides, and leaders. The structure is still collegial. But by the second half of the second century an authoritative bishop emerges, Dionysius, in Corinth. Clement argues that the office (*episcopé*) is transmitted by succession and lasts a lifetime. The ministers must be blameless in leading the "flock of Christ," a concept repeated several times in chapter 44. The Letter considers the various ministers—bishops and deacons —as those who carry out a *leiturgia* (a public work), in Latin a *munus*. The ministers carry out a permanent, stable and vital *leiturgia*.

According to Justin Martyr, who wrote around 150 in Rome, it is the president of the Sunday assembly who preaches: "When the reader has ceased, the president verbally instructs, and exhorts to the imitation of these good things. Then we all rise together and pray, and, as we said before, when our prayer is ended, bread and wine and water are brought, and the president in a similar way offers prayers and thanksgivings, according to his ability, and the people assent, saying Amen."[143] Preaching takes place within a liturgical assembly on a specific day, the day of the sun, that is, the Christian Sunday, and takes place after reading a passage from the New Testament (the memoirs of the apostles) or a prophetic text, that is, from the Old Testament. In the time of Cyprian of Carthage († 254) preaching is the duty of the bishops—the preaching bishops (*tractantes episcopi*).[144] In some cases, even a presbyter authorized by the bishop can preach. Cyprian was still a presbyter when he preached.

It is a profound conviction that the bishop is chosen by God who is the foundation of his authority in the church. The bishop's ordination prayers emphasize the divine choice of the ordaining pastor. The document referred to as the *Apostolic Tradition* notes: "Grant, O Father, who knows hearts, to this servant of yours whom you have chosen for the episcopate."[145] The candidate for the episcopal or priestly ministry does not affirm the choice or discern with the help of wise guides that he has a "vocation" and that he has been called. Therefore, one does not conceive of a vocation in the modern sense: it is God who calls someone to ministerial life. No one feels called by an inner inspiration which must be evaluated and verified according to their situation and qualifications. The call to ministry is manifested through the precise will of the Christian community which chooses its own ministers. Whoever calls directly and publicly is the living church here and now in a certain place. The will of the community gathered in prayer is the actual and verifiable manifestation that someone has been chosen by God to ministry. Bishop Cornelius (251-253) in Rome was elected "by the judgment of God and his Christ."[146] Augustine writes, "God put the office of clergyman on his shoulders for a service to his people and it is more a burden than an honor."[147] If the community wants someone to be ordained, it is God Himself who wants him. The will of the chosen one does not count because whoever has been called in this way cannot and must not put up resistance. Otherwise he is going against God's will. Moreover, the ecclesial community calls ministers for pastoral service according to need in relation to its size and its environs. God manifests his will through various signs such as the appreciation and the testimony of the people, their unanimous consent, as well as the approval of the neighboring bishops.

In practice, however, the community does appoint someone. The community can designate a candidate even if the candidate is *invitus*, i.e. unwilling. We know of several people who were elected but did not want to accept the office because it was not what they wanted. Augustine and Ambrose were acclaimed and ordained despite their resistance and eventually succumbed to the new office. Paulinus of Nola was ordained by popular compulsion.[148] The famous monk Ammon, who lived in the desert but was knowledgeable about the Scriptures, was requested as a bishop. He decisively refused but his refusal was ignored. So he cut off one of his ears in order to create an impediment that would not allow him to be ordained. The bishop Timothy, however, declared that such an impediment applied to the Jews, not to him who was willing to ordain him with other mutilations. They finally left Ammon alone because he threatened to cut out his tongue.[149] In the case of monks, the monks usually preferred their quiet life and did not willingly accept the episcopate.[150]

But sometimes this reluctance, which we find in the sources, is just a literary tool (*topos*). Today's rule for a valid ordination requires the full freedom of the one who is chosen to accept or refuse the call. In ancient times, the will of the community was the important factor, not the recipient's consent. The *Apostolic Tradition* further specifies: "He who is ordained as a bishop, being chosen by all the people, must be irreproachable. When his name is announced and approved, the people will gather on the Lord's day with the council of elders and the bishops who are present. With the assent of all, the bishops will place their hands upon him. . . ."[151] Cyprian of Carthage († 258) gives us even more details: "For this reason it is necessary to respect with care the divine tradition and apostolic practice—tradition and practice that are also found among us and in almost all the provinces. That is, in order to proceed according to the law of ordination, the closest bishops belonging to the same province must intervene in the community in which the election takes place. The bishop must be chosen in the presence of the people. People truly know the life of each one and know how to appreciate conduct by living together."[152] The role of the three components —the people, the local clergy and the neighboring bishops—is not specified here.

In Rome the same procedure was followed, as Cyprian writes, speaking of the election of Pope Cornelius, who was elected according to the righteousness of God and his Christ by the almost unanimous consent of the clergy, by the approval (*suffragium*) of the gathered *plebs* and by the assembly of bishops.[153] Cyprian judges that the same procedure was followed in Rome as in the Carthaginian church. The choice of God is manifested by these two indispensable signs: the choice of the people and the clergy of the local church, and the approval of the bishops of the region. But it is God who made him a bishop.[154] The life of the ordained, in this case Cornelius, was the confirmation that the choice really proceeds from God. Cyprian's extended *Letter 55* repeats several times and in different ways that the divine will has decided the choice of Cornelius, because the divine authority (*auctoritas*) has established that the choice of the candidate be made in the presence of all. The Lord himself elects his priests in the church and gives them his assistance.[155] Cyprian's insistence that each community must have only one bishop is directed against the schismatics or heretics ordaining of other bishops. His statement is peremptory and repeated elsewhere as well: "No heresies have arisen nor schisms grown from any other cause than this: that obedience is not yielded to the priest of God. No one in a church is a bishop or a judge for the time being, as if he were temporarily occupying the place of Christ."[156]

Human discernment must be careful, scrupulous and public, to avoid any subtle maneuvering. The "witness" given by the clergy, which guides the opinion of the people, is fundamental in discerning the divine election and blessing which are in evidence through the joint action of the entire local Christian community. The culminating moment is the approval of the Christian people gathered in a public assembly, in which all the faithful (*fideles*) are invited to participate. Only then is the ordination considered valid and legitimate.[157] The divine election, manifested through the explicit will of the community, is the visible sign of the "calling." As stated earlier, the feelings of the one who is called are of no consequence. We should note here that Cyprian is simply expressing the practice of his own church in the ordinations of the local clergy.[158]

In Origen's controversy with Celsus, he offered a rather ideal picture of what happens in Christian communities when they choose people in authority in the church. He wrote:

> Those who are ambitious we reject; but we constrain those who, through excess of modesty, are not easily induced to take a public charge in the church of God. And those who rule over us well are under the constraining influence of the great King, whom we believe to be the Son of God, God the Word. And if those who govern in the Church, and are called rulers of the divine nation (that is, the Church) rule well, they rule in accordance with the divine commands, and never allow themselves to be led astray by worldly policy.[159]

Origen reminds us that there are ambitious people who want to occupy important positions in the church. We also learn that it was the practice of the early church at times to force some to accept leadership roles. His observation is interesting: the latter are better in leadership because they act for the common good of the church in order to build it up.

The procedure varies according to time and place. In the fourth century it underwent an evolution in restricting the role of the people (*plebs*) who nevertheless in many cases imposed their will. Whatever we might think of this procedure, it was the best they could come up with and we would certainly agree that it could be improved. It did lend itself to dramatic and numerous abuses. It was often a source of schisms, because frequently the different factions elected their own candidates, creating devastating divisions. The history of the Roman church, in ancient times, suffered for centuries from continuous schisms and the presence of two bishops in its bosom, starting with Novatian in 251; then Felix II in 356; at the time of Damasus there was also Ursinus (366). And the list could go on. Influential and powerful people controlled the choice of the candidate, and often imposed that choice upon the church, even resorting at times to physical violence.

In the third century, the wealthiest women often supported a candidate and were able to have him elected because these women were an important and significant part of the Christian communities. In these same communities the powerful men were often in the minority, for social as well as political reasons.[160] Jerome observed that the system that was followed led to the worthiest candidates being sidelined because they were less intriguing than the ambitious and less desirous who sought after these honorific positions.[161] If there were people who, in order to get ahead socially, aspired to the clergy,[162] it is necessary also to allow that others were forced to accept the pastoral ministry. There was, for instance, the African Castorius, whom Augustine and Alypius begged to accept the episcopal office, because they considered him worthy: "We beseech you by the divinity and humanity of Christ, and by the peace of that heavenly city where we receive eternal rest after laboring for the time of our pilgrimage, to take your place as the bishop of the Church of Bagai which your brother has resigned."[163]

It is also important to win the support of the Christian people.[164] The system for choosing a bishop almost naturally involved a certain type of propaganda, so that the best candidates escaped from office while the ambitious were elected.[165] As Damasus says, "Money, service, or the favor of the people" are all elements that can be used to be elected.[166] A Roman synod of 499 found that "because of the frequent intrigues and debilitating greed involved, those without title who sought after the episcopate caused the desolation of the Church and the discord of the people."[167] The same thing is said in the synods of 501 and 502.[168] The second canon of the Ecumenical Council of Chalcedon (451) was very strict in condemning the practice of simony in ordinations.

Reasons of pride, prestige or economics pushed the ambitious to fight for election by resorting to corruption and bargaining. In the first three centuries there was no clear instance of simony. It developed from the fourth century when, due to the imperial concession of benefits connected with clerical functions, some aspired to enter the clergy—especially the upper levels of clerical office. Moreover, there was most likely also the influence of the age-old practice of using large sums of money to buy one's way into certain public offices, from which then considerable economic, social and political benefits would be obtained. The attainment of the ecclesiastical ministry in an irregular manner could take place in different ways: the applicant might make a payment in some way, there might be intimidation of lay and ecclesiastical voters, or recourse to powerful people, intrigue, distribution of money, promises to give rewards once elected—to name only a few. Augustine writes that disputes over the election of a new bishop were frequent in the churches of Africa—and elsewhere as well.[169]

This custom occurs above all when the *clarissimi* families, that is, members of the senatorial class, become Christians. However, for social, political and ecclesial reasons, the role of the people in the election of their bishop increasingly was reduced when it served the advantage of the provincial ecclesiastical hierarchy, the pope and the emperor. Perhaps already in the fourth century the people's normal and recognized role was only to acclaim the candidate proposed by the clergy, as happened in the Roman secular realm. A typical example was when Augustine proposed the designation of his successor to his community. The stenographer reports acclamatory phrases of the genre several times: "The faithful then shouted thirty-six times: Thank God! Praised be Jesus Christ! Three times: Christ, hear us! Live Augustine! Eight times: You, for father, you, for bishop! Twenty times: He (the successor Heraclius) is worthy and just! Five times: It is worthy. It is worthy! And six times: He is worthy and just!"[170]

In the fourth century a complex canonical and civil legislation was defined, but in practice it was also quite diversified, often differing from the legislation. Therefore, we can indicate some elements of a general nature for the fourth to sixth centuries with references to real cases, keeping in mind that the non-observance of certain rules for election and ordination often gave rise to bitter disputes about the legitimacy of a bishop and the acts surrounding his election.

The local reality was complex. There was no homogeneity in episcopal elections throughout the Empire. They were quite diverse in the various regions and in large ecclesial communities.[171] By now the bishop was becoming the pillar of the local communities and a crucial figure in Late Antiquity. The figure of the metropolitan was the most important in authority. The local bishops, often of small communities, grew fewer in number until there were hardly any. In the first centuries a more charismatic and capable figure was elected. Since the fourth century, other factors also came into play. However, many great personages do get elected for their extraordinary qualities: Ambrose, Augustine, Chrysostom, Maximus of Turin, Basil of Caesarea, Theophilus of Alexandria, and others.

A distinctive method of electing the local bishop was practiced in Alexandria, Egypt. Until the late third century an Alexandrian priest was elected by the other priests and was enthroned in the presence of the corpse of his predecessor, along with popular approval.

When the episcopate spread in Egypt, other bishops also participated. The first case was that of Heracles in 233. It was not so much an ordination as an installation of the one elected. Athanasius, on the other hand, was elected even though he was only a deacon, a novelty that was challenged. Subsequently the rules of Nicaea were followed, but the monks and the ruling classes also became involved. The Alexandrian bishop was the only head for the whole of Egypt. In the fourth century, this authority would also extend to Ethiopia and then to Nubia.

Many elements played a specific role, such as local traditions or, more importantly, regional ones. For example, the office holder would suggest the name of his successor. Other elements that might affect the choosing of a bishop included doctrinal tendencies, conflicts, canonical norms, imperial politics,[172] local social situations, administrative problems, civil laws, the role of the people who intervened with acclamations, the candidate's notoriety, his charisma, his wealth, corruption, local notables, local struggles, the interests of dominant groups, the will of the metropolitan who becomes more and more influential, as well as other factors. Normally it was thought (incorrectly) that the dominant factor was the intervention of the emperor or of some king, especially for the larger dioceses. In some cases, this might have been true, but in practice they too needed to consider the will of the people and the reaction of the bishops.

The emergence of a Christian aristocracy was also expressed in the fact that bishops were often chosen from their own class, sometimes completely ignoring the people. Simony was condemned, but it did occur. This was more the case for large venues than for unknown local communities. Here the interventions of the imperial authorities were practically null and void. Local conflicts, riots and violence—at times excessive—in episcopal elections marked ancient Christian history. Some scholars would like to explain the spread of violence in the late antique city as a consequence of the emergence of the figure of the bishops.[173] This is a one-sided view, since violence and uprisings due to fiscal problems, oppression, or various other reasons (including religious ones) were common.[174]

Many texts trace the figure of the ideal bishop who is holy and learned. The majority, however, was neither holy nor learned. Nevertheless, the bishop remained in office for life, hence the tendency to elect people of a certain age who offered guarantees. For example, in the West, the rule was established that the bishop must be at least 45 years old, which is an advanced age for those times.[175] The fact that this standard was required is an indication that it was often done differently.

For the Latin countries, at least theoretically, the rule of the *Ancient Statutes of the Church* remained in force through the Middle Ages. The statutes established that the bishop was elected "with the consent of the clergy and laity and the assembly of bishops from the entire province, especially the metropolitan."[176] The wealth of the candidate was sometimes a reason the people requested the ordination of a certain candidate. The *Canons of Athanasius* often observed that many were chosen because they were rich, while the saints were rejected because they were poor.[177] Having a rich presbyter meant that his assets made the local community rich. Or, being a powerful man, he could better protect his people and intervene with the civil authorities.

It is difficult to say when, but perhaps already in the fifth century, the metropolitan chose candidates that were proposed by the clergy, the decurions (who were the members of the local senate), and the notables of the city.[178] A definitive norm was reached at the second Council of Nicaea in 787 (can. 3), which reserved the election to the bishops only. The people could be considered a valid guarantor of the dignity of the chosen person, but in some cases, the people let themselves be guided by their own vested interests or other concerns. In the period of the Roman Empire's disintegration, the people were led to elect someone who could defend them politically and socially, and divisions and popular struggles were not uncommon among supporters of different candidates.

The elected bishop did not necessarily have to belong to the clergy of the city but he must at least be known there. Even lay people could be elected, but from the fourth century legislation was oriented towards choosing candidates from among the clergy, according to canon 10 of the Council of Serdica of 343 where Hosius of Cordoba proposed that in order for someone to be a bishop he must have first been a lector and deacon or presbyter. It became a universal fact at the end of the 4th century that it was no longer possible to access the episcopate directly, even if we know of various exceptions. Leo the Great once again strongly affirmed that lay people could not be ordained bishops without first having gone through the progressive steps (*cursus*) leading up to the bishop's office as a guarantee of their preparation. In this period, however, the practice of ordaining hermits and monks—categories then not belonging to the clergy—expanded with the hope that they would have greater preparation and above all be observers of the continence requirement.

As mentioned earlier, the bishop was the center of the life of the community. He was the one who chose all the other members of the lower clergy. To help him with this, he looked for advice from others, especially the priests. Cyprian writes: "When it comes to ordaining clerics, we usually consult you before their ordination and examine the morality and merits of each in the course of a public assembly."[179] Origen too mentions that the minor ministers were appointed by the bishop.[180] Also from the third century, the *Didascalia* attributes the choice to the bishop alone,[181] but in general the later testimonies require the collaboration of all the clergy. The people also intervened for the nomination of priests, but most likely not always. Sometimes the ordination of the presbyter took place through pressure from the people, as was the case with Paulinus of Nola, Augustine, Paulinianus, and Jerome's brother, Nepotianus. There was an ecclesiastical norm that when presbyters die, they must leave their property with their church. This is one reason for forcing rich people to be ordained, as was the case with Pinianus in Hippo.[182]

The difficulty of recruiting people specifically prepared for the ministry gave rise to the idea of preparing future clerics, as suggested by the letter of Pope Siricius to Himerius of Tarragona in 385 as well as others like Augustine, sensing the needs of the times. In the *Pastoral Letters* we find indications, especially of a moral nature, for the choice of a good bishop (*Titus* 1:6-7; *1 Tim* 3:2-7). Moreover, a new Christian (a neophyte) was not allowed to be a bishop, nor could someone who had married twice. Already in the third century anyone who had done public penance was not to be admitted to the clergy (episcopate and lower orders), nor was anyone who had made a voluntary mutilation or received baptism during a serious illness (the *clinici*). Both ecclesiastical and civil bans on admission to the clergy during the fourth century became numerous and severely limited the choice of candidates. The church did not admit those who practiced certain professions, such as actors, state officials, soldiers baptized before military service, or administrators of the property of others before they had given final account to the master. Neither slaves nor freedmen were admitted to the clergy because they did not have full civil freedom.

Due to economic concerns, beginning with Constantine imperial legislation prohibited certain categories of people from entering the clergy such as slaves and tenant farmers (*coloni adscripticii* or *originales*). In Rome in 365 bakers were prohibited entry into the clergy[183] and in 445 all members of corporations had the same restriction; in 452 the *collegiate* from other cities (members of some corporations) were similarly banned.[184] In addition, pork butchers, subordinate officials of different public services, employees of imperial factories, the vast middle class of the *curiales*, i.e. the members of the city council and their families, were also banned. Under Justinian (ruled 527-569), the rules were relaxed somewhat so that the slaves and tenant farmers (*coloni*) could be considered for the ministry but they needed the written permission of their patron (*patronus*).[185]

With the granting of exemptions many people were admitted to the clergy, which explains Constantine's several interventions. Those who possess sufficient wealth cannot enter into ecclesiastical service, because "it is fitting that the rich subsidize worldly needs so that the poor be sustained by the riches of the church."[186] Constantine's legislation, with adjustments, was also proposed by the successive emperors and included in the Theodosian Code of 438. This legislation was consistent with the Constantinian policy towards other social groups during those years.

Therefore, there were not many social classes from which clergy could be drawn. *Clarissimi*, the senatorial class, were allowed to enter the clergy but it was not socially expedient for them, and the church was not particularly attractive for such people. We know of a few cases, which in their time, caused a great stir, and those few from high society who did embrace ecclesiastical life immediately became bishops. There were also a few members of the clergy from the professional classes, namely professors and lawyers, and the latter were not all that much appreciated by the church because of their activities.

Moreover, since Christianity in most parts of the Empire was a mainly urban phenomenon, it was not possible to recruit members from the farmers and peasants. Only the poor craftsmen of the city remained, and it is to be assumed that this category constituted the backbone of the clergy of the fourth and fifth centuries. But a social survey of the clergy during these centuries remains to be accomplished and there is still a lack of adequate instruments for research. One should not think, however, that the indications given by ecclesiastical and civil legislation were absolute and rigidly observed. The monotonous repetition of similar laws is a sign that they were often violated, and we know of too many exceptions and adaptations to changing situations.

A Council in Africa in 420, at the time of Augustine, complained about the painful situation that this legislation produced. Augustine writes: "Now, in the council so many complaints arose about the shortage of clerics because of the law—which obliges them to return them to the civil obligations proper to their social condition—that the brothers summoned to the council were forced to send messengers to the imperial court."[187]

Pope Innocent also presents a list of people who cannot be admitted to the clergy: in addition to the members of the local senate, who are then called to their secular obligation, also administrators, lawyers, and military personnel.[188] Several times the popes intervened to exclude unworthy people from the clergy and sometimes used real examinations (*scrutinia*) to ascertain the conduct and faith of the candidate. In fact, the pastoral ministry required a suitable theological preparation and a certain knowledge of the rhetoric for preaching. However, there were no specific schools for the preparation of the clergy. This was obtained by a quasi apprenticeship acquired through frequent attendance at liturgical celebrations, familiarity with the bishop and other priests, personal study and the exercise of the orders received.

For example, in Gaul in the 5th/6th century at the moment of greatest need for qualified clergy for the mission field, the situation grew worse because the permission of the king or governor was necessary to enter the clergy. This rule was set at the Council of Orléans of July 10, 511 (can. 4), because the king did not want to deprive himself of qualified people. One solution to make up for the lack of clergy with a certain cultural background and an irreproachable life was to appeal to monks who already had left everything to live in the monasteries.

The examination required before ordination, however, was aimed at assessing the moral qualities needed to belong to the church's spiritual ranks (*militia spiritualis*) and not so much for gauging their intellectual preparation. Of course, these provisions which became stricter with Popes Siricius (384-399) and Zosimus (417-418) applied above all to young people, but also to those advanced in years. And so, this resulted in certain requirements that one follow the progression through the various ministerial offices. We know of exceptions that are enlightening: Augustine and Ambrose, for instance. Similar cases, writes Gregory of Nazianzus, are frequent.[189]

In some cities there was a school of readers (*schola lectorum*), from which some of the higher clergy were chosen. The age of aggregation varied: Epiphanius of Pavia was made a lector at 8 years of age. Popes Siricius, Innocent and Zosimus say that baptized children are included in the number of lectors even before puberty. The office of lector, generally, constituted the beginning of the sequence of clerical offices (*cursus clericalis*) in the spiritual ranks (*militia spiritualis*). These indications, as mentioned before, should not be generalized.

Diodore, the future bishop of Tarsus, directed a school in Antioch that offered theological teaching and ascetical formation. Augustine founded a monastery of clerics in Hippo where they could receive adequate training. The bishops who came from his monastery did the same and their example was imitated elsewhere. Something similar already existed in Vercelli with Eusebius († 371), and in Gallia (Gaul) numerous bishops came from the monastery on the island of Lérins. At the Council of Vaison of 525 it was prescribed that the parish priests, following the custom existing in Italy, must instruct the office of lectors. Normally the young people would learn the rites, ceremonies and ecclesiastical norms under the assiduous supervision of the local bishop. It was not unusual for the children of a bishop or a priest to become priests and bishops in turn. There were many instances of this. Here is just one example: In Laodicea, Combusta (Phrygia; today Ladik), the presbyter Aurelius Firmius had a tomb built for himself and his two sons Conon and Alexander who were also presbyters.[190] The deaconess mother's son was a lector; a subdeacon was the son of a subdeacon.[191] On the island of Milos, an inscription commemorates a mother, Eutychia, who was the mother of three priests, a deaconess and two consecrated virgins.[192] The presbyter's son memorializes his mother, the deaconess.[193] The collective burial of clerics and women suggests that it was a family tomb. Gregory of Nazianzus was the son of a bishop, also named Gregory, who built a beautiful and large cathedral church in Nazianzus.[194] In Armenia the episcopate passed from father to son, or as happened in Cappadocia we have an exceptional Christian family, from whom Basil of Caesarea and two of his brothers become bishops (Gregory of Nyssa and Peter of Sebaste).

Attempts at training could only do so much since there were no real organizational structures for clerical education. All the great fathers insisted that the clergy have a secular but above all Christian cultural background. After all, they themselves were trained in the best profane schools of the time, but they were often self-taught in terms of religious knowledge. For this reason, they insisted on a careful reading of Scripture, since the priest was both a preacher and a teacher of scripture.[195] It was forbidden to ordain clerics who did not have a minimum of education: "Those who are ignorant of letters should not dare to aspire to sacred orders."[196] But the clergy of the fourth and fifth centuries must normally have been quite ignorant: "Illiterate people are frequently elected by judgment of God and the popular vote. Once they are ordained as priests, however, they should at least try to learn God's law so that they can teach it, and not be ashamed to learn from the laity who know what concerns the office of the priest" writes Jerome.[197] The exercise in each clerical rank allowed learning and preparation for a higher rank, especially for the diaconate and presbyterate.[198] The length of time in the reception of individual orders was useful in view of the progressive formation of the individual's experience of discipline (*experientia disciplinae*).[199]

Augustine makes a similar observation about the clergy of the African countryside, "crowded with rural and illiterate priests,"[200] but even the urban clergy left much to be desired. We do not know what degree of preparation was required for individual orders, and there are no studies in this regard. The Council of Seleucia-Ctesiphon (410) in Mesopotamia prescribed that the subdeacon must at least know how to read the Psalter.[201] The Breviary of Hippo also requires that clerics should know the sacred Scripture—without specifying the degree of knowledge they needed to have, however.[202] The *Ancient Statutes of the Church* required the bishop to be learned (*litteratus*), i.e., he should know the Scriptures: "Let whoever is to be ordained a bishop be first examined [to determine] if he is prudent in nature, if he is teachable, temperate in his habits, chaste in his life; if he is sober, if he always [tends] to his own business; if he is affable to men of humbler status, merciful, literate, and learned in the Lord's law; if he is attentive to the meanings of Scripture; if he is trained in the Church's teachings."[203] Later information, obtained from the Councils of Spain and Gaul, offers a survey of an even more ignorant clergy in the West. In the East things were not much better, according to Justinian's *Novellae*[204] and the second canon of the second Council of Nicaea in 787. Already in the West, however, schools for bishops were beginning to appear.

In addition, in the fourth century, we see the beginning of church legislation (necessarily still fluctuating) concerning the age required for access to various orders. Although the legislation reaffirmed general principles, it was not uniform. Canon 11 of the Council of Neocaesarea in Pontus 314/319 required a person to be thirty years of age in order to enter the priesthood. This age was the most consistent in the variety of orders for clerical office and would remain normative for the following centuries. There was, however, no strict prescription for canonical age in general. Inscriptions and other sources offer us a wide variety of situations. The norms cited here from several councils were not widely known, or even scrupulously observed.

LEGAL CONDITIONS FOR JOINING THE CLERGY

Earlier it was mentioned that in order to enter the clergy, legal and personal freedom was required according to Roman law. A person must be a free person (*sui iuris*), not subject to certain obligations under the law. We shall now focus further attention in particular on the slaves. Their admission to the clergy was a demonstration of equality within the Christian community because the cleric slave or priest acquired an honor (*dignitas*) and dispensed the sacraments to their masters. However, there were several serious difficulties that could not be easily overcome. The slave did not possess legal freedom, inasmuch as he was the "property" of another. He did not have the *dignitas* since he was indeed a slave and was consequently lacking in preparation. The clear division between slave and free in late antiquity was different than today. The condition of numerous people, although free, was actually worse than that of many slaves.

The practice of admitting slaves into the clergy expanded in the 4th century throughout villages and estates. There was little canonical or imperial legislation and the legislation we do know is occasional and local. The main concern of admitting slaves into the clergy was their freedom. Even a freedman found it difficult to enter the clergy after the Council of Elvira (can. 80). He needed permission to leave his obligations from his previous master (*dominus*).[205] A pagan master committed to his pagan beliefs would no doubt oppose a Christian freedman entering the clergy.

In Spain, the 10th canon of the Council of Toledo of 400 states: "Those who are slaves by legal contract or by family origin cannot be ordained clerics, unless their conduct is irreproachable and have the consent of those who have power over them." But was this rule observed? Only in the 6th century do we find other local councils in Gaul prohibiting the admission of slaves, as is the case for example in canon 8 of the Council of Orléans (411). In Rome, Pope Boniface (418-422) established that "slaves or subjects to the *curia* and the like should not become clerics."[206] In a circular letter to the Italian bishops, Leo the Great opposed the admission of slaves to orders and to the episcopate.[207] The letter gave several reasons for the prohibition: (1) The slaves did not have the *dignitas* of birth or custom; (2) They had not been able to obtain freedom from their masters; (3) The demeaning nature of being a slave (*vilitas servilis*) did not allow them to achieve the highest degree of priesthood (*fastigium sacerdotii*); (4) Those who were not approved by their master could not be approved by God; (5) Such a promotion would effectively usurp the authority of their masters. No one was allowed to be in the clergy if he was subject to the authority of any person—especially if that person had not given his consent. Pope Gelasius even intervened several times on the subject because of numerous abuses.[208]

In the West, the ordination of slaves and of *coloni* (tenant farmers), who were required not to abandon the land, was widespread. But the same was also true in the East. The *Apostolic Canons*, an appendix to the *Apostolic Constitutions*, include the following norm: "We do not permit any servants to be ordained to the clergy without the consent of their masters which might otherwise upset the masters who own them. For this would cause upheaval in the households. But if any servant should appear to be worthy to be ordained to any rank, as our own Onesimus did, and their masters are willing to permit it, and grant them their freedom and allow them to leave home, let him be so ordained."[209]

Basil and Gregory of Nazianzus tell of an episode that highlights the problem. A slave of a rich mistress, Simplicia, was made bishop. She claimed the right to her slave but was rebuked by Basil.[210] A few years later, she asked for her slave but was firmly refused by Gregory who offered to reimburse the cost.[211] We do not know the outcome of the dispute. But the practice of repaying the owner continued to apply even in later times. After the middle of the 5th century, different practices and legislation were created in the East and the West.[212]

There was no difficulty, at least theoretically, for the slaves of the church (*servi ecclesiae*). They were the property of the church. They were the heirs of the public slaves (*servi publici*). There were in fact different categories of slaves within the church: (1) Personal slaves of clerics who were their property; (2) Slaves of a single local church; and (3) Slaves of monasteries. Some people donated slaves to the monasteries to be laborers on the farms. The slaves of the church, if they were freed became the freedman (*libertus*) of the church, but their condition was not the same as it had been a few centuries before.[213] The Roman church had many slaves in Sicily who worked in the cultivation of the land. Even as recent as two centuries ago the church held slaves in America in the 1800s.

The lack of freedom also created problems for the entry of slaves into monasteries. If the owner allowed it, then it was possible. But if he did not allow it, tensions and disputes were bound to occur. Not all Christian authors offered the same solution to this issue. Sometimes fugitive slaves took refuge in the monasteries. Basil offered a solution for such a situation. The slaves must be encouraged to accept their servile condition and be sent back to their master, who would be asked to forgive them and then accept them.[214] If instead the monastery accepted them because the master was being unjust to the slaves, then the monastery would have to deal with the master directly. The position taken by Basil shows the prudence of the practice followed by the ancient legislators of monasticism.[215] This phenomenon was also linked to the refuge given to slaves in the church (*ad ecclesiam confugere*). The Theodosian Code contained three laws regulating asylum in churches.[216] The first states that certain categories of people, including slaves, who have taken refuge in churches and are ordained to the clergy, must be returned to their prior condition (*pristinae condicioni*). The same law is reported in Justinian's Code, where it speaks only of the condition for slaves of members of the curia.[217] The second law specifically concerned slaves who had fled to churches. The clerics must inform their master within one day and ask for his forgiveness. If the slave is armed, then he can be forcibly removed.[218]

Gelasius summarized the tradition and the reasons against the ordination of slaves in a circular letter issued as a decree. In that same letter, however, he was very concerned about the serious shortage of clergy and therefore the lack of spiritual assistance:

> The fact that there are slaves here and there—even those who have been slaves from birth—who flee from the rights and property of their masters under the pretext of religious life and enter into the monasteries or are indifferently admitted even with the connivance of the bishops to the ecclesiastical service—this practice must at all cost be avoided. This shame must be removed in every way so that it does not appear that the rights of others are violated, or public order is subverted in the name of Christian institutions. Above all, it is not appropriate that the very dignity of the clerical ministry be tarnished by such an impediment. The ministry should not be challenged by the status and condition of those who influence it, nor should it appear—may it never be!—a source of danger. Forbid these things with authority and with prompt prohibition: any bishop, presbyter, deacon or any of those who know how to preside over monasteries who keeps such persons close to him, believing that he should not hand them over to their masters or who might even use them in the service of the Church or of religious congregations —unless these same persons have first been freed by the will of the masters with a written document or with a legitimate transaction—no one should doubt that such clergy will incur the loss of their office and of the same communion, if some proven complaint on this matter reaches us.[219]

RITES AND SYMBOLS FOR THE TRANSMISSION OF AUTHORITY

We read in the church orders:

> Let the bishop be ordained after he has been chosen by all the people. When his name is announced and approved by all, let him, with the presbytery and such bishops as may be present, assemble with the people on a Sunday. While all give their consent, the bishops shall lay their hands upon him, and the presbytery shall stand by in silence. All indeed shall keep silent, praying in their heart for the descent of the Spirit. Then one of the bishops who are present shall, at the request of all, lay his hand on him who is ordained bishop, and shall pray as follows, saying: God and Father of our Lord Jesus Christ, Father of mercies, God of all consolation . . . And when he is made bishop, all shall offer him the kiss of peace, for he has been made worthy.[220]

But when a presbyter is ordained, the bishop shall lay his hand upon his head along with the other presbyters, and he shall speak similar to what was said above concerning the bishop, praying and saying: God and Father of our Lord Jesus Christ, look upon your servant here, and impart the spirit of grace and the wisdom of presbyters, that he may help and guide your people with a pure heart, just as you looked upon your chosen people, and commanded Moses to choose elders, whom you filled with your spirit which you gave to your attendant. . . . Now, Lord, unceasingly preserving in us the spirit of your grace, make us worthy, so that being filled we may minister to you in singleness of heart, praising you, through your Son Christ Jesus, through whom to you be glory and might, Father and Son with the Holy Spirit, in your Holy Church, now and throughout the ages of the ages. Amen.[221]

The deacon, when he is ordained, is chosen according to what was said above, with the bishop alone laying his hands upon him in the same manner. When the deacon is ordained, the bishop alone shall lay his hands upon him because the deacon is not ordained to the priesthood but to serve the bishop and to carry out the bishop's commands. He does not take part in the council of the clergy. He is to attend to his own duties and to make known to the bishop what he needs to know. He does not receive that Spirit that is possessed by the presbytery in which the presbyters share. He receives only what is entrusted to him under the bishop's authority. This is why the bishop alone shall make a deacon. But on a presbyter, however, the other presbyters shall lay their hands because of the common Spirit and similar duty. Indeed the presbyter has only the authority to receive. He has no authority to give. For this reason, a presbyter does not ordain the clergy, but at the ordination of a presbyter he seals while the bishop ordains. Over a deacon, then, he shall say as follows: O God, you who have created all things. . . .[222]

The hands are not imposed on the subdeacon, rather, he is nominated because he is at the service of the deacon.[223] "The lector is appointed in the act of the bishop handing him the book. He does not have hands laid upon him."[224]

These formulas show a full development of previous traditions concerning the investiture of those in the community who perform leadership roles. This investiture entailed an elaborate and precise rite filled with theological meaning that also included clear terminological distinctions. The investiture of bishops, priests or deacons necessarily involved the imposition of hands (or a single hand) (*cheirotonia*), while the others enter their roles via an appointment (*katastasis*) but without the imposition of hands.

The imposition of hands (Gk. *Cheirotonein – cheirotonia*), albeit with some variations, will become a technical term to indicate the installation of a candidate into an ecclesial office through consecration, accomplished by the laying on of hands and the prayer of invocation to the Holy Spirit, known as the epiclesis. Already from the third century the corresponding

Latin technical term is *ordinatio* (in English *ordination*), which in the Christian language acquires a new meaning distinct from the parallel Greek terminology. Consecration (*consecrare /consecratio*) is another term that is also used by the Latin church. When the author of the *Apostolic Tradition* discusses why only words are used in the appointment of widows, he provides the basic reason for the difference between the two rites:

> When a widow is appointed, she shall not be ordained but is chosen by name. . . . The widow shall be appointed by word alone, and then she may join the other widows. Hands shall not be laid upon her because she does not offer the oblation nor does she have a liturgical duty. Ordination is for the clergy on account of their liturgical duty, but the widow is appointed for prayer, and prayer is the duty of all. The reader is appointed by the bishop's giving him the book. He does not have hands laid upon him.[225]

The rites and prayers of the *Apostolic Tradition* had an enormous influence on the canonical-liturgical documents of the following centuries. The prayer of the ordination of the bishop has recently been taken up again both by the Catholic liturgy and by the American Episcopal Church. In the Western tradition, the laying on of hands and the prayer of ordination are considered necessary, although the practice varies according to the bishop or minister who is ordaining.

In Africa, Cyprian speaks of the imposition of hands on the schismatic Novatian but does not mention a prayer connected with the rite.[226] The contemporary anonymous author of *De aleatoribus* states in chapter 3: "For by the imposition of the hand we have received in the dwelling of the heart the episcopate, that is, the Holy Spirit." There is an identification between the episcopate and the reception of the Holy Spirit through the imposition of hands. But the same bishop, then, transmits the Holy Spirit to the newly baptized with the laying on of hands as well.[227] The rite of the impositions of the hands is common in the Christian sphere. Its meaning, whether in an ordination, in an exorcism, in a baptism, or in the reconciliation of penitents can be deduced from the context and from the prayer that accompanies it.

At the time of Augustine in Africa the laying on of hands (or of the hand) certainly took place along with an invocation of the name of God over the one being ordained. But, Augustine adds: "Nevertheless their admission is accompanied by variations such as seem convenient to the peace and the usefulness of the Church."[228] Elsewhere he also notes: "The invocation of the name of God on their heads when they are ordained bishops is the work of God, not of Donatus."[229] In one of his letters he also speaks of the laying on of hands to ordain a presbyter: "I, on the other hand, did not know how to decide whether to lay hands on that individual for ordination."[230]

The *Ancient Statutes of the Church*, composed in Gaul in the fifth century, present the rite of episcopal ordination as follows: "When a bishop is ordained, let two bishops place and hold a book of the Gospels (*evangeliorum codex*) on the nape of his neck. With one bishop pouring out the blessing (*fundente benedictionem*) above him, let all the remaining bishops who are present touch his head with their hands."[231] For the other ordinations they prescribe the following rite:

> When a priest is ordained, a bishop shall hold his hand above the head [of the one being ordained] and offer a blessing, while the priests who are present shall hold their hands close to the hand of the bishop above the head of the one [who is being ordained]. When a deacon is ordained, a single bishop shall bless him and place his hand above his head, since he is not being consecrated into the priesthood (*sacerdotio*) but into a ministry (*ministerium*).[232]

The Statutes then present the rites of the other ordinations, which take place without the imposition of hands: the subdeacon receives from the bishop an empty paten and an empty chalice; an acolyte, instructed by the bishop, receives from the archdeacon a candle holder with a candle; an exorcist receives from the bishop the book of exorcisms; the lector receives the book of biblical readings.

The rite is different in the East since John Chrysostom considers the imposition of hands as essential to ordination.[233] According to Basil it is a rite that confers the Spirit and the reception of a special power.[234] The Book of the Gospels (*evangeliarium*) is also handed to the one being ordained as a symbol of authority and commitment in the preaching of the Gospel.[235] For Jerome the ordination of a bishop consists only in the rite of having a simple priest sit on the episcopal chair.[236]

The origin of these rites and their Jewish or pagan background are discussed by contemporary scholars. It is commonly thought, following Lohse,[237] that Christian ordination was structured on the model of Jewish ordination (*semikhah*), while receiving a new meaning in the early church. But this opinion of the scholarly community (*opinio communis*) was challenged by the American rabbi L. Hoffman.[238] He holds that the dependence of Christian ordination on rabbinic ordination has not yet been proven. In fact, no Palestinian tannaitic text, that is, before 200 CE proves that there was an imposition of hands in Jewish ordination. Rather, it seems that the rabbi acted in his functions only by means of the word. In Babylonian Judaism there is no rite of s*emikhah*, and yet he receives the title of *rav* (rabbi) with authority to issue legal and religious decisions. Rabbis are established as doctors and jurists, but not as presidents of the community. Moreover, Christ instituted the apostles by word alone, while the apostles instituted the seven deacons by the laying on of hands and by prayer (*Acts* 6:6). The same happens with Paul and Barnabas in Antioch (*Acts* 13:3), but we do not know much about the importance of these gestures as far as their role in granting a mandate. The rite of laying on hands is specified only in the pastoral epistles (*1 Tim* 4:14; *2 Tim* 1:6, etc.)

The person, thus invested with authority, receives a charism, that is, a power to fruitfully exercise his ministry. He is symbolically given a mandate during a liturgical assembly to equip him for the ministry of speech and leadership of the community by persons who already exercise that mandate. The imposition of hands,[239] which we have seen so frequently in antiquity, has a multi-purpose function as well as having a pagan and Jewish prehistory. It already had different meanings and took place in different contexts in the Old Testament. Also, in the New Testament it was used as a gesture of blessing (*Mk* 10:16) or healing, for example, with Jesus (*Mk* 6:5; *Lk* 4:40) or the disciples (*Mk* 16:18; *Acts* 28:5). It also served to confer a ministry as was the case with the seven deacons of *Acts* 6:1-6, as well as in the two *Letters to Timothy* referred to above (*1 Tim* 4:14; *2 Tim* 1:6).

Epiclesis is the literary genre of the prayers of ordination. It includes an invocation addressed to God to send the Holy Spirit to the person to be ordained so that this person, strengthened by the gift of the Spirit, may fulfill his duties. In this way the bishop and the priest receive the ministry (service) of the sacraments, of the word and more generally of being pastors of the community. According to Augustine, the priest is the minister of word and sacrament (*minister verbi et sacramenti*).[240] During the performance of his office, the minister constantly remains under the influence of the Spirit to guide the community by allowing himself to be guided by that same Spirit. It is the Spirit, given in ordination, who establishes the authority of the minister in the community and gives power to carry out his duties.

In the *Apostolic Tradition* those known as confessors since they confessed the faith during persecution were frequently promoted to the ecclesiastical offices without receiving the ordination that conferred the Spirit because, according to the ancient conception, they had suffered for the faith and so they already possessed the Spirit. But this exception is not valid for the episcopate, which seems to result from a compromise between the conferral of the divine charism and the rite of institution. This disappears soon, though. The rites described in the *Apostolic Tradition* will substantially remain in all later canonical-liturgical documents. Later documents will only add clarifications and embellishments of other elements of the rite. In the West the distinction the *Apostolic Tradition* makes relating to the rite of the imposition of hands that is reserved for the making of a bishop, a presbyter and a deacon, is still maintained. In the East the rite is extended to the subdeacon, the lector and the deaconess. Indeed in the church of Antioch it also is extended to other offices.[241]

In the fourth century, when a bishop was ordained, the imposition of the book of the Gospels on his shoulders was added as part of the rite. In the fifth century we see the addition of the use of the crozier, i.e., the shepherd's staff. Later in the Frankish period, symbols and objects were multiplied with anointings, the bestowal of the pectoral cross and ring as well as the miter. Each of these elements has its own meaning. Sociologically, the rite of assuming an office is enriched with new elements and the obligations of the office. Theologically, each symbol becomes an expression of a different aspect of the pastoral office.

There are also rites for the creation of minor orders such as lector, exorcist, doorkeeper, among others,[242] for some of which there is little information for the first few centuries. From the first documents in our possession, such as the fifth century *Ancient Statutes of the Church*, the rite consists of an admonition, the handing over of one's own instruments, symbols of the office, and a blessing.[243] The third century *Apostolic Tradition* already notes at that time that, "The lector is appointed when the bishop gives the book to him. He does not need hands laid upon him."[244] According to the *Statutes*, the subdeacon receives the chalice and the paten, the acolyte the candelabrum, the doorkeeper a key, etc.

Ordination of the bishop must always take place on Sundays during a Eucharistic assembly,[245] while that of priests and deacons takes place in Rome on the Saturday evening of the ember (fasting) days.[246] When a bishop is ordained, bishops of the same province must be present according to canon 5 of the Council of Nicaea. Their presence is a sign of approval and demonstrates the communion in the faith of the whole church, not only with those of the immediate area, but with the churches scattered throughout the world.

Relative ordinations were prohibited. The term refers to ordinations made in such a way that the ordained person was not bound to a ministerial office assigned to a particular community or place. In other words, one cannot be ordained a bishop or priest to the church at large, but must be united to a particular diocese as one who is *incardinatus*, i.e., attached to a local church. Canon 6 of the Council of Chalcedon of 451 also prohibited the transfer of a bishop to another episcopal see. The provision stems from the fact that many bishops did not remain tied to the place for which they were ordained, aspiring to go to a more prestigious episcopal see. The conception of the nature of ordination as being ordained into a ministry which is meant to be in service to the community rather than for personal honor is virtually lost. In the fifth century there were many roaming clergy (*clerici vagantes*) or *vagi*, a term that in the Middle Ages will have another meaning. It is also plausible that Chalcedon's canon 6 was issued to regulate monastic orders.[247] There are cases of priestly ordinations made to confer honor on the ordained.[248] The legislation established that the cleric was ordained for a service to be rendered in one place, whether it be a monastery, martyrium or a church. In the western language *titulus* becomes synonymous with a church whose founding member was ordained there (*titulus paupertatis, incardinatio*, etc.). In addition, there is also concern especially in subsequent centuries that the cleric also has the means to support himself, and so the term *titulus* evolves to indicate the means of support (*titulus beneficii, titulus patrimonii*).

The provision that a minister be connected to a parish is not entirely new and also comes into effect in the West. Previously, we know of various exceptions, such as Paulinus of Nola, who writes: "I was taken suddenly and with great strength by the multitude . . . and I was ordained a priest. This happened out of my reluctance."[249] Jerome and others were ordained without a strict connection to a church. Subsequently, the practice of ordaining someone to the church at large is mainly found in Ireland.

Women in the ancient Christian tradition were always excluded from the office of bishop and presbyter. Nevertheless, according to Epiphanius, there were ordinations of women that took place among the heretical groups of the Montanists and the Collyridians.[250] Normal practice was consistent enough that the 44th canon of the Council of Laodicea at the end of the fourth century merely recalls that women should not approach the altar.

CONCLUSION

In this chapter we have seen the development of the ministry in general with its various offices during the first five centuries of the church. It often developed in answer to the needs of the various places and times. Often there were "exceptions" to the rules of what the church established. But the church was searching for a consistent approach for how to serve its people in an ever changing environment. While not all ministers were up to the task, and many were opportunists, there was a consistent push for faithfulness to the call of the Gospel. In the chapter which follows we will examine in more detail how the church buttressed its ministry in terms of the hierarchical structure that developed out of the *cursus honorum* discussed above.

---

1. Cf. J.D.G Dunn, *Christianity in the Making:* Vol. 1 *Jesus remembered* (Grand Rapids, MI: Eerdmans, 2003).
2. Justin, *1 Apology* 66.3; *Dialogue with Trypho* 100.4.
3. See *1 Pet* 2:10; *Acts* 15:14; *Gal* 6:16; *Rom* 9:1-13; *Mt* 26:28.
4. *Rom* 9:25; *2 Cor* 6:16; *Gal* 3:29.
5. See *Gal* 4:29; *1 Cor* 10:18.
6. *Rom* 9:1-9.
7. *Gal* 6:16.
8. *1 Thess* 2:14; *2 Thess* 1 4; *1 Cor* 1:1; 10:32.
9. *Mt* 26:28.
10. Justin, *Dial* 123.7.
11. *Letters of Barnabas* 4.6; Justin, *Dial* 19.2; Augustine, *Comm. on the Psalms* 56.9.
12. *1 Cor* 1:2; 10:32; 11:6; 15:9; *2 Cor* 1:1; *Gal* 1:13; *1 Thess* 2:14; *2 Thess* 1:4.
13. Cf. *Ep.* 58: *plebi Thibari consistenti:* Yvette Duval, "La plebs chrétienne au 'siècle de Cyprien' jusqu'à la paix de l'Église," *Rev. Ét. Augustiniennes* 47 (2002): 251-82; 48 (2002), 23-78; Yvette Duval, *Les chrétiens d'Occident et leur évêque au IIIe siècle. Plebs in ecclesia constituta (Cyprien, Ep. 63)* (Paris: Institut d'études augustiniennes, 2005); (see the remarks of P. Mattei, *Revue d'Histoire Ecclésiastique* 102 (2007): 972-81).
14. Cyprian, *Ep* 52.2.3; 58.1.1.
15. Cyprian, *Ep* 66.8.1; 69.14.2.
16. Lactantius, *Inst.* 4.26.21.

17. V. Loi, "Populus Dei-plebs Dei. Studio storico-linguistico sulle denominazioni del "Popolo di Dio" nel latino paleo-cristiano," *Salesianum* 27 (1965): 604-28.
18. *Cyprianus presbyteris et diaconibus, item plebi universae* (Cyprian, *Epp.* 38; 39; 40).
19. *deseruerunt plebes suas*: *Ep.* 228.5 and passim.
20. Bauer, Arndt, Gingrich, Danker, 2nd ed. *A Greek-English Lexicon of the New Testament and Other Early Christian Literature* (Chicago: Univ. of Chicago Press, 1979), 435.
21. See *Acts* 1:17; 8:21; 26:18; *Col* 1:12.
22. Clement Al., *Quis dives* 42; Origen, *Hom.* 11.3 *in Jer*; *Exp. in Prov.* 26:7; Tertullian, *De exhort. cast.* 7.
23. Cyprian, *Ep.* 45.2; *De unit.* etc., 17; Anonymous, *De rebat.* 12; *De sing. clericorum*; Ambrose, *Ep.* 18.14; *Apostolic Const.* 6.17. 3; Council of Ancyra of 314, can. 3.
24. Jerome, *Ep.* 60.10.
25. CTh 16.2.2.
26. *clerici omnes qui in ecclesiastici ministerii gradibus ordinati sunt*, (Isidore, *Ecc. off.* 2.1). The elaboration of the doctrine that took place in the first centuries is effectively summarized by the Catechism of the Catholic Church: "Integration into one of these bodies in the Church was accomplished by a rite called *ordinatio*, a religious and liturgical act which was a consecration, a blessing or a sacrament. Today the word "ordination" is reserved for the sacramental act which integrates a man into the order of bishops, presbyters, or deacons, and goes beyond a simple election, designation, delegation, or institution by the community, for it confers a gift of the Holy Spirit that permits the exercise of a "sacred power" (sacra potestas) which can come only from Christ himself through his Church. Ordination is also called *consecratio*, for it is a setting apart and an investiture by Christ himself for his Church. The laying on of hands by the bishop, with the consecratory prayer, constitutes the visible sign of this ordination" (Canon 1538).
27. Augustine, *Enarr. in Ps.* 67.19.
28. Y.M.-J. Congar, *Jalons pour une théologie du laïcat* (Paris: Éditions du Cerf, 1954), 24-25.
29. The Catechism of the Catholic Church summarizes the evolution and meaning of the term: "The word order in Roman antiquity designated an established civil body, especially a governing body. *Ordinatio* means incorporation into an *ordo*. In the Church there are established bodies which Tradition, not without a basis in Sacred Scripture, has since ancient times called *taxeis* (Greek) or *ordines*. And so, the liturgy speaks of the *ordo episcoporum*, the *ordo presbyterorum*, the *ordo diaconorum*. Other groups also receive this name of *ordo*: catechumens, virgins, spouses, widow" (Canon 1537).
30. *Post transacta sollemnia dimissa plebe* (Tertullian, *De anima* 9).
31. Tertullian, *Exhortation to Chastity* 7.3.
32. Cyprian, *Epp.* 45.2; 14.4; 58.1; 67.5.
33. Cyprian, *Ep.* 63.14.4.
34. *quis hoc unquam presbytero suo coram plebe imperavit episcopus? Ep.* 2.5. Civil law, enshrined in the Theodosian Code, also speaks of the *ordo ecclesiasticus* (CTh 16.5.26).
35. *ordo episcoporum, ordo presbyterii, ordo viduarum, ordo virginum*, etc.
36. Augustine, *Ep.* 82.4.32.
37. Cf. Augustine, *De civ. Dei* 20.9.2; *sermons* 46 and 47.
38. Augustine, *Ep.* 21.3.
39. Augustine, *Sermon* 304.1.1.
40. Augustine, *De moribus* 1.32.69.
41. Augustine, *Ep.* 23.3.
42. Leo the Great, *Ep.* 12.4.
43. Cf. Gregory of Nyssa, *Oratio* 18.33 (PG 35:1027); *Oratio* 43.25 (PG 36:531).
44. Council of Rome, 465, can.3, *Brev Hipp*, can 3; council of Seleucia -Ctesiphon of 410, can.26, Mansi 7, 1181, *Statuta ecclesiae antiqua*, etc., prologue; Jerome, *Comm. on Haggai* 2.11, Augustine, *Ep.* 202A, 3.7; *Novellae* 6.4 and 123.12.
45. Augustine, *Ep* 20, Divjak 4; cf *Ep.* 209.
46. *In ecclesia istae (episcopus et presbyter) sunt dignitates*. (*Tract. in ps.* 14.4. Homily 5 in modern translations).
47. Leo the Great, *Ep.* 6.6 (PL 54:620A); 12.4 (PL 54:649ff).
48. Ambrose, *De officiis* 1.82.
49. Celestine, *Ep.* 4.2.

50. G. Marconi, "La sostanza dell'effimero. L'abbigliamento dei chierici nell'Italia teodericiana," in *Pensando tra gli oggetti. Dai Greci ai giorni nostri*, ed. by G. Falaschi (Perugia: Morlacchi, 2012), 77-90.
51. Thus, expresses Paul or one of his disciples, *Eph* 2:2, "In him the whole building is joined together and grows into a holy temple in the Lord."
52. Ignatius, *To the Magnesians* 7.2.
53. Justin, *1 Apology* 65-67.
54. Justin, *Dialogue* 41.1-3; 117.14.
55. Irenaeus, *Advers. haer.* 5.34.3.
56. *Didache* 14; Justin, *Dial* 41; Irenaeus, *Adv. haer.* 4.17.5.
57. M. Bévenot, "'*Sacrdos*' As Understood by Cyprian," *JTS* 30 (1975): 413-428, see esp. 415ff.
58. Irenaeus, *Adv. haer.* 4.18.5; L.M.R. Tillard, "La 'qualité sacerdotale du ministre chrétien," *Nouvelle Revue Théol.* 95 (1973): 481-514.
59. Y.M.J. Congar, *Jalons pour une théologie di laïcat*, 170ss.
60. Augustine, *De civ. Dei* 20.10; Prosper of Aquitaine, *In Ps.* 131.16: PL 51:38.
61. P. Mattei, "Habere ius sacerdotis. Sacerdoce et laïcat au témoignage de Tertullien De Exhortatione Castitatis et De Monogamia," *RevSR* 59 (1985): 200-221.
62. *sacerdotalia munera* = priestly gifts.
63. Tertullian, *De praesc.* 41.8. Cf. P. Mattei, 219-21.
64. Tertullian, *De pudic.* 20.10.
65. Tertullian, *Apol.* 17.5.
66. *praesident probati seniors;* Tertullian, *Apol* 39.
67. *summus sacerdos, si qui est episcopus.*
68. Tertullian, *On Baptism* 17.1-2.
69. Tertullian, *De Fuga* 11.1-3.
70. Tertullian also uses the term *episcopatus*.
71. Tertullian, *De corona* 3.3.
72. Tertullian, *De praescrip.* 43.3.
73. Tertullian, *De praescrip.* 41.6-8.
74. Cyprian, *Ep.* 61.3.1.
75. *Apostolic Tradition* 3.
76. Origen, *De oratione* 29.9-10.
77. Origen, *Homily 11 in Exodum* 6 (PG 12:380-81D).
78. *hiereus = sacerdos; archiereus = summus sacerdos.*
79. D. Spataru, *Sacerdoti e diaconesse: La gerarchia ecclesiastica secondo i Padri Cappadoci* (Bologna: ESD, 2007), 91ff.
80. Ambrose, *De officiis* 2.69.
81. Jerome, *Ep.* 82.11.
82. Jerome, *Ep* 60.
83. Jerome, *Ep.* 123.5.
84. Siricius, *Ep.* 1.7; 1.8; 1.12.
85. Innocent, *Ep.* 17, intr. Di Berardino A. (ed.), *I concili della chiesa antica*, vol. II, *Decretali pontificie e canoni di Serdica*, 144.
86. Innocent, *Ep.* 17.1-2.
87. Innocent I, *Ep.* 17.3.
88. Mansi 2.625.
89. This limit is also found among other fathers: John Chrysostom: *In Ep. Philip hom.* 1.1 (PG 62:183); Jerome, *Ep.* 146.1 (CSEL 56:308); *Ep.* 69.3 (CSEL 55:683).
90. Cf. *De septem ordinibus Ecclesiae* (PL 30:155-57).
91. John the Deacon, *Ep. ad Senarium* (PL 59:403); cf. Ambrosiaster, *In 2 Tim* 3.10 (PL 17:406).
92. Augustine, *De civ. Dei* 20.10.
93. *episcopus, presbyter, diaconus.*
94. Augustine, *Ep.* 73; 173A.
95. Augustine, *Ep.* 142.
96. Siricius, *Ep.* 1.15.19 (PL 13:1145).

97. Augustine, *Retract.* 2.1.
98. Optatus of Milev, *De schismate* 1,13; Innocent, *Ep.* 25, in some manuscripts there is *sacerdotes secundi ordinis*: Sidonius Apollinaris, in the epitaph for the priest Claudianus Mamertus, writes: *Antites ordine in secundo* (*Carmina* 4.11); in the Roman prefaces for the ordination. In an inscription for the archbishop Adeodatus of Nola it is said that: "*sedet in sacerdotali ordine ann(os) L*" (Diehl, 1123, line 9) and *sacerdos*.
99. Cf. *Dictionnaire Antiquités Grecques et Romaines* 4.1:576-78.
100. Tertullian, *De pudicitia* 1.6.
101. Pontius, *Vita Cypriani* 9.5 and 11.8.
102. PL 8:761 and 762.
103. PL 13:81-82, 577, 1141, 1147, 1208, 1210, 1211; PL 16:579; PL 21:602.
104. CTh 16.1.2 of February 27.
105. CTh 16.1.3 of 381; 16.5.13 of 384.
106. PL 13:101.
107. PL 20:633D.
108. *pontifex et episcopus, quem oportet esse sine crimine* (PL 22:611).
109. PL 22:553, 594, 663, 665, etc.
110. PL 22:530C, 535, 536, 664, 743, 791, 882, 904.
111. PL 23:667.
112. PL 23:179 (see PL 13:1215); PL 22:663.
113. PL 23:406D.
114. PL 23:488D.
115. PL 20:782, 783.
116. PL 33:126.
117. PL 21:13.
118. Cassian, *Institutiones* 2.5.1.
119. Fulgentius, *De veritate Praed* 2.31.
120. PL 45:1145.
121. PL 33:253, 263, 286.
122. PL 51:919-20; 53:289; 58:576, 612; 67:311.
123. Diehl, 990; 1761b; 1838; 1770; see Vol. III:388-89.
124. Diehl, 1077; 1079.
125. *Pontifices vocantur pastores gregis, ita et patres plebis pro cura et patria solicitudine* (PL 40:1312, a sermon attributed to Augustine).
126. PL 54:154.
127. PL 20:644; 50:773; 52:964; 58:576; 67:263; 101:1203.
128. *Passio Perpetuae* 13; in Cyprian, *Epp.* 102; 103; 105, etc.; Augustine, *Ep.* 31.8 (for Ambrose); Jerome, *Epp.* 81; 102; 103; 105, etc. Cf DACL 13,1097-1111 (also in epigraphy); the bishops of the Council of Arles refer to Sylvester with the title of "Papa" (Munier, SC 241:40).
129. *sacerdotes secundi ordinis*.
130. See Cyprian, *Ep.* 48.1.
131. Laodicea, can. 24.
132. Ambrosiaster, *Opus imperf. in Matt.* (PL 56:884).
133. *Sit amoris officium, pascere dominicum gregem*; Augustine, *In Iohan. Tract.* 123.5.
134. Augustine, *In Ioh. tr.* 123.5.
135. Augustine, *Ep.* 43.1.1.
136. Augustine, *Contra Cresconium* 2.11.13.
137. *Didache* 8.11.
138. Polycarp, *To the Philippians* 5.
139. E. Cattaneo, "L'origine apostolica dell'episcopé nella Lettera di Clemente ai Corinzi (1Clem 40-44)," *Rassegna di Teologia* 53 (2010): 357-78. Some authors anticipate the letter to be over twenty years earlier, even before the 70s, cf. E. Cattaneo, "I 'vota' della Chiesa romana per l'adventus di Vespasiano nel 69 A.C (*1 Clem* 60.4-61,3)," *Rassegna di Teologia* 52 (2011): 533-53.
140. *1 Clement* 47.3.

141. *1 Clement* 42.4.
142. *1 Clement* 44.4.
143. Justin, *I Apology* 67.3-5.
144. Cyprian, *Ep*. 58. 4.1; cf. Irenaeus, *Adv. haer*. 3.3.1.
145. *Apostolic Tradition* 3.
146. *de Dei et Christi eius iudicio;* Cyprian, *Ep*. 55.8.4.
147. Augustine, *Sermon* 355.6.
148. Paulinus of Nola, *Ep*. 1.10.
149. Palladius, *Historia Lausiaca* 11.
150. Cf. Cassian, *Institutes* 11.4 and 8; J.H. Dalmais, "Sacerdoce et monachisme dans l'Orient chrétien," *La vie spirituelle* 80 (1949): 37-49.
151. *Apostolic Tradition* 2.
152. Cyprian, *Ep*. 67.5.1.
153. Cyprian, *Ep*. 55.8.4.
154. Cyprian, *Ep*. 55.8.1.
155. Cyprian, *Ep*. 48.4.2: *Dominus sui sacerdotes sibi in ecclesia sua eligere et constituere dignatur, electos quoque et constitutos sua voluntate atque opitulatione tueatur.*
156. Cyprian, *Ep*. 59.5; cf. *Ep*. 3.3.2; 66.5.1; 49.2.4 of Cornelius to Cyprian. *Non aliunde haereses obortae sunt, aut nata schismata, quam inde quod sacerdoti Dei non obtemperatur, unus in ecclesia ad tempus sacerdos et ad tempus iudex vice Christi cogitatur.*
157. Cyprian, *Ep*. 67.4.2: *sit ordinatio iusta et legittima quae omnium suffragio et sudicio fuerit examinatua.*
158. Cyprian, *Ep*. 38.
159. Origen, *Contra Celsum* 8.75.
160. Cf. Jerome, *Comm. in Thess*. 3.3.
161. Jerome, *Adversus Iovinianum* 1.34.
162. Jerome, *Ascension of Isaiah* 3:23-27; Augustine, see *Sermon* 255.6; *Ep*. 21.1.
163. Augustine, *Ep*. 69.2.
164. Pelagius, *Com. in ep. ad Galatas* 1.1.
165. Cassiodorus, *Variae* 9.15.
166. *pecunia, gratia,* or *favor popularis;* Damasus, *Ad Gallos* 5.13. Cf. Jerome: *Ep* 69.9: *favorem populi. pretio redimere*; Pelagius, *Comm in ep ad Galatas* 1.1.
167. MGH AA 12:403.
168. MGH AA 12: 426-37; 438-55.
169. Augustine, *Ep*. 22.5 Divjak; *Ep*. 213.1.
170. Augustine, *Ep*. 213.2.
171. *Episcopal Election in Late Antiquity*, ed. by Johan Leemans et al. (Berlin: De Gruyter, 2011). Many scholars have collaborated on this precious volume, which shows the variety of the elections with essays on different cases.
172. P. Norton, *Episcopal Election 250-600: Hierarchy and Popular Will in Late Antiquity* (Oxford: Oxford University Press, 2007), ch. 2.
173. R. MacMullen, *Changes in the Roman Empire: Essays in the Ordinary* (Princeton: Princeton University Press, 1990), 205-76; P. Brown, *Power and Persuasion in Late Antiquity: Towards a Christian Empire* (Madison, WI: Univ. of Wisconsin Press, 1992), 85-95.
174. *Episcopal Election in Late Antiquity*, 12-13.
175. Siricius, *Ep*. 1.13; Zosimus, *Ep*. 9.5.
176. *Statuta ecclesiae antiqua*, prologue.
177. *Canons of Athanasius,* can. 4; cf. 5 and 9.
178. *Code of Justinian* 1.3.41.
179. Cyprian, *Ep*. 38.1. Cf. *Breviarium Hipponense* 20; *Statuta ecclesiae antiqua* can. 10; *Apostolic Constitutions* 8.16. 4.
180. Origen, *In Matthaeum* 16.21-22.
181. *Didascalia* 2.34.
182. Augustine, *Ep*. 126.3.
183. CTh 16.3.11.
184. Valentinian, *Novella* 20.

185. A.H.M. Jones, *The Later Roman Empire,* Vol. 2 (Baltimore: Johns Hopkins Univ. Press, 1964), 921.
186. Code of Theodosius 16.2.6: cf. 16.2.3. A. Di Berardino, "The Poor Should be Supported by the Churches (Constantine, Codex Theodosianus 16.2.6)," in *Prayer and Spirituality*, vol. 5 (Strathfield: St. Pauls Publications, 2009), 249-68. See below for more details.
187. Augustine, *Ep.* 22.1 Divjak.
188. Innocent, *Ep.* 3.
189. Gregory of Nazianzus, *Or.* 18.33 (PG 36:1027); *Or.* 43.25 (PG 36:531).
190. Monumenta Asiae Minoris Antiqua 1,207; S. Destephen, "L'émergence de l'Église dans les inscriptions d'Orient," *Acta XVI Congressus internationalis archeologiae Christianae* (Vatican City: Pontificio Istituto di archeologia Cristiana, 2016), vol. 2:1250; S. Destephen, *Prosopographie du diocèse d'Asie (325-641)* (Paris: Association des amis du centre d'histoire et civilisation de Byzance, 2008), 404. Another inscription of a woman "from a family of priests", Destephen, *L'émergence de l'Église*, 1250.
191. Destephen, *L'émergence de l'Église*, 1252-53.
192. G. Kiourtzian, *Recueil des inscriptions grecques chrétiennes des Cyclades* (Paris: De Boccard, 2000), 87-88; Destephen, *L'émergence de l'Église*, 1249-50.
193. Monumenta Asiae Minoris Antiqua 7.113. S. Destephen, *Prosopographie*, 93.
194. Gregory of Nazianzus, Or. 18.39.
195. *scripturarum tractator et doctor*; Augustine, *On Christian Doctrine* 4.6.
196. Council of Rome of 465, can. 3.
197. Jerome, *Comm. on Haggai* 2.11.
198. Cf. Leo the Great, *Ep.* 6.6 (PL 54:620A); 12.4 (PL 54:649ff).
199. Leo the Great, *Ep.* 12.4.
200. Augustine, *Ep.* 202.3, 7.
201. Mansi 7:1181: can. 26.
202. *Breviarum Hipponense,* can. 2.
203. *Ecclesiae antiqua Statuta,* prologue.
204. Justinian, *Novellae Constitutiones* 6.4 and 123.12.
205. Modestinus, *Digestum* 25.3.6.1. Cf. CTh 4.10.1 of 326, which is in Justinian Code CI 6.7.2. The freedman can be forced back to the condition of a slave.
206. *Liber Pontificalis,* ed. Duchesne, 227, *nec seruum clericum fieri, nec obnoxium curiae vel cuiuslibet rei.*
207. Leo, *Ep.* 4.1.
208. Gelasius, *Ep.* 14.2. J. Gaudemet, *L'Église dans l'Empire romain (IVe-Ve siècles* (Paris: Sirey, 1958), 138-39.
209. *Apostolic Constitutions,* canon 82.
210. Basil, *Ep.* 115.
211. Gregory of Nazianzus, *Ep.* 79.
212. A. D. Manfredini, "Sugli schiavi ordinati 'invito domino,'" *Atti Acc. Rom. Costantiniana* 10 (1995): 529-40.
213. M. Melluso, *La schiavitù nell'età giustinianea. Disciplina giuridica e rilevanza sociale* ([Besançon]: Presse Universitaire, Franc-Contoises, 2000), 264-67.
214. Basil, *Regulae fusius* 11 (PG 31:948).
215. G. Barone Adesi, *Monachesimo ortodosso e diritto romano nel Tardo Antico* (Milan: Giuffrè, 1990), 297-306.
216. CTh 9.45.3 of 398; 9.45.4 and 5 of 431.
217. *Codex Iustinianum* 1.3.12.
218. G. Barone Adesi, "'Servi fuggitivi in ecclesia'. Indirizzi cristiani e legislazione imperiale," *Atti Acc. Romanistica Cost.* 8 (1990): 695-741; M. Melluso, "'Servi fugitivi in ecclesia' in età giustinianea: le 'bullae Sanctae Sophiae,'" *Labeo* 48 (2002): 339-69.
219. Di Berardino A. (ed.), *I concili della chiesa antica*, II,1 *Decretali, concili romani e canoni di Serdica.*
220. *Apostolic Tradition* 2-4. *The Apostolic Tradition of Hippolytus,* trans. by Burton Scott Easton (Cambridge: Cambridge University Press, 1934).
221. *Apostolic Tradition* 7.
222. *Apostolic Tradition* 11.
223. *Apostolic Tradition* 13.
224. *Apostolic Tradition* 11.
225. *Apostolic Tradition* 10-11.

226. Cyprian, *Ep.* 67.5.2.
227. Tertullian, *De bapt.* 8; *De resurrect. carnis* 8; Cyprian, *Ep.* 73.9.2.
228. Augustine, *Contra. Crescon.* 2.11.13.
229. Augustine, *Sermo ad plebem Caes.* 2.
230. Augustine, *Ep.* 78.3.
231. *Statuta ecclesiae antiqua,* can. 90.
232. *Statuta ecclesiae antiqua,* canons 91-92.
233. Chrysostom, *In Tim.*3:8 *hom.* 2 (PG 62:553).
234. Basil, *Ep.* 188.
235. Cf. PG 56:397, by Severian of Gabala; Palladius, *Vita Chr.*, 14 (PG 43:43).
236. Jerome, *Ep.* 146 (PL 22:1194; CSEL 56:316).
237. E. Lohse, *Die Ordination in Spätjudentum und im Neuen Testament* (Gottingen: Vandenhoed & Ruprecht, 1951).
238. L.A. Hoffman, "L'ordination juive à la veille du christianisme," *La Maison-Dieu* 138 (1979): 7-49.
239. M. Paternoster, *L'imposizione delle mani nella Chiesa primitiva. Rassegna delle testimonianze bibliche, patristiche e liturgiche, fino al sec.* (Rome: Edizioni Liturgiche, 1977) (21983); G. Cavalli, *L'imposizione delle mani nella tradizione della chiesa latina: un rito che qualifica il sacramento* (Rome: Pontificium Athenaeum Antonianum, 1999); NDPAC 2:2546-47.
240. Augustine, *Ep.* 21.4; 228.2; 261.2. Cf. E. Lamirande, "Le rôle du ministre de la Parole et des sacrements," *Bibliothèque augustinienne: Oeuvres de saint Augustin* 32 (1965): 745-46.
241. *Apostolic Constitutions* also includes the confessors, cf. 7.23. 1-3.
242. Their functions will be discussed more fully later.
243. *Statuta ecclesiae antiqua,* canons 93-97.
244. *Apostolic Tradition* 11.
245. Leo the Great, *Ep.* 10.6.
246. Gelasius, *Ep.* 15.3. Ember days were days of fasting and prayer that were established in the four seasons of the liturgical year (Pentecost, per annum - in September - in December and Lent), which were called *Quatuor tempora* and date back to the time of Pope Siricius (384-399).
247. P. Canivet, *Le monachisme syrien selon Théodoret* (Paris: Beauchesne, 1977), 233.
248. Peter L'Huillier, *The Church of the Ancient Councils: The Disciplinary Work of the First Four Ecumenical Councils* (Crestwood: St. Vladimir's Seminary Press, 1996), 224-25.
249. Paulinus of Nola, *Ep.* 1.10.
250. A sect widespread in Arabia and elsewhere, whose members pay Mary excessive worship; one of their rituals is on certain days to put some bread on a cloth, which they then offer to Mary. In the end, they all feed together. Epiphanius, *Panarion* 78.1.1.

CHAPTER 5
MINISTERIAL HIERARCHY OF THE EARLY CHURCH

MAJOR ORDERS

THE BISHOP

THE TERM *HIERARCHY*, WHICH LITERALLY MEANS "SACRED AUTHORITY," IS A TERM THAT dates to the 6th century and is used by Pseudo-Dionysius the Areopagite. Among its various meanings, it primarily refers to the Christian ministry aimed at the consecration of men to God and their sanctifying work in building up the church of God. The Christian ministry is therefore defined in relation to its purpose, the economy of salvation, that is, God acting on our behalf in the sense that, in order to realize his saving plan God uses human beings who are "ministers of Christ and stewards (*oikonomoi*) of the mysteries of God" (*1 Cor* 4:1). Among these ministers, the bishop serves in a critical role as the "steward of God" (*theou oikonomos; Tit* 1:7). Instead of rulers, the ministers are to be simple servants and dispensers of the mysteries of God through their words and actions. As such, their virtue par excellence is faithfulness. Gregory of Nazianzus refers to this divine work of salvation through God's ministers when he writes: "All of us who preside are its servants and fellow workers (*sunergoi*)."[1] Therefore, there is the divine initiative as well as human cooperation. "It is God who works through him."[2]

The term *ministry*, on the other hand, expresses the condition and function of a person who performs a service. *Minister* derives from the Latin *minus (minor; parvus)*, which means a service that is performed by servants and those of lesser status. Other terms such as *office*, *function* and *helper* are related to it. In the Christian language the term ministry is enriched with many nuances: preaching is a ministry, worship is a ministry, almsgiving is a ministry. Ministry is exercised by a minister, by someone who is inferior. Before God all are inferior and render service to him in many ways. The corresponding word in Greek for minister is *diakonia*, and the one who serves is a deacon. The first deacon in this sense is Christ.

The term *hierarchy* when applied to how Christian leadership is organized, indicates the various offices of deacon, priest and bishop. Each office has its own rules which develop from the beginning of the apostolic witness concerning the apostles, the deacons, the prophets, the teachers, the guardians, and the missionaries. There are also people who have a certain authority depending on the situation because they serve as "leaders" (*hegumens*), "pastors," "presidents," or "guardians." The source of their authority is Christ who is the "guardian of our souls" (*1 Pet* 2:25) and the first true shepherd. The authority is passed on to subsequent generations through apostolic succession, as Clement of Rome wrote towards the end of the second half of the first century:

> Our apostles knew through our Lord Jesus Christ that there would be strife over the office of the bishop. This is why, after they had received complete foreknowledge, they appointed those [ministers] already mentioned, and afterwards gave instruction that if these should fall asleep, other approved men should succeed them in their ministry. Those therefore who were appointed by them, or afterward by other eminent men, with the consent of the whole Church, and have blamelessly ministered to the flock of Christ humbly, peacefully and modestly, and have for a long time possessed a good opinion from everyone—we consider these to have been unjustly removed from the ministry.[3]

Such apostolic succession was foreshadowed in the Old Testament. Succession is an apostolic norm, even though the establishment of the office of leadership and supervision dates to the time of the apostles.

In ancient times it was constantly repeated that the Christian ministry is a service that branches out into a multiplicity of ministries and roles that are hierarchically arranged. Already in the New Testament there was a variety of ministries adapted according to places and times that reflected a spirit of creativity and suitable to various needs. First, we have the community of Jerusalem, led by the Twelve who were placed into the ministry by Jesus himself. They are also called apostles, but this name can also be applied to other people such as Paul and Barnabas. Since the community dedicated to preaching the message was composed of Palestinian Jews and those of the diaspora (Hellenists), disagreements eventually arose between the two. To address this division, a group of seven was created to serve the needy, which only centuries later will be considered the prototypes of the deacons. In *Acts* 6 it is said that these deacons were intended to serve tables. In reality they served as courageous and dynamic preachers. The demands of preaching dispersed the two groups, the Twelve and the Seven, and so the terms themselves gradually lost their original meaning.

A few years later the community of Jerusalem appears to be structured differently. James is the head of the community, assisted by elders (presbyters), similar to the council of elders in the synagogues. The elders have both doctrinal (*Acts* 15:2-29) and charitable (*Acts* 12:23-30; *James* 5:14; *Gal* 2:10) roles. The Book of *Acts* speaks of elders also in Pauline communities (*Acts* 14:21-23; 20:17-30) and as having managerial functions. Other ministries also appear, so that the New Testament church appears to us to be articulated in a variety of functions: "God has appointed in the church first apostles, second prophets, third teachers; then miracles, then gifts of healing, helping, administration, and various kinds of tongues" (*1 Cor* 12:28). "And his gifts were that some should be apostles, some prophets, some evangelists, some pastors and teachers" (*Eph* 4:11). The undisputed Pauline letters certainly do not mention the elders.[4] In addition to the ministries mentioned in the *Letter to the Corinthians*, there were also bishops and deacons: the former with the office of oversight (*episcopé*), the latter with the office of service (*diakonia*). These are the new ministries linked to the local communities coming from paganism. They were stable ministries compared to the itinerant ministries of the apostles and the prophets. The predominantly Jewish communities, on the other hand, had a structure like that in Jerusalem: a single head and a council of associate leaders. The *Third Letter of John* also portrays a model of a church with a single head. In contrast, the *Didache*, from the second half of the first century, reflects a fluctuating and evolving situation within Christian communities coming from paganism: "Appoint for yourselves, bishops and deacons worthy of the Lord, men who are meek and not lovers of money, truthful, and proven. For they also render to you the service of prophets and teachers. Therefore, do not despise them, for they are your honored ones, together with the prophets and teachers."[5]

The *Pastoral Epistles* present communities who have leaders such as Titus and Timothy. They serve as the organizers of all of church life. They are in charge of teaching and appointing presbyters/bishops (overseers). We do not know exactly whether these two titles of presbyter and bishop indicate different functions in these letters, or whether they are equivalent terms and serve as synonyms. It is a debatable point as to whether the traditional Jewish term of *presbyters* (elders) and the new Greek term of *bishop* are used to indicate the same function. They constitute the council of the local community, have authority over it, and are responsible for teaching and supervising doctrine. They are entitled to compensation. The author of the *Pastoral Epistles* insists on outlining the ministerial and moral formation of the presbyter-bishop. More or less the same qualities must be possessed by deacons. This short sketch portrays for us a variety of organization and terminology which are gradually becoming more precise, similar to the growth of a child who begins to assume the personality and bodily characteristics of an adult.

Eusebius of Caesarea writes: "And when they (the apostles) had only laid the foundations of the faith in foreign places, they appointed others as pastors, and entrusted them with the nurture of those that had recently been brought in, while they themselves went on again to other countries and nations, with the grace and the co-operation of God."[6] Eusebius demonstrates the movement from the condition of a community with itinerant ministers to that of permanent ministers who take care of a specific community. In other words, itinerant ministers are ultimately replaced by permanent ones. Clement of Rome in his day could speak of ministers who were stable and elected for life, and who could not be replaced at will. Christianity presented itself first of all as an urban phenomenon where the leadership of individual communities had a rather collegial character, but within these communities there was a great variety of situations. At different times, local authority over a community was concentrated in the hands of the bishop.

There are two kinds of sources for outlining the figure of the bishop that was being constructed between the second and third centuries. The first source of information tends to trace the ideal image of the bishop as the saintly bishop. The second source is both more varied and abundant, offering information on various bishops' deficiencies and aberrations, including among other things their greed and ambition.

During the second century we still find presbyters, teachers and prophets, but already with Ignatius of Antioch the triad bishop-presbyter-deacon appears well defined at the head of the church, even if their functions are not very clear yet. The three ministries now form forever the fundamental hierarchical structure and leadership of the church. In the course of the third and fourth centuries their functions will be clarified and delimited both theologically and legally. In the meantime, other offices of a lower level were established with specific tasks and a different legal status, so that two groups were created. The first was the superior orders of clergy (*clerici superioris ordinis*), made up of bishops, presbyters, and deacons. It is found in every church and the three orders are always mentioned in documents with the same descending or ascending order. They constitute the leadership of the church by authority and culture. Their social impact is very strong, as evidenced by the abundant imperial legislation in their regard. The second group, the inferior orders of clergy (*clerici inferioris ordinis*), vary in number, tasks, and importance according to the various provinces. They tend toward the humblest offices, even culturally, and are socially less relevant. They have quite different rights, responsibilities, and duties which will be referred to in the pages which follow. Here we limit ourselves to a brief exposition on the *clerici superioris ordinis*, the clergy who are in positions of leadership.

The episcopate, presbyterate, and deaconate are ministries usually conceived almost exclusively in terms of their liturgical component. This is a medieval conception, however. In ancient times, they embraced the whole of Christian life: teaching, worship, religious life, assistance of every kind and administration of the goods of the community. Gregory of Nyssa writes that by his ordination the minister, "is constituted tutor, president, teacher, and mystagogue of the invisible mysteries."[7] The considerable variety of terminology used to indicate the minister's various roles may be disconcerting, but it does not concern so much the unity of the ministry itself as its many functions. The economic element, for example, is not unimportant because there are widows, the poor, foreigners, and sick people to help. Therefore, the indications mentioned here, although they refer above all to bishops, also concern presbyters and deacons, even if to a lesser extent.

The figure of bishop as the chief guardian of the church is elaborated and developed slowly. When the bishop is considered as the only guardian—the office comes to be referred to as "the monarchical episcopate"—he is the sole head of the community. His power grows because he is the teacher who teaches (his symbol is the *cathedra*, a special chair), the liturgist who celebrates the liturgy and instructs the faithful with homiletical preaching, and the judge who administers justice in the community. The bishop is the head of the community in all its manifestations. Already Ignatius, at the beginning of the second century wrote:

> See that you all follow the bishop, even as Jesus Christ does the Father. And follow the presbytery as you would the apostles. Reverence the deacons as being the institution of God. Let no one do anything connected with the Church without the bishop. Let that be deemed a proper Eucharist which is [administered] either by the bishop or by one to whom he has entrusted it. Wherever the bishop shall appear, there let the multitude [of the people] also be present, even as wherever Jesus Christ is there is the Catholic Church. It is not lawful either to baptize or to celebrate a love-feast without the bishop. But whatever he shall approve of, that is also pleasing to God, so that everything that is done may be certain and valid.[8]

Each community has only one bishop who also represents it in relation to other churches or in the various synods. He decides who to admit, expel, or readmit to the community. He cannot be transferred to another place, even if we know many exceptions. According to canon 16 of the Council of Nicaea (325) he is obliged to reside in his diocese. He cannot carry out ordinations outside his diocese, nor ordain persons from other dioceses or those excommunicated by other bishops. He administers justice within the community and cares for the poor and all those in need. He must worry about all the clergy and their behavior, including the monks. The presidency he holds has the aim of building up the holy people, the community as the body of Christ. In a word, he must feed the flock entrusted to him.

Through the chain of succession, the local bishop is connected all the way back to the time of the apostles, and through ordination he is inserted into a network of relationships at the present. The metropolitan normally ordains a bishop. The ordination generates a sort of adoption between the church of the ordaining bishop and the church of the ordained bishop. The ordination transmits the Holy Spirit, who is the Spirit of authority. The ordinand is chosen by God; to oppose him is to resist God himself. Whoever is not with the bishop is not in the church. The bishop must account to God for his conduct on judgment day. Augustine continually has this concern in his mind. He is God's representative in the community. For this reason, the bishop is required to possess the virtues and abilities necessary to set an example to all and to fulfill his numerous duties. As already mentioned, legislation was becoming increasingly demanding for admission to the episcopate. He must be a "mirror" of the divine life for everyone. He governs his church until his death and cannot be deposed except in the case of serious sin, unworthiness, or heresy, and his deposition is generally carried out by a provincial council.

The first and foremost function of the bishop is preaching. This task is reserved for him in particular. He must instruct the faithful, preserve the purity of their faith, remove them from error, and correct the wandering. Even if all this is a thankless burden, he must not abandon it. It is a divine precept. Most of the Christian population did not read books. They had no other opportunity to deepen their faith except by listening to the homilies during the liturgy. The ancient Christian literature which has been preserved consists mainly of preached texts which have sometimes been reworked in preparation for publication. Sometimes the texts handed down preserve the liveliness of the living speech which was collected by stenographers (*exceptores, notarii*) during the sermons.[9] The text was recorded through a special type of symbols that were used which were then transcribed and corrected by proofreaders or by the author himself and then published. Augustine often mentions notaries, or stenographers, who used special signs: "To this class also belong shorthand characters. Those who are acquainted with them are called stenographers [*notarii*]."[10] The church has its own stenographers (*notarii ecclesiae*) which perform various functions[11]: "The stenographers of the church, as you see, are taking down what we are saying. They are taking down what you say, and my words and your shouts of approval do not fall to the ground."[12]

The second half of the fourth century and the first half of the fifth are the times of maximum flowering with Christian oratory. The great preachers improvised, which is why they needed stenographers to take notes. "Often it happened that the improvised sermon, written in shorthand at the time, was transcribed into current writing and published without revision either by the author or by others."[13] A great speaker like Augustine could easily improvise. It is estimated that he delivered about five thousand sermons. Only a small portion of them is preserved because when the stenographers recorded his sermons they did not keep them all in one place. He also explains the reason for the importance of improvisation. The preacher follows the reactions of the crowd and can use other words and images in order to be understood. He must worry that the crowd understands what he says because he cannot ask questions:

> And this must be insisted on as necessary to our being understood, not only in conversations, whether with one person or with several, but much more in the case of a speech delivered in public.... On this account the speaker ought to be especially careful to give assistance to those who cannot ask it. Now a crowd anxious for instruction generally shows by its movements if it understands what is said. And until some indication of this sort be given, the subject discussed ought to be turned over and over, and put in every shape and form and variety of expression, a thing which cannot be done by men who are repeating words prepared beforehand and committed to memory. As soon, however, as the speaker has ascertained that what he says is understood, he ought either to bring his address to a close or pass on to another point.[14]

In addition, the bishop is the center of the liturgy. He presides over the Eucharist, administers the sacraments of initiation, readmits penitents, and consecrates virgins, widows, churches, and the oil for chrism. But many of these functions later become the purview of the presbyter as the number of the faithful increases more and more in combination with the expanding structures of the local church. The expansion of Christianity into rural areas led to the creation of the *chorepiscopus*, the country bishop, in some provinces of the Empire as early as the third century. He served under the bishop of the nearby city. He was inferior in rank and could not ordain presbyters and deacons without the urban bishop's permission. Legislation in the fourth century sought to limit the number of *chorepiscopoi* along with their powers. For this reason, in the East his position became increasingly diminished to the point where he was deprived of his episcopal dignity in the eighth century. The same is true in the West, where the beginning of the institution dates to the fifth century, and its full expansion to the eighth and ninth centuries in the Frankish and Germanic countries.

The government of a religious community entrusted to a single person for its entire life is something not found in other ancient religious associations, not even in Judaism. The bishop has great authority, and greater authority generates greater temptation.[15] If the norm is a certain required behavior, then the transgressions and deficiencies of the bishop end up making news. The development of the bishop's office is well described in the prayer of ordination contained in the 3rd century *Apostolic Tradition*. It provides a synthesis of the duties of the bishops. He asks God: "Pour out upon him the power which is from you, the princely Spirit, which you gave to your beloved Son Jesus Christ, which he gave to your holy apostles, who founded the Church in every place as your sanctuary, for the glory and endless praise of your name."[16]

The *Didascalia*—of which a portion is also preserved in Latin—dedicates a special section to the treatment of bishops:

> You also then today, O bishops, are priests to your people, and the Levites who minister to the tabernacle of God, the holy Catholic Church, who stand continually before the Lord God. You then are to your people priests and prophets, princes and leaders and kings, mediators between God and his faithful and receivers of the word. You are preachers and proclaimers of that word. You are those who know the Scriptures and the utterances of God and are witnesses of his will. You bear the sins of all and are to give an answer for all. You are they who have heard how the word sternly threatens you if you neglect and do not preach God's will, who are in dire peril of destruction if you neglect your people.[17]

> For they are your high priests; but the priests and Levites now are the presbyters and deacons . . . but the Levite and high priest is the bishop. He is minister of the word and mediator. But to you he is a teacher, and your father after God, who begot you through the water. This is your chief and your leader, and he is your mighty king. He rules in the place of the Almighty. But let him be honored by you as God, for the bishop sits for you in the place of God Almighty. But the deacon stands in the place of Christ, and you should love him. And the deaconess shall be honored by you in the place of the Holy Spirit. And the presbyters shall appear to you in the likeness of the Apostles. And the orphans and widows shall be considered by you to be in the likeness of the altar."[18]

For this reason the anonymous author insists on the qualities of the bishop and on his conduct, so that he ". . . be proved when he receives the imposition of hands to sit in the office of the bishopric."[19] Concerning the duty of teaching and studying the Scriptures we read: "Know how to interpret the Law and the Second legislation well, explaining and showing what the law of believers is."[20] The bishop must also be an honest judge and he must correct sinners while at the same time being welcoming towards them.

The archbishop is a title that comes from the fourth century. It is used to designate the bishops of the great Sees of Alexandria, Antioch, Constantinople, Jerusalem and Rome—the Sees that will eventually constitute the five Patriarchates. In some cases it also applies to the metropolitans and bishops of important episcopal sees such as Ephesus, Caesarea of Palestine, Thessalonica, and Seleucia-Ctesiphon.[21] The term, however, has no legal meaning. Canon 19 of the Council of Constantinople (869) distinguishes the archbishops from the metropolitans. In the West, the term spread slowly and generally it did not indicate a precise hierarchy. Isidore of Seville divided bishops into four categories: bishops, metropolitans, archbishops and patriarchs. He calls the archbishop the chief of bishops (*princeps episcoporum*)[22] who "presides over both metropolitan and other bishops."[23] But the reality was often different. Only later did the term become synonymous with *metropolitan*. In the common language of the ancient church we use the term *archbishop* to indicate the metropolitan.

Presbyters

THE PRESBYTERS constituted the senate of the bishop known as the *presbyterium* (presbytery) which was formed on the model of the administration of Greco-Roman cities and assimilated to the apostolic college. The term presbyter occurs twelve times in the New Testament. *Presbyter* is a comparative adjective derived from *presbys* that indicates the oldest by age, a mature person by wisdom, or things or persons earlier in time. Its original meaning is that of elder, but soon in the first Christian community it becomes a technical term to indicate not age but a person with leadership responsibility who possesses wisdom and authority. In the Jewish tradition, the elders are those who have local authority. In the time of the Maccabees the elders were those who ruled in the cities and villages, especially in Jerusalem. They were the men of the Law.[24] During the Second Temple period, the Jewish communities were served by a college of presbyters known as a *gerousia*. In Jerusalem it was called the *Sanhedrin* which was composed of 70 elders and the high priest. In the diaspora the number of members of the college of the elders varies according to the size of the community. There were 70 in Alexandria, 35 in Cyrenaica, and commensurate numbers in other ancient cities.

In the first Christian community those who had authority were the "apostles and the elders (presbyters)" (Acts 15:2-6, 22-23; 16:4). In Jerusalem presbyters actively participated in the administration of the community (*Acts* 15 and 16:4) and were associated with James (*Acts* 21:18). Paul and Barnabas nominated presbyters on their first trip: "After having appointed for them elders (presbyters) in each church, and having prayed and fasted, they recommended them to the Lord, in whom they had believed" (*Acts* 14:23). In Miletus Paul "sent to Ephesus to call the presbyters of the church" (*Acts* 20:17), who were later called bishops (20:28). Presbyters were important and prominent figures in the *Pastoral Epistles* which speak of, "the laying on of hands from the college of presbyters (elders)" (*I Tim* 4:14) and hold the presidency (*I Tim* 5:17; cf. *I Pt* 5:5). They must be constituted in each city (*Tit* 1:5).

The *Pastoral Epistles* specify the qualities that the principal leaders, bishops and deacons must have (*I Tim* 3:2-12). The same qualities are required for presbyters (*Tit* 1:5-9). In *Titus* the two terms *episcopos* and *presbyteros* are both used. In the Latin translation they are merely transliterated and used interchangeably. The *Letter of James* exhorts that the presbyters of the church are to be called when someone is ill (5:14). Clement of Rome writes that the apostles appointed presbyters in every city where they had preached, "after having tested them in the

Spirit."[25] They then received the episcopate.[26] The selection process for presbyters then moved from apostolic nomination to election by the congregations.[27]

Polycarp, who presents himself as the head of the church of Smyrna, writes to the Philippians together with the presbyters and also feels it his task to appoint deacons.[28] He criticizes the presbyter Valens of Philippi who has taken advantage of his position: "I was exceedingly grieved for Valens, who previously was a presbyter among you, because he is so ignorant of the office which was given to him."[29] With Ignatius of Antioch, as mentioned previously, the distinction of a triad of leaders appears very clear: bishops, presbyters, deacons. The bishop is surrounded by his presbytery. In the Christian texts there is never mention of a *gerousia* (assembly of the elders), perhaps to put the emphasis on individual rather than collective duties. However, even in the later language of the fathers the term *presbyter* continues to have a non-technical meaning, that is, it serves to indicate an elderly and wise person. In addition, other terms are sometimes used such as shepherd or guardian. Therefore, in the oldest Christian texts the term *presbyter* has a plurality of meanings including that of an elderly man, a wise and venerable man, but the term can also be applied to an apostle or employed as a synonym for bishop. It can refer to a member of the bishop's council or to a witness to the Christian tradition. It is not easy to grasp the meaning in the individual texts because the non-technical usage persisted. Irenaeus speaks of a succession of presbyters as well as a succession of bishops for the Roman church.[30] The two terms are interchangeable; later authors realized that presbyter had actually become an outdated term.[31]

In the third century, the Latin translation of Firmilian's letter to Cyprian also uses non-technical terminology, using elders (*maiores natu*) for presbyters[32] and elders and supervisors (*seniores et praepositi*) for presbyters and bishops.[33] Later, the technical meaning becomes increasingly imposed to clarify precisely what their role is in the Christian community as distinct from that of bishop and deacon.

First, they serve as the advisers of the bishop who uses their advice in leading the community. They also serve together with him in the liturgy as they are involved in baptism, in the celebration of the Eucharist, in the reconciliation of penitents and in the ordination of other presbyters. They are recognized for their priestly character and are eventually called priests in the Middle Ages up to modern times, but they do not act on their own. They always work in close collaboration with the bishop.[34] This collegial aspect is sometimes attenuated for occasional reasons, such as the persecution and absence of the bishop. And then, because of the expansion of Christianity both in the cities and in the countryside there is also a multiplication of places of worship such as parish churches in the cities and in the countryside, as well as the construction of *martyria*.[35]

Collegiality between presbyter and bishop, however, remains a fixture both theoretically and often in practice on numerous occasions, at least into the fourth and fifth centuries.

Already in the third century presbyters could celebrate the Eucharist, baptize, and reconcile penitents with the explicit permission of the bishop. In the following centuries, these practices tend to become normalized for the presbyter in the places previously mentioned where the bishop cannot be present. However, the development is not uniform and depends on the number of bishops present in the region. In Africa or in central-southern Italy the excessive number of bishops present in each town does not provide space for the individual apostolate of presbyters. In northern Italy or in Gaul they have greater autonomy and were there to ensure the necessary religious services took place in various places.

In the East there was the figure of the itinerant presbyter, the *periodeuta*, who visited the areas where there were no permanent presbyters. He served under the bishop of the city similar to the *Chorepiscopus*. This institution dates back to the third century and is found in the eastern provinces of Asia Minor, Syria and especially in Egypt where the bishop is not easily reachable because he resides only in the capitals of the districts or is far away for other reasons, as in the case of persecution.[36] The fifty-seventh canon of the Council of Laodicea at the end of the fourth century established that for the villages and the countryside it was not necessary to consecrate a bishop. Rather, they would have someone assigned to them for only a period of time who had no fixed residence and he would take care of the Christians of more than one village, especially in dioceses with a vast territory and with Christian villages.[37] The figure of the *periodeuta* is closely linked to that of the *chorepiscopus* and so from the fourth century there is a tendency to decrease the number of *chorepiscopoi* and increase that of the *periodeuti*, while the presence of a bishop is more appropriate among nomadic populations.

The *archpresbyter* (archpriest), the oldest presbyter, already existed in the middle of the fourth century in the cathedral churches. Initially he was the senior presbyter without any specific authority. With the expansion of the *presbyterium* his function became that of head of the presbyters and he replaced the bishop when he was absent for ordinary pastoral activities, while the archdeacon was in charge of administrative and financial activities. There was only one archpriest for every episcopal church: "Each church has only one bishop, one archpriest, one archdeacon."[38] Canon 7 of the *Ancient Statutes of the Church* prescribes that the archpriest (or archdeacon) must care for widows, orphans, and pilgrims. Merovingian Gaul had a vicar archpriest in the villages[39] who served as the presbyters in charge of a parish where there is other clergy.

The preaching of the word, which was typically the responsibility of a bishop, becomes entrusted more to presbyters. The Arian heresy was begun by the preaching of a presbyter in Alexandria. According to the historian Socrates, presbyters did not initially preach in Alexandria, but began to do so at the time of Arius. He does not mention whether they preached in the presence of the bishop.[40] In the third century even some lay people preached, causing protests among the bishops.[41] Origen is one such example who preached even before being ordained a presbyter. After Theoctistus and Alexander of Jerusalem invited Origen, still a layman, to preach at Caesarea, Origen's bishop Demetrius protested. The two justified themselves, saying:

> [Demetrius] has stated in his letter that such a thing was never heard of before and that laymen have never before preached in the presence of bishops. I do not know how he can say what is plainly untrue. For whenever persons able to instruct the brothers are found, they are exhorted by the holy bishops to preach to the people. Thus, in Laranda Euelpis was urged to preach by Bishop Neon; and in Iconium, Paulinus preached at the direction of Bishop Celsus; and in Synada, Theodorus was urged by his bishop Atticus to preach—all our blessed brothers. And probably this has been done in other places unknown to us.[42]

The deacon Ephrem of Edessa criticized the successful presbyter Paulinus, his disciple, who was an educated man and a great improvisational preacher.[43] In the East in the fourth century it was already customary for presbyters to preach since the same Antiochene prayer of ordination mentions this duty. John Chrysostom also mentions it.[44] Egeria also testifies to the practice, stating that available presbyters preach first and then the bishop—making the ceremony very long.[45] In fact, many presbyters preached. Basil preached as a presbyter in Caesarea. John Chrysostom did the same in Antioch as did Atticus in Constantinople and Hesychius in Jerusalem. It seems that sometimes the success of the presbyter in preaching caused envy in the local bishop, as happened in Caesarea with Basil.[46]

Rich from his eastern experience, Jerome blamed the Western custom that presbyters do not preach in the presence of the bishops.[47] Ambrose allowed presbyters to preach, but not in his presence.[48] In Africa, Augustine was the first presbyter to preach before the bishop and then the example was followed elsewhere. Possidius writes: "[Bishop Valerius] attributed to Augustine also the faculty to preach the Gospel in his presence, in the church, and to do it very often. However, this was against the traditional use of African churches. Therefore, some bishops also began to criticize it."[49] What Possidius has written does not exclude the practice of preaching presbyters in Africa, but that they preach before the bishops. Other eastern authors also criticized the western practice, such as the two historians Socrates and Sozomen.[50]

In other western provinces, this practice was slower in being introduced. The tendency to transfer episcopal functions to the presbyter was such that in the second half of the fourth century some wanted to equate presbyters with bishops and consider the distinction only juridical. Jerome writes: "In reality, if you do not look at the office received, what else does a bishop do that cannot be done by a presbyter?"[51] At the beginning, he observes, there was no other distinction between the two offices. It was to avoid schism that only the bishop was elected to preside over the community. However, the assimilation between the two orders, even if it is supported by many fathers, was also commonly rejected with different arguments.

At the end of the fourth century, in order to raise the status of presbyters, Jerome and Ambrosiaster lowered the profile of deacons, who in some cities like Rome, had gained considerable power. More than one council prohibited deacons from celebrating the Eucharist, from giving communion to presbyters or from putting themselves ahead of the presbyters. During the liturgy in Rome, presbyters sat, deacons stood.[52]

Deacons

CHRISTIAN DEACONS ARE NOT the successors of the seven chosen in the *Acts of the Apostles*, even if later it was understood as such from the end of the second century, since the apostles had delegated to the seven some of their activities, in particular, the ministry (*diakonia*) of assistance, reserving for themselves the *diakonia* of preaching.[53] But then we see that Stephen and Philip, two of the Seven, did indeed preach. Philip behaved like an apostle who preaches, heals, and baptizes (*Acts* 8:5-40). "Philip was found at Azotus and passing on he preached the gospel to all the towns till he came to Caesarea" (*Acts* 8:40).

In general, the term deacon refers to a person who carries out an activity under the authority of another person or in the name of an authority. He acts as an agent, an executor, or a minister. The term indicates a function not a title. It is widely used in the Christian context and indicates different functions such as that of service in general (*Mt* 20:26), of service at table (*Mt* 22:13) or simply as a helper (*Col* 4:7). Paul presents himself as a servant of justice (*2 Cor* 11:15), of Christ (*2 Cor* 11:23), of God (*2 Cor* 6:4), of the Gospel (*Eph* 3:7), and of the Church (*Col* 1:25). "Christ became a *diakonos* to the circumcised to show God's truthfulness, in order to confirm the promises given to the patriarchs" (*Rom* 15:8). The earthly authorities are servants of God in righteousness (*Rom* 13:4). The term *diakonos* occurs twenty-four times in the New Testament. Paul describes himself as a "messenger (*diakonos*) of a new covenant, not of the letter but of the Spirit" (*2 Cor* 3:6). Paul also speaks of the "*diakonia* (ministry) of reconciliation" (*2 Cor* 5:18). There are also "deacons of Satan" (cf. *2 Cor* 11:15). Therefore, in the New Testament the term covers a plurality of functions or activities that are both profane and religious. The term is used in the initial greeting to the church of Philippi in the technical sense of ministers of the church who are greeted together with the bishop: "Paul and Timothy, servants of Jesus Christ, to all the saints in Jesus Christ who are in Philippi, with the bishops and deacons." The *Letter to Timothy* (*1 Tim* 3:8) indicates the characteristics and qualities of the deacon but does not indicate any aspects of their ministry. The deacon is not identical to a servant (*servus; doulos*) who is a slave without rights.

When communities organize themselves, the deacons of the New Testament texts seem to perform only service functions and do not have a specific liturgical role. With Ignatius of Antioch they come in third place on the hierarchical scale, subject to the bishop and presbyters. Not servants of food and drink but of the Church of God, they help the bishop and must be respected by the faithful. The *Apostolic Tradition* strongly emphasizes that they are not ordained to the priesthood, but to the service of the bishop with the task of carrying out his orders. In fact, they take part in the council of presbyters, but administer and inform the bishop of what needs to be done.[54] Cyprian also insists on these concepts, since deacons "are ministers of the episcopate and of the Church."[55] A text by the *Shepherd* of the Roman Hermas, around 150, is very significant when he speaks metaphorically of the deacons:

> The beasts that have the spots are deacons that exercised their office poorly, and plundered the livelihood of widows and orphans, and made gain for themselves from the ministrations which they had received to perform. If then they remain in the same evil desire, they are dead and there is no hope of life for them. But if they turn again and fulfill their ministrations in purity, it shall be possible for them to live.[56]

Were these Roman deacons he was referring to? They were therefore charged with providing financial aid to the needy, widows and orphans, and they took advantage of the goods they handled. The eternal temptation of money corrupts even those who exercise professions that mete out generosity.

In another contemporary text, the *Didascalia*, we read, "But let them have very free access to the deacons and let them not be troubling the head at all times, but making known what they require through the ministers, that is through the deacons."[57] The laity must not address the bishops directly but should first approach the deacons who serve as intermediaries. "Let the bishops and the deacons, then, be of one mind; and shepherd the people diligently with one mind. For you ought both to be one body, father and son. For you are in the likeness of the Lordship. And let the deacon make known all things to the bishop, even as Christ to His Father. But what things he can, let the deacon order, and all the rest let the bishop judge. Yet let the deacon be the ears of the bishop, and his mouth and his heart and his soul. For when you are both of one mind, through your agreement there will be peace also in the Church."[58] "But of the deacons let one stand always by the oblations of the Eucharist and let another stand outside by the door and observe those who come in. Afterwards, when you offer, let them minister together in the Church."[59]

Since the third century, there were only seven deacons in Rome with each one overseeing a region of the city, while the presbyters were assigned to the *tituli*, the future titular parishes of Rome. Deacons were to administer the goods and take care of the assistance of those in need, as the martyr Lawrence did, for example. At the beginning of the fourth century, the 15th canon of the local council of Neocaesarea in Pontus states: "The deacons ought to be seven in number, according to the canon, even if the city be large. Of this you will be persuaded from the *Book of the Acts*." What was the extent and importance of this rule? We do not know. Even in the seventh century Isidore of Seville quoted it.[60] We do not see it observed as much in the East. The Council of Chalcedon states that in the Church of Edessa there were fifteen priests and thirty-eight deacons.

Because deacons worked closely with the bishop, and in large cities their numbers were kept small in proportion to the presbyters, they had more power. Their number may vary. Some large churches adhered to the canonical number of seven, which was not to be exceeded. This is why their number was considerably lower than the ever-increasing number of presbyters. But in 5th century Constantinople in the East there were one hundred deacons, and Emperor Heraclius brought the number to one hundred and fifty.[61] Deacons influenced and determined the decisions of the bishop much more than the college of presbyters. They had a wide range of liturgical functions, but above all they oversaw assisting the needy, administering the goods of the community, and other tasks entrusted to them by the bishops. They were men who were experts in government and finance. They enjoyed prestige, which is why in Rome the pope, in general, was chosen for many centuries from their rank. It is therefore only natural that they should make claims to non-traditional rights and honors. There are countless texts that remind deacons of their rank and not to forget that their office is a ministry, a service, according to the original meaning of the Greek word *diakonos*. Canon 18 of the Council of Nicaea (325) highlights this: "Deacons are the servants of bishops and inferior to presbyters." Perhaps that is why Ambrose prefers the word *minister* or *servant* to *deacon*, because it is more indicative to the ear of a Latin speaker of the specific role that belongs to its holder, rather than the Greek word Latinized.

Already in the third century Cyprian recalled that the diaconate was indeed an apostolic institution, but not one made by the Lord: "Deacons must not forget that the Lord himself chose the apostles, that is, the bishops and heads of the Church, while it was the apostles after the Ascension of the Lord who instituted the deacons to be the ministers of their episcopate and of the Church. Therefore, no more and no less can we do something against God who makes the bishops, neither can they do anything against us, who make them deacons."[62] The aspiration of deacons to be equated with presbyters must have been a constant in Christian antiquity, if the bishops felt they needed to intervene among those gathered in Arles in 314 and even more so those of Nicaea in 325. The Western bishops in Arles note that in many places the practice of deacons celebrating the Eucharist was widespread. Canon 16 reads: "With regard to the deacons of whom we have been informed that in many places they offer the Eucharistic sacrifice, it has been decided that this must absolutely not happen." The celebration of the Eucharist was reserved for bishops and in some cases for presbyters. In canon 18, the council reminds the Roman deacons: "That they do not presume too much for themselves, but reserve honor for the presbyters, so that they do nothing of importance without the presbyter's knowledge." The Ecumenical Council of Nicaea (325) does not mention the celebration of the Eucharist by deacons, but does indicate in canon 18 that there were a number of abuses such as giving communion to presbyters, because they "do not have the faculty to consecrate the Eucharist." Deacons were also receiving the Eucharist before the bishops, and so the council insisted the deacons must remain within their limits because "they are ministers of the bishop and inferior to the presbyters." They also must not sit among the presbyters, which they were apparently doing.[63] In fifth century Gaul, the *Ancient Statutes of the Church* still have to reiterate: "May the deacon know that he is at the service of both the presbyter and the bishop."[64] They even add several requirements for deacons concerning their treatment of presbyters.

The increase in the size of the communities led to an increase in the number of ministers. Then some functions of deacons began to be delegated to other people. For instance, the figure of the sub-deacon was born with the aim of "assisting the deacon."[65] It is the same with the acolyte, a minor order that is attested first in Rome, then elsewhere.[66]

Among the deacons the first place was occupied by the archdeacon, who was their president and the closest to the bishop. The term was coined in the fourth century along with specifying its function. Optatus of Milevis was the first witness to the term and used it to indicate Caecilian's office in Carthage before the episcopate.[67] A few decades later Athanasius was called archdeacon of Alexandria.[68] He was the *senior* deacon, but since his office was of considerable importance, he was not elected by the other deacons but appointed by the bishop regardless of his age.[69] Both the term and the institution of the archdeacon appear and develop during the 4th and 5th centuries, both in the East and in the West.

While the number of deacons may vary for individual churches, the archdeacon is unique: "Each church has only one bishop, one archpresbyter, one archdeacon."[70] When his bishop wants to remove him "under the appearance of honor" (*sub honoris specie*), he promotes him to the presbyterate.[71] The archdeacon plays a liturgical role. In Alexandria he read the Gospel, while in Constantinople he could delegate another to do so.[72] He was the closest confidante of the bishop.[73] In addition to being the head of the deacons, he supervised all the administration and assistance to the needy. In the absence of the bishop he controlled the ministerial ordinations and the liturgy. Often he succeeded the bishop in office. He was in charge of the ecclesiastical business (*ecclesiastica negotia*),[74] indeed of the administration of every decision of the curia (*dispensatio totius causae et curiae*),[75] and in a particular way of the entire public assistance to the community.[76] He supervised the course of discipline,[77] controlled the ordinations and took care of the young clergy.[78] He took the place of the bishop in his absence[79] and could represent him also in the councils where he also took the floor.[80] This is why he often became the successor of the local bishop, especially in Rome.

MINOR ORDERS AND OTHER FUNCTIONARIES

In a letter to Victricius of Rouen Pope Innocent I (401-417) distinguished the clerics of the *superior ordo* from those of the *minor ordo*.[81] Having already talked about the first category, we now move on to the second, pointing out that it varies greatly depending on time and place and that many details still escape us, so it is worthwhile to propose only a comprehensive overview.

Subdeacon

THE OFFICE of the subdeacon is an assistant to the deacon and he carries out different tasks according to the needs of the communities. Two Latin terms are used for this minor ministry: *subdiaconus* and *hypodiaconus*; the second word is simply the Greek for the first word, written in Latin characters. But Greek fathers also used the term *hyperetes*.[82] The latter term may, however, refer to any minor ministry. Cyprian of Carthage normally used the term *hypodiaconus*.[83] If the name specifies the office, then the subdeacons must be at the service of the deacons and help them in their liturgical functions. This function can push some subdeacons to arrogate to themselves the prerogatives of the deacon. This kind of ambitious move was opposed by the so-called Council of Laodicea (363-364).

According to the medieval *Liber Pontificalis*, Pope Fabian († 250) divided the city of Rome into seven regions entrusted to seven deacons and he also appointed seven subdeacons.[84] Cyprian often appointed subdeacons with different functions such as serving as letter carriers.[85] The office of the sub-diaconate is the most important among the minor orders. The *Apostolic Tradition* prescribes that subdeacons do not receive the imposition of hands (*ordination*) but are only appointed, because they "assist the deacon."[86] The *Canons of Hippolytus* have a similar prescription. The *Apostolic Constitutions,* however, do require the laying on of hands[87] contrary to what Bishop Theodore of Mopsuestia says.[88] According to the prayer of the *Apostolic Constitutions*, it seems that their office was involved with taking care of the sacred vessels.[89] In the Eucharistic liturgy they brought water for the ablutions of the presbyters. They also were in charge of the doors where the men entered,[90] while the deaconesses were in charge of the doors where the women entered. This office seems to correspond to the doorkeepers of the Latin church and reflects a different behavior for women and men in different locations. The Council of Antioch of 341 (*in Encaeniis*) allows the subdeacon to be ordained by the *chorepiscopus* (can. 10). For the West, at the end of the fifth century, the *Statutes of the Ancient Church* state: "When a subdeacon is ordained, since he does not receive the laying on of hands (*manus impositionem*), let him receive an empty paten (*patena*) and an empty chalice from the bishop's hand, as well as an empty flask (*urceolum*) with a water basin (*aquamanile*) and a hand towel (*manutergium*)" (canon 93). The difference in the liturgical rites must be interpreted in the context of the time, but it does not mean that the subdeacons were ordained like deacons. The Council of Neocaesarea (314-319) established that a deacon who had committed a carnal sin before ordination must be downgraded to the rank of subdeacon (can. 10). The so-called Council of Laodicea stated that the subdeacons must honor the deacons (can. 20) and "must not occupy the place intended for deacons (*diaconicon*) or touch the sacred vessels" (can. 21). They cannot "wear the deacon's stole" and must remain at the doors (can. 22), which "they should not abandon even for a short time and devote themselves to prayer" (can. 43). They "cannot distribute the blessed bread, nor bless the chalice" (can. 25). This prohibition was intended to suppress abuses. In Visigoth Spain it was the subdeacons who could take the sacred vessels to the altar.[91] According to canon 43 of the Council of Braga (561) the subdeacons must be in charge of the doors.

The decrees of some popes recall that the subdeacons belong to the minor clergy.[92] In the meantime, celibacy was also being imposed on subdeacons in the West. Already in Carthage in 419 it was established that married subdeacons, like the other members of the superior clergy, must abstain from their wives (*ab uxoribus continere*).[93] The Council of Toledo (397-400) did not allow the widowed subdeacon to remarry (can. 4). The Council of Gerona (517) forbad cohabitation with the subdeacon's "former wife, who has now become a sister" (can. 6).

Isidore of Seville sums up the ministry of the subdeacons which is similar to the *Statutes of the Ancient Church*. They receive the offerings from the people and they hand the sacred vessels to the deacons at the altar. They must be chaste and continent (*continentes*). At ordination they do not receive the imposition of the hands but only the paten and the chalice from the hands of the bishop and from the archdeacon they receive the water basin, the tray, and the manuterge (towel).[94] The Gallican liturgy tells us the rite and blessing of the subdeacon occurred with the delivery of the empty chalice and the paten.[95]

Thus far we have seen numerous testimonies that demonstrate the variety of subdeaconate activities according to different places and times, also demonstrating the evolution of the ministry in general. Ultimately, the subdeaconate was abolished in the Latin Church in 1972 by Pope Paul VI, after the Second Vatican Council.[96]

Acolyte

The acolyte was at the service of the deacon or subdeacon and was an almost exclusively

Western ministry. The Latin term from which our English word acolyte derives is *acoluthus* (Gk. ἀκολουθος), indicative from the Greek of the service of "one who follows." The term acolyte refers to a minor order which in ancient times was not tied to any specific service and in the ordering of the minor orders came after the subdeacon. In Latin we also find variant spellings such as *acolythus, acolithus,* among others.[97] The office of the acolyte seems to have been established in the first decades of the third century because of the increase in the number of the faithful. The deacons needed helpers besides the subdeacons. The earliest clear testimonies to the presence of acolytes come from Carthage and Rome. Cyprian mentions the acolytes (*acoluthi*) several times, referring to them as bearers of money,[98] or letters,[99] or as distributors of alms and aid.[100] In 251 in Rome there were 42 acolytes.[101] Since the city of Rome was divided into seven regions, it is likely that each region had six acolytes. Eusebius of Caesarea mentions the presence of acolytes at the Council of Nicaea.[102] The *Constitutum Silvestri* (ca. 501) mentions that Pope Sylvester had created 45 acolytes, 22 exorcists, and 90 lectors.[103] The same *Constitutum* qualifies the seven deacons as "cardinal deacons."[104] They became the cornerstones of the regional administration.

In 385 Pope Siricius specified that one must first be appointed an acolyte and a subdeacon in order to gain access to the deaconate and only if he has married a virgin.[105] No one who had married a widow could be ordained.[106] Pope Innocent wrote in 416 to Decentius of Gubbio that in Rome the acolytes were charged with bringing the *fermentum* (a particle of the consecrated host) on Sundays to all the titular churches.[107] Pope Gelasius also mentions the acolyte when speaking of the *cursus clericalis*.[108] In 6th century Rome, the acolytes assisted deacons and presbyters during liturgical services.[109] The *Ordines Romani* attest to their presence in the papal procession, bringing oils, the gospel, tablecloths, and bags for offerings.

Exorcist

THE EXORCIST IMPOSES his hands on the catechumens and the sick and has the task of doing exorcisms to free the possessed from the diabolical presence, according to the beliefs of the time. Exorcism was widespread in pagan and Jewish antiquity. In Christianity, demons were driven out in the name of the Lord Jesus Christ (*exorcismum agere*).[110] In their controversy with the pagans, Christians said that although they were less educated, they had more power over demons, which at that time they considered to be present everywhere, as we do today with viruses. The infestation was everywhere, affecting places and people. They caused all kinds of illnesses, both spiritual and physical, in the mind and body.[111] Exorcism healed body and soul. The Christian had the power to defeat demons and make them flee. Indeed the demons would even confess the Christian God as the true God. As Tertullian writes:

Yet all this rule and power of ours over them derives its strength from the naming of Christ, and from the mention of those things which they look for as impending over them from God, through Christ the Judge. Fearing Christ in God and God in Christ, they are subject to the servants of God and Christ. Thus from our touch and from our breath being carried away by the thought and vision of that fire, they even leave the bodies of men at our order, unwilling and embarrassed and ashamed at your [Christ's] presence.[112]

Because of the importance of exorcism in the context of those beliefs and practices, the Church required good spiritual dispositions of the exorcists. Exorcism could be practiced on many occasions through words and rites. But above all it was accomplished during the period of the catechumenate and then in close preparation for baptism. The true exorcist knew when there was a diabolical presence.[113] The Theodosian Code placed the exorcists after the subdeacons and before the lectors.[114] In the rite of ordination, he receives the book of exorcisms as a sign of his office. This order was not widespread in every region, and it seems that it disappeared towards the sixth century.

Reader/Lector

The ministry of the reader (*lector: officium lectoris, gradus lectoris*) has been mentioned a number of times already. This is because it was very important in ancient Christian communities and is linked to the synagogue tradition.[115] Not many people knew how to read a text with "continuous script" (*scriptio* or *scriptura continua*),[116] a continuous sequence of letters without interruption or spaces, and without distinction between the various letters. There were no chapters or paragraphs. The lector must first distinguish the individual words and then construct the sentence with the appropriate punctuation. This took a lot of mental energy since the lector had to have already memorized the text according to the division of words. Augustine observes:

> He who reads to an audience pronounces aloud the words he sees before him. He who teaches reading does it that others may be able to read for themselves. Each, however, communicates to others what he has learned himself. Just so, the man who explains to an audience the passages of Scripture he understands is like one who reads aloud the words before him. On the other hand, the man who lays down rules for interpretation is like one who teaches reading, that is, shows others how to read for themselves.[117]

Therefore, the lector must understand the text and pronounce it so that it can be understood. This requires a greater effort with the eyes to pay attention to individual words and phrases.[118] The reading was not done like we do today, but almost sung. The change of voice distinguished one sentence from another. In other words, a musicality is combined with rhetoric. A strong and clear voice was also essential in order to be heard among all the noise (*in tumultu*) in the absence of microphones as the text was proclaimed from the ambo (*pulpitum* or *tribunal*).[119] The lector must have cultural, physical and spiritual qualities because they allow us to hear the voice of God.[120] Isidore of Seville goes on to explain the characteristics required of a lector. He must respect the rules of phonetics, know when a sentence ends and where to place the accent, among other things.[121] Medical doctors recommend exercise, today we might take a walk. In this period they would recommend reading, that is, reciting out loud with arm motion. The text was written not so much to be read, but to be proclaimed and listened to. Similar principles are involved when one reads alone and for oneself. Reading aloud occurs more slowly than reading quietly, similar to the recommended way of reading the liturgy of the hours. If recited in private it must also be done with the movement of the lips.

In the middle of the second century, Justin writes that the lector reads the memoirs of the apostles or of the prophets and is a minister distinct from the president of the assembly.[122] It is a minor office but one that is found in all the communities. Tertullian placed the lector with the bishop and the deacon.[123] Origen preached on the texts proclaimed by the lector, as repeatedly mentioned in the *Homilies on the Judges*.[124] Lectors are also mentioned during Diocletian's persecution with some rather curious cases being recorded. In a papyrus, a lector of a church in an Egyptian village did not sign his statement on ecclesiastical goods because he was illiterate. It may indicate that he could not write Greek or that he refused to for religious reasons.[125] In Cappadocia the lector Ariston and cantor Severianus were accused of having written a defamatory *libellus* against the emperors.[126]

Cyprian placed the lector among the clerics.[127] In 303 in Cirta (today, Constantina, Algeria) the police requisitioned the sacred books which were kept by the lectors. There were seven of them, who were also known by the pagan authorities so the commission of inquiry could easily go to their homes.[128] In the fourth century, at least in some geographical areas, the office of lector became a step for entering into ecclesiastical service.[129] Augustine often alludes to his lectors, who read Scripture in church and sometimes read a different passage from the one he had prepared for preaching.[130] Although the lector was considered a member of the lower orders, the laity were also allowed to read the Scriptures publicly: "The office of lector . . . as we know, is usually granted also to the laity in case of necessity."[131] In this letter, Augustine is talking about a certain Donantius, whom he had established as a doorkeeper of the church of St. Theogene. He had been demoted because he had been ordained deacon in another diocese against ecclesiastical norms. Even though a certain Privatio was not a lector, he had read non-canonical texts in church which was not allowed.[132]

In liturgical assemblies Augustine often associated the office of the lector with that of the *disputator* (the preacher or expositor), especially in comments on the psalms and sermons.[133] "The psalm is sung, the Gospel is read, the voice of the lector is echoed, the commentator insists."[134] Sometimes the lector or cantor makes mistakes: "I was prepared for the exposition of a short psalm, also commanding the lector to sing it to us. Suddenly, however, he must have gotten confused and read one instead of another."[135] If the one who proclaims the psalm sings it, then even a boy could learn it by heart without necessarily having to have read it.

In the African church the lector was considered clergy (*clericus*).[136] Lectors who were approaching puberty either married or made a profession of continence. They could read in church until puberty was reached, then it was no longer allowed.[137] They could not get married a second time.[138] The Synod of Milevis of 402 states: "Whoever has exercised, even if only once, the functions of lector in a particular church can no longer later receive an ecclesiastical ministry in another church."[139]

In the time of Cyprian, as we have seen, lectors also read the Gospel. In Augustine's day in some cases they read the Gospel, but we do not know if this was regular practice. But lectors did not provide a greeting to the assembly since that was reserved for the one who was presiding.[140] Jerome advises that the lector, as well as the acolyte or the psalmist, be dressed decently.[141] We know from the inscriptions that many lectors died when they were young, some when they were nine or twelve years old.[142] The lector did not need the laying on of hands but received the book as a sign of the institution.[143]

Porter/Doorkeeper

ANOTHER MINOR MINISTRY was that of the porter who served as the doorkeeper or doorman. The letter of Pope Cornelius († 253) sent to Fabius of Antioch mentions the existence in Rome of doorkeepers (*ostiarius, ianitor*; in Greek *pylorus* or *thuroros*). It does not mention how many but there were most likely at least seven. In 258 in Rome, the doorkeeper Romanus was killed at the same time as the deacon Lawrence.[144] The *Liber Pontificalis* presents two lists for the orders of the clergy (*cursus clericalis*). The first list recorded during the reign of Pope Gaius (283-296) places the doorkeeper as the first step in the hierarchy of orders.[145] The second list recorded during the reign of Pope Sylvester (314-335) omits the doorkeeper altogether,[146] but does appoint a guardian of the martyrs' shrines (*custos martyrum*). The office is mentioned in the *Constitutum Silvestri*,[147] in the *Apostolic Constitutions*[148] and in a letter of Pseudo-Ignatius.[149] It is not a compulsory step in the ecclesiastical *cursus*. This begins with the other orders. Paulinus of Nola counts the doorkeeper among the clergy.[150] In 377 the emperor Gratian exempted the doorkeepers from personal duties (*munera personalia*).[151] In the *Didas-*

calia it is the deacons who perform the functions of the doorkeeper.[152] While according to the so-called Council of Laodicea the subdeacons are in charge of the doors in general (can. 43), according to the *Apostolic Constitutions* only the subdeacons are in charge of the doors where the men enter, whereas the deaconesses are in charge of the doors where the women enter.[153]

In Milan, a doorkeeper prevented Monica from "carrying porridge, bread and wine to the tombs of the saints."[154] He is mentioned by Pope Gelasius.[155] For Pope Pelagius I († 561) the ministry of the doorkeeper is the lowest and the bishop is the highest in the ecclesiastical hierarchy.[156] There are records of doorkeepers in Trier,[157] Salona,[158] Jerusalem,[159] and in Hippo where Augustine appointed a needy doorkeeper to the church of St. Theogene.[160] In ancient times their office in the Roman church was replaced, according to Duchesne, by the *mansionarius*.[161] The *mansionarius* (the sacristan) oversaw the church where he lived, or he was in charge of the cemetery—but he did not belong to the clergy. The office of porter/doorkeeper was abolished in 1972 by Pope Paul VI, after the Second Vatican Council.[162]

OTHER MINOR MINISTRIES

There are also other minor ministries, depending on the regions. In the *Statutes of the Ancient Church* we have the order of cantors according to Eastern practice and other churches, where there are two different offices: the lector and the psalmist or the cantor. Severianus, quoted above, was a cantor from Cappadocia. The gravediggers (*fossores*; *copiatae*) belonged to the clergy. They were responsible for digging the tombs of the deceased in the catacombs and cemeteries and performed all the works of beautifying and upkeep of the grounds as well as taking care of the administration of these places. They were organized into business groups. Civil law had taken an interest in the gravediggers, as they were of considerable social and economic importance. In their work, which they learn in a practical way, they are helped by engineers and specialized personnel. Initially they lived off the offerings of the faithful and at the expense of the community,[163] but later they sold the graves themselves directly. In the fourth century they were a very compact social and economic group and found a lucrative trade in selling tombs. Because of the abuses that ensued, their office was suppressed, perhaps in the fifth century. Gregory the Great (590-604) abolished every kind of fee on burials.[164]

In Rome, Leo the Great (440-461) also established the office of *cubicularius* (chamber servant) for the special custody of the two tombs of the apostles, but this office is documented only for this city. In the many bilingual churches of the Greek-Syriac East, there is an official figure belonging to the clergy who oversees the translation during the liturgy. At the end of the fourth century, in dealing with the Easter liturgy in Jerusalem Egeria writes that the bishop speaks in Greek and a presbyter translates into Syriac after him, while for those who spoke Latin one relied on someone of good will.

Martyrs and Confessors

A SPECIAL HONOR was reserved for confessors who, however, did not belong to the clergy. They were called *confessors* because they had confessed their faith during the persecution. In the first two centuries the terms *martyr* and *confessor* are considered synonymous. It was only later that a precise distinction was established between the martyr, who died during torture, and the confessor who survived. But both were united in suffering to free themselves from the present world for the love of Christ by sharing in his passion. They could make their confession of faith only by virtue of the Spirit of God which was in them: "since neither can we suffer on behalf of God except there be in us the Spirit of God."[165] "The Spirit of God the Father, who does not abandon or leave confessors, speaks and is crowned" in them.[166]

Martyrdom was considered a divine gift. That is why the martyr had visions, performed miracles, and remained serene during his or her suffering. Not only the martyrs, but the confessors too were venerated by the community and held in high esteem. They were recognized as having effective power to intercede for the faithful, to intervene in the life of the church, and to forgive sins. The *Apostolic Tradition*, which perhaps reflects a widespread custom, admitted among the clergy the true confessor without rite of ordination: "If a confessor has been placed in chains for the Name of the Lord, hands are not laid upon him for the office of deacon or presbyter. He has the honor of the office of a presbyter through his confession. If he is instituted as a bishop, then hands will be laid upon him."[167] Confession of faith therefore replaced ordination and designation by the community, which only examined the authenticity of the suffering incurred for the faith. The imposition of hands was only required for the episcopate. Even Cyprian himself, while defending the rights of the hierarchy, attributed great value to the witness given by confessors and admitted them to the clergy because they did not need "a human witness when it was preceded by divine approval."[168] However, it was the bishop who decided on admission and completed the ordination that he considered necessary in each case. Even for the remission of sins, Cyprian recognized the confessor's power to intercede and to contribute to forgiveness, but reserved to the hierarchy the decision and the readmission in fact, also in order to avoid numerous abuses.

During the persecution of Decius (250) there were many lapsed (*lapsi*) who had not confessed the faith, and many confessors (*confessors*) as well. The lapsed desired reconciliation with the Church and so sometimes they turned to the confessors for help who in turn provided a certificate of peace (*libellum pacis*) as a sign of reconciliation. Cyprian, and in general the episcopate, while recognizing the importance of the intervention of confessors, demanded that sinners submit to a due penance proportionate to the gravity of the sin of apostasy.

The term *confessor* was broadened in the fourth and fifth centuries and also included people who had fought for the faith in the broadest sense, such as the great bishops involved in the Arian crisis, or all those who were committed to living Christianity in a more radical way. The term eventually became synonymous with the ascetic.

Other Secondary Ministers

IN THE CHURCH of the first centuries we meet other people who dedicated themselves to its service and growth besides the institutional ministries. There were the prophets and the *doctores* (teachers or theologians) who, however, had already disappeared as dominant figures by the third century. In the New Testament writings, the charismatic prophets were influential figures who pronounced "words of edification, exhortation and consolation" (*1 Cor* 14:3) and had a liturgical role (*1 Cor* 14:3-3).[169] They spoke under the inspiration of the Holy Spirit (*Acts* 21:11). In Antioch, five men were called prophets and teachers (*Acts* 13:1). The prophet as a man of God performed a function for the benefit of all. He was the man inspired in a special way and directed by God. This is why he enjoyed free reign and whatever he did was not questioned. But the rise of false prophets discredited the prophetic ministry and so the prophet needed to provide proof of the authenticity of his charism and to submit it to the judgment of the community. His conduct was a litmus test of his qualification as a prophet to see if he had "the way of life of the Lord."[170] Hermas specified the criteria for distinguishing false prophets from true ones. "The false prophet ruins the minds of the servants of God, that is, he ruins the minds of the uncertain, not of the true faithful."[171] The author repeatedly speaks of the false prophets, perhaps because there were a lot of them in the Roman community of the first half of the second century. Justin also knew of false prophets.[172] In the second century there was still the rare prophet and prophecy was still appreciated although looked at with a certain suspicion. Montanists helped to devalue it and cause it to disappear.

Another eminent personage was the *didaskalos* (the teacher, the doctor) who was listed immediately after the apostles and prophets.[173] He was not to teach any of his own doctrines but only the official teachings of the community. He also served as their catechist. This office continued into the ensuing centuries. In the *Passion of Perpetua and Felicity* there were two individuals mentioned who taught the faith. There was Saturus who was referred to as the one who "instructed us in the faith" (*aedificaverat*), and Aspasius, who was qualified as a teaching presbyter.[174] Since Saturus was addressed as neither a presbyter nor a deacon, he must have been a layman. Therefore, in Carthage there were lay catechists and presbyters, the *presbyteri doctores*.[175] In *Letter* 29 [23], Cyprian speaks of *doctores audientiem* as those who instructed catechumens (the hearers, *audientiem*) in the pre-baptismal period as well as teaching presbyters (*presbysteri doctores*). They seem to have been two distinct categories. In the *Apostolic Tradition* the teachers prepared and instructed the catechumens for baptism.

In addition to the official institution of teachers there were also private teachers who opened their schools and taught Christian doctrine independently on a par with pagan philosophers. Justin, Rhodon, Pantaenus, and Clement of Alexandria were examples of such private teachers. Origen saw himself first and foremost as a teacher, referring to himself as a teacher of the church (*doctor ecclesiae*).[176] Even the laity, whether they were teachers or not, had a huge influence on the spread of Christianity. But the fight against heresy gradually led to an ever-increasing insistence on the true doctrine and tradition that were transmitted through episcopal succession. Thus, the teacher par excellence in the community became the bishop, and his *cathedra* was the symbol of his teaching office. Even the functions of prophet and teacher ended up being subsumed under the figure of the bishop.

Briefly, there were also other personnel connected in some way to the life of the community which became more and more articulated and complex after Constantine. In Alexandria and then in Constantinople there was an association of men who were dedicated to the care of the sick. They were called *parabalani*, that is, those who risk their lives. According to the Theodosian Code the *parabalani* must care for bodily sick patients.[177] We do not know exactly the nature of their work. We are also ignorant of when they started, but already at the beginning of the fifth century they constituted a powerful organization which sometimes could even cause unrest in the city. For this reason, after the death of Hypatia—which they may or may not have been involved with—Theodosius in 416 reduced their privileges and their activities not specifically related to welfare. He also prescribed that they must have come from a poor family and their number must not exceed 500—a number that two years later was raised to 600.[178] They must not meddle in public affairs such as the city government or courts for fear of interfering in the judgments rendered. According to the law of 418, the *parabalani* were under the control of the bishop of Alexandria. On certain occasions they may have been his right arm, as in the un-ecumenical Council of Ephesus of 449.[179] The *parabalani* enjoyed certain privileges of the clergy, but even though in the Theodosian Code they were listed under the title *de clericis*, we are not sure whether they actually belonged to the clergy. Some of the legislation of the Theodosian Code also passed into the Justinian Code.[180]

In Africa there were lay elders (*seniores laici*), a kind of board of directors consisting of qualified lay personnel at the service of the bishop and in charge of the administration of his property. Another figure, which only came about gradually, was that of the *defensor ecclesiae* (defender of the church), that is, a sort of lawyer, initially secular and then obliged to have a tonsure from the time of Pope Gelasius (492-496).[181] In 367. some *defensores* helped Pope Damasus write a petition addressed to the emperors.[182] At the time of Pope Innocent (†417) they acted to expel the heretical Photinians from Rome.[183] Possidius, bishop of Calama (403-437), spoke of a *defensor ecclesiae* of Calama whose task it was to defend the church against the abuses of the Donatists.[184] Pope Zosimus, in a letter of 418, wrote to *defensores ecclesiae* who were chosen from among laymen.[185] The emperor Honorius spoke of lawyers who were employed for the benefit of the church.[186] Originally, the task of the *defensor* was to defend the interests of the church in the courts. But he soon became a collaborator of the bishops in various temporal tasks. This was already the case at the beginning of the 5th century. According to Pope Pelagius II († 590) the duties of the *defensor* concerned procedural activities and examination of irregularities.[187] At the time of Gregory the Great (590-604) in Rome there were seven *defensores* who carried out various tasks of a judicial and administrative nature. They could contract regular marriages and sit among the clergy at councils (*in conventu clericorum*) and they received a salary from the Church.[188]

Civil and Religious Privileges of the Clergy

THE MINDSET of the ancient world held religion to be an essential component of society and therefore contributed to the welfare of public society. There was no distinction between the private and public spheres in religion. Religion was an integral part of social and political life, not so much in terms of belief as in the official cultic ceremonies which were part and parcel of public life. Religion was above all about ritual, not faith. Our difficulty in understanding ancient religions is that we start from the concept of faith and belief in the gods. The ancients were only interested in worship in its various expressions, whether it be by sacrifice, a libation offering, or other rites. The ceremonial rite itself was essential to the life of the city. We can distinguish various types of religious practice in the ancient world. These can be summarized in the ancient distinction between private and public *sacra*. *Sacra* pertains to the ritual that was done in the official name of the "State" or various groups. Public worship, the official worship that established the religious identity of each city, must therefore be funded by the public and performed by public officials, whether magistrates or priests, in public temples.

The purpose of public worship was to pacify the gods (*pax deorum*). The peace of the gods was viewed as the foundation of the political community and also ensured success in war. Since one of the fundamental aims of civic worship was that of pleasing the gods (*placatio deorum*), if a citizen did not contribute to the appeasing of the gods (*pax deorum*) he was considered a potential cause of their anger.

Immediately after the victory of Constantine over Maxentius at the Milvian Bridge on October 28, 312, Constantine showered an array of concessions, subsidies and benefits on the Catholic Church, starting from the beginning of 313. First, he granted an exemption for Catholic clergy from having to perform public duties (*munera*). He wrote to Anulinus, Proconsul in North Africa:

> It is my wish that those who play an official role in the Catholic Church in the province entrusted to you in the Catholic Church over which Caecilian presides—those who exercise a role in worship and who are generally called clergy—that they should be completely exempt from every public responsibility (*leiturgiai, munera*) so that they are not distracted by some error or sacrilegious deviation of the worship owed to the divinity but that without any disturbance they dedicate themselves in conformity with their own law. For when they render the highest veneration to the divinity, it seems they confer incalculable benefits on the affairs of the state.[189]

Thus, ministers who lead worship "should act in accordance with their own law." That means the emperor perceived an incompatibility in the lifestyle of the clergy—particularly in religious affairs—with the permanent position of the governing Roman *curia* which was still almost completely pagan. In October 313, when he reconfirmed the exemption of the clergy, Constantine recalled the qualifications and activities of those exempted as, "Those who devote their service to the divine cult as ministers of religion" (*qui divino cultui ministeria religionis impendunt*).[190]

According to the law, what specific things became exempt for clergy? First and foremost, they were no longer required to be members of the *curia* (called *curiales*) or municipal assemblies and they were freed from civic responsibilities (*munera civilia or publica*), that is, from those duties that the *curiales* must fulfill in the administration and organization of the cities (*civitates*.) The *curia* named the local magistrates in charge of administration, and their functions varied according to the city and the region. Furthermore, they had responsibility for taking care of the shrines, theaters, aqueducts, streets, baths, markets, and other public venues. The clergy were moreover exempt from *mumera sordida*, that is, from a variety of services that were to be rendered to the community. They were also exempt from taxes owed on the assets of the church, per capita taxes as well as certain extraordinary taxes. Clergy who had commercial interests did not have to pay the tax owed by fellow merchants (*collatio illustralis*).

In the general framework of his religious policy, Constantine favored the catholic Christian clergy, which assumed ever greater importance in the sphere of the empire. At first, the privileges granted concerned just the clergy of the western part of the empire, privileges that were then extended in the East after the victory over Licinius in 324 when Constantine abolished Licinius' legislation against the Christians.[191] He extended the application of the laws published in the West into the East, but with caution, ensuring continuity with the previous administration to achieve uniformity with the West.[192] The Law of September 1, 326[193] specified that the privileges granted for the consideration of religion (*contemplatione religionis*) to the clergy applied only to those who followed the catholic rule (*catholicae legis*), and therefore heretics and schismatics were excluded. Eusebius tells us about the application of these religious laws in the East: "Laws full of humanity of the victorious emperor were promulgated everywhere, as well as laws that bore witness to his munificence and true piety. Thus, every tyranny was abolished, and only Constantine and his children were left with the empire, which belonged to them, safe and unchallenged."[194] This sentence closes the *Ecclesiastical History* in the last edition.

The catholic clergy were organized according to their own rules. The emperor did not interfere with the internal ecclesial organization, which was respected and recognized by the empire. The same ecclesial organization, now well-structured and established, was the same for the whole empire in its essential elements. Already within the church there was a distinction between the various categories of people, with a precise hierarchy, as has been amply demonstrated above. The emperor granted certain privileges to members of the higher ecclesiastical ranks. In this way the civil authorities helped to differentiate and distinguish the various hierarchical levels and established them as a separate group from the common faithful.

Constantine in 319 reiterated in a rescript addressed to Octavian that only those of the clergy had the right to exemption of *munera* "who devote themselves to worship and are clearly called clerics."[195] The concessions concerned people who devoted themselves expressly and specifically to worship—the cult that was so important for the preservation of public life (*salus rei publicae*)—and were specifically called "clerics" by the Christian community itself. The civil authority was not able to make an individual investigation as to who these clergy were, so it had to be satisfied with the list offered by the bishop who was a clearly identifiable and indisputable authority.

The exemptions granted to clerics by Constantine immediately led to an influx into the clergy greater than expected. This adversely affected the staffing of necessary public services (*munera*) as many tried to take advantage of the exemption from public service. The number of clerics grew significantly and immediately in the space of a few years. In his invective against the Melitians, Athanasius criticized those who, though pagans and members of the curia, become Christians and almost immediately bishops in order to escape public service while also collecting subsidies.[196] The attraction to the episcopal office also shows how, in addition to the privileges it was allowed to acquire, it was perceived as an obvious sign of social promotion at a time when the church was perfectly integrated into state structures and participated in its power.

Starting in the year 325, Constantine, who previously had been generous in granting exemption from the *curia* for various categories of people, began a policy of limiting escape from this office. He radically changed politics and from 329 initiated a change in fiscal policy towards clerics as well. It was a very restrictive legislation, which for the first time also dealt with the way in which the clergy were recruited. A constitution of 329 marked a radical turning point in politics towards the catholic ministers of the Christian religion.[197] The Theodosian Code contains two laws of the Emperor Constantine which concern who, how, and when one can enter the catholic clergy. One law was addressed to Bassus, the praetorian prefect in the West from 318 to 331 (Consul in 331),[198] and the second was addressed to Ablavius, praetorian prefect in the East from March 329.[199] The second law on this subject carries the dating of the first of June 326; it is in fact dated prior to the first. The following is the translation of the Theodosian Code 16.2.6:

> The same emperor Augustus to Ablavius praetorian prefect: Exemption from public services should be conferred neither by popular request nor on any persons at all petitioning under pretext of being clergymen. And great numbers should not be added to the clergymen heedlessly and beyond measure. Rather, when a clergyman shall have died, another should be selected to take the deceased person's place who shall have had no familial connection with municipal senators and who does not have the wealth of resources, which can endure very easily public functions. If there is any doubt between the community and the clergy over anyone's name, if equity ascribes him to public services and if he is known to be suitable as a municipal senator because of family or patrimony, he should be excluded from the clergy and should be assigned to the community. For it is proper that the rich should sustain the necessary expanses of the present age, but that the poor should be supported by the churches' wealth. Posted on June 1, Constantine Augustus for the seventh time and Constantius Caesar being consuls (June 1 of [326] 329).[200]

What does this law really establish? 1) The exemption must not be granted by popular request (*vulgari consensu*). 2) The law does not even recognize the fact of belonging to the clergy (an ordination that has already taken place), in the sense that the election and ordination took place only within the ecclesial community and then the *fait accompli* is presented to the civil authorities. 3) Moreover, it states that it is not necessary to have a large clergy beyond measure (*citra modum*). Does Constantine consider that by now the number of clergy is more than enough for pastoral needs? 4) An individual can join the clerical order only in order to replace a deceased cleric. Therefore, the number must remain stable. Ecclesial communities do not have freedom of choice. In fact, the main purpose was so that the municipal senate would not be weakened. The emperor was interested only in the *curiales*, not so much in others who were not forced to be members of the curia. 5) The new cleric must not be of senatorial origin (*progenie municeps*[201]) because, even if young, he is already or will later be a member of the municipal senate. The right and duty of belonging to the *curia* now passed from father to son, as an obligation. Membership was hereditary. 6) The last restriction states that the candidate must not possess patrimony, which would have made him fit to bear the civil functions (*munera civilian*). A citizen with enough assets (*patrimonio idoneus*), and therefore suitable to be a member of the senate, could not enter the clergy. In case of disagreement or doubt, the requests of the municipal assembly must be confirmed on the grounds of equity (*aequitas*). The legislator adds a consideration of social and civic responsibility. Those who have earthly goods must provide for the needs of the present age (*Opulentos enim saeculi subire necessitates oportet*), while the poor must be sustained by the goods of the church (*pauperes ecclesiarum divitiis sustentari*). Of course, the clerical poor were not the poor in the modern sense, but were those who did not have enough wealth to be suitable for the local senate.[202] The amount of wealth required varied from city to city, depending on its size. Constantine assumed that the individual churches now possessed sufficient economic opportunities to sustain their clergy (*ecclesiarum divitiis*), having accumulated their wealth through donations.[203] This restrictive legislation has been preserved throughout antiquity.

The Constantinian legislation was too radical for those people who, motivated by sincere intentions, wanted to embrace the clerical state. That is why over time it was partially mitigated. Valentinian I, in September 364 on the one hand reiterated the idea that the rich plebeians should not be clergymen, but at the same time introduced a great novelty which sought to favor those who truly intended to put themselves at the service of the church: those seeking to enter the clergy would abandon their property so that the interests of the city were not harmed.[204] Valentinian's new solution to the age-old conflict between the municipal senate and the clergy was successful, so much so that it was accepted by his successors, especially Theodosius I.[205]

The main consequences of the legislation of Constantine, corrected by Valentinian, are the following: 1) These laws, which imposed strong limitations on "vocations," did not facilitate the mission of the church, especially because of the increasing number of Christians in cities and the expansion of Christianization in villages and estates. 2) As a result of their application, clerics (bishops, presbyters, deacons, etc.) were often called to the municipal senate and therefore to be members of the municipal council. 3) They fostered less qualified clergy who must be chosen from among the poor and who thus had not been able to obtain a proper secular education since normally only the children of the local senators could attend the schools at some higher level. The recruitment of clergy was a sensitive area when it came to the cultural acumen of the clergy.

Moreover, since Christianity in most parts of the Empire was urban, it was not possible to recruit members from the peasant countryside. Only the poor craftsmen of the city remained, and it is to be assumed that this category constituted the backbone of the clergy of the 4th and 5th centuries. One should not think, however, that the strictures provided by ecclesiastical and civil legislation were absolute and rigidly observed. The monotonous repetition of similar laws is a sign that they were often violated.

Deaconesses[206]

The term deacon (minister, servant, or helper) comes from the Greek *diakonos,* which was transliterated into Latin as *diaconus*. The verbal form is *diakoneo* (to serve, to assist, to serve at table) and, as mentioned above, is indicative of the ministry of Christ himself who came to serve (*Mt* 20:28). The term *deacon* has a wide range of meanings in the New Testament as well. The term itself in Greek can be either masculine or feminine. The gender is indicated by the feminine or masculine article. Canon 19 of the Council of Nicaea used the feminine term of *deaconess*. There is always the danger of understanding this term with the technical meaning it took on later. So, we can be mistaken in our translation and understanding.

Women were very important in the origins of Christianity, with their actions often quiet but effective in spreading the faith. They were the faithful followers of Jesus who helped with their contributions.[207] Commenting on the text of *1 Cor* 9:5, Clement of Alexandria observed that by women accompanying the apostles, it helped their mission as "it was through them that the Lord's teaching penetrated also the women's homes without giving rise to slander."[208] Paul recommended Phoebe (*Rom* 16:1), a zealous *diakonon*—there is no feminine form—of the church of Cenchreae (Corinth). What role did she play? Was she just a benefactress? Since Phoebe was connected to a local community, she must have played some role. Origen, almost two centuries later, commenting on this passage, writes that this diaconate of women can be accessed by those who have given "assistance to many and with their good works have deserved the praise of the apostles."[209] The first letter to Timothy describes the qualities that deacons must possess (3:8-10). Verse 11 goes on to say: "women likewise must be serious, not slanderers, but temperate, faithful in all things." One wonders if the eleventh verse also refers to deaconesses. This is indeed how it was interpreted by some ancient authors.[210]

Governor Pliny the Younger, in his letter to Trajan (*Ep.* 10.96.8) written around 111 CE, speaks of the tortures to which two *ministrae* had been subjected in order to extract from them information about their co-religionists. We do not know what their duties were and whether the term already had a specific meaning. In this case Pliny, a pagan, interpreted a Greek term which he translated into Latin according to his religious sensitivity and according to the tasks that women performed in pagan worship. The first text that speaks extensively about women and their ministry is the *Didascalia*, composed in Syria in the first half of the third century. It speaks of deaconesses in many of its chapters, stating such things as: "The deaconess will instead be honored by you in place of the Holy Spirit."[211] Their function was almost parallel to that of the deacon. They worked closely with the bishop and were freely chosen by him. Deaconesses visited women who were sick and washed them when they begin to feel better. They could enter houses where the presence of deacons or presbyters, on the other hand, might have occasioned slander or scandal. They anointed the bodies of women in baptism and instructed them, and so there were also practical reasons for the presence of deaconesses.[212] This section of the *Didascalia* concludes with these words:

> This is why, O bishop, you are to appoint workers of righteousness as helpers who may cooperate with you in leading people to salvation. Those that please you out of all the people are the ones you shall choose and appoint as deacons—a man for the performance of most things that are required, but also a woman for the ministry of women. For there are houses where women live where you cannot send a deacon, on account of the heathen, but may send a deaconess. Also, because in many other matters the office of a woman deacon is required. In the first place, when women go down into the water they ought to be anointed by a deaconess with the oil of anointing. And where there is no woman at hand, and especially no deaconess, he who baptizes must of necessity anoint her who is being baptized. But where there is a woman, and especially a deaconess, it is not fitting that women should be seen by men but with the imposition of hand you should anoint the head only. . . . And when she who is being baptized has come up from the water, let the deaconess receive her, and teach and instruct her how the seal of baptism ought to be (kept) unbroken in purity and holiness. This is why we say that the ministry of a woman deacon is especially needful and important. For our Lord and Savior also was ministered to by women ministers, Mary Magdalene, and Mary the daughter of James and mother of Jose, and the mother of the sons of Zebedee [Mt 27:56], as well as other women. And you also have need of the ministry of a deaconess for many things, for a deaconess is required to go into the houses of the heathen where there are believing women, and to visit those who are sick, and to minister to them in that of which they have need, and to bathe those who have begun to recover from sickness.[213]

Why this strong exhortation to the local bishop? Is it perhaps because many bishops did not have deaconesses to help them with these types of service? The anonymous author writes that their service was needed even more because of the rigid separation of the sexes at that time, especially among those churches of the East. Nothing is mentioned in the Latin texts. According to the *Apostolic Constitutions*, as we saw above, all that was said was that subdeacons were in charge of the doors where men entered, while deaconesses were in charge of the doors for the women.[214] And deaconesses also were involved with distributing charity as part of their office.

The *Didascalia* does not mention that they were ordained. A century later, however, the *Apostolic Constitutions* present a rite that includes the laying on of hands and prayer, analogous to the ordination of deacons.[215] But the deaconess does not assist the bishop in the celebration of the Eucharist, nor does she distribute communion. She also does not baptize but assists in the administration of baptism. The deaconess does instruct the women after their baptism[216] even as the *Apostolic Constitutions* strictly speaking do not allow women to teach, referring to *1 Tim* 2:12.[217] But the deaconesses were the bishop's intermediaries to the women of the congregation.[218]

While as we saw earlier, the Council of Nicaea (325), in canon 19, prescribed: "the deaconesses . . . have no imposition of hands and are to be numbered only among the laity," canon 15 of the Council of Chalcedon (451) a little more than a century later speaks of the imposition of hands for the diaconal ordination of women as a normal fact: "A woman shall not receive the laying on of hands as a deaconess under forty years of age, and then only after searching examination. And if, after she has had hands laid on her and has continued for a time to minister, she shall despise the grace of God and give herself in marriage, she shall be anathematized as will the man united to her."[219] The Council in Trullo only mentions that a deaconess is not ordained before 40 years of age (canon 14).

Basil of Caesarea states that if the deaconess has committed a sin of fornication with a pagan, she must complete seven years of penance to return to her office.[220] The canon assumes the existence of celibacy, as does the Council of Chalcedon of 451 mentioned above. Some inscriptions attest to the existence of married deaconesses, such as Nonna in Lycaonia who dedicated the inscription to her son Alexander, a presbyter.[221] In the same region there was a deaconess Matrona who was the mother of Thecla. Euthymius the Great was the son of a deaconess who offered her son at the age of three to Bishop Otreius of Melitene, who immediately baptized him and made him a lector. There is also the case of Pentadia who became a deaconess when her husband died.[222] Theodoret of Cyr sent a letter of condolence to the deaconess Casiana upon the death of her husband.[223]

The female diaconate spread in the Middle East especially from the fourth century to the eleventh century, particularly in the Syrian and Persian regions. It seems that there was a greater need for deaconesses in those areas because relations between men and women were more reserved—similar to today in the Middle East. The canons attributed to Maruthas of Martyropolis (Maypherqaṭ, early 5th c.), Catholicos Isoyahab III (580-596) and the Synod of Catholicos George I (676 CE), required the deaconess to serve as a helper during the rite of baptism. However, in the period after, the figure of the deaconess disappears also in the

Middle East. In the Byzantine tradition, the canonist Theodore Balsamon (late 12th c.), affirmed that the office of the female diaconate had devolved into an honorary title for certain nuns,[224] and that they had no access to the altar.[225] The office of deaconess had never existed in the Coptic church until recently and is spreading to Egypt and elsewhere.[226]

In the West this ministry was hardly present, albeit with some exceptions. The fact that some councils in Gaul condemned their ordination is an indication that in some cases bishops did ordain them. For example, the Council of Nîmes of 396 commented in canon 2: "It seems that women—we do not know where—have been elevated to the diaconal ministry, something that ecclesiastical discipline does not admit because it is inconvenient." The prohibition is repeated in canon 26 of the Council of Orange in 441: "They must not be ordained deaconesses."[227] There were also some later councils that condemned deaconesses. Canon 22 of the Council of Epâone in the Burgundian Kingdom of 517 ruled: "Let us completely renounce the consecration of widows called deaconesses throughout our territory. If they wish to convert, only the penitential blessing must be imposed on them." This ruling however was not about real deaconesses, it was about an honorary title.[228] And then there was the Council of Orléans of 533, can. 17. The repetition of the condemnation reflects an Eastern influence in some dioceses. In other cases, there were no deaconesses to begin with, in the strict sense. Venantius Fortunatus writes that Bishop Medardus, in 544, consecrated Queen Radegonda as a deaconess (?).[229] From the previous prohibition it seems correct to understand that he consecrated her to God and not as a deaconess in the technical sense.

Literary and archaeological evidence abounds on the presence of deaconesses in the early church. We mentioned the literary documentation; there is also epigraphic documentation which is equally precious.[230] From this it emerges that the western attestations are very rare; most come from the East. Felle collected the epigraphic documentation from western Asia Minor and from some Greek islands.

Were they part of the clergy? According to the research of Martimort, they were not. The 8th century *Euchologion Barberini Gr. 336* records a prayer for the ordination of deaconesses. It should be noted that the gesture of the imposition of hands could mean many things and its significance could usually be derived from the words that were spoken.[231]

The term deaconess becomes a technical term, but it always retains a certain ambiguity because in some cases it meant a widow serving in charity or a consecrated woman. For example, canon 20 of the Council of Tours of 567 ordered: "In truth, if a presbyter is found with his *presbiteria*, a deacon with his *diaconissa* or a subdeacon with his *subdiaconissa*, he is excommunicated for a whole year and is deposed from every clerical office."[232]

Deposition and Reduction of the Clergy to the Lay State

ONE OF THE CONSEQUENCES of the lacerating Decian persecution of 250 was the action of bishops and guilty clerics who wanted to be reintegrated into all their activities. As there was no sure and recognized practice, different solutions were developed. The practice of reducing the cleric to the lay state was adopted after adequate penance had been demonstrated, the requirements of which were more radical for the clergy, including the loss of the clerical condition and its privileges.[233] The Bishop Fortunatianus of Assuras was reduced to a layman and then tried to get his office back.[234] It was the same with Bishop Evaristus.[235] An African synod in 252 reproached Bishop Terapius for having readmitted the former presbyter Victor to the peace of the church (*pax ecclesiae*) with too much haste after he had admitted to worshiping a pagan god.[236] According to Cyprian, Cornelius had also decided on admission to penance and reduction to the lay state of lapsed (*lapsi*) clerics.[237] In the Roman Council of the summer of 251 Cornelius and the other bishops readmitted an entire community to the *pax ecclesiae* while its bishop Trophimus remained in the lay condition.[238] Cornelius employed a similar treatment in receiving back into his community in the lay condition a bishop who had ordained Novatian.[239] However, in some cases the Roman church was more indulgent as, for example, their readmission of the schismatic *confessores* and the readmission of the presbyter Maximus into the clergy.[240] Cornelius left the presbyter and confessor Maximus in office even though he at first had supported Novatian,[241] perhaps because he was a well-known *confessor* during the persecution and Cyprian himself had urged him to abandon the schism.[242] However, Rome and Carthage differed in their practices, both in the case of the presbyter Maximus and with the Spanish bishop Basilides of León-Astorga and Martial of Mérida who were accused of apostatizing at the time of the Roman bishop Stephen I († 257). The solution to the problem posed during Decius' persecution of downgrading the clerics remained fluid in the period that followed. At the Council of Rome in 313, Miltiades was ready to welcome the bishops ordained by Majorinus, and "established that in all the places where two bishops of the two parties were, the one ordained previously should be confirmed and that the other should be assigned other faithful to govern."[243] Canon 13 of the Council of Arles (314) reduced the lapsed clerics (*lapsi, traditores*) to the lay state but considered the ordinations they had done valid. The Council of Ancyra (314) established that apostate presbyters retained their *honor* but were reduced to the lay state (can. 1). Deacons were reduced to the lay state at the discretion of the bishop (can. 2). Apostate catechumens, if baptized, could be ordained (can. 12). Canon 8 of the Council of Nicaea (325) established that the followers of Novatian who converted could remain in the clergy after having received the imposition of hands,[244] and retained their rank if there was no bishop or a catholic presbyter in the same place. But if a bishop or presbyter was already in place it was advisable to find another solution. Nicaea's position was contrary to African tradition and open to future solutions. Canon 62 of the *Apostolic Canons* reduced the apostate cleric to the lay state. The *Epistula ad Gallos* of Damasus reduced to the lay state those who changed dioceses.[245] In the context of the Donatist controversy, strategies for adoption were being developed.[246] Augustine noted that there was a different practice for clerics ordained in the schismatic church than for those who had been ordained in the Catholic Church and who, having converted to Donatism had since returned to the Catholic Church.[247] Donatus both re-baptized and reordained.[248] But at the time of Augustine the Donatists welcomed clerics in the condition of lay catechumens[249] who, after baptism, could also be reordained.[250] Since the Catholics, on the other hand, did not repeat baptism, they also did not reordain because "the Order had remained intact in them."[251] They only subjected converts to penance.[252] The imposition of hands on clerics did not take place in public.[253] Perhaps one explanation is because of the lack of clergy to facilitate the conversion of the Donatist clergy which had retained its functions.[254] Whereas, according to an ancient tradition, if apostates who returned to the Catholic Church had been Catholics before they became apostate, they could not belong to the clergy, and if they were lay people they could not be ordained.[255] But not all bishops observed this rule.[256] However, as Vogel has shown, apart from the exceptions, ancient doctrine considered the ordinations of heretics and schismatics null, according to the principle of Pope Innocent I that those who come to the Catholic Church obtain only the layman's condition (*laica communio*).[257]

Another aspect emerges in this controversy of the *lapsi* clerics and their reduction to the lay state.[258] Did the clerics lose their sacramental state of ordination? This aspect was not examined in depth, since they did not think in terms of a sacrament that confers the sacramental character. However, they were considered unworthy of exercising the ministry and were referred to as pseudo-bishops[259] or adulterers.[260] In 256, Cyprian wrote to Stephen that it was decided in the synod that if the clergy who had left the church and had joined the heretics or schismatics, such as those who had been ordained in those sects, wanted to return to the Catholic Church, they could only be received in the lay state.[261] Therefore, the ordination was initially valid, but when he left the Catholic Church, the ordained was no longer a cleric.[262] Nor was someone ordained for a place that already had a valid cleric.[263]

Another question that was raised was whether an ordination performed outside the Catholic Church was valid? Cyprian's answer is clearly negative and contrary to the later theological development of the indelible character of the ordained.[264] It is an unlawful ordination (*ordinatio illicita*), that is, an ordination that goes against ecclesiastical practice and also occurs outside the Catholic Church. It is also an invalid ordination (*ordinatio irrita*), and therefore it is as if it had never happened, while those who have received a lawful ordination (*ordinatio licita*), if they become apostate, a schismatic, or heretic they lose their clerical state.[265] Cyprian's position is based on his ecclesiology. Cyprian repeatedly affirmed the conviction that "he who does not possess the unity of the Church does not possess ecclesiastical ordination."²⁶⁶

As we noted, in the case of the Novatians, they had received baptism and ordination in their sect, but because they had the right doctrine, only the laying on of hands was required for them to remain in the clergy according to the Council of Nicaea (325). Was the rite a new ordination, as some claim?²⁶⁷ The difficulty arises in interpreting the gesture of the imposition of hands, which is extremely ambiguous and is specified by the words that accompany it. If the followers of Paul of Samosata converted, they were required to be rebaptized and reordained if they were clergy (can. 19). In the same council it is established that the Melitians, if ordained in the sect, must be reordained and then continue in the clergy in a lower condition. If the clergy of the titular church died where they served, they could assume his place. Canon 7 of the synod of Laodicea required the rebaptism of the converted Montanists. Canon 7 of the so-called synod of Constantinople²⁶⁸ required rebaptism of numerous converting sects. The Council of Serdica considered the ordination of someone from another diocese invalid. The long-lasting Donatist controversy over the validity of the sacraments in the fourth century was resolved in mutual recognition: Catholics considered valid the ordinations of Donatists who accepted the return to the Catholic Church. Augustine supported a doctrine totally contrary to Cyprian's: "And just as the baptized, moving away from unity, does not lose the sacrament of baptism, so the ordained, moving away from unity, does not lose the sacrament of giving baptism."²⁶⁹

The later Roman Catholic conception of the *indelible character* bestowed at ordination will be worked out in the Middle Ages from the 11th century. Only at the Council of Trent, on June 15, 1563, will it be defined that the sacrament of order, like baptism, gives a character that cannot be cancelled or abolished. The question of the validity of ministerial ordination, as it was set out in the third century, is extremely delicate and is still the focus of attention today because it is of great ecumenical importance.²⁷⁰

---

1. Gregory of Nazianzus, *Or.* 2.26; PG 35:436A.
2. Chrysostom, *Comm. in 2 Tim.* 2.2; PG 62:610.
3. *1 Clement* 44.4.
4. Outside the *Pastoral Epistles*, whose authorship by Paul has been disputed.
5. *Didache* 15.1.
6. Eusebius, *HE* 3.37.3.
7. Gregory of Nyssa, *In diem luminum*: PG 46:581D.
8. Ignatius, *To the Smyrnaeans* 8.
9. S. Lilla, *La brachigrafia italo-bizantina* (Vatican City: Biblioteca apostolica vaticana, 1981); H. C. Teitler, *Notarii and exceptores. An inquiry into role and significance of shorthand writers in the imperial and ecclesiastical bureaucracy of the Roman Empire (from the Early Principate to c.450 A.D.)* (Amsterdam: J.C. Gieben Publisher, 1985).
10. Augustine, *De doctrina chr.* 2.26.40.
11. Augustine, *Ep.* 213.2.

12. Augustine, *Ep.* 238.1; *Gesta coll. Carth* 3.1.
13. F. Gori, "L'oratoria cristiana antica. Dall'improvvisazione alla ripetizione. Il ruolo della memoria," in *Nuovo e antico nella cultura greco-latina del IV-VI secolo*, ed I. Gualandri, F. Conca, R. Passarella (Milan: Cisalpino, 2005), 351-70, see esp 353; F. Gori, "L'edizione critica delle Enarrationes in Psalmos graduum: questioni specifiche," *Augustinianum* 41 (2001): 102-12; *EAC* 3:273-93.
14. Augustine, *De doctrina chr.* 4.10.25.
15. Cyprian list the deficiencies of the bishops as does Origen, *Hom. in Num.* 22.4.
16. *Apostolic Tradition* 3. In the translation of the Ethiopian text made by A. Bausi we read: "pour out the truth that comes from you, the guiding spirit, which you granted to your beloved Son Jesus Christ" in *Christianity in Egypt: studies in honor of Tito Orlandi* (Rome: Institutum Patristicum Augustinianum, 2012), 29.
17. *Didascalia* 2.25.7.
18. *Didascalia* 2.26.3-7.
19. *Didascalia* 4.2.2.
20. *Didascalia* 4.2.5.
21. City south of Baghdad; also called Mahoze (twin capital), Mahoza Rabba (the great capital) or Mdinatha d'Beth Aramaye (the cities of Beth Aramaye).
22. Isidore of Seville, *Etym.* 7.12.10.
23. Isidore of Seville, *Etym.* 7.12.6.
24. *I Macc* 7:33; 11:23; 12:6 and 35; 14:20; *II Macc* 1:10; 4:44; 11:27; 13:13.
25. *I Clement* 42.4-5.
26. *1 Clement* 44.1; 44.3 and 5.
27. *1 Clement* 44.2-3.
28. Polycarp, *To the Philadelphians* 1.1; 5.2; 6.1.
29. Polycarp, *To the Philadelphians* 11.1.
30. Irenaeus, *Adv. haer.* 3.2.2.
31. Chrysostom, *Hom. 1.1 in Phil.*
32. PL 3:1209A.
33. PL 3:1206; cf. Tertullian, *De pudic.* 14.16: *praesidens*.
34. The collegial character not only of the priesthood, but of the whole Christian ministry is highlighted very well by Alberto Vilela for the third century: *La condition collégiale des prêtres au IIIe siècle* (Paris: Beauchesne, 1971).
35. A shrine, oratory, or church built in memory of a martyr.
36. Cf. Phileas, *Ep ad Meletium*: PG 10:1566B.
37. Cf. Athanasius, *Apol.* 85: PG 25:400.
38. Jerome, *Ep.* 127.15; 146.1-2.
39. Cf. Council of Tours of 567, can. 20.
40. Socrates, *HE* 5.22: PG 67:639.
41. Eusebius, *HE* 6.19.16-18.
42. Eusebius, *HE* 6.19.17-18. Translation modified.
43. Gennadius, *De viris ill.* 3: PL 58:1063.
44. Cf. Chrysostom, *In epist. I ad Cor.*, *hom.* 36.4; *Philogon.* 3: PG 48:752, lines 47-50; see also *Ap. Const.* 2.57.9.
45. Egeria, *Itinerarium* 25.1.
46. J. Bernardi, *La prédication des Pères Cappadociens : le prédicateur et son auditoire* (Paris: Presses universitaires de France, 1968), 58-59; 188, endnote 5.
47. Jerome, *Ep.* 5.7.
48. R. Gryson, *Le prêtre selon saint Ambrose* (Louvain: Édition orientaliste, 1968), 138.
49. Possidius, *Life of Augustine* 5.3.
50. Socrates, *HE* 5.22; Sozomen, *HE* 7.19. Cf. A. Olivar, *La predicación cristiana antigua* (Barcelona: Herder, 1991), 528-54.
51. Jerome, *Ep.* 146.1.
52. Jerome, *Ep.* 147.2.
53. R. Cabié, "Quand les "Sept" deviennent les diacres," *Bulletin de littérature ecclésiastique* 97 (1996): 219-225
54. *Apostolic Tradition* 8.
55. Cyprian, *Ep* 3.1.

56. Hermas, *Shepherd*, Parable 9.26.2.
57. *Didascalia* 2.28.6.
58. *Didascalia* 2.44.3-4.
59. *Didascalia* 2.57.6.
60. Isidore of Seville, *De ecclesiasticis officiis* 2.8.
61. Justinian, *Novella* 3.1.
62. Cyprian, *Ep.* 3.3.
63. Cf also *In Trullo* 7.
64. *Statuta ecclesiae antiqua*, can. 57.
65. *Apostolic Tradition* 13.
66. Ch. Pietri, *Roma Christiana* (Rome: École Française de Rome, 1976), 690-96; MEFRA 89(1977), 392-93.
67. Optatus of Milevis, *Against the Donatists* 1.16; PL 9:916.
68. Gelasius of Caesarea, *HE* 2.7.44: PG 85:1244A.
69. Anatolius of Constantinople, *Ep.* 132.2 [among the letters of Leo the Great]; Theodoret, *HE* 1.26.3; Sozomen, *HE* 6.30; 8.9; Palladius, *Vita Chr.* 2.
70. Jerome, *Ep.* 125.15.
71. Jerome, *Comm. ad Ez.* 14.48, PL 25:484; Leo the Great, *Ep.* 111.2. In other words, when the bishop wants to get rid of his archdeacon, but is having trouble doing so, the bishop gives the deacon the "honor" of becoming a presbyter, which was really no honor at all since archdeacons exercised more power than presbyters in most situations.
72. Sozomen, *HE* 7.19.6.
73. *Apostolic Const.* 2.57.16; Palladius, *Vita Chr.* 2; PG 47:9.
74. Leo the Great, *Ep.* 112.1.
75. Leo the Great, *Ep.* 111.2.
76. Council of Carthage of 398, can. 17; Isidore of Pelusium, *Ep.* 1.29, PG 78:200C; *Statuta ecclesiae. ant.* 7; Gelasius, *Ep.* Fr. PL 59:100.
77. Optatus, *Against the Donatists* 1.16; Leo the Great, Ep. 111.2.
78. *Statuta ecclesiae. ant.* 94.
79. Council of Chalcedon ACO II.1.2 p. 42, line 8.
80. Mansi VI, 568; 569; 616; VII, 404; 433.
81. Innocent I, *Ep.* 2.3: PL 20:472.
82. Basil, *Ep.* 54: PG 32:400C.
83. Cyprian, *Epp.* 9.1; 29.2; 34.4; 36.1; 45.4; 47.2; 69.1.
84. *fecit VII subdiaconos*: *Liber Pontificalis* 1.148 ed. Duchesne.
85. Cyprian, *Epp.* 9.1; 20; 36; 45; 77; 79.
86. *Apostolic Tradition* 13.
87. *Apostolic Constitutions* 8.21.1-4.
88. Theodore of Mopsuestia, *In Ep. Pauli Com.*, ed. Swete 1982, Vol 2:123-24.
89. *Apostolic Constitutions* 8.21.
90. *Apostolic Constitutions* 8.11.11-12.
91. Councils of Braga of 561: can. 10; of 572: can. 41.
92. Siricius, *Ep.*1.11: PL 13:1144; Sylvester, *Ep.* 15: PL 8:848; *Ep.* 7: PL8:835; Innocent, *Ep.* 37.5: PL 20:604; Zosimus, Ep. 11.1: PL 20:642.
93. Munier, *Concilia Africae*, CCL 149:108, 126, 142.
94. Isidore of Seville, *De off.* 2.10: PL 83:790-91.
95. PL 72:319.
96. *Ministeria quaedam*, in *Enchiridion Vaticanum* 4:1749-70.
97. Cf. Jerome, *Ep.* 52.5; *Concilia Africae*: CCL 149:344.
98. Cyprian, *Ep* 7.2.
99. Cyprian, *Epp.* 45.4.3; 52.1; 59.1.
100. Cyprian, *Epp.* 77.3.2; 78.1.1; cf. also *Epp.* 34.4.1; 49.3; 59.9.
101. Eusebius, *HE* 6.43.11.
102. Eusebius, *Life of Constantine* 3.8.

103. Mansi 2, 620; PL 8:831.
104. Mansi 2,627 and 629.
105. *Ep. ad Himerium* 9 in Di Berardino A. (ed.), *I concili della chiesa antica*, vol. II, *Decretali, concili romani e canoni di Serdica*, 72.
106. In order to avoid criticism of Ambrose's ordination, Paulinus of Milan insinuated the idea that he received the various ministries in a week: "It is said that [Ambrose] exercised all the functions of the ecclesiastical ministry, and on the eighth day he was ordained bishop." Paulinus of Milan, *Vita Amb.* 9.3.
107. Innocent, *Ep. ad Decentium* 5.
108. *Ep. ad episcopos Lucaniae* III,3, in *I canoni dei concili*, 202.
109. John the Deacon, *Ep. ad Senarium*: PL 59:495.
110. Tertullian, *De praescr.* 41; *De spect.* 26; Cyprian, *Sent.* 37; Augustine, *Contra Iul.* 3.9.18.
111. Cf. Tertullian, *Apologeticum* 22-23.
112. Tertullian, *Apologeticum* 23.15.
113. Augustine, *Gen. litt.* 2.36.
114. *Theod Cod* 16.2.24.
115. C. Perrot, "Luc 4,16-30 et la lecture biblique de l'ancienne Synagogue," *Revue Sciences R.* 47 (1973): 324-40.
116. P. Saenger, *Space Between Words: The Origins of Silent Reading* (Stanford: Stanford University Press, 2000).
117. Augustine, *De doctrina chr., prol.* 9.
118. See Quintilian, *Inst. orat.* 1.1.33-34. G. Stefani, "La recitazione delle letture nella liturgia romana antica," *Ephemerides Liturg* 81(1967): 113-30.
119. Isidore, *Etym.* 2.11.5: PL 83:791.
120. Augustine, *En. in Ps.* 93.9.
121. Isidore of Seville, *Etym.* 2.39.1: PL 83:790-91.
122. Justin, *I Apology* 67.4.
123. Tertullian, *De praescr. haer.* 41.8.
124. "The lector of the present reading has read" (1.1); "for us has been proclaimed the reading" (2.1); "as the reading that has been proclaimed has explained" (3.1).
125. E. Wipszycka, "Un lecteur qui ne sait pas écrire ou un chrétien qui ne veut pas se souiller (P.Oxy XXXI-II,2673)," *Zeitschrift für Papyrologie und Epigraphik* 50 (1983): 17-21
126. P. Maraval, *La passion inédite de S. Athénogène de Pédachtho, en Cappadoce (BHG 197b)* (Brussels: Société des Bollandistes, 1990).
127. Cyprian, *Ep.* 38.
128. In *Optatus Milevi*, ed. Ziwsa, CSEL 26, (Vienna 1893), 186-87.
129. Cf. Gregory of Nazianzus, *Ep.* 11: PG 37:44.
130. Augustine, *In ps. 138 enarr.*, 1; *Ep.* 29.4; *Ep.* 71.3; *De doctr. christ.* 4.6.
131. Augustine, *Ep.* 26.2 Divjak.
132. Augustine, *Ep.* 64.2-4.
133. E. Paoli Lafaye, *Les lecteurs des textes liturgiques*, in: A. M. La Bonnardière, *Saint Augustin et la Bible*, *Bible de tous les temps*, vol. 3 (Paris: Beauchesne, 1986), 59-74.
134. Augustine, *Enar. in ps.* 63.19.
135. Augustine, *Enar. in ps.* 138.1.
136. *Brev. Hipp.* 19, Munier 39.
137. *Conc. Hipp.*, can. 2, Munier, 20; *Brev. Hipp.* 18, Munier, 38; cf. Canons in the case of Apiarius 16, Munier, 138; Ferrandi *Brev.* 129, Munier, 298.
138. *Con. Hipp*, Munier 21.
139. *Reg. etc.Carth* . 90, Munier, 208.
140. *Brev. Hipp.*, can. 1, Munier, 33.
141. Cyprian, *Ep.* 52.
142. Cf. E. Diehl, *Inscriptiones latinae christianae veteres*, vol. III, indice.
143. *Apostolic Tradition* 11.
144. *Liber Pont.* 1, p. 155, ed. Duchesne.
145. *Liber Pont.* 1. p. 161, ed. Duchesne.
146. *Liber Pont.* 1. p. 171, ed. Duchesne.

147. Mansi 2,623; PL 8:836.
148. *Apostolic Constitutions* 8.11.11-12.
149. Ps. Ignatius, *Ad Antioch.* 12: PG 5:908.
150. Paulinus of Nola, *Carmen* 1.10; 19.447.
151. CTh 16.12.24.
152. *Didascalia* 2.57.6; 2.58.1.
153. *Apostolic Constitutions* 2.25.26; 2.28.5; 3.11.1-3; 6.17.2.
154. Augustine, *Conf.* 6.2.
155. Gelasius, *Ep.* 14.2: Thiel 363.
156. *Liber Pont.* 1.303; cf. 1.309.
157. 13, 789; Diehl 1288.
158. CIL 3, 13142; Diehl 1289; cf. index of Diehl, vol. III, 374.
159. DACL 14, 1532-33.
160. Augustine, *Ep.* 26, Divjak.
161. L. Duchesne, *Origines du culte chrétienne* (Paris: De Boccard, 1925), 365, n.3; for the *mansionarii* see Diehl 1290 and 1290.
162. *Ministeria quaedam*, in *Enchiridion Vaticanum* 4,1749-70.
163. Tertullian, *Apologeticum* 36.3; *Apostolic Tradition* 40.
164. Gregory the Great, *Ep.* 8.3; *EAC* 2:60-61.
165. Tertullian, *Adversus Praxeam* 29.
166. Cyprian, *Ep.* 58.5.
167. *Apostolic Tradition* 9.
168. Cyprian, *Ep.* 38.1.1.
169. Cf. *Didache* 11 and 13.
170. *Didache* 8, 12.
171. Hermas, *Shepherd, Mandate* 1.1-2.
172. Justin, *Dialogue* 35.5; 51.2; 69.1; 82.1-2.
173. Ulrich Neymeyr, *Die christlichen Lehrer im zweiten Jahrhundert. Ihre Lehrtätigkeit, ihr Selbstverständnis und ihre Geschichte* (Leiden: Brill, 1989), 2015.
174. *Passion of Perpetua and Felicitas* 4.5 and 13.1.
175. Cf. Cyprian, *Ep.* 29 [23].2. The ANF edition numbers this as *Letter* 23.
176. Origen, *Homil. in Ezech.* 2.2.
177. CTh 16.2.43.
178. CTh 16.2,.42 and 43.
179. Mansi 6,828. Leo referred to this council as the Robber Synod.
180. CI – Justinian Code; CTh 16.2.42 = CI 1.3.17; CTh 16.2.43 = CI 1.3.18.
181. Galasisu, *Ep.* 141; R.M. Frakes, *Contra Potentium Iniurias: The Defensor Civitatis and Late Roman Justice* (Munich: C.H. Beck, 2001), 182-94.
182. *Collectio Avellana*, Ep. 6; *Enciclopedia dei Papi*, 1:363.
183. Innocent, *Ep.* 41: PL 20:607A.
184. Possidius, *Vita Augustini* 12.5.
185. Zozimus, *Ep.* 9.3: PL 20:673.
186. CTh 16.2.38.
187. Pelagius, *Ep. et dec.* 8: PL 72:745.
188. Gregory the Great, *Ep.* 1.42.
189. Eusebius, *HE* 10.7.2.
190. CTh 16.2.2.
191. Cf. CTh 15.14.1 of December 16, 324.
192. J. Gaudemet, "Constantin, restaurateur de l'orde," in *Studi in onore di S. Solazzi* (Naples: E. Jorene, 1948), 653-74. Cf. C. Dupont, "De quelques problèmes découlant de la conquête de l'Orient par Constantin. Leur solution par ce prince," *Revue Int. Des droits de l'Antiquité* 18 (1971): 479-500.
193. See CTh 165.1.
194. Eusebius, *HE* 10.9.8-9 and *Vita Constantini*.

195. Th 16.2.2.
196. Athanaius, *Hist. Arr.* 78.1-3.
197. CTh 16.2.6.
198. CTh 16.2.3.
199. CTh 16.2.6.
200. Trans. Coleman-Norton, alt.
201. *Municeps:* indicates the *civis* of a *municipium* or any city, but, as in this case, a *curialis* (Paulus, *Digestum* 50.16.228; CTh 1.15.12; 12.1.89).
202. The word *Pauperes* indicates the social origin of the clergy from the patrimonial point of view.
203. There was no property that belonged to the church as such, but to individual ecclesial communities.
204. CTh 16.2.17.
205. CTh 12.1.104.
206. A.G. Martimort, *Les diaconesses* (Rome: C.L.V.-Edizioni liturgiche, 1982); Martimort states that deaconesses do not belong to the clergy; A.D. Salapatas, "The Liturgical Role of the Deaconess in the Apostolic Constitutions," *OCP* 68 (2001): 561-78; John Wijngaards, *No Women in Holy Orders? Ancient Women Deacons* (Norwich: Canterbury Press, 2002) - he considers deaconesses members of the clergy; C. Osiek, Margaret Y MacDonald; Janet H Tulloch, *A Woman's Place: House Churches in Earliest Christianity* (Minneapolis: Fortress Press, 2006); D. Spataru, *Sacerdoti e diaconesse. La gerarchia ecclesiastica secondo i Padri Cappadoci* (Bologna: ESD, 2007); Moria Scimmi, *Le antiche diaconesse nella storiografia del XX secolo. Problemi di metodo* (Milan: Glossa, 2004).
207. Angelo Di Berardino, "Women and the Spread of Christianity in the First Centuries," *Augustinianum* 55 (2015): 305-37.
208. Clement of Alexandria, *Stromata* 3.6.53.
209. Origen, *Comm. In Rom.* 10.17.
210. Clement of Alexandria, *Stromata* 3.6.53; John Chrysostom, *In Epistula 1 ad Timotheus* 3, *hom.* 11,1,
211. *Didascalia* 2.26.6; see *Apostolic Constitutions* 2.26.
212. *Didascalia* 3.12.1-2.
213. *Didascalia* 3.12.3.
214. *Apostolic Constitutions* 8.11.The Latin translation of the *Didascalia* uses the term "diaconissa." (Erik Tidner, ed., *Didascaliae apostolorum, Canonum ecclesiasticorum: Traditionis apostolicae, versiones latinae,* (Berlin: Akademie-Verlag, 1963), 42, 59, 111.
215. *Apostolic Constitutions* 8.3.20.
216. *Didascalia* 3.12.3.
217. *Apostolic Constitutions* 3.6.1-2.
218. *Didascalia* 2.26.6.
219. Balsamon, at the end of the 12th century, commenting on this canon, notes that the practice is no longer in use.
220. Basil, *Ep. can.* 44.
221. Monumenta Asiae Minoris Antiqua VII, 113 nr. 539 e 143: sec. IV.
222. Chrysostom, *Ep.* 94: PG 52:657.
223. PG 83:1195.
224. *Scholia in concilium Chalcedonense,* in PG 137:441.
225. *Responsa ad interrogationes Marci* 35, in PG 138:988.
226. *Coptic Civilization: Two Thousand Years of Christianity in Egypt,* ed. Gawdat Gabra, (Cairo: American University of Cairo Press, 2014), 265-67; C. Chaillot, "Deaconesses in the Coptic Orthodox Church," *Ecclesia Orans* 35 (2018): 307-25, spec. 316ff.
227. These two councils use the Latin term *diacona.*
228. Cf. R. Barcellona, "Le vedove cristiane tra i Padri e le norme," *Annuarium historiae conciliorum* 35 (2003): 167-85.
229. *manu superposita, consecravit diaconam: Vita Radegundis reginae* 12: PL 88:502.
230. U.E. Eisen, *Women Officeholders in Early Christianity: Epigraphical and Literary Studies* (Collegeville: Liturgical Press, 2000) (very incomplete for epigraphy). There is a better article by A. Felle, "Diaconi e diaconissae tra Oriente e Occidente. L'apporto della documentazione epigrafica," in Διακονία, *diaconiae, diaconato. Semantica e storia* (Rome: Institutum Patristicum Augustinianum, 2010), 489-537.
231. C. Vagaggini, *L'ordinazione delle diaconesse nella tradizione greca e bizantina*: Orientalia Christiana Periodica 40 (1974), 145-89.

232. *I concili gallici*, vol. II, ed. P. Pellegrini(Rome 2011), 217f; EUNOMJA 2,350; the word *presbitera* in the Council of Auxerre (561-605), can. 21; Gregory the Great, *Dialogi* 4,12; CIL 10,8079.
233. Cf. Cyprian, *Ep* 67.6.3; *Ep*. 72.2.
234. Cyprian, *Ep*. 65.1.1.
235. Cyprian, *Epp*. 50.1.2; 52.2.1.
236. Cyprian, *Ep*. 64.1.1.
237. Cyprian, *Ep*. 67.6.2.
238. Cyprian, *Ep*. 55.11; cf. Peter of Alexandria can 10; PG 18:488-89; P.-P. Joannou, *Discipline générale antique*, vol. II, (Grottaferrata: Tipografia Italo-Orientale "S. Nilo", 1963), 46-47.
239. Eusebius, *HE* 6.43.10.
240. Cyprian, *Ep*. 49.2.
241. Cornelius, in Cyprian, *Ep*. 49.2.
242. Cyprian, *Ep*. 46; cf. *Ep*. 55.5.
243. Augustine, *Ep*. 43.16; cf. *Ep*. 185.47.
244. What is the meaning of this "laying on of hands"? A new ordination? Cf. Peter L'Huillier, *The Church of the Ancient Councils*, (Crestwood, NY: St. Vladimir's Seminary Press, 1996), 58ff. According to some authors, no real re-ordination was required, but L'Huillier is of contrary opinion.
245. Can 16. Cf. canons 17-19.
246. Cf. Albert C de Veer, *L'admission aux fonctions ecclésiastiques des clercs donatistes convertis*: Bibliothèque augustinienne 31 (1968), 766-71. For the readmission of the clergy in the Donatist controversy: Bibliothèque augustinienne 31, 791-92; Bibliothèque augustinienne 28,737-38; Bibliothèque augustinienne 31,766-771 (bibliography); Bibliothèque augustinienne 31,842-45; Bibliothèque augustinienne 31,771-73; Bibliothèque augustinienne 32,743-45.
247. Augustine, *Contra Cresconium* 2.16.19.
248. Cf. Optatus of Milevis, *Contra donat*. 1.24.
249. Augustine, *De unico bapt*. 11.19.
250. Augustine, *Contra Petilianum* 3.38.44; *Ep*. 108.6.19.
251. Augustine, *Contra ep. Parmeniani* 2.13.28.
252. Cf. G. Bavaud, *Le don de l'esprit par l'imposition des mains* : Bibliothèque augustinienne 29,600-605.
253. Augustine, cf. *Contra ep. Parmeniani* 1.1.2; *De baptismo* 1.1.2.
254. Crespin, *Ministère et Sainteté : Pastorale du Clergé*, o.c. pp. 55-60.
255. Cf. Cyprian, *Ep*. 65; Council of Arles, can. 13; Council of Nicaea, can. 10.
256. Cf. Augustine, *De baptismo* 1.1.2; *De unico bapstimo* 12.20.
257. *Ep ad Rufum*, IV,9.
258. H.E.J. Cowndrey, "The Dissemination of St. Augustine's Doctrine of Holy Orders During the Later Patristic Age," *JTS* 20 (1969): 448-81; C. Vogel, "Laica cummunione contentus," *Revue Sc. Religieuses* 47 (1973): 56-122.
259. Cyprian, *Ep*. 59.9.1; G. D. Dunn, "Cyprian's Rival Bishops and their Communities," *Augustinianum* 45 (2005): 61-93.
260. Cyprian, *Ep*. 45.1.2.
261. Cyprian, *Ep*. 72.2.1. Augustine discusses this letter in *De bapstimo contra donatistas* 6,15,25.
262. G. D. Dunn, "Schism and Heresy According to Cyprian of Carthage," *JTS* 55 (2004): 551-74. Cyprian does not exactly distinguish between heresy and schism, therefore he could not accept the Augustinian position on the Donatists (Cf. SC 519:129ff.).
263. Cf. Cyprian, *Ep* 44.3.2; 55.8.4-5.
264. G.D. Dunn, "Validity of Baptism and Ordination in the African Response to the 'Rebaptism' Crisis: Cyprian of Carthage's Synod of Spring 256," *Theological Studies* 67 (2006): 257-74.
265. Cyprian, *Ep*. 72.
266. Cyprian, *Ep*. 55.8.3.
267. Cf. Peter L'Huillier, *The Church of the Ancient Councils*, (Crestwood, NY: St Vladimir's Seminary Press, 1996), 58ff.
268. It is not a canon of the Council of Constantinople of 381, but an extract from the letters of the church of the capital to Martyrius Antiochene (cf. P. L'Huillier, *The Church of the Ancient Councils*, 131).
269. Augustine, *De baptismo c. donatistas* 1.2.1. N. Häring, "The Augustinian Axiom: Nulli sacramento iniuria facienda est," *Medieval Studies* 16 (1954): 87-117.
270. *Les Pères de l'Église et les Ministères,* ed. P.-G. Delage, (La Rochelle: Association Histoire et Culture, 2008).

CHAPTER 6

AUTHORITY, ORGANIZATION AND ECCLESIAL COMMUNION

AUTHORITY IN THE CHURCH

THE EXPRESSION "MINISTRY OF LEADERSHIP" USED IN THE PREVIOUS CHAPTER IMPLIES THE existence of people who have authority in the church. "For a long time, the idea prevailed that the New Testament church from the beginning had a purely charismatic constitution and had been governed exclusively by people elected in a charismatic manner and endowed with charismatic prerogatives. Since the charisms subsequently faded until they ceased altogether, the law of man would be established in the church. The latter could therefore be considered an emergency, but it would be contrary to the essence of the church. Although such a rigid opposition may not fit, the relationship between Spirit and ministry is a problem in the history of the church of origin and perhaps always."[1] For this reason there would be a break between the first Christian generation and the time after the Apostles, that is, between the primitive community with a purely charismatic character and that with a hierarchical structure and institutions which followed. When this shift occurs, the Catholic Church is birthed as a community of believers with a hierarchy, an organization, and a division of roles. Such an interpretation arises from the opposition between charism—a sign of creativity and spontaneity—and institution. But since such opposition is not fully reflected in the New Testament, this schema has in part been abandoned. However, it has served to better understand the evolution of the organization of the ancient church, its various ministries and their evolution. When Schelke wrote the quoted passage above, there was a heated dispute over the opposition between charism and institution—with disastrous consequences. On the one hand there were those who were inflexible in their attachment to tradition; and on the other there were those who wanted radical change. Today a greater balance has been achieved among scholars belonging to different Christian confessions.

Certainly, the church of the first two centuries knew a wealth and variety of charisms and people. There were apostles, missionaries, evangelists, prophets, doctors, all of whom enjoyed great prestige. But they were controlled by the small, close-knit communities who made them, in different ways, participate in the offices involved with oversight of the community. Charismatic members and leaders complemented one another, even if at times there were disputes or misunderstandings. Far from slavishly following charismatic or democratic anarchy, the first communities were much more influenced by the synagogues and priestly, Essene or other traditions. They formed themselves into communities and churches under the direction of the responsible leaders, with their own authority.[2] The insistence that some older Christian texts place on order and harmony among all followers of Jesus is a sign of the difficulties but also of the ideals they aspired to.

Already in the New Testament we hear of those who had authority and required received obedience from the community. There were apostles who were in charge of and established bishop-presbyters, deacons and other ministers who had responsibilities. All of these were identified with various names, such as leaders, guides, teachers, and other similar terms. Obedience was a common emphasis: "But we appeal to you, brothers and sisters, to respect those who labor among you, and have charge of you in the Lord and admonish you; esteem them very highly in love because of their work. Be at peace among yourselves" (*1 Thess* 5:12-13). "Obey your leaders and submit to them, for they are keeping watch over your souls and will give an account. Let them do this with joy and not with sighing—for that would be harmful to you" (*Heb* 13:17).[3] The community must obey, but at the same time it must also hold its leaders accountable. There is no opposition between charism and institution because leadership, understood as service, is also considered a charism. There is the charism of spontaneity, but there is also the charism of order whereby the prophets are judged by the community and its leaders (cf. *1 Cor* 14:29-30). There is a dialectical relationship between the community, the *ecclesia*—that is, the assembly of baptized summoned by the Lord—and those who exercise responsibilities. Institutional realities and charisms cannot be separated because they are complementary and conditioned by each other. After the apostolic period we have a progressive unification of the characteristics of authority which previously and at various times belonged to different ministries. This coalescence of the different aspects of authority takes place in the person of the bishop, who is the head of the community, as well as its pastor, teacher, liturgist and priest, prophet and the man of the Spirit. These roles he obtained through ordination in service to the church (*ecclesia*). The bishop—according to the original meaning of the term—is the overseer who ensures fidelity to the tradition and unity of the church. The establishment of the canon, which developed during the second century, is also an important element in ensuring fidelity to trustworthy doctrine. It also helps bishops in carrying out their activity of oversight, especially at the time of the emergence of so many texts, which actually introduced other doctrines, or works attributed to the apostles that were full of imagination. Marcion himself, with his selection, contributed in a positive sense to the selection of those texts to be preserved from the Old and New Testaments.

An important Roman writer of the fourth century, referred to as Ambrosiaster, makes a keen observation when commenting on a text from the *Letter to the Ephesians* on charisms (*Eph* 4:11). He affirms that the progress of evangelization and the spread of Christianity entailed a specialization of the various ministries, but that at the beginning everyone could preach and baptize. In his own day, when the church had by then been firmly established, he recognized that, unlike at the beginning, no cleric would dare exercise an office in an established ecclesial community if he was not ordained to that office.[4] We should note that when discussing the ecclesial community, instead of using a more specialized term, the author uses the more generic Latin term *conventicula*, as do some other authors of his day.[5] Our image of the local ecclesial community comes from Cyprian. He sees it as the faithful and clerics gather around their bishop who serves as the vital center of the community: "The Church consists of people who remain united with their bishop, it is the flock that stays by its shepherd."[6] He sees it as a well built and tightly organized community. In reality the church was still in a period of experimentation, searching for solutions to many problems discussed in churches and among churches such as the issue of how to deal with sinners and apostates, the validity of baptism, the dignity of ministers, sinful clergy, and the list goes on.

In the previous chapters we described these developments and variations. Churches, in the absence of precedents, had to improvise and used ideas and examples from civil society. That is why it is naive to think that only one model of local organization had developed. The essential elements are unity and harmony, but decentralization is also another facet of the local organization not only due to local influences but also because of what they inherited in practice from itinerant missionaries who originally established the communities.

Clement of Rome, writing to the Corinthians at the end of the first century speaks firmly to the community there—albeit with a delicate and pastoral tone—exhorting them to follow and obey their leaders: "We proclaim that they cannot unjustly be dismissed,"[7] because the foundation of their authority is their succession from the apostles sent by Christ. Here Clement already clearly insinuates the fundamental idea of apostolic succession.[8] It is clear from the whole letter that the Christian community is hierarchically organized and is closely identified with the church established by Christ. At the beginning of the second century, Ignatius of Antioch even more forcefully reiterates the idea of unity and submission to the ministers, especially to the bishop, who is the visible representative of the invisible bishop,

Christ himself. Resisting the bishop is resisting God.[9] Irenaeus emphasizes the role of the bishops in the community: "It is incumbent to obey the presbyters who are in the Church—those who, as I have shown, possess the succession from the apostles; those who, together with the succession of the episcopate, have received the certain gift of truth (*charisma veritatis certum*), according to the good pleasure of the Father."[10]

Any discourse on authority in the ancient church must consider several factors, including the various ministries, ecclesiological doctrines, the historical context, their previous Jewish heritage, the role of Scripture, and above all considerations of geographical space and chronological time. As we have seen in chapter two, the great transformations took place gradually during the third and fourth centuries. The differences were sometimes quite noticeable but would diminish with the passage of time. An example is the feast of Easter where both the date of the celebration and its theological significance developed over time. Another example is in the field of Christology which recorded dramatic changes over time. There were also numerous disciplinary, liturgical and sacramental rules that experienced similar divergence and development in the ensuing centuries in various places. Many differences eventually disappeared as a result of the influence of the larger ecclesial communities, creating geographical areas of a certain homogeneity in both doctrine and discipline in their orbit.

We have talked so far about the existence of authority in the church in the singular, and not of authorities in the plural, because most of these explanations we have been discussing are dependent on the idea of a singular authority. Moreover, it seems that the concept of *authority* should be distinguished, at least theoretically, from that of *power*, according to the famous expression of Pope Gelasius in the letter written in 494 to Emperor Anastasius: "There are two orders, O August Emperor, by which the world is principally ruled: the sacred authority of the pontiffs and the power of the king."[11] Power entails the possibility of influencing and controlling the actions of others, while authority is the right, and even the duty in certain cases, to exercise that power. Already at the time when Cyprian was writing to Bishop Rogatianus, he set about distinguishing the two concepts: "You had the power (*potestas*) of punishing him (a deacon) immediately by virtue of the strength of the episcopate (*vigore episcopatus*) and the authority of your see (*cathedrae auctoritate*).[12] Because of the office he exercises, the bishop has authority and can take measures to ensure that authority is carried out.[13] In this affirmation the term *vigore* (strength) expresses precisely the authority connected to the office of bishop, while the *cathedra* confers the validity of his teaching.[14] In the second century the accent was placed on the bishop, considered as a *teacher*, who possessed the true tradition by means of succession. His *cathedra* became a symbol of his teaching and thus of his very episcopal authority.

Due to the changes that took place inside and outside the church after Constantine, the meanings of the two terms have tended to be confused. The supreme and ultimate authority, of course, is divine and is realized in Christ and in his teaching. Christ's teaching in turn is manifested in Scripture and in the Apostolic Tradition. Recourse to both of these is a consistent theme in Christian antiquity and in every circumstance. As Cyprian notes: "If in fact we return to the source and origin of divine tradition, human error ceases. . . . If the truth has given way at some point and vacillated, we must go back to our source and Savior, to the tradition of the gospels and the apostles. The motivation for our action must derive from this because this is where our order and origin come from."[15] More briefly Cyprian expresses the same concept when he writes: ". . . we return to evangelical authority and apostolic tradition with sincere and religious faith."[16] In this sentence two fundamental bases of authority in the church are mentioned: Scripture and the Apostolic Tradition.

Scripture refers to divine authority which is the basis of doctrinal truth expressed in the rule of faith, in morals and also in the juridical realm.[17] The apostles ensured the integral transmission of the deposit of faith (*depositum fidei*) through succession, which in turn ensures the permanence of apostolic authority in Christian communities.[18] As time passes witnesses to this faith, who are successors of the bishops, as well as others (the fathers) acquire authority themselves, as do the decisions of bishops gathered together in synods.[19]

As mentioned, above, for the fathers the ultimate source of authority is divine,[20] according to the biblical schema: the Father sends the Son who in turn sends the apostles (cf. *Jn* 20:21; 17:18). In addition to the apostles, the bishops are soon added as an authority. We see this already in Clement of Rome,[21] and even more in Irenaeus[22] and Tertullian who summarized the concept in this way: "We advance, each one of us, sure in this rule of ours, that the Churches received from the Apostles, the Apostles in turn drew from the voice of Christ, and Christ from God."[23]

The mediated foundation of all authority in the church, however, is the apostles. The concept of apostolicity, which became established during the second century, became a fundamental category for understanding the ancient church. It is mentioned by Clement of Rome and is present in the episcopal lists of Hegesippus. Elaborated in particular by Irenaeus, Hippolytus, Tertullian and Cyprian, it became for them an indispensable conceptual tool both in doctrinal elaborations and in daily practice. The succession of the bishops is connected to it. The two concepts refer to each other and include each other. Apostolicity concerns both the origin of the church and its doctrine along with episcopal succession. The latter is proven historically by the drawing up of verifiable episcopal lists of churches for apologetic needs,[24] and also biblically and theologically by recourse to quotations from Scripture.

In the profession of faith, which became richer from the second century onwards, there is included a statement of belief in the apostolic church. The adjective "apostolic" refers directly to the apostles as a historical reality. But very soon it assumed doctrinal and institutional significance in relation to the term "catholic" as well. The Catholic Church was to be considered the authentic church because it traced its origins back to the apostles and faithfully transmitted their teaching as the first and true witnesses to the teaching of the Lord who founded the church and made the decisions that would govern its future ministerial organization. The mission received by Christ from the Father is entrusted to his disciples, who are called to be faithful witnesses through succession from the apostles to those who will take their place in the mission of proclaiming the Kingdom of God. When Christians included the terminology of apostolicity in the Creed, they wanted to affirm the historical, verifiable continuity of the faith of the church and of individual believers, and also to demonstrate that the church's ministry was in continuity with that of the apostles. The two terms *apostolic* and *catholic* are integrated in that *apostolic* expresses unity and continuity with the church's origins, while *catholic* expresses fellowship (*koinonia*) and unity with the present. Moreover, the term *catholic* is not primarily a geographical term referring to the *territory* of the whole earth so much as a term that is meant to address all *people* of every nation, country, time and place.

Historical contingencies, such as the fight against heretics who referred to a secret tradition, led to the insistence on episcopal succession. Irenaeus explicitly recalls this when he writes that "the bishops instituted by the apostles and their successors" until his time have never taught the doctrines attributed to the Gnostics.[25] In order to demonstrate that the true doctrine is found only in the Catholic Church, Tertullian bases his argument in his *Prescription Against Heretics* precisely on the episcopal succession existing in the Christian communities and dating back to the apostles. He adds the even finer point:

> Therefore, the Apostles (whose title denotes their being sent), having added to their number by lot a twelfth, Matthias, in the place of Judas, on the authority of a prophecy in a Psalm of David, and having obtained the promised power of the Holy Spirit for miracles and for utterance, bore witness to the faith in Christ Jesus first throughout Judaea. And, having founded churches there, they went out into the world and spread abroad the same doctrine of the same Faith to the nations. And, following the same pattern, they founded churches in every city, from which the rest of the churches hereafter have derived the transmission of their faith and the seeds of their doctrine and are daily deriving them in order to become Churches. Thus, these churches themselves are also considered Apostolic because they are the offspring of Apostolic churches.[26]

His contemporary, Hippolytus of Rome,[27] writes: "The Holy Spirit bequeathed to the church what the Apostles who had first received the message have transmitted to those who have rightly believed. But as their successors and participants in this grace, high-priesthood, and office of teaching—as well as being reputed guardians of the Church—we must not be found deficient in vigilance or disposed towards suppressing correct doctrine."[28] Cyprian has extremely precise and strong expressions, some of which suggest that bishops and the apostles have identical functions: "The Lord chose the apostles, that is, he chose the bishops and the leaders."[29] "Christ . . . says to the apostles and, through them, to all the bishops who succeed the apostles and become their vicars by order of succession: Whoever hears you, hears me" (*Lk* 10:16).[30]

We see the apostles putting in place from the beginning certain structures that would ensure continuity in their teaching and ministry. They established guides and safeguards[31] and the bishops should do the same.[32] And so, on the one hand there is the idea of a doctrine to be jealously guarded[33] and on the other there is the idea of continuity of ministry through the legitimate succession of leaders of the community.[34] This idea, already present in Clement of Rome, develops in Irenaeus who refers to "those who were instituted by the apostles as bishops and their successors down to us."[35] This idea reaches its full formulation with Hippolytus and Tertullian. In this subtle interweaving of ideas, episcopal lists—i.e. lists of bishops of churches drawn up chronologically—come about as historical proof of succession, which in turn serves as a guarantee of the orthodoxy of the teaching of a community inasmuch as through the uninterrupted succession of its bishops it can trace its authority back to its origins. In this regard, it should not be forgotten that in the second century there was a greater identification of a local church with its bishop, who was considered as the spokesman of his community. In addition, the succession was also a guarantee of the authority of a bishop and the priests who were in communion with their local bishop.

By the third century the doctrine of apostolic succession is constantly affirmed and assumed and does not require further confirmation; it did, however, need some further clarification. Cyprian's expression *vicaria ordinatione* helps us to understand the meaning of apostolic succession as a succession of the pastoral ministry which is supplementary and dependent on the foundation of the apostles—but with the same authority they had, all of which was derived from Christ. The fathers constantly remind us that Christ is present in his ministers, first and foremost in the bishops who are his servants and representatives who make Christ present and visible in the community. The fathers use various expressions to indicate this, such as referring to them as the vicars of Christ,[36] or the images and icons of Christ[37] who are the "mouth of God."[38]

Apostolic succession is the bridge that unites the unrepeatable moment of the apostles with the present time, and such apostolicity concerns not only the bishops, but the whole church, all Christians.[39] Since "the bishop is in the church and the church in the bishop,"[40] the apostolic succession is expressed visibly and concretely in him. For this reason the rite of ordination, of which we have already spoken in the previous chapter, plays an important role and is the title that is inserted in the line of succession which, it should be noted, is succession into an office of authority not by direct consecration by the predecessor, but by divine and ecclesial designation.

The laying on of hands in the rite of ordination bestows the Holy Spirit who must inwardly transform the ordained in order for them to be effective models for the people. It also confers on them the necessary and effective authority to carry out their tasks. Even when the bishop is elected by the whole community, he never considers himself—this must be emphasized—a delegate of the electorate. His authority does not come from below, but from above, from the Spirit. If, however, he is not faithful to his mission as leader and pastor, because he fails in faith or behavior, he can be deposed by his congregation and especially by the other bishops. The episcopate is not the culmination of the clerical *cursus* (progression) in a city, as is the case with city magistrates. A *cursus* forms in the fourth century for the purpose of preparation, even if sometimes they pass from baptism to episcopate by popular choice, without adequate preparation. The popular choice, based on the city's model of elections, in some cases favored the most notable and wealthiest people, which is not always a bad thing.

AUTHORITY AS SERVICE

Authority and service[41] are two opposite terms in our contemporary language. The term "authority" (*auctoritas*) comes from *augeo* which, in its original meaning, does not mean "to increase," or "to grow," but "to produce," "to raise." "Every word pronounced with authority determines a change in the world, creates something."[42] Those with authority have the right to issue rules to be observed. It may also exempt you from their observance. According to Hannah Arendt, authority must be distinguished from coercion,[43] but coercion still can be used. Service, on the other hand, comes from *servus* (slave or servant), someone whose very existence is at the full discretion of the master. In our case, he is in the service of his master. Several times in the previous chapter there was reference to clerics who must be people at the service of the faithful and others. The term "ministry" expresses the condition and function of a person who serves. It derives from *minus,* which means "minor" or "small." In other words, a minister is one who performs a service as a servant for others, something which is normally said of an inferior person (a *famulus*, a slave). This is the type of "authority" ministers were meant to have.

The kind of authority ministers have, in other words, is not autonomous but dependent on that of the apostles and is always conceived in terms of *diakonia*, which in Latin is rendered by the term *ministerium*, i.e., service. Although this term does not exclude a moral connotation, unfortunately today we are led to restrict it to this aspect only, distorting the original theological sense. In fact, the Greek term *diakonia* attempts to express the nature of authority in the church in general according to the evangelical spirit: "So Jesus called them and said to them, 'You know that among the Gentiles those whom they recognize as their rulers lord it over them, and their great ones are tyrants over them. But it is not so among you; but whoever wishes to become great among you must be your servant, and whoever wishes to be first among you must be slave of all."[44] The Gospels not only present Jesus as a subversive of certain current conventions and ideas in Palestine, but as one who came to serve: "For the Son of Man came not to be served but to serve, and to give his life a ransom for many."[45] The washing of the feet is a subversive gesture of the relationship between masters and servants. The first disciples understood that well. Paul describes his authoritative apostolate with these words: "Nor did we seek praise from mortals, whether from you or from others, though we might have made demands as apostles of Christ. But we were gentle among you, like a nurse tenderly caring for her own children. So deeply do we care for you that we are determined to share with you not only the gospel of God but also our own selves, because you have become very dear to us."[46] "I exhort the elders among you to tend the flock of God that is in your charge, exercising the oversight, not under compulsion but willingly, as God would have you do it not for sordid gain but eagerly. Do not lord it over those in your charge, but be examples to the flock."[47]

These passages and ideas are foundational concerning life in the church. But we also know that the reality from the beginning was a bit different: there were Christians who served and Christians who pretended to serve. In ancient times, as in later periods, the words of William of Auvergne in the 12th century could be applied: "The church is more like Pharaoh's chariot than God's! It hurtles down into the abyss of wealth and sensuality, even into sin. The wheels of the church's teachers have come off the track and are far removed, in their unlikeness, from Christ. . . . Today the chariot of the Church is no longer moving ahead but falling behind, because its horses are running backward and dragging it after them."[48] The idea of the *diakonia* is taken up by Ignatius of Antioch[49] and by the letter of the Christians of Lyon[50] and is also still found in the following period, even if expressed differently.

Origen says: "He who is called to the episcopate is not called to the command of the whole church but to its service."[51] Cyprian refers to himself as one "who every day serves the brothers."[52] Jerome specifies: "Bishop, priest and deacon are not terms indicating merits but offices."[53] Likewise, Augustine: "Bishop is a name of service, not of honor."[54] John Chrysostom writes: "The Lord has explicitly said that the concern for his flock was a proof of love for him."[55] Augustine defines the bishop as a "servant of Christ and of the servants of Christ."[56] This expression is referred to in the much-used formula by Gregory the Great: *servus servorum Dei*—servant of the servants of God. Christian epigraphy is also rich in similar expressions, such as *servus sanctorum*—servant of the saints. Augustine often emphasizes this idea of service that he must render to the community, of which he is a member: "From the moment this burden, about which such a difficult account must be rendered, was placed on my shoulders, anxiety about the honor shown me has always indeed been haunting me. . . . Where I'm terrified by what I am for you, I am given comfort by what I am with you. For you I am a bishop, with you, after all, I am a Christian. The first is the name of an office undertaken, the second a name of grace; that one means danger, this one salvation."[57] "You see, we whom the Lord has deigned, thanks to no merits of ours, to set in this high station (about which a very strict account indeed has to be rendered) have two things about us that must be clearly distinguished: one, that we are Christians, the other, that we are placed in charge (*praepositi*). Being Christians is for our sake; being in charge is for yours. It is to our advantage that we are Christians, only to yours that we are in charge. And there are many people who reach God as Christians."[58]

Jesus' question to Peter, as reported by John, strikes the heart of Peter as well as many pastors: "Simon, son of John, do you love me more than these?" And then he adds: "Feed my lambs."[59] These words have certainly caused great discomfort for those tasked with pastoral care. Those who have commented on this passage, such as Augustine, have pointed out that the authority is *Officium amoris pascere dominicum gregem*, i.e., it is a ministry of love to pasture the flock of the Lord.[60]

With the Constantinian peace the bishops became increasingly like Roman magistrates with greatly expanded powers and authority, which also had civil implications. One can easily imagine that some clergy handled this better than others. Our historical-theological treatment carried out so far has not included the sociological aspects that the ecclesial authority sometimes assumed in its exercise. From the very beginning we encounter complaints about the existence of ministers unworthy of both doctrine and behavior.[61] Origen often spoke of bishops who were proud, hypocritical and who accumulated wealth.[62] Cyprian painted many of his contemporaries in dark colors during the Decian persecution. The canonical legislation of the 4th and 5th centuries suggests a less than encouraging picture.

From the New Testament writings up to the time of Gregory the Great, the constant refrain was that bishops needed to have the moral qualities necessary to hold a managerial office if they were to be considered worthy of the episcopate. This insistence—sometimes obsessive as in the case of Origen—could imply that the church thought that the effectiveness of the sacraments depended on the holiness of the minister. The consequences of bishops not living up to the ideal were often dire for the life of the community. The numerous divisions and struggles that arose in ancient times are a sad consequence of this.

When the bishop, the man filled with the Spirit in ordination, is no longer a spiritual and charismatic figure, an expectation develops in the conscience of the people, especially in the East, of an exclusively spiritual character for their church leaders, proper to the man of God (*vir Dei*). One went to him for the needs of the soul.[63]

Experience shows from the very beginning of Christianity that there were unworthy ministers who were taken with domineering and this-worldly desires,[64] or who did not teach the right faith or ended up becoming schismatics. Was their ordination valid? Did their administration of the sacraments confer grace? These problems were already addressed during the debate on the validity of the baptism administered at the time of Cyprian in the middle of the third century. The doctrine elaborated for baptism is also valid for ordination and the administration of the sacraments.[65] The foundation of validity is Christ. This is why the unworthiness of the minister does not touch the substance of the sacraments, as Augustine forcefully puts it:

> He who is a proud minister is considered in league with the devil; but the gift of Christ is not contaminated. What flows through the minister remains pure, the liquid which passes through him reaches fertile soil. . . . For the spiritual power of the sacrament is like the light: it is received pure by those who are to be enlightened, and if it passes through the impure it is not stained. Let the ministers certainly by all means be righteous, and seek not their own glory but the glory of the One whose ministers they are. Let them not say, 'The baptism is mine,' for it is not theirs.[66]

THE ECCLESIAL COMMUNITY AND SIGNS OF ITS KOINONIA

From the very beginning, the church has been seen as a group of believers who have a fellowship of life with God through Jesus Christ in the Holy Spirit and fellowship with one another.[67] In his first letter, John writes: "We declare to you what we have seen and heard so that you also may have fellowship with us; and truly our fellowship is with the Father and with his Son Jesus Christ."[68] John emphasizes how the communication of faith generates ecclesial communion, which in turn is an indispensable condition of communion with God. The two aspects are essential and constitutive of the *ecclesia* and are expressed in the New Testament with the term *koinonia* (communion) and similar terms or expressions. *Koinonia* finds no correspondence in modern languages since it can indicate either a community that exists through a participation and sharing of goods or a communion that unites us together.[69]

The spiritual aspect of union with God and with others is the basis for the visible and material union among believers who consider one another as brothers and sisters inasmuch as they share in the same faith and the same sacraments, especially in the Eucharist. It is a spiritual but also a social communion among the members and is therefore under jurisdiction as a canonist would say. The idea of being a member of a *koinonia* is a fundamental category for understanding the institutions and life of the ancient church. Leaving aside its primary theological and ecclesiological significance, we must here give a little attention to what it means for one's life in the church. A brief text by Augustine summarizes the patristic vision of the problem: "Now, through what is common to the Father and the Son, they wanted us to be united among ourselves and with them, and through this gift to gather us together in unity through the one gift they have in common, that is, through the Holy Spirit, who is God and the gift of God."[70]

In the fathers, as in the New Testament, the concept of communion is expressed through numerous terms. The most frequent are terms such as *communio - communicatio, concordia, societas, unitas, caritas, consortium, fraternitas* and their Greek counterparts. Only in the late Middle Ages did the word communion narrow down to indicating participation in the Eucharist. For ancient Christians the term did not only connote affection and good feeling toward one another, but also and above all it had a binding and semi-legal aspect to it, both internally (*foro interno*) in terms of the individual conscience and externally (*foro externo*) in one's relations with others. The distinction between *foro interno* and *foro externo* is not patristic, but scholastic. Still, both are present in the idea of *communio*, because this is a communion of both faith and conduct. To fail in either the Christian faith or morals excludes one from ecclesial and sacramental communion. The community, especially the bishop, must take measures to exclude the guilty party, even socially, from other believers.

The church is a communion but it is also an organization, and as such the *koinonia* has its ways, its forms, its places and its times for expressing itself.[71] To use the language of the fathers, the church is a communion of faith, sacraments and discipline. In other words, it is a community that has a common faith and follows rules as it also fosters social relationships. Justin expressed what a communion of faith looks like: "All those who are convinced and believe that what we teach and say is true, and undertake to live accordingly are instructed to pray and entreat God with fasting . . . and are then brought by us to where there is water where they are regenerated." [72] And then, after instruction and baptism, these new Christians are allowed to participate in the Eucharist. It is a common idea from Irenaeus onwards, as we have seen in the previous paragraph, that the churches founded by the apostles, through episcopal succession, remain in communion with the apostles themselves and among themselves, and transmit the faith to other new churches so that all churches are apostolic and have the same faith and the same Tradition, which must be held on to and jealously guarded.

Fellowship in the faith was configured both diachronically and synchronously through apostolic succession and the union they had at the time among the churches scattered throughout the various regions. Already by the second century they had their ready response at hand for the heretics: "Let them set forth the earliest beginnings of their churches. Let them unfold the roll of their bishops coming down by succession from the beginning in such a manner that their first bishop had for his guarantor and predecessor one of the Apostles or those Apostolic men who never deserted the Apostles."[73] Those churches that cannot boast of direct apostolic origin, and therefore of doctrinal communion with the apostles, have no guarantee from the apostolic churches, as Tertullian effectively expresses it: "According to this standard, consequently, they will be tested by those churches which can produce perhaps no Apostle or Apostolic man for their founder, since they are of much later foundation—those, for instance, that are being daily founded. Yet since they agree in the same faith, they are none the less accounted Apostolic by virtue of the bloodline of their doctrine (*pro consanguinitate doctrinae*). . . . But indeed, the [heretical churches] are not like this, nor can they prove themselves to be what they are not, neither are they received into communion and fellowship by churches which are in any way Apostolic, seeing that they are in no way Apostolic because of their divergence in doctrine."[74] The expression *consanguinitas doctrinae* cannot be perfectly translated, but it is a very strong phrase to indicate intimate union, a biological union through the same blood.

The church of the first centuries is obsessed with the desire for unity precisely because in many respects it is evolving—doctrinally, liturgically, in discipline and in its organization. As the number of churches increases, and their membership grows, especially in large cities, it is necessary to find adequate tools to meet the new challenges.

Celsus, an external observer of the late second century who was hostile to Christianity, observed a swarm of sects with the Christian name that were in competition with each other.[75] He writes: "The most tremendous insults, speakable and unspeakable, are hurled at one another; nor will they give in on the slightest point for the sake of harmony."[76] Among the various currents that are in competition and struggle with one another, Celsus gives primacy of place to the sect that seems to him to be the largest in number of members and doctrinal importance, calling it "the great church."[77] The expression endured and is still used by historians today, with different meanings, to distinguish the Orthodox Church from heretics and marginal groups in doctrine and behavior. Christianity—the great church—in the time of Celsus is not monolithic in its structure, in its teaching or in its liturgy.

Now, observing these communities of the "great church" from within, one can see that they felt bound together by a deep sense of belonging to a unique, essential and constitutive reality. They experienced a close bond with God, who constitutes and establishes the union among all the *fideles* and between their communities of faith. It is the "we" of the local church and the universal church. The idea of the "communion of the saints" is based on this concept, both in its meaning as participation in the "holy things" (Eucharist) and as a community "of the saints," that is, of the faithful. Salvation comes from God as his gift and creates communion above all with him. This soteriological basis establishes communion both among individual believers who are in a particular community which is presided over by its bishop, and among the communities scattered throughout the known world (*oecumene*).

The church has its origin and its foundation in God, so one can also talk about the preexistent church. "It is the Spirit, or God the Trinity, who founds the origin of all churches and thus constitutes the permanent principle of their unity."[78] Cyprian of Carthage (†258) wrote a work on the unity of the church where he defined the church as the "sacrament of unity."[79] This unity must also be achieved at the social level among local church communities, as well as at the doctrinal level with unity of faith as expressed in the sacraments and ecclesial discipline. Concerning these latter two, there is a whole canonical-liturgical literature which evolves and adapts according to time and place. The doctrinal criteria also changes over time, moving from broad elasticity to greater rigidity. The criterion of a righteous and true faith acquires ever greater importance for ecclesial communion, especially in the Trinitarian and Christological discussions of the fourth through the seventh centuries and leads to the development of a symbol of common faith as a Christian identity marker in relation to the variety of heresies. The very term *symbol* is understood as a sign of recognition among Christians.[80] "It is called *symbol* because Christians are recognized in it."[81] In fact, it is sometimes written on tablets as an apotropaic sign.

The Arian crisis of the fourth century, with its councils, mutual excommunications, struggles, etc., highlights well how important it is to agree in the same confession of faith in order to be in communion with one another. This is why there was such an intense exchange of letters preceding the Nicene council. In practice, the criterion is quite simple: to receive or grant letters of fellowship (*litterae communionis*)[82] to a person means sharing the same faith since the peace (*pax*) is exchanged with that person. Since there is no unique and exclusive center of reference, it is necessary for the individual churches to have continuous contact with one another, especially with the most important ones, in order to ensure unity in faith and discipline. Therefore the bishops make use of the exchange of letters and journeys to address common issues. Tertullian uses the verbal form *contessero* to refer to the full cohesion and connection existing between the Roman church and the African churches.[83] His recourse to the classical juridical language relating to contracted bonds of association is adapted by him to express the idea of belonging to the same faith and to the same society. Cyprian notifies his colleague Cornelius, bishop of Rome, of the names of the African orthodox bishops so that not only the Roman but also the other bishops may know whom they should deal with for the reception and dispatch of letters of communion.[84] The African bishops have always been concerned about communion with other churches, but proud of their autonomy, even in the third century, and especially towards Rome.[85] The episode of dissent in the case of Apiarius in the years 416-419 and that of Pelagius clearly reveal their attitude. The fierce defenders of Roman primacy in the Middle Ages transformed and overturned the African rulings and sources from those years.[86]

Communion in faith makes possible communion in the sacraments, particularly in the Eucharist which, as a participation in the body and blood of Christ, establishes that communion and at the same time is its expression. When Polycarp went to Rome to discuss the date of Easter with Anicetus, even though they disagreed on this point Anicetus had him preside over the celebration of the Eucharist to signify the peace between them.[87] Ignatius wrote to the Christians of Smyrna: "Let no man do anything connected with the Church without the bishop. Let that be deemed a proper Eucharist which is [administered] either by the bishop or by one to whom he has entrusted it."[88] Receiving the Eucharist from a bishop means being in communion with him as well in faith. This is why heretical bishops forced catholics to receive their Eucharist, while they themselves abstained from partaking.[89] Ambrose informs us about his brother Satyrus who had arrived in Sardinia after a shipwreck and then wanted to receive baptism. First, however, "he informed himself diligently (as to whether the local bishop) was in communion with the catholic bishops, that is, with the Roman church."[90] In Rome there is the use of *fermentum*, a word that indicates that part of the host consecrated by the bishop in the Sunday liturgy is sent to other churches in the city as a sign of communion between all the churches of Rome.

Another visible sign of communion between the churches and, therefore, of sharing the same faith was the diptychs. These were originally made up of two tablets joined together by a hinge so that they could be folded together enclosing a message inside on a wax tablet, while the outside was adorned with an image. Diptychs were increasingly used in the church as catalogues of deceased and living persons including martyrs, benefactors, bishops who succeeded one another in an Episcopal see, other bishops of the province, or those with whom one is in communion—especially the name of the pope and the name of the emperor.

The names in the diptychs are remembered during the liturgical celebration, especially in the Eucharistic synaxis.[91] The terms that are used to indicate them vary, the most common of which are *tabellae*, *codices*, and above all *diptyca*, which becomes a technical term. Some names become fixed depending on the church and its needs, while others change according to the times especially if they are recording the names of individuals recently alive but now dead or those who are still alive and needing prayers. For this reason, diptychs were subject to continuous growth and updating, as for example is the case with listing the bishops of the same See. Cyprian himself testifies that there was a tradition of praying for the dead[92] and, above all, he was concerned with drawing up lists of those who had died for the faith, in order to remember them.[93] The inclusion of names of living people was born of the same conviction that prayer was also good for them, but it also acquired another deeper meaning. It expressed the communion that exists in the Christian community, even among people in distant lands. In this regard, Dionysius the Areopagite observes: "For it is not possible to be gathered together toward the One and to partake of the peaceful union with the One while divided among ourselves. If, however, we are illuminated by the contemplation of and knowledge of the One, we are enabled to be united and to achieve a truly divine unity."[94]

For this reason, having one's name written in the sacred diptychs[95] of both the living and the dead is a sign of communion with those named as well as judgment on their orthodoxy which is why they are sometimes also referred to as the book of life (*liber vitae*).[96] When one enters into communion with the bishops of another episcopal see the act of receiving the name into the diptych (*nomen in diptyca recipere*) is performed.[97] When someone's name is removed from the diptychs it is a sign of condemnation.[98] This inclusion or removal can also be done retroactively, so that the names of bishops judged heretical are erased and, at times, no longer read in subsequent centuries.[99] During disputes, the inclusion or exclusion of names in diptychs was an indication of a breach of fellowship between churches and of excommunication of a bishop. Pope Hormisdas affirms this, "promising that in the future the names of those separated from the communion of the Catholic Church, that is, those not agreeing with the Apostolic See, shall not be read during the sacred mysteries."[100] The diptychs were read by the deacon during the Eucharistic celebration at different times according to the various local traditions. In the fourth century Jerome also records that the "deacon in the church publicly recites the names of donors."[101]

Another sign of communion came to be and still is expressed in the rite of episcopal ordination. Already at the end of the second century it was customary for more than one bishop to be present at episcopal ordinations.[102] This use was made obligatory by the Council of Nicaea, which required that all the bishops of the province be present and that those prevented send letters of agreement. It further stipulated that at least three bishops must be present (can. 4). The rule evidenced here does not have so much a ritual and liturgical character as seeking to express the idea that in the ordination of the new bishop the whole church is present and at the same time welcomes him into the communion of the universal church.

The dispute over the day of Easter celebration in the second century was on the brink of causing a schism in the church between those who followed the Sunday custom and those who instead adhered to the Jewish use of the 14th day of Nisan, the aptly named *quartodecimans*. The latter were accepted or at least tolerated in the second century depending on the case, although they were excluded from ecclesial communion by the Council of Nicaea in 325. Still in the late fourth century a few Christian communities such as the Audians (Anthropomorphites) followed another Easter calendar. The celebration of Easter on the same date was very important as a sign of unity within the church and in relation to the outside world. The matter was dealt with at the Council of Arles in 314 and especially at the Council of Nicaea in 325.[103]

The forgiveness to be granted to those who apostatized (*lapsi*) during persecution in the third century, the question of the repetition of baptism administered by heretics, and the rules for a valid episcopal ordination all had different applications according to the where and when they happened. Cyprian did not in any way approve of Martianus of Arles who did not readmit the *lapsi*, while he defended the African tradition of rebaptizing those who came from heresy which was in conflict with the Roman tradition. On that particular occasion, Cyprian said that, "while retaining the right of communion" (*salvo iure communionis*)," it was permitted to follow different opinions and traditions. Indeed, this idea of Cyprian was held with deep conviction and quite common throughout Christian antiquity, even though there was a great diversity of rites and practices in different regions and sometimes even in the same city. In the fourth century the less capable might think that behind this diversity there was a difference in faith. When Januarius explained his perplexity over this, Augustine replied:

> But there are other practices that vary from place to place and region to region. . . . And whatever else of the sort one notices, this whole kind of practice is open to differing observation according to choice, nor is there any discipline in these matters better for a serious and prudent Christian than to act in the way he sees the church acts to which he may have come. For what is proved to be neither contrary to the faith nor contrary to good morals should be regarded as indifferent and should be observed in accord with the society of those with whom one is living.[104]

Even though there were numerous differences—all defended and safeguarded—there was nonetheless a tendency towards uniformity in this period which would only continue and increase in the centuries that followed, albeit within homogeneous geographical areas. The differences between the various geographical areas, on the other hand, were also multiplying due to lack of linguistic communication and the fragmentation of the Roman Empire. In the East there were different geographical churches that were linked to specific regions and their languages such as Armenian, Egyptian, Syriac, Georgian, among others. What divided the churches in these regions was whether they were Chalcedonian or non-Chalcedonian churches, i.e., did they follow the decisions of the Council of Chalcedon (451) or not.

Prior to Chalcedon, the communion between the churches was expressed by every means possible since it was lived on such a profound level. First of all, there were personal relationships between the various churches, both at the level of their bishops and of simple Christians. To be in communion with the bishop of a community meant to share the same faith and vice versa. For this reason, letters of fellowship[105] were exchanged, as we have seen. Each bishop had a constantly updated list of other bishops with whom he was in communion. When there were three bishops simultaneously in Antioch (Meletius, Vitalis and Paulinus), Jerome, who was living there at the time found himself in difficulty and wrote to Pope Damasus "I beg your beatitude, by the cross of the Lord . . . tell me with whom I must communicate in Syria."[106] In the same period, Basil of Caesarea in Cappadocia only recognized Meletius out of the three: "My church has always remained in communion with Meletius and, may it be pleasing to God, we will always be so."[107]

Keeping in constant contact was a common practice—a fact that should not be overlooked. In fact, Basil himself complains to Damasus: "Why is it that we do not receive a letter of consolation, nor visits from brothers, nor any other help that is due to us by the law of charity?"[108] In general, letters of fellowship/communion were sent to the bishops of the principal Sees who acted as intermediaries between the various regions. In this way a structure with the character of a hierarchical communion was created. Even for the simple Christian to be in communion with a local church implied recognition and legitimacy for him or her among all other churches in communion with his or her own. There was also the well-established rule that "he who is excommunicated (by a bishop) must not be readmitted by anyone else."[109] The same canon prescribes that in the Synod during Lent in every province "all discord be removed and the gift (the Eucharist) be offered with a pure heart."

According to the theology of the episcopate, the bishop was responsible for his own community but also in some way for the whole church, as is evidenced with the main bishops of the second century. Clement of Rome, Ignatius, Polycarp, Dionysius of Corinth, Irenaeus, and Victor of Rome all wrote letters and intervened in other church's affairs on various occasions. The same thing happened in the third century. Interventions were also made to depose local bishops or examine their faith. Sometimes synods were called for this purpose, as happened with Privatus of Lambaesis, Beryllus of Bostra, Novatian in Rome and Paul of Samosata in Antioch. This awareness of episcopal responsibility was not limited to one's own community but extended to all the churches and was explicitly affirmed and applied. Origen insisted that whoever was called to the episcopate was not called to domination but to service —but it was service to the whole Church.[110] Cyprian was the bishop who in the third century had the strongest expressions in this regard, as evidenced in what he writes to Pope Stephen about Martianus of Arles: "Now, dearly beloved brother, there is good reason why our body of bishops is at once so generously large and yet so tightly bound together by the glue of mutual concord and by the bond of unity. It is so that should anyone from our sacred college attempt to form a heretical sect and thus to savage and devastate the flock of Christ and cause harm, the others must intervene and, as useful and merciful shepherds, must bring the Lord's sheep back to his flock."[111]

The fathers spoke a great deal about the unity of the church which they continually sought after and, when attained, made sure it was maintained, as Ambrose writes: "We must preserve intact the prerogatives of the ancient members of communion whose good relations are very dear to us."[112] Their language could generate the opinion that they perceived Christianity as a federation of local churches with a certain hierarchy among them. Nothing could be less true. Theirs was more an ecclesiology of communion than of hierarchical authority, and the visible unity of the church was manifested not so much in the acceptance of one or more visible leaders as in the communion between Christians and their bishop and at the same time between all the bishops. For this reason, they spoke more of unity, of harmony, of peace than of obedience, as Tertullian writes: "Therefore these Churches themselves are also reckoned as Apostolic.... In this way all are primitive and all are Apostolic. They are proven to be one, in unbroken unity, by the peaceful communion (*communicatio pacis*), the title of brotherhood[113] and their common pledge of hospitality—privileges which no other rule governs than the one tradition of the selfsame Bond of Faith."[114]

PATTERNS OF *KOINONIA* IN THE EARLY CHRISTIAN CENTURIES

What tools were in place to preserve this harmony and unity that was so desired?[115] Christian writers represent doctrinal divisions, that is, heresies as a deviation from their very simple origins. The Father sent the Son who preached and founded the Church. Christ then sent the apostles to spread the truth everywhere. At the instigation of demons, however, there were evil people who introduced heresies in the post-apostolic period—a period considered pure and innocent. The second century Hegesippus was already sure of this in his own age:

> In addition to these things the same man (Hegesippus), while recounting the events of that period, records that the Church up to that time had remained a pure and uncorrupted virgin since, if there were any that attempted to corrupt the sound norm of the preaching of salvation, they lay until then concealed in obscure darkness. But when the sacred college of apostles had suffered death in various forms, and the generation of those that had been deemed worthy to hear the inspired wisdom with their own ears had passed away, then the league of godless error took its rise as a result of the folly of heretical teachers, who, because none of the apostles was still living, attempted from that point on with a bold face to proclaim, in opposition to the preaching of the truth, the knowledge which is falsely so-called.[116]

The presentation of the heresy and the attitude of the heretics exposed by Hegesippus in the cited passage and in others reported by Eusebius are repeated more or less by all in antiquity. In fact, various aspects of the account were later enriched and expanded upon such as the simplicity and purity of the initial faith, the hidden teaching of heretics, the deception, their misconduct. However, we know that historically things went very differently and it was a much more complex situation. In any case, polemics, persecution, opposition and social exclusion forced the early Christians to close ranks, or rather to encourage a more convinced awareness of their own identity despite the numerous liturgical, doctrinal and disciplinary differences among the various local and regional communities. However, Christian identity had to be affirmed on different fronts. Moreover, in a hostile and suspicious society, it was essential for Christians to present their true nature and identity, while clarifying their own history, doctrines and way of life.

The Christians of the first centuries discovered and practiced different patterns of the faith that preserved and promoted communion, unity of faith and discipline among the many communities scattered especially within the Roman Empire and in the political autonomy of the following centuries. Such patterns were more or less useful and effective, but they were also indispensable because there was such a variety of expressions of faith out there at the time and some of these expressions were strongly accentuated and drew more attention to themselves. Moreover, the communication and the circulation of ideas were very problematic as well. The organizational forms that sought to ensure unity of thought and practice forcefully evolved to the point where they became the definitive expressions and configurations of the faith. For this reason, let us examine some of these instruments that promoted ecclesial communion and cohesiveness.

First, however, it seems fitting to offer a preliminary observation. In the process of ensuring ecclesial peace (*pax*) the laity became increasingly marginalized, whereas in the earlier days of the church they played anything but a secondary role. For example, in the third century, councils were held in public assembly and the laity were also vigilant over their bishop's orthodoxy. But how could the simple faithful be sure of his orthodoxy? The answer was simple. If he personally was in communion with his own bishop, and his bishop in turn was in communion with other bishops, in particular with the great apostolic see—then he must be orthodox.

Epistolary Solicitude and Travels

One of the most common tools used to preserve the harmony and unity of the church was communication. From the earliest times, it was important to get and stay in touch with other Christian communities, especially the oldest and most venerable, in order to verify that one's faith and ecclesial practice were in line with the catholic faith. A prime example is Paul who went up to Jerusalem fourteen years after his conversion, bringing with him Barnabas and Titus so that he could meet the other apostles and compare his teaching with theirs, "I went up by revelation; and I laid before them (but privately before those who were of repute) the gospel which I preach among the Gentiles, lest somehow I should be running or had run in vain."[117] Ignatius of Antioch testifies to his knowledge of the communities with which he came into contact on his journey as a prisoner to Rome; he also sends letters to many communities. In the second century many went to Rome, some to spread their doctrine, others to cultivate contacts with the Roman church and compare their teaching. Justin, Abercius,

Tatian, Polycarp, Montanus, Hegesippus, Irenaeus, Origen, Valentinus, Marcion, Theodotus of Byzantium, and Noetus are just a few examples of the many prominent personages from other parts of the empire who came to Rome for these various reasons. Irenaeus expresses the idea of comparing one's teaching with what other churches are teaching when he writes:

> It would be very tedious, in such a volume as this, to count up the successions of all the Churches . . . by indicating that tradition derived from the apostles of the very great, the very ancient, and universally known Church founded and organized at Rome by the two most glorious apostles, Peter and Paul. We could also do this by pointing out the faith preached among the people which can be found even up to the present day by means of the successions of the bishops. For it is a matter of necessity that every Church, that is, the faithful everywhere, should agree with this Church because of its preeminent authority inasmuch as the apostolic tradition has been preserved continuously by those who exist everywhere.[118]

The eastern father Hegesippus went first to Corinth and then also to Rome, where he remained for a few years. He wrote his "Memoirs" of his journey, during which "he had conversations with many bishops and always found the same and identical doctrine among all of them."[119] The frequent contacts between the churches were necessary not only for the comparison of the doctrines received in order to reject the erroneous ones, but also to confirm each other in the same faith.

The Development of a Common Symbol of Faith[120]

The many short doctrinal formulas of the first two centuries are too diverse to record here. The Trinitarian formula of Matthew 28:19 which is connected with the baptismal rite in the text itself grew in size and content over the first two centuries. At the same time, a Christological confession of the faith linked to teaching and preaching developed which dealt with the human history of Jesus. It too, perhaps, was used in the administration of baptism and was also used on other occasions. The exact place and time of when the two formulas merged together to produce a synthesis of thought which ended up constituting the nucleus of the Apostles' Creed is unknown, but we do find that synthesis in many Christian writers of the second and third centuries.[121] However, the various formulas, whether brief or extensive, differed from community to community. In the course of the second century another type of doctrinal summary formula was born which is found in many authors but is not linked to baptism. It summarized the faith and teaching of the communities in which it was found. Tertullian offers a detailed outline. The order and content corresponded to the Roman symbol of the fourth century, but in reality it was the outline of the teaching provided to the catechumens.[122] It was referred to in a number of different ways, such as the canon of truth, the rule of faith, the rule of piety, and other such terminology.

Although the doctrinal formula varied at certain points from church to church, it also served as proof of a true and upright faith. In other words, it became the focal point by which brothers and sisters in the faith found themselves in fellowship among themselves and with God. But it was equally used as an instrument of exclusion for those not considered to hold the same faith. In an instance where there was doubt as to whether someone held the true faith, a public confrontation was initiated within the church, as witnessed in the *Dialogue* of Origen with Heraclides. In order that he might dispel any doubt about his orthodoxy after the Council of Nicaea, Eusebius of Caesarea sent a profession of faith to his church affirming that he professed the same faith which he had studied in his catechumenal formation and that his profession of faith did indeed coincide with the symbol elaborated at Nicaea. The numerous Councils of the fourth century were simply working out formulations that could serve as a sign of their doctrinal identity. They were concerned to find a formulation that everyone could identify with. At a certain point the symbol of the Council of 381[123] became normative when it was accepted by the Council of Chalcedon in 451. And while it was meant to be an instrument of fellowship and unity, it had the unintended consequence of also becoming an instrument for conflict with the introduction in the West of the *filioque*.

Episcopal Assemblies and Ordinations

Episcopal synods were created and developed as a natural way to respond to the needs of the Christian communities from early on. The practice of holding Councils, which were always regional at first, developed slowly. The first evidence for one of these important assemblies dates back to the second half of the second century in an eastern environment. In the Roman province of Asia (the western part of the Anatolian peninsula) synods of bishops were held to combat Montanism. The dispute over Easter at the time of Pope Victor (189? -199) gave rise to meetings of bishops also, in Italy. That is why Victor of Rome was putting pressure on the bishops of Asia Minor. Tertullian refers to them when he writes that in the eastern regions there were "councils formed by all the churches in which the most important questions were dealt with in common."[124]

Victor's strong intervention failed. Irenaeus, who had exhorted him to tolerance in the name of union, elsewhere maintained that we must agree with the faith of the Roman church "because of its preeminent authority": *Ad hanc enim ecclesiam, propter potentiorem principalitatem*.[125] The significance of these last three words in Latin which we have translated "because of its preeminent authority" has generated much debate. But everyone should be able to agree that in light of this quote and the one we provided a few pages earlier, Irenaeus perceived the Roman church had a superior origin and a more excellent foundation. Therefore, its tradition had greater value and validity. Victor based his claim on the prestige of the Roman church due to its glorious origins. Irenaeus follows the phrase we just quoted with the list of Roman bishops who prove its antiquity and fidelity to the apostolic tradition. In the third book of his *Against Heresies,* Irenaeus often mentions Paul together with Peter as founders of the Roman church.

The church is built on the tradition received, which is the highest authority. Tradition is transmitted orally through the episcopal succession beginning from the apostles. In this sense the whole church is apostolic and therefore one and the same, notwithstanding the different local traditions. The bishops draw the strength of their authority from the fact that they are elected by the people and therefore by God himself, and from the fact that they succeed the apostles.

The Council's activities developed and were better organized during the third century. This practice was used first by Emperor Constantine to resolve the Donatist question with councils in Rome (313) and Arles (314), and then the Arian and Easter questions at Nicaea in 325. For both doctrinal and disciplinary reasons, the activity of the fourth century Councils reached paroxysm without resolving the problems debated. The solution for these problems was entrusted to theological discussion and the agreement of the bishops of the important sees. Yet, there was no other way for a fruitful dialogue to occur than to encourage meetings of bishops. The Council of Nicaea required synods to be held two times a year so that all the bishops of the same province could gather together for the same purpose in order to discuss their common problems. Canon 19 of the Council of Chalcedon of 451 reiterated the same requirement in order to deal with "many of the ecclesiastical affairs that would need reform."

While the provincial and plenary councils—i.e. those made up of several provinces—ensured limited communion, the ecumenical councils of the first millennium were meant to guarantee the communion of the entire Christian world (*orbis christianus*) even though they all took place only in the East. After the Council of Chalcedon (451), many Eastern Christians, including the Miaphysites, the Nestorians and the Armenians, no longer participated in the peace (*pax*) of the church.

The bishop of Rome was the interlocutor with the Christian East, in so far as he had become the conscience of the West in relation to an ever more distant East. Today, attention is usually focused on the Old and the New Rome while the whole Christian world beyond the Proto-Byzantine Empire is neglected. Eastern Christians are almost totally ignored today although their reasons for autonomy were important Christological issues. For them it would be easier, if they were to establish contact at all, to do so with Old Rome.

Episcopal Ordination

Episcopal ordinations were important moments that allowed for the meeting of the bishops of the same ecclesiastical province who could deal with common problems on such occasions while preserving and increasing the fellowship of their communities. There were significant exceptions, such as the bishop of Alexandria who had authority over the whole of Egypt, Libya, and Cyrenaica. In Numidia there was no metropolitan, but they did have a primate who would have been the oldest bishop by ordination. In Syria the bishops of several provinces depended on the see at Antioch. The Council of Chalcedon specified the criteria for episcopal ordination: the bishop of Constantinople was to ordain all the metropolitans in his area of responsibility which included Pontus, Asia, and Thrace. Those metropolitans in turn conferred ordination on the bishops of their own provinces (can. 28). In addition, the bishop of Constantinople also ordained bishops in barbarian territories. Such episcopal ordination seals and cements a relationship of dependence between the various churches and their sees while also creating a *de facto* hierarchy.

The Solicitudo Omnium Ecclesiarum (The Care of All Churches)

The expansion of Christianity lead to the creation and establishment of new communities, generating a heartfelt and vital relationship between mother churches and their daughter churches. Apostolicity was transmitted throughout the generations in the faith and thus all churches were apostolic and catholic. Those churches that preserved a stronger memory of having been founded by an apostle—also because of their strategic situation in the Roman political system and location—enjoyed greater authority. In this way the great apostolic sees (*sedes apostolicae*) developed with mutual esteem and respect for one another. The Council of Nicaea recognized Rome, Alexandria, and Antioch (can. 6), without any intention of ordering them by rank, however. Their rank among the cities of the empire had also been recognized in the civil realm. The canonical decision was the result of previous practice since those churches had already exercised oversight and aid with other communities apart from their own—sometimes even in communities that were quite distant. The decision of the sixth canon of Nicaea gave rise to the theory of the three apostolic sees. Peter was the founder of the churches of Antioch and Rome, and his disciple Mark, called a disciple or son of Peter (*discipulus* or *filius Petri*), founded the church of Alexandria.[126] In other words, the pre-eminence of the three Sees stemmed from the importance of Peter and therefore from apostolic and not political reasons.

Individual churches were not independent entities. They also needed to be concerned about other churches, as Cyprian theorized already in the third century. For this reason, he also intervened in other geographical areas and asked the Bishop of Rome to do the same.

INSTITUTIONAL FORMS OF AUTHORITY

In the following two paragraphs we will examine in more detail the application of the doctrine of *communio* and fellowship in the life of the church.

The expression of authority in the ancient church had been structured according to need, external influence and ecclesial life. It had approached its definitive form already in the third to fourth century period. Earlier it was the apostles who had the greatest authority. As we have already seen, other ministers had also joined them in that authority. At the end of the second century the episcopate, for instance, was fully developed. The bishops were the supreme ministers of their respective communities. Their authority embraced all aspects of local ecclesial life. In the second century the episcopal *cathedra*, on which only the bishop could sit, was the only external indication of his authority and it became synonymous with his function. The late second century Muratorian canon wrote concerning Hermas: "Sitting in the seat (*cathedra*) of the church of the city of Rome [was] Bishop Pius, his brother."[127] *Cathedra* was already being used as a technical term. During the same century the bishop appeared above all as a teacher of the community in opposition to sects that were spreading false doctrines. In antiquity, the *cathedra* was a special seat that indicated the function of teaching. In the third century, the emphasis instead was placed on the bishop as a liturgist, that is, the center of ecclesial life. The bishop sat on the chair because only he was authorized to speak during the liturgical celebrations. Only rarely were priests allowed to preach in the East at least until the fourth century when the practice became more wide spread. Only later were priests allowed to preach in the West.

In the prayers for episcopal ordination, the powers of the bishop are summarized in the terms of his role as teacher, pastor and liturgist. We have no extant record of early episcopal legislation in the first few centuries, but we do have numerous traces of it in the vast anonymous canonical-liturgical literature which presents itself as apostolic. This literature extends from the *Didache* to the *Didascalia*, to the numerous compilations of the fourth century such as the *Apostolic Constitutions*, the *Testament of our Lord Jesus Christ*, the *Octateuch of Clement*, and various collections of canons.[128]

THE COUNCILS AND THE BISHOP OF ROME'S AUTHORITY

Having discussed the role of the bishop, we now focus our attention on the two other institutional forms of authority: the Councils and the special position of the Bishop of Rome.

The assemblies of bishops who as *doctores* and *pastores* must preserve faith and discipline, are called in Greek *synodos* and in Latin *concilium*. Ambrose was the first to use the term *synodus* in Latin, transliterating it from Greek.

After the apostolic experience in Jerusalem and the widespread practice in the Roman civil administration of carrying out *concilia*, it seemed natural that the bishops should meet to discuss and decide doctrinal matters and other concerns of a more general character. Already in the second century councils were held in Asia on the question of the Montanists. Pope Victor (193-203) invited the bishops to meet in councils in Pontus, Palestine and Syria to determine the date of Easter.[129] Episcopal meetings were also held in Rome. In Africa, around 220 Agrippinus gathered a council to declare the baptism administered by heretics null and void. Cyprian often brought together the bishops of the African provinces that included proconsular Africa, Numidia and Mauritania in order to initiate discussions with them in the presence of the faithful. The same applied in Rome to the case of Novatian. Also noteworthy is the Council of Antioch in 268 which was called to depose the bishop of the city, Paul of Samosata. But the era of the truly great flowering of the Councils was the fourth and fifth centuries. The first great western council was that of Arles in 314 which was called by Constantine. Canon 5 of the Council of Nicaea (325), which he also called, established that in each ecclesiastical province two Councils were to be held per year.

The breadth of participation determined the quality of the council. Councils could be provincial, where they took place with bishops attending from a single province. They might also be patriarchal if they were called by one of the patriarchs of Alexandria, Antioch or Constantinople. There were also plenary councils as, for example, took place in the African, Spanish or Gallic episcopates. There were also the so-called ecumenical councils, that is, those with the bishops of all Christianity in attendance: Nicaea (325), Constantinople (381), Ephesus (431), and Chalcedon (451). They are recognized by Roman Catholics, Orthodox and almost all Protestants. Gregory the Great compared them to the four Gospels: "Let us accept the four councils of the holy universal church as the four books of the holy Gospel."[130] They were summoned by the emperor and held in the East. Their decisions became the law of the state.

The syntagma or phrase "Ecumenical Council" is a theological concept, not a historical one, since it is not the number of participating bishops that makes it ecumenical but its reception by the church. For example, the Council of Rimini in 359[131] convened by the Emperor Constantius had a large episcopal participation of about 400 bishops and was presided over by Restitutus of Carthage. At first this Council reaffirmed the Nicene doctrine, but then the emperor and the Arians opposed this reaffirmation and forced all bishops to sign a generic formula which could also be interpreted in an Arian way. The second Council of Ephesus held in 449, referred to as the Robber Synod (*latrocinium ephesinum*) also had large episcopal participation. And yet, neither of these two councils are considered ecumenical, while that of Constantinople in 381 is accepted as ecumenical even though there were only around 150 bishops present and there was no representation from Rome. After a period of almost absolute silence for seventy years, it acquired the designation of "ecumenical" because its profession of faith was received by the Council of Chalcedon (451). Only in 519 was it recognized by Pope Hormisdas. The pope did not take part personally in the councils held outside Rome. Instead he would usually send delegates to represent him.

The historian records a very high number of councils. Those referred to as ecumenical have great normative value; others are acknowledged for the regulations they impose or are simply relegated to the past, while still others were finally rejected for various reasons. As we saw, it was not the number of participants which determined the significance of a council. The record is somewhat enigmatic on what made a council perdure in the memory of the church. Each case has its own history and could include such factors as its deliberations and decisions about doctrine, its reception by the church, the prestige of the participants, imperial support, and other such considerations. The councils generally affirmed that the Holy Spirit had spoken through the bishops gathered in the assembly, or they invoked the text of Matthew, "Where two or three are gathered together in my name, there am I in the midst of them."[132] These supported the claim that the council's authority had divine sanction because the decisions were made by the participants inspired by the Holy Spirit: *placuit nobis sancto Spiritu suggerente*.[133]

In the fourth and fifth centuries the Council of Nicaea held the highest authority and was often referred to as the holy and great council, a term it had coined for itself in its own canons 14 and 19. It was sometimes also referred to as ecumenical by such figures as Eusebius and Athanasius,[134] but the adjective did not yet have the technical meaning that it would assume later on. The Council of Ephesus in 431 established that the decisions of Nicaea could not be changed because the fathers had legislated their decisions together with the Holy Spirit. Sieben[135] has demonstrated that the reason for this success, despite the strong opposition of the fourth century, was because its teaching was recognized to be according to tradition. However, its participants were aware that they were commencing a new and wide-ranging experience which is why they made numerous disciplinary decisions concerning the universal church which would become the basis for subsequent ecclesiastical legislation.

There is a more general question that needs to be addressed. What authority does any council have since some of them were fiercely contested while others were totally ignored? St. Augustine tried to order the authority of the councils by saying that the regional or provincial councils were superior to the plenary ones and among the regional or provincial councils the most recent were to be considered more authoritative.[136] The Roman church of the fifth century then began to elaborate the doctrine of the *causae maiores* which referred to major cases on which only the Pope could render decisions, sometimes referred to in the literature as his *reserved powers,* i.e. authority for decisions that only the pope can make.[137] This was the doctrine that then passed into Western canon law—not, however canon law in the East—and would become valid and normative for the Latin churches.

Y. Congar and H. Chadwick deepened our understanding of the concept of how councils were received by the church and in particular by the Roman see: when a council is accepted and received, only then does it acquire value.[138] The development of the reception of councils was a similar phenomenon in part to the formation of the canon of Scripture. While in the early days it was mainly based on the truth contained in the decisions of the council and how closely they corresponded to Scripture and to the faith received, more and more authority was transferred to the council itself because it was accepted and approved by the church. It was then assumed that the council expressed the traditional faith in a spirit of continuity.

The abundant, albeit incomplete, council legislation from the fourth and fifth centuries gave rise to a number of problems such as how their decisions should be interpreted or over what geographical territory they could be applied—an issue which would have more weight if the decisions had the emperor's approval and became part of the civil laws. There was also the concern as to whether those who did not participate or rejected the council's decisions were bound by them. Where there is a kind of geographical-ecclesiastical unit, as in Africa and Egypt, these problems were not really an issue.

THE BISHOP OF ROME

The bishop of Rome played a prominent role in the ancient Christian community,[139] a role which has only grown over time to where it today has become one of the reasons for the deep division of Christianity and is actually an obstacle to reunion for many Christians. Here we want to briefly explain its function in the ancient church and the doctrine underlying its authority.

We do not know when Christianity arrived in Rome, perhaps already at the beginning of the life of the church (*Acts* 2:10). It was already present at the time of the emperor Claudius (41-54) who drove out the Jews from Rome around 48 CE: "He expelled from Rome the Jews who, by instigation of Chrestus, were a constant cause of disorder."[140]

Paul's Letter to the Romans, written around 57-58 indicates the importance of the Roman community as early as the middle of the first century, around 25 years after the death of Jesus. A few decades later, Clement's letter to the Corinthians (ca. 96) was an intervention to quell disagreements that had arisen in the Corinthian church. The tone of the letter is fraternal but firm. It includes a reference to the martyrdom of Peter and Paul in Rome (ch. 5) and insists on apostolic succession as legitimating ministry. These will be offered as some of the reasons and bases for subsequent interventions by the Bishop of Rome. A few years later Ignatius' letter to the Romans refers to the presence of the two apostles having issued orders in Rome as apostles and recognizes the Roman church for both its steadfast faith and charity, as well as its teaching authority (ch. 3). First Hegesippus and then Irenaeus give us an early list of the Roman bishops, although certainly not reliable or set in stone.[141]

Irenaeus' list and its meaning are important for the historical reconstruction of the Roman church, but the list presents some difficulties when compared with others. It is fundamental that we ask why he offers such a list. He did so in order to demonstrate the apostolic succession of Rome, the importance of the Christian community living there which has the dignity and authority to speak to all churches and to express authentically the faith of all.[142] It is also a wealthy community that is able to provide economic help even to the Christians of other provinces.[143] Abercius of Hierapolis came to Rome in the second half of the second century and described the Roman church with great imaginative admiration while limiting himself to naming only a few of the other communities that he visited. He was struck by Rome's importance and prestige.[144]

The Petrine foundation cannot be proven, much less that of Paul. The two apostles however are still considered the foundation for the authority of every bishop of Rome via succession. But in the third century, Paul's name begins to drop out and we only hear of Peter. To justify the primacy that belongs then to Peter and therefore to his successors, the text of Matthew is invoked: "I tell you, you are Peter, and on this rock I will build my church, and the gates of hell shall not prevail against it. I will give you the keys of the kingdom of heaven, and whatever you bind on earth shall be bound in heaven, and whatever you loose on earth shall be loosed in heaven."[145]

There were numerous interventions of the Bishop of Rome outside his territory from the second century onward. He was moved by his desire to help the entire church (the *sollicitudo omnium ecclesiarum*; 2 *Cor* 11:28) in matters concerning faith and discipline as well as helping churches in need. The Roman church was distinguished by being the custodian of faith and discipline (*custodia fidei et disciplinae*).[146] The influence of Rome largely depended on the personality of its bishop. It was not until Pope Damasus (366-384) that a doctrine of the Roman primacy was fully elaborated with respect to all the other bishops—a doctrine defended and deepened by his successors such as Siricius, who first applied the concept of *sollicitudo* to the papal office, as well as Anastasius I (399-402), Innocent I (402-417) and above all Leo the Great (440-461).[147]

As we have seen, deference to Rome began already with Clement's intervention with the church at Corinth. There were also other churches or individuals in the second and third centuries who appealed to Rome. Even Cyprian requested Roman intervention in some cases. The Council of Serdica in 343 established the appeal to the Bishop of Rome in canons 4 and 5.

Although these two canons are included in the Byzantine collections, they had no influence then or in the later period on the Eastern church. These canons also created serious disagreements with the African bishops over the situation with Apiarius of Sicca in the early fifth century. His appeal to Rome was quite controversial. Other Western churches, however, simply ignored the canons more often than not. Decretals issued by Roman bishops starting with Damasus were usually directed to quite specific situations rather than more general pronouncements. The legislation of the decretals continued to develop with Popes Innocent I (401-407), Celestine (422-432), Leo the Great (440-461), Gelasius (492-496) and Hormisdas (514-523), all of whom helped in elaborating further the doctrine of the primacy of Rome, founded on the phrase, "You are Peter."[148]

For instance, Pope Gelasius wrote: "What the Apostolic see has established in a Council endures forever; what it has refused cannot have any force."[149] Pope Leo was expressly and insistently requested by the participants and the emperor to confirm the acts of the Council of Chalcedon (451). In this period there was also the common practice of requesting Roman authorization in order to celebrate a synod. In fact, Leo's legate to the Council of Chalcedon, Lucentius, reproached Dioscorus, Bishop of Alexandria, for breaking with this practice.[150] Normally, however, if one was in communion with the Roman church that was sufficient for being in communion with all the western churches.[151]

A new way of intervening came about with the papal decretals. These were letters in which Rome responded to disciplinary questions addressed by bishops or communicated decisions. The decretals (*epistolae decretales*) were of a more general nature and were drawn up in the form of a letter containing rules to be followed. They were issued in the name of the pope but were elaborated by a kind of Roman council. There have been numerous Roman assemblies, but they have not always issued canons, or the canons issued have not always been incorporated into the decretals. The first decretal is considered to be the *Epistula ad Gallos* from the time of Damasus (366-384). Dionysius Exiguus made the first collection of pontifical letters in Rome, which then inspired later collections. We know about the decretals mainly through their reception and transmission in the canonical collections. Therefore, we only know of those that the compilers preserved in their collections, not necessarily all those that were actually published.

The Council of Constantinople (381) established that the church of New Rome had the same rights as that of ancient Rome. Canon 3 reads: "The Bishop of Constantinople, however, shall have the prerogative of honor after the Bishop of Rome, because Constantinople is New Rome."[152] In the past the episcopal see of Constantinople was dependent on the see of Heraclea. Canon Three of Constantinople based the importance of the episcopal see on a political factor: the identity between the political and the religious city.[153] The following year, Damasus reaffirmed the authority of the Roman church. This is where the beginning of the differences between the two Sees must be placed. The Roman church based its authority on the apostolic foundation while the Constantinopolitan church based its authority on its political and civil status.[154]

In Leo's time, in referring to canon 3 of the Council of Constantinople of 381, the Council of Chalcedon (451) published an extended excursus in canon 28 which recognized the privileges of Constantinople mainly for political reasons.[155] It notes that in 381:

> Following in all things the decisions of the holy Fathers, and acknowledging the canon, which has been just read, of the One Hundred and Fifty Bishops beloved-of-God . . . we also do enact and decree the same things concerning the privileges of the most holy Church of Constantinople, which is New Rome. . . . For just as the Fathers rightly granted privileges to the throne of old Rome, because it was the royal city . . . equal privileges are given to the most holy throne of New Rome,[156] justly judging that the city which is honored with the Sovereignty and the Senate, and enjoys equal privileges with the old imperial Rome, should in ecclesiastical matters also be magnified as she is, and rank next after her; so that, in the Pontic, the Asian, and the Thracian dioceses only the metropolitans and such bishops also of the Dioceses aforesaid as are among the barbarians, should be ordained by the aforesaid most holy throne of the most holy Church of Constantinople.[157]

The jurisdiction of the imperial see extended only to the three civil dioceses of Pontus, Asia and Thrace. These were dioceses as understood in the Roman administrative sense and therefore not of the entire eastern church but only a small portion of it. It seems that the control over those three dioceses was the main purpose of the canon, which intended to sanction by right what had already been the practice starting from the interventions of John Chrysostom. The canon was not in any way intended as an attack on the position of the Roman church. The authority of the bishop of Constantinople was later extended, but the extent of his authority was the subject of discussion for centuries. He for instance had no authority over other churches in the East, such as Antioch and Alexandria. Indeed, the Council of Ephesus in 431 had granted autocephaly to the church of Cyprus from the church of Antioch. Only in 927 did the church of Bulgaria obtain autocephaly from Constantinople.[158]

Canon 28 deserves further attention. Leo's delegates were absent during the session that formulated the text and so the next day they protested vigorously, with the protest being inserted into the proceedings.[159] Leo was asked to confirm the canon, but his opposition was vociferous and he refused to confirm it because it went against previous canons and upset the existing hierarchical order of the Sees while also usurping the rights of those other Sees. In addition, he noted, Constantinople did not have an apostolic foundation. This is why at some point defenders of the new see imaginatively romanticized that it dated back to the apostle Andrew.[160] All the explanations sent to Leo seemed to minimize the content of the canon, but the increased rise of the authority of the bishop of Constantinople led to unforeseen consequences in the coming years. At first, everything was peaceful and for some time the canon was not included in the collections of the ecumenical councils. But it soon came to be applied to the advantage of the new patriarchate. In 545 Justinian (*Novella* 131) acknowledged the bishop of New Rome—this was the wording that was normally used in the canons—in the second place after the Roman pope. The Quinisext Council (or *in Trullo*) of 691 reaffirmed the Chalcedonian canon in its entirety (can. 36).

More than previous councils, the Council of Chalcedon (451) did recognize that the Roman pope enjoyed a primacy which however was understood differently in the East and in the West. Leo claimed for himself full sovereign authority (*plenitudo potestatis*)[161] and saw himself as head of the universal church by virtue of being bishop of the Roman church which in turn is the head of all the churches.[162] While respecting the authority of local bishops, the *plenitudo potestatis* attributed to the pope a universal authority to teach as well as a legislative power that was implemented by means of decretals. He also interpreted the meaning of the conciliar canons while exercising control over discipline. Therefore, a centralizing and absolute conception was proposed which tended to impose on everyone what the pope had decided or elaborated in a synod.

This conception of the papacy was arrived at via complex events and doctrinal reflections. Theologically the doctrine of Roman primacy is based on the Petrine succession and on the continuity of Peter's ministry in the popes who followed. The Roman church was called the see of the Apostles (*sedes apostolica*) par excellence, even with respect to the other apostolic foundations of other churches. However, there were many factors which contributed to the prestige of Rome. The apostolic origins and the presence of Peter and Paul in Rome, the tombs of the two apostles resided there as a destination of pilgrimages. It was ancient (*antiquitas*)—a concept dear to the ancients—in its founding at least with respect to the Western churches. It was also faithful to the Council of Nicaea. In addition, there are political and social factors one should consider. Rome was the capital of the Empire and served as the crossroads for Christians especially in the second century. There is also the idea of the eternal city (*urbs*) along with the decline of other centers in the West, such as Carthage and Milan. Rome also was home to strong personalities, especially as found in its bishops.

The effectiveness of the intervention of the Bishop of Rome varied according to region and each province marked that history differently. Geography was an important factor, as was distance and the time it took to travel to and from Rome. Until the beginning of the fourth century Roman ecclesiastical intervention rarely crossed Italian borders. In the middle of the fourth century the interventions took the form of decretals which widened its sphere of influence. The influence was exercised mainly in Gaul and Spain. In Africa, which enjoyed great autonomy, the recourse of bishops and priests to Rome was forbidden by a council held in Carthage in 418, but relations with Rome were still close from the third century. Rome had little influence on the British Isles, accentuated by the arrival of the missionary Augustine († 604) at the time of Gregory the Great. In the Germanic countries Rome exerted its influence only from the time of St. Boniface (ca. 675-754).

The pallium (ecclesiastical vestment) was sent from Rome to the metropolitans of the Latin-speaking regions as a sign of their dependence on Rome. The western *Illyria* was under the direct influence of Rome, which had its own vicar in Thessalonica. The patriarchal Sees of Alexandria and Antioch were strongly autonomous, but became somewhat subordinate to the Patriarch of Constantinople in the fifth century—albeit only those who followed the Chalcedonian faith. In the papal registers published by Jaffè-Wattenbach[163] there are 1,100 documents issued up to 1198 by the Roman church, of which about one hundred concern Illyria and only about three hundred all the Eastern churches, thus implying those churches enjoyed the widest canonical autonomy. When a new patriarch was elected, he immediately communicated his election via a letter (*synodicon*) to the pope, who then responded with congratulations. This gesture of communion was considered essential for the newly elected. Pontifical interventions in the East were mainly concerned with issues of fellowship (*communion*) and faith (*fides*).

In the East the ecclesial attitude was more collegial, which is why they did not readily accept *ex auctoritate* orders. Even though they recognized in Rome a certain primacy, the Eastern Christians insisted on the more general concept of fellowship and thought that the most important decisions needed to be made together. Even while admitting the Petrine succession, they never identified the pope with Peter. For this reason, they did not accept that the major ecclesiastical cases (*causae maiores*) should be decided in Rome. They never considered the papal decrees as sources of ecclesiastical legislation, as happened in the West.

These observations now allow us to better understand the conception of the Roman primacy in antiquity and that it should be seen in the context of the different doctrinal perspectives of the East and the West. A *potentior principalitas* was recognized to inhere in the Roman church due to the presence of Peter and Paul there in the beginning. In this way the Roman church served as a point of reference for the faith and for all the other churches. It was considered the privileged place of universal fellowship (*communio universalis*) in faith, in the sacraments and in grace. The Roman bishop was at the service of this fellowship and presided over the *agape*.[164] This was the justification for his intervention in the other churches. However, there was still not a full legislative mindset included in the Petrine Ministry. The difficulty lies in using a term such as "primacy" that has experienced much accretion over the centuries, creating a somewhat different reality than it had initially. Hence our present misunderstanding.

At the center of this fellowship, or communion, is the Roman church because "from this church come the rights of communion that must be respected by all the churches."[165] Leo himself, who insisted on primacy to the full, still also emphasized episcopal collegiality.

At the time of Leo the Great, there were at least two disagreements with the Alexandrian church on the date of Easter. In 444 according to the Roman cycle, Easter should have been on March 26, but according to the Alexandrian cycle it should have taken place on April 23.[166] In 455 the matter was more complex and was better known thanks to the involvement of Emperor Marcian (450-457) to whom Pope Leo had written an important letter. Leo wanted Easter to be celebrated together by all Christians on the same day and believed it was a grave omission not to do so: "It would not be a matter of levity, left undone, if the universal Church did not hold to the demands of truth and unity in the principle of the sacramental mystery."[167] In both cases, he accepted the Alexandrian dating. For the Easter date of 455 he wrote to the bishops of Gaul, Spain and other Western provinces to celebrate Easter on April 24 as a sign of peace and unity.[168] He did not neglect to make known his frustration to the emperor but accepted the Alexandrian proposal nonetheless for the supreme good of unity.[169] He did not impose himself on the basis of the authority of the Apostolic See. He did not do so because it did not seem appropriate to him. Instead, he appealed to tradition and to the previous fathers who enjoyed authority in the life of the Church. While seeing that the proposed date was against this tradition, as a man of dialogue and peace, he placed the unity of the Church above his convictions and Roman traditions.

In the meantime, Roman theology expanded on the meaning of what it meant to be the head (*caput*) of all churches.[170] The East, on the other hand, continued to attach greater importance to the local church as a starting point for larger organizations. They saw unity deriving not from above, but from below where the drive to create harmony originates. In this way they preserved greater local, regional and patriarchal autonomy. Decisions about faith or important disciplinary matters needed to be made together. The third Council of Constantinople (680-681), the richest in praise and expressions of deference to the pope, did not simply accept the dogmatic letter of Pope Agatho who condemned Monothelitism. It agreed with his decision, but also considered every issue to be an open question deserving of further in-depth examination. The same council had received his letter with great respect because it was "written by the supreme authority of the apostles."[171] Having seen that its content was in conformity with the traditional faith, only then did the bishops say "all of us are, by inspiration of the Holy Spirit, unanimous and of the same feeling, and we offer our commitment to the dogmatic letter of Agatho, our most holy father and pope."[172]

In the Council there were several Eastern bishops who admitted a true primacy for the pope—even though he had limited himself to recognizing his privileged position and not his absolute authority.[173] The Eastern Church was more conditioned by political situations as is evidenced in canon 28 of the Council of Chalcedon.[174] Meanwhile, the political situation in the West gave greater importance to the religious authority which could then affirm the superiority of the spiritual authority over the temporal. In the Byzantine East, this could never happen, and so the emperor continued to legislate in ecclesiastical matters. In the West, such power was increasingly being reserved for the Pope. In other geographical areas, the situation was totally different. Every area, in fact, had its own diverse issues to deal with. While most Eastern churches would recognized the pope as having a primacy—which was something more than a simple primacy of honor or a *primus inter pares*—it still was not understood in the same sense as it was in the West. The pope was the *primus* in the context of the fellowship of all the churches. It was the bishop of a particular community who exercised authority and was the center of the local communion, while the metropolitan, the patriarch, and the pope—always at the highest and widest level—shared in the concern for all the churches in their area and were the centers and bonds of communion at the provincial, patriarchal and universal level.[175]

The *apostolic see* is an expression that was addressed earlier as a term which arose to indicate those episcopal sees that were of apostolic origin (*sedes apostolicae*). The succession of bishops that occurred in those places was a guarantee of transmission of the evangelical truth. They were the seats of witness, as Tertullian wrote:

> Apostolic Churches are where the very thrones of the Apostles to this very day preside over their own districts, where their own genuine letters are read which speak their words and bring the presence of each before our minds. If Achaia is nearest to you, you have Corinth. If you are not far from Macedonia, you have Philippi. If you cannot travel into Asia, you have Ephesus. Or if you are near Italy, you have Rome, where we too have an authority close at hand. What a happy Church is that whereon the Apostles poured out their whole doctrine together with their blood; where Peter suffers a passion like his Lord, where Paul is crowned with the death of John (the Baptist), whence John the Apostle, after being immersed in boiling oil and taking no hurt, is banished to an island. The African Church was not founded by an Apostle, but from Italy: Rome was therefore its natural authority.[176]

And, of course, concerning Rome, there is the well-known text by Irenaeus that we have already mentioned several times.[177] At a later time the syntagma would be applied in particular to the Roman See, which became the apostolic *sedes* par excellence, expressing the ultimate criterion of catholicity.[178] In the fourth century it became commonplace to call it the See of Peter (*sedes Petri*).[179] These two expressions are the most common, alongside similar ones such as *prima cathedra* or *ecclesia principalis*. However, there is another wording that although rarely used in late antiquity becomes common by the Middle Ages: the Holy See (*sancta sedes*).[180]

THE CHURCH'S TERRITORIAL STRUCTURES

The Christian movement born in the land of Israel from the middle of the first century slowly moved towards the great cities of the Mediterranean world along the great roads and maritime routes, becoming an urban phenomenon while simultaneously expanding into the villages and countryside in some areas, as evidenced by Pliny's letter to Trajan regarding Bithynia in the beginning of the second century.[181] Jews, on the other hand, were only present in the major cities and not in the countryside or more marginal areas. Certainly, the network of synagogues proved useful for Christian expansion, as Tertullian already recognized when he noted its spread "under the shadow of a most famous religion, or one that is at any rate permitted by law."[182]

Bearing in mind this strong mobility, we must think of Christian travelers, whether they were unknown missionaries or simple believers in Christ. They built up a network of communities both large and small that sought to preserve unity among themselves through a shared faith, the exchange of news, mutual exhortations and exchange of information on the life of the various churches. They focused on in-depth study of Scripture and doctrine along with discussions revolving around the problems of various church's respective practices in order to verify and compare doctrinal traditions. While in the same inhabited space as unbelievers, they did not separate themselves into a separate community as was the Jewish practice. Christians chose to live in a common public space while differentiating themselves on the basis of the behavior which grew out of their religious and moral convictions.

Cities and Episcopal Sees

Cities became the place where the Christian faith spread most prolifically in the early centuries of the church's existence which accounts for the common view today that it was largely an urban phenomenon. But this was not always the case, because there are testimonies that it was also present in the villages as we noted, for instance, in Pliny's letter above.[183] In the first century, the structure of the Roman Empire was based on the cities, which had a political, administrative, religious and urban organization very different from that of the beginning of the fourth century, at the time of the Council of Nicaea (325). Cities, especially the capitals of the provinces, were a point of reference for a wide territory. Eusebius of Caesarea captured this aspect well when he wrote:

> For indeed most of the disciples of that time ... starting out upon long journeys performed the office of evangelists, being filled with the desire to preach Christ to those who had not yet heard the word of faith, and to deliver to them the divine Gospels. And when they had only laid the foundations of the faith in foreign places, they appointed others as pastors, and entrusted them with the nurture of those who had recently been brought in, while they themselves went on again to other countries and nations, with the grace and the co-operation of God. For a great many wonderful works were done through them by the power of the divine Spirit, so that at the first hearing whole multitudes of men eagerly embraced the religion of the Creator of the universe.[184]

In this way, local communities were born and felt a connection with each other even as they remained independent of one another. At different times, depending on the places and the size of the communities, they organized themselves more completely into a single entity. They did this by focusing their leadership on one individual, the bishop, who became the focal point in his identification with his community and exercised all of its authority in an exclusive sense, so that in each center there could only be one Christian community, which must have only one bishop. Each community thus became autonomous, having the requisite facilities to operate as a church.

The intuition of Theodore of Mopsuestia is precise: "Originally there were usually two bishops, or at most three, in each province, a situation that prevailed in most of the western provinces until just recently, and that can be found in several still today. But with the passage of time the bishops were ordained not only in the cities, but also in very small places."[185] The proliferation of episcopal sees, both for political and religious reasons, increased. For each civil province, the number of episcopal sees was in relation to the degree of evangelization, the density of the population and the number of towns, whether city or municipality, as reflected in the Roman municipal structure. In Africa, in Asia Minor, in *suburbicaria* Italy there were more episcopal sees than in Gaul, Egypt, or the Balkan peninsula, for instance.

In the beginning, the local communities were referred to as the "church that is in Corinth" or "of Corinth," for instance, or the "church that is in Carthage" or "of Carthage." Only in the course of the third century does the Greek word *parochia* (or *paroecia*) appear to indicate the local church. At the beginning of the fourth century it begins to indicate the territory of a bishop and becomes synonymous with diocese. In the course of the fifth and sixth centuries it takes on its present meaning, but is restricted to rural churches and not to those of the city.

In order to oppose the multiplication of episcopal sees, the Council of Serdica of 353 established that in villages or small towns it was enough for them to have a priest. There was no need to resort to appointing a bishop (can. 6). Whether urban or rural, however, those churches that did not have episcopal sees had little autonomy since only the cathedral had the baptistery and that was where the faithful normally convened and were baptized.

Local communities nonetheless felt they were an integral part of the universal church, understood not as a federation of local churches but as a unity in its origin and being. Although the local churches remained both autonomous and distinct, they still sought other means of mutual communion beyond their local diocese to preserve this unity. The bishops as personifications and representatives of their respective churches retained equal rights but also acknowledged their mutual dependence. This idea is expressed in the very rite of ordination. However, another idea emerged which held that some of the bishops exercised a privilege of honor over their peers, either because their church had an apostolic foundation or because their city was considered as important for political, cultural, economic or religious reasons.

It may be helpful at this point to clarify some of the terminology. The term *diocese* which was used in antiquity comes from the sphere of Roman political administration. The Latin term is a transcription from the Greek *dioikeo*, which means to administer. *Dioecesis* thus indicated a vast administrative territory. At the time of Diocletian, it referred to a homogeneous area which included several provinces all under the control of a *vicarius*. Only later did it enter into ecclesiastical use, passing from the term *church*—which itself came to take on the meaning of a building of worship—to that of *paroikia* (Greek) and *paroecia,* from which we get our English word *parish*. In his letter to Decentius of Gubbio, Pope Innocent referred to churches in the countryside as parishes.[186] However, phrases or syntagma such as *ecclesia*, *territorium, fines episcopatus* and *dioecesis* were still being used as well. The term *plebs* could refer to both a diocese and a parish. Since the seventh century it has been customary in the west to use the term *dioecesis* to indicate the territory under the jurisdiction of a bishop. However, even during the Middle Ages the meaning of the term fluctuated, and its exact meaning can only be deduced from the context. For example, the Council of Épaone in 517 speaks of a priest in charge of a diocese (= parish) (can. 8). In the same Rome of a century earlier the *titulus* was considered a *quasi dioecesis*.

Parishes[187]

As we saw in the fourth chapter, the bishop had become the center of the community. Our image of the most widespread local community is that presented by Cyprian. He speaks of the faithful and clerics gathered around their bishop, the vital center of the community who serves as their priest and their shepherd.[188] He is entrusted primarily with the ministries *of koinonia* in his community, i.e., with preaching and with administering the sacraments. As the number of faithful in the cities and the countryside increased, many of these functions were gradually transferred to the presbyters as the structures of the local church expanded. A more complex and divided local community emerged over against what had previously been more unified. As these urban and rural parishes emerged, pastoral care was tailored towards the individual needs of each community in their respective geographical areas.

Therefore, pastoral care developed differently in different areas. For example, in Egypt where there were only a few bishops, the figure of the *periodeuta,* or visiting presbyter, emerges who visits the villages. In other areas, *chorepiskopoi* (country bishops) were created to help fill the void of pastoral care.[189] Other parishes were created that were administered by presbyters. In Roman Africa where bishops abounded these types of parishes would arise only later. In Augustine's vast diocese in Numidia there were priests in some smaller towns who carried out liturgical functions.[190] Some were killed by Donatists.[191]

We find the beginnings of the parish system in Egypt as early as the end of the third century. In large cities such as Rome, Alexandria, Antioch, Milan, as well as in medium-sized towns, such as Nicomedia, several edifices for worship were built. The administrative and pastoral duties in these large cities became decentralized. Rome for instance was divided into pastoral districts, each of which had a *domus ecclesiae,* i.e., a building for worship which also included a place for the clergy to live. In the fourth century such a building was called a *titulus.*[192] In addition, in the same century oratories and rural churches were built in small towns, i.e. in the *villae* (estates), in the *vici* (villages), especially in the very large dioceses so that the population had a place for worship. Some examples are, for instance, the churches of Jerusalem which have an intense liturgical activity, as testified by Egeria. Another example was near Antioch, in Daphne, where there was a *martyrium* of Saint Babylon complete with clergy to welcome the pilgrims. The sanctuary of Thecla in Seleucia of Isauria is a further example as well as the various Roman martyr churches.

In the West, the parish system spread in Spain and Gaul during the fifth and sixth centuries.[193] During the sixth century the parish system acquired greater autonomy and presbyters performed many functions such as celebrating the Eucharist, baptizing and reconciling sinners. They were, however, considered as clergy who had been delegated by the bishops for these tasks, as we mentioned in the fourth chapter.[194] Thus the office of preaching was extended also to presbyters, especially in Gaul from the fourth century. To obviate their insufficient competence, some bishops beginning with Augustine prepared texts that could be used by the presbyters. In addition, others such as Faustus of Riez towards the end of the 5th century and Caesarius of Arles (†542) published collections of homilies known as homiliaries which presbyters could read during the celebration.

Pastoral work also took place in other locations frequented by Christians, such as sites where the cult of martyrs was observed, urban and rural oratories, large sanctuaries that attracted crowds of pilgrims even from afar, and *memoriae* erected on the larger estates that also housed a contingent of the local clergy. Monasteries also became centers that radiated outward and furthered Christianization.

ECCLESIASTICAL PROVINCES

Since already in the second century there was a lack of a unifying and decision-making center, there was no real uniformity at least for the foundational elements of the Christian faith. Therefore, some important episcopal sees emerged as beacons of reference. Moreover, Christianity as a movement that spread throughout the vast Roman Empire and aspired to a certain unity in doctrine and experience necessarily required exchanges of letters and written texts. "This double impulse for uniformity and organizational structure is truly one of the most distinctive characteristics of Christianity."[195]

Christianity quickly moved beyond its founding center to extend throughout the four corners of the earth. Although Jerusalem had been at the center of the first generation of Christians, especially for some of the apostles such as Peter, James and Paul, it decreased in importance. There is a stark contrast between the Jerusalem of the second century which Hadrian had turned into a secular city called *Aelia Capitolina* and the mid-first century Jerusalem of Paul. Jerusalem had been the mother community for the fledgling group of Christians but soon found itself in dire straits. Its importance for Paul is shown in that he went to Jerusalem several times, collected money for "the saints in Jerusalem,"[196] and wrote to the Romans: "For the moment I am going to Jerusalem to serve that community."[197] As Jerusalem decreased in importance other cities gained more prominence as Christianity expanded outward.

An inscription of Abercius, found in 1882/1883 in Hierapolis (today Koçhisar) in *Phrygia Salutaris*,[198] helps us understand the network of churches that had been created at the end of the second century. The Bishop Abercius leaves from a remote country in the Roman province of Asia ultimately arriving at Rome in the West. In the East he had to cross the plain of Syria, reaching the city of Nisibis, on the border of the Roman Empire, which in 192 had become the capital of the province of Mesopotamia. Understand that Abercius had made a round trip of about 8,000 km (almost 5,000 miles)—certainly not for tourism! He did not go to Jerusalem, the mother church, but to Rome as well as other communities. But why did he go on such a long journey to Rome? Was it because of the question of Easter, so much debated in those years? Or the Montanist question? Was it to confront or meet with others to discuss the faith of their respective communities, as Hegesippus had done? Christians in other words had an interest in travelling around in order to compare the faith of different distant churches, which we see not only with Hegesippus, but also with Irenaeus and Origen. There was also the stature of the Church of Rome that drew people to it, as many people came to Rome even from very distant lands in the context of this network of relationships. There was a common heritage of faith and rituals that bound members, scattered though they might be. We see the creation of a common identity now distinct from the original Jewish matrix despite the ethnic and linguistic diversity—an identity that has moved beyond Jerusalem as a point of reference.

The documentation we have for churches of the second and third centuries chronicle the differences between them. Even in the West where the bishop of Rome enjoyed great prestige there was no disciplinary or organizational uniformity. The triad of bishop, presbyters, and deacon was held in common, but the other functions and ministries were not equally widespread. Participation in councils in the third and fourth centuries helped to create greater uniformity in civil dioceses and in large geographical areas. The different liturgical traditions that we can document in later times reflect a tradition that had been formed by the influence of the great See.

Despite so many differences, many centralizing characteristics slowly progressed during the third century in order to combat this dispersion and division. The episcopal see of a more important city conferred on its bishop a prestige, a certain privilege of honor, which included a certain authority, since the nearby churches referred to the bishop of that city for episcopal ordinations and synodal assemblies. These meetings were composed of bishops from the same territory, which may or may not have coincided with the Roman administrative structure epitomized in the civil province. This is how ecclesiastical provincial federations arose already in the third century, although not in every part of the empire. These federations did not always follow the borders of the provinces. In fact, a city like Antioch had influence which extended from Palestine to the Black Sea. Alexandria embraced all of Egypt up to Cyrenaica, and Carthage emerged as an ecclesiastical authority over all Roman Africa up to the *Mauritania Tingitana*.

Canon 6 from the Council of Nicaea admits and actually establishes this supra-diocesan structure complete with its metropolitan circumscriptions, even giving the churches of Rome, Alexandria and Antioch greater rights than the other churches. Traditionally, it was thought that Canon 6 from Nicaea, in a certain sense, had already admitted the patriarchates of these cities, an interpretation endorsed by the Council of Constantinople in 381 with an evident forcing of the text.[199] More recent studies, however, have demonstrated that Nicaea recognized only the metropolitan structure, that is, it was simply recognizing the capital city of the civil province, granting some exceptions over a wider geographical area. The Council of Nicaea often refers to the metropolitan organization. For instance, in each province (eparchy) synods are to be held twice a year (can. 5). In episcopal ordinations all the bishops of the province must agree, if possible, and the consent of the metropolitan (can. 4), that is, the bishop of the metropolis, the capital of the province, is required.[200]

The title of *archbishop* (*archiepiscopus*) was not a synonym for *metropolitan*. And yet, until the end of the fifth century it was used to indicate the bishops of the great Sees and was nearly synonymous with *patriarch,* although this latter term then became employed in a more technical sense, and furthermore at times was applied to the bishops of a *metropolis*, or of other important sees.[201] The Metropolitan is the center of the provincial communion (*eparchy*):

> The bishops in every province must acknowledge the bishop who presides in the metropolis, and who has to take thought for the whole province; because all men of business come together from every quarter to the metropolis. Wherefore it is decreed that he have precedence in rank, and that the other bishops do nothing extraordinary without him. . . . For each bishop has authority over his own parish to manage it with piety. . . . But let him undertake nothing further without the bishop of the metropolis, neither the latter without the consent of the others.[202]

This canon provides even more specificity: the metropolitan has the care of the entire province and has the place of honor and no bishop can operate outside his territory.

The *Apostolic Canons* state: "The bishops of every region must acknowledge him who is first among them and consider him as their head and do nothing of consequence without his consent. But each may do those things only which concern his own parish. . . . But neither let him (who is the first) do anything without the consent of all, for in this way there will be unanimity and God will be glorified through the Lord in the Holy Spirit" (can. 34). The principle of "territorial accommodation" is being affirmed, that is, that the ecclesiastical organization is modeled on the civil one, whereby if the juridical state of a city changes, the same thing happens in the ecclesiastical ambit as well, as canon 17 of the Council of Chalcedon makes clear.[203] The consequence of this is that this principle can also be extended to the metropolitan organization. In other words, if the imperial authority divides a region into several provinces, the same thing can happen in the ecclesiastical organization, even if the ecclesiastical side tries to preserve the previous form. This is what Basil tried to do on the occasion of the division of Cappadocia.[204] Having recourse to the imperial authorities, he initiated the process of dividing the civil province in which he was located into two ecclesiastical provinces.

Before proceeding further, there is a methodological point to consider. Normally we generalize disparate and fragmentary texts, presenting a false picture. Or we imagine a homogeneous situation in the absence of information to the contrary. Or perhaps we project subsequent ecclesiastical rulings onto earlier situations in order to provide an explanation. When the ancient authors read the sources that we also read today and use, they had no critical editions—an obvious point but one that rarely enters into the conversation. Another relevant point that is often overlooked is that the meaning of the terms used such as metropolitan, diocese, catholicos, patriarch, bishop, primate, primacy, etc., changes over the years and they often had a different meaning then than they have today.

Returning now to the explanation, ancient documents especially those in Greek used the word *honor* (*timê*) to indicate the authority of the metropolitan to create new bishops, establish provincial councils, be the arbiter for those who made an appeal to him, as well as all inter-diocesan affairs. The development of the metropolitan organization was not homogeneous throughout the Roman Empire. Here, too, the East preceded the West. In *Africa Proconsularis,* the metropolitan—referred to as the primate—was the bishop of Carthage while in the other provinces he was simply the oldest bishop by ordination. The administrative restructuring of Rome had consequences for the ecclesiastical organization, so that the reunion or subdivision of provinces or the change made to a civil metropolis would have immediate consequences for ecclesiastical structures, resulting in quarrels and difficulties between bishops. Often in such cases a compromise was sought in order not to cause an inordinate disruption to situations that had only recently come about. While the synodal requirements reflected the situation in some eastern provinces, they also expressed guidelines for the future for other geographical areas.

In Spain, the metropolitan system was only partially implemented in the second half of the fourth century.[205] Pope Siricius wrote to Himerius of Tarragona, asking him to bring his answers to the knowledge of "all our brethren in the episcopate and not only to those who are established in your diocese, but also to all the Carthaginians, of the Baetica, the Lusitanians and the Galicians, and also to all those who belong to provinces in any way close to you."[206] The system was better implemented in the fifth century and by the sixth century the Council of Gerona (517) had established that all the communities of each province must celebrate the Eucharist according to the same practice as the metropolis (can. 1). In Gaul, the metropolitan system developed during the fourth century in relation to the civil provinces, but there were still disputes at times in the fifth century and the metropolitan see did not always find its territory coinciding with the provincial capital.[207]

The anonymous author of the fifth century *De septem ordinibus*, considered metropolitan governance a recent innovation that was imposed for reasons of discipline. At the end of the fourth century, few cities in northern Gaul had episcopal sees. Christianity was practically unknown, especially in the central and northern countryside, and the people had to go to the city to come to know and venerate Christ.[208] Martin of Tours († 397) is known to be the great missionary—or Christianizer—of the vast territory of Tours (*Civitas Turonorum*), preaching in villages, destroying pagan temples, and cutting down sacred trees and idols of various kinds. The territory of Gaul was divided into two civil dioceses and did not have an administrative geographical unit. But on several occasions the Gallican episcopate was seen as a whole, as happened for instance in the Council of Paris of 360 gathered by Hilary, as well as in the Priscillian affair, the Council of Aquileia in 381, the decree *Ad Gallos episcopos,* and in the Council of Turin in 398 which was convened for the bishops of the "provinces of Gaul."

PATRIARCHATES[209]

The Council of Nicaea brings some order to the organizational structure of the higher ranks of the ecclesiastical authorities, but leaves several problems unresolved, because in general it tried to render mandatory what had been created in the East and not in the West. Subsequent councils also behaved in a similar way. This method of proceeding gave rise to ambitious bishops who introduced novelties and abuses which would later be legitimized in future councils. It is interesting to note how the councils or other authorities in every circumstance declared—with a rather boring monotony—that they wanted to remain faithful "to the custom and canons of the Fathers." Sometimes the very canons expressly mentioned are forced to take on a new meaning. A typical example of this way of proceeding concerns canon 6 of the Council of Nicaea (325) that has already been featured often in this chapter. The Council of Constantinople (381) revised and expanded this canon in order to grant the see of the Constantinopolitan Episcopate the second place after that of Rome (canons 2 and 3) and the Council of Chalcedon (451) utilized it to found the patriarchate of New Rome (can. 28). Carthage, which in fact had an influence that extended over the whole of Africa, never reaches such a level. In the West, no see receives this right except for the Roman church.

From the years of the Council of Nicaea in 325 to the Council of Chalcedon in 451, the supra-metropolitan structure evolved and settled, resulting in the consecration of five patriarchates (pentarchy), with their respective areas of influence. The councils also recognized there were new situations and problems Nicaea had not had to confront, such as the recognition of an authority superior to that of the metropolitans. *Metropolitan* remained the initial term used, but already in the middle of the fifth century the term *Patriarch* was introduced, which became the definitive term leading up to the time of Justinian (527-565).

By the middle of the fifth century the great ecclesiastical Sees ranked by decreasing order of honor were: Rome, Constantinople, Alexandria, Antioch and Jerusalem. The bishop of Rome was first on the scale in relation to all the churches and was considered the patriarch of the West, with his various spheres of influence.[210] The bishop of New Rome—the preferred terminology from the Council of Chalcedon—was the patriarch of the civil dioceses of Thrace, Pontus and Asia. His authority had been steadily growing and extending, first as we saw at the Council of Constantinople (381) and then even more so at Chalcedon (451).[211] Several factors contributed to the rise of Constantinople. There was the action of its bishops who, out of zeal or ambition, depending on the case, exercised power beyond the borders of the province. Another factor was the potential for imperial support, with the presence of the imperial throne with its senate which could and would lead to caesaropapism. There was also the honor of the city itself, having been founded by Constantine and now serving as the imperial residence. In just 70 years, from the suffragan diocese of Heraclea of Thrace, the see of Constantinople became the first and highest see in the whole East. Many bishops went to the capital for the most diverse reasons. They went to make appeals—appeals addressed to the emperor—who instructed the bishop to provide solutions or resolutions to the issues that came before him. In fact, the bishop of Constantinople presided over the so-called permanent synod (*synodos endemousa*), composed of bishops passing through as well as those present in the capital.[212] Thus one passes from the simple title of bishop of Constantinople to bishop of Constantinople as New Rome, and then to archbishop.

While, as we've seen, the importance of a see like Rome was based on its apostolic foundation by Paul and Peter, now a political criterion is officially introduced at the very moment when the eastern capital had become truly important by virtue of it housing the residence of the emperor. Before Arcadius, an emperor rarely stayed long in New Rome. The first time that the title of "Ecumenical Patriarch of New Rome" appears in an official document is found in a letter of John II (518-520) to Pope Hormisdas—but it was not accompanied by any anti-Roman spirit.[213] The Code of Justinian states that the name "Rome" indicates both cities, the old and the new.[214]

The Roman church refused to recognize this novelty for quite some time,[215] considering the previous hierarchy of Sees which were linked to the apostle Peter. There was Rome where Peter had died; Alexandria, founded by Mark, Peter's disciple; and Antioch, where Peter had been for a certain period of time. From the time of Boniface (418-422) the bishop of Rome accepted only the triarchy of Rome, Alexandria, and Antioch. The pentarchy was only formally recognized by the Pope over eight hundred years later at the Fourth Lateran Council of 1215.

Canons 9, 17 and 28 of the Council of Chalcedon of 451 demonstrate that the council recognized what was at stake and, despite the opposition of Rome, Constantinople became not only the see of the patriarchate of the dioceses of Pontus, Thrace and Asia, but the second degree of jurisdiction after Rome, with an effective power, even if not always definable, for the whole East.[216] By the middle of the fifth century the term *ecumenical* began to be used for some patriarchs. The Greek term *oikoumene* was translated into Latin as *universalis*.[217] As bishop of Constantinople, Acacius (471-489) used it habitually after his schism from Rome which became known as the Acacian schism. His successors also used it as did the Emperor Justinian himself when he was referring to the Constantinopolitan patriarchs. Pope Pelagius II (579-590) received the Acts of the Synod of Constantinople of 587 wherein the title of *ecumenical* for the patriarch was used by John the Faster († 595), who then used it regularly.[218]

Pelagius did not approve of this title because he thought it indicated an act of pride and that it was being used to express the prestige of the bishop of the Byzantine capital for the East. Gregory, Pelagius' successor, protested strongly and more than once. He even brought it to the attention of the emperor Mauritius (†602), along with the other Eastern patriarchs, but to no use. And so, the title continues to be used even unto the present day.

The patriarchate of Alexandria—although the term *patriarchate* itself was not used until later—has a history dating back to the third century when its authority extended far beyond the boundaries of the great city and the surrounding territory.[219] In fact, it extended at that time as far as Cyrenaica and all of Egypt; later it would also include Ethiopia and later still Nubia.[220] Its authority was built on historical elements, but also upon ambition and legends such as its foundation by the evangelist Mark. There were also cultural, commercial and religious interactions between the various regions that contributed to Alexandria's ascendency. The Nicene Council of 325 ratified a de facto situation, stating that "in Egypt, Libya and the Pentapolis (Cyrenaica and Libya) the ancient custom applies, whereby the bishop of Alexandria has authority over all these provinces." The custom, it is said, is ancient. In this vast territory there were no independent metropolitans, at least from the fourth century onwards, even though it was divided into provinces and a portion of it was even beyond the borders of the Roman Empire. There was a metropolitan office in Cyrenaica, that of Ptolemais, as can be seen from the letters of Bishop Synesius. The Metropolitan controlled the bishops of the province, but it was always dependent on Alexandria. Cyrenaica had another special feature in that its bishops could be ordained either by the Alexandrian Patriarch or by three local bishops, as was the case elsewhere. In Egypt however only the Patriarch, the Bishop of Alexandria, consecrated all the bishops, although in rare cases he might delegate someone to represent him. The patriarch summoned the councils and presided over them often making decisions unilaterally that applied to all under his jurisdiction. These rights recognized by the Council of Nicaea (can. 6) are confirmed later on. Alexandria had a non-hierarchical structure in that the Alexandrian bishop would choose, upon presentation by the local church, and personally consecrate all the bishops north of the First Cataract of the Nile, creating a personal relationship with all of them and also ensuring their subordination to and dependence on him. At Chalcedon, Alexandria was degraded to third in rank and so its bishop also moved down to the third place of honor in the rankings.

Antioch had seen its rights recognized without geographical specifications at Nicaea, and extended its jurisdiction in the vast civil diocese of the East and theoretically as far as India. Its influence, however, was minimal beyond the confines of the Roman Empire. Its territory was immense but its authority was rather precarious in the more distant areas. The fifth-century schisms at Antioch created two subdivisions: one for western Syria and another for eastern Syria. Today this see has five patriarchs of its own—three Catholic and one from the Greek Orthodox tradition with the other from the Syrian Orthodox tradition.

Jerusalem's fortunes, on the other hand, were rather bleak for the first few centuries, having been turned into the pagan city *Aelia Capitolina* by Hadrian. Her recognition as a patriarchate had a rather troubled history. A shadow of its former self, it depended on the metropolitan of Caesarea in Palestine, despite having received certification of its honor from the Council of Nicaea (canon 7), which recognized in her a primacy of honor.[221] Jerusalem had little political importance during this time and her name and reputation were only restored under Constantine when it also became a center of pilgrimage. Cyril of Jerusalem promoted her prestige as the holy city and an apostolic see that could trace its roots back to James the brother of the Lord.[222] In the first half of the fourth century Jerusalem shook off its pagan moorings and took on a Christian character with the construction of large basilicas and monasteries. Its liturgy also underwent development that included processions to the holy sites, as well as pilgrimages by the faithful.[223]

Cyril's successor, John, received a letter of reproach in 386 from Jerome for boasting of possessing the *apostolica cathedra*,[224] which implied greater prestige for Jerusalem as having an apostolic foundation. He was even harsher in another text: "You who seek ecclesiastical norms and use the canons of the Council of Nicaea, and commit yourself to using clerics from outside belonging to other bishops, answer me: What relationship does Palestine have with the bishop of Alexandria? If I am not mistaken, it has been established (in Nicaea), that Caesarea is the metropolis of Palestine and Antioch of the whole East.[225] Well, either you should have had recourse to the bishop of Caesarea . . . , or, if it was really necessary to go and seek an opinion further away, it would have been better to address your letter to Antioch."[226] John had neglected to consult his metropolitan which, to Jerome, smacked of ambition.

At the Council of Ephesus in 431, Jerusalem's Bishop Juvenal (bishop since 422) sought to obtain authority over all Palestine, Phoenicia and Arabia. We know about these maneuvers, including the use of false documents, through a letter from Cyril of Alexandria sent to Pope Leo.[227] Juvenal managed to avoid excommunication, but he carried out various abuses in his ordinations. His machinations were filled with intrigue and ambition in order to get what he wanted at the Council of Ephesus in 449 (*latrocinium ephesinum*).[228] Later he reached a compromise with his opponent, Maximus of Antioch, at the Council of Chalcedon, against the acquired rights of the Patriarch of Antioch. The provinces of Phoenicia and Arabia would belong to Antioch, the three provinces of Palestine to Juvenal. The compromise was accepted in the Council and Jerusalem became the fifth patriarchal See, against the protests of the Roman delegation.[229]

So too in this case—notwithstanding the Roman opposition—the geographical circumscription and juridical settlement carried out at the Council of Chalcedon became fully integrated into the synodal and state structure of the East. It received its definitive imperial sanction from Justinian who provided copious legislation that helped define the legal implications of the structure and the respective responsibilities of the various Sees. In 553 he convened a council—the fifth in the series of so-called ecumenical councils—on a strict patriarchal basis, in opposition to and without consulting Pope Vigilius. This council was recognized by Rome only later.

In the West, Aquileia claimed the title of patriarchate in the sixth century for a time. Due to this, the title was later attributed to the bishop of Venice in the eighth century. After this, other episcopal offices would eventually claim the title of patriarch also for their bishops.

CONCLUSION

At this point, some general considerations need to be made. The higher ecclesiastical structures of the Christian communities located outside the confines of the Roman Empire, which had been forming since the fourth century, were deliberately left out, places such as Armenia, Georgia, Persia, Ethiopia, and Ireland. Each region was so varied that it is almost impossible to present a unified picture. Moreover, even the exposition made so far has more of a theological-canonical character than a historical one, considerably simplifying the canonical conciliar dispositions which themselves present many difficulties of harmonization. Their legislation was always in process (*in fieri*) and tended to set their current situations into law, that is, customs that more or less became consolidated and codified.

It is very difficult to trace historically the first five centuries in order to see how such situations were created because one would end up outlining a history of anarchies, claims, rejections, struggles and ambitions, zeal for good—altogether mixed with theological and exegetical speculations along with the historical arguments.

In order to defend acquired rights or reject the claims of a metropolitan see upon an episcopal or patriarchal see—either way, the rite of episcopal consecration assumed absolute importance. It conferred a kind of maternity and, therefore, dependency on the seat of the consecrating bishop compared to that of the one who was being consecrated. This is why at the canonical-liturgical level the history of groupings of local communities in larger circumscriptions is reduced to the history of episcopal ordinations. Nonetheless, the historian should, in any case, seek to understand why and how a certain situation of supremacy and dependency on the episcopal sees occurred among the various sees. The system of ecclesiastical provinces that developed first with metropolitan and then patriarchal sees does not coincide with the administrative subdivisions of the Empire, even if in fact there were many similarities. The political factor was generally decisive, but other elements came into play such as apostolicity, culture, and the prestige of the city.

Such an ecclesiastical organization does not produce anything approaching a divine right —except in the case of the Bishop of Rome who as the successor of Peter traced the institution back to Christ himself, although in reality it was born out solely from the need for greater ecclesial communion and to resolve problems of faith and discipline on an ever wider level.

---

1. K. H. Schelkle, *Teologia del Nuovo Testamento*, vol. IV: *Ecclesiologia, escatologia* (Bologna: Dehoniane, 1980), 48-49; Engl. Translation: *Theology of the New Testament. 4, The Rule of God: Church, Eschatology* (Collegeville, MN: Liturgical Press, 1978).
2. *EAC* 1:306.
3. Cf. *1 Cor* 16:16; 13:1; 13:24; etc.
4. Ambrosiaster, *Comm. in Eph.* 4.11: CSEL 81:89-90: *Ut ergo cresceret plebs et | multiplicaretur, omnibus inter initia concessum est et evangelizare et baptizare. At ubi omnia loca circumplexa est Ecclesia conventicula sunt constituta, ut nullus de clericis auderet, qui ordinatus non erat, praesumere officium.* (It was to allow people to grow and multiply that at the beginning everyone was allowed to evangelize, to baptize, and to expound the Scriptures in the church. But when the church became established in every place, congregations were formed and rectors and other officials were appointed with the result that after that no clerk who was not ordained would dare perform a function which was not appointed or assigned to him. (*Ambrosiaster: Commentaries on Galatians-Philemon*. Edited by Gerald Lewis Bray (Downers Grove: IVP Academic, 2009), 49.
5. Ex. Augustine, *Ep. ad catholicos c. donatistas* 6, 11; the term can also indicate an edifice: Ps.-Cyprian, *Ep. ad Tur.* 3; Lactantius, *De mortibus* 15 and 36. 3; *Institutiones* 5.11.10; Arnobius, *Adv. nationes* 4.36; Augustine, *Comm. ad Gal.* 35. This sometimes had a negative connotation.
6. *Ecclesia plebs sacerdoti unita et pastori suo grex adhaerens* (*Ep.* 66.8: CSEL 3.2:732; *Ep.* 69.8: PL 4:403).
7. *1 Clement* 44.2.
8. Cf. *1 Clement* 42.
9. Cf. *Letters to the Magnesians* 3.1-2; *to the Trallians* 3.1; *Letter to the Ephesians* 5.3.
10. Irenaeus, *Adv haer.* 4.26.2.
11. *Duo quippe sunt, imperator auguste, quibus principaliter mundus regitur: auctoritas sacrata pontificum et regalis potestas*: *Ep.* 8.2: PL 59:42; G. Mancuso, "'Auctoritas Sacrata Pontificis' e 'Auctoritas Principis,'" *Apollinaris* 68 (1995): 193-204.
12. Cyprian, *Ep.* 3.1. Cf. also Cyprian's declaration to the council of Carthage of 256 (Hartel III, 1:435-36).
13. L.I. Scipioni, *Vescovo e popolo. L'esercizio dell'autorità nella chiesa primitiva (III secolo)* (Milan: Univ. Cattolica del Sacro Cuore, 1977).
14. Cf. E Cattaneo, *I ministeri nella Chiesa antica: testi patristici dei primi tre secoli* (Milan: Edizioni Paoline, 1997), 520; R. Seagraves, *Pascentes cum disciplina* (Fribourg: Éditions universitaires, 1993), 230-36.
15. Cyprian, *Ep.* 74.10; cf. Augustine, *On Baptism against the Donatists* 5.26.37.
16. *si ad evangelicam auctoritatem atque ad apostolicam traditionem sincera et religiosa fide revertimur.* Cyprian, *Ep.* 73.15.2; cf. *Ep.* 69.12.1.
17. Tertullian, *Adv. Marc.* 4.12.3.
18. Tertullian, *De praescript.* 21.1; *Adv. Marc.* 4.2.1.
19. Cf. Cyprian, *Ep.* 59.4.13; Cf. Leo the Great, *Ep.* 6.2.
20. Here we talk about the authority of the church. Every authority according to Paul (*Rom* 13:1f.) derives from a divine source—a concept which also corresponds to the ancient imperial conception of authority; cf. P. De Francisci, *Arcana Imperii*, vol. III, 2. (Rome: Bulzoni, 1970), 86-135.
21. *1 Clement* 40-44.
22. Irenaeus, *Adv. haer.* 3.3.3; 4.26.2-5.
23. *in ea regula incedimus quam ecclesiae ab apostolis, apostoli a Christo, Christus a Deo* (Tertullian, *De Praescrip.* 37.1; cf. 21.4.)
24. Through Eusebius of Caesarea (*HE.* 4.22.2) we know that Hegesippus redacted some episcopal lists in the second century. Cf. Irenaeus, *Against Heresies* 3.3.3 for the Roman Church. On the importance of these lists see: C.H. Turner, "The Early Episcopal Lists," *JTS* 1 (1900): 529-53; J. Dubois, "Les listes épiscopales, témoins de l'organi-

sation ecclésiastique et de la transmission des traditions," *Rev. Hist. Ecc. De France* 62 (1972): 9-23. A. Di Berardino, *EAC* 1:832-34 (with bibliography).
25. Cf. Irenaeus, *Adv. haer* 3.3.1.
26. Tertullian, *De praescript.* 20.4-7.
27. The anonymous Roman author of the work entitled *Refutation of all heresies (Philosophoumena)*, who opposed Callixtus.
28. Hippolytus, *Refutation of All Heresies*, Prooemium.
29. Cyprian, *Ep.* 3.3.
30. *apostolis vicaria ordinatione succedunt;* Cyprian, *Ep* 66.4.
31. *Acts* 14:23; 20:17-35; *1 Tim* 4:14; *2 Tim* 1:6.
32. *Tit* 1:5-9; 2:1-15; *1 Tim* 5:17-22.
33. *1 Tim* 4:12-16; 6:20; *2 Tim* 1:13ff.; 2:15; 3:14-4:5.
34. *1 Clement* 42 and 44.
35. *eos qui ab apostolis instituti sunt episcopi et successores eorum usque ad nos*: *Adv. haer.* 3.3.1; cf. 3.3.4; 4.26.2.
36. *vice Christi;* Cyprian, *Ep.* 59.5; 63.14; 68.5.
37. Ignatius, *To the Trallians*, 3, 1; Ambrose, *Comm. to Ps.* 63.14; John Chrysostom, *Homilies on 2 Timothy*.
38. *Didascalia* 2.28.9. The biblical bases which are most frequently cited are: *Mt* 10:40 (whoever receives you receives me, ...); *Mt* 28:18-20 (And Jesus, having drawn nigh unto them, said: all power in heaven and on earth has been given to me ...); *Acts* 1:8.
39. Cf. the cited texts in these paragraphs of Tertullian; so too in the confession of the faith (the *credo*) there is a reference to the entire church and not just to the bishops, which is an affirmation of the church's apostolicity.
40. Cyprian, *Ep.*66.8.
41. I. Petriglieri, *Autorità come servizio: figure e ruolo del vescovo nei Padri della Chiesa* (Vatican City: Libreria editrice vaticana, 2009); not useful of our subject.
42. É. Benveniste, *Le vocabulaire des institutions indo-européennes*. II. *Pouvoir, droit, religion* (Paris: Les Èditions de Minuit, 1969, 2001), 398.
43. H. Arendt, *Between Past and Future: Eight Exercises in Political Thought* (New York: The Viking Press, 1968), 130-46.
44. *Mk* 10:42-44.
45. *Mk* 10:45; cf. *Lk* 22:27.
46. *1 Thess* 2:6-8.
47. *1 Pet* 5:2-3.
48. Text quoted by H. U. von Balthasar, *Spouse of the Word* (San Francisco: Ignatius Press, 1991), 195.
49. Ignatius, *To the Philippians* 1.1.
50. Eusebius, *HE* 5.1.29.
51. Origen, *In Isaiam hom.* 6.1; *In Math. Comm.* 16.8.
52. *Ego qui cotidie fratribus servio*" *Ep.* 66.3.2.
53. Jerome, *Contra Iovinianum* 1.34: PL 23:270.
54. *episcopus nomen est operis, non honoris*; Augustine, *City of God* 19.19.
55. Chrysostom, *De sacerdotio* 2.4; PG 48:635.
56. *servus Christi servorumque Christi*; Augustine, *De peccatorum meritis* 3.1; *Ep.* 130.
57. Augustine, *Sermon* 340.1.
58. Augustine, *Sermon* 46.2. Y. Congar studied this point in "La hiérarchie comme service dans le Nouveau Testament et les documents de la tradition," *L'Épiscopat et l'Église universelle* Y. Congar and Bernard-Dominique Dupuy (Paris: Éditions du Cerf, 1962), 67-99, Ibid, *Quelques expression traditionnelles du service chrétien*, 101-32.
59. *Jn* 21:15.
60. Augustine, *Tractates on the Gospel of John* 124.
61. Cf. *3 Jn*.
62. Cf. Origen, *Comm. In Matth.* 16.8; 21.9.
63. Cf. Y. Congar and J. M. Todd, *Problèmes de l'autorité* (Paris: Éditions du Cerf, 1962), 156-57.
64. *cupiditas dominandi* or *cupiditas huius mundi*.
65. Cf. chapter 4.
66. Augustine, *Ioh. evang tr.* 5.15.
67. Cf. *1 Cor* 1:9; 10:16; *2 Cor* 13:13.

68. *1 Jn* 1:3.
69. John of Damascus explains: "It is called Koinonia, and truly it is, because through it we commune with one another and are mutually united" Cf. *On the Orthodox Faith* 86, IV, 13, Ed. Kotter n.197, 168-69.
70. Augustine, *Sermon* 71.12.18.
71. Juan Gil-Tamayo and Aldaz Ruiz. *La communio en los padres de la Iglesia* (Pamplona: Ediciones Universidad de Navarra, 2010).
72. Justin, *1 Apology* 61.1.
73. Tertullian, *De praescript.* 32.1-2.
74. Tertullian, *De Praescript.* 32.4-5.
75. Origen, *Contra Celsum* 5.61-62.
76. Origen, *Contra Celsum* 5.63.
77. Origen, *Contra Celsum* 5.59.
78. H.-J. Sieben, *DSp* 7.1751.
79. Cyprian, *De unitate* 4 and 7; *Epp.* 45.1; 69.6; 73.11, etc.
80. Cf. Rufinus of Aquileia, *Comm. on the Creed* 2.
81. Augustine, *Sermon* 213.2.
82. See J. Vilella, *Letters of communion*, EAC 2:557-59.
83. Tertullian, *De praescriptione*, 36.4.
84. Cyprian, *Ep.* 59.9. J. Vilella, *Letters of communion*, 557.
85. M.-E. Mombili Thumaini, *L'aspect d'autonomie et de communion dans la praxis africaine des recours à Rome (IIIe-Ve siècles): essai d'interprétation du comportement ambivalent de l'épiscopat africain* (Rome: Pontificia Università gregoriana, 2001).
86. Charles Munier, *Vie Conciliaire el Collections Canoniques en Occident, IVe-XIIe siècles* (London: Variorum Reprints, 1987), 49 and 122.
87. Eusebius, *HE* 5.24.17.
88. Ignatius, *Letter to the Smyrnaeans* 8.
89. Cf. C. L. Hertling, *Communio e primato* (Rome: Herder, 1961), 18-19.
90. Ambrose, *On the death of his brother Satyrus* 1.47.
91. Epiphanius, *Panarion* 75.3: PG 43:508A; *Liturgy of James*, PO 26:212.12.
92. Cyprian, *Ep.* 1.2.
93. Cyprian, *Ep.* 12.2.
94. Ps. Dionysius, *Ecc. hier.* 3.3.8.
95. *nomen in sacris diptycis scriptum.*
96. Facundus of Hermiane, *Defens.* 4.1: PL 67:608.
97. Rusticus, ACO I. 4.90.2; Atticus, *Ep.* 75 [among the letters of Cyril]: PG 77:352B.
98. Justinian, *Conf.*: PG 86:1027C; Theodore Lect., fr,.: PG 86:220B; Evagrius, *HE* 3.34: PG 86:2674AB.
99. Facundus of Hermiane, *Defens.* 4.1: PL 67:609; Mansi 8,1044 and 1051 5.; see DACL 4:1054.
100. *Libellus professionis*; Denzinger 172; *Collectio Avellana* p. 800.
101. *publice diaconus in ecclesia recitat offerentium nomina*; Jerome, *In Ezek* 4.18; PL 25:175. EAC 1:723-25; V.L. Guidetti, "I dittici nelle liturgie d'Oriente e d'Occidente," *Studi sull'Oriente cristiano* 20 (206): 61-147.
102. *Apostolic Tradition* 2; Cyprian, *Ep.* 67.5.
103. A. Di Berardino, "L'imperatore Costantino e la celebrazione della Pasqua," in *Costantino il Grande* (Macerata: Università degli Studi di Macerata, 1992), 363-84.
104. Augustine, *Ep.* 54.2.2; WSA 2.1:210-11.
105. *litterae communionis - koinonikà grammata.*
106. Jerome, *Ep.* 15.5: PL 22:355.
107. Basil, *Ep.* 258.3: PG 32:951.
108. Basil, *Ep* 242.2; PG 32:901.
109. Council of Nicaea, can. 5.
110. Origen, *In Isaiam hom.* 6.1; *Comm. on Math* 16.8.
111. Cyprian, *Ep.* 68.3.2.
112. Ambrose, *Ep* 12.4; PL 16:989.

113. Perhaps the English translation loses effectiveness; here is the Latin text: *Probant unitatem communicatio pacis et appellatio fraternitatis et contesseratio hospitalitatis.*
114. That is, the Creed. Tertullian, *De praescript*. 20.4.
115. In this paragraph I will partially take up and complete one of my texts: A. Di Berardino, "Patterns of Koinonia in the First Christian Centuries," in *Concilium* 37 (2001): issue 3:46-58.
116. Eusebius, *HE* 3.32.7-8.
117. *Gal* 2:2.
118. Irenaeus, *Adv. haer.* 3.3.2. Regarding this text, one should especially consult: M. Maccarrone, *Apostolicità, episcopato e primato di Pietro* (Rome: Fac. Theol. Pontif, 1976), 42-63.
119. Eusebius, *HE* 4.22.1.
120. J. N. D. Kelly, *Early Christian Creeds*, (London: Longman, 1972).
121. Cf. for example Irenaeus, *Adv. haer.* 1.10; 3.4.
122. Tertullian, *De praescript*. 13.
123. Formula from the Nicene Council of 325, revised and amplified by that from Constantinople of 381 with the inclusion of the Holy Spirit.
124. Tertullian, *De ieiunio* 13.6.
125. Irenaeus, *Adv. haer.* 3.3.2.
126. Cf. PL 13:374D-376A; PL 54:1007.
127. *sedente in cathedra urbis Romae ecclesiae Pio episcopo fratre eius.*
128. For the canonico-liturgical literature cf. A. Di Berardino, "Canonica e liturgica, Letteratura," in *Letteratura Patristica*, eds. A. Di Berardino, G. Fedalto, M. Simonetti, (Milan: Cinisello Balsamo 2007), 222-49.
129. Eusebius, *HE* 5.23; 5.16.
130. Gregory, *Ep.* 3.10: PL 77:613.
131. Cf. M. Simonetti, *La crisi ariana nel quarto secolo* (Rome: Institutum Patristicum Augustinianum, 1974), 313-25; A. Miranda, "Chiesa "orientale" ed "occidentale" nel sinodo di Seleucia-Rimini," in *I concili della cristianità occidentale, secoli III-V* (Rome: Institutum Patristicum Augustinianum, 2002), 461-70.
132. *Mt* 18:20.
133. Cyprian, *Ep.* 57.5.
134. Eusebius, *Life of Constantine* 3.17; Athanasius, *Apology c. arr.* 59
135. H. J. Sieben, *Die Konzilsidee der Alten Kirche* (Paderborn: Schöningh, 1979); cf. R. B. Eno, "Pope and Councils: the Patristic Origins," *Science et Esprit* 28 (1976): 183-211.
136. Augustine, *On baptism* 2.3.4.
137. Pope Innocent I (402-417): *Ep.* 2,3: PL 20:47.
138. Y Congar, "La réception comme réalité ecclésiologique," *Revue Sc Philosoque et Théol.* 56 (1972): 369-403; H. Chadwick, "Un concetto per la storia dei concili. La ricezione," *Cristianesimo nella storia* 13 (1992): 475-92.
139. The term *papa* from the Greek pappas, papas = father, daddy was an affective title given to bishops and then too to Abbots and priests. In Egypt, however, the *pappas* was par excellence the Bishop of Alexandria. Applied to the bishop of Rome, it began in the third century. The council of Arles in 314 called Silvester of Rome, *gloriosissimus papa*. Thereafter this usage became more and more common.
140. *Iudaeos impulsore Chresto assidue tumultuantes Roma expulit*; Suetonius, *Claudius* 25.11.
141. Irenaeus, *Adv. haer.* 3.3.3. H. Holstein "'Propter potentiorem Principalitatem' (Saint Irénée, 'Adversus Haereses', III, 3, 2), *Recherche de science religieuses* 36 (1949): 122-34; P. Lampe, *From Paul to Valentinus: Christians at Rome in the First Two Centuries*. Trans. by Michael Steinhauser (Minneapolis: Fortress Press, 2003), 404-6.
142. For a synthesis of the significance of this excerpt from Irenaeus *Adversus haereses* 3.3.2 see in SC 210: 223-36.
143. A. Di Berardino, "La solidarietà: forme ed organizzazione a Roma (secoli IV-V)," *La comunità cristiana di Roma. La sua vita e la sua cultura dalle origini all'Alto Medio Evo*, (Rome: Libreria editrice vaticana, 2000): 83-112.
144. *EAC* 1:8; M. Guarducci, *Epigrafia greca*, vol. IV, (Rome 1978), 337-86; "L'iscrizione di Abercio e Roma," *Ancient Society* 2 (1971): 174-203; "L'iscrizione di Abercio" *Ancient Society* 4 (1973): 271-79 E. Wirbelauer, "Aberkios, der Schüler des reinen Hirten, im römischen Reich des 2. Jahrhunderts," *Historia* 51 (2002): 359-82; M.M. Mitchell, "Looking for Abercius: Reimagining Contexts of Interpretation of the Earliest Christian Inscription," in *Commemorating the Dead: Texts and Artefacts in Context*, ed. Laurie Brink, Deborah Green (Berlin: Walter de Gruyter, 2008), 303-36.
145. *Mt* 16:18-19.

146. Cf. Leo the Great, *Ep.* 115.1.
147. W. Kasper, ed., *The Petrine Ministry: Catholics and Orthodox in Dialog* (New York: Newman Press, 2006).
148. *Tu es Petrus.*
149. *Quod firmavit in synodo sedes apostolica, hoc robur obtinuit; quod refutavit, habere non potest firmitatem*; *Tract.* 4.9: (Thiel, 565).
150. Mansi VI, 581; *Acta conc. oecum.* II, I, 1.65.
151. Leo the Great, *Ep.* 147-149.
152. The political principle was criticized by Rome but consolidated in the East. The canon principally was against the see of Alexandria. The principle of the importance of a see is based on religious reasons such as the apostolic foundation or the place of martyrdom of some apostle.
153. V. Monachino, "Anno 381: il canone 3° del Concilio Costantinopolitano I", in *Roma Costantinopoli Mosca* (Napoli: Edizioni Scientifiche Italiane, 1983), 253-260. Gelasius I, *Ep.* 26, in *Epistolae romanorum pontificum genuinae*, recensuit et edidit Andreas Thiel, 1, (Brunsbergae, 1868), 174-220, 393-413.
154. K. Baus, E. Ewig, "L'epoca dei Concili (IV-V secolo),", *Storia della Chiesa*, ed. H. Jedin, vol. 2, trad. it, (Milan: Edizioni Opera della Regalità di Nostro Signore Gesù Cristo, 1977), 275-77; G. Dagron, "Constantinople, la primauté après Rome," in *Politica retorica e simbolismo del primato: Roma e Costantinopoli (secoli IV-VII)*, ed. F. Elia (Catania: CULC, 2002), pp. 23-38. See F. Elia, *Sui privilegia urbis Constantinopolitanae*, 79-105.
155. V. Monachino, "Il Canone 28° di Calcedonia e S. Leone Magno," *Gregorianum* 33 (1952): 531-65; Peter L'Huillier, *The Church of the Ancient Councils: The Disciplinary Work of the First Four Ecumenical Councils* (Crestwood, NY: St. Vladimir's Seminary Press, 1996), 267-96.
156. Constantine had founded Constantinople on the model of Rome, with a senate and an administration that was similar.
157. He is speaking of the civil dioceses.
158. S. Runciman, *The Emperor Romanus Lecapenus and his Reign* (Cambridge: Cambridge University Press, 1988), 99.
159. *The Acts of the Council of Chalcedon*, vol. III, eds. Richard Price, Michael Gaddis (Liverpool: Liverpool University Press, 2005), 67-103; *Leo's Letter*, 144-45.
160. Cf. Francis. Dvornik, *Byzance et la primauté romaine* (Paris: Éditions du Cerf, 1964), 73-77.
161. Cf. Leo the Great, *Ep.* 14.1: PL 54:671.
162. Mansi 7, 9.
163. *Regesta pontificum romanorum ab condita ecclesia ad annum post Christum natum MCXCVIII*, edit Ph. Jaffé, G. Wattenbach curaverunt S. Löewenfeld, F. Kaltenbrunner, P. Ewald, (Lipsiae1885-1888). Cf. *Pontificia Commissio ad redigendum Codicem Iuris Canonici Orientalis, Fontes*, Series III, Acta Romanorum Pontificum a S. Clemente (a.c. 90) Caelestinum III (1198), I, (Vatican City 1943).
164. Cf. Ignatius, in the preface to the *Letter to the Romans.*
165. Ambrose, *Ep.* 11.4: PL 16:946.
166. The divergence occurred due to calculations regarding the lunar cycles (called by the Greeks "epact"). Cf. PL 54:603, endnote.
167. Leo the Great, 121.3; PL 54:1058; cf. *Ep.* 127. *Non leviter delinquitur si in principio sacramenti veritas et unitas ab universali Ecclesia non tenetur.*
168. Leo the Great, *Ep.* 138: PL 54:1101-1102: *Quia ergo studio unitatis et pacis malui Orientalium definitioni acquiescere, quam in tantae festivitatis observantia dissidere, noverit fraternitas vestra die octavo kalendas Maias ab omnibus resurrectionem Dominicam celebrandam, et hoc ipsum per vos aliis esse fratribus intimandum: ut divinae pacis consortio, sicut una fide jungimur, ita una solemnitate feriemur.*
169. Leo the Great, *Ep.* 137.1: PL 54:1101: *non quia hoc ratio manifesta docuerit, sed quia unitatis, quam maxime custodimus, cura persuaserit.*
170. Leo the Great, *Ep.* 14.11.
171. Mansi, 11,660.
172. Mansi 11, 664 B.
173. W. de Vries, *Orient et Occident: Les structures ecclésiales vues dans l'histoire des sept premiers conciles œcuméniques* (Paris: Éditions du Cerf, 2011), 212; 218-20.
174. F. Dvornik, *Byzance et la primauté romaine*, 19.
175. Cf. *Apostolic Canons*, can. 34; *Council of Antioch* of 341, can. 9.
176. Tertullian, *De praescript.* 36.

177. Irenaeus, *Adv haer* 3.3.2.
178. The expression *Sedes Apostolica* is used for the first time by Liberius to designate the Roman *cathedra*, shortly after the Council of Arles in 353 (*Ep. ad Eusebium* 1.1, PL 8 :1350; CCL 9 :121); P. Batiffol, *Cathedra Petri: études d'histoire ancienne de l'Église* (Paris: Les Éditions du Cerf, boulevard de La Tour-Maubourg, 1938), 152-53; M. Maccarrone, "'Sedes Apostolica' et 'Sedes Apostolicae'" in *Acta congressus internationalis de theologia Concilii vaticani* II (Vatican City: Typis polyglottis Vaticanis 1968), 144-66; C. Alzati, "Ripensando alle vices Apostolicae Sedis nelle lettere di papa Leone I al presule di Tessalonica. Contributo alla storia dell'ecclesiologia," in *Occidente: Synthesis* 4 (2015): 1-34.
179. Augustine, in his discussions with Petilianus, asked: *cathedra tibi quid fecit Ecclesiae Romanae, in qua Petrus sedit et in qua hodie Anastasius sedet? (C. litt. Petil.* 2.51.118). This expression is found often in Augustine. Cf. A. Trapè, "La Sedes Petri in S. Agostino," *Miscellanea A. Piolanti*, II (Rome: Facultas Theologiae Pontificiae Universitatis Lateranensis, 1964), 1-19; M. Maccarrone, *"Cathedra Petri" e lo sviluppo dell'idea del primato papale dal II al IV secolo*, II, 37-56.
180. J. Delmulle, "A quando risale l'uso dell'espressione "sancta sedes" per designare la Chiesa romana?" in *Costellazioni geo-ecclesiali da Costantino a Giustiniano: dalle chiese principali alle chiese patriarcali* (Rome: Institutum Patristicum Augustinianum, 2017), 449-62.
181. Pliny the Elder, *Ep.* 10.96.
182. Tertullian, *Apologeticum* 21.1.
183. W. A. Meeks, *The First Urban Christians: The Social World of the Apostle Paul* (New Haven: Yale University Press, 1983); *After the First Urban Christians: The Social-Scientific Study of Pauline Christianity Twenty-Five Years Later*, ed. by Todd D. Still and D. G. Horrell (London: T&T Clark, 2009).
184. Eusebius, *HE* 3.37.3.
185. Theodore of Mopsuestia, *Comm. in I Ep. ad Timotheum.* ed. Swete 2, 122.
186. *Ep. ad Decentium* 5. A. Chavasse, *Le sacramentaire gélasien*, (Paris/Tournai: Desclée, 1958), 83-85.
187. Vincenzo Bo, *Storia della parrocchia: I secoli delle origini (sec. IV-V)*, (Roma: Edizioni Dehoniane, 1992), vol. II: *I secoli dell'infanzia (sec. VI-XI)*, (Rome: Edizioni Dehoniane, 1990).
188. *Illi sunt Ecclesia, plebs sacerdoti unita et pastori suo grex adhaerens* Cyprian *Ep.* 69.8.
189. A. Martin, "Topographie et liturgie : le problème des 'paroisses' d'Alexandrie," in *Actes du XIe Congrès international d'archéologie chrétienne* (Rome: École française de Rome, 1989), pp. 113-14.
190. Augustine, *Ep.* 83; *Ep.* 139.1.
191. Augustine *Ep.*133.1; *Ep.*134.1.
192. Ch. Pietri, *Régions ecclésiastiques et paroisses romaines*, in *Actes du XIe Congrès International d'Archéologie Chrétienne*, 1035-62; now also in *Christiana Respublica* (Rome: Ecole française de Rome, 1997), 173-200.
193. Anne Lunven, "Christianisation and Parish Formation in Early Medieval France: A Case Study of the Dioceses of Rennes, Dol and St Malo," in *Making Christian Landscapes in Atlantic Europe: Conversion and Consolidation in the Early Middle Ages*, ed., Tomás Ó Carragáin (Cork: Cork University Press, 2016), 325-44.
194. *Alle origini della parrocchia rurale, IV-VIII sec.*, ed. Philippe Pergola (Vatican City 1999).
195. R. S. Bagnall, *Early Christian books in Egypt* (Princeton: Princeton University Press, 2009), 2.
196. *1 Cor* 16:1-4; *2 Cor* 8-9; *Rom* 15:25-29; cf. *Gal* 2:9.
197. *Rom* 15:25
198. This is a different city than the Hierapolis of Papias, which is today called Pamukkale.
199. Cf. H. Chadwick, "Faith and Order at the Council of Nicaea: A Note on the Background of the Sixth Canon," *Harvard Theological Revue* 53 (1960): 171-95; P. L'Huillier, *The Church of the Ancient Councils*, 45-53.
200. The bishop of a metropolis is called *metropolitanus, metropolites*; in Africa there is also *primas, episcopus primae cathedrae* (cf. Augustine *Epp.* 43.5.15; 53.2.4; 88.3; *Contra Cresc.* 3.27.30).
201. Cf. *EAC* 2:86-88.
202. Council of Antioch of 341, can. 9.
203. Cf. F. Dvornik, *Byzantium and the Roman Primacy* (New York: Fordham University Press, 1966), passim.
204. Gregory of Naz., *Oratio* 22. Sophie Métivier, *La Cappadoce (IVe-VIe Siècle): Une histoire provinciale de l'Empire romain d'Orient* (Paris: Publications de la Sorbonne, 2005).
205. D. Mansilla, "Orígenes de la organización metropolitana en la Iglesia española," *Hispania Sagrada* 12 (1959): 255-90; Idem, in *Diccionario de Historia Eclesiástica de España* (Madrid: Instituto Enrique Flórez, Consejo Superior de

Investigaciones Científicas. 1972), 983-85; D. Mansilla, "Antiguas divisiones político-administrativas de España," *Burgense* 30 (1989): 433-75.

206. *Ep. to Himerius* 15. *I canoni dei concili della Chiesa antica*, ed. A. Di Berardino, II, *I concili latini*, 1, *Decretali, concili romani, ed* by Teresa Sardella (Rome: Institutum Patristicum Augustiniaum, 2008), 77.

207. H.J. Schmitz, "Die Rechte der Metropoliten und Bischöfe in Gallien vom 4. bis 6. Jahrhundert," *Archiv für kathol. Kirchenrecht* 72 (1894): 3-49.

208. Cf. *the poem De mortibus boum* by Endelechius, who wrote that the cross came to be venerated only in the great cities (*Signum, quod perhibent esse crucis Dei, Magnis qui colitur solus in urbibus* (vv. 105-106).)

209. Cf. *EAC* 1:770-72; 3:86-88.

210. Cf. paragraph 6 regarding the bishop of Rome.

211. G. Dagron, "Constantinople, la primauté après Rome," in *Politica retorica e simbolismo del primato: Roma e Costantinopoli (secoli IV-VII)*, ed. F. Elia (Catania: Catania CULC, 2002), 23-38; cf. F. Elia, *Sui privilegia urbis Constantinopolitanae*, 79-105.

212. J. Hajjar, *Le synode permanent (Synodos endēmousa) dans l'Église byzantine des origines au XIe siècle* (Rome: Institutum Orientalium Studiorum, 1962).

213. V. Grumel, *Les Regestes des Actes du Patriarcat de Constantinople*, I (Paris: Institut français d'études byzantines, 1947), 86, n. 212.

214. Code of Justinian 1.17.1.10: *Romam autem intellegendum est non solum veterem, sed etiam regiam nostram, quae deo propitio cum melioribus condita est auguriis.*

215. Cf. Leo the Great, *Ep.* 106.5.

216. *Urbis constantinopolitanae, quae Romae veteris praerogativa laetatur*, cf. Code of Theodosius 16. 2.45.

217. For Leo the Great: Mansi 6,895; for Pope Agapetus: Mansi 8.895.

218. V. Laurent, "Le titre de patriarche œcuménique et la signature patriarcale: Recherches de diplomatique et de sigillographie byzantines," *Revue des études byzantines* 6 (1948): 5-26; A. Tuillier, "Grégoire le Grand et le titre de patriarche œcuménique," in *Grégoire le Grand*, ed. J. Fontaine et al. (Paris: Editions du Centre national de la recherche scientifique, 1986), 69-70.

219. A. Camplani, "L'identità del patriarcato alessandrino, tra storia e rappresentazione storiografica," *Adamantius* 12 (2006): 8-42; E. Wipszycka, "The Origins of the Monarchic Episcopate in Egypt," *Adamantius* 12 (2006): 71-90.

220. For the Egyptian church, the work of Ewa Wipszycka is fundamental, *The Alexandrian Church: People and Institution* (Warsaw: Journal of Juristic Papyrology, 2015). This rich volume is the final fruit of decades of research and publications by this Polish scholar.

221. Canon 7: "Since custom and ancient tradition have prevailed that the Bishop of *Aelia* should be honored, let him, saving its due dignity to the Metropolis, have the next place of honor."

222. Sozomen, *HE* 4.25.

223. Cyril of Jerusalem, *Catech.* 13.7.

224. Jerome, *Ep.* 82.10.

225. That is, of the civil diocesis of the East.

226. Jerome, *Contra Iohannem Hier.* 37: PL 23:407.

227. Leo the Great, *Ep.* 119; PL 54:1044.

228. E. Honigmann, "Juvenal of Jerusalem," *Dumbarton Oaks Papers* 5 (1950): 211-79.

229. *The Acts of the Council of Chalcedon*, vol. I, Richard Price, Michael Gaddis (Liverpool: Liverpool University Press, 2007), 244-49 (cf. Hefele-Leclercq II, 735-40).

CHAPTER 7
MONASTICISMS AND CHRISTIAN MONASTICISM

General Elements

RECENT STUDIES HAVE CALLED ATTENTION TO MONASTICISM AS A PHENOMENON COMMON to several religions and possessing numerous substantially corresponding characteristics, even amid the particular diversity of each religion. Such correspondences justify the adoption also of a "monastic" vocabulary to designate the various elements with terms such as monk, abbot, novitiate, monastery, rules, among others, for the various monasticisms. Constitutive elements exist that also give rise to some common structures of monastic life of a psychosocial character.

First of all, monasticism presents itself as a phenomenon of solitary or communally living individuals, separated from the surrounding environment not only psychologically but also by ways of life particular to them. Entering into the group means a progressive religious and ascetic initiation, with a novitiate and a religious profession which seals the definitive admission. In the communal life, once one has entered, failings are punished in grave cases with exclusion from the community through expulsion. Separation from others can be expressed in various ways such as a more or less strict enclosure, a special habit, poverty, cutting the hair, a new name, to name a few. Other constitutive elements are practices such as temporary or perpetual celibacy which we find almost everywhere, poverty expressed by the sharing of goods as a sign of interior detachment though not among solitaries. The poverty, however, has more of an individual character to it and is not necessarily considered a practice of the whole community as such. There are also a variety of ascetical practices as well as various forms of prayer.

The communities hold themselves to certain rules and are directed by a superior to whom obedience and submission are due. The three traditional vows for western monasticism are poverty and the sharing of goods, celibacy, and the obligation of obedience to a superior. These are the basis of every form of monasticism. What has been said so far leads us to the conclusion that monasticism is a fruit of man's religiosity, an attitude of the human spirit in search of *what is above* man himself which can be attained through a liberation from earthly realities. The "renunciations" are only means, or rather consequences of a fundamental attitude.

> It is appropriate to say that monasticism must not be considered simply as the haphazard product of historical influences, whether these are simple or complex. Alongside the ideological motivations inherited from others one must allow a large space for the psychological motivations that arise from religious awareness. This is why monasticism could be considered to coincide with a spontaneous creation to the degree in which it expresses the need for unity, the exclusivism that derives from adherence to an absolute which, by its very nature, relativizes and tends to exclude all the rest. In this way monasticism, which appears to be a religious phenomenon provided with its own particular structure, could be born in other times and in other places, beyond every influence of either Hellenism or Judaism.[1]

Therefore, monasticism as a social phenomenon is not something specifically Christian. The essential elements are those that constitute the *vows* in the Catholic tradition, that is, the commitment to poverty, chastity, and obedience. Nevertheless, in various monasticisms the motives differ, sometimes profoundly. Naturally the terms used are not identical either, but pertain to the individual religion.

In the Mediterranean basin we know of the Pythagoreans, the Essenes of Palestine, the Therapeutae[2] of Egypt described by Philo of Alexandria († 41 CE), the *katochoi* (recluses) dedicated to the cult of Serapis in Egypt and mentioned in Memphian papyri. Later on there are the Manichees, and the Sufi monks in the Middle Ages. For middle-eastern Asia the most well-known are the Hindu and Buddhist monasticisms. Once one admits the possibility that monasticism can be the fruit of an attitude of man's religious spirit, the question of various reciprocal influences loses the polemical character which it had in the past, and one's interest moves more toward the implied motivations that are inherent in the various monasticisms. Here the differences are radical and each monastic form has its specific motivations. This does not take away the possibility of there also being shared motivations, above all that of seeking the transcendent and union with it. These motivations depend generally on the religious creed, on the social and cultural conditions of the various peoples, and can vary within the same religion itself.

Therefore, the figure of the Christian monk—in his psychology, in the image he has of himself, in his aspirations, in the proposed models of life, as also in his external behavior— is a figure who is born and develops in the midst of a fervent human and religious transition in the course of the fourth century. He is a new figure in the social and religious context, and in the social panorama of the Roman Empire he reveals a new manner of life lived either alone or with others.[3] Nevertheless, the figure of the monk is a natural development of various forms of Christian asceticism practiced by numerous believers in the period before Constantine and also during the fourth century. Two typical figures were "the virgins of Christ" (note, they are "of Christ") and the *continentes*, that is, men who practiced celibacy and asceticism.

The motives adopted by the ancient Christian monks are a recovery and a development of primitive Christian ascesis, and at times a Christianization of ideas and practices of other origin.[4] In some geographical areas, common Christians were called the "just," while the "perfect" were the ascetics.[5] Perhaps in these contexts the term "monk" fills in for that of *teleios*, the "perfect." In the course of the first centuries there were already motives being elaborated for justifying the ascetic forms of virginity, celibacy, renunciation, and poverty. Even so, the basic and principal motivation always makes strict reference to Christ, an element that distinguishes it from the asceticism of non-Christians.[6]

A typically Christian motivation is the imitation of Christ and following him, as is dramatically shown in Anthony's decision as handed on by Athanasius:

> Before six months had passed [since his parents' death] it happened that while he was on his way to church as usual, he came to think of how the apostles had rejected everything to follow the Savior and how many people, as it says in the Acts of the Apostles, had sold their possessions.... Turning these things over in his mind, Anthony entered the church. It happened that just at that moment the Gospel passage was being read in which the Lord says to the rich man, 'If you wish to be perfect, go and sell everything you possess and give it to the poor and come, follow me and you will have treasure in heaven.' ... Believing ... that this passage of Scripture had been read out for his sake, he immediately went home and gave away his possessions among his neighbors.... On another occasion when Anthony had gone to church and heard the Lord saying in the Gospel, 'Take no thought for the morrow,' he distributed also the rest of his wealth to the poor.[7]

The *sequela Christi* (follower of Christ) inspires a certain kind of life, according to Jesus' own invitation to the rich young man: "Come and follow me."[8]

Renunciation of goods and of one's self is an important condition, like a presupposition for following Christ. In this alone does perfection consist, not in the renunciation as such. All are called to the *sequela Christi*, but monks in a more radical way.

Wanting to follow Christ concretely, the monk does so:

> ... by imitating his virginity, his renunciation regarding any earthly interest, his submission to the Father's will and his love for Him; one wants to participate in his mystery by uniting oneself in a particular way to his cross, reproducing some of his actions, like solitude in the desert, his fasting, his struggle against demons, his long moments of prayer. One wants to respond to the call to penitence, to conversion, to changing one's life and way of thinking that he addressed to us. One wants to realize in a radical way the task one has accepted in his regard with baptism, surely to obtain the forgiveness of sins, fully to receive his Spirit, abundantly to acquire his grace, to enter into that relationship of bridegroom and bride of which the Gospels, St. Paul, and the Apocalypse speak, to demonstrate that one could suffer for Him like the martyrs and serve his Church with the same generosity with which his first disciples had done it. All these themes came directly from the Gospel and the apostolic writings.[9]

Christian monasticism always makes reference to Christ and is inconceivable without him. Recalling the first community of Jerusalem is the point of inspiration for the Augustinian rule. In fact, for Cassian the cenobitic life found its first expression and particular incentive among the first Christians.[10] The monastic life comes to be linked back up with martyrdom and is the way in which the new heroism is expressed in the Church. While martyrdom was the suffering of a moment, the monastic life is a continual martyrdom, a daily martyrdom (*cotidianum martyrium*).[11] The monastic commitment also comes to be referred to as a second baptism, insofar as it is a more effective renunciation of Satan that already had been completed in baptism. Moreover, it comes to be conceived as a continual fight, a *militia spiritualis* against wicked habits and especially against demons who, according to ancient belief, lived particularly in the deserts. Anthony ventures there to unearth them and engage in battle with them on their own terrain. For this reason, the monk commits himself "not to the peace, not to security, but to fight, to the struggle, to the battle" (*non ad quietem, non ad securitatem, sed ad pugnam, ad certamen, ad agonem*).[12] He cannot be perfect in his homeland,[13] which is why it is necessary to separate oneself from one's environment and take oneself elsewhere (*xeniteia*), according to the example of Abraham: "Go from your country and your kindred and your father's house" (Gen 12:1). The change of life in monasticism implies a change of residence and a detachment from what went before. It is also a spiritual exodus.

The monk can restore the paradisal condition of Adam and lead an angelic life, in the sense of the contemplative life, prayer, innocence of life, and the harmony reached within oneself. For this reason, the intense asceticism he undergoes is not the fruit of a dualistic conception or of scorn for the body — aspects present in the Neoplatonists or in heretical Christian sects. Rather, it is an aspiration toward a greater realization of the Christian calling in view of the primitive paradisal condition.[14] The monk, however, does not just turn his focus towards his inner self. In his solitude he is a help for the brothers in the faith. "The monks give thanks for all humankind as if they were the fathers of all of humanity. They thank God for everyone and practice true brotherhood."[15] "The monk is the one who is separated from all and united to all."[16]

Like the asceticism of the first centuries, the monasticism begun in the fourth century had a fundamentally lay character rather than priestly. However, in time, two currents evolve: one allowed the existence of the monk-priest or monk-bishop, while the other excluded it because, according to this spiritual vision, the monk is one who dedicates himself to ascesis understood as a conquest, and to contemplation, while the priesthood implies the active life. Nevertheless, many monks, especially in certain regions, were called to the episcopate or priesthood, and the practice became more and more diffuse in the fifth and sixth centuries. This was the case of the monk-bishops.[17] Certain churches that were often visited by the faithful or by pilgrims were tended to by a religious community which dedicated itself to the liturgy. Later on, this became a notable characteristic of monasticism, in the sense that the monks committed themselves to conduct liturgical celebrations, insofar as these were considered the image of heaven on earth.

The monk, especially in the East, is one who through long and continual effort becomes the "man of God." Therefore he acquires great authority over the faithful which is parallel to, but not opposed to that of the bishop. He can carry out spiritual direction, not like a master who teaches but like a true spiritual father. He does not need the priesthood to carry out this function in the church but rather his own prayer and the people's trust in him. Spiritual direction naturally flowed into confession. Often one confessed to a monk who was not a priest—a practice found in some places in the East but not in the West. The monk was the preeminently free man, a frontiersman in every sense. He was the charismatic person who had spiritual authority, unlike the bishop or priest who had institutional power.

THE ORIGINS OF MONASTICISM

It is impossible to determine the origins of Christian monasticism, as if we could trace it back to a specific founder or organizer. Upon attentive consideration, however, there emerges the recognition that monasticism arises and develops as a marginal phenomenon both in a spatial sense in going out to the desert to be in solitude, and in a sociological sense with respect to the Great Church and to the society of the time. In the course of the fourth century we see, in the setting of a lively fermentation, the spontaneous and uncontrolled flourishing of an extraordinary number of persons dedicated to an intense asceticism. We name them "monks" out of convenience and as those who exemplify this type of dedicated life which they lived especially in the eastern areas of the Roman Empire. The desire to radicalize their belonging to Christ drove numerous people to search for very personalized ways of living, ways that are very different and exceptional in their strong demands and also quite original most of the time.

But what in the fourth century drove so many people to dedicate themselves fully to unyielding and extreme forms of asceticism, or total solitude? What motivated them to seek refuge from every contact with other individuals—and for all this to happen, especially in marginal social settings like with the agricultural class of Egypt and Syria? Why then did these ideals of life so quickly fascinate people who were cultured and engaged politically and socially? Many answers have been given, but they are often not entirely convincing to us. Are the motivations that they themselves elaborated sufficient? In any case, since those persons called themselves Christians, it was necessary not to marginalize them even more from the Christian community. Great men like Athanasius saw it as their task to recover this phenomenon, at least in the majority of cases, and integrate it into the Great Church. Others tried to discipline and organize this ascetic movement, which was sometimes uncontrollable.

Moreover, this movement often presented itself as an uncivilized phenomenon, in the sense that it did not follow the normal rules of civil or ecclesial coexistence. The proliferation of numerous groupings around some charismatic personality, coupled with an eremitism that was sometimes crude and ill-advised—but also characterized by a high spiritual commitment which was the fruit of a refined human and Christian experience—all of this makes for a disturbing picture of the late Roman Empire.

The recovery and integration of monks into civil society or into ecclesial communities was the work of a few eminent personalities. This recovery was not always completely carried out.[18] Discernment then became a noteworthy spiritual and intellectual category entailing a proper capacity of certain people who knew how to identify and verify positive aspects of a movement. "It fell to the bishops, holders of authority in the Church, to 'evangelize' this spontaneous monasticism, to verify its evangelical inspiration, to purify it, to consolidate it, as the case demanded."[19] Discernment, therefore, was truly an important element for the constitution and acceptance of monastic life into the heart of the Church. In the fourth century there was an attempt to discipline and provide concrete norms of behavior to these various types of ascetics and virgins in an effort to help them in discernment and to serve as guides of their lives. Asceticism and monasticism were spontaneous phenomena that arose and developed at the margins of the Great Church. Ecclesiastical authority approved some forms and rejected others according to the criteria of evangelical authenticity. "Christian monasticism was, from the very beginning, a wild phenomenon that it was necessary to domesticate; it was a manifestation of 'marginality,' which needed to be 'recuperated,' integrated into religious and secular society."[20] This would be the task of the bishops, which is what Athanasius did for the eremitism of Anthony and his followers, what Basil did with his *Asceticon*, what the councils of Asia Minor aimed for in regard to the followers of Eustathius of Sebaste or the Messalians.[21] It was also what Augustine, Sulpicius Severus, and even the imperial laws themselves aspired to working in conjunction with ecclesiastical authority.[22] The individuals or movements recognized were those who had relationships of respect, collaboration, and submission to the bishops and which, though living at the margins of the Christian community, influenced it by contesting the morality current at the time. These individuals and movements proposed higher ideals of life without practicing a false dualism between themselves as the perfect, and the others who were the sinners. The phenomenon of gradual inclusion of these individuals and communities was highly visible in the work of Athanasius of Alexandria, as evidenced with both Athanasius himself and his visit to the Pachomian monasteries of the Thebaid (Egypt).

What these monastic movements were all about depended on whether you were one of the members who belonged to it—thus an inside perspective—or you were one of those from the outside looking in. Those outside the monastic movement viewed it with an intellectual and spiritual attitude that understood there was a possible risk associated with such movements—albeit a risk still viewed as worth taking—coupled with a variegated range of subtleties that progressed from identifying with the monastic ideal on the one hand to a complete rejection of that ideal on the other. The witness from outside often ended up idealizing monasticism while also failing to understand what it was really about, like Libanius (†394) who criticized the life and behavior of the monks of Syria in his day; or like Rutilius Namatianus († after 416) and his critique in *De reditu*. There were others, however, also from the outside, who engaged with monasticism, sought to purify it, and elaborate on the ideal of the monk which they transformed into a model and example to propose to others. In some biographies, the examples elaborated in the course of the fourth century imposed themselves in a rather boisterous way that drew attention to it while simultaneously increasing membership in these communities.

We know some of the most eminent examples of monks who fascinated the imaginations of people especially through the idealized presentation of some writers. This happened with Anthony due to the shrewd work of Athanasius, with Martin of Tours through the presentation of Sulpicius Severus, and Benedict with the literary reconstruction provided by Gregory the Great in his *Dialogues*. Thus, we can ask how much of such a literary presentation or such an idealizing reconstruction as presented by these three writers corresponds to the truth, and how much, on the other hand, is only an interpretation in view of the ideal model of the monk that had been created. Furthermore, even the Egyptian anchoritism which exercised such fascination in antiquity did not survive in its original form, and yet it has left as an inheritance an ideal of monastic and spiritual life which has served as a reference point for subsequent monasticism, epitomized in the attitude of prayer that was fostered, the ideal of the angelic life, the emphasis on humility, the practice of discernment of the heart and the passions, renunciation, and the attentive examination of what happens in the human psyche. All of these were lasting achievements that fed into the awareness of the religious individual.

In successive centuries reference was always made to that image of the monk created in the course of the fourth century—that figure who emerged from certain writings received by the Christian community—which then became the obligatory reference point even amid the diversity of successive historical situations and the birth of different monastic forms. Even today entirely new forms of monastic life are inspired by it and draw inspiring nourishment from it for a different religious and human experience that is being pursued.

Numerous testimonies show us that personalities dedicated to asceticism already existed before the first years of the fourth century. Not only do Anthony and Pachomius refer to the fathers, but we know there is already a Melitian monasticism present around 330. Furthermore, in the religious fervor of the fourth century there were various ways of practicing asceticism, so that the ancients speak of varieties (*genera*) of monks.[23] Cassian, who was well acquainted with Egyptian monasticism, writes, "In Egypt there are three types of monks, two of which are optimal while the third is lukewarm at best and in every way to be avoided."[24] This last group was known as the Sarabaites,[25] a name of Coptic origin. The name is meant to indicate monks who do not trust in God for the necessities of life but rather accumulate riches to satisfy their greed. They do not submit to a superior and they bear the name of monk but do not embrace the monk's life. In the first years of the sixth century Benedict of Nursia begins his *Rule* by describing four categories of monks: the cenobites who reside in a monastery and follow a Rule under the guidance of an abbot; the anchorites or hermits who lead a solitary life; then "third, there are the Sarabaites, the most detestable kind of monks, who with no experience to guide them, no rule to try them as gold is tried in the furnace, have a character as soft as lead. Still loyal to the world by their actions, they clearly lie to God by their tonsure. Two or three together, or even alone, without a shepherd, they pen themselves up in their own sheepfolds, not the Lord's. Their law is what they like to do, whatever strikes their fancy."[26] The fourth kind of monk was known as the Gyrovagues[27] because they were constantly wandering and never stayed in one place.

I am convinced that using the ancient terminology (*genera monachorum*) fits much better with the reality of those times and the multiplicity of lifestyles rather than just reducing the categories to just eremitism and cenobitism. An anonymous author writes: "This manner of life can be observed as multi-faceted and the types of monks can be found under various names."[28] A variegated picture is offered to us also by the critiques that many others, like

Augustine, make of people who are called monks but then lead a very free life that proved scandalous to pagans and Christians alike. The monastic rules were born precisely from this concern to regulate the lives of those who desired to follow Christ.

At the beginning of the fourth century, Eusebius of Caesarea realized that a new reality was emerging and that it had been developing since the second half of the third century. Various forms of Christian asceticism had begun to develop from the very first Christian generation, assuming a more organized character only gradually. In succeeding centuries not only is continual reference made back to the models of the fourth century to draw on the inspiring motives for the subsequent Christian monasticism that developed, but in monastic history recourse to the origins of the movement has always been about renewal and of fidelity to an ideal, a way of life. The idea of reaching back to the experience of the primitive Christian community of Jerusalem, as described in the *Acts of the Apostles*, was rich with inspiration for Augustine and Cassian. Their influence has been immense in western monastic spirituality.

The Lutheran Reformation condemned monastic vows and monastic life.[29] At that time two trends of interpretation of the ancient monastic phenomenon arose. On the one hand there was the Catholic and Eastern Orthodox view which held to the tradition but with a greater tendency toward comparative historical research and toward the general context. The other trend was embodied in the Lutheran perception which denied monasticism's evangelical roots and devalued Christian monasticism, reducing it to a series of external influences. The research of scholars of the past century has led to the overcoming of the Lutheran position and to a greater sensibility in Catholic studies to the broader context of the ancient world and of the Christian experience of the first centuries starting with Jesus himself. On the Lutheran side Karl Heussi brought about a change of perspective, leaving behind Luther's condemnation of monasticism so that the study of monasticism is no longer done from a polemical perspective.[30] He sees monasticism as the point of arrival of a process of development of ascetical practices that had already begun in primitive Christianity.

Today monasticism is studied not only in the context of spirituality and of Christian asceticism, but also as a great social and religious phenomenon of late antiquity. Peter Brown influenced these studies with his in-depth analysis of the concept of the *holy man* and of the *vir Dei*, the divine man or man of God.[31] Such studies have been useful for understanding the social rather than institutional role played by a person considered holy and bearing the divine. In the last few decades numerous studies on individual persons, on the monastic movement in general, and on the movement in individual provinces of the Roman Empire and beyond its eastern frontier have renewed interest and opened new tracks of study. Noteworthy are the volume edited by Giovanni Filoramo and the special issue of the journal *Adamantius*.[32]

First of all, the thesis that monasticism was a consequence of the slackening of Christian life with the arrival of religious liberty and the enrichment of the institutional church under the emperor Constantine who allowed the churches to accept donations no longer holds sway. Even the two persons described by Athanasius and Jerome, Anthony the Hermit (252–356) and Paul of Thebes, can trace their origins back to the pre-Constantinian period.[33] Paul of Thebes, whose historicity is contested, would be even earlier than Anthony. The thesis of a homogeneous development of a unitary phenomenon needs to be dropped. The developments were gradual and differed according to the geographical areas, the local influences, the religious sensibility of the regional population, the religious experiences actually lived out and the theological reflection evidenced in the various accounts.

There were already urban forms of monasticism at the beginning of the fourth century in Egypt. An important figure, though largely unknown, is Hieracas of Leontopolis who began an urban asceticism of a cultured character on the model of a school.[34] Since the members deprecated marriage, only the continent could participate in their liturgy. They accepted only a spiritual resurrection and identified the Holy Spirit with the figure of Melchizedek. The group was marginalized by Bishop Peter of Alexandria († 311). It was a conflict between a Christianity of a scholastic character and one that was episcopal and universal. Athanasius also blamed the influence exercised over the ascetics of Alexandria in his *First Letter to Virgins*, in which he condemned spiritual marriage, a practice lived out among the followers of Hieracas.[35]

Non-Christian ascetic forerunners or similar monasticisms born from other religious convictions are manifestations of a shared religious need, and today it is no longer an issue whether or not they influenced nascent Christian monasticism. To justify their manner of life the first Christian monks went back to biblical models and to motives inherent in the New Testament. The influence on monastic literature of ideas coming from Greco-Roman culture, however, is undeniable, just as it cannot be excluded that particular social and political conditions, at least in certain cases, drove some to seek refuge in monasticism. In reality, the monasticism of the fourth century should be placed in the line of development and organization of those forms of asceticism that already existed since New Testament times. "Therefore, it is impossible to make these great saints (such as Anthony and Pachomius in Egypt) into initiators, founders in the proper sense of the word. History sees their vocation as that of a judicious discernment in the midst of an intense ferment. This is what an attentive reading finds in the sources which praise more the discernment of spirits than revolutionary initiative or, in a broader sense, an autonomous creation, a new and personal project of an Anthony or a Pachomius."[36]

Primitive Christian communities practiced ascetic forms with notable moral rigorism, even if, at least in some groups, this was more a matter of principle than something really lived out. We know of the existence of persons who embraced celibacy or virginity and were called virgins (women) and continents (men). Afterwards they were called ascetics which derives from the Greek work *askeo*, meaning to train oneself. In the second century, Athenagoras of Athens writes that there exist among Christians "men and women who grow old in virginity at the heart of our community in order to unite themselves more intimately with God."[37] While the men enjoyed greater freedom, the Church took special care of the virgins and the widows[38] who committed themselves to remain as virgins. Their fundamental characteristic was celibacy, but they committed themselves to some ascetic practices as well such as vigils, prayers, and fasts.

The original significance of the term "monk" was precisely that it initially referred to a celibate person before it went on to mean a person living apart from others. Eusebius of Caesarea writes at the beginning of the fourth century:

> In the Church of Christ there are two types of lifestyle; the first overcomes nature and normal conduct by excluding marriage, child-bearing, riches, possessions; separating oneself completely from the common manner of life, one dedicates oneself exclusively to the worship of God, full of an immense love for heavenly things. These people, as if separated from this mortal life, remaining on earth only in their body, are in heaven through their feelings and thoughts. . . . The lifestyle of the many, on the other hand, is less perfect. . . . For such there is established a time for the exercises of piety and certain days are consecrated for religious instruction and reading of the law of God.[39]

This group about whom Eusebius speaks with such admiration consisted precisely of the "virgins of Christ" and those who exercised sexual continence. At that time these ascetics did not live apart from other Christians. The whole community had a certain regard for them—and in a particular way for the virgins. As soon as one felt the need to separate oneself, to live apart from the community perhaps as solitaries or in a group, then monasticism would arise which presents itself in the fourth century as a movement parallel to the traditional asceticism, which was of an individual character yet was recognized by the Church. "The similarity between the pre-monastic ascetics and the monks themselves and their institutions is such that it is difficult to say with certainty if certain individuals or groups should be classified among the former or the latter."[40]

In the first centuries we recognize a variety of ascetics by their rules of life that varied according to the various regions, and even within a particular area. The Syrians tended to be more rigorous than their western counterparts. In fact, there was a tendency among them to admit to baptism only those who, if married, nevertheless renounced the marital act. Perhaps their descendants were the celibates of the fourth century—the so-called "sons of the covenant"—who served the community. In the fourth century there were also the gyrovague monks mentioned earlier, who were not tied to one specific place and were often criticized by those who possessed a greater sense of discernment and balance. Even in the schismatic Melitian group opposed to Athanasius in Egypt there were some monks who in turn organized Melitian communities. These continued to exist until the eighth century. We know them through sources who were opposed to their way of life and their doctrines.[41]

Moreover, the great monastic personalities were also engaged in channeling the centrifugal forces and disciplining their better aspirations. These characteristics come to be expressed with the technical term "discernment" (*diakrisis* in Greek; *discretio* in Latin) which is what is admired and praised about them in the sources. When monasticism is spoken of, it usually refers to Egyptian monasticism, born in Egypt as eremitism with Anthony and transformed by Pachomius into cenobitism where they practiced a communal life which later underwent further reform under Basil of Caesarea. This monasticism in turn was disseminated throughout the world.

This traditional historical reconstruction has come to be commonly rejected today because of the fact that the ancients themselves spoke of "different classes of monks" who existed independently of their historical-geographical origins. In her late fourth century *Itinerarium*, Egeria refers to all the various types of ascetics she meets on her pilgrimage in the East as monks. Thus monasticism, expressed in antiquity in a notable variety of manners of life, arose in different regions as the mature fruit of an asceticism that was already being practiced everywhere. It cannot therefore be traced back to a single creative mind. In this, however, Egypt has the merit of having given two great models in Anthony and Pachomius, who were known more than others in the Christian world due to specific literature written about them that was broadly read and translated. This assured that they would not only become well known but transformed them into archetypes of monasticism itself.[42] Another problem often discussed was the orthodoxy of the first monastic forms. This is a problem that moderns pose themselves, but the first monks thought more about their way of life than about doctrinal debates current in the first half of the fourth century.

EASTERN MONASTICISM

A vast ancient literature[43] informs us of the eremitism that developed in the desert regions of Lower Egypt.[44] This consists for the most part of the compiled memories of foreign visitors drawn by the hermits' fame. The collection of the sayings of the great hermits (*Apophthegmata Patrum*)[45] such as Anthony, Arsenius, Macarius, Sisoes, Paphnutius, and Poemen, among others, were key. These sayings, substantially authentic, put us in contact with the spiritual world of the anchorites. The first writing, however, that became the most well known was the *Life of Anthony* written by Athanasius after the hermit's death († 356) for the purpose of offering a model to imitate for other monks. Only seven letters of Anthony's remain to us, today considered authentic and preserved in their entirety only in Georgian.[46] These were written between 330 and 337. They preserve the spirituality of Origen according to the Alexandrian tradition. Important aspects of his life are the fight against demons, a rigorous asceticism, and the insistence on divine knowledge which enables the discernment of spirits. The problem of Origen's heterodoxy arose only later in Egypt.

Anthony was not the first anchorite for we know of others before him. But he was certainly the most well-known because of Athanasius who spread his ideal and maintained relationships with him and with other monks. Born in the village of Koma (today Qumans) around 251, Anthony, having renounced everything, submitted himself to the teaching of an anchorite and dedicated himself to ascesis, to meditation on Scripture, and to work: and these will be the fundamental elements of the eremitic life. An important aspect of Anthony's spirituality was the battle against demons and this battle becomes a special element of monastic life when it first starts out.[47] After receiving advice for his formation from other spiritual persons and testing his abilities sufficiently, he went out into the desert for the first time around 285. Initially he lived for about twenty years in an abandoned fortress on Mount Pispir [now Der-el-Memun], which would come to be known as the "outer" mountain, where there was a spring of water. But then he went further into the desert searching for greater solitude arriving at Mount Kolzim. In the meantime, a host of disciples sought to imitate his life. They turned to him as the inspirer, not the founder, of a broad spiritual movement. Thus colonies of hermit cells began to arise: "He led many others to the love of spiritual exercises; and since his words had an immediate fascination, numerous dwelling-places arose of people who led the solitary life and he supervised them all as a father."[48] This all happened before 312, that is, before the freedom obtained by the Church. Athanasius transforms Anthony into a champion of orthodoxy, while Hieracas comes to be considered a heretic. Athanasius' intent is to reinforce his episcopal authority, to unite Christians around the Nicene faith, and to combat the fragmented and freer, more disordered devotional forms that had arisen. Moreover, he intended to integrate monasticism into the life of the organized church.

The hermits established themselves especially in the desert situated on the western bank of the Delta, particularly at Nitria, Scete, and Kellia (the Cells), in addition to Pispir where Anthony was. Ammonas, considered by tradition as the successor of Anthony at Pispir, has left *Letters* and another work called *Teachings*. In their content he depends on the teaching of Anthony his master. He is concerned that the monastic communities need to be better organized, condemning those monks who separated themselves from their spiritual masters to be masters and guides themselves. He wanted to avoid dispersion of the monks.

The first three localities were linked to the figures of Ammon of Nitria and Macarius called the Egyptian. Around 330 Ammon, a recent widower, first took retreat in Nitria, accompanied by many disciples, and then at a certain distance, more to the south, he founded a second center, called Kellia (the Cells), following the advice of Anthony, who had gone to visit him. Macarius the Egyptian established himself even further south, where he founded the monastic center of Scete (Wadi-el-Natrum). Many writings have been attributed to Macarius. Only the *Letter to Sons*—one of the first documents of Egyptian monasticism—can actually be linked to him.

And so villages, as it were, were formed with some common service for all. Their reference point was the church as the center of worship. "And thus, appeared dwellings of solitaries on the mountains and the desert becomes a city of monks who have abandoned their goods and inscribed themselves in the citizenship of heaven."[49] There was no truly common life; rather, solitaries gathered under the spiritual guidance of an *apa* (father), who gathered them together on feast days for liturgical celebrations, common meals, and discussion of their common problems.[50] The period of maximum flourishing of Egyptian anchoritism pushes toward about 450, leaving to posterity a great lesson on spirituality. It was not pure eremitism nor anchoritism, precisely since there was this communal element. The desert became a city of monks who abandoned their goods to live a religious experience, which had its own rules for living.

Another great Egyptian personality of the fourth century is Pachomius (†346), a convert from paganism in 313 and a soldier under Maximinus Daia. After a few years of eremitic life under the tutelage of Palaemon, around 324, he founded a true monastery in the vicinity of Tabennisis, in Upper Egypt, on the eastern bank of the Nile, halfway between Pbow and Chenoboskion. He began a new experience that met with broad success by promoting monks living together in communal life, what came to be known as cenobitism. He himself had gradually passed from an eremitic or semi-eremitic life to the cenobitic life which is characterized by the sharing of time, of daily prayer, of work, and of meals taken together. Pachomius' sister Maria was also associated with his work, on account of which a monastery for women was also constructed. Other monasteries quickly arose, including the most important monastery of Pbow which was established around 330 on the right bank of the Nile about 60 km north of Luxor. The monasteries grew in number and in wealth. The vision of a new life together fits precisely with a charismatic person who knows how to attract to himself hosts of others who are willing to follow this life and accept his manner of thinking and of living. The monastic life was also intended for service to one's brothers, as Pachomius himself had been served by Christians during his imprisonment. This conception was new in the history of monasticism.

The founder enjoyed undisputed prestige, but at some point the shared life needed to address practical considerations and stricter control. So Pachomius detailed a rule—if indeed it is his—that came to maturity through experience and the demands of the development of federated communities. Some bishops brought charges against him in the so-called Synod of Latopolis (today Esna, in the Thebaid) perhaps because of his gift of seeing visions. He was acquitted, however, shortly afterward he died of the plague. Upon his death (†346) there were already nine male and two female monasteries in Egypt. The Pachomian monastery was not built in the desert and seems to have mirrored the structure of a Roman military camp. There was a wall surrounding it, a gatehouse, living quarters for 20–40 monks, various services, and a meeting place. They were communities (*koinoniai*) with many members—at least a few hundred, although the sources mention thousands—all under the guidance of a shared superior and other subordinate superiors over various groups. As the monasteries multiplied, a type of superior general came into being whose residence was at Pbow, in the Thebaid.

The so-called Pachomian rule imposed equality among its members who were in general not priests. It also imposed individual poverty, obedience to the superior, work, prayer, and a biblical formation with the concomitant expectation that everyone must know how to read. But it especially emphasized that there be a fraternal communion among the members. Cenobitism became like a well-organized institution, perhaps reflecting Pachomius' own military experience. Scripture was the heart and soul of Pachomian cenobitism.[51] Pachomius named Petronius his successor, who died quickly, and who in his turn named the elderly Orsiesis in 381 (he lived c. 305–c. 390) during a moment of crisis among the monasteries regarding problems of poverty and of reciprocal assistance among them for necessity's sake. In Latin there is preserved a *Liber Horsiesi*,[52] translated by Jerome, and lost in its Greek and Coptic forms. It is a kind of spiritual testament with admonitions addressed to superiors. Jerome translated one of his letters along with other works of Pachomius and Orsiesis. Recently two other letters dealing with disciplinary and moral problems have been found in Coptic that were composed on the occasion of the annual meetings of the Pachomians.

Considering himself not up to the task, Orsiesis named the charismatic and capable Theodore (†368) as his vicar to serve as the superior of the monastery of Tabennisis and head of the Pachomian monasteries in general. Between 350 and 368 Theodore managed to reestablish order and tranquility among the monasteries, providing for the communities' growth both internally and externally while also fostering good relations with the bishop of Alexandria. A letter of his concerning the Pascha is preserved among the letters written for the annual meeting held on the 20th of Mesore.[53] At the death of Theodore, Orsiesis would return to his post.

Also pertaining to the formative period of the Pachomian communities is a corpus of works translated by Jerome into Latin from Greek, in its turn translated from Coptic. The development of these texts shows how the charism of a founder could slowly be replaced by a body of norms for regulating the common life. Another later work needs to be added here, a work preserved only in Coptic, a collection known as the *Regulations* which is difficult to attribute to a particular author. Other texts of solitary ascetics came to be transmitted first orally and then in written form. This is how the *Sayings* (or *Apothegms*) *of the Desert Fathers* (*Apophthegmata Patrum*) emerged, an alphabetic collection developed by the disciples of Poemen (c. 340–450), the most frequently mentioned Abba (Father) in the collection, who lived at Scete. Nomadic incursions on Scete caused the dispersion of the monks who nonetheless preserved the memory of the great masters.[54]

There were other cenobia in the same period in Egypt. The most famous was the great *White Monastery* at Sohag in the Thebaid where Shenoute of Atripe (†466)[55] was abbot, along with his successor Besa who wrote his biography. The monastery was founded by his uncle Pkiol as a double monastery in which in two distinct complexes there lived 2,200 monks and 1,800 nuns. In 431, Shenoute accompanied the Bishop Cyril to the council of Ephesus. He was the most important author of Coptic literature, treating spiritual and practical topics for the monks and the region's inhabitants while maintaining relationships with the civil authorities as well. He engaged also in helping the population of the area on the occasion of incursions by Blemmi nomads. His writings are preserved only in Coptic in a shoddy manuscript tradition. They are organized into a corpus subdivided into two parts: the so-called *Canones* in nine books, and the *Logoi* in seven books.

The cenobia usually had some groups of solitaries who depended on them for support while leading a semi-eremitic life. After the council of Chalcedon in 451 Egyptian cenobitism[56] became almost entirely monophysite and lost the prestige it had enjoyed up till then, being greatly affected by the theological battles that developed around that council. Anchoritic monasticism in general receded. There was a greater integration of monks and clergy into the cenobia with the presence of ordained monks. John Moschus deserves mention in this regard. He was originally from Cilicia but took retreat in Palestine. He made two journeys to Egypt, one with Sophronius around 580 and the second between 604 and 607. After he left Egypt in 614, he wrote about the orthodox monasticism in Egypt in his work *The Spiritual Meadow*.[57] On the other hand, there are other Coptic texts, the so-called *Plerophories*,[58] which serve as testimonies of those who opposed the Chalcedonian doctrine. The subsequent history of Egyptian monasticism is little known. Even today there are only a few Coptic monasteries still in existence that serve men and women—in all scarcely fifteen.

When the pilgrim Egeria went to Sinai towards the end of 383, she found hermits dwelling near the top of the mountain along with four small churches for liturgical service. It was prohibited to live on the very top of the *mons Dei*.[59] On her visit Egeria is accompanied by local monks and presbyters (*deductores*), who show her all the places where the events narrated in Exodus were located. Sinai becomes not only a place of pilgrimage then, but also a desirable place for hermits. Important writers lived in the monastery of St. Catherine, like John Climacus, Anastasius of Sinai, and Nilus of Ancyra. In the seventh century the episcopal see of Pharan was transferred to Sinai due to Arab attacks. Only in the ninth century did the monastery take the name of St. Catherine († 307), whose body according to legend had been transported there by angels. As a place of pilgrimage, it had an international character. In the sixth century it housed three abbots who spoke Latin, Greek, Coptic, and Ge'ez.[60] The monastery of St. Catherine still exists today in the Melchite tradition[61] which can be traced back to the emperor Justinian I.

Monasticism also developed around Gaza in southern Palestine, and Gaza became an important center for monasticism with various monastic writers having lived there, such as Isaiah of Gaza (†488), Barsanuphius († c. 520) and Dorotheus of Gaza (†660). The flourishing city of Gaza had remained pagan up to the end of the fourth century when it became Christian.

Palestine was already a land of pilgrims by the fourth century. In the first half of that century the laura of S. Charito emerged; the laura consisted of a central nucleus of common service buildings surrounded by the cells of solitaries.[62] This typically Palestinian monasticism was expanded especially by Euthymius († 473) of Melitene (today Malatya on the Euphrates) in Lesser Armenia. Euthymius arrived in Palestine in 405 at the age of 29 accompanied by his disciple Saba of Cappadocia. After his death, the laura of Euthymius was transformed into a cenobium with an organized common life. The cenobium was recently brought to light at Khan al-Ahmar, between Jerusalem and Jericho. His life was told by Cyril of Scythopolis (today Beit She'an), who lived in the monastery of Euthymius from 544 until 555. In 557 Cyril went to the Great Laura, that of Saba, and remained there until his death. He is very useful for the knowledge of Palestinian monasticism and of the life of the lauras, since he wrote seven biographies of monks of the Judean desert. The two most important biographies are those of Euthymius (†473) and of Saba (†532), who organized Chalcedonian monasticism in the Judean desert.

In this desert, at a distance walkable from Jerusalem in a day, there was an impressive number of monasteries (lauras). Hirschfeld managed to identify 64 of them, located at a distance of a few kilometers, and joined by paths between them. The furthest away was the laura of San Saba, still extant as a Greek orthodox community which is found about 30 km from Jerusalem. It was founded in 439. In the seventh century it was inhabited by about 4,000 monks. John of Damascus lived his whole life there.[63] When Palestine came under the rule of the Arabs, the laura of San Saba became an active center of translation from Greek to Arabic, promoting the birth of Christian literature in Arabic, the influence of which extended beyond Palestine, all the way to Mt. Sinai.

In Palestine an urban monasticism also developed around the great sanctuaries visited by pilgrims in connection with the route of the holy places (*Loca Sanctorum*). Here there were also monasteries founded by and for westerners. The Roman Melania the Elder went to Egypt after the death of her husband, meeting Rufinus of Aquileia there. She then traveled to Palestine and founded a monastery on the Mount of Olives around 380. Jerome, who had previous anchoritic experience, and the wealthy Paula the Elder founded a men's and a women's monastery in Bethlehem along with a guesthouse. The members of the monastery were subdivided according to social rank. Jerome oversaw the male house which served also as a center of high Latin culture and exercised an influence on western monasticism. The very wealthy Romans Pinianus and Melania the Younger, who was niece of the other Melania, traveled to Africa around 410 where they met Augustine. In 417 they established themselves in Jerusalem, leading an ascetic life there. After her husband's death, Melania founded a women's monastery and a men's monastery near the church of the Ascension, under the guidance of Gerontius who then wrote her biography. In these monasteries interest for biblical and theological culture was vibrant.

When we speak of Syriac monasticism, we mean that which developed in Roman Syria, in Mesopotamia, and in what is today Kurdistan.[64] The common language was Syriac before the imposition of Arabic. After the council of Chalcedon in 451 the Christian communities fractured into a West-Syrian and East-Syrian Church, along with the Chalcedonian churches. The two cities of Nisibis and Edessa were the centers of Syriac Christianity. Christians of the Syriac language tended in a particular way toward asceticism. First we find some rigorists there, the Encratites, and subsequently "the sons and daughters of the covenant." Aphraates addressed his sixth *Demonstration* towards them.[65] Susan Ashbrook Harvey maintains that "the daughters of the covenant" had a special task in Syriac Christianity, noteworthy (and perhaps unique) in their public ministry of sacred music performed for liturgical purposes in city churches. The Syriac tradition has attributed the constitution of these choirs of virgins to Ephrem the Syrian. Jacob of Sarug's homily on St. Ephrem presents these choirs as a soteriological model with eschatological significance for the greater ecclesial community.[66] Often, even from the first centuries as has already been noted the admission to baptism included—although it did not mandate—a preference for the renunciation of married life. Baptism leads to the heavenly wedding ceremony. The manner of living out one's asceticism varied. In general, however, the ascetics were integrated into the ordinary life of the local church. It seems that the origin of Syriac monasticism is autochthonous; nevertheless, quite early on it underwent Egyptian and Greek influence. The figure who came to be considered as the root of a special and severe ascetic life is Jacob, Bishop of Nisibis, who participated in the council of Nicaea in 325. His successors, Babu and Vologese, also followed his style of life.

Jerome withdrew into the desert of Chalcis, east of Antioch, and the pilgrim Egeria knew of Mesopotamian monasticism. In his *Historia Philothea*, Theodoret of Cyrrhus († c. 466) acquaints us with both Syrian cenobitism and the eremitic life which took strange and eccentric ascetic forms.[67] Some practiced a return to the primitive life, refusing not only meat but also bathing and clothing, covering themselves in chains and standing upright for extended periods of time. In western Syria the *stylites* flourish. These were solitaries who lived on top of a column or tower. The most famous is Simeon Stylites who lived for years in a small shelter placed on the top of a column, which then itself became a cultic center. It was a vertical eremitism, as opposed to the horizontal eremitism of the desert. All these practices manifested a control of the body, not its negation as if it were a sign of being able to overcome the normal human condition, but rather as an action of grace in the birth of a new world. Manual labor was not an important aspect of this monastic life, as it was for Egypt. The monk who lived outside of normal habitation was sustained by the nearby Christian communities, but he lived not in the isolation of the desert but near the roadside. In Syria too we find semi-eremitic forms of life. The cenobitic monasticism of Syria in the fourth and fifth centuries was not of a cultivated character, yet it provided the church with many bishops and was held in high esteem by the people. It was distinguished also by its evangelizing and charitable activity. It was not rare to find bilingual monasteries in Syria too. In the neighborhood of Zeugma there was the famous monastery of Publius (or Paulus). In the territory of Antioch, although not in the city itself, there were various monastic centers, as was the case also in the neighboring regions.

Behind the city of Nisibis was the massif of Tur 'Abdin ("mountain of the servants of God") with Mt. Izla (Izlo; *Izala* in Greek). The mountain was populated by monasteries from the time of the evanescent and important figure of Mar Eugenius (Awgin). Many subsequent monasteries look back to him as their founder. From 363 until Justinian, this was a Roman district on the empire's frontier. Ammianus Marcellinus writes that some nuns were captured by the Sassanid King Shapur in the territory between Amida and Mardin[68] around 363. In the sixth century monasticism flourished at Tur 'Abdin, especially on account of Abraham of Kashkar (c. 492–586) who founded a new monastery around 571 called "the Great Convent." He reformed and spread East-Syrian monasticism with the foundation of new monasteries by his disciples. "With Abraham arises a monasticism that is more structured, anti-Messalian, and strongly rooted in not only the institutions but also the theology of the Church of Persia. The Rules composed by him are preserved, which were then modified with a stronger doctrinal emphasis by his first successor Dadišo'. Perhaps the reform of the monastic *eskimâ* can be attributed to him, which consisted of the introduction of the monastic tonsure (*subbârâ*) instead of baldness, which was typical of Monophysite monks."[69]

The area is still very important for the Syrian Orthodox (Jacobites) as its numerous monasteries and churches testify to a very ancient Christianity. About 20 km southwest of Midyat there is still today the important and grandiose monastery of Mar (Mor) Gabriyel (near the village of Qartmin), known in ancient times as Mor Simeon, the most ancient monastery founded by the monk Samuel at the end of the fourth century and seat of the metropolitan bishop. Six kilometers from the city of Mardin the monastery of Mor Hananyo[70] still stands which dates back to the end of the fifth century.[71]

In central and southern Mesopotamia monasticism dates back to the late fourth century. This is an anchoritic and missionary monasticism that included itinerant monastic groups as well as those who take up residence in villages and cities.

In western Syria and eastern Asia Minor a monastic movement spread in the fourth century called the *Messalians*—those who pray. The term is of Syriac origin. They were also called in Greek the Euchites.[72] The Messalians had no specific or structured organization; rather they presented themselves in groups with a head leader. They insisted on the importance of prayer. They valued baptism less than prayer because they believed that at birth, through the sin of Adam, everyone received a demon from whom one could be liberated only by continual prayer. Itinerant monks demanded for themselves the alms of the faithful intended for orphans and the poor. Ephrem in Syria with his *Hymns on Heresies* around 360 and Epiphanius of Salamis around 374 denounced the dangers of the Messalians for the Christian life. The bishops tried to discipline the members of such a complex movement, which is why the Messalians were condemned by multiple councils of the time. We refer to it as a complex movement because the term *Messalian* indicates a varied collection of practices, beliefs, and activities, which the heresiological literature consolidates under a single term. Their founder is considered to be the monk Adelphius who was active in Edessa[73] in the first half of the fourth century. The most well-known exponent is Macarius/Simeon whose *Asceticon* was condemned at Constantinople (426), then at the council of Ephesus (431), and several more times in Syria and Armenia.

Various ascetic groups such as the Apotactics, Marcionites, Encratites, and Saccophoroi spread from the second century on throughout Asia Minor which was a complex and diverse world at the time. In the region of Pontus in the fourth century the disciples of Eustathius of Sebaste (ca. 300 – ca. 380) also prospered to the east of Caesarea. They held themselves to a severe ascesis and did not allow clerical marriage. Eustathius had a troubled life because of his doctrinal fluctuations and ways of life. In Cappadocia, as head of contesting groups he was deposed several times—first of all by his own father Eulalius because when he was a priest he wore clothing that was unbecoming someone in the church.[74] The council of Gangra around 341 condemned Eustathius and his followers for forbidding marriage and relations between husband and wife, for not receiving communion from married priests, for remaining virgins not for virtue but because they despised matrimony, for holding their own assemblies, for dressing in such a way as to set themselves apart, for despising wealth, for organizing themselves like a separate church, and the list goes on. We do not know if all these practices are to be attributed to the Eustathians, or perhaps, also reference other groups. Some Eustathians were clergy. The members of Basil's family embraced sexual continence and were influenced by the movement. As a young man Basil of Caesarea came into contact with Eustathius, though he didn't participate in the asceticism of the movement until after his studies at Athens. Even as a clergyman in Caesarea he remained a follower of his friend and master. From 372 onward their relationship deteriorated to the point of a complete break in 375 for theological reasons.[75] After the break the followers separated, some remain faithful to Eustathius, others followed Basil. Upon Basil's death his relatives and friends portray Eustathius negatively and present Basil as the founder of the monastic life. Certainly, he was a great organizer.

After visiting the monks of the various eastern regions and after his personal cenobitic experience, Basil of Caesarea drew up a first formulation of norms for the ascetic life (the *Little Asceticon*)[76] and afterwards a second and fuller compilation that was subdivided into two parts: the short and the long rule. For Basil, the goal of monastic life is the love of God which is realized only in the common life (= *koinos bios*: cenobitism), hierarchically organized under the guidance of a superior and assisted by a council, and where labor is important for living and for works of charity. Scripture must be the monk's object of meditation. The humanity and balance of the rules assured enormous success for Basilian cenobitism in the Byzantine world. Rufinus of Aquileia translated the *Little Asceticon* into Latin (*Regulae brevius tractatae*), assuring Basil great prestige in the West and Benedict of Nursia does indeed draw upon it.[77] Among the ascetic writings of Basil the *Great Asceticon* (*Regulae fusius tractatae*)[78] is important, and is more commonly known as the *Rule*. It assimilates the earlier work.[79]

Constantinople, the capital of the Empire in the East, also flourished as a monastic center. In fact, in 448 there were already 23 monasteries which increased to around 76 in 536. The monastery of the *acoemetae* (*akoimetoi*) was a renowned community founded by Alexander the Acoemete († c. 430). The acoemetae (the sleepless ones) prayed constantly in turns to sanctify the twenty-four hours of the day. The great monastery of the studites descended from the acoemetae.[80] Monasticism spread quickly beyond the boundaries of the Roman Empire in the East, in Persia and from there into Central Asia, but in particular in Armenia,[81] in Georgia, and Albania (today Azerbaijan) which are adjacent to each other. Cyril of Scythopolis wrote that a group of four hundred Armenians of Militene, traveling from Jerusalem to the Jordan River visited Euthymius, who had founded a laura. In fact, three Armenian brothers became his disciples there and others who could celebrate in their own language also joined in. The same occurred in the monastery of Saint Saba. While an Armenian monasticism developed in Palestine, the same happened in Armenia itself under Syrian influence even before Mashtots' in the first years of the fifth century—a monasticism that was ascetic as well as solitary and cenobitic. The latter type developed more and was encouraged by the bishops because they could control it better than the lauras. The Benedictine Rule was translated into Armenian in the twelfth century by Nerses of Lambron, exercising a notable influence on Armenian monasticism. The monasteries become the main cultural centers for religious and secular studies.

WESTERN MONASTICISM

The sources for learning about western monasticism in the first centuries are scarce and fragmentary compared with the abundant eastern sources. They are insufficient for understanding its spread, its impact on society, and the variety of experiences involved. These sources are almost exclusively literary and were intended to edify rather than inform, similar to the hagiographical literature that narrated only the actions of some "men of God." For this reason, the vast majority of our questions about the concrete life of monks in Latin areas remains without answers.

Forms of ascetic life were widespread in the West too even before Constantine. But the transition from this form of life to monasticism seems to have happened under eastern influence. In the West there was no rich blossoming of eremitism. There were no true deserts there either and, furthermore, Christianity was more of an urban reality than a rural one except for a few regions. The evangelization of the countryside happened at a later time. Thus, for example, in Italy hermits first withdrew onto the small islands of the Tyrrhenian Sea and then moved on to the Adriatic. In Rome there were domestic communities of ascetics by the second half of the fourth century. Augustine knew about a female community and male communities around the year 387 that included a superior and the obligation to work. Jerome also touched upon the existence of numerous monks in the city. He has a particular way of presenting female ascetic groups which, however, were not all that popular and tended towards the aristocratic as well as familial connections. To live out their ideal the ascetics withdraw to the countryside on their own lands, but often they went to the East and founded monasteries in Bethlehem or in Jerusalem. This is what Melania the Elder, Paula, Melania the Younger and her husband Pinianus did.[82]

Jerome's ascetic preaching in Rome stirred up a strong anti-monastic reaction, which we know about from his own works, particularly in the persons of Helvidius and Jovinian. This movement of thought rightly wanted to reevaluate the married life, accenting the importance of faith and baptism while at the same time denying special merits for virginity and ascetic practices. They held that there was one reward in the kingdom of heaven for all who had kept their baptismal vow.[83] The anti-monastic trend was not only a Roman phenomenon, however, insofar as there were those within the sphere of Christianity itself in Africa and Antioch who opposed it, not to speak of the pagans like Libanius, Eunapius of Sardis, and Rutilius Namatianus. An unusual phenomenon occurred in Rome as well between 430 and 470: popes began founding men's monasteries near certain basilicas such as St. Lawrence, St. Sebastian, and St.

Peter and included an obligation for the monks to celebrate the divine liturgy. By the year 800 there were 46 monastic institutions in existence in the city.

The first monastic foundation known in Italy was that of Eusebius of Vercelli where he was bishop in the middle of the fourth century. He led the common life with his clergy who were all dedicated to prayer and to the study of Scripture as well as manual labor and ascetic practices. During his residency in Milan, Augustine knew about the existence of a monastery outside the city walls, while the Bishop Ambrose demonstrated great concern for the virgins. There were groups of virgins in Bologna and Verona. Rufinus touches upon the existence of a male group of virgins at Aquileia around 370. He translated the first rule of Basil (*The Little Asceticon*) into Latin with the intent of offering the monasticism arising in Italy a unified direction without, however, achieving the goal. In 396 Paulinus of Nola founded a community in Campania where men and women lived in separate sections of the same complex.

From these few hints of monasticism one can discern how scarce the information is for the fourth century about monasteries existing in Italian territory, even if Rufinus shows us that there must have been quite a few monasteries by the end of the century. We can say the same for the fifth century. We are better informed about the sixth century because of the *Dialogues* and letters of Gregory the Great who mentions various monasteries.

The second book of the *Dialogues* is dedicated to Benedict of Nursia, who founded the monasteries of Subiaco and Montecassino. Gregory himself founded a monastery on the Celian Hill in Rome that was dedicated to St. Andrew. This was the same monastery from which the forty missionary monks with Augustine were sent off to England. Other information about the Italian situation concerns Cassiodorus (†583) who founded the monastery of *Vivarium* in Calabria, and Eugippius († after 533) who had been a disciple of St. Severinus at *Favianis*.[84] After his death around 488 Severinus' disciples, among them Eugippius, abandoned Noricum (Danubian Austria) and brought the saint's body with them and established themselves near Naples, founding the monastery of Severinus *in casto Lucullano* on the hill of Pizzofalcone. Eugippius was its abbot; he died sometime between 532 and 543. Towards the end of his life he also compiled a *Rule* as well as a cento[85] of previous material containing the entire *Rule* of Augustine. He constructed summaries of Basil and of the *Institutiones* of Cassian, as well as the so-called *Regula Magistri*.

There has been both long and heated discussion in the research involved with studies in late antiquity about the changes that occurred in monasticism, even in the realm of the evolution of western monasticism and the so-called *Regulae* of various provenance from the *Praeceptum* and *Ordo Monasterii* of Augustine onward. This research has shown that the anonymous *Regula Magistri* was written before the *Rule of St. Benedict*, and it was composed in central Italy in the first decades of the sixth century. Thus, a traditional conviction was overturned and many discussions were clarified.[86]

There were also some ascetics in Gaul at the beginning of the fourth century, but monasticism proper began with Martin, Bishop of Tours (316–397), who established himself as a hermit first at Ligugé, eight kilometers south of Poitiers, surrounded by other hermits. Then, after being chosen as bishop, in about 371 he founded the monastery of Marmoutier (= *magnum monasterium*) near Tours. The two monasteries resemble the Palestinian lauras. Their monks did not dedicate themselves to manual labor but to pastoral work and were sustained by the Christian community or by contributions from wealthy people who embraced the monastic life. There was no written rule. Various disciples of Martin were chosen as bishops. At his funeral in 397 there might have been two thousand monks present. The biographer of Martin, Sulpicius Severus, founded a community at Primullac (Périgord) after the model of Martin's. Victricius, Bishop of Rouen, commissioned other monasteries to be built.

At the beginning of the fifth century monasticism in Provence thrived with the community of Lérins (two islands off the coast of Cannes) that was founded by Honoratus in 410, along with the community of St. Victor founded at Marseilles in about 415 by John Cassian († c. 435) who also founded a female monastery there. Numerous bishops came out of the monasticism of Lérins, which had a more disciplined and cultivated character than that of Martin because of the aristocratic provenance of its members. Although John Cassian highly esteemed the eremitic ideal, he preferred communal life within the city and favored theological study that no doubt aided his involvement in many of the theological debates of the time.[87] His own writings have had an enormous influence on western monastic spirituality. Cassian was born in Scythia (Dobrugia) and received an excellent education. He was deeply familiar with the monasticism of Bethlehem and Egypt. Between 420 and 430 he compiled the two works destined to have great influence, the *Institutes* (*Institutiones*) and the *Conferences* (*Conlationes*) that would relay the authentic tradition of eastern monasticism (especially Egyptian) to the West.[88]

Another monastic center arose in Jura, a territory between France and Switzerland. Monasteries multiplied in Gaul during the Merovingian period, but they did not always have written monastic rules at the beginning and the situation fluctuated greatly. Slowly the Benedictine rule was imposed, especially through the effort of Charlemagne (†814) and Louis the Pious (†840). At the end of the century it is estimated that there were a thousand monasteries in Gaul.

We know that monks existed on the Iberian Peninsula in the second part of the fourth century, but we do not know their number, which was no doubt very small. The writer Bachiarius († 425) was an itinerant monk and author of a *Libellus fidei*. We know that the Priscillianists, who had been condemned by the Church, practiced a rigorous asceticism. But we know little else, which is also the case for the fifth century. Iberian monasticism developed only in the second half of the sixth century under Victorianus (†558), Martin of Braga,

Leander, and his brother Isidore of Seville. There were also the seventy monks who came from Africa with Donatus. Monasticism prospered in the following century with Braulio of Saragossa (†651), a friend of Isidore, who wrote the *Life of St. Emilian*, a Spanish hermit.

There were numerous virgins in Africa in the course of the fourth century who were exhorted to live in community by the council of Hippo in 393 and of Carthage in 397. The first known female monastery was that associated with Hippo where Augustine's sister was the superior. Such female monasteries expanded little by little in the fifth century into much of Africa.[89] There were also hermits and numerous *continentes* who lived on their own in different parts of Africa. We know of the existence of male monasteries both in Carthage and in Hadrumetum in the time of St. Augustine. There is no information about how they began, although they were certainly not Augustinian. When Augustine was in Milan he read the *Life of Anthony* by Athanasius[90] and thus was interested in the monastic life present in the city and in Rome, and was interested in a similar type of monasticism for himself. Upon his return to Africa in the years 388/389 he gathered a group of friends in Thagaste, but it was only in Hippo in 391 that he founded his first monastery. He was already a priest by that time and so conducted pastoral ministry and the running of the monastery simultaneously.

Once consecrated a bishop, Augustine also founded a monastery for the clergy under his episcopal oversight. In this way he was able to realize the union of monasticism with the priesthood in service to the local church. He fully integrated them, instead of leaving monasticism at the margins as generally happened elsewhere. Various friends and disciples of Augustine who were members of his monastery followed his example when they became bishops by founding monasteries of men and of women.

Augustine proposed a few essential and fundamental ideals to his monks such as having fellowship with one another in community in order to realize the love of God concretely by the full sharing of goods, demonstrating human compassion, prayer, and study—all conducted against the backdrop of a spirit of friendship which must pervade the religious life lived together. The Augustinian *Rule* known as the *Praeceptum* or *Regula ad Servos Dei*[91] profoundly influenced all western monasticism, both medieval and modern. His biographer Possidius writes that Augustine left monasteries to the African church that were filled with religious fervor and monastic life continued in Africa after Augustine, encountering every kind of difficulty from the Vandal invaders but still thriving into the seventh century. There are numerous monasteries about which we have some information for the fifth to seventh centuries, but after this Roman Africa came to be occupied by Muslim Arabs with the consequent disappearance of not only monasticism but also Christianity.

Irish monasticism was the last to emerge in the West. It traces its roots at least in some way to St. Patrick (†461) who was a native of Britain who made his residence in Armagh in the north of Ireland. The first monastic communities about which we have some information date back to the end of the fifth century and the beginning of the sixth and are linked to the work of Enda and Firmianus. There was remarkable growth in the number of monasteries in the course of the following century. Various Irish dioceses were organized on a monastic basis. The abbot of the religious community also served as the bishop of the diocese. Some monasteries (*paruchiae*) kept other foundations strictly connected to them as if they were a kind of congregation—especially their daughter-houses. In the monasteries there were few members who were priests. The superior in fact could be a lay abbot, a priest, or a bishop. Nevertheless, for the needs of the worshiping community, there was always a bishop or priest in their fold. These monasteries were quite complicated affairs because of the presence not only of numerous monks, but also of lay people, of lodgers, of students and pilgrims, and of residents who resided within the vicinity.

The Irish monasteries had schools not only for their own members but also for lay people some of whom came from a great distance. The principal interest in their schools was indeed religious, but the profane classical Latin culture was also cultivated. In this way they contributed a great deal to the Carolingian cultural renaissance. These communities also produced numerous missionaries such as Columbanus, Fursa, and Killian who went out to evangelize or to found more monastic communities on the continent.

MONASTIC RULES

Beginning with the *Didache,* a canonical and liturgical literature developed which sought to discipline the life of the community, the clergy, and those who wanted to practice a consecrated life. When organized communities arose in the fourth century they felt the need to draw up texts—today we call them *Rules*—in order to discipline the members' life together for the good of all. Naturally those groups or movements that were more or less free had no need of norms, like the Messalians of whom we have spoken. These were itinerant groups without any formal organization.

The ancient concept of a rule is quite different from ours, since it is not a legislative instrument with precise norms. Those attributed to eastern monasticism were very generic and more like suggestions and guidelines than rules for spiritual growth—like St. Basil's *Rules* or the Pachomian texts. The rules in western monasticism are shorter and of a more general character. The so-called *Rules* of ancient times were more general in character while modern religious who follow them have developed more detailed norms which go by the name of *Constitutions.* For modern foundations the base text is the opposite. The *Constitutions* indicate the charism and the general norms while the *Rule*—or Rules—went into greater detail. Ancient *Rules* continually refer back to biblical texts and served as an application and an explanation of those texts.

The works of Pachomius and Basil were translated into Latin and have had a vast influence on western monasticism. The rules are quite varied among themselves as to length, form, and structure, and the subsequent rules depend on the preceding ones in a complex interweaving. In fact, some were just anthologies or *centos* of preceding texts with no originality of their own. Some were intended for a specific monastery even if they then spread elsewhere, while others had a more general character. And yet, a monastery could pass from one rule to another or also use multiple rules according to its needs. In that period there was no thought at all about the particular charism an order or monastery might have; such an idea implied fidelity to founding prescriptions and a single rule.

In the preceding section the writings of Pachomius and Basil of Caesarea were examined. With the growth in the number of communities and of their members Pachomius wrote some norms for community life which I have already fully treated. The works of the two authors came to be translated in Latin respectively by Rufinus of Aquileia and by Jerome, who call such monastic legislation *regulae*, rules in the plural. Quite soon, however, the term would be used in the singular to designate the program of life lived out in the monastery—even if the texts designated with the term *regula* were often different in form and content, as was already noted with the *Liber Horsiesi*. The charism of the abbot was important in the Pachomian communities. The Basilian texts have had a great influence in the eastern and western world. Benedict referred to him as "our holy father Basil." He was a great defender of the cenobitic life. "I find that in many aspects it is more useful to live together. Above all, because none of us is sufficient by himself, not even for the needs of the body, but we need each other to provide what we need. . . . But more than that, also on account of the love of Christ it is not permitted for each one to look to his own interest. It is written: Love does not seek what is its own. The solitary life, however, has a single goal: that each one provides for his own needs. This is in evident contrast with the law of love that the Apostle fulfilled by seeking not what was good for him, but for many, that they might be saved."[92]

We are used to considering Benedict as the father of western monasticism. In reality the Benedictine Rule spread and was imposed only during the ninth century at the time of Charlemagne and of Louis the Pious. Before that, numerous rules were in circulation. Augustine was considered secondary. The *regulae*, of western and Latin origin, which have some legislative character for the monastic life, are about thirty in number. Since the literary genre is very fluid, it is not always easy to say if a text is a rule or not.[93]

The most ancient texts in Latin were those connected with Augustine of Hippo, who wrote and preached about the religious life and lived as a monk in his episcopal house.[94] In his *Retractions* (*Retractationes*), Augustine and his biographer Possidius do not mention any Augustinian rule. The first to do so was Eugippius (c. 465–539), who began his compilation by putting together two texts both by Augustine, separating them with an "amen." The two texts were: *Ordo monasterii* (*Ante omnia, fratres carissimi*) and the *Praeceptum* (*Haec sunt quae observetis*). The first text was also called the *Regula secunda*, while the second was referred to as the *Regula prima*. His *Letter* 211 (paragraphs 5–16) was addressed to the nuns where his sister was the superior. It reads the same as the *Praeceptum* except that it was addressed to women instead of men. The occasion of the letter is a troubled situation in that community.

The *Regula recepta* consists of the first phrase from the *Ordo monasterii* "Before everything, most beloved brothers, love God, then your neighbor, because these are the precepts that have been given to us" (*Ante omnia, fratres carissimi, diligatur Deus, deinde proximus, quia ista sunt praecepta nobis data*) followed by the *Praeceptum*. This is the masculine version of *Letter* 211. We do not know whether the masculine or the feminine is the earlier text. Today it is thought that the masculine version is earlier. The Augustinian rule became popular in the eleventh century when it was adopted by the Lateran Canons founded by Pope Alexander II (1061–1073). It was also adopted by other reformers like St. Norbert (Premonstratensians or Norbertines), the Knights of St. John,[95] the Teutonic Knights, and then by St. Dominic.

It is evident, therefore, that the Rules composed in the East and the Augustinian texts influenced later compositions.[96] In the fifth century there was a flourishing of texts for regulating the religious life of monasteries. We see a multiplication of rules within Latin monasticism up until the seventh century. These rules mark the development of the institution itself, beginning with the first eastern rules of Pachomius and Basil translated into Latin, as well as the Latin rule of Augustine. The authority of the Word of God stands above the rule, as does the authority of the local bishop. Everyone, especially bishops as well as abbots, can draw up a text which is not strictly normative and exclusive as it will be later on. Every rule has had its history: some have had a more local usage, others were employed more broadly such as the *Regula Basilii*, the *Corpus Pachomianum*, and the *Regula Augustini*. The custom of gathering multiple rules together emerged, which was especially the case with the shorter rules (the *corpora regularum*), which most often were arranged in chronological order, or sometimes in order of importance. They were often read together and observed in one and the same monastery. This type of compilation was referred to as the *regula mixta*.[97] Thus, the small rules included in the *corpora* crossed the strict local boundaries for which they had been written. The *corpus regularum* of a monastery then could expand with time as additional rules were added. The *Regula Benedicti* was one of the many rules that emerged. It was imposed in the Carolingian period due to its intrinsic value.

The ancient monastic rules were not homogeneous texts. There was noticeable diversity among them, starting with their breadth. Sometimes the rules cited were very brief, offering only some normative prescriptions. Others were quite broad, like the *Rule of the Master* (*Regula Magistri*), which was unrivaled in its explanation of the details of the religious life in all its organization. As to content, some were limited to a few practical prescriptions, others gave greater importance to ascetic exhortation. In the context of the cenobitic life the abbot and prior were key because they served as the true guides of the community. Even amid the diversity of rules, from the sixth century onward western monasticism demonstrated a remarkable homogeneity in its ascetic understanding, in its organization of life together, and in the communal or private practices of religious communities.

The vocabulary was also variable. It developed and gained precision, although the same term used throughout a given document would still need to be viewed in the context of where it occurred in the document, as was the case for example with *praepositus*. Yet there were many other texts that were related to the rules and sounded like ascetic exhortations. Some rules' authors were identified, while others remained anonymous. We provide here a list of those composed by bishops and monks: (1) Caesarius of Arles (c. 470–543), the great reformer in southern Gaul who also founded a monastery for women in 512. He drew up the *Regula ad virgines* for them, taking inspiration especially from Cassian. He was continually perfecting the rule. He insisted on communal life and on the stability of the members. (2) Benedict of Nursia (480/490 – Montecassino, 550/560). He drew up his famous rule around 540, taking inspiration from the preceding tradition which included Augustine, John Cassian, Basil, Pachomius, Caesarius, and the anonymous *Regula Magistri*.[98] The current text is a redaction that occurred over time and was the fruit of correction and improvements based on experience. It consists of a prologue and of seventy-three small chapters, with digressions, organized according to a coherent and detailed plan for the organization of the community which functioned as a cenobitic society. (3) Towards the end of his life Eugippius (460/467 – before 543) drew up a *Regula* intended for the monks of his monastery.[99] In reality it is a cento of other authors which included Augustine, Cassian, Basil, and the *Regula Magistri*. (4) Leander of Seville and his brother Isidore [100] composed some rules. The first was a text for women addressed to their sister Florentina; the second was a rule intended "for the holy brothers residing *in coenobio Honoriacensi*." (5) After various incidents in different European countries, the Irishman Columbanus founded a monastery at Bobbio where he later died in 615. He also wrote a rule which was composed of ten chapters that dealt with obedience, silence, fasting, rejection of worldly goods, rejection of vanity, chastity, prayer, discretion, mortification of arrogance and pride, and living an exemplary life. This text was completed by the *Regula coenobialis*, which was formed as a series of penitential chapters concerned with the faults of the monks. (6) Numerous other authors composed monastic rules for men or women, such as Fructuosus of Braga in Galicia (†651), and Donatus in Gaul (†ca. 600).

There were numerous anonymous rules. Among the most important were: (1) *Regulae Quattuor Patrum*.[101] This was the oldest anonymous rule on which the other four depend. It is difficult to locate geographically and in time, but might be traced back to Lérins. It takes its name from a meeting of four interlocutors: Serapion, Macarius, Paphnutius, and the other

Macarius. These were famous figures of Egyptian monasticism. The rule expounds on their ideas for organizing the common life of monasteries. This Rule was disseminated not only in Gaul but elsewhere, including in Italy. It was known to the author of the *Regula Magistri* and to Benedict. The initial version was probably expanded with the addition of norms about corrections and preferential treatment of certain individuals. Four other anonymous rules are dependent on this one: (a) *Regula patrum secunda*; (b) *Regula Macarii*; (c) *Regula orientalis*; (d) *Regula patrum tertia*. (2) The *Regula Pachomii brevis*[102] was compiled in Italy in the first half of the fifth century. It is practically a compilation and adaptation of Pachomian legislation for the West. It was translated by Jerome into Latin in 404 and includes a preface he inserted. (3) The *Regula Magistri*[103] received its name from Benedict of Aniane because it was formulated as questions from the disciples and responses by their Master. The fact that many compilers and authors evidence a dependence on this text, beginning with Benedict, is an indication of its richness, breadth, originality, importance, and antiquity. The unknown author was a true spiritual master who desired a well-organized, hierarchical, and spiritually rich community in the context of ecclesial life. He confronted all the various aspects of cenobitic life and sometimes also provided further details for their ordered life together.

The Benedictine rule drew abundantly from this text, especially concerning spiritual matters which are the subject of the prologue and the first ten chapters. The Master understands the monastic life, or "school," to be based on three pillars: the rule, the monastery itself, and the abbot, and his treatment turns upon these. The three essential virtues are obedience to the abbot and to the superiors, silence, and humility. The Rule is composed of a prologue and 95 chapters. The first section is of a more general character and confronts themes that concern the spiritual life; then follow norms regarding the structure of the monastic community such as finances, schedule, meals, hospitality, the sick, norms of conduct on journeys, and the like. The next section concerns the admission of new members and the rules for succession in choosing the next abbot. The rule closes with chapter 95 which deals with the topic of the porter, or doorkeeper. The author draws on earlier monastic texts, but not on Augustine. He also draws on other non-monastic texts such as the passions of the martyrs. Since the Benedictine rule depends heavily on the *Regula Magistri*, and in fact sometimes seems to want to correct it, one must admit that it had been composed at least a few decades earlier, and thus at the beginning of the sixth century, south of Rome.[104]

MONASTICISM AND INSTITUTIONS

When monasticism started out it seemed like it was an extremely free and spontaneous phenomenon, and thus in complete contrast with the normal way of living at the time, both in society and at least to some extent in the Christian community itself. Monasticism existed at the margins of society due to the radicalism inherent in the new ideals it posed for living. Abuses within the monastic movement were not infrequent, because in certain cases there was a very narrow margin of difference between the monk in his highest realization, and the brigand or the dissolute. This is why eremitism, which always remained the ultimate aspiration of much ancient monasticism, came to be replaced almost entirely by cenobitism, although pockets of eremitic monasticism endured in various places. Cenobitic monasticism allowed for regulation of the community and granted less freedom of movement compared to what the hermits experienced with their absolute freedom and independence. The regulation stems from a three-fold direction: from the monks themselves who wrote the monastic rules, from ecclesiastical authorities who intervened with their own regulations that sought to normalize monastic life, and lastly from civil authority with its own set of legislative arrangements for checking abuses.

At the beginning of the monastic movement there were no written rules. It was thought that the monk's life must be learned through an intimate encounter with someone who already lived that life and could provide instruction. The first monks considered themselves members of the local Christian communities and consequently submitted to the authority of their respective bishops, even if they lived quite far from these communities. Sacred Scripture and the examples contained in them were the constant reference point for every type of monasticism at the time and for what followed later on as well. The written norms that arose later on in no way presumed to replace the earlier rules, but only sought to be of further help.

The *Life of Anthony*, written by Athanasius, comes to be received as a monastic rule, "promulgating the precepts of the monastic life under the form of a story."[105] This life had an enormous influence, as we have noted more than once in the preceding pages. The *Sentences* or *Sayings of the Fathers* (*Apophthegmata Patrum*), a collection of the maxims of certain monks that were first transmitted orally and then put down in writing, also constituted a fixed reference point. There is a vast and varied ascetic literature in these early centuries because the greater part of the Christian writers of the period were either monks themselves or were influenced by monastic spirituality. The authors of the specifically monastic rules were not at all planning on founding a religious order in the modern sense, and so they cannot be called founders or legislators as is commonly thought or written.

The monastic rule of Pachomius (†346),[106] compiled in Coptic and then translated into Greek, and that of Basil of Caesarea served to discipline ascetic aspirations. As we have already mentioned, Basil was the one who had the most influence on monasticism, particularly Byzantine monasticism, with his series of writings that take on a monastic character. Among the Palestinian lauras we can name the *Typikos* attributed to Saba (†532) which served as guidelines for the monastic and liturgical life. In the Syrian area numerous rules arose, among which was that of Rabbula who would afterwards become bishop of Edessa (†436).

The Latin West made use of translations of eastern writings, but it soon produced its own rules for governing cenobitic life, such as the texts of Augustine, the *Regula Magistri* compiled in Italy, Benedict of Nursia († c. 550/560) with his *Regula monasteriorum*, along with rules written by bishops like Caesarius of Arles, Aurelius of Arles († 551), Isidore of Seville, and others such as Columbanus who were experts on the cenobitic life.

In the seventh and eighth centuries in the West there was a certain monastic unification with the adoption of the Benedictine rule, especially through the effort of Benedict of Aniane († 821) who made a collection of all rules known to him. At that time there was great freedom: abbots could choose the rule they wanted to follow and could change it as they please. There was no regulation and even less fixity. The first interventions of ecclesiastical authority did not have a legislative character, but rather sought to establish order in order to avoid abuses, and thus they implicitly recognized the validity of the monastic ideal. The juridical condition of the monk was not well defined. He was normally a layperson, but he could also be a cleric, and in fact the number of clerical monks increased with time. Religious vows did not exist; only consecrated virgins professed a public commitment to virginity that was then recognized by the Church. Because of ecclesial and civil arrangements, slaves could be admitted only with the consent of their respective masters. The monk committed himself to chastity, to poverty, and to obedience, but not by a legal act, on account of which abandoning the monastic life is condemned and the monk can be submitted to public penance. A marriage contracted by a monk, as also by a consecrated *virgo*, came to be considered always valid even if the one contracting it was excommunicated or submitted to penance—a discipline that changed afterwards.

The rules insist on obedience to the superior, while the council of Chalcedon (can. 24) speaks of obedience to the local bishop. In effect all the faithful depended on the diocesan bishop both for the directing of the Christian life and for the liturgy and ordinations. In practice, however, everything depended on the concrete situation of the monastery, including its distance from the city, whether or not it had been founded on family property, its ties to a cultic center, whether it had been founded by the bishop himself, as well as other concerns. The first known case of the exemption of a monastery from episcopal jurisdiction is that of Bobbio in 628, conceded by Pope Honorius I (625-638) who set it under his own authority.

With the exception of some interventions by local councils, only the council of Chalcedon intervened in monastic life, for various reasons, particularly in canons 4 and 24 in which it was prescribed that monks could not erect a monastery without the consent of the bishop. Once they had been erected and consecrated, they must remain as they were and not become common living quarters. The monks must submit to the local bishop and dedicate themselves to the specific practices of their life, and therefore could not commit themselves to worldly affairs. They also could not leave their residence without the bishop's permission because he was the overseer of them all.

One need not, however, naively believe that these arrangements were immediately and everywhere observed. Also, there were not only conciliar interventions. There were also those interventions enacted by popes, especially Gregory the Great who organized various monasteries. Civil authorities also legislated in specific cases, but only rarely did they do so before Justinian. In 370 Valens ordained that those who joined monasteries to avoid curial obligations should be prosecuted.[107] For reasons of public security, in 390 Theodosius prohibited monks from residing in cities—an arrangement revoked in 392—because some of them were instigating uprisings because of fanaticism.

In 471 the Emperor Leo prohibited monks from leaving their monasteries and staying in the city. The emissaries of the monasteries, however, were allowed to stay in the city if they promised not to discuss religion. In this case too, the motive that inspired the law was more than clear. Justinian (525-565) published numerous instructions regarding monks which are found in the first book of the *Codex* and of the *Novellae*. These instructions concerned entering the monastery and leaving it, the election of the abbot, the separation of monks and nuns, the common life, and certain patrimonial aspects. The laws of Justinian applied only within the sphere of the Byzantine Empire. As far as the patrimonial aspect is concerned, individual monks could not possess anything, but the community itself could have goods in common that might derive from donations, from the monks' labor, or from property offered by those who entered the monastery whenever other arrangements had not been made before. Individual monks were poor but the monasteries, capable of ownership as juridical entities, become increasingly wealthy, accumulating extensive landed properties. Furthermore, since these monasteries were not subject to the hereditary apportionment characteristic of movable goods, but only to the possibility that other goods be added to them, at times they became like fiefs, contributing in this way to giving the medieval countryside a particular character.

---

1. A. Guillaumont, *Aux origines du monachisme chrétien: pour une phénoménologie du monachisme* (Bégrolles en Mauges: Abbaye de Bellefontaine, 1979), 218.
2. Subsequent tradition considered them Christians, but in reality, they belonged to the variegated Jewish world of the first century.
3. For many centuries, monasticism was the only form of religious life in the Christian sphere and still today it is characteristic of the Christian East, while in the West other forms of religious life have developed as adaptations of monasticism from which they took numerous elements that are still prevalent today.
4. Peter Nagel, *Die Motivierung der Askese in der alten Kirche und der Ursprung des Mönchtums* (Berlin: Akademie-Verlag, 1966).
5. The Greek term *ascesis* is not very descriptive of the ascetic phenomenon of Christianity which is more of a renunciation in order to follow Christ and dedicate oneself to the service of others, but we have no other terminology.

6. The *Liber graduum* makes this distinction. While the first must observe all the commandments, the second need not work but remove themselves from the discipline of the Church. Another view is that of A. Kowalski, *Perfezione e giustizia di Adamo nel Liber graduum* (Rome: Pontificium Institutum Orientale, 1989).
7. Athanasius, *Life of Anthony* 2–3.
8. *Mt* 19:21.
9. J. Leclercq, *Dizionario Istituti Perfezione* 5 (Rome: Edizioni paoline, 1974-2003), 1679-80.
10. Cassian, *Conferences* 18.5; SC 64:14-16.
11. Jerome, *Ep.* 3.5; 108.31.
12. Faustus of Riez, *Sermo* 23, CSEL 21:314.
13. Jerome, *Ep.* 14.7.
14. Cf. D.J. Chitty, *The Desert a City: An Introduction to the Study of Egyptian and Palestinian Monasticism under the Christian Empire* (Oxford: Blackwell, 1966), 4.
15. John Chrysostom, *In Matth.* 55.5, PG 58:547.
16. Evagrius, *Treatise on Perfection (On Prayer?)* 124; PG 79:1193C.
17. Claudia Rapp, *Holy Bishops in Late Antiquity: The Nature of Christian Leadership in an Age of Transition* (Berkeley: University of California Press, 2005).
18. The fearful group of the Circumcellions in Africa, though with strict similarities to monks, is a mistaken and not integrated monastic form. So also other groups, like the Apotaktoi and Saccophoroi (cf. Codex Theodosianus 16.5.5 and 11, laws from 381 and 383). The view presented by the council of Gangra in 341 on Eustathius of Sebaste, who encouraged insubordination. There were also the Messalians. Cf. G. Barone Adesi, *Monachesimo ortodosso d'Oriente e diritto romano nel tardo antico* (Milan: Giuffrè, 1990).
19. J. Leclecq, *Dizionario Istituti di perfezione* 5:1680ff.
20. Ibid, 6:1681.
21. Basil first wrote the *Little Asceticon*, composed of 203 answers, and translated into Latin by Rufinus of Aquileia with the name of *Rule*, which was the only writing of Basil known in the West. Then Basil redacted the *Greater Asceticon*, which is a shuffling and expanding of the first and is subdivided in turn into *Lesser Rules*, 55 questions, and *Greater Rules*, 313 questions.
22. For example, Codex Theodosianus 16.5.7, 11.
23. Cf. Jerome, *Ep.* 22.34, among whom are the Remnuoth (a coptic term), gyrovagues, and sarabaites (a coptic term); Cassian, Coll. 18.4ff. On the topic: A. de Vogüé, *Histoire littéraire du mouvement monastique dans l'antiquité* (Paris : Cerf, 1991), 288-325; see especially J.-M. Besse, *Les moins d'Orient antérieurs au concile de Chalcédoine (451)* (Paris: Cerf 1990), 19-57.
24. *tria sunt in Aegypto genera monachorum, quorum duo sunt optima, tertium tepidum atque omnimodis evitandum.* Cassian, *Collationes* 18.4. Jerome also distinguishes three kinds (*Ep.* 22.34).
25. M.J. Blanchard, "'Sarabaitae' and 'remnuoth': Coptic considerations," in *The World of Early Egyptian Christianity: Language, Literature, and Social Context*, eds. J. E. Goehring, J. Timbie, D. W. Johnson, (Washington: Catholic University of America Press, 2007), 49-60.
26. *Rule of St. Benedict* 1.
27. From the Latin *Gyrus* = circular + *vagus* = wandering, implying they were wandering around in circles.
28. *Multiplex enim observantiae istius forma est, ac sub nomine diversa genera monachorum* This is from *Consultationes Zacchaei et Apollonii*, cf. J.-L. Feiertag, *Les Consultationes Zacchaei et Apollonii: étude d'histoire et de sotériologie* (Fribourg: Editions universitaires, 1990), 97-109.
29. M. Luther, *De votis monasticis iudicium*, of 1531. See also Art. 28 of the Augsburg Confession (1530).
30. Karl. Heussi, *Der Ursprung des Mönchtums* (Tübingen: Mohr, 1936), repr. Aalen 1986.
31. Cf. Peter. Brown, *Society and the Holy in Late Antiquity*, (Berkeley: University of California Press, 1982); *Authority and the Sacred: Aspects of the Christianisation of the Roman world* (Cambridge: Cambridge University Press, 1995); "The Rise and Function of the Holy Man in Late Antiquity," *JECS* 6 (1988): 353-76.
32. *Monachesimo orientale: Un'introduzione*, ed. Filoramo Giovanni, Morcelliana, (Brescia: Morcelliana, 2010); "Storia della Chiesa e monachesimi (secc. IV-VI)," *Adamantius* 17 (2011): 6–153, in collaboration with Monaci Castagno, Adele, *Storia della Chiesa e monachesimi* (secc. IV-VI) / Collab.: F. Thelamon, O. Andrei, R. Alciati, S. Boesch Gajano, A. Martin, M. C. Giorda, R. M. Parrinello.
33. Jerome wrote the *Life of Paul of Thebes*.

34. *EAC* 2: 232; J. E. Goehring, *Ascetics, Society, and the Desert: Studies in Early Egyptian Monasticism* (Harrisburg, PA: Trinity Press Intl, 1999), 110-35.
35. S. Elm, "Athanasius of Alexandria's "Letter to the Virgins": Who Was Its Intended Audience?" *Augustinianum* 33 (1993): 171-83
36. J. Gribomont, "Il monachesimo orientale," in *Dizionario degli Istituti di perfezione*, vol. V,1964. This vast dictionary is of noteworthy scholarly value and offers an excellent treatment of all the arguments considered in this chapter; it also treats some particular persons in an ample and exact way.
37. Athenagoras, *Embassy* 30.
38. In the next chapter, I will treat fully of virgins and widows.
39. Eusebius, *Demonstratio evang.* 1.8; PG 33:76.
40. G. M. Colombás, *Dizionario Istituti di Perfezione* 1:922.
41. Cf. Alberto Camplani, *Atanasio di Alessandria, Lettere festali* (Milan: Paoline, 2003).
42. In the Latin world the most well-known were the Egyptian monasticism and in part the cenobitic monasticism of Basil. Syrian monasticism, though extremely important, was virtually unknown; even lesser known was Armenian monasticism.
43. Tito Orlandi, *Vita dei monaci copti* (Rome: Città Nuova, 1984).
44. A. Camplani, ed., *L'Egitto cristiano: aspetti e problemi in età tardo-antica* (Rome: Institutum Patristicum Augustinianum, 1997).
45. *Vita e detti dei Padri del deserto*, ed. by Luciana Mortari (Rome: Città Nuova, 2012).
46. Samuel Rubenson, *The Letters of Saint Antony: Monasticism and the Making of a Saint* (Minneapolis: Fortress Press, 1995).
47. David Brakke, *Demons and the Making of the Monk. Spiritual Combat in Early Christianity* (Cambridge: Harvard University Press, 2006).
48. Athanasius, *Life of Anthony* 15. The followers of Anthony did not live together in the sense of leading the communal life, but were simply hermits.
49. Athanasius, *Life of Anthony* 14.7.
50. Cf. L. Regnault, *La vie quotidienne des Pères du désert en Egypte au IVe siècle* (Paris: Hachette, 1990); English translation *The Day-to-Day Life of the Desert Fathers in Fourth-Century Egypt* (New York: Fordham University, 2002).
51. Douglas Burton-Christie, *The Word in the Desert: Scripture and the Quest for Holiness in Early Christian Monasticism* (New York: Oxford University Press, 1993).
52. The text is inserted into the *Codex Regularum* of Benedict of Aniane with the title: *Teaching of the Holy Abbot Orsiesis of Tabennisi on Monastic Formation*.
53. Paul C Dilley, *Monasteries and the Care of Souls in Late Antique Christianity: Cognition and Discipline* (Cambridge, UK: Cambridge Univ. Press, 2017), 225.
54. William Harmless, *Desert Christians: An Introduction to the Literature of Early Monasticism* (New York/Oxford: Oxford University Press, 2004).
55. T. Orlandi, *Shenoute d'Atripè*: DSp 14:797-804; Coptic Encyclopedia 7:2131-2133; Patrologia V, ed. by A. Di Berardino, 544-551; David Brakke, A. Crislip, translated with introduction, *Selected Discourses of Shenoute the Great. Community, Theology, and Social Conflict in Late Antique Egypt* (Cambridge: Cambridge University Press, 2015).
56. M. C. Giorda, "Il monachesimo egiziano tra il concilio di Calcedonia (451 d.c.) e l'arrivo degli Arabi (VII secolo)," in *Monachesimo orientale: Un'introduzione*, ed. Filoramo Giovanni (Brescia: Morcelliana, 2010), 93-138.
57. Giovanni Mosco, *Il Prato*, ed. R. Maisano (Napoli: M. D'Auria, 2002); John Moschus, *The Spiritual Meadow* (Piscataway, NJ: Gorgias Press, 2010).
58. A collection of anecdotes, stories, memories, episodes against the council of Chalcedon. Cf. L. Perrore, "Dissenso dottrinale e propaganda visionaria: Le Pleroforie di Giovanni di Maiuma," *Augustinianum* 29 (1989): 451-95; Corneilia B. Horn, *Asceticism and Christological Controversy in Fifth-Century Palestine: The Career of Peter the Iberian* (Oxford: Oxford University Press, 2008), passim.
59. Cf. also the anonymous *Itinerarium Plac.* 37ff.
60. Anonymous, *Itinerarium Plac.* 37.4.
61. The name *Melchite* (= imperial) was given to the Christians of Syria who were faithful to the faith of the council of Chalcedon and were accepted by the court of Constantinople. It was meant as an act of derision on the part of the other Christians who were devoted to monophysitism.

62. Laura (= throat, narrow passage) in the ancient world meant a collection of little cells, or caves, for monks. The laura had a central church and sometimes also a refectory. The monks were not hermits, insofar as they had moments of common life in church, nor were they cenobites who lived together. The priest had contact with outsiders. Today the term *laura* (*lavra*) in orthodox Christianity indicates a monastic complex (a large monastery).
63. During the crusades, the saint's body was taken to Venice. In 1964, his body was returned to Mar Saba.
64. V. Berti, "Il monachesimo siriaco," in *Monachesimo orientale: Un'introduzione*, ed. Giovanni Filoramo (Brescia: Morcelliana, 2010), 139-92.
65. Aphraates, *Dem.* 6, D. I. Parisot (ed.), *Aphraatis sapientis persae demonstrationes*, in *Pat. Syriaca* 1, R. Graffin (ed.) (Paris, 1894), 241-311; J. Gwynn (trans.) in NPNF 2 13:362-75.
66. S. Ashbrook Harvey, "Revisiting the Daughters of the Covenant," *Hugoye: Journal of Syriac Studies* 8 (2005): 125-49.
67. Pierre Canivet, *Le monachisme syrien selon Théodoret de Cyr* (Paris: Beauchesne, 1977).
68. *Historiae* 18.10.4.
69. Sabino Chialà, *Abramo di Kashkar e la sua comunità* (Magnano, BI: Qiqajon Edizioni, Bose 2005).
70. Kurkmo Dayro in Syriac and Dairu 'l-Zaʻfarān in Arabic.
71. It was the seat of the patriarch until 1932.
72. The Messalians also came to be called Euchites, Enthusiasts, Adelphians, and other names. Messalian comes from the Syriac *mṣallyānā*, which means 'praying'.
73. Şanlıurfa today, between Turkey and nearby Syria, in Osroene.
74. Socrates *HE* 2.43.
75. Cf. Basil, *Ep.* 119; 223.
76. Cf. D.J. Chitty, *The Desert a City*, 4ff.
77. A. de Vogüé, "L'influence de saint Basile sur le monachisme d'Occident," *Revue bénédictine* 113 (2003): 5-17.
78. L. Cremaschi, *Basilio di Cesarea. Le regole. Regulae fusius tractatae. Regulae brevius tractatae di Basilio* (Magnano, BI: Qiqajon Edizioni, 1993; 2013).
79. *Basilio – Opere ascetiche*, ed. U. Neri (Torino: UTET, 1990).
80. In the city of Constantinople around 422 a cenobium called *Studion* was founded, named after its founder. This cenobium had great prestige in the centuries which followed.
81. N. G. Garsoïan, "Introduction to the Problem of Early Armenian Monasticism," *Revue des Études Arméniennes* 30 (2005-2007): 177-236.
82. Cf. the preceding section, where monasticism in Palestine is discussed.
83. *esse omnium qui suum baptisma servaverint unam in caelorum remunerationem.* Jerome, *Contra Iovinianum* 1.2.
84. Today Mautern an der Donau, Austria.
85. A collection of sayings.
86. B. Steidle, ed., *Regula magistri. Regula s. Benedicti* (Rome: Herder, 1959); I.M. Gómez, *Regla del Maestro, Regla de S. Benito* (Zamora: Monte Casino, 1988); A. de Vogüé, "Regula Magistri," *Dizionario degli Istituti di Perfezione* 7:1582-87; Ibid, "New Views on the Rule of the Master and the Dialogues of Gregory the Great," *American Benedictine Review* 66 (2015): 419-32.
87. A.de Vogüé, *Histoire littéraire du mouvement monastique dans l'Antiquité. Première partie: Le monachisme latin*, vol. VI: *Les derniers écrits de Jérôme et l'oeuvre de Jean Cassien (414-428)*, (Paris: Editions du Cerf, 2002); R. Alciati, "Quarant'anni di studi cassianei," *Rivista di Storia del Cristianesimo* 7 (2010): 229-48.
88. John Cassian, *The Conferences*, translated and annotated by Boniface Ramsey (New York: Paulist Press, 1997); *The Institutes*, translated and annotated by Boniface Ramsey, (New York: The Newman Press, 2000).
89. John Gavigan, *De vita monastica in Africa septentrionali inde a temporibus S. Augustini usque ad invasiones Arabum* (Torino: Mariett, 1962), 74-93. This volume is rarely cited, but is very rich in dates and information not easy to find elsewhere.
90. This biography had two Latin translations in the fourth century: the anonymous one read by Augustine, and another translation made by the presbyter Evagrius, who then became bishop of Antioch. This translation is found in PG 26:837-976.
91. Augustine *Ep.* 211 contains a version of the *Regula ad Servos Dei* but the epistle references the feminine rather than masculine, and was written later. It is composed of two parts: *Obiurgatio*, paragraphs 1-4; the second part, paragraphs 5-16, the rule for nuns. L. Verheijen, *Règle de Saint Augustin*, 2 vol. (Paris: Etudes augustinienne, 1967);

Adolar Zumkeller, *Augustine's Ideal of the Religious Life* (New York: Fordham University Press, 1986); N. Cipriani, *Sant'Agostino, La Regola. Introduzione e note* (Rome: Institutum Patristicum Augustinianum, 2006); G. Lawless, *Augustine of Hippo and his Monastic Rule* (Oxford: Clarendon Press, 1987); *Saint Augustine, The Monastic Rules*, foreword by G. Lawless, commentary by Gerald Bonner, translation and notes by Sister Agatha Mary and Gerald Bonner, ed. by Boniface Ramsey (Hyde Park: New City Press, 2004).

92. Basil of Caesarea, *Le Regole*, ed. L. Cremaschi, (Magnano (BI): Qiqajon Edizioni di Bose, 1993); *Regole Diffuse*, D. 7:99-100; Anna M. Silvas, *The Asketikon of St Basil the Great* (New York: Oxford University Press, 2005).

93. Cecilia Falchini, *Abitare come fratelli insieme - Regole cenobitiche d'Occidente*, (Magnano (BI): Qiqajon Edizioni di Bose 2016).

94. Saint Augustine, *The Monastic Rules*, foreword by George Lawless; commentary by Gerald Bonner; translation and notes by Sister Agatha Mary and Gerald Bonner; ed. by Boniface Ramsey, (Hyde Park: New City Press, 2004).

95. Later known as the Knights of Rhodes and then as the Knights of Malta.

96. Adalbert de Vogüé, "Regole cenobitiche dell'Occidente," in *Dizionario degli Istituti di Perfezione* VII (Rome: Edizioni Paoline, 1981), coll. 1420-28, and the smaller volume *Les règles monastiques anciennes* (Turnhout: Brepols, 1985).

97. See Gregory of Tours, *Hist. Franc.* 10:20; *Regula Pauli et Stephani*, ed. J.E.M. Vilanova 124; 195-197; 203-204; *Regula Fructuosi*, PL 87:1109.

98. Adalbert de Vogüé, *La règle de saint Benoit. Commentaire doctrinal et spiritual* (Paris: Édition du Cerf 1977); *The Rule of Saint Benedict: A Doctrinal and Spiritual Commentary* (Kalamazoo, MI.: Cistercian Publications, 1983). *The Rule of Saint Benedict*, ed. and trans. by Bruce L. Venarde (Cambridge, Mass: Harvard University Press, 2011); *St. Benedict's Rule for Monasteries*, trans. by L. J. Doyle (Collegeville, MN: Liturgical Press, 2016).

99. Eugippius, *La regola*, ed. B. Degórski and L. Mirri (Rome: Città Nuova, 2005); L. Krestan, L. Bieler, *Eugippius: the life of Saint Severini* (Washington: Catholic University Press, 1965).

100. *Regole monastiche della Spagna visigota*. Abbazia di Praglia (Bresso di Teolo (PD): Scritti monastici, 2014). (Leander of Seville, Fructuosus of Braga, Isidore of Seville).

101. PL 103:435-442; SC 297:180-204; 2ed SC 298:580-602.

102. PL 50:271-302.

103. CPL 1558; PL 88:943-1051; SC 105-106.

104. Many other rules are anonymous or are of uncertain attribution. For all these, refer to my *Patrology*, vol. 4, (Marietti: Casale Monferrato, 1996).

105. Gregory of Nazianze, *Oratio* 21.5; PG 35:1088.

106. Armand Veilleux, trans., *Pachomian Koinonia: The Lives, Rules, and Other Writings of Saint Pachomius and His Disciples*, 3 vols. (Kalamazoo: Cistercian Publications, 1980-1982); L. Cremaschi, ed., *Pacomio e i suoi discepoli: regole e scritti* (Magnano (BI): Qiqajon Edizioni di Bose,1988).

107. *Codex Theo.* 12.1.63.

CHAPTER 8

VIRGINITY, WIDOWHOOD AND ABSTINENCE (CELIBACY)

VIRGINITY

THE TERM VIRGIN[1] COMES FROM THE LATIN *VIRGO* AND SERVES BOTH AS A NOUN AND AN adjective. It indicates a person, either a man or woman, who has never had sex. Usually, however, it refers to women and only rarely to men who more often are identified as *asceti* or *singularis*.[2] The latter recalls the solitary life of those who have no wife. Especially in the past it was synonymous with a girl or a young woman. The term celibate, on the other hand, which comes from the Latin *caelebs* (*coelebs*) indicates a man who has not taken a wife or who is not currently married. An example would be a widower or someone who abstains from sexual relations perhaps because he has taken a vow. Celibacy is the condition of a celibate person and the term, as applied to the clergy in major orders, has had a technical meaning since the twelfth century.

For the ancients, the concept of virginity was based on the physical integrity of women. For Tertullian *virginitas* meant a triple physical integrity: a *nativitate*, from birth; *a lavacro*, from baptism; a *morte coniungis*, from the death of a spouse with whom one was monogamous.[3]

In the New Testament writings, virginity is praised and highly recommended. It is a gift from God that has value if it is chosen in view of the kingdom of heaven and not as a purely physical fact of abstention from sexual activities. Indeed, those who rejected marriage out of contempt were condemned (*1 Tim* 4:3). Virginity that allows us to serve the Lord more freely was considered a sign of a future reality, of a future life, especially now that we are in the last times. Marriage, on the other hand, is a reality of the present world and for this reason is transitory. Virginity in the ancient world was not valued, except that which was practiced, for religious reasons, among the vestal virgins of Rome. It soon became established among Christians. In Rome, Justin († ca. 165) extolled virginity in comparison to pagan corruption, writing that "many men and women who were disciples of Christ from childhood still remain pure in their sixties and seventies. I am proud that I can provide examples from every social class."[4] At the same time in Athens, Athenagoras makes a similar observation: "You could find among us many men and women who have aged without getting married in the hope of being closer to God. If remaining in the state of virginity or sexual abstinence brings us closer to God, while the mere conception of thoughts and desires moves us away from him, then let us even more rightly avoid the actions whose thoughts we flee."[5]

Christian authors of the first two centuries would revisit the fundamental motivations for virginity expressed in the New Testament texts. Sometimes in their exaltation of virginity they would insinuate arguments, however, that went beyond strictly biblical reasons. In this they derived their thinking from concepts current at the time: ritual purity, the Platonic devaluation of the body, the Stoic conception of *ataraxy* (serenity), along with the Aristotelian idea that marriage was a minor thing that often only brought annoyances and troubles for those engaged in it. Some authors described the difficulties of married life in gloomy hues in order to exhort their audience to remain virgins. But only a few heterodox sects despised and totally rejected marriage. The fathers condemned these sects and claimed that marriage was a good thing—and yet, virginity was a better and superior good than marriage.[6] On the other hand, they noted that virginity was a gift from God; it was not obligatory.[7] In this we begin to see a movement towards the later distinction between counsel and commandment: religious vows were considered a way to offer evangelical counsel to those seeking it.

When the Christian considered virginity as a gift from God rather than a personal achievement, he or she felt better equipped to resist any kind of temptation. There was a danger that virgins would feel privileged and think that they were part of a superior class. The fathers opposed this kind of attitude that was fostered in exclusive groups who considered themselves to be perfect and true Christians—thinking of themselves as the true guardians of the Gospel. According to Flavius Josephus, even the Essenes despised marriage for themselves, but "they did not condemn marriage in itself or procreation, but wanted to protect themselves from the lust of women because they were convinced that no woman could remain faithful to just one man."[8]

The author of the *First Letter to Timothy* writes: "They forbid marriage and enjoin abstinence from foods which God created to be received with thanksgiving by those who believe and know the truth" (*1 Tim* 4:3-4). This is why Irenaeus exhorted the church to distinguish and reject those heretics "who follow Saturninus or Marcion, proving themselves hostile to marriage by their hatred of the creator who made man and woman. They preach abstinence from marriage and so void God's pristine creation and indirectly reprove him, who made both male and female, for generating the human race. They also introduce abstinence from what is called by them animal food, being thus ungrateful to the God who made all things."[9] This Christian group, generically referred to as the *Encratites,* wanted sexual abstinence to be mandatory. The movement was quite widespread, spanning several regions. The *Acts of Paul and Thecla* (5-6) exalt the purity of the body and heart:

> Blessed are the pure in heart, for they shall see God. Blessed are they who keep their flesh undefiled, for they shall be the temple of God. Blessed are the temperate, for God will reveal himself to them. Blessed are they that abandon their secular enjoyments, for they shall be accepted of God. Blessed are they who have wives, as though they had them not, for they shall be made angels of God. . . . Blessed are the bodies and souls of virgins, for they are acceptable to God and shall not lose the reward of their virginity, for the word of their Father shall prove effectual to their salvation in the day of his Son, and they shall enjoy rest forevermore. Blessed are the bodies and souls of virgins, for they are acceptable to God and shall not lose the reward of their virginity, for the word of their Father shall prove effectual to their salvation in the day of his Son, and they shall enjoy rest forevermore.[10]

The *Acts of Thomas* follow a similar line. A married couple is told: "Remember, my children, what my brother said to you, and to whom he commended you. Know this, that if you abandon this filthy intercourse you become holy temples, pure and free from afflictions and pains—both those that are evident and those that are hidden. And you will not be weighed down with cares for life and for children, the end of which is destruction."[11]

Even Orthodox bishops are sometimes very demanding. In fact, Dionysius of Corinth, in the second half of the second century, wrote to Bishop Pinitus of Knossos "not to impose the command of chastity on the brothers as a serious necessary burden but to take into account the weakness of most."[12] Pinitus claimed that we must offer the faithful a more solid food.

We must distinguish between virgins and *continentes* (those who refrain from sexual activity) the latter of which could be either men or women. Tertullian acknowledged that he was a sinner, but then he practiced sexual abstinence: "I for my part am aware that it was not with some other flesh that I committed adulteries, and that it is not now with some other flesh that I am striving towards continence."[13] He distinguished *virgines* from *continentes,* who he notes can be either males or females, even among the pagans.[14] Married people, or people still living in marriage, could also practice sexual abstinence.[15] There are two well known cases: Paulinus of Nola and his wife Terasia, and Melania and her husband Pinianus.

The idea of spiritual marriage in which the husband and wife voluntarily renounce sexual activity for reasons of piety began to spread. It is assumed that it emerged as a paradigm modeled on the chaste union of Mary and Joseph. It started out as a spontaneous practice; however, it aroused the suspicion of the ecclesiastical authorities who pointed out various dangers with the practice. Many others, however, extolled its virtues.[16] The concept of spiritual marriage so understood is different from that which mystics such as John of the Cross and Teresa of Avila speak about. John of the Cross writes: "The spiritual marriage of the soul and the Son of God now remains to be accomplished. This is beyond all comparison a far higher state than that of betrothal, because it is a complete transformation into the Beloved; whereby they surrender each to the other the entire possession of themselves in the perfect union of love, wherein the soul becomes divine, and, by participation, God, so far as it is in this life."[17] Rather, this marriage is called mystical, which is quite different from the chaste cohabitation between two spouses.

The idea of some type of divine marriage existed prior to Christianity. Similarly, there were examples of married couples living as brother and sister. For some Christian authors such as Ambrose, Methodius of Olympus, Gregory of Nyssa, and the author of the Acts of the Martyrs, death took on the connotations of spiritual marriage.[18] Tertullian coined the expression *sponsa Christi* to designate the Christian virgin, as already mentioned.[19] The expression was a great success.[20] But this concept concerns spiritual intimacy with Christ. The expression *sponsa Christi* also applies to the Church, considered the fruitful bride of Christ, as Clement of Alexandria writes: "The Church marries no one else, for she has her husband."[21]

There were two models: couples who decided to live chastely forever, or couples who at a certain moment considered themselves brother and sister. Normally the initiative was taken by the woman. Augustine criticizes a Catholic woman, Ecdicia, who had vowed sexual abstinence without the permission and consent of her husband; her disobedience to her husband made her responsible for his adultery. She had abandoned her usual attire as a married woman to wear widow's clothing.[22]

> But this great evil—the husband's adultery—has occurred because you have not treated his heart with the prudence that you ought to have. For, even if by agreement with each other you were not having sexual intercourse, as a wife you still ought to have been mindful of your husband in other matters out of marital obedience, especially since you were both members of the body of Christ. And if you had had a husband who was not a believer, even then you ought to have acted submissively toward him in order to win him for Christ, as the apostles directed. . . . I omit the fact that I know that you took up a life of sexual abstinence not in agreement with sound teaching when he was not yet willing. For he should not have been deprived of the debt of your body that you owed him before his desire had also joined yours for that good which surpasses marital chastity. Or had you perhaps not read or heard or paid attention to the apostle saying, It

is good for a man not to touch a woman, but on account of fornication let each man have his own wife and each woman her own husband."[23]

Previously, they had decided by common agreement to abstain from marital relations: "For the more religiously he granted you something so great by imitating you, the more humbly and obediently you ought to have yielded to him in your domestic life. After all, he did not cease to be your husband because you agreed together to refrain from carnal intercourse; quite the contrary, you remained married to each other in a holier way to the extent that you harmoniously observed holier promises."[24]

Jerome distinguished various conditions of people: virgins, continents, monks, clerics, husbands, widows, continents in marriage.[25] A law issued by Valentinian I in 370 that was recorded in the Theodosian Code legislated that "ecclesiastics or those among the ecclesiastics who preferred to call themselves by the name continents, must not approach the homes of widows or orphans"[26] because they would take advantage of them and steal their property.

Respect for marriage was always defended, albeit in various ways by different Christian authors, against the extremists. Clement of Alexandria offered a very balanced position against the Encratite currents. "We therefore embrace chastity out of love for the Lord and his intrinsic beauty, sanctifying the temple of the Lord. . . . But those who, out of hatred for the flesh, wish to free themselves from conjugal relationships and the use of ordinary food, showing ingratitude, are ignorant and ungodly, and their sexual abstinence is not rationally motivated."[27] Modesty must be observed in every condition of life: "Purity occupies the first place among the virgins, the second place among those who observe sexual abstinence, the third place among the married persons. Yet purity, with its several degrees, is truly glorious in all three classes."[28] St. Ambrose writes: "No one who has chosen marriage blames integrity (virginity), and neither do those who follow virginity condemn marriage. All opponents of this norm have long been condemned by the church, that is, those who dare to dissolve the conjugal bond."[29] And John Chrysostom noted: "I am convinced that virginity is preferable to marriage, which is why I do not consider marriage to be something bad, indeed I praise it wholeheartedly."[30] Augustine writes: "By divine right sexual abstinence in itself is more excellent than marriage and consecrated virginity more excellent than marriage."[31] However, in this work dedicated to extolling the virtue of virginity, Augustine seems more concerned with defending the dignity of marriage than with defending virginity itself. We have cited three works with the same title, indicating the vast literature dedicated to the subject. We could also add that of Gregory of Nyssa, the brother of Basil of Caesarea. Gregory emphasized the coexistence in human existence of the present and the future; marriage belongs to the present age; virginity is the beginning and prophecy of the future. "The sacred aspect of virginity is truly precious in the judgment of all those who make purity the parameter of beauty; but it belongs to those whose only struggle to obtain the object of noble love is favored and helped by the grace of God."[32] Virginity is a participation in the incorruptibility of God. And Gregory of Nyssa who was himself married offered poetic praise for it.

For the fathers, virginity has value if it is freely entered into and combined with righteous faith, but not just valued in and of itself. "If we honor virgins, it is not because they are virgins, but because they are virgins consecrated to God by virtue of sexual abstinence."[33] This is why the virginity of Roman vestal virgins is not considered a virtue since it is temporary and only physical. The large number of men and women living in chastity was already proposed by apologists of the second century as an argument to show the high Christian morality that aroused admiration even from the pagans, as has already been mentioned. According to the fathers, the heretical virgins, on the other hand, should be condemned because they despise marriage, the work of God, and are unwilling to work with the creator.

Christian virginity is a form of perpetual life and of an ascetic character. Asceticism is necessary to preserve it, and it fosters freedom for contemplation. It has no active, charitable, or other purpose. It is the same personal holiness that is of benefit to the whole church. However, there is no proof that in the first three centuries there was a public vow of virginity, nor a special rite of consecration, as will be witnessed from the fourth century onwards. The first canonical sanctions against those who fail in the commitment dates back to the canons from the councils of Elvira (ca. 306) and Ancyra (314). In the fourth century the exaltation of virginity was opposed by some dissonant voices, such as Jovinian who thought that marriage and virginity had the same value. The monk Jovinian rebelled against the excessive asceticism that was taking hold in Roman Christian society at the end of the fourth century. He even convinced some virgins in Rome to get married. His position and his followers caused a lively reaction.[34]

The excessive exaltation of virginity generated in virgins a sense of superiority with respect to the common faithful. Hence the continuous call to humility as early as the second century. "If anyone is able to abide in chastity to the honor of the flesh of the Lord, let him so abide without boasting. If he boasts, he is lost; and if it be known beyond the bishop, he is polluted."[35] Augustine was very attentive to the pride of the virgins as well as the place they occupied in the church and the esteem they enjoyed from the whole community. "Mark this, virgin dedicated to God: you refused marriage, which is permitted; but now you are haughty, which is not permitted. A humble virgin is better than a humble matron, but a humble matron is better than a proud virgin. If she turns her eyes towards marriage, she is not condemned because she wants to marry, but because she had already gone beyond that, and becomes a Lot's wife by looking back."[36]

He writes concerning virgins:

> You will find undisciplined nuns; but does that mean the consecrated life itself is brought into disrepute? . . . They are proud; they are too free both with their tongues and in their drinking. Virgins they may be, but of what use is bodily integrity if the mind is debauched? . . . What good is their physical integrity if their soul is corrupt? Family life combined with humility is much more excellent than superb virginity. If, in fact, such a nun was married, she would not have the title that makes her go proud and would have a restraint that would moderate her.[37]

Women living in virginity are called holy virgins, the virgins of Christ, or the wives of Christ and God (*nubere Deo; sponsa Christi; nupta Christo*). Already in Tertullian's time the idea was elaborated of marrying Christ and the failure to do so was qualified as adultery. Origen, on the other hand, introduced the concept of spiritual fecundity which was typical of virgins who were considered excellent members of the body of Christ, that is, of the church. Since they also practiced asceticism they were compared to—or rather equated with—martyrs and thus deserved the crown of virginity just as the crown of martyrdom existed for the martyrs. This is why they occupied a reserved place in the liturgical assemblies and in the life of the church. They belonged not to the ministerial hierarchy but to the spiritual hierarchy of the church; they were a kind of spiritual aristocracy.

Cyprian of Carthage insisted on the behavior of virgins especially in public, concerned with the way they dressed so that it was without display of riches, luxury and ornaments. If their clothing was expensive and luxurious he thought that wealth and luxury should be used for the poor and not to embellish themselves but rather to create a treasure in heaven. They should not attend wedding banquets because on such occasions shameful things happened with strong words and drunkenness and lasciviousness.[38] They also should not go to mixed baths which were frequented by naked men and women.

> For this reason, therefore, the Church frequently mourns her virgins; she moans at their scandalous and detestable stories. The flower of her virgins goes out, the honor and modesty of sexual abstinence are wounded, and all her glory and dignity are desecrated. Thus, the hostile besieger insinuates with his arts; so, with the dangers that deceive by secret means. Thus, while virgins wish to be more carefully adorned, and wander with more freedom, they cease to be virgins, corrupted by stealthy dishonor; widows before being married, adulteress, not with their husband, but with Christ. In proportion as they were virgins destined for great rewards, so will they experience great punishments for the loss of their virginity.[39]

The texts and inscriptions praised the *univira—monandros* in Greek which meant the wife of a single man[40]—but the texts do not speak of a man who is the husband of a single woman.[41] *Univira* indicated the woman who after her husband has died has not remarried. In a Jewish environment it was normal to remarry after the death of the spouse, therefore the *univira* was worthy of admiration.[42] The phenomenon was especially frequent among Christians because they were advised not to remarry. The widows who were the poorest were the object of careful care by the communities. Literary texts and inscriptions demonstrating a high regard for them appear everywhere. The widow was also called *vidua Dei, Deo vixit,* meaning she was a widow of God or that she lived for God. Male mortality was higher than female mortality, and many men were also soldiers. Widowhood involved the free decision of the woman, the appreciation of the community, and economic help. One of the fundamental duties of the episcopal ministry, as was mentioned in chapter four, was the care of orphans and widows. This obligation was continually repeated to affirm one of the most important bishops' duties.

Tertullian wrote a short treatise *On the Veiling of Virgins* first in Greek and then in Latin where he discussed the veil that women should wear.[43] In Carthage at the beginning of the third century women beyond puberty—i.e. more than twelve years old—had to wear something on their heads when they were out on the street, unless they were prostitutes.[44] In church married women always covered their heads while girls did not, but the position of unmarried women was less clear. Tertullian suggested that unmarried women other than girls should be veiled in church, just as adult married women were. The veil should only cover the head and not the whole face as was already the case in Arabia at that time.[45] Tertullian considered this total coverage of the face totally barbaric[46] and entirely inappropriate. Instead, the recommended veil was the one we see in the portraits of the Roman matrons: a part of the garment covered the head and fell on both sides over the ears and onto the nape of the neck up to the shoulders.

In fourth century Western Christianity the rite of the *velatio* (imposing the veil) was introduced which, according to Pope Siricius (384-399), was to take place at Christmas, at Epiphany and at Easter. The public ceremony involved the imposition of a veil, the change of dress and a brief speech by the bishop, to whom the direction of the ceremony was reserved. At the time of the official recognition ceremony, the virgins received a veil: *sacred velamine tecta es.*[47] *Velatio* would become synonymous with public virginal consecration officially recognized by the church.[48] Ambrose's sister, Marcellina, consecrated herself to virginity before Pope Liberius in St. Peter's Basilica on Christmas Day around the year 353. The ceremony included a change of dress and a speech to the newly professed virgin:

> It is time, holy sister, to reconsider those teachings of Liberius of holy memory which you used to talk over with me. . . . For on the Nativity of our Savior in the church of the Apostle Peter

[St. Peter's Basilica] you signified your profession of virginity by your change of attire. What day could have been better to do this than the day on which the Virgin received her child! You did this with many virgins (*puellae Dei*) surrounding you who all enjoyed each other's company. This is when Liberius said to you: You my daughter have chosen an excellent marriage. Look at the great crowd that has come together for the birthday of your Spouse and no one has gone away without food.[49]

In his letter *Ad Gallos*, Pope Damasus speaks of the veiled virgins and the ceremony:

They questioned us about the veiled virgins. In case they abandoned their purpose they asked us how they should be judged as a result of this. Let us take the case of a virgin already veiled in Christ who, after having publicly professed her vow of virginity, received the veil from the bishop with the prayer of blessing—but it was found out that she has secretly committed an illicit act and wanting to defend her crime calls her husband her accomplice in adultery, in effect transforming those who were members of Christ into members of a prostitute. In this way, she who had been the bride of Christ was then called the wife of a man. In a woman of this type there are as many crimes as there are accusations: the purpose of virginity has changed, the veil was abandoned and the first promise has been betrayed and thwarted.[50]

This virgin is considered a sinner subject to severe penance. Then there was the case of the virgin who had not yet received the *velatio*. "Likewise, for a virgin who has not yet been veiled, but had intended to remain a virgin though she is not yet veiled in Christ,[51] for she had still promised she would do so, and even though she is not yet veiled by marriage in Christ the wedding must be called clandestine, for she has not kept the purpose of divine marriage, driven by blind passion toward lust."[52]

The *velatio* is an imitation of the Roman marriage rite and expresses the mystical marriage of the virgin with Christ and, as we mentioned, becomes a technical term to indicate the consecration of virgins. The veil must be imposed only on young girls who have been well formed in faith and who have behaved in an impeccable manner; it covers their head and shoulders and must be worn both in church and outside. Consecrated virgins would live with their families. That is why a whole code of conduct we heard about earlier is inculcated in them. Besides dressing modestly, not participating in wedding banquets or going to the baths, they were to devote themselves to ascetic practices and prayers. In the fourth century some of them began to live together in private houses or monasteries, giving rise to a custom that is often confused with the origins of female monasticism; others instead continued to live on their own.

Among the men, we know of the *continentes,* a technical term, which referred to all who refrain from all sexual activity, including those who struggled to preserve their chastity or married people who abstained from sexual relations for ascetic reasons. In this context we should consider a phenomenon that lasted several centuries: the *agapetae* (beloved) also called a little contemptuously the *virgines subintroductae* (the intruders, virgins introduced in secret). This term refers to virgins who consecrated themselves to God to live in chastity while also living with laymen or clerics for mutual support. This way of living later resulted in abuses and scandals, so much so that councils of the fourth century forbade it. Later this also included the cohabitation of a widow with an ascetic or cleric where the sole purpose of the cohabitation was mutual material and spiritual support, while excluding sexual intercourse. We do not know if this behavior was inspired by the idea of spiritual marriage, nor are we aware of details regarding its actual proliferation. What is certain is that this form of living together lent itself to abuse of all kinds and so there were many interventions by the fathers or councils starting from the second century onward. The critiques and denunciations are found over a vast span of time and space and the condemnations were made in quite harsh language. The numerous writings and reprimands are a sign that the phenomenon was very widespread and deeply rooted. As we already noted, men who practiced sexual abstinence did not constitute a special order (*ordo*), like virgins. Some of them could be admitted among the clergy whose members were mostly married, as can be deduced from the admittedly paltry testimonies we have from before the time of Constantine. In fact, as far as we know there was no law before the fourth century which obliged the clergy to observe celibacy, although there was a growing movement of thought in favor of celibacy already in the third century. Only second marriage if one's lawful wife died was forbidden; but even this rule was sometimes disregarded.

Paul chose celibacy for himself in order to better serve the Lord in his ministry (*1 Cor* 7:32-33). Clearly the primary motive was not ascetical but rather freedom for ministry. The idea of celibate clerics slowly asserts itself but for various reasons. The motives put forward by Tertullian and Origen for preferring an unmarried clergy were of a more cultic nature as opposed to the preference for virginity, which was largely motivated by biblical and spiritual arguments. Clement of Alexandria also added pastoral reasons. The *First Letter to Timothy* already required that the bishop and the deacon be married only once (3:3). The book of *Revelation* demonstrated a certain diffidence towards married people because only virgins follow the Lamb, who "are not contaminated with women, are indeed virgins and follow the Lamb wherever he goes" (14:4). The author thus testifies to the increase in the number of those living a celibate life. A similar rigorism was affirmed especially in Syria for admission to baptism.

Chastity relates to virginity. According to Isidore of Seville the adjective *castus* (chaste) describes those who practice perpetual abstinence not just from sex but also from lust (*qui perpetuam libidinis abstinentiam pollicebantur.*)[53] Chastity refers to a sexual lifestyle practiced by virgins, celibates and married couples. Chastity in this sense is also a value in the Greco-Roman world. In Christian texts it is often closely connected with virginity or celibacy, and also widows who are advised to remain chaste. Sometimes it was taught that marriage was so indissoluble that a second marriage was referred to as "respectable adultery." Athenagoras notes: "You would find many among us, both men and women, growing old unmarried in hope of living in closer communion with God. . . . A person should either remain as he was born or be content with one marriage, for a second marriage is only a specious adultery."[54] When we read texts about second marriage we must keep in mind the context as, for example, if one is speaking of remarriage for reasons of divorce or repudiation, or when the spouse is deceased. As Clement of Alexandria observes: "(Scripture) considers remarrying adultery while one of the separated spouses is still alive."[55]

Origen notes that in the past some leaders of the Church, in order to avoid more serious consequences, allowed remarriage while the other spouse was still living.[56] He does not reject marriage but advises the practice of sexual abstinence through the mortification of the flesh.[57] On the contrary, he criticizes the husband who could be the cause of his wife's adultery: "Whoever refrains from relations with his wife often makes himself responsible for her adulteries when he does not satisfy her desires, even if he does so under the appearance of being more chaste and self-controlled."[58]

WIDOWS AND DEACONESSES

Many texts associate orphans and widows as persons who deserve special care and attention from the bishops and the whole community. In the chapter on ministries this was one of the duties specifically mentioned as a responsibility of bishops. In chapter 14 we will further address the special assistance required of widows and orphans. In this chapter, however, we are dealing with complementary aspects of the presence of widows in the community.

In older texts, there is some uncertainty regarding widows as to whether they are the only persons needing assistance as recipients of the church's charitable service, or whether they also carried out a ministry or a service.[59] Context helps us determine the meaning. In the Gospels, Jesus' attitude towards women is quite free and positive as opposed to the way women were normally treated in his environment. He places the emphasis on equality between men and women in marriage and sexual ethics. Women follow him from Galilee to Judea. In some cases, the services that women render to Jesus and his disciples are mentioned (*Mt* 27:55; *Lk* 8:3). Luke writes: "And the twelve were with him, and also some women who had been healed of evil spirits and infirmities: Mary, called Magdalene, from whom seven demons had gone out, and Joanna, the wife of Chuza, Herod's steward, and Susanna, and many others, who provided for them out of their means" (*Lk* 8:2-3).

In other texts of the New Testament the presence of women for the work of the Gospel is very well attested: women welcome meetings at home, they are prophetesses, they provide various services; they too have "struggled" and "worked" for the Lord (*Rom* 16:1-16). In the following centuries a group of widows was officially recognized by the church and had a special place in the liturgical assemblies. They had to meet the requirements of the first letter to Timothy, which included having reached their sixtieth birthday, married only once, having the testimony of good works, being disposed to hospitality, having brought up the children well, and having helped those in need. The widow "places her hope in God and consecrates herself to prayer day and night" (*1 Tim* 5:5). Supported by the community, they certainly dedicated themselves to good works, to advising the young, and to a more intense ascetic practice. They were asked to be sexually continent and to dedicate their lives to prayer and asceticism. The term "widow" therefore indicated both a social condition and an ecclesial position complete with rights and responsibilities.

Ignatius of Antioch writes: "I greet the families of my brothers with their wives and children and the virgins called widows."[60] The sentence is not clear and is subject to different interpretations. One interpretation could be that widows were assigned to take care of orphans for the sustenance of the church and for their conduct of life as an example for virgins; or perhaps simply the widows were called virgins because they observed sexual abstinence. Polycarp writes: "We teach that our widows must be sober-minded as touching the faith of the Lord, making intercession without ceasing for all men, abstaining from all calumny, evil speaking, false witness, love of money, and every evil thing, knowing that they are God's altar, and that all sacrifices are carefully inspected, and nothing escaped Him either of their thoughts or intents or any of the secret things of the heart"[61]—perhaps meant in the sense of their dedication to prayer. The idea that the widow is an "altar of God" was also repeated by the *Didascalia*, which adds: "For the altar of God does not turn in all directions but is fixed in one place."[62] It also states that a woman be "established" as a widow and must be at least fifty years old, so that she is not tempted to marry.[63] She must worry about praying for her benefactors and for the whole Church. She should not receive the laying on of hands in her institution.[64]

From this emerges the idea that the term "widow" also indicated a special category of people within communities. Their function was not clear but they must have had precise requirements according to the text of the *First Letter to Timothy* (5:9-16), to which the teaching of the fathers refer. To be enrolled in the register of widows she must be at least 60 years old, married only once (*univira*), of impeccable conduct, but she also must show that she has done good deeds including the raising of children, the practice of hospitality and generosity towards others. Young widows should not be accepted into the "order" because they are in danger of remarrying again.[65] A daughter remembers her sweet mother in a Roman burial inscription (390-425): Regina, widowed for 60 years, and *univira* (faithful to a single husband), was particularly deserving because she had not lived at the expense of the community.[66] She died at the age of 80.

An order of widows (*ordo viduarum*) was formed who, according to Tertullian, were closely connected with clergy. They occupied a special place in liturgical assemblies. The bishop celebrated the liturgy or the Eucharist surrounded by widows who were married to only one husband.[67] Even penitents prostrated themselves before widows and priests to implore forgiveness.[68] Widows did not perform a liturgical task, but their service (*diakonia*) was that of prayer and assistance. Together with virgins and ascetics they prefigured monasticism in a certain sense.

They also carried out activities within the Church, especially for women, such as preparing them for baptism,[69] being present at their baptism, anointing them, covering them with a veil when they descended into the baptismal font. They visited the sick[70] but above all they dedicated themselves to asceticism and prayer.[71] In the East they were gradually replaced by deaconesses. Some widows gathered virgins and widows in their own palace and devoted themselves to a spiritual and ascetic life, such as Marcella and Paula in Rome.[72] Others had an important role in the upbringing of children such as Anthusa who as a young widow brought up her son Chrysostom, or Monica who took care of Augustine. They played an active role in Christianizing society.

In ancient times, the widow's condition was generally very precarious. They were quite marginalized and were included among the categories of the poor. For this reason, it was a constant of Christian teaching to demand that they be supported by the community.[73] One of the main duties of the bishops was to care for them.[74]

The female diaconate can be dated to the third century at least in some churches. It was a group separate from the widows, an innovation which partly replaced the functions of widows as well as adding new ones.[75] Although it is commonly believed that deaconesses were the widows, it must rightly be observed that while widows embraced a condition of life the others were dedicated to service tasks. According to the third century *Didascalia*, the deaconess and the widow carried out the same functions of assistance but the deaconess also carried out liturgical tasks relating to the catechumens and the baptism of women. The bishop needed to choose female helpers who would serve the women when visiting them in their private homes, and during baptism:

> ... when women descend into the [baptismal] water, are anointed with anointing oil by the [female] deacon.... But if there is a woman, and especially a female deacon, it is not convenient for women to be seen by men; ... it will be the [female] deacon, as we said before, who will do the anointing of women.... When she who is baptized comes out of the water, let her be

received by the [female] deacon who will instruct her and educate her. . . . That is why we say that the ministry of a female deacon is highly required and necessary. In fact, even our Lord and Savior was served by women such as Mary Magdalene. . . . In fact, for you [O bishop], the ministry of women as deacons is necessary in many things.[76]

From this text emerges the role of women in pastoral activities, simply because of the greater privacy of women and the greater separation between men and women that occurred in the Semitic world. In the western environment such concerns did not arise because there was more freedom and people were more accustomed to the nakedness of the public baths (*thermae*).

The fourth and fifth centuries were the period of greatest flourishing for deaconesses, especially in Syriac-speaking environments. Canon 19 of the Council of Nicaea (325) mentions the deaconesses of a heretical group that returned to the Catholic Church. The *Ecclesiastical Canons of the Apostles*[77] sometimes called by other names, was a compilation of texts prior to the fourth century which discussed female ministries in canons 24-28, albeit fictitiously reporting the opinions of the Apostles. They conclude with a sentence from James: "How then can we assign a ministry to women, if not that only ministry which consists in comforting women in need?" (can. 28). The *Apostolic Constitution,* which was composed around 380, perhaps in Antioch, takes up the *Didascalia* with some clarifications on widows and deaconesses: "Let the deaconess be a pure virgin, or at the very least a widow who has only been married once and who is faithful and honorable."[78] They assigned different functions to deaconesses in connection with women but also denied them some activities: "The deaconess does not bless or do anything that priests and deacons do, but watches over [women's] doors and assists priests during the baptism of women because of decency."[79]

In the West, the institution of the deaconesses had no success, while the institution of widows continued to exist in the East. In Syria, deaconesses, chosen from among the virgins or widows, belonged to the clergy and were ordained by the imposition of the hands by the bishop. They had a type of authority and they carried out some very specific liturgical functions such as the reception of women into the church and the anointing of women, visits to the sick, an elementary catechesis and assistance to women. They were the intermediaries between these women and the clergy. It seems, however, that the female diaconate in Eastern regions was not understood as the promotion of women, as recent publications would lead us to believe, but rather as a sign of detachment and separation between the clergy and the women themselves.

The age of the deaconess varied. The emperor Theodosius established the age of sixty. Later, the civil legislation also aligned itself with the disposition of the Council of Chalcedon (451) which fixed the age at 40 years old. Whenever we talk about written rules, however, one must always ask: "Were these rules actually applied?" We have no answers. In an Orthodox environment woman were never given the office of the presbyterate or episcopate.

ECCLESIASTICAL CELIBACY

The celibacy of the clergy has been studied historically, but normally with unbalanced attitudes on the part of both Protestants and Catholics. The former are very critical, the latter sometimes too apologetic.[80] It seems that today there is more balance except for the Protestant Phipps who presents his reconstruction as sure and certain but is actually quite sectarian.[81] In fact, in some Protestant circles, the principle of a progressive corruption of Christianity from the pure and immaculate beginnings to the present corrupted church has persisted. Today this position is dismissed by almost all scholars who tend to highlight the variety of Judaism of the first century from which Christianity came, and the variety of Christianity itself that came about through external influences. Historical research shows that the pure Christianity envisioned never existed.

We propose here a brief historical summary. Jesus spoke of disciples who leave their homes, wives, children, and relatives to follow him and that they would be rewarded in the Kingdom of Heaven (*Lk* 18:28-30). This request of Jesus is radical but in no way refers to the celibacy of the clergy. In fact, at least some apostles were married and carried out missionary activity together with their wives. The Apostle Paul writes to the Corinthians: "Do we not have the right to bring with us a wife who is a sister (i.e. a believer), as do the other apostles and the Lord's brothers and Cephas?" (*1 Cor* 9:5). This short text raises several problems, many of which are not related to celibacy. He strongly defends his apostolic action and his title of apostle and all his rights connected with that office. Luke alludes to the wives of the apostles, acknowledging that some are married like Peter and Philip. In the seventh chapter Paul had just said that he was not married, wishing that others would be like him (*1 Cor* 7:7). But he is aware that not everyone has the gift of celibacy. The so-called pastoral letters of Paul (*Titus* and *Timothy*) mention bishops, priests (the elders), and married deacons, but there is no mention of a need for sexual abstinence on their part.[82]

Tertullian was the first author to praise a celibate clergy, an attestation of a novelty because, he says, some have obtained ecclesiastical honors because of their chaste life; he does not, however, require sexual abstinence from all clerics.[83] Tertullian often talked about a single marriage for all members of the clergy as an important requirement. His main concern was that laity too only be allowed a single marriage because if they could contract a second marriage, this would shrink the pool from which the members of the clergy could be chosen. "If everyone is not required to contract a single marriage, where should we seek people who are married only once, in order to bring them into the clergy? A special order of people married only once should be established from which to choose priests."[84] He intended to refute the opinion of those who, according to the Apostle, thought that monogamy was only for clerics and not for all. Tertullian did not require sexual abstinence for married clerics. Sexual continence for bishops in the Eastern churches later on became a requirement.

In the same period Clement of Alexandria allowed for married clergy and that they should be allowed to live a normal married life.[85] A few decades later, Origen preferred a sexually continent clergy but did not speak of it as a requirement.[86] He writes: "Not only fornication, but also second marriages exclude us from ecclesiastical dignity. In fact, neither bishop, priest, nor deacon, nor widow can be married twice."[87]

The increase in the responsibilities and commitments of the bishops perhaps more than anything else influenced the choice of an unmarried clergy, i.e., a clergy that was fully committed and therefore supported by the community. Writing to the Christian community of Furnos,[88] Cyprian of Carthage (†258) demanded that the clergy devote themselves fully to prayer and divine service. This was a period of transition and not of homogeneous practice. There were concerns about how to handle the difference between clerics who must work to support themselves and clerics who were paid monthly.[89] Previously, receiving any type of sustenance was considered scandalous.

The demand for greater holiness was another reason, especially the need for a ritual purity to celebrate the Eucharist, an ancestral heritage in ancient religions and not only in the Old Testament. Ascetical motives and some expressions found in the New Testament also influenced the choice of celibacy. An anonymous text by an African bishop, attributed to Cyprian, was intended to persuade clerics, perhaps priests, who lived with women, the so-called *virgines subintroductae*, to desist from such coexistence. In an acute and detailed manner, he demonstrated the numerous difficulties in observing chastity in this kind of arrangement where they were living together, and he responds to all the objections raised by these clerics who were cohabitating.[90] Even in the case of where the cohabitation was innocent, the author highlights the scandal inherent for the faithful who would not understand the arrangement. The fact that this phenomenon already existed testifies to the existence of an unmarried clergy. Moreover, it exalts "celibate chastity" for its great spiritual advantages (chap. 39-41) while also admitting the cohabitation of clerics with "mothers or daughters or sisters or wives or relatives" (chap. 44).

The *Didascalia*, an oriental text from the first half of the third century, accepted for episcopal ordination both unmarried and married persons with families if they have governed their own homes well. But it does not prohibit sexual relations in the married clergy. Perhaps the first Western testimony that forbids them for all clerics is canon 33 of the Council of Elvira (Granada): "The bishops, the priests, the deacons who exercise the sacred ministry, must absolutely abstain from their wives and not generate children. Those who do not respect this prohibition should be deprived of the dignity of the clerical office." But when was this text written? In the early fourth century or much later? It was almost virtually ignored for centuries. The prohibition of marriage for the clergy was founded on the concept of ritual purity.[91]

At the Council of Nicaea there were plans to introduce more restrictive rules regarding celibacy for the clergy, but these were not accepted because of the opposition of Paphnutius.[92] The request of bishops—we don't know how many—who wanted to impose celibacy on higher ministers manifests the development of the concept. However, canon 3 of the council stated: "The Great Council absolutely forbids a bishop, or a priest, or a deacon, or in general a member of the clergy, to have a woman to live with them, unless it is the mother or a sister or an aunt, or one of those people above suspicion." This text has given rise to discussions on its interpretation, but it seems to indicate only women other than the cleric's wife who can live with him. Eusebius of Caesarea, who had participated in the council, wrote that clerics must refrain from marriages.[93] Civil law also sought to impose this same rule of cohabitation with women, other than mothers, daughters or sisters. It condemned the practice, widely criticized by the fathers, of the so-called *virgines subintroductae*, or *agapetae*i (*consortio sororiae appellationis*) which concerned priests and those who were clerics. The law was issued in the West by the emperor Honorius in 420 and was introduced into the Theodosian code in 439.[94]

The Council of Ancyra of 314, canon 10, introduced a new concept: the public announcement of intent to marry before ordination. It states: "They who have been made deacons, declaring when they were ordained that they must marry, because they were not able to abide so, and who afterwards have married, shall continue in their ministry, because it was conceded to them by the bishop. But if any were silent on this matter, undertaking at their ordination to abide as they were, and afterwards proceeded to marriage, these shall cease from the diaconate." This new concept was the basis for canon 1 of the Council of Neocaesarea that was held between 314 and 325 in Pontus. The canon expelled any married priest from the clergy. It did not, however, refer to the previous decision, which was supposed to be known.

This rule of celibacy began to be imposed on the whole West at the end of the fourth century with the decrees of Popes Siricius and Innocent and was taken up by numerous councils. The texts disagree, however, on the question of the cohabitation of a member of the clergy with his wife. In the East, Epiphanius[95] viewed sexual abstinence as the normal state of life for the members of the superior clergy, even for those who were married, including the subdeacons, but added the comment that "things are not so everywhere." Synesius of Cyrene who was elected Metropolitan of Ptolomais in Cyrenaica against his will, understood that he had to separate himself from his wife.[96] Justinian obligated bishops to remain unmarried or to place their wives in convents. Priests and deacons were ordered to live in chastity. He no doubt did this partly for economic reasons but also out of respect for church tradition.

In the fourth century Western church married men were still admitted to the major orders, provided, however, that they were of excellent moral character and had not committed serious sexual sins. In addition, at the time of their marriage both spouses were required to be virgins. Men who had been remarried or married to a woman who was not a virgin, such as a widow, were generally not allowed to be clerics.

Ambrose of Milan states that clerics must refrain from marital relations because they must keep the ministry pure and immaculate and they were "not to violate it with any marital relationship." But at the same time, he mentions that there were those who thought differently based on an ancient custom.[97] Augustine writes:

> The sacrament of marriage in our time has been reduced to the union between a single man and a single woman; and consequently, it is not lawful to ordain a minister of the Church except for those who have had only one wife. Some say that one should not even ordain those who have had a second wife as a catechumen or as a pagan. For it is a matter of sacrament, not of sin. . . . He who has had more than one wife has not committed sin, but in relation to the sacrament has lost a requirement, essential not to achieve the merit of a virtuous life, but to receive the seal of ecclesiastical ordination.[98]

In his letter to the bishops of Gaul Pope Damasus (366-384) takes up and strongly defends the principle of ritual purity to celebrate the divine mysteries: "For this reason, my dear friends, I admonish you, as respect for the same religion suggests, so that such impure and infidel men, in whom the holiness of the body appears contaminated by impurity and incontinence, may not be entrusted with the divine mysteries."[99] He goes on to justify his argument knowing full well that many acted differently, also appealing to previous texts unknown to us.[100]

Pope Siricius (384-399) proposed a similar rule with two letters, one to Himerius of Tarragona for all the Spanish bishops, and the other, the fruit of a Roman Council in 386 (can 9) which was sent to inform the bishops of the African provinces. The rule he promulgated was imitated by all his immediate successors. In his letter to Himerius, Siricius recognized that some by ignorance—and others fully conscious of what they were doing—did not observe sexual abstinence. The first were to be forgiven and left in their own office. However: "from now on," he wrote, "any priestly bishop or deacon who will have been found [to be sexually active]—which we hope will not happen—he should understand that from now on we are excluded from any possibility of offering forgiveness, since it is necessary to cut with iron the wounds that do not respond to the remedies of the medicines."[101]

In those same years cases concerning celibacy were discussed such as the one dealt with by Jerome in a letter to Oceanus written in the year 397.[102] Oceanus, his young friend from Rome, asked him a question about ecclesiastical discipline for married clergy. Jerome wrote: "You remember the question that you proposed. It was this: a Spanish bishop named Carterius, old in years and in the priesthood has married two wives, one before he was baptized, and, she having died, another since he has passed through the baptism. And you are of the opinion that he has violated the precept of the apostle who in his list of episcopal qualifications commands that a bishop shall be 'the husband of one wife.' I am surprised that you have pilloried an individual when the whole world is filled with persons ordained in similar circumstances; I do not mean presbyters or clergy of lower rank, but speak only of bishops of whom if I were to enumerate them all one by one I should gather a sufficient number to surpass the crowd which attended the synod of Ariminum (Rimini)."[103] Jerome, in derisive and strong language, criticizes this interpretation and adds: "He (Paul) not only says that a bishop must be the husband of one wife, but he has commanded that he must be blameless, vigilant, sober, of good behavior, given to hospitality, apt to teach, moderate, not dedicated to wine, not brutal, not quarrelsome, not stingy and not a neophyte. Yet to all these requirements we shut our eyes and notice nothing but the wives of the aspirants."[104] However, not everyone accepts this interpretation. According to Theodore of Mopsuestia and Theodoret of Cyr in their exegesis on 1 *Timothy* 3:2 and *Titus* 1:6, the apostle would not forbid the members of the clergy from getting married again but would ask them to be examples of fidelity to their spouse. Moreover, we know that in Syria in the fourth century there were bishops who had remarried.

The insistence on ritual purity by some ancient authors has prompted several modern scholars to consider it the cause of the insistence on sexual abstinence for the major clerics.[105] The topic certainly has some value, but it is not unique. In two letters Pope Innocent († 417) took up the themes of Siricius, showing the difficulty of imposing the new discipline:

> You asked me how to behave towards those who have been ordained into the ministry of deacons or into the office of priests when they reveal that they are sexually incontinent or have generated children. The teaching of the divine laws is clear in this regard, and the evident warnings of Bishop Siricius of blessed memory recall that if someone is incontinent, those who are in such ministries are deprived of all ecclesiastical honor. They are also not admitted to that ministry, which can only be carried out if one is sexually abstinent.[106]

In Africa, canon 3 of the Council of Carthage of 390 states: "We all agree that the bishop, the presbyter, and the deacon should be custodians of chastity, and also that those who serve at the altar should refrain from having relations with their wives, so that chastity is respected in all respects by all."

Leo the Great extends sexual abstinence also to the subdeacons and allows married clerics to remain with their wives but as brothers and sisters (*caritas connubiorum*). We see the gradual establishment of this practice throughout the West in this period as evidenced in numerous local councils, although there are numerous exceptions. The ordination of monks, who were already unmarried, promoted the implementation of celibacy as well. Numerous norms were elaborated so that sexual abstinence (or celibacy) was observed and protected—norms concerning the cohabitation of ministers with women who could only be close relatives or were bound by the vow of chastity.

In fact, since the beginning of the fourth century we have found both in the East and in the West an extremely varied and complex range of indications and prescriptions on this subject which are difficult to summarize. This is proof that celibacy or sexual abstinence did not immediately enter into practice and that on this point one proceeds through the data by trial and error. The so-called *Apostolic Canons*, which were so successful and composed around 380, prescribed in canon 6: "Let not a bishop, a priest, or a deacon cast off his own wife under pretense of piety; but if he does cast her off, let him be suspended. If he continues in this practice let him be deprived." In canon 51 it further states: "If any bishop, or presbyter, or deacon, or indeed any one of the sacerdotal list abstains from marriage, or flesh, or wine, not because of religious restraint but because he abhors these things, forgetting that 'all things were very good,' and that 'God made man male and female,' and blasphemously abuses the creation, either let him reform, or let him be deprived, and be cast out of the Church; and the same for any of the laity." But marriage was not possible after ordination: "Of those who come into the clergy unmarried, we permit only the readers and singers, if they have a mind, to marry afterward" (canon 26). In the fifth century the historian Socrates notes that in Thessaly:

> If a clergyman in that country, after taking orders, should sleep with his wife, whom he had legally married before his ordination, he would be deposed. In the East, indeed, all clergymen, and even the bishops themselves, abstain from their wives: but this they do of their own volition, and not by the necessity of any law; for there have been among them many bishops, who have had children by their lawful wives during their episcopate.[107]

Therefore, we can only present some general lines of thought which show substantial divergences between the two parts of the Church from the fourth century onwards, whereas previously both had the same practice. The reasons given, which were elaborated in Rome in the fourth and fifth centuries, were largely biblical but these texts were often interpreted unilaterally and taken out of context. The aim was to provide a theological justification for an already established practice and to give a biblical basis to the conviction deeply rooted in the mentality of the time that sexual purity was a necessary and daily condition for prayer so that the prayer would be answered. The same was true for the administration of the sacraments. However, there were other practical considerations such as pastors being available for everyone, the example they provided as a demonstration of spiritual fatherhood, the imitation of Christ the Virgin who was both priest and victim. There were also economic implications because the goods of the church would go not only toward the cleric's care but would also need to be shared among his children.

In the Greek-speaking churches it was established that celibates who were admitted to the major orders such as the diaconate, presbyterate and episcopate could no longer marry after ordination.[108] This legislation sometimes also applied to subdeacons but not to other members of the lower orders who were permitted to contract marriage. If, on the other hand, they were already married at the time of ordination, they could continue to live together in marriage. It is true that there were also rigorous tendencies on this point. The Council of Gangra of 340/341 condemned those who did not want to receive the sacraments from the married clergy.

The emperor Justinian defended clerical sexual abstinence as a rule. In 530, close to the beginning of his government, he published an extensive law concerning the celibacy of the clergy. "Though the sacred canons allow neither the God-beloved priests, nor the most devout deacons or subdeacons to marry after such ordination—but concede this to only the most devout cantors and lectors—we still see certain clergy despising the sacred canons and procreating children from certain women who, according to sacerdotal ordinance, they cannot marry."[109] Up to this point he cites ecclesiastical law. He orders that this ecclesiastical law should also become the civil law of the state. He adds, that beyond expulsion from the clergy, their children are not considered legitimate, being of ignominious descent. "For we determine them to be such as the laws define as born from incestuous or nefarious marriages, so they should not be considered natural children or base-free." The law goes on to say that they cannot receive inheritances because "in all ways interdicted and unworthy of succession to parents, neither they nor their mothers nor through immediate persons are they able to accept a donation from them." The alienation of church property is also at stake, in the case of married bishops.[110] Bishops should preferably be chosen from unmarried clerical candidates or monks.[111] Married bishops without children must live separated from their wives.[112]

The joining together of Eastern ecclesiastical and civil practice finds its official and definitive consecration at the Council in Trullo (or the Quinisext Council) in 691. There are several rules governing the matter,[113] but we need only highlight a few. In the sixth canon of the council it states: "Since it is declared in the apostolic canons that of those who are advanced to the clergy unmarried, only lectors and cantors are able to marry, we too maintaining this determine that from now on it is not in any way lawful for any subdeacon, deacon or presbyter after his ordination to contract matrimony. But if he shall have dared to do so, let him be deposed. And if any of those who enter the clergy wishes to be joined to a wife in lawful marriage before he is ordained subdeacon, deacon, or presbyter, let it be done."[114] Canon 13 of the same council says:

> Since we know it to be handed down as a rule of the Roman Church that those who are deemed worthy to be advanced to the diaconate or presbyterate should promise no longer to cohabit with their wives, we, preserving the ancient rule and apostolic perfection and order, will that the lawful marriages of men who are in holy orders be from this time forward firmly established, by no means dissolving their union with their wives nor depriving them of their mutual intercourse at a convenient time. And so, if anyone shall have been found worthy to be ordained subdeacon, or deacon, or presbyter, he is by no means to be prohibited from admittance to such a rank even if he is living with a lawful wife. Nor shall it be demanded of him at the time of his ordination that he promise to abstain from lawful intercourse with his wife—in order that we do not negatively affect the institution of marriage constituted by God and blessed by his presence, as the Gospel says: 'What God has joined together let no man put asunder.'... But we know, as those who assembled at Carthage (who were concerned about the honest life of the clergy) said, that subdeacons who handle the Holy Mysteries, and deacons, and presbyters should abstain from their wives according to their own way of administering the sacrament. So that what has been handed down through the Apostles and preserved by ancient custom, we too similarly maintain, knowing that there is a time for all things and especially for fasting and prayer. For it is proper that those who assist at the divine altar should be absolutely abstinent when they are handling holy things, in order that they may be able to obtain from God what they ask in sincerity.[115]

The text acknowledges the legislative divergence with the Roman church and confirms it—but at the same time testifies that married people were still ordained in the West.

The background to the whole disposition is a clear polemic against the rigorists. But even then it appears quite rigorous when it specifies that conjugal relationships are to be avoided on the days of fasting, prayer, and participation in the Eucharistic celebration. These days are not few. A married bishop is not allowed to live with his wife. The Council in Trullo (Quinisext) orders that he must leave his wife by mutual consent after episcopal ordination. The former wife must live in a monastery far from the episcopate and be supported by her spouse. The dispositions of the Council in Trullo have been followed in the Byzantine Church up to the present day.

In the West, Roman discipline was defined at the beginning of the fifth century. In this regard, it should be borne in mind that in ancient times celibacy was not the requirement so much as sexual abstinence. Therefore, a marriage contracted after ordination remained valid. Despite the commitment of the popes, the observance of celibacy was rather uncertain and depended on local situations. For example, canon 8 of the Council of Turin of 398 states: "With regard to those who have been ordained in spite of being interdicted or have had children during their ministry, the authority of the Council has decreed that they cannot be promoted to higher degrees of dignity." This decision does not allow the promotion of the cleric, but it also does not establish celibacy and recognizes the existence of married clerics with a regular married life.

The later local councils tried to generalize the Roman discipline as happened for example in the council of Agde (Gaul) in 506, which referred to the popes Siricius and Innocent (canon 9) and various Iberian canons. [116] Married clerics continue to be ordained, but the discipline was oriented towards having the spouses live separately—although it still allowed them to live together chastely. But this practice generated suspicion and reporting. Still, many clerics continued to live with their wives or concubines.

In the Latin literature after the 4th century and in the Middle Ages we find terms such as *episcopa*, *presbytera* (presbyter), *diaconissa* (*diacona*), *subdiaconissa*; [117] they are the wives of the ordained ministers with their names corresponding to their husbands' roles. These terms, depending on the time and place, may indicate women with different marital situations. They're married to clerics, and they run the houses and the family, and they're publicly respected. They could also be the widows of clerics.

In the Carolingian era, with the emperors' approval, the discipline became more stringent but was never completely observed. In fact, there were numerous legal and recognized marriages of clerics.[118] In the eleventh century there was a strong movement of renewal in the western church. In the context of the "Gregorian reform" of the eleventh century church, the celibacy of the clergy was a fundamental point of the reform. It abolished married clergy and no longer permitted their cohabitation with concubines, even if such cohabitation was legal.[119] There were two main reasons for the establishment of celibacy: doctrinal reflection and practical considerations. The celebration of the Christian mysteries required a personal purity not stained by sexual relations. There were practical reasons as well: the cost of a married clergy, the appropriation of ecclesiastical property as family property, and the creating of clerical dynasties. The champion of clerical celibacy and a great reformer was St. Peter Damian (1007-1072). In the eleventh century, the strength and influence of the reforming current in the Church prevailed.[120] The consequence was that the thought of the reformers was now transformed into canon law with numerous social and legal consequences that would be solved by the jurists.[121] Until then, the numerous repetitions of regulations had substantially sought to regulate the marriage life of clerics. Many were not married. But how many were married or simply living together with a woman, especially in small towns and in the countryside?

In canon 21 of the first Lateran Council of 1123 the clerics were forbidden to marry and any marriage that had been contracted was declared invalid.[122] It states: "We absolutely forbid priests, deacons, subdeacons and monks to have *concubines* or to contract *marriages*. We adjudge, as the sacred canons have laid down, that marriage contracts between such persons should be made void and the persons ought to undergo penance."[123] A marriage that in the past was considered illegal but valid was now considered invalid or void. Canon 6 of the Second Lateran Council of 1139 repeated the prohibition and nullity of marriage and prohibited the faithful from attending their Masses. Further, canon 7 prescribed: "Nobody is to hear the masses of those whom he knows to have wives or concubines." These texts make use of the provisions of previous popes.[124] From this moment on, ecclesiastical celibacy became increasingly important. The synthesis of canonical thought from this period can be found in *Distinctio* 28, *Prima Pars*, of the *Decretum Gratiani*. For the decretist[125] Roland Bandinelli (later Pope Alexander III) it was the solemn vow made at the laying on of hands by the bishop that made the marriage of the clergy null and void.[126]

* * *

Appendix on the Other Eastern Churches

THE GREEK-BYZANTINE CHURCHES still adhere today to the legislation arrived at by the Council in Trullo (Quinisext). This legislation is considered settled and therefore mandatory for the future. All the churches, both Orthodox and Eastern Catholic of Byzantine rite, follow these rules

The other Eastern churches had already separated at the time of the Council in Trullo in 691 and therefore did not accept those canons and prescriptions, nor did they accept Justinian's legislation on celibacy. They have developed their own tradition which mainly follows the regional practice of the first centuries. Their norms are also followed in the present day by Catholics belonging to those rites such as the Armenians, Syrians, Copts, Chaldean Catholics, and others.

We offer here a preliminary observation to help illuminate what may seem an inconsistency. In these churches just enumerated bishops and priests were often chosen from among the monks, who were not married, and so, the majority of bishops and priests were not married—but there still were and still are some clergy that are married, following the early regional practices that had been established in the ancient church. The Catholic Church has recognized the full legitimacy of the Eastern tradition having married priests, or *uxorati*, respecting the local custom. The modern legislation is in the Code of Canon Law for Eastern Churches.

In addition, the strong migration of Catholics of Eastern rites—i.e. Ukrainians and Ruthenians, Chaldean Catholics—to other continents before 1900 and especially in North America, raised the question of the ministry of the Catholic married clergy. In the past, rules had been published according to which the ministry could not be carried out by married ministers. It is estimated that about 200,000 returned to Orthodoxy as a result of this ruling. This situation, however, is currently regulated by a new document published in 2014. The document states that married priests can also exercise their ministry outside their traditional territories in places such as the Middle East and Eastern Europe—that is, they can follow their faithful to the countries where they have immigrated and even be ordained there. In India the Syro- Malankarese Orthodox Church adheres to the traditional discipline of Syrian Christians. That is, the bishop must be celibate and they have always had simple celibate priests alongside married clergy. A new marriage is not allowed, however, after the death of the spouse. There is also an obligation of abstinence when it comes to celebration of the Eucharist. The Syro-Malankarese Catholic Church which met in Rome in 1930, on the other hand, accepted the celibacy of the clergy, and so the candidates for the diaconate and presbyterate must be celibate. The Syro-Malabar Catholic Church also in its legislation has established that candidates for the diaconate and priesthood must be unmarried. Other churches of the Byzantine tradition such as the Bulgarian and Albanian churches have also chosen celibacy. The Catholic churches of the Middle East adhere to their traditions for the married clergy. Pope Benedict XVI in his 2012 Post-Synodal Apostolic Exhortation *Ecclesia in Medio Oriente*, recalled and encouraged "the ministry of married priests who are an ancient component of Eastern traditions" (n. 48).

In the Coptic Church, the bishop is chosen from among unmarried people who had never been married before. It traces the prescription back to the Council of Nicaea. The required celibacy is no doubt the reason they choose a monk as bishop. The reader (lector), known as the *Ognostis*, can marry and remarry if his legitimate wife dies. Priests can be married, but only once, because once they have a family they will have to deal with family problems (and one family's problems is enough). If he becomes a widower, he cannot marry another woman, "because he is the father of all women, and he is not allowed to marry one of his daughters." The subdeacon—or deacon's assistant—may marry but if the deacon is not married before ordination, he must remain unmarried. A married man can be ordained a deacon but if his wife dies he cannot remarry.

The Armenian Apostolic Church followed the same practice. There was no obligatory celibacy. All catholicoses were married and the throne of the catholicos was hereditary in the family until Isaac (Sahag) Bartev (354–439), who had no son to succeed him. For monks who lived in the monasteries celibacy was mandatory. Celibate monk-priests were not allowed to leave their monasteries and live in towns or villages. They had the opportunity rather to dedicate their lives to study the Bible, literature, copying manuscripts, translations, and painting. Because of their lack of culture, married priests were mere functionaries performing ministerial services. Only the celibate priests had the higher hierarchical positions within the church. Many married priests and bishops lived in the monasteries, as was the case in the Monastery of Etchmiadzin in the city of Vagharshaphat, Armenia until the last century.

It is evident that the freedom of choice concerning clergy marriage in the Armenian Church has become the norm. Married priests who are called Der Hayr (Reverend Father) and celibate priests called Hayr Soorp (Holy Father, very reverend Father) have exactly the same hierarchical rank and identical duties and responsibilities. The wife (Yeretzgin) of the priest generally plays an active role in the parish.

Overall, we can affirm that the Oriental churches still follow the ancient customs on the celibacy of the clergy.

---

1. These topics are mentioned in several chapters in relation to specific themes. For example, in the chapter on ministries for the continence of some ministers; in the chapter on assistance for widows and virgins and clerics. There are also further references in the chapter on monasticism or in the chapter on marriage. Therefore, what is said must be completed with the other information in those chapters.
2. Cf. Tertullian, *Exhortation to Chastity* 1.1; Ps. Cyprianus, *De singularitate clericorum*.
3. Tertullian, *Exhortation to Chastity* 1.4.
4. Justin, *I Apology* 15.6.
5. Athenagoras, *Embassy* 34.2.
6. From the beginning of Christianity there were those who were opposed to marriage such as the Encratites, Marcionites, Montanists, some Gnostics, Manichaeans, etc.
7. Origen, *Comm. in Mt.* 14.25; *Comm. in Rom.* 10.14.
8. Flavius Josephus, *De bello iudaico* 2.120-21.
9. Irenaeus, *Adv. haer.* 1.28.1.
10. Ch. 5-6; see 12.
11. Ch. 12, trans. H.J.W. Drijvers.
12. Eusebius, *HE* 4.23.7.
13. Dionysius, *Resurrectione* 59.3.
14. Tertullian, *De exhort.* 13.2; *De praescr.* 40.5.
15. Jerome, *Ep.* 49.2.
16. Dyan Elliott, *Spiritual Marriage. Sexual Abstinence in Medieval Wedlock* (Princeton, NJ: Princeton Univ. Press 1993).
17. John of the Cross, *Canticle of Spirituality*, 22.3.
18. A.C. Rusch, "Death as a Spiritual Marriage: Individual and Ecclesial Eschatology," *Vigiliae Chr* 26 (1972): 81-101.
19. Dyan Elliott, "Tertullian, the Angelic Life, and the Bride of Christ, in Gender and Christianity" in *Gender and Christianity in Medieval Europe: New Perspectives*, ed. Lisa Bitel, (Philadelphia: University of Pennsylvania Press, 2008):16-33. See Tertullian, *Ad uxorem* I.4.4; *De resurrectione*. 61.6; *De virginibus vel.* 16.4.
20. *EAC* 2: 694.
21. Clement of Alexandria, *Stromata* 3.74.2. R.J. DeSimone, *The Bride and the Bridegroom of the Fathers: An Anthology of Patristic Interpretations of the Song of Songs* (Rome: Institutum Patristicum Augustinianum, 2000); D.G. Hunter, "The Virgin, the Bride, and the Church: Reading Psalm 45 in Ambrose, Jerome, and Augustine," *Church History* 69:2 (2000): 281-303.

22. Augustine, *Ep.* 262.9-10.
23. Augustine, *Ep.* 262.1-2.
24. Augustine, *Ep.* 262.4.
25. Augustine, *Ep.* 48.2 and 3.10; see *Ep.* 48.10: *Si virgines primitiae Dei sunt, ergo viduae, et in matrimonio continentes, erunt post primitias, hoc est, in secundo et tertio gradu. In secundo et tertio gradu viduas ponimus et maritatas: et haeretico furore dicimur damnare nuptias?*
26. *ecclesiastici aut ex ecclesiasticis vel qui continentium se volunt nomine nuncupari, viduarum ac pupillarum domos non adeant*: CTh 16.2.20.
27. Clement of Alexandria, *Stromata* 3.59.4 -60.1.
28. Novatian, *In Praise of Purity,* 4.1.
29. Ambrose, *De virgin.* 6.34.
30. Chrysostom, *De virgin.* 9; PG 48:539.
31. Augustine, *De sancta virgin.* 1.1.
32. Gregory of Nyssa, *De virgin.* 1.
33. Augustine, *De sancta virgin.* 10.11.
34. Y.M. Duval, *L'affaire Jovinien : d'une crise de la société romaine à une crise de la pensée chrétienne à la fin du IV et au début du Ve siècle*, (Rome: Institutum Patristicum Augustinianum, 2003).
35. Ignatius, *To Polycarp* 5.2.
36. Augustine, *Enarr. in Ps.* 75.16.
37. Augustine, *Enarr. in Ps.* 99.13; cf. *Sermo* 354.9.
38. Cf. Cyprian, *De habitu* 18.
39. Cyprian, *De habitu* 20.
40. *1 Timothy* 3:2 and 12.
41. Majorie Lightman - William Zeisel, "Univira: An Example of Continuity and Change in Roman Society," *Church History* 46 (1977): 19-32; Bernhard Kötting, "Univira in Inschriften," in *Ecclesia peregrinans: das Gottesvolk unterwegs* (Münster: Aschendorf 1988), 345-55.
42. H.J. Leon, *The Jews in Ancient Rome* (Philadelphia: Jewish Publication Society of America, 1960), 122-30.
43. P. A. Gramaglia, *Tertulliano, De virginibus velandis: la condizione femminile nelle prime comunità cristiane* (Rome: Boria,1984).
44. Tertullian, *On the Veiling of Virgins* 13.
45. Tertullian, *On the Veiling of Virgins* 17.4.
46. *barbarior*: Tertullian, *On the Veiling of Virgins* 15.6.
47. Ps.-Ambrose, *Laps. virg.* 5.20.
48. Ambrose, *De virgin.* 39.
49. Ambrose, *De virgin.* 3.1.1.
50. Damasus, *Ad Gallos Episcopus* n.3.
51. *Velatio* and the term *coniugium* refer to the marriage between a man and a woman, but by extension they can also refer to the divine wedding.
52. Damasus, *Ad Gallos* 4. T. Sardella, "Vincoli e divieti matrimoniali nelle prime decretali papali e reato nell'adulterio della sponsa Christi," in *Il matrimonio dei cristiani: esegesi biblica e diritto romano* (Rome: Institutum Patristicum Augustinianum, 2009), 309-30.
53. Isidore of Seville, *Etymologies* 10.33.
54. Athenagoras, *Plea for the Christians* 33.4-5.
55. Clement of Alexandria, *Stromata* 2.145.2.
56. Origen, *Com. in Matthaeum* 14.23.
57. Origen, *In Hom. Num.* 24.2.
58. Origen. *Com. in Matthaeum* 14.24.
59. A. Nazzaro, "Figure di donne cristiane: la vedova," in *La donna nel mondo antico. Atti del II convegno*, ed. R. Uglione (Torino: Regione Piemonte, Assessorato alla cultura, 1989), 187-219; B. Thurston Bowman, *The Widows: A Women's Ministry in the Early Church* (Minneapolis: Fortress Press, 1989).
60. Ignatius, *To the Smyrnaens* 13.1.
61. Polycarp, *Letter to the Philippians* 4.3.
62. *Apostolic Constitutions* 3.6.3; cf. 2.26.8.

63. *Apostolic Constitutions* 3.1.1.
64. *Apostolic Tradition* 10.23.
65. U. E. Eisen, *Women Officeholders in Early Christianity: Epigraphical and Literary Studies* (Collegeville, MN: Liturgical Press, 2000), 143-57.
66. *Rigine vene merenti filia sua fecit / vene. Rigine matri viduae que sedit vidua annos LX et eclesa / numqua gravavit unibyra que /vixit annos LXXX mesis V / dies XXVI*. ILCV 1581; ICUR 9,24120; C. Carletti, *Iscrizioni cristiane di Roma: testimonianze di vita cristiana (secoli III-VII)* (Firenze: Centro internazionale del libro, 1986), 146-47; U. E. Eisen, *Women Officeholders*, 145-46.
67. Tertullian, *Exhortation to Chastity* 11.2.
68. Tertullian, *Exhortation to Chastity* 13.7.
69. *Statuta eccl. ant.* 12.
70. Cf. *Testamentum Dom.* 1.40; 2.4 and 8.
71. *Didascalia* 3.5.2; *Test. Dom.* 1.41; Chrysostom, *Vidua eligatur* 1.
72. Cf. Jerome, *Epp.* 127 and 108.
73. Cf. *Acts* 6; *Ap. Tradition* 50; Ignatius, *To the Smyrnaeans*.
74. *Didascalia* 2.4.1; 2.26.1-3.
75. U. E. Eisen, *Women Officeholders*, 158-98.
76. *Didascalia* 3.12.1-4.
77. CPG 1739.
78. *Apostolic Constitutions* 6.17.4.
79. *Apostolic Constitutions* 8.28.6.
80. Christian Cochini, *Origines apostoliques du célibat sacerdotal* (Paris: Lethielleux, 1981); A.M. Stickler, *Der Klerikerzölibat: Seine Entwicklungsgeschichte und seine theologischen Grundlagen* (Abensberg: Kral Verlag, 1993), (English Trans., *The Case for Clerical Celibacy: Its Historical Development and Theological Foundations* (San Francisco: Ignatius Press, 1995).)
81. Cf. W.E. Phipps, *Clerical Celibacy: The Heritage* (New York: Continuum, 2004).
82. Sydney Page, "Marital Expectations of Church Leaders in the Pastoral Epistles," *Journal for the Study of the New Testament* 50 (1993): 105-20.
83. Tertullian, *Exhortation to Chastity* 13.4.
84. Tertullian, *De monogamia* 12.
85. Clement of Alexandria, *Stromata* 3.12.90.
86. Cf. Origen, *Hom. in Lev.* 6.6.2-3.
87. Origen, *Hom. in Lucam* 17.10.
88. Cyprian, *Ep.* 1.
89. Cf. Cyprian, *Ep.* 39.5.2.
90. Ps. Cyprian, *De singularitate clericorum*, CSEL 3.3:173-220. Italian trans. C. dell'Osso, *Pseudo-Cipriano, Trattati* (Rome: Città Nuova, 2013), 219-71.
91. Cf. R. Gryson, *Les origines du célibat ecclésiastique du premier au septième siècle* (Gembloux: Duculot, 1970), 39-42.
92. Socrates, *HE* I.11. G. Rossetti, "Il matrimonio del clero nella società altomedievale," in *Il matrimonio nella società alto medievale* (Spoleto: Presso la sede del Centro, 1977) (Settimane 24), 473-567, also 482-485; 491-493.
93. Eusebius, *Demon. evang.* 1.9.
94. Theodosian Code 16.2.44; cf. Gryson, *les origines du célibat*, 101-2; 110-16. J. Dumortier, *Jean Chrysostome, Les cohabitations suspectes. Comment observer la virginité* (Paris: Société d'édition "Les belles lettres," 1955).
95. Epiphanius, *Panarion* 59.4.
96. Synesius, *Ep.* 105 to his brother.
97. Ambrose, *De officiis* 1.249.
98. Augustine, *De bono con.* 18.21.
99. Damasus, *Ad Gallos* 7.
100. D. Callam, "Clerical Continence in the Fourth Century: Three Papal Decretals," *Theological Studies* 41 (1980): 3-50.
101. Siricius, *Letter to Himerius* 7.
102. Oceanus is called *filius* and *frater*, an intimate of Jerome (see *Ep.* 61.3) who writes to him several times.
103. Jerome, *Ep.* 69.2.

104. Jerome, *Ep.* 69.9.
105. R. Price in TRE 36 (2004) 724 (valid argument); D. Hunter, *Marriage, Celibacy, and Heresy in Ancient Christianity: The Jovinianist Controversy* (Oxford: Oxford University Press, 2007), 213-17, recognizes its importance, but does not consider ritual purity as the primary topic.
106. Innocent, *Ep. to Exuperius* 1; cf. *Ep. to Victricus* 12
107. Socrates, *HE* 5.22: PG 67:639.
108. R. Cholij, *Clerical Celibacy in East and West* (Leominster, Herefordshire: Fowler-Wright Books, 1988). R. Girgis, "Il clero coniugato nelle disposizioni antiche delle chiese orientali," *Studia Or. Christiana* 44 (2011): 81-168.
109. *Codex Iustinianus* 1.3.44. P.R. Coleman-Norton, *Roman State and Christian Church: A Collection of Legal Documents to A.D. 535* (London: S.P.C.K., 1966), 1078.
110. *Codex Iustinianus* 1.3.41.
111. *Novella* 6.1.
112. *Novella* 123.29, of 546.
113. R.M.T. Cholij, "Married Clergy and Ecclesiastical Continence in Light of the Council of Trullo (691)," *Annuarium Historiae Conciliorum* 19 (1987): 71-230; 241-99.
114. NPNF 2 14:364 (slightly altered).
115. NPNF 2 14:371 (slightly altered).
116. See Gerona in 517, canons 6 and 7; the Council of Toledo in 527, canon 1; the III Council of Toledo in 589, canon 5; the Council of Seville in 590, canon 3; etc. Tours (567), canons. 13 (12), 20 (19). Corpus Christianorum 148 A, 180-1, 183-4. Auxerre (561-605), c. 21. Ibid, 268.
117. Cf. A. Souter, *A Glossary of Later Latin to 600 A.D.* (Oxford: Clarendon Press, 1949), s.v.; CIL 10,8079 = Diehl 1192; M. Buonocore, *Inscriptiones Christianae Italiae* (Bari: Edipuglia, 1987), 24; *Codex Diplmaticus Lang.* 125.11; Atto episcopus Vercellensis 303.23; Gregory the Great, *Dial.* 4.2. Du Cange, *Glossarium mediæ et infimæ latinitatis* 6.488-89; J.F. Niermayer, *Mediae latinitatis lexicon minus* (Leiden: E.J. Brill, 2002), 2:1091-92.
118. G. Rossetti, *Il matrimonio del clero*, 533-537; T. di Carpegna Falconieri, "Il matrimonio e il concubinato presso il clero romano (Secoli VIII-XII)," *Studi Storici* 41 (2000): 943-71.
119. Pope Gregory VII (1073-1085), which begins a reform of the church, and in particular of the high and low clergy.
120. J.A. Brundage, *Law, Sex and Christian Society in Medieval Europe* (Chicago: University of Chicago Press, 1987), 212-23.
121. F. Liotta, *La continenza dei chierici nel pensiero canonistico classico: Da Graziano a Gregorio IX* (Milan: A. Giuffrè, 1971).
122. The date of this canon is discussed in J. Gaudemet, "Le célibat ecclésiastique. Le droit et la pratique du XIe au XIIIe siècle: Zeit. der Savigny-Stiftung für Rechtsgeschichte," *Kanonistische Abteilung* 99 (1982): 1-31.
123. https://www.papalencyclicals.net/councils/ecum09.htm.
124. C. Alzati, "A proposito del clero coniugato e uso del matrimonio nella Milano alto medievale," in *Società, istituzioni, spiritualità. Studi in onore di C. Violante* (Spoleto: Centro italiano di studi sull'alto Medioevo, 1995), 79-92; St. Dusil, "The Emerging Jurisprudence, the Second Lateran Council of 1139 and the Development of Canonical Impediments," in *The Use of Canon Law in Ecclesiastical Administration, 1000-1234*, ed. Melodie Eichbauer and Danica Summerlin (Leiden: Brill, 2019), 140-58.
125. In canon law this term refers to one specializing in the study of decretals.
126. Comment to the *Causa XXVII*, see also *Decretum Gratiani*.

CHAPTER 9

THE SINNER, PENANCE, EXCOMMUNICATION AND ANOINTING OF THE SICK

ECCLESIAL PENANCE IN THE FIRST THREE CENTURIES

THE EARLY CHRISTIAN COMMUNITY UNDERSTOOD ITSELF AS A LIVING COMMUNION BOTH among its members and with God, and so it is the place of salvation. It is a "communion of saints," "a chosen people," because it is a community of people freely forgiven by God. Divine forgiveness belongs to the core of the gospel and bringing that gospel to everyone is at the heart of the mission of the church: "And in [Christ's] name repentance for the forgiveness of sins shall be preached to all nations, beginning with Jerusalem" (*Lk* 24:47).[1] The human being's response to the offering of divine forgiveness must be that of a new life, of a radical reorientation. However, even after the bestowal of forgiveness through baptism, the congregation experiences the fact that human and divine fellowship can be broken by some through infidelity even though they are close to Jesus (*Mt* 18:22, 25). These repentant people, too, can obtain forgiveness again, which therefore concerns not only those who convert for the first time but also the members of the community.[2]

In granting forgiveness or in refusing forgiveness, the community plays a role: "If another member of the church sins against you, go and point out the fault when the two of you are alone. If the member listens to you, you have regained that one. But if you are not listened to, take one or two others along with you, so that every word may be confirmed by the evidence of two or three witnesses. If the member refuses to listen to them, tell it to the church; and if the offender refuses to listen even to the church, let such a one be to you as a Gentile and a tax collector. Truly I tell you, whatever you bind on earth will be bound in heaven, and whatever you loose on earth will be loosed in heaven" (*Mt* 18:15-18).[3]

Now if Jesus' disciples have the authority to forgive they also have the authority not to forgive.[4] Historically speaking, one cannot deduce apodictically from the biblical texts the institution of the sacrament of penance, as it was understood later by the Church. But neither do the scriptures exclude it—indeed in some ways they established it. It is certain, however, that from the very beginning many texts have been invoked to legitimize the penitential practice of granting forgiveness.

In the apostolic and post-apostolic period, the granting of forgiveness and the readmission to the full life of the community of Christians who had seriously sinned was not an issue. Since the communities were small, full of enthusiasm and close knit, infidelity in faith or behavior was rather rare—but there were exceptions. When public sin did occur, the whole community was concerned about the repentance of the guilty party,[5] praying for him[6] and correcting one another.[7] Community leaders were more involved than others in bringing the sinners to repentance.[8] All failings were forgivable without exception: "For after you have made known to them these words which my Lord has commanded me to reveal to you, then shall they be forgiven all the sins which in former times they committed, and forgiveness will be granted to all the saints who have sinned even to the present day, if they repent with all their heart, and drive all doubts from their minds."[9] This same attitude was expressed in almost all the writings of the first and second centuries, including the apocryphal writings.[10] On the contrary, it seems that penance could be repeated, both because there was no testimony contrary to its repetition and because church practice at the time was clearly open to offering forgiveness repeatedly. In fact, Tertullian attests that Marcion was expelled several times from the community and reintegrated before his definitive expulsion.[11] If the guilty party did not show signs of repentance, he was excluded from the community.[12] This exclusion carried out by its leaders was a manifestation of the power to bind and loose, that is, to exclude or readmit the guilty.[13] Clement's *Letter to the Corinthians* explicitly speaks of the judgment of the community:

> Who then among you is noble-minded? Who compassionate? Who full of love? Let him declare, 'If on my account sedition and disagreement and schisms have arisen, I will depart, I will go away wherever you desire, and I will do whatever the majority commands. Only let the flock of Christ live on terms of peace with the presbyters set over it.' He that acts in this way shall procure to himself great glory in the Lord and every place will welcome him. For 'the earth is the Lord's, and the fullness thereof.' Those who live a godly life that is never to be repented of both have done and always will do these things.[14]

The judgment of the community was important because, since it was a place of salvation, divine forgiveness was linked to readmission or exclusion from the *ecclesia*: "For it is better for you that you should occupy a humble but honorable place in the flock of Christ, than that, being highly exalted, you should be cast out from the hope of His people. For thus speaks all-virtuous Wisdom."[15] Ignatius writes something similar to the Christians of Philadelphia: "All those who belong to God and to Christ are united to the bishop, and all those who do penance and come to the unity of the church will also belong to God."[16]

These general observations concerning the first and early second centuries introduce us to one of the most delicate problems of the ancient church: the penitential question which from the middle of the second century became more complicated and evolved until the practice stabilized in the third and fourth centuries in both the Eastern and Western churches. In the Latin speaking countries a radical change took place in the sixth and seventh centuries, and in the twelfth century penance took on features that have endured up to the present day. Even in the Eastern church, as we will see, there was a development almost parallel to that of the West.

Penance in ancient Christianity can be studied from various angles: historical, theological, sociological, or liturgical. Choosing one of these means limiting its broader understanding. On the other hand, a coordinated exposition according to the four views requires more space than is allowed here. I believe, however, at the cost of leaving important elements in the shadows, that this is the best approach, and I will try to follow it, taking care to highlight more of the many problems that were gradually posed and solved—or not solved.

As the number of members of the Christian community grew, including the introduction of people baptized at an early age, there was a loss of internal cohesion and a certain decrease in fervor. In this context, the cases of serious shortcomings of those who "fall into the condition of the pagans" were not exceptional.[17] An unknown preacher of the second century defined the church as "a den of thieves."[18] Hermas repeatedly denounced the conduct of many Christians, referring to them as apostates, traitors of the church, slanderers, people who have grown rich and become arrogant and proud, who "have abandoned the truth, have separated from the just, have lived with the pagans and have found the pagan's way of life more comfortable."[19] It is in the context of these developments that the first major problem for the community arose: Is there the possibility of a post-baptismal penance and consequent readmission into the church? A very uncompromising stream of thought answered this question: There is no possibility of granting any forgiveness:

> I have heard, Sir, from certain teachers, that there is no other repentance except that which took place when we went down into the water and obtained remission of our former sins. He said to me: You have heard well, for so it is. For whoever has received remission of sins ought no

longer sin but live in purity. But since you accurately enquire about everything, I will declare to you this also so as to give no excuse to those who shall believe from this point on, or those who have already believed in the Lord. For those who have already believed, or shall in the future believe, have no repentance for sins, but have only remission of their former sins."[20]

This testimony concerns Rome, but the same was true of Pontus where Bishop Palmas of Amastris[21] was exhorted by Dionysius of Corinth "to receive (in the church) those who repent of any fall, whether it be an [ordinary] sin or even a sin of heresy."[22] Despite this opinion reported by Hermas and circulating in Rome, we know that those who sinned were readmitted—the two most notorious cases being that of Marcion and that of Natalius.[23] Because Marcion persisted in what he taught he was excommunicated at a certain moment. In chapter 8 of the *Acts of Peter* those who do penance immediately obtain forgiveness—even those who followed Simon Magus and apostatized. The same chapter also reports that a certain Marcellus, a great benefactor of the poor of every kind, at a certain point also followed Simon Magus. Peter then lashes out against Satan, after the community has interceded for him. Then many repent.[24] In chapter 18 we read that Eubula also converted. Peter tells her that she will be saved in Christ if she does penance with all her heart.

A few decades later at the beginning of the third century Tertullian, who had previously admitted the possibility of reconciliation, fiercely criticized the practice of readmission into the church in a pamphlet titled *De pudicitia*, written precisely with this in mind. In the same years in Rome, the author of a work against heresies—the authorship is usually identified with Hippolytus—attacked Bishop Callistus[25] for similar reasons. The rigorist perspective presents a range of nuances, ranging from those who refuse forgiveness for all sins considered serious, to those who exclude only some specific faults such as adultery, apostasy or the like. However, the rigorist teaching has no serious biblical or theological arguments in its favor but only psychological justifications, since it assumes that indulgence can open the door to other sins, as Tertullian himself recognizes in a moment of sincerity: "The church can forgive sins, but I will not do so for fear that others will then be committed."[26]

Although the rigorist perspective ended up being rejected in its entirety and in its motivations, it still left its mark on the penitential discipline that was elaborated in the last decades of the second century and at the beginning of the third.[27] Despite the differences between the local communities, the larger church continued to admit the possibility of forgiveness but did end up accepting the innovation that we find in Hermas for the first time, that is, that post-baptismal penance was considered possible only once in life for truly serious sins: "One who sinned and repented must be received, yet not often, for there is but one repentance for the servants of God."[28] This affirmation became a fixed norm throughout antiquity up to the Middle Ages in both the West and the East. Pope Siricius († 26 November 399) acknowledged that there were no exceptions: "They do not have the remedy of penance," he wrote.[29] Canon 11 of the Council of Toledo in 589 refused to grant a second pardon. For recidivists, forgiveness from God was not excluded but the church no longer reconciled them with itself.[30]

The only dissonant voice in the third century for this severe practice seems to have been the *Didascalia*, which has beautiful pages devoted to the duties of the bishop towards sinners and in no case speaks of a single forgiveness. Perhaps this work echoes an older tradition and is not yet imbued with rigorism.[31] At the end of the second century the discipline of penance developed in tandem with the catechumenate.[32] The discipline was both rigorous and extended over a long period of time. It was commonly referred to as ecclesiastical or canonical penance in order to distinguish it from personal penance or that practiced by the catechumens. It involved fasting, prayers, almsgiving and other mortifications staggered over a period of time. Tertullian writes:

> In this second and only (remaining) penance, the procedure is more rigorous and the probation period more laborious in order that it may not be exhibited in the conscience alone, but may likewise be carried out in some (external) act. This act, which is more usually expressed and commonly spoken of under a Greek name, is *exomologesis*, whereby we confess our sins to the Lord, not indeed as if He were ignorant of them but inasmuch as by confession satisfaction is settled, of confession repentance is born; by repentance God is appeased."[33]

In ancient terminology it is also called *poenitentia secunda* (second penance) in contrast to baptismal penance, which is considered the first penance. This is why penance must always be seen in relation to baptism where the forgiveness of sins (Gk. ἄφεσις) is free, while now penance is "severe and [offered] in tears.[34]

The parallel with baptism reinforces the idea of the uniqueness of post-baptismal penance: "For as there is only one baptism, so there is only one course of penance, so far as the outward practice goes" (*sicut unum baptismum, ita una paenitentia quae tamen publice agitur*).[35] But true biblical arguments in favor of only one course of penance cannot be invoked, and so Augustine himself honestly recognized that unrepeatability was only for prudential and psychological reasons.[36] Furthermore, great importance was attached to external penitential acts (*satisfactio*) both to obtain divine forgiveness and to demonstrate to the community the sincerity of one's repentance.[37]

But what value do individual elements such as the internal acts, external acts, reconciliation, or absolution have in the penitential process? The ancients did not underestimate the internal aspect of conversion,[38] and so a repentant sinner in grave danger of death was generally granted reconciliation even with the obligation, once healed, that he or she would fulfill external practices. However, by stressing these acts (*satisfactio*) that were considered essential, they used the term penance to express the whole process. During the eighth and ninth centuries of the Middle Ages the emphasis shifted to the confession of sins, considered in itself already as a *satisfactio*. It is thus understood that during that time there was a possibility that one could confess to a layman in case of necessity or lack of a priest—although the layman had no power to absolve. In this context of theological reflection, the term *confessio* began to replace the older term of penance. The ancient discipline was slowly being overturned as periodic confession was introduced, with the consequent shift of *satisfactio* occurring after confession and reconciliation (*absolution*) had taken place. In the popular mind this last point about reconciliation has always remained alive, so that even today elderly women use the word reconciliation for confession. With the recent reform of the second Vatican Council, a certain return to the old terminology has been proposed.

A more delicate problem concerns the very forgiveness of sins itself. It was a common belief that God would grant forgiveness only after personal atonement had been made. What, therefore, is the function of ecclesial reconciliation? This question is actually more of a medieval and modern problem since the ancients did not use these terms in the questions they asked. For them, both the personal element and the act of reconciliation granted by the church were essential, according to the classic expression of Leo the Great:

> The dispositions of divine goodness are made in such a way that God's forgiveness cannot be obtained except by the prayers of priests (bishops). The mediator between God and men, the man Jesus Christ, gave the leaders of his church the power to grant penance to repentant sinners and to readmit them, through reconciliation, to the communion of the sacraments, as soon as they have purified themselves with a salutary atonement (*satisfactio*). The Savior himself is continually involved in this work of salvation, and is never a stranger to what his ministers do. For he has said: "And behold, I am with you every day until the end of the world - *Mt* 28:20."[39]

While not excluding in general that the repentant sinner can obtain divine forgiveness, the fathers argue that the *pax ecclesiae* should not be absent either, because only those who are living members of the church can obtain salvation.[40] The church is a mediator and a place of salvation for which its forgiveness is essential.[41] Augustine deepens the doctrine of reconciliation with an example: God alone works the resurrection of Lazarus, but it is the church that frees him from the bandages, that is, from the guilt of sin (*reatus peccati*).[42] He expresses this even more clearly elsewhere: "The peace of the Church looses sins, and estrangement from the Church retains them, not according to the will of men, but according to the will of God and the prayers of the saints who are spiritual, who 'judge all things, but themselves are judged of no man.'"[43]

Since the beginning of the third century, the texts used to justify this authority have varied. The text from Matthew 16:18-19 is one such text: "I tell you, you are Peter, and on this rock, I will build my church, and the powers of death shall not prevail against it. I will give you the keys of the kingdom of heaven, and whatever you bind on earth shall be bound in heaven, and whatever you loose on earth shall be loosed in heaven." Matthew 18:18, already mentioned above, is another text in which the same concept is repeated but extended to others who also have the same authority as Peter in binding and in loosing.[44] Augustine points out that this authority belongs to the whole church:

> For the whole body of the saints, therefore, inseparably belonging to the body of Christ, and for their safe pilotage through the present tempestuous life, did Peter, the first of the apostles, receive the keys of the kingdom of heaven for the binding and loosing of sins. And for the same congregation of saints, in reference to the perfect repose in the bosom of that mysterious life to come did the evangelist John recline on the breast of Christ. For it is not Peter alone but the whole Church that binds and looses sins.[45]

However, the binding and loosing was exercised by the head of the community, that is, by the bishop and only rarely by his delegate, the simple priests. This is a constant datum of the ancient tradition.[46] But from the fourth and fifth centuries onward, the delegation of this binding and loosing to priests became more and more frequent, until it later became the norm.

The only discordant voice on episcopal authority is that of Tertullian after he had converted to Montanism. He asserts that this authority belongs to the Church of the Spirit.[47] Leaving aside this polemical statement, we know that the martyrs and confessors in the first three centuries were considered to be filled with the Spirit. They played an important role in the readmission of sinners into the church. Perhaps at the beginning they could even grant the *pax ecclesiae*, that is, reconciliation, but the role recognized and approved was only that of "interceding" for the guilty. In the Byzantine East the role of the martyrs was assumed by the *viri Dei*, by the monks, who, as men filled with the Spirit of God, could receive the confession of sinners and grant forgiveness.[48]

Ancient ecclesiastical penance was public as far as *satisfactio* was concerned—certainly not because of a public confession of sins before the community, even if in some cases this did happen. It was also done in public for serious sins that were not obvious. In this case it was necessary for sinners to confess their sins to the leaders of the community in private or in public. This already appears clear at the beginning of the third century: "The sinner is not ashamed to confess his sin to a priest of the Lord and ask for remedy."[49] Elsewhere Origen himself advised to look carefully for the person to whom the faithful should confess his sin, because such a person must be like an expert physician.[50] Leo the Great condemned the practice of revealing secretly confessed sins in public: "This is a way of acting contrary to the apostolic dispositions, a way that has been unduly established, as I knew earlier, and whose suppression I order. . . . It is sufficient, in fact, that the faults be indicated to the bishop only, in a secret conversation."[51] The existence of a completely private or secret ecclesiastical penance, the subject of countless controversies between Catholics and Protestants, is today commonly denied, and rightly so. It was only introduced in the early Middle Ages.

For what sins was this laborious penance necessary? We can find in the fathers a terminology similar to ours, which distinguishes between mortal sins (*peccata mortalia, capitalia, graviora*, etc.) and venial sins (*peccata leviora, venialia, quotidiana*, etc.). Ecclesiastical penance was necessary for mortal sins even if they were hidden. For everyday venial sins, the daily penance which every good Christian had to do with fasting, almsgiving, prayers, etc. was sufficient.[52] And so they drew up lists of sins, inspired by those of the New Testament and the Decalogue. There was no homogeneity among the various lists offered to us by the fathers since they all had different ways of dealing with them. Among the capital sins (*peccata capitalia*), they placed in descending order the following: apostasy, idolatry, murder, adultery and fornication, perjury, circus performances, etc., normally excluding sins committed only in thought. Despite the similarity of terminology between antiquity and today, there is a considerable difference in the conception of what constituted a grave sin. Our modern sensibilities are much more demanding and would not hesitate to include among the grave sins those which occur in the heart or mind—sins which the ancients would have considered only *venialia*.

THE EVOLUTION OF PENANCE IN THE FOURTH TO SIXTH CENTURIES

A methodological error in the reconstruction of the history of penance is the generalization of some texts and practices. I have to say to myself often that I must be careful not to generalize too much. For Christian antiquity there are no manuals on morals, or treatises on theological ethics, or even canon law. There are only scattered norms derived from local councils. These rules were truly local and were not widely used elsewhere. Rules established by Eastern local councils only came to be known in the West in the fifth century, and those of the Western councils would never be known in the East. The exceptions are texts of African Councils which were translated into Greek in the sixth century. Any reconstruction is therefore impressionistic.

After Constantine, penitential discipline developed and established itself with more precise and homogeneous rules compared to the previous period. The new political and social situation also brought about a change in the members of the ecclesial community. Augustine (†428) was disconsolate when he observed: "How many seek Jesus for no other object but that

He may bestow on them a temporal benefit! One has a business on hand, he seeks the intercession of the clergy; another is oppressed by one more powerful than himself, he flies to the church. Another desires intervention in his behalf with one with whom he has little influence. One in this way, one in that, the church is daily filled with such people. Jesus is scarcely sought after for Jesus' sake."[53] Already in the third century Origen regretted the primitive fervor and noted at the time a sharp drop in the ethical standard of Christians: "Once upon a time there were few faithful, but they were truly faithful, following the rigorous and narrow path that leads to life. Now that we are many, since it is not possible that there are many chosen . . . among the multitude, to whom the true worship of God is taught, there are very few who come to the election of God and to the beatitudes."[54] At the time of Augustine, things had changed considerably for the worse than at the time of Origen, as can be seen from the text cited above.

In addition to political and social factors, the extension of the administering of baptism to children—and this even more so in the following two centuries—also influenced the fact that they were not well trained in Christian doctrine and morals and did not experience the intense catechumenal process that adult converts experienced.[55] Moreover, the Christian community itself was no longer a closed group where people watched over one another, and possibly even corrected each other fraternally—so that the greater the number of sinners, the less control there is. Fewer people embraced penitential discipline than those who would need it. Augustine complained that so many gravely illicit behaviors had entered among Christians that it was getting to the point of becoming normal, for which the ecclesiastical authorities themselves had become more tolerant: "So that for such sins not only do we not dare to excommunicate a lay person, but not even degrade a cleric."[56]

The change and lowering of the ethical standard of Christians did not correspond to an adaptation of penitential discipline to ways more suited to the new situation. On the contrary, there was a move towards making penitential discipline even more rigid and structured. The result was that for all intents and purposes it ended up being reserved mainly for the dying. Very severe penitential forms that were appropriate for heroic situations and for communities with strong internal unity cannot be applied to large and amorphous masses. Unfortunately, however, this is what was claimed was needed, so that those forms became practically unusable. In fact, those that had been attempts at a solution in the previous two centuries now tended to become legal norms: numerous Eastern and Western Councils issued canons.[57] In order to respond to new situations and needs, some fathers wrote letters or treatises on penance. The first treatises in the East acquired great canonical value. In the West there were the decrees of the popes, especially of Siricius († 399), Innocent († 417) and Leo the Great († 461). These decrees had no general effect at the time, something which they would acquire only much later and only in the Latin West.

The difficulties of reconciliation for the sins committed after baptism led to the postponement of penance indefinitely. Already in the third century some postponed penance until the moment of death[58] or when afflicted with a serious illness with little hope of a cure, thus making it almost a sacrament reserved for the dying. Moreover, this situation also pushed people to postpone baptism as much as possible. Some chose to remain catechumens, such as Ambrose and Augustine, rather than be baptized. Some even postponed baptism to the point of death, as evidenced by numerous funerary inscriptions of neophytes. Those who were baptized at the time of death or during a serious illness were referred to as *clinici*. In moments of invasion by barbarians or of common dangers, we know of catechumens "for life" who crowded the churches to receive baptism.[59] The fathers therefore urged that baptism should not be delayed too long, while the councils concerned themselves with the seriously ill, allowing even a simple believer to administer penance to them. Usually, once healed, the laying on of hands by the bishop was required to give the gift of the Holy Spirit.

Having also mentioned the theological aspects related to the discussions on penance, it is now time to focus more attention on its sociological and liturgical aspects, keeping in mind that penance in its essential structure remained the same: unique, public, with exclusion from the Eucharist, completion of various penances and final reconciliation. The practice was as follows: the guilty person asked for penance (*paenitentiam petere*),[60] then received the laying on of hands and his penance was specified in terms of what he must do (*dare paenitentiam*). He thus became part of the *ordo paenitentium*, a group that occupied a special place reserved for them in the assembly. Those who had been officially incorporated into this *ordo* could be present at the Eucharistic liturgy, unlike the catechumens, who had to leave after the liturgy of the word. The penitents, however, had to remain on their knees while the faithful stood.[61] The entrance into the *ordo* of penitents usually took place at the beginning of Lent since reconciliation took place before the celebration of Easter. This great feast was a moment of great celebration because many were baptized during the Easter vigil the night before, and those penitents judged worthy were readmitted to the Eucharist on Holy Thursday. In this way everyone could celebrate Easter with great joy.

During the probationary period, the community prayed for them and they also received a laying on of hands:

> There are a great many penitents here. When hands are laid on them, there is an extremely long line. 'Pray, penitents—and the penitents go out to pray.' I examine the penitents and I find people living evil lives. How can you be sorry for what you go on doing? If you're sorry, don't do it. If you go on doing it, though, the name's wrong, the crime remains. Some people have asked for a place among the penitents themselves (*locus paenitentiae*) while others have been excommunicated by me and reduced to the penitents' place. And those who asked for it themselves want

to go on doing what they were doing, and those who have been excommunicated by me and reduced to the penitents' corner don't want to rise from there, as though the penitents' corner was a really choice spot. It ought to be a place for humility, and instead it becomes a place for iniquity.[62]

Unlike in the West, in Asia Minor penitents were divided into two categories. There were the *flentes* (the weepers) who remained outside the church begging the faithful who were entering to pray for them. And then there were the real penitents who, in turn, were divided into three subcategories: the *audientes* (the hearers) who, like the catechumens, could only participate in the liturgy of the word and then were dismissed; the *substrati* (those lying on the ground); and finally the *stantes* (those who stood with the faithful). Only *the stantes* remained in the church for the whole time of the Eucharistic liturgy, naturally without being able to receive the Eucharist.

In the fourth century, a casuistry began to emerge concerning the duration of time that one spent as a penitent according to the various types of sins. The duration could be several years or longer depending on the gravity of the sin. For example, canons 21 and 22 of the Council of Ancyra of 314 imposed a lifetime penance for willful murder and ten years for an abortion, while for sexual sins and idolatry the duration of the penance ranged from two to thirty years, depending on the circumstances. Basil prescribed ten years for an abortion and twenty years for murder. The fourth century Syrian *Apostolic Constitutions* were much more indulgent. In the West there was even more rigor because in both the fifth century and the sixth there were prescribed penances that lasted a lifetime.

In the absence of a common canon law, the bishops had great freedom in determining the length of penance, taking into account above all the subjective conditions of the guilty party, because "if one has committed such a crime as to deserve to be separated from the body of Christ, in doing penance one must not look so much at the amount of time as at the intensity of the pain."[63] "In what concerns the evaluation of their sins, it is up to the bishop to do so. Consider the accusation against the penitent, but also his tears and his moans."[64] In a letter to Paulinus of Nola, Augustine set out his concerns in this regard. The following is an excerpt:

> What shall I say about punishing or not punishing? For we want all of this to contribute to the salvation of those who we judge should be punished or not punished. What a deep and dark question it is: what the limit in punishing should be, not only in terms of the quality and quantity of the sins, but also in terms of the particular strength of minds—what anyone might endure or what he might refuse—for fear not only that he might not make any progress, but also that he might give up! Of those who fear an impending punishment, which human beings generally fear, I do not know whether more are corrected than take a turn for the worse. What shall I

say about the fact that it often happens that, when you punish someone, that person perishes, but if you leave him unpunished, someone else perishes? I myself admit that I sin daily in these matters.[65]

Canon 13 of the Council of Nicaea of 325 had established the following concerning those who were dying:

> Concerning those who are likely departing, the ancient and canonical law is still to be maintained that, if anyone be at the point of death, he must not be deprived of the last and most indispensable Viaticum. But, if anyone should be restored to health again who has received the communion when his life was despaired of, let him remain among those who communicate in prayers only. But in general, and in the case of anyone who is likely to die and who asks to receive the Eucharist, let the bishop, after examination made, give it to him.

This rule was imposed only gradually since it upset not only the practice of various churches, but also the very conception of penance which required a long previous expiation. For example, in rigorist Gaul it only came into force in the fifth century, especially through the interventions of Popes Innocent I (†417) and Celestine I (†432).

In the West penance became particularly burdensome and intolerable to the faithful due to a series of interdicts affecting those under penance. Such interdicts remained valid even after the penitents had been reconciled. Among these lifetime prohibitions we find inadmissibility to civic office or military service, and prohibition from any involvement in trade or the clerical state. Another stipulation might be perpetual sexual abstinence, even for married people. These strict prohibitions were particularly applied in Gaul and Spain, while Leo the Great on the other hand tried to be more indulgent.[66] The result of such severity was that almost no one accepted canonical penance except in the final phase of their lives. Indeed, the important Council of Gaul in 506 took note of the situation that had arisen and established that "it would be difficult to grant penance to those who were still young because of the weakness of their age."[67] There were also substitutes for public penance, such as embracing monastic life—so highly esteemed at the time that it was considered a second baptism. Or one could become a *conversi*, that is, one who leads a private ascetic life. In both cases, once these states of life had been embraced, a long period of reparation was not necessary and one was immediately readmitted to the Eucharist. However—and this is important—since there was no centralized church, these norms were not always applied according to the rigor of the actual text that contained them.

From the beginning of the fourth century, the higher clergy both in the West and in the East were not granted penance, Instead, they were demoted, which would later be accompanied by retreat in solitude which usually took place in monasteries: "It is contrary to the customs of the Church that ordained clerics, priests or deacons, may receive the remedy of penance for their sins by the laying on of hands. . . . In order to deserve the mercy of God, the sinful clergy must ask to be admitted to retreat in solitude."[68]

By this time public penance had reached a dead end which is why from the sixth and seventh centuries the so-called "tariff" penance that was propagated by the Irish and Anglo-Saxon monks who went to the European continent as missionaries spread so easily. One of the great missionaries for the re-evangelization of Europe was Saint Columbanus, who died in Bobbio (†615). It consisted of a precise confession of the various faults and a fixed imposition of penance (in days, months, years), consisting above all in fasting, with the possibility of substituting other works that could also be done by other people, such as monks for example.[69] Penance was now private and could be repeated for other faults. Because of this, the idea of uniqueness and unrepeatability, which was one of the presuppositions from the ancient discipline, began to fall away. Moreover, penance was now administered regularly by a priest and no longer reserved for the bishop, as was the case before. The result was that frequent confession was introduced which subsequently became not only periodic but indeed compulsory: *saltem semel in anno* (at least once in a year).[70]

We know much less about the penitential development in the Eastern churches. Even in the Byzantine regions around the eighth century it resulted in a system similar to the western one, but due to difficulties inherent in its application, it almost completely receded.[71] In the Orthodox tradition a new form developed in the tenth century, although it is attributed to the sixth century's John the Faster, patriarch of Constantinople (†582).[72] This text, according to van de Paverd, was the result of four successive interventions.[73] The system of auricular confession and absolution is also developed in this work, and the priest is seen as the witness of repentance for reintegration into the Body of Christ. A "general" confession is also permitted for certain circumstances which was not meant to be a substitute for individual confession. Monasticism influenced the penitential system in the eighth century. The monks served as confessors and also became the spiritual guides of individuals. The laity confessed their sins to them and received a penance which served as a form of medicine prescribed to address the condition of the penitent's life. In reality, "the Byzantines seldom go to confession, at least in the secular world,[74] for in the monasteries . . . confession is regularly practiced. But is this confession, or is it a direction of conscience of simple laymen by their spiritual father? Both practices exist and, in the monasteries, are indistinguishable from one another."[75] Books on penitential discipline also came out of this tradition.[76] The texts speak of penances of various kinds for certain sins, "but, except in [the] case of 'mortal' sins—murder, apostasy, adultery—followed by formal excommunication, it is nowhere evident that a priest's absolution is necessary to seal the act of repentance. On the contrary, numerous sources describe absolution given by non-ordained monks, a practice which has survived in Eastern monasteries until our own day."[77] The Orthodox priest and scholar Paul Meyendorff, son of the great Orthodox theologian John Meyendorff, confesses that he had not grown up with the idea of going to confession. He discovered confession in old age when he offered his first confession. In the various formulas, "absolution is expressed through prayer, and, even if a declarative formula is used it implies that the remission of sins is attributed to God Himself."[78] In Russia, one must confess every time one wants to receive communion during Mass. The confession thus becomes a legalistic fact, as the liturgists of Russian tradition recognize. For today's practice, see Enrico Morini and Basilio Petrà.[79]

The other Eastern churches such as the Coptic, Armenian, and Syrian churches have also developed their own discipline. The Christians of Egypt and Ethiopia (Copts) have a system very similar to the Catholic Church. They confess to a priest showing concrete signs of repentance and then the priest pronounces the words of absolution because he is considered as a physician who cures spiritual diseases. In cases of serious sins, he can impose special penances such as fasting or almsgiving.

In the Armenian Apostolic Church, the Sacrament of Penance for reconciliation with God requires the confession of sins to the priest.[80] Confession is considered a return to baptism when full communion with the Lord has been achieved. The three conditions required are (1) sincere repentance, (2) confession as recognition of repentance of sins committed and (3) absolution. The confessor assigns the acts of penance to be performed by the penitent according to the seriousness of the faults. But this personal confession is not very widespread; it is in fact rather rare. There is instead a "public" and general confession in the sense that a text of confession is recited before communion which, if read in its entirety, takes about ten minutes. In any case, both private and public confession are often used together with personal and private confession being practiced more in Armenia than elsewhere.

Penitents and Their Ecclesial Community

An interesting aspect of the penitential procedure is the fact that during the period of *satisfactio* by the penitents, the whole community is involved through fraternal correction, counsel and above all prayer. Already at the beginning of the third century Tertullian observed: "The penitent for the most part, however, feeds his prayers with fasting, to groan, to weep and make outcries unto the Lord your God, to bow before the feet of the presbyters and kneel before God's dear ones, to enjoin on all the brothers to be ambassadors to bear his deprecatory supplication (before God)."[81]

The body cannot feel gladness at the trouble of any one member. It must necessarily join with one consent in the grief, and in laboring for the remedy. In a company of two there is the church; but the church is Christ. When, then, you cast yourself at the brothers' knees, you are handling Christ, you are entreating Christ. Similarly, when they shed tears over you, it is Christ who suffers, Christ who prays the Father for mercy. What a son asks is ever easily obtained.[82]

We have the texts of prayers, such as those for the catechumens that the community recited during the liturgical assemblies. There were prayers as well for penitents who also received the laying on of hands. The final reconciliation and the consequent readmission to the Eucharist (the *pax ecclesiae*) were accomplished through a final ritual:

Lay hands upon this man, while all pray for him, and then bring him in and let him communicate with the Church. For the imposition of hands shall be administered to him in place of baptism. For whether by the imposition of hands, or by baptism, they receive the transmission of the Holy Spirit. Wherefore, as a compassionate physician, heal all those who sin, go about with all skill, and bring healing to bear to help with their lives. And you shall not be ready to cut off the members of the Church, but instead employ the bandages of the word.[83]

The minister, bishop or presbyter who confers reconciliation accompanies the gesture of the laying on of hands with a prayer. This rite already took place in Italy on Holy Thursday in the fourth century: "As for those who . . . do penance, they will be reconciled on Holy Thursday, according to the custom of the Roman church,"[84] while in Spain it happens on Fridays. Of course, for cases of necessity there is no fixed time. In the East, it is also customary to anoint the penitent. However, no formula of absolution is used (such as: *I absolve you*...), which was introduced later into the Latin church and spread with the Lateran Council IV (1215).[85] Canon 21 of this Council also established annual confession and communion at least at Easter:

All the faithful of both sexes shall after they have reached the age of discretion faithfully confess all their sins at least once a year to their own (parish) priest and perform to the best of their ability the penance imposed, receiving reverently, at least at Easter, the sacrament of the Eucharist. They shall do this unless perchance at the advice of their own priest they may for a good reason abstain for a time from its reception. Otherwise they shall be cut off from the Church (excommunicated) while they are living and be deprived of Christian burial in death.

It also imposed absolute secrecy on the priest.

It is precisely the case that due to the theological reflection of scholasticism, penance was included in the list of seven sacraments. All churches considered penance to be one of the seven sacraments. In the West another distinction was made between *attritio* (simple repentance for the sins committed) and *contritio* (full repentance).[86] In ancient times, penance paralleled baptism in relation to the remission of sins for salvation. Jerome[87] called it *secunda tabula post naufragium*,[88] according to a previous tradition which considered penance as a second possibility for the forgiveness of sins.[89]

By its very nature, the penitential institution was complex, since it was the union of various elements: it was personal, it affected one both internally and externally, it involved the community and relied on the mercy and goodness of God. According to the cultural and theological values of the time to which we refer, one can place particular emphasis on one of these elements, which in turn affects the liturgical and sociological form of this sacrament. By placing too much importance on *satisfactio*, the ancients made penance acceptable only to those brave or stout enough to put themselves under such discipline. On the other hand, in our own time there is so much emphasis placed on the internal act of repentance and divine bounty and mercy, that penance has become easy and almost routine.

I have tried to offer a more or less complete vision of penance in the ancient church, even if for reasons of space I limited myself to a brief outline. However, it is important to note that a new methodology needs to be applied to this subject compared to what has been done so far. It is essential to study it from various points of approach, possible today thanks to the progress made in many sciences. Due in general to theological or apologetic needs, scholars in the past have tended to collect countless elements of information and evidence in order to offer a unified picture of the ancient practice of penance. For our historical methodology we use the same elements to offer a new chromatic vision. In other words, antiquity presents many variations in continuous evolution reflecting differences from place to place. Since these are not easily traceable to a particular structure, modern scholars have preferred to favor only some characteristics because they are better known than others. In fact, on this specific topic, as in others, we realize today that there were greater differences than we thought existed in the past and particularly in the first three centuries. These are differences that were attenuated later, for example, by the influence of conciliar legislation, rather than becoming more diverse as previously believed. Hence the difficulty of reconstructing the discipline of penance, especially for the earlier period.

Exclusion from Communion (Excommunication)[90]

The English term "excommunication" and the phrase "to excommunicate" come from the Latin *excommunicatio* and *excommunicare*, words typically used in Christian vocabulary and by Christians from the fourth century onwards—by Jerome and especially by Augustine. Their basic meaning is the "exclusion or expulsion from the communion of the church" (*exclusio vel expulsio a communione ecclesiae*). Such exclusion implies above all exclusion from the Eucharist. Therefore, since the *ecclesia* is conceived as a *communitas fidelium*, we can then speak of depriving someone of communion (*communio*) with the faithful in the liturgical community. The canonical terminology of the fourth and fifth centuries was rather imprecise and fluid; it did not yet have the clarity of later canon law because there was not yet any unified canon law. All that existed were individual sentences issued in individual cases for application in specific contexts.

The term excommunication today is often used in common parlance and can be found frequently in publications such as newspapers. It always has a negative connotation and a tinge of controversy directed towards the ecclesiastical authorities.[91] If, on the other hand, a bibliographic survey is carried out, one would quickly notice that historians do not like to talk about excommunication. On the contrary, they prefer to talk about *koinonia* or *communio*. The bibliography on the subject is abundant, especially concerning the earliest centuries of the church, since the primitive church is considered to be the inspiration for that of every time and place. The two terms are just as pleasing as the underlying idea of unity and harmony. A rich volume published in Spain a few years ago presents an overview of the situation of communion in the fathers for those interested in further research.[92]

In the pagan world there was no excommunication in the religious sense, but certain forms of ritual impurity could exclude one from participation in religious rites. In the ancient political world, there was what was known by the modern term of *damnatio memoriae*, literally the condemnation of memory, whereby the memory of a person was to be scrubbed from official public records and commemorations.[93] It was reserved for those who were considered *hostes*, enemies of the Senate and of Rome. It concerned above all the leaders of the community (*principes*), whose memories and any memorials in their honor (*memoriae*) must be erased. Excommunication, on the other hand, was a Jewish legacy passed on to Christianity and taken up for religious rather than political reasons.

The twelfth blessing (Shema),[94] the *Birkat Ha Minim* of the synagogue liturgy, which according to the Talmud was written by Samuel the Younger towards the end of the first century, contains an exclusion from the synagogue. The one used currently is taken from the Babylonian Talmud, but there is also an ancient version found in the Genizah of Cairo which says: "For the apostates let there be no hope. And let the arrogant government be speedily uprooted in our days. Let the noẓrim and the minim be destroyed in a moment. And let them be blotted out of the Book of Life and not be inscribed together with the righteous. Blessed art thou, O Lord, who humblest the arrogant." The minims (heretics or dissidents), and more specifically the nozrim, the Nazarenes, i.e., the followers of Jesus of Nazareth, were excommunicated.

Doctrinal differences were already occurring within Christianity from the very beginning.

Which differences were acceptable and which were to be rejected? The dilemma was not easy to resolve. Fidelity to the apostolic teaching remained the foundation, but as a living community composed of men and women the community developed in its organization, doctrine and rituals. On his way to Jerusalem, in Miletus Paul gave the elders of Ephesus a moving speech. Among other things, he added: "Keep watch over yourselves and over all the flock, of which the Holy Spirit has made you overseers, to shepherd the church of God that he obtained with the blood of his own Son. I know that after I have gone, savage wolves will come in among you, not sparing the flock. Some even from your own group will come distorting the truth in order to entice the disciples to follow them" (*Acts* 20:28-30). The elders, that is, the guardians of the community were placed there by the Holy Spirit to watch over themselves and to feed not their own church but that of God the Father—a church purchased with the blood of his own Son. A great responsibility was entrusted to them because the flock belongs to God. This text is the spiritual testament of Paul. The elders—here it is not a question of age but of leadership—were not chosen for their own benefit but for the benefit of others.

The elders who will later be the priests and bishops are charged with watching over the flock. The *episcopos*, in its original meaning, was a magistrate, a supervisor with the task of ensuring that things were done correctly and as they should be. He was to be a curator, a guardian and a superintendent. The *First Letter to Timothy* specifies in the first part of chapter one more precisely the qualities of the *episcopos* which must watch over false teachers (1:3-7). He then adds: "By rejecting conscience, certain persons have made shipwreck of their faith; among them are Hymenaeus and Alexander, whom I have turned over to Satan, so that they may learn not to blaspheme" (1:19-20). They blasphemed by teaching false doctrine (cf. *Rom* 2:24).

Some important Christians in Ephesus had "made shipwreck of their faith" by uttering blasphemies. Faith is like a journey. It is full of dangers, and during that journey shipwreck is possible. Therefore the sailor and the helmsman need to pay attention. The e*piscopos* is the helmsman, who must be vigilant. Paul, using a Semitic expression, separates them from the community. This sentence of Paul, or whoever the author of the letter is, together with other texts of the New Testament,[95] expresses not only disappointment but also little tolerance for doctrinal and ethical deviations which already were confronting the first Christian generations. One can go as far as total exclusion of the guilty from the community, handing them over to the hostile outside world—handing them over to Satan. Timothy must always remember that "wicked people and impostors will go on from bad to worse, deceiving others and being deceived" (*2 Tim* 3:13).

Expulsion as a practice of discipline began quite soon in the Christian community.[96] We already hear of it in chapter five of the *Acts of the Apostles* with Ananias and Sapphira. Even more intriguing is the case of Simon Magus (*Acts* 8), to whom Peter said: "May your silver perish with you, because you thought you could obtain God's gift with money! You have no part or share in this, for your heart is not right before God" (*Acts* 8:20-21). In ancient literature and legends Simon has had a long history. I dare say that the case of Simon Magus can be considered as an act of excommunication in the New Testament. Chapter five of Paul's first letter to the Corinthians also requires: "Let him who has done this be removed from among you" (5:2). In the second letter to the Thessalonians the separation has a remedial function: "Take note of those who do not obey what we say in this letter; have nothing to do with them, so that they may be ashamed. Do not regard them as enemies but warn them as believers" (*2 Thess* 3:14-15). While in the Old Testament the guilty person could even be subject to the death penalty, we see that person now deprived only of the citizenship of the new community with this exclusion having a clearly educational and corrective purpose.[97] The same attitude can be seen in the period after the New Testament.[98]

It was not easy to expel someone from the community in the second century because the boundaries between heresy and orthodoxy were not very clear and defined. Many doctrines still needed to be clarified. That was why exclusion from communion (excommunication) was not easy to apply.[99] Excommunication, as physical exclusion, required the support of the local community. The creation of *ostiarii* (doorkeepers) among other things addressed this function of exclusion.

In the late second and early third century we learn from Tertullian that within the Christian community there were still punishments and censorships. After lengthy consideration, a punishment would be imposed corresponding to the gravity of the guilt:

> Exhortations, corrections, and godly judgments are also pronounced [during the service]. For our judgment too is delivered with great weight, as among those who are sure that they are acting under the eye of God, and there is the greatest anticipation of the future judgment so that if anyone has so sinned, they are banished from the communion of prayer and assembly and all holy fellowship. We are governed by the most approved elders, who have obtained this office not by purchase, but by testimony; for indeed nothing of God is obtainable by money.[100]

A few decades later Origen observed that "there are therefore also today, in all the Churches which are under heaven, several judges, to whom the judgment not only of actions but also of souls has been entrusted."[101] He says elsewhere, "It may therefore happen that the judge of the Church does not always wield the sword, that is, does not always make use of the austerity of the word and the bit of the correction. . . . But perhaps our people will say: when is the Church of God without a judge? Even if the previous one fails, another one is given!"[102]

In the third century Gregory the Wonderworker, on the occasion of a Gothic invasion of Pontus, proceeded severely against those who had taken advantage of the confusion by taking possession of the property of others: "Greed is a terrible thing, and it is not possible in a single letter to quote the divine Scriptures wherein robbery is denounced not only as something to be avoided, but also as something that is positively horrible. But in general, greediness and laying hold of what belongs to others with a view to filthy lucre, and every such offender, is to be banished from the Church of God."[103] However, as we have already seen at the beginning of this chapter, there was also the possibility for them to be readmitted after due penance. In most of the churches, if the sinners were born or baptized in heresy, readmission did not require *satisfactio*, but only the laying on of hands.

According to the ancient doctrine, separation deprived the faithful of the fullness of grace, of the possibility of praying together, of participating in the sharing of the same bread and the same chalice. The first canon of the first canonical letter of Basil of Caesarea summarizes this teaching. It notes that the separated (schismatic) communities from the communion of the church do not receive grace when kinship is broken because they no longer possess the Holy Spirit, "because the origin of separation arose through schism, and those who had apostatized from the Church had no longer on them the grace of the Holy Spirit, for it ceased to be imparted when the continuity was broken."[104]

The continuous exchange of information with other churches via letters and other means was primarily aimed at having the churches conform to the agreed upon doctrine and the biblical canon. But it also helped exclude doctrinal deviances and heretics from the orthodox churches. The first step was to convince as many bishops as possible, at least those of the important sees. Excommunication was first applied locally and then elsewhere. The bishop was part of a network of episcopal relations through communication and communion. A capillary collegiality was emerging. Only with the rise of the great episcopal assemblies did excommunication acquire greater force and greater dissemination, although not always. Councils at various levels had more authority and more capacity for exclusion. It was only from the fourth century onwards that more effective and binding rules were drawn up. There were of course always some welcoming bishops. But the local bishop was primarily responsible for the penance of sinners as well as their reconciliation. Unreconciled sinners would be socially excluded from the community without, however, recourse to physical force.[105]

The Christian tradition, up to Constantine, opposed the recourse to civil authorities to regulate internal differences. However, the first known case of appeal is narrated by Eusebius of Caesarea concerning Bishop Paul of Samosata[106] who was deposed by a council in Antioch, around 268, with the appointment of a successor named Domnus: "But as Paul refused to surrender the church building, the Emperor Aurelian was petitioned. He decided the matter most equitably, ordering the building to be given to those to whom the bishops of Italy and of the city of Rome should adjudge it. Thus, this man was driven out of the church, with extreme disgrace, by the secular power."[107] Eusebius points out that only the power of this world which utilized force had managed to enforce the episcopal sentence, which otherwise would have remained ineffective. The Emperor Aurelian († 275) was the first case of an emperor deploying political intervention in the internal affairs of the church since Bishop Paul did not want to abandon the church in his possession.

Things changed when from the end of 312 Christianity first became the religion of the emperors and then, slowly, the official religion of the empire. Since we cannot deal with the evolution of this policy, we can proceed to the end of the fourth century when it was definitively realized by Theodosius I (379-395) and his sons. The practice of condemning some members of the church was perfected during the course of the fourth century. It seems to me that it was more a matter of practice than of clear written rules. Also, the excommunications decided in some local council, even if there was ample participation, did not have a widespread effect because frequently the dissemination of their decisions and their applications was local without wider implications.

The condemnation of an ecclesiastic could be imposed by the civil authority, the ecclesiastical authority, or both together. The first question we must ask is: Which civil authority? Which ecclesiastical authority? The level of juridical authority was a prerequisite for any condemnation to be effective and enforceable. The excommunication imposed by a bishop could only be effective in his diocese. A disciplinary measure imposed by a group of bishops of an ecclesiastical province or a civil diocese, that is, a group of several civil provinces, had a wider area of application. Naturally the greater the number of bishops who signed a condemnation, the greater the possibility of its execution and enforcement in a larger area. The dissent among the bishops was always lurking in the background, however. If the civil authority did not intervene for other reasons, the enforcement of a judgment remained rather uncertain.

Moreover, the observance of a sentence was conditioned by its reception in other geographical regions, including those close by where relations and communications were easier. Arius was condemned in a synod in Alexandria perhaps in 321, but he was received, acquitted and supported in Palestine and elsewhere. His bishop responded by initiating a vast campaign of letter writing in order to gain the support of the most important episcopal sees.[108] The same goes for Arius who had recourse to powerful protectors.[109] Arius was sent into exile by Emperor Constantine, who in 327 rehabilitated him. But Arius was not readmitted to the church in Alexandria. Throughout the Arian affair, the numerous excommunications imposed on an incredible number of people on several occasions were only effective if they were supported by the imperial authorities, which sometimes were also divided among themselves.

Often a condemnation issued by the Western Church was not accepted in the East, and vice versa. This was not only because sometimes the decision taken was not communicated, but also because of disagreements between bishops. It was considered enough for the sentenced person to travel elsewhere, outside his region. Even if there was no real excommunication between the churches, sometimes relations were cut off with the exclusion of names from the liturgical diptychs, that is, bishop's names were excluded from mention in the liturgy where there was dissidence or disagreement on doctrine or church practice. It was not a true excommunication between the churches, but the sign of the separation that existed between them.

Normally the ecclesial communities did not use force nor did they have any type of enforcement apparatus and so the execution of a sentence was sometimes entrusted to chance, other times to negotiations between episcopal sees. There were still other situations where the intervention of the civil authority was required, but they were not always interested in executing ecclesiastical sentences so as not to create unpleasant reactions, or because the same local civil authority was of a different opinion or of a different religious orientation. An ecclesiastical *crimen* such as heresy could also be considered a crime by the imperial authorities, but one could not always count on this. The civil authorities in charge of law enforcement were provincial and local and were sometimes not interested in creating unfortunate situations since their main purpose was to ensure order and peace. Normally they agreed with the majority of the population. The Theodosian Code records law after law against heretics. A prime example was the legislation directed against the Donatists and their doctrines. Yet, in fact, many of these laws were dead letters and frequently ineffective as evidenced by the same boring repetition of the same legislation over and over. Therefore, the civil effectiveness of a sentence depended on several concomitant factors which did not always occur: the force of pressure exerted by the bishops to obtain not only the law but its actual application; the geographical dissemination of the law; the personnel in charge of ensuring it was observed, as well as difficulties of various kinds, including the size of the group of heretics in a place, their capacity for opposition, and the like.

Constantine introduced the concept of *haereticus* in religion into legislation. In 326 he excluded heretics and schismatics from the privileges previously granted to the clergy in 313.[110] Only members of the Catholic community could access the economic benefits granted by the emperors. This constitution began a *titulus de haereticis* which included 66 laws in the Theodosian Code.[111]

Augustine observed that belonging to the right faith was only a fiction if the interior faith was lacking: "It cannot even be said that he is in the Church and belongs to the communion of the Spirit who mixes with the sheep of Christ only physically and hypocritically."[112] The possible shortcomings for exclusion could vary greatly. Some were considered grave, which would then result in exclusion from Eucharistic communion. After appropriate penance, however, full reintegration was possible. From the fourth century onwards, exclusion also became more social and public because of moral and doctrinal deviations that were considered to be highly serious.

It may be instructive to examine the canons of the so-called Council of Elvira, which, as some scholars claim is a later collection.[113] The canons help us to realize the uncertainty of terminology, the vagueness of terms and what type of ancient institution actually existed in terms of penance. Of the 81 canons, 56 contain sanctions which amount to 72 types of various penances. For instance, concerning an adult Christian who goes to a pagan temple for sacrifice canon 1 states: "It has been decided that he cannot receive communion even at the point of death." There is a similar punishment in canon 2 for the *flamines* (priests of the ancient Roman religion) who make a sacrifice: "Not even at the point of death can they receive communion." If, instead, he makes only an offering without sacrifice, after due penance, communion at the point of death is granted according to canon 3. A baptized person who causes the death of someone by means of witchcraft cannot receive communion even at the point of death, according to canon 6. A similar penalty was imposed in many other cases as well. There were also many other failures for which an extended period of penance was imposed with the length of the period depending on the severity of the fault. For example, according to canon 13 consecrated virgins who repeatedly violated their vow "may not be granted communion even at the point of death," but if, instead, they violated their vow only once, then they were required to do penance for the rest of their lives and then "may receive communion at the point of death." On the other hand, a girl who had united herself to someone who then married her needed only one year of abstention from communion without penance (*sine paenitentia*). But if instead she was intimate with other men as well, then the duration of the penance was five years according to canon 14. Parents who gave their daughter in marriage to a heretic (there is no mention of schismatics) or a Jew were according to canon 16 "denied communion for five years." The responsibility of any clergy who committed the same fault was considered greater and therefore the guilt was greater and made them liable to more severe penalties. Bishops, priests, and deacons who committed adultery "should not receive communion even at the point of death," according to canon 18. Instead, according to canon 20, one who, despite the admonition, continued to practice usury was to be cast out from the church (*ab ecclesia esse proiciendum*). Those in the church who wrote defamatory letters were to be anathematized (*anathematizentur*) according to canon 52. This is the only instance in these canons where the term *anathematize* appears, while it appears four times in the Council of Zaragoza of 378/380.[114] There were two types of deprivation concerning Eucharistic communion. One concerned only the communion held on Sunday (*dominica communio*) while the other involved the communion of the church (*communio ecclesiae*), which by its very nature included the first.

The ancient councils of Gaul from the beginning of the fourth century also dealt with the issue of the social separation of some from the Christian communities.[115] The Council of Arles of 314[116] contains numerous exclusions from Eucharistic communion using phrases such as "to abstain from fellowship" (*a communione abstineri*) (canons 3 and 13), "to be separated" (*separari*) (canons 4, 5, 12), "are excluded" (*excludantur*) (canon 7), "is not to have fellowship" (*non communicare*) (canon 15), "is not given fellowship" (*non dandam communionem*) (canon 22). While in its fifth canon the Council of Turin (395) speaks of Eucharistic communion, in canons 6 and 7 it speaks instead of inclusion or exclusion from the community as such—canon 6 has "to be received in peace by the community" (*pacis consortio suscipere*); canon 7 has "to bring back into communion" (*recipere in communionem*.) The term *excommunicatus* was first used in the Council of Paris of 361/362 in the third canon in relation to some Arians.[117] The verb *excommunicare* is what is usually found in the Ancient Statutes of the Church,[118] which on the whole manifest a terminology that had by that time become established. The term *excommunicatio* is found in many later councils and there were also other terms used to express separation from the ecclesial community. The term *anathema,* however, was quite rare.[119]

The African Councils "especially of a later period focused less on repressive measures than those councils of Gaul and Spain. . . . The Councils of Carthage of 348 and 390 are more concerned with providing norms than with prescribing penalties."[120] The Council of Carthage of 348 which was presided over by Gratus utilized the term *excommunicare*, but also the phrase "to be separated from fellowship" (*a communione separari*) (can 3) or "to be deprived of communion"(*communione privari*) (can. 14). Due to the nature of the deficiencies taken into consideration, the terms and phrases concern exclusion from the community and deprivation from the Eucharist. Indeed, the penalty for the same fault is again different for the layman, who is to be excommunicated (*excommunicetur*), whereas the cleric is reduced to the lay state (*clerici honore priventur*).[121] There is a restorative element as well, however, consisting in reconciliation (*reconciliatio*) but conceding to no participation in the celebration of the Christian mysteries. This *reconciliatio* is more frequent for moral and disciplinary reasons. Therefore, excommunication consists mainly in the denial of participation in the Eucharist or in denial of communion with other bishops or, in the case of lower clergy, having no fellowship with his community. If clergy were excommunicated they lost their ecclesiastical privileges. The *excommunicatio* required a formal act on the part of the bishop or the assembly of bishops. The reconciliation of the Donatists was done differently in the African and Roman churches. For example, a Roman Council established that if Donatist clerics came to the Catholic church they could not be readmitted to the clergy. The African church, on the other hand, preferred to leave the final decision to the local bishop as to whether to accept them.

Augustine was part of the African tradition and frequently used the terms *excommunicare* (34 times) and *excommunicatio* (14 times). There were also other terms that he used such as condemnation, reproach, repentance (*damnatio, correptio, poenitentia/paenitentia*) to indicate the procedure as well. First of all, excommunication was to be used as a "spiritual punishment pronounced by the bishop against a member of his community guilty of a notorious grave fault such as impurity, idolatry, murder (*impudicitia, idololatria, homicidium*)—such enumeration is not exhaustive since he also used other terms such as accusation, trespass, sin (*crimen, delictum, peccatum*), etc."[122] Augustine sets out this idea in his letter to Macedonius: "We turn away from the communion of the altar those whose sins are manifest, although they were released from your severity, in order that by doing penance and by punishing themselves they may appease him whom they held in contempt by sinning. For someone who truly repents does nothing else but makes sure that the evil he did does not go unpunished."[123]

In order for exclusion from ecclesial communion to be more effective and more intimidating it must apply not only in the community where it is imposed, but also in other communities in communion with one another. This is the reason for the development and diffusion of the letters of fellowship (*litterae communionis*) which someone must have in order to be received elsewhere.[124] These were precautionary so that the excommunication would be effective not only in the place where it was issued, but also in other provinces and dioceses. In fact, those excommunications only imposed by a bishop or by a local or provincial council were not easily known elsewhere—evidenced in the fact it was repeated insistently that the excommunicated person must not be received elsewhere. The sentences, in fact, were not widespread except in the case of famous heretics or to check the spread of a wide-ranging doctrine. Sometimes the removal of an excommunicated person from his place or region was more than enough. Normally, it was not expected that a local sentence would be observed elsewhere. Exile was enough.

As imperial and ecclesiastical legislation developed together, their mutual geographical area of influence and application diversified. After Chalcedon the rules were different in Roman controlled Egypt where there were often two patriarchs. Much of the West was out of Roman control, however, where they were ignorant of most imperial norms. The Iberian Peninsula had already been invaded by the barbarians in the first decade of the fifth century. Britain was completely cut off while with the Vandal invasion of 429/430 North Africa was no longer under the rule of the emperor of Ravenna. The same applies to Armenia and the Christian world beyond the city of Nisibis (Nusaybin, Turkey) east of the Euphrates River. The dissemination of a law is essential for its application along with the willingness to apply it.

Therefore, in the patristic period we can distinguish three types of exclusion from communion. When these were applied by the bishop special minutes were drawn up:[125] 1) The first entailed complete exclusion and total rupture of any relationship with the guilty person. It concerned above all apostates, heretics and schismatics, that is, those cases in which sin was also considered a crime which then broke all the bonds of communion. Excommunication involved both liturgical exclusion, that is, non-participation in worship, and social exclusion whereby other Christians were forbidden from having relations or contact with the excommunicated.[126] 2) The other type of exclusion, on the other hand, was only of a cultic nature involving worship and not involving the breaking up of social relations. That is why some speak of liturgical excommunication which concerned both sinners who were not subject to the penitential regime and those who had begun the journey of reconciliation. This type involved exclusion from the Eucharist and gave official penitents a special juridical status —a reserved place in liturgical assemblies accompanied sometimes by a special regimen, prayers, or various other injunctions. 3) Another type of excommunication was introduced in the fourth century that was not connected with ecclesial penance and was applied for less serious offenses. This involved only the refusal of the Eucharist as happened for example in the case of a girl who was unable to guard her virginity as we hear about in canon 14 of the Council of Elvira. The bishops applied this kind of excommunication at their discretion, and so Leo the Great in a letter to the bishops of southern Gaul exhorted them to be prudent:

> No Christian should be denied communion lightly, nor should it be done by the will of an angry bishop. . . . We have in fact ascertained that some have been cut off from the grace of communion by trivial actions and words, and that the soul for which the blood of Christ has been shed has been exposed to the attacks of the devil and wounded, so to speak, unarmed and stripped of all defense with the imposition of a punishment so virulent as to fall an easy prey to Satan.[127]

Until the fourth century, the excommunication itself was so closely linked to the liturgical excommunication that it was generally impossible to distinguish one from the other. Therefore, we often fail to separate it from penance.[128] With the decline of the penitential system that by this time was reserved for exceptional cases, and the introduction of private absolution, the link between penance and excommunication was partly dissolved. Excommunication, therefore, became a penalty with an independent corrective purpose. After Constantine, however, it was increasingly seen only as the ecclesial exclusion from the visible community of Christians and therefore came to be distinguished from penance so much so that in modern canon law it is considered only as an external remedial punishment.

Exclusion from the Christian community was expressed in different terms which themselves manifest a differentiated practice among the churches.[129] This diversity stems from the fact that canonical criminal law was being developed and was not yet uniform, but it especially stems from a lack of distinction between internal and external forums, to use a later language of canonical law.[130] The *forum* is the place of the administration of justice in Roman antiquity, i.e. the place where official legal acts were carried out. In Christian communities the term comes to indicate the place where the power to judge is exercised and, in the scholastic period, the *locus conscientiae*, that is, the place where the forgiveness of sins is granted. In Christian antiquity, in relation to sins there is still no difference between penitential procedure according to local practice and judicial procedure. Every deficiency considered serious was considered at the same level. The canonists warn that there is a mutual invasion of the field between the two forums and therefore inevitable conflict. In 1967 the first synod of bishops formulated as the second inspiring principle in the revision of the Code of Canon Law a greater harmonization and clarity between the internal and external forums. The internal forum concerns the sphere of conscience and morals, the external forum the public and outwardly known sphere. But conflicts cannot be entirely eliminated between the publicly punitive and sacramental points of view.

This problem that is so much discussed by modern day canonists did not exist in ancient times. The local bishop was responsible for the penance of sinners, the reconciliation of sinners, and their social exclusion from the community without recourse to physical force.[131]

ANOINTING OF THE SICK

The sacrament of anointing of the sick is also related to the doctrine of penance for the forgiveness of sins.[132] In the West in the eighth through the eleventh centuries the anointing of the sick began to be administered only to the dying, and so it was called *extreme unction* (*extrema unctio*) beginning in the twelfth century. That term has now been abandoned in favor of the older terminology. It is no longer linked to death, but to illness and old age, which itself is a disease. In the Greek East it is called *euchelaion* (the oil of prayer). These names and others used over the centuries put the emphasis on one aspect, leaving others in the background. Theological reflection itself is historically linked to these changes. Today, in this area, as in many others, we are witnessing an abundant recovery of the sources of ancient Christianity, so we are trying to have a more global and less unilateral view of this practice.

Stories of the sick who meet Jesus and his disciples constitute a significant part of the Gospels. The sick call for their care and attention. They ask for and obtain healing which is done through prayer and, at times, is accompanied by other symbolic gestures such as the laying on of hands (*Mt* 9:12 and 18; 9:13; *Lk* 5:31-32; *Mk* 7:32) and anointing with oil (*Mk* 6:13). Healing from illness is part of the mission entrusted by Jesus to his disciples (*Mt* 10:8; *Lk* 10:9; etc.). In the Bible oil is used for various purposes including healing of wounds (*Is* 1:6), and thus acquires the meaning of healing. The only text in the Gospels that mentions anointing with oil is *Mk* 6:7-13.[133] The evangelist reports that the Twelve had been sent by Jesus on their first mission, "So they went out and preached that men should repent. And they cast out many demons and anointed with oil many that were sick and healed them" (*Mk* 6:12-13).[134] This text was widely used in ancient times to justify the practice of anointing the sick.

The biblical text that can best support the practice of anointing the sick is found in the letter of James: "Is any among you sick? Let him call for the elders of the church, and let them pray over him, anointing him with oil in the name of the Lord; and the prayer of faith will save the sick man, and the Lord will raise him up; and if he has committed sins, he will be forgiven. Therefore, confess your sins to one another, and pray for one another, that you may be healed. The prayer of a righteous man has great power in its effects" (5:14-16).[135] Various aspects are highlighted in this text. The sick person has an illness of a certain gravity because he cannot go personally to the presbyters but must call them to come to him. According to the context, the presbyters are the leaders of the community which are certainly of Jewish extraction. They make the symbolic gesture of anointing accompanied by prayer based on faith, since prayer is more important than anointing to obtain salvation. The oil, certainly olive oil, is not used as a medicine, a common practice in ancient times, but with a specifically religious-symbolic purpose. The sick person who according to the Semitic mindset is conceived as a unity of body and soul will receive a benefit in his person without further specification. The sick person can obtain the forgiveness of sins if he needs it and for this reason it is necessary to confess those sins. The rite of anointing is not a private gesture reserved only for some people, but is an official act of the community manifested through the presence of presbyters. It is therefore of an ordinary character and not linked to the gift of healings that existed in ancient Christianity. It is meant to be a sign that the whole church cares for the sick.

The author of the letter does not seem to have created on his own initiative this symbolic gesture of religious content. It had to have been disseminated elsewhere even before the drafting of the letter. In fact, we know that the use of the anointing of the sick was also present in an environment where the letter of James was not recognized as canonical. Moreover, although the meaning of the passage seems so clear to us today, it was not cited in the first centuries to justify the practice of anointing the sick but rather for the remission of sins in the church.[136] In this regard it does not seem to have been used before the fifth century. In the West it was remembered by Pope Innocent in 416 and in the East by the Canons of Hippolytus, apparently written in the first half of the fourth century.

The first testimony referring to an anointing of the sick is found in the *Apostolic Tradition* and is a prayer of consecration for the oil: "If someone makes an offering of oil, the bishop shall give thanks in the same manner as for the oblation of the bread and wine. He does not give thanks with the same words, but quite similar, saying: Sanctify this oil, God, as you give holiness to all who are anointed and receive it, as you anointed kings, priests, and prophets, so that it may give strength to all who taste it and health to all who use it."[137] The oil of which we speak here is intended for the sick who can ingest it as well as use it for anointing—James' letter does not specify one or the other. Moreover, this oil is distinct both for its blessing and for its use. It can be used for exorcism and for thanksgiving and is linked to baptism, of which the author of the *Apostolic Tradition* speaks in chapter 21. The text of the *Apostolic Tradition* was widely circulated and passed on in the Eastern canonical-liturgical documents that depend on it such as the *Apostolic Constitutions*, *Canons of Hippolytus*, and the *Testament of Our Lord*. The *Testament of Our Lord* (*Testamentum Domini*) also reports a long invocation for the consecration "of the oil for the healing of those who suffer." The *Apostolic Constitution* also contains a prayer for the blessing of water and oil, recited by the bishop or a priest.

Another liturgical document referring to the blessing of the oil is the euchology of Serapion († after 362). For the Syrian church of the fourth century we have the testimonies of Aphrahat († after 345) and Ephrem the Syrian. If we look at Latin-speaking countries, the first explicit and clear mention occurs in 416 with Pope Innocent in his letter to Decentius of Gubbio.[138] He first mentions explicitly James' text with reference to the anointing of the sick and adds that such anointing is done with oil blessed by the bishop, and can be done both by the bishop and by presbyters and laity. Moreover, it cannot be conferred on penitents since, being a kind of sacrament (*genus sacramenti*), it cannot be received by those to whom the other sacraments are not administered.[139] Innocent's letter was widely circulated and was included in the Western canonical collections. However, there is little evidence of the anointing of the sick for subsequent centuries either in the West or the East. This lack of data is not an indication that it was not practiced. Since anointing was the normal practice, there was no reason to talk about it. For example, Caesarius of Arles three times advises the use of anointing in case of illness instead of resorting to magic formulas.[140] The sacramentaries of Gelasius and Gregory report the formula of the consecration of the oil. The text of the blessing mentions three uses of it: the anointing, as something to be ingested, and for different uses.[141]

The oil absolutely had to be blessed since the prayer of blessing in the form of an epiclesis made it effective. In the West the blessing was reserved for the bishops, while in the East it could also be carried out by presbyters, a practice also followed in Gaul and Milan. In the East the rite of anointing was reserved for the bishop and presbyters, becoming ever more solemn. In the West, on the other hand, it was also allowed to be done by lay people who were excluded only later on due to the influence of the exegesis of the letter of James, which in turn determined the theological reflection on the practice. This is a typical case in which Scripture does not establish the institution, but rather, the institution is an aid to understanding the Scripture, and this understanding in turn affects the institution.

---

1. Cf. also *Lk* 15:22; *Mk* 16:16; *Jn* 20:21-23,
2. *2 Cor* 2:5-11; 12:21; *2 Thess* 3:14; *1 Tim* 1:20; *Jas* 5:14-16; the entire book of *Revelation*.
3. See also *Mt* 16:17-19; *Jn* 20:21-23. These biblical texts are fundamental to the penitential doctrine of the ancient Church. See the article of B. Rigaux, "Lier et délier. Les ministères de réconciliation dans l'Eglise des temps apostoliques," *La Maison-Dieu* 117 (1974): 86-135, especially 117.

4. See *Mt* 16:19; 18:17-18; *Jn* 9:22; 12:42; 16:2; 20:23; *1 Cor* 1:5:13; *Rev* 2:2-20.
5. See *1 Clement* 2.4-6; *2 Clement* 17.1-2.
6. *1 Clement* 56, 59.2-4; Ignatius, *Smyrnaeans* 4.1.
7. *Didache* 4.3; 15.3; Barnabas, *Ep*. 19.4; *2 Clement* 17.2; Polycarp, *Ep*. 11.4; etc.
8. Barnabas, *Ep*. 19.4.
9. Hermas, *Shepherd, Vision* 2.2.4.
10. See Ignatius, *Philadelphians* 3.2; 8.1; *Smyrnaeans* 4.1; 5.3; *1 Clement* 51.1; *Epistle of the Apostles*, 47-50; *Acts of Peter* 2.8-10; *Acts of John* 48-54. However, the text of *Heb* 6:4-6 (see 10, 26-27) constituted and constitutes a difficulty for the penitential doctrine, which affirms the impossibility of a new conversion with penance and therefore the text would speak of the irremissibility of the sin of apostasy. In Christian antiquity it was used by some (Montanists and Novatians) to deny the possibility of reconciliation and generally by the fathers to assert the impossibility of repeating baptism. See M. Goguel, "La doctrine de l'impossibilité de la seconde conversion dans Épître aux Hébreux et sa Place dans l'évolution du Christianisme," *EPHE* 40 (1930): 3-38.; A. Schökel, "Heb. 6, 4-6: eis metanoian anastaurountas," *Biblica* 56 (1975): 193-209; M. Ciccarelli, "Un pentimento impossibile. L'apostasia nell'Epistola agli Ebrei e nell'Halakhah mishnaica," *Bibbia e Oriente* 52 (2010): 171–226.
11. *De praesc. haer.* 39.2-3.
12. *Titus* 3:10; *Didache* 4.3; Ignatius, *Smyrnaeans* 4.1; 7.2; *Ephesians* 7.1; Barnabas, *Ep*. 19.4; *2 Clement* 17.3 and 5.
13. Elsa Marantonio Sguerzo, *I delitti contro la fede nell'ordinamento canonico: secc. I-V*. (Milan: Giuffrè, 1979), 108.
14. *1 Clement* 54.1.
15. *1 Clement* 57.2.
16. Ignatius, *To the Philadelphians* 3.2.
17. Polycarp, *Ep*. 11.2.
18. *2 Clement* 14.1.
19. Hermas, *Shepherd, Similitude* 8.7.2; see 8.1; 8.6.4-5; 9.1.
20. Hermas, *Shepherd, Mandate* 4.3.1.
21. Today Amasra, in Turkey, on the Black Sea.
22. Eusebius, *HE* 4.23.6.
23. Eusebius, *HE* 5.28.8-12.
24. See *Acts of Peter* 9ff.
25. Hippolytus, *Philosophoumena* 9.12.
26. Tertullian, *De pudicitia* 21.5.
27. Tertullian never claimed that there was only a triad of unforgivable sins (idolatry, murder and adultery), since it is precisely in *De pudicitia* that he offers lists of many serious sins, all unforgivable. However, in ancient times certain expressions of Tertullian also influenced the fourth century, so some fathers limited the canonical penance to that triad: *nonnulli putant tria tantum crimina esse mortifera* (Augustine, *Specul. de script. sacr.* 29).
28. Hermas, *Shepherd, Mandate* 4.1.8.
29. Siricius, *Ep*. 1.5: *suffugium non habent paenitendi*.
30. Augustine, *Ep*. 153.3-8; Victor of Cartenna: Mansi 9, 995.
31. See *Didascalia* 2.10-13.
32. Tertullian, *De paenitentia* 7.2.10-12; 12.2 and 9.
33. Tertullian, *De paenitentia* 9.1-2.
34. Augustine, *sermo* 352.3.8; see Cyprian, *Ep*. 55, 22; *De opere et elem*. 2.
35. Ambrose, *De paenitentia* 2.10.95.
36. Augustine, *Ep*. 153.7.
37. Cyprian, *De lapsis* 15.17; Augustine, *Enchiridion* 17.5; Leo the Great, *Ep*. 18.3-5: PL 54:1012-13.
38. This is the only point in which ancient, medieval and modern are in full agreement; in the Middle Ages, however, the concepts of *contritio* and *attritio* were introduced, indicating a gradual intensity and motivation for repentance.
39. *Ep*. 18.2: PL 54:1011.
40. Cf. Poschmann, *Pénitence et onction des malades* (Paris: Editions du Cerf, 1966), 58-91. See Origen, *In Iesu Nave* 3.5: PG 12 :841; Augustine, *Enchiridion*, 17.65: *recte constituuntur ab iis qui Ecclesiis praesunt tempora paenitentiae, ut fiat satis etiam Ecclesiae, in qua remittuntur ipsa peccata ; extra eam quippe non remittuntur. Ipsa namque proprie Spiritum sanctum*

pignus accepit, sine quo non remittuntur ulla peccata, ita ut quibus remittuntur, consequantur vitam aeternam ; cf. M. Righetti, *Storia liturgica* (Milan: Ancora, 1953), vol. IV, 147-49; 161-67.

41. Cyprian, *Ep.* 4.2; 16.2; 17.2; 57.4; 55.13, passim.
42. See Augustine, *Tract. in Ioan.* 22.7; 49.24; *sermo* 67.1.2; 98.6; 352.3.8.
43. 1 Cor 2:15; Augustine, *De bapt. contra Donatistas* 3.18.23.
44. See Tertullian, *De pudicitia* 21.9; *Didascalia* 2.11; Cyprian, *Ep.* 73.7. Between Catholics and Protestants there has been much discussion on this verse to determine its true meaning: that is, whether that plural of the text should be referred to the heads of the community or to the whole community in its entirety; cf. J. Schmid, *The Gospel according to Matthew* (Brescia, 1962), 354-55. and B. Rigaux, cited in note 1.
45. Augustine, *Tract. in Ioan.* 124.7; *sermo* 99.9, passim.
46. *Didascalia* 2.10-13; *Apostolic Tradition*, 3; Leo the Great, *Ep.* 18.2.
47. Tertullian, *De pudicitia* 21.17.
48. Cf. L. Ligier, "Il sacramento della penitenza secondo la tradizione orientale," in *La penitenza* (Torino, 1968), 151; Basilio Petrà, *La penitenza nelle chiese ortodosse. Aspetti storici e sacramentali* (Bologna: Dehoniane, 2005).
49. *cum (peccator) non erubescit priests Domini indicate peccatum et quaerere medicinam*: Origen, *In Leviticum, homil.* 2.4: PG 12:418.
50. Cf. Origen, *Hom. II.6 in Ps.* 37: PG 12:1386 AB.
51. Leo the Great, *Ep.* 168.2.
52. Cf. Augustine, *sermo* 252.2.7.
53. Augustine, *Tract. in Ioan.* 25.10.
54. Origen, *In Ierem. hom.* 4.3.
55. Augustine denounces this state of affairs: there are baptized children who then do not receive enough Christian education, for which they are *nescientes omnino quid christiana discipline iubeat aut vetet* (ignorant of what the norm of Christian living commands and what it prohibits: *Epistolae ad Rom. Inch. Expos.* 16). In this period also there were lax currents which claimed that those who remained in the true church would still have been saved in the end. See A.-M. La Bonnarrdière, "Pénitence et reconciliation des pénitents d'après saint Augustin," *Revue des Études Aug.* 13 (1967), 31-53; 249-83; esp. 273-74.
56. Augustine, *Enchiridion* 21.80.
57. For the East there was Gregory Thaumaturgus († 270); Peter of Alexandria († 311); Basil of Caesarea and Gregory of Nyssa. In the West there was Tertullian, Pacianus of Barcelona and Ambrose. The ancients preferred to speak of *canones*, as rules of behavior, and not of *leges* (laws). Cf. I. Anastasiou, "Ecclesiastical Discipline in the Life of the Believer" Concilium 11 (1975/7), 80. The term canon also meant an observed but not written tradition, as can be seen from the Council of Nicaea of 325.
58. Cf. Cyprian, *Ep.* 55.23.4.
59. Augustine, *De urbis excidio*: PL 40:722.
60. Sometimes the bishop himself could place someone in the state of penance, but not oblige him by physical force, because in this field there was no secular intervention. See below the letter of Augustine to Paulinus of Nola; *sermo* 392.5. See F. van der Meer, *Augustine the Bishop: The Life and Work of a Father of the Church* (London: Sheed and Ward, 1962).
61. *Statuta eccl. ant.* can. 80.
62. Augustine, *Sermo* 23.8.
63. Augustine, *Enchiridion* 17.65.
64. Pope Innocent, *Ep.* 1.7.
65. Augustine, *Ep.* 95.3.
66. Leo the Great, *Ep.* 167.9-19.
67. *Agde,* can. 15.
68. Leo the Great, *Ep.* 167.2; cf. Augustine, *Enchiridion* 21.80.
69. Numerous penitentials were drafted, that is, lists of sins with the precise determination of the *satisfactio* to be performed for each of them. Penitentials, abundant in the West, were also found in the Byzantine East.
70. Lateran Council IV of 1215, chap. 21.
71. Cf. L. Ligier, *Il sacramento della penitenza,* 146, 164.
72. N. Uspensky, *Evening Worship in the Orthodox Church* (Crestwood, N.Y.: St. Vladimir's Seminary Press, 1985), 227-28.

73. Frans van de Paverd, *The Kanonarion by John, Monk and Deacon and Didascalia Patrum* (Rome: Pontificio Istituto Orientale, 2006).
74. Not secular in our modern sense, but referring to the world outside the monastery.
75. J. Pargoire, *L'Église byzantine de 527 à 847* (Paris : V. Lecoffre,1905), 32; J. Meyendorff, *Byzantine Theology: Historical Trends and Doctrinal Themes* (New York: Fordham University Press 1974), 195-96.
76. M. Arranz, *I penitenziali bizantini: il Protokanonarion o Kanonarion primitivo di Giovanni monaco e diacono e il Deuterokanonarion o "Secondo kanonarion" di Basilio monaco* (Roma: Pontificio Istituto Orientale, 1993); Frans van de Paverd, *The Kanonarion by John, Monk and Deacon and Didascalia Patrum* (Rome: Pontificio Istituto Orientale, 2006).
77. J. Meyendorff, *Byzantine Theology*, 196.
78. A. Almazov, quoted by Meyendorf, 196.
79. E. Morini, *La Chiesa ortodossa: storia, disciplina, culto* (Bologna: Edizioni Studio domenicano, 1996), 300-3; B. Petrà, *La penitenza nelle chiese ortodosse: Aspetti storici e sacramentali* (Bologna: Dehoniane, 2005).
80. *La disciplina della penitenza nelle Chiese orientali*, ed. Georges-Henri Ruyssen, (Rome: Pontificio Istituto Orienale, 2013).
81. Tertullian, *De paenitentia*, 9.4.
82. Tertullian, *De paenitentia*, 10.5-6.
83. *Didascalia* 2.41.
84. Innocent, *Ep.* 25.7.
85. Cf. Poschmann, 190; Ligier, 153-55.
86. *Dictionnaire de Spiritualité* 2:1312-1321; 12:971-973.
87. *Ep.* 84.6: PL 22:1115; cf. *Ep.* 130.9. Jerome repeats the same concept with several words: *Illa quasi secunda post naufragium miseris tabula sit*. The formula is then rejected by the Council of Trent (Denzinger 912).
88. The expression is based on a sentence by Tertullian, who invited penance, saying: "O sinner . . . do you so hasten to, so embrace, as a shipwrecked man the protection of some plank" (*ita invade, ita amplexare ut naufragus alicuius tabulae fidem*) (*De Paenitenta* 4.2).
89. Penance as sacrament in ancient Christianity, cf. *Dictionnaire de Spiritualité* 12:963-65.
90. Marcel Metzger, "Une Église peut-elle excommunier? Le témoignage de la Bible et de l'Église primitive," *Revue de droit canonique* 56 (2006): 7-32; A. Di Berardino, "La condanna di Giuliano: l'incidenza ecclesiale e civile di una condanna ecclesiastica nel tardoantico," in *Giuliano di Eclano e l'Hirpinia cristiana*, ed. S. Accomando and R. Ronzani (Avellino: Editoriale Todisco, 2012), 237-76.
91. Cf. A. Di Berardino, "L'eretico nell'antichità cristiana," in *L'altro, il diverso, lo straniero*, ed. G. Barbaglio et al, (Bologna: EDB, 1993), 247-63.
92. Juan Antonio Gil-Tamayo, Juan Ignacio Ruiz Aldaz, eds. *La communio en los padres de la Iglesia* (Pamplona: Ediciones Universidad de Navarra, 2010).
93. R. Delmaire, "La "damnatio memoriae" au Bas-Empire à travers les textes, la législation et les inscriptions," *Cahiers du Centre Gustave-Glotz* 14 (2003): 299-310. Eric R. Varner, *Mutilation and Transformation: Damnatio memoriae and Roman Imperial Portraiture* (Leiden: Brill, 2004).
94. Ruth Langer, *Cursing the Christians? A History of the Birkat HaMinim* (New York: Oxford University Press, 2011).
95. Mt 18:15-17; 1 Cor 5:5; 2 Cor 2:5-11 and 2 Thess 3:14-15.
96. J. Bernhard, "Excommunication et pénitence-sacrement aux premiers siècles *de l'Église*. Contribution canonique," *Revue de Droit Canonique* 15 (1965): 318-330; 16 (1996): 41-70; M. Metzger, "Une Église peut-elle excommunier? Le témoignage de la Bible et de l'Église primitive," *Revue de Droit Canonique* 56 (2009): 7-32.
97. *Didascalia* 2, 39; Augustine, *De fide* 11, 3: PL 40:199.
98. Barnabas, *Ep.* 19, 4; Ignatius, *Smyr.* 4, 1; 7, 2; *2 Clement* 17, 3 and 5; *Codex eccl. afric.*, can. 38; 76; 80.
99. E. Thomassen, "Orthodoxy and Heresy in Second-Century Rome," *Harvard Theological Review* 97 (2004): 241-56.
100. Tertullian, *Apologeticum* 39.4.
101. Origen, *Homilies on Judges* 3.2.
102. Origen, *Homilies on Judges* 4.3.
103. Gregory Thaumaturgus, *Ep. can.* 3
104. P.P. Joannou, ed. *Discipline générale antique* (Grottaferrata: Tipografia Italo-Orientale "S. Nilo," 1962), vol II, 93-99.
105. Cf. M. Metzger, *Constitutions apostoliques*, SC 329 (Paris: Éditions du Cerf, 1986), 97-105.

106. Today Samsat, southeastern Turkey which is now a submerged city.
107. Eusebius, *HE* 7.30.19.
108. Cf. Theodoret, *HE* 1.3.
109. Theodoret, *HE* 1.4.
110. CTh 16.5.1.
111. CTh 16.5.
112. Augustine, *Sermo* 71.19.32.
113. J. Vilella, P.-E. Barreda, "Cánones del concilio de Elvira o cánones pseudoiliberritanos?" *Augustinianum* 42 (2006): 285-373.
114. Josep Vilella Mesana, "Las sanciones de los canones pseudoiliberritanos," *Sacris Erudiri* 46 (2007): 5-87, here 28, n. 85.
115. C. Vogel, "Les sanctions infligées aux laïcs et aux clercs par les conciles gallo-romains et mérovingiens," *Revue Droit Canonique* 2 (1952): 5-29; 171-194; 311-328 ; now in, *En remission des péchés : Recherches sur le système pénitentiels dans l'Église latine*, ed A. Faivre, (Aldershot: Variorum, 1994); R. W. Mathisen, "Les pratiques de l'excommunication d'après la législation conciliaire en Gaule (Ve-VIe siècle)," in *Pratiques de l'eucharistie dans les Églises d'Orient et d'Occident (Antiquité et Moyen Âge)*, vol I, ed. D. Rigaux, (Paris: Institut d'études augustiniennes, 2009), 539-60.
116. The original canons are 22 in number.
117. *Auxentium et Ursacium ac Valentem, Gaium, Megasium et Iustinum excommunicatos habemus secundum litteras vestras ut certe, et diximus iuxta.*
118. *Statuta ecclesiae ant.*, canons 17; 30; 31; 33; 40; 74; 86. Cf. *I Concili Latini*. 2. *I Concili gallici*, vol. 1, edited by R. Barcellona and M. Spinelli (Rome: Institutum Patristicum Augustinianum, 2010), 96ff.
119. Augustine frequently uses the term *anathema* to condemn the doctrinal errors of the various groups.
120. J. Gaudemet, *Note Sur Les Formes Anciennes De L'excommunication*. Vol. 23, vol. 1/2, (1949), 71.
121. Augustine also uses the term *degradatio* (cf. *C. Cresconium* 3.48.52).
122. Cf. C. Munier, "Excommunicatio," in *Augustinus Lexikon* 1:1169.
123. Augustine, *Ep.* 153.2.6.
124. Cf. "Letters of communion," in *EAC* 2:557-59.
125. Cf. Augustine, *Ep.* 250.1 and 3.
126. Numerous texts that can be used: see Elsa Marantonio Sguerzo, *I delitti contro la fede nell'ordinamento canonico: secc. I-V.*, (Milano: Giuffrè, 1972), 112-39, especially 114ff. Origen qualifies the condition of the guilty person with these words: "to be cast away from the assembly of good people, to be separated from the society of the camp of the saints, his conversation it shall be outside the camp" (*abici a conventu bonorum, segregari a coetu castrisque sanctorum, extra castra erit conversatio eius* (*In Levit*. 8.10: PG 12:502-4. In the fourth century provisions were also issued concerning possible appeals against the excommunication imposed by a bishop (Cf. Council of Nicea, can. 5; *Apostolic canons* 36 (38); *Codex etc. Africanae*, can. 133).
127. *Ep.* 10.8: PL 54:535.
128. A. Di Berardino, "Risoluzione dei conflitti tra i cristiani (episcopalis audientia)," in *Nessun giusto entrerà nel regno dei cieli*, ed., R. Scognamiglio and C. dell'Osso (Bari: Ecumenica Editrice, 2010), 29-38.
129. A. Di Berardino, *Risoluzione dei conflitti*.
130. F. A. Cappelletti, *"Sagesse" e "honnêteté": la dicotomia "Forum internum" e "Forum externum" nella tematica del saggio da Montaigne a Méré*, (Pisa: University of Pisa, 1988); M. Visioli, *Il diritto della chiesa e le sue tensioni alla luce di un'antropologia teologica* (Rome: Pontificia Università Gregoriana, 1999), (chapter 4).
131. Cf. M. Metzger, *Constitutions apostoliques*, SC 329, (Paris: Èditions du Cerf, 1986), 97-105.
132. *Recovering the Riches of Anointing: A Study of the Sacrament of the Sick: An International Symposium*, Kevin Tripp ... [et al.]; ed. by G. Glen, (Collegeville, MN: Liturgical Press, 2002); Jean-Philippe Revel, *Traité des sacrements. VI. L'onction des malades. Rédemption de la chair et par la chair* (Paris: Èditions du Cerf, 2009).
133. The parallel texts do not mention oil but have the same meaning.
134. *Mk* 16:18 mentions the laying on of hands on the sick for their healing.
135. B. Reicke, "L'Onction des malades d'après Saint Jacques," *Maison-de-Dieu* 113 (1973): 50-56.
136. Origen often compares sin to illness and in this regard cites the passage of James 5:14-6 in a penitential context: see *In Levit. hom*, 2.4: PG 12:417. In the East, during the rite of reconciliation, the anointing of the penitent and the laying on of hands were used.
137. *Apostolic Tradition* 5.

138. M. Monfrinotti, ed. *La Decretale di papa Innocenzo I al vescovo di Gubbio Decenzio: atti del Convegno internazionale (Roma, 18 March 2016)* (Rome: Pontificio Ateneo Sant'Anselmo, 2017).
139. Innocent, *Ep.* 25.8.
140. *Sermons* 13; 52 and 184. The texts of the Latin tradition are collected by A. Chavasse, "Étude sur l'onction des infirmes dans l'Église latine du II au XI siècle," *Revues Sc. Religieuse* 20 (1940): 64-122.
141. M. Righetti, *Manuale di storia liturgica*, vol. IV (Milan: Ancora, 1953), 232.

CHAPTER 10
MARRIAGE AND FAMILY

THE CHRISTIAN VISION OF MARRIAGE IN THE ANCIENT CONTEXT

THE CHRISTIAN DOCTRINE OF MARRIAGE STEMS FROM A REFLECTION ON SCRIPTURE accompanied by the considerable and decisive influences of Roman law as well as the philosophical theories of the time—above all Platonic and Stoic—that were part and parcel of the ancient mentality and praxis. It is therefore the result of biblical revelation, theological reflection and cultural models. In Christianity the equality of man and woman is affirmed in full because both spouses are children of the same Father and on the way to a single life in the hereafter where there will no longer be a distinction of sexes: "God created the man in his image, in the image of God he created him: male and female he created them" (*Gen* 1:27). Scripture places the human couple of man and woman at the origin of humanity on which all later human beings depend, according to the explicit command: "Be fruitful and multiply, fill the earth and subdue it" (*Gen* 1:27-28). The Palestinian Judaism of the time of Jesus had different positions on relations between the sexes, defending the superiority of man over the naturally inferior woman who was obliged to chastity before marriage and fidelity after. Only she commits adultery. The man does not. And only the man can give a certificate of divorce without showing cause and the certificate can be given for almost any reason. Generally, in the time of Jesus marriage is monogamous even if previously there had been polygamy.

Philo of Alexandria (ca. 20 BCE– ca. 45 CE) is representative of Hellenistic Judaism in holding that marriage has procreation as its goal, therefore marital relations are legitimate only for this purpose. He advised moderate sexual relations between spouses as well as not marrying a widow who was certainly sterile and not having relationships with a pregnant wife or having intercourse during menstruation or when she has reached menopause. He favored moderation in light of asceticism and spiritual progress. Due to their eschatological outlook, the men of Qumran practiced their asceticism in view of the final struggle for the triumph of the kingdom of God and of the victory of the children of light against the children of darkness. Their members, who were 25 years and older, were required to practice full abstinence in order to fight the holy war.

Returning to the Christian vision of man and woman, we note that the apostle Paul states: "There is no longer Jew nor Greek, neither slave nor free, nor male or female for you are all one in Christ Jesus" (*Gal* 3:28). "In the Lord the woman is not independent of the man, nor man independent of the woman" (*1 Cor* 11:11). Therefore, the human being is only one, being diversified into two different existences, into two related realities that give rise to the human world. Man and woman are the two faces of the same and the only reality: the human being. According to the aforementioned expression of St. Paul to the Galatians, the antinomies born of human history, of whatever kind they are, will have to recompose in Christ in a superior and definitive reconciliation—even the same fundamental fracture (*sexus/sectus*) will have to disappear. In ancient Judaism there was a difference in the exercise of sexuality between men and women. The difference was even greater among Greek and Roman society. Sexual relations took place outside of a context of love—even among teenagers. Sex was meant to satisfy one's instinct. The girls were still very young when given in marriage, and therefore without any experience of this kind.

The fathers, in principle, admitted the equality of man and woman, but their thinking developed on different levels. In the theological context they admitted the overcoming of the sexes in the kingdom of heaven where there will be no hierarchical distinction, but perfect equality, in the sense that differentiation has no relevance. And so virginity was the anticipation of the future condition common to all the elect. Even in the present world there was a fundamental equality: "For if the God of both is one, the master of both is also one; one church, one temperance, one modesty . . . And those whose life is common, have common grace and a common salvation; they have a common virtue and a common way of life."[1] Even many pagan authoritative voices affirmed the equality between men and women and the beauty of marriage. The Christian novelty—totally original—was the strong affirmation of conjugal fidelity from both spouses and the exaltation of the widowed woman who was married only once (*univira*).

Now in the Scripture there are two different traditions: one (*Gen* 1:27) affirming that Eve is not distinguished from Adam except by a sexual characteristic, while the other speaks of the creation of woman after man (*Gen* 2:18-25) as a companion to him and taken from his rib. Besides this there is the famous text of Paul in his letter to the Ephesians, who says: "The husband is head of the wife as Christ is head of the Church, his body, of which he is the Savior. Therefore, as the Church is subjected to Christ, so too wives should be subject to their husbands in all things" (*Eph* 5:23-24). In biblical texts nowhere is it affirmed that the woman is inferior with respect to man as a person; rather, only a hierarchical order is presented within the family and the church, and therefore expressive only of a social order. Along this line of thought and practice, starting from the Scriptures and in contrast with the widespread view of their time which tended to devalue the woman as a person, the fathers elaborated and explained their teaching which tended to underline the fundamental equality: "This is also the work of God's grace, that for women there are limits only in temporal matters—or better yet, not even in them. In fact, women carry a significant part of the societal organization, providing among other things domestic care.... Therefore, also in this [societal] realm, the part of the woman is not small, let alone in the spiritual realm."[2] This theoretical approach did not completely escape the cultural conditioning of both the Old Testament and their own time and place. Expressions also abound in the writings of the fathers that underline the inferiority of women in the physical and social realms as well as the cultural and spiritual spheres.

The teaching of Jesus took place within the debate of the religious schools of that period. Jesus who was born of a woman (*Gal* 4:4), with all his behavior and teaching, considered marriage an original datum of human existence, desired by God to achieve "one flesh" (*Mk* 10:6-9). Recalling the original purpose "at the beginning," Jesus affirmed the need—inconceivable for the entire ancient world—for the indissolubility of marriage.[3] At the same time he considered marriage as a reality of the present world destined to disappear with the resurrection.[4] The spouses form only one flesh and so divorce had been tolerated because of the hardness of hearts, but no longer—even if one admits an exception, that of fornication (*Mt* 19:9). This new vision of marriage and relations between the sexes is what troubled the disciples the most, so much so that to them it seemed better not to marry at all (*Mt* 19:10). Jesus had placed men and women on the same level, in effect challenging Jewish law by allowing even a woman to leave a man for the cause of fornication.

Jesus also introduced an upsetting novelty with respect to the "be fruitful and multiply" of Genesis (1:28), proclaiming with a mysterious sentence, "Let him who is able to accept this, accept it" in speaking of voluntarily becoming a eunuch for the sake of "the kingdom of heaven" (*Mt* 19:12)—in other words, he was speaking about virginity and celibacy.[5] As we can see, Jesus only provided fundamental indications without presenting a complete exposition of the problems related to marriage. Paul also followed this doctrine and recommended it. In fact, he recommended celibacy to unmarried Corinthians as a form of life to be preferred for eschatological reasons and for making oneself available to be totally devoted to God (*1 Cor* 7:26).

Through the teaching of Paul and the Synoptic Gospels we can reconstruct the teaching of Jesus and the practice of early Christians on marriage and its indissolubility.[6] It is observed that the formulation of Mark has in the background the Roman law in force during the first century while also reflecting the different traditions.

Paul, who wrote before the evangelists, specified that his teaching derived from Jesus himself: "To the married I give this command, not I but the Lord, that the wife should not separate from her husband—but if she does, let her remain single or else be reconciled to her husband—and that the husband should not divorce his wife" (*1 Cor* 7:10-11). He was referring to an authentic teaching of Jesus. Paul also addressed conjugal duties between the husband and wife. He spoke of mixed marriages by providing what he referred to as advice rather than a precept of Christ: "To the rest I say, not the Lord, that if any brother has a wife who is an unbeliever, and she consents to live with him, he should not divorce her. If any woman has a husband who is an unbeliever, and he consents to live with her, she should not divorce him" (*1 Cor* 7:12-13). Paul is answering the questions of the Corinthians on marriages performed before their conversion to Christianity. He worries about the Christian spouse, because "God has called you to live in peace" (*1 Cor* 7:15). He is concerned also because there is the possibility that the non-believing spouse will convert. The later canon law was based on his statements to create "the Pauline privilege," which admits in this case the dissolubility of a legitimate marriage.

In the same context Paul considers virginity as more convenient to the present situation (*1 Cor* 7:26). "I think that in view of the impending distress it is well for a person to remain as he is. Are you bound to a wife? Do not seek to be free. Are you free from a wife? Do not seek marriage. But if you marry, you do not sin, and if a woman marries she does not sin. Yet those who marry will have worldly troubles, and I would spare you that" (*1 Cor* 7:26-28). The whole of the final part of this chapter deals with the question of virginity which frees us from the worries of this world.

While affirming the goodness of marriage—the original order of creation—Jesus makes it clear also through his own behavior that the renunciation of marriage for "the kingdom of heaven" is a more radical attitude, but also that this abstinence is not something absolute and a value in itself, but relative to the coming of the kingdom. Marriage and abstinence are goods that are not mutually exclusive, but one of which is better than the other.[7] This ideological patrimony was a constant of the Great Church. In this regard, John Chrysostom wrote: "Whoever condemns marriage also deprives virginity of its glory; those who praise it, make virginity more admirable and luminous. What appears to be good only when compared with something bad is not all that valuable. But when it surpasses things that everyone else highly values, then indeed it is universally recognized as the best and highest good."[8]

The exaltation of the superiority of abstinence with respect to marriage runs through all the abundant eschatological literature, albeit with different accents. It was further enriched with Jewish, Hellenistic, Gnostic and popular motifs which tended to devalue the body, family commitments and women.[9] Thus abstinence became charged with new meanings that were not always positive because in order to affirm its beauty, marriage was sometimes put in a bad light although its fundamental benefit was still recognized. Sometimes arguments and accents were emphasized that today would create serious doubts. Such sentiments as the following, expressed by Gregory of Nazianzus, were unfortunately rare: "Marriage does not distance us from God; indeed, it draws us near to him because it is God himself who urges us to it."[10]

Following the example of Jesus, but above all for other reasons that are not always "Christian," ascetic currents and thoughts that were contrary to marriage soon arose, for which the author of the Pastoral Epistles condemns those who "will forbid marriage" (*1 Tim* 4:3) and advises young widows to remarry (5:14). These currents punctuate, with a timely onset, every moment of the history of ancient Christianity. Encratism, Marcionism, Gnosticism, Messalianism, Novatianism, Priscillianism, and Manichaeism are just a few examples. The phenomenon cannot be fully explored here since it is too vast to attribute only to these marginal groups. On the contrary, it is an indication of the widespread embarrassment of ancient Christianity in the face of marriage and sexuality—an embarrassment that partially influenced subsequent Christian doctrine.

Christians of the first centuries did not live apart from society but lived within their context although following a different manner of behavior. Like everyone else they too brought children into the world.[11]

At the beginning of the third century, the editor of the *Passion of Perpetua* describes Perpetua as *honesta nata, liberaliter instituta, matronaliter nupta*.[12] How should we translate this Latin sentence? It is not easy. Its meaning is something like this: "nobly born, liberally educated, a lawful wife." Such a translation does not represent the entire meaning, however. Perpetua was born from a family of *honestiores,* which indicates those of a higher class, but we do not know which class (senatorial, *curialis*). She had a good grasp of classical culture and was married (*matronaliter,*) i.e., is a real wife legally married under Roman law (*iustum matrimonium*), as opposed to a concubine for instance, and therefore had the right to the honors associated with legal marriage (*honor matrimonii*).

Globally, the Greek, Latin and Eastern fathers fought extremism, defending the institution of marriage and at the same time the ideal of virginity and celibacy. It was not easy to preserve the balance and the tension between the two ways of life.[13] Irenaeus of Lyon and

Clement of Alexandria associated Encratism with Gnosticism, but as F. Bolgiani has shown, the reality was more complex and intertwined. Indeed, some Christians resumed practices and speculations with roots in Jewish ascetic currents.

Certainly the great fathers took care to provide a careful and balanced approach with discernment.[14] For example, Ambrose wrote: "None of those who have chosen marriage blames virginity, and none of those who follow virginity condemns marriage. All the adversaries of this norm, those who dare to dissolve the conjugal bond, have long been condemned by the Church."[15] For them marriage is a way of saving people—even if a more difficult way—for a variety of human and worldly relationships.[16] However, "those who have an obstacle in marriage know that marriage itself was not the impediment, but their free will which used marriage badly."[17] Clement of Alexandria, who had already been fighting the widespread practice of the pagan world to avoid marriage for its "slavery," exalted marriage's advantages and defended its necessity: "We must marry for our country's sake, for the succession of children and also, as far as we are concerned, to bring the world to perfection. . . . [Those who do not marry] have an ungodly behavior because they destroy the divinely created human race. It is also unmanly and weak to escape living with a wife and children."[18] On the other hand, the church, which cares about orphans ensures that they marry worthily and it is the duty of the bishops to try to favor marriage.[19] The fathers therefore have energetically refused both antimatrimonial tendencies more or less heretical, and the prevailing custom of escaping from marriage for selfish reasons.[20]

Augustine was the theologian who surpassed all others in his theological reflection on marriage. He had more influence on the West although his influence has often been judged negatively. But as far as we can see, such judgment has almost never considered the totality of his mature thought and his final reflections on marriage, so that in this context we often notice a reductive and partial interpretation of his thought. His influence was decisive, as a fine scholar writes, for two reasons:

> The Fathers had predominantly ascetic interest when comparing marriage and virginity. Augustine has more theological interest when writing on marriage. Marriage for the first time begins to be considered in itself and not in comparison with virginity. The titles of his two works (*On the Good of Marriage* and the *On Marriage and Concupiscence*) reveal this new theological perspective. After the disappearance of the eschatological urgency of the first centuries, the evaluation of marriage was mainly natural, that is, based on nature and creation. Augustine sees marriage is also and above all historical, in relation, of course, to the history of salvation.[21]

Augustine takes into consideration not the man who is the fruit of the pure creation of God, but the one who has confronted his inherent original sin with his freedom.

Since Augustine has had a great influence in the West, he deserves special attention. His reflection on marriage developed over time. For example, in the *Soliloquies* he considered marriage as an impediment to his contemplative life: "I believe that for the serenity of my soul—with due justice and good reason, I think—I have enjoined myself not to desire, not to seek and not to take a wife."[22] His conception of marriage was related to the problems discussed in his time in opposition to Manichaeism, Pelagianism, Jovinian and others, but always starting from Scripture. Since some authors by exalting virginity devalued marriage, as Jerome did, Augustine first of all defended its goodness.

He then elaborated more fully the reasons for the goodness of marriage, reducible to three goods (*tria bona*) which constitute its essential nature. The good of marriage "is threefold: fidelity, offspring, and the sacrament. What fidelity (*fides*) means is that neither partner should sleep with another person outside the marriage bond; the offspring (*proles*) means that children should be welcomed with love, brought up with kindness and given a religious education; that marriage is a sacrament means that the union should not be broken up, and that if either husband or wife is sent away, neither should marry another even for the sake of having children."[23] The *sacramentum* has a transcendent meaning in human relationships and varies according to the unfolding of the history of salvation as is found in both the Old and the New Testament: "Just as the multiple marriages of that time symbolically signified the future multitude subject to God in all peoples of the earth, so the single marriages of our time symbolically signify the unity of all of us subject to God which is to be in one heavenly City."[24]

He admonishes consecrated persons not to despise marriage, as often happened at that time: "I admonish both men and women who have embraced perpetual continence and holy virginity to prefer their blessing to marriage in such a way that they not consider marriage an evil and that they acknowledge that the Apostle did not say falsely but in all truth, 'He who gives his virgin in marriage does well, and he who does not give her does better.'"[25] In Augustine, and throughout the patristic period, we cannot find the concept of marriage as a sacrament, that is, one of the seven sacraments, in the later sense of Scholasticism and of the Council of Trent; nevertheless, he has set all the conditions for getting to that point.

While placing the accent on the procreative aspect of marriage, the fathers did not neglect to emphasize also its unitary implications, utilizing expressions not common in their contemporary pagan environment, such as the biblical phrase that the two become one flesh (cf. *Gen* 2:24). Tertullian uses very delicate expressions:

> How shall we be able to find words enough to describe fully the happiness of that marriage which the Church arranges, the oblation confirms and the blessing signs and seals, at which angels attend as witnesses, and to which the Father gives his consent? For even on earth children

do not rightly and lawfully wed without their fathers' consent. How beautiful then is that yoke of two believers, two who are one in hope, one in desire, one in the discipline they follow, one in the religion they serve? They are brother and sister, both fellow servants of the same Master. There is no difference between them of either spirit or of flesh. No, they are truly 'two in one flesh.'[26] Where there is but one flesh there is but one spirit too. Together they pray, together they worship, together they observe their fasts. They teach each other, encourage each other, sustain each other. They accompany each other when they visit the Church of God and partake of the banquet of God together. Side by side they confront difficulties, face persecutions, as well as share their consolations. They have no secrets from each other nor do they avoid each other's company, and they never bring trouble to the other. Unencumbered, the sick are visited and the indigent relieved. Alms are given without anxiety and the Sacrifice[27] is attended without difficulty. Daily diligence in piety is discharged without impediment: they need not make the sign of the cross in secret nor is there any timid greeting of the brothers and sisters, or silent asking for a blessing. The singing of Psalms and hymns echoes between the two and they mutually challenge each other over who will more beautifully chant praises to their Lord. When Christ sees and hears such things, he rejoices. To such as these he gives his own peace. Where there are two together, there he himself is also present,[28] and where He is, there the Evil One is not.[29]

Over and above the theological aspect of marriage, the fathers were mainly concerned with its ethics, even more so than any juridical or liturgical rules. The Christian novelty concerning marriage was above all its moral nature. First of all, there was its insistence on the indissolubility of marriage, founded biblically on the New Testament.[30] This was in full and radical contrast to the laws and behavior of ancient societies—including even the Old Testament—with its total refusal of any kind of divorce due to infertility, imprisonment of the spouse, illness, etc.

Already at the end of the first century and during the second a uniform teaching was developing. Women were exhorted to submit to their husbands, but not in the Old Testament sense. The *Letter to Titus* includes the so-called domestic code and domestic ethics: "Bid the older women likewise to be reverent in behavior, not to be slanderers or slaves to drink; they are to teach what is good, and so train the young women to love their husbands and children, to be sensible, chaste, domestic, kind, and submissive to their husbands, that the word of God may not be discredited. Likewise urge the younger men to control themselves" (*Tit* 2:3-6). The author of the *First Letter to Timothy* also inculcates an exhortation to women about their decent and modest conduct of good works (2:9-11): "I also want women to adorn themselves modestly and sensibly in seemly apparel, not with braided hair or gold or pearls or costly attire but with good deeds, as befits women who profess religion. Let a woman learn in silence with all submissiveness." The author does not accept that women speak during liturgical assemblies, teach men or dictate laws to them. This text today is frequently discussed—sometimes rather heatedly. Even the *First Letter of Clement* has instructions regarding women, who were charged "to perform all their duties with a blameless, reverent and pure conscience, cherishing their own husbands, as is right." They were to "abide by the rule of obedience, and to manage the affairs of the house with dignity and discretion."[31]

The paraenesis of the *Letter to the Colossians* became a basis for subsequent Christian domestic ethics. There is a very well-known text in the letter that reflects the composition of a normal ancient family composed of parents, children and slaves: "Wives, be subject to your husbands, as is fitting in the Lord. Husbands, love your wives, and do not be harsh with them. Children, obey your parents in everything, for this pleases the Lord. Fathers, do not provoke your children, lest they become discouraged. Slaves, obey in everything those who are your earthly masters, not with lip-service, as men-pleasers, but in singleness of heart, fearing the Lord" (*Col* 3:18-22).

This is the line taken by a text of Polycarp of Smyrna, which reflects the teaching of Christian communities at the beginning of the second century:

> Then teach your women to walk in the faith they have received, in charity and chastity, sincerely loving their husbands and having for everyone else an affection without preferences and perfectly pure. Teach them to raise children in the discipline of God's fear. The widows must be wise in the Lord's faith, pray incessantly for everyone, guard against all slander, false testimony, love of money and every evil; remembering that they are the altar of God which examines everything in detail and to which nothing escapes, neither of reasoning, nor of thoughts, nor of the secrets of the heart.[32]

Even his contemporary Ignatius of Antioch speaks of the family. He is the first to exhort that conjugal union, like his model of the union between Christ and the Church, be concluded with the bishop's assent:

> Recommend to my sisters, that they love the Lord, and be satisfied with their husbands both in the flesh and spirit. Similarly exhort my brothers in the name of Jesus Christ to love their wives as the Lord loves the church. If anyone can continue in a state of purity, to the honor of Him who is Lord of the flesh, let him so remain without boasting. If he begins to boast, he is undone; and if he considers himself greater than the bishop, he is ruined. But it is proper for both men and women who marry to form their union with the approval of the bishop so that their marriage may be according to God, and not after their own lust. Let all things be done to the honor of God."[33]

He implicitly refers to the fifth chapter of Paul's *Letter to the Ephesians*. This is an important text for the theology and ethics of marriage and Ignatius' letter, in its brevity, presents the church's teaching on marriage.

THE CHRISTIAN EXPERIENCE OF MARRIAGE

The second-century apologists whose task it was to defend the Christian religion against the slander of the pagans stressed the conduct of Christians, their proven morality, respect for the order of the Empire, and in particular their emphasis on sexual morality and family. In this argument the philosophy of the time also served as an ally. Athenagoras of Athens who lived in the second century mentioned the accusations against the Christians: "Three crimes are alleged against us: atheism [the non-acceptance of the pagan gods], Thyestean feasts [meals where children's meat was eaten], Oedipodean intercourse [incest]. But if these charges are true, spare no class: proceed at once against our crimes; destroy us root and branch, with our wives and children, if any Christian is found to live like the brute."[34] Of these accusations, the first is the most dangerous, because it had very strong political and social implications.

In fact, the same Athenagoras worries about the first accusation. He defends the moral life of Christians who, out of love and fear of God, do not harm others, consider themselves brothers and sisters, do not seek pleasure and preserve pure thought. He adds:

> Having the hope of eternal life, we despise the things of this life, even to the pleasures of the soul, each of us reckoning her his wife whom he has married according to the laws laid down by us, and that only for the purpose of having children. Just as the farmer, once he has sown the field awaits the harvest without coming back to sow, so also for us the measure of concupiscence is the procreation of the offspring. You would find many among us, both men and women, growing old unmarried, in hope of living in closer communion with God. But if remaining in virginity and in the state of a eunuch brings one nearer to God, while the indulgence of carnal thought and desire leads away from Him, in those cases in which we shun the thoughts even much more do we reject the deeds. For we bestow our attention not on the study of words, but on the exhibition and teaching of actions, holding that a person should either remain as he was born or be content with one marriage. For a second marriage is only a specious adultery. 'For whosoever puts away his wife,' says He, 'and marries another, commits adultery'; not permitting a man to send her away whose virginity he has brought to an end, nor to marry again. For he who deprives himself of his first wife, even though she is dead, is a cloaked adulterer who resists the hand of God—because in the beginning God made one man and one woman—and destroying the union of flesh with flesh that was meant for the propagation of the race.[35]

In this text of Athenagoras we see the lights and shadows of the Christian communities of the second century.

The abundant so-called apocryphal literature[36] which we can classify as a literature of edification flourished in the second and third centuries with its encratic and ascetic motifs. The *Acts of Paul and Thecla*, from the end of the second century, composed by a presbyter in the Roman province of Asia, is an exhortation to continence, to escape from the slavery of married life and to commitments in the education of children to fan exterior and interior freedom. Thecla remains fascinated by Paul's teaching on virginity and refuses marriage at the cost of her death. Today, scholars are attracted by these texts, seeing also a manifestation of the freedom of women, virgins and widows in ancient Christianity. Sometimes it is an individual freedom outside the control of ecclesiastical authorities and the normal life of an organized community.[37]

The ancient Christian tradition is unanimous in affirming respect for life, because it is a gift from God. There is unanimous condemnation of abortion, of the exposure of children and their abandonment, and a rejection of suicide. Christians denounce immorality, prostitution, pederasty, adultery of men and women and the immorality associated with pagan gods. Their stringency was also employed for apologetic purposes. Christian communities were small and so there was more control exercised by the community leaders with the mutual consent of the people. Now, since one of the burning problems was the penitential question dealing with the sins committed after baptism, it is evident that Christians also failed in sexual and family morality.

The interpretation of the text of Matthew raised problems: "I say to you that everyone who divorces his wife, except on the ground of unchastity, makes her an adulteress; and whoever marries a divorced woman commits adultery" (*Mt* 5:32; 19:9). Here it should be restated that in the Christian context the term adultery was applied to both men and women rather than only to woman, as it was for Jewish and Greek-Roman law. The fathers admitted that the innocent spouse could divorce the one guilty of adultery—in fact, some considered it obligatory to do so[38]—but sometimes it was advised that the couple resume cohabitation after repentance. Justin refers to a case of a converted Roman Christian woman who, having failed to obtain the conversion of her husband, wanted to separate from him for his infidelities. But the brothers in the faith exhorted her to be patient with the hope of a future conversion. Instead, the husband denounced her to the authorities together with her teacher Ptolemy, who was put to death. It seems that the woman belonged to the superior class of society.[39] Justin does not tell us what happened to the woman after her husband's denunciation.

The problem of living with an adulterer was debated in Rome in the middle of the second century. Hermas asked this question of the Shepherd:

> Sir, I say, if a man who has a wife who is faithful in the Lord detects her in adultery, does the husband sin in living with her? So long as he is ignorant—the Shepherd replied—he does not sin; but if the husband knows of her sin, and the wife does not repent, but continues in her fornication, and her husband lives with her, he makes himself responsible for her sin and an accomplice in her adultery. What then, Sir—Hermas asked—shall the husband do if the wife continues in this case? Let him divorce her—the Shepherd answered—and let the husband remain alone. But if after divorcing his wife he shall marry another, he likewise commits adultery."[40]

But he adds that if the woman repents after being expelled, the husband must take her back, otherwise he commits sin, "because we must welcome those who have sinned and repent." In Justin's account the woman was innocent; in Hermas' account, however, the woman was considered a sinner. Therefore, there is absolute equality between the sexes, and not inequality as in Jewish practice. In the first case the solution was to wait and be patient; in the second, separation and at the same time the acceptance of the repentant person were commanded.

In the first case is it possible to remarry after the separation or divorce from the innocent party occurs? According to Hermas, the innocent person cannot remarry after separation or divorce. Theoretically the fathers always defended the most rigid indissolubility, but we do not know well the application of the principle in daily practice. Origen notes that, contrary to Scripture and tradition, some bishops did allow a new marriage to women while their husbands were still alive, and not without valid reasons. But for Origen the new marriage was only apparent.[41] This pastoral understanding must not have been widespread and was more open to men than to women. At the end of the fourth century, the West would take the path of absolute rigor while the East would be more tolerant. According to the teaching of Paul, the fathers defended the indissolubility of marriage, and only death could separate what God has united.[42] This biblical basis was the foundation of their common teaching. The practice of the Old Testament was a problem, however, which was resolved by affirming that it was valid for the Jews but was not valid anymore for the members of the New Covenant.

CHRISTIAN MARRIAGE AND CIVIL LEGISLATION

The imperial law on divorce changed in the Late Antique period with restrictions limiting it as a possibility. For Christians, the matrimonial bond remained even after separation: "So enduring, indeed, are the rights of marriage between those who have contracted them, as long as they both live, that even they are looked on as man and wife still who have separated from one another, rather than they between whom a new connection has been formed."[43] In

Augustine the term *divortium* can mean both the separation of spouses and divorce in our modern sense.

The Roman legislation from Constantine onwards never accepted the total indissolubility of marriage but did make unilateral divorce more difficult. Constantine introduced legislation against divorce which, in the first phase, was directed against unilateral divorce. The emperors fixed certain legal grounds called *iustae causae* (just causes) to be met by the party dissolving the marriage. But the marriage was, nonetheless, still able to be dissolved. The dissolution of a marriage by mutual consent, on the other hand, had always been allowed up to the time of Justinian with no legislation being introduced against such a divorce. Constantine's legislation requiring compelling motivations (*iustae causae*) to leave a spouse were initiated in legislation he proposed in 323,[44] establishing three lawful causes of unilateral divorce for each gender: The woman could divorce her husband if he was (1) homicidal, (2) a poisoner, or (3) a violator of sepulchers. The man could divorce his wife if she was (1) an adulterer, (2) a poisoner, or (3) a procurer of women. If the woman was guilty of any of these, she lost her dowry and wedding gift which had been given to the husband and was condemned to deportation to an island (*deportatio in insulam*). If the man was guilty of any of the crimes listed, he had to give back the dowry and could not take a second wife. If he did take a second wife, the first wife could claim all the assets of the ex-husband as well as the dowry of the second wife.

These rules were accepted about two centuries later by the Roman law of the Burgundians and the edict of Theodoric, but in the Empire, they lasted only up to the time of Emperor Julian the Apostate (†363) who re-established the regime of freedom. In 421 in the West, Honorius partially returned to the legislation of Constantine[45] by requiring serious reasons (*graves causae*) for a divorce before granting it; while divorce without cause (*sine causa*) or for minor faults was punished and not granted. Theodosius II[46] was even less severe. The law lists a number of reasons for allowing marital separation. Now for the first time the motivation of the *favor liberorum* (the good of the children) was introduced in order not to dissolve the marriage: the good of the children requires that the dissolution of the marriage be made more difficult.[47] The allowance for divorce by mutual consent, however, remained.[48] Justinian, on the other hand, progressively made divorce increasingly difficult.[49] The restrictions were increased in 542 with Novella 117, and continued along the same line. The later western legislation continued the Roman tradition.[50]

In the Christian sphere, the teaching on monogamy was affirmed also for persons who were left widowed, who were normally advised against remarrying and even forbidden by some fathers to contract a second marriage. The variety of opinions I mention here, show that there was no single teaching nor were there any general legal rules. These would be formed slowly in the various geographical areas, hence the differences existing still today in the various Christian churches.

In the middle of the second century, Hermas affirmed the lawfulness of the second marriage for both spouses, but considered widowhood much more meritorious.[51] Starting from the fact that the clergy did not remarry, Tertullian wanted to impose the single marriage also on the laity, because if they could contract a second marriage it would not be easy to find suitable candidates for the clergy "If everyone is not obliged to contract only one marriage, where should we look for people married only once to bring them into the clergy? Will it be necessary to establish a special order of once-only married persons in order to choose priests from its ranks."[52] The motivation is specious and factitious. While criticizing the Encratites who denigrated marriage, Clement of Alexandria quoted Paul who advised young people to remarry. He adds: "Certainly the apostle admits that 'the man who marries only one woman,' whether he is a presbyter, a deacon or a layman, if he blamelessly uses the marriage will be saved by raising children."[53]

Even Origen discouraged the possibility of second marriage for everyone. He observed that the second nuptials constituted an impediment to the orders (bishop, presbyter, deacon, widow):

> Women, look at the testimony given by Anna, and imitate her. . . . It is a good thing, and above all else, if a woman can preserve the grace of virginity. If she cannot and then happens to lose her husband, it is good that she should remain a widow. She should have such an idea in mind, in fact, not only after the death of her husband, but also while he lives. Then, if what she wants and proposes does not occur, she will be crowned by the Lord and can say, "If something happens in the course of my life, even if I do not want it to happen, I shall do nothing else but persevere in widowhood." Today, however, there are people in the Church who marry two, three and even four times—and I dare not speak about even more. We know that such a union will exclude us from the kingdom of God. Not only fornication but also second marriages exclude us from an office in the church. In fact, neither bishop, nor presbyter nor deacon nor widow, can be married twice.[54]

Origen adds:

> I believe that those who have married only once, those who have remained virgins, and those who persevere in chastity, are of the Church of God. Those who have married twice, despite their good conduct and all their other virtues, are not part of the Church or of that the number 'who have neither stain nor wrinkle or any such defect.' Such persons are placed in a second rank and among those 'who invoke the name of the Lord.' They are saved in the name of Jesus Christ, but are not crowned by him.[55]

Even the author who we usually identify as Hippolytus criticized Callistus for several times accepting married people into the clergy.[56] His position, however, was different from Tertullian and Clement of Alexandria, who demanded monogamy also from the laity.

These authors mention twice married people several times. Does this indicate that there was a high rate of mortality? Or is it an indication of the devastation of war? Or was it an indication that the richer widows could remarry more easily and were in higher demand? The thinking goes that men died more easily (due to wars) and so more women were widowed and exposed to the possibility of a second marriage. A sociological reason, however, explains much better why there was an abundance of widows. Men married at a relatively late age, between 20 and 25 years, while women married between the ages of 18 and 20, and often even earlier as we will see later. Ancient sources attest that military life made it difficult to reconcile the needs of married life with those connected with military discipline. For the *comitatenses*—a mobile line of troops traveling from one province to another—the limitations and difficulties for cohabitation were even more difficult especially as they would be gone sometimes for many years.[57] But when the men left, they were already advanced in age to begin with and they married very young girls. Since their life expectancy was much shorter than ours, these girls/women were relatively old by the time they acquired full autonomy after the death of their husbands (*paterfamilias*).[58] We forget that many people—too many—could not be married for a wide variety of reasons. None of the great mass of slaves could contract a *matrimonium iustum* (a valid marriage). At most, a cohabitation between a male slave and a female slave might allowed. And even this cohabitation was difficult due to the housing situation and also because they could be separated by the owner at any time and for any reason, such as, for example, one of the two being sold.

A second marriage was an impediment for men to enter into the clergy. Even marrying a widow was an obstacle. The norms that we read about in the authors above or in the canons of the councils suggest that those norms were not much observed however.

The fathers point out the contrast between the church and the state when dealing with conjugal morality: "The laws of the Caesars are different from the laws of Christ. Papinianus' legal system is different from that of our Paul. In their code we can say that there is no brake on the immorality of men. . . . In our code, however, there is full equality: if something is not lawful for women, it is not lawful even for men; and since they are of equal condition, the bond is the same."[59] A sermon attributed to Augustine, but considered spurious, speaks of the *iura fori* (the laws of the court) and of the *iura coeli* (the laws of Heaven) on the subject of marriage.[60] The same idea is also found elsewhere, however, in Augustine, for example in *Sermon* 355.5 where he distinguishes the two: *sed iure fori, non iure caeli*. Augustine insists on the contrast between the Christian norm and that of society in particular on fidelity and matrimonial chastity between men and women.[61] In *Sermon* 153.6 he speaks of the law of the world that is different from the law of the creator of the world.[62]

In a speech regarding marriage given in the church in Constantinople and in the presence of the imperial court,[63] Gregory Nazianzus says that "the laws are unequal and irregular. For what was the reason why they restrained the woman, but indulged the man, and that a woman who practices evil against her husband's bed is an adulteress, and the penalties of the law for this are very severe; but if the husband commits fornication against his wife, he has no account to give? I do not accept this legislation; I do not approve this custom. They who made the law were men, and therefore their legislation is hard on women, since they have placed children also under the authority of their fathers, while leaving the weaker sex uncared for. . . ." He continues: God does not do this. He tells us to honor your father *and* mother. . . . Notice the equality of legislation."[64] Later in the sermon he notes: "Now the law grants divorce for every cause; but Christ does not grant divorce for every cause; He allows only separation from the whore."[65] Gregory says nothing about if it is possible to remarry after the divorce which is allowed only in this case. How is it possible, Gregory asks, to demand chastity from one but not from the other? Christ saved both man and woman; he became flesh to save man and woman. Gregory asks for equal treatment.[66] Christianity fails to offer equality in its perpetuation of the divorce laws of the state. Gregory categorically rejects legislative disparity. He disapproves of the second marriage: "The first is the law, the second is indulgence, the third is transgression."[67] He wants changes in the penal legislation about adultery and in the legislation that promotes inequality between father and mother in their relationships with their children.[68]

Augustine expresses the same thought but with different words, because his preaching is addressed to Christians, not to authorities. He does not criticize human laws as such, but the Christians who follow them:

> But when we tell them these things, they not only are unwilling to back down at all from their severity, but moreover they are angry against the truth. They respond by saying: But we are men! Then will the dignity of our sex have to endure this affront of being put on par with women in the punishment to be suffered if we have relationships with other women besides our wives? On the other hand, precisely because they are men, even more should they be able to keep the illicit lusts under control. . . . On the contrary, they are indignant if they feel that adulterous men are subject to the same punishment of adulterous women. They should be punished much more severely, as it befits them to surpass the virtue of their wives and to govern them by their example. . . . However, there are some who are not pleased at the fact that, in the matter of chastity, there is a single norm for both husband and wife."[69]

As I have already mentioned, in ancient practice only the woman was considered adulterous. Jesus, however, already considered the man as an adulterer too and Christians in general when they speak of adultery refer especially to men. Here is a passage from Augustine:

> What has taken more of my time is that evil which spreads its tentacles widely, which more keenly exasperates that adversary who is making such a fuss just because he wants sooner or later to be a friend. Complaints in this matter are a daily occurrence, even though the women themselves don't yet dare to complain about their husbands. A habit that has caught on everywhere like this is taken for a law, so that even wives perhaps are now convinced that husbands are allowed to do this but wives are not. They are used to hearing about wives being taken to court, found perhaps with houseboys. But a man taken to court because he was found with his maid, they have never heard of that—though it's a sin. It is not divine truth that makes the man seem more innocent in what is equally sinful, but human wrongheadedness."[70]

The Latin fathers and especially Augustine while describing the spiritual advantages of widowhood are much more flexible than the Eastern fathers. He writes: "This in the first place you ought to know, that by the good which you have chosen second marriages are not condemned, but are set in lower honor."[71] Indeed he even admits more possibilities for remarrying by showing himself so much more open than the current ideas of his time dictate.

In our period there is not yet a corpus of canonical or liturgical norms that regulate marriage. It will be formed slowly under the influence of various cultural, political and legal factors. In the period before the council of Nicaea (325), the teaching about marriage was elaborated and the practice then implemented according to local practical norms. The norms were inculcated during catechesis in preparation for baptism. However, since the beginning of the fourth century the conciliar assemblies enacted more specific and precise rules and began to sanction those that fell short.

Legal Aspects of Marriage

In Roman law, children had no legal freedom when they were under the authority of the head of the family (*patria potestas*). The father was the absolute authority. This situation was eased over time to give more freedom to the children. At the same time the mother also assumed a greater role. The model of the extended family under the authority of the father evolved because of the attenuation of his authority which occurred during the rise of the Empire.

For Christians, even with the limits of law and tradition, parents took on greater responsibility. It was the parents who chose the person their child would marry. Ambrose writes: "It is not convenient for the modesty of a virgin to choose her husband."[72] Even for widows he has this to say: "But you too, or married women, if someone still young, having soon lost her husband, fears that she is soon deceived by her own weakness and wants to marry, she is only married in the Lord, entrusting her husband's choice to her parents because they do not seem motivated by brash desire, claiming to themselves the choice regarding their own wedding."[73] In the absence of the father, according to Augustine, the mother must also act in this way: "For, perhaps, the mother of the maiden will also come forward, though in the meantime she does not make herself known, and to a mother's wishes in regard to the giving away of a daughter nature gives in my opinion the precedence above all others, unless the maiden herself be already old enough to have legitimately a stronger claim to choose for herself what she pleases."[74]

The Church accepted the practice of engagement with its Roman legal elements, making the promise more demanding and sacred since it was considered as an anticipation of marriage itself and thus also influenced the imperial legislation of Late Antiquity.[75]

According to recent research, the adage "consent makes the marriage" (*consensus facit nuptias*) belonged to the period of the first centuries of our era. In other words, the *affectio maritalis*[76] consisted in the intent by the spouses to consider their union a true marriage with all the social and juridical consequences. Ulpian states: "It is not the copulation that constitutes marriage, but the marital will."[77] Therefore, it is the consent that produces the matrimonial juridical bond, and not the physical relationship between the spouses (*copula carnalis*) as it was for the oriental and then Germanic traditions. In marriage a continuous consent is demanded, so when the *affectio maritalis* fails in one or both of the spouses, one has the option of divorce (*divortium*) which too is an essential aspect of the concept of marriage. Marriage presupposes the existence of divorce: free union and free separation.

The fathers did not bother to deepen the aspect of sexual intercourse in marriage. However, influenced by Scripture they attached greater importance to the physical relationship than Roman law did. To preserve the validity of the marriage of the Virgin with Joseph, they placed the emphasis on consensus, thus contributing to the solutions of later Canon Law. Augustine clarified this aspect, discussing it on several occasions. In the fifth book against Julian, he repeatedly affirmed that Mary was a true wife of Joseph and that she generated a son without having relations with him.[78]

> She is called a bride for her first engagement, without Joseph having known her or planning to know her by carnal union. The title of bride had not failed nor had it been deceitfully preserved, despite the fact that there had not been a carnal union. . . . In Christ's parents, therefore, all the properties of marriage have been realized: offspring, fidelity and sacrament. We recognize the

offspring in the same Lord Jesus; fidelity, in the fact that there was no adultery; the sacrament, because there was no divorce. Only the conjugal act was absent.[79]

Compared to the Roman tradition, Christians insisted on marriage as a public event in order to avoid the practice of concubinage. A public ceremony testified to God's will and intent. The union of the sexes goes back to the original will of God concerning procreation.[80] This is why Christians put the accent on the free will of the spouses. As Tertullian wrote: "Marriage is born from the will" (*matrimonium perficitur ex voluntate*). In practice, however, he did not always follow his own advice. Ambrose and others considered the will as foundational: "It is not the deflowering of virginity that produces marriage, but the conjugal covenant" (*non defloratio virginitatis facit coniugium, sed pactio coniugalis*).[81] However, according to Roman law, when one of the parties violated this marital will and covenant the union ceased and divorce became the consequence. For Christians, the initial consent remains forever, even if the will can change. It creates an alliance without a term limit. In this period there is no doubt about the failure of consent and the total freedom of the ones contracting the marriage.

The Bishop of Narbonne, Rusticus, posed a series of questions to Leo the Great (440-461), for which we have Leo's replies. One of his answers concerns the conditions of marriage according to how it was viewed in that period. The answer of Pope Leo is very interesting:

> Not all women who are united to a man are his wife, as every child is not his father's heir. But the bond of marriage is legitimate between a freedman and a person of the same condition. This was established by the Lord long before the Roman law had its beginning. And so, a wife is different from a concubine,[82] since one is the slave and the other is her mistress.[83] For this reason, also the Apostle, to show the difference between these people, quotes from Genesis, where it is said to Abraham: 'Cast out the slave and her son: for the son of the servant will not be heir with my son Isaac' (*Gen* 21:10, *Gal* 4:30). And therefore, since the bond of marriage from the beginning was so constituted, besides the union of the sexes, to symbolize the mystical union of Christ and his Church (*Eph* 5:32), it is undoubted that that woman is not bound in a true marriage, as the mystery of marriage has not been realized. Consequently, a cleric of any rank who has given his daughter in marriage to a man who has a concubine, should not be considered to have consigned her to a married man, unless the other woman has become free, has received the dowry according to the law and publicly celebrated the wedding.[84]

Leo accepts the tradition that marriage is between legally recognized equals and that a marriage is not possible between a slave and a free person. The elements constituting the marriage for Leo are (1) the free condition, (2) the dowry and (3) its public nature.

Christians married according to the laws existing in the various regions where they lived, whose legal practices varied from place to place both inside and outside the Roman Empire. Athenagoras had written already in the second century: "Each of us marries according to the laws and customs received."[85] But they also found themselves increasingly observing Roman law which gained in acceptance along with the parallel expansion of Roman citizenship. Christians were concerned with rejecting only those elements that were incompatible with Christian ethics and doctrine—including those elements that were of a ritual nature. The author called Hippolytus accused Callistus of admitting into his community women who "were not married according to Roman laws."[86] The fathers followed Roman law coupled with elements of Jewish tradition in dealing with various prohibitions for marriage. They prohibited contracting a marriage between relatives, marriages where the age of the spouses was an issue or the two spouses came from different social backgrounds or did not share the same religion.[87]

According to Roman law, the woman was normally *alieni iuris*, that is, dependent on another person whether it be her father, husband or a guardian. If she was not under her father's authority (*patria potestas*) or under the *manus* (power) of a husband she was considered in the condition of *tutela mulierum* which meant that she was legally incapable of carrying out certain legal acts, similar to the legal status of a prepubescent child (*impuberes*). Men and women were not legally recognized as equals under Roman law. The woman always had to be under a guardian (*tutor*) of some sort. This was the law up to the time of Diocletian (emp. 284-305). After him we have no more mention of it. According to the law, women were inferior to men and so they were placed under guardianship, which was understood as a protection of the patrimony, i.e. the inheritance and property of the family. But women were considered inferior even in other contexts. Ulpian writes: "Women are excluded from all civil or public offices. Therefore they cannot be judges, perform the duties of magistrates, bring suits in court, intervene in favor of another or serve as a procurator."[88] During the imperial period, especially from Constantine onwards especially in the time of Justinian, many aspects were changed in order to provide equality between the two sexes. Some elements, such as the *fragilitas sexus* (weakness of sex) that were earlier invoked to exclude women from certain functions were now invoked in a favorable sense. The clergy were forbidden to be guardians (*tutors*) of women as early as the third century.[89]

A final observation concerns concubines, which were allowed under Roman law while fornication (*fornicatio*) was condemned. A concubine was a woman with whom a man lives permanently, but she was not legally his wife since some legal conditions were lacking such as the *affectio maritalis*, the *honor matrimonii* and, of course, the special clothing of a wife. And concubinage was also practiced by the emperors. It is considered by jurists as "an unequal marriage" (*inaequale connubium*). The marriage legislation of Augustus (emp. 27 BCE - 14 CE) had the aim of favoring stable marriage and children but also produced an increase in concubinage. Concubines were of a lower class and legal status than men were. In the fourth century, concubinage, thus understood was not as prominent, since the status of the concubine was lowered, and the children of the concubine were considered *liberi naturales* (natural children). In 336 Constantine prohibited donations to the concubine and to her children.[90] Later legislation intervened several times in the case of donations, stability and legitimizing of natural children.[91]

A text attributed to Augustine is very clear on what Christians thought about all this: "I therefore say to the baptized: There is no lawful fornication. Your wife must suffice or you must do without it, but you are forbidden to keep a concubine. If you are deaf to this command that I give you, there is God who listens; if you do not want to accept the warning, the angels of God listen. There is no lawful concubine. Even if you do not have wives, there is no law to hold a concubine, to be dismissed later to take a wife. Even more serious will be your condemnation if you want to keep a concubine and a wife."[92] Sometimes a concubinage was transformed into a marriage.[93] The concubinage itself was not accepted, however, even if the purpose was for having children.[94]

Jerome points out the frequency of the union of masters with slaves who were treated as if they were wives.[95] Stable cohabitation was more common among non-wealthy people while immorality was common among the wealthiest. Something similar occurs today in extended cohabitations before marriage or with those who live together without a legal or religious marriage. The Council of Toledo (400) issued a practical norm in canon 17 which was concerned about marital fidelity and stability: "If a married Christian has a concubine, he is excluded from communion. But whoever has no wife and, instead of his wife, has a concubine, he is not excluded from communion provided that it is enough to have a single woman who may be a wife or concubine, whichever he prefers."

There is one last consideration to undertake in this section. It concerns slaves who are not citizens and thus could not contract a true marriage. Their unions or cohabitation depended on the will of the master. If both were the property of the same master, cohabitation was possible and easier. But they did not have much of a private life as a family. It was not easy to overcome this difficulty if they depended on two different masters. In this case the problem of the sons (*vernae*) also arose. Who do they belong to? To which master?

Christian communities had to take account of these legal situations. It was easier for them to tolerate or even allow the union between a free person and a freedwoman, or even a slave. Marital fidelity and stability were essential to them.

Mixed Marriages

What did Christians think about the marriages of people practicing different religions?

What was their attitude? For Roman antiquity such a problem did not exist. The religious element was completely foreign to a juridical and polytheistic mentality. Simply put, the problem of mixed marriages on a religious basis did not exist in the pagan Roman world or in other ancient societies, nor does the issue of racial bias even arise in any of these when it came to marriage. On the other hand, the legal situation of the individual within Roman society was decisive. Roman legislation did not allow certain types of matrimonial unions such as those between different classes or that between a Roman citizen and a non-citizen. The idea and practice of disallowing some marriages for exclusively religious reasons comes from the Hebrew Bible and from the Jewish tradition already in force at the time of Jesus. Testimonies in this regard attest to the existence of the prohibition and the difficulty of unions among Jews with non-Jews. A man or a woman was not free to marry just anyone; rather, there were ethical, biological and ritual purity impediments that could prevent certain marriages (see *Deut* 7:3-4).

For the first time the question was discussed by Paul in the seventh chapter of his *First Letter to the Corinthians*. In this case too, as in marriage, Jewish tradition was disrupted by a Jew (Paul). The great novelty is spelled out in another one of his letters: "... where there is no distinction between Greek and Jew, circumcised and uncircumcised, barbarian, Scythian, slave and freeman, but Christ is all, and in all" (*Col* 3:11). The difficulties were many in mixed marriages for religious and ethical reasons. In the following pages only some of these difficulties emerge. Most of them come from the pagan environment of that time since religion was a component of social and family life—although religion was also an integral part of politics. For Christians the ethical conception of marriage was an essential component of their identity, and included conjugal fidelity and the severe condemnation of adultery. The problem of mixed marriages because of the religion of spouses in a polytheistic context makes no sense. Rather, the idea of the rejection of such marriages comes from the Old Testament which alternates between a rigorous and a more relaxed approach.

In the first two centuries of the patristic era we do not find explicit testimonies about mixed marriages, although they were not forbidden by the Church or by the books of the New Testament. The question was often dealt with in the fathers of the Church in different ways. Many simply did not talk about it, perhaps because they considered the issue irrelevant for the purposes of a Christian life. One thing is certain: we must distinguish the practice of the Christian laity from the preaching of the bishops. We also must recognize that the legal distinction between an *impedient* impediment (a marriage that is illicit but valid) and a *diriment* impediment (which makes a marriage invalid)[96] is not a distinction the ancients made. Rather, this dates back to the end of the 12th century and is the work of jurists like Gratian, Peter Lombard and others.

The principle of Roman civil law, *partus sequitur ventrem*, (that which is brought forth follows the womb) means that the civil condition of the child follows and is tied to the legal status of the mother. It also holds true in Jewish law, since one is considered a Jew only if born of a Jewish mother. Determining one's citizenship for a true marriage was just as important for the Romans as it was for the Jews, with both tracing it through the mother. This brings up an observation that may also prove useful in understanding the spread of Christianity. Usually modern scholars investigate the arguments put forward by Christian authors to discourage mixed marriages. Mixed marriages, however, were very frequent between Christians and non-Christians. I think that marriage was the place for tolerance among people, more than any other situation of cohabitation. And this was also true in marriages with mixed religious backgrounds.

Some authors of the third century rejected mixed marriages, such as Tertullian whose counsel on the matter was quite strict: "If these things are so, it is certain that believers contracting marriages with Gentiles are guilty of fornication and are to be excluded from all communication with the brotherhood, in accordance with the Letter of the apostle who says that 'with persons of that kind there is to be no taking of food even.'[97] . . . Is it not adultery that he forbids? Is it not fornication?"[98] He continues with this very strong tone.[99] Tertullian's idea that mixed marriage was adultery has never been accepted.

In the first four centuries there was an abundance of Christian girls and a scarcity of Christian boys. This situation created problems especially for women who wanted to get married, a subject which the council of Elvira took up in canon 15: "Because of the abundance of young girls, do not give Christian virgins as brides to the pagans, so that the imprudence of their young age does not lead them to the adultery of the soul." In third century Syria the *Didascalia* advised bishops to marry girls (virgins) to young Christians.[100]

The historical analysis presented by Augustine is useful:

> Blessed Cyprian . . . is not silent about another thing—thus confirming that it belongs to the same bad habits—that is, contracting marriage with non-believers—asserting that is nothing else than prostituting the members of Christ with the Gentiles. In our times these things are no longer considered as sinful. Since the New Testament does not prescribe anything in this regard, it is believed to be lawful or left as a doubt. Equally uncertain is whether Herod had married his dead or living brother's wife. This is why it is not clear what illicit behavior John was reproaching him for. Even with regard to a concubine who has declared that she no longer wants to join any man, if she is sent away by the one to whom she is linked, it is right to doubt whether she should not be admitted to receive baptism.[101]

As can be deduced from the quoted text, Augustine is quite lenient. So is Chrysostom in the East. In the West Ambrose is more severe towards unions with pagans, heretics, and Jews as are other authors like Jerome.[102] Both local Western and Eastern councils addressed the issue.[103] The so-called Elvira Council (Granada, Spain)—a collection of canons composed at different times—contains several canons on different prohibitions that dealt with the difference of religion, a difference of Christian confession (heretics),[104] kinship, previous relationships, being in the condition of a slave or that of an official penitent, and also prohibitions concerning certain members of the clergy. All these testimonies denounce the frequency of unions with non-Catholics. In the Greek East, it was only in the seventh century that the important council in Trullo of 692 (canon 72) declared for the first time that marriage with a heretic was invalid. It introduced a new idea in the conception of Christian marriage which at that time had no influence on the Latin world. Both in the West and in the Greek East it reemerged in the Middle Ages—in the East in particular with the canonists Zonaras and Balsamon when the Church had already established complete jurisdiction on matrimonial matters.

The main reason for the opposition by some members of the Church and some later councils for mixed marriages was the intention to safeguard the faith of the Christian spouse, the purity of the ecclesiastical community and the Christian education of children born of marriage.[105] Alongside these topics, the authors also point out the theological dimensions of Christian marriage—a kind of union between Christ and the Church—which was in danger in the case of a mixed marriage. In Late Antiquity the Church worried about mixed marriages of any kind, even those with Jews. Christian emperors, on the other hand, did not legislate on the legitimacy of marriages between Christians and pagans, but only marriages with the Jews. The law of 339[106] punished with death a very small group for reasons that were most likely not religious but economic, while the law of 388[107] sanctioned all these unions for religious reasons with capital punishment by putting them on the same level of punishment as that received for adultery: "No Jew shall take a Christian woman in marriage, nor shall a Christian enter into marriage with a Jewish woman. If someone has done such an act, the crime is considered in the same way as adultery and anyone is allowed to file a public prosecution." In short: a Jew cannot marry a Christian; a Christian cannot marry a Jew. This provision is also found in the Visigoth *interpretatio* which adds nothing special. The law is also reported a second time in the Theodosian Code at 9.7.5, which in turn is taken up by the Justinian Code at CI 1.9.6 without adding anything significant either.

This law has had numerous interpretations of its purpose and application. Some thought that it was published as a request by church officials in defense of Christian marriage, or as the result of an anti-Semitic attitude against the Jews, or even as legislation without a religious character at all, similar to the law prohibiting marriage with the barbarians. The law directly concerned men and indirectly also women. As noted above, such a union was considered in the same way as adultery but with this exception: only close relatives could accuse someone of adultery, but those who married Jews could be accused by anyone, without limitations.

Personally, I accept the interpretation of O. Odrobina who recently, in a large and well-documented study, asked the question: *cui prodest* (who benefits) from this law? He rejects any anti-Semitic interpretation as well as the idea of an explicit request from bishops. Examining the rabbinical tradition, he advances the hypothesis of a Jewish origin of the law in the sense that Jewish exponents, in the interest of the Jewish nation, were not only able but desirous to apply for such a law. It was not easy to preserve the ritual purity in a Jewish home with a Christian wife. Inevitable problems would arise. Likewise, there were difficulties for a Christian who married an observant Jewish wife, whose children would be considered Jews. The law then "is the legitimate continuation, through Roman law, of rabbinical practice."[108]

CELEBRATION OF MARRIAGE

The celebration of marriage was not a question of law, as it is today, both in the civil society and in the Christian community. It was simply a social and family event founded on two important elements: the cohabitation of the spouses and the so-called *affectio maritalis*, that is, the enduring will of the spouses to live as husband and wife—which is not the same thing as "love" as understood today. The expression *affectio maritalis* cannot be translated as "marital affection." This desire to be considered husband and wife was more an expression of the will to remain together—an expression that was to be made publicly, although there was no standard legal form of public celebration. Marriage, rather, was considered a private affair with public and legal consequences.

The celebration of the wedding, both in the Jewish and Roman spheres, also involved external rituals, some of which were religious. Even in this case, Christians accepted all the rites, according to the various local traditions, eliminating only what was pagan, because "whether we take a wife, or if we write a will . . . we do not act according to our law, but according to what they have prescribed."[109] We do not know of any specifically Christian rites, places, or ministers involved in the celebration of weddings in the first few centuries. These were celebrated in private homes and the presence of the clergy was not required. Ignatius of Antioch advised that the marriage be done with the approval of the local bishop for the honor of God.[110] However, a trend emerged from the beginning of the third century that considered marriage not only as a social event, but also as a religious and Christian phenomenon. In this context the traditional Roman *tabulae nuptiales* or *matrimoniales* (tablets of marriage) were becoming more important. The conditions of ownership related to marriage, the dowry of the bride, and the procreation of children were all recorded in these tablets. The dowry—*ad sustinenda onera matrimonii*—was one of the conditions of marriage and was considered fundamental by Pope Leo.[111] However, the requirement of the dowry—consisting of movable and immovable property—evolved in Roman law.[112] In Late Antiquity it became mandatory. In the event of dissolution of a marriage, the principle of restitution of the dowry was also mandatory.

The *tabulae nuptiales* were used everywhere during the time of the Roman Empire. Augustine informs us precisely what the situation was:

> Anyone who desires his wife's body for more than is prescribed by this limit—the purpose of procreating children—is going against the very contract (tablets) with which he married her. The contract is recited, it's read out in the presence of all witnesses, and what's read out is this: 'for the sake of procreating children,' and this is called the matrimonial contract. Unless this were what wives are given away and taken for, who with any sense of shame would give away his daughter to another's lust? But to save parents from being ashamed when they give away their daughters, the contract is read out, to make them fathers-in-law, not whoremongers. So, what's read out in the contract? 'In order to procreate children.' The father's brow clears, his face is saved when he hears the words of the contract. We observe the face of the husband who takes the woman as wife.[113]

Augustine often refers to the tablets being read to remember that the purpose of marriage is procreation and not carnal satisfaction: "The text of the contract comes to tell you: to give life to children. Unless you have a generation of children in sight, if you can, observe continence. If you make passion prevail, you do not respect the law and the contract. Is it not evident?"[114]

The scholars of Roman law attribute to the *tabulae* the value of a declaration to take a woman as wife and therefore they constitute the legal act of a true marriage. Or they consider the *tabulae* from an ethical and social standpoint as the point when the woman is assumed to the rank of wife with all her rights and she receives the honors associated with marriage (*honor matrimonii*).[115] In marriage a *virgin* passes to the status of *uxor* (wife.) Tertullian talks about this rite of passage: "Recognize the woman—recognize that she is married by both the testimonies of body and of spirit which she experiences both in the conscience and in the flesh. These are the first tablets on which nature has engraved the engagement and the wedding. Externally impose a veil to her which is already internally covered. The lower parts are already covered, now they also cover the upper parts with the veil."[116]

The marriage is preceded by the official engagement (*sponsalia*), a preliminary ceremony that takes place in the house of the *nubenda* (bethrothed). The domestic and family ceremony consisted in the promise of the engaged couple's intent, given in front of their parents, relatives and friends. This was followed by a banquet. According to Jewish and Hellenistic rites, marriage takes place in two distinct and essential moments with a space of time between the engagement and the actual marriage ceremony. In Roman law, on the other hand the engagement (*sponsalia*) was an important moment but not essential because it did not produce a legal bond and thus did not oblige one to consummate the marriage. The Old Testament too had some prescriptions about engagement. Its rules were more stringent than Roman law and that stringency may have also influenced later Christian legislation.[117]

In the engagement an exchange of gifts was also introduced which had legal value, and was supported by the church itself by strengthening it with a moral obligation as well.[118] The man gave the woman several gifts depending on the possibilities, a ring of gilded iron or gold for the ring finger.[119] Christians gave a new meaning to the ring.[120] Juvenal and the Christian Tertullian both considered it a pledge (*pignus*), but now it is seen as a pledge of affection and a symbol of fidelity, as Ambrose expresses when referring to it as "the seal of genuine faithfulness and an expression of love.[121] In later Roman law, gifts also acquired legal importance (*arrha sponsalicia*), and so if the marriage did not materialize through the fault of one or both of the parties, the gifts were not given back. There were also legal consequences if the promised marriage sealed with a ritual kiss (*osculo interveniente*) was dissolved without a valid reason.[122]

Jewish tradition influenced the development of the importance of engagement in Christianity, according to which the engagement, i.e., the formal promise of marriage generated a bond that constituted a semi-relationship with the boyfriend acquiring special rights with regard to the girl. Siricius writes to Himerius of Tarragona about the breaking of the marriage commitment: "You have also asked, regarding the wedding veiling (*velatio*), if it is possible that someone marries a girl who had already been promised to another. We absolutely forbid this to happen."[123] The ceremony of engagement continued in Italy until a few decades ago. Canon law and the texts of moral theology dealt with the theme for the obligations and consequences that arose.

The choice of the day for the celebration of the wedding had to be made carefully (*dies nuptialis*) because according to the Roman calendar it was not allowed to be held on certain days, especially on the so-called "religious" days during certain festivals (*feriae; dies festi*). These days were *nefasti*, i.e., they were the days reserved for the gods, and not for men.[124] Ovid observed that he had a daughter and wanted her to live a long and full life and so he needed to get the correct information about which days he could have her marry.[125] The reason why marriage could not be contracted on these days was explained by Macrobius: on those days no violence can be done to anyone.[126] Did Christians follow these traditions? I suppose they normally followed them, as they did with so many other traditions.

The Marriage Ceremony

The ancient authors described the marriage ceremony in detail. In the numerous pagan and Christian images that have been preserved, the ceremony was solemnized with the joining of the right hands (*dexterarum iunctio*). The gesture expressed the marital harmony into which they were entering. In Christian iconography this scene was no different from the pagan ceremony. It was interpreted as Christian from the context: the spouses were turned towards each other and the right hand was outstretched. The groom normally held the scroll containing the *tabulae nuptiales* in his left hand. Following the kiss (*osculum*), a crown was placed on each of the heads of the couple and further ceremonial acts followed. Constantine freighted the kiss with even more significance.[127] Another ritual that was quite common was the placing of a veil on the bride (*velatio*, spousal veil).[128] This rite was already in use in Rome and Milan in the fourth century together with a blessing.[129] Sometimes the bride alone wore the veil, as Pope Siricius writes (384-399) to Himerius; sometimes both spouses[130] wore the veil. In his letter Pope Siricius mentioned a blessing which the priest pronounced: "You also asked about the wedding *velatio*, if it is possible for someone to marry a girl who has already been promised to another. We absolutely forbid this happening because if the blessing that the priest gives to the bride is violated by a transgression, it is held by the faithful as a sacrilege."[131] Many Latin sources confirm the existence of this blessing.[132] Pope Innocent I (401-417), writes to Victricius of Rouen: "It is taught that the blessing which the priest pronounces on those who marry does not provide the remedy for sin but rather preserves the form of the Law established by God in ancient times."[133] Pope Gelasius (492-96) noted that the "bride had accepted the pledge and received the veil that was to be put on her head."[134] Augustine also mentions an oath of matrimonial fidelity. On the unions between Catholics and Donatists, he affirms: "Do we not grievously lament that husband and wife do in most cases, when marriage makes them one flesh, vow mutual fidelity in the name of Christ, and yet tear asunder Christ's own body by belonging to different sects?"[135] Canon 101 of the *Ancient Statutes of the Church* of fifth century Gaul prescribes: "Although brides and grooms should be blessed by a priest, they can be offered to each other by their parents or by groomsmen (*paranymphi*)."

Another important and essential element was the conducting of the woman into the husband's house (*deductio in domum mariti*).[136] This procession was a public statement that was also reflected in the language: to lead the wife (*uxorem deducere*), as an expression itself of the marriage relationship, was seen as synonymous with marrying (where the woman is given to a husband). Only then was the couple considered truly married. The entry into the husband's house was the definitive proof of the conclusion of the marriage and of the *affectio maritalis*. This ceremony could also take place with the absence of the groom. The evening procession to the husband's house (*deductio*) went through the town or village accompanied by relatives and friends under the light of torches and with the throwing of walnuts. It involved very licentious elements along with strange acclamations which Christian authors such as John Chrysostom condemn in rather harsh terms.

We do not know when the blessing recited during the wedding ceremony itself was introduced. At a later time, it was reserved for the clergy, if one was present. It became obligatory in the East only towards the seventh century.[137] The first text that speaks of a Eucharistic celebration as part of the ceremony dates back to the fifth century.[138] The Church was also concerned that marriage be observed as a public event celebrated in front of the community and its representatives, and not just a private family ceremony which was forbidden. As Tertullian notes: "That is why we execrate secret unions, even those of a permanent nature; I mean those not announced before to the church. They are of the same peril as adultery and fornication."[139] The marriage contract was signed in front of the bishop, according to Augustine: "It is true: these contracts are signed by the bishop: your wives are your servants, you, the masters of your wives."[140] However, the sacredness of Christian marriage for the fathers was not the result of the form and shape of the celebratory rites, but derived rather from its very essence, inasmuch as it was a divine institution and living symbol of Christ's love for the Church, in line with the Pauline expression "This is a profound mystery—but I am speaking with reference to Christ and the Church" (*Eph* 5:32). Since "from the beginning God appears to have made special provision for this union,"[141] it is sacred in its beginning and throughout the span of its permanence, as Clement of Alexandria expresses: "The marriage, then, that is consummated according to the word, is sanctified, if the union be under subjection to God, and be conducted 'with a true heart, in full assurance of faith.'"[142] This natural sacredness associated with marriage is the founding basis of marital Christian ethics with its demands for indissolubility, fidelity and mutual love: "It is not something human; rather God has sown this love."[143]

Duchesne notes that: "With the exception of haruspicy [the art or practice of divination] all the Roman wedding ritual has been preserved in Christian usage, including the crowns.... The Church, essentially conservative, in this kind of thing only modifies what is incompatible with its beliefs."[144] In the pagan ceremony the haruspex served as a witness; in the Christian ceremony the presence of the priest served as a simple witness. On the other hand, Christian teaching regarded some elements of the Roman wedding ritual as essential, in particular the doctrine on the importance of consent, on the need of the dowry and on the importance of the wedding blessing.

The Family and Its Duties

The teaching of the fathers on the family is based on the biblical texts, according to which the marriage union flows from the heart (*kardia*),[145] while the disunion is the result of hardness of heart (*sklerokardia*). Consequently, the connective element must be love, understood as agape.[146] Indeed the love of Christ for the Church constitutes its supreme ideal (see *Eph* 5:32), and marriage itself is a figure of the link between Christ and the Church (*2 Cor* 11:2). Strangely, the texts of the New Testament speak more of the duties of the parents towards the children than of the obedience and love that the children must give to them—exhibiting a great sympathy towards the children (*Mt* 19:13).[147] Children must obey their parents, but "in the Lord" (*Eph* 6:1) and parents have a duty to educate them firmly but with love. The children have the duties of obedience, respect and filial love and, if they are of mature age, also of parental care. But parents must be concerned with raising them physically healthy, culturally aware and, above all, foster their religious growth based on love and the fear of God, so as not to be "spiritual murderers" of their children.[148]

The poet Juvenal (ca 60–ca 140) writes: "The child is due the utmost respect" (*Maxima debetur puero reverential.*)[149] This sentence has become the motto of many modern associations. Juvenal dealt with the education of children through the example of the virtuous life of the parents. Although the Roman period was the best for children and the elderly, ancient society in general was not a paradise for the elderly and children. First, there was a high infant mortality. Those who survived the first terrible years often became orphans due to the death of the father and often also of the mother. An often neglected aspect in all of this was the children of marriages between brothers and sisters[150] and the offspring of bigamous marriage or divorced parents.

The rights of the father as noted above had already experience a downsizing in imperial society. Christianity further reconfigured those rights inasmuch as, while recognizing the *patria potestas* (fatherly authority), Christianity preferred to speak of *patria pietas* (fatherly affection).[151] It went even further in affirming the family as "a small church,"[152] where its members prayed together and listened to the explanation of Scripture: "The house thus becomes a church, so that the devil, the enemy of our salvation, is put to flight. Let the grace of the Holy Spirit rest upon everyone and all peace and harmony protect those who dwell in the house."[153] In this small domestic church, the father played his role not with the spirit of domination—as recognized by law—but with that of service. He was the domestic bishop: "So, brothers, when you hear the Lord saying 'Where I am, there also my servant will be,' do not think only of worthy bishops and priests. You too, each in his own way, can serve Christ by living well. . . . And so, each head of the family also acknowledges in this name that he owes fatherly affection to his family. Let each head admonish all of his own for Christ's sake and for eternal life. Let him teach, admonish, correct, employ good will and exercise discipline. In this way, in his own house he will fulfill in a way a churchly and episcopal function, serving Christ so that he may be with him forever."[154]

Jesus taught that husband and wife "are no longer two but one. What therefore God has joined together, let not man put asunder" (*Mt* 19:6; *Mk* 10:9-10). This teaching formed the basis of the patristic teaching on the family, with the aim of highlighting its sacred character as well as its needs. John Chrysostom writes: "The men must listen to this, and women must also listen to it too! Women, so that they manifest their inclination towards their husbands and do not put anything before their health; men, so that they have much kindness toward their women and act in everything as if they had a single soul with their wife and form one single flesh with her. We have a true marriage when a similar harmony reigns among the spouses and the bond is so close that they are in this way linked by love. . . . Where harmony prevails, every good is present. There is peace and love, and spiritual harmony reigns."[155] Therefore, compared to the contemporary pagan mentality and practice, the Christian family bond was placed on a different basis founded on love and faith. This is how Ignatius of Antioch expresses himself: "Tell my sisters to love the Lord and to be content with their husbands in flesh and in spirit. Similarly, also charge my brothers in the name of Jesus Christ to love their wives, as the Lord loved the Church."[156] Mutual affection (*mutuus affectus*) and matrimonial love (*caritas coniugalis*) are both part of the essence of marriage.

As a personal encounter "marriage is the seal of an unbreakable friendship . . . the unique drink from a fountain enclosed, that does not allow strangers to imbibe."[157] But this "mystery of love" (*agapes mysterion*)[158] has a profound sacred dimension in its origin and in its development because it comes from God and is lived according to his word and its end goal is eternal salvation. Therefore, Christianity goes beyond the current mentality, partly in re-evaluating the subjective aspect of the encounter between two persons, and fully in offering the deepest and most radical motivations for conjugal coexistence.

However, although the marriage bond is based on *caritas* it also generates a mutual submission. It "is really a bond . . . because it forces the spouses to a mutual subjection that is far more serious than that of any servant . . . as the feet of the fugitive slaves are bound each one for themselves and also linked one to the other."[159] For these reasons, in their common life together the spouses are on the same level as far as their rights are concerned, owing to each other fidelity, mutual assistance, and conjugal relations. The latter are sometimes forbidden in certain periods for cultural reasons.

This parity that is found especially in the realms of soteriology and the mutual affection of the spouses still does not exclude a hierarchy. The husband is the undisputed leader and so his wife and children are on a subordinate level. The very structure of the ancient family, codified in law and in custom, is otherwise inconceivable even for Christians. The fathers however add biblical and theological motivations to it that reference the story of humanity's creation in Genesis and also Paul. The woman was taken from the man and molded in his image. She sinned first while also inducing the man to sin.

The relevance of a social factor, normally neglected by scholars, concerning the age difference between spouses at the time of marriage of a gap of at least a decade should be considered when speaking of the dependence of women on men. According to Roman law, for a marriage to be valid the boys must be at least 14 years old and the girls twelve, because at that age they are considered capable of procreating. It was common in the ancient period to give young girls in marriage while they were still small. The father (*pater*) could also promise a baby girl to a man, and even give her in marriage before the age of twelve (*iusta aetas*, proper age). Despite knowing when the woman was able to bear children, both lawyers and legislation chose an arbitrary minimum age when they could have sexual relations and could therefore marry. They were called *virpotens*. This term indicates both a girl capable of having sexual intercourse and one who can marry. It was not a biological but a juridical judgment. In fact, "the statements of the jurists on the female puberty age did not stop the widespread use of unions with girls not yet twelve, unions qualified by most scholars as 'early marriages.'"[160] Augustine tells us of his own mother Monica's betrothal: "When she had arrived at a marriageable age, she was given to a husband whom she served as her lord."[161] The language is significant: she was given.

This kind of legislation can be illustrated by the example of Augustine's life. When his father Patricius discovered that his son had grown up and was already "becoming a man, he, as if from this anticipating future descendants, joyfully told it to my mother." His sensitive mother was worried about the sins he could commit: "She privately warned me, with great solicitude, 'not to commit fornication; but above all things never to defile another man's wife.' These appeared to me but womanish counsels, which I should blush to obey."[162] In Milan, when Augustine sent back the woman of his heart[163] because she was an obstacle to a *matrimonium iustum* according to the law, "Active efforts were made to get me a wife.... Yet the affair was pressed on, and a maiden sued who was two years under the marriageable age; and, as she was pleasing, she was waited for."[164] The girl was only ten years old. Monica died "the fifty-sixth year of her life, and thirty-third of mine, that blessed and holy soul departed from this earth."[165] Monica gave birth to Augustine at the age of twenty-three. How long before this had she been married? Even today in Africa there are marriages that take place at an early age.

The lawyers mention cases of girls before the age of twelve who are taken to their husband's house. These cases are recorded in relation to problems of ownership, dowry and adultery. This is why the husbands are urged to be like guides and protectors for their wives who are considerably younger than they and less prepared both socially and culturally. Even in the family context, the contribution of Christianity did not aim to change the society of the time, but rather to change the hearts of men in order to create a new human relationship. And so the church in the early centuries did not care about the legal problems and assets governed by Roman or local law because Christians married "according to the customs of the country they inhabit" (*secundum consuetudinem illius regionis quam incolunt*).[166] Christianity later changed some rules concerning marriage, as it did in other fields as well when it replaced the State. The canonical matrimonial law was based on Roman law. Even today, the minimum allowable age for marriage for boys is sixteen and for girls is fourteen—although the ecclesiastical authority can make changes and has recently proposed moving that age to sixteen for girls as well.

In many other fields Christians accepted the Roman legal norms. For example: children born of two slaves were also slaves themselves. Also, natural born children inherited the status of their mother and the children of two free persons were free and not slaves.

Conclusion. It was not always possible to realize the Christian ideal in the family because in ancient Christianity at least until the late fourth century there was a strong predominance of women. These women were often forced to contract marriage with pagans if they did not want to embrace the state of virginity—although in general they were advised against doing so. Family solidarity, however, was not normally affected since extensive religious and cultural tolerance reigned in the fourth century. And so it seems quite clear that the Christian attitude towards marriage was initially only of an ethical and religious nature, so it was only natural that it also influenced the Roman law being elaborated in Late Antiquity.[167] It was only after our period, however, that a canonical corpus was established that replaced the Roman one—albeit a corpus reliant on that previous Roman legal experience it had encountered and lived by.[168]

Abortion Practices

Abortion practices[169] were very widespread at that time and were severely and unanimously condemned since the beginnings of Christianity. Abortion is equated with murder because that which is conceived is a living being and has the right to life, so that those who practice it will be gravely condemned by God.[170] From the quotations of the footnote it is clear that the condemnation goes back to the origins of Christianity. Tertullian writes: "But to us, to whom homicide has been once for all forbidden, it is not permitted to break up even what has been conceived in the womb, while as yet the blood is being drawn (from the parent body) for a human life. Prevention of birth is premature murder, and it makes no difference whether it is a life already born that one snatches away, or a life in the act of being born that one destroys. That which is to be a human-being is also human; the whole fruit is already actually present in the seed."[171] When abortion was practiced by some Christians, the Church imposed exclusion from the Eucharist for them: "For the woman who deliberately procures an abortion the penalty of murder is imposed. Do not let us argue as to whether the fetus is formed or not. . . . However, one must not let the penitent remain in a state of penance until death but keep within the measure of ten years: inner healing is established not by the length of time, but by the quality of penance."[172]

The Christian attitude was promoted by a new idea: respect for life since it comes from God. Therefore it must be protected from anything that would threaten it. This is why even the abandonment of newborns—a custom legally permitted by the state until the fourth century[173]—was strongly rejected, as was their sale. Instead Christians recommended adoption.

* * *

Appendix: Spiritual Marriage

THE USE of the phrase "spiritual marriage" expresses an analogy with the practice of a marriage between a man and a woman. The mystic John of the Cross defined it this way: "The spiritual marriage between the soul and the Son of God is incomparably more than spiritual marriage (engagement), because it is a total transformation in the Beloved. In it the one part gives itself to the other in total possession with a certain consummation of the union of love, in which the soul is made divine and God by participation, as much as possible in this life."[174]

This idea is ancient, going back even before Christianity. The prophets presented the relationship between Yahweh and Israel as a marriage. Already Philo of Alexandria spoke of the intimacy of contact with God and of receiving a spiritual seed.[175] The Song of Songs—an erotic text—gave rise to different interpretations of the union of God's people with himself (e.g. Hippolytus) or of the soul with Christ/God (Origen).[176] The book of the Apocalypse ends with the wedding of the Lamb (Rev 19:7-9). Origen develops the concept of marriage, looking at it from the divine perspective:

> Right from the start, we find that the union of man and woman in the divine realm refers to the union of Christ with the church, the first union representing and indicating the second union. But if one considers the matter from above, from the summit and not from the base, it is not the union of Christ and the church that derives from the creation of the human couple, but on the contrary it is the man-woman relationship at the core of marriage that has in the Christ-church union its practical and living archetype, the supreme reason for its existence.[177]

Even the Church is presented as a bride of Christ and therefore also as mother. "It was especially Origen in the *Commentary and Homilies on the Song of Songs* and in other works who heavily orchestrated this double meaning of the spouse, Church and soul, thus creating the theme of mystical marriage: the Christian soul is a spouse because it makes up part of the Church/spouse: the Church progresses in its quality as spouse through the progress of souls in the Church."[178]

At the end of the second century the concept of the "bride of Christ" is affirmed, that is, of the virgin who gives her whole self to God. Tertullian is the first to use such a term regarding widows and virgins.[179] He demands that the virgins wear the veil.[180] Then this theme is developed (e.g. Methodius of Olympus and Ambrose) and we reach the consecration of virgins through the imposition of the veil (*velatio*), as if it were a wedding celebration. The public imposition of the veil, with the change of dress, is for a young girl, mature in faith and in virtue: "You are covered by a sacred veil" (*sacro velamine tecta es*.)[181]

A totally different phenomenon that was widespread in the East and in the West, which we introduced earlier in the chapter, was the so-called *virgines subintroductae*, also called *agapeti*, referring to ascetics of both sexes who cohabit together. Sometimes one of the two was a celibate cleric and the other was a virgin. Cohabitation was a way, perhaps, to provide support and mutual help, but it also raised legitimate suspicions. This type of cohabitation was condemned by many fathers, beginning with Cyprian, and continued to be condemned during the fourth century by councils and bishops. A quote from Jerome will suffice:

> I blush to speak of it, it is so shocking; yet though sad, it is true. How comes this plague of the *agapetæ* [beloved] to be in the church? Whence come these unwedded wives, these novel concubines, these harlots, so I will call them, though they cling to a single partner? One house holds them and one chamber. They often occupy the same bed, and yet they call us suspicious if we fancy anything amiss. A brother leaves his virgin sister; a virgin, slighting her unmarried brother, seeks a brother in a stranger. Both alike profess to have but one object, to find spiritual consolation from those not their relatives; but their real aim is to indulge in sexual intercourse.... Can one go upon hot coals and his feet not be burned? We cast out, then, and banish from our sight those who only wish to seem and not to be virgins.[182]

---

1. Clement of Alexandria, *Pedagogue* 1.4.1-2.
2. John Chrysostom, *Homilies 2 letter to Tim* 10.3: PG 62:659.
3. See *Mk* 10:9-12, *Mt* 5:31-32;19:3-9.
4. *Mt* 19:12: 22:30, *Mk* 12:25, *Lk* 14:26; 19:29.
5. Rabbinical Judaism considered marriage as an obligation and a duty to generate a lineage. The ancient church, even if in some cases it understood a eunuch as someone who experienced physical castration, the term was normally interpreted in a metaphorical way. Nonetheless, the church refused to ordain evirated people to the ministries. See *Theological Dictionary of the New Testament*, 2:487.

6. Pietro Dacquino. *Storia del matrimonio: cristiano alla luce della Bibbia* (Torino: Elle Di Ci, 1984); Gillian Beattie, *Women and Marriage in Paul and His Early Interpreters* (London: T&T Clark International, 2005); D. G. Hunter, *Marriage, Celibacy, and Heresy in Ancient Christianity: The Jovinianist Controversy* (New York: Oxford University Press, 2007); D.G. Hunter, *Marriage in the Early Church* (Minneapolis: Fortress Press, 1994); *Il matrimonio dei cristiani: esegesi biblica e diritto romano: XXXVII incontro di studiosi dell'antichità cristiana* (Rome: Institutum Patristicum Augustinianum, 2009); W.R. Loader, *Making Sense of Sex. Attitudes towards Sexuality in Early Jewish and Christian Literature* (Grand Rapids MI: Eerdmans, 2013).
7. The Apostle Paul defends the goodness of marriage, according to the words of Genesis, and exhorts the Christians to live it in its fullness. However, he advises celibacy as best suited to the present time (cf. *1 Cor* 7:1-40; *Col* 3:18-19).
8. John Chrysostom, *Virginity* 10; PG 48:450.
9. See R. Cantalamessa, ed., *Etica sessuale e matrimonio nel cristianesimo primitivo* (Milano: Vita e pensiero, 1976), pp. 434s; Charles Munier, *L'Église dans l'Empire romain (IIe - IIIe siècles)* (Paris: Éditions Cujas, 1979), 7-13; H. F. Hägg, "Continence and Marriage: The Concept of *Enkrateia* in Clement of Alexandria," *Symbolae Osloenses* 81 (2006): 126–43.
10. Gregory of Nazianzus, *Poemata moralia* 1.275-76: PG 37:543.
11. Athenagoras, *Embassy* 33; *Diognetus* 5; Tertullian, *Apology* 42.
12. *Passion of Perpetua* 2.1.
13. Claude Rambaux, *Tertullien face aux morales des trois premiers siècles*, (Paris: Les Belles lettres, 1979), 204-62; Pier A. Gramaglia, *Il matrimonio nel cristianesimo preniceno: Ad uxorem, De exhortatione castitatis, De monogamia*, (Roma: Borla, 1988); A. R. Guffey, "Motivations for Encratite Practices in Early Christian Literature" *The Journal of Theological Studies* 65 (2014): 515-49.
14. B. Gain, "La défense du mariage en Asie Mineure et en Syrie au IVe siècle," in: *Les Pères de l'Église et la chair. Entre incarnation et diabolisation, les premiers chrétiens au risque du corps*, ed. Pascal Delage. (Royan: Caritas Patrum, 2012), 315-36
15. John Chrysostom, *Virginity* 6.34.
16. See John Chrysostom, *Virginity* 43-44; 57-58.
17. John Chrysostom, *Hom. in Hebr.* 7.4.
18. Clement of Alexandria, *Stromata* 2.140-46.
19. *Didascalia* 4.2; *Apostolic Constitutions* 4.2.
20. The Emperor Augustus enacted laws to promote marriage and procreation, which remained in force until Constantine. Cf. for this ancient procreation mentality, Clement Alex., *Stromata* 2: 140-46. For Christians instead, continence has value as a free choice of consecration to God, therefore with a functional character and not as a status, condition of life, or as a biological fact. Virginity "if it is worthy of honor, is not for itself, as such, but because it is consecrated to God," Augustine, *De sancta virg.* 8.8 and in this sense is an anticipation of the future kingdom: "the intention to preserve enduring corruption while in corruptible flesh" (Augustine, *De sancta virg.* 13.13).
21. R. Cantalamessa, *Etica sessuale*, 437-38.
22. Augustine, *Soliloquies* 1.10.17.
23. Augustine, *De Genesi ad litteram* 11.7.12.
24. Augustine, *The Good of Marriage* 18.21.
25. *1 Cor* 7:38; Augustine, *On Holy Virginity* 18.
26. Cf. *Gen* 2:24, *Mt* 19:6; *1 Cor* 6:16.
27. A reference to the Eucharist—language which was deliberately chosen to contrast with the pagan sacrifices that were being offered.
28. Cf. *Mt* 18:20.
29. Tertullian, *To His Wife* 2.8.
30. *Mt* 5:32; 19:9; *Mk* 10:11-12; *1 Cor* 7:10-11.
31. *1 Clement* 1.
32. Polycarp, *To the Philippians* 4.2-3.
33. Ignatius, *To Polycarp* 5.
34. Athenagoras, *Embassy* 3.1.
35. Athenagoras, *Embassy* 33.2-6.
36. The numerous *Acts of the Apostles*, called *apocrypha*, written in the East.

37. Jean-Daniel Kaestli, "Fiction littéraire et réalité sociale: que peut-on savoir de la place des femmes dans le milieu de production des Actes apocryphes des Apôtres?" *Apocrypha* 1 (1990): 279-302; *A Feminist Companion to the New Testament Apocrypha*, ed. Amy-Jill Levine, Maria Mayo Robbins (New York: T&T Clark International, 2006).
38. These Christians writers based their thinking on *1 Cor* 6:16; see Hermas *Shepherd, Mandate* 4.4-5; Tertullian, *Adv. Marc.* 4.34.5; Novatian, *De pudic.* 5-6; Origen, *Fragm. in 1 Cor.* 35; Idem, *Comm. in Matth.* 28.25.
39. Justin, *Second Apology* 2. A. Di Berardino, "Scuole e maestri cristiani nella Roma del secondo secolo. Relazioni tra l'Ecclesia e i Didaskaleia," in *Rivista di Archeologia cristiana* 2019 (forthcoming.)
40. Hermas, *Shepherd, Mandate* 4.4-7.
41. Origen, *Comm. on Matthew* 14.23-24.
42. Cf. Augustine, *De bono coniugali* 32.
43. Augustine, *On Marriage and Concupiscence* 1.11.
44. CTh 3.18.1.
45. CTh 3.16.2.
46. CI 5.17.8.
47. *solutionem etenim matrimonii difficiliorum esse favor imperat liberorum.*
48. CI 5.17.9.
49. See CI 5.17.10, completed in Novella 22.
50. *Lex Romana Burgundiorum, Lex Romana Visigotorum*, the edict of Theodoric.
51. Hermas, *Shepherd, Mandate* 4.
52. Tertullian, *On Monogamy* 12.2-3.
53. Clement of Alexandria, *Stromata* 3.12.90.
54. Origen, *Hom. in Lucam* 17.10.
55. Origen, *Hom. in Lucam* 17.11.
56. Hippolytus, *Against Heresies* 9.12.
57. P. Garnsey, "Septimius Severus and the Marriage of Soldiers," *California Studies in Classical Antiquity* 3 (1970): 45-53; P.P. Onida, "Il matrimonio dei militari in età imperiale," *Diritto@Storia* 14 (2016): 1-36.
58. B.D. Shaw, "The Family in Late Antiquity: The Experience of Augustine," *Past & Present* 115 (1987): 3-51; cf., F. Lamberti, "La storiografia sulla 'familia' romana fra inquadramenti tradizionali e nuove tendenze," in *La famiglia tardoantica. Società, diritto, religione* ed. Neri V., B. Girotti (Bologna: LED, 2016), 11-29; N. Geoffrey, *The Family in Late Antiquity: The Rise of Christianity and the Endurance of Tradition* (New York: Routledge, 2012).
59. Jerome, *Ep.* 77.3. See Jerome, *In epist. ad Eph.* 3.5, see also 21-22; PL 26:563-64.
60. Augustine, *Sermon* 392.2; CPL 285.
61. "Mundi legibus subditi esse quam Christi, quoniam iura forensia non eisdem quibus feminas pudicitiae nexibus viros videntur obstringere [...] Si haec observanda sunt propter decus terrenae civitatis, quanto castiores quaerit caelestis patria et societas angelorum?" (*De coniugiis adulterinis* 2.8.7).
62. *Sed in foro, non in caelo; in lege mundi, non in lege Creatoris mundi.*
63. Gregory of Nazianzus, *Oration* 37; SC 318.
64. Gregory of Nazianzus, *Oration* 37.6.
65. Gregory of Nazianzus, *Oration* 37.8.
66. Gregory of Nazianzus, *Oration* 37.7.
67. Gregory of Nazianzus, *Oration* 37.8.
68. J. Bernardi, *La Prédication des Pères cappadociens: Le Prédicateur et son auditoire* (Paris: Presses Universitaires de France, 1968), 220-22.
69. Augustine, *De coniugiis adulterinis* 2.8.7.
70. Augustine, *Sermon* 9.4; WSA 3.1:263.
71. Augustine, *De bono viduitatis* 5.6.
72. Ambrose, *De Abraham* 1.9.91.
73. Ambrose, *De Abraham* 1.9.91.
74. Augustine, *Ep.* 254; NPNF 1.1:591.
75. See Tertullian, *De orat.* 22.10 ; *Apology* 6.4; Council of Elvira, canon 54; see J. Gaudemet, *L'Église dans l'Empire Romain: IVe-Ve siècles* (Paris :Sirey, 1958), 521-24.
76. The intent to be married, also sometimes rendered as marital affection, but primarily concerned the intent.

77. *non enim coitus matrimonium facit, sed maritalis affection. Digestum* 24.1.32.13. Olis Robleda, *El matrimonio en derecho romano: esencia, requisitos de validez, efectos, disolubilidad* (Roma: Libreria editrice gregoriana, 1970), 59-71; C Fayer, *La familia romana*, 2:344ff. *Digestum* 35.1.15 = 50.17.30: *Nuptias non concubitus, sed consensus facit.*
78. Augustine, *Answer to Julian* 5.12.46 – 5.16.62.
79. Augustine, *On Marriage and Concupiscence* 1.11-12.13.
80. Augustine: "The true and living God is the creator of human beings, that marriage is good, that God instituted it by the creation and union of both sexes and blessed it with the gift of fertility" (*Answer to Julian* 4.1.1). "Since the two sexes were created for this purpose and a human being is born only as a result of their union, spouses for this purpose make a good use of that evil. But if they also seek pleasure from sexual desire, they make a bad, but pardonable use of it (*Answer to Julian* 5.12.46).
81. Ambrose, *De inst. Virg.* 6.41.
82. According to Roman law, a concubine was not a wife but a woman with whom one lives together.
83. Here he is talking about the social and legal status of the two people.
84. Augustine, *Ep.* 167.4; PL 54:1204-05.
85. Athenagoras, *Embassy* 33.
86. Irenaeus, *Against heresies* 9.2.
87. The fathers speak little of these topics, since, as has been said, their main concerns were with ethical behavior.
88. *Feminae ab omnibus officiis civilibus vel publicis remotae sunt et ideo nec iudices esse possunt nec magistratum gerere nec postulare nec pro alio intervenire nec procuratores existere* (Digestum 50.17.2pr).
89. See Cyprian, *Ep.* 1.
90. CTh., 4.6.2.3.
91. Dante Gemmiti, *Il concubinato nel diritto romano e giustinianeo: Con appendice sul diritto bizantino* (Napoli: LER, 1993); Riccardo Astolfi, *Il matrimonio nel diritto romano classico* (Milano: CEDAM, 2014), 128-41.
92. Augustine, *Sermon* 392.2.
93. Augustine, *De bono coniugali* 17.
94. Augustine, *De bono coniugali* 14.16.
95. Jerome *Ep.* 69.5.
96. For the Canon Law, see 1073ff.
97. Cf. 1 *Cor* 5:11.
98. Tertullian, *To His Wife* 2.3.1. C. Micaelli, "'Matrimonium' e 'stuprum' in Tertulliano Cast. 9.1-4: osservazioni su un brano controverso," *Sileno* 36 (2010): 79-102.
99. Tertullian, *De corona militis* 13; *De monogamia* 7; Hippolytus, *Elenchos* 9.12; Cyprian, *De lapsis* 6; *Testimoniorum libri* 3.62; Origen, *Fragm. in 1 Cor* 7:34-36.
100. *Didascalia* 17.2. The *Didascalia* advises bishops to adopt an orphan girl, and to marry her to his son, if he has one.
101. Augustine, *De fide et operibus* 19.35 see *De coniugiis adulterinis* 1.25.31.
102. Ambrose, *De Abraham* 1.9.81-86; *Ep.* 62 *ad Vigilium*; *Expositio Evangelii secundum Lucam* 8.2-4; *Expositio psalmi* 118.20.48; Jerome, *Commentarii in IV epistulas Paulinas, Ad Ephesios* 3.5; *Epistula* 107.1-2; *Commentarii in Isaiam* 7.19.23; *Ep.* 123.5.
103. Elvira (306), cann. 15-16 (17); Arles (314), can. 11; Hippo (393) can. 12; Laodicea (second part of Fourth Century.) can. 10 and 31; Chalcedon (451) can. 14; Agde (506), can. 67; Orléans II (533), can. 19; Clermont (535), can. 6; Orléans III (538), can. 13; Toledo III (589), can. 14; Toledo IV (633), can. 68.
104. Canon 16: "To the heretics who did not wish to pass to the Catholic Church should not be given in brides Catholic girls; neither to the Jews nor to the heretics can be given, because there can be no communion between a believer and an infidel. If the parents violate this decree, they are denied communion for five years."
105. Tertullian, *De corona militis* 13; *De monogamia* 7.5; *Ad uxorem* 2; Ps. Hippolytus, *Elenchos* 9.12; Cyprian, *De lapsis* 6; *Testimoniorum libri* 3.62; Origen, *Fragm. in 1 Cor* 7:34-36; Epiphanius, *Adv. haereses* 2.1.61.5; Zenon of Verona, *Hom.* 2.7; Chrysostom, *Hom. in Eph.* 20.5; *Hom. in 1 Cor* 19.3; Ambrosiaster, *Comm. in 1 Cor* 7.15; Ambrose, *De Abraham* 1.9.81-86; *Ep.* 62 *ad Vigilium*; *Expositio Evangelii secundum Lucam* 8.2-4; *Expositio psalmi* 118 20.48; Jerome, *Commentarii in IV epistulas Paulinas, Ad Ephesios* 3.5; *Epistula* 107.1-2; *Commentarii in Isaiam* 7.19.23; *Ep.* 123.5; Augustine, *De fide et operibus* 19.35; *De adult. coniug.* 1.25.31, *Epp.* 23; 33; 220; 252-55; 258.
106. CTh 16.8.6.
107. CTh 3.7.2.

108. L. Odrobina, *Le CTH 3,7,2 et les mariages mixtes* (Szeged: Hungaria, 2007), 300.
109. John Chrysostom, *Hom. ad Ant.* 16.4: PG 49:164.
110. Ignatius, *To Polycarp* 6.
111. Leo, *Ep.* 167.4: PL 54:1204-5.
112. R. D'Ancona, *Il concetto della dote nel diritto romano: Studio storico-giuridico* (Rome: L'Erma Di Bretschneider, 1972); A. Arjava, *Women and Law in Late Antiquity* (Oxford: Oxford University Press, 1998); J. Evans Grubbs, *Women and Law in the Roman Empire* (London: Routledge, 2010), passim.
113. Augustine, *Sermon* 51.22; *Sermons* 9.11.18; 278.9; 292.39.
114. Augustine, *Sermon* 278.9.
115. C. Foyer, *La familia romana: aspetti giuridici ed antiquari*, vol. II (Rome: L'Erma Di Bretschneider, 2005), 373.
116. Tertullian, *On the Veiling* 12.1; see, *To his Wife* 2.3.1.
117. John Chrysostom, *Hom. In Genesim* 48 and 56.2 (PG 54:443 and 448).
118. See Council of Elvira, canon 54: "Parents who break their children's marriage promise, abstain from communion for three years; however, their behavior will be justified if the promised spouse or the betrothed had incurred a serious fault." Judith Evans Grubbs, *Law and Family in Late Antiquity: The Emperor Constantine's Marriage Legislation* (Oxford: Clarendon Press, 1995), 156-83.
119. Augustine, *On the Gospel of John* 8.4: "Who will make such offerings to his bride? Men may offer to a bride every sort of earthly ornament, gold, silver, precious stones, houses, slaves, estates, farms, but will any give his own blood? For if one should give his own blood to his bride, he would not live to take her for his wife."
120. L. Anné, "La conclusion du mariage dans la tradition et le droit de l'Eglise latine jusqu'au VIe siècle," *Ephemerides theologicae Lovanienses* 12 (1935): 513-50; M. Sordi, "Da Ambrogio al Boccaccio: l'anello simbolo della fede," *Rendiconti dell'Istituto Lombardo Accademia di scienze e lettere* 114 (1980): 116-22; P.C. Finney, "Images on Finger Rings and Early Christian Art," *DOP* 41 (1987): 181-86.
121. *Sincerae fidei signaculum et expressio caritatis.* Ambrose, *Expositio in Ev. sec.Lucam* 7.231.
122. See CTh 3.5.2; 3.5.6 of Constantine; CI 5.3.16; *Digestum*, 19.5.17. 5; 16.3.25; 23.1.
123. Siricius, *Ep.* 4.
124. Marriages were not celebrated in the calends, nones and ides of each month; in May, on February 13-21, 1-20 March, June 5-15, etc.
125. Ovid, *Fasti* 6.219-20.
126. Macrobius, *Saturnalia* 1.15.21.
127. CTh 3.5.6.
128. Tertullian, *De virginibus velandis* 11.7: PL 2:905.
129. Ambrose, *Ep.* 23.5; PL 16:984.
130. Paulinus of Nola, *Carmen* 25.227-28.
131. Siricius, *Ep* 1.4. The imposition of the veil (*velatio*) concerned both consecrated and married women. In the former it expressed an ascetic choice in which the *velatio* expressed metaphorically, on a spiritual level, the marriage of the virgin with Christ (*sponsa Christi*). In this passage Siricius refers not to a marriage between a man and a woman, but to a promise of marriage. The word *velatio* now had acquired a new meaning.
132. Ambrose, *Ep.* 19.7 (PL 16:984); Peter Chrysologus, *Sermon* 157 (PL 52:616).
133. Innocent, *Ep* 2.6.9.
134. P. Dacquino, *Storia del matrimonio cristiano*, 190-91.
135. Augustine, *Ep* 23.5.
136. Danielle Gourevitch and Marie-Thérèse Raepsaet Charlier, *La femme dans la Rome antique* (Paris: Hachette Littératures, 2001); also *La donna nella Roma antica* (Firenze: Giunti, 2003), 80-82.
137. P. Jounel, "La liturgie romaine du marriage," *La Maison Dieu* 50 (1957): 30-57; I.H. Dalmais, "La liturgie du mariage dans les Eglises orientales," *La Maison Dieu* 50 (1957): 58-69.
138. See *Praedestinatus* 3.
139. *occultae coniunctiones, id est non prius apud ecclesiam professae.* Tertullian, *On Modesty.* 4.4. See also Tertullian, *De virg. velandis* 12.1; Jerome, *Ep.* 58.5; Augustine, *Sermo* 332.4; see Ignatius of Antioch, *To Polycarp* 5.2: "It becomes both men and women who marry to form their union with the approval of the bishop."
140. Augustine, *Sermon* 332.4.

141. John Chrysostom, *Hom. in Eph.* 20.1; see Fulgentius of Ruspe, *Rule of Faith* (42) 85; in the fragment of the sarcophagus of Villa Albani, there is the effigy of Christ with the gesture of crowning the spouses to express the idea that it is he who unites them.
142. Clement of Alexandria, *Stromata* 4.126-129.4.
143. John Chrysostom, *Hom. quales ducendae sint uxores* 3; PG 51:230.
144. Louis Duchesne, *Origines du culte chrétien, étude sur la liturgie latine avant Charlemagne* (Paris: Albert Fontemoing, 1909), 419.
145. See *Mt* 5:27f; 19:8, *Mk* 10:4.
146. See *Col* 3:18ff; *Eph* 5:22ff.; *l Pet* 2:18ff.; Anders Nygren, *Agape and Eros,* trans. by Phillip S. Watson (New York: Harper & Row 1969).
147. See *Col* 3:21; *Eph* 6:4; *Tit* 2:4; *Lk* 15:11-32.
148. Augustine, *Ep.* 98.3 (to Boniface).
149. Juvenal, *Satires* 14.47.
150. W Scheidel, "Incest Revisited: Three Notes on the Demography of Sibling Marriage in Roman Egypt," *The Bulletin of the American Society of Papyrologists* 32 (1995): 143-55; Idem, "Brother-Sister Marriage in Roman Egypt," *Journal of Biosocial Science* 29 (1997): 361-71.
151. See Tertullian, *Adv. Marc.* 2.13; M. Roberti, ""Patria potestas" e "paterna pietas,"" *Studi in memoria di Albertoni*, vol. I, (Padova: CEDAM, 1935), 257-70.
152. John Chrysostom, *In epist. ad Eph.* 20.6: PG 62:143; more texts see P. Rentinck, *La cura pastorale in Antiochia nel IV secolo* (Rome: Università Gregoriana editrice, 1970), 277-80; see Augustine, *Ep.* 188.3; *Sermo* 94: PL 38:581.
153. John Chrysostom, *Homilies on Gen.* 2.4.
154. Augustine, *On the Gospel of John.* 51.13.
155. Chrysostom, *Homilies on Genesis* 45. For more quotations, see Ambrose, *Hexameron* 5.18-19; Jerome, *In epist. ad Eph.* 3.5, v. 25ff; Lactantius, *Divinae inst.* 3.21; Augustine, *sermo* 51.13; *Contra Faustum* 19.26; 23.8, etc.
156. Ignatius, *To Polycarp* 5. See Irenaeus, *Adv. haer.* 4.20.12; 5.9.5.
157. Gregory of Nazianzus, *Carmina moralia* 1: 270-71; PG 37:543.
158. See John Chrysostom, *In epist. ad Col.* 12.5.
159. John Chrysostom, *De virginitate* 40; Ambrose, *De virginate* 6.33; *Hexameron* 5.7.18.
160. C. Fayer, *La familia romana* 2:440.
161. Augustine, *Confessions* 9.9.19.
162. Augustine, *Confessions* 2.3.6; 2.3.7.
163. Augustine, Confessions 6.15.25: "Meanwhile my sins were being multiplied, and my mistress being torn from my side as an impediment to my marriage, my heart, which cleaved to her, was racked, and wounded, and bleeding. And she went back to Africa, making a vow unto You never to know another man, leaving with me my natural son by her."
164. Augustine, *Confessions* 6.13.23.
165. Augustine, *Confessions* 9.11.
166. Mansi II.1037 can. 4.
167. B. Biondi, *Il diritto romano cristiano*, 3 vols. (Milan: Giuffrè, 1952-1954); J., Gaudemet, "Droit romain et principes canoniques en matière de mariage au Bas-Empire," in *Studi in memoria di Emilio Albertario*, vols. 2 (Milan: Giuffrè, 1950), 173-96.
168. As already mentioned in the previous pages, we only have a limited understanding of matrimonial canon law in this period. This is why we need to talk here more about doctrinal than legal aspects.
169. M. J. Gorman, *Abortion and the Early Church. Christian, Jewish and Pagan Attitudes in the Greco-Roman World* (Downers Grove, Il: InterVarsity Press, 1992); J.M. Riddle, *Contraception and Abortion from the Ancient World to the Renaissance* (Cambridge, MA: Harvard University Press, 1992); K. A. Kapparis, *Abortion in the Ancient World* (London: Duckworth, 2002); B. Petrà, "Basilio il grande e l'aborto: l'insufficienza dell'interpretazione tradizionale e la necessità di andare oltre," *Nicolaus* 37 (2010): 247-66.
170. See *Didache* 2.2; 5.2; *Ep. Barnabas* 19.5; 20.2; Justin, *Apology* 1.27.1 and 29.1; Athenagoras, *Embassy* 35; Tertullian, *De anima* 37.2; Minucius Felix, *Octavius* 30.2; Clement of Alexander, *Paedagogus* 2.96.1; *Stromata* 2.88.4; Origen, *C. Celsum* 8.55.
171. Tertullian, *Apology* 9.8.
172. Basil, *Ep.* 88.2. See also Councils: Elvira, can. 63; 68; Ancyra, can. 21.

173. See Justin, *Apology* 1.27 and 29; Athenagoras, *Embassy* 35; *Diognetus* 5.6; Tertullian, *Ad nationes* 1.15.3.
174. John of the Cross, *Spiritual Canticle*, 22.
175. Philo, *De cherubim*, 42-52.
176. R.J. DeSimone, *The Bride and the Bridegroom of the Fathers: An Anthology of Patristic Interpretations of the Song of Songs* (Rome: Institutum Patristicum Augustinianum, 2000).
177. T. Špidlík, in *EAC* 2:694.
178. H. Crouzel, in *EAC* 3:629; D. Faul, "Ecclesia, sponsa Christi. Orígenes y Agustín ante la exégesis de Eph. 5,27," *Augustinus* 15 (1970): 263-80; H. Crouzel, "Le thème du mariage mystique chez Origène et ses sources," *Studia Missionalia* 26 (1977): 37-57.
179. Tertullian, *To His Wife* 1.4.4; *On the Resurrection* 61.6; *On the Veiling* 16.4.
180. Tertullian, *On the Veiling* 3.
181. Ps.-Ambrose, *Laps. virg.* 5.20; Ambrose, *De virginitate* 39; *De virginibus* 3.1.1. See R. Metz, *La consécration des vierges dans l'Église romaine: étude d'histoire de la liturgie* (Paris: Presses Universitaires de France, 1954); H. Crouzel, *Virginité et mariage selon Origène* (Paris-Bruges: Desclée de Brouwer, 1963).
182. Jerome, *Ep* 22.14.

CHAPTER 11

THE LITURGY: ORIGIN AND DEVELOPMENT

Christians seemed to be a very strange people in the eyes of their contemporaries in the first three centuries. They did not practice their religion in the usual forms observed by everyone else—even the Jews were performing sacrifices up to the year 70. The pagans' confusion was summarized by Minucius Felix in this way:

> A race of people who flee from the light, silent in public, talkative in hidden corners; they despise the temples as if they were tombs, they insult the gods, mock the sacred rites, and, miserable themselves, if they can be called such, they show pity for the priests.[1] ... Why do they not have altars in temples or recognized images, why do they not speak in public, why never freely gather with others, if not because what they honor and keep hidden is worthy of punishment or a reason for embarrassment? ... And if that is not enough—what strange and monstrous things the Christians invent! That god of theirs, which they can neither show nor see, closely investigates the behavior of everyone?[2] ... You, meanwhile, stand there anxiously undecided and in great apprehension, abstaining from every honest pleasure, you do not attend the spectacles, do not participate in the processions (*pompae*), abhor the sacred games, the foods set apart according to the rite and whatever remains of the libations poured on the altars. To such a point are you struck by fear for gods whom you deny! You do not adorn your head with flower garlands.[3]

Minucius returns to this topic elsewhere.[4] Tertullian mentions the reason why the pagans persecuted the Christians:

> You say: 'You do not honor the gods and do not offer sacrifices for our emperors.' – It follows that we do not sacrifice for others because we do not even sacrifice for ourselves, once and for all not honoring the gods. Thus, we are tried as guilty of impiety and treason. This is the main point of our case, or rather is the whole case: truly worth being known, if it is not presumption or injustice that judges, the one despairing and the other refusing to bring the truth out clearly. We stopped honoring your gods when we learned that they are not gods. Thus, you must demand of us that we prove that they are not truly gods, and thus are not worthy of being honored, because only if they were gods should they have been honored.[5]

Tertullian records that Christians do not value the temples and monuments.[6] These ideas were widespread: Christians had no temples or altars for offering sacrifice.[7] Augustine cites Porphyry, who asserts: "Christians blaspheme—says Porphyry—the sacrificial rites, the victims, the grains of incense, the other ceremonies observed in the cult of our temples, while —he says—the same cult was begun by them or by the God adored by them since ancient times, in which a God who needed first-fruits presents himself to us."[8]

In fact, in the fourth century an entire imperial legislation tends to overturn the ancestral system, with the suppression of pagan rites and sacrifices. In the beginning of the fourth century, Arnobius asserts that Christians did not construct sacred buildings,[9] but in reality, they were constructing buildings for their assemblies.

In the preceding chapters I have discussed various liturgical themes: Christian initiation (baptism and confirmation), the rites of ordination, penance, and anointing of the sick, as well as the celebration of Christian marriages. In a following chapter I will consider Christian burial. In this chapter I intend to treat other topics connected with the rise and development of the liturgy: the relations with the Jewish and pagan tradition, the sources of the ancient Christian liturgy and the liturgical books, the Eucharistic celebration (its origins and development, its locations), the variety of liturgical traditions in different geographical areas, liturgical furnishings and gestures of prayer; and finally, the Eucharistic prayers. In a subsequent chapter I will treat the rise and diffusion of a Christian calendar that organizes Christian social time.

THE CHRISTIAN LITURGY

The liturgy permeates many aspects of Christian life, institutions, and organization. It expresses the whole sacramental life of Christian communities. The liturgy is a rite and manifests itself as a rite, but it is founded on a theology that underlies every sacrament and sacramental act. The way of praying, of reciting communal and personal prayers also constitutes the heart of the liturgy. The richness of the liturgy has grown in time and in space; I say in space because of the birth of numerous so-called liturgical families even in antiquity.

We commonly use the term "liturgy" (the term "cult" has a broader meaning) which is a Latin calque of the respective Greek term *leitourgia*, which means the public service freely rendered by citizens to the civic community.[10] This service includes many activities, covering popular feasts, theater, competitions, Olympic games, etc., among which there is also the cultic service in the official temples. In the Roman world, the term *munus* (*munera*) was used to indicate services that were meant to benefit the civic or imperial community—spectacles, repairing streets, bridges, and aqueducts, oil for temples, welcoming imperial officials, etc.—which at a certain point were made obligatory for the more well-off. Less tax was paid than in our time, but in return the citizens had to attend certain services at their own cost such as the spectacles, repairing bridges and roads, etc. The Christian use of the term goes back to the Septuagint Greek translation based on the two Hebrew words *charat* and *'avodah* which referred to the cultic service performed by the ministers of the Old Covenant. With the word "liturgy," then, the Jews indicated the cult offered to God by some members of the community in order to benefit the people. In the case of the Jews, it was the Levites who were responsible for the service of the temple and served as mediators between the God of Israel and the people. Thus both God and the people remained distant from each other in the encounter. When carried out correctly, that is, in the minute attention to detail required in the ceremonies on the part of the Levites, the "liturgy" was meant to express the entire religious significance of the Jews' relationship with the divine. It was a work (*ergon*) which was to be offered on behalf of the people (*leiton*) but only in the temple and not by everyone (only by the Levites). The polemic of the New Testament writings is entirely contrary to this rather formal conception of cult.

Nevertheless, Judaism in the Diaspora for those Jews who lived outside of Palestine recognized a worship accepted by God on the same level as the temple worship. This worship occurred in the many synagogues erected, everywhere there was a significant increase of Jewish citizens. In the synagogue, worship is rendered to God by "worshipers of Wisdom" (*Sir.* 4:14). The worship was of a spiritual nature that unfolded in prayer accompanied by explanations of the word of God which had been read—but without any offering of sacrifices. Christianity certainly assimilated this religious dimension of Judaism that was not strictly tied to the ritualism of the temple.

The *Didache* (14.1), a text of the second half of the first century, used the Greek term *thysia* to indicate the Eucharistic sacrifice, as did also other later texts. From the fourth century on, *leiturgia* designated the Eucharistic celebration more particularly; its religious value was often reinforced through the qualifying adjective "divine liturgy." This was translated into Latin with *servitium, ministerium*, and above all *officium*. The Greek term would be transcribed from the Renaissance onward as a technical term for indicating the acts of organized cult under the responsibility of ecclesiastical authority and regulated by it insofar as they were public acts of the church. This use, however, became generalized only from the 19th century onward and one had to wait until 1947 for the supreme magisterium of the Catholic church to propose a doctrinal definition,[11] repeated and elaborated by the Second Vatican Council (*Sacrosanctum Concilium* 7).[12] The use of this term is widespread among other Christian churches too. Latin authors, including both Cyprian and Augustine and many others, also used the term *dominicum* to indicate the celebration of the Eucharist from the third century onward.[13] In the *Passion of Sts. Saturninus, Dativus*, etc.[14], the term *collecta* was frequently used to indicate the assembly of Christians gathered to celebrate the Eucharist.

The original Greek meaning of the term "liturgy" and then the Latin meaning of *munus* are maintained in Christian usage too because liturgy is meant to signify a public cultic act of the Church, of the *ecclesia* as an assembly of those called, and not a private act of individuals or a group. Liturgy is an act of the ecclesial community as such, and so it is the Church of Christ as a whole that accomplishes a priestly ministry. Stripping the term of its previous restrictions, Christians intended *leiturgia* in the sense of "approaching God, coming close to Him," through the unique mediation that is possible only in Jesus Christ, who is the "minister of the true tabernacle" (*Heb* 8:12). In Him all human beings are "ministers" who can approach God. Jesus Christ becomes the means for a religious relationship between God and every human being—not just when the experience takes place in particular religious meetings or specific locations. Rather the encounter occurs in the daily life of Christian existence by emphasizing the influence every cultic gathering—particularly the celebration of the Eucharist[15]— is to have on living a life pleasing to God. The Christian conception of the liturgy is that it is not tied to the possibilities of a few and to moments and places, but rather to a life lived in relation to God, as happened with Jesus of Nazareth. Such a radical religious revolution made Christians vulnerable to accusations of atheism and impiety by the pagans.[16] They were judged as innovators who opposed themselves "against ancient institutions and ancient customs."[17]

Paul considered his missionary activity a public work (*leiturgia* or *munus*), referring to himself as "a minister of Christ Jesus to the Gentiles in the priestly service of the gospel of God, so that the offering of the Gentiles may be acceptable, sanctified by the Holy Spirit" (*Rom* 15:16). He considers himself a priest due to his evangelical preaching and on account of the sacrificial offering ("acceptable offering": *Rom* 15:16b) of the pagans who, with their conversion, assume their death (faith and baptism) with Christ. A new priesthood arises, then, which is celebrated also in the preaching of the Gospel which calls one to faith and solidarity with the mystery of Christ.

The commentaries on the Our Father offer an initiation into the prayer life of the Christian as the early Christians fostered a catechesis organized around Christian worship. This catechesis specified a new form of understanding religion based on the one taught to us by Jesus Christ himself. It inculcated a new understanding of the cultic acts which took place in worship which, as we noted, were no longer celebrated exclusively by some for others who were precluded from approaching God personally. Religion was not restricted to the ritual acts in themselves, nor to determined moments and places. And, finally, the offering was not to be made with inanimate or irrational things, but by man himself, who, relating himself to God in his concrete existence, is a "minister." Such a vision does *not* nullify the service offered in the liturgical assemblies by those in charge of the communities. Rather, some Christians were ordained for this purpose. This service offered on the part of appointed members was not, however, to be received in the manner of the Levitical and pagan priests, who were considered true intermediaries by their followers, but rather in the manner of a ministry enacted for the service of the community.

Tertullian helps elucidate this point in his commentary on the Our Father, written at the end of the second and beginning of the third century. He organizes his conception of liturgy, that is, worship of God utilizing the text of John 4:23 where Jesus speaks to the Samaritan woman of the "true worshipers of the Father." For the theologian of Carthage, the true worshipper is Jesus Christ and those Christians who are united to and in Him who then repeat the adoration Christ himself expressed towards God. He writes:

> This is the spiritual offering which has abolished all the ancient sacrifices. . . . The Gospel teaches well what it has asked of us. It is written: 'A time will come when true worshippers will worship the Father in spirit and in truth and such worshipers does he seek.' We are the true worshippers and the true priests: praying in spirit, we make our sacrifice of prayer in spirit, an offering which is God's own and acceptable to him. This is the offering which he has asked for, and which he has provided for himself.[18]

This and other similar texts of other authors[19] constitute a whole series of testimonies in relation to human life lived in the spiritual line of Jesus, which, per se, is worship of God.

Alongside these there is then another series of testimonies (*1 Pet* 2:4–10; *Rev* 1:6; 5:10; 20:6) that portray the Christian people as honored with a royal priesthood. This title, which is of Old Testament origin (*Ex* 19:6), depicts a fulfillment in the New Testament of a promise made to the Jewish people who would one day be "a kingdom of priests." In the letter of Peter and in the Book of Revelation, those baptized in the name of Christ are referred to as kings and priests when they are gathered together.[20] In antiquity the sacred constitutes the place of access for an encounter always mediated by a priest who is, precisely, the man of separation and at the same time of mediation with the divine. Because he is marked with a royal priesthood, the Christian comes to be indicated as the one who approaches God directly, without need for further mediation: in this sense he is a priest. The baptismal context puts emphasis on this aspect: one is consecrated to God,[21] receiving that anointing of the Spirit that, in line with the anointing of Christ, enables one to approach God—in other words, to be a priest. Within the realm of priesthood as a Christian reality that is able to relate to God in Jesus Christ, ancient Christianity also knows a diversity of ministries which, on the concrete level, reflect a hierarchical structure of the Church, particularly the deacon, presbyter, and bishop.

The first Christian generation referred only to Christ as "priest," or rather "high priest." It did not use such a title for its leaders, instead using only administrative titles such as deacon, presbyter and bishop. However, shortly thereafter Christians did begin to move in the direction of calling their leaders "priests." For instance, toward the end of the first century Clement of Rome intervened in a dispute within the church community of Corinth. The church had dismissed its presbyters, and Clement countered this action by juxtaposing the role of the *episcope,* with its connotation of overseeing, with the Aaronic priesthood, thus beginning an interpretation of the ministry of those in charge of the Christian community in a Judaic-sacerdotal key in tune with the priesthood of Aaron.[22] It then becomes common from the fourth century on to refer to the bishop as a "priest." Later on, the same thing happens with the presbyter, perhaps in consideration of his presiding in the Eucharistic assemblies in the absence of the bishop. The presence of an entire hierarchy of ministers within the community was very developed in the pre-Nicene church, especially in the Latin church and particularly in the African church. There were bishops, presbyters, deacons, subdeacons, acolytes, exorcists, lectors. The laity too were divided into catechumens, the baptized or faithful, penitents, widows, virgins, and confessors—i.e., those who survived persecution inflicted upon them for their faith in Christ.[23] The whole ecclesial structuring avoided creating opposition between the various levels. The whole community, in fact, in its every order and level, was called to global co-responsibility. The most eloquent evidence related to this has been left by Cyprian, who wrote to the clergy of Carthage. "Dearest brothers, I made a rule for myself from the beginning of my episcopate, not to decide anything without your counsel and the input of the people."[24] And again: "It is fitting to the discipline and to our very life together that we must determine that whoever presides in the assembly, with the clergy and in the presence of those of the people who have not fallen and who must be honored for their faith and fear of God (the confessors), can decide everything, keeping to a common council."[25]

The Jewish and Christian Liturgy

Christian liturgical institutions cannot be separated from their Jewish matrix since Jesus and his disciples were of Jewish origin, and Christianity arose within the Judaism of that time as a new Jewish sect. Beyond the Jewish feasts that took on Christian meanings, the Christians read the Old Testament, prayed with the psalms and other traditional prayers. And so, in the field of cultic worship we see not so much an abolition of the Old Testament rituals as their fulfillment, as the Gospel of Matthew insists (*Mt* 5:17), along with further adjustments in the prophetic direction. Christian worship made a conscious decision not to fall into the ritualism of the temple. The spirituality of Christian cultic worship, rather, was linked to the synagogues of the diaspora whose worship was centered in the reading and explaining of the Word of God, while also cultivating family spirituality. The feast of Passover, for instance, is itself a feast celebrated in the family.

In polemic with the Jewish followers of the temple worship, Christians explored more deeply the idea of God's presence confined to a place such as the temple in Jerusalem which had been destroyed in the year 70. God's presence thus was not tied to a material place, but rather is embodied in Jesus Christ and those who believe in Him and gather in his name. The place of God's presence, then, becomes the person, the man, the God-man, the community which gathers in the name of the one sent by God, Jesus of Nazareth, who has now become recognized as Lord.[26] With such a change in perspective the history of religious cultic observance was turned on its head: in the relationship with God, the person would now come to substitute definitively for the conception of sacred place and material offering accepted by the divinity. On the Christian side, what is recovered from Judaism is not so much the ostentatiousness and minute attention to temple ceremonial, but the religious heart and soul that discovers links with its God everywhere: in the synagogues of the diaspora and in family intimacy. The blessing given before and after meals—especially that of the Sabbath and the Passover meals—is but one example.

There are two trends evident among scholars: one tends to exaggerate the influence of the Jewish liturgy on the Christian liturgy while the other affirms the Christian liturgy's originality. There is also the difficulty of not knowing the Jewish liturgy of Jesus' time well—a liturgy that would have been practiced by his first disciples both in attending the Temple and in praying in their private assemblies. Furthermore, which Jewish liturgy would serve as the exemplar for comparison? The temple's or the Essenes', or that of other groups such as the diaspora's, since there is a great variety of ways of being Jewish?[27] Or might it be that which the rabbis of later centuries codified? Many Jewish sources come from a period later than that under consideration. The Jewish liturgy itself, like the Christian one, underwent development.[28] In fact, the studies of Jewish scholars cast much light on the evolution of the Jewish liturgy, and thus some shadows over the reconstructions of Christian authors. The relationship of the Christian liturgy with its Jewish cousin needs to be studied in different ways depending on the Christian liturgical families, since there is not a single Christian liturgy either, but many, although they agree in the essential components. There are different traditions concerning Sabbath observance, fasts, days of celebration, etc., along with different Eucharistic prayers, local influences, different terminologies, etc. that all must be taken into account.

The synagogue liturgy would be a product of the period after the destruction of the Temple when it had to adapt many practices that had previously been carried out in the Temple. At the time of Jesus, the synagogues were places of study, not of prayer which only came about later. The annual feasts were not celebrated in the ways described in later rabbinic literature. The *seder* of Passover[29] also did not exist during the period of the Second Temple.[30] Therefore, the similarities with the celebration of the Christian Eucharist that are posited are debatable. The same caution also applies for the other Christian prayers. For example, a comparison between the Jewish prayer *Birkat ha-mazon*—the prayer of thanksgiving given after meals on special festive occasions—and the text of the *Didache* is not valid because the oldest witness of the Jewish text goes back only to the ninth century AD. Certainly, such a Jewish prayer existed, but the text and its ways of being performed are simply not known to us. Also, Christian prayers of intercession are different from the Jewish prayers of the *'Amidah*[31] (prayer while standing), which are also called in Hebrew *Tefillah* (prayer in general), that are recited three times a day. Every blessing ends with the expression, "Blessed are you, O Lord, etc."

The reason so many doubts and uncertainties arise, comes from the fact that Jewish as well as Christian prayers emerged spontaneously from the people, sometimes also improvised on the numerous occasions for gathering. This is where their variety and diversity come from. The synagogue prayers themselves were not a creation of the rabbis in their academies. Only later did the rabbis proceed towards a revision, rejecting some and accepting others, and establishing which prayers were to be recited and on what occasions. Rather, the rabbinical traditions that came together later in the Mishna and Talmud to form Jewish orthodoxy were, according to various scholars, only marginal in the first century. The same is true for Christian origins as well. If we consider that Christianity followed an exclusively Pauline trend in the first century, we are mistaken. Rather, most Christians coming from Judaism were not Pharisees and almost none of the first missionaries were followers of Paul.

Some Christian practices have been considered as a reaction to Jewish practices in order to distinguish themselves from Judaism. For example, the *Didache* urges fasting on Wednesday and Friday, while the Jews fasted on Monday and Thursday. Why choose those days? The different practice could derive from the Essenes.[32] When the Jews prayed they faced toward Jerusalem, while the Christians faced east.[33] It was a very widespread custom to face toward the East both in private prayer[34] and in the liturgy, such as the baptismal[35] and Eucharist liturgies.[36] The *Acts of Paul* attest that Paul "turned toward the East, lifted his hands to heaven, and prayed at length."[37] Could this new attitude not have derived from some Jewish group?

Therefore, many Christian traditions could have derived from the practices of different Jewish groups that have not been preserved in later rabbinic Judaism. The texts of Qumran should be kept in mind as well. Normally scholars focus on the Jewish origins of the Christian liturgy. But were there also later influences? This question relates to the debated topic of when the separation between the Christian church and the Jewish community came about. Briefly, one can affirm that the separation happened at different moments according to the place and the circumstances. The Roman authorities distinguished between the two groups quite early on. But, there were also quite a few Christians who followed Jewish traditions—the so-called Jewish Christians, and these were not a homogeneous group themselves either. A dialogue also existed between Jews and Christians and so a Christian influence on Judaism[38] is also evident, and there were also some Christians even in the fourth century who still attended the synagogues. Paul Bradshaw wonders if the form of every Jewish prayer with the final formula, "Blessed are you, Lord God, etc." could have undergone Christian influence as it was handed down.[39] Or perhaps it was the result of an independent and parallel development. In cases of literary similarity, one must not always immediately jump to the conclusion of dependence of Christians on Jews, or vice versa. Rather, both may have simply been inspired by their shared Scriptures. Even some traditions regarding the Temple customs transmitted by the Mishna could just be projections into the past of what must have been, according to the redactors, but never in fact were.

For example, the *Apostolic Constitutions*, a work of the second half of the fourth century, demonstrates Jewish influences for instance in its prayer that is similar to the *Amidah*.[40] The *Sanctus* acclamation that emerged in the Christian liturgy is another example of where there is debate as to when and how it entered into the Eucharist anaphora.[41] The Quartodeciman tradition, widely followed in many geographical areas, with its Jewish roots was slowly marginalized and ultimately rejected as the Christians worked to develop their calendar in a way independent of Judaism.

Bradshaw concludes his review of studies and research by affirming that a Jewish influence certainly existed, but not to the extent supposed in the past and not in all aspects,[42] just as one should not expect to find the same formulations in Jewish and Christian liturgies where sometimes Christians sought to distinguish themselves from the Jews. As noted above, the possibility of a Christian influence on the Jewish liturgy, and certain liturgical traditions deriving from groups that have now disappeared, are also possibilities.

Pagan Religions and Christian Liturgy

When I studied at the state university it was fashionable to derive many aspects of the Christian religion—especially its cultic acts, symbols, prayers, common beliefs, festivities, etc.—from the pagan religion of the time.[43] This view emerged primarily in a Protestant context in order to demonstrate how Christianity had fallen from its original and biblical purity into a certain form of transformed paganism. This view has been left behind today for four fundamental reasons: (1) due to the study of the connection of nascent Christianity with its biblical and Jewish roots; (2) there are new methodological approaches, that recognize Christians adopted many pagan elements by giving them new meaning;[44] (3) sometimes the similarities with pagan cultic practices were mere coincidences, as the feast of Christmas was and other Christian celebrations; (4) at other times certain attitudes and practices pertained simply to what a religious person would do (*homo religiosus*), without needing to postulate dependences. For example, it was normal for all to pray toward the East where the direction was laden with symbolism.[45]

The view of ancient pagan critics of Christianity was completely contrary to any idea that Christians had co-opted pagan rites.[46] In fact, one of the main accusations was that Christians had abandoned the ancestral tradition, committing apostasy from the rites of pagan ancestry. In his letter to Trajan, Pliny focuses on religious and cultic aspects, noting the separation from the tradition as well as what made Christians different from their pagan neighbors. The Christian response was to demonstrate the innocence of their ritual activities, shifting the discourse to the moral quality of their life.[47] Minucius Felix summarized all these criticisms of Christians' religious distinctiveness,[48] as did Tertullian with the brief phrase: *divortium ab institutis maiorum* (breaking with the ancestral traditions).[49] Christian authors accented prayer which took the place of every kind of sacrifice: "For this is the spiritual victim, which abolishes the former sacrifices" (*Haec est enim hostia spiritalis, quae pristina sacrificia delevit.*)[50] Pagans performed sacrifices for the emperor and the empire; Christians offered the spiritual sacrifice of prayer from the heart.

When we use the term "pagan," we employ a word already in use but with a further Christian meaning. It was the Christians who invented the pagans. The pagans didn't know they were pagans. In the first centuries there were many cultic forms which we include under the single term. In the Roman Empire there was a great variety of local religions, of groups, of associations and civic religions, with their respective gatherings. Polytheism made room for different cults. There was not competition among them. The same person could practice different cults and have some personal ones as well. With the term "pagan" we refer then to all these various religions.[51] Cultic worship was essential to the life of the city where we can distinguish various types of religious practice which can be summarized in the ancient distinction between *sacra privata* and *sacra publica*.

The *sacra privata* were of various kinds: (a) familial and domestic cults (*sacra familiaria*), (b) cults of districts in cities; (c) cults of associations; (d) cults in the great religious sanctuaries. The religion common to all was fundamental. It was the religion of the city—the *sacra publica*, the distinctive cult of the city, of each city, which had its polyadic (from *polus*, many) divinities.[52] In the *sacra publica* the cultic acts were public not only in the sense that they were performed before the citizenry in open places, but because they were financially supported by the city, officiated by public functionaries, and were meant for everybody in the city. The officiants were the magistrates, that is, the public authorities who along with the priests were chosen for this office by the authorities and by the citizen assemblies. The priesthood was not a matter of sacramental ordination or for one's whole life, but was temporary and tied to the office.

Civic religion was not a personal matter. For this reason, many sought proper spaces in the private sphere, in the intimacy of the individual conscience, where the mysterious presence of God was felt. In this religious distress the eastern mystery and spiritual cults were reborn in the Empire with their focus on individual soteriology, and Christianity as we noted came to compare itself with these. Christians too emphasized the personal element in their being religious, but they also noted its social aspect and impact. If Pliny found out about it through the normal sort of judicial interrogations, this is owed to the fact that, in the ranks of Christians they were being educated in open polemic with the pagan way of being religious. The Christian was being educated to give weight to his own religious faith which found its great expression in the practice of worship itself, to the point of becoming a principle of action for life itself.

The evidence of a polemic that arose in this regard in the second century between a Christian and a pagan sufficiently informs us about the different conception of religion and cult. A Christian accused a Greek of the uselessness of his lament regarding the son who is attacking his marriage, in the following way: "Why do you, who are a Greek (= in religion), get angry with your son if he, imitating Jove, has laid traps for your marriage, or rather has stolen it from you? Why do you consider him your enemy when you venerate one who behaves in the same way? As regards to us Christians, our emperor, the divine Word, who assiduously presides over us, wants from us a pure soul equipped with holiness and the badges of our king, divine actions."[53]

One of the debated questions concerning all of this is the relationship of Christian liturgy with the pagan mysteries, that is, the rite as "mystery" in the pre-Nicene liturgy—in particular the mystery religions and the Jewish rites. As to whether there was such a relationship with the rites of pagan religiosity—demonstrating influences, dependence or priority—Christian apologists rejected any such connection. They considered the liturgies of the mystery cults as diabolic works and judged the similarities as the mystery cults copying and counterfeiting the Christian rites.[54] They often put in the same category the manipulation of Christian rites made by heretics.[55] This decisive reaction arose, ironically, from the very recognition of a similarity between the Christian rites and the non-Christian rites.

The Alexandrians Clement and Origen used the Greek terminology of initiation: mystery, rite, initiate into the mysteries, and mystagogy (*mysterion, teleté, myeo, mystagogeo*). Since these terms had connections with the mystery religions, the fathers normally sought to avoid them in order to distinguish themselves and Christianity from those religions. The apologists often tried to deny any possible similarities or sought to demonstrate that the pagans mimicked Christian rites.[56] In reality, in putting forth all this effort to distance their celebrations from the pagan ones, they actually still found themselves sharing in the same common lot with the mystery religions who celebrated their common religious rites in honor of a god as well. If we take out from consideration the acts of public worship rendered to the gods in the whole Roman Empire, the mystery initiations which were all off a soteriological character had the same common denominator: the concept of "mysterious" participation in the world of the divine through an initiation and a celebration of a god invoked as benefactor and savior of man. The term *mysterion*, which the Latins translated sometimes as *sacramentum*,[57] was already present in Paul who provided a threefold explanation of what it meant: (1) the will of God to save humanity in Christ (*Col* 1:26); (2) the realization of that plan in the calling of the gentiles together with the Hebrews (*Eph* 1:1–19); (3) Christ himself as the "great mystery of religion" (*1 Tim* 3:16). In the second century, this last significance of "mystery" became, with Justin, the common denominator for indicating the historical events of the life of Christ, which in fact came to be called *mysteria*. These included his incarnation, birth, passion, death, resurrection, and ascension in which one participates in the liturgical gatherings celebrated in his name. Beyond the baptismal literature, the evidence of Eucharist liturgies, particularly the *Apostolic Tradition*, reveal such a direction of understanding. After Justin, especially in Alexandrian Christianity, the whole divine economy in relationship to the world is expressed with the idea of *mysterion*.

Thus, the *mysterion* came to be understood as a hidden reality that manifests itself and lets itself be received by someone capable of doing so, that is, by the person who comes and is initiated into the *mysterion*. The concept of initiation into the mystery lies behind the entire understanding of Christian catechesis, explained through the interventions of God in human history as they are narrated to us in the Scriptures. These came to be read through the lens of the *mysterion* that was to be discovered in order to make the mystery one's own. The "mysterious" category drew into its semantic field the terms "image, symbol, sign, truth, type–antitype," and became the key for reading both the Old and the New Testament as liturgical celebrations. These came to be understood together as a *mysterion* which indicated Christ in his concrete person as the primordial mystery. The Church was the place where the mystery of Christ was revealed and realized through the cultic rites as a whole and especially those involved in initiation: baptism, chrismation and then the Eucharist as well. With the appropriation of the religious category of "mysterious" participation, Christianity created a bridge with the whole of ancient religiosity and made it converge in Christ, the one mediator for human beings to be able to approach God the Father. The master and initiator of this dialogue was Clement of Alexandria, and then Origen who developed its theoretical conception in the pre-Nicene Church.

However, in Christianity not of Alexandrian but of Asiatic derivation that was more tied to groups of Jewish extraction, the same category of participation in the mystery was carried out by the celebration of the Eucharist as the Christian Passover. This came to be considered the true Passover in contrast with the Jewish Passover which, according to the Christians was already emptied of its religious meaning because, according to the promises of the Old Testament, its significance was ultimately found in Jesus Christ.[58] Melito of Sardis, Irenaeus of Lyon and, later, Apollinaris of Laodicea were the principal spokesmen of this tradition, which has been preserved for us mainly in the Easter homilies of the second century. These have assumed a not insignificant interest in recent years from the point of view of our knowledge of the Jewish-Christian dialectic and the theological development in that area and that time, as well as the gradual formation of the Christian festivities and their meaning beginning from the celebration of Passover.

An important aspect was the pagan cultic terminology used by Christians.[59] The traditional words took on a new meaning in order to indicate a different reality in the liturgical language, whether it be Greek, Latin, Syriac, or Coptic, etc. Christian compositions, or Jewish ones read in a Christian spirit, pagan texts reused and adapted by Christians in all the ancient languages—all of these favored the change in meaning for the existing pagan words along with the creation of new words. Often the terms came to be marked by other languages and adapted for another language. Christian communities sang psalms, along with chants composed by authors such as Ambrose and Prudentius. They also composed and sang hymns for various hours of the day, as well as antiphons and responses. Some compositions arose from the people or from individuals and then were standardized into acclamations, doxologies, litanies, or hymns. Numerous Hebrew words passed into the liturgy such as amen, alleluia, the Trisagion – Holy, Holy, Holy is the Lord, God of hosts! – maranatha and hosanna. Some Greek terms were transliterated into Latin such as Kyrie eleison.

In the canon of the Mass cited in Ambrose of Milan's *De Sacramentis* one can clearly identify the tendency to use stylistic devices from old Roman sacred language; but it is above all in the so-called *Sacramentum gelasianum* that the stylistic forms of this prayer are applied systematically, determining that style of solemn hieratic prayer that would shape the euchological forms of the Roman liturgy for centuries: i.e., a liking for precise juridical formularies, a constant striving for measured cadences in the structure of sentences, a tendency to build up synonyms, the presence of antithetic and synonymous parallelism, and an attempt to make the language sonorous by alliteration and rhyme. But if the stylistic structure of the prayer was influenced by the sacral tradition of Rome, the vocabulary and images of the Christian liturgical language were combined with the tradition of ancient Christian prayer, so that liturgical Latin remained faithful to Christian Latin, in fact becoming an important form of it.[60]

Documentation

The evidence[61] concerning the liturgy of the first centuries of Christianity up to the Council of Nicaea in 325 is rather meager. It becomes more abundant from the beginning of the fourth century. The Christian period before and after Constantine was greatly changed and the liturgy shows this with precision. We can draw fragmentary information from the writings of the fathers, from catechetical works, and from a series of small works, generally anonymous, which we organize under the title of canonical-liturgical literature. This text genre is typically very repetitive and of a juridical character. The works, which are not conciliar decrees, are normally anonymous and very different from one another in content and value. One cannot call these documents of the first four centuries canon law, which is a later development. Their content ranges from ethical norms to practical advice with directives of an organizational character. It is difficult to use them, since their provenance is usually unknown or merely hypothetical. Even information about where and when they were applied is unknown and those texts that emerged and spread in a precise location are still sometimes a hodgepodge of the ancient that was already obsolete, along with the new. Texts born elsewhere and adapted in a different geographical and organizational context raise more questions than answers, because one cannot offer an explanation as to why the adaptation was not completed for the new historical and geographical situation.

We are accustomed to reconstructing the institutions of the ancient Church using this literature and the conciliar canons, both ecumenical and local. The local canons pose similar problems because we do not know about their reception or how and whether they were enforced. For example, as noted in an earlier chapter, the canons of the Eastern Greek councils, except those of Nicaea, were entirely unknown in the West in the fourth century.[62] The Western canons were never known in the East after the sixth century, except for the so-called

Council of Carthage of 419. Were the anonymous works of the *Collectio Veronensis*, i.e., *Traditio Apostolica*, *Didascalia*, *Apostolic Constitutions*, disseminated in the West? It seems not, because we know of only a single palimpsest manuscript of a translation made in the fourth century. In the eighth century the parchment was reused because its content was considered useless. The living oral tradition of individual churches which we are not capable of reconstructing, along with the concrete practice used and lived which is learned with practice and experience —these are what determined the institutional organization and the liturgy. The almost total lack of manuscripts in the early Middle Ages for the Eastern non-Greek churches is an important clue both for reevaluating their oral tradition, which in many areas was very traditional and venerable, and for not giving excessive importance to the more ancient, written canonical-liturgical documentation.

If a social or religious movement wants to survive, it cannot entrust itself only to the spontaneity of its emergence and its founding charismatic figures. Rather, it must resort to organizing itself with more or less binding norms for its members, and also commit itself to some sort of hierarchy. This need is expressly emphasized in one of the most ancient documents, the *Apostolic Constitutions* (beginning of the fourth century). The anonymous author writes that Jesus ordained the Apostles to make provision for various necessary ministries.[63] The text reinforces the validity and compulsory nature of the various prescriptions—not just because of Jesus' command or their apostolic origin, but also in view of the final judgment of God on each one's observance. All the members of the community in their various proper roles must remain faithful to these prescriptions which come from the very beginnings of the Christian faith.

The text of the *Apostolic Constitutions* presents a community that is already well organized. The complex of norms, which at the beginning were reduced to those that were essential, grew according to the needs of the community's development, and these norms were transmitted orally within the various communities. Thus, every community, or the communities of a specific region, went on creating and developing their particular disciplinary, organizational, and liturgical patrimony. In other words, each community was creating its own tradition that was transmitted orally—a tradition that was continually enriched and expanded under practical impulses and influences of various provenance. For example, we can tell from Tertullian's and especially Cyprian's references to tradition, what the tradition of the African church of the third century was. It was a tradition whose various phases of development we are not capable of reconstructing, nor can we establish how this tradition expanded and was modified in the course of the fourth century. Through an examination of their works, as V. Saxer has done,[64] we are only able to know what these men witnessed about the traditions where they were. We do not know other disciplinary and liturgical points not touched on by them, however. The African church did not compile a practical manual that assembled their local tradition. It was oral transmission that allowed for continuity even among the novelties that were introduced with the passing of time. This phenomenon occurs in all Christian communities. Even in the cases when specific works were compiled to assemble those particular norms, or, in the fourth and fifth centuries, if councils were held that decreed norms designed for resolving specific situations—in either case, the oral transmission of each community's patrimony always remained fundamental, insofar as the conciliar decisions had a limited dissemination.

The first pieces of information about tradition we have come from the texts of the New Testament itself, in particular St. Paul, who tells us of the tradition he received about the Eucharist (1 Cor 11:23) and the Gospel message itself (1 Cor 15:3). We hear other useful information about early Christian practices and beliefs from the pagan ruler Pliny the Younger, governor of Bithynia and Pontus in the years 111–113. In the first centuries the local *consuetudo* (custom) was transmitted orally and was expanded. What Tertullian writes is significant: after having spoken of baptismal practice, norms for receiving the Eucharist, fasts, rites of prayers, the frequent use of the sign of the cross, he adds: "If, for these and other customs, you look for biblical prescriptions, you will find none."[65] In less than two centuries a patrimony and tradition of rites, norms, and customs had already developed.

Two centuries later Augustine writes:

> Regarding, however, the prescriptions that are not written but that we observe as having been handed on through the tradition and that are observed in the whole world, it is easy to see that they are maintained insofar as they were established and recommended by the Apostles themselves or by plenary councils, whose authority is most useful for the salvation of the Church. Of such a sort are the feasts celebrated on the occasion of the Passion, Resurrection, and Ascension of the Lord.[66]

He writes in another letter: "Other practices, then, vary according to place and region, like those by which some fast on Saturday and others not, some receive the body and blood of the Lord every day, but others receive it on determined days. In some places not a day is allowed to pass without offering the Sacrifice, in others it is offered on Saturday and Sunday, and in still others only on Sunday."[67]

It is also worth noting that the liturgical texts for which we have written evidence were generally anonymous.[68] With the passing of time and the growth of communities, which became ever more complex and structured, the prescriptions also increased, which in their turn were put into writing. Later texts reuse these earlier ones with omission of elements that were no longer in use. They also added or relocated sections and integrated and interpolated others. Sometimes they tried to correct a more archaic theology spread here and there in the text. This type of text, precisely because of its practical utility, pertains to a genre that we can define as "living texts." These texts were subject to continual regional and local adaptations, not only successive ones but even contemporary ones according to the local church. One must not forget when dealing with these anonymous written texts that one does not know how much was invented by the author and how much, on the other hand, goes back to the specific character of the community to which the author himself belonged.

The process of re-adaptation began already with the most ancient of our documents, the *Didache*, which was reused in other texts. In the *Didache* the Jewish elements come to be assumed into a Christian context. The *Apostolic Constitutions*, in book seven, adapt the *Didache* with interpolations, adding other biblical citations, reducing the norms for receiving itinerant missionaries (chs. 11–12), and adding significant alterations in the administration of baptism and in the liturgy. The blessing of oil, which we also find in the Coptic text, is introduced in the tenth chapter. The phenomenon of adaptation can be observed well also in the translations both of the *Didache* and the *Didascalia* into other languages, where the text remains substantially the same.[69] Another significant example can be drawn from the systematic and point-by-point comparison of the *Canons of Hippolytus* (first half of the fourth century) with the so-called *Apostolic Tradition*.[70]

The rewriting of a text becomes necessary when it is reread within a different liturgical and canonical tradition. In this way, an attempt is made to reconcile different traditions, and the rewritten document preserves the aura of antiquity and authority in both the old part and the new. Since the rewriting often takes place during a translation into another language, the text's prestige grows, and it is received with veneration. When a work can be traced back to a well specified and concrete author, it comes to be respected and considered untouchable. A kind of psychological copyright protects it from falsifications and adaptation because, with no printing press in existence, it was easy to introduce any type of alteration and interpolation into it. By contrast, this type of text, embodied in the *Didache* and the *Didascalia*—although associated with high apostolic authority that guaranteed acceptance and validity—was subject to continual rewriting in order to confront the new religious, social, liturgical, and organizational needs of its users. A minimal degree of adaptation could consist in the substitution of some expressions in order to make the text comprehensible to a new audience, and this updating could employ biblical terminology or imagery in order to aid the process of normalization. In using the *Didache,* in its seventh book the compiler of the *Apostolic Constitutions* abandoned the archaic and approximating form of New Testament citations and substituted them with expressions taken directly from the New Testament. The theology of the earlier document, especially its Trinitarian and Christological theology, gets revised in accordance with the doctrine accepted later. Sometimes the same tradition, disseminated earlier elsewhere and in other contexts, and thus without a strict literary dependence, shows up in later documents, like the doctrine of the two ways, already used in Jewish circles. The most substantial and noticeable adaptations are on the level of institutions where the adaptations develop, grow more precise, and expand. Some disappear, such as the figure of the prophet in the *Didache* (10.6), who becomes a presbyter in the *Apostolic Constitutions* (7.26.6). Some new things appear such as the various levels of the clergy and what that demands, the ritual of initiation and the Eucharist, larger and more complex Christian assemblies, conciliar meetings, territorial ecclesial organizations, etc. One and the same text can also be managed differently in different documents. The typical case is the so-called *Apostolic Tradition* which is treated in the *Apostolic Constitutions*, in the *Octateuch of Clement*, and in the *Epitome* of the eighth book of the *Apostolic Constitutions*.

The process of revising a text in later eras often entailed the marginalization of the older text, with its consequent disappearance in its original redaction. In this entire literature—both the older anonymous sort and successive conciliar collections—an implacable principle is at work: that the later product, considered better, eclipses the earlier one which is considered no longer usable. The *Apostolic Tradition*, widely employed up to the fourth century, became obsolete and thus disappeared in its original Greek form. This phenomenon explains the disappearance of ancient texts originally written in Greek and their preservation in other languages. A whole, vast canonical-liturgical literature goes under the aegis of apostolic origin, but there are also many texts that pass under the name of Clement, who is an apostolic personality, such as the *Apostolic Constitutions*, the *Pseudo-Clementines*, *Octateuch of Clement*, *Apocalypse of Peter*.[71] Others are attributed to Hippolytus. These texts, I repeat, are anonymous even if one seeks to attribute certain works to specific persons.

The titles given to works of primitive canonical and liturgical literature vary from scholar to scholar, especially in the past. Today the tendency is toward uniformity in naming. Still, the habit of indicating the various works with different titles causes no small confusion in the reader, especially in the different translations and recensions in ancient languages. A typical case, which is a real brainteaser, is what happens with the *Ecclesiastical Constitution of the Apostles* (see below). Here I keep to the titles used by A. Faivre and Bruno Steimer with the indication of the *Clavis Graeca* or *Latina*.

(1) *Didache (Teaching of the Twelve Apostles)*.[72] The literary genre of the Didache is debated in relation to the esteem of the document itself. For some, the *Didache* stands at the moment of passage from a prevalently charismatic church to a hierarchically organized one with ministers and sacraments: from a proto-catholicism (*frühkatholizismus*) to the catholicism of the later second century. This document offers us a series of details, even if incomplete, about various aspects of Christian communities and their organization. In each case it had influence and was reused by successive canonic-liturgical documents. The text is known by slightly different titles: a shorter one (*Didache of the Twelve Apostles*) and a longer one which is at the

beginning of the text (*Didache of the Lord to the Nations Through the Twelve Apostles*); but the work was also known as *Didache of the Apostles* (Latin: *Doctrina Apostolorum*). If we accept the shortest title—which seems more ancient—then the hypothesis fails that the author/s put it under apostolic authority, who, in this case, were itinerant missionaries and this was their manual for catechesis. The *Didache*, then, does not originally have a pseudepigraphical character. Rather, the expansion of the title with the addition of the "twelve" transforms it in the eyes of the reader and it becomes a canonical-liturgical text.

The *Didache* presents itself as a short codex of ethical indications and guidance for the life of the community; it was used for the instruction of catechumens. Athanasius, for instance, recommends using it for the instruction of catechumens.[73] The current text is already a compilation composed and not well blended from different traditions, especially Jewish ones, but also Christian. The first six small chapters cover the doctrine of the *Two Ways, of Life and of Death* (already present at Qumran, in the wisdom and rabbinic literature). It presents archaic rules for the life of a community regarding the catechumenate, baptism, and the Eucharist. The *Didache* was held in high esteem in the first Christian centuries, so much so that it was held to be Sacred Scripture by Clement of Alexandria[74] and Origen.[75] Then it was reused in other fuller and more expanded texts, like the *Didascalia* and the *Apostolic Constitutions* (7.1–32).

Chapters 9–10 still give us the most ancient Eucharistic Prayer. I include a small passage:

As this broken bread was first scattered over the hills and, once gathered, became one; so also let your Church be united from the ends of the earth into your kingdom. For yours is the glory and the power, through Jesus Christ, for all ages! Let no one eat or drink of your Eucharist, except those baptized in the name of the Lord" (ch. 9). "But after you are satisfied with food, thus give thanks: We give thanks to you, O Holy Father, for your Holy Name which you have made dwell in our hearts, and for the knowledge and faith and immortality which you have made known to us through Jesus your servant. To you be glory forever. You, Lord Almighty, created all things to the glory of your Name, and have given food and drink to men for their comfort, that they might give thanks to you; but on us you have bestowed a spiritual food and drink and eternal life through your servant" (ch. 10.1–4).[76]

(2) The *Epistula Apostolorum* (140–160) contains a creed of faith with a three-part construction, along with references to the remission of sins in the Church and mention of the Eucharist which comes to be called the Passover: "The Lord said: celebrate the memorial of my death, that is, the Passover" (ch. 13).

(3) Justin, *1 Apology* 65-67, offers us many elements concerning the manner and meaning of baptism and the Eucharist. Regarding the latter we have the first indication of how it was

celebrated, both after baptism and on Sundays: the reading of the memorials of the Apostles, the presentation of the offerings, the Eucharistic Prayer said by the presider of the assembly according to his abilities to formulate it, the distribution of the Eucharist to those present and the sending of it also to the absent who could not come, and the collection of offerings to set aside for the use of the needy. We include what we have in ch. 67, which is the first explicit evidence about the way the Eucharist was celebrated in the second century:

> And on the day called Sunday, all who live in cities or in the country gather together to one place, and the memoirs of the apostles or the writings of the prophets are read, as long as time permits. Then, when the reader has ceased, the president verbally instructs, and exhorts to the imitation of these good teachings. Then we all rise together and pray out loud. Then, when our prayer is ended, bread and wine and water are brought, and the president in like manner lifts to heaven prayers and thanksgivings, according to his ability, and the people assent, saying Amen. And there is a distribution to each, and a participation of that over which thanks has been given, and to those who are absent a portion is sent by the deacons.

(4) The *Apostolic Tradition* (*Diataxeis*) is the most important document for understanding the ancient Christian liturgy. The work is no longer attributed to Hippolytus and is not even identified by the title which is found on the base of the statue "of Hippolytus" in the Vatican Library: *On Charisms, the Apostolic Tradition*. Determining a place of composition also influences its interpretation. There is debate also about its title and content. There is agreement, however, about the date of composition which is placed in the first half of the third century. Studying other earlier documents and using the eastern traditions (Arabic and Coptic) and the Latin fragments of Verona, Botte had attempted a Latin reconstruction of the archetype rather than from the lost Greek original for which some fragments remain. The result was a selection of passages that could be attributed to the *Apostolic Tradition*, creating a *textus receptus* on which the modern translations are based. Since the successive documents were composed according to local needs, real or ideal, the difficulty arises of reconstructing the archetype because it is hard to distinguish the elements of the archetype from the adaptations and the interpolations that were made and the interpolations. Hanssens, on the other hand, limited himself to presenting the various witnesses side by side in a Latin version, without trying to reconstruct an archetype or original. Bradshaw, Johnson, and Phillips recently did likewise, presenting the recensions and reworkings of the *Apostolic Tradition*. Many later texts directly or indirectly depend on it including the *Testament of our Lord Jesus Christ* which was translated from the original into Syriac, Arabic, and Ethiopic (Ge'ez), the *Canons of Hippolytus* existing in Arabic through Greek and Coptic, the *Apostolic Constitutions*, the *Epitome* (*Constitutiones per Hippolytum*) which exists in Greek and Eastern versions, the

Synodos Alexandrina, the *Optateuch of Clement*, and the *Canons of St. Basil* (according to Kretschmar without mediation.) And through these texts it has profoundly influenced the practice of all Christian communities. The *Apostolic Tradition* drew particular attention after the last world war, influencing the conciliar liturgical reform. The current second Eucharistic prayer and the ordination rites are still witnesses to it: the distinction between *cheirotonia* (laying on of hands) and installation into a ministry, well outlined in the *Apostolic Tradition*, is still the current teaching in the Christian churches.

In these documents, some of which are translations, others reworkings, there is a common element often containing the same words. Recognizing this, efforts have been made to reconstruct the content of the original Greek text, also through the Latin fragments of the collection of Verona first published by Hauler and then by Tidner. In a few places the Eucharist is spoken of. Its liturgy reflects a substantial urban community in which many social categories are represented. Since the various prescriptions are short it was easy afterwards to transform them into canons. Some repetitions and prescriptions that are simply put side by side reveal that this document is already a mix of earlier elements.

A recent discovery of an Ethiopian manuscript[77] published by Bausi which derives from a Greek original (c. fifth century), includes both the *Apostolic Tradition*, in an independent version similar to the fragments of Verona, along with *On Charisms*.[78] This discovery is very important because it is substantially parallel to the Latin, and is more ancient and archaic compared to the other eastern traditions. The *Apostolic Tradition* is much used by liturgists and historians today—and yet the reader of a text like this, as it is presented today in the reconstruction of Botte, must never forget that it is a hypothetical reconstruction even if it does have solid foundations.

Here is the Eucharistic prayer from the *Apostolic Tradition*:

The Lord be with you: And with your spirit. Lift up your hearts: We lift them up to the Lord. Let us give thanks to the Lord: It is right and just. We give you thanks, O God, through your beloved Son Jesus Christ whom you sent us in the fullness of time as Savior, Redeemer, and Messenger of your will. He is your inseparable Word through whom you created all things and in whom you have placed your delight. You sent him from heaven into the womb of the Virgin, in her womb he was incarnate; he was manifested as your Son, born of the Holy Spirit and the Virgin. He did your will and, to acquire a holy people, opened his arms in the passion to free from suffering all who believe in you. When he willingly consigned himself to suffering to destroy death and break the chains of the devil, to crush hell beneath his feet, to enlighten the just, to ratify the covenant, and to manifest the resurrection, he took bread and, giving thanks to you, said: 'Take and eat, this is my body which is broken for you.' He did the same with the chalice, saying: 'This is my blood which is spilled for you. When you do this, do it in memory of me.'

Mindful, then, of his death and his resurrection, we offer you bread and wine, giving thanks that you have held us worthy to stand in your presence and minister to you. We ask you to send the Holy Spirit on the offering of your Holy Church. Grant to all your saints who, as you unite them, receive this offering, that they be filled with the Holy Spirit to confirm their faith in truth, so that they may praise you and glorify you through your Son Jesus Christ.[79]

(5) *Didascalia Apostolica* (or *Apostolorum*). The *Didascalia* (teaching) was composed in Syria close to 230 and presents itself as a transcription of the Apostles' commands in a council in Jerusalem. The original Greek text is lost, except for some fragments. The work has reached us in its rewritten form through the *Apostolic Constitutions* and in different translations including Latin (partial), Coptic, Arabic, Ethiopic, and Syriac (which is complete and therefore referred to as the *Didascalia Syriaca*). Its anonymous author, likely a bishop, gives a full picture of the norms that should regulate the life of a Christian community around its bishop, who is its center and spiritual and administrative guide. He is the teacher of all and dispenser of the Word; he is the central personality of the community which was already well organized by this time.

(6) Tertullian and Cyprian are precious sources for knowledge about the African liturgy, referring to baptism, the Eucharist, penitential practices, and how church assemblies were conducted. The *De Oratione* of Tertullian is useful for learning about many customs relating to the Eucharist. An important passage in the third chapter of the *De Corona* describes how baptism was carried out and gives a description of a Christian assembly gathered to celebrate the Eucharist.

(7) There are numerous works of the fourth century that take advantage of and reuse earlier works, that return to and adapt them. I collect a few of them here, some of which have been cited earlier: (a) *Ecclesiastical Constitution of the Apostles*. This, cited with various names by different scholars, is preserved in its original Greek text and in various translations. Its redaction is placed in the first years of the fourth century in Syria or more likely Egypt. Its structure is in the form of canons (rulings). (b) *The Testament of our Lord Jesus Christ*. Published for the first time in 1899 by Rahmani from a Syriac manuscript, but whose original must have been redacted in Greek in the fifth century. (c) *Canons of Hippolytus*. A collection of 38 canons, preserved only in Arabic, going back to the middle of the fourth century. (d) *Apostolic Constitutions and dependent works*. This famous compilation of pseudepigraphic texts takes up and reworks earlier documents, particularly the *Didascalia Apostolica* (1–6), the *Didache* (7.1–32), the *Apostolic Tradition* (8.3–45), with a final addition of the *Apostolic Canons*, but of other texts too including the *1 Clement*, the Pseudo-Clementines, apocryphal texts, liturgical formularies, liturgical practices from its own times and environs, as well as biblical citations. Chapters 33–38 of the seventh book include five prayers that seem to be adaptations of Jewish prayers. The

compiler presents the work as if it were Clement's (8.47.13; 8.47.85). It does not limit itself to the simple juxtaposition of existing texts, but presents them with omissions, interpolations, and additions. In this way all the different ecclesiastical institutions and every subdivision of its content can only be summarized, since the various themes come back elsewhere too. The themes include: Christian conduct, the hierarchy, reconciliation of penitents, Christian initiation, ordinations, the liturgical year, widows, orphans, martyrs, schisms, charisms, Christian ethics and the Eucharist. Other later texts depend on the *Apostolic Constitutions*.[80]

LITURGICAL BOOKS

The liturgical literature that was used primarily for worship purposes is useful for learning about the life of Christian communities in both its social and religious contexts, along with the expression of its faith. While the prayers and hymns can sometimes also have noteworthy literary value, in general liturgical books have only historical value. The most ancient period is characterized by spontaneity and creative freedom rather than written texts. Improvisation was the norm, which was accompanied by the creation of ritual and liturgical language and the proliferation of various rites according to the variety of cultural and linguistic environments. Improvisation by the celebrant was slowly replaced by the written text composed by others which offered a greater guarantee of orthodoxy.

The most ancient liturgical books are the sacramentaries and *ordines*, all dating to after Gregory the Great (+604). The *Apostolic Tradition*, which has already been noted, mixes liturgy with disciplinary norms. The *Libelli Missarum*, short formularies of Masses for various occasions, constitute the preparatory phase of the sacramentaries into which they were combined later on. The other liturgical books are after our period. The various *lectionaries*, either as lists of biblical pericopes to be read or with the complete text, are not relevant to our theme. The same is true of the homiliaries which were later collections of sermons from more ancient authors that were useful for preaching. Although the homilaries are very important for reconstructing the works of the fathers, they do not tell us much about how they were used. The sacramentary was a book reserved for the celebrant alone—whatever level of clergy he was. It included all the elements necessary for the presider of the assembly such as collects, *secreta*, post-communion prayers, and the prayers for the administration of the sacraments and for other occasions. The most ancient is the so-called *Leonine Sacramentary* (or *Veronense*), composed toward 560 at the time of Pope John III (561–574) with texts from the Roman archives and thus more ancient than the time of their final redaction. The *Old Gelasian Sacramentary* (*Vat. Reg. lat. 316*), also of Roman origin but not from Pope Gelasius (492–496), composed before Pope Sergius I (687–701), is of the presbyteral type. At the time of Pepin the Short, the *Gelasian Sacramentary of the Eighth Century* (*Frankish Gelasian* or *Gelasian of Pepin the*

Short) was immediately disseminated in Gaul, but was later replaced by a sacramentary of the Gregorian type.

The *Ordines* contained rubrics that were to be followed for conducting Mass, baptisms, ordinations, etc. These became more important when the Roman liturgy of the eighth century started replacing local liturgies. *Ordines* themselves could contain older texts going back to the seventh and eighth centuries which were usually quite brief.

The three centers that influenced the formation of the eastern liturgies were Antioch, Alexandria, and Jerusalem. Jerusalem especially influenced the Armenian, Georgian, and Constantinopolitan liturgies (but also others). Antioch, on the other hand, though it influenced the Constantinopolitan liturgy as well, had special influence in the eastern regions. Alexandria influenced the Ethiopian liturgy. As we mentioned previously, the birth of liturgical books was rather late; those of the Byzantine tradition are well known, but much less is known about the liturgical books of other traditions because sometimes that have not yet been edited.[81]

Among the eastern liturgies are the following:

1. **Byzantine** liturgical books: (1) *Euchologion* that includes the elements reserved for the deacon, presbyter, and bishop, as well as the rubrics, liturgical elements (the liturgy of St. John Chrysostom, and sections of St. Basil's liturgy), the sacraments and sacramental; (2) *Horologion* which is a book of hours with the main elements of the office.
2. **Eastern Syrian** liturgical books: (1) *Hudra* which contains texts for all the offices of all feasts; (2) *Gazza* used for the offices of vigils; (3) *Warda* (antiphons); then there are three lectionaries, etc.
3. Among the numerous **Coptic** liturgical books is the *Euchologion* which contains the three anaphoras of St. Cyril, St. Basil, and St. Gregory, along with Matins and Vespers.
4. **Ethiopian** liturgical books: *Missal* (the anaphoras); texts for penitential books, for marriage, for anointing of the sick, etc.
5. **Armenian** liturgical books: (1) *Horhrdatetr* containing the missal with the liturgy of St. Athanasius; (2) *Tonac`oyc`* (similar to the Greek *typikon*), the lectionary; (3) the Zamagirk` (liturgy of the hours).

CHRISTIAN ASSEMBLIES

As we have noted, evidence about the pre-Nicene Christian liturgy is not abundant.[82] Two activities however were important: the baptismal liturgy and the Eucharistic liturgy. Both see a development from the simpler to the more complex. I wrote amply on baptism in the third chapter. Here I will discuss the Eucharist, defined by Ignatius as "the medicine of immortality" already at the beginning of the second century: ". . . with an undivided mind, breaking one loaf, which is the medicine of immortality, and the antidote which wards off death but yields continuous life in union with Jesus Christ" (*Eph* 20). In the same letter he expresses the necessity of the Eucharist for life: "Let no one be deceived: if one is not at the altar, he is deprived of the bread of God" (5.2).

Some texts were written for the Christians themselves, others to defend them from the accusations of the pagans, especially concerning the Christian's secret meetings. These texts form the apologetic literature but were not meant to describe their assemblies in detail. Following the suggestion of *1 Peter*, the authors had to be respectful and use comprehensible language: "But in your hearts sanctify Christ as Lord. Always be ready to make your defense to anyone who demands from you an accounting for the hope that is in you; yet do it with gentleness and reverence" (*1 Pet* 3:15–16). Lactantius reproves Cyprian, who uses the Bible to defend Christians, argumentation that is not fitting for the pagans. One must not speak to the ignorant of what is difficult to understand because they are spiritual matters and only the faithful can understand them.[83]

To know Christian assemblies better we must pay attention to some formal aspects that develop from the beginning onward: the organization, the order of execution, the times, the places, the directing person, and the components of the whole action of the assembly which included readings, teaching, preaching, song, prayer over the offerings, the distribution of the bread and wine, etc. These are conducted among the people of God (*populus Dei*),[84] or, as Augustine refers to them, the people of Christ (*Christi populus*).[85]

The first disciples of Jesus attended the Temple in Jerusalem, which still existed, and then held their prayer gatherings only among themselves. Elsewhere, some of those of Jewish origin attended the local synagogue, but then participated in the prayer of the Christian community. Others did not go to the synagogue at all. The gatherings of Christians of the first two centuries must be studied according to the religious context of the time, not just the Jewish context. As with other things, Paul is the most ancient source on the first Christian gatherings. The *Acts of the Apostles*, the *Pastoral Letters*, and the *Didache* give us other information.

The Pauline communities and others met in the evening, weekly, and shared prayers, readings—they read the letters of Paul—a meal. They taught each other in turn under some guides. Paul himself describes these gatherings (*1 Cor* 10:16–23; 11:17–14:40). His intention was to impose a model for the gatherings that would include a meal and other actions mentioned, like praying, singing, preaching, and teaching (*1 Cor* 14:13–15, 19, 26, 29–31). In the twentieth chapter of the *Acts of the Apostles* too, a double structure appears: a meal and then discourses and prayers. Luke implies that the gathering was held on the night of Sunday, insofar as he speaks of the first day of the week (*Acts* 20:7). The *Didache* describes the gathering, beginning by saying: "Regarding the Eucharist, give thanks in this way" (9.1). Then it offers a model of prayer and a series of practical recommendations. And it further adds: "On the Lord's day, gathered together, break bread and give thanks after having confessed your sins, so that your sacrifice be pure" (14.1). Ignatius of Antioch gives several exhortations in his letters not to miss the gatherings with bishops and priests, and also to give thanks and pray together. But he does not offer further information about how this would take place: "Try to gather together more frequently to celebrate God's Eucharist and to praise him. For when you meet with frequency, Satan's powers are overthrown and his destructiveness is undone by the unanimity of your faith. There is nothing better than peace, by which all strife of heavenly and earthly powers is done away."[86] The *Didascalia* insists heavily on attending the gatherings, and strongly exhorts not to miss them.

A model for gathering develops so that it can be organized better. Christians develop one model typically for themselves because of internal needs, according to the comprehension and interpretation of their ritual practices, and also to create their own identity and reinforce their cohesion. The standard scholarly opinion used to be that Christians limited themselves to following the synagogue model, but recent studies show that it was not so. Certainly, they took over some elements, for example the periodic gathering according to the Jewish week, the system of readings and explanations and some prayers.

Around 111–112, the pagan Pliny the Younger proved to be a precious non-Christian source, offering us a view from outside according to a pagan lens. In a letter to Trajan, he informs us about the Christians' liturgical gatherings:

> They [the interrogated Christians] asserted, however, that the sum and substance of their fault or error had been that they were accustomed to meet on a fixed day before dawn and sing responsively a hymn to Christ as to a god, and to bind themselves by oath, not to some crime, but not to commit fraud, theft, or adultery, not falsify their trust, nor to refuse to return a trust when called upon to do so. When this was over, it was their custom to depart and to assemble again to partake of food—but ordinary and innocent food. Even this, they affirmed, they had ceased to do after my edict by which, in accordance with your instructions, I had forbidden political associations. Accordingly, I judged it all the more necessary to find out what the truth was by torturing two female slaves who were called deaconesses. But I discovered nothing else but depraved, excessive superstition. I therefore postponed the investigation and hastened to consult you. For the matter seemed to me to warrant consulting you, especially because of the

number involved. For many persons of every age, every rank, and also of both sexes are and will be endangered. For the contagion of this superstition has spread not only to the cities but also to the villages and farms. But it seems possible to check and cure it.[87]

He had no way to specify further what type of meeting the two deaconesses were talking about.

The text of Pliny offers us six pieces of information about Christian liturgical gatherings before Nicaea: (1) Christ is invoked as God; (2) they sang in alternating choirs, which probably disturbed their neighbors; (3) they met early in the morning on a set day (Sunday); (4) they strove on the basis of their religion to behave rightly in daily life; (5) they met again for an innocent meal (agape); (6) this provoked many absences from the ceremonies in use in pagan temples. The last issue was a new way of expressing one's religiosity, by attending habitual meetings which took place at the temples on the part of many citizens. The pagan Pliny noticed the importance the issue of meetings had in strict relation to a citizens' way of life, both social and religious, and as a Roman administrator he naturally was concerned. According to Pliny, the Christians met early in the morning on a set day which the Christians call "the Lord's day." Naturally at that hour they cannot consume a meal. So instead they met again at another time, in the evening, and had a meal in common as was normal in other religious associations. None of the texts mentioned where they met and Pliny does not say. For this reason, it is supposed that the meetings were held in private houses of persons who had enough room for a group, but it is possible that they may have also used a reserved location.

The periodic Christian assemblies developed over time in the manner of how they met as well as in their organization and in the locations of the gathering. And all this depended on the cities, towns, or small inhabited areas where they occurred. This development also presupposes the evolution of the ministerial orders which were discussed in earlier chapters. After the Constantinian peace a new pastoral effort arose with more time and space provided, and thus the liturgy was enriched and became more elaborate. In fact, the Eucharistic celebration was moved to a later time, toward nine in the morning. The preaching within the celebrations also became more solemn.

In the pre-Constantinian era, the Christians organized their religious and social life according to their religious rhythm, especially with the Sunday celebration. This implied notable difficulties both because of the fixed recurrence of the Christian day and because of the working rhythms imposed by society. Thus, Christians were normally constrained to meet before dawn. In social life they abstained from the public religious celebrations observed by the population. Because of this absence they were accused of being anti-social and of not participating in the rhythm and demands of civic life, and of not contributing to the *pax deorum*, by their social and religious absenteeism.[88]

THE LITURGY: ORIGIN AND DEVELOPMENT

Their assemblies resembled the voluntary religious meetings widespread throughout the Roman Empire, and yet they were different in content and manner of conducting their meetings. In the pagan religious meetings, no discourse was heard, unlike the Christian meetings. The following is an important passage from a homily on Genesis by Origen, who speaks of the assemblies and their minister in an extended discourse:

> Rebecca goes out to get water and a servant of Abraham meets her. Isaac, says the Scripture, was growing and becoming strong, that is, joy was growing for Abraham, who considered not the visible things. . . . But I fear that the Church still gives birth in sadness and lamentation: is it not sadness and lamentation for her when you do not come together to hear the word of God, and with difficulty get yourselves to church on feast days, and even then, not so much out of desire for the word but rather in looking for solemnity and to obtain in some way the public remission of sins? . . . What then must I do, who have been entrusted with the ministry of the word? I who, though a useless servant (*Lk* 17:20), still have received from the Lord the 'measure of grain to distribute to the Lord's household.' But consider how the Lord's discourse ends: 'A measure of grain, he says, to be distributed at the right time.' What then must I do? Where and when should I find the time that works for you? The greater part of it, or really almost all of it, you use in worldly occupations, one part you consume in the forum, another for business; one has time for a campaign, another for trials, and no one or very few have time to hear the word of God. . . . But why do I blame you for your occupations? Why do I lament over the absent? Even you who are present, and who are in church, are not attentive but usually exchange banal chatter and turn your backs to the word of God and the divine readings. I fear that the Lord will say to you too what he said through the Prophet: They have turned their backs to me, and not their faces (cf. *Jer* 2:27). What then must I do, who have been entrusted with the ministry of the word? The things that are read are mystical and need to be explained through the mysteries of allegory. But can I make the pearls of God's word penetrate into deaf and ill-disposed ears? The Apostle did not do so. In fact, consider what he says: 'You who read the law and do not hear the law. . . . Perhaps I will seem too rigid to you, but I cannot plaster a falling wall; and I fear what is written: "my people, those who call you blessed seduce you and confuse the paths of your feet; I warn you as my dearest sons.' I marvel if you have not yet known the way of Christ; if you have not even heard of this, that the way that leads to life is not large and spacious but hard and narrow; and so you, then, enter through the narrow gate, leave the wide space to those who are perishing. The Apostle commands us to pray without ceasing; you, who do not gather to pray, how do you accomplish without ceasing what you always omit? But the Lord also commands: Watch and pray, not to enter into temptation. That if not even those who watch and pray and always adhere to the word of God have escaped from temptation, what do they do who only come to church on solemn days? If the just man is saved with difficulty, what will happen with

the sinner and the impious? . . . So, if you do not come every day to the wells, if you do not obtain water every day, not only will you not be able to give something to drink to others, but you too will suffer thirst for the word of God. . . . It is quite necessary for us to castigate for a short time with patience those who neglect the gathering and avoid hearing the word of God, who do not desire the bread of life nor the living water, who do not come out of the encampment and do not leave the houses of mud to collect manna, who do not come to the rock to drink, from the spiritual rock. In fact, the rock is Christ, as the Apostle says. I tell you, have a little patience; our discourse is addressed to the negligent and to those who are sick. . . . Tell me, you who come to church only on feast days, are the other days not feast days? Are they not the Lord's day?[89]

Origen's attitude about people's church attendance becomes only more pessimistic the older he gets, as evidenced from comments he makes initially in his commentary on the episode of the purification in the Temple (*Commentary on John Bk. 10*) compared with when he later comments on Matthew's account of the same event (*Commentary on Matthew Bk. 16*).

Eucharistic celebration

What should we call the first Christian celebrations? The Lord's supper (*coena domini*), the breaking of the bread (*fractio panis*), the Eucharist (*Eucharistia*), i.e. the thanksgiving (which is the most frequently used term)? As has been noted, the model developed for celebrating the Eucharist included prayers, readings, preaching, but also other activities, as Justin describes in his *First Apology*, in chapters 65 and 66. He describes two Eucharistic assemblies: one after the baptism of the catechumen and another weekly assembly which occurred on Sunday. These two descriptions are addressed to the pagans to excuse the Christians from every defaming accusation, and thus they are partial and apologetic. They do not offer the details a historian would want. Here is part of the text:

But we, after we have thus washed him who has been convinced and has assented to our teaching, bring him to the place where those who are called brethren are assembled, in order that we may offer hearty prayers in common for ourselves. . . . Having ended the prayers, we salute one another with a kiss. There is then brought to the president of the brethren bread and a cup of wine mixed with water; and he taking them, gives praise and glory to the Father of the universe, through the name of the Son and of the Holy Spirit, and offers thanks at considerable length for our being counted worthy to receive these things at His hands. And when he has concluded the prayers and thanksgivings, all the people present express their assent by saying Amen. This word Amen answers in the Hebrew language to γένοιτο [so be it]. And when the president has given

THE LITURGY: ORIGIN AND DEVELOPMENT 439

thanks, and all the people have expressed their assent, those who are called by us deacons give to each of those present to partake of the bread and wine mixed with water over which the thanksgiving was pronounced, and to those who are absent they carry away a portion. It is the body and blood of Jesus incarnate. And this food is called among us Εὐχαριστία [the Eucharist], of which no one is allowed to partake but the man who believes that the things which we teach are true, and who has been washed with the washing that is for the remission of sins, and unto regeneration, and who is so living as Christ has enjoined. For not as common bread and common drink do we receive these; but in like manner as Jesus Christ our Savior, having been made flesh by the Word of God, had both flesh and blood for our salvation, so likewise have we been taught that the food which is blessed by the prayer of His word, and from which our blood and flesh by transmutation are nourished, is the flesh and blood of that Jesus who was made flesh. For the apostles, in the memoirs composed by them, which are called Gospels, have thus delivered unto us what was enjoined upon them; that Jesus took bread, and when He had given thanks, said, This do in remembrance of Me, this is My body; and that, after the same manner, having taken the cup and given thanks, He said, This is My blood; and gave it to them alone. (ch. 65–66)

And on the day called Sunday, all who live in cities or in the country gather together to one place, and the memoirs of the apostles or the writings of the prophets are read, as long as time permits; then, when the reader has ceased, the president verbally instructs, and exhorts to the imitation of these good things. Then we all rise together and pray, and, as we before said, when our prayer is ended, bread and wine and water are brought, and the president in like manner offers prayers and thanksgivings, according to his ability, and the people assent, saying Amen; and there is a distribution to each, and a participation of that over which thanks has been given, and to those who are absent a portion is sent by the deacons. And they who are well to do, and willing, give what each thinks fit; and what is collected is deposited with the president, who offers help to the orphans and widows and those who, through sickness or any other cause, are in want, and those who are in bonds and the strangers sojourning among us, and in a word takes care of all who are in need. But Sunday is the day on which we all hold our common assembly, because it is the first day on which God, having wrought a change in the darkness and matter, made the world; and Jesus Christ our Savior on the same day rose from the dead. For He was crucified on the day before that of Saturn (Saturday); and on the day after that of Saturn, which is the day of the Sun, having appeared to His apostles and disciples, He taught them these things, which we have submitted to you also for your consideration. (ch. 68)

In these two lengthy citations we see the structure of the Eucharistic assemblies in Rome in the middle of the second century. In the second text some different elements are added:

readings, preaching, the presider says a prayer from memory as he is able. Fixed Eucharistic prayers do not exist yet, like the one included in the *Apostolic Tradition*. Here too it is affirmed that the meeting happens on Sunday, that is, on a fixed day, and the reasons are also given. In the *Dialogue with Trypho*[90] Justin offers some other details explaining the Eucharist as a memorial of Christ, the refusal of bloody sacrifices, the offering by Christians of a bloodless and pure sacrifice. The text of Malachi 1:10–12 on the refusal of sacrifices is already employed: "For from the rising of the sun to its setting my name is great among the nations, and in every place, incense is offered to my name, and a pure offering; for my name is great among the nations" (*Mal* 1:11). Then this text is repeated by other authors such as Irenaeus (*Adv. Haer.* 4.18.3). Irenaeus also speaks of the Eucharist, but does not offer details on the manner of its celebration.[91]

About sixty years after Justin, Tertullian tells us about the assemblies held in Carthage on various occasions. In his *De Corona* of 211, after having spoken of the administration of baptism, he adds: "As concerns the sacrament of the Eucharist, the Lord celebrated it in the evening during supper and entrusted it to all, and we too celebrate it during the night assemblies before dawn and receive it only from the hands of those who fulfill the ministries of presiding. We make the offerings for the dead on the anniversary of their death as if it were the day of their birth. We consider it an impiety to fast or adore God on one's knees on Sunday.[92] Because of the same need to abstain from penitential practices, we feast and rejoice from the day of Easter until Pentecost. We are concerned, then, and troubled if some drop of the chalice or even some crumb of our bread falls to the ground."[93]

In his *Apology* addressed to the pagans, Tertullian adds other elements:

We meet together as an assembly and congregation, that, offering up prayer to God as with united force, we may wrestle with Him in our supplications. This violence God delights in. We pray, too, for the emperors, for their ministers and for all in authority, for the welfare of the world, for the prevalence of peace, for the delay of the final consummation. We assemble to read our sacred writings, if any peculiarity of the times makes either forewarning or reminiscence needful. However it be in that respect, with the sacred words we nourish our faith, we animate our hope, we make our confidence more steadfast; and no less by inculcations of God's precepts we confirm good habits. In the same place also exhortations are made, rebukes and sacred censures are administered. For with a great gravity is the work of judging carried on among us, as befits those who feel assured that they are in the sight of God; and you have the most notable example of judgment to come when any one has sinned so grievously as to require his severance from us in prayer, in the congregation and in all sacred intercourse. The tried men of our elders preside over us, obtaining that honor not by purchase, but by established character. There is no buying and selling of any sort in the things of God. (39.2–4)

The *Apostolic Tradition* asks that much attention be paid to the Eucharist in receiving it and reserving it. The following excerpt is from the Ethiopian text translated by Bausi:

> Regarding the matter of receiving the Eucharist before all else, let every faithful person seek to receive the Eucharist before tasting anything; if he receives it with faith, even if there is someone who gives him something lethal, after that it will prevail over him. . . . Let all make sure that one who does not believe not taste of the Eucharist, nor mice or domestic animals, and that not even a little falls and is ruined, because it is the body of Christ, food for the faithful, not to be wasted. Regarding the chalice, that it not be poured. Indeed, having blessed it in the name of Christ, you have received as it were the image of the blood of Christ. For this reason, do not spill it lest some unrelated spirit lick it up as if you had despised it: you will be guilty of blood, as if you had despised its worth, with which you have been redeemed. Let all the deacons with the presbyters gather where the bishop has ordered, early in the morning, and let the deacons not fail to be present every time, unless they are impeded by some illness. Once they are gathered, let them communicate this to the church and thus, after having prayed, let each one do what is just.[94]

Place and Time of the Assemblies

Where the Christians Met Together[95]

Worship gatherings of many people need common and shared places and times in order for them to work. In the earliest days of the church it seemed normal to gather in the private houses of people who had sufficient space. In the beginning the meetings did not need special spaces and temples. They were totally free from every link with a specific place (*Jn* 4:23-24), unlike the Jews whose worship was strictly tied to a unique Temple. The Christians only had the command to keep a memorial of Jesus: "Do this in remembrance of me" (*Lk* 22:19; *1 Cor* 11:25). This command could be fulfilled anywhere and everywhere. The new temple of God was to be the church-community, the body of Christ, and the Christian too in his turn becomes a temple. In fact, the first small communities met in private or in rented houses. In Rome, "Paul lived for two whole years in a house he had rented" (*Acts* 28:30.)

The names for the meeting places of Christian communities in the first two centuries are unknown.[96] Today we use the phrase "house church" (*domus ecclesiae*), a phrase that is found in the Latin translation of Origen.[97] More specific terms appear only at the beginning of the third century, such as *ecclesia* (earlier it meant just an assembly), *basilica*, *aula* (earlier it referred to a courtyard or palace). The term "house of prayer" never occurred before in Greek until Eusebius,[98] but in Latin there was house of prayer (*domus orationis*; εὐκτήριον),[99] and house of

God (*domus Dei*). The term *basilica* is the most closely connected to the secular tradition. Tertullian speaks of meeting places, which he calls *ecclesia*—*in ecclesiam venire*[100]—and also *domus Dei*.[101] Hippolytus, the author of *On Daniel*, speaks of meeting places known to the pagans and Jews (1.32), which he calls "the house of God" (1.20). Origen refers to the meeting place as a "synagogue."[102] The author of *Against All Heresies* (*Philosophoumena*) writes that the bishop of Rome, Zephyrinus (†217), "having elected Callixtus as his associate and coadjutor in the governance of the clergy, set him in charge of the cemetery" (9.12), a cemetery that still exists, which at that time belonged to the community or to some private person. We can say the same about the places for liturgical celebrations. As the number of the faithful grew it was necessary to procure larger spaces.[103] Eusebius notes that because of the rapid growth of Christians spacious buildings had to be built: "Since the earlier buildings were not sufficient, then in every city large and spacious churches were raised from the foundations up."[104] "Feasts of dedication were held in every city and consecration of buildings of prayer that had just been built."[105] I think that the dedication of a building, in imitation of what happened with the Temple in Jerusalem and with pagan buildings, supposes a history with precedents in the third century.

The shift of the term *ecclesia* from an assembly and community to a specific building is expressed in an effective way by Clement of Alexandria: "For is it not the case that rightly and truly we do not circumscribe in any place that which cannot be circumscribed; nor do we shut up in temples made with hands that which contains all things? What work of builders, and stonecutters, and mechanical art can be holy? . . . For it is not now the place, but the assemblage of the elect, that I call the Church. This temple is better for the reception of the greatness of the dignity of God."[106] In this text the term "church" already assumes the meaning of a meeting place as well. Some decades later Origen speaks of the house church—*domus ecclesiae*, literally, house of the church.[107] The expansion of meaning is normal. For example, "synagogue" progresses from meaning a gathering to indicating a building. In Latin the term *curia* means a municipal assembly, but goes on to include the meaning of a building as well. At the beginning of the fourth century in the West, at a popular level the term *dominicum* is used which is a translation from the Greek *Kyriakon*. The anonymous author of the *Itinerarium Burdigalense*, from the years 333–334, actually explains the term *basilica* in this way: *ibidem modo iussu Constantini imperatoris basilica facta est, id est dominicum, mirae pulchritudinis* (in that place, by command of the emperor Constantine, there was built a basilica, that is, a *dominicum*, of amazing beauty).[108] He is speaking of the basilica of the Holy Sepulcher. The term is also used by the fathers: Hilary, *Ad Const.* 2.2; Jerome, *Chron. ad an. 327*; Augustine, *Sermon* 32.25, to name only a few. The term *dominicum* is also used in Rome. The inscription on the collar of a fugitive—whether slave or beast—speaks of *dominicum Clementis* and of *acolytus*.[109] The term *martyrium* also is used for some types of building.

In the first communities which the texts of the New Testament speak of, the believers gather in one of their houses which offers a sufficiently large place, to hear instruction, pray, and celebrate worship.[110] We find similar expressions several times in the first decades: "The community that gathers in their house," "Greet those of the house of Narcissus who are in the Lord," "Hermas and the brothers who are with them. Greet Philologus and Julia, Nereus and his sister and Olympas and all the believers who are with them" (*Rom* 16:5, 11, 15). In other letters too, Paul mentions those who meet in some private house. Thus, in Rome there are already various meeting places in the year 58 such as at Troas: "On the first day of the week, when we met to break bread, Paul was holding a discussion with them. . . . There were many lamps in the room upstairs where we were meeting" (*Acts* 20:7-8).

The *Letter of James* tells us of a greater organization in a place with different positions for the people: "For if a person with gold rings and in fine clothes comes into your assembly, and if a poor person in dirty clothes also comes in, and if you take notice of the one wearing the fine clothes and say, 'Have a seat here, please,' while to the one who is poor you say, 'Stand there,' or, 'Sit at my feet'" (2:2-3).

In small cities there was only one meeting place; in the large cities there were more. In the second century there must have been several meeting places in Rome since the first communities arose where the Jews lived. The catacombs outside the city help us locate them within the city: the populous neighborhood on the river, known today as Trastevere; near the crowded Porta Capena, before the Porta San Sebastiano; in the Campus Martius, on the two sides of the Via Lata, which is the modern Via del Corso in Subura, and on the Aventine. Since they could not travel long distances for worship, there had to be one or more meeting places in each district. Justin affirms to the prefect of Rome that the Christians meet where they can: "Where each one prefers and can, since undoubtedly you imagine that we all meet in the same place. But it is not so, for the God of Christians is not circumscribed in a single place, but, being invisible, fills heaven and earth and is adored and glorified everywhere by the faithful."[111]

The *domus ecclesiae* theory supposes that the wealthy families offered their houses and so that it was these families who had large houses with large rooms. If in the second century the Christians were still "meeting wherever they prefer and can," there was no delay in having their own buildings. At any rate, the places of worship and meeting could not only be private houses, as has been maintained in the last decades in the English-speaking world. Rather, they met any sort of place, as long as it was fit for the purpose. It could be a shop, a large living room, a building readapted according to the necessities of the worship life and the large number of the members of the individual community. When the community met in a private house, it was more significantly controlled by the patron and had little independence. Thus, it was better to have a building or place that was not under the control of some private person.

The first known place is found in distant Edessa, in Mesopotamia, destroyed by a flood in 201. Tertullian speaks of meeting places but not of private houses.[112] Elsewhere he observes that these places are simple and open, while those of the heretics are hidden: "The house of our dove is simple, always in high places and open spaces; the symbol of the Holy Spirit loves the east, symbol of Christ."[113] In *On Daniel,* Hippolytus speaks of meeting places known to the pagans and Jews (1.32). Origen also mentions places of gathering and of prayer where he preaches.[114] The numerous apocryphal *Acts* report about meeting places in private houses; so also do the Pseudo-Clementine writings.

The discovery of an early building for Christian worship in a small military center named Dura-Europos in Syria on the river Euphrates helps us understand how the assembly place could have been arranged. This building was modified around the year 230 and was destroyed by the Persians in 256. There is a spatial separation between the place for baptism and the place for meeting. This room where the faithful assembled is capable of holding about seventy people. It is constructed with the axis from west to east; there are signs of a platform on the eastern wall. How many buildings like this or even much larger ended up totally destroyed? After the persecution of Valerian, his son Gallienus in 260 had the cemeteries and cultic places that had been confiscated from the Christians restored to them.[115] The *Didascalia* describes in detail where the participants in the assembly must sit in order to observe correct order: the presbyters sat in the eastern part with the bishop's seat at their center; the men and women sat in separate places; the young people sat in other places as did also the elderly; families with small children sat in a place assigned to them as did also the widows and old women. Some remained standing. When the deacon entered he had to ensure that everyone was in his or her proper place.[116] From this description one deduces that it was not a living room, not even a large one, but a place that had already been modified for assemblies and participants that were rather numerous.

From these small hints one can infer that the liturgy must have determined the form and structure of the internal space because, compared to pagan worship, Christian worship now took place inside and not outside.[117] We also learn: (a) the assembly was gathered in a hierarchical form in the meeting place—the *quadratum populi*—according to the ranks and the functions of the various participants; (b) there was a special position for the reading, the proclamation of the texts, and preaching; (c) the gaze of the participants was directed toward the presider and his assistants; (d) there was a special position for the table or altar where the offering of the Eucharist was placed. There was also special provision made for the place for baptism and confirmation (baptistery). In the fourth century, as in St. John Lateran, the baptistery is a separate building.[118] In this period the great Constantinian basilicas were built which became models for other buildings both small and large. The Roman *basilica forensis,* with adaptations and flexibility according to liturgical demands, fully accommodated the needs of Christian communities.

In Rome some titular churches such as *titulus Clementis, titulus Byzantis, titulus Equitii,* and *tutulus Gaii,* could have come from these places of worship, from private places that became community property. For Rome the most ancient archeological evidence could be under the church of St. John and Paul.[119] In 2005 a Christian place of worship was discovered in Palestine[120] at Kefar 'Othnay (Lat. *Caparcotani*) near Tel Megiddo. It was used as a place of prayer by soldiers. In the building dated to before the persecution, there is a 54-square-meter mosaic with the Christian symbol of the fish and three inscriptions in Greek. One commemorates a soldier who contributed to the construction, one honors three women and a fourth who donated the altar table as a memorial of Jesus Christ, with the inscription in Greek: "Akeptous, a lover of God, offered the table to God Jesus Christ as a memorial." In distant Mauritania Caesariensis (today north-west Algeria), for example, in the city of Altava (modern Ouled Mimoun, 30 km east of Tlemcen) there is a military fortress for the cavalry and infantry of the *cohors II Sardorum* in which a *basilica dominica* (house of the Lord) was built in 309, as attested by an inscription.[121] If in these marginal areas buildings were constructed for Christian gatherings, all the more must it have been the case in the cities. These buildings were already impressive at the end of the third century.

In his first edict Valerian prohibited gatherings of Christians and entry into their cemeteries, and he confiscated these places. Valerian was imprisoned by the king of Persia and was still living in slavery when his son Gallienus restored this real estate to the Christian communities by rescripts.[122] In the second half of the third century larger churches were built, also because of the increased number of Christians. The pagan Porphyry (†305) wrote that Christians possessed impressive buildings where they met: "The Christians, imitating the construction of the temples, build huge houses, inside of which they meet to pray, even though nothing prevents them from doing this in their houses, because it is clear that the Lord listens everywhere."[123] Since he spent most of his time at Rome during the second part of his life and died there, he knew the Christians of Rome and certainly their Christian buildings in order to talk about them in such a way.

Eusebius narrates an episode that probably took place at the time of Gallienus concerning the soldier Marinus in Caesarea, his city, who was brought into church—which Eusebius called an *ecclesia*—by his bishop and made to stop near the altar.[124] Thus, in Caesarea there was a specific church building. During the persecution of Diocletian, Eusebius speaks many times of the existing churches which he also calls houses of prayer.[125] One can affirm with great probability—although the sources are lacking—that up to the end of the third century Christians did not build specific buildings, limiting themselves instead to adapting existing ones. The *Recognitiones* mention a certain Theophilus who turned his house into a large church.[126]

Eusebius affirms that the first edict of Diocletian ordered that the churches be razed to the ground and the Scriptures destroyed with fire.[127] Lactantius mentions the destruction of the church of Nicomedia in the enforcement of the first edict of Diocletian. It was on high ground and was easily visible from the imperial palace.[128] A trial was written up on May 19, 303 in the city of Cirta (later Constantina) in the presence of the clergy in the "house where the Christians meet."[129] This house could be what Optatus of Milevis will call a basilica.[130] A presbyter declares that he had deposited the money before the episcopal throne (*ante cathedram episcoporum*).[131]

As the communities grow, they begin to construct buildings suitable for their worship. In fact, at the end of the persecution Gallienus wrote in the so-called edict of Serdica of April 311: "So that there be Christians once again and once again buildings be constructed in which they were accustomed to meet."[132]

Eusebius appraises the situation a few years after the conversion of Constantine:

And we especially who placed our hopes in the Christ of God had unspeakable gladness, and a certain inspired joy bloomed for all of us, when we saw every place which shortly before had been desolated by the impieties of the tyrants reviving as if from a long and death-fraught pestilence, and temples again rising from their foundations to an immense height, and receiving a splendor far greater than that of the old ones which had been destroyed.[133]

Liturgical Space

Our knowledge of the places[134] for liturgical assemblies in the period before the peace of the Church, as has been said many times, is very scarce. We know the liturgical space of churches very well in the period that followed. These churches vary greatly in size. Generally, they have a rectangular room with three aisles, with an apse and a main entrance on the opposite side facing the apse. Some of the larger churches could have even five or seven aisles, or nine. Sometimes the smaller ones had several aisles in order to support the structure.[135]

In the ancient conception the orientation of the buildings has a religious character. Vitruvius writes that a temple must have an east-west orientation such that the statue of the god looks toward the western quarter of the sky (*ad vespertinam caeli regionem*), and the faithful who look at the statue make sacrifices towards the eastern portion of the sky (*ad partem caeli orientis*).[136] In prayer one also directs oneself east, both in private and in public prayer, both in the East and in the West.[137] And one prays with open arms.[138]

The orientation of the building is also related to the performance of the liturgy,[139] because the presider and the people move at certain moments, turning themselves east or west. The apse where the clergy are seated determines the orientation of the building. In some regions the apse is placed in the westernmost part of the church, as is the case in Rome for example, while in other churches the apse is placed in the easternmost part. "In Cyrenaica—an intermediate zone—basilicas facing west are as numerous as those facing east, for no apparent reason. Finally, there are anomalous orientations, e.g., north-south, where buildings were adapted to topographical situations."[140] At any rate, one need not consider the orientation as always observed; archeology testifies to a variety of situations. During the celebration the assembly turns to the west to renounce Satan, to the east to profess acceptance of Christ, the light (*ex oriente lux*).

The church of Dura-Europos of the third century discussed earlier is a simple room, while the baptistery is well decorated with a basin. The architects of Christian buildings used existing models, adapting them to the liturgical needs that were developing. Among the most ancient buildings known are the remains of the basilica built by Theodore in Aquileia and the description given by Eusebius of the great church of Tyre in 315, of which there is no archeological evidence, and which was built on a prior building. According to the description a large colonnaded courtyard with four fountains, surrounded by a wall, stands before the three entryways that face toward the east.[141] "For when the bishop had thus completed the temple, he provided it with lofty thrones in honor of those who preside, and in addition with seats arranged in proper order throughout the whole building, and finally placed in the middle the holy of holies, the altar, and, that it might be inaccessible to the multitude, enclosed it with wooden lattice-work."[142] The placement of the components of the assembly reflect an ecclesiological conception, in particular the position of the presider.[143]

The structure of the room must account for the organization of the community in its various components. In other words, the liturgical space was conceived according to the idea of how a Christian community functions (ecclesiology) and of the performance of cultic action. The position of the bishop and of his greater clergy—presbyters and deacons—and of the lesser—acolytes, lectors, etc.—has a central and visible placement seated around the altar. Then there is the section reserved for the seating of the faithful, along with other sections reserved for the order of widows, of consecrated virgins, of catechumens, and of penitents. In the western church the faithful remained standing since there were no seats, while in some regions of the Middle East there was seating where the faithful could sit. There were also furnishings for the liturgical service: tables and ambos along with the episcopal throne. In the fourth century the liturgical space grew larger and was better organized according to regional variations.[144] The altar (*mensa*) in ancient churches was never located at the back of the apse.

That place was reserved for the episcopal throne around which the seats of the clergy were situated. The altar in fact was located outside of the apse, with it sometimes being located in the center of the church.

In order to demonstrate how the assembly was organized before the time of Constantine, we include a segment of the *Apostolic Tradition* in the Ethiopian edition translated by Bausi:

> Regarding the prayer of the auditors: After the catechumens have left the teacher, they are to pray separately from the adult Christians. Let the women remain standing by themselves. Let the adult Christians not exchange the sign of peace with the catechumens as holy ones, for they are not yet holy for their part. Let the adult Christians kiss each other, men with men and women with women. Let them kiss each other on the mouth. Let all the women veil themselves with a veil for their head, not of soft linen, because it is not a covering. But let the virgin not veil herself on account of the fact that she knows that she openly declares herself a believer. (ch. 14)[145]

> Regarding prayer: In church, you who are presbyters and deacons whose task is to teach in each community, on the Sabbaths you are to set up the places for worship, having arranged everything for the brothers with every care and exactness. If one is found to have seated himself outside of the rule, let him be rebuked because the Lord has made our church like his own dwelling place. As we see that speechless animals such as cows, horses, goats, and sheep who stand each according to their own species even when they are woken up and milling around do not separate from each other, so also in church the youths should sit on their own if there is a place for them; if not, they should stand. The adults too should stand in their own place, and if they have children let them watch over them. Virgins, then, should stand in their own area as well, and if there is no place set apart for them, let them stand for this reason in front of the other women. Those who have children and are married should sit in their own place; and the church widows and lay widows in their own place. If some brothers or sisters have come from other districts, a deacon should come and check if the sister has a husband. If they are lay widows, make them enter and have them each sit in their place; and the presbyters should also sit in their proper place. If another bishop has come from some other district let them receive him in a place suitable for him. But if some other man or woman has come in secular attire, whether from the area or from outlying districts, as brothers, you, presbyter, while you speak the word of the Lord or while you have them listen or while you read, do not show partiality and do not leave your service to indicate their places to them, but stay still; and let the brothers receive them. But if there is no place, it is a charitable action of fraternal love that, having stood up, you give him your place. And if while the youths remain seated an older man has gotten up, or an older woman, to give

him a seat, you, deacon, having paid good attention to a youth among those who remain seated or otherwise among the youths, have him get up, make the other sit there, or that one who has left her place. And the one you had stand up you should put at the door, so that the others be rebuked and yield to those who are greater than themselves. Take care to arrange large churches, and if a poor man or woman comes who is from the area or from one of the neighboring districts, and there is no place, you, presbyter, make then a place for such persons wholeheartedly, even if you end up having to sit on the ground, so that there be no partiality toward human beings, but only toward the Lord (ch. 38).[146]

In the fourth century the great basilicas and churches were built everywhere, as also were some great baptisteries. These monuments have been studied as works of art, along with their building techniques and materials used, and other aspects. Today's interest, however, also considers the relationship between buildings and the liturgy that took place in them, and how the liturgy influenced the structure of the buildings.

When Did They Gather?

Christians, as the author of the *Epistle to Diognetus* says in the fifth chapter, share the spaces and social life of all:

Christians are indistinguishable from other men either by nationality, language or customs. They do not inhabit separate cities of their own, or speak a strange dialect, or follow some outlandish way of life. Their teaching is not based upon reveries inspired by the curiosity of men. Unlike some other people, they champion no purely human doctrine. With regard to dress, food and manner of life in general, they follow the customs of whatever city they happen to be living in, whether it is Greek or foreign. And yet there is something extraordinary about their lives. They live in their own countries as though they were only passing through. They play their full role as citizens, but labor under all the disabilities of aliens. Any country can be their homeland, but for them their homeland, wherever it may be, is a foreign country." On the other hand, it was well known both to the authorities and to the common people that they observed a special time for their meetings. Christians were easily visible also because of the observance of their calendar, which conferred a communal identity on them. Since the places and times for meetings were known to the authorities, too, they could easily be arrested in case of persecution. The preoccupation of Christians was the question: "How can we meet? How can we celebrate the solemnity of the Lord's day?" (*Sed quomodo colligemus? quomodo dominica sollemnia celebrabimus?*).[147]

From this arose the necessity to pay off the soldiers in order to be left in peace.[148]

In his investigation, Pliny had already found out that the Christians met "*stato die*," on a precise day.[149] As explained by Justin and Tertullian, that day was the *dies solis*, which is why Christians came to be confused by some with sun-worshippers.[150] Origen writes that the pagans know "our celebrations that happen on determined days, the Sundays, Easter, or Pentecost."[151] On that day they often were arrested or harassed at their meetings, as Hippolytus and Tertullian write. Hippolytus says:

> For when the two peoples conspire to destroy any of the saints, they watch for an appropriate time and then enter the house of God while all there are praying and praising God, and seize some of them, and carry them off, and keep hold of them, saying, 'Come, consent with us, and worship our Gods; and if not, we will bear witness against you.' And when they refuse, they drag them before the court and accuse them of acting contrary to the decrees of Caesar, and condemn them to death.[152]

Tertullian mentions the practice of paying the police not to disturb their meetings:

> But how shall we assemble together? Say you; how shall we observe the ordinances of the Lord? To be sure, just as the apostles also did, who were protected by faith, not by money; which faith, if it can remove a mountain, can much more remove a soldier. Let your safeguard be wisdom, not a bribe. For you will not have at once complete security from the people also, should you buy off the interference of the soldiers. Therefore, all you need for your protection is to have both faith and wisdom. If you do not make use of these, you may lose even the deliverance which you have purchased for yourself; while, if you do employ them, you can have no need of any ransoming. Finally, if you cannot assemble by day, you have the night, the light of Christ luminous against its darkness. You cannot run about among them one after another. Be content with a church of threes. It is better that you sometimes should not see your crowds, than subject yourselves (to a tribute bondage). Keep pure for Christ His betrothed virgin; let no one make gain of her.[153]

From the New Testament it seems one can deduce that Christians met in the evening. In Palestine the meeting at first probably took place on the evening of the Sabbath, after the synagogue services, but which would have already been the first day of the week for the Jews (Sunday). Everything was evolving. Paul already mentions the collection to be made in Corinth "every first day of the week" (*1 Cor* 16:2).[154] Therefore in Corinth a day had already been established for the meetings. The *Acts of the Apostles* also speaks of "the first day of the week" (*Acts* 20:7).[155] According to the Jewish system the first day of the week began—and still does so today—after the sunset of the Sabbath. Is it, then, the Sabbath evening or Sunday morning? John places the disciples' meetings on two Sunday evenings (*Jn* 20:19, 26). The author of the book of Revelation already speaks of the "Lord's day," which in pagan language is the day of the sun and in Judaism is the first day of the week. The phrase "the Lord's day" became common in the second century in Christian language.[156]

Latin authors usually translate this as *dies dominicus*, starting with Tertullian,[157] who in the *De ieiunio* uses the term *dominicus* as a noun.[158] Often, instead of saying *dies dominicus*, they just say *dominicum*.[159] The Lord's day soon becomes the common expression in Christian language. In fact, when the *Gospel of Peter* narrates the resurrection of Jesus, it no longer uses the Gospel wording, "the first day of the week," but "the Lord's day" (35; 50). This means that this new terminology is what Christians are using. A few decades earlier, however, the *Epistle of Barnabas*, addressed to the Jews, speaks of the eighth day of the week: "For this reason we pass the eighth day in joy, on which Jesus rose from the dead and, having manifested himself, ascended to the heavens."[160] Tertullian also attests that this day is joyful for Christians,[161] as do other authors, like Minucius Felix.[162] The *Didascalia* prescribes: "The first day of the week you must pass entirely in joy; in fact whoever afflicts his soul on the first day of the week is made guilty."[163]

The new typical Christian term also indicates the day for Christian meetings. The *Didache* (14.1) prescribes: "Gathered on the Lord's day, break bread and give thanks." The text of Pliny cited earlier speaks of meetings early in the morning on a set day, which we interpret as Sunday. But they also have an evening meeting. This is the first evidence of a weekly morning meeting. But this meeting became ever more frequent, until it became daily. What character does it have? Is it a liturgy of the word as some suggest? When was there the separation between the Eucharistic celebration and the agape? Ignatius insists that one must live according to the Lord's day and according to the Sabbath.[164]

In the middle of the second century in Rome, Justin bears witness that the meeting takes place on Sunday. He writes that the reading of biblical texts extends as long as time permits. The expression can imply that the necessity of going to daily activities does not leave much free time.[165] When he describes the Eucharistic meeting of Christians, Justin does not say that it takes place in the morning or in the evening, but indicates only the day of the week. The same thing happens in Corinth, as its bishop Dionysius attests in the second half of the same century, writing to the Romans: "Today, then, we have celebrated the holy day of the Lord, in which we have read your letter, which we shall always continue to read."[166]

Thus, from the beginning Christians met on Sunday, because of the Lord's resurrection, the first day of creation, as Justin says, when God transformed the darkness into light and created the world.[167] Christians consider Sunday the replacement for the Jewish Sabbath, and for this reason it is also called the eighth day, the day of fulfillment.[168] Cyprian adds other meanings: "Because the eighth day, which is the first after the Sabbath, would be the day on which God arose, giving us life and spiritual circumcision, this eighth day, which is the first after the Sabbath and is the Lord's day, has been anticipated in prefiguration."[169] A rich symbolism converges around the number eight: the resurrection, the new kingdom, the new creation, the day of purification, the day of the manna in the desert, the pledge of the future kingdom, the new circumcision, the day of the Lord and the day of judgment.[170] Our Sunday, according to Origen, has been prefigured in the descent of the manna, on account of which "on our Sunday the Lord always makes the manna come down,"[171] which is the word of God read and proclaimed during the worship service.

One final question remains: At what time did they meet in the morning or evening? The most ancient sources do not give the hour, but only the day. Even Justin, who is otherwise so detailed, makes no mention of it, even if normally one used to think that he referred to the morning.[172] Authors presuppose the evening: some think of Saturday evening which as we just noted was already the first day of the week for the Jews, while others think of Sunday evening. When Pliny speaks of a morning meeting, some think that this is an agape meeting, or rather is a liturgy of the word and of reciting prayers.

Tertullian offers numerous pieces of information about Christian meetings and how they were conducted, and yet doubts remain about how the rite was conducted.[173] In the *De Corona* (3.3) he explicitly refers to a Sunday morning Eucharistic celebration: "We receive the sacrament of the Eucharist in nocturnal assemblies, which are celebrated before dawn by those who preside, even if the Lord entrusted it to all in the hour of the supper." Since Sunday was a common day, Christians were forced to meet early in the morning, and thus Tertullian speaks of "gathering before dawn" (*antelucani coetus*). Novatian also confirms this tradition.[174]

Tertullian considers the morning celebration normal.[175] He criticizes those Christians who refuse to receive the body of the Lord in order not to break the fast. For him, rather, it is a greater glory of God to participate in his altar. In Carthage the morning Eucharistic celebration took place not only on Sunday but also on weekdays. Such a practice was not uniform, as with many other aspects of the liturgy. Thus, the Eucharist was celebrated at the hour of the resurrection or, quite rarely, on Saturday[176] or Sunday[177] evening. At any rate it would seem that one must also keep in mind the different system for calculating the day: from morning to the following morning, from evening to the following evening, or in the Roman practice from midnight to the following midnight.

In distant Syria the *Acts of Thomas* bear witness to a morning meeting for various days.[178] The *Apostolic Tradition* also speaks of morning assemblies before work.[179] Its author writes that, in the evening, the bishop should not say "lift up your hearts" at the moment of introducing the lamp-lighting, because it is said in the offering.[180]

Cyprian, who was bishop from 249–258, speaks of the morning sacrifice (*sacrificial matutina*), in which the blood of Christ is consumed.[181] One need not fear "to smell the Lord's blood through the taste of the wine." Some suggest offering only water in the morning, while offering a chalice mixed with water and wine in the evening, as the Lord did in the Last Supper. From the evidence of Cyprian, it becomes clear that, among small groups, the daily Eucharist in Carthage was still connected to an evening meal, although he expresses his disapproval of the hour of the celebration and institutes that the time for the Eucharist should be the morning. In his letter he condemns the so-called "Aquarians" who only use water.[182] For him the most fitting time is the morning, and not the evening, and this follows a long tradition.

Christians pray in the morning to celebrate the Lord's resurrection,[183] and they receive the Eucharist every day.[184] The first evidence of the daily celebration of the Eucharistic at Carthage is found in *Letter* 57.2 where he writes: "We priests who every day celebrate sacrifices for God, a sacrificial victim to God."[185] One must distinguish between the Eucharistic celebration and reception of the Eucharist, which can also happen at other times, whenever he takes the consecrated bread with himself to a house.[186]

By now the practice was habitual, but the fact remains that the early morning created problems. In 321, Constantine arranged for the *dies solis*, that is, Sunday, to be a day of rest for the inhabitants of cities. It was not easy to implement this different way of organizing time. But it favored Christian pastoral ministry, since the bishops were able to shift the celebration to a more convenient hour, around the third hour, that is, nine in the morning.[187]

LITURGICAL FURNISHINGS

Historical studies on the origin and development of the Christian liturgy normally make no mention of liturgical furnishings[188] or to the garments used during the cultic ceremony.[189] These topics, like others that are mentioned in this chapter, are treated by archeologists. Here we limit ourselves to some hints; for a fuller treatment one can look at the three articles in the *Encyclopedia of Ancient Christianity* indicated in the notes, which have a full bibliography.

The furnishings were numerous, insofar as they included all that was needed for the correct performance of the liturgy. The *Liber Pontificalis*, the latest edition of which was redacted around 535, gives us detailed information about the donations of Constantine to various churches. It lists the objects and also their size and quality. Some furnishings were portable while others were fixed in place. Among the portable furnishings were, for example, the basins (*scyphi*), chalices, patens, *amulae* (or *amae*, which were like flasks), the Paschal candle, books for readings or chants, the furniture, which included seats for the clergy, portable lamps, tables, etc. Among the fixed objects were the episcopal throne, the lamps (since the building must be well lighted inside),[190] the ambo, as well as other furnishings.

It is more difficult to address the liturgical clothing in which both liturgists and scholars of clothing are interested. Certainly, in the first two centuries specific consecrated vestments were not used. In this aspect they were not the heirs of the Old Testament, which prescribed vestments for the cult. The practice was to use common, but decent vestments. The affirmation of the *Liber Pontificalis* that Pope Stephen I (254–257) established that the sacred vestments not be put to daily use (*constituit sacerdotes et levitas ut vestes sacratas in usu cottidiano non uti, nisi in ecclesia*), needs to be understood as saying that at the time of the redaction of the text there had already been an evolution in practice by the middle of the third century.

When, in the fourth century, the clergy became ever more important in society, the bishops of the main cities especially began to wear costly and precious vestments.[191] They began to distinguish themselves from the normal people not with vestments peculiar to them but with those that would be found in high society. The clothing indicates their higher role. Furthermore, the clergy did not wear special vestments, insofar as they were not distinguished from the common faithful. The use of special vestments emerged slowly, with differences in the various geographical areas. In the fourth century it was especially the monks who wore special vestments as a sign of their life. Such vestments might include a dark tunic, clogs, a wool cincture as a sign of their life dedicated to God. Iconography shows us monks who wore tunics with long or short sleeves. They wore them on every occasion, in the liturgy as well as in daily life.[192] The monastic rules also dealt with the topic.

Augustine and his monks dressed in a simple way. He preferred not to wear precious garments:

> I do not want, for example, that a precious mantle be offered to me. Perhaps it is fitting for the bishop but not for Augustine, a poor man, born of poor people. They would say right away that I am wearing precious clothes that I would not have been able to have from my father's house or from the profession that I undertook in the world. It is not right for me. I must have a garment that I could give to a brother if he did not have one; a garment that a presbyter could have, that a deacon could wear with dignity, or a subdeacon. . . . If a finer garment is offered me I sell it: that is what I am used to doing because the profit of the sale can be used in common while such a vestment cannot be used in common. I sell and give to the poor. If someone really wants to give me a garment as a gift let him give me one that does not embarrass me. I confess to you, I am ashamed of a garment that is too beautiful; it does not suit my ministry, my teachings, my poor physical body, my white hair.[193]

Pope Celestine reproved the bishops of Gaul for the vestments that distinguished them.

The phenomenon occurs because people who had held important posts in society continued on with the same vestments when they entered the ministry. Celestine admonishes:

> Where does this way of life in the Churches of Gaul come from, on account of which a custom has changed into another way of life that lasts for so many years and pertains to so many bishops? We must distinguish ourselves from the people and from all others for our doctrine, not for our habit, for our conduct, not for our manner of dressing, for the purity of our mind, not for our lifestyle. In fact, if we begin looking for novelties, we will trample the rules handed down to us from the Fathers.[194]

From the sixth century on, the shift in clothing was introduced both in the daily life of the clergy and in the liturgy, particularly through the influence of new invading peoples.[195]

COMMUNAL PRAYER AND GESTURES

As Origen observes, prayer is an act of the soul and of the body in space and in time.[196] Above all the inner dispositions are fundamental. Christian authors speak about them a great deal: to be at peace, to be repentant, to practice brotherhood, to have feelings of mutual love, not to suffer disturbances of soul, freedom from sins, freedom from the passions, not to nurture anger, etc. Here is a passage from Origen: "He who prays must lift his hands that he will keep pure if he forgives all who have done him offense, if he makes the feeling of anger leave his soul, nor is angry with anyone. Likewise, in order for the mind not to be polluted by other thoughts, it is necessary during the time of prayer to forget all that is foreign to prayer."[197]

The same Origen, as Perrone observes many times, spiritualizes the gestures and is not very concerned with them. He writes:

> I think it not out of place to add, by way of completing my task in reference to prayer, a somewhat elementary discussion of such matters as the disposition and the posture that is right for one who prays, the place where one ought to pray, the direction towards which one ought except in any special circumstances to look, and the time suitable and marked out for prayer. The seat of disposition is to be found in the soul, that of the posture in the body. Thus Paul, as we observed above, suggests the disposition in speaking of the duty of praying without anger and disputation and the posture in the words lifting up holy hands, which he seems to me to have taken from the Psalms where it stands thus—the lifting up of my hands as evening sacrifice; as to the place I desire therefore that men pray in every place, and as to the direction in the

Wisdom of Solomon: that it might be known that it is right to go before the sun to give thanks to you and to intercede with you towards the dawn of light.[198]

The gestures[199] performed during cultic acts vary according to the sacraments and sacramental (to use the modern terms): the catechumenate, baptism, confirmation, exorcisms, penitential process, ordinations. About these rites I have already spoken in various chapters. One of the more important is the imposition of hands. As today so also then numerous gestures were performed together from ancient tradition; others are new according to the various cultures. We know them only in part. Some of these come from the Jewish world, others from other influences. For example, praying to the east is not of Jewish origin—in Judaism one faces toward Jerusalem—but from other cultures. Another example is the gesture of washing one's hands before prayer, which is commended but only if one is also pure on the inside.[200]

Praying Towards the East

The gesture of praying toward the east was performed in the communal assembly, but it was also done in private:

A few words may now be added in reference to the direction in which one ought to look in prayer. Of the four directions, the North, South, East, and West, who would not at once admit that the East clearly indicates the duty of praying with the face turned towards it with the symbolic suggestion that the soul is looking upon the dawn of the true light? Should anyone, however, prefer to direct his intercessions according to the aperture of the house, whichever way the doors of the house may face, saying that the sight of heaven appeals to one with a certain attraction greater than the view of the wall, and the eastward part of the house having no opening, we may say to him that since it is by human arrangement that houses are open in this or that direction but by nature that the East is preferred to all the other directions, the natural is to be set before the artificial. Besides, on that view why should one who wished to pray when in the open country pray to the East in preference to the West? If, in the one case it is reasonable to prefer the East, why should the same not be done in every case? Enough on that subject.[201]

The last words of Origen manifest his preoccupation with spiritualizing and not treating secondary things. In addition, he offers a reason as well since the redemption comes from the east, from where the light is born that banishes the darkness and from where the sun of justice comes.[202]

The fact that Christians pray turned toward the east means that the pagans think they are worshippers of the sun: "Lastly the suspicion arises from the knowledge that we turn to the east in prayer. But many of you too with an affectation of sometimes worshiping heavenly bodies move your lips towards the rising sun. Likewise, if we give rein to joy on Sundays, we do so in a far different way from sun worship."[203]

Praying with Open Arms Extended and While Standing

Prayer with open arms (*expansis manibus*) and hands lifted up is documented by many sources both literary and archeological. The figure of the *orans* of ancient tradition is very diffuse since even texts of the Old Testament say: "All day do I call you, Lord, to you I extend my hands" (*Ps* 89:10; 119:48). The Odes of Solomon too speak of hands lifted in prayer (28 [27].2; 63.5; 21.1; 35.7; 37.1; etc.). On many Roman coins one also finds a female figure as an *orans* with writing that explains its meaning (*Pietas, Pietas publica, Pietas augusta, Pietas Augusti*, etc.). This image is picked up without alteration by the Christians, giving it another interpretation. In paleo-Christian art the figure of the Good Shepherd and the *orans* are encountered together. Many biblical characters are represented as praying (*orantes*), as also dead people sometimes with their names, or martyrs, and still others.[204]

Prayer while standing is already attested in Irenaeus: "The practice of not praying on one's knees during the Lord's day is a symbol of the resurrection, by means of which we have been freed, thanks to Christ, from sins and death which has been put to death by him."[205] Origen observes: "One cannot doubt that, however many the positions of the body may be, to be preferred to them all is that consisting of lifting the hands and turning the eyes on high; for in this manner the body in prayer bears the image of the qualities which suit the soul in prayer." Canon 20 of the council of Nicaea reaffirms the tradition of prayer while standing on feast days: "Since there are some who kneel on Sunday and the days of Pentecost, to observe complete uniformity in all dioceses it has seemed good to this holy council that prayer to God be addressed while standing." One sees that not all pray while standing, at least in communal assemblies. This tradition of standing during the liturgy is still followed in many churches in the east (although the elderly are allowed to sit).

The posture of the tax-collector in the gospel of Luke (18:9ff.) also inspires certain counsels of Tertullian and Cyprian: to pray with humility without lifting the eyes too much, or the voice, without making others hear one's own requests, etc.[206] Kneeling expresses humility of spirit and the sense of penitence, because "one is to be accused before God of one's own sins, supplicating him to remit them."[207] On weekdays it is normal to pray on one's knees or genuflect, especially on fast days. In the fourth century, Basil attests that: "Only on the first day of the week do we make our prayers while standing; not everyone, however, knows the reason."[208] On Saturday too, in fact, there was kneeling, according to tradition, even if some small group abstained.[209] Praying on one's knees during feast days and during the period after Easter up to Pentecost was absolutely forbidden: "Fasting or adoring God on one's knees on Sunday we consider an impiety,"[210] because these days are to be passed in joy and not in sadness. "Only on the day of the Lord's resurrection, according to our tradition, must we abstain not only from this practice of praying on our knees, but also from every posture that implies anxiety. . . . The same is true for the feast of Pentecost which is characterized by the same festive exultation."[211]

Did they sit on some occasions? Origen suggests that if someone cannot stand on their feet because of sickness or some other reason, he should just be seated: "Effectively in such occasions it is permitted sometimes to pray conveniently while staying seated as, for example, when one has a foot problem that cannot be ignored; or staying in bed because of fever or other similar infirmities. Analogously, if, for example, we are on a ship or the carrying out of duties does not permit us to retire for the required prayer, one can pray without having the air of prayer."[212] The *Apostolic Tradition* and the *Syrian Didascalia*—two texts already cited—prescribe sitting for almost everyone. This supposes that there were sufficient seats, unlike the Latin churches, which did not have seats for the people.

The Sign of the Cross

An important gesture that came to be associated with prayer and which became quite common was the making the sign of the cross: "If we set out on a journey, if we exit or enter, if we get dressed, if we wash up or go to table, in bed, if we sit ourselves down, in these and in all our actions we sign our foreheads with the sign of the cross."[213] Such a sign is common in many cultures, but for Christians it becomes their distinctive sign. At the time of Tertullian, it was already a habitual gesture and assumed different meanings. It could be used for apotropaic purpose such as for providing protection like signing one's forehead before sleeping or also signing the bed.[214] The first Christian evidence is found in the *Odes of Solomon* mentioned earlier. The *Odes of Solomon* are a collection of prayers in verse dating from the second century AD. The *orans* prays with arms open, like the form of the cross: "I extended my hands/and proclaimed that my Lord is holy./The stretching out of my hands is the sign of him/and my standing straight, the straight wood."[215] In other words, when we pray with open arms, we become the sign of the cross, we are the sign of the cross. For Justin the symbol of the cross is the greatest symbol of God's strength and power. The cross can be seen in many situations such as on a ship, in the figure of a man praying with open arms, on trophies, in the world itself.[216] This symbol is also found in the Old Testament.[217] The cross is also a cosmic symbol, insofar as the four arms of the cross represent the four corners of the world.[218]

For Tertullian, following Justin, the cross reflects the structure of the human body.[219] The *Apostolic Tradition* advises making the sign of the cross in every circumstance, because it is a defensive weapon:

> Always be concerned to sign your forehead, because it is a manifest sign of the Passion, against Satan, and it is evident, if it has been done with faith, not only so that you be recognizable to men, but you equip yourself with the sign as if with a suit of armor. And once the adversary has seen the power of man that is in his heart, made with certainty in the likeness of a washing, he will flee trembling for fear, not because of the spitting but because of the breath. . . . Signing then our forehead and eyes with our hands, we keep ourselves far from him who plots to bring on death. While one knows this with grace and right faith, he will give edification in the church and eternal life to all those who believe: because as all listen to the apostolic tradition, heresy will not arrive to draw any righteous one into error.[220]

The sign of the cross is connected with the Passion of Christ; for this reason, it is a force against the adversary. In Christian tradition it becomes a gesture of protection, of exorcism, of blessing, of prayer, an apotropaic gesture, and the like. It gets traced on persons and on things; it especially gets depicted, also under the form of the Tau.[221] The Latin verb *signare* and the noun *signatio* mean making the sign of the cross. In the *Acts of John*, the apostle John, "with his gaze turned toward the East, praised God and, entirely immersed in light, signed himself completely with the sign of the cross" (ch. 115).

When the catechumen starts his journey, he is signed on the forehead; it is a *consignation* carried out in a solemn manner: *solemniter utique signandus est*.[222] With this rite he becomes a Christian, but not one of the faithful.[223] "We ask a catechumen: Do you believe in Christ? I believe, he will respond, and will make the sign of the cross; he already bears the cross of Christ on his brow and is not ashamed of the cross of his Lord."[224] "Moreover, because you had no doubts, because you had no shame, when you began to believe, you received the sign of Christ on your forehead, which is like the seat of modesty. Think back to what you have on your forehead, and you will not fear another's tongue."[225] Even the emperors at the time were not ashamed to carry the sign of the cross on their forehead: "Now the wicked kings have disappeared, they have become good; they too have believed, they already bear the sign of Christ's cross on their forehead, a sign more precious than any gem of their crown."[226]

Augustine often speaks of the sign of the cross, and the Christian also makes it on strange occasions, as in the circus: "They—those absent from the Eucharist—if by chance, while they are in the circus, for some reason are frightened, immediately sign themselves, and carrying that sign on their forehead they remain there, in the place from which they would have withdrawn if they had borne that sign in their heart."[227] It seems that some also bore a tattoo of the cross.[228]

The Kiss of Peace

Another sign and liturgical gesture which accompanied prayer and certain rites is the kiss of peace. Paul already mentions the kiss of peace to be exchanged during the Eucharistic gatherings. This is above all a sign of brotherhood and unity[229] and goes right back to the origins of Christianity (*Rom* 16:16; *1 Cor* 16:20; *2 Cor* 13:12; *2 Thess* 5:26; *1 Pt* 5:14). As we saw earlier, the kiss of peace is exchanged during the liturgy, but only among the faithful and not with the catechumens, the lapsed, or the penitents,[230] and without distinction of sex.[231] Since, in a later era, the sexes were separated in the assembly, as a consequence the kiss of peace came to be exchanged only among persons of the same sex.[232] The exchange occurred at different moments in different regions; in the west the custom was established of kissing one another before the communion,[233] moreover, the kiss was exchanged on other liturgical occasions as well, where it was always considered the seal on something that had already happened: after baptism,[234] after the ordination of a bishop,[235] in the nuptial rite during the act of "betrothal,"[236] since the kiss also took on a juridical value.[237]

Tertullian criticizes those who introduced a new tradition by abstaining from the kiss of peace during the communal prayer because of a private fast: "What prayer is complete without the kiss of peace, which is the seal of prayer?"[238] Tertullian also mentions various gestures during prayer. In the *Apology* he writes: "We Christians, lifting our eyes, with hands outspread, because we are innocent, with uncovered head, because without shame, and finally without a prompter, because we pray from the heart, we always found ourselves praying for long life for all the emperors" (30.4). "Not only do we lift our hands, but we lift them in a cross like Our Lord in his passion, and with this posture we confess Christ."[239] Origen also speaks of the proper position of the body: "with the palms open and the eyes lifted to heaven."[240] But instead he offers other interpretations of the gesture, of a moral character, without associating it with the image of the cross.[241]

EUCHARISTIC PRAYERS AND ANAPHORAS

Justin affirms that the presider at the assembly prays as he can, in other words, he has in mind some ideas and formulas but expresses himself freely. Here, I quote some ideas from the *Encyclopedia of Ancient Christianity:*

In respect to the formulation of prayers (=*euchology*) and rites, the paleo-Christian era has two basic tendencies, which in turn relate to different periods: that of creativity, spontaneity and liberty of liturgical expression, followed by a gradual linguistic and ritual formulization resulting in fixed forms and formulas. Of course, the two periods cannot be clearly distinguished. The first period (1st–3rd/4th c.) saw improvisational prayer, spontaneous creativity and varied forms of proliferation of rites. Although the different traditions all came from a common Jewish-Christian origin, in adapting to new cultures into which Christianity came they took shape under the influence of the particular religious instincts of the converted peoples. Similarly, creativity in prayer, with the movement from Aramaic to Greek, to Coptic and Syriac, and with that from Greek to Latin, progressively gave way—for various reasons—to a period of compilation and standardization of written formulas. This then is the second period (3rd/4th–6th/7th c.), that of the production of set prayers, in the context of the great Latin-Roman and Greek-Eastern literary traditions, the influence of the great Eastern Fathers (Basil, John Chrysostom, etc.) and Western (Ambrose of Milan = Ambrosian liturgy; Leander = Hispanic-Visigothic liturgy; Leo, Gelasius, Gregory = Roman liturgy; Peter Chrysologus = Ravennan liturgy; Chromatius = Aquileian liturgy), as well as of the principal metropolitan sees (Jerusalem, Antioch, Alexandria, Constantinople; Rome, Milan, Seville, Lyons, etc.).[242]

Every improvisation, however, occurs within certain fixed and traditional elements of biblical inspiration. One must always remember that culture and tradition were transmitted in the practice of orality, common in that time.

The earliest preserved Eucharistic prayer is found in the *Apostolic Tradition*, already included earlier. Not all were capable of composing a prayer, even using some previously developed expressions and the biblical repertoire. Some presiders at assemblies were inadequate. The lack of preparation could lead them to say inexact or even heretical things. For African churches we have the canons from two African councils, that of Hippo in 393 inserted into that of Carthage in 397 (canons 21–28), and that of Milevis from the council of Milevis in 416. In the meantime, some texts were composed as well such as the so-called *libelli missarum*,[243] witnessed by the *Sacramentarium Veronense* [*Leonianum*]).[244]

In the preceding paragraph I included a selection from the scholar Triacca which explained the initial improvisation and then the birth of fixed formulas, which we call "Eucharistic prayers"[245] and anaphoras. The term "anaphora" has numerous meanings. In the liturgy, starting already with the *Letter to the Hebrews* 13:15 and the *First Letter of Peter* 2:5, the anaphoric prayer takes on the meaning of a cultic sacrifice. We learn of the different ways the term "anaphora" was employed from Gelsi in an article in the *Encyclopedia of Ancient Christianity*:

Anaphora includes four principal meanings: (1) the act of offering the Eucharist; (2) the formulary employed in the Eucharistic act; (3) the material offered in the Eucharist (equivalent to προσφορά); and (4) the liturgical veil that covers the Eucharistic species. The meaning most used in a technical sense in liturgical language is anaphora as the priestly Eucharistic prayer. Christian antiquity found the term so incisive that liturgies celebrated in languages other than Greek did not translate it.[246]

Thus, after improvisation some formulas of priestly Eucharistic prayers continually evolved in the same Christian communities, in the various languages used and in the various geographic areas.[247] In areas we know about in the fourth century, the improvisation still continued which could produce unorthodox prayers. In Africa the councils prescribed the use of prayers that conformed to the right faith and were approved by competent persons.[248] "Their great number, and the richness and variety of their content show that they derive from periods of liturgical freedom and creativity; such a process did not culminate in anarchy but in the unity of inspiration of the great anaphorical compositions. Anaphoras form liturgical families, not to be confused with the homonymous institutional or confessional families: e.g., the Alexandrian or St. Mark anaphora is virtually unused in the patriarchate of Alexandria; the churches of the Byzantine branch use the anaphora of St. Basil of Caesarea and St. John Chrysostom, Antiochene in structure; the Ethiopian church currently uses the Syriac anaphora adopted during the medieval liturgical reforms carried out under the influence of the Syrian church. The most commonly accepted classification includes three families: (1) Syro-Eastern (improperly called Chaldean), (2) Antiochene (or Syro-Western), and (3) Alexandrian."[249]

CONCLUSION

In this chapter we have seen both uniformity and diversity in liturgical practice. The uniformity revolved around the core content of the Gospel and its orthodox formulations. The diversity came from local expressions informed by the talent, theological acumen and ingenuity of the various geographical areas into which the church had spread. As the church grew and experienced doctrinal challenges there were calls for greater uniformity and orthodoxy in liturgy and proclamation.

Church meetings and assemblies started out from simple structures, first occurring in people's homes or perhaps rented buildings. Even before Christianity was legalized, however, the archaeological and written witnesses inform us of church buildings being constructed to meet the increasing needs of the church community and her catechetical, liturgical and sacramental life. The liturgy, too, evolved from the simple instructions we find in the *Didache* and other early liturgical documents, to more complex liturgies which met the needs of the ever growing Christian community. Various traditions also developed that were meant to confirm everyday Christians in their faith and aid their worship and practice. The church, her institutions, her leaders, her liturgy, her traditions, her catechesis—even the time and place of worship—were all derived in various ways from Scripture and the *regula fidei* and the faithful themselves. The church and her liturgy were being shaped, formed and structured to glorify God, serve his people and challenge the culture and society of the day, even as those same forces also shaped the church.

---

1. Minucius Felix, *Octavius* 8.4.
2. Minucius Felix, *Octavius* 10.2-5.
3. Minucius Felix, *Octavius* 12.5-6.
4. Minucius Felix, *Octavius* 4.
5. Tertullian, *Apologeticum* 10.1-3.
6. Tertullian, *De spectaculis* 13.
7. Athenagoras, *Suppl.* 13.1; Origen, *Contra Celsum* 7.62; 8.17; Cyprian, *Ad Demetrianum* 12; Lactantius, *Div. Inst.* 7.26.9-10.
8. Augustine, *Ep.* 102.16.
9. Arnobius, *Adv. Nationes* 6.1; *in hac enim consuestis parte crimen nobis maximum impietatis adfigere, quod neque aedes sacras venerationis ad officia construamus, non deorum alicuius simulacrum constituamus aut formam, non altaria fabricemus, non aras, non caesorum sanguinem animantium demus, non tura neque fruges salsas, non denique vinum liquens paterarum effusionibus inferamus.*
10. A. Romeo, "Il termine leitourgia nella grecità biblica," *Misc. Mohlberg, II* (1949): 467-519; P. Fernández Rodríguez, "El término liturgia. Su etimología y su uso," *Ciencia Tom.* 97 (1970): 143-63; S. Rossi, *Un popolo di sacerdoti* (Rome: LAS, 1999), 71-79 (bibliography).
11. *Mediator Dei* 20.
12. H.-D. Dalmais: *EAC* 2:584.
13. Cyprian, *De operis et el.* 15; *Ep.* 38,17; *Ep.* 63,16: *dominicum post cenam celebrare debemus?*; *Ep.* 63. 16; Augustine, *Brev. Collat.* 3.17.32; *Acta sanctorum Saturnini etc: celebrantes dominicum* (2.6); i martiri '*qui contra interdictum imperatoris et caesarum collectam sive dominicum celebrassent*' (5.1); '*qui non potest intermitti dominicum, lex sic iubet*' (11.4; cf. 9.4 ; 12.3); '*in domo mea egimus dominicum*' (12.1); '*Quasi christianus sine dominico possit, aut dominicum sine christiano celebrari*' (13.5). See J. Leal, *Actas latinas de mártires africanos* (Madrid: Ciudad Nueva, 2009).
14. Abitinae (today Chouhoud al-Bâtin, near Medjez el-Bab in Tunisia).
15. Justin, *1 Apol.* 67.
16. Justin, *2 Apol.* 3.
17. Justin, *1 Apol.* 40.
18. Tertullian, *De Or.* 28.1-2.
19. E.g. Minucius Felix, *Octavius* 32; Cyprian, *Or. Domin.* 2; *Ep.* 77.2.
20. The New Testament expression *regale sacerdotium* derives from the Septuagint Bible. The original Hebrew text of Ex 19:6 has *regnum sacerdotum* (a kingdom of priests) instead of *regale sacerdotium* (a royal priesthood). The text of Peter is the following: "Come to him...and like living stones, let yourselves be built into a spiritual house, to be a holy priesthood, to offer spiritual sacrifices acceptable to God through Jesus Christ. ... You are a chosen race, a royal priesthood, a holy nation, God's own people, in order that you may proclaim the mighty acts of him who called you out of darkness into his marvelous light."
21. Justin, *1 Apol* 61.
22. *1 Clem.* 43-44.
23. For these topics see chapters four and five.
24. Cyprian, *Ep.* 14.4.

25. Cyprian, *Ep.* 19.2.
26. This evolution is present in the *Acts of the Apostles* and constitutes the meaning of the stoning of Stephen (Acts 6–7). See F. Hahn, *Der urchristliche Gottesdienst* (Stuttgart: Verlag Katholisches Bibelwerk, 1970), tr. It., *Il servizio liturgico nel cristianesimo primitivo* (Brescia: Paideia, 1976). Hahn asserts that at the beginning Christians were free from Jewish practices, but afterwards reintroduced them. The affirmation is only partially valid and only in individual aspects. For example, in later centuries they reintroduced some Jewish practices such as the feast day rest, impurity of women after birth, etc.
27. I recently asked an American Jew, who considered himself deeply Jewish and explained many things to me, what it means to be Jewish. He tells me he is a "secular Jew." I asked him what this means. He answered me by describing the great variety of Jews; basically, each person feels Jewish but observes the prescriptions in his or her own way.
28. Daniel K. Falk, "Jewish Prayer Literature and the Jerusalem Church in Acts," in Richard Bauckham, ed., *The Book of Acts in its Palestinian Setting* (Grand Rapids: William B. Eerdmans, 1995), 267-301.
29. The ritual performed by the community in the celebration of Passover.
30. Cf. Joshua Kulp, "The Origins of the Seder and the Haggadah," *Currents in Biblical Research* 4 (2005-2006): 109-34, especially 114ff.
31. *Shemonè esrè* are also said, the *Eighteen* [blessings] with reference to the original number, but they became ten.
32. Thomas J. Talley, "The Eucharistic Prayer of the Ancient Church According to Recent Research: Results and Reflections," *Studia Liturgica* 11 (1976): 138-58, here 149.
33. M. Righetti, *Storia liturgica* I, 278-313; G. Ladocsi, *EAC* 1:760-61.
34. Basil, *De Sp. sancto* 27; Methodius of Olympus, *Symposium* 11.2.
35. Ambrose, *De Myst.* 7; Cyril of Jerusalem, *Catecheses* 19.11.
36. *Const. Apost.* 2.57.
37. *Martyrdom of Paul* 5.
38. I. J. Yuval, "Easter and Passover as Early Jewish-Christian Dialogue," in Paul F. Bradshaw & Lawrence A. Hoffman, eds, *Passover and Easter: Origin and History to Modern Times* (South Bend: University of Notre Dame Press, 1999), 98-124, Christian influence is discussed on 103-4.
39. P. Bradshaw, "Jewish Influence on Early Christian Liturgy: A Reappraisal," in *Liturgies in East and West: Ecumenical Relevance of Early Liturgical Development*, Hans-Jürgen Feulner, ed., (Berlin: Lit Verlag, 2013), 47-59, here 58, published on the site: Jewish-Christian Relations. Insights and Issues in the ongoing Jewish-Christian Dialogue.
40. D. A. Fiensy, *Prayers Alleged to be Jewish: An Examination of the Constitutiones Apostolorum* (Chico, CA: Scholars Press, 1985); P. W. van der Horst, "The Greek Synagogue Prayers in the Apostolic Constitutions, Book VII," in J. Tabory, ed., *From Qumran to Cairo: Studies in the History of Prayer* (Jerusalem: Orhot Press, 1999), 32-36.
41. Cf. P. F. Bradshaw, M. E. Johnson, *The Eucharistic Liturgies: Their Evolution and Interpretation* (Collegeville, MN: Liturgical Press, 2012), 111-21. The bibliography is vast, cf. B. Spinks, *The Sanctus in the Eucharistic Prayer* (Cambridge: Cambridge University Press, 1991), 1-121; Y. de Andia, "L'hymnologie céleste. Le 'Sanctus' et la vision d'Isaïe dans l'Orient chrétien du IIIe au Ve siècle et la 'Hiérarchie céleste' de Denys l'Aréopagite," *Connaissance des Pères de l'Église* 137 (2015): 2-26.
42. P. Bradshaw, *Jewish Influence*, 59.
43. A few comments in P. Bradshaw, *The Search for the Origins of Christian Worship* (London: SCPK, II ed. 2002), 21-23.
44. In paleo-Christian art it is normal.
45. C. Vogel, "Sol aequinoctialis. Problèmes et techniques de l'orientation dans le culte chrétien," *Revue Sciences Religieuses* 36 (1962): 175-211.
46. L. Perrone, "For the Sake of a 'Rational Worship': The Issue of Prayer and Cult in Early Christian Apologetics," in *Critique and Apologetics. Jews, Christians and Pagans in Antiquity*, ed. Jörg Ulrich, David Brakke and Anders-Christian Jacobsen (Tübingen: Peter Lang 2012), 231-64.
47. L. Perrone, "Christianity as 'Practice' in Origen's *Contra Celsum*," in *Origeniana nona* (Leuven: Peeters, 2009), 293-317.
48. Minucius Felix, *Octavius* 10.2, 5.
49. Tertullian, *Ad Nationes* 1.10.3.
50. Tertullian, *De Oratione* 28.1.

51. The meaning of the term: *EAC* 3:2-3; *paganus* from *pagus* (village) = a) village, country, rustic; [*paganus*, κωμήτης, *qui in pagis habitat*]; b) civil as opposed to military (*Pagani saepe opponuntur militibus*). c) Christian authors: *paganus* = *Gentilis*; pagan.
52. Every city or village had its patron deity who took care of the wellbeing of the community as such, not of individuals. The civil community took care of the relationship with its particular divinity through the public cult adapted to each divinity (sacrifices, spectacles, etc.).
53. Pseudo-Justin, *To the Greeks* 4–5: PG 6:238-39.
54. Cf. Justin, *1 Apol.* 62.1; 66.4. "The wicked demons, by imitation, said that all this happened in the mysteries of Mithras too. In fact, you already know, or can comprehend, how in the initiation rites bread and a cup of water are introduced, while some formulas are pronounced." See also Tertullian, *De Bapt.* 5.1.
55. This was the accusation made against Marcion, emphasized by Tertullian, and against the Gnostics, highlighted by Irenaeus. We also find it in Justin.
56. P.-M. Gy, "La notion chrétienne d'initiation. Jalons pour une enquête," *La Maison-Dieu* 132 (1977), 33-54; M. Metzger, "Katechumenat," *Reallexikon Antike und Chr.* 20 (2003): 509-10. A.D. Nock, *Christianisme et Hellénisme*.
57. See V. Loi, "Il termine 'mysterium' nella letteratura latina cristiana prenicena," *Vigiliae Christianae* 12 (1966): 85-107. *Sacramentum* is mostly used to render the liturgical and sacramental sense. The African Latin translation of the Bible (the *Afra*) prefers *sacramentum* to *mysterium*, while the Latin translation called the *Itala*, or *Vetus Latina*, prefers *mysterium* to *sacramentum*. G. Trettel, G., *Mysterium e sacramentum in san Cromazio* (Cittadella: Bertoncello, 1979); G. Francesconi, *Storia e simbolo. Mysterium in figura, la simbolica storico-sacramentale nel linguaggio e nella teologia di Ambrogio di Milano* (Brescia: Morcelliana, 1981).
58. For these issues see Vittorino Grossi, "La Pasqua quartodecimana e il significato della croce nel II secolo," *Augustinianum* 16 (1976): 557-71; and the recension of the *Letter of Barnabas* (Corona Patrum 1, SEI-Torino 1975); *Biblica* 58 (1977): 274-78. The texts about Passover are in an Italian translation by R. Cantalamessa, *I più antichi testi pasquali della Chiesa* (Rome: Edizioni liturgiche, 1972).
59. Chr. Mohrmann, "Le latin liturgique," *La Maison D.* 23 (1950): 5-30; P. Bernard, "Les latins de la liturgie (antiquité tardive et Moyen-Age). Vingt-cinq années de recherches (1978-2002)," *ALMA* 60 (2002): 77-170; *EAC* 2:524-27.
60. V. Loi, *EAC* 2:593. Chr. Mohrmann, "Le latin liturgique," *La Maison D.* 23 (1950): 5-30; *Medieval Latin: An Introduction and Bibliographical Guide*, edited by F.A.C. Mantello and A.G. Rigg (Washington, D.C.: The Catholic University of America Press, 1996), 157-82; P.Bernard, *Les latins de la liturgie*, 77-170; Antoine A. R. Bastiaensen, "Biblical Poetry in Latin Liturgical Texts," in *Poetry and Exegesis in Premodern Latin Christianity: The Encounter Between Classical and Christian Strategies of Interpretation*, ed. by Willemien Otten and Karla F. L. Pollmann (Leiden: Brill, 2007), 265-74; Uwe Michael Lang, *The Voice of the Church at Prayer: Reflections on Liturgy and Language* (San Francisco CA: Ignatius Press, 2012).
61. Marcel Metzger, *L'Église dans l'Empire Romain. Le culte, vol. I: Les institutions* (Rome: Pontificio Ateneo Sant'Anselmo, 2015), 72-184.
62. See Chapter 1 Subheading "Dissemination and application of the texts."
63. Cf. Chapter one in our present volume.
64. V. Saxer, *Vie liturgique et quotidienne à Carthage*.
65. *Harum et aliarum eiusmodi disciplinarum si legem expostules scripturarum, nullam invenies* (*De corona* 4.1; concerning *consuetudo*, cf. *De virginibus velandis*, passim).
66. Augustine, *Ep.* 51.1.1.
67. Augustine, *Ep.* 54.2.2.
68. Joseph G. Mueller, "The Ancient Church Order Literature: Genre or Tradition?" *JECS* 15 (2007): 337-80.
69. For the *Didache*, cf. *SC* 248: 98, especially 114; for the *Didascalia*, Nau, *La Didascalie*, 12-13.
70. *The Canons of Hippolytus*, ed. P.F. Bradshaw.
71. Cf. S. Grébaut, "Littérature éthiopienne pseudo-clémentine," *Revue de l'Orient chrétien* 12 (1907): 285-97; 380-92; 13 (1908): 166-80, 314-20; 15 (1910): 198-214, 307-23, 425-39; A. Jaubert, *SC* 167: 20-23.
72. *The Teaching of the Twelve Apostles* = (Didache), introduction, critical text, trans., notes, appendices, and indices by Willy Rordorf and André Tuilier; trans. by Maria Benedetta Artioli, 2 ed. revised and expanded (Bologna: EDB, 2009).
73. Athanasius, *Festal Letter* 39.
74. Clement of Alexandria, *Pedag* 2.10.89; *Strom.* 1.20.100.4.
75. Origen, *De Princ.* 3.2.7; *Hom. Iud.* 6.2.

76. Some authors tend to diminish the strictly Eucharistic character of such prayers in the Christian sense, and link them back to the prayers of blessing that the Jews recited before and after meals.
77. An Ethiopian translation was already known, published by G. Horner, *The Statutes of the Apostles or Canones Ecclesiastici* (London: Williams and Norgate, 1904) edited with Translation and Collation from Ethiopic and Arabic MSS.; also a Translation of the Sahidic and Collation of the Bohairic Versions; and Sahidic fragments, (London 1904), 10-48 [text], 138-86 [trans.]; H. Duensing, *Der äthiopische Text der Kirchenordnung des Hippolyt* [Abhandlungen der Akademie der Wissenschaften in Göttingen. Philologisch-historische Klasse 3/32], (Göttingen: Vandenhoeck & Ruprecht, 1946).
78. A. Bausi, *La Nuova versione etiopica*, 19-69.
79. *La tradition apostolique: d'après les anciennes versions*, ed. B. Botte (Paris: Éditions du Cerf, 1984), 10–17.
80. For a wider treatment of this literature, see A. Di Berardino, *Letteratura canonica e liturgica*, 222-49. Or in the individual entries in the *EAC*, ed. A. Di Berardino.
81. For eastern liturgical books, cf. M. Nin, *Patrologia*, vol. V, ed A. Di Berardino (Genova: Marietti, 2000), 677-83.
82. M. Metzger, *L'Église dans l'Empire Romain. Le culte, vol. I: Les institutions*, 297-388; F. Cassingena-Trévedy, *Les Pères de l'Église et la liturgie* (Paris: Desclée de Brouwer, 2009), 35-92; B. Amata, "Testimonianze di Arnobio Afro sulle assemblee liturgiche agli inizi del IV secolo," *Ephemerides Liturgicae* 98 (1984): 513-25.
83. Lactantius, *Divinae Instit.* 5.1.26: *sacramentum ignorantibus non potest, quoniam mystica sunt quae locutus est, et ad id praeparata ut a solis fidelibus audiantur.*
84. Cyprian, *De patientia* 24; *De ecclesiae unitate* 7.24.
85. Augustine, *De vera religione* 7.12.
86. Ignatius, *Ephesians* 13; cf. *Magnesians* 7.2; *Philadelphians* 6.2.
87. *Ep.* 10.96.
88. A. Di Berardino, "I cristiani e la città antica nella evoluzione religiosa dei primi secoli," in E. dal Covolo – R. Uglione, (eds.), *Cristianesimo e Istituzioni politiche, Da Costantino a Giustiniano* (Rome: LAS, 1997), 45-79.
89. Origen, *Homilies on Genesis* 10.
90. Chapters 41; 70; 117.
91. Cf. Irenaeus, *Adv. Haer.* 4.18.3, 6; 5.2.3.
92. In the *Apologeticum* (16.6) Tertullian addresses the pagans and uses the term *dies solis*; here he addresses Christians and uses the expression *dies dominicus*.
93. *De Corona* 3.3-4. Other texts are collected by R. Cantalamessa, *La Pasqua nella Chiesa antica* (Torino: Società editrice internazionale, 1978), 59.
94. A. Bausi, *La Nuova versione etiopica*, 19-69, here 35.
95. M. Metzger, *L'Église dans l'Empire Romain. Le culte*, 185-295.
96. Chr. Mohrmann, "Les dénominations de l'église en tant qu'édifice en grec et en latin au cours des premiers siècles chrétiens," *Revue Sciences Rel.* 36 (1962): 155-74; G. Herbert de la Portabarré-Viard, "Recherches sur les dénominations des édifices du culte chrétien dans les textes latins à l'époque constantinienne et post constantinienne," in *Acta XVI Congressus Internationalis Archeologiae christianae, Costantino e i Costantinidi* (Vatican City: Pontificio Istituto di archeologia cristiana, 2016), Pars II, 1359-77.
97. Origen, *Homilies on Exodus* 2.2.
98. G.J.M. Bartelink, "Maison de prières comme dénomination de l'église en tant qu'édifice, en pariculier chez Eusèbe de Césarée," *Revue des Études Grecques* 84 (1971): 101-18.
99. In a work of Ps-Cyprian, *De singularitate clericorum* of the middle of the third century.
100. Tertullian, *De idol.* 7.1.
101. Tertullian, *Ad uxorem* 2.8.8.
102. Origen, *Homilies on Jeremiah* 4.3.
103. A. Nestori, "Riflessioni sul luogo di culto cristiano precostantiniano," *Rivista arch. Cristiana* 75 (1999): 695-709. He collects text concerning places of worship.
104. Eusebius, *HE* 8.1.5.
105. Eusebius, *HE* 10.3.1.
106. Clement of Alexandria, *Stromata* 7.5.
107. Origen, *Homilies on Exodus* 12.2.
108. *Itiner. Burdigalense*, in *Itineraria romana*, eds. Otto Cuntz, Gerhard Wirth (Stutgardt: in aedibus B. G. Teubneri, 1929), 23.

109. CIL 15:7192 (*Tene me quia fugi et reboca me Victori acolito a dominicu Clementis*). Jerome knew a church in Rome that was preserved into his own time and was linked to Clement: *nominis eius memoriam usque hodie Romae extructa ecclesia custodit* (Jerome, *De viris ill.* 15).
110. E. Adams, *The Earliest Christian Meeting Places: Almost Exclusively Houses?* (London: T&T Clark, 2013).
111. *Acts of Martyrdom*, recension A, 3.
112. Tertullian, *De idolol*. 7.1; *Ad uxorem* 2.8.8.
113. *Nostrae columbae etiam domus simplex in editis semper et apertis et ad lucem amat figuram spiritus sancti orientem Christi figuram*. (*Adv. valentinianos* 3.1).
114. Origen, *Homilies on Exodus* 2.2; 12.2; *Homilies on Leviticus* 9.9; *Homilies on Joshua* 2.1.
115. Eusebius, *HE* 7.13.1.
116. *Didascalia Ap.* 2.57; this text is collected in the Ethiopian translation of the *Apostolic Tradition*, ed. A. Bausi, ch. 38.
117. Sible de Blaauw, "A Classic Question: The Origins of the Church Basilica and Liturgy," in *Acta XVI Congressus internationalis archeologiae Christianae*, 553-62.
118. O. Brand, "Constantinian Baptisteries," in *Acta XVI Congressus internationalis*, 583-610.
119. M. Trinci Cecchelli, "Osservazioni sul complesso della 'domus' celimontana dei ss. Giovanni e Paolo," in *Atti IX Congresso Internazionale di archeologia cristiana*, 550-62.
120. Yotam Tepper and Leah Di Segni, *A Christian Prayer Hall of the Third Century CE at Kefar 'othnay (legio): Excavations at the Megiddo Prison 2005* (Jerusalem: The Israel Antiquities Authority, 2006).
121. Cf. C. Gebbia, "Ancora Altava," in *L'Africa romana XVI*, eds M. Akerraz, P. Ruggeri, A. Siraj, C. Vismara, (Rome: Carocci, 2006), 495-505; M.A. Ruiu, "La Cohors II Sardorum ad Altava (Ouled-Mimoun, Algeria)," in *L'Africa romana*, (Rome: Carocci, 2004), 1415-32; J. Marcilet, *Les inscriptions d'Altava*, (Gap: Éditions Ophrys, 1968); C. Lepelley, *Les cités de l'Afrique romaine au Bas-Empire*, Vol. 2 (Paris: Études augustiniennes, 1981), 522-34.
122. Eusebius, *HE* 7.13.
123. G. Muscolino, ed., *Porfirio, Contro i cristiani. Nella raccolta di Adolf von Harnack* (Milan: Bompiani, 2009), fr. 76, 355.
124. Eusebius, *HE* 7.15.4.
125. G.J.M. Bartelink, "Maison de prières comme dénomination de l'église en tant qu'édifice, en pariculier chez Eusèbe de Césarée," *Revue des Études Grecques* 84 (1971): 101-18.
126. PG 1:1452.
127. Eusebius, *HE* 8.2.4-5.
128. Lactantius, *De mortibus* 12.3.
129. ed. Ziwsa, CSEL 26: 186.20.
130. DACL 3:1914.
131. ed. Ziwsa, CSEL 26:194. Y. Duval, *Chrétiens d'Afrique à l'aube de la paix Constantinienne - Les premiers échos de la grande persécution* (Paris: Institut d'études augustiniennes, 2000), 77-78.
132. Eusebius, *HE* 8.17.9; Lactantius, *De mortibus* 42.
133. *HE* 10.2.1.
134. For an optimal summary of the current debates, cf. O. Brand, "The Archaeology of Roman Ecclesial Architecture and the Study of Early Christian Liturgy," *Studia Patristica* 71 (2014), 21-52.
135. N. Duval, *Church Buildings*; *EAC* 1:524-37.
136. *De arch.* 4.5.1-2.
137. C. Vogel, "Sol aequinoctialis. Problèmes et techniques de l'orientation dans le culte chrétien," *Revue Sciences Religieuses* 36 (1962): 175-211; E. Peterson, "La croce e la preghiera verso oriente," *Ephemerides Liturgicae* 59 (1945): 53-68; *EAC* 1:760-61 (with bibliography); Uwe Michael Lang, *Turning Towards the Lord: Orientation in Liturgical Prayer* (San Francisco CA: Ignatius Press, 2004, 2009).
138. V. Saxer, "Il étendit les mains à l'heure de sa Passion. Le thème de l'orant/-te dans la littérature chrétienne des IIe et IIIe siècles," *Augustinianum* 20 (1980): 335-65.
139. S. de Blaauw, *In vista della luce: Un principio dimenticato nell'orientamento dell'edificio di culto paleocristiano*, in *Arte medievale: Le vie dello spazio liturgico*, ed. Paolo Piva (Milan: Jaca Book 2012), 15-45 (*Art médiéval. Les voies de l'espace liturgique* (Paris: Picard, 2015), 15-45).
140. N. Duval, *EAC* 1:527.

141. Ch. Smith, "Christian Rhetoric in Eusebius' Panegyric at Tyre," *Vigiliae Christianae* 43 (1989): 226-47; J.M. Schott, *Eusebius' Panegyric On The Building Of Churches (HE 10.4.2-72): Aesthetics And The Politics of Christian Architecture* (Leiden: Brill, 2011).
142. Eusebius, *HE* 10.4.44; cf. also 10.4.66.
143. R. M. Jensen, "À la redécouverte de l'ecclésiologie des premiers siècles chrétiens : emplacement de l'autel et orientation de la prière dans l'Église latine primitive," *La Maison-Dieu* 278 (2014): 51-81, here 62-67.
144. N. Duval, "L'espace liturgique dans les églises paléochrétiennes," *La Maison-Dieu* 193 (1993): 7-29; R. M. Jensen, *À la redécouverte de l'ecclésiologie des premiers siècles chrétiens*, 51-81.
145. A. Bausi, *La Nuova versione etiopica*, 41.
146. Ibid, 67-69.
147. The expression *domenica sollemnia* occurs multiple times in Tertullian and could mean either the Sunday worship or the worship rendered to the Lord.
148. Tertullian, *De fuga* 14.1.
149. *Ep*. 10.96.7.
150. Tertullian, *Ad nationes* 1.13.1. The Christians of the first centuries named Sunday in three or four ways: *dies dominicus*, *dies solis* (especially when speaking with pagans), and the first day of the week; sometimes the "eighth day" occurs. Further, they also use the expression "the day of the resurrection."
151. Origen, *Contra Celsum* 8.22.
152. Hippolytus, *Hom. Dan.* 1,20.
153. Tertullian, *De fuga* 14.1-2.
154. W. Rordorf, *Sunday: The History of the Day of Rest and Worship in the Earliest Centuries of the Christian Church* (Philadelphia: Westminster Press 1968), 193ff. S.R. Llewelyn, "The Use of Sunday for Meetings of Believers in the New Testament," *NovT* 43 (2001): 205-23, esp. 210-13.
155. J. Tromp, "Night and Day. A propos Acts 20:7," in *Jesus, Paul and Early Christianity*, eds. R. Buitenwerf, H.W. Hollander, J. Tromp (Leiden: Brill, 2008), 363-75.
156. *Didache* 14.1; Ignatius, *Magnesians* 9,1; *Epistle of the Apostles* 18; *Gospel of Peter* 35; 50; Dionysius of Corinth, in Eusebius, *HE* 4.23.9; Clement of Alexandria, *Ex. ex Theod.* 63.1; *Stromateis* 5.106.2; Eusebius, *HE* 3.27.
157. Tertullian, *Idololatria* 14.7; *Corona*. 3.4.
158. *On Fasting* 15.2: *exceptis scilicet sabbatis et dominicis*,
159. Cf. Augustine, *Epp.* 36.8, also 19 and 23; 65.2; *Enar. in ps.* 150.1.
160. *Ep. Barn.* 15.9.
161. Tertullian, *Ad nationes* 1.3.1.
162. Minucius Felix, *Octavius* 9.13.
163. *Didascalia* 5.20; cf. 5.10.1.10.
164. Ignatius, *Magnesians* 9.1.
165. Justine, *1 Apo*. 67.3.
166. Eusebius, *HE* 4.23.11
167. Justin, *1 Apol* 67.7.
168. W. Rordorf, "Origine et signification de la célébration du dimanche dans le christianisme primitif," *La Maison Dieu* 149 (1981): 103-22, anche in *Liturgie, foi et vie des premiers chrétiens. Études patristiques* (Paris: Beauchesne, 1986), 29-48.
169. Cyprian, *Ep.* 64.4.3.
170. Cf. W. Rordorf, *Sabato e domenica nella chiesa antica* (Torino: SEI, 1979), index 253f; J. Daniélou, "Dimanche comme huitième jour," in *Le Dimanche* (Paris: Éditions du Cerf, 1965), 61-89; in Gnostic literature (ogdoad): *EAC* 2:952-53; G.W. Clarke, *The Letters of St. Cyprian of Carthage*, Vol. 3 (Mahwah, NJ : Paulist Press), 312; baptisteries in octogonal form.
171. Origen, *Homilies on Exodus* 7.5.
172. H. Lietzmann, *Mass and Lord's Supper* (Leiden: Brill, 1979) (*Messe und Herrenmahl*, Bonn: Marcus and Weber, 1926), 211.
173. P. F. Bradshaw, *Eucharistic Origins* (London: SPCK, 2004), 97-103.
174. Tertullian, *De Spectaculis* 5.5.
175. Tertullian, *De Oratione* 19.1.

176. *Second Apocalypse of John*, 7, in *Rev. Bibl.* 11 (1914), 209-21, here 215: the text says that God blesses those who observe Sunday, ceasing to work at the ninth hour of Saturday and going to church "the evening of the holy Sunday," (according to the Syriac manner of calculating the day it corresponds to Saturday evening). This apocalypse pertains to a group of texts that support the Sunday observance and the obligation of rest: cf. *Rev. Bib.* 11 (1914), 213, n. 4 and 215 n. 4.
177. E. Dekkers, "L'Église ancienne a-t-elle connu la messe du soir?" in *Miscellanea Liturgica in honorem L. C. Mohlberg* (Rome: Edizioni Liturgiche 1948), I, 1238-57; Ibid, "La messe du soir à la fin de l'antiquité au moyen âge. Note historique," in *Sacris Erudiri* 7 (1955): 98-130; W. Rordorf, *Sunday: The History of the Day of Rest and Worship*, 250-55; 271-73; I. M. Alçada Cardoso, "La sinassi eucaristica domenicale: vespertina e/o mattutina?" in *Tempo di Dio, tempo dell'uomo*, XLVI Incontro di Studiosi dell'Antichità Cristiana (Rome: Institutum Patristicum Augustinianum, 2019), 645-53; A.C. Stewart, *The Transfer from Sabbath to Sunday*, 655-57.
178. *Acts of Thomas* 27-29.
179. *Apostolic Tradition* 22, 25, 27, 35-37.
180. *Apostolic Tradition* 22, Ethiopian ed.
181. Cyprian, *Ep* 63.15.
182. Cyprian, *Ep.* 63.13-16.
183. Cyprian, *De Oratione* 35.
184. *Eucharistiam quotidie accipimus* 18; cf. Cyprian, *Ep.* 58.1.2.
185. Cf. Cyprian, *De lapsis* 26; *Ep.* 58.1.2. Cf. V. Saxer, *Vie liturgique à Carthage*, 46f; *DTC* 3:515-17.
186. Cf. Tertullian, *De Oratione* 6.2; 19.1ff.; *Ad Uxorem* 2.5.2; *De Idolol.* 7.3. See also the anonymous *De centesima*: PL suppl. 1,63; V. Saxer, *Vie liturgique à Carthage*, 47.
187. A. Di Berardino, "La cristianizzazione del tempo nei secoli IV-V: la domenica," *Augustinianum* 42 (2002): 97-125.
188. M. Cecchelli, "Liturgical Furnishings" in *EAC* 2:578-81; S. De Blaauw (ed.), *Arredi di culto e disposizioni liturgiche a Roma da Costantino a Sisto IV* (Rome: Van Gorcum, 2000); F. Guidobaldi, "Strutture liturgiche negli edifici cristiani di Roma dal IV al VII secolo," in Margherita Cecchelli (ed.), *Materiali e tecniche dell'edilizia paleocristiana a Roma* (Rome: De Luca, 2001), 171-90.
189. Cf. E. Pavan, "Color – Liturgical" in *EAC* 1:1122-25; Idem, "Vestments, Liturgical" in *EAC* 3:889-95; P. Rossi, *Vesti e insegne liturgiche: Storia, uso e simbolismo nel rito romano* (Milan: Lampi di stampa, 2003); *Omnia parata. Le vesti liturgiche tra passato, presente e futuro*, eds. L. Palmeri, C. Piro, M. Vitella (Trapani: Liber Artis, 2006); S. Piccolo Paci, *Storia delle vesti liturgiche* (Milan: Àncora Editrice, 2008).
190. Cf. *EAC* 2:578-81.
191. R. Martorelli, "Influenze religiose sulla scelta dell'abito nei primi secoli cristiani," *Antiquité tardive / Late Antiquity* 12 (2004): 231-48; Valerio Neri, "Vestito e corpo nel pensiero dei Padri tardoantichi," *Antiquité tardive / Late Antiquity* 12 (2004): 223-30
192. M. Mossakowska-Gaubert, "Tuniques à manches courtes et sans manches dans l'habit monastique égyptien (IVe - début VIIe siècle)," *Antiquité tardive / Late Antiquity* 12 (2004): 153-67.
193. Augustine, *Sermo* 356.13; *Ep.* 263.1.
194. Celestine, *Ep.* 4.1.2.
195. M. C. Miller, *Vestire la Chiesa. Gli abiti del clero nella Roma medievale* (Rome: Viella, 2014).
196. Cf. L. Perrone, *La preghiera secondo Origene* (Brescia: Morcelliana, 2011), 145-74.
197. Origen, *De Oratione* 9.1; cf. 31.2.
198. Origen, *De Oratione* 31.1.
199. M. Righetti, *Manuale di storia liturgica*, Vol. 1 (Milan: Ancora 1964), 362-415; *Gestes et paroles dans les diverses familles liturgiques* (Rome: Edizione Liturgiche, 1978; J. Dubuc, *Il linguaggio del corpo nella liturgia* (Milan: Edizioni Paoline, 1989); H F. Stander, "The Clapping of Hands in the Early Church," *Studia Patristica* 26 (1993): 75-80; *EAC* 2:135-36; P. Prétot, "La liturgia, un'esperienza corporale. Indicazioni per una 'grammatica' del corpo nella liturgia," *Rivista Liturgica* 96 (2009): 968-985; *Dizionari San Paolo, Liturgia*, eds. D. Sartore, A.M. Triacca, C. Cibien (Milan: San Paolo 2001), 859-77 (rich bibliography).
200. Tertullian, *De Oratione* 13.1; *De baptismo* 15.3; *Apostolic Tradition* 41; Clement of Al., *Stromateis* 4.141.4; Ps. Clement, *Homilies* 11.28-29.
201. Origen, *De Oratione* 32.
202. Cf. Origen, *Homilies in Leviticus* 9.10. Also see C. Vogel, "La croix eschatologique," in *Noël, Epiphanie, retour du Christ*, eds B. Botte, E. Mélia (Paris: Éditions du Cerf, 1967), 85-108.

203. Tertullian, *Apologeticum* 16.9-10.
204. V. Saxer, "Il étendit les mains à l'heure de sa Passion": le thème de l'orant dans la littérature chrétienne des IIe et IIIe siècles," *Augustinianum* 20 (1980): 335-65.
205. Frag. 7, Harvey 2.478. R. Cantalamessa, *La Pasqua nella Chiesa antica* (Torino: Società editrice internazionale, 1978), 59, text and translation.
206. Tertullian *De Oratione* 17; Cyprian *De Oratione* 6.
207. Origen, *De Oratione* 31.3.
208. Basil, *On the Holy Spirit* 26.67.
209. Tertullian, *De oratione* 23.1. Cf. Rordorf, *Sabato e domenica*, 57, and note 1. What Tertullian describes may have only been in the African churches, although it is difficult to say.
210. Tertullian, *De Corona* 3.4. Augustine also notes this tradition, writing that, during the Paschal period, the alleluia is sung, and adding: "As for the custom of praying while standing during these fifty days and on all Sundays, I am unaware if it is a universal practice" (*Ep.* 55.32).
211. Tertullian, *De Oratione* 23.2.
212. Origen, *De Oratione* 31.2.
213. Tertullian, *De Corona* 3.4.
214. Tertullian, *Ad Uxorem* 2.5.2.
215. *Odes of Solomon* 27.1-3.
216. Justin, *1 Apo.* 55.2-3; 60.1-7.
217. Justine, *Dialogue with Trypho* 138.2; 91.4; 40.3; 25.4. T. Piscitelli, "La croce negli scritti cristiani dei primi due secoli." *Koinonia* 38 (2014): 165-192; Boris Ulianich, ed., *La Croce. Iconografia e interpretazione (secoli I – inizio XVI)*, 3 vols. (Naples: Elio de Rosa Editore, 2007).
218. J. Daniélou, "Le symbolisme cosmique de la croix," *Maison Dieu* 75 (1963): 23-36.
219. Tertullian, *Ad Nationes* 1.12.7.
220. *Apostolic Tradition* 42.1-5; Bausi translation, 35, 61, 63.
221. Cf. Augustine, *Quaestiones in iudices* 37.
222. Augustine, *De catech. rudi.* 26.50.
223. C. Vogel, "La signation dans l'Eglise des premiers siècles," *La Maison-Dieu* 75 (1963): 37-51.
224. Augustine, *Tract. in Evan. Ioan.* 11.3.
225. Augustine, *Serm.* 215.5.
226. Augustine, *Enarr. in Ps.* 32 2.2.13.
227. Augustine, *Enarr. in Psalm.* 50.1.
228. Henri Rondet, "Miscellanea augustiniana; la croix sur le front," *Rech. Science Religi.* 42 (1954): 388-94.
229. Tertullian, *Ad Uxorem* 2.4; *De Oratione* 18, 24; Ambrosiaster, *In 1 Cor.* 16.20.
230. Cf. *Apostolic Tradition* 18; Council of Laodicea, can. 19; Augustine, *Contra Litt. Petil.* 2.23.
231. Cf. Justin, *1 Apol.* 65; Athenagoras, *Legatus* 32; Clement of Alexandria, *Paed.* 3.11; Council of Laodicea, can. 19.
232. *Apostolic Constitutions* 2.57.17; 8.11.9.
233. Cf. Pope Innocent, *Ad Decent.* 25; PL 20:553.
234. *Apostolic Tradition* 21; *Testament of our Lord Jesus Christ* 2.9; *Canons of Hipp.* 19; Cyprian, *Ep.* 59.
235. *Apostolic Tradition* 4; *Apostolic Constitutions* 8.5.10.
236. Tertullian, *De Virg. Vel.* 11; Ambrose, *Ep.* 41.18.
237. *Kiss, Holy, EAC* 2:507-508, with bibliography.
238. Tertullian, *De Oratione* 18.5.
239. Tertullian, *De Oratione* 14.
240. Origen, *De Oratione* 31.2 Cf. DACL 12,2: 2291-2322.
241. L. Perrone, *La preghiera secondo Origene*, 165-66.
242. A. Triacca, *EAC* 2:594-95 (with bibliography).
243. E. Romero Pose, *EAC* 2:562.
244. A.M. Triacca, "'Improvvisazione' o 'fissismo' eucologico. Asterisco ad un periodico episodio di pastorale liturgica," *Salesianum* 32 (1970): 149-64; E. Cattaneo, *Il culto cristiano in Occidente. Note storiche* (Rome: C.L.V.-Edizioni liturgiche, 1978), 17-183; B. Neunheuser, *Storia della liturgia attraverso le epoche culturali* (Rome: Edizione Liturgiche, 1983), 15-55; A. Budde, "Improvisation im Eucharistiegebet. Zur Technik freiein Betens in der Alten Kirche," *Jahrbuch Antike und Chr.* 44 (2001): 127-41.

245. E. Mazza, *L'anafora eucaristica. Studio sulle origini* (Rome: Edizioni Liturgiche, 1992); [*The Origins of the Eucharistic Prayer* (Collegeville, MN: 1995)]; Ibid, *La celebrazione eucaristica. Genesi del rito e sviluppo dell'interpretazione* (Cinesello Balsamo: San Paolo, 1996) [*The Celebration of Eucharist: The Origin of the Rite and the Development of Its Interpretation* (Collegeville, MN: Pueblo, 1999)]; Ibid, *La celebrazione eucaristica: genesi del rito e sviluppo dell'interpretazione* (Cinisello Balsamo (Milano): San Paolo, 2003.)
246. D. Gelsi, *EAC* 1:110.
247. A. Hänggi-I. Pahl, *Prex eucharistica* (Fribourg: Éditions universitaires, 1968).
248. M. Klöckener, "Les réformes liturgiques dans l'histoire," *Maison Dieu* 277 (2014): 33-66, esp 43-44.
249. D. Gelsi, *EAC* 1:110.

CHAPTER 12
THE ORIGINS OF THE CALENDAR AND CHRISTIAN FEASTS

In the preceding chapters, especially in the tenth, I have spoken of the liturgy, of Christian assemblies, of the Eucharist, of prayers, and of ritual gestures. Christians not only organized the social and religious life within their own assemblies, but, in time, especially from the fourth century on, they had a profound influence on the organization of public time, including social, political, religious, judicial, recreational, and working time. Much of what they initiated is still observed up to our own day in predominantly Christian countries. Today this calendar, still observed in many respects, is being overturned due to our multicultural and religiously pluralistic society. Public time is coming to be fragmented and more personal. Computers and cell phones have imposed an organization of time that is lived out in a universal and coordinated way. Even amid the diversity of national and religious calendars, all these instruments use the Julian-Gregorian calendar, with some small adjustment.

After treating some general elements about the calendar and about the measurement of time, I will dedicate more space to the birth of Christian feasts and the organization of time according to these feasts. Since the central feast of the Christian liturgical year is Easter, a demanding task in the first centuries was prediction of the date of its celebration in the future. From this arose the science of the Easter *computus*.

Today we speak of the liturgical year, but this phrase was not used in Christian antiquity, but is a later development. It implies the idea of an integral and well-structured annual cycle of feasts with either movable or fixed dates. In the later period the *anni circulus* is spoken of, an expression that one finds in the Gelasian Sacramentary and in the Gregorian Sacramentary. But the development of the concept occurs in the twelfth century and is found in the *Golden Legend* of Jacobus de Varagine.[1]

SOME GENERAL ELEMENTS

The term *calendar* derives from the Latin term *kalendae*, the first day of each month.[2] The term *calendar* can indicate: a) the conventional system of calculating time by various methods, for example the year (solar or lunar, etc.; the month; etc.); b) an instrument that presents a list of days, or something else, with indications of events (feasts, or something else); c) an order of activities (scholastic, judicial, athletic, meetings, etc.). A few days ago my watch stopped; without my watch I felt lost; I could not manage to locate myself in the passing of time. How many times a day do we look at the time? Up to a few generations ago, no one had a watch. The mechanical watch was invented only around 1300. With the watch was born official time that was marked by the official city clock. In the churches there were bells that marked the liturgical and religious time for Christians.

Normally people regulated themselves by the sun, moon, and stars. By day the sun was fundamental: with the shadows of trees and buildings and the position of the sun they calculated the time with a certain precision. They knew all the variations of shadows. They knew the starry sky with great precision as well. The Romans spoke of night-watches (of soldiers on guard). There were other instruments: the rooster's crowing was the time to rise. They also observed the behavior of animals.

Today we eat according to schedules. At one time the best clock was the stomach. Every group of people as well as each person needs to measure time by units of duration. The choice of this unit is important, depending on the area. In certain situations, it can be approximate (in the early afternoon); in others it must be extremely precise (on high-speed trains; on flights; in the coupling of satellites). Thus, one can study the history of creating temporal measurements.

Many ancient cultures developed their calendar to regulate their religious life, social and religious time, and also aspects of society such as taxes, agriculture, and assemblies. The points of reference were the sun and the moon. When the sun returned to the same constellation, that duration of time was known as a year. With the moon, when the first new moon appeared, that duration of time was known as a month. The lunar or synodic month, from their experience, was not less than 29 days and not more than 30 days. The system of lunation was common, except in the Egyptian calendar and then in the Roman calendar reformed by Julius Caesar. With the system of lunations the month always began with the new moon and ended when the next new moon arrived.

Marking time is an essential component in the unfolding of human life. Such marking or measurement of time determines the social, political, and religious relations of a community. It highlights the difference between profane and religious time. It is human beings who determine the characteristic and nature (*qualitas*) of human time. This distinction was very important for the pagan world, and even more so for the Jews with, for example, their Sabbaths and feast days. For Christians too the *qualitas* of time slowly became the regulator of religious life. For example, the *qualitas* of the Lenten period demanded also a renewal of conduct, prolonged fasts, intense prayers, generous almsgiving, and even the abstaining from sexual relations between spouses.[3] There was also the prohibition of marriage celebrations (Council of Laodicea, etc.) and other human actions.

In more ancient times there were no watches. The instruments used to tell time were hourglasses that could be used for short spaces of time—something might have a duration of one hourglass or two hourglasses, for instance. They also used sundials which, by their very nature, were a more local instrument. People knew how to orient themselves by other means as well: shadows of the sun, the crowing of the rooster, or the position of the stars. People knew the starry vault very well. There was no light pollution back then, nor was there any artificial light, only lamps of various kinds. They kept track of the change of seasons, the flowering of plants, the withering of leaves, the maturation of grapes, and the like. In the Middle Ages the almanac came into being. It was a calendar with astronomical tables, as well as tables for seasons and religious feasts. Their dissemination was possible only with the printing press. Time was local, according to the movement of the sun. And so, there were different times in different cities in the same geographic area. The sun rises at different times depending on the different geographic areas. The creation of time zones in the 1800s permitted global coordination, and the calculation of time grew more and more precise. In the past, sundials were useful on sunny days. The hours were adapted to the sun, that is, to the duration of light. Since the relation of sun and Earth changes depending on the seasons and the locations, the hours would change too. They lengthen or shorten in relation to the sun, insofar as the night always had twelve hours and the day twelve hours.[4]

With the spread of watches and time pieces since the beginning of the nineteenth century, the perception of time changed and greater regularity was sought. Speed becomes a virtue along with punctuality and regularity. While for other measurements such as weight, length, and volume, there are still many differences across cultures and countries, for time alone a single system of measurement has been reached.[5] The search for precision expands, and especially for globalization, where everything is connected, everything happens in real time. The tiny second is subdivided into billionths of a second (nanosecond) or a picosecond (a thousandth of a nanosecond), with still other even smaller units being created.

The organization of time in ecclesiastical use (*supputatio temporis*) varies from century to century. Currently it is regulated by the Canon Law in effect for the Catholics (canons 200–

203). These canons are of a general character, and thus admit exceptions, as is expressly said both in the Code itself and in other norms such as the liturgical ones. In the Codex of 1917 there were greater indications. The canons concern "continual time," the length of the day starting from midnight, the week, the year, etc. In years past, there was no distinction between legal time and solar time. In canon law the day lasts twenty-four hours; in the liturgical sphere it normally lasts twenty-four hours as well; but it can also be longer. This came to be called the *dies ecclesiasticus* which runs from the first vespers of the day to midnight of the following day (the anticipated mass; indulgences, etc.)

THE BASIS OF THE CALENDAR

All societies in antiquity sought to organize social time, public time, religious time, and political time. The social time of a community is arranged to make it collaborative according to the shared values, beliefs, and ideals. This organization of social time orders the times of individuals or small groups, along with cosmic and natural time and biological time. A calendar is created which, though based on astronomical data, alternates mainly between sacred and profane time. In fact, among all ancient peoples the calendar was developed primarily by priests. The week (of seven days, eight days, etc.) was not based only on an astronomical fact, but accounted for other religious, symbolic, and socio-cultural values.

In our society too, the calendar is an essential instrument for organizing social time. Now the more complex a society is the more it needs calendars and ways of organizing shared time. Numerous calendars are in use at the same time and must be harmonized. In the western world the religious calendar is the original calendar; many other particular and localized calendars come into being (civil, scholastic, financial, liturgical, work, entertainment, etc.), which must be articulated not only by month, week, and day, but also by hour and minute, with ever greater attention to precise timing.

The solar calendar considers only the sun for the day and the solar year (the Roman calendar); the lunar calendar is based only on the moon (Hebrew, Islamic calendars). The lunisolar calendar is of two types: (1) The first type is based primarily on the solar calculation with some lunar adjustments (our calendar, and the Christian calendar). The months however have little connection with the lunar phases and are simply artificial. And yet there are still twelve months, in honor of their lunar origin. There could also be a year without months since it could be sufficient to simply count the days, or the year could be comprised of more months of a different length. (2) The second type relies more on the moon, with adjustments made for the sun. In this case, there are twelve or thirteen months. The lunisolar calendar thus considers both the moon and the sun, similar to the Christian calendar and, to a degree, the Hebrew calendar.

There are three basic components of which the calendar is comprised:

1) The *day* (from the Latin *tempus diurnum*) was used with different meanings. It can mean the space of twenty-four hours; the period of daylight; an imprecise unit of time, such as when we speak of a day's walk. It also can be used more generically to refer to, for instance, a day of sun, a day of rain, a day of work, or a day of rest. As mentioned previously, in more ancient times there was no instrument for measuring time. The first instruments were sundials such as the meridian, gnomon, and other types, which indicated local, not general, time. There were also water-clocks (clepsydrae): *ex aqua fecit horarium*.[6] This type of clock was very useful for trials when to each party the same time to speak was given: one clepsydra, two clepsydrae....

There were also various expressions for the time of day used in common speech: *gallinicum* (cockcrow), *quarta castrensis vigilia* (the fourth watch),[7] *diluculum* (dawn), *mane* (early morning), *ad meridiem* (late morning), *de meridie* (afternoon), *crepusculum* (twilight, dusk), *vespera* (evening), and other approximate terms. In Roman antiquity as well as the Gospels both the night and the day were divided into twelve hours, as is noted in the text from Censorinus. Their length varied according to the seasons and the places. For example, in Rome in December an hour was less than forty-five minutes and in summer was about seventy-five minutes. In the army the night hours were subdivided into four *vigiliae*, the same term which is used in the Gospels. The day hours began with the rising of the sun (*hora prima*) and went to the ninth hour (*hora nona*). The Christian liturgy takes the subdivision of the hours from this terminology. In practice the day was divided into two parts. In the New Testament the hours are also spoken of in an approximate way. In the Gospel of John it is said that the day has twelve hours (*Jn* 11:9). The beginning of the day also varied from people to people.[8]

2) The *month* was always based on the movement of the sun around the earth. This system is no longer universal, but is rather only used for certain calendars such as the Islamic and Hebrew calendars. The span of time between one new moon and another is called a lunar month or synodic month, the average length of which is currently 29.5305889 days, because it is not equal in all months. Since a solar year is 365.242190 days, twelve lunations (twelve full moons) make a shorter lunar year (354 days, 8 hours, 48 minutes). A lunar year also does not coincide with the civil year; therefore sometimes a day needs to be added. In lunar calendars that nevertheless account for the sun, as for example the Hebrew calendar, every two or three years a month needs to be added—what is referred to as an embolismic month. Such years have thirteen months according to the Metonic cycle. The Metonic cycle takes its name from the Athenian astronomer Meton who lived in the fifth century B.C. He discovered that in the cycle of nineteen solar years, which is approximately 235 lunations, the new and full moons return to the same dates as when they started the cycle. The Christian and the Hebrew calendars follow the Metonic cycle but not the Islamic.

3) For us today the *year* is based on the rotation of the earth around the sun. The tropical year is the time that the sun takes to return to the same point. Around 1900 it was 365.242190 days; toward 2010 it was 365.242184. Within the year, there are various days which serve as markers. For the northern hemisphere[9] there is the winter *solstice* which is the shortest day of the year, near December 21, when the sun is at its lowest point, toward the south. The summer *solstice* designates the longest day of the year, near June 21. The term comes from Latin: *sol* (sun) and *stare* (to stand still). It is the other way around for the southern hemisphere, although for Easter the point of reference is still the vernal equinox of the north. The summer solstice is when the sun, around June 22, is found in the first part of Cancer and stops rising above the celestial equator. Another marker within the calendar year is the vernal *equinox,* when night and day have the same length. It occurs near March 21; the autumnal equinox occurs near September 22. As an example of these four markers, in 2019 the vernal equinox occurred on March 20 at 21:54; the summer solstice occurred on June 20 at 15:54; the autumnal equinox happened on September 22 at 07:50 and the winter solstice took place on December 21 at 04:19.

The length of the year varies according to the points of reference, which could be, for example, the length of time between the two vernal equinoxes, or the two winter solstices. By convention the solar or tropical year is considered to be 365 days. Every four years a day is added—what we call in North America a "leap year" when February has 29 days instead of 28. Now since the reckoning of months according to lunations, on the other hand, does not correspond to the solar cycle, it creates a shorter year of around 354 or 355 days—an anticipated shortfall of eleven days every year with consequent shifting of the seasons and feasts every year as well—as happens in the Islamic calendar which is exclusively lunar. Therefore, one needs to find an agreement between the moon and the sun at some point: twelve lunations do not coincide with a solar year (365.2492 or 365¼). After three years, thirty-three days add up to a little more than a regular month. In Mesopotamia, where astronomy was more developed, they thought to introduce by imperial decree a supplemental month known as an intercalary month. In order to introduce that intercalary month, they had to make certain solar calculations while also making reference to the constellations.

ANCIENT CALENDARS

In antiquity as we have seen there were different units of measurement. There were also very many different calendars, mostly local. A few, however, had wider dissemination. Knowledge of local calendars used by ancient authors in epigraphy and in documents is very useful to avoid giving incorrect dates and incorrect reconstructions of events. In the eastern Mediterranean the Syro-Macedonian calendar received many adjustments. The Bishop Epiphanius of

Salamis († 403) presented the birth and baptism of Jesus according to many local calendars including Roman, Egyptian, Antiochene, Paphos, Arabia, Macedonian, Cappadocian, Athenian, and Judean. His account begins thus: "Christ was born in the month of January, that is, on the eighth day before the ides of January—in the Roman calendar this is on the evening of January 5 or the beginning of January 6; according to the Egyptian calendar the birth occurred on the eleventh of Tobi; according to the Syrian or Greek calendar it is the sixth day of Audynaeus; according to the calendar of Cyprus or Salamis it is on the fifth day of the fifth month; according to the Macedonian calendar it is the sixteenth of Apellaeus; according to the Cappadocian calendar it is the thirteenth of Atartes; according to the Athenian it is the fifth of Maemacterium; according to the Judean it is the fifth of Tevet."[10] "Jesus went to John in the eleventh month, in the time of the consuls Silanus and Nerva, and was baptized in the River Jordan . . . on the sixth day before the ides of November, that is, on the twelfth day of the Egyptian month Hathor, the eighth of the Greek month of Dios. . . ."[11]

The main calendars were the following:

THE MACEDONIAN CALENDAR

The conquest of the Middle East by Alexander the Great also meant the dissemination of the Macedonian calendar, one of the many calendars of ancient Greece. The original lunar Macedonian calendar is almost unknown. It mixed with the local calendars of Asia Minor, in Syria, and in Egypt; it came to be called "the Greek one." Julius Africanus writes that, from the beginning of the third century, the Jews, like the Greeks, intercalate three months every eight years.[12] Thus, they followed a cycle of eight years. By "Greeks" he means the inhabitants of Syria and Palestine who spoke Greek in his time. Since the Babylonian calendar, also lunar, spread in the Middle East with the Achaemenids, the two were assimilated, insofar as the Greek months took the names of the Babylonian months which are similar, but not identical, to the Judaic ones. The reality is much more complicated because the documentation is scarce. Also, there was no central office that managed the intercalation, which happened at the local level instead. Since the month begins with the new moon when it is visible, who decides that a new month has started? Discrepancies between one place and another easily arose, also because there was no written text that signaled the beginning of the new month.

This calendar also spread in Palestine and in the province of Arabia until the sixth century, but with local adaptations.[13] Many calendars also had different names for the months.[14] The passing of the kingdom of the Seleucids favored the proliferation of local calendars.[15] Josephus Flavius[16] presents the correspondence between the Judaic months and those of the Macedonian calendar and, in order to be understood, usually used the Macedonian names. In his *Church History*, Eusebius of Caesarea used the Macedonian calendar of Antioch, which was the most wide-spread. It was made official by the patriarchate in the fifth century. He often has his dating coincide with the Roman calendar, as is seen in the *De martyribus Palestinae*, where he uses the calendar of Caesarea.[17] Furthermore, the calendar of Antioch coincided exactly with the Roman calendar, as is seen in the *Hemerologia*, a harmonization of multiple calendars.[18]

THE EGYPTIAN CALENDAR

Leaving aside the more ancient calendars,[19] the Egyptian calendar had a year of twelve months of thirty days each, for a total of 360 days; at the end of each year five days were added. Thus, it reached 365 days. The calendar was solar, unlike the other calendars which were lunar and empirical, and so could be manipulated with the addition of an intercalary month. The Egyptian names of the months were used by Christians too. Even with the additional five days added this solar calendar was short by a day every four years, so the first month of the year began a day early every four years. The reform of Julius Caesar spread in Egypt too, where the year began on August 29; in a leap year it began on August 30. The first month of the year was Thoth. The festal letters of Athanasius follow the Egyptian calendar with Coptic names provided for the months.[20] The Coptic Church today still starts the year on August 29, starting from the era of the martyrs, or of Diocletian, that is, 284. The era of the martyrs is still used by the Copts. Today four calendars are used in Egypt: (1) the Coptic; (2) the Islamic; (3) the Julian/Gregorian, which is used by the Greek Orthodox who have fixed feasts like our own and movable feasts scheduled according to the Julian calendar; and (4) the Gregorian. In the Coptic Christian calendar, which follows the Julian calendar, the year starts on September 11, and on September 12 in leap years.[21]

THE HEBREW CALENDAR

We know the history of the Jewish world from the Bible. Archeology and other sources tell a different story. It seems rather strange that our information about their calendar is scarce for the most ancient period. There are only a few pieces of information which are interpreted, in turn, in various ways. Throughout their history the Israelites used a variety of calendars depending on times and places. The first certain information about the Jewish calendar dates back to the second century BCE. Sacha Stern summarizes the creation and evolution of the Jewish calendar up to the creation of the current rabbinical calendar: "From the second century BCE to the first century CE, solar and lunar calendars are both attested in the sources; whereas from the first century CE the Jewish calendar becomes exclusively lunar. From this point until at least the sixth century CE the lunar calendar was reckoned by different communities in a wide variety of forms. But by the tenth century, at the end of our period, a single lunar calendar had taken shape, that of rabbinic Judaism. This rabbinic calendar may still have been challenged by the Karaites; but in the course of time, it was to become universal and standard throughout world Jewry."[22] The current Jewish calendar is substantially lunar because it does not take the sun, but the seasons, into consideration; the function of the sun for the intercalations is marginal.

The sources for reconstructing the calendar of the first century, other than Philo and Josephus Flavius, come from the rabbinic texts of the *tannaim*, the sages who were the experts in the Law and lived in the first century CE up to 220. But it is not easy to know exactly which period their information belongs to. Philo considers Tishrei the first month of the year, but he also emphasizes the importance of the month of Nisan, which is the seventh month of the solar year but the first of the liturgical calendar. Josephus Flavius affirms that the month of Nisan (March/April) was the beginning of the religious year, while the month of Tishrei (September/October) began the civil year for the secular calendar,[23] but he always counts the months from Nisan to Adar. This is true also for the most ancient part of the Mishna. In the second century months start to be counted from Tishrei, which becomes the first month, from which the years and months are then counted. "From the first century CE onwards, solar calendars disappear entirely from all Jewish sources. The Jewish calendar, in Philo, Josephus, rabbinic, and Christian sources, as well as in documents and inscriptions, is only and exclusively lunar. This suggests that the lunar calendar had emerged, by the first century CE, as the only calendar in use among the Jews."[24]

In the lunar calendar, the month begins with the birth of the new moon; that is, when the appearance of a small sliver of the new moon's birth is officially declared after sunset at the end of the twenty-ninth or thirtieth day of the current month. It was necessary for two witnesses to see it in an empirical way, with their own eyes. If it was not visible, or if there were clouds, then the beginning was postponed to the following sunset. It was known that the average month was about 29.5 days, so the legal month had twenty-nine or thirty days. The names of the months are of Assyrian-Babylonian origin. To maintain a relationship with the seasons, recognizing that the feasts are linked to the seasons, it was necessary as we noted earlier to insert a supplementary month once in a while known as an intercalation or an intercalary month. Such an addition could be made empirically, or according to precise mathematical calculations.

The principal Jewish feasts at the time of Jesus and in later Judaism were: 1) The Sabbath, which was a typically Jewish observance, known to the pagans, who criticized it. Christian texts from the New Testament onward often refer to it. There was a polemic between Jesus and the Jews who called for its rigid observance which included abstaining from work (the most important thing); attending the synagogue which was then a place of instruction, not of prayer; meals consumed together either with family or with others. Abstaining from work was specified in many details including economic activities, transporting burdens outside the house and travel. But one could study the Torah without it being considered work. 2) The celebration of Passover (Pesach) has a long history.[25] The term Pesach came to be translated by the LXX as *Pascha*, and from this came the translation in Latin and in many modern languages. In the Judaism of the time of Jesus the term could indicate a precise act on Nisan 14, or the entirety of the observances of Passover including the following seven days of unleavened bread. The feast of the Passover itself was a nocturnal celebration. In the Jerusalem of the first century the celebration of Passover was connected with the Temple, and the celebration outside of Jerusalem was conducted without the sacrifice in the Temple. At the time of Jesus, the slaughtering of the lamb was done from at least mid-afternoon (3:00 PM) until sundown. The fifteenth of Nisan began the feast of unleavened bread which lasted seven days. 3) Pentecost[26] was also called the Feast of Weeks or Shavu'ot. It had two components: the gathering of grain and the gift of the Law on Sinai. The celebration was connected with the Temple. 4) The Day of Atonement known as Yom Kippur, celebrated on the tenth day of the month of Tishrei. 5) The Feast of Booths, also known as Sukkot, celebrated on the fifteenth of the month of Tishrei.

The feasts involving a pilgrimage to the Temple of Jerusalem were Passover (Pesach), Feast of Weeks (Shavu'ot), and the Feast of Booths (Sukkot). After the destruction of the Temple the pilgrimage was no longer obligatory, in expectation of the rebuilding of the Third Temple. But today many inhabitants of Jerusalem go to the western Wall. In any case, there were and are other feasts: Rosh Hashanah which celebrates the New Year; Hanukkah which commemorates the dedication of the Temple at the time of Judas Maccabaeus in 164 B.C.; and Purim in observance of the salvation of the Hebrews from the plot of Haman, the minister of King Ahasuerus, whose plan was foiled by Esther.

According to all the New Testament sources, Christ died the day before the Sabbath (Friday) and rose the first day after the Sabbath (Sunday; cf *Mk* 15:42; *Mt* 27:62; *Lk* 23:54; *Jn* 19:31, 42). All agree that Jesus had a last meal with his disciples before his death. Now, while for the Synoptic Gospels that Friday was the fifteenth of Nisan, having already eaten the Passover meal the day before, for John that Friday was the fourteenth of Nisan. According to the Synoptic Gospels Jesus celebrated the dinner as a paschal meal toward sundown at the beginning of the fifteenth of Nisan, since the day ran from sunset to sunset (*Mt* 26:17–19; *Mk* 14:12; *Lk* 22:8–13) and he died on the day before the Sabbath, which would have been the day of Pesach. Mark specifies that the death occurred on the evening before the Sabbath: "When evening had come, and since it was the day of Preparation, that is, the day before the Sabbath" (*Mk* 15:42). Note that he did not mention the Passover. Did this meal have the characteristics of a Passover meal? For the Synoptics it was indeed a Passover meal. The Johannine chronology is different, however. Jesus dies on the day of "preparation" (*parasceve*), that is, Friday which was the day of preparation for both the Passover and the Sabbath, which would start after sunset. At the beginning of this day, that is, what we today would call the prior evening which would serve as the beginning of the fourteenth of Nisan, Jesus had his last supper (18:28; 19:14). Thus, in John's reporting Jesus did not celebrate the Hebrew ritual Passover, but a last meal. The crucifixion happened then at the same moment as they were cutting the paschal lambs' throats in the Temple, which would have occurred during the afternoon of the fourteenth of Nisan, on Friday, so that they could eat them after sunset, when the fifteenth of Nisan and the Passover meal would begin.

What is the solution to these chronological and theological differences? There are various attempts at a solution and many theories have been developed.[27] The most common are: (a) a first option is to give credit to the chronology of the Synoptics and not John, which is what Jeremias and Barrett do; (b) another is to credit John's chronology; (c) the third seeks a reconciliation based on the use of different calendars between the Synoptics and John.[28] The last author I saw in this sense is Humphrey, who also considers astronomy.[29] He maintains that John uses the official lunar calendar of the Temple of Jerusalem (not the solar one of Qumran) which is the calendar of the priests, which records the day from sunset to sunset. The other Evangelists used another lunar calendar with the day beginning from sunrise to the next morning. Such a calendar was used by the Samaritans, Zealots, and Galileans. The Last Supper was a Passover meal according to the pre-exilic calendar. The meal, according to Humphreys, would have occurred on Wednesday, April 1, and the Crucifixion on Friday, April 3, of the year 33 which, as Humphreys also points out, was one of the dates when a lunar eclipse would have been visible in Jerusalem. This solution of course flies in the face of millennia of church tradition which has placed the meal on a Thursday, Maundy Thursday.

The Julian and Gregorian Calendar

The ancient term for the calendar was *Fasti*, which indicated the table that recorded days of religious observance and assemblies as well as official commemorations. This was also the term used in the Christian sphere as well.[30] Only in Late Latin did it begin to take on its modern meaning (Isidore of Seville). It could also be used to refer to the list of saints (martyrology) or to an almanac. The term does not refer to the passing of time which is more of a social construct.

The most ancient Roman calendar existing today is in the Museum of the Palazzo Massimo. It is the *Fasti Antiates*, so named since they were discovered at Anzio. Days are marked by various letters: C (*comitialis*) indicates days on which assemblies can be held, along with elections and certain judicial proceedings; F (*dies fastus*) stands for the days on which tribunals are open; N (*dies nefastus*) refers to religious occasions on which no secular activities could take place, trials could not be held in the tribunals, nor could any public official transactions occur because these days were dedicated to the gods. NP (*feriae*) refers to feast days in the Roman sense, that is, public holidays established by a magistrate to mark a special occasion (*qualitas*).

In the Roman month, the Kalends, the Nones, and the Ides marked time. In a certain sense they were like our week, since they were points of reference for activities, for appointments, and for numerous activities. The *nundinae* were a type of week but functioned only for markets and not for organizing public or private time, which is what the Kalends, Nones, and Ides were for.

The reform of Julius Caesar, with the help of Sosigenes of Alexandria, created an exclusively solar calendar. It eliminated the need for an intercalary month. Caesar sought to alter the months as little as possible, for religious, political, and judicial reasons. The Ides of each month became the reference point for religious celebrations. Caesar reorganized the length of the months. The new calendar had four months of thirty days: April, June, September, November; and seven months of 31 days: January, March, May, July (*Quintilis*), August (*Sextilis*), October, December; and one month, February, of 28. Every four years between February 23 and 24 a day was added so that for that year February would have 29 days. This day was variously referred to as: 23,[31] the sixth [day before] the first of march (*sexto kalendas martias*); 23bis, the sixth [day before] the first of March, twice (*bis sexto calendas martias*); 24, the fifth [day before] the first of March (*quinto calendas martias*). Thus, the year which contained these combined two days, a *bis sexto* (lit. six twice), was called *bisextus*[32] or later *bisextilis*. These two days were computed and counted as a single day.[33] One might wonder why Caesar did not regularize the length of all the months so that they were the same. It seems he did not do it for religious reasons, since it would mean changing the dates of some festivals. The names *Quintilis*, *Sextilis*, etc. clearly indicate that the beginning of the civil year was March when the principal magistrates (the consuls) took office. Caesar, however, decided that the beginning of the year was to begin with January,[34] which is still the case up to the present day. To arrange this, he greatly lengthened the year 46 BC–*annus ultimus confusionis*—making it 444 days (or 443 days in other sources). The reform entered into force on January 1, 45 BC. After the death of Julius Caesar in 44 B.C. the senate changed the name of the month *Quintilis* to *Iulius* (July). At that time the vernal equinox fell on March 25.

In the first years of applying the new calendar an error occurred in interpreting the rules established by Sosigenes. In the year 8 B.C. Augustus decreed that the bissextile year would happen every four years. For that time, the calculations of Sosigenes seem incredible in their precision. The solar year of Julius Caesar is 365 ¼ days: 365 days with the addition of one day every four years (leap year), where the average is 365 days and 6 hours. It should rather be 365 days, 5 hours, 48 minutes, and 46 seconds. It is longer than that by 11 minutes and 12 seconds. On account of this difference it accumulates an excess of one day every 133 years.

The structure of the Julian calendar, up to today, has not undergone significant modifications, except for the small correction in the computation of the leap years in 1582 (the Gregorian calendar). The names and lengths of the months today are still those instituted by Caesar and by Augustus.

In antiquity Christians fought among themselves about celebrating Easter correctly in relation to the moon and sun. At a certain point it was discovered that there was an increasing offset with respect to the seasons and especially in relation to the vernal equinox, according to which the date of Easter was calculated. The reference point was the vernal equinox, which first was set as March 25, but at the Council of Nicaea was set as on March 21. Now from 325 until 1582 the difference was 9.7 days.[35] The Julian year was slightly longer with respect to the length of the tropical year, on account of which the vernal equinox fell even earlier than March 21 (the reference point for Christians), thus causing confusion for the dating of Easter.

After centuries of controversy the Council of Trent (held from December 13, 1545 to the 25th session held on December 4, 1563) ordered the reform of the breviary and missal. The reform meant also attending to the calendar. In 1572 Pope Gregory XIII was elected (after whom the Pontifical Gregorian University is named). He had participated in the Council of Trent as a jurist and so knew its regulations. A commission prepared the reform utilizing the work of the Jesuit Christophorus Clavius who in turn based his work on Luigi Lilio, and implemented the reform. In 1582 Pope Gregory published a bull entitled *Inter gravissimas* which imposed the reform which was referred to as the "new style," against the "old style."[36]

The content of the reform had several components. The leap year was counted every fourth year, similar to what was done previously, but if it fell in a centenary year, it was considered a normal, not bissextile, year. Every four centenary years, the fourth centenary was to be considered a leap year. Thus, it is arranged as follows: 1600 remained a leap year while 1700, 1800, 1900 were not considered leap years, but the year 2000 would be considered a leap year (this was explicitly said in the Bull). The leap day was transferred from the twenty-fourth to the twenty-ninth of the month. Ten days were abolished in October of 1582—from October 4 it skipped to October 15. With this system the equinox then would fall between March 19 and March 22. The rules for calculating Easter also changed. The whole reform centered on the leap year. The reform was still not perfect however because it did not manage to coincide perfectly with the solar year—a difference of only about 30 seconds. Depending on the calculation of the solar year, an extra day needs to be accounted for every 3,000 years (or 10,000 years). The reformed calendar of Gregory was based primarily on the Christian festivals

(Easter) and Sunday. The calendar was published on March 3 in Rome, on the doors of St. Peter's, the Basilica of St. Lawrence in Damaso, and in Campo dei Fiori. The instruments of communication were slow, however, and did not permit immediate dissemination. The sending out of copies began at the end of May 1582.

The reform was immediately adopted by Catholic countries such as Italy, Portugal, Spain, Poland, and Bavaria, among others.[37] Very strong opposition was raised by the Protestants of Germany. Even if some accepted the reform, there was still opposition by others on religious grounds. A professor at Tübingen said that Satan was lurking behind it all, which is why one had to disobey even the civil authorities that imposed it. Sometimes in Germany magistrates even stopped Catholics from applying the reform; chaos and rebellions were the result.

Christians of the Eastern rite still hold to the Julian calendar. In the modern period the Gregorian calendar has been imposed on most of modern life, especially due to the demands of communication involved in banking, stock markets, airplanes, trains, computers and the internet.

SUNDAY AND EASTER

There were two primordial Christian celebrations: the annual Easter and the weekly Sunday. Both were linked to the Passion and Resurrection of Christ. The first, with its annual repetition, was in relation to the solar and lunar cycle and thus was on a movable date, while Sunday was linked to the week of seven days, an entirely conventional temporal rhythm. The two celebrations did not have the festive character of pagan and Jewish celebrations. They served to confirm Christians in the faith and in behavior[38] through liturgy, biblical readings, and catechetical instruction, and to reinforce their bonds of brotherhood. Likewise, these feasts created and reinforced the sense of belonging to a community with the consequent distinction from others, from those who had another temporal rhythm. Attendance at the celebrations made the social Christian identity clear, not only with respect to the pagans but also in relation to the Jews from whom the Christians took their origin.

The Christians of the first centuries referred to Sunday in three or four different ways[39]: the Lord's day (*dies dominicus*), the sun's day (*dies solis*) when speaking particularly to pagans which was the first day of the week; sometimes they also used the name "eighth day" or the expression "the day of the resurrection."[40] As Justin writes: "We hold this common assembly of ours on the day of the sun because it is the first day, on which God, having disturbed darkness and matter, created the world, and because Jesus Christ our Savior rose from the dead on this same day."[41] Sunday, the first day of the week and the eighth, is the day of creation, the day of resurrection, and quite soon would also be called the day of the annunciation or of the incarnation. Sunday was enriched not only with new meanings but also with gestures and acts:

it was also the main day of preaching and Christian instruction. They take up not only the Jewish system with its rhythm of seven days along with the names they used for the days, but also earlier meanings which they expand. When Justin addresses the pagans, he uses the name *dies solis*,[42] but when he speaks with the Jew Trypho, he says, "first day after the sabbath" (*prima sabbati*).[43] In his works addressed to pagans, Tertullian uses the term *dies solis*,[44] while in those addressed to Christians, he uses the expression *dies dominicus*.[45] Taking back up the Hebrew tradition of the joyful Sabbath, for Christians too Sunday was a day of joy. The *Epistle of Barnabas* writes: "Therefore we also celebrate the eighth day with gladness, for on it Jesus arose from the dead, and appeared, and ascended into heaven" (15.9). "The first day of the week you must pass entirely in joy; in fact, whoever afflicts his soul on the first day of the week makes himself culpable," as the *Didascalia* affirms.[46]

Jesus and his followers followed the Jewish calendar and lived according to its temporal rhythm, including participation in the traditional feasts. When the followers of Jesus separated themselves from the Jews and were perceived as their own sect (*airesis;* Acts 28:22) they still did not immediately found their own form of worship, as we have seen in the previous chapter. The first Christians, who lived in Palestine, because they participated in the religious life of their time according to the Jewish calendar, placed the resurrection of Jesus on the first day after the Sabbath (*Mt* 28:1; *Mk* 16:2, 9; *Lk* 24:1; *Jn* 20:1, 19). This is the first day of the Hebrew week, while Saturday is the last day. This same terminology was also used by the first Christians outside of Palestine (*Acts* 20:7; *1 Cor* 16:2), maintaining the Jewish expression even for Christians converted from paganism. Besides, the temporal cycle of seven days named after the planetary week was not yet widely disseminated at this time.

In the first century of the Christian era, in the sphere of the Roman Empire, the planetary week did not mark the rhythm of social and religious time, but only astrological time. From the second century on, the planetary week became well known in the pagan sphere, but it had no effect on the organization of public time. The Jews followed a social and religious temporal rhythm that was entirely their own, well known and visible that included rest and Sabbath worship. This was recognized and accepted by the Roman authorities, even if it was criticized by pagans. Christians also organized their religious and social life according to their own religious inflections, especially with the Sunday celebration. This meant notable difficulties both for the fixed occurrence of the Christian day and for the work rhythms imposed by society. The Christians, therefore, were normally constrained to meet before dawn. In social life, on the other hand, they abstained from the public religious celebrations observed by the population. For this reason, they were accused of being anti-social and of not participating in the rhythm and demands of civic life, and did not contribute to the *pax deorum* because of their social and religious absenteeism.[47] On the other hand, it was well known by the authorities and by the common people that Christians observed a special time for their gatherings.

Christians were quite visible also because of their calendar observance, which granted them a communal identity. Pliny already recognized, in his investigation, that Christians met "*stato die*," on a set day.[48] On account of their celebrating their assemblies on the *dies solis* the Christians came to be taken for sun worshippers.[49] The pagans, Origen writes, know "our celebrations that occur on determined days, on Sundays, at Easter, at Pentecost."[50] Often Christians were arrested or disturbed in their meetings, as Hippolytus[51] and Tertullian[52] write.

Since Sunday was a normal day Christians were constrained to meet early in the morning, as Pliny already gives witness to,[53] as do Christian authors like Tertullian, who speaks of the meeting before dawn (*antelucani coetus*).[54] But how, why, and when did they shift immediately to Sunday morning? Was it just for convenience or because they wanted to place the emphasis on the resurrection of Christ? We do not have a sure answer. I think that two elements could have been influential: the desire to commemorate the resurrection of Christ and the Roman system of marking the day, from midnight to midnight. The first seems more convincing. The *dies dominicus* began only after midnight, and so the celebration must not precede that hour. For a different temporal rhythm even an earlier time, still after sunset, was the Lord's day. The fact that they lived in a pagan environment where the *dies solis* began at midnight meant that the *dies dominicus* had the same temporal articulation.

For many Christians the Sunday meeting was a strongly felt need, as the martyrs of Abitina, a village of proconsular Africa near Carthage, confirm during the persecution of Diocletian, in 304, declaring that they could not live without the Eucharist: "Because the Lord's supper cannot be skipped, because the law commands thus"; "Because we cannot go without the Lord's supper."[55] The reason is that the Christian does not exist without the Eucharistic meal (*dominicum*), and this does not exist without the Christian. A text of the second century also speaks of the need for the Eucharistic celebration, the *Epistula Apostolorum*: "And we told him: Lord, is it then necessary that we must take the chalice again and drink?[56] He told us: Yes, it is necessary, until the day I return, with those who have suffered death for my sake" (ch. 16).

Now before going any further we must address the question: Does the celebration of Sunday come first and then that of Easter, or vice versa?[57] Some maintain that we first have the celebration of Easter, to which the name "Lord's Day" is applied and which term is then assimilated into the weekly celebration that occurs. There is no certain testimony about the celebration of the Christian Easter in the first century or in the first decades of the second. The first pieces of evidence which come from the middle of the second century, concern a profound and serious divergence between the practice of the annual Sunday Easter and the Quartodeciman observance which had spread not only into Asia Minor but also into Syria and Mesopotamia. Thus, the celebration of Easter was already confirmed and wide-spread. Meanwhile there was no divergence in the celebration of the *dies dominicus*, which was universal not only in the West and in the Greek East, but also in the Syrian East, according to the ancient testimony of Bardaisan which we have from the beginning of the third century: "For all of us, wherever we are . . . gather together on the first day of the week."[58] In fact, one finds no group that does not observe the Sunday celebration. Thus, it seems more likely that the annual observance of Easter was derived from the weekly observance, which is the primordial Christian celebration, which in a second moment also becomes the annual celebration of Easter. The first evidence for the Christian Easter comes after the evidence for Sunday. Hamman has shown that Justin is silent about Easter, though he speaks amply of Sunday.[59] Talley writes that there are various scholars who affirm that "there was no annual observance of *pascha* before it was instituted by Soter around 165 under Eastern influence, where the celebration of Easter Sunday instituted in Jerusalem around 135 spread from that city to Alexandria and everywhere in Hellenistic Christianity."[60]

A few points are certain. The first pieces of evidence from various regions attest that, in the first half of the second century, Sunday is a universal celebration. It is observed by all communities, both of pagan and of Hebrew origin. It seems reasonable to deduce that Sunday worship arose before missionary expansion beyond Jerusalem rather than being imposed afterwards. Perhaps the first evidence of the observance of Sunday comes from Egypt, from the *Epistle of Barnabas*: "It is not the Sabbaths of the present time that are acceptable to me, but the one I have made, in which I will give rest to all things and make a beginning of an eighth day, which is the beginning of another world. Therefore, also we celebrate the eighth day with gladness, for on it Jesus arose from the dead, and appeared, and ascended into heaven."[61] Christians chose to meet as a group on the first day of the week—once a week, and not each month or yearly—perhaps because, since they originated from the Jewish religion with its Sabbath, once a week seemed natural. Furthermore, commemorating the resurrection of Christ seems to be founded on the fact that it occurred on the first day of the week. Now if Christian origins are Palestinian and the first communities in Palestine were made up of Christians of Jewish origin, it would have been impossible that Sunday would have been observed for reasons of sun worship which was a pagan practice.[62] Notice, conversely, that the Council of Jerusalem also did not impose Sabbath observance on the pagans (*Acts* 15:19).

If, on the one hand, the Lord's Supper was celebrated on the *dies dominicus*, on the other hand celebration of the Lord's Supper was not indissolubly tied to Sunday but could also take place on other days and in other moments. The few sources that we have tend to consider the origin of the Sunday worship as tied to the memory of the Lord's resurrection in the Palestinian community of the initial period. The universal agreement and practice of the Sunday celebration that we see in the first centuries, without exceptions, confirm this hypothesis. Whether missionaries were addressing the Palestinian Jewish world, the diaspora, or the pagans, they did nothing other than implement the practice of the Palestinian mother church.

Perhaps Eusebius's testimony about the Ebionites can cast some light on what happened at the beginning. He distinguishes two groups, although in reality there were many Ebionite sects. One of them observed the entire Jewish tradition while the other observed both the Sabbath and Sunday as a "memorial of the Savior's resurrection."[63] Thus, this is how it must have happened in Jerusalem in the beginning. The first Christians of Jewish origin attended synagogue, as *Acts* explicitly attests (13:42, 44; 16:13; 17:2; 18:4) and they practiced the prescribed traditional Sabbath rest. Meanwhile, the Christians of pagan provenance left the Sabbath observance behind and concentrated on the meeting that commemorated Christ's resurrection. The missionaries attended synagogue, as long as it was possible, in order to be able to proclaim Jesus Christ there while commenting on "the words of the prophets that are read each Sabbath" (*Acts* 13:27). The synagogues were the initial support network for the Apostles and missionaries in the diaspora for the spreading of Christianity. The increase in the number of Christians coming from paganism, along with the separation between Christians and Jews, made the Sabbath observance fall out of practice to the complete advantage of the "first day of the week." The shift was not easy because of the presence of Jewish nostalgia, as we see in Ignatius of Antioch.[64]

As we move further into the second century, in the sphere of communities converted from paganism, the Sabbath was normally not observed. In fact, strong criticism was aimed at those who did observe the Sabbath, using expressions such as Judaizers or Sabbath observers.[65] This happened because there were always a few who preached and demanded such observances, and this was still the case in the fourth century. Even amid the criticisms and diversity there was tolerance too, however.[66] Nevertheless there was no intention theological or otherwise that Sunday, the first day of the week, should replace the Sabbath or that the third [fourth] commandment be applied.[67] This phenomenon occurred later on and is even found in the Apostolic Letter of John Paul II, *Dies Domini*. Nor was moving from the Sabbath to Sunday considered something anti-Jewish since, for Christians, the Eucharistic celebration was always central to their worship rather than emulating Jewish practices. Sunday was not a feast day, at least not as that was commonly understood by pagans and Jews, but was functional for the gathered assembly that especially performed the *anamnesis*, the fundamental element of the community itself, commemorating the dead and risen Christ and proclaiming his message which it actualized through those rites that repeated the Last Supper, the Paschal one. For this reason, the "memoirs" of the Apostles were read.

Resting, a special characteristic of the Jewish Sabbath, was not a requirement in Christian worship and as we noted was in fact sometimes criticized by Christians: "So we no longer observe the Sabbath in the way in which the Jews do, nor do we put our joy in inactivity."[68]

The concept of rest prescribed by the Mosaic commandment instead gets spiritualized: the Christian rests from sin or from doing evil. We see this as early as the *Epistle of Barnabas* (15.1-9) which emphasizes holiness rather than rest. While there is no evidence for the application of the Sabbath prescriptions to the Christian Sunday, sometimes comparisons are made between the Sabbath and Sunday, naturally with the affirmation of the latter's superiority, but the Sabbath legislation is not applied to it. That only happens later on.

Having discussed how Sunday was observed in its relationship to Judaism and Easter, we now move on to Easter itself. Easter observance literally explodes in the second half of the second century, becoming the center of Christian cult. With its biblical and soteriological content, it wins ever greater attention, and thus undergoes an enormous liturgical and organizational development, especially in the fourth century. Its time expands disproportionately with the passing of decades, with an ever longer time of preparation embodied in Lent,[69] followed by an extended period of time after Easter with Sunday adorned liturgically in white (*in albis*) through the fifty days up to Pentecost. The period after Easter, starting from the Sunday of the resurrection, comes to be seen and celebrated as a single festival day. Easter day is the heart of the liturgical year, with a preparatory period which in some sense anticipates it, and an observance of fifty days afterward which prolong it. This whole long period of over ninety or so days is enriched with numerous elements: preparation of catechumens, reconciliation of penitents, baptism at the Easter Vigil, prayers, fasting, intense preaching,[70] postbaptismal instruction, festive celebrations after Easter, with the institution of the feast of the Ascension after it (4th century).

The whole period comes to be considered a celebratory unit. Augustine describes it as *tota Paschalis solemnitas*.[71] Egeria writes about Jerusalem: "When Easter time comes, it is celebrated thus. Among us forty days are observed before Easter, but here, instead, eight weeks before Easter are observed. Eight weeks are observed because there is no fasting on Saturday and Sunday, except for one Saturday, the one of the Easter Vigil on which one must fast."[72] In successive centuries, up to the fourth, there is a further prolonging of the celebration with quinquagesima, sexagesima, and even septuagesima. The specific character (*qualitas*) of the Lenten period also demands a renewal of conduct, serious fasts, intense prayer, generous alms, and even abstaining from sexual relations among spouses,[73] all because, "it is with his passion that the Lord 'passed' from death to life and opened for us believers the way toward his resurrection, so that we might pass from death to life."[74]

A deeply felt and debated problem was the dating of Easter, which we discussed briefly towards the beginning of this chapter and now will go into more detail. In the second century we find two traditions concerning the day of the Easter feast. The first, which spread in Asia Minor and Syria, followed the Jewish calendar, celebrating Easter on the fourteenth of the lunar month which is the first month of the Jewish year of the time, called Nisan. The Easter celebration could fall on any day of the week, and it could even happen that there would be fasting on Sunday and then the beginning of the Easter Vigil in the evening. The followers of this practice came to be called Quartodecimans,[75] because they celebrated on the fourteenth day of the month of Nisan, according to the Jewish calendar. The month begins with the rising of the new moon so that by halfway through the month, on the 14th day, there was a full moon.

The other tradition followed by the Romans and Alexandrians, along with numerous other churches both Western and Eastern, celebrated the Easter resurrection of Christ on the following Sunday, but still according to the Jewish calendar. The difference of date also had doctrinal implications such as the soteriological meaning of the Passion, as well as disciplinary concerns such as the fast and penitential acts that were to be observed. Irenaeus makes mention of disagreements between the Church of Rome and that of the Roman province of Asia.[76] Eusebius of Caesarea recounts that in order to solve the difficulty several synods were held.[77] Perhaps in Rome itself there were different communities who celebrated Easter on different days. Rome was after all a cosmopolitan city. Persons from the whole Empire came there, especially from the Eastern provinces: writers, doctors, slaves, freedmen, merchants, and the like. A merchant of Hierapolis came to Rome 72 times according to the inscription on his tomb. Eastern Christians also resided in Rome. Immigrants lived among the Christians of Trastevere in the zone of Porta Capena,[78] the Aventine. As happened with European emigrants in the Americas who lived together and had their own churches, so it must have happened in Rome. Their main language was Greek. As immigrants they followed their own traditions which no doubt was also the case for Easter. So in Rome itself there may have been two traditions. And so it happened that some were fasting and others feasting, celebrating Easter on different days.

The crisis becomes particularly acute at the time of Pope Victor and the bishop of Ephesus Polycrates.[79] The intervention of Irenaeus of Lyons helped to overcome the difference. Irenaeus agreed with the Roman tradition perhaps because he lived in the West, but advised against a rupture in the church. There was no excommunication issued, but in those years the Quartodeciman Blastus was condemned as a heretic and was listed as such by some Western authors. The question remained open and debated, although a there was a gradual convergence toward the Sunday when Easter was to observed.

The council of Nicaea in 325 faced the question directly and resolved it by deciding that Easter should be celebrated on the Sunday after the full moon after the vernal equinox.[80] This is also the practice of all churches today. The current divergence arises from the equinox's being placed on different dates since some churches still follow the Julian calendar. According to this calendar the equinox falls about thirteen days after it does on a solar calendar, as followed by the Julian-Gregorian calendar. In later periods there were other polemics about the different forms of ecclesiastical *computus,* i.e., about how to properly calculate the day of Easter.

It was necessary to know the date of Easter ahead of time in order to organize the calendar and the preparation for the celebration of the great feast. Already at the Council of Arles in 314 the western bishops asked of Pope Sylvester (314–335), "that among us and in every place the feast of Easter be observed on the same day and at the same time; and that you address letters to all according to the custom." Many more or less competent authors[81] dedicated themselves in the following centuries—although it happened even before Nicaea— to developing cyclical systems of calculations to determine a precise date for when Easter should be celebrated in the future. The Council of Nicaea seems to have decided that the Alexandrian church was tasked with calculating the date of Easter ahead of time. It communicated that date to the principal churches, who then disseminated it in their local areas of jurisdiction. Several times in the fourth century the Roman dating did not coincide with the Alexandrian. For example, in 387 a great discrepancy is noted, since the Alexandrian church proposed April 25 as the date while the Roman church preferred the earlier date of April 18 in order not to have to observe the fast on April 21, a day of great celebrations for the founding of Rome. In Milan the Bishop Ambrose chose April 25 when Augustine was to be baptized; in Gaul, on the other hand, Easter was observed on March 21. This divergence was repeated in the time of Leo the Great as well. He did everything possible to have a celebration of Easter on the same day across the church, but was unsuccessful.[82]

The Easter feast was actually extended a week further, during which the instruction of the newly baptized continues. They were instructed about the sacraments they had just received: baptism, anointing with chrism, and the Eucharist. These instructions came to be called mystagogical because once a person was baptized and thus enlightened the lectures introduced them to the understanding of the mysteries they had just participated in. Only the enlightened could understand them. On the first Sunday after Easter, called *in albis* (in white) or *quasimodo geniti* (from the Latin of the text read that day, *1 Pet* 2:2 "like newborn infants"), the newly baptized put off the white garment. A vast wealth of homilies connected with Easter and this following Sunday is preserved.[83] In antiquity the administering of baptism was normally allowed only at the Easter Vigil and on Pentecost. In other cases, only in case of emergency.

OTHER CHRISTIAN FEASTS

The celebration of Pentecost is connected with Easter. Tertullian calls it a most joyful period (*laetissimum spatium*) for conferring baptisms, clarifying a little later, "and Pentecost, which is properly a feast day" (*et pentecostes, qui est proprie dies festus*),[84] and also referring to it elsewhere as the "period of Pentecost" (*spatium pentecostes*).[85] The period of fifty days, seven weeks according to the Jewish tradition, must be a period of joy and for that reason the *alleluia* is sung and the *Acts of the Apostles* are read.

The feast of the Ascension, as distinct from Pentecost, was more widely disseminated in the second half of the fourth century. Toward the 380s the feast of the Ascension was already fairly widely known in various regions, so we can suppose that its institution was somewhat earlier than those years. In fact, for the area of Antioch, the *Apostolic Constitutions* (5.20.2) consider it a great feast. It is the same for John Chrysostom, who offers several testimonies.[86] The most ancient homily on the feast of the Ascension that has been preserved is that given in 388 by Gregory of Nyssa.[87] Basil of Caesarea, on the other hand, never speaks of a feast on the fortieth day after Easter. Jerusalem celebrated Pentecost in the years 420–430.[88] Chromatius of Aquileia witnesses to it in the West. We have extant his Pentecost sermon[89] which speaks of it as a *solemnitas*.[90] Filaster of Brescia (who died before 397) list four major feasts (*festivitates maiores*): Christmas, Epiphany, Easter, and Ascension; he does not include Pentecost.[91] On the occasion of the feast of the Ascension in Africa Augustine preached several sermons in Hippo as well as in Carthage, speaking of a *solemnitas*.[92] We do not know when Pentecost began to be celebrated in Rome. According to Coebergh it was already celebrated in 419, a date that seems too late with respect to many other regions.[93] Eight discourses of Pope Leo on the feast of the Epiphany are preserved which explain the meaning of the celebration.[94]

Christmas, as its Latin name *Nativitas* itself indicates, almost certainly arose in the West in Rome and perhaps North Africa,[95] and then spread in the East in the course of the fourth century. Epiphany, as the name indicates, arose in a Greek language environment perhaps in Egypt, but the first evidence for it as an important feast comes in 361 from Gaul—not from a Christian but a pagan.[96] Another very ancient piece of evidence comes from Spain.

Other evidence for the date of the celebration of Epiphany and of Christmas comes from Augustine who says in a sermon that the Donatists do not celebrate the feast of Epiphany,[97] but do celebrate Christmas. Separated from the Catholic Church around 312, they maintained the earlier customs and did not take up the new ones coming from the Catholic Church. That explains why they did not celebrate Epiphany. If they celebrated Christmas, then it must go back, at least in Africa, to before the schism, while Epiphany was introduced afterwards and thus was not accepted by the Donatists.

Another ancient indication of the two feasts could be the fact that they were also celebrated by Latin-language Arians, as shown by the sermons published recently by R. Étaix, as well as by the Arian sermons from Verona.[98] In both series of sermons the content of the feast is the commemoration of the birth of Jesus at Christmas and the adoration of the Magi, while at Epiphany it is the baptism. Gregory of Nazianzus refers to the Arian emperor Valens observing the feast of the Epiphany.[99] If this reasoning has any validity, the feast of Christmas arose earlier in the West, perhaps before that of Epiphany, which could have arisen between 312 and 325. This does not mean that the feast of Epiphany might not, at least in some locations, be still earlier than 312. Since it was observed both by Catholics and by Arians, it certainly goes back to before 325.

The Roman calendar of 336 known as the *Depositio martyrum*, starts the list of the memorials of the martyrs with the birth of Christ on December 25, and thus puts it at the beginning of the list of Christian celebrations. The text says nothing about how the memorial was celebrated, however. The *Depositio* is part of the so-called *Chronograph of 354*. In this collection of documents, on another occasion the birth of Christ on December 25 is affirmed,[100] while, at the beginning of the list of bishops of Rome, his death is placed at March 25.[101] If a text published by Martine Dulaey[102] is authentic, the date of Christmas is earlier. A chronological fragment attributed to Victor of Petovium († 304) also speaks of the birth of Christ on December 25.[103]

One current of research posits that the date was chosen at Rome on the same day on which the feast of *Sol Invictus* was celebrated, as instituted by the emperor Aurelian in 274, when he made the week begin with the *dies solis*. But this thesis has not been proven. I consider it a pure coincidence. Here I point out a short work that makes an entire chain of reasoning of a symbolic and chronological character. A 4th century work that is very useful for understanding dates which have a symbolic value is the *De aequinoctiis et solstitiis* (On the Equinox and Solstice). This text places the annunciation to Zechariah in the Temple on September 24, and the birth of John the Baptist on June 24; the Annunciation to Mary on March 25 and the birth of Christ on December 25 (*octavo kalendas ianuarias*). The conceptions occur on the two equinoxes—March and September—while the two births occur on the two solstices—June and December.

When does the feast of Epiphany arise in the East? The name itself, which is Greek, hearkens back to the environment of its origin, which is Greek and not Latin or Semitic. In Latin it went forward only as a transcription, which preachers often have to explain. The feast of Epiphany may have arisen even before 325 because it was already an established feast among both the Eastern and Western Arians. This feast, which we say is of Eastern origin, is attested for the first time, as has already been noted, by a pagan author, Ammianus Marcellinus, who writes that Julian, in 361, went to church in the city of Vienne, in Gaul, "on the feast day which the Christians celebrate in the month of January, calling it Epiphany; after praying solemnly to their God he went away."[104] Thus Julian went into the local church, where Epiphany was a *dies feriarum*, that is, a feast day.

What does this expression of Ammianus "*dies feriarum*" mean? Does it refer only to a feast for Christians, or does it refer to a feast for all citizens that is recognized also by the imperial authorities? Ammianus uses the traditional pagan expression for a feast day, *dies feriarum*, paired with the Christian terminology, with the Greek word transcribed into Latin. But how widespread was this feast in Gaul?[105] The first official recognition by an emperor of Epiphany and Christmas as days on which shows could not be held belongs to Honorius (393-423).[106]

Christians of the fourth century had to clarify the content of the two feasts, which seemed to be the same. The East had to clarify what Christmas was about and the West had to clarify what Epiphany was about. The liturgical content of the two feasts varied according to geographical areas as well. There are certain aspects of Epiphany and Christmas that almost seem the same—thus the difficulty of imposing Epiphany as a celebration in the West and the same with Christmas in the East. Filaster who was bishop of Brescia († 387) noted that, in his time, there was discussion about whether to celebrate the feast of Epiphany at all, insofar as they considered it a repetition of Christmas.[107] Augustine's preaching intimates that at Epiphany one celebrates the adoration of the Magi, while at Christmas the adoration of the shepherds.[108] The Roman church and the African church celebrated the birth of the Savior on December 25 and the adoration of the Magi on January 6. The memorial of the massacre of the Innocents, mentioned by Matthew,[109] is celebrated after Christmas in Rome, but is connected with the Epiphany in Africa. There were divergent traditions in Northern Italy too, which go on being clarified and unified. In Gaul the principal content of January 6 is the baptism, to which the miracle of Cana is connected, and sometimes the multiplication of the loaves.

In Constantinople the feast of Christmas was celebrated at the time of Gregory of Nyssa in 381, although he observes that there is some objection to it.[110] In Antioch around 380, the feast of Christmas was already being celebrated according to the *Apostolic Constitutions*, which already considered it a great feast, as did John Chrysostom,[111] who attributed particular importance to it as the root of all the other feasts.[112] In Syria, Ephrem knows about the feast of Christmas. The lack of clarity about the two feasts made their diffusion more difficult. Christmas spread in the Greek and Byzantine world, but not in the Coptic or Armenian world. No evidence is known from the church of Egypt that there they celebrated Epiphany at the beginning of the fourth century. Rather, the first testimony comes from a Latin, John Cassian, who placed it on January 6, with the double significance of the birth of Jesus and of his baptism.[113] This brings us close to the year 400.

The majority of Christians celebrate the feast of Christmas associated with the birth of Christ, and Epiphany associated with his manifestation to the Gentiles, which includes his birth, baptism, and the Magi's adoration. Even still there is a divergence among Christians regarding the date of the Christmas celebration: Catholics and Protestants celebrate Christmas on December 25, following the Gregorian calendar; the Orthodox, who follow the Julian calendar, celebrate Christmas on January 7. The Copts celebrate Christmas on January 7 and Epiphany on January 19. The Armenians, on the other hand, only celebrate the feast of Epiphany—the Theophany—which also includes Christmas. There are also Armenians who follow the Gregorian calendar, for example those in Canada, who celebrate Epiphany on December 25, and still others who celebrate it on January 6 (or 7). Those who follow the Julian calendar celebrate Epiphany on January 19.

To conclude this section, there are in Christian churches seven great Christological feasts: The Annunciation, Christmas, Epiphany, Palm Sunday, Easter, the Ascension, and Pentecost.

MARIAN FEASTS[114]

The anonymous voyager who visited Palestine around 560—the *Anonymous Placentinus* (5.2)—notes about Nazareth: "The house of St. Mary is now a basilica and many are the beneficial effects that come to one who manages to touch her garments."[115] Recent excavations made in the basilica have brought to light remnants from the first centuries including a place of worship, then a church which—the preceding edifice being destroyed with only the grottoes preserved—was built as a basilica with mosaics. The graffiti announces a cultic presence. One of the examples of graffiti, going back to the second or third century, recites the *Khaire Maria* (Hail Mary), with evident reference to the greeting of the angel.[116] Thus, at Nazareth there was veneration for Mary in the place believed to be the house of the Annunciation. A papyrus text from Egypt which contains the oldest Marian prayer that is known, as Under Your Protection (*Sub tuum praesidium*),[117] seems to belong to the same period, i.e., the second half of the third or early fourth century. Numerous documents which go under the name of the Dormation of Mary or the Translation of Mary (*Dormitio Mariae* or *Transitus Mariae*), affirm that Mary was laid in a "new tomb," in the Kidron Valley near the garden of Gethsemane.[118] In this location is where we find the church of the Tomb of Mary. The emperor Theodosius I had a church built there dedicated to the Madonna where toward the middle of the fifth century a feast of the Virgin was celebrated.[119]

In the same period in which Juvenal of Jerusalem lived and was bishop (451–458), another church is mentioned that was four kilometers from Jerusalem at Kathisma (which means *rest*) on the road to Bethlehem. It was built "in honor of the Immaculate Theotokos and ever virgin Mary."[120] Such locations are important for at least two reasons. First of all, to distinguish the much more ancient veneration for Mary from the actual liturgical cult which developed somewhat later. Furthermore, they help us toward a more precise view of the content of the liturgical celebrations themselves. To celebrate the feast in a certain place meant, then, to celebrate a certain mystery; something similar must have happened, therefore, for the celebrations at Kathisma and the Tomb of Mary. And these places had the earliest Marian celebrations, at least that we know of. Churches named for the Madonna existed, but no liturgical feasts are known before the first years of the fifth century.

Why is there this discrepancy between the liturgy and between theology and preaching about Mary where she is often spoken of and spoken of in glowing terms?[121] This question becomes even more forceful when one keeps in mind the numerous commemorations of the martyrs or the celebration of the birth of St. John the Baptist which was already being observed in liturgical celebrations, and often with a special solemnity as well. What could have been the motive for the delay in the rise of the Marian feasts? Perhaps two considerations can direct us toward an eventual solution. The first concerns the cult of the martyrs that arose and developed in relation to the memory of their *dies natalis* (the day of their birth into Heaven) and their relics; while, for the Madonna, we have no news about these. Indeed, the apocryphal sources speak of her assumption, or rather, as the more ancient texts express it, the translation of her body to heaven.[122] Nevertheless, for the Madonna, too, more or less the same phenomenon happened that provided the basis of the Marian cult. It arose in relation to her *memoriae*, that is, the places and times of her life. In Jerusalem at Gethsemane her *Dormitio* was celebrated, i.e., her *dies natalis*. The texts that deal with the assumption/dormition were intended to be read in church on the occasion of the memorial feast, as one of them asserts.[123]

We meet a notable uncertainty and confusion about the origin of the Marian feasts. If on the one hand our sources provide us with some light, on the other they create problems of interpretation. In the last few decades notable progress in historical knowledge about Mary and the feasts associated with her has been made. But a complete clarification has not yet been reached. It is possible, however, to outline a satisfactory reconstruction with notable accuracy.

The erection of buildings dedicated to Mary, along with the decisions of the Council of Ephesus, favored the rise of Marian celebrations. It seems that in the first half of the fifth century there was a commemoration at Kathisma as we mentioned above to honor the Theotokos. It was a feast of general character, celebrated on August 15.[124] From the liturgical texts and homilies one can deduce that the content of the feast concerned the divine motherhood. It seems in some way related to the Council of Ephesus (431).[125] A homily of Hesychius of Jerusalem († c. 433) is preserved that was preached on such an occasion at Kathisma. The preacher shows himself to be entirely concerned with praising precisely the divine motherhood of the Virgin. Another sermon by Chrysippus on the same theme demonstrates his dependence on Hesychius' sermon. Chrysippus was a Cappadocian who lived in the laura of St. Euthymius, ten kilometers from Jerusalem.[126] In any case this Marian liturgical celebration seems to be the most ancient one known. For some scholars there exists no other testimony of any other feast celebrated elsewhere.[127] Nevertheless, for the same period and that which followed, we find Marian commemorations, more than proper Marian feasts, sometimes but not always in relation to the celebration of Christmas that are connected to the pre-Christmas Gospel readings, occurring on the Sunday preceding that feast.[128] Already from before the Council of Ephesus we have an indication from Proclus of Constantinople who delivered a discourse in that city in the presence of Nestorius.[129] The shrines of Kathisma and of the Tomb of Mary are at the origin of the Marian cult, as is the celebration of the *Memorial of Mary* which was a memorial also celebrated outside of Palestine on different dates.[130]

As Aubineau rightly pointed out, the still very incomplete research about Greek homilies make way for rather different hypotheses on the date of discourses, and thus of the festivities on which they were delivered.[131] One can likewise make deductions from other information, like lectionaries and calendars.[132] We have various dates for the various regions. In any case, for the fifth century we have a notable wealth of forms of worship and expression of praise toward the Madonna,[133] which then find their more complete realization in the four Marian feasts which establish themselves in the course of the sixth century in Constantinople: Hypapante on February 2, the Annunciation on March 25, the Nativity on September 8, and finally that honoring the Theotokos of August 15.[134]

In the second half of the sixth century Marian devotion received a great impulse in the very capital of the Byzantine Empire with the dedication of new churches to the Madonna,[135] as well as in feasts, in poetry, in preaching, and in the religious life in general. This significant role of Mary in the religious and civil life of the city culminates in the threat of 626, when the city was besieged by the Avars. On that occasion Mary was seen and considered as the true protector and savior of the capital.[136] In this period, Averil Cameron points out, Mary came to be invoked mainly for her potent work of mediation with God.[137]

In the West, in Rome we cannot document a Marian feast in the fifth century. Klauser maintained that the Roman church was against the Marian cult until the introduction of the eastern feasts in the seventh century.[138] This is too rigid a position and is disproved by two important facts. First of all, there is the great Church of St. Mary Major dedicated to the Virgin in order to exalt her divine motherhood (Theotokos). This dedication goes back at least to the time of Sixtus III (†440) and constitutes the interpretative key for its mosaics, where the Virgin is represented with the vestments of a princess.[139] Moreover, in the *Communicantes* of the Eucharistic prayer, which many scholars place in the fifth century even before Leo the Great, mention is already inserted of the *gloriosae semper Virginis Mariae, Genetricis Dei et Domini Nostri Iesu Christi* (always glorious Virgin Mary, Mother of God and our Lord Jesus Christ).[140]

In Jerusalem the celebration at Kathisma was transferred to Gethsemane, the burial place of the Virgin. It then assumed the specific meaning of the memorial of the *Dormitio Mariae*,[141] which was the original title of the feast of the Assumption in the West too. Some scholars consider this feast as the foundation of the Marian liturgical cult.[142] We do not know the date for the transfer of the feast of August 15 from Kathisma to the Tomb of Mary with the new meaning associated with the assumption. The vast apocryphal literature, which goes under the name of *Transitus Mariae*, insists that a commemoration of her *koimesis* (*dormitio*) be celebrated. This literature locates the celebration precisely in this place, i.e. Gethsemane. The first evidence of the existence of the feast of the Assumption goes back to Theotecnus who lived between the sixth and seventh century and was bishop of Livia, a city on the other side of the Jordan. The emperor Maurice (582–602) extended this feast to the entire Byzantine Empire as it grew in importance and came to be known as the *Dormition of Mary*.[143]

From the seventh century on in the eastern churches (if we leave out the Nestorian and Jacobite churches) the doctrine of the Assumption of Mary became common both in liturgical texts and in homilies on the occasion of the feast of August 15.[144] The feast was introduced in Rome in the course of the seventh century. From Rome it spread quite soon to western countries. Roman liturgical texts, however, from the eighth century on already speak of the "Assumption" and no longer of the "Dormition." At the end of the seventh century, according to the *Liber Pontificalis*, at the time of the pontificate of Sergius I (687–701), the liturgies of the Annunciation of the Lord,[145] of the Dormition, of the Nativity of Mary, and of St. Simeon (Hypapante – February 2 or 14) which were of Syrian origin were celebrated. These were the only Marian feasts celebrated in Rome until the fourteenth century.[146] On the other hand the feast of the Conception of Mary was wide-spread before the first half of this same century.[147]

In Palestine, perhaps in Jerusalem, a feast of the birth of Our Lady arose in the course of the sixth century, celebrated on September 8. The motive for choosing this date is unknown.[148] The content of the feast was inspired by the *Protoevangelium of James*, which goes back to the second half of the second century. And so it is a very ancient source.[149] That text tells us about Mary's parents, Joachim and Anne, but especially about Mary as the central figure of the whole narrative.[150] The text was widely used in the eastern liturgy.[151] Now a feast of the Nativity of the Virgin does not exist in the West in the first years of the fifth century, as Augustine explicitly observes.[152] In his time, they celebrated only the birth of Christ and of John the Baptist, on whose feast he delivered several discourses. Afterwards the feast is attested by the *Martyrologium Hieronimianum*.

Like the other ancient Marian feasts, the feast of the Conception of Mary arose in the East. The first feast to come into being was that of the *Conception of Anne, mother of the Theotokos* on December 9. Perhaps this arose at Constantinople where her relics had been brought. Afterwards the contents of such a feast were further refined, both in East and West, as the Conception of Mary who was born without the guilt of sin. In the East in such churches as the Byzantine and Armenian the feast has always remained on December 9. In many Catholic communities united to Rome it is celebrated on December 8.[153] The first subject of this feast was the miraculous birth of Mary from her mother Anne who was sterile according to the story of the *Protoevangelium of James*. The first evidence for the celebration of the feast goes back to the seventh century to Andrew of Crete (c. 660 – 740)[154] and John of Euboea (from c. 740)[155] whose sermon carries the title "The Conception of the Holy Mother" (*in Conceptione sanctae Deiparae*). Other similar sermons were given by George of Nicomedia,[156] Euthymius of Constantinople, and Peter of Argos. The feast was included in the *Nomocanon* of Photius (883). The emperor Leo the Philosopher (896–903) extended it to the whole Byzantine empire.

In Rome, at the end of the seventh century, the Nativity of Mary was an important feast, inasmuch as a procession was prescribed for it at the time of Pope Sergius I (687–701).[157] Hence it was one of the four great Marian feasts, originated in fact specifically to celebrate Mary. For quite some time, the Roman church celebrated only these four Marian feasts that were named in the *Liber Pontificalis* at the time of Pope Sergius I, and celebrated them all with a solemn procession. Only two of them have specifically Marian titles, however. In Rome there were several churches dedicated to Mary, among them the Pantheon, which became a church dedicated to her on May 13, 609 due to the efforts of Pope Boniface IV who had requested it from the eastern emperor Phocas.

CHRISTIAN FEASTS AND LATE ANTIQUE SOCIETY

The organization and rhythm of social and religious time in the Roman Empire was marked by calendars, which also conferred an identity on communities and on individuals.[158] Beyond the general and official calendar for the army and the administration, there were numerous local calendars, especially in the East in Asia Minor, Egypt, and Syria.[159] Religious calendars and their observance varied in different cities. The Roman feast of the new year, with its carnival atmosphere, spread throughout the whole Roman Empire and became the most popular and shared feast in the fourth century. Christians also gave rhythm to their religious and social life according to their religious commitments. For this reason, as we noted earlier in the chapter, they were accused of being anti-social and of not participating in the rhythm and demands of civic life including the rites associated with the *pax deorum* which they did not attend for social and religious reasons.[160] As we further noted, the pagan cult was expressed publicly in the streets, in the plazas, in the places of spectacle and of worship. The Christian cult on the other hand was more intimate, personal, and took place inside buildings and out of sight to most people. Christians then were distinguished above all by their abstaining from the public worship and from other forms of socialization.

In the ancient city the great moments of socialization consisted of worship, sacrifices, processions, public banquets, and spectacles in which Christians, at least the heads of families, were obliged to take part. Refusal or abstention was noted and criticized. Everyone was supposed to take part, from the children to the elderly, even if the heads of family alone were strictly "obligated." And whoever did not participate in the public worship put himself or herself at the margins of society. Everyone would know about it, feelings would be hurt and inevitable conflicts would result. But Christians could not participate in these public solemnities or attend the public banquets that were of a religious character. Hence the accusation of being anti-social, and more.

As we discussed elsewhere, the civic religion in all its forms, both of individual cities and of The City (*urbs*, i.e. Rome), was considered essential for the salvation and prosperity of the Empire and of the cities, and was indispensable for assuring the cohesion of all inhabitants. The *pax deorum* was the foundation of the political community. It was also the key for assuring success in war, defeating plagues and avoiding public calamities such as floods and earthquakes. By rejecting the official religion Christians put themselves outside the context of where they lived and were considered potentially subversive because they became the cause for the gods' anger and hence responsible for the worst misfortunes for society. Since one fundamental purpose of the civic cult was to placate the gods (*placatio deorum*), abstaining from the public cult was not considered a private act of conscience but rather an affront to the whole society, a failure to contribute to the *pax deorum*, and hence a potential cause of the gods' wrath.

In the fourth century the organization of public, social, political, and religious time changed profoundly with the progress of conversion to Christianity and the diffusion of Christian feasts. If citizens of the third century who had participated intensely in the cultural and religious life of his city had found themselves walking through the same city in the first years of the fifth century, they would be quite confused. In part this was because city planning itself had changed, but above all they would not find, or at least not with the same intensity, certain habitual places of socialization like the feasts, and certain great moments of collective participation in the same traditional framework of streets and plazas. This was in fact the experience recounted in the legend of the seven sleepers of Ephesus.[161]

With the arrival of Constantine and through the influence of the Christian religion, the old Roman calendar began to be transformed radically because its foundations were made up of a different conception of time and of religion—a conception that determined the *qualitas* of sacred and profane time, insofar as time for the Romans as well as the Jews was not only a temporal numeric quantity but had its own specific quality of purpose.

The instituting of the Christian articulation of social and religious time was a slow and complex process effected in different ways: 1) institution of the Christian feast days as public festivals (*feriae publicae*), begun by Constantine and continued afterward with the increase also in the number of feast days. 2) The recognition of certain days and periods of the year for the fulfilling or abstaining from certain acts *ratione temporis* (e.g. Lent). 3) The slow but steady abolition of public pagan sacrifices. 4) The removal and destruction of the pagan idols in the temples and hence the decline of the related feasts. 5) The closing, destruction, and reconversion of pagan temples and the confiscation of their goods. 6) The abolition of the *feriae* linked to pagan celebrations which then became *dies iuridici*, that is, normal working days. 7) The prohibition of spectacles on Christian feast days. 8) The conservation and secularization of the spectacles for the entertainment of the people. 9) The creation of a civic ritual that replaced the preceding pagan religious ritual.

We cannot follow the entire slow and lengthy process that ensued toward implementing the articulation of religious and public time in relation to Christian feasts. Rather, we limit ourselves to two important moments: the beginning with Constantine in 321[162] and the almost complete fulfillment with Theodosius II in 425.

a) *Institution of the Christian Liturgical Calendar*. The first law that required a day of rest for feasts was issued by Constantine and goes back to 321, Codex Justinianus 3.12.2, not preserved in the Codex Theodosianus. If the date of its posting (the city is not specified, but it could be Rome) is March 3, it was issued some time earlier, when Constantine was in Illyricum. My translation: *The Emperor Constantine to Elpidius. All judges and urban populations and workmen must rest on the venerable day of the Sun. Farmers, however, employed in the cultivation of fields, should freely and without impediment attend to agriculture, since often it happens that no other day is more suitable for entrusting the grain to the furrows or the vines to the trenches, so that the favor granted on that occasion by heavenly providence not be lost. Issued March 3, Crispus and Constantine being consuls for the second time.*

The extract preserved in the Codex Justinianus is part of the copy addressed to Elpidius, whose office is not indicated, but who at that time (321–324) was the vicar or deputy of the city of Rome (*vicarius urbis Romae*). Analogous copies were addressed to the "governors of every province commanding that they must give reverence to the Lord's day."[163] Constantine required abstention from work only of the urban populations, especially of the judges who, on the *dies solis*, must not administer justice. In the text there is nothing said of worship, and even less of sacrifices or other external cultic acts, yet the law does not have a social, but only a religious, purpose. Eusebius presents it in the sense that the *dies solis* is a day of prayer for all.[164] The historian Sozomen also affirms the arrangements made by Constantine for the purpose of *"rendering worship to the divinity with prayers and supplications."*[165]

b) *Passing from Rescript to Law*. Under the title "Concerning Feasts" (*de feriis*) in the second book of the Codex Theodosianus it passes from a rescript of 321 directed to the same Elpidius, to a law of 386 with a blank of sixteen missing laws, according to the edition of Mommsen, laws which should nevertheless have been present in the Codex and would have been very instructive for our research. Only in 386 does a legislative text first speak of the Lord's day (*dies dominicus*), even if this nomenclature is coupled with the traditional expression *dies solis* (*solis die, quem dominicum rite dixere maiores*; day of the sun, more correctly referred to as the Lord's day),[166] to be understood better. The law directly favors Christians, who carry out their cultic acts especially on Sunday which is the cornerstone of their worship.

The law of 386, issued at Aquileia by Valentinian II, is repeated in three different places in the Codex Theodosianus:[167]

> The emperors Gratian, Valentinian, and Theodosius, Augusti, to Principius, Praetorian Prefect. On the day of the sun, which has rightly been called the Lord's day by our ancestors, let us abstain entirely from every action of legal disputes, from trials, and from citations in the tribunal. Let no one demand the payment of his public or private debt. There should not even be an investigation about disputes, not even among the arbiters themselves, whether requested in tribunal or freely chosen. Whoever has deviated from the inspiration or rite of the holy religion should be considered not only infamous (*notabilis*) but also sacrilegious. Published November 3 at Aquileia, received in Rome November 24, the most noble child Honorius and Evodius being consuls.[168]

The Visigothic *Interpretatio:*

> On the day of the sun, which rightly is called the Lord's day, every legal action should be suspended, on account of which no debt, whether public or private, should be called in, and no judicial act be done, public or private. Whoever does not observe this law should be considered sacrilegious.[169]

This law was issued at Aquileia[170] by Valentinian II on November 3, 386 and received in Rome on the twenty-fourth of the same month, in the name of Gratian (*senior Augiustus*), Valentinian, and Theodosius. In reality Gratian had already been killed by Magnus Maximus at Lyons on August 15 of 383, and laws were still being published under his name. In the Codex Theodosianus the law is given a full three times, a sign of its importance: 2.8.18; 8.8.3 under the rubric *De executoribus* (here it says *data*, i.e. published) where there is also the *interpretatio*; 11.7.13 under the rubric *De exactionibus*, although here no mention is made, as in the other two texts, of the law's reception at Rome. The law is severe and qualifies the transgressor as *sacrilegus*, to whom, therefore, the laws of sacrilege are applied. But there is no knowing what application or efficacy it had. One must always distinguish between the text of a law and the concrete application, which normally requires a lot of time and the will of the governors to apply it.

Because of the significance it assumes in Christian spirituality, the Lenten and Easter period was received by the civil authorities with two very humanitarian measures: the Easter amnesty and the suspension of torture during the Lenten period, although with no mention of the liturgical specificity of those days in Christian spirituality and life. In 367 the emperor Valentinian[171] issued a law with which he concedes a general amnesty on the occasion of Easter each year.[172] The Easter amnesty, conceded for the first time in 367 with a general law with no spatial limits, is valid for that year only and is limited in time, and its application is not immediate in all provinces. Afterward the amnesty became regularized.

Right after the publication of the *Cunctos populos* on March 3, 380, Theodosius, still in Thessalonica, published the law,[173] also preserved in the Codex Justinianus,[174] but under the title *de feriis*. This law recognized the Christian Lent with an extended expression, and ordained that in that period every penal process be suspended, hence also the search for evidence, which usually took place through torture. The motive for the suspension of every process is due to the *qualitas* of the pre-Easter time, as a special time of preparation for Easter.

The fathers of the Church recognize and appreciate this imperial legislation. The humanitarian arrangement is *ratione temporis*,[175] that is, *pro reverentia religionis* (due to the reverence for religion), as the *interpretation* says: Lent is a specifically Christian time that had been developing in the course of the fourth century, but with differences in length and organization in the various churches. Even if it would be little observed by the competent authorities, the law adapted the judicial calendar for the administration of justice to the rhythms of the Christian liturgy.

The complete organization of the division of time and of the calendar for tribunals and summer holidays was accomplished by Theodosius I on August 7, 389, during his stay in Rome. He did this together with Valentinian II, including a law that specified the entire feast-time judicial system.[176] The law[177] (of 389) reaffirmed that legal actions were not permitted on feast days (*feriae*), but at the same time it reworked a new list of *feriae* (cf. Digest 2.12).

c) *The Completed Reform*. On February 1, 425[178] Theodosius II issued a disposition at Constantinople that reorganized the whole system of the calendar of days on which spectacles were prohibited, in relation to the Christian liturgical calendar, according to the principle: *aliud esse supplicationum noverint tempus, aliud voluptatum* (*Let them know that there is one time for prayers, another for entertainments*). The number of Christian feast days on which spectacles were prohibited was increased since the feasts of Epiphany and Christmas were also included —two feasts that, in 425, were celebrated both in Rome and in Constantinople—along with the days of the Easter period.[179]

Theodosius Augustus and Valentinian Caesar to Asclepiodotus, Praetorian prefect. All theater and circus entertainments are forbidden to the populations of all cities: Sunday, which is the first day of the whole week, and on the days of Christmas and the Epiphany of Christ, and on the days of Easter and of Quinquagesima—when the garments that imitate the splendor of the light of the heavenly bath, are evidence of the new illumination of holy baptism—and also when the commemoration of the Apostolic passion, teacher of all Christianity, is celebrated by all according to the norm, insofar as all the minds of faithful Christians are occupied with the worship of God. If anyone is still prisoner of the madness of Jewish impiety or of error or of the insanity of stupid paganism, let him know that there is one time for prayers and another for entertainments. Thus let no one consider himself constrained to honor our numen as if of a necessity higher than our imperial office, and if, with spite toward the divine religion he dedicates himself to spectacles, perhaps he will have to undergo the offense wrought upon Our Serenity, if he will have shown toward us less devotion than he was accustomed; thus let no one doubt that Our Gentleness is honored in a particular way by the human race, when the service is rendered to the virtues and merits of almighty God. Given on the Kalends of February at Constantinople, Theodosius being consul for the eleventh time and Valentinian Caesar for the first (February 1, 425).[180]

The law is also contained in the Codex Justinianus,[181] which is a reworking with passages of laws issued at different times: CTh 15.5.5 of 425[182] of Theodosius II on the days of spectacles, CTh 8.8.3 of 386 issued at Aquileia by Valentinian II to make it complete, keeping in mind the evolution of the civil and religious calendar that happened after 389.[183] The Justinian reworking is always attributed to Valentinian II and is dated to 389. Moreover, it includes a passage whose source is not known, which calls for the deferment in the fifteen or so days of Easter of the *compulsio* and of the exaction of the Annona (a Roman tax consisting of foodstuffs) and of public and private debts. Perhaps the inclusion of the feasts of Christmas and Epiphany in the law of 425 had already happened earlier on an unspecified date. This was not only, as they used to say, a reform of the judicial calendar, since years earlier, and precisely in 395,[184] a law of general character had been issued, addressed to Heraclianus, governor of Paphlagonia, in which it was said that the pagan solemnities must not be numbered among the feast days on the basis of a preceding law.

Issued in the East in 425, the regulation of CTh 15.5.5 concerned the prohibition of spectacles on Christian feast days, which are: (1) Sunday, as the first day of the week, a typically Christian expression (and not part of the week-end or the end of the week). (2) Christmas and Epiphany (it uses the plural *epiphaniorum Christi*). (3) The days of Easter (a week before and after Easter). (4) Quinquagesima, that is, the period after Easter.

This regulation of Theodosius II was the culmination and bringing together of the changes that took place in a century of religious evolution. In the decades that followed other festivities would be added, but not that of the Ascension, even if in the ecclesial sphere it was already a solemnity.

PILGRIMAGES

The Hebrew tradition celebrated the feasts of pilgrimage[185] to the Temple of Jerusalem. Especially at Passover the city was filled with foreigners as well as Jews coming from far away. Christians of the first centuries were not interested in the biblical locations, insofar as they were more interested in a spiritual religion that was centered on their way of life. The first known Christian pilgrim is the Bishop Alexander, who went to Jerusalem from Cappadocia in the first years of the third century, "to pray and to visit the (holy) places."[186] But other people went to Jerusalem, like Melito of Sardis and Origen. The development of the pilgrimage to Jerusalem accelerated at the beginning of the fourth century when, as Eusebius observes: "All those who believe in Christ gather here (in Jerusalem) from every part of the world, not, as in the past, to admire the splendor of the city or pray at the ancient Temple, but they stop here to marvel at the effects of the conquest and destruction of Jerusalem . . . and to pray over the city on the Mount of Olives . . . where the Savior's feet stood."[187]

Pagans also made pilgrimages, going to the most famous sanctuaries. Some of these preserve evidence of pilgrims' votive memorials as graffiti.[188] The pilgrim is one who travels out of devotion to places which are considered to have a special holiness and to receive some benefit from them.

Helen, the mother of the emperor Constantine, went to Jerusalem and Palestine as a pilgrim.[189] Moreover, through imperial initiative numerous churches were constructed which drew pilgrims even from far away. An anonymous pilgrim from Bordeaux went to Jerusalem in 333, leaving us the itinerary of his voyage. Thus, we come to know that pilgrims visited not only the places of Jesus' life but also the important ones of Jewish history.

The diary of Egeria, a wealthy pilgrim who came from Spanish Galicia, offers us rich details about the places visited, the liturgies, the monasticism, and what was done in the places visited. Egeria also visited other places not connected with biblical history such as the tomb of St. Thecla at Seleucia in Isauria, which is in western Cilicia. She went to Mount Sinai and even to far away Edessa in Mesopotamia. At the end of the fourth century numerous westerners went to Jerusalem and its surroundings. Some took up residence there, founding monasteries, like Jerome and Paula, at Bethlehem, and Melania. Paula also founded a guesthouse for Latin guests. Someone in love with the biblical places like Jerome writes: "Anthony and the whole array of monks . . . did not visit Jerusalem, and nonetheless the gates of paradise were opened for them."[190] The numerous studies by Maraval collect abundant documentation. *Letter* 46.9–10 of Jerome contains a long list of regions from which the most representative persons come, from the farthest west to eastern regions. Whoever goes to Jerusalem certainly also goes to Bethlehem.

There were no printed guidebooks. The Bible was the official guide. At the location then there were local guides who entertained the pilgrims with stories. The text of Egeria is very useful for us, because it tells what was visited, how it was visited, and how one did it. Later on, texts helpful for pilgrims were also compiled. Other than Jerusalem which was the most famous pilgrimage destination in the East, there were also great shrines like that of Thecla at Seleucia (today Silifke in Turkey) in Isauria. A few ruins of the shrine remain still to this day in a place called Meriamlik. Egeria notes in her diary: "In that place, near the church (the shrine of St. Thecla) there was nothing other than innumerable monasteries of men and women . . . ; at the center, a wall that surrounds the church, in which the martyr's shrine is found. . . . Having come to that place in the name of the Lord, and having prayed at the shrine, and having read also the *Acts of St. Thecla*, I gave infinite thanks to Christ."[191]

Not only were the biblical places pilgrimage destinations, but so were persons known for their holiness, especially in the East. In particular the monks of Skete and of Nitria in Egypt were visited, along with the Syrian stylite monks who lived on columns, such as Simeon the Elder in Qal'at Sem'ān (†459), and Simeon the Younger near Antioch (†592).

In the fourth century a rapid transformation of the religious landscape came about, not only because of the rapid spread of Christianity, but also because of the structural transformation of cities and the surrounding areas. Contributing to this was the great diffusion of the cult of the martyrs and of their relics, the widespread construction of larger or smaller churches for their cult, and the enthusiasm of the people for going to places connected with the martyrs. In the beginning of the fifth century there were thousands of them. They were not simple places of prayer and meeting, like traditional churches, but places on which the presence of the relics conferred a special strength (*virtus*). The *martyria* were the places of victory—like trophies—for the martyrs who had triumphed through God's gift, as well as places of *memoria* where their martyrdom was remembered and commemorated.

Augustine observed:

> Think, brothers, of what happens when the news of the martyrs' feast is given to the people, or some holy place selected for gathering together on a determined day to celebrate the feast there: how the whole people gets excited and, exhorting each other, says: Let's go, let's go! If one asks them: Where are we going? they respond, there, to that place, to that shrine. Thus, they speak to each other and, enkindling each other, so to say, they both form one flame; and this one flame, born from the one who, speaking, spreads the fire with which he burns to another, makes all flow together to that holy place, and the holy intention sanctifies them. If thus a pure love

manages to transport [the faithful] to a material shrine, how much more sublime must that love be which lifts to heaven the heart of one who, living in harmony, can exchange with his brother the words: *Let us go to the house of the Lord!*[192]

Augustine puts this example forward to encourage his listeners to run toward the heavenly Jerusalem.

One of the pilgrimage centers was Rome. For various reasons, in the second century very many people came to Rome from every part of the Empire including Palestine (Hegesippus and Justin), Assyria (Tatian), Asia Minor (Abercius), and Gaul (Irenaeus), to name only a few. A significant example comes from the *memoria apostolorum* (today the site of the basilica of St. Sebastian built in the 16th c.) on the ancient Apian Way (Via Appia Antica). Earlier it had been a much visited place for the cult of the two apostles, Peter and Paul, who had been martyred in Rome.[193] This small shrine, which received its name *memoria apostolorum* from the excavators, was built between 244 and 258 on top of three decorated mausoleums that were subsequently buried in preparation for the basilica Constantine built there. The part that was slightly elevated and porticoed in a trapezoidal form was covered with a canopy; this was called a *triclia* by Styger who was the one in charge of the excavations.[194] This site was much visited after it had been built and was used for about fifty years up to the beginning of the fourth century. The lack of the Constantinian monogram is a sign of its antiquity. The quantity of graffiti etched into the walls in the short span of fifty years, although numerous have been lost, is an indication of the large number of pilgrims who went to venerate the two apostles before there was religious freedom. But many pilgrims perhaps did not leave any trace of their visit. Now on the east plaster wall of the *triclia* about 640 graffiti have been discovered, with invocations and prayers to the two apostles.[195] Some of them go back to about 260. Some are written in Greek, a few are in Latin but written in Greek letters, but the great majority are in Latin (over 80%). The visitors had made a journey, had prayed in the small place, and had a funeral banquet—known as a *refrigerium*—about which I will speak in the following chapter. Among the pilgrims who came from afar there is one who came from Benevento,[196] another from Sardinia.[197] Some graffiti record prayers for good travel by sea[198] (*rogo quot bene navigant*),[199] which means some probably came from Africa where the term *navigare* meant to go to Rome.

In the beginning of the fifth century crowds of pilgrims poured into Nola on the occasion of the feast of St. Felix.[200] Augustine also sent two of his monks, one already a priest, to Nola from Hippo to the tomb of St. Felix to ascertain the truth. "I chose then a middle way and exhorted them to take upon themselves with mutual accord the obligation to go to a shrine, where the thought of awesome miraculous interventions worked there could more easily bring to light which of the two had a guilty conscience and would constrain him to confess the fault, either through some punishment or fear of it."[201]

In Italy other famous tombs of martyrs also drew pilgrims, even if to a lesser degree, like those of Agatha at Catania, Januarius at Naples, and Victorinus at Amiterno. The same phenomenon occurred everywhere. In Gaul the most famous center was the tomb of St. Martin at Tours.[202] A little known shrine was that of Stephen at Uzalis (El Alia, in Tunisia), the most important in the African provinces, where several existed. This shrine drew pilgrims even from afar and the town's inhabitants were proud of their protector. People who obtained healing there had come from various parts of Proconsular Africa including *Membositanus locus,*[203] *Utica,*[204] *Hippo Diarrhytus,*[205] *Pisitana civitas,*[206] and even from as far away as Carthage. Vitula and her daughter Megetia,[207] and Florentius,[208] all from Carthage, preferred to go to Uzalis even though there were some relics in Carthage in a women's monastery (*monasterio puellarum*) where, around 434, a miracle had occurred in the presence of the bishop.[209] For those who came from afar and stayed for a few days there must have also been some places of accommodation. Sometimes the sick remained in church, even during the night, intent on prayer and supplication. The *De miraculis Sancti Stephani* narrates events in a time span that covers several years. The various miracles concern daily life such as healings of various illnesses, liberation from prison, soured wine that becomes good again, a favorable trial in court. The text offers us information about the language and life of small centers, and about the life of the Carthaginian aristocrats at the beginning of the fifth century. The *De miraculis* provides us with a cross-section of popular devotion, of enthusiasm, and of participation in various events. The people already considered Stephen as their fellow citizen[210] and their protector.[211]

CONCLUSION

In this chapter we have seen an intimate relationship between Christians and time that is evident in how the calendar developed from its initial moorings in Roman reckonings and Jewish festivals through the ecclesiastical rhythms of the early church, many of which have endured up to the present day. The calendar was tied to nature itself in its vernal equinoxes and solstices, reflecting the ebb and flow of times and season in the created and the ecclesial worlds. The various ecclesial feasts that are highlighted in the calendar of the church were meant to convey the history of God's redemption in Jesus Christ that enervates the Christian life lived until his return. As such, it regulated the lives of the faithful, guided their paths through life on their way to their own *dies natalis*.

1. Susan K. Roll, *Toward the Origins of Christmas* (Kampen: Kok Pharos, 1995), 42-45; W. Evenepoel, "La délimitation de "l'année liturgique" dans les premiers siècles de la chrétienté occidentale, caput anni liturgici," *Revue d'histoire ecclésiastique* 83 (1988): 601-16.
2. *Kalo, calo*, from Greek καλεῖν *to call; calo* can have three meanings: *to name, to invoke, to call. Calo* relates to any type of convocation of people in assembly. The ancients linked it with the convocation of the people in the *Curia Calabra* or the *comitia*. Explanations vary, but all are uncertain.
3. Cf. Augustine, *Sermones* 210.6.9; 105; 107; 108; 109; 110; 10.5; 116.3; 141.3; 142.7. Basil recommends abstinence to spouses: *De ieiunio hom*.1, PG 31:181. In the Orthodox world the practice remains of abstaining from conjugal relations when one is to receive communion.
4. Censorinus, *De die natali* 23: *Qui a media nocte ad proximam mediam noctem in his horis quattuor et viginti nascuntur eundem diem habent natalem. In horas XII diem divisum esse noctemque in totidem vulgo notum est. Sed hoc credo Romae post inventa solaria observamus*. Cf. Macrobius, *Saturnalia* 1.21.13.
5. In 1960 there came into being *Coordinated Universal Time*; today time is established by the *International Atomic Time* (TAI from the French *Temps Atomique International*), which added a one-second delay on July 15, 2015.
6. Censorinus, *De die nat.* 23.
7. Censorinus, *De die nat.* 23: *Alii diem quadripertito, sed et noctem similiter dividebant; idque similitudo testatur militaris, ubi dicitur vigilia prima, item secunda et tertia et quarta*.
8. Pliny writes (*Naturalis Historia* 2.69.188): *Ipsum diem alii aliter observavere: Babylonii inter duos solis exortus, Athenienses inter duos occasus, Umbri a meridie ad meridiem, vulgus omne a luce ad tenebras, sacerdotes Romani et qui diem finiere civilem, item Aegyptii et Hipparchus a media nocte in mediam*. Other ancient authors also affirm the same thing (e.g. Censorinus, *De die natali* 23).
9. Equinox from Latin *aequinoctium*, a combination of *aequus* (equal) and *nox* (night; solstice from Latin *solstitium*, made of *sol* (sun) and the verb *stare* (to stand still).
10. Epiphanius, *Panarion* 51.24.1-3.
11. Epiphanius, *Panarion* 51.24.24.4.
12. Cf. Eusebius, *Demonstr. Evang.* 8.2.3; Jerome, *In Danielem* 3.9.24: CCL 75A:868.
13. Cf. Grumel, *La chronologie* (Paris: Presses Universitaires de France, 1958), 168-69; 172-75.
14. S. Stern, *Calendars in Antiquity: Empires, States, and Societies* (Oxford: Oxford University Press, 2012), 247, n. 35.
15. Ibid, 250-53; Y. Meimaris, *Chronological systems in Roman-Byzantine Palestine and Arabia. The Evidence of Dated Greek Inscriptions* (Athens: Kentron Hellēnikēs kai Rōmaikēs Archaiotētos Ethnikon Hydryma Ereunōn, 1992), 38ff.
16. S. Stern, *Calendars in Antiquity*, 255-59.
17. Cf. 1.2; 7.1. J. P Rey-Coquais, "Le calendrier employé par Eusèbe de Césarée dans les Martyrs de Palestine," *Analecta Bollandiana* 96 (1978): 55-64.
18. S. Stern, *Calendars in Antiquity*, 260.
19. Ibid, 125-66.
20. Cf. A. Camplani, *Atanasio di Alessandria, Lettere festali* (Milan: C.I.M., 2003).
21. Cf. Otto F.A. Meinardus, *Christian Egypt: Ancient and Modern* (Cairo: The American University in Cairo Press, 1977), 70-74; (with the list of feasts, pp. 74ff.); Roger S. Bagnall and Klaas A. Worp, *The Chronological Systems of Byzantine Egypt* (Leiden: Brill, 2004); Otto F.A. Meinardus, *Two Thousand Years of Coptic Christianity* (Coptic calendar 285-309 on the fixed celebrations; starts with 1 Thoth, 11 = September in the Gregorian); Christian Cannuyer, *Les Coptes* (Turnhout: Brepols, 1990), liturgical calendar 204-10; 301-305.
22. S. Stern, *Calendar and Community: A History of the Jewish Calendar, 2nd Century BCE to 10th Century CE* (Oxford: Oxford University Press, 2001), VI.
23. *Antiquities* 1.81.
24. S. Stern, *Calendar and Community*, 18.
25. Cf. what is said in the *EAC* 1:561-63. It is the mixing of two distinct celebrations. The first of the lamb, an apotropaic rite linked to pastoral life. On the other hand, the rite of unleavened bread supposes a sedentary and agricultural life.
26. Thus, it was translated into Greek by the LXX.
27. Cf. for a summary, J.J. Meier, *Un ebreo marginale* (Brescia: Queriniana, 2008), 1:377-401; Étienne Nodet, "On Jesus' Last Supper," *Biblica* 91 (2010): 348-369; S. Saulnier, *Calendrical Variations in Second Temple Judaism. New Perspectives on the "Date of the Last Supper" Debate* (Leiden: Brill, 2012). J. Jeremias, *Eucharistic Words of Jesus*, trans. by Norman

Perrin (Philadelphia: Fortress Press, 1997), 17-22 gives a long list of scholars. This book is of great value, one of those books that never goes out of date. Étienne Nodet, "Chronologies de la passion: leur sens," *Revue biblique* 118 (2011): 362-407, 365-68.
28. Cf. R. T. Beckwith, *Calendar, Chronology and Worship: Studies in Ancient Judaism and Early Christianity* (Leiden: Brill, 2005), 291ff.
29. Colin J. Humphreys, *The Mystery of the Last Supper. Reconstructing the Final Days of Jesus* (Cambridge: Cambridge University Press, 2011).
30. E.g. Tertullian: *fasti Iudaici*, *De Iei.* 13; *Adv. Marc.* 4:3.
31. Others think it is between February 24 and 25, cf. *Enciclopedia Italiana* 8:399.
32. When? Isidore, *Etymologiae.* 6.7; 6.4: *annus bissextilis*; Augustine, *Ep.* 55.7.13 PL 33:210: *bisextus annuus*; Isidore, *Etymologiae* 6.17.25 *Bisextus dies*.
33. The jurist Celsus, *Digest* 50.16.98
34. Ovid, *Fasti* 2.48.51.
35. Cf. *Gregorian Reform of the Calendar: Proceedings of the Vatican conference to Commemorate its 400th Anniversary*, eds. Hoskin, M. A. and O. Pedersen (Vatican City: Pontifica Academia Scientiarum, Specola Vaticana, 1983), 186, note 28 and 29; esp. 211.
36. *Gregorian Reform of the Calendar*. This fundamental volume is available online as a PDF. http://www.casinapioiv.va/content/dam/accademia/pdf/es3.pdf
37. For the diffusion, cf. L. von Pastor and Angelo Mercati. *Storia dei Papi dalla fine del Medio Evo. 1592-1605 11, 11* (Rome: Desclée, 1958), 11:180ff.; *Gregorian Reform of the Calendar: Proceedings of the Vatican Conference to Commemorate its 400th Anniversary*, 243-80.
38. Cf. Pliny, *Ep.* 10.96.
39. B. Botte, "Les dénominations du dimanche dans la tradition chrétienne," in *Le Dimanche* (Paris: Éditions du Cerf, 1965), 7-18; W. Rordorf, *Sabato e domenica nella Chiesa antica* (Torino: SEI, 1979), 133, note 1, from which I draw this summary, according to which it has been affirmed that *kuriake hemera* first meant Easter (Strobel); Jan van Goudoever, *Biblical Calendars* (Leiden: E.J. Brill, 1959), 169ff; C.W Dugmore, "Lord's Day and Easter," *Neotestamentica et Patristica* 6 (1962): 272-81 (the day of the Lord means the day of the Lord's resurrection, that is, Easter). Such a thesis is not sustainable, cf. W. Rordorf, *Sunday: The History of the Day of Rest and Worship in the Earliest Centuries of the Christian Church* (Philadelphia: Westminster Press, 1968); C.S. Mosna, *Storia Della Domenica dalle origini fino agli inizi del V secolo* (Rome: Libreria editrice dell'Università gregoriana, 1969), 19ff.
40. Eusebius, *Com. Ps.* Text in Rordorf, *Sabato*, n. 44, 83. See also the discussion in the previous chapter on liturgy.
41. Justin, *1 Apol.* 65.7.
42. Justin, *1 Apol.* 63:2, 7.
43. Justin, *Dialogue* 41:4.
44. Tertullian, *Ad nationes* 1.13; *Apologia* 16.
45. Tertullian, *De idol.* 14: PL 1:759; *De corona* 3; 11: PL 2:99, 112.
46. *Did. Apost.* 5.20.11, ed. F.X. Funk 1905, 298; W. Rordorf, *Sabato e domenica*, n. 104.
47. A. Di Berardino, "I cristiani e la città antica nella evoluzione religiosa dei primi secoli," in *Cristianesimo e Istituzioni politiche, Da Costantino a Giustiniano* ed. Enrico Del Covolo and R. Uglione (Rome: LAS, 1997), 45-79.
48. Pliny, *Ep.* 10.96.7.
49. Tertullian, *Ad nationes* 1.13.1.
50. Origen, *Contra Cels.* 8.22.
51. Hippolytus, *Comm Dan.* 1.20, in SC 14:10ff.
52. Tertullian, *De fuga* 14.1
53. Pliny, *Ep.* 10.96.7.
54. Tertullian, *De corona* 3.3. Cyprian, bishop in 249-258, writes: *Nos autem resurrectionem Domini mane celebramus* (*Ep.* 63.16.2).
55. *Quia non potest intermitti dominicus. Lex sic iubet* (ch. 10 and 11); *Quoniam sine dominico non possumus* (ch. 12), P. Franchi de' Cavalieiri (ed.), *Note agiografiche*, Studi e Testi 65 (Rome: Tipografia Vaticana, 1935), 57-58. On these martyrs cf. Augustine, *Brev. Conl. cum donatistis* 3.2.32, in PL 43:643; P. Franchi de' Cavalieri, *Note agiografiche*, 3ff; for other Sunday meetings during the persecution, cf. 24, note 3. J. Leal, *Actas latinas de los mártires africanos*, (Madrid: Ciudad Nueva, 2009), 326-30.
56. Lord, did you not complete the Paschal drinking? Is it then necessary that we complete it again? *Ethiopic*.

57. Cf. the discussion is summarized by R.J. Bauckham "Sabbath and Sunday in the Post-Apostolic Church," in *From Sabbath to Lord's Day: A Biblical, Historical and Theological Investigation,* ed. By D.A. Carson (Grand Rapids, MI: Zondervan, 1982), 230ff.
58. Bardaisan, *On Fate.*
59. A. Hamman, "Valeur et signification des renseignements liturgiques de Justin," *Studia Patristica* 13.2, TU 116, (1975): 364-74.
60. Julian Talley, "Le temps liturgique dans l'Eglise ancienne. Etat de la recherche," *Maison-Dieu* 147 (1981): 29-60, 33.
61. *Epistle of Barnabas* 15.8-9.
62. W. Rordorf discusses this point in *Sunday, The History of the Day of Rest,* 24-38; 181-82.
63. Eusebius, *HE* 3.37.5.
64. Ignatius, *Ep. ad Magn.* 9.1-2, in SC 10:88-89.
65. Cf. Ignatius, *Ep. ad Magn.* 9.1.
66. Cf. Justin, *Dialogo* 47; W. Rordorf, *Sabato e domenica nella Chiesa antica* (Torino: SEI, 1979), n. 23, 41
67. *The Dictionary of the Later New Testament,* ed. L.P. Martin, P. H. Davids (Downers Grove: InterVarsity Press, 1997), 683.
68. Pseudo-Ignatius, *To the Magnesians* 9: PG 5:767.
69. There is debate about the origin of Lent, which undergoes great development in the fourth century. Its duration varied according to region: in Jerusalem around 380 "Lent" lasted eight weeks: "Among us are observed forty days before Easter, but here, on the other hand, eight weeks before Easter are observed" (*Egeria, Peregr.* 27.1; 45.2). Cf. *EAC* 2:538-49.
70. Egeria, explaining Lent in the Holy City, speaks of Wednesday preaching: "So that the people be always instructed in the law, the bishop and a presbyter preach assiduously" (*Pereg.* 27.6). Elsewhere there is also preaching during the weekdays: cf. F. Sottocornola, *L'anno liturgico nei sermoni di Pietro Crisologo* (Cesena: Centro studi e ricerche sulla antica provincia ecclesiastica ravennate, 1973), 144 and 199.
71. Augustine, *Sermo* 210.7.9; cf. John Chrysostom, *Hom. 4 de statuis* 6.3: PG 49:84.
72. *Pereg.* 27.1.
73. Cf. Augustine, *Sermo* 210.6.9; cf. DACL 2:2151-52.
74. Augustine, *Enarr. In Psal.* 120.6; cf. *De civ. Dei* 16.43.
75. Quartodeciman is made up of quarto (4) and decem (10) which, added together equal 14. Augustine writes: [these] "celebrate Easter on the fourteenth day of the moon, whatever day of the week it might be, and if it coincides with Sunday, on that day they hold the vigil and fast" (*De haeresibus* 29). Cf. *EAC* 3:363-64.
76. Eusebius, *HE* 4.14.1; 5.24.26.
77. Eusebius, *HE* 5.23.2.
78. Today east of the Circus Maximus, in Suburra, the Campus Martius (Via Lata, today Via del Corso).
79. Eusebius, *HE* 5.23.3; 24.2-17.
80. Angelo Di Berardino, "L'imperatore Costantino e la celebrazione della Pasqua," in *Costantino il Grande, Dall'antichità all'umanesimo,* ed. Giorgio Bonamente, Franca Fusco (Macerata: Università degli studi di Macerata, 1992), 363-84.
81. Cf. "computus, ecclesiastical" in *EAC* 1:583-584. There are many other entries regarding this subject.
82. Angelo Di Berardino, *Leone Magno e il calendario cristiano: tra Oriente e Occidente,* in: http://docplayer.it/19861953-Leone-magno-e-il-calendario-cristiano-tra-oriente-e-occidente.html
83. Cf. "Easter homilies," *EAC* 1:764-66.
84. Tertullian, *De bapt.* 19.2.
85. Tertullian, *De oratione* 23.2.
86. John Chrysostom, *Hom. De Ascensione* 2: PG 50:444; cf. 441.
87. PG 46:689D-693C; CPG 323-327. J. Daniélou, "Grégoire de Nysse et l'origine de la fête de l'Ascension," *Kyriakon, Festschrift J. Quasten* (Münster: Aschendorff, 1970), 663-66.
88. A. Renoux, *Le Code Arménien Jérusalem 121* (Turnhout: Brepols, 1969-71), 336-39.
89. Sermon 8; cf. Lemarié, SC 154:96.
90. Another word for festal celebration, or solemnity.
91. Filaster, *Haer.* 140.2; cf. 141.
92. *Sermo* 261.1; 265.1; 265A.1; 265F.1.
93. C. Coebergh, "L'Épiphanie à Rome avant S. Léon. Un indice pour l'année 419," *RevBén* 75 (1965): 304-307.

94. M.A. Vannier, "L'Épiphanie dans le monde latin d'après S. Augustin et de S. Léon le Grand," *Connaissance des Pères de l'Église* 80 (2000): 32-36.
95. We know of more than twenty Nativity scenes (mangers) of the fourth century on sarcophagi, which come from Roman workshops. Cf. Dino Milinovic, "L'origine de la scène de la nativité dans l'art paléochrétien (d'après les sarcophages d'Occident): Catalogue et interprétation," *Antiquité Tardive* 7 (1999): 299-329.
96. Ammianus Marcellinus, *Rerum gestarum* 21.2.5.
97. Augustine, *Sermo* 202.2: PL 38:1033.
98. Raymond Étaix, "Sermons ariens inedits," *Recherches augustiniennes*, 26 (1992): 143-79 (12 sermons from a Freising MSS). See also Roger Gryson (ed). *Scripta Arian Latina*, CCL 87 (1982) that contains 15 sermons from a Verona MSS.
99. Gregory of Nazianzus, *Oratio 43, In laudem Basilii* PG 36:561.
100. *Fasti consulares*, ed. Mommsen, 56.
101. Ibid, 73.
102. M. Dulaey, "Le fragment chronologique de Victorin de Poetovio et la culture grecque aux confins de l'Empire dans la seconde moitié du IIIe siècle," in *Cristianesimo Latino e cultura greca sino al sec. IV* (Rome: Institutum Patristicum Augustinianum, 1993), 127-45.
103. PL 129:1369.
104. *feriarum die, quem celebrantes mense Ianuario Christiani Epiphania dictitant, progressus in eorum ecclesiam sollemniter numine orato discessit. Rerum gestarum* 21.2.5.
105. In the same era, or a little later, in Africa, Optatus of Milevis does not mention it. Then, it is attested simultaneously by the Council of Saragossa (380), by Filaster of Brescia, and by Siricius (*Ep.* to Imerius of Tarragona: Jaffé 25) as *apparitio Christi*; as the adoration of the Magi by Augustine, Paulinus of Nola, and Prudentius; by Polemius Silvius and Peer Chrysologus as a feast in memory of "three miracles" (Magi, Cana, baptism). It is in this span of time that the theme of the feast is fixed in the West.
106. CTh 2.8.24 of 400 [405].
107. Filaster, *Haer* 140.1.
108. Augustine, *Epiphany*: Serm. 199-204; 373-75.
109. Also, by Macrobius, *Saturnalia* 2.4.11: "When Augustus heard news that, in Syria, Herod, King of the Hebrews, had all the children under two years (*intra bimatum*) killed, and among them his own son, he observed: It is better to be one of Herod's pigs than his son."
110. PG 46:1148C-1149C.
111. E. Theodorou, "Saint Jean Chrysostome et la Fête de Noël," in *Noël, Épiphanie retour du Christ*, ed. B. Botte, E. Mélia, etc. (Paris: Èditions du Cerf, 1967), 195-210.
112. PG 48:703.
113. Cassian, *Conferences* 10.2.
114. I. Calabuig, "The Liturgical Cult of Mary in the East and West," in *Handbook for Liturgical Studies: Liturgical Time and Space*, Vol. 5 (Collegeville, MN: Liturgical Press, 2016), 219-97; *Storia della mariologia*, Vol. 1 (Rome: Città Nuova Editrice, 2009); C. Maggioni, "Le feste mariane nell'antichità e nel primo medioevo: Theotokos," *Rivista interdisciplinare di mariologia* 16 (2008): 127-54; Philippe Beitia, "La vierge Marie dans les martyrologes latins," *Bulletin de littérature ecclésiastique* 109 (2008): 153-72; Michael O'Carroll, *Theotokos: A Theological Encyclopedia of the Blessed Virgin Mary* (Eugene, OR: Wipf and Stock Publishers, 2000); Bäumer, Remigius. *Marienlexikon* (St. Ottilien: EOS-Verl, 1988-1994), six volumes.
115. C. Milani, ed., *Itinerarium Antonini Placentini. Un viaggio in terra Santa del 560-570 d.C.* (Milan: Vita e pensiero, 1977).
116. E. Testa, *Maria Terra Vergine* (Jerusalem: Franciscan Printing Press, 1984), 26.
117. G. Giamberardini, "Il "Sub tuum praesidium" e il titolo "Theotokos" nella tradizione egiziana," *Marianum* 31 (1969): 324-62; *EAC* 3:644.
118. Stephen J Shoemaker, *Ancient Traditions of the Virgin Mary's Dormition and Assumption* (Oxford: Oxford University Press, 2002, repr. 2006), 98-99; S.C. Mimouni, *Les traditions anciennes sur la Dormition et l'Assomption de Marie: études littéraires, historiques et doctrinales* (Leiden: Brill, 2011).
119. Ps.-Dioscorus of Alexandria, CSCO 416, vol. 42, cc. VII-X (especially pp. 38f.; 47)
120. D. Baldi, *op. cit.*, 106; E. De Moreau, "L'Orient et Rome dans la fête du 2 février," *Nouvelle Revue théologique* 62 (1935): 5-20. Cf. E. Testa, *Maria Terra Vergine*, 146. Now especially S.J. Shoemaker, *Ancient Traditions*, 78-106.

121. G.M. Roschini, *Maria Santissima nella storia della salvezza*, vol. IV, *Il culto mariano* (Isola dei Liri: Pisani, 1969), 43.
122. Cf. *Il Libro del riposo etiopico* 4.89, *Gli Apocrifi del Nuovo Testamento* I.2, ed. M. Erebetta ([Torino]: Marietti, Casale Monferrato, 1983), 440. Cf. now E. Norelli, *Marie des apocryphes. Ce que la bible ne dit pas sur la Mère de Jésus* (Geneva: Labor et Fides, 2008).
123. *Transito della beata Vergine dello Ps. Melitone* (Erbetta, 2.1, 498). The fact that these texts were read publicly in the gathered community indicates that they were living texts and thus subject to further development and adaptation according to the theological tendencies of the communities themselves.
124. Kathisma could be the place where Mary, having dismounted from the donkey, rested on a stone (*Protoevangelium of James* 17.2–3). Cf. M. Aubineau, *Les homélies festales d'Hésychius de Jérusalem* (Bruxelles: Société des bollandistes, 1978), 136f.
125. J.A. De Aldama, "La primera fiesta de nuestra Señora" *Estudios Eclesiásticos* (cit. later as *Estudios Ecc.*) 40 (1965): 43-59.
126. M. Aubineau, *Les homélies festales*, 149f.
127. De Aldama, 46-51.
128. De Aldama, 52, for example, for Constantinople, the homily of Proclus is evidence; likewise, from the sermons of Peter Chrysologus for the church of Ravenna; perhaps also for Milan.
129. F.J. Leroy, *L'homilétique de Proclus de Constantinople* (Vatican City: Biblioteca apostolica vaticana, 1967), 66–67.
130. S.J. Shoemaker, *Ancient Traditions*, 115.
131. F.J. Leroy, *op. cit.*, 133f.
132. E. Russo, "L'affresco di Turtura nel cimitero di Commodilla, l'icona di S. Maria in Trastevere e le più antiche feste della Madonna a Roma," *Bulletino dell'Istituto Storico Italiano per il Medio Evo e Archivio Muratoriano* 88 (1979): 35-85; 89 (1980-1981): 71-150 (esp. 72-78).
133. D.M. Montagna, "La lode alla Theotokos nei testi greci dei secoli IV-VII," *Marianum* 24 (1962): 453-543.
134. E. Russo, 89 (1980-81): 78; S.C. Mimouni, *Dormition et assomption de Marie: histoire des traditions anciennes* (Paris: Beauchesne, 1995), 376-77.
135. Id., Paris, 1969, II ed., 156 ff. In two of these churches the relic clothing of the Madonna is venerated: cf. N. Baynes, "The Finding of the Virgin's Robe," in *Byzantine Studies and Other Essays* (London: University of London, Athlone Press, 1955), 240ff.
136. A. Cameron, "The Theotokos in Sixth-century Constantinople. A City Finds its Symbol," *Journal of Theological Studies* 29 (1978): 79-108.
137. Ibid., 104 and 106ff.
138. Th. Klauser, "Rom und der Kult der Gottesmutter," *Jahrbuch für Antike und Christentum* 15 (1972): 120-35 (esp. 121-26).
139. E. Russo, "L'affresco di Turtura nel cimitero di Commodilla," 83ff. This instance of St. Mary Major is the first indication of the theme of *Maria Regina*, a theme which develops in the course of the sixth century first in Rome and then in the East; in particular with Venantius Fortunatus. Cf. beyond this ample article by E. Russo, also M. Lawrence, "Maria Regina," *Art Bulletin* 7 (1924-1925): 150-61; A. Cameron, *The Theotokos in Sixth-century Constantinople*, 79-108 (spec.. 84f).
140. "The ever glorious Virgin Mary, Mother of God and of our Lord Jesus Christ." E. Russo, 87ff.
141. B. Capelle, "La fête de la Vierge à Jerusalem au Ve siècle," *Le Muséon* 56 (1943): 1-33 (now also in *Travaux Liturgiques*, vol. 3, Mont Césars/Louvain, 1967); I.-H. Dalmais, "Les Apocryphes de la Dormition et l'ancienne liturgie de Jérusalem," *Bible et terre Sainte* 179 (1979): 11-14.
142. P. Jounel, A.G.Martimort, *La Chiesa in Preghiera*, vol. IV, *La liturgia e il tempo* (Brescia: Queriniana, 1984), 158.
143. Niceforo Callisto, *Historia Ecclesiastica*, 17,28, *PG* 147:292A. The evidence is late. Cf. A. Cameron, 87 and 95f.
144. More indications for Syria are found in B. Capelle, "L'Assunzione e la liturgia," *Marianum* 15 (1953): 241-76 (esp. pp. 253f.).
145. On the importance of this feast, cf. M. van Esbroek, "La lettre de l'empereur Justinien sur l'Annonciation et la Noël en 561," *Analecta Bollandiana* 86 (968): 351-571; Ibid, "Encore la lettre de Justinien. Sa date: 560 et non 561," *Analecta Bollandiana* 87 (1969): 442-44. This last article offers more precise details about the letter, which is to be dated to 560, not 561.
146. A. Chavasse, *Le Sacramentaire gélasien*, 376-402.
147. M. Lamy, *L'Immaculée Conception: étapes et enjeux d'une controverse au Moyen-Âge (XIIe-XVe siècles)* (Paris: Institut d'études augustiniennes, 2000), 339-443.

148. The hypothesis is the dedication of a church to the Nativity of Mary: cf. *La preghiera della Chiesa*, vol. IV, ed. A.G. Martimort (Brescia: Queriniana, 1983), 158.
149. E. Cothenet, "Le Protoévangile de Jacques: origine, genre et signification d'un premier midrash chrétien sur la Nativité de Marie," *ANRW*, II, 25:5 (1988): 4252-69.
150. M. Erbetta, *Gli apocrifi del Nuovo Testamento*, 20-27.
151. E. Amman, *Protoévangile de Jacques et ses remaniements latins* (Paris: Letouzey et Ané, 1910), 109ff; 164ff.; M. Erbetta, 20.
152. Augustine, *Sermo* 290.2: PL 38:1313; *Ser.* 292.1: PL 38:1320.
153. D.M. Sartor, *Le feste della Madonna. Note storiche e liturgiche per una celebrazione partecipata* (Bologna: Edizioni Dehoniane, 1998), 61.
154. PG 97:1305-16. R. García, "Andrés de Creta: Doctor de la Inmaculada Concepción y teólogo clásico de la Asunción de María a los cielos," *Studium: Cuatrimestral Revista de filosofía y teología* 10 (1970): 3-52.
155. PG 96:1474-75.
156. PG 100:1335-1402.
157. *Liber Pontificalis*, I, 376, ed. Duchesne.
158. For some aspects this section refers back to A. Di Berardino, *I cristiani e la città antica nell'evoluzione religiosa del IV secolo*, 45-79; now also in: *Chiesa e Impero. Da Augusto a Giustiniano*, ed. E. dal Covolo and R. Uglione (Rome: LAS, 2001), 209-243; Ibid, "La cristianizzazione del tempo nei secoli IV-V: la domenica," *Augustinianum* 42 (2002): 97-125.
159. A.E. Samuel, *Greek and Roman Chronology. Calendars and Years in Classical Antiquity* (München: Beck, 1972), 171-77.
160. Cf. Minucius Felix, *Octavius* 12.5-6.
161. Cf. *EAC* 3:561-62.
162. Cf. A. Di Berardino, "La cristianizzazione del tempo nei secoli IV-V: la domenica," *Augustinianum* 42 (2002): 97-125.
163. Eusebius, *Vita Const.* 4.23.
164. *Vita Const.* 4.18. Eusebius repeats these motivations also in *Laudes Constantini* 9.10; PG 20:1437, cf. *De sepulchro Christi* 17.14: PG 20:1368 (part of the *Laudes Constantini*).
165. *Hist. Ecc.* 1.8.11; PG 67:880; SC 306:146.
166. CTh 2.8.18.
167. CTh 2.8.18: only here is there the *interpretatio*; 11.17.13.
168. CTh 2.8.18.
169. CTh 8.8.3.
170. CTh 2.8.18.
171. Cf. A. Di Berardino, *Tempo cristiano e la prima amnistia pasquale di Valentiniano I*, in: Miscellanea S. Pricoco, Soneria Mannelli 2003; Idem, "Christian Liturgical Time and Torture (Codex Theodosianus 9,35,4 and 5)," *Augustinianum* 51 (2011): 191-220.
172. CTh 9.38.3.
173. CTh 9.35.4.
174. CI 3.12.5.
175. In the law CTh 2.8.24 games are prohibited on Sundays, *religionis intuitu*.
176. CTh 2.8.19, preserved but expanded in the Codex Justinianus 3.12.6; cf. also the law of Theodosius II 15.5.5 of 425. A *Ratione tempers* refers to the effect of the passage of time on a tribunal's power or legislation.
177. CTh 2.8.19.
178. CTh 15.5.5.
179. In Egypt or in Jerusalem only the feast of Epiphany was celebrated, as the birthday of Christ.
180. CTh 15.5.5.
181. CI 3.12.6, under the rubric *De feriis*.
182. From the law of 425 it takes back up the feasts of Christmas and the Epiphany of Christ, as well as the proscription of spectacles on Christian feast days; from the law of 386 the norm on *iuridici* days.
183. CTh 2.8.19.
184. CTh 2.8.22.
185. It could be helpful to read this section in connection with the last section of the preceding chapter. E.D. Hunt, *Holy Land Pilgrimage in the Later Roman Empire A.D. 312-460* (Oxford: Clarendon Press, 1982); P. Maraval, *Lieux*

Saints et Pélerinages d'Orient. Histoire et géographie des origines à la conquête arabe (Paris: Cerf, 1985); *Akten des XII Internationales Kongress für christliche Archäologie* (Bonn: Aschendorffsche Verlagsbuchhandlung, 1995) (various contributors); D. Frankfurter, ed., *Pilgrimage and Holy Space in Late Antique Egypt* (Leiden: Brill, 1998); G. Otranto, "Il pellegrinaggio nel cristianesimo antico," *VetChr* 36 (1999): 239-57; *Pellegrini e luoghi santi dall'antichità al Medioevo*, ed. M. Mengozzi (Cesena: Il Ponte vecchio, 1999); J. Elsner and I. Rutherford, *Pilgrimage in Graeco-Roman and Early Christian Antiquity: Seeing the Gods* (Oxford: Oxford University Press, 2005); G. Otranto, "Caratteri identirari del pellegrinaggio dei cristiani nel rapporto con i "santuari," *Annali Storia Esegesi* 22 (2005): 99-117; *Pèlerinages et lieux saints dans l'Antiquité et le Moyen Âge: mélanges offerts à Mélanges Pierre Maraval*, ed. B. Caseau et al (Paris: Association des amis du Centre d'histoire et civilisation de Byzance, 2006).

186. Eusebius *HE* 6.11.2.
187. Eusebius, *Demonst. evang.* 6.18.23.
188. W. Eck, "Graffiti nei luoghi di pellegrinaggio dell'impero tardoantico," in *Tra epigrafia, prosopografia e archeologia* (Rome: Quasar, 1996), 107-123; Jas Elsner and Ian Rutherford, *Pilgrimage in Graeco-Roman and Early Christian Antiquity: Seeing the Gods* (Oxford: Oxford University Press, 2012); *Excavating Pilgrimage. Archaeological Approaches to Sacred Travel and Movement in the Ancient World*, ed. by Troels Myrup Kristensen, Wiebke Friese (Oxford: Routledge, 2017).
189. Eusebius, *Vita Const.* 3.42.
190. Jerome, *Ep.* 58.2.
191. Egeria, *Diary* 23.2-5. Gregory Nazianzus withdrew to that place for a few years in a monastery next to the sanctuary. (*Poem on his own Life* 545-551).
192. Augustine, *Enarr. in Ps.* 121.2.
193. Anna Maria Nieddu, *La Basilica Apostolorum sulla via Appia e l'area cimiteriale circostante* (Vatican City: Pontificio istituto di archeologia cristiana, 2009), 7-9.
194. The term was suggested to him by a graffiti interpreted as a list of provisions. For Ferrua, however, it is a list of pilgrim's clerics (ICUR 5:12911).
195. For the texts cf. A. Ferrua, ICUR 5:12907-13090.
196. ICUR 5:12966l.
197. ICUR 5:12911.
198. ICUR 5:12973.
199. ICUR 5:12959.
200. Paulinus, *Carmen* 27.
201. Augustine, *Ep.* 78.3.
202. Ch. et L. Pietri, "Le pèlerinage en Occident à la fin de l'Antiquité," *Les Chemins de Dieu: Histoire des pèlerinages chrétiens des origines à nos jours*, ed. Henry Branthomme and Jean Chélini (Paris: Hachette, 1982), 79-118.
203. *De miraculis* 1.5. PL 41:833-54; J. Meyers, *Les miracles de saint Etienne: Recherches sur le recueil pseudo-augustinien (BHL 7860-7861), avec édition critique, traduction et commentaire* (Turnhout: Brepols, 2006).
204. *De miraculis* 1.12.
205. *De miraculis* 1.11.
206. *De miraculis* 1.13.
207. *De miraculis* 2.2.
208. *De miraculis* 2.5.
209. Quodvultdeus, *De prom., Dim. Temp.* 9: SC 102:606.
210. *Uzalensis sum*: 1.14; PL 41:841.
211. *Patronum nostrum Stephanum primum martyrem*: Prol., PL 41:833.

CHAPTER 13
DEATH AND BURIAL OF CHRISTIANS AND THE CULT OF MARTYRS AND SAINTS

The Death of a Christian

When considering how Christians dealt with death, there are various elements that must be taken into consideration, such as the attitudes, words, aspirations, prayers, and gestures of the dying person and those connected to him or her. The combination of these elements gives Christian death its concrete meaning. Some of these were combined over time, influencing future generations' attitudes toward death. We have detailed knowledge of the last moments of death for at least some Christian such as the first martyr, Stephen, whose account is recorded in Luke's reconstruction in the *Acts of the Apostles*. There are also accounts of the many martyrs, such as Cyprian,[1] and the deaths of others such as Monica, Augustine, Ambrose, Martin of Tours, Macrina the sister of Basil, and Gregory of Nyssa, and others. These became the model for how to view death. Gregory of Nyssa describes the last hours of his sister Macrina: "She was not speaking with us who were near her, but kept her eyes fixed on her beloved. Her bed was turned toward the east. . . . She addressed words to God alone. She supplicated him with her hands, with a faint tone of voice, hardly perceptible."[2] Then he includes her prayer, which he actually wrote himself.

There are two main sources for reconstructing early Christians' attitudes toward dying: (1) literary sources which are in general written by pastors, and (2) archeological sources, especially those found in epigraphy which involves the study and interpretation of ancient inscriptions. These latter sources show us more concretely how death was lived out in the daily experience of various social classes, in various regions, in various contexts, and at various times. There is certainly an imbalance between theories and the actual life of persons regarding so personal and complex an aspect of life.

The Christian conception about life, death, the body of the deceased, the resurrection, and the life to come (eschatology)[3] distinguishes them from the pagan world and also from the Jewish world, if in a lesser way.[4] This has a determining influence also on funerary practices and customs. Right from the beginning Christianity presented itself as a religion of salvation.[5] Other religions of the time such as the mystery cults,[6] also sought to bestow salvation, a *soteria* amidst the difficulties of life achieved through initiation—a rebirth. The idea of rebirth is also found in the Mithras cult, through the *taurobolium*, a purification and rebirth brought about through the blood of a bull slain in a ritual manner.[7] Once the rite was complete, the initiate was reborn for eternity (*renatus in aeternum*).[8] Christian certainty about the life to come, on the other hand, was based on the resurrection of Christ who died and rose for us (*1 Cor* 15:20–23; cf. *Rom* 1:4; *2 Tim* 2:11–12). Christ conquers and destroys death.

Christian acceptance of martyrdom was founded on the idea of victory and eternal life. It was incomprehensible to the pagans that Christians would be able to face death for something not empirically verifiable. Ignatius of Antioch, who died in Rome around the year 111, demonstrates enthusiasm for being chosen to die and thus reach endless joy. In his *Letter to the Romans* he earnestly, almost impatiently, desires to give his life for Christ; "It is good for me to die in Jesus Christ rather than reign to the very ends of the earth. I seek him who died for us. I desire him who rose for us. Rebirth approaches me" (6.1). Belief in the resurrection of the whole human person, an idea entirely incomprehensible in a pagan context, constituted the basis of hope and of the capacity to face death even in the most excruciating forms of martyrdom. This conviction was derided by the pagan authorities during the trials in the tribunals. In the *Acts of the Martyrs* little is said of the resurrection, but Christians forcefully affirm their hope to live. The dialogue in Rome between Justin and the prefect Rusticus toward the year 165 remains a model for such an attitude: "The prefect said to Justin: – If you were whipped and beheaded, do you think you will ascend into heaven? Justin responds: – I trust to obtain it with my perseverance, if I do not cease to persevere. I know that this is reserved to those who have lived uprightly, but only at the complete conflagration of the world."[9]

The bodies of the martyrs of Lyon in 177 were left out on display for six days, subjecting them to ridicule. Then they were burned and the ashes were dispersed in the Rhone, "because, as they said: – they could not really hope in that resurrection, convinced by which they bring an unusual and strange religion into our cities and show spite for every torment and run ready and joyful to death. Let us see now if they will rise up again."[10] The ashes of other Christian martyrs were dispersed as well.[11] Was this gesture of the authorities motivated only by spite for the Christians or were there also other reasons too? The practice was to return the remains of the bodies of those slain, even of criminals, for burial. Christians were sensitive to and engaged in the burial of their martyrs.[12] The Roman practice and Roman law were not obligatory on this point. When there was an explicit request the bodies of the executed were given back—but at the authorities' discretion.[13] The case of Polycarp is illustrative. Nicetas, an important person in the province, asked the proconsul of Asia to deny the restitution of Polycarp's body "lest forsaking the one that was crucified, they begin worshiping this one." Others also were opposed to the restitution of his body. So the proconsul had Polycarp burned and allowed the Christians to collect the ashes to bury them.[14] The Christians of Smyrna collected the remains of the burned corpse of Polycarp:[15] "And thus, in the end, having gathered those bones that are more precious than rare gems and purer than fine gold, we put them where they rightfully belonged. And gathering together in this place with exultation and joy every time it will be possible; the Lord will grant us the opportunity to celebrate the anniversary of his martyrdom."[16] This is the first evidence of a commemoration of the day of a martyr's death—the *dies natalis*—since the day of death was considered the actual day of true birth. The churches drew up lists for these days. The *depositiones* of martyrs and bishops of the Roman church are preserved, having been drawn up before 336.[17]

In contrast to Polycarp, Cyprian's body had the honor of an almost solemn funeral, as we read in the biography written by Pontius. There was an even greater preoccupation with the burial of the martyrs, as we will discuss later in this chapter when dealing more fully with Cyprian. Eusebius calls the martyrs, "the soldiers of the new religion."[18] For Christians, as Augustine writes, it was their duty to bury the dead, but if it was not possible to bury them, the failure to do so did not constitute a difficulty for the future resurrection.[19]

Pagan epigraphy provides little hint of a future life in the fullest sense. Rather it begins with a dedication to the spirit or spirits of the dead. In Latin this is rendered as *di manes, or diis minibus*. The formula is normally abbreviated in the epigraphy as DM, or DMS (*dis manibus sacrum*). This formula also spread gradually into the provinces. Some inscriptions speak also of eternal sleep, of eternal memory, or of an eternal rest.[20] The inscriptions seem to aim to give consolation to the deceased, but in reality were addressed to the living. In Christian texts too, the conception of death as sleep was common.[21]

The significance of death and how one dies also conferred meaning on life. Thus, a specifically Christian way of dying also developed accompanied by such questions as: How does a person intend to die? How do they prepare for it? How do they live out the last moments of their earthly life? What gestures and rites are to be performed as death approaches? It is also necessary to observe how others live out another's death and what gestures they perform. Were certain gestures that we find in the lives of the martyrs and saints common? Prayers to accompany the death of a believer also arose at this time. A gesture that appeared early on was that of lifting one's eyes to heaven, or praying like Stephen: "Lord Jesus, receive my spirit" (*Acts* 7:59).

The council of Nicaea of 325 provides a rule and norm both for the reconciliation of the dying and concerning the communion to be given them. If they recovered, they must abstain from communion for a certain period of time (canon 13). Such a practical directive attaches itself to a traditional practice. The canon then begins to take on a more general character in its application, and this is where its innovative force is found, namely, to extend to all the possibility of receiving communion at the point of death.[22] In case of death baptism was administered at any time; the administration of baptism implied also the administration of confirmation and the Eucharist. The viaticum (reserved sacrament) must be administered to those who are dying and not to the dead, a practice condemned by the council of Hippo of 393 (canon 4). These more general observations will have to suffice for now as space will not allow us to go into the development of the numerous local observances that surrounded the death of a believer and his or her funeral.

BURYING THE DEAD

After Harnack, various scholars cite a phrase of the emperor Julian's who, in an effort to restore and reform the pagan cult, observed that the charitable work and care for the dead favored the spread of Christianity. "Do we not see that what especially contributed to the growth of atheism has been the philanthropy for strangers and care to bury the dead."[23] The cities and local or imperial authorities also sometimes concerned themselves with burying the dead, no doubt also for hygienic reasons.[24]

People in ancient times sought a burial place, as fitting as possible, attaching a great importance to it—much more so than even we do today. Thus, the Christians also considered it an urgent duty of charity to properly bury the indigent dead. How and where you were buried mattered. In his *Satyricon*, Petronius expressed the mentality of the ancient Romans by narrating how Trimalchio, who was anxious about his own death, was to have a stupendous monument and how he instructed the builder in all its numerous details, informing him of the inscription that should adorn his tomb (ch. 71). The anxiety to survive at least in memory characterized Roman or ancient humanity. Numerous inscriptions attest that many of their tombs were built while they were still alive, as still happens in some parts of Italy today. Here is one example from an agreeable pagan Roman: "Lucius Lectorius Pimitius, while alive, made this for himself and for his wife, rich in merits and devoted as she was, who lived with any arguments with her spouse, and for the devoted freedmen and freedwomen."[25] The domicile they were in now at their death would be their "forever house," as opposed to the temporary home they occupied while alive. The tomb was an *aeterna domus* for the deceased.[26]

A beautiful inscription for a freedman can explain well the importance of the tomb, in which the deceased leaves the image and impression he wants the reader to have of him:

> Stranger, stop and look left at this mound where the bones of an honest, merciful man are contained, a lover of the poor; I pray you, O passerby, do nothing ill to this monument. In this monument is buried C(aius) Ateilius Euhodus, freedman of Caius Ateilius Serranus, seller of pearls near the Via Sacra, O passerby I greet you. On the basis of his testament, it is not permitted that anyone be placed secretly into this monument, except those freedmen to whom I have given and granted it on the basis of the testament.[27]

Often the relatives or heirs constructed the tomb for their dear ones. Associations of a religious nature also had the responsibility of ensuring worthy burial for their members. A matter of intense scholarly debate is whether Christians in the first centuries also had recourse to the juridical fiction of being a funerary association (*collegium tenuiorum*).[28] In Christian circles, beyond the duty of individuals, there was an obligation of the communities to provide for burial.[29] In 177/178 the Christians of Lyon were troubled that they had not been able to bury their martyrs worthily.[30] Other authors also emphasize the Christian's special care for the deceased.[31] In the first half of the second century, Aristides of Athens writes that, when someone dies, Christians strive to collect the resources to be able to bury him or her [32] "If then they see a dead poor person, they bury him, contributing generously according to their own abilities."[33] Like other authors, Aristides lists some works of mercy typical of Christians as a community.

Lactantius writes: "There is a final service of piety of great importance, and that is the burial of travelers and the poor."[34] In Jerusalem there was already a communal effort to bury foreigners. Tertullian tells us of a "shared fund"[35] which, among other helpful works, served also for the burial of the poor (*egenis humandis*).[36] The *Apostolic Tradition* from the beginning of the third century, attributed to Hippolytus but of unknown origin, confirms this organization and these goals. The text shows us the communal organization for burial. Pseudo-Hippolytus speaks of the deacon Callixtus being in charge in Rome of the *koimeterion,* a Greek term rendered into Latin as *coemeterium* (from which we get our English word "cemetery").[37] Tertullian affirms that Christians also used costly herbs and spices to honor the body of the deceased: "If the Arabian lands complain, let the Sabaeans know that in greater quantity and at greater expense than for sending smoke to the gods their wares are used for burying Christians."[38]

Some authors such as Cyprian and Dionysius of Alexandria emphasized how, during the outbreak of plague in the middle of the third century, Christians took care to bury not only their co-religionists but all the dead. Cyprian exhorted his followers to bury everyone.[39] The same was true in Alexandria.[40] Eusebius praised the Christians' spirit of zeal for all, even for non-Christians.[41]

According to the *Apostolic Constitutions* (3.7) there were people in charge of burying the dead in a decent way. Alexandria had a whole organization for this service.[42] Ambrose considered burial, along with the ransom of prisoners,[43] such an important work that it was permissible and necessary to sell the sacred vessels to accomplish it.[44] Care for the deceased, so advanced and documented in Rome, remained a highly visible testimony to the Christians' care and concern for their neighbor, whether Christian or not.

According to Roman law the tomb was considered a religious object (*res religiosa*) and a religious place (*locus religious*).[45] The violation of graves has always been considered a most serious crime. A much studied inscription, for instance, is the so-called Nazareth inscription against the violation of tombs. Beginning sometime in the second century, sometimes funerary inscriptions bore the threat of a sepulchral fine (*multa sepulchralis*),[46] the payment of which was allotted to the tax office, the vestal virgins, the city government, or the treasury.[47] Sometimes curses were unleashed on violators.[48] Under the heading *De sepulchris violatis* the Theodosian Codex drew together seven laws, making no distinction between violation of a grave and violation of a corpse. The fines in inscriptions, the curses, and the laws suggest that violation of graves was frequent in the fourth century. In later times one sees that the fine is paid to the church.[49] Curses for violators were indeed, as we noted, inscribed on many tombs;[50] Christians, however, did not employ such curses, instead pointing out an eventual judgment by God[51] or a monetary penalty to be paid, as the inscription of Abercius prescribes: "No one should put anyone else in my grave, otherwise he will pay 2,000 gold coins to the treasury of the Romans and 1,000 to my beloved homeland."

In the fourth century another phenomenon occurred. Tombs were opened not to be violated but in order to transfer the occupant's bones—a practice connected to the widespread cult of the martyrs. Christians started removing the martyrs' bodies and transporting them elsewhere, what became known as the *inventiones* and *translationes* of relics.[52] This new practice contrasted with the prohibition against touching tombs and the obligation to place the bodies of the dead outside the city walls.[53] Even for the simple *translatio* (moving of the bones) the imperial authority's permission was necessary. Imperial prohibitions at any rate did not stop the phenomenon.[54] The cult of the martyrs' relics, which arose already in the second century was expanding in an impressive way by the fourth century. The greatest change consisted in the unification of the city of the living and the city of the dead with the transferal and burial of the dead inside the walls.

The Body of the Dead

Christians, unlike Jews, Greeks, and Romans, established a serene and even joyful relationship with the bodies of the dead. The dead were not a cause of religious impurity or even of fear, as we shall see. Today we do not know much about the bedrooms and kitchens of ancient homes, but we actually know more about the places where they laid their dead. There was great concern for having a dignified tomb. Ancient ritual differences reflect the religious and social conceptions deriving from prescriptions of religious purity and from the conception of life after death.

A first consideration was: cremation or burial?[55] During the Roman Empire two ways of treating the bodies of the dead were prevalent: cremation and burial. Mummification as the physical preservation of the body was relatively rare but was still practiced in Egypt. That tradition was followed by the Coptic Christians too. In cremation the body of the deceased is burned, and the ashes are gathered in an urn or are scattered. Much ancient mortuary evidence attests to this practice. Burial included the preparation of the body for burial. The Roman tradition followed either of the two rites of cremation or burial. For the remains of cremation, they used the *cineraria*, while for burial they used various forms of sarcophagi or other arrangements. In the first century, burial was considered a Roman custom, *Romanus mos*.[56]

The Jewish tradition preferred burial,[57] except in special cases; cremation was utilized only in certain instances (*Jer* 34:5; *2 Chron* 16.14). This tradition was followed by Christians. Minucius Felix writes: "Nor, as you believe, do we fear any loss from sepulture, but we adopt the ancient and better custom of burying in the earth. See, therefore, how for our consolation all nature suggests a future resurrection."[58] It is not an absolute refusal of cremation, but is done out of respect for the body that had been inhabited by the soul.

In the near East the preoccupation with impurity caused by the corpse was wide-spread (*Num* 19:16; *Deut* 21:22–23). Contamination came about through contact with a human corpse and with animal corpses (*Lev* 5:2–3; 11:24–27). The priests especially must maintain ritual purity and must not contract an impurity from a corpse (*Lev* 21:1–5, 22:8; *Num* 6:6–7). Later on, the rabbis tried to delimit the scope of impurity from the corpse of the deceased.[59] In the pagan Roman world the corpse also created impurity. Cicero speaks of the purification of members struck with impurity that was produced with the death of one of their members. The rite was necessary for reintegrating them into the civil community.[60]

Christians disregarded all these prescriptions.[61] They did not consider the bodies of the dead as means of transmitting impurity. On the contrary, the cult of martyrs spread as well as that of the non-martyr saints. Then again, a somewhat even festive rapport was also established with the bodies of normal Christians. The bodies of some martyrs particularly acquired a special protective value and became sources of holiness. Hence the practice of being buried as close as possible to a special tomb, ideally next to the body of a dead martyr (*Ad sanctos*).[62] This custom was completely antithetical to the concept of any type of impurity arising from the dead. The practice of not considering the corpse impure is confirmed by some literary texts as well. The first is found in the *Didascalia,* a text of the first half of the third century (26.8; 6.21.8; 6.22.1). Among other things it adds: "Gather in cemeteries to read sacred Scripture and offer your prayers and your rites to God, disregarding the (Jewish) observances, and to offer an acceptable Eucharist, figure of the royal body of Christ."[63] The *Apostolic Constitutions* (Syria ca. 380), include these same ideas, and affirms: "Without any observation, gather together in cemeteries to read the holy books and sing psalms, for the martyrs who have fallen asleep, for all the saints who have been from the beginning of the world, for your brothers who have fallen asleep in the Lord."[64] The author goes on to affirm that the body is holy and not even the clergy is contaminated by it. I think that the two texts, if on one hand they demonstrate a Christian practice of behavior in relation to funerals and corpses, on the other hand they are polemical texts against traditionalists and followers of Jewish traditions. Christians break down the wall of separation between the living and the dead, so as not to distinguish the city of the living and the necropolis which is the city of the dead, to the point of bringing the bodies of the deceased *intra muros,* that is, within the walls.

Around certain special tombs a crowd of the dead was created on all sides. From the tomb of a martyr in the subterranean cemeteries, burial areas branch out in all directions, which come to be called *retrosanctos*. There was even a sort of competition for a prime spot, according to what is said in a Roman inscription on a woman's tomb in 382 (the actual date is indicated): *sepulchrum intra limina sanctorum, quod multi cupiunt et rari accipiunt* (here lies a grave on the threshold of the saints, which many desire and few receive).[65] She managed to obtain this privilege since she was an *amator pauperum* (lover of the poor). This not always satisfied desire was still obtained by two women, Valeria and Sabina, who during their life bought the place for two bodies from Apro and Victor in the new crypt behind the saints.[66] It could happen that tomb-sellers would profit from them by creating as many tombs as possible in a small space, while also reusing earlier tombs.

This practice was widespread in the East and in the West because it was considered efficient. In his small work *De Cura pro Mortuis Gerenda*, addressed to Paulinus of Nola who wanted to learn from him what benefit there was for someone to be buried near the *memoria* of a saint, Augustine summarizes Paulinus's thought in this way: "You add that the ancient practice of the universal Church to pray for the dead cannot be without meaning; and from this practice one can deduce that it is also beneficial for man, after death, if the affectionate care of his dear ones in burying his body also allots him a place that expresses in itself the desire of the saints' protection."[67] Augustine answers that the quality of life lived before death has value, because the Lord recompenses according to the works completed. The prayers said during the Mass and personal prayers for the dead can be of help to the dead, if they can receive help, and can also help the living.

Pagans considered this practice disgusting, like that of venerating a corpse (Christ) or the martyrs. The most well-known attitude was that of the emperor Julian, called the Apostate. To avoid *pollutio*[68] he prohibited the celebration of funerals during the day and issued an edict against it on February 12, 363, when he was in Antioch (CTh 9.17.5).[69] Elsewhere he observed that Christians "have filled the world with tombs and graves,"[70] referring to the cult of the martyrs.

The reasons for the regulation of Julian are explained in Letter 136b, since through law he wanted to reestablish the ancient custom. For him, having a funeral in the daily life of a city was absolutely unacceptable. Seeing a funeral bier was a sinister omen. It was not permissible for biers to pass near temples; moreover, the cult for the infernal gods (the gods that resided in the inferno of hell) was practiced at night.

Funerary Rites

These rites varied according to culture and religion in relation to their conception of life and death. Christians usually eliminated whatever did not fit with the Christian faith. Often they accommodated themselves to the local practice, giving new meanings to certain traditional gestures; while in other cases, they just accepted them as is. Some rites were not strictly connected with religion, and these could be preserved. At any rate, local traditions were important to the Christians, even if some spread more widely if they originated from the great churches. Others disappeared. The living people wanted to preserve the memory of the dead and establish a positive or sometimes negative relationship with them.

Some of these rites, which can be reconstructed using various types of evidence such as literary, epigraphic, and archeological evidence, concern the treatment of the corpse before burial, while others are connected with the tomb of the deceased. All are related to the concept of death and of the body of the deceased. In the fourth century cremation disappeared almost entirely. Thus with the spread of the practice of burial, the rites associated with it also underwent transformation. More attention was paid to the body of the deceased, hoping that it would in some way be preserved.

In the New Testament there are a few, brief mentions of the dead and their burial: that of the deacon Stephen, and of Ananias and Sapphira. The body of the deceased was washed and sprinkled with perfumes, as happened with the burial of Jesus. Various pieces of information come from Acts and from the Passions of the martyrs. Others we can find in texts and the numerous tombs that still exist.

Among the ancients, when the person was thought to have expired, to be certain of his death, his name was shouted (*conclamatio*), a rite that could last a long time and is represented on sarcophagi. Dirges were played and recited. Christians, however, prayed.[71] The dead person's eyes were closed, the body washed with warm water and wrapped in linen cloth, and perfumes were also used.[72] The corpse was crowned with flowers—a custom condemned by Tertullian—and covered in a shroud if the person died in the afternoon or evening; otherwise the corpse was buried the same day. Gregory of Nyssa writes about the death of Macrina: "I remembered the desire she expressed to me that I be the one to close her eyes and to attend to the customary care of the body."[73]

Eusebius includes a passage from a letter of Dionysius of Alexandria that narrates what the Christians did in the city during the plague of 252, purifying the eyes of the dead: "The best of our brothers—presbyters, deacons, and laypeople. . . grasped the bodies of the holy ones to their chests, purified their eyes and closed their mouths, then carried them on their shoulders and arranged the corpses; close to them, they embraced them, washed them, decorated them with vestments."[74] Augustine closed his mother Monica's eyes.[75] John Chrysostom criticized the practice of using aromatic herbs that was still practiced in his time at Antioch.[76] He too mentions, however, the normal rites of preparation for the corpse.[77] Augustine limited himself, as in other aspects, to emphasizing the uselessness of certain rites and certain expenses, like the use of perfumes.[78] Because of the decrease in importing costly products in the fourth century, only the rich could afford and use them. Normal people contented themselves with less or with just a little sprinkling.[79]

The remains were wrapped in a cloth or also with costly garments, as Lactantius says.[80] Augustine also refers to the African practice: "[The deceased] bears with himself the shroud in which he was wrapped, and that which was spent for him, to construct a precious sepulcher of marble and to inscribe the stones."[81] Jerome also mentions the use of a sheet to wrap the corpse.[82] Traces of costly garments are also found in the catacomb burials. The long galleries of niches on both sides in the catacombs contained bodies wrapped in sheets, in the folds of which lime had sometimes been spread for disinfection and for an inexpensive embalming. The niche was then enclosed with tiles or with one or more slabs of marble carefully secured with lime. I still remember that, in my part of Italy, the elderly were concerned with purchasing new and suitable clothes in which to dress their dead body. Thus, the corpse was laid in the tomb, sometimes a very simple one, sometimes very rich, like certain sarcophagi, but without the use of a wooden casket.

A description of the preparation of the body is found in the *Passion of Peter* (4th c):

> And then, when all the people answered 'Amen' in a loud voice, Peter surrendered his spirit. And immediately Marcellus, without waiting for anyone's opinion, but seeing that the blessed

Apostle had breathed his last, took down the sacred body from the cross with his own hands, washed it with milk and the best wine, and grinding 1500 minas of mastic and aloe, with myrrh and silphium (?), and oil of myrrh along with the various other spices—another 1500 minas—he embalmed him most lovingly. He also filled a new sarcophagus with Attic honey and placed the body, anointed with the perfumes, in it.[83]

Some objects connected with the life of the deceased were then placed within the tomb. Sometimes a coin was also put inside the burial space or inserted into the mouth of the deceased or into his hand. This pagan custom goes back to the tradition that the coin was good for paying Charon to ferry the deceased across the Styx. The coin in the tomb could also have other meanings or be part of the funerary endowment.[84] Jerome recalls that various flowers were also put on the tomb, while Pammachius honored his wife with works of charity.[85]

Aristides of Athens, who wrote between 124 and 126, spoke of how Christians behaved at the death of one of their own: "If a just one among them dies, they rejoice and give thanks, they pray for him and accompany him as if he had made a journey."[86] Tertullian notes the prayer made by a presbyter near the body of a deceased woman.[87] Furthermore, in other works such as the *De Corona*, he notes the *Oblationes pro defunctis, pro nataliciis, annua die facimus* (we make offerings for the dead, we keep the feast of the martyrs' anniversary).[88] More than once Cyprian confirms this practice of celebrating for the dead. Yet if a presbyter has died, without having observed the ecclesiastical rules, then the sacrifice should not be offered for him, *pro dormitione defuncti*, as is said about a presbyter of Furni.[89] It is necessary to register the dates of the martyrs' deaths because "to commemorate them we make offerings and sacrifices that we will soon celebrate as a group."[90] "For them we always offer sacrifices, every time we celebrate with a commemoration of the passions and the anniversary days."[91] For the martyrs they celebrated a commemoration to remember their *dies natalis*, as on the Roman feast of the *parentalia* in February.[92] The Christian vision developed quite rapidly as something different from the pagan tradition. Origen, as early as the first decades of the third century, writes: "Supplication may be addressed only to the saints (martyrs), if someone is found to be a Peter or a Paul so as to help us by making us worthy to share their authority of forgiving sins."[93]

Rich archeological evidence comes from the *memoria Apostolorum* on the Via Appia Antica that we spoke about in the previous chapter. Here, from 258 on, a commemoration of Peter and Paul is held on June 29.[94] The cemetery basilica *ad Catacumbas* was built in the first decades of the fourth century, perhaps by the emperor Constantine. Earlier, there was a place for the cult of the two apostles that was frequently visited.[95] This small sanctuary, as we noted, was built between 244 and 258 on three decorated mausoleums that were buried. Much of the graffiti on the walls consists in requests for the two apostles' intercession[96]: Peter and Paul pray for (name) (*Petre et Paule petite pro* (name);[97] Peter and Paul, keep in mind, in your prayers (*Petre et Paule in mente [h]abete in orationibus vestris*).[98] "Keep in mind" (*in mente habete*) recurs about sixty times. Sometimes it is a family group that makes the request[99] or for friends.[100] They pray for the living and the dead and they might also record the fulfillment of a vow.[101] One graffito reads, *X kl. Iulias Paule Petre in mente habete Sozomenum, et tu qui leges* (July 22, Peter and Paul remember Sozomen and you too who are reading this).[102] The writer asks for the intercession of Peter and Paul and asks for a prayer from the reader. Peter's name generally precedes Paul's in most literature, but in Greek graffiti Paul's name precedes Peter's when the two apostles are invoked together.

Augustine observes that such commemorations are done in order to stir up the imitation of the living and to seek intercession.[103] Numerous inscriptions are addressed to the martyrs to ask for their intercession. In Eastern Christianity we have the evidence of Eusebius: "These honors are perfectly fitting, after death, to those who are beloved of God, who can quite rightly be defined, without fear of refutation, as the soldiers of the true religion."[104] Gregory of Nyssa whom we have already mentioned describes in detail the moments of prayer, first around the dying person and then around her body. It is clothed with garments of white linen as if it were a bride. Then everyone sings "as is usual on the feast of the martyrs." A large procession makes its way toward the place of burial, and the bier is carried by the clergy. They did not use closed caskets. The entombment is accompanied by continual chants and prayers in the very tomb of the parents, whose remains are visible.[105] The *Apostolic Constitutions* mention chants and prayers to be recited on the anniversary days and how the clergy should behave when they participate in the commemoration of the dead.[106]

Augustine also speaks of a Eucharistic celebration on the death of his mother at Ostia in 387.[107] The council of Hippo in 393 prescribes: "I hold it opportune to prohibit anyone from daring to celebrate the Eucharist in the presence of bodily remains, or to give part of the Holy Body to a lifeless cadaver."[108] This prohibition relates perhaps to the custom referred to by the *Life of Melania*, where the Latin text mentions that it is a custom of the Romans to have the *communion Domini* at the moment that the soul leaves the body.[109]

When Monica died in Ostia in the summer of 387:

> Evodius took up the Psalter and began to sing, with the whole household responding, the psalm, 'I will sing of mercy and judgment unto you, O Lord.' And when they heard what we were doing, many of the brothers and religious women came together. And while those whose office it was to prepare for the funeral went about their task according to custom, I discoursed in another part of the house, with those who thought I should not be left alone, on what was appropriate to the occasion. . . . So, when the body was carried forth, we both went and returned without

tears. For neither in those prayers which we poured forth to you, when the sacrifice of our redemption was offered up to you for her—with the body placed by the side of the grave as the custom is there, before it is lowered down into it—neither in those prayers did I weep.[110]

Augustine emphasizes that everything is done according to local custom. By contrast, concerning the death of a young man of Uzalis in Africa, he includes the letter of Evodius: "We had quite an honorable and worthy funeral for such a noble soul. For three days we praised the Lord in chorus with hymns, above his burial place, and on the third day we offered the sacrifice of our redemption."[111] At the death of Augustine himself a Mass was celebrated: "In our presence a sacrifice was offered to God for him to entrust him to God in his departure, and he was buried."[112]

A period of mourning known as the *tempus lugendi* followed the burial. It was a time for weeping during which in Roman law it was forbidden for the widow to remarry. During this period the deceased was commemorated on the third, seventh, or ninth day, and on the thirtieth and fortieth, with a funeral banquet during which Christians also celebrated the Eucharist.

Dies Natalis and *Refrigerium*

Christians used a new language to speak about death, although they still partially used some pagan terminology. They also created new symbols too, which they placed on the tomb. Sarcophagi reveal this shift, with their biblical depictions, symbols of the resurrection, and the cross as a sign of victory. Death itself becomes a *natalis*, a birth, and the anniversary day is a *dies natalis* to remember.[113] The phrase is first found in about the middle of the second century, in the *Martyrdom of Polycarp* (18.3). The idea is already present in Ignatius of Antioch in his letter to the Romans: "I desire him who has risen for us. My rebirth is near."[114] Tertullian speaks of the *natalicia* of the martyrs.[115] At Rome the official term used was *depositio* (deposition), as in the deposition of martyrs and bishops (*depositiones martyrium* and *depositiones episcoporum*). Jerome used the term *dormitio* (to fall asleep) because death is like falling asleep and rest: "Indeed it is not called death but sleeping and rest."[116] Thus, in his consolatory letters he normally uses the term dormition (*dormitio*).

The deceased was buried right away so that the day of death and of burial coincide. In this case the *depositio* and the *dies natalis* occur on the same day and so the two terms indicate the same thing.[117] However, when burial came to be deferred in the fourth century, some inscriptions make note of the gap.[118] The expression *dies natalis* came after the *depositio*. In the earlier period before the fourth century one normally used the single term *natalis*.

The pagans celebrated people's *natalicium*, that is, their birthday, the most important being that of the *paterfamilias*. In Paulinus of Nola, however, this term indicates the *dies natalis* of St. Felix, that is, his death. On the occasion of the anniversary of his death, every January 14, he composed a poem, and in total there are fourteen *Natalicia*. Augustine also used this term often on the *dies natalis* of the martyrs.[119] The same phrase *dies natalis* meant, for the pagans, the day of birth, but for the Christians, as we have seen, the day of death, that is, their birth to heaven.

Cyprian encouraged the noting down of the exact day to be able to recall it in the future.[120] In Carthage there was a register of names and of dates of death (burial) of martyrs for liturgical commemoration through the offering of the Eucharistic sacrifice.[121] The list of dates, the *fasti* calendar, had to be kept up to date. Cyprian's *Letter* 80 mentions the recording of the death of Pope Sixtus and his four deacons.[122] Likewise, the Acts (or *gesta*) must be taken care of so that they are read.[123] This attention has preserved for us a rich patrimony of African hagiographic texts.

A text of Augustine's from the beginning of the fifth century helps explain many things:

> May the Holy Spirit inspire in us what would be best to say in this circumstance: we should indeed say something in praise of Cyprian, a most glorious martyr, whose Nativity we celebrate today, as you know. The Church frequently repeats this term, that is, 'birthday,' to the point of calling the precious deaths of the martyrs Nativities. Thus, I repeat, this manner of speaking is so customary for the Church that even those who do not pertain to the Church repeat it along with her.[124]

In late antiquity the day of death (*dies mortis*) is noted in line with pagan practice, instead of the *dies natalis*.[125]

On such a day, there was among Christians, as I have mentioned, a liturgical commemoration for the martyrs and afterwards for the saints. The meetings or assemblies have a different character, and not all are the same, according also to the time and place. One can celebrate the Eucharist and thus make it a commemorative gathering, as Augustine says in a sermon.[126] This custom is attested in various places from the third century on[127] and in the East too.[128] During mass the diptychs were read, and the names of the deceased were also mentioned.[129]

When a meal was eaten provision was made so that the dead could participate in some way in order to offer them relief. Hence the name *refrigerium*—which means relief, refreshment, or comfort—was used for these convivial gatherings.[130] The term *refrigerium* mainly means physical relief but comes to mean also a spiritual relief and the future happiness of paradise. The first mention is found in Tertullian: "In reality she prays for his soul and invokes relief (*refrigerium interim*) for him for the period of waiting and of enjoying his company in the first resurrection. She makes offerings on the day of his *dormition*."[131] In another work as well

Tertullian recalls the prayer of a husband for his deceased wife: "So you pray for her spirit and every year offer anniversary oblations for her."[132]

Other rites were also performed at tombs, but these could also degenerate into less than sacred affairs. Food and drink such as wine or milk were poured through holes or pipes built into the tomb itself in order to feed the dead. Archeology has preserved many traces of this rite. Naturally these banquets must be performed with much joy and celebrating.[133] The most ancient indications of this practice were found under the afore-mentioned basilica of St. Sebastian on the Via Appia Antica. Here about ten graffiti record that a *refrigerium* had been celebrated there.

In a beautiful Christian mosaic in the vicinity of Tipasa (Algeria), from the end of the fourth century, various fish were depicted to indicate a funerary banquet. The inscription reads: "In (the name) of Christ our God let peace and concord rule in our banquet" (*in Chr[isto] Deo, pax et concordia sit convivio nostro*).[134] The two terms "peace" and "concord" must evoke the atmosphere that should preside during the banquet to express the coexistence that links the living and the dead.[135]

Cyprian himself condemned a traditional custom followed by Christians too. Near the tombs of the dead, funerary banquets were held that were considered to be immoral, which he characterized as "vile and rich pagan banquets."[136] Earlier Tertullian had already condemned them only insofar as they were idolatrous.[137] Libations were made and food was offered to the dead. In the years of Cyprian, in Pontus, Gregory Thaumaturgus permitted them in order to facilitate the conversion of the pagans.[138] In reality, over a century later, Basil of Caesarea still had to fight against certain abuses. He criticized women who transformed the cemetery into a place of obscene amusements.[139]

To avoid abuses, the bishops actively fought against them. Ambrose's action is well known, since he mentions the abuses at Milan concerning "those who take chalices to the tombs of the martyrs to drink them until evening in that place."[140] Monica, who held to the African tradition, wanted to follow the same practice in Milan too.[141]

In Africa, Augustine, along with the other bishops, especially Aurelius of Carthage, energetically battled against the degeneration of these banquets for funerals or in honor of the martyrs while praising also their positive aspects. He deplored and combatted against the abuses done in relation to the celebration of the martyrs from 392 onward[142]: "The revelry and drunkenness, in fact, are considered permissible and licit to the point that they are celebrated even in honor of the most blessed martyrs, not just on solemn days (and who on earth does not see that this is deplorable, as long as he does not observe them only with the eyes of the flesh?), but even daily."[143] Augustine spiritualizes and offers another dimension: "Ultimately, we think we can be helpful to the dead only by interceding for them devoutly with the Eucharistic sacrifice, with prayers, with alms."[144] But the Christian tradition of offering alms and doing charitable deeds to help the poor for the sake of the dead had already been affirmed.[145] In Rome on the feast of the *cathedra Petri* (February 22), the *caristia* which came at the conclusion of the *parentalia* was celebrated where people brought food offerings to the tombs of the deceased.

These banquets subsided with the transferal of tombs to the area within the cities, themselves already reduced in size, and through the spread of sentiments proposed by many bishops like Augustine who said, "These [the outward forms that accompanied burial] are more solace for the living than any comfort for the dead" (*magis sunt vivorum solatia, quam subsidia mortuorum*).[146] Moreover, typically Christian practices that became associated with the burials spread as well, such as prayer and the Eucharistic sacrifice.[147]

CHRISTIAN CEMETERIES

Early on Christians were buried in the same places[148] as everyone else, that is, in burial grounds—necropolises—or along the roads that branched out from the cities. The physical separation of the tombs came about slowly, in different moments and different places. The inscription of Abercius, in Hierapolis in Phrygia Salutaris, was placed along the street and those passing by could read the inscription that he had composed while alive. The author of the *Epistle to Diognetus* affirmed that "Christians, living in Greek and barbarian cities, however it happens for each person, are not distinguished from other men by their attire, adapting themselves to the customs of the place in dress, food, and the rest."[149] Paul was buried in a pagan necropolis. The Vatican necropolis, where Peter was buried, was also pagan. Other Christians were also buried there. When the pagan family of the Julii became Christian, they decorated their funerary chamber with mosaics of a Christian character. In the necropolis of Portus there was the tomb of the Christian Telesphorus.

Thus, if there are not specifically Christian elements present with the tombs, it is hard to distinguish a Christian from a pagan tomb. Even the most ancient Christian epigraphy followed the style of the time and only slowly acquired typically Christian characteristics. The place where the burial inscriptions are found indicates the condition of the deceased Christian, but a strict distinction in burial between Christians and pagans did not exist, especially in the first two centuries, and not even all that much in the following centuries.

Archeologists distinguish between private and communal burial places, that is, those burial places that were under communal control and were for all Christians. The anonymous *Apostolic Tradition* speaks of the obligation of burying the destitute as a duty of the ecclesial community.[150] Some tombs were also reserved, for example, for a family (*sepulchra familiaria*) and also for heirs (*sepulchra ereditaria*). The founders who established the tomb decided who could be buried there. An inscription from the end of the third century, in the Catacomb of

Domitilla in Rome, says: "M. Antonius Restitutus built the hypogeum for himself and for his relatives who believe in the Lord."[151] In a hereditary burial place it was not allowed to exclude heirs on religious grounds.

Burial places including Christian cemeteries were located outside the city walls. If the city later grew and expanded, such burial places ended up on the inside of the city walls. Not all provincial cities respected the norm of distinguishing the city of the living from the city of the dead (necropolis).

Christian cemeteries arose in Rome because of the beneficence of wealthy families who supported the burial of other believers on their properties outside the city walls. The private catacombs of Domitilla, Priscilla, and Praetextatus, for example, were expanded in order to make room for the tombs of other people as well. Some catacombs could themselves be expansions of private pagan burial places, as in the case of Domitilla's. Others, however, arose through the initiative of the local community. In Caesarea of Caesarean Mauritania (today Cherchel, Algeria), a lover of the Word (Christ) built a burial place at his own expense: "An adorer of the Word donated the area for burial / and built the cell (=tomb building) entirely at his own expense. / He left this monument to the holy church. / Hail, my brothers of pure and simple heart. / I, Evelpius, greet you in the Holy Spirit. / The church of the brothers restored this *titulus* of Marcus Antonius Julianus [?] Severianus, of the most noble rank. Composition by Asterius."[152] In Caesarea the presbyter Victor also built a tomb for the burial of various people.[153] Other tombs, especially outside Rome, arose through the work of the local community and were their property. A certain Faltonia Hilaritas had a *coemeterium* built—a tomb—at her own expense and donated it to "this religion." [154]

The cemeteries could be above ground, especially along roads, or underground when the terrain lent itself to being excavated easily. The underground cemeteries are called *catacombs* today, a term that, in antiquity, indicated a single underground cemetery of Rome along the Via Appia, called *ad Catacumbas*, under the basilica of St. Sebastian.[155] It was only in the Middle Ages that the rumor spread that Christians hid in the catacombs during the persecutions—an absurd and impossible thing. The cemeteries above ground have almost all been destroyed; the underground ones, on the other hand, are better preserved,[156] even if through the centuries they have been systematically plundered of mortal remains and artifacts. The pillagers were particularly interested in the bodies of saints.

Construction of a cemetery underground begins at one point and can then branch out in different directions with progressive expansion; you can move to a lower level with the same system of galleries linked together and arranged in a regular scheme. That all supposes an initial plan that foresees an almost indefinite expansion. All the spaces are intentionally planned out to maximize the area for burial. There were also privileged spaces for some people to construct monumental tombs, for example the so-called crypt of the Popes in the catacomb of Callixtus, where nine bishops of Rome were buried. Five original Greek inscriptions are preserved for five bishops: Pontian (230 – 235), Anterus (†236), Fabian (†250), Lucius I (†254) and Eutychianus (†283); the others are in Latin (e.g. Cornelius, †253).[157] The inscriptions carry just the name with the addition of EPI(SCOPOS), and two carry the label of martyr. Nearby is the crypt of St. Cecilia who was buried in a sarcophagus.

In antiquity the term cemetery (*coemeterium*) is used by both Jews and Christians. In the pagan world it means the place in the house where one sleeps. Some Christian authors dwell on its etymological meaning, like John Chrysostom, for whom the resurrection is viewed as a waking up from sleep.[158] In the pagan world death was also compared to sleep, but in terms of an endless sleep. The word *depositio* when used by Christians meant that the laying down of the body is only temporary, in anticipation of the resurrection.[159] Christians noted the date of death on the tomb, which became important for commemorating the dead, and in the process discounted the date of birth. This is a major innovation, even if it can be understood in relation to a tendency that is being affirmed in a pagan sphere as well.

The discussion about the emergence of the first places reserved for Christian burials depends on the meaning one attributes to the term *cemetery*. In Christian language it certainly meant a "place of rest," or "a sleeping chamber," but did it also mean a cemetery in the technical sense, as is usually said? É. Rebillard has shown that it initially meant only the tomb of a martyr and is a synonym of *martyrium*.[160]

The first evidence that Christians had their own places for burial is found in Tertullian, who includes a request from pagans: "Let the places of burial be taken away from the Christians." He wrote this around 212 and the Latin term he uses here for burial places is *areae*.[161] This much debated expression does not mean that they already had their own cemeteries, but they had at least some burial area. The first evidence of a communal Christian cemetery, perhaps just for martyrs, comes from Rome. The deacon Callixtus († 222) was the official responsible for it.

It seems that in Carthage and elsewhere in the middle of the third century there were burial places that were reserved for Christians. Cyprian considered it inconceivable for Christians to be buried along with pagans. Thus, it was a scandal for him that the Spanish Bishop Martial had buried his sons along with pagans of a *collegium* (i.e. a civic or religious organization) through non-Christian rites.[162] The scandal arose from the fact that on certain occasions pagan ceremonies were held in those places.[163] Perhaps that is the reason for his indignation and not the fact that they had been buried with pagans. The poet Commodian, who writes in the second half of the third century, criticized Christians who sought a sumptuous funeral, having recourse even to the *collegia*.[164] The *Acta Cypriani* (1.7 and 5), however, are sure evidence for Christian burial locations.[165] Valerian had ordered Christians not to go into cemeteries. Since he speaks of meetings with the clergy, such cemeteries could be just *martyria*. One of the main reasons to have exclusive burial places for the faithful was the fact that the practice had arisen of celebrating the Eucharist in connection with the tombs. The sense of solidarity with the poor, the importance of having a decent burial, and the greater economic resources of the large communities favored the construction of cemeteries reserved for Christians.

In Rome in the first years of the third century, communal cemeteries arose under the control of the clergy. Callixtus, later bishop of Rome, was put in charge of the cemetery that bears his name by Zephyrinus (198/199–217). Then other Roman cemeteries arose, the catacombs, which were under the clergy's control. But some Christians were also buried in family tombs. Or there were private cemeteries, as was the case with the catacomb of Via Latina, where pagans and Christians were both buried.[166]

Even though they were plundered, the catacombs have given us a great quantity of pictures, objects, and inscriptions. In larger spaces more costly tombs were created, with simple pictures of biblical scenes that suggest the idea of salvation: e.g. Jonah, the youths of Babylon saved from the fire, Daniel in the lions' den, Noah saved from the flood, and the resurrection of Lazarus. Many symbols were adapted to express Christian beliefs, such as the fish which was a symbol of Christ,[167] the anchor which symbolized the firmness of faith, a dove which symbolized the peace of paradise, and the figure of the good shepherd who cares for his sheep, for example. Today we are surprised also by the excessive number of small niches for infants. The phenomenon however is explained by the high infant mortality rate.

When the cult of martyrs developed in the fourth century alongside the traditional cult of the dead, large churches connected to the catacombs were built. To facilitate pilgrims' access, even from the time of the great cultivator of the martyrs Pope Damasus (366–384), new entrances were opened up and additional routes through the catacombs were constructed along with skylights that allowed light and air to enter. Restrooms were constructed and even written guides were prepared for the visitors to the catacombs. The young Jerome visited the catacombs in Rome and recalled: "Often we entered into the galleries, excavated in the flesh of the earth, completely lined with tombs and so dark that the prophetic saying seemed to be realized, 'Let them descend living into hell' (Ps 54:16). A few rays of light coming from above ground attenuated the darkness a little, but the illumination was so slight that it seemed to come from a crack and not from a skylight. You went slowly, one step after another, completely shrouded in darkness."[168]

For Augustine, who reflects the African tradition, not even catechumens could be buried with the faithful.[169] The reason for the prohibition—no other reasons were given—was that the Eucharist was celebrated alongside the tomb. This prohibition was repeated in the strongest of terms.

The creation of a Christian epigraphic language came about slowly.[170] With some exceptions the heading DM, *diis manibus* (to the spirits of the dead [Manes]) was abandoned, a sign of the difficulty of assuming a totally Christian attitude. The term "peace," which parallels the Hebrew *shalom,* becomes more common[171] although the formulations would vary: *Pax tibi*; *pax tecum*; *Leonti pax a fratribus vale*,[172] *pax tecum sit*; *pax tibi cum sanctis*; *decessit in pace*; etc.[173] Another term that was used was the verb, *vivere*, which refers to life: *vivas in Deo*, *vivas in aeternum*, etc. Sometimes the epigraphy tells us whether the deceased was a virgin, was consecrated, or was a maidservant of God (*ancilla Dei*). The term faithful (*fidelis*) qualified a baptized believer, not a catechumen; many inscriptions included the fact that the deceased was a neophyte.

Some typically Christian expressions included the deceased being asked to pray for us; but sometimes it was the deceased who would ask us to pray for him: "you who read this pray for me" (*qui legis ora pro me*).[174] These types of concepts and expressions introduced the idea of the communion of saints which exists between those still on this earth and those who belong to the kingdom of God.

THE CULT OF THE MARTYRS, SAINTS, AND RELICS

In the preceding sections I spoke of the cult of the martyrs and of the dead at different points,[175] because they were closely connected in origin and development. The cult of the dead was traditional in antiquity and predated Christianity. The cult of the martyrs was grafted onto it and is related to it, as one can deduce from the archeological evidence and inscriptions. It was a form of the cult of the dead in origin and partly in its rites. Later the cult of non-martyrs would arise, those whom we call saints. Still another development would be the cult of relics, through which the power of the martyrs and saints continued to manifest itself. The first evidence concerns Polycarp in the second century. Cyprian, as has been seen, insisted that the date of the martyrs' death be noted in order to keep their memorial.[176] For Rome we have two lists, one of the martyrs (*Depositio martyrum*) and one for the Roman bishops (*Depositio episcoporum*).

The cult of the martyrs was not practiced by a group or a family, as happens with the cult of the dead, but by the whole local community, presided over by a presbyter or bishop when the Eucharist was celebrated. This cult was linked to the burial place and to the date of the *dies natalis*, that is, the date of their death. The Roman *Depositio martyrum* bears witness to the same practice. Inscriptions and graffiti attest that the martyrs, especially the apostles, were invoked for their intercession.

The rites of the cult of the dead and of the martyrs were intertwined with pagan elements too, with varying intensity depending on the place. The most focused action of the bishops was to eliminate all these legacies—which was not an easy thing to do. For the West, Augustine was the one who strove the hardest toward this goal. He was concerned with the way the cult was celebrated, seeking to eliminate acts and gestures that were not fitting and he was also very concerned about the meaning in the gestures and in the cult itself.

In the second half of the fourth century the anniversary of the martyrs began to be celebrated with great solemnity and with great popular participation. Basilicas dedicated to them were built in connection with their tombs. This fact is also a further reminder that the cult of the martyrs was a development of the cult of the dead. A specific preaching associated with the cult was developed which sang the praises of the martyr and invited imitation. We still have many bishops' homilies for these solemn occasions:

> I am urged to speak to your graces by the courage of the holy martyrs, courage that was not only heroic but also dutiful—that, after all, is the useful sort of courage, or rather the only true sort, properly called courage, when it serves in God's army. So, I am urged to speak to your graces and urge you to celebrate the feast of the martyrs in such a way that you also take delight in imitating them by following in their footsteps. The fact, after all, that they turned out to be so brave was not something that derived from themselves. That source, moreover, from which they drew their courage didn't only flow as far as them. The one who gave it to them is also powerful enough to give it to us; since one price was paid for all of us.[177]

"So the thing you have particularly to be reminded of, to remind yourselves of time and again, and to think about all the time, is that the martyr of God is not such on account of the punishment but the cause."[178] "This is why in the Church one does not pray for them. One prays for the other faithful departed, but for the martyrs one does not pray. In fact, they have left in such a purified way that they are not our wards but our advocates. And not on account of themselves, but in Him to whom, as Head, the perfect members are closely connected."[179]

In *The City of God*, Augustine offers a summary of his thought on the cult of the martyrs and saints:

> But, nevertheless, we do not build temples, and ordain priests, rites, and sacrifices for these same martyrs; for they are not our gods, but their God is our God. Certainly, we honor their reliquaries, as the memorials of holy men of God who strove for the truth even to the death of their bodies, that the true religion might be made known, and false and fictitious religions exposed.... But who ever heard a priest of the faithful, standing at an altar built for the honor and worship of God over the holy body of some martyr, say in the prayers, 'I offer to you a sacrifice, O Peter, or O Paul, or O Cyprian?' For it is to God that sacrifices are offered at their tombs—the God who made them both men and martyrs, and associated them with holy angels in celestial honor; and the reason why we pay such honors to their memory is, that by so doing

we may both give thanks to the true God for their victories, and, by recalling them afresh to remembrance, may stir ourselves up to imitate them by seeking to obtain similar crowns and palms, calling to our help that same God on whom they called. Therefore, whatever honors the religious may pay in the places of the martyrs, they are but honors rendered to their memory, not sacred rites or sacrifices offered to dead men as to gods. And even such as those that bring food—which, indeed, is not done by the better Christians, and in most places of the world is not done at all—do so in order that it may be sanctified to them through the merits of the martyrs, in the name of the Lord of the martyrs, first presenting the food and offering prayer, and thereafter taking it away to be eaten, or to be in part bestowed upon the needy. But he who knows the one sacrifice of Christians, which is the sacrifice offered in those places, also knows that these are not sacrifices offered to the martyrs. It is, then, neither with divine honors nor with human crimes, by which they worship their gods, that we honor our martyrs; neither do we offer sacrifices to them or convert the crimes of the gods into their sacred rites.[180]

With the persecution over in the fourth century, there were only a few martyrs, like the three martyrs of Val di Non (Trent).[181] The new witnesses would be those who defended the faith through their writings and life. In Rome the *Depositio episcoporum* preserved in the *Chronography of 354* already includes a list of Roman bishops of whom they made memorial, from Lucius I (†254) to Sylvester I (†335) and Julius I (†352). Their names are inserted into the diptychs recited during the celebration of mass.[182] The Carthaginian Calendar, from the first years of the sixth century, also includes bishops who are not martyrs. Thus, there comes about an equivalence between witnesses of the faith through martyrdom and witnesses of the faith through life. The phenomenon occurs in all the churches, even if at different times. These are famous bishops and great ascetics, like the monk Anthony about whom Athanasius wrote a biography, as well as great bishops in the East like Athanasius, Basil the Great, or the ascetics like Hilarion, Symeon, and the like.

Another phenomenon that originates and develops during this time is the cult of relics, which initially was identified with the cult of the body of the martyrs or saints. Indeed, the Christians of Smyrna, as I already mentioned, write: "And gathering together in this place with exultation and joy every time it will be possible, the Lord will grant us the opportunity to celebrate the anniversary of his martyrdom."[183] They hold a celebration, although we do not know what kind, in the place where some remains of the martyr were found. And this is what would normally happen in later centuries as well. According to ancient norms that were reinforced also with imperial laws in late antiquity, the body which was placed intact in the tomb, could not be removed, divided, or transferred elsewhere. This rigid attitude was found very much in the west but not so much in the east. In the second half of the fourth century, however, the use and preservation of relics spread, which might be small pieces of the martyr's bones or also of the soil of his or her tomb.

And so, against the laws and customs that had been established, the mortal remains of the martyrs are not just transferred and even brought inside the cities' walls, but they are also broken into fragments. Already by the end of the fourth century, the partitioning and diffusion of martyrs' relics in a way that also involved commercial activity assumed a scandalous form. Imperial authorities prohibited it in 386 with a law published in Constantinople.[184] In the first decades of the fifth century the religious sensibility changed and the diffusion of relics became an accepted practice, but one that demanded vigilance against abuses. The council of Carthage of 401 recommended destroying the false memorials of the martyrs (*falsae memoriae martyrum*), because *memoriae* (smaller or larger martyrial monuments[185]) were being set up everywhere in fields and roads without even elements of the martyrs' bodies.[186] The bishops, however, realized that it would not be easy because of popular opposition (*si autem tumultus populares non sinitur*), so it would be necessary to admonish the people not to visit them and not to yield to superstition. The altars (*altaria*) built on account of various dreams or revelations were to be rejected. In the same year of the council, Augustine also criticized *vagantes* monks (wandering monks) who sold body parts of so-called martyrs.[187] As early as 392 and onward he deplored and combatted the abuses committed in relation to martyr celebrations.

A typical and emblematic case was the discovery of the tomb of Stephen the Protomartyr.[188] On December 26 of 415, the day of the saint's feast (*VII kalendas Ianuarias*), John of Jerusalem in holy procession transferred the discovered relics—a few bones along with soil mixed with the dust of their flesh— to the church of Holy Sion in Jerusalem, leaving the presbyter Lucian, who had discovered them, a few small relics. Their distribution favored the spread of the cult of Stephen, both in the East and in the West, with the construction of many centers of cult and pilgrimage in places such as Constantinople and Rome (where the church of Santo Stefano Rotondo dedicated to St. Stephen goes back to about 450), various places in Africa, such as Uzalis, Carthage, Hippo, and Calama, to name a few, as well as in the African countryside at the *fundus Audurus*. There are also centers in Ancona (central Italy), in the Balearics, and in Gaul (Bourges).

The bodies of the martyrs or also of the saints were considered means of protection. The local populations were very attached to them. In tribulation they entrusted themselves to them. The relics were also useful for detaching the faithful from superstitious behaviors. Augustine preached sermon 318[189] in 425 on the occasion of the deposition of the relics of Stephen the Protomartyr in the *memoria* near the *Basilica Maior*. This sermon was important for being able to understand why he favored the cult of Stephen: "It can happen that one of the faithful gets sick; behold the tempter is there. For the sake of a cure one promises him an illicit sacrifice, a reproachable and sacrilegious amulet, a nefarious incantation, a magical rite, saying: This or that person was in bigger trouble than you and in this way they were freed from it; behave like this if you want to live; you will die if you do not do it. Note whether this is not the same as 'you will die if you do not deny Christ.'... You have found the same struggle, so win an authentic victory. You are in a bed and you are in an amphitheater; you are lying down and you are engaged in battle. Persevere in faith; and, while you strain yourself you are victorious. Therefore, dearly beloved, you have no small comfort: a place of prayer. Here may the martyr Stephen be venerated, but, in honor of him, let him be adored who crowned Stephen."[190]

The cult of the martyr had a specific function: to be a path to God amidst the various adversities of life, which is the goal of every cult. The chapel of the martyrium was a place of prayer and of comfort. Augustine attributes the greater importance to miracles in general, and those performed through the intercession of Stephen the Protomartyr have the purpose of reinforcing the Christians' faith and of urging them to imitate the saint. In the sermons on Stephen he emphasizes the relationship between Christ and Stephen, and that the faithful Christians must imitate this servant (*servus*), because all are fellow servants of Christ. It is a practical purpose that leads to no theoretical reflection.

Because of the desire to have something especially connected to the saint, importance was also given to elements that were quite marginal compared to the actual relics.[191] The concept of the relic expanded to include not just the tiniest part of the body, but everything connected to it, with or without having had actual contact with the body. In the episode of Uzalis,[192] it is evident that the population was against being deprived of even a part of the relics, which had been put into a silver capsule; the Bishop Evodius had to yield and put everything back in its place.

Pilgrims would bring souvenirs back with them, like eulogia, flasks[193], or *brandea*. The eulogia were any object used for devotion, be they relics of holy places, lamp oil acquired in Palestine and kept in flasks, water, or the bread of an exorcism. The most well-known flasks were those of the martyr St. Menas which came from the sanctuary of Abu Mena near Alexandria. The *brandea* were pieces of fabric that had been put in physical contact with the relic—for example, the body—from which the fabric received a sacred character. These are described by Gregory of Tours (†594) thus: "If one desires to take away some relic from the tomb, the pilgrim must carefully weigh a piece of fabric and hang it inside the tomb. Then pray ardently and, if his faith is strong enough, the fabric, once removed from the tomb, will be so full of God's grace that it will be much heavier than before."[194] But there were other connections with martyrs as well. For example, the use of flowers that had perhaps touched the relics' container,[195] a tunic that had been in the place of the martyr's relics,[196] flowers that had been on the altar where the relics were kept,[197] or oil from the martyr chapel.[198]

The relics were also useful for the missionary work among other peoples. Gregory the Great wrote a letter to Mellitus, whom he had sent to Britain with this instruction of a pastoral character.[199] Much has been written about the spread of relics, about the abuses that took place on the part of the laity and of the clergy—we could even say of that paganism that was connected with the cult of the martyrs. But I think that, if on the part of some there was an intentional promotion of profit and actual commerce, more often than not the abuse was due to ignorance, even on the part of religiously sensible people.

---

1. See V. Saxer, *La vie liturgique et quotidienne à Carthage vers le milieu du IIIe siècle* (Città del Vaticano: Pontificio Istituto di archeologia cristiana, 1969), 264-328.
2. Gregory of Nyssa, *Life of Macrina* 23.
3. J.A. Gaytán Luna, *Fin del mundo y destino final del hombre. La exégesis escatológica de I ad Corinthios 7,31, y 15,50, en la literatura cristiana antigua* (Frankfurt am Main: P. Lang, 2014).
4. Christian symbolism on tombs and the scenes carved or depicted transmit the message of the Christians' conception of death and burial.
5. *Pagani e cristiani alla ricerca della salvezza (secoli I-III): XXXIV Incontro di studiosi dell'antichità cristiana, Roma, 5-7 maggio 2005* (Roma: Institutum Patristicum Augustinianum, 2006).
6. U. Bianchi and M.J. Vermaseren, ed., *La soteriologia dei culti orientali nell'Impero Romano*, ed. (Leiden: Brill, 1982).
7. Cf. NDPAC 3:5204-05.
8. CIL 6:510.
9. *Acts of Justin* 5.1-5.
10. *Acts of the Martyrs of Lyon* 63.
11. Yvette Duval, *Auprès des saints, corps et âme. L'inhumation "ad sanctos" dans la chrétienté d'Orient e d'Occident du IIIe au VIe siècle* (Paris: Etudes Augustiniennes, 1988), 24-25.
12. V. Capocci, "Sulla concessione e sul divieto di sepoltura nel mondo romano ai condannati a pena capitale," *SDHI* 22 (1956): 366-410.
13. An exhaustive study is Barbara Fabbrini, "La Deposizione di Gesù nel sepolcro e il problema del divieto di sepoltura per i condannati," *SDHI* 61 (1995): 97-178; especially 159-60. It also treats fully the cases of martyrs' bodies.
14. *Martyrium Polycarpi* 17.2-3.
15. The author of the martyrdom narrative gives precise references about the date, which can be February 22 of 156, or February 23 of 167.
16. *Martyrium Polycarpi* 18.2-3.
17. *EAC* 1:693-94.
18. Eusebius, *Praeparatio Ev.* 13.11.2.
19. Augustine, *City of God* 1.13.
20. M.B. Ogle, "The Sleep of Death," *Memoirs of the American Academy in Rome* 11 (1933): 81-117.
21. Jeremiah Mutie, *Death in Second-Century Christian Thought: The Meaning of Death in Earliest Christianity* (Cambridge: James Clarke & Company, 2015).
22. Lorenzo. Perrone, "Da Nicea (325) a Calcedonia (451). I primi quattro concili ecumenici istituzioni, dottrine, processi di ricezione," in *Storia dei concili ecumenici*, G. Alberigo, ed. (Brescia: Queriniana, 1990), 42-43.
23. Ep. 84.429d. W. Koch, "Comment l'empereur Julien tacha de fonder une église païenne," *Revue Belge de philologie et d'histoire* 6 (1927): 123-46; 7 (1928): 49-82; 511-50; 1363-1385.
24. Éric Rebillard, "Les formes de l'assistance funéraire dans l'Empire romain et leur evolution," *Bibliothèque de l'Antiquité Tardive (BAT)* 7 (1999): 269-282, here 229-276.
25. A. Ferrua, "Iscrizioni antiche viste dal Torrigio," *Rivista Storia Antica* 5 (1975): 167-168, n. 22; *Année Epigraphique* (1976), 976 (1); *Année Epigraphique* (1976), 0101 (2).
26. An example: *Leo et Annibonia domu eterna se vivi fecerunt cum suis* (ICUR 4.11938).

27. CIL VI.9545; CIL I.1212; ILS 7602. Cf. Guy de la Bédoyère, *The Real Lives of Roman Britain* (New Haven: Yale University Press, 2015), VI-IX.
28. Éric Rebillard, *Religion et sépulture. L'église, les vivants et les morts dans l'Antiquité tardive* (Paris : Editions der l'Ecole des hautes études en sciences sociales, c2003), 51-71.
29. Robert Wilken, "Christianity as Burial society," in *The Christians as the Romans Saw Them* (New Haven: Yale University Press, c2003), 31-47.
30. Eusebius, *HE* 5.1.61.
31. Origen, *Contra Celsum* 5.14; 8.30; Minucius Felix, *Octavius* 34.10.
32. Aristides, *Apology* 15.6.
33. Aristides, *Apology* 15.7.
34. Lactantius, *Div. Inst.*: Ultimum illud et maximum pietatis officium est peregrinorum et pauperum sepultura 6.12.25; cf. 6.12.39.
35. R. Staats, "Deposita caritatis. Die alte Kirche und ihr Geld," *Zeit. Theol. Kirche* 76 (1979): 1-29.
36. Tertullian, *Apologeticum* 39.6.
37. Ps. Hippolytus, *Philosophoum.* 9.12.14.
38. Tertullian, *Apologeticum* 42.7.
39. Pontius, *Vita Cypriani* 9-10.
40. Eusebius, *HE* 7.22.8.
41. Eusebius, *HE* 9.8.14. Rodney Stark, "Epidemics, Networks, and the Rise of Christianity," in *Social networks in the Early Christian Environment: Issues and Methods for Social History*, ed L.M. White (Atlanta: Scholar Press, 1992), 159-75.
42. A. Di Berardino, *Parabalani*: *EAC* 3:63.
43. Ambrose, *De Off.* 2.15.70ff.
44. Ambrose, *De Off.* 2.28.142. For other pieces of evidence cf. Rebillard, *Religion et sépolture*, 131-39.
45. Gaius, *Institutiones* 2.6-7.
46. Cf. *Amendes (dans le droit funéraire)*; DACL 1 :1575-98.
47. Anna Maria Rossi, "Ricerche sule multe sepolcrali romane," *Rivista distoria dell'antichità* 5 (1975): 118-59.
48. Cf. André Parrot, *Malédictions et violations des tombes* (Paris: Geuthner, 1939).
49. Taxes paid to the church of Salona (Dalmatia): *Année Epigraphique* 1892, 32; CIL 3:2654; 14905; cf. DACL 1:1581. CIL 3:9535 and ILCV 3837: quiscumque extraneus voluerit alterum corpus ponere det ecclesiae catholicae Salonitanae auri Tres.
50. Cf. Lyuba Radulova, Rita Sassu, "Funerary Imprecations in the Balcan Provinces," *Academic Journal of Interdisciplinary Studies* 4 (2015): 468-78 (the text is in Italian).
51. Ibid, 475-78 for Christian texts.
52. Hippolyte Delehaye, *Les origines du culte des martyres* (Bruxelles: Société des bollandistes, 1933), 50-99.
53. CTh 9,17,6 of 30 July 381.
54. The law is the one of 386: CTh 9.17.7. *Storia del cristianesimo*, vol. II, *La nascita di una cristianità (250-430)*, ed. C. and L. Pietri (Rome: Città Nuova, 2000), 567.
55. Cf. *Thesaurus Cultus et Rituum Antiquorum* (ThesCRAo) (Los Angeles: Getty Publications, 2012), Vol. 6: 204-8 (inhumation and cremation); J.M.C. Toynbee, *Death and Burial in the Roman World*, repr. (Baltimore: Johns Hopkins University Press, 1996), 26ff.
56. Tacitus, *Annales* 16.6.
57. E.R. Goodenough, *Jewish Symbols in the Graeco-Roman Period* (New York: Pantheon Books, 1953), 61-177.
58. Minucius Felix, *Octavius* 34.10. Éric Rebillard, "Sépulture et construction de l'identité chrétienne aux IIe et IIIe siècles," *Annali di storia dell'esegesi* 21 (2004): 131-46, esp.135-38.
59. Hans G. Kippenberg, G.A. Wewers, *Testi giudaici per lo studio del Nuovo Testamento* (Paideia: Brescia, 1987), 265-68.
60. Cicero, *De legibus* 2.55.
61. Moshe. Blidstein, *Purity, Community, and Ritual in Early Christian Literature* (New York: Oxford University Press, 2017), 92-104.
62. DACL I :479-509 ; Duval, *Auprès des saints*; Paula Rose, *A Commentary on Augustine's De cura pro mortuis gerenda: Rhetoric in Practice* (Leiden/Boston: Brill, 2013), 558-70.
63. *Didascalia* 6.22.2.
64. *Apostolic Constitutions* 6.30.1-2.

65. Diehl, I ILCV 2148; ICUR 1.3127; C. Carletti, *"Quod multi cupiunt et rari accipiunt:* A proposito di una nuova iscrizione della catacomba dell'ex vigna Chiaraviglio," in *Historiam pictura refert: miscellanea in onore di padre Alejandro Recio Veganzones O.F.M.* (Città del Vaticano: Pontifico istituto di archeologia cristiana, 1994), 111-26.
66. ICUR 7.19432 = ICLV 2153: *In cr<y>pta no<v>a retro san/ctus emeru<nt> se vivas Baler/a et Sabina (e)meru<nt> loc/u(m) biso<um> ab Aponte et a / Biatore.*
67. Augustine, *De Cura pro Mortuis Gerenda* 1.1.
68. R.C.T. Parker, *Miasma, Pollution and Purification in Early Greek Religion* (Oxford: Oxford University Press, 1983, 2ed., 1996).
69. It does not appear clearly in the law what the intent was against Christians, but in letter 136 it is seen clearly.
70. *Contra Galilaeos*, fr. 81 Masaracchia.
71. Today the *conclamatio* takes place for the death of a Pope.
72. Tertullian, *Apologeticum* 42.4-7.
73. Gregory of Nyssa, *Life of Macrina* 25.
74. Eusebius, *HE* 7.27.8-9.
75. Augustine, *Conf.* 9.12.29.
76. Chrysostom, *Hom. in Ioannem* 85.5; PG 59:465-68.
77. Chrysostom, *Hom. in Job* 1.
78. Augustine, *Enarr. in Psalmos* 33.2, 25.
79. Cf. Prudentius, *Cathemerinon*, Hymn 10.51.
80. Lactantius, *Divinae Institutiones* 2.4 CSEL 19:109.
81. Augustine, *Enarr. in Psalmos* 48.2.7.
82. Jerome, *Ep.* 1.12.
83. Ps. Linus, *Passion of Peter* 16.
84. C. D'Angela, "L'obolo a Caronte. Usi funerari medievali tra paganesimo e cristianesimo," *Quaderni Medievali* 15 (1983): 82-91.
85. Jerome, *Ep.* 66.1.
86. Aristides, *Apology* 15.9.
87. Tertullian, *De anima* 51.6, CCL 2:857. Cf. also a discourse attributed to Ambrose: 57.1; PL 17:745; CCL 23:28.
88. Tertullian, *De Corona* 3.3. V. Saxer, *Morts, martyrs, reliques en Afrique chrétienne aux premiers siècles. Les témoignages de Tertullien, Cyprien et Augustin à la lumière de l'archéologie africaine* (Paris: Beauchesne, 1980), 70-73.
89. Cyprian, *Ep.* 1.2.1. Cf. V. Saxer, *Vie liturgique*, 301.
90. Cyprian, *Ep.* 12.1.
91. Cyprian, *Ep.* 39.3.1.
92. The *dies parentales* (ancestral days) lasted nine days in honor of the ancestors, starting on February 13.
93. Origen, *On Prayer* 14.6.
94. A.E. Felle, "Alle origini del fenomeno devozionale cristiano in Occidente. Le inscriptiones parietariae ad memoriam Apostolorum," in *Martiri, santi, patroni per una archeologia della devozione*, Coscarella, A., De Santis, P., ed. (Arcavacata di Rende: Rende Università della Calabria, 2012), 477-502.
95. Anna Maria Nieddu, *La Basilica Apostolorum sulla via Appia e l'area cimiteriale circostante* (Vatican City: Pontificio istituto di archeologia cristiana, 2009), 7-9.
96. A. Ferrua, "Rileggendo i graffiti di San Sebastiano," *Civiltà Cattolica* 116/III (1965): 428-37; 116/4 (1965): 134-41.
97. E.g. ICUR 5.12931; 12966; 12970; 12989.
98. Ibid, 5:12912.
99. Ibid, 5:12955; 12930.
100. Ibid, 5:3024.
101. Ibid, 5:12932; 12907.
102. Ibid, 5:12980.
103. Augustine, *Sermo* 159.1; cf. *In Ioh. tr.* 84.1.
104. Eusebius, *Praeparatio ev.* 13.11.2.
105. Gregory of Nyssa, *Life of Macrina* 25-35.
106. *Apostolic Constitutions* 8.42.1-3 and 8.44, SC 330:260-61.
107. Augustine, *Confessions* 9.12.32.
108. *Conc. Hipp.* 4, CCL 149:21.

109. Chapters 55 and 66-67 Elizabeth A. Clark, *The Life of Melania the Younger* (New York: E. Mellon Press, 1984), 68 and 79.
110. Augustine, *Confessions* 9.12.31 and 32.
111. Augustine, *Ep.* 158.2.
112. Possidius, *Vita Aug.* 31.5.
113. Cf. Augustine, *Sermo* 335C.1: *Quia beati martyris natalis illuxit dies quem voluit nos Dominus celebrare vobiscum.* Jos Janssens, *Vita e morte del cristiano negli epitaffi di Roma anteriori al sec. VII* (Rome: Università Gregoriana Editrice, 1981), 276-84.
114. Ignatius, *To the Romans* 6.1.
115. Tertullian, *De Corona* 3.3.
116. Jerome, *Ep.* 74, to Theodora (PL 22:685); *Neque enim mors, sed dormitio et somnus appellatur.*
117. A text attributed to Ambrose, but of another author: *Nam ideo haec dies* (depositio) *pro celebritate maxima procuratur; quia vere est summa festivitas monuum esse vitiis, soli vigere justitiae; unde et depositionis ipsa dies natalis dicitur, quod delictorum carcere liberati* (*Sermones S. Ambrosio hactenus ascripti*, 57.1: PL 17:745; CCL 23:28).
118. ILCV 303.
119. Augustine, *Sermo* 4.33.36: *per natalicia martyris sui Vincentii.* Cf. *Sermones* 35C.11; 345.6, etc. 299A.3: *apostoli quorum hodie natalicia celebramus.*
120. Cyprian, *Ep.* 12.1.
121. Cyprian, *Ep.* 39.1.
122. Cyprian, *Ep* 80.1.4.
123. Cf. Cyprian, *Ep.* 77.2.1; *Ep.* 22.2.2.
124. Augustine, *Sermo* 310.1.
125. C. Carletti, "Dies mortis-depositio: un modulo 'profano' nell'epigrafia tardoantica," *Vetera Christianorum* 41 (2004): 21-48.
126. Dolbeau 7.1.
127. Tertullian *De Cor.* 3.3; *De exh. cast.* 11.1; *De monog.* 10.1.
128. Palladius, *Hist. Laus.* 21; *Const. App.* 8.42, Evodius, in Augustine, *Ep.* 158.2.
129. Victor Saxer, *Morts, martyrs, reliques en Afrique chrétienne aux premiers siècles*, 105-107, 171-173.
130. R.M. Jensen, "Dining with the Dead: From the Mensa to the Altar in Christian Antiquity," Brink Laurie, ed., *Commemorating the Dead: Texts and Artifacts in Context: Studies of Roman, Jewish, and Christian Burials* (Berlin; New York: Walter de Gruyter, 2008), 107-43.
131. Tertullian, *De monogamia* 10.5.
132. Tertullian, *De exhor.* 11.1.
133. *Paule Dulciti deus te refrigeret cui vixit annis undeci mens(ibus) sex dies tredici* (ICUR 10.26781).
134. *L'Année épigraphique*, 1979, n. 682.
135. Cf. P.-A. Février, "A propos du repas funéraire: culte et sociabilité, *'in Christo Deo, pax et concordia sit convivio nostro,*" *La Méditerranée*, vol. 1 (Milan: École Française de Rome, 1996), 29-45.
136. *gentilium turpia et luculenta convivia*; Cyprian, *Ep.* 67.6.2.
137. Tertullian, *De Spect.* 13.
138. PG 46:953B.
139. Basil, *Homily* 14.1; PG 31:445-46.
140. Ambrose, *De Elia et ieiunio admonitio* 17.62; PL 14:719.
141. Augustine, *Confessions* 6.2.2.
142. Cf. Saxer, *Morts et martyrs*, 138-49.
143. Augustine, *Ep.* 22.3.
144. Augustine, *Ep.* 18.22.
145. Cf. Paulinus of Nola, *Ep.* 13; Jerome, *Ep.* 66, two letters addressed to Pammachius.
146. Augustine, *de Civ. Dei.* 1.12; the same words were also used by Caesar Augustus centuries earlier.
147. Cf. *EAC* 2:75-86.
148. Cf. *EAC* 1:482-87, with a rich bibliography; *EAC* 2:817-26 (Epigraphy). V. Fiocchi Nicolai, D. Mazzoleni, F. Bisconti, *Le catacombe cristiane di Roma: origini, sviluppo, apparati decorativi, documentazione epigrafica* (Regensburg: Schnell & Steiner, 1998).
149. *To Diognetus* 5.2.

150. *Apost. Trad.* 40.
151. ILCV n. 1597.
152. CIL 08:9585; 08 :20958; ILCV 1583. DACL 3:1275f.; Y. Duval, *Loca sanctorum Africae, Le culte des martyrs en Afrique du IVe au VIIe siècle* (Rome: École française de Rome, 1982), 380-83, n.179; Éric Rebillard, "Les areae carthaginoises (Tertullien, Ad Scapulam 3.1): cimetières communautaires ou enclos funéraires de chrétiens?" *MEFRA* 108 (1996): 175-89.
153. CIL 8:9586; ICLV and 1179.
154. ILCV 3681; cf. G. Mancini, "Scoperta di un antico sepolcreto nel territorio veliterno, in località Solluna," *Notizie degli scavi di antichità* (1924): 341-53. Année épigraphique (1925): 21 s. n. 84.
155. In antiquity the catacombs were called *cryptae* (Jerome, *In Ezech.* 12.40; Prudentius, *Perist.* 11.154).
156. Not only in Rome, but in many Italian regions, in Malta, in Africa, in Paris.
157. His inscription in Latin could be later.
158. Cf. e.g. John Chrysostom PG 49:393.
159. Lucrezia Spera, "Depositus in Christo. Valenze soteriche nella ridefinizione cristiana del mondo funerario," in *Pagani e cristiani alla ricerca della salvezza (secoli I-III)* (Rome: Institutum Patristicum Augustinianum, 2006), 765-77.
160. Éric Rebillard, *Religion et sépulture. L'église, les vivants et les morts dans l'Antiquité tardive* (Paris: Editions der l'Ecole des hautes études en sciences sociales, 2003), 12-17.
161. Tertullian, *Ad Scapuluam* 3. According to Rebillard, the term does not indicate a Christian cemetery, but some Christian *sepulchrum familiare*: Éric Rebillard, *Les areae carthaginoises*, 175-89.
162. Cyprian, *Ep.* 67.6.2.
163. A. M. Milazzo, "Causa funeris e 'causa religionis': spunti ricostruttivi sui sacra praticati dai collegia funeraticia," in *Religione e diritto romano: la cogenza del rito*, ed. Salvo Randazzo (Tricase: Libellula Ed., 2014), 305-30.
164. Commodianus, *Instructiones* 2.29. See the fine comment of J.-M. Poinsotte, *Commodien, Instructions*, CUF, SL 392 (Paris: Belle Lettres, 2009), 460-64.
165. For other burial places for Christians see G.E. Clarke, *Letters of Cyprian of Carthage* (New York; Ramsey, N.J.: Newman Press, 1984), 252; S.T. Stevens, "Commemorating the Dead in the Communal Cemeteries of Carthage," in Brink Laurie, ed., *Commemorating the Dead: Texts and Artifacts in Context: Studies of Roman, Jewish, and Christian Burials* (Berlin, New York: Walter de Gruyter, 2008), 79-103.
166. For mixed burials, cf. M. J. Johnson, "Pagan-Christian Burial Practices of The Fourth Century: Shared Tombs?" *Journal of Early Christians Studies* 5 (1997): 37-59.
167. The Greek letters in *Ichthys* stand for Jesus Christ Son of God Savior.
168. Jerome, *In Ezech.* 12.40.
169. Augustine, *Sermo Dolbeau* 7.1.
170. Charles Pietri, "La mort en Occident dans l'épigraphie latine. De l'épigraphie païenne à l'épitaphe chrétienne, IIIe-VIe siècles," *La Maison-Dieu* 144 (1980): 25-48.
171. E. Dinkler, "Schalom – Eirene – Pax. Jüdische sepulkral Inschriften und ihr Verhältnis zum frühen Christentum," *Rivista di archeologia cristiana* 50 (1974): 121-44.
172. ICUR 9.25319 (ILCV 2300); cf. ICUR 1.1261, 692; 2.7274; 4.12839; 6.15871; 7.21527; 9.26037. C. Carletti, *Epigrafia dei Cristiani in Occidente dal III al VII secolo. Ideologia e prassi* (Bari: Edipuglia, 2008), 150; Pietri, *La mort*.
173. "Peace be to you; Peace be with you; Peace to Leontius, farewell from your brothers; may peace be with you; peace to you with the saints; depart in peace." Also, similar terms: *requiescere*, or *quiescere*.
174. ILCV 2353.
175. The treatment in this section can be completed adequately with the last part of chapter eleven.
176. Cyprian, *Ep.* 12.2, 39.3.
177. Augustine, *Sermo* 285.1.
178. Augustine, *Sermo* 285.2.
179. Augustine, *Sermo* 285.5.
180. Augustine, *De civitate Dei* 8.27.
181. Three Christians who came from Cappadocia and dedicated themselves to the evangelization of the valleys (Anaunia): the deacon Sisinius, the lector Martyrius, and his brother Alexander, an ostiary. They were killed during a pagan feast on May 29, 397.
182. Cf. DACL 4:1051, 1063.

183. *Martyrium Polycarpi* 18.3.
184. CTh 9.17.7.
185. Cf. V. Saxer, *Morts, Martyrs, Reliques en Afrique chrétienne*, 126-33.
186. Ed. Munier, CCL 148:204-5.
187. Augustine, *De op. monach.* 28.36.
188. A. Di Berardino, "Guarigioni nel contesto della traslazione delle reliquie di S. Stefano al tempo di S. Agostino," in *Salute e guarigione nella Tarda Antichità*, ed. Hugo Brandenburg – Stefan Heid, Christoph Markschies (Vatican City: Pontificio istituto di archeologia cristiana, 2007), 227-43.
189. Cyrille Lambot, "Collection antique de sermons de saint Augustin," *Revue Bénédictine* 57 (1947): 104-7.
190. Augustine, *Sermo* 318.1–3.
191. Such an Esperius in Fussala had some soil taken from the place of Christ's resurrection in Jerusalem (Augustine, *De civ. Dei* 22.8.7); *Letter* 52.2 also mentions the importance of soil brought from the East: "If you bring the Donatists a little soil from those regions they venerate it."
192. *De miraculis Sancti Stephani* 1.7; PL 41:838.
193. Chiara Lambert and Paola Pedemonte Demeglio, "Ampolle devozionali ed itinerari di pellegrinaggio tra IV e VII secolo," *Antiquité Tardive* 2 (1994): 205-31.
194. *Gloria martyrum* 27.
195. Augustine, *De civitate Dei* 22.8.11.
196. Augustine, *De civ. Dei* 22.8.13; 22.8.17 and 18.
197. Augustine, *De civ. Dei* 22.8.14.
198. Augustine, *De civ. Dei* 22.8.19.
199. See Bede, *Eccl. History* 30.

CHAPTER 14

ECONOMIC AND SOCIAL CONSIDERATIONS

Historical and Social Background

The concept of poverty and what it means to be poor is relative to different societies. Someone who is considered poor in one society may be referred to by a different term and enjoy a different social status in another. It is also an abstract concept, under whose roof are many applications and meanings. The difference in meaning creates a certain ambiguity of understanding. Thus, the Latin term *pauper* and other similar ancient terms refer to something other than our word 'poor' today; it has a broader spectrum of meanings, although it mainly indicates one who does not belong to the dominant class of citizens (*ordines*).[1] It does not indicate a person who is truly needy or destitute. Marcellus Nonius, a grammarian who lived between the fourth and fifth centuries, notes that *paupertas dicta est a pecunia parva* (poverty is spoken of one who comes from little money).[2] Of course, as Seneca observes, poverty is also a personal perception: *Non qui parum habet, sed qui plus cupit pauper est* (it is not the poor who possesses little, but the one who desires more who is poor).[3] Ambrosiaster says that the *pauperes* [...] *qui publici egeni sunt* (the poor ... are those who are publicly in need).[4]

Here is an example from Augustine of the use of the Latin term *pauper*. He defines himself and his parents as poor: "Perhaps it suits the bishop but not Augustine, a poor man born of poor people."[5] Patricius, his father, belonged to the curia of Thagaste, and so he was not poor. In fact he had to contribute to the city's expenses.[6] He made sacrifices for his son's education with the help of a benefactor. Augustine himself had some land, although we do not know how much; he inherited some of it, which he then sold,[7] but did his brother and sister also own a share of the property? If so, the ownership had to be substantial. The clerics who lived with him were sustained by the goods of the church. They did not have any possessions of their own. They were *pauperes Dei*,[8] but not poor (*inopes*). The same goes for the monks in his monastery. Elsewhere he uses the term *pauper* in the sense of a true poor man and there are any number of times where he uses the term in the sense of those who are needy, as in those who receive support from others. Sometimes he calls the truly needy *inopes vel mendici* (poor or beggars).[9]

At the time of the Roman Empire, society was hierarchical, organized in the shape of a pyramid. Societies were structured by unparalleled juridical condition, according to the *qualitas*—social and juridical status—of people, not their wealth.[10] A freedman could be much wealthier than a free citizen. Even a slave could own property, but he would not enjoy the rights of the citizens. It was a society of inequalities consisting in legal and social status, different clothing that marked one's position, marriages that were contracted depending on one's social status, the application of the law and the different penalties meted out depending on one's station in life.

The Theodosian Code published in 438 provided a range of terms in relation to poverty and wealth. The *pauper* is the one who cannot obtain everything necessary for his daily subsistence. The *egenus* (= *indigens*), on the other hand, is in an even lower economic condition, being deprived of the minimum necessary to live. The term *inopes* is the opposite of one who is rich (*opes*), while *tenuis* (*tenuior*) indicates both the one who is of humble origin and the one who possesses little. The term *mendicus* referred to a beggar who had physical impediments.[11]

Even more important for the understanding of the terms "poor" and "wealthy" is to keep in mind that ancient authors do not speak in economic and statistical terms. The two terms are rather vague and refer to people who own things versus those who cannot meet even basic needs. In each text we need to look at which wealthy people or which poor people it is talking about. But both words also have a moral meaning—and the poor are the ones who are inferior. Christel Freu[12] in a documented study examines the Latin terms for wealthy and poor in late antique Italian texts; they cover a wide variety of situations. The two terms change in meaning depending on the type of text. Terms, of course, must be seen in relation to each other in the same textual and social context. The wealthy are those who either oppress or help the poor; the wealthy are those who give, the poor are those who receive. The poor are also the marginalized in a hierarchical society.

Basil, in a brilliant text, speaks of a poor man who asks for a loan to meet his needs, and a rich man who lends money in order to earn money; in reality the so-called poor man provided himself with a beautiful life, with entertainment, sumptuous banquets, and the like.[13] "The "poor" of patristic texts in other words were not necessarily poor. Nor is it certain that the poor were everywhere and more numerous in Late Antiquity than in the first centuries of the

Empire.[14] Here, too, one needs to pay attention to the time and place in these discussions. At the time of the invasions of barbaric tribes which occurred in the second half of the fourth century and in the first half of the fifth, a large portion of the population lost its property. In Roman Africa there was still great prosperity, but when the vandals arrived many left and their properties were confiscated. The fact that Christian preachers talked frequently about almsgiving and the needy gives the impression that the number of poor and needy had increased considerably.[15]

A. de Tocqueville, in the mid-nineteenth century, after a trip to wealthy England and the poor nations of Spain and Portugal, notes that among the most civilized peoples the lack of a multitude of things causes misery, while in less civilized countries poverty consists only in not finding something to eat. In other words, in the most civilized countries, "needs" increase and diversify endlessly. The opportunity to be exposed to some of these becomes more frequent every day.[16] In my opinion, these same interpretative criteria can be applied during the period of the Roman Empire to the relationship between the great city and the towns of the provinces, and even more in relation to the countryside. In rural areas something to eat is available or hunger can be satisfied, even if only with vegetables. In the "megalopolis" of Rome, and in the other great cities such as Antioch, Alexandria, and Caesarea of Cappadocia, it was difficult for many people to satisfy basic needs of subsistence. The percentage of poor in the modern sense increased in relation to the number of inhabitants. After the crisis of the third century, even in small towns the number of those in need was increasing.

There are no reliable statistics for city dwellers at that time. Nor do we know the proportion between rich and poor. I do not know if a page of John Chrysostom may help us when, speaking of the situation in Antioch, he states in a sermon:

> I believe that the wealthiest make up a tenth of the inhabitants of this city, and that the poor are another tenth, while the rest constitutes the middle class. . . . For the number of the very rich is small, but those that come after them is large; and the poor, in turn, are a limited number compared to them. Yet, although there are many people who can feed the poor, many go to sleep hungry not because those that have are not able with ease to help them, but because of their great barbarity and inhumanity. For if the rich and the well-off shared amongst themselves the task of helping those in need of food and clothing, scarcely would one person fall to the share of fifty men or even a hundred. Consider how many widows and virgins the Church helps and sustains every day, despite having an income equal to that of one of the least well-off in this city, not the richest. The list reaches the figure of three thousand virgins and widows. The Church also helps those who are in prison for the faith, the sick in hospitals, convalescents, pilgrims, the mutilated and all those who come here every day to ask for help.[17]

Chrysostom does not specify the number of those in need, those who are somehow marginalized and are rescued by the church, but their poverty is extreme because they need the minimum necessary to survive, that is, only something to eat and some clothing. That concept of poverty is different from ours, which we discussed previously.

In the big cities, especially in Rome, which is actually the only real megalopolis of the period, many people, who elsewhere would live on the land, devoted themselves to satisfying non-essential needs such as the numerous shows in the theater. And many people, without working productively, lived off imperial aid and contributions. There was therefore a huge non-productive mass of the population, which was not the case in small towns. In addition, wealth was concentrated in the hands of large families who possessed wealth scattered throughout the Empire. The city, however, then as now, beckoned and attracted: the destitute hoped that the crowded city might offer opportunity and hope in possibly receiving help from its many inhabitants—but above all receive consolation in the shared circumstances of indigence and disease.

Entertainment and all kinds of shows were offered by wealthy families. These are the traditional *liberalitates*, although theoretically free, in practice made compulsory for the wealthy classes. The organization of various types of shows—free for the people, but also of enormous expense for the rich citizen—was criticized by Christian preachers, even if sometimes it was Christians in public office who offered them free to the people. Among the many critics, Ambrose writes: "It is prodigal to consume one's substances to win the favor of the people, as do those who squander their assets in the games of the circus or even in theatrical performances and gladiators or even in hunts of beasts, to overcome the fame of those who preceded them."[18] Lactantius establishes a contrast between pagan *liberalitas* and Christian charitable forms.[19] Those same people, Chrysostom observes, who do not give to the poor, instead spend enormous sums of money on public liberalities, from where political and social prestige is obtained.[20]

Another way to show the superiority of the rich and powerful were the figures of the *patronus* and the *cliens*. There is a hierarchical relationship, but the relationship also consisted of mutual obligations. The patron was a protector and benefactor (*patrocinium*) of the client. They could even be of the same social order, but the second was inferior in wealth, power, prestige, or other power dynamics. One's patron would play the role of representing the client in court, lend money, political support, support in elections, help to occupy posts, etc. Clients, on the other hand, must respect and pay homage. They also enjoyed privileges such as exemption from witnessing in trials. The *patronatus* was also important for Christians, especially in the first three centuries: the owner—or mistress—of huge houses would make them available to the Christian communities. Cities also had their *patronus*, an influential person at the imperial court (hence the figure of the patron saint).

The concept of *patronus* and *patronatu*s becomes applied to the saints who become the patrons of cities.

In Greek and Roman antiquity, local notables and patrons made voluntary gifts to cities, which sometimes were not voluntary, such as buildings, foundations, shows or food distribution. They paid little tax, but the rich also redistributed their wealth. The emperor also performed the same gestures. The phenomenon arose in the Greek world, but then spread throughout the West, becoming a fundamental element in civic life. The recipients were the citizens as such, and not the poor, although there was the occasional if rare possibility of a donation for humanitarian reasons. Donors were benefactors, they received accolades, and were the subject of honorary inscriptions and statues. The superiority of the wealthy class thus was also affirmed in this way.[21]

Andrea Giardina observes that "The *euergetes* (benefactor) donates to mark his social distinction, patriotism, civic sense; his gesture addresses the reality of this world. The Christian donor puts his charity into practice in order to acquire merits from the Lord; his generosity looks to a different world which is not the real one. The *euergetes* addresses the people as a group of citizens; the Christian donates to the 'poor,' understood as a social and moral category, not a civic one."[22] The *eugergetes* was a benefactor who performed works that would reflect well on his public image in order to be honored and admired in his own city.

The poor, in the sense of indigent, were rejected by Roman society or at the most were tolerated, as a Pompeian graffito expresses: "I hate the poor. If anyone wants something for nothing, he is insane. He has to pay it."[23] And Plautus writes: "He deserves ill of a beggar who gives him what to eat or to drink; for he both loses that which he gives and prolongs for the other a life of misery."[24] However, we must not generalize. There were compassionate people, like a certain C. Ateilius Euhodus whose epitaph can be found on the Appian Way, a few kilometers from Rome, where it says he was "a good man, merciful, a friend of the poor" (*homo bonus, misercors, amans pauperis*).[25] Stoic morals and Christian teaching spread the idea of helping the poor, but they did not animate the traditional civic institutions which remained as they were in the Christian empire, like the various *liberalitates*, with their traditional characteristic of civic privilege, while daily the poor were killed (*quotidie pauper occiditur*).[26] As a scholar who is attentive to social issues observes, "The impermeability of the *annona* institution (the corn supply system) to the new moral concerns will therefore be no more surprising than the survival of the Amphitheater games organized by Christian magistrates throughout the fifth century."[27] The new moral sensibility remained alien to public institutions.

There was a widespread tendency among the upper classes to identify the nobility of birth with the nobility of spirit, consequently considering the poor as potential criminals or at least of a lower moral character. Traditionally, poverty was considered shameful, and the poor were viewed as a miserable lot, even morally. Poverty took on an ethical coloring. Even in a trial the testimony of a *plebeius* (a citizen, but of the lower class) or an *egens* (a needy individual) had less value or no value, because it was thought the testimony could be corrupted out of a desire for money.[28] The poor did not have the *dignitas* (dignity) or the *existimatio* (reputation) of the members of the upper class.[29] When Christians were characterized as poor, the Christian Minucius Felix replied that: "When it is said that most of us are poor, it is not to our infamy but to our glory. . . . On the other hand, how can he be poor if he has no needs, if he does not long for others, if he is rich before God?"[30] And again: "Our poor have found wisdom and have taught others. From this we can see that ingenuity is not given by wealth nor is it acquired through study."[31] Within Christianity, poverty was often associated with holiness. Saints were by their very nature poor.[32]

In Late Antiquity, the continuous call to almsgiving and giving to the poor by Christian preachers—such calls were addressed above all to people of the same faith—along with the scarcity of pagan sources in this regard seems to give the impression that the category of "the poor" was invented by those Christian preachers. The poor did not constitute a social class. They had no voice and yet they existed even before Christians came on the scene. The Christian approach, rather, highlights the contrast and even opposition between the poor and the rich (the *pauperes* and the *divites*) precisely because that opposition is inspired by a whole biblical tradition. As will be seen below, the centrality of almsgiving in Christian ethics as a duty for all including both rich and poor must be seen in light of one's eternal salvation. Previously, relief for the poor could be an act of mercy, of *humanitas*, of *pietas*, and for some even a sign of their belonging to a higher class. The teaching of most of the church, with the exception of a few bishops, argued that its properties are for the *bona pauperum* (the good of the poor). Even objects of value were considered to be for the poor.

A CHRISTIAN PERSPECTIVE

Christianity[33] introduced new concepts and ideas along with a new anthropology. Every human being was created in the image of God and therefore there were no distinctions of worth. Within the Christian community there was a distinction between the *fideles*, that is, the baptized and the catechumens who aspired to baptism. Between the faithful, distinctions of orders were created between the clergy and the *plebs*, but all had access to the same sacraments, whether one was free, a noble, or a slave. All were brothers and sisters in Christ. Around 310, the layman Lactantius summed it up as follows:

> Some will say, Are there not among you some poor, and others rich; some servants and others masters? Is there not some difference between individuals? There is none, nor is there any other cause why we mutually bestow upon each other the name of brothers, except that we believe

ourselves to be equal. For since we measure all human things not by the body, but by the spirit, although the condition of bodies is different, yet we have no servants, but we both regard and speak of them as brothers in spirit, in religion as fellow-servants (*spiritu fratres, religione conservi*). Riches also do not render men illustrious, except that they are able to make them more conspicuous by good works. For men are rich, not because they possess riches, but because they employ them in works of justice. And those who seem to be poor, on this account are rich because they are not in want and desire nothing. Therefore, although in lowliness of mind we are equal—the free are on an equal footing with slaves, as are the rich with the poor—nevertheless before God we are distinguished by virtue.[34]

He echoes Tertullian who affirms that Christians are *fratres et conservi* (brothers and fellow servants).[35] One may wonder if Lactantius was expressing only an eschatological ideal or if this was propaganda written to the pagans to accentuate the contrasts. Certainly, the statement is against what was the actual reality in his time.

The name that Christians gave each other—or even when bishops qualified all the members of a community as brothers—expressed a way of thinking, even if in reality things were different.[36] At the beginning of the second century, because the Christians said that all were brothers in the faith, some slaves pretended to be freed and the community then paid for their manumission. Ignatius writes: "Do not despise either male or female slaves, yet neither let them be puffed up with conceit, but rather let them submit themselves the more, for the glory of God, that they may obtain from God a better liberty. Let them not long to be set free [from slavery] at the public expense, that they be not found slaves to their own desires."[37]

Many Latin terms were reserved for members of the upper class to indicate their social, political and economic status and to mark their distinction from members of other classes. For example some of the terms used by the upper class were: *dignitas, nobilitas, honor, gravitas, honestas*. Christian authors now began to apply them to the *fideles*, as members of the body of Christ. This process is referred to as an ascending metaphorical ennoblement.[38] The words of Pope Leo in a Christmas sermon are well known: "Be aware, O Christian, of your dignity. You have been elevated to communion with the divine nature and you do not want to devolve into the baseness of your former conduct. Remember which Head and which mystical body of which you are a member. Think about the fact of your liberation from the power of darkness and your transfer into the light and kingdom of God."[39] In the new vision, "all are hired servants, all are workers" (*omnes mercenarii, omnes operarii*) of Christ.[40] In another sense, all Christians are also beggars of Christ (*mendici Christi*).[41] This is an expression dear to Augustine, since every Christian is a *mendicus Christi* or *Dei*.[42] Even social relations appear to be ennobled. Christian inscriptions, for instance, do not mention people's high positions or honors, which are normal aspects in pagan epitaphs. On the other hand, there are frequent indications of their professions including what trades they plied, even those that were not at all prestigious, as in the catacomb of San Callisto where a certain Valerius Pardus built the tomb of his wife and included the symbols of the peasant.[43] The freedman Secundus also constructed the tomb of his worthy mistress, Marcia Rufina, in the crypt of Cornelius with the insignia of the workshop: a hammer and anvil.[44]

The social binary which gradually evolved in the Roman Empire, with many local varieties, was itself gradually overtaken by Christians with another mainly economic binary that partly replaced it: that of the rich and the poor. Of course, the two new categories were understood in different temporal, regional and authorial contexts. Between the two categories there was also that of the *mediocres* (ordinary).

Christians employed traditional concepts widely to speak of an identity and a belonging, referring to their heavenly citizenship and acknowledging that while on earth they were only pilgrims with no abiding home. The new citizenship was acquired through baptism. Christians did recognize, however, that they had dual citizenship in that they must render to Caesar what is Caesar's and to God what is God's. The *Epistle to Diognetus* which we have quoted elsewhere, notes for instance:

> Christians are indistinguishable from other men either by nationality, language or customs. They do not inhabit separate cities of their own, or speak a strange dialect, or follow some outlandish way of life.... With regard to dress, food and manner of life in general, they follow the customs of whatever city they happen to be living in, whether it is Greek or foreign. And yet there is something extraordinary about their lives. They live in their own countries as though they were only passing through. They play their full role as citizens, but labor under all the disadvantages of aliens. Any country can be their homeland, but for them their homeland, wherever it may be, is a foreign country. Like others, they marry and have children, but they do not expose them. They share their meals, but not their wives. Living in Greek and barbaric cities, as it has happened to each one of them, and adapting to the customs of the place in its dress, in its food and in the rest, they testify to an admirable and undoubtedly paradoxical method of social life. They live in their own country, but as strangers; they participate in everything as citizens and from everything they are detached as foreigners. Every foreign homeland is their homeland, and every homeland is foreign.[45]

SCRIPTURAL UNDERSTANDING OF RICH AND POOR

READING THE TWO TESTAMENTS TOGETHER

Christians mined the Old Testament to express the binary between rich and poor, but only utilized those texts that were useful for their purpose. The oldest Jewish tradition considered Sheol, the realm of the dead, as an equalizing place where the dead gathered without distinction of rank, social or moral condition. It included the rich and the poor, the pious and the impious, the old and the young, the master and the slave (*Ezek* 32; *Is* 14; *Job* 23). Rewards and punishments were received while on earth. Wealth and well-being in this life were signs of divine blessing, but since there were endless exceptions to this rule there were searches for better explanations, such as that found in the book of Job or in apocalyptic literature. Jewish piety attended to the poor with mercy as well as mandating almsgiving. It developed the idea of a future reversal and the overturning of the situation of individual disadvantaged persons. Development of Jewish belief in the afterlife, after the invasion of Palestine by Alexander the Great about 333 BCE along with its subsequent occupation, was reflected in *Daniel* 12, the *Wisdom of Solomon* 5, and 2 *Maccabees* 7. In Palestine there were people who chose poverty in order to dedicate themselves to God, such as was the case with the Qumran community.

This is the milieu in which Jesus arrived on the scene, placing the Kingdom of God and the transience of all things in this world at the center of it all. He counseled his followers to seek first his kingdom and his righteousness. He spoke of the poor in spirit as blessed (*beati pauperes in spiritu* of *Mt* 5:3) so that the term "poor" took on a new positive meaning in the Latin translations of the New Testament, having a spiritual connotation. Does *pauperes* in Latin have the same meaning as the original Greek text, *ptōchoi*, which referred to those who were dependent on others for support, and saw the poor as beggars?[46] *Pauperes* and many similar terms such as *mendicus, humilis, pupillus,* became associated with spiritual virtue in relationship to God. A connection was established between being poor and being humble. The poverty of Christ, according to Paul's words, is inspiring: "For you know the grace of our Lord Jesus Christ: though he was rich, he became poor for your sake, so that you through his poverty might become rich" (*2 Cor* 8:9).[47] Augustine often exalted the poverty of Christ; he was deeply struck by it.[48] *Sermon* 14 illustrates what poverty he wants to talk about:

> Let's look for the poor, let's look for the orphan. It is no wonder that I invite you to look for what we see everywhere and experience being there in abundance. Aren't they all places full of the poor? Aren't all the places full of orphans? . . . There are poor people who have no money, who barely find daily food, who are so in need of the compassion and help of others, who are not even ashamed of begging. . . . And what other hope would we have if we were not abandoned in the one who does not abandon us?[49]

Before we proceed further, there's a question that comes up. Isn't there a contradiction between the vision of the Old Testament and the teaching preached by Jesus? Of course, there is an evolution in the same Jewish tradition. The pagan Celsus saw an irreconcilable contrast on this point. He points out how Jesus, predicated as the Son of God, teaches the opposite of what Judaism teaches. While the God of the Jews exhorts us to be rich, to become powerful, to fill the earth, and to kill, Jesus teaches that the rich, those who aspire to domination, those eager for fame cannot access the Father. Again: "that one must worry about food or the pantry no more than the crows do, or about clothing less than the lilies do."[50] He is using the gospel of Luke and intends to highlight the contrast between the two Testaments. Origen replies that in Scripture there is a deeper sense than the literal one; based on this principle he explains the various biblical statements.

But what is the Christian attitude? We must never generalize and think that all pagans are bad, and all Christians are good. The exhortation to alms, the criticism of the rich, the condemnation of unfair wealth, the provisions against the stingy, selfish and usurious clergy constitute the negative aspects. A change of perspective is undeniable. The Christian attitude towards the poor and poverty manifests a change of values in the life of the late antique city. Christian preaching, which is the primary instrument of Christian communication, is rich in references to poverty and its social forms and to the various categories of the needy: from the prisoner, to the sick, to the orphan and widow, to the prostitute, and the list goes on. This preaching influences the creation of a new sensitivity and therefore new concerns. The vocabulary for the poor was also changing.[51] "The Christian author normally avoided those words that had political, social or moral nuances—*infamis, ignobilis, insufficiens, humilior, tenuior* —*miser* takes on a spiritual connotation."[52]

For Christians, who prefer to use the term *pauper*, the poor are those who are hungry, thirsty and cold, and therefore need to be helped in these elementary needs. Lactantius asks polemically: "What is the reason why [the pagans] do not think they should help those who are hungry, thirsty and cold? . . . The only certain and genuine task of liberality is to sustain the needy and useless."[53] Lactantius' remark introduces us in some way to the sensitivity and values of that society, so distant from us. They are not worried about facing a theoretical or theological reflection, but in dealing with the problems of everyday life and therefore to change the mentality of the time about the poor, that is, the people right in front of them. Historical contexts and concrete situations are different in the second century than the fourth century, and so the preaching and teaching of the fathers adapt to the new demands of the times. But it is also true that the family and social background can help us to place individual Christian authors in a better position to understand them better.

From the beginning, the attitude of Christians towards the rich and riches presents a range of nuances. The evangelist Luke, for instance, more than the other evangelists, uses the term 'poor' in the concrete sense of truly poor people. To begin with, Jesus and the disciples are poor; and the heirs of the kingdom are concretely poor. Luke describes the idyllic situation of the communion of goods prevalent in Jerusalem, but such a communion of goods is only a voluntary act and done only by some and is not obligatory for all.[54] However, the presence of a community structure that tends towards equality between the various components is undeniable: everyone puts themselves under the authority of the Twelve, the breaking of bread (*fractio panis*) is something they all hold in common, they all offer their assistance to the needy with the provision of those who are the wealthiest. But the experience of Jerusalem, the extent and breadth of which we do not know, was suppressed by persecution.

The *Letter of James*,[55] on the other hand, reflects a bitter controversy against the rich and their wealth, highlighting the dangers for salvation they face (*James* 1:10-11; 5:1-6). The social situation was different because there was someone in their midst from the upper class, like the one who comes into the assembly with the gold ring on his finger: "For if a man with gold rings and in fine clothing comes into your assembly, and a poor man in shabby clothing also comes in, and you pay attention to the one who wears the fine clothing and say, 'Have a seat here, please,' while you say to the poor man, 'Stand there,' or, 'Sit at my feet,' have you not made distinctions among yourselves, and become judges with evil thoughts?" (*James* 2:2-4; cf. 1:9-10). The letter ends with an invective against the rich landowners who have accumulated wealth at the expense of the workers (*James* 5:1-6). The workers will be their condemnation (*James* 5:2). The message is that of a certain equality and the sharing of material goods and mutual help to create harmony.

The *Didache*, from the second half of the first century, exhorts in various ways to give alms to the needy according to Jewish tradition. Almsgiving is an aspect of justice and a good thing for the recipient and also for the giver.[56] In the following chapter the author repeats his exhortations not to close your heart to the needy; and again: "But if you do not have a prophet, give to the poor."[57]

Towards the end of the first century, Clement of Rome writes: "The rich should help the poor, and the poor person in turn thanks God because he gave him those who begged for his poverty."[58] This message of sharing is also repeated by other authors such as Hermas in the *Shepherd* of Hermas.[59] Even giving requires discernment, as in other deeds.

Some Judeo-Christian sects at the time tended to exalt pauperism: poverty was magnified for its own sake and considered necessary for salvation. Even at the end of the fourth century and the beginning of the fifth there were some groups, such as the Manicheans, the Pelagians and others who were against owning property and considered poverty essential for salvation.[60] Some groups absolutely denied carnal relationships, marriage and any physical union. Normally they considered wealth as not a detriment in itself, but an obstacle and a burden to rid oneself of materiality. Wealth could be the cause of sins, but poverty on the other hand promoted adherence to God. We find this sentiment for instance in the *Acts of Thomas* which tended toward an Ebionite worldview:[61] "[I] do not even possess wealth like some others, which, being useless at all and being left on the earth from which it comes, ultimately ruins whoever is its master."[62] Marcion, who preferred the Gospel of Luke, concedes that "the richness of creation belongs to the god of this world and therefore prevents the acceptance of the pure goodness of the God revealed in Christ, who is poor."[63] For him, wealth and poverty had no ethical value because they were not able to obtain God's free revelation.

In fact, in the first and second centuries, the Christian community was made up of a large majority of poor or middle class, so that in the eyes of the pagans *pauperes* were Christians, as Minucius Felix testifies.[64] And Christians were not ashamed at this identification: "Most are called poor" (*plerique pauperes dicimur*).[65]

The conversion of the rich was more difficult both for political reasons because of difficulties in making a career in the *cursus honorum,* and for social reasons due to the difficulty of Christians inserting themselves into the social life of the city of that time—both for the obligations of brotherhood which they were to show to all, even slaves, imposed by the new religion, and also because of the possibility of being blackmailed by their own slaves or others who might denounce them for being adherents to Christianity.[66] Thus Lactantius notes: "It happens that the poor and the humble believe in God more easily than the rich."[67]

Among Christians, some chose voluntary poverty for ascetical reasons, without particular social or community significance. This must have caused a lively debate within the community since numerous writings point out the dangers of wealth which blinds and distances us from the Christian life.[68] However, the prevailing doctrine, which will later become common to the whole church, taught that wealth was not an evil in itself, and was ethically irrelevant; indeed, it was to be considered as a gift from God.[69] On the other hand, with a few exceptions, poverty was never considered a good in itself. To someone who could have thought of it in this way, the *Pseudo-Clementines* answer:

> Do we not see many impious men poor? Then do these belong to the saved on this account? And Peter said: Not at all; for that poverty is not acceptable which longs for what it ought not. So that some are rich as far as their choice goes, though poor in actual wealth, and they are punished because they desire to have more. But one is not unquestionably righteous because he happens to be poor. For he can be a beggar as far as actual wealth is concerned, but he may desire and even do what above everything he ought not to do. Thus, he may worship idols, or be a blasphemer or fornicator, or he may live indiscriminately, or perjure himself, or lie, or live the life of an unbeliever.[70]

One can therefore possess things, but must refuse greed, avarice, and a thirst for riches.[71]

"God did not forbid one to be honestly rich, but did forbid one to be rich in an unjust and insatiable way."[72] Therefore, the sin was in one's attachment to wealth.[73]

Christianity insists on the detachment from wealth, stressing the duty to help those in need. This aspect was one of the most relevant characteristics of ancient Christianity both in doctrine and in one's actual life lived out in faith. All the authors who mention the subject speak of it, especially when commenting on the Gospel episode of the rich young man—and there are many authors who comment on the episode.[74]

Mention should be made of Clement of Alexandria († ca. 215), who knew many of the rich people of Alexandrian society at the beginning of the third century. He was the first writer to deal with the theme of wealth and poverty in a broad and articulate discourse in his treatise entitled *Who of the Rich Can Be Saved* (*Quis dives salvetur?*) The title alludes only to the problem of wealth, although he also speaks of penance. The title raises the question of whether the rich can be saved, as if the rich person cannot be saved. He recognizes that wealth is a danger:

> ... because, although wealth is of itself sufficient to puff up and corrupt the souls of its possessors, and to turn them from the path by which salvation is to be attained, [those who praise the rich] stupefy them still more, by inflating the minds of the rich with the pleasures of extravagant praises, and by making them utterly despise all things except wealth, on account of which they are admired; bringing, as the saying is, fire to fire, pouring pride on pride, and adding conceit to wealth, a heavier burden to that which by nature is a weight, from which somewhat ought rather to be removed and taken away as being a dangerous and deadly disease.[75]

The flatterers of the rich are corrupters because they help to divert them from the faith. The saying of the Lord: "'that it is easier for a camel to go through the eye of a needle than for a rich man to enter into the kingdom of heaven,' (*Mt* 19:24) despair of themselves as not destined to live, surrender all to the world, cling to the present life as if it alone was left to them, and so diverge more from the way to the life to come, no longer inquiring either whom the Lord and Master calls rich, or how that which is impossible to man becomes possible to God."[76] His exegesis of this text understands that lack of goods is not something admirable in itself; on the contrary, it can constitute an obstacle to a serene life devoted to the things of the spirit.[77] Likewise, it is not a particular merit to strip oneself of all goods and then to preserve one's desire or longing for them and one's attachment to them.[78] Wealth is a gift from God and even helps us to fulfill the precepts of the Lord.

Wealth and poverty as such have no ethical qualification and are therefore not decisive for the attainment of salvation. Both the rich and the poor can be full of longings, desires and coveting of wealth. For this reason, Clement's ethical and religious judgment focuses on the way in which goods are obtained, whether the behavior was honest or not,[79] and on their use according to the will of Christ.[80] Clement insists on charity.[81] Wealth should not be thrown away; but it all depends on how it is used, for good or for evil. The rich must learn how to use wealth because God desires the salvation of all. The text is a discourse on conversion. This is why it also includes the account of the conversion of the robber who had been a disciple of the Apostle John, but fell away.

Clement is important, because his ideological positions influence the subsequent reflection which follows substantially the same line of thought, despite the variety of emphases and variations. Given that wealth is viewed in a largely positive light—which has no relevance from an ethical point of view—the judgment instead focuses on the manner of how it is attained and used. Other areas of focus include one's attachment to wealth, the needs of charity and the use of wealth from time to time motivated by the gospel expressed in love for others. Detachment from wealth, views on wealth in terms of justice along with a tendency towards a certain leveling of social classes existing within the community are some of the other ways wealth is examined. Moreover, if all the fathers agreed on the need for emotional detachment from goods, there were still always those in the ancient church (and not only then) who also practiced the most austere forms of effective detachment, such as certain forms of monasticism and pauperism. The common thought of the church was concerned with the social and spiritual aspect of renunciation of wealth, and in the preaching of the fathers of the second half of the fourth century ascetic motives were also grafted in, since many of them had received monastic formation. The legitimacy of owning private property, however, was never questioned.

At the beginning of the fifth century when many very rich families became Christians and dedicated themselves to asceticism, one strong voice was that of the Pelagian author of *On the Riches* (*De divitiis*). He made the following distinction, "Every person is to be considered rich, or poor, or sufficient to himself,"[82] which is a very rudimentary sociology based on a biblical quotation from Matthew 6:34. He is a champion of sufficiency, of possessing what is necessary according to nature. The inspiration for saying this is the imitation of Christ's poverty: "If I am not mistaken, it is in poverty, not in wealth, in humility, not in the glory of the world, not with longing, but with contemplation [that Christians are to be engaged].[83]

He is scandalized by the fact that Christians, to whom the same law (*eadem lex*) was given, oppress and harass others. There are so many varieties of Christians! The poor Christian, like Christ, stand before the judge in court, while the rich Christian sits in the tribunal (*in tribunal*) as a corrupt judge.[84]

LABOR

As I mentioned earlier, the term *pauper* has a range of meanings and does not correspond to our term 'poor'; the same must be said for the word *work*.[85] There is no such term that corresponds to what we think of when we hear the term *work*. The Greek term *ergon* designates a completed work, while the Latin word *labor* (Gk. *pónos*) indicates effort and fatigue. The ancients talk about professions in everyday life. Whoever does a job is dependent on the one who pays, so he is not a free man. The farmer, on the other hand, is a free man, but is not necessarily rich even though he makes a considerable physical effort, and not all those who work in the countryside are free people either.[86]

The modern concept of work, understood in a general sense, comes instead from the industrial revolution. The ancients do not have any discussions about the ethics of labor, or trade, or earning a living. The great Greek philosophers such as Plato and Aristotle already considered manual laborers to be inferior and at the service of their masters. A quotation by Cicero[87] sums up the mentality of the aristocrats:

> Now regarding trades and other means of livelihood, which ones are to be considered becoming to a gentleman and which ones are vulgar, we have been taught, in general, as follows. First, those means of livelihood are rejected as undesirable which incur people's ill-will, as those of tax-gatherers and usurers. Unbecoming to a gentleman, too, and vulgar are the means of livelihood of all hired workmen whom we pay for mere manual labor, not for artistic skill; for in their case the very wage they receive is a pledge of their slavery. Vulgar we must consider those also who buy from wholesale merchants and sell at retail immediately; for they would get no profits without a great deal of downright lying; and truly, there is no action that is meaner than misrepresentation. And all mechanics are engaged in vulgar trades; for no workshop can have anything liberal about it. Least respectable of all are those trades which cater to sensual pleasures: Fishmongers, butchers, cooks, those who keep chickens, and fishermen, as Terence says. Add to these, if you please, the perfumers, dancers, and the whole *corps de ballet*. But the professions in which either a higher degree of intelligence is required or from which no small benefit to society is derived—medicine and architecture, for example, and teaching—these are proper for those whose social position they become. Trade, if it is on a small scale, is to be considered vulgar; but if wholesale and on a large scale, importing large quantities from all parts of the world and distributing it to many without misrepresentation, it is not to be greatly disparaged. In fact, it even seems to deserve the highest respect, if those who are engaged in it, satiated, or rather, I should say, satisfied with the fortunes they have made, make their way from the port to a country estate, as they have often made it from the sea into port. But of all the occupations by which gain is secured, none is better than agriculture, none more profitable, none more delight-

ful, none more becoming to a freeman. But since I have discussed this quite fully in my *Cato Major*, you will find there the material that applies to this point.[88]

Other authors confirm this view, such as Seneca in his *Letter* 88.21 and *De vita beata* 22.

The Apostle Paul, on the other hand, is proud that he provides for his needs with his own work and that he does manual labor. "We work hard with our hands" (*1 Cor* 4:12); "You remember our labor and toil, brothers and sisters; we worked night and day, so that we might not burden any of you while we proclaimed to you the gospel of God" (*1 Thess* 2:9); "But we urge you, beloved, to do so more and more, [11] to aspire to live quietly, to mind your own affairs, and to work with your hands, as we directed you, so that you may behave properly toward outsiders and be dependent on no one" (*1 Thess* 4:11-12); "Thieves must give up stealing; rather let them labor and work honestly with their own hands, so as to have something to share with the needy" (*Eph* 4:28); "For you yourselves know how you ought to imitate us; we were not idle when we were with you, and we did not eat anyone's bread without paying for it; but with toil and labor we worked night and day, so that we might not burden any of you" (*2 Thess* 3:7-8). Luke already in the *Acts of the Apostles* expresses in his own way the attitude of the Apostle: "In all this I have given you an example that by such work we must support the weak, remembering the words of the Lord Jesus, for he himself said: It is more blessed to give than to receive" (*Acts* 20:35). This saying of Jesus is recalled by later authors such as Clement of Rome (*1 Clement* 2.7); Clement of Alexandria (*Quis dives* 31.7), Epiphanius (*Haer.* 74.5) and the author of the *Apostolic Constitutions* (5.3.1).

Because Christians did not take part in certain categories of professions, pagans considered them to be *infructuosi negotiis*, i.e. unprofitable in terms of the commercial activity in the cities. Tertullian responds to this objection in his *Apology*:

> But we are called to account also on a different charge and are accused of being unprofitable in business matters. How can this be true of men who live with you, who enjoy the same food, have the same manner of life, and dress and are under the same necessities of existence? For we are neither Brahmins nor Indian gymnosophists who dwell in the forests and exile themselves from ordinary life. We remember the gratitude we owe to God our Lord and Creator. We reject no fruit of his works, though it is true we refrain from the excessive or wrong use of them. Consequently, we live together with you in the world, foregoing neither the forum, nor the slaughterhouses, nor your baths, shops, workshops, taverns, fairs or other places of commerce. We also sail with you, and serve in the army with you, and till the ground with you, and engage in trade as you do. Even in the various arts we make our work publicly available to you for your benefit.[89]

The moral teaching of the fathers can arouse wonder in the modern reader: the insistence on the necessity of work and the rejection of idleness. The fathers often speak of the obligation to work, following Paul's teaching: "For even when we were with you, we gave you this command: Anyone unwilling to work should not eat" (*2 Thess* 3:10). And yet there are also many biblical texts of the Old and New Testaments which refer to work (*Gen* 2:15; *Ex* 20:9; *Sir* 38:29-35; etc.; *Mk* 6:3; *Mt* 10:10; 13:1ff; 24:45-51). The *Didache* echoes Paul's words:

> But receive everyone who comes in the name of the Lord and prove and know him afterward; for you shall have understanding right and left. If he who comes is a wayfarer, assist him as far as you are able; but he shall not remain with you more than two or three days, if need be. But if he wants to stay with you, and is an artisan, let him work and eat. But if he has no trade, according to your understanding, see to it that, as a Christian, he shall not live with you idle. But if he wills not to do, he is a Christ-monger. Watch that you keep away from such.[90]

This first century text already expresses the two lines on which later exhortation will move: the need to work to be able to live and the escape from idleness as the father of vices. In fact, these two aspects are generally combined, as for instance in the *Didascalia* (1.4.5). The same prescription is also valid for the rich who, however, if they already have what they need, dedicate themselves to the study of Scripture.[91]

The fathers sometimes exalt the dignity of work as a participation in God's creative work. Irenaeus writes that human beings have, "received from God the hands to affirm and work. He who participates in the art and wisdom of God also shares in his power,"[92] but they also strongly emphasize his irreplaceable dignity and greatness. Through his work, human beings share in the work of the Creator, and thus give a personal seal to their accomplishments. They become aware, in the work accomplished, of what they are made of, their know-how and the talents they have received. Clement of Rome describes the satisfaction of the worker who has done his job well."[93] We must do our work well, like the builders of the tower in Hermas' vision.[94]

The fathers were not interested in the economy of labor, in production systems, or in the causes of wealth and poverty. Rather, their concern was man as such, rich or poor, and for the ethics of certain trades, as well as mutual responsibility. In general, they do not elaborate a theology of labor, limiting themselves to offering only indications of a moral nature, inasmuch as we are created for work (*creati ad laborem sumus*).[95] Augustine writes a work against those monks who reject manual labor and claim to be fed by the offerings of good people. His teaching is an explication of the teaching of Saint Paul and of his way of living and is in perfect harmony with the Gospel.[96]

When Augustine wrote these lines, the composition of the Christian community had changed sociologically compared to the first two centuries. If at the time of Tertullian and Origen, Christians were almost all craftsmen, traders, small businessmen, slaves, and soldiers; still, the majority was composed of women, both young and old. They worked at home doing domestic work, but they were also the ones who did weaving, sewed clothes, made sweaters and all kinds of clothing. At that time there were no clothing or shoe stores and not many professions like we have in modern times; many of the trades that did exist then exist no longer. Everyone basically lived off the work they did.

The many Christian epitaphs express the pride and merits of many manual workers.[97] The fathers, on the other hand, directed their attention to the morality of certain trades, especially to those that were not suitable for Christians. The *Apostolic Tradition* provides us with a list of them that included builders of idols and things destined for idolatrous worship, as well as all the actors and others involved in the theater due to their immoral and idolatrous content.[98]

The work of the monks deserves a separate discourse. There were two tendencies which emerged. The first, widespread in Egypt and in the West, allowed for manual labor; the other, prevalent in Syria, considered the more perfect life as one reliant on alms and the full trust of Providence, devoting themselves to prayer and other spiritual works. The *Statutes of the Ancient Church* (can. 29) obliged clerics to work, but in such a way that it did not detract from their ministry. Bishops such as Fulgentius of Ruspe also prescribed that clerics should work.[99]

PRIVATE PROPERTY

What has been said so far allows us to overcome a problem frequently debated concerning whether the fathers allowed or denied the right to own property.[100] They did not raise the question of the legality of the economic system of their time and only rarely addressed the theoretical aspect of property law. They limited themselves to more practical situations since they were concerned more with changing the individual than society, and more with the rich than the poor where property was concerned. Moreover, as a methodological principle, each text must be read in its historical context and in the current conceptions of the time. The concept of private property, as it is understood today especially in Western society, is a modern idea—that is, an absolute and unconditional power over what is possessed, without conditions and without limits. Private property ownership is a consequence of the secularization of law. In the biblical and Christian tradition, only God has absolute power over men and over all creation. The conclusion of the modern idea of ownership is expressed in the common saying, "My body is mine." Therefore, I have the right to every kind of freedom: to abortion, to sexual change, to assisted suicide, to be assisted at every need, over earthly things, etc. (*ius utendi et abutendi*).[101]

For Christianity, life is sacred in all its stages as a gift from God and must always be preserved. Since many people suffer, they must be helped in their suffering and need. Christians do not intend to change social and political structures, but to generate the new man. In fact, early Christians did not even call for the abolition of slavery—the existence of which is a scandal for us—although they did call for new relationships between persons, including slave owner and slave. The same must be said of the economic structures. The fathers do not seek the reasons for the existence of poverty but preach the application of the evangelical precepts of fraternal love and to help those in need of clothing and food. The economy is to be at the service of man and not vice versa.

Ambrose was a member of the aristocracy and aware of the disastrous situation of so many oppressed people and the dishonesty of the rich, who used any means to extort from even the poorest of the poor. But the other bishops of the same period in northern Italy also said had similar concerns, even if in a less effective way, such as Zeno of Verona, Gaudentius of Brescia and Maximus of Turin. The bishops preached the moralization of economic life in their time.[102] Previously, aristocrats as men of power (*potentiores*) did the same thing, but now there were people in their own class who could make their voices heard to alleviate the suffering of land workers, but also of city dwellers who could not afford to live there.

From the texts cited exhorting to charity it is evident that there were people in the community who owned properties. Their number increased as conversions of people in the upper classes increased. Their right to possess property was not disputed, but they were encouraged to be generous and fraternal. Even the strongest expressions, which seem to deny the right to own property, must be read in the context of a moral and religious parentage.

> Do not be someone who stretches forth the hands to receive and then draws them back when it's time to give. If you have anything, through your hands you shall give ransom for your sins. Do not hesitate to give, nor complain when you give; For you shall know who the good paymaster of your reward is. You shall not turn away from him that is in need but shall share with your brother in all things and not say that anything is exclusively your own. For if you are fellow partakers in that which is imperishable, how much more so in the things which are perishable?[103]

An even stronger expression of this sentiment is found in the *Shepherd* of Hermas: "The rich of this world, if they do not lose their riches, will not be able to be useful to the Lord."[104] The same phrase of the *Didache* is found almost verbatim in the *Epistle of Barnabas* (19.8). The episode of Ananias and Sapphira in the Acts of the Apostles clearly shows that one was not obligated to put everything in common (*Acts* 5:1-11; 11:29) and this freedom was never questioned (*1 Cor* 16:1-2; *2 Cor* 8:1; *Acts* 11:29). The full and absolute freedom of the donor also stands out in the continuous exhortation to charity and in explicit attestations. Justin writes: "The rich who have the ability, each according to his own ability, give what they want."[105] Tertullian insists on precisely this type of freedom of offering compared to pagan associations, where one was obliged to pay a fee.[106]

However, we note that the commitment and insistence to put things in common for the needs of all was diminishing with the enlargement of the communities and the lowering of the initial fervor and the reduction of eschatological tension. And yet, the repeated condemnation of not wanting other people's possessions and not stealing is an indirect confirmation of the right to own. After the Gothic invasion of Pontus in the middle of the third century, Gregory the Thaumaturge wrote a letter that was later included in the canonical collections which condemned a wide spectrum of cases of appropriation, abuse or neglect of the property of others.[107] Moreover, many of the clergy in that period were given to the accumulation of wealth.[108] The communities themselves owned their own properties, which in the course of the fourth century grew enormously. Clement of Alexandria vigorously rejected the theory of Epiphanius, son of Carpocrates who, arguing that the terms "*mine* and *yours* were introduced by the laws," admitted a complete commonality of goods and life, even in sexual relations.[109]

The new vision of goods offered by Christianity, in addition to their use, also concerned the way in which they were purchased. The fathers do not care if they come from inheritance, personal work or otherwise, provided they were procured honestly. They counsel agriculture and those professions that do not compromise their faith.[110] Any kind of dishonest gain was condemned, even the alteration of prices in the market,[111] and above all usury.

According to a traditional trend of thinking, dishonesty was linked to the trades or professions, as emerges from the quoted text of Cicero cited earlier. Augustine, on the other hand, linked it to the person. He reports a kind of dialogue with a merchant who imports goods from afar, who sells by telling lies, committing perjury and more, asserting that it is the merchant as such that is sinful.[112] This applies to all professions. Augustine, however, seeks to rehabilitate the trade, against the Ciceronian tradition[113] and against the anonymous author of the Commentary *In Matthaeum*.

In recent times, some have posed the problem of private property by studying the strong expressions of Ambrose, John Chrysostom and the three Cappadocians (especially Basil) and Augustine. Some statements seem to point in the direction of a certain communal ownership. For example, Ambrose says: "God has ordered all things to be produced, so that there should be food in common to all, and that the earth should be a common possession for all. Nature, therefore, has produced a common right for all; private possession on the other hand is produced by greed."[114]

The foundation of the fathers' statements is found in the biblical texts and in the doctrine of creation. The common idea of the fathers is that property does not come from a natural right, but from the human desire (*cupiditas*), which takes possession of common goods. Basil of Caesarea also preached:

> Think, O rich man, of your Benefactor; return to yourself, remember who you are, what goods you administer, from whom you received them as a custodian and for what reasons you were chosen among many others. You are the executor of the orders of God the Benefactor, the bursar of those who have the same fate as you, and do not think that everything is destined for your stomach: use the goods you have in your hands as if they belonged to others.[115]

This concept is repeated several times.

I shall dwell briefly on Augustine. For him only God is the possessor, the sole and supreme administrator of all the goods of this world:

> All those (animals) you do not own are mine, and these that you do own are mine too. If you are my servant, all your personal property belongs to me. If the property a slave has gained for himself belongs to his master, it cannot be the case that property the Master has created for the servant does not belong to its Creator. The forest animals that you have not caught are mine, and so are your cattle that graze upon the mountains, and the oxen that feed at your manger. They are all mine, because I created them.[116]

God is the donor of every earthly good.[117] However, in relation to individuals, there is a right to own property, a right that comes from natural law, as stated in the commentary to *Psalm* 57:1-2, based on the principle of not doing to others what we do not want to be done to us. Don't commit adultery, don't steal, don't covet the things of others. His teaching is against some groups who taught that poverty was essential to salvation.[118]

More relevant is how the goods were obtained under Roman law, whether by donation, trade, inheritance, or exchange.[119] If one possesses something in good faith, he is a legitimate owner (*possessor*), but he is not so when he discovers that he possesses it illegally.[120] Ambrose's quoted phrase above that "private possession is produced by greed" goes against Roman tradition, which claims the opposite.[121] Ambrosiaster, who was known to Augustine, also maintained that "everything is common to all" (*omnia . . . communiter omnibus*).[122] For Augustine riches generate avarice, which then causes one to refuse to share them.[123] Avarice makes us desire more at the expense of others.[124] One desires more and more and the rich are corroded by their possessions and the desire to possess.[125]

In conclusion Augustine admits the right to private property but affirms its limits and dangers. He condemns the so-called '*apostolici*,' because "they do not admit to each other who has contracted marriage and who possesses a private patrimony."[126] The Catholic Church also legitimately possesses its goods based on human right:

> By human law, however, one says: this estate is mine, this house is mine, this servant is mine. By human law, therefore, is by right of the emperors. Why so? Because God has distributed to humankind these very human rights through the emperors and kings of this world. Do you wish us to read the laws of the emperors, and to act by the estates according to these laws? If you will have your possession by human right, let us recite the laws of the emperors; let us see whether they would have the heretics possess anything. But what is the emperor to me? you say. It is by right from him that you possess the land. Or take away rights created by emperors, and then who will dare say: that estate is mine, or that slave is mine, or this house is mine?[127]

USURY

In Latin there are several terms to indicate loans with interest: *usura, fenus, centesima, impendium, hemiòlion*. The two terms *usura* (generally in the plural: usurae) and *fenus* (*foenus, faenus*) often overlap although they each have a different meaning. *Usura* indicates the interest earned, i.e., the profit; while *fenus* refers to the loan of money made for profit, the capital invested by the *faenerator*.[128] But Augustine notes: "The Latin word *feneratur* indicates both the lender and the receiver." He immediately adds that this double meaning, which he is using in preaching, is not according to the grammar: "It is better that you understand with our barbarism, rather than with our eloquence you remain abandoned."[129]

At present, usury means a loan of high interest, which easily turns into exploitation; while in the period in which Saint Augustine lived, it means, on the part of the fathers, any loan: *quodcumque sorti* (sors = capital) *accedit usura est*,[130] that is, any return that is added to the money lent is a form of usury. Jerome presents the following definition: "Usury consists in receiving more than one has lent."[131] Augustine instead offers different definitions that have a more descriptive character of the phenomenon. In a sermon he states: "But do you know what usury is? Give a lower sum and receive more."[132] Loans are made not only in money, but in small towns, especially "in grain, wine or oil."[133]

The Roman law allowed the loan at a low interest rate, but limited itself to fighting abuses, setting only the criteria.[134] In the fourth century the phenomenon of interest-bearing loans, given the unfavorable economic conditions, had become more widespread, and it was used by the neediest in case of emergency. For these reasons, the condemnation of the fathers emerges strongly. Those who have taken goods with interest are often unable to repay the debt. While the preaching of the fathers severely condemned the usury exercised by Christians, without distinction, the Council canons of Late Antiquity severely condemned only that exercised by the clergy. The fathers of the Church, even if they added considerations taken from the Greco-Roman ethical tradition, based their absolute condemnation of all forms of usury, that is, of any interest-bearing loan, on the biblical texts, especially those in the Old Testament.

Before that period there were only sporadic references in Christian writers, perhaps because less use was made of loans. The fathers condemned any kind of loan intended to receive more than what had been lent: *usura est plus accipere quam dare*.[135] To us today it seems natural and perfectly legitimate to lend at a low interest rate, while for the ancient Christians, "the profit of money is the death of the soul" (*fenus pecuniae funus est animae*).[136] Already Clement of Alexandria, in the third century, clearly formulated the Christian attitude: "The law prohibits lending with interest to the brother. By saying 'the brother,' means not only the one who was born of common parents, but also who is of the same race and the same doctrine, and is a participant in the same Logos."[137] This text implies that one *can* exercise usury towards those who are not of the same race and community of faith.

Cyprian in the *Testimonia*[138] collects some biblical texts to demonstrate that one should not lend with interest (*non faenerandum*). At the same time, others go even further, asserting that even charity is not acceptable to God for usurers.[139] Especially in the fourth century, the fathers were against usury, understood in an ancient and not a modern sense. There are two homilies on the subject, one by Basil and the other by Gregory of Nyssa.[140] In the West, the intervention of Leo the Great is particularly significant as he vigorously condemns it in a letter addressed to various bishops; the essential passage then passed into the canonical collections (*Hadriana*), strongly influencing the later moral judgment until the condemnation of the Third Lateran Council of 1179, which denies the ecclesiastical burial to usurers (can. 25). Already in the fourth century interest loans were condemned by numerous councils, sometimes even imposing excommunication and deposition for the clergy, as evidenced at the councils of Elvira (can. 20); Arles (can. 12); Nicaea (can. 17); Carthage of 348 (can. 13), and others.[141] The reasons given by the fathers for such severity are based not only on the Old Testament but also on humanitarian reasons of charity and the needs of the poor.

Following the teaching of the Councils, among which is that of Hippo in 393 in which Augustine had participated as a presbyter, Augustine in line with the teaching of Ambrose's *De Tobia* which he had read, first of all condemns usury and loans practiced not only by clerics but any type of loan issued by anyone. The condemnation I found both in the sermons and in the letters. In his letter he writes:

> What about the interest earned with usury, which the same laws and judges command us to repay? Which is crueler? Perhaps the one who steals something from a rich man, or the rich man who ruins a poor man with usury? These and other income of this kind are undoubtedly

possessed unjustly and I would demand their return; but there is no judge by which they can claim themselves.[142]

In a sermon he is very severe.[143]

Augustinian teaching has had a great influence. In order to explain usury, Gratian takes up the Augustinian definition that is given in the commentary on Psalm 36.[144] In this passage Augustine distinguishes between consumer loans (*mutuum*) and interest-bearing loans (*fenus*); he speaks both of the loan of money and of other goods, but in any case, receiving more than the loan is to be condemned. He distinguishes the simple loan from the actual usury: "And you will lend to many nations. Scripture refers to money given as a loan as *fenerationem* (lending with interest), even if no interest (*usurae*) is received." (*et fenerabis gentes multas. fenerationem scriptura dicit mutuo datam pecuniam, etiam si usurae non accipiantur*).[145]

SLAVERY AND CHRISTIANITY

The structure of a society of inequalities, as has been said—not only in daily lives, but in the legislation itself of the society—is immediately obvious to us today.[146] The existence of slavery on a large scale is always striking, something which the early church did not fight against, although it did try to humanize it since the clergy had their slaves and even the churches had slaves who worked for the ecclesial community. However, slavery was above all a legal fact and not just a social one. The slave was one who was not *sui iuris*, independent and free, but he still could nonetheless be rich and credentialed as a doctor, scribe, courier, schoolteacher, famous cook and wealthy—or, on the other hand, one condemned to a miserable life of despair.

According to the Roman tradition, "Slaves are either already born or become slaves. They are born of our female slaves; they become so by right of the people, that is, by captivity, or by civil law" (*servi autem aut nascuntur aut fiunt. Nascuntur ex ancillis nostris: fiunt aut iure gentium, id est ex captivitate, aut iure civili*);[147] that is, the slave is born of a slave mother, even if the father is a free man, or he loses his freedom for various reasons, such as imprisonment or being taken captive. There is a corrective to slavery through manumission, where through a legal process the slave becomes *libertus* and acquires his freedom, but is still linked to the *patronus*. The freedman becomes a citizen but does not yet enjoy full civil rights. The slave does not always want to be manumitted and acquire freedom, especially when he is doing well in a family or with a master. Freedom was not always an advantage in ancient society. The slave's health was an investment for the master. Like objects, slaves could be bought and sold under certain conditions. I quote in the endnote an example of a tablet, a real contract with witnesses, found in Romania in Alburns Maior (Roşia Montană), which deals with the purchase of a slave under certain conditions.[148] This example of a slave purchase, certainly commercial as evidenced in the details, is written in the year 137.[149]

Roman jurists recognized that freedom is a natural right. But the laws were appalling for runaway slaves. Some improvements were of benefit not only to the slaves, but also to the masters. Allowing unions between slaves promoted the birth of slaves at home, and so it was actually a less expensive way to obtain them. Since slavery was a legal fact, there was a huge disparity among the slaves themselves. There were slaves who were privileged because they had certain skills and were more enterprising; some were in fact wealthy and might even possess other slaves. Some slaves were even in a better position that those who were free.

In the New Testament there were Christians who possessed slaves. But in all the texts a new spirit of equality and fraternity transpires.[150] The equality of all men before God is affirmed. There are no distinctions of race, sex, social, political or legal condition.[151]

The *Letter to the Colossians* teaches how Christian slaves must behave: "Slaves, obey in everything those who are your earthly masters, not with eye service, as men-pleasers, but in singleness of heart, fearing the Lord. Whatever your task, work heartily, as serving the Lord and not men, knowing that from the Lord you will receive the inheritance as your reward; you are serving the Lord Christ" (*Col* 3:22-24). And concerning the masters he commands: "Masters, treat your slaves justly and fairly, knowing that you also have a Master in heaven" (*Col* 4:1). Slaves and masters are subject to the same Lord as all and they must live in harmony and in mutual respect.[152] From these texts the idea emerges that while Christians try to regulate human relations ethically, they do not abolish slavery. Rather, they address both the masters and the slaves, indicating their mutual duties. Their main concern is not ecclesial or social discipline, but the salvation of individuals in their own context lived in the world; this is true for both masters and slaves. The moral and inner life are at the core of their teaching because slaves are not "things" (*res*) that are possessed but have an inner life and a personal and moral religious experience. This conception is extremely subversive in that society because the dignity of a person is at stake who by human right is a slave, that is, not a free person.

A passage from the *Epistle to the Ephesians* seems to be fundamental: " Slaves, obey your earthly masters with fear and trembling, in singleness of heart, as you obey Christ; not only while being watched, and in order to please them, but as slaves of Christ, doing the will of God from the heart. Render service with enthusiasm, as to the Lord and not to men, knowing that whatever good we do, we will receive the same again from the Lord, whether we are slaves or free" (*Eph* 6:5-7). The masters are such according to the flesh and the slave also must not be hypocritical. He is a slave of the Lord from whom he receives the reward; even the master in this is equal to the slave and must not command with threats.

Dauvillier's consideration was clarifying: "It should be noted that the Apostles do not say a single word that justifies slavery—unlike the authority exercised by the prince over the state, the father over the children, the husband over the wife. This means that they do not believe that this institution is based on the natural order and should remain unchanged."[153]

The biblical tradition of the Old Testament does not condemn slavery. Therefore, even the Jews had and would continue to have slaves—at least those who could afford them. This background affects the teaching of the early Christians, as it is an uncontested institution. One can compare the attitude of the Jews with that which was prevalent in the same period throughout the Mediterranean world.[154] The emperor Constantine in fact allowed for the possession of slaves by the Jews, but forbade them to circumcise Christian and even non-Christian slaves.[155] And so, Jews were not forbidden to have Christian slaves, but they were forbidden to circumcise them. Moreover, they had to allow Christian slaves to practice their religion, according to a provision of Honorius (415).[156]

Christianity, inspired by biblical teaching, affirmed that all are children of God and destined for eternal salvation. The message was not about social or political change. No biblical text in fact mentions the abolition of slavery. Even though they sometimes conceived of a society without slavery, Christians still had not been able to free themselves mentally from the existing social structures. Instead they focused on moral norms and human relationships. Some generous Christian could offer himself for the liberation of slaves, according to Clement of Rome: "We know that many of us offered ourselves to the chains to free others; many offered themselves to slavery and with the income fed others."[157]

Christian communities made no distinction between slave and free, if baptized, because they were all members of the same community. All participated together in the same sacraments and in the same liturgical assemblies. Since slaves were subject to the master and enjoyed little freedom, the consent of the master was sometimes required for baptism, if they were pagan.[158] Everyone was buried in the same cemeteries and everyone could get married. Roman law did not consider it a real marriage, however. Slaves also could be admitted to ecclesiastical functions. The first example is that of Callistus in Rome elected bishop of the capital. The Council of Elvira forbids the admission among the clergy of a freedman, whose *patronus* still lives (can. 80). Therefore we see that Christianity does not preach a social or political revolution, but a moral one.

The Christian attitude of equality and brotherhood was of course an ideal, one that was expressed by Lactantius: "There are no servants or masters among us; there is no other reason if we call ourselves brothers."[159] Of course, I suppose this vision is ideal. Already in the second century a pagan who mocked Christians, Lucian of Samosata, observed from the outside: "Their legislator persuaded them to be all brothers."[160]

Slaves and free persons were united in the same martyrdom and venerated as holy martyrs. Such was the case with Blandina in Lyon and Felicity in Carthage. A pagan slave even denounced his Christian masters in order to receive a buy-back:

The Christian religion began to spread during the reign of Tiberius and the truth pulled down upon itself a world of hatred in its very cradle. For it had as many enemies as there are men outside of the pale of revelation. And even those within the pale, in particular the Jews—and most expressly so—were enemies out of a blind passion for the law. The soldiers too were violent towards our people out of hate for our religion. Even the very servants in our households —out of base motivations—are just as bent on our destruction as the Jews and soldiers. Thus are we daily besieged, daily betrayed—and even caught by surprise as we are often taken in the middle of our public meetings and assemblies.[161]

Tertullian's statement was confirmed by the Christians of Lyon in 177:

And some of our heathen servants also were seized, as the governor had commanded that all of us should be examined publicly. These, being ensnared by Satan, and fearing for themselves the tortures which they beheld the saints endure, and being also urged on by the soldiers, accused us falsely of Thyestean banquets and Oedipodean intercourse, and of deeds which are not only unlawful for us to speak of or to think, but which we cannot believe were ever done by men.[162]

Along the lines of Paul's *Letter to the Colossians*, Christians urged mutual respect between masters and slaves, so that slaves were not to abuse their master and vice versa.[163] The slaves must respect their masters, but they cannot claim to be manumitted at the expense of the community. But there were slaves who abused the climate of fraternity and required that the community pay in order for them to become free. Similar to the *Didache*, the author of the *Letter to Barnabas* writes: "Be submissive to masters in modesty and fear, as to a symbol of God; you shall not command in bitterness your slave or handmaid who hope on the same God, lest they cease to fear the God who is over you both; for he came to call those whom the Spirit has prepared, without respect of persons."[164] These three texts set the tone for patristic teaching that is repeated by subsequent authors.[165] Clement of Alexandria further adds: "Those who are negligent or who are guilty of faults should not be corporally punished, but should be corrected with patience."[166]

The Council of Elvira counsels spiritual punishment for the violent mistress who, "inflamed by anger, violently flogs her handmaiden" (can. 5). During Diocletian's persecution, some Christian masters who were forced to sacrifice sent their slaves to perform the rite,[167] or they asked the pagans to do it in their name (can. 5).[168]

Sometimes the idea emerged that since slaves had equal Christian dignity with their masters, they must rebel against their servile condition. The small council of Gangra held between about 340 and 358, in Paphlagonia, northern Turkey, condemned those who, "teach the slaves to despise their master and to flee, or not to serve him in good faith" (can. 3).[169]

Mutual respect continued to be taught, but moralists demanded more humane behavior from the owners. Someone even demanded the release of the slaves. Melania and Pinianus, for instance, wanted to free their thousands of slaves; but many refused to be freed because they would have been worse off.

Church fathers such as Basil, Augustine, Chrysostom and many others were critical of slavery and the behavior of the masters. They too did not condemn slavery as such, even if it was considered an injustice. Ethical reasons along with the fact that they need to coexist in Roman society inspired their teaching. They accepted Roman law and, in general, did not dispute it. They instead tried to explain the causes that created slavery. For instance, Lactantius speaks of justice: "Neither the Romans nor the Greeks have preserved themselves in justice because they have established different degrees of the human condition among men. When not everyone is equal, there is no equity. Inequality excludes justice, whose strength lies in this: to make all men equal, who received life in the same condition."[170] I have mentioned this chapter of Lactantius several times because it summarizes many contrasts between how society actually was versus how it should be.

We can collect many texts that have a similar tone and others that are even more radical. The same preachers, some of whom were very wealthy, had an abundance of slaves on their lands and in their homes. And the churches they lead also owned slaves. I limit myself to a quotation from Augustine,[171] which links everything to sin which makes us slaves:

> He did not intend that His rational creature, who was made in His image, should have dominion over anything but the irrational creation—not man over man, but man over the beasts.... The origin of the Latin word for slave is supposed to be found in the circumstance that those who by the law of war were liable to be killed were sometimes preserved by their victors and were thereafter called servants. And these circumstances could never have arisen save through sin.... The prime cause, then, of slavery is sin, which brings man under the dominion of his fellow human being.... But by nature, as God first created us, no one is the slave either of man or of sin. This servitude is, however, penal, and is appointed by that law which enjoins the preservation of the natural order and forbids its disturbance; for if nothing had been done in violation of that law, there would have been nothing to restrain by penal servitude. And therefore, the apostle admonishes slaves to be subject to their masters, and to serve them heartily and with good-will, so that, if they cannot be freed by their masters, they may themselves make their slavery, in some sort, free.[172]

It was mentioned previously that slaves were also admitted to the ecclesiastical hierarchy. This was a demonstration of equality within the Christian community, because the slave who is a cleric or priest acquires a *dignitas* and dispenses the sacraments to their masters. I have spoken extensively on this subject in an earlier chapter.

Roman practice had always admitted the granting of freedom in various ways. In the fourth century Constantine established that freedom could be granted to the slaves in the church under the gaze of the community and in the presence of the bishop.[173] This introduced a new mode of manumission. Manumission is the granting of freedom to a slave, freeing him from the hand (*manus*) or authority of his master (*dominus*), with the concession of citizenship. Constantine created a new kind of manumission. The conditions for the validity of his type of manumission were that it take place on public holidays, in the presence of the people and the bishop, with the signature of the master and of the bishop. This legislation had a social character to it and would have considerable effects when people of immense wealth devoted themselves to an ascetic life towards the end of the century. Manumission was made during a liturgical function, i.e. on public holidays. The Theodosian Code preserved only one law; the Justinian Code preserved two of them. In 316 (if this is the correct date) it was declared that already earlier—*iam dudum*, which may mean 'not long ago' or 'already long ago')—manumission had been allowed in the church.[174] Augustine provides us with an example of how manumission was performed during a festive celebration.[175]

CHURCH FINANCES

Overview

An important opening premise that we must consider before proceeding is methodological, concerning how we read the sources. These sources are local and concern local and not general situations. Why had no general rules been issued for all the churches in its early days? Part of the reason is that it was not yet possible because holding councils was not yet common practice, and because the individual churches did not yet possess great wealth, as they did in later times. However, rules were still necessary even if many were in actuality doing the opposite of what the rule itself required. More importantly, a law must be widespread and known in order to be applied. We do not know what kind of dissemination conciliar law had—at the ones we are going to mention—nor do we know whether the local authorities were interested in its application. A rule sheds light on the current situation, but we pretty much remain in the dark about what was happening before the rule was enacted or how it was observed after.

A second premise that is no less important concerns the fact that the fathers preached honesty, righteousness and charity according to the moral teachings of the commandments and evangelical texts. They did so as much in the economic realm as in other areas of life such as relationships within the family, community or society. These teachings were concerned with all manner of economic activities and trade because, at the time, businesses were easily identifiable by name and surname. This is almost impossible today for many activities, due to the anonymity behind public limited companies and corporations. The fathers looked above all at the ethics of human actions although they were also obliged to consider the legal aspects. Augustine very often referred to Roman laws in this regard. Many authors observed and subsequently denounced social and economic imbalances. The contrasts were strident between the many who were poor versus the palpably observable ostentation of wealth evident in clothes, in houses, and in the sheer cost of prestige and image, as exemplified in the shows, sumptuous weddings, and the like.[176] Since there was no Christian manual of social ethics, it was necessary to rebuild a certain consensus through a variety of sources from some of the most sensitive and qualified authors.

A final consideration that emerged from the beginning of the third century was that the church now had places of worship, where previously worship had perhaps taken place in private houses, cemeteries or other properties until it gradually grew out of those spaces. During the period of persecution, many of these were confiscated, but later returned.[177] However, while the sources for the beginning of the third century speak largely only of cemeteries and places of worship, at the beginning of the fourth century Christian communities also owned houses and lands. Since before Constantine, Christianity was not legal (*religio illicita*), modern historians have put forward numerous hypotheses on the legal title of possession of goods by Christian communities. Some of them refer to the successful hypothesis developed by De Rossi who in the nineteenth century maintained that communities could appear before the State as associations of a funerary nature, a so-called *collegia tenuiorum*. It seems, however, that there were no particular difficulties for local communities to possess real estate as a group of individuals instead of as a legal entity.[178] The property belonged to the individual local churches presided over by their respective bishops, and not to the universal church as such. It was not the church in its *universalitas* that had ownership, but the individual local communities. This is also proved by the imperial laws, which often address an individual bishop or bishops of a region under the guidance of its metropolitan.

On what legal basis then did they own real estate? If Christianity was not officially allowed, which is what *religio illicita* means, it makes the solution of the legal problem insoluble. How is it possible that an unrecognized and sometimes persecuted group could legally own property? How can we understand the information in the *Historia Augusta* that Emperor Alexander Severus (d. 235) had given back to the Christians a place in Trastevere? Eusebius reports that the emperor Aurelian in Antioch presided over a property dispute between the heretical Bishop Lucian of Samosata and the Catholic community of Antioch. He writes: "But as Paul refused to surrender the church building, the Emperor Aurelian was petitioned. And he decided the matter most equitably, ordering the building to be given to those to whom the bishops of Italy and of the city of Rome should adjudge it. Thus, this man was driven out of the church, with extreme disgrace, by the worldly power."[179] This information confirms that the communities possessed property *de facto*.

Constantine and Licinius decided with the so-called Edict of Milan (313) to return the real estate that had been confiscated to the *corpus christianorum*—the text also uses the phrase *persona christianorum*. This was an imperial decision and the text was written by jurists. They certainly knew what they were doing. Modern scholars cannot find a satisfactory solution.[180]

We do not know what the ecclesiastical properties consisted of before the edict of Milan of 313; they must not have been much. This edict constituted a watershed in recognizing both the fact of church ownership and establishing the principle of restitution for confiscated church property:

> With respect to the Christians, we formerly gave certain orders concerning the places appropriated for their religious assemblies. But now we decree that all persons who have purchased such places, either from our exchequer or from anyone else, do restore them to the Christians, without money demanded or price claimed, and that this be performed peremptorily and unambiguously. . . . All those places are, by your intervention, to be immediately restored to the Christians. And because it appears that, besides the places appropriated to religious worship, the Christians did possess other places, which belonged not to individuals, but to their society in general, that is, to their churches (*ad ius corporis eorum id est ecclesiarum, non hominum singulorum, pertinentia*), we comprehend all such within the regulation aforesaid, and we will that you cause them all to be restored to the society or churches—and to do so without hesitation or controversy: Provided always, that the persons making restitution without a price paid shall be at liberty to seek indemnification from our bounty.[181]

The *corpus Christianorum* possessed real estate which had been confiscated by Diocletian that must be returned to the individual communities. In addition, the edict and other subsequent laws specify how it should be returned and any compensation to the owners.

An imperial constitution of 321 allows that: "Everyone has the capacity, at the point of death, to leave what he wants of his own goods to the most holy and venerable council of the Catholic Church."[182] The Council of the Catholic Church, an expression that is not precise, refers to the local community, presided over by the bishop. The jurists discuss whether it is the community as a legal person—today we would refer to this as a diocese—or the very person of the bishop as the sole person responsible for it. The discussion stems from the fact that the Roman jurists did not yet have a clear notion of the legal person.[183]

In the course of the 4th an 5th centuries, ecclesiastical ownership increased dramatically, at least for some churches. This dizzying development was due to various causes. First of all, the munificent imperial donations from Constantine, his family and then his successors, of grandiose buildings, supplies, money and real estate, with various contributions to the Roman church and other churches.[184] Imperial donations continued through the fourth century, but decreased in the fifth due to the general economic situation, especially in the West. Since the sixth century, the church has been able to count on its own strength and on the faithful.

Subsequently, during the rule of Constantine and his successors, temples and pagan places of worship were also given to the churches.[185] Not all temples were immediately given to the churches, however. In Carthage, the temple of the goddess *Caelestis* was taken peacefully by Bishop Aurelius.[186] The Pantheon, on the other hand, only came into Christian possession in 609. Material from other temples was reused to build new churches. In Africa, the goods of the Donatists passed to the Catholic Church after 411.[187] Their property was substantial. Not only the churches, but also the adjoining properties were handed over to the Catholic Church. The process of transfer was slow and did not occur immediately. In fact, even as late as 417, the Donatists complained about the transfer of goods.[188] Donatists had also received donations; a woman had left many goods to a Donatist bishop before 411.[189]

The ecclesiastical patrimony was slowly building up as communities grew in number and size. There were three ways of acquiring property: (1) small offerings from the faithful in liturgical assemblies, especially in the early days; (2) euergetism (donations by those with high status and wealthy benefactors); and (3) large or small donations from the fourth century onwards. We use these distinctions only out of convenience, because it is not easy to distinguish the different kinds of donations. In addition, the situations were different from one church to another, which makes it hard to generalize. In order to survive, every institution needs economic support—in the case of the church it was the generosity of the faithful that sustained the church. This generosity could be expressed in a thousand different ways and in different quantities, as Paul wrote to the Corinthians: "Every first day of the week let each one put aside what he has earned" (*1 Cor* 16:2).

The First Two Centuries[190]

The primitive ecclesiastical economy was based on free will offerings. Since the time of Jesus there had been a common fund (*Jn* 12:6; 13:29) that served both for the needs of the group as well as for the needy. For the period after Pentecost Luke presents, in a rather idealistic way, the common life of the first Christians: "All who believed were together and had all things in common; they would sell their possessions and goods and distribute the proceeds to all, as any had need" (*Acts* 2:44-45). The apostles appear to us as those who are charged with receiving the offerings and distributing to each as needed (*Acts* 4:34-35). This practice of giving to the leaders of the communities continued over the following centuries, and the faithful were continually urged to give alms either privately or by handing their gifts over to the leaders who then distributed what was donated to the needy in the manner that will be seen in what follows.

Precisely because of its deep welfare character, the economic dimension in the life of the church was one of the characteristic aspects of the ancient Christian communities. However, there are only fleeting hints of welfare which make it hard to know the extent or breadth of the dispersal of the communal funds. Ignatius suggests the existence of a common fund: "[The slaves] should not seek to be freed from the community so as not to be slaves of desire."[191] Justin was the first writer to offer some hints about the collection of funds: "They who are well to do, and willing, give what each thinks fit; and what is collected is deposited with the president, who helps the orphans and widows and those who, through sickness or any other cause, are in want, and those who are in bonds and the strangers sojourning among us, and in a word takes care of all who are in need."[192] This collection took place during the Sunday Eucharistic celebration but Justin does not specify the nature of the offerings, which may have been in money, clothes,[193] or first fruits of any kind.[194] The Christian community worked together, and these gestures fostered unity. They always insisted on acting collectively and those who didn't were called out. Polycarp, in the eleventh chapter of his letter to the Philippians, asks for mercy for the presbyter Valens and his wife who had been stained with an inordinate love of money.

A happy intuition of Mario Mazza[195] links this attitude of communal support to a passage of the pagan Aelius Aristides (†180), from western Asia Minor, who writes: "But their disbelief and greed must not know of anything entrusted to a deposit; in fact, they take everything they can. When they steal, they say that they share. They call their envy 'philosophy' and their mendacity 'disdain of worldly goods.'"[196] The passage refers to Christians because in the same speech he speaks of those of Palestine and offers a very harsh criticism of their way of life.

Tertullian provides us further information:

You cannot buy and sell the things of God. We do have our treasure-chest though, although it is not made up of purchase-money as though our religion had a price you could pay to buy it. On a given day each month, if he likes, each person puts in a small donation—but only if he wants to and only if he is able. We don't compel anyone. Everything is voluntary. These gifts are, as it were, piety's deposit fund. We don't take them and spend them on feasts, drinking-bouts, or fancy restaurants. Instead we use them to support and bury poor people, to supply the needs of boys and girls who have no means and no parents. We support the elderly confined now to their homes. We also help those who have suffered shipwreck. And if there happens to be any in the mines, or banished to the islands, or shut up in the prisons—for nothing but their fidelity to the cause of God's Church—they then become the nurslings of the confession they hold [as we take them in to help them]."[197]

Tertullian explained to the pagans the way of mutual assistance of Christians, an assistance that was born out of mutual love.

While Justin, a witness to Roman custom, speaks of a weekly offering, Tertullian refers to a monthly custom for Africa, where Cyprian also attests to the existence of a fund administered freely by the bishop, who makes it available to the clergy for the needy of all kinds.[198] He adds that if this is not enough, he can draw on his private property. The *Didascalia* repeatedly exhorts the faithful to offer gifts to the bishop, because he knows who is in need,[199] exhortations repeated in part by the *Apostolic Constitutions*.[200] The canonical-liturgical and conciliar texts contain various references to what is to be offered and when.[201] The free oblations linked to worship continue to be offered even in the fourth and fifth centuries, even though in this period we see sporadic cases of constraint on the part of the clergy towards the faithful.[202]

The self-financing of Christian communities, with the growth in number and therefore in activity, was a problematic fact of life. It required more gifts as well as more staff. In his *Letter to the Philippians* (6.1), Polycarp exhorts priests to pastoral activity with these words: "Let priests care, being merciful to all, reproaching errors, visiting all the sick, without neglecting widows, the orphan and the poor, always being solicitous for good before God." This activity also required economic expenses both for the support of priests and for charitable activities. If there were few widows, orphans and the poor in Philippi, the problem would have been easy to solve, but if there were many, the resources also needed to be substantial. The Roman church in Cornelius' time could help about 1500 people and of course the clergy, if they did not have another job, and could help other churches.[203] The information comes from a known source. Dionysius of Rome (259-269) was able to help the Christians of Caesarea Cappadocia by providing for the ransom of the prisoners.[204] And he not only helped them, but there is "the whole of Syria and Arabia to which you send help when needed."[205]

Rome in the middle of the third century had a large population that included many people in need of assistance. Of course, there were always those who took advantage of the community's generosity. Pope Cornelius († 253), writing to Cyprian and the African bishops, writes that a certain Nicostratus, guilty of numerous crimes, defrauded his mistress—therefore a freedman guilty even before Roman law—and the church's administrator, moreover, "... stole from the Church the considerable sums of money that had been deposited."[206] Nicostratus had been a confessor during the persecution, and now he had fled Rome with the stolen money. But was this about money deposited with the community and not owned by it? In

Letter 52 addressed to Cornelius, Cyprian still refers to this case and gives us some further information: "Nicostratus . . . has not returned the deposits to the widows and orphans."[207] Cyprian distinguishes between widows' deposits and the Church's furnishings or movable property.

For Christians trust and responsibility are at the core of their ethics. Refraining from stealing applies to everyone, but especially to those who are in charge of taking care of the money of others or money intended to help those in need. Fraud and robbery, which Cyprian mentions in his *Letter* 41 (1.1), is particularly hateful. Already in the early part of the second century, Pliny was struck by the fact that Christians took an oath to return deposits left with someone.[208] Is the *depositum* a kind of personal account of some believer, or is it the community's account that is used for common expenses? Fraud is one of the most serious sins.[209] In his canonical letter, Gregory the Wonderworker severely condemns thieves and looting, particularly in canons two and three. He condemns the root cause of such behavior, namely greed which is the source of all evil, for "through greed they accumulate the wrath [of God] upon themselves and upon all the people." This is the central argument of the letter, which expresses a moral and Christian condemnation, but also which demands the restitution of the goods of others to their proper owners.[210]

Other contributions to the common fund are first fruits and tithes. Sometimes these two kinds of offerings are distinct, sometimes they are mentioned together.[211] The practice of tithes has a Jewish provenance tied to the maintenance of the Levites, priests and the Temple.[212] In the New Testament there is no indication of paying tithes. In the agricultural areas there was a system of tithes and first fruits, particularly in Palestine and Syria,[213] while the churches in the cities already in the second century began to give a salary (*salarium*) to the bishop.[214] When the authors quote the Old Testament, that is when they are more likely to mention tithing. But it also happens that the texts on tithing are explained allegorically, as Irenaeus does: "Instead of simply paying tithes, we should distribute our goods to the poor."[215] Irenaeus again: "The law will not require the tithe from him who has consecrated all his goods to God, has abandoned his father and mother and his family."[216] Although there is some information from the non-Syriac world such as the *Apostolic Tradition* 31, the other sources that speak about tithing are above all from Syria.[217] It seems that the practice of tithing was not that widespread because it is possible to tithe only in an agricultural environment, while Christianity, in the first four centuries, especially in the West, was largely an urban phenomenon. In Gaul, the fifth canon of the Council of Mâcon in 585 wanted the custom of tithes to be re-established, but it was an isolated voice. Moreover, since goods in nature are easily perishable, they must be distributed with some urgency, lacking the structures for extended preservation.[218] Donated non-perishable items could be stored for distribution to people in need.

There is a rather interesting and significant example of what church possession might have looked like from 303 when the Roman authorities made an inventory of the objects owned by the local community of Cirta—later called Constantina by the Emperor Constantine, in Numidia. There were many objects of gold and silver, property of the community.[219] Substantial donations came from wealthy people who, on special occasions, could offer the church considerable sums and even real estate. Such benefactions can be traced back to the very beginning of the church. When Marcion came to Rome from Pontus, he donated 200,000 sesterces to the Roman community.[220] However, because he was preaching doctrines that were not acceptable, the community returned the sum given by him.[221] The eighteenth chapter of the *Didascalia* speaks widely on this subject:

> You, the bishops and the deacons, must be constant therefore in the ministry of the altar of Christ—we mean the widows and the orphans—so that with all care and with all diligence you make it your endeavor to search out concerning the things that are given, (and to learn) of what manner is the conversation of him, or of her, who gives for the nourishment—we say again—of 'the altar'? For when widows are nourished from (the fruits of) righteous labor, they will offer a holy and acceptable ministry before Almighty God through His beloved Son and His Holy Spirit: to whom be glory and honor for evermore.[222]

The author provides a long list of people unworthy of their activities, from whom they should not accept benefactions:

> From rich persons who keep men shut up in prison, or ill-treat their slaves, or behave with cruelty in their cities, or oppress the poor; or from the lewd, and those who abuse their bodies; or from evildoers; or from forgers; or from dishonest advocates, or false accusers; or from hypocritical lawyers; or from painters of pictures; or from makers of idols; or from workers of gold and silver and bronze (who are) thieves; or from dishonest tax-gatherers; or from spectators of shows; or from those who alter weights or measure deceitfully; or from inn-keepers who mingle water (with their wine); or from soldiers who act lawlessly; or from murderers; or from spies who procure condemnations; or from any Roman officials, who are defiled with wars and have shed innocent blood without trial: perverters of judgement who, in order to rob them, deal unjustly and deceitfully with the peasantry and with all the poor; and from idolaters; or from the unclean; or from those who practice usury, and extortioners. Now they who nourish widows from these (sources) shall be found guilty in judgement in the day of the Lord.[223]

Cyprian puts it succinctly: "The sacrifices of the wicked are not accepted."[224] The twenty eighth canon of the Council of Elvira says: "The bishop must not receive any offering from those who are not in communion." This conception of honest wealth to donate continues even in the later fathers.

Cyprian († 258) complains of the lack of generosity of the faithful: "Now, instead, we do not even give the tithes of our own."[225] The 'we' of the African bishop does not concern only the laity, but also the clergy, who devote themselves to lucrative and commercial activities. In the African church there was a custom that at the moment of baptism an offering was made to the community.[226] Perhaps the twentieth chapter of the *Apostolic Tradition* refers to this practice when it notes that "the baptized should carry nothing with them except what each one carries for the Eucharist. It is good, in fact, that those who have become worthy should make the offering at the same time." The Council of Elvira opposed this practice: "It is necessary to correct the custom, observed until now, according to which the baptized put money in the tray, so that the bishop does not seem to grant what he has received for free upon payment."[227] The text confirms traditional practice, but at the same time calls for its abolition for the Iberian Peninsula.

Julian the Apostate notes that in the church of Antioch Christian women replenish its coffers. This is why he reproaches their husbands for the excessive freedom granted to their wives.[228] He learns that in Edessa the Arian community had taken possession of the goods of the small Valentinian community, which had appealed to him.[229] The emperor ordered the seizure of stolen property. In addition, the emperor began a policy of depriving the clergy of receiving benefactions; in other words, he attempted to abolish previous favorable legislation. Complaints arose over this policy.[230]

Chrysostom noted the insufficiency of the collections for the work of the church, which was shameful.[231] He complained that "there are faithful who do not want to make even the smallest offering to the poor and suffering Christ, deprived of the indispensable nourishment."[232] He contrasts the search for human glory, which for Christians becomes a vain and ephemeral glory, with the needs of the people. The seekers of such glory spend a great deal of money needlessly in order to be acclaimed in the theater or at the circus: but there is a dear price to be paid for applause.[233] A few years earlier Zeno of Verona had praised the generosity of his faithful.[234] But the criticism of vainglory was the more common theme in the fathers of the Church. Augustine too highlighted the vain search for applause, financed with great expense and sometimes even with debt.[235]

The offering must be freely given, and it is given to the president, that is, to the bishop, who personally will help those in need. Augustine reminded the faithful when there was a shortage of funds for the needy,[236] that is, he reminded them that the *gazophylacium* (treasury) was empty. In Rome, the traditional days of fasting, on *Tempora* and Lent, were considered the suitable time for almsgiving. The collection took place during the episcopal liturgical celebration, when the offerings were placed on seven large tables.[237] According to Leo the Great, it was a very ancient institution: "With foresight and piety, therefore, dearly beloved, the holy fathers have arranged for a few days, at different times, to be dedicated to excite the devotion of the faithful people to a public collection in the churches—so that all those who are in need may have recourse above all to the church—and from the possibilities of the many a voluntary and holy collection may take place that serves the necessary expenses, to be borne by the ecclesiastical authority."[238] "Next Sunday, then, there will be a collection. I exhort and admonish your holiness that you all remember the poor."[239] The various offerings of Christians and the oblations constituted the fund of charity. By the fourth century the sense of solidarity involving the entire Christian community that Justin earlier had written about was probably lost.

At the same time ecclesiastical properties increased especially through wealthy benefactions. The goods were used to cover all expenses and also for Christian charity.[240]

Euergetism[241]

According to the thousands of inscriptions documenting *euergetism* (doing good deeds) in pagan cities, it assumed a variety of donations.[242] Such donations were given in many ways: to the whole city, to an institution, to a religious *collegium* or to an association. And the gift could take many forms: a distribution of money; free shows; public *convivia*—which had a religious character; building of monuments including statues, decorations, mosaics, temples; public services; religious festivals and the like. The donor was "doing good" (*benefacere*) and so affirmed his social position in his city or elsewhere among the ruling group. The Latin for *benefacere* does not mean giving alms. The benefits of the donor were for his or her fellow citizens and not specifically donated to the poor.[243] The euergetes gives, but expects something in return—perhaps honor, glory, a statue, a special place in the circus, or a dedication in an inscription.

Christian charity, on the other hand, requires no reciprocity. The Christian looks toward his reward in heaven rather than on this side of eternity. Augustine's patron, Romanianus, however, received a statue from Thagaste because he had provided a great show for the people. The richer a person was, the more he could be—and was expected to be—generous in order to attain a type of immortality, albeit a transient and earthly glory that was the most that could be achieved. Romanianus himself was a benefactor of Augustine who dedicated his work *Contra Academicos* to him. The Christian euergetes, whether secular or bishop, who does not limit himself to making an anonymous gesture of almsgiving, but builds a building of any kind, pursues both the glory of God and his social prestige. In the dedications and inscriptions, he represents himself as one who has been proven to be generous; and he relies on the future to remember him. It is these types of individuals who left their mark on the evolution of the ancient city with the construction of Christian buildings.

The multiplication of buildings of worship—even in pagan cities—was not always motivated by the practical needs of worship, but by the desire to honor some saint and show special devotion. Christian buildings changed the ancient urban landscape. In a small town in Gerasa (modern Jerash in northern Jordan), about twenty churches were built. The greatest of them, St. Theodore, was built by Bishop Aeneas, who is commemorated in the structure itself.[244]

The common people expected wealthy people to give. The people did not themselves request such gifts in order for the bishop or wealthy person to rule over the subjects, but such giving was inevitably necessary in order for the bishop or ruler to be accepted, loved and thanked. The donation of something played a social, political and religious role. Today, in order to have a number of services, we must pay taxes and fees even for television, which becomes a public service. Taxes are also levied to finance cinema, theatre, music and other public goods. Being public services, the people have the right to them; in ancient times they were funded by donations, and therefore there was a greater sense of thanks. There was also an economic aspect for the benefit of those employed in these activities.

I quote an interesting inscription from Sicca Veneria (modern Le Kef, Tunisia) that was inscribed around the year 170 or so, to better understand the spirit of the time and to appreciate the values prevalent then.[245] It intends to honor Publius Licinius Papirienus, who had made a donation in the sum of one million three hundred thousand *sestertii*. With the annual income from the principal, there was included an obligation to feed 300 male children up to the age of 15, and as many girls up to the age of 13. In the event of someone's death, his or her place would be occupied by another in order to always keep the number of 600 children. Were all the children poor? I doubt it; they were for sure citizens.

Pagan euergetism also inspired Christian euergetism even if exercised in a different way, with donations and buildings.[246] The pagan euergetism has a playful and alimentary character with its donations of provisions. Christian benefaction is geared primarily towards charitable purposes or for the benefit of the community through common works. The ancient tradition allows the great development of the ecclesiastical buildings, the decorations of the churches, the mosaics, even the construction of public buildings in service to the community. The countless inscriptions testify to the practice. Bishops, priests, deacons, or lay people left evidence of what they had done. Eugene of Laodicea Combusta, in Pisidia (modern Ladik) included the following in a famous inscription on a large sarcophagus: "son of *curialis*; member of the local provincial government at the time of Maximinus Daia; tortured; then bishop for 25 years: built the church with porches, paintings, fountains and mosaic decorations." He had to be very wealthy to have done all that work.[247]

The change in the urban landscape of cities during the fourth and fifth centuries was the result of this Christian, secular and ecclesiastical euergetism. Many Christian inscriptions still bear witness to the generosity of rich donors, with the same spirit as pagan donors, but to be recognized and appreciated by the communities. If there is a similarity between pagan and Christian euergetism, there is also a difference in motivation. The purpose of ancient society was to receive here and now glory and honor in the form of applause, statues, various dedications and the like. But Christians were supposed to desire only the glory of God, the otherworldly reward and service to the community of brothers and sisters. Of course, this is an ideal. In practice, who is not happy to receive honors? Even the holy preacher, taken from the zeal of souls, is happy with the applause, as the author of the novel Lazarillo of Tormes suggests: "We say, 'The Doctor preaches very well and he is one who desires much the welfare of souls,' but ask him whether he is much offended when they say, 'How wonderfully your reverence has done it!'"[248]

Yet another difference may also be that it is only the rich who can afford to give such large gifts to receive honor and fame. Even the poorest Christians can in different ways help to raise the poor, to build a church, to carry out a common work. Their names are not inscribed on any gravestone, but in heaven. Christian charity is not occasional, or every now and then, but becomes customary and ordinary and comes both from private people and from the church authorities.[249] It concerns not only the citizens, but also the marginalized of all kinds.

Numerous dedicatory and votive inscriptions on the mosaics show us the spread of the phenomenon.[250] They indicate that the rich put their goods to the benefit of the believing community for a service to God in the liturgy. The term *dedicatio* takes on a religious connotation: a gift is made to God and the church; the dedicator expects a reward of a spiritual order, unlike the pagan euergetes who expected an honor, an acclamation, a statue, or other forms of praise. In the pagan dedications one reads something similar in an abbreviated way: *de pecunia sua fecit* (similar: *de suo fecit, ex suo peculio, ex sua pecunia*), which means he made the gift with his own money. Christians use another formula: *de donis dei, de dei dono* (from the gifts of God). The sentence expresses a distinct Christian conception of the world. One of the oldest (313-319 CE) is by Theodore of Aquileia, who built the basilica. The mosaic inscription is quite beautiful: *Theodore felix, adiuvante Deo omnipotente et poemnio*[251] *caelitus tibi traditum (!) omnia [b]aeate(!) fecisti et gloriose dedicasti*.[252] (O happy Theodore, with the help of Almighty God and the flock entrusted to you by heaven you have blessedly made and gloriously dedicated everything).[253] Here it is the community itself—which contributed to the construction of the basilica—that praises its bishop. Theodore, we presume, was still alive.

In Aquileia, numerous inscriptions attest to the fact each donor was responsible for a portion of the overall construction of a monument. Sometimes the fulfillment of a vow was the reason for the donation. An example of this comes from Lucera (Foggia). Two people made a gift to the local church: *Bictorius et Iusta promissa sua e(cclesiae) l(ucerina)e solberunt* (Victor and Justa fulfilled their promise to the church of Lucera).[254] Also in Grado: *servus Christi Laurentius diaconus votum fecit* (the servant of Christ, the deacon Lawrence, fulfilled his vow).[255] In the cathedral of Santa Maria del Fiore in Florence there is a mosaic inscription in the old cathedral that shows many donors who had each financed a portion of the cathedral.[256]

John Chrysostom exhorted wealthy owners to build churches and bear the costs of the clergy in charge. The construction of Christian buildings was a tool for the Christianization of urban and extra-urban space. In addition, it offered the opportunity for farmers and people living far from the center of worship to participate in religious services.[257] In a homily on the *Book of Acts*, John Chrysostom addresses the rich:

> Many build squares and spas, but not churches. They do everything but this. I warn you. I beg you. And I ask you for a favor. Better yet, I suggest to you as an obligation that no one own a villa—in the sense of a large estate—without a church. Don't say: '[The church] is nearby, it's next door, the expenses are many and the income few.' If you have something to spend on the poor, spend it on this. This act is better than the other. It feeds a teacher, feeds a deacon or a group of priests. As you behave with the daughter you grant in marriage, so you must act with the church: give her a dowry. In this way your villa will be full of blessing.[258]

The exhortation of Chrysostom stems from his desire that the rich commit themselves concretely to the evangelization of the people—settlers or slaves—who work on their property.

The traditional way of seeking social glory and prestige through *liberalites* of every kind corrupted many Christian bishops in the fourth century. In fact, they are remembered more for their construction than for their charitable work. There are discordant voices raised concerning these bishops known for their building because of their resemblance to pagan donors in search of honor. The author of the *Opus imperfectum in Matthaeum* is very critical of the clergy dedicated to building activities while neglecting the poor:

> For one who builds a martyr's shrine (*martyria*) and adorns churches seems to do a good work, but if they also keep the righteousness of God at other times, if paupers enjoy their goods, and if they do not acquire other people's property through violence or deceit, know that they build for the glory of God. But if at other times they do not keep the righteousness of God, if paupers never enjoy their benefaction, and they acquire other people's goods through violence or deceit, who is so senseless that he does not understand that they do not build those buildings for the glory of God but for the good opinion of people? . . . For the martyrs do not rejoice whenever

they are honored by those monies for which the poor beg. . . . Do you wish to build a house of God? Give to poor believers the means to live, and you have built a reasonable house of God.[259] For people live in buildings, but God lives in saints. . . . Therefore, is not it better that we build buildings that all people look at, not only currently, but also in posterity? For as long as a building remains, the memory of the builder is mentioned.[260]

Palladius of Helenopolis also criticized the bishops as those suffering from *"pharaonic litomania."* He notes:

For many so-called bishops, anxious to rid themselves of the quite reasonable hatred in which they are held owing to their own characters and their indifference to spiritual things, do but exchange one evil affection for another, covetous of vain-glory. While with one hand they do wrong without interruption for the sake of unrighteous gain, with the other they set elaborate tables, and raise pillars for lofty buildings in order to gain a reputation for being good and laborious workers and win honor instead of dishonor. . . . In saying this, I do not include in my condemnation those who build reasonably, and out of necessity, or beautify Church property. I am thinking of those who waste the money of the poor on hanging corridors, and water-cisterns raised into the air three stores high, and disreputable baths, hidden from sight, for effeminate men; or spend their gifts of energy upon buildings, either as an excuse for collecting more money, or again, to win the esteem of popular favorites. That is simply to sacrifice everything to give pleasure to sinners.[261]

Palladius is targeting Theophilus of Alexandria who was a great builder.[262]

Augustine, as Possidius says, "never had the urge to build new buildings . . . but he did not forbid those who wanted to build them to do so, provided they did so in moderation."[263] In Edessa, in the first half of the fifth century, concrete measures were put in place to help foreigners, the poor and the needy of all kinds. The *Life of Alexis* (Legend of the Man of God),[264] an apology of Bishop Rabbula, and The *Life of Rabbula* outline what the figure of the bishop should be, who instead of devoting himself to construction should commit himself to helping foreigners and those in need.[265]

The wealthy bishop became the *euergetes* of the cities.[266] They were also sometimes concerned about public works. Theodoret of Cyr not only took care of buildings of worship, but also of buildings of public utility: "I have consciously spent part of my ecclesiastical revenue in erecting public arcades. I have built two large bridges. I have taken care of the functioning of public baths and, finding a city lacking in water—even though it had a river that ran alongside it—I have built an aqueduct. And so a dry city is filled with water."[267]

Constantine the emperor and his family financed the construction of numerous large religious buildings in many cities, particularly in Rome and Jerusalem.[268] Even in small peripheral towns, such as Cirta (Numidia), he financed the construction of two churches. The desire to build, and therefore to achieve glory, has multiplied the number of churches disproportionately, without a real concern for the needs of the faithful. Thousands and thousands of churches, generally not very large, are scattered everywhere for the joy of archaeologists. Archaeological research has brought to light a great many buildings. For this aspect I refer only to a few bibliographical titles in the note.[269]

Rome is the most studied because many churches are designated with the term *titulus* followed by a name of a person. *Titulus* is a legal term of possession, and may indicate, at least in many cases, a donor or founder. These can be men, women or clerics who of course have many resources available to fund the building.[270]

Donations

I have already mentioned the imperial donations of real estate to the local churches for the maintenance of the clergy, for the sustenance of the poor, for the various charitable activities and for various constructions. The *Acts of Peter* reports that after her conversion Eubula gave her goods to charitable causes. Benefactions from private citizens, especially wealthy families, became more common in the fourth century.

Constantine, making an innovation in Roman testamentary law, allowed the making of a will in favor of the Catholic church,[271] so that it was possible to leave the entire property to it, or at least the *pars Dei* (portion for God), and thus the church could be considered as a member among the heirs. Many fathers advise this second way in the case of children who are heirs: "If you inscribe Christ among the heirs and give him the rightful part."[272] The clergy and bishops were also advised to leave their property to the local church. Canon 81 of the Council of Carthage of 419 prescribes that the goods of the members of the clergy acquired during their stay in office, if they were not the source of the inheritance or donation, at the death of the owner pass to the church. This norm was accepted in the East by Justinian[273] and in the West by Gregory the Great.[274]

Imperial benefactions were important, but from the fifth century on there were not as many in the West. Already from the beginning of the fifth century in many regions they disappeared altogether. We can document that they still happened in the East, but in fewer and fewer regions, starting with Italy. The Justinian Code still offers us documentation, but the size of the Empire was drastically reduced.[275]

The conversion of the rich senatorial families favored donations.[276] They, who were previously in search of 'vainglory', were now urged to charity towards the poor and generosity towards the church. They were moved to Christianize their estates, encouraging the conversion of workers. This also involved the construction of small churches in the *latifundia* and a local clergy, although poorly prepared, to officiate over worship. Generosity generates a treasure in heaven. The rich were urged to invest in generosity by giving in order to find their treasure with God. The Roman Paula was very generous: "She gave her money to each according as each had need, not ministering to self-indulgence but relieving want. No poor person went away from her empty handed. And all this she was enabled to do not by the greatness of her wealth but by her careful management of it."[277] She was also prudent, leaving part of her property to her children.[278] Marcella, a widow after seven months of marriage, in order not to oppose her mother Albina, left the movable property to relatives and did works of charity living in voluntary poverty.[279] The rich young widow Furia was exhorted by Jerome to leave her possessions to the church: "To whom then are you to leave your great riches? To Christ who cannot die. Whom shall you make your heir? The same who is already your Lord. Your father will be sorry, but Christ will be glad; your family will grieve but the angels will rejoice with you."[280] Even her mother Titiana had been generous with donations. "Clothe the naked, feed the hungry, visit the sick. Every time that you hold out your hand, think of Christ. See to it that you do not, when the Lord your God asks alms of you, increase riches which are none of His."[281] He advises Hedibia to share her goods with her own children and "let Christ be co-heir with your children."[282] The same is suggested to his friend Julian.[283] History has handed down to us the names of generous matrons, but it omits those who are victims of Jerome's criticism.[284] In Rome, men also generously practiced that charity. Jerome extols Nebridium[285] and Pammachius[286] for their generosity.

A law, issued by Valentinian II and Theodosius in 390 in Milan, perhaps fits into this climate of donations from rich widows who donate their goods to churches or the religious. They wish to become deaconesses. They must leave their property to their children, but they can have usufruct, i.e. the right to enjoy the use and advantages of the property as long as they leave it intact. And so they're free to do whatever they want with their personal property, but there are many limitations with regard to movable property such as jewels, furniture and money.[287] This provision is related to a stricter legislation concerning the church of Rome and published by the father of Valentinian II in 370 and addressed to Pope Damasus. This law was to be read in churches.[288] The legislative measure had caused confusion and was also recalled by Ambrose[289] and Jerome, "Shameful to say, idol-priests, play-actors, jockeys, and prostitutes can inherit property: clergymen and monks alone lie under a legal disability, a disability enacted not by persecutors but by Christian emperors. I do not complain of the law, but I grieve that we have deserved a statute so harsh. . . . It is the glory of a bishop to make provision for the wants of the poor; but it is the shame of all priests to amass private fortunes."[290]Clerics or monks were forbidden to go to the homes of widows or minors; they were forbidden to receive wills, not even through intermediaries, under a threat of confiscation and exile.[291]

An advantage for the local community was having wealthy bishops from upper class families. Sometimes this phenomenon is emphasized, but there were not many, indeed very few in comparison with the mass of faithful bishops who had to provide for their subsistence also through manual labor. The reason for this poverty of the clergy is given by the fact that, "according to recent laws . . . if a priest sought the privilege of avoiding curial offices, he would have to renounce the goods of his father and ancestors and all his substance."[292] Indeed, the Christian minister could not receive legacies or donations.[293]

The personal belongings of the clergy needed to be kept distinct from those of the church precisely so that they did not go missing.[294] Already at the time of Cyprian he had distinguished the goods of his community from those that were his personal property which he used in case of need for the needy.[295] Canon 40 of the *Apostolic Canons* summarizes the practice and guidelines to be observed:

> Let the private goods of the bishop, if he have any such, and those of the Lord, be clearly distinguished, that the bishop may have the power of leaving his own goods, when he dies, to whom he will, and how he will, and that the bishop's own property may not be lost under pretense of its being the property of the Church. For it may be that he has a wife, or children, or relations, or servants. And it is just before God and man that neither should the Church suffer any loss through ignorance of the bishop's own property, nor the bishop or his relations be injured under pretext of the Church: nor that those who belong to him should be involved in contests, and cast reproaches upon his death.[296]

Imperial law also established that the property of clerics, monks and nuns who had died without a will and without close relatives for heirs must, under certain conditions, pass to the church.[297] On the part of the Church, wishing to preserve intact the ecclesiastical patrimony belonging to the community—which is why they were called the goods of God—those who take possession of them were condemned.[298] The increase in ecclesiastical wealth, all available to the bishop, could easily cause personal enrichment of clerics. The one who was most exposed was the bishop.[299]

Canon 32 of the Council of Carthage in 419 was very attentive to this. It was approved that:

> If any poor cleric, no matter what his rank may be, shall acquire any property, it shall be subject to the power of the bishop. It also seemed good that bishops, presbyters, deacons and any other of the clergy, who when they were ordained had no possessions, and in the time of their episco-

pate or after they became clerics, shall purchase in their own names lands or any other property, shall be held guilty of the crime of entrenching upon the Lord's goods, unless, when they are admonished to do so, they place the same at the disposal of the Church. But should anything come to them personally by the liberality of anyone, or by succession from some relative, let them do what they will with it; if, however, they demand it back again, contrary to what they proposed, they shall be judged unworthy of ecclesiastical honor as back-sliders.

The concern was to protect the integrity of ecclesiastical property. Canon 33 says the following:

It also seemed good that presbyters should not sell the ecclesiastical property where they are settled without their bishop's knowledge; and it is not lawful for bishops to sell the goods of the Church without the council or their presbyters being aware of it. Nor should the bishop without necessity usurp the property of the maternal Church (cathedral) [nor should a presbyter usurp the property of his own cure (*tituli*)].[300]

Similar legislation had been in the East for many decades.[301]

This law applied both to the presbyter who administered a parish and to the bishop. At the same time, the Imperial authority supported ecclesiastical property, granting churches exemption from certain taxes.[302] All these factors favored the progressive growth of ecclesiastical property; however, Jones notes:

We possess very few figures for ecclesiastical revenue earlier than the sixth century. The wealth of the churches grew enormously between the beginning of the fourth century and the sixth, but there is no means of estimating how rapid the growth was. There were at all times great contrasts between the richest and poorest sees, and they were probably accentuated with the progress of time, since the great sees attracted more numerous and larger benefactions.[303]

There was a practice, at least in some areas, that when someone was ordained a presbyter his goods should belong to the church for which he was ordained. Augustine writes on the subject: "When one is ordained a priest (*clericus*), he must belong to the Church in which he is ordained, all that belongs to him by virtue of the right of legitimate possession."[304]

The wealth of a church was advantageous for both the bishop and the people. But the people were convinced that the bishop could do what he wanted, "whose power seems to them to surpass all limits because it is thought that they can use and enjoy the goods of the Church as owners and masters."[305] Augustine refers to a well-established practice, that of leaving the goods to the local church. He doesn't always accept them, however. He mentions two specific cases. "Instead, I have not accepted the legacy of Boniface, commonly known as Fatius: in this case not out of compassion, but out of fear. I did not want the Church of Christ to become a shipping society. . . . Every day the poor, who ask, complain and urge us. There are many of us who must leave many of them in sadness, because we have nothing to give to all."[306] A second case is that of a father without children who left his property to the church of Hippo. Augustine returned the inheritance to him when a son was born to him.[307]

Augustine preached in the church of Hippo Diarrhytus (modern Bizerte, Tunisia), where the community had grown in number and the church building was still small and so there was need that a new one be built: "And yes, now we are in this basilica: it is narrow, you feel a sense of narrowness. And the bishop has decided to make another one, and this one will have to be torn down."[308] Of course, the bishop must ask for offerings to build the new basilica. A bishop from Tipasa in Mauritania left a testimony for a splendid construction, that, "it was not the work of notables,"[309] implying that it had been funded by the regular church members.

Donations could be small or large. Some of the donations were enormous assets granted to the churches. In order to dispel some criticism, Augustine states in a speech: "I assure you that I accept good offerings, holy offerings. . . . But certainly, if he does what I have often urged people to do—he has one child. Let him consider Christ a second child. Do you have two? Consider him a third. Do you have ten? Consider Christ the eleventh, and I'd accept the eleventh. So, I have already done in some cases."[310] This procedure of Augustine is confirmed by Possidius, who relates numerous details in chapter 24 of his biography. The mostly widespread diffusion of the cult of the martyrs in Africa favored the spread of private *euergetism* in the construction of *martyria*, churches, even on small properties. As well as causing the spread of rural dioceses or parishes, it is also assumed that they also had the means of subsistence.[311]

As we have just seen, during the fourth century donations were suggested in which Christ was declared the heir.[312] These were also donations made for the good of their soul (*in bonum animae*) by the deceased.[313] Jerome exhorts his friend Julian, who in a short time had lost his wife and two daughters and had lost many goods through a barbarian raid,[314] with the following advice:

> Provide good things for your children who have gone home before you to the Lord. Do not let their portions go to swell their sister's fortune but use them to ransom your own soul (*in redemptionem animae tuae*) and to give sustenance to the needy. These are the necklaces your daughters expect from you; these are the jewels they wish to see sparkle on their foreheads. The money which they would have wasted in buying silks may well be considered saved when it provides cheap clothing for the poor. They ask you for their portions (*Repetunt a te partes suas*). Now that

they are united to their spouse, they are loath to appear poor and undistinguished: they desire to have the ornaments that befit their rank.[315]

Julian was already a generous benefactor of the poor and needy and had given "a great deal to the churches."[316]

Another terminology employed is that of pious causes (*piae causae*), a syntagma that dates to Justinian's time. There is a religious motivation in these donations that must serve charity or worship purposes. These are all those bequests destined for charity that were encouraged by the Christian authorities and then recognized by post-Classical Roman law.

CONCLUDING THOUGHTS

Some of the larger churches came to own vast estates in many regions of the Empire. The wealth of the churches varied according to the donations received. Here I do not discuss individual churches but briefly discuss the Roman church.[317] Even the church in Milan already at the end of the fourth century possessed immense wealth in various Roman provinces.

The *Liber Pontificalis* lists many of these donations starting with Pope Sylvester,[318] and so there are many of them in Italy and elsewhere.[319] The first great basilica, known as the Lateran Basilica, was perhaps completed in 324 and was financed by Constantine. It was an immense five-aisle basilica. The emperor not only had churches built, but also gave them furnishings and funds.[320] An even larger basilica is St. Peter's Basilica. The Roman church was certainly the wealthiest and most well-known. It also had possessions in distant regions such as Sicily, Africa,[321] Corsica, Sardinia, Gaul, Dalmatia and even in Asia Minor.[322] Over time, this immense wealth took on the designation of the patrimony of Saint Peter (*Patrimonium Sancti Petri*): "A patrimony, therefore, vast, of which, however, it is difficult to determine the exact extent, even if we manage to get an idea from some partial data emerging from the ... Gregorian epistolary."[323] Gregory the Great (590-604) tried to make these vast estates that were considered the patrimony of St. Peter productive,[324] not for his own advantage but for all the poor. In addition to wealthy churches, such as Rome and Alexandria, there were many poor churches, such as that of Bishop Musonius of Meloe of Isauria, who practiced the much-disapproved usury in order to survive.[325]

Even small churches, such as that of Cappadocian Caesarea owned real estate outside the diocesan territory with possessions in Taurus, and so problems arose with Anthimus of Tyana.[326] Gregory of Nyssa said that his church was poor, but he still was able to build a new church (*Ep.* 25). Chrysostom implied that his church had fewer revenues than some of the less wealthy families in his city but yet was still expected to help so many people.[327] Augustine, on the other hand, observed that his church possessed a patrimony twenty times greater than his father's.[328] Even in Africa there were families of immense wealth.

Administration of Ecclesiastical Goods

This topic is not easy to deal with except in a localized sense and over a limited time frame, offering at best an impressionistic reconstruction with fragments of information which are put together and generalized. I am increasingly convinced of this by reading Ziche's very informative article which does its best with quite scattered information. In the same issue, there is also an article by Leone that focuses only on Africa, and for that very reason it is very instructive.[329] Towards the end of this section, I will deal briefly with the administrators of the assets, in addition to the bishop, who was usually the primary person responsible. Scholars have managed to collect a few, albeit quite rare, artifacts of information.

In the community of Jerusalem, the apostles, helped by the Seven, were responsible for the administration of the common goods (*Acts* 6:1ff). In Justin's *Apology* (ca. 150), it was the president of the local community who was in charge of receiving and distributing,[330] but who also had assistants, especially deacons.[331] Hermas criticizes the 'deacons' who take advantage of the funds of the community.[332] This criticism and other information about deacons or priests appropriating common goods suggests that there was already a certain organization of the distribution of Sunday offerings.

The *Didascalia* repeatedly affirmed the freedom of the bishop in the distribution of goods and in their use.[333] One must not take advantage of the goods of the church to lead a comfortable life, however; one must rather give them to all those in need:

> But you too should also be nourished and live from the revenues of the Church; yet do not devour them by yourselves but let them that are in want be partakers with you, and you shall be without offense with God. For God upbraids those bishops who greedily and by themselves make use of the revenues of the Church and make not the poor to be partakers with them. . . . For the bishops ought to be nourished from the revenues of the Church, but not to devour them.[334]

> As then you have undertaken the burden of all, so also ought you to receive from all your people the ministration of food and clothing, and of other things needful? And so again, from these same gifts that are given to you by the people who are under your charge, you should also provide nourishment for the deacons and widows and orphans, and those who are in want, and strangers. For it behooves you, O bishop, as a faithful steward to care for all. For as you bear the

sins of all those under your charge, so shall you beyond all men receive more abundant glory of God.[335]

The bishop administers the goods of the church at his complete discretion; neither should he be held accountable, because he is accountable to God.[336] In the larger communities, on the other hand, even at the time of Cyprian, the administration became more organized, as we see in Rome with Pope Cornelius[337] and also in Carthage itself.[338] At the beginning of the third century it was a matter of administering, in general, food and clothing offered by the faithful. The administration later became more complex as the church received real estate assets it needed to manage so that they would bear fruit.

Augustine did not like to manage the property of his episcopal church because it absorbed too much of his time in administrative affairs. During his episcopate property had grown considerably. He would have preferred to be done with it, especially to avoid the criticism of his faithful.[339]

> God is my witness that, as for the whole management of those ecclesiastical revenues over which we are supposed to love to exercise lordship, I only bear it as a burden which is imposed on me by love to the brethren and fear of God: I do not love it. In fact, if I could, without unfaithfulness to my office, I would desire to be rid of it. God also is my witness that I believe the sentiments of Alypius to be the same as mine in this matter.[340]

His biographer Possidius says that he delegated and entrusted to clerics, alternately, the administration of goods. These clerics had to be diligent to note everything, and "at the end of the year they read the report to him, so that he was informed."[341] He trusted his administrators but alternated between them to avoid abuse. Basil of Caesarea, who came from a rich senatorial family, personally inspected the properties of his church,[342] but he still needed assistants. From Possidius' information we can infer that others were not behaving in the same way. They preferred to act personally because they were men of action and not of thought, like Augustine. In 426, Augustine delegated Heraclius to take care of his diocese, in order to devote himself totally to study and prayer. A very young bishop, like Antoninus of Fussala who was appointed by Augustine, took advantage of the office to abuse the property of his small community.[343]

The so-called Council of Antioch (341) was very detailed on the behavior of the bishops in the administration of ecclesial property and the care they must have for it.[344] What follows are two significant quotations from that Council. The first is from canon 24:

It is right that what belongs to the Church be preserved with all care to the Church, with a good conscience and faith in God, the inspector and judge of all. And these things ought to be administered under the judgment and authority of the bishop, who is entrusted with the whole people and with the souls of the congregation. But it should be clear as to what is church property, with the knowledge of the presbyters and deacons about him; so that these may know assuredly what things belong to the Church, and that nothing be concealed from them, in order that, when the bishop may happen to depart this life, the property belonging to the Church being well known, may not be embezzled nor lost, and in order that the private property of the bishop may not be disturbed on a pretense that it is part of the ecclesiastical goods. For it is just and well-pleasing to God and man that the private property of the bishop be bequeathed to whomsoever he will, but that for the Church be kept whatever belongs to the Church; so that neither the Church may suffer loss, nor the bishop be injured under pretext of the Church's interest, nor those who belong to him fall into lawsuits, and himself, after his death, be brought under reproach.

The second quotation is from canon 25:

Let the bishop have power over the funds of the Church, to dispense them with all piety and in the fear of God to all who are in need. And if there be occasion, let him take what he requires for his own necessary uses and those of his brothers sojourning with him, so that they may in no way lack anything, according to the divine Apostle, who says, 'Having food and raiment, let us therewith be content.' And if he shall not be content with these, but shall apply the funds to his own private uses, and not manage the revenues of the Church, or the rent of the farms, with the consent of the presbyters and deacons, but shall give the authority to his own domestics and kinsmen, or brothers, or sons, so that the accounts of the Church are secretly injured, he himself shall submit to an investigation by the synod of the province. But if, on the other hand, the bishop or his presbyters shall be defamed as appropriating to themselves what belongs to the Church (whether from lands or any other ecclesiastical resources), so that the poor are oppressed, and accusation and infamy are brought upon the account and on those who so administer it, let them also be subject to correction, the holy synod determining what is right.

I have cited these two long canons for several reasons. The bishop and the other members of the clergy were not only responsible to God and their conscience, but there was already a provincial synod to which they must report. In addition, these canons expressed the common feeling and practice that was emerging. Canon 38 of the *Apostolic Canons* also required bishops to take care in the administration of the goods of their diocese and not to keep them for himself or his relatives. In addition, canon 41 required the bishops to seek assistance from others in the administration of the goods of the church.

Almost at the same time as the Council of Antioch, the Council of Serdica (343) at which many bishops were present, ordered:

> Bishop Hosius said: Since no case should be left unprovided for [let this also be decreed]. There are some of our brother-bishops, who do not reside in the city in which they are appointed bishops, either because they have but little property there while they are known to have considerable estates elsewhere, or, it may be, through affection for their relatives whom they want to take care of. Let this much be permitted them, to go to their estates to superintend and dispose of their harvest, and [for this purpose] to remain over three Sundays, that is, for three weeks, if it be necessary, on their estates; or else, if there is a neighboring city in which there is a presbyter, in order that they may not be seen to pass Sunday without church, let them go there, so that [in this way] neither will their private affairs suffer loss from their absence, nor will they, by frequent trips to the city in which a bishop is resident, incur the suspicion of ambition and place-seeking. All said that this was approved by them.[345]

This is further evidence that there were rich dioceses and poor dioceses.

Canon 4 of the *Apostolic Canons* mentions that certain foods should no longer be brought to church but given directly to clerics such as the bishop, presbyter, deacon and others. Therefore, the offer of the first fruits disappears, at least in the environment of its author. Canon 18 of the *Breviariun Hipponense* still mentions the first fruits, but specifies that they are milk and honey and offered only on special occasions.

The goods of the church were considered the patrimony of the poor, as Ambrose expresses it: "The possession of the Church is the maintenance of the poor" (*possessio ecclesiae sumptus est egenorum*).[346] For this reason, care and attention had to be taken in the collection and administration of these goods. The ecclesiastical patrimony that was slowly being built up required an ever more complex system of administration.

In addition, the Council of Chalcedon (451) issued various canons for the administration of assets. First, there was always the separation of the goods proper to the bishops from those of the diocese, as already mentioned. At the death of the bishop it sometimes happened that the clerics took possession of those goods. This is the implication of canon 22: "It is not lawful for clergymen, after the death of their bishop, to seize what belongs to him, as has been forbidden also by the ancient canons; and those who do so shall be in danger of degradation from their own rank." Note that the text refers to previous decisions.[347] Already canon 15 of the Council of Ancyra (314), before the Council of Nicaea (325), had dealt with this subject, that is, of presbyters who had sold the property belonging to the church.

These general rules were the result of both experience and abuse. The cited text of the Council of Serdica (343), canon 15, informs us that bishops, certainly of small dioceses as the great majority in Africa were, could be absent in order to take care of the administration of personal property in another place. African legislation, which mirrored what was happening elsewhere, exhorted the clerics: "Those who are in the service of God and are clerics should not hold the office of delegates, administrators or procurators of goods."[348] The proponent of the rule initially notes that it may displease some people. The observation refers to those who devote themselves to such activities which distract them from their ministry and expose them to the dangers of deeds not conforming to Christian ethics. This text is in the line of Cyprian who, in the middle of the third century, wrote that several bishops became procurators of secular interests (*rerum saecularium*), neglecting their ministry.[349] The rule of 345/348 is repeated in canon 15 of the *Breviariun Hipponenese*: "Bishops, priests and deacons cannot be contractors or private procurators, nor can they earn a living from an activity that forces them to travel or diverts them from their ecclesiastical commitments." For economic reasons or for reasons of power some bishops also took possession of the territory of other dioceses.[350] Given the widespread system of the *emphyteusis* in the fourth century, which entailed a perpetual right to the enjoyment of a property as long as the owner took proper care of it, including payment of tax and rent, even imperial estates were administered by some clerics.[351]

There were wealthy bishops, but there were also those who were poor. Ammianus Marcellinus, who had visited many provinces during his travels, criticized the bishop of Rome for his splendor, noting that there were many poor "bishops of the provinces . . . who are content with the smallness of food and can drink with great parsimony and wear inexpensive clothing."[352] Some bishops were not able to attend the Council of Rimini (359) because they did not have the financial means to travel. Even from Tripolitania there were difficulties in going to Carthage for the councils because of their poverty.[353]

The number of employees involved in administration depended on the size of the community and the extent of the assets to be administered. Some churches possessed land that was located in distant regions, and so there was also the difficulty of people having to travel in order to maintain control of the property and bring the produce or goods from the property to the main office. Much of the merchandise had to be taken to the main town. According to the *Liber Pontificalis*, Constantine gave donations for the Lateran baptistery from funds in Africa, whose income was calculated in terms of the solidus, the gold coin used during his reign.

The administration of ecclesiastical goods ranged from the familial and patriarchal administration prominent in the smaller communities to that of large cities such as Rome and Alexandria. As we noted earlier, in the middle of the third century the Roman church took care of about 1500 people in various need along with the clergy. It was also able to send aid to other communities in Africa and the East. For this work it needed different specialized and organized personnel. The same applied to Alexandria where administrative staff had been around since the third century.[354] With the increase in wealth in the fourth and fifth centuries, the administrative structure also expanded and diversified according to the various needs and regions. Greater responsibility was granted to the clergy.[355]

While retaining his freedom on principle, the bishop still must be accountable to God and so was increasingly obliged not to manage the administration directly, but to make use of other people. Canon 41 of the *Apostolic Canons,* a text that had been widely circulated, gives the following prescription:

> We order the bishop to have power over the goods of the church. In fact, if the precious souls of men are entrusted to him, it is all the more necessary to place temporal goods in his hands, so that under his power all may be distributed to the needy, with the help of priests and deacons according to the fear of God and with all compassion. The bishop, if he needs it, has the right to take these goods for his own needs and for the needs of his host brothers, so that nothing is missing from them; for the law of God commands that those who serve the altar should have part of the altar [1 Cor 9:13].

The bishop in some regions already at the beginning of the fourth century utilized assistants. Canon 6 of the Council of Gangra of 340 speaks of "the one to whom this service is entrusted." In canon 8 it repeats the same idea in relation to the distribution of goods: "the one who was in charge of the administration of charity." Basil worked with several people in the administration of the church's possessions,[356] and his brother Gregory of Nyssa also had people in charge of the administration of real estate,[357] but we otherwise know very little about individual churches. When Gregory of Nazianzus arrived in Constantinople, he found a confused situation. He writes:

> As for the great riches, of which there was much talk, which the greatest sanctuaries in the world had been accumulating since time immemorial, precious objects and entries from all over the world, I did not find any distinction of any kind in the registers of those who had been before me the head of the church or even with the new administrators on whom business depended. I was then content with this situation and did not want to hire any strangers.[358]

Chrysostom discovered unnecessary expenses and waste in church management, where the administrators took every opportunity to steal.[359] Domitian, a presbyter and bursar, was also in charge of virgins and widows.[360] In his church there was also an assistant to the administrator.[361] His successor Nectarius discovered that the financial administration was well organized with a distinction between the expenses of the bishopric and those of the bursar.[362]

Theophilus of Alexandria had two people in charge.³⁶³ Isidore of Pelusium accused the bursar Martinianus of abuse and asked Cyril of Alexandria to name another.³⁶⁴ The Acts of the Council of Ephesus (431) appointed the bursars of various churches such as Constantinople, Ephesus, Philadelphia, and Arabia.

The larger churches were supposed to have several administrators, as they had much furnishings and many properties. But sometimes even the small churches, such as that of Perrhe in Syria, had several administrators, who were mistreated by the local clergy.³⁶⁵ Its bishop Athanasius had the full support of Cyril of Alexandria³⁶⁶ and his case was also dealt with in the Council of Chalcedon in 451. The church of Edessa had considerable riches in coins and precious objects.³⁶⁷ Since Bishop Ibas was accused of abuse, he assured them that he wanted to follow the system of the great church of Antioch, appointing clergy administrators.³⁶⁸

These rules were necessary not only for administrative reasons but also to avoid the unauthorized dispersal of ecclesiastical goods for personal profit, and above all, to avoid confusion between the personal property of the bishop and that of his community. Some fathers complained that their priests were required to devote time to these tasks at the expense of their ministry.³⁶⁹

In some churches the head of administration was the archdeacon; in others, especially in the East, there was the *oikonomos* who was a member of the clergy. The *oikonomos* was an office made compulsory by canon 26 of the ecumenical council of Chalcedon (451) which states: "Forasmuch as we have heard that in certain churches the bishops managed the church business without stewards, it has seemed good that every church having a bishop shall have also a steward from among its own clergy, who shall manage the church business under the sanction of his own bishop; that so the administration of the church may not be without a witness; and that thus the goods of the church may not be squandered, nor reproach be brought upon the priesthood. And if he [i.e., the bishop] will not do this, he shall be subjected to the divine canons."³⁷⁰

This decision is echoed in the West in the *Ancient Statutes of the Church*, which ordered in canon 3: "That the bishop should not return himself to the care of his family's affairs, but that he should be free of so much [of these matters] for reading, prayer and preaching the Word of God."³⁷¹

---

1. J. Leclercq, "Pour l'histoire du vocabulaire latin de la pauvreté," *Parole de l'Orient* 3 (1967): 293-308; D. Grodzynski, "Pauvres et indigents, vils et plebeines (une étude…sur le vocabulaire des petits gens dans le CTh)," *Studia et Doc. Hist. Iuris* 53 (1987): 140-218.
2. *De compendiosa doctrina*, ed. J. Bailey, II, 106.
3. Seneca, *Letters to Lucilius* 3.6.
4. Ambrosiaster, *In II Cor.* 9:9, ed. Vogels, 268.

5. *Hominem pauperem, de pauperibus natum.* Augustine, *Sermo* 356.13.
6. Possidius, a friend and biographer, writes: "Augustine was born of parents of honorable and Christian status, belonging to the curial class. He was brought up and raised by them with care, diligence and sacrifice" (*Vita Aug.* 1.1).
7. Augustine, *Sermon* 355.2.
8. Augustine, *Sermon* 356.9.
9. Augustine, *Ep* 126.7.
10. There is an extensive discussion in Géza Alföldy, *The Social History of Rome*, trans. by David Braund and Frank Pollock (Baltimore: John Hopkins Press, 1988).
11. Chiara Corbo, *Paupertas: La legislazione tardoantica (IV-V sec. d. C.)* (Naples: Satura, 2006).
12. Christel Freu, *Les figures du pauvre dans les sources italiennes de l'Antiquité tardive* (Paris: De Boccard, 2007).
13. Basil, *Hom. 2 on Psalm* 14.
14. Antoine Hérouard, Jean-Marie Salamito, Marie-Hélène Congourdeau, and Jacky Marsaux. *Riches et pauvres dans l'Eglise ancienne* (Paris: J.-P. Migne, 2011), 19.
15. Cf. Peter Brown, *Power and Persuasion in Late Antiquity: Towards a Christian Empire* (Madison: University of Wisconsin Press, 1992).
16. A. de Tocqueville, *Il pauperismo*, ed. Mario Tesini (Rome: Lavoro, 1998), 115.
17. *Comm. in Matthaeum* 66.3; PG 58:630. Cf. Ottorino Pasquato, *I laici in Giovanni Crisostomo: Tra chiesa, famiglia e città* (Roma: LAS, 1998), 165.
18. Ambrose, *De off.* 2.21.109.
19. Lactantius, *Div. Inst.* 6.11.
20. Chrysostom, *Comm. in Matthaeum* 66.3; PG 58:630.
21. Yvette Duval and Lucc Pietri, *Evergétisme et épigraphie dans l'Occident chrétien (IVe-VIe s.)* (Paris: Publications de la Sorbonne, 1997); Christer Bruun and Jonathan Edmondson, *The Oxford Handbook of Roman Epigraphy* (New York: Oxford University Press, 2015), 495-558.
22. A. Giardina, "Carità eversiva. Le donazioni di Melania la giovane e gli equilibri della società tardoromana," *Studi Storici* 29 (1988): 127-42; *Hestiasis: Studi di tarda antichità offerti a Salvatore Calderone* (Messina: Sicania, 1986), 2:77-102, here 77.
23. *CIL* 4,9839b.
24. *Trinummus* 2.2.58ff.
25. *CIL* VI, 9545. Cf. Guy de la Bédoyère, *The Real Lives of Roman Britain* (New Haven: Yale University Press, 2015), vi-ix; Andrea Giardina, ed., *L'uomo romano* (Rome, Bari: Editori Laterza, 1989), 291-92.
26. Ambrose, *De Nabuthae* 1.
27. J.-M. Carrié, "Les distributions alimentaires dans les cités de l'empire romain tardif," *MEFRA* 87 (1975): 995-1101; 1100; cf. G. Ville, "Les jeux de gladiateurs dans l'empire chrétien," *MEFRA* 72 (1960): 273-335.
28. *Digest* 22.5.3.
29. Cf. *Digest* 22. 5.3.1.
30. Minucius Felix, *Octavius* 36.3.
31. Minucius Felix, *Octavius* 16.5.
32. Cf. William Den Boer, *Private Morality in Greece: Some Historical Aspects* (Leiden: Brill, 1979), 168.
33. L. William Countryman, *The Rich Christian in the Church of the Early Empire: Contradictions and Accommodations* (New York: Edwin Mellen, 1980); Susan R. Holman, *The Hungry Are Dying: Beggars and Bishops in Roman Cappadocia* (Oxford: Oxford University Press, 2001); P. Allen, B. Neil, W. Mayer, *Preaching Poverty in Late Antiquity: Perceptions and Realities* (Leipzig: Evangelische Verlagsanstalt, 2009); *Povertà e ricchezza nel cristianesimo antico (I-Vsec.)* (Rome: Institutum Patristicum Augustinianum, 2016).
34. Lactantius, *Divinae Inst.* 5.16.
35. Tertullian, *De paenit.* 10.4: *ceterum inter fratres atque conservos, ubi communis spes metus gaudium dolor passio, quia communis spiritus de communi domino et patre.*
36. Cf. Michele Dujarier, *L'église-Fraternité. L'ecclésiologie du Christ-Frère aux huit premiers siècles*, 2 vol. (Paris: Cerf, 2013).
37. Ignatius, *To Polycarp* 4.3.
38. J.-M. Salamito, "Excellence chrétienne et valeurs aristocratiques: la morale de Pélage dans son contexte ecclésial et social," in *Du héros païen au saint chrétien*, eds. Gérard Freyburger and Laurent Pernot, Laurent (Paris: Institut d'études augustiniennes, 1997), 139-57.

39. Leo the Great, *Sermo I in Nativ. Dom*; PL 54:192-93.
40. Ambrose, *Ep.* 7.36; Maurini 2:36.
41. Commodian, *Instr.* 2.35.
42. Augustine, *Sermons* 53A.9 ;56.6.9; 61.4; 83.2.2; 123.5. *Omnes enim quando oramus, mendici Dei sumus*: 83.2.2.
43. ICVR IV: 9450.
44. ICVR IV: 9415.
45. *Ep. to Diognetus* 5.4-5.
46. *2 Cor* 8:9. *A Greek-English Lexicon of the New Testament and Other Early Christian Literature*, 3rd Edition, ed. Frederick William Danker, based on Walter Bauer's and previous English Editions, (BDAG) (Chicago, IL: University of Chicago Press, 2000), 896, 3.
47. For the Cappadocian fathers' commentary on this passage, see: G. A. Nigro, "L'esegesi di 2 Cor 8,9 nei Padri Cappadoci," *Vetera Christianorum* 51 (2014): 197-212.
48. Jean Leclercq, "'Il s'est fait pauvre'. Le Christ, modèle de la pauvreté volontaire d'après les Pères de l'Eglise," *La vie spirituelle* 117 (1967): 501-18.
49. Augustine, *Sermon* 14.1.
50. Origen, *Against Celsus* 7.18.
51. Ch. Pietri, "Les pauvres et pauvreté dans l'Italie del'Empire chrétien (Ive siècle)," *Christiana Respublica*, Vol. 2 (Rome: Ecole française de Rome, 1997), 837f; 844f; 859ff; V. Neri, *I marginali nell'Occidente tardoantico: poveri, "infames" e criminali nella nascente società cristiana* (Bari: Edipuglia, 1998); E. Patlagean, *Pauvreté économique et pauvreté sociale à Byzance* (Paris: Mouton, 1977), 17-35.
52. English translation: ill repute, unknown, insufficient, lowly, mean— wretched. Pietri, *Les pauvres*, 844.
53. Lactantius, *Div. Instit.* 6.11; PL 6:72 and 76. In the same chapter Lactantius criticizes the squandering of money to organize shows. This theme often occurs in the later fathers, but not in the earlier ones. This is an indication of the new social situation of the Christians themselves.
54. *Acts* 2:44 ff.
55. A. D'Incà, "Divitiae vestrae putrefactae sunt (Iac 5,2). Tra rivendicazioni sociali e letteratura apocalittica. Contrasto tar ptokoi e plousioi," in *Povertà e ricchezza nel cristianesimo antico (I-V sec.)* (Rome: Institutum Patristicum Augustinianum, 2016), 81-89.
56. *Didache* 4.5-8. F. Rivas Rebaque, "La limosna redentora en la Didaché," in *Povertà e ricchezza nel cristianesimo antico (IV sec.)* (Rome: Institutum Patristicum Augustinianum, 2016), 91-100.
57. *Didache* 13.4.
58. Clement of Rome, *Letter to the Corinthians* 38.2.
59. Hermas, *Shepard, Mandate* 2.4.
60. Cf. Augustine, *Contra Faustum* 5.10; *Ep.* 157.23-39; *Contra Petilianum* 2.99.227.
61. C. Schiariti, "Povertà e ricchezza negli Atti di Tommaso. Suggestioni e ipotesi interpretative," in "Atti del XLII Incontro di Studiosi dell'Antichità Cristiana, Roma 8-10 maggio 2014," *Studia Ephemeredis Augustinianum* 145 (2016): 121-30.
62. *Acts of Thomas* 66.
63. M. Girolami, "Povertà e ricchezza secondo la dottrina della creazione di Marcione," in *Povertà e ricchezza nel cristianesimo* (Rome: Institutum Patristicum Augustinianum, 2016), 101-9, here 108f.
64. Minucius Felix, *Octavius* 36.
65. Tertullian, *Ad uxorem* 2.8.
66. The letter of the Christians of Lyons reports that pagan servants accused their Christian masters (Eusebius, *HE* 5.l.14). Tertullian writes that our enemies are *domestici nostri (Apology* 7). For other cases see U. Benigni, *Storia sociale della Chiesa*, Vol. I (Milan: Casa editrice F. Vallardi, 1906), 359.
67. *Divinae Inst.* 7.l. *eo fit ut pauperes et humiles Deo credant facilius ... quam divites.*
68. *Didache* 5.2; *1 Clement* 16.10; *Barnabas* 20.2; Hermas, *Shepherd, Vision* 3.6.5-7; *Mandate* 10.l.4; *Parable* 9.20.1-2.
69. *Didache* 1.5; *1 Clement* 39.3; Hermas, *Shepherd, Mandate* 2.4; *Parable* 2.7; *Diognetus* lo.6; Clement of Alexandria, *Quis dives* 16.
70. *Hom.* 15.10.
71. Polycarp, *Ep.* 11; Tatian, *Ad Graecos* 11; Tertullian, *De idolol.* 11; *Apostolic Constitutions* 4.4.
72. Clement of Alexandria, *Stromata* 3.6.56.
73. *Mk* 10:29; Irenaeus, *Adv. haereses* 4.30.

74. Giuseppe Visonà, *Per foramen acus. Il cristianesimo antico di fronte alla pericope evangelica del 'giovane ricco'* (Milan: Vita e Pensiero, 1986).
75. Clement of Alexandria, *Qui dives salvetur* 1.3.
76. Clement of Alexandria, *Qui dives salvetur* 2.1-2.
77. Clement of Alexandria, *Qui dives salvetur* 12-14, esp the end of 14.
78. Clement of Alexandria, *Qui dives salvetur* 13.
79. Clement of Alexandria, *Paedagogus* 1.11.
80. Cf. Clement of Alexandria, *Quis dives salvetur* 14 and 18.
81. Clement of Alexandria, *Qui dives salvetur* 32.
82. *De divitiis* 5.1: *omnis namque homo aut dives, aut pauper, aut sufficiens sibi esse censendus est.*
83. *De divitiis* 10.1: *In paupertate, nisi fallor, non in divitiis, in humilitate, non in gloria saeculi, non concupiscendo, sed contemplando.*
84. S. Toscano, "Ille ante tribunal: i Cristiani e le rappresentazioni del potere," *Mediterraneo Antico* 1 (1998): 311-61; 635-57.
85. Cf. *EAC* 2:510ff; De Robertis, F. M., *Storia sociale di Roma. Le classi inferiori* (Rome: L' Erma di Bretschneider, 1981), 158-210; B. Van den Hoven, *Work in Ancient and Medieval Thought: Ancient Philosophers, Medieval Monks and Theologians and Their Concept of Work, Occupations and Theology* (Amsterdam: Gieben, 1996); K. Verboven, C. Laes, ed. *Work, Labour, and Professions in the Roman World* (Leiden; Boston: Brill, 2016); Marcone, A. and E. Cascio, *Lavoro, lavoratori e dinamiche sociali a Roma antica: persistenze e trasformazioni* (Rome: Castelvecchi luglio, 2018).
86. Cl. Mosse, *Le travail en Grèce et à Rome* (Paris: P.U.F., 1996).
87. E. Narducci, "Valori aristocratici e mentalità acquisitiva nel pensiero in Cicerone," *Index* 13 (1985): 93-125, especially 116; now in *Modelli etici e società. Un'idea di Cicerone* (Pisa: Giardini, 1989), Ch. 6.
88. Cicero, *De officiis* 1.150-51.
89. Tertullian, *Apology* 42.1-3.
90. *Didache* 12.
91. *Didascalia* 6.
92. Irenaeus, *Adv. haer.* 5.3.2; 33.2; cf. Clement of Alexandria, *Protrept.* 115.1.
93. *I Clement* 34.1; Ch. Munier, *EAC* 2:510.
94. Hermas, *Shepherd, Vision* 3.6.5-7; *Mandate.* 10.1.5.
95. Ambrose, *In ps. 114* exp. 14.9; cf. *De Cain et Abel* 2.2.8.
96. Augustine, *The Work of the Monks* 16.19.
97. F. Bisconti, *Mestieri nelle catacombe romane. Appunti sul declino dell'iconografia del reale nei cimiteri cristiani di Roma* (Rome: Pontificia commissione di archeologia sacra, 2000).
98. I mentioned these things in the chapter on Christian initiation.
99. Ferrandus, *Vita Fulgentii* 59.
100. P. Christophe, *L'usage chrétien du droit de propriété dans l'Ecriture et la tradition patristique* (Paris: P. Lethielleux, 1964); Ch. Avila, *Ownership. Early Christian Teaching* (Maryknoll: Orbis Books, 1983); C. Leyser, "Homo pauper, de pauperibus natum. Augustine, Church Property, and the Cult of Stephen," *Augustinian Studies* 36 (2005): 229-37.
101. F. Piccinelli, *Studi e ricerche intorno alla definizione 'Dominium est ius utendi et abutendi re sua, quatenus iuris ratio patitur'* (Firenze 1886, reprint Naples: Joneve, 1980).
102. J.-M. Salamito, "Christianisme antique et économie : raison et modalités d'une rencontre historique," *Antiquité Tardive* 14 (2006): 27-37.
103. *Didache* 4.8ff.
104. Hermas, *Shepherd, Visions* 3.6.6.
105. Justin, *1 Apology* 67.
106. Tertullian, *Apologeticum* 29.
107. A. Di Berardino, "Gregorio Taumaturgo e l'epistola canonica," in *Il Giusto che fiorisce come palma. Gregorio Taumaturgo fra storia e agiografia*, eds. B. Clausi and V. Milazzo (Rome: Institutum Patristicum Augustinianum, 2007), 57-72.
108. Cf. Cyprian, *De lapsis* 6.
109. Cf Clement of Alexandria, *Stromata* 3.2; PG 8:1108.
110. Aristides of Athens, *Apology* 15; Tertullian, *Apologeticum* 41; *Apostolic Tradition* 15-16.
111. Clement of Alexandria, *Pedagogue* 3.11.

112. Augustine, *Enarr. in ps.* 70.1.17.
113. Cf. Cicero, *De officiis* 1.150-51.
114. Ambrose, *De officiis*, 1.28.132: *Natura igitur ius commune generavit, usurpatio ius fecit privatum.*"
115. Basil of Caesarea, *Homilia* 6; *De avaritia* 2.
116. Augustine, *Enarr. in ps.* 49.17; 21.2.31; 34.7; *De civitate dei* 5.26.1; *In Iohan tr.* 79.14.2.
117. Augustine, *Sermon* 50.2.
118. Cf. Augustine, *Contra Faustum* 5.10; for the rigorous Pelagians: *Ep.* 157.23-39; some Donatists, like Petilian: *Contra Petilianum* 2.99.227.
119. Augustine, *De libero arbitrio* 3.15.42; *In Iohn tr.* 6.25; *De civ. Dei* 15.16.2.
120. Augustine, *De fide et op.* 7.10.
121. The concept is also found in *Exp. in ps. 118, Sermo* 8.22; *Sermo 64, de temp.* Cf. Cicero, *De offic.* 1.20-24; Seneca, *Epistulae morales* 90.3-6.
122. Ambrosiaster, *Comm.in Ep. II ad Cor. 9*, (verse 9); PL 17:332.
123. Augustine, *Sermon* 61.9.10; cf. *Sermon* 85.3.5.
124. Augustine, *De Gen. ad litt.* 11.15.19.
125. Augustine, *De civ. dei* 5.10.
126. Augustine, *De haeres.* 40.
127. Augustine, *In Ioan, Ev. tr.* 6.25-26.
128. See Ambrose, *De Tobia* 3.11 and passim.
129. Augustine, *Enarr. in ps.* 36, *sermo* 3.6.
130. Ambrose, *De Tobia* 14.49.
131. Jerome, *Breviarium in psalmos* 54; PL 26:1042.
132. Augustine, *Sermon* 239.4: *Minus dare, et plus accipere.*
133. Augustine, *Enarr. in ps.* 36, *sermo* 3.6.
134. CTh 2.33.1.
135. Ambrose, *Brev. in ps.* 54; PL 16:982.
136. Leo the Great, *sermo* 17; PL 54:181.
137. Clement of Alexandria, *Stromata* 2.19; cf. *Pedagogue* 1.10.
138. Cyprian, *Treatise* 12, *Testimonia* 3.48.
139. Commodianus, *Instructions* 2.20: CCh 128.59.
140. V.M. La Matina, "Basilio di Cesarea, Gregorio di Nissa e le passioni dell'usura," *Pan* 15-16 (1998): 131-68.
141. Cf. R. P. Maloney, "The Teaching of the Fathers on Usury: An Historical Study on the Development of Christian Thinking," *Vigiliae Chr.* 27 (1973): 241-63; E. Bianchi, "In tema di usura. Canoni conciliari e legislazione imperiale del IV secolo," *Athenaeum* 61 (1983): 321-42; 62 (1984): 136-53; M. Solidoro Maruotti, "Sulla disciplina degli interessi convenzionali nell'età imperiale," in *L'usura ieri ed oggi*, ed. by S. Tafaro (Bari: Cacucci, 1997), 177-212; C. Lepelley, "Facing Wealth and Poverty: Defining Augustine's Social Doctrine," *Augustinian Studies* 38:1 (2007): 1-17.
142. Augustine, *Ep.* 153.25.
143. Augustine, *Enarr. In ps.* 54.14.
144. Augustine, *Enarr. in ps.* 36, *sermo* 3.6; cf. *Decretum Gratiani*, Causa XIV, q. III, c. I, *Corpus Iuris Canonici*, ed. Aemilius Friedberg, (Lipsaie 1922), 735f. Cf. J. Gaudemet, *Le droit romain dans la littérature chrétienne occidentale du IIIe au VIe siècle* (Mediolani: Typis Giuffrè, 1970), 140-41.
145. Augustine, *Locutionum libri septem* 5.39.
146. Paul Allard, *Les esclaves chrétiens depuis les premiers temps de l'Eglise jusqu'à la fin de la domination romaine en Occident* (Paris: Didier, 1876; reprinted, Hildesheim 1974); Gervase Corcoran, *Saint Augustine on Slavery* (Rome: Augustinianum, 1985); P. Garnsey, *Ideas of Slavery from Aristotle to Augustine* (Cambridge: Cambridge University Press 1996); Jennifer A. Glancy, *Slavery in Early Christianity* (Oxford: Oxford University Press, 2002); Ilaria Ramelli, *Social Justice and the Legitimacy of Slavery: The Role of Philosophical Asceticism from Ancient Judaism to Late Antiquity* (Oxford: Oxford University Press, 2016).
147. Digestum I,1.3.4 (Marcianus).
148. Translation: "Mamiximus of Bato buys and acquires—with 205 denarii—his emancipation from Dasius of Verzo; (of origin) Pirust of Kavieretium, a child (slave) by the name of Passia or another name, at the age of about six years, taken (that is, entered the property of the seller) as a child found (*empta sportellaria*)." The signatures follow.

149. CIL, III, 936 and 2215; V. Arangio-Ruiz, *Fontes iuris Romani Anteiustiniani: Pars III Negotia,* (Florence: Barbèra, 1943), 283-85.
150. *1 Cor* 7:20-24; *Eph* 6:5-8; *Col* 3:22-25, 4:1; *1 Tim* 6:1-2; *Tit* 2:9-10; *1 Pet* 2:18-20; *Philemon.* G. Barone Adesi, "Istanze servili alle liberalitates: alle origini della disciplina costantiniana de his qui in ecclesiis manumittuntur," *IVRIS ANTIQVI HISTORIA* 5 (2013): 89-120.
151. *1 Cor* 7:32; *Gal* 3:28; *Eph* 6:5-8; *Col* 4:1.
152. M. Sordi, *Paolo a Filemone, o, della schiavitù* (Milano: Jaca Book, 1987); J. A. Harrill, *Slaves in the New Testament: Literary, Social, and Moral Dimensions* (Minneapolis: Fortress Press, 2006).
153. Jean Dauvillier, *Les temps apostoliques* (Paris: Sirey, 1970), 442.
154. C. Hezser, *Jewish Slavery in Antiquity* (New York and Oxford: Oxford University Press, 2005).
155. CTh 16.9.1.
156. CTh 16.9.3.
157. *1 Clement* 55.2.
158. *Apostolic Tradition* 15; *Testam. Dom.* 2.1.
159. Lactantius, *Institutiones div.* 5.15.
160. Lucian of Samosata, *The Death of Peregrine* 13.
161. Tertullian, *Apology* 7.3; cf. *Ad Nat.* 1.7.15.
162. Eusebius, *HE* 5.1.14.
163. *Didache* 4.10; Ignatius *Ad Polycarpum* 4.3.
164. *Epistle of Barnabas* 19.7.
165. Clement of Alexandria, *Paedagogus* 3.34-38; cf. 3.26 and 30; *Stromata* 4.65.3; 4.69.
166. Clement of Alexandria, *Pedagogue* 3.93.
167. Peter of Alexandria, Canons 6 and 7, ed. Joannou, 40.
168. Cf. ed. Joannou, 38.
169. T.D. Barnes, "The Date of the Council of Gangra," *JTS* 40 (1989): 121-24 (he supposes 358); A. Laniado, "Note sur la datation conservée en syriaque du Concile de Gangres," *Orientalia Christiana Periodica* 61 (1995): 195-99, also 343.G. Barone Adesi, *Monachesimo ortodosso e diritto romano nel Tardo Antico* (Milano: Giuffrè, 1990), 120 and 295-96.
170. Lactantius, *Div. Institutiones* 5.15
171. François Decret, "Augustin d'Hippone et l'esclavage. Problèmes posés par les positions d'un évêque de la Grande Eglise face à une réalité sociale dans l'Afrique de l'Antiquité tardive," *Dialogues d'histoire ancienne Année* 11 (1985): 674-85.
172. Augustine, *City of God* 19.15; PL 41:644.
173. F. Fabbrini, *La manumissio in ecclesia* (Milan: Giuffrè, 1965); J. Albert Harrill, *The Manumission of Slaves in Early Christianity* (Tübingen: Mohr Siebeck, 1998); G. Barone Adesi, "Istanze servili alle liberalitates: alle origini della disciplina costantiniana de his qui in ecclesiis manumittuntur," *IVRIS ANTIQVI HISTORIA* 5 (2013): 89-120.
174. CI 1.13.1.
175. Augustine, *Sermon* 21.6-7.
176. B. Biondi, *Il diritto romano cristiano* (Milano: Giuffrè, 1952), II:327-34. John Chrysostom, *In Matt. Hom.* 66.3; cf. A. M Harteny, *John Chrysostom and the Transformation of the City* (London: Duckworth, 2004), 132-81.
177. Cf. 'Hippolytus', *Philosoph.* 9.7; Tertullian, *Ad Scapulam* 3.1; *Historia Augusta, Alex. Sev.* 49; Origen uses the word translated as *dispensator*: PG 13:1696-97; rescripts of Gallienus: Eusebius, *HE* 7.13; 30.19; for Galerius, cf. Lactantius, *De mortibus pers.* 34; Eusebius, *HE.*, 8.17.9.
178. For some opinions cf. G. Bovini, *La proprietà ecclesiastica e la condizione giuridica della chiesa in età precostantiniana* (Milano: Giuffré, 1949); idem, in *Enciclopedia Cattolica* 3:1504-06.
179. Eusebius, *HE* 7.30.19.
180. Ch. Munier, *L'Église dans l'Empire Romain, IIe et IIIe siècles* (Paris: Cujas, 1979), 271-74.
181. Lactantius, *De mortibus* 48.7-9.
182. CTh 16.2.4 = CI 1.2.1.
183. P.G. Caron, "Proprietà ecclesiastica nel diritto del Tardo Impero," in *Atti dell'Accademia Romanistica Costantiniana* 9 (1993): 217-30, esp. 219-25.
184. Ch. Pietri, *Roma Christiana. Recherches sur l'Église de Rome, son organisation, sa politique, son idéologie de Miltiade à Sixte III (311-447),* I (Rome: Ecole Francaise de Rome, 1976); E. Wipszycka, *The Alexandrian Church: People and*

Institutions (Warsaw: Journal of Juristic Papyrology, 2015), 171-93. *Acta XVI Congressus Internationalis Archaeologiae Christianae (romae 22,28-9-2013): Costantino E I Costantinidi: L'innovazione Costantiniana, Le Sue Radici E I Suoi Sviluppi*. ed. by O. Brand, V. Fiocchi Nicolai, (Vatican City: PIAC, 2016).

185. Quodvultdeus, *Liber de prom*. 3.38.44 ; cf. 3.38.43. cf. Theodosian Code 16.10.20 of 415; 16.10.25 of 435.
186. Quodvultdeus, *Liber de prom*. 3.38.44 ; cf. 3.38.43.
187. CTh 16.5.54.
188. Augustine, *Ep*. 185.9.35.
189. Augustine, *Contra litt. Parm*. 1.12.19.
190. DACL 5:689-697 for a brief orientation.
191. Ignatius, *Polycarp* 4.3.
192. Justin, *1 Apology* 67.
193. *Oracles syb*. 8.402-5.
194. *Didache* 13.3-7.
195. M. Mazza, "Deposita pietatis. Problemi dell'organizzazione economica in comunità cristiane tra II e III secolo," *Atti dell'Accademia Romanistica Costantiniana* 9 (1993): 187-213, esp.197; S. Benko, *Pagan Rome and the Early Christians* (Bloomington, IN: Indiana University Press, 1984), 46 and 53.
196. Aristides, *Oratio* 46.308.1ff; Keil 2:394. On this text see S. Benko, "Pagan Criticism of Christianity During the First Two Centuries AD," ANRW 2.23.2, 1055-1118, spec. 1097ff.
197. Tertullian, *Apologeticum* 39.5-6.
198. Cyprian, *Ep*. 7.1.
199. Cf. *Didascalia* 2.27.3-4; 2.34.5-7; 2.36.4-6.
200. Cf. *Apostolic Constitutions* 2.36.3-8; 2.57.3; 5.20.18.
201. Cf. A. Hamman, *Vie liturgique et vie sociale* (Paris: Desclée, 1968), 262-82.
202. Cf. *Code of Justinian* 1.3.38, par. 2.
203. Cf. Eusebius, *HE* 6.43.11.
204. Basil of Caesarea, *Ep. ad Damasum*.
205. Eusebius, *HE* 7.5.2.
206. Cyprian, *Ep*.50.
207. Cyprian, *Ep*.52.2.
208. *Ep*. 10.96.
209. Cf. Tertullian, *De pudicitia* 19.25; *Adv. Marcionem* 4.9.6.
210. A. Di Berardino, "Gregorio Taumaturgo e l'epistola canonica," *Il giusto che fiorisce come palma: Gregorio il Taumaturgo fra storia e agiografia*, ed. by B. Clausi and V. Milazzo (Rome: Institutum Patristicum Augustinianum, 2007), 57-72.
211. Cf. *Didache* 13.3 (the first fruits to be given to the prophets); *Apostolic Const*. 2.22.6 (handing over the first fruits to the bishop); *Apostolic Const*. 8.30.2. (the first fruits for the clergy, the tithes to the poor); cf. *Apostolic Canons* 4; *Apostolic Tradition* 28; Origen, *In Num. Hom*. 9.2 (the first fruits to be given to the preachers of the gospel. Cf. R. M. Grant, *Early Christianity and Society* (London: Collins, 1978), 134-45.
212. L. Vischer, *Tithing in the Early Church* (Philadelphia: Fortress Press, 1966); Ivo Fasiori, "La dîme du début du deuxième siècle jusqu'à l'édit de Milan (313)," *Lateranum* 49 (1983): 5-24; Idem, "Storia della decima dall'editto di Milano (313) al secondo concilio di Mâcon (585)," *Vetera Ch* 23 (1986): 39-61; M. Del Verme, *Giudaismo e nuovo testamento: Il Caso delle decime* (Naples: M. D'Auria Editore, 1989).
213. Cf. A. Vilela, *La condition collegiale des prêtres au IIIe siècle* (Paris: Beauchesne, 1971), 110ff., includes quotations of Origen on the first fruits to be given to preachers of the gospel.
214. We do not know if the singular incident of the Natalius' salary episode stemmed from the excessive sum he received or from the fact that a bishop was paid (cf. Eusebius, *HE*. 5.28.8-12).
215. Irenaeus, *Adv. haer*. 4.13.3; cf. 4.18.1. Cf. S. Mazzarino, *L'Impero Romano*, II:464 and endnote 20.
216. Irenaeus, *Demonstratio Ap*. 96.
217. *Didache* 13.1-7; *Apostolic Constitutions* 2.25-30; 8.30.
218. In the United States, today, there is a system of tithes in many Protestant and Pentecostal communities, that is, the tenth of the salary or earnings every month must be given to churches by every single believer.
219. *Gesta apud Zenophilum*, in Opatatus of Milevis: CSEL 26:187. Yvette Duval, *Chrétiens d'Afrique à l'aube de la paix constantinienne. Les premiers échos de la grande persécution* (Paris: Institut d'études augustiniennes, 2000).

220. Tertullian, *De praescr.* 30.
221. Tertullian, *Adv. Marcionem* 4.4; *De praescr.* 30. Cf. P. Lampe, *From Paul to Valentinus: Christians at Rome in the First Two Centuries* (Minneapolis: Fortress Press 2003), very useful for the knowledge of the Roman community.
222. *Didascalia* 18.4.5.
223. *Didascalia* 18.4.6-9.
224. Cyprian, *Treatise* 12, *Testimonia* 3.111.
225. Cyprian, *De unitate ecclesiae* 26.
226. Cf. Jerome, *De viris* 67, about Cyprian.
227. Can. 48; cf. Council of Braga of 572, can. 7.
228. *Misopogon*, 363B. Concerning Julian, see his *Letters* 84 and 89, where he speaks of the charitable works of Christians. E. Kislinger, "Kaiser Julian und die (christlichen) xenodocheia," in *Byzantios: Festschrift fur Herbert Hunger zum 70*, ed. W. Hoerander (Vienna: Becvar, 1984), 171-74.
229. Julian, *Ep.* 115 *to the Edessenians*; G. Rinaldi, *Povertà e ricchezza dei cristiani*, 588-93.
230. Julian, *Ep.* 114; G. Rinaldi, *Povertà e ricchezza dei cristiani*, 598-99.
231. Chrysostom, *Hom. in Matth.* 32.6; 66.3.
232. Chrysostom, *De inani gloria* 12.
233. In John Chrysostom this criticism is repeated: *In ep. ad Tim, hom* 10.3: PG 62:552; *In epist. ad Rom. Hom* 17.3: PG 60:568. Cf. F. Leduc, "Le thème de la vaine gloire chez saint Jean Chrysotome," *Proche-Orient chrétien* 19 (1969): 3-32.
234. Zeno, *Tractatus* 1.4.
235. A.-G. Hamman, *La vie quotidienne en Afrique du Nord au temps de Saint Augustin* (Paris: Hachette, 1979).
236. Possidius, *Vita Aug.* 24.14 and 17.
237. Cf. Pauline of Nola, *Ep.* 34.1; Ambrose, *Expl. Ps.* 118, prol. 2; Hamman, *La vie quotidienne*, 262-63.
238. Leo the Great, *Sermon* 11; cf. *Sermon* 10.6.
239. Leo the Great, *Sermon* 6.
240. Ambrose, in his speech against the Arian bishop Auxentius, refuting the various accusations made against him, at a certain point exclaims: "The Church pays taxes for her fields; if the emperor wants them, he has the power to take them, none of us will resist. The offerings of the people may suffice for the poor" (*Sermo contra Auxentium* 33; PL 16:1017).
241. In order to provide some clarification: the term euergetism is a modern term, even if it derives from the Greek εὐεργετέω (*eueregete*). It was introduced into the French lexicon in the 20th century by historian A. Boulanger, then by H.I. Marrou, and especially from Paul Veyne. The Latin terms are *munificentia*, *liberalitas*. The term *munificentia* that we find written on many papal or other inscriptions refers to this Roman practice of the *munificentia principis*. Giving becomes almost a moral obligation.
242. F. Jacques, *Le privilège de liberté. Politique impériale et autonomie municipale dans les cités de l'Occident romain (161-244)* (Rome: Ecole Française de Rome, 1994), 692-786.
243. A.R Hands, *Charities and Social Aids in Greece and Rome* (London: Thames & Hudson, 1968).
244. R. Raja, "Bishop Aeneas and the Church of St. Theodore in Gerasa," in *Group Identity and Religious Individuality in Late Antiquity*, eds. Eric Rebillard, Jörg Rüpke (Washington: Catholic University of America Press, 2015), 270-92.
245. CIL 08, 01641 = ILS 6818; Année Épigraphique 2004, 01877. Arangio-Ruiz, FIRA III, (Florence 1943), 167-68, n. 55b; M. Christol, A. Magioncalda, "La fondazione di P. Licinio Papiriano da 'Sicca Veneria' (CIL VIII, 1641). Nota preliminare," in *Africa Romana* VIII (Sassari: Gallizzi, 1991), 321-30; A. Magioncalda, *Documentazione epigrafica*, 61-70; L. Gagliardi, *Mobilità e integrazione delle persone nei centri cittadini romani. Aspetti giuridici. Vol. 1: La classificazione degli incolae* (Milan: Giuffrè, 2006), 268-70; I. Cao, *Alimenta. Il racconto delle fonti* (Padova: Il poligrafo, 2010), 221-31.
246. L. Cracco Ruggini, *Spazi urbani*, esp. 167ff.
247. DACL 5,694-700; M. Guarducci, *Epigrafia greca* (Roma: Ist. Poligrafico dello Stato, 1978), Vol. 4:394-98.
248. *The Life of Lazarillo de Tormes*, trans. by Clements Markham (London: A. & C. Black, 1908), 2.
249. P. Brown, *Power and Persuasion in Late Antiquity*, 130ff.
250. Y. Duval et L. Pietri, "Évergétisme et épigraphie dans l'Occident chrétien," in *Actes du Xe Congrès international d'épigraphie grecque et latine* (Paris: Publications de la Sorbonne, 1997), 371-96.
251. Instead of the Latin word *grex*, the transcription of Greek word *poimnion* is used.

252. ILCV 1863; D. Mazzoleni, *Epigrafi del mondo cristiano antico* (Rome: Lateran University Press, 2002), 158-61; C. Carletti, *Epigrafia dei cristiani in Occidente dal III al VII secolo. Ideologia e prassi* (Bari: Edipuglia, 2008), 256-57 J.-P. Caillet, *L'évergétisme monumental chrétien en Italie et à ses marges d'après l'épigraphie des pavements de mosaïque (IVe-VIIe s.)* (Paris: École française de Rome, 1993), 137-39, nr. 4.
253. Another translation is possible: "... with the help of Almighty God, for the flock entrusted to you from heaven all these things you have happily and solemnly made the consecration". Cf. Mazzoleni, *Epigrafi del mondo cristiano antico* 159.
254. C. Carletti, "Lucera paleocristiana: la documentazione epigrafica," *Vetera Chr* 20 (1983): 427-41.
255. CIL 5, 1594 ; ICVL 1210.
256. Caillet, *L'évergétisme monumental*, 25-28.
257. M.-Y. Perrin, "Il nuovo stile missionario: la conquista dello spazio e del tempo," in *Storia del Cristianesimo*, II. *La nascita di una cristianità (250-430)*, ed. by Ch. and L. Pietri, ital. edition ed. by A. Di Berardino (Rome: Città Nuova, 2000), 549-84, in part. 566ff.
258. Chrysostom, *Hom. in Acta apost.* 18.6.
259. *Vis domum Dei aedificare? Da fidelibus pauperibus unde vivant, et aedificasti rationabilem domum Dei* (PG 56:886).
260. *Opus Impferfectum in Matthaeum* 45; PG 56:885f; trans. Kellermann. Cf. Teresa Sindona, "Aspetti sociali nell'Opus Imperfectum in Matthaeum," *Koinonia* 20 (1996): 79-105.
261. Palladius, *The Dialogue on the Life of St. John Chrysostom* 13.
262. Palladius, *The Dialogue on the Life of St. John Chrysostom* 6.
263. Possidius, *Vita Aug.* 24.13.
264. A young Roman from a rich family refuses to marry and goes to Edessa where, unknown, he leads a poor life and dies as a poor man; Rabbula, the bishop, discovers the truth only at his death.
265. Han J. W. Drijvers, "The Man of God of Edessa, Bishop Rabbula, and the Urban Poor Church and Society in the Fifth Century," *JECS* 4 (1996): 235-48.
266. Peter Brown, *Power and Persuasion in Late Antiquity*; Jean-Pierre Caillet, *L'évergétisme monumental chrétien en Italie et à ses marges d'après l'épigraphie des pavements de mosaïque (IVe-VIIe s.)* (Rome: Ecole française, 1993).
267. Theodoret of Cyr, *Ep.* 81.
268. Richard Krautheimer, "The Ecclesiastical Building Policy of Constantine," in *Costantino il Grande: dall'antichità all'Umanesim*, ed. G. Bonamente (Macerata: Università degli studi di Macerata, 1993), 509-52.
269. Ch. Pietri, "Évergétisme et richesses ecclésiastiques dans l'Italie du IVe à la fin du Ve s. L'exemple romain," *Ktèma III* (1978), 317-37; now in: *Christiana respublica* (Rome: École Française de Rome, 1997), 813-33; B. Hamarneh, "Evergetismo ecclesiastico e laico nella Giordania bizantina ed ommayade nel V-VIII secolo: testimonianze epigrafiche," *Vetera Chr* 33 (1996): 57-75; R. Haensch, "Le financement de la construction des églises pendant l'Antiquité tardive et l'évergétisme antique," *Antiquité tardive* 14 (2006): 47-58. Especially, the Proceedings of the International Congresses of Christian Archaeology. Most important is the last one, published on 2016.
270. J. Hillner, "Clerics, Property and Patronage: The Case of the Roman Titular Churches," *Antiquité Tardive* 14 (2006): 59-68.
271. CTh 16.2.4.
272. Chrysostom, *Hom. in Matth.* 45.2; PG 58:474. Cf. P. Rentinck, *La cura pastorale in Antiochia nel IV secolo* (Rome: Universita Gregoriana, 1970), 314; E. F. Bruk, *Kirchenväter und soziales Erbrecht* (Berlin: Springer-Verlag, 1956).
273. *Novella* 131 of 545.
274. Gregory the Great, *Ep.* 4.36.
275. G. Barone-Adesi, "Il sistema giustinianeo delle proprietà ecclesiastiche," in *La proprietà e le proprietà*, ed. by E. Cortese (Milan: A. Giuffre, 1988), 75-120.
276. M. Salzman, *Making of a Christian Aristocracy: Social and Religious Change in the Western Roman Empire* (Cambridge, MA: Harvard University Press, 2002), 139-77.
277. Jerome, *Ep.* 108.16.
278. Jerome, *Ep.* 108.5-6; cf. 16. If Paula in Palestine continues to give alms it means that she had kept part of her vast heritage. For women cf. F.E. Consolino, "Modelli di comportamento e modi di santificazione per l'aristocrazia femminile in Occidente," ed. A. Giardina, *Società romana e impero tardoantico*, 1 (Rome/Bari: Editori Laterza, 1986), 272-73; E. Giannarelli, *La tipologia femminile nella biografia e nell'autobiografia cristiana del IV secolo* (Rome: Istituto storico italiano per il Medio Evo, 1980).

279. Jerome, *Ep.* 127.4. He is speaking of relative poverty, as she has retained some property in order to live with dignity (Cf. Jerome, *Ep.* 124.8 and 13).
280. Jerome, *Ep.* 54.4.
281. Jerome, *Ep.* 54.12.
282. Jerome, *Ep.* 120.1.
283. Jerome, *Ep.* 118.
284. Jerome, *Ep.* 22.32: "Today you may see women cramming their wardrobes with dresses, changing their gowns from day to day, and for all that unable to vanquish the moths. Now and then one more scrupulous wears out a single dress; yet, while she appears in rags, her boxes are full. Parchments are dyed purple, gold is melted into lettering, manuscripts are decked with jewels, while Christ lies at the door naked and dying. When they hold out a hand to the needy, they sound a trumpet." B. Feichtinger, *Apostolae apostolorum: Frauenaskese als Befreiung und Zwang bei Hieronymus* (Franfurt am Main: P. Lang, 1995).
285. Jerome, *Ep.* 79.2 and 5.
286. Jerome, *Ep.* 66.5.
287. CTh 16.2.27.
288. CTh 16.2.20.
289. Ambrose, *De officiis* 1.20.87.
290. Jerome, *Ep.* 52.6.
291. R. Martini, "Su alcuni aspetti della 'testamenti factio' passiva dei chierici," *Atti Accademia Romanistica Costantiniana* 9 (1993): 325-30.
292. Ambrose, *Ep* 18 =73.13.
293. Cf. Jerome, *Ep.* 73.14.
294. Council of Antioch of 341, can. 24.
295. Cf. Cyprian, *Ep* 7.2.
296. Di Berardino A. (ed.), *I concili della chiesa antica*: vol. I, *I concili greci*, 377.
297. Theodosian Code 5.3.1 of 434; Justinian Code 1.3.20.
298. Cf. Council of Antioch, can. 25; *Apostolic Canons* 38.
299. A. Barzanò, "La questione dell'arricchimento dei vescovi e del clero da Cipriano a Damaso tra polemica anticristiana, autocritica ecclesiale e legislazione imperiale," *Rivista di storia della chiesa in Italia* 47 (1993): 359-67.
300. *I concili della chiesa antica*, ed. by Angelo Di Berardino, II, *I concili Latini*, 4, *I concili africani*, new edition, 137.
301. Council of Antioch can. 15 and 25. Di Berardino A. (ed.), *I concili africani*, 157.
302. Cf. CTh 16.2.15: exemption from property tax; however, we do not know how long it lasted; the exemption from the *Munera extraordinaria et sordida* was also granted: CTh 11.16.15.
303. A. H. M. Jones, *The Later Roman Empire, 284-602* (Oxford: Oxford University Press, 1964), 904.
304. Augustine, *Ep.* 83.4.
305. Augustine, *Ep.* 125.2.
306. Augustine, *Sermon* 355.5.
307. Augustine, *Sermon* 355.5.
308. Augustine, *Sermon* 15A.8.
309. CIL 8:20903.
310. Augustine, *Sermon* 355.4.
311. A. Leone, "Clero, proprietà, cristianizzazione delle campagne nel Nord Africa tardoantico: 'status quaestionis'," *Antiquité Tardive* 14 (2006): 95-104.
312. Augustine, *Sermon* 355.4; Jerome, *Ep.* 118.
313. J.L. Murga Gener, *Donaciones y testamentos 'in bonum animae' en el derecho romano tardío* (Pamplona: Universidad de Navarra, 1968).
314. Jerome, *Ep.* 118.2.
315. Jerome, *Ep.* 118.4.
316. Jerome, *Ep.* 118.5.
317. Ch. Pietri, *Roma Christiana. Recherches sur l'Église de Rome, son organisation, sa politique, son idéologie de Miltiade à Sixte III (311-447)*, I (Rome: Ecole Française, 1976); D. Moreau, "Les patrimoines de l'Église romaine jusqu'à la mort de Grégoire le Grand," *Antiquité tardive* 14 (2006): 79-93 (with literature).
318. Ed. Duchesne, according to the various popes from 313.

319. D. De Francesco, "Le donazioni costantiniane nell'Agro Romano," *Vetera Christianorum* 27 (1990): 47-75; A. Leone, "Clero, proprietà, cristianizzazione," 95-104.
320. H. Geertmann, *Hic fecit basilicam: Studi sul Liber Pontificalis e gli edifici ecclesiastici di Roma da Silvestro a Silverio*, ed. by S. de Blaauw (Leuven: Peeters, 2004).
321. The *Liber Pontificalis* has a long list of Constantine's donations to the Roman church and numerous funds in Africa.
322. Celestine, *Ep.* 33.432.
323. V. Recchia, *Gregorio Magno e la società agricola* (Rome: Edizioni Studium, 1978), 12. R.A. Markus, *Gregory the Great and His World* (Cambridge: Cambridge University Press, 1997).
324. Gregory the Great, *Ep.* 10.22.
325. Cf. Severus of Antioch, *Ep.* 1.4.
326. Gregory of Nazianzus, *Ep.* 36; PG 37: 572AB.
327. O. Pasquato, *I laici in Giovanni Crisostomo: tra chiesa, famiglia e città* (Rome: LAS, 2006).
328. Augustine, *Ep.* 126.7.
329. H. G Ziche, "Administrer la propriété de l'Église: l'évêque comme clerc et comme entrepreneur," *Antiquité Tardive* 14 (2006): 69-78. A. Leone, *Clero, proprietà, cristianizzazione*, 95-104.
330. Justin, *1 Apology* 67.12.
331. Ignatius, *To Trallians* 2-3.
332. Hermas, *Shepherd, Simil* 9.26.2.
333. *Didascalia* 2.24-25.
334. *Didascalia* 2.25.
335. Ibid.
336. Cyprian, *De lapsis* 6.
337. Eusebius, *HE* 6.43.
338. Cyprian, *Ep.* 76.1. 3; Pontius, *Vita Cypr.* 6.4; 9.5-7; 15.3.
339. Cf. Augustine, *Sermons* 355 and 356.
340. Augustine, *Ep.* 126.9.
341. Possidius, *Vita Augustini.* 24.1; cf. Possidius, *Vita Aug.* 23.2; 24.10; Augustine, *Ep.* 126.9.
342. Gregory of Nazianzus, *Or.* 43,58.
343. Cf. Augustine, *Ep.* 20 Divjak.
344. The original text of Greek canons is in Di Berardino A. (ed.), *I concili della chiesa antica*: vol. I, *I concili greci*.
345. Can. 15, from Latin redaction.
346. *Ep. Ep* 18 =73,16: PL 16:1018.
347. See Council of Nicaea, canons 15-16; *Apostolic Canons* 15; Council of Antioch (341), can. 3; Council of Serdica. (343), canons 15-16; Council of Carthage (419), canons 54 and 90.
348. Council of Carthage of 345-348, can. 6.
349. Cyprian, *De lapsis* 6.
350. Can 10; Council of Carthage of 390, can. 11.
351. See Augustine, *Contra litt. Parm.* 2.83.184; 2.98.228.
352. *Res gestae* 27.3.13; G. Rinaldi, "Povertà e ricchezza dei cristiani nel giudizio dei pagani," in *Povertà e ricchezza nel Cristianesimo antico (I-V sec.)* (Rome: Institutum Patristicum Augustinianum, 2016), 565-616, here 586-87 and 596.
353. *Canones in causa Apiarii* 14; Di Berardino A. (ed.), *I concili della chiesa antica*: vol. 4,1, *I concili africani*, II ed., 126.
354. Origen, *Comm. Series in Mt.* 61; PG 13:1697.
355. Council of Antioch can. 25; *Apostolic canons* 41; Gelasius, *Ep.* 17.1.
356. Basil of Caesarea *Ep.* 237.1.
357. Basil of Caesarea *Ep.* 225.
358. Gregory of Nazianzus, *Carmen de vita sua* 1479ff.
359. Palladius, *Dialogue on the Life of John* 12.32.
360. John Chrysostom, *Ep.* 217.
361. Palladius, *Dialogue on the Life of John* 20.78.
362. The scanty information is well exploited by G. Dagron, *Naissance d'une capitale. Constantinople et ses institutions de 330 à 451* (Paris: Presses universitaires de France, 1974), 489-91.
363. Socrates, *HE* 6.7.

364. Cyril of Alexandria, *Ep.* 2.127.
365. Perrhe today in Turkey near Adıyaman. Johan Leemans et alii, eds., *Episcopal Elections in Late Antiquity* (Berlin: De Gruyter, 2011), 67-69; R. Price, M. Gaddis, *The Acts of Council of Chalcedon* (Liverpool: Liverpool University Press, 2005), Vol 2:290.
366. Cyril of Alexandria *Ep.* 77; CPG 5377.
367. R. Price, M. Gaddis, *The Acts of Council of Chalcedon,* Vol 2: 283-85.
368. Cf. P. L'Huillier, *The Church of the Ancient Councils: The Disciplinary Work of the First Four Ecumenical Councils* (Crestwood, NY: St. Vladimir's Seminary Press, 1996), 265; ACO II,1,3, 15-16 (374-375); R. Price, M. Gaddis, *The Acts of Council,* 263.
369. Cf. Basil, *Ep.* 285; PG 32:1021A; Augustine, *In Iohan. trac.* 6.25; John Chrysostom, *Hom. in Matth.* 85.4.
370. See *Apostolic Canons* 38-39.41; Council of Ancyra (314), can.15; Council of Antioch (341), canons 24-25; Council of Gangra (ca. 340), can.7); Council of Carthage (419), can.26; Theophilus of Alexandria, can. 10; Cyril of Alexandria can. 2 (CPG 279 ff.). The best comment on this canon is found in Philip Schaff, *The Seven Ecumenical Councils*, NPNF 2 14:286. See also G. W. H Lampe, *Greek Patristic Lexikon.*
371. *I concili della chiesa antica*, ed. by A. Di Berardino, *I concili della Gallia*, 1, 97.

CHAPTER 15
CHARITABLE AND SOCIAL WORK

THE PRESENT TOPIC DISCUSSES WHAT CHRISTIANS TAUGHT ON ALL KINDS OF TANGIBLE HELP for the needy, including the sick, orphans, prisoners, those who are persecuted, and paupers who could not afford burial. It is a very sensitive subject and susceptible to rhetoric on the one hand and beautiful expressions of compassion on the other. Christian charity is based on a theological foundation and on the teaching of Jesus. Practice, however, could be quite different—perhaps more so than with other matters dealt with in this book. We must make a distinction between the ethics that were preached and those that were practiced, between the duty to be a Christian and the everyday life lived by all Christians, but especially by clerics and their bishops. In the ancient city, people lived in more confined spaces where they all knew each other. In smaller communities, the bishop could know the truly needy individually. This turns out to be more difficult in large communities, however, or when Christianity becomes the religion of most of the population. So "when the bishop loves the poor, there are no poor in his city, because the church in the city is rich."[1]

Both the Old and New Testaments recommend generosity towards the needy and the poor of all kinds. Sometimes they advise followers to sell everything and distribute it to the poor (*Mt* 19:21); to invite to dinner those who cannot reciprocate because they have nothing (*Lk* 14:12-14). There is no expectation of reciprocity; one must give free of charge. The first disciples of Jesus immediately felt the need for solidarity with those in need. Normally, the texts speak of individual persons exhorted to generosity. Paul, in his *Letter to the Galatians*, writes that in Jerusalem, in the so-called Council of 49, the apostles present asked him, "only one thing, that we remember the poor, which was actually what I was eager to do" (*Gal* 2:10).[2] We do not know in detail his charitable activity. Instead, we know more about his great concern for collecting a sum in the churches of Asia, Macedonia, and Achaia that was to be brought to the poor of Jerusalem. He often spoke about this.[3] Paul's gesture was not only personal but involved many communities. Giving with generosity and without ostentation was a gesture "worthy of praise from God, and he who does it with such simplicity will live with God."[4]

Private charity was highly commended, but soon organized charities arose among the individual communities. Because the community of Jerusalem was poor, many churches organized a collection of money to support the Christians of Jerusalem. There were collections in Antioch (*Acts* 11:29), in Galatia (*1 Cor* 16:1-2), in Macedonia (*2 Cor* 8:1) and in Achaia (*2 Cor* 9:2). Caring for the poor was a prime focus of the early church (*Gal* 2:10). While the main mission of the apostles was the ministry of the word (*ministerium verbi*) embodied in their preaching, no less important was the ministry of the poor (*ministerium pauperum*).[5]

These were not just words, but words embodied in concrete actions:

> And he, who has, gives to him who has not, without boasting. And when they see a stranger, they take him into their homes and rejoice over him as a very brother, for they do not call them brothers after the flesh, but brothers after the spirit and in God. And whenever one of the poor passes from the world, each one of them, according to his ability, gives heed to him and carefully sees to his burial. And if they hear that one of their numbers is imprisoned or afflicted on account of the name of their Messiah, all of them anxiously minister to his necessity, and if it is possible to redeem him, they set him free. And if there is among them any that is poor and needy, and if they have no spare food, they fast two or three days in order to supply to the needy their lack of food.[6]

I have already mentioned this in the previous chapter, but mention it here for further emphasis.

From the very beginning of Christianity, we find personal Christian charitable acts provided at their own discretion concerning how much to give and being directed primarily towards those in need. We find the common action of a community as such, which must organize itself for this purpose. This presupposes the generosity of the faithful and the personal responsibility of caring for others in the community's name.

In what follows, we will first address individual charity work which we normally call almsgiving, and then will move on to the charity work of the church as the body of Christ.

ALMSGIVING

The term 'almsgiving'[7] comes from the Greek *eleemosyne*, which in Latin is transcribed as *eleemosyna*. It means to have mercy on someone. Its object, however, is not so much the poor but rather has the more general meaning of almsgiving (*alms*, in English) in the Jewish or Christian sense. There was no exhortation in the ancient world concerning giving alms to the poor. It was appreciated when one was generous, but one's generosity did not necessarily target the poor. Not even religious communities pushed for the care of the poor.

Jewish and Christian teaching on the matter differed significantly. The spirit that animated Christian communities from the beginning was that of mutual solidarity, especially as a brotherhood, and as persons created by God in his image. Luke in the *Acts* has perhaps somewhat idealized the community of Jerusalem in its sharing of goods and the institution of deacons for the service of widows and the poor with the community having everything in common (*Acts* 6:1-7; 4:32). But a network of solidarity did exist. Strong evidence of this solidarity is the collection that Paul organizes in great detail and which he brings personally to Jerusalem as a sign of solidarity and sharing with brothers so far away. The collection takes place in Achaia, Macedonia, and Galatia for the sake of the 'saints' in Palestine.[8]

Paul implies that donations are as much a benefit for those who give [it is a good thing for you: *2 Cor* 8:10] as for those who receive: "For the time being, may your abundance make up for their poverty, so that their abundance may also make up for your poverty, and may there be equality" (*2 Cor* 8:14). The reason for mutual benefit is well illustrated by Hermas in a text which will be quoted in detail later. One might also note that the only time the New Testament uses the term religion (*threskeia*) is in reference to the care of widows and orphans (*Jas* 1:27).

This premise serves to introduce us to the spirit of Christian almsgiving. A motivation continually repeated by writers and preachers concerns almsgiving as a means of obtaining the forgiveness of sins: "If you can do good, do not postpone it, for almsgiving frees you from sin."[9] In fact, it occupies the first place: "Beautiful is almsgiving as the repentance of sin. Fasting is better than prayer, and almsgiving [better] than both. . . ; almsgiving is the relief of sin."[10] For Cyprian, the subject is so fundamental for him that he dedicates a brief treatise to almsgiving (*De opere et eleemosynis*)[11] in order to underline its importance and the reasons for practicing it. Despite God's benevolence and mercy, human beings continue to sin and could not be saved unless God "had not paved the way for him to obtain salvation and to be able to purify through alms any contamination of sin that might dwell in our hearts."[12]

Almsgiving was considered the main means for the salvation of the donor. In the English context, the syntagma '*redemptive almsgiving*'[13] is used. Almsgiving as a path to eternal salvation was a widespread and repeated concept in the early church. Almsgiving which provided material help to the needy erased sin more than other acts such as fasting and prayer. Early on the *Didache* (4.5) already exhorted: "If you have something thanks to the work of your hands, you will give it in expiation of your sins." *The Epistle of Barnabas* (19.11) also speaks of rewards to the giver: "Do not hesitate to give and do not mumble when you give; you will know that he is your rewarder."

The insistence on the salvific value of giving to the poor arises first of all from the biblical tradition itself, from the preaching of Jesus, from Paul, and from other sources of the New Testament. Some sentences also from the *Book of Tobias* are often quoted: "For all those who do it, almsgiving is a precious gift before the Most High" (4:11); "A good thing is prayer with fasting and almsgiving with justice. Better the little with justice than wealth with injustice. It is better to give alms than to set aside gold" (12:9). The Latin translation of the Vulgate lends itself better to the exhortations of the fathers: "Prayer with fasting and almsgiving is better than collecting treasures of gold, because almsgiving frees from death and it is that which cleanses sins and will attain eternal life."[14]

But there are also certain expressions in the mouth of Jesus that are germane: "Looking around, Jesus said to his disciples, 'How difficult it is for those who possess wealth to enter the kingdom of God!' The disciples were disconcerted by his words, but Jesus resumed and said to them, 'Children, how difficult it is to enter the kingdom of God! It is easier for a camel to pass through the eye of a needle than for a rich man to enter the kingdom of God.' They were even more amazed and said to each other, 'And who then can be saved?'" (*Mk* 10:23-26). Concerning Jesus himself, Paul says, "Though he was rich, yet for your sakes he became poor so that you though his poverty might become rich" (*2 Cor* 8:9).

At the end of the second century Clement of Alexandria speaks of an exchange that occurs through almsgiving: "What a beautiful exchange! What a divine contract! One purchases immortality for money, and by giving the perishable things of this world receives in exchange for these an eternal mansion in the heavens! . . . Do not spare yourself perils and labors so that you may purchase here the kingdom of heaven."[15] Almsgiving comes across as a loan to God.[16]

The importance of almsgiving to all is amply explained by Cyprian in his *De opere et eleemosynis*. In his *Letter 55* (*On Work and Mercy*) Cyprian makes a precious clarification on the liberation from death that occurs through almsgiving: "*Almsgiving frees us from death*, and, there, is clearly meant not deliverance from that death which the blood of Christ has quenched once and for all and from which the saving grace of baptism and of our Redeemer has delivered us, but deliverance from that death which afterward creeps in through sin."[17] I believe that the clarification is important; it is not made by other preachers. Speaking of the enormous gravity of the sin of apostasy and of the works to be done to obtain forgiveness, he adds: "You must prefer fasting; be earnest in righteous works, whereby sins may be purged; frequently apply yourself to almsgiving, whereby souls are freed from death."[18] John Chrysostom affirms: "Even doing many other good works to enter the kingdom of heaven is impossible without alms."[19]

Another expression used to express the importance of almsgiving for the forgiveness of sins is in the *First Letter of Peter*: "Love covers a multitude of sins" (*1 Pet* 4:8). The theme of love runs through all ancient Christian preaching. The *Letter to the Hebrews* still offers a link to the Jewish tradition of almsgiving as a sacrifice. The abolition of the bloody sacrifice in the Temple is now replaced by almsgiving. The first was addressed to God, the second to the servant of God who is called to serve his neighbor: "Do not neglect to do good and to share what you have, for such sacrifices are pleasing to God."[20] The bloody sacrifice is now over. "Let us honor the Creator of all things, recognizing, as we have been taught, that he does not need blood, libations or perfumes."[21] Justin refers to teaching received from others. Cyprian also observes: "These works of charity are offerings presented to God and that whoever performs them can deserve grace from God. . . . The one who has compassion for the poor lends to God."[22] In this new view of sacrifice widows become the altars of the offerings: "Religion that is pure and undefiled before God, the Father, is this: to care for orphans and widows in their distress, and to keep oneself unstained by the world" (*Jas* 1:27). They are among the first recipients of alms precisely because of their social condition, as Cyprian himself affirms shortly before the text cited.

In his *Homily on Matthew*, Chrysostom shows that to honor Christ is not to despise the poor, but to honor him in the poor:

> Do you want to honor the Body of Christ? Do not despise him when he is naked. Do not honor him here in the church, with silk fabrics, while you leave him outside to suffer in the cold for lack of clothes. Because whoever said: 'This is my body' (*1 Cor* 11:24), and whoever understood it by saying this, is he who said: 'You saw me hungry, and you didn't feed me' (*Mt* 25:42), and also: 'Truly I tell you, just as you did not do it to one of the least of these, you did not do it to me' (*Mt* 25:45). Here the Body of Christ does not need clothes, but pure souls; there, it needs much solicitude.[23]

This text is interesting because John Chrysostom combines the two biblical texts of the *First Letter to the Corinthians* on the Eucharist 'This is my body' and *Mt* 25:45 on the identification of Christ with the 'least' or 'poor' and the last judgment. Chrysostom preached often about almsgiving and helping the poor since the time when he had become a presbyter.[24]

Almsgiving for the remission of sins is a common and repeated theme. I limit myself to an observation of Augustine: "When I say 'suitable,' I mean that they are not to be unfruitful in almsgiving; for Holy Scripture lays so much stress on this virtue. . . . Almsgiving is not enough to erase unprecedented crimes in which one perseveres. . . . One's life must be changed for the better, and almsgiving must be used to propitiate God for past sins, not to purchase impunity for the commission of such sins in the future."[25] Augustine, in my opinion, corrects a common and widespread opinion about the saving power of alms as such. For him, this teaching is true, but personal conversion must accompany it along with an interior change.

Other reasons are also given for exhorting almsgiving. It is like a loan made to God, so that he who gives to the needy "may know that he offers to God all that he offers."[26] "In the same way as he makes Christ a sharer in earthly goods, so will Christ make him a partaker in the kingdom of heaven."[27] We see an identification between the poor and Christ: "You see Christ in the needy, Christ who has so commended the poor to us that in them we clothe, welcome and feed him in person."[28] Besides these specifically Christian motivations, other purely humanitarian reasons are not lacking, since the poor are needy brothers and sisters.[29] For this reason, almsgiving should be given to all without distinction.[30] In some authors, especially those from the monastic tradition, ascetic reasons are given for detachment from wealth and for its use for the benefit of the poor.

At the end of the fourth century, the rich and influential in particular made amazing gestures in distributing enormous wealth. Paulinus of Nola was not an isolated case, nor was that of Melania and Pinianus.[31] The great expense for the armies guarding the borders, the increase of the bureaucracy, and the rampant corruption absorbed huge resources, and taxes of various kinds increased. Many were impoverished. Peter Brown estimates that 90% of the population had to struggle to survive, while 10% enjoyed great wealth. It's hard to know how to value these statements since there is no basis given for any of these statistics.

Some wealthy Christians followed the politics of ostentation, while other Christians chose the path of helping the needy. These were the two extremes. People with few possessions were those who made up the backbone of the Christian communities. The role of the rich was in their ability to make large donations. Some of them benefited the poor, while others encouraged the growth of ecclesiastical foundations, which I spoke about in the previous chapter.[32]

The term *almsgiving* was used almost exclusively in a Christian environment. It had a strong religious resonance, since it was often linked to the liturgical celebration during which free-will offerings were collected.[33] For this reason, it was considered part of the service rendered to God.[34] It could be practiced by all, within the limitations each had, because what mattered was the intention: "The poor, therefore, also have their own gain in this trade in mercy and take from their substance, however small, something that does not sadden them, for the sustenance of the needy. The rich should be more abundant in their gift, but the poor should not be inferior in their soul."[35]

The exhortation to alms was valid for all. But for the fathers, there was a close relationship between the one who gave and the one who received, not only in terms of charity but also in terms of a spiritual bond. In this context, a new interpretation of charity was elaborated: the one who gives to the poor receives in return his prayers and the reward of heaven, and so they help each other. This doctrine was already formulated in detail by Hermas in the first half of the second century, with the comparison of the sterile elm tree that has a vine clinging to it which bears its fruit only if supported by elm tree. Hermas concludes this long comparison by writing:

> These two trees [elm and vine] he said-symbolize the servants of God.[36] I would like to know the symbolism of these trees of which you speak. . . . The vine bears fruit; the elm is a tree without fruit. But if that vine does not go up on the elm, it cannot bear fruit in abundance by lying on the ground, and the fruit it bears rots if it is not suspended from the elm.[37] When, therefore, the vine is twisted with the elm, it bears fruit on its part and on the part of the elm. See, then, that even the elm bears much fruit, no less than the vine, indeed even more. . . . The rich man possesses the substance but is poor in the eyes of the Lord. Since he is worried about his wealth, he makes too brief a prayer and confession to the Lord, and what he does is weak, brief, and has no other power. When, therefore, the rich man relies on the poor man and gives him what is necessary, he believes that if he works on behalf of the poor man, he will be able to receive the reward from God; because the poor man is rich in his prayer and confession, and his prayer has great power with God. . . . Both, therefore, carry out a task: the poor man dedicates himself to prayer, which is his wealth, which he has received from the Lord and which he renders to the Lord in favor of the one who helps him. Similarly, the rich man offers to the Lord on behalf of the one [the poor man] who helps him. Similarly, the rich man offers the poor without hesitation the wealth he has received from the Lord. And this work is great and pleasing to God because the rich have reflected on their wealth, have worked for the poor with the gift of the Lord, and have perfectly fulfilled their service. . . . Thus, also the poor, turning to the Lord on behalf of the rich, perfect the riches of these and, in their turn, the rich, providing what is necessary for the poor, perfect their souls. Therefore, both share in the right work. And so he who does these things will not be abandoned by God, but his name will be written in the books of the living. Blessed are those who have goods and understand that wealth comes from the Lord, for he who understands this will be able to do a good service.[38]

The long quotation is very important for Christian spirituality in relation to wealth, poverty, material, and spiritual solidarity. The author does not frame his speech in terms of economic or social concerns but spiritual interests.

What follows is a rough outline of the various Christian conceptions concerning wealth and of the reasons for taking up offerings for the poor. In addition, we will also discuss the emphasis placed by Christians on the benefit that the rich receive from helping the poor that is subsequently expanded and developed, resulting in the recommendations of the fathers of the fourth and fifth centuries to make a last will and testament, thinking above all of one's own soul through bequests to the poor and to the Church, and also in supporting religious communities that devote themselves to prayer.

Origen follows this line of thought when he writes: "If, for his salvation, he who shares with the poor is helped by their prayer, receiving help for his spiritual poverty from the spiritual wealth of those who are poor in material things . . . to whom else could this happen and be helped with such great assistance since God answers the prayers of so many of the poor who are lifted up?"[39] Clement of Alexandria advises us to give to all because it is difficult to discern the worthy from the unworthy, so as not to "neglect some that are loved by God. . . . But by offering to all in turn who are in need, you must of necessity, by all means, find someone of those who has power with God to save."[40] The poor help the rich enter heaven: "You aspire to dwell in the heavens, and to reign with God. A man imitating God will give you this kingdom. By receiving a little here, there through all ages he will make you a dweller with Him."[41] The poor are the benefactors of the rich and their defenders. Paulinus of Nola wrote to Pammachius that the poor are the patrons of our souls.[42]

Yet another reason is given for the duty of almsgiving, and this reason has the character of social justice. The fathers of the fourth century strongly denounced social injustices and the exploitation of the poor, from Basil to Ambrose, from John Chrysostom to Augustine.

From these hints, it can be inferred that it is possible to reconstruct a whole theology of almsgiving in the life and preaching of the ancient church for the richness, variety, and diversity of motivations put forward. The insistence—obsessive in some cases—on the necessity, importance, and effects of almsgiving manifests one of the lesser-known aspects of the life of the ancient communities. Chrysostom observes that some might reproach him "that his daily discourse concerns almsgiving and mercy."[43]

A quotation from Augustine explains in what ways alms could be given:

> Not only, then, the man who gives food to the hungry, drink to the thirsty, clothing to the naked, hospitality to the stranger, shelter to the fugitive who visits the sick and the imprisoned, ransoms the captive, assists the weak, leads the blind, comforts the sorrowful, heals the sick, puts the wanderer on the right path, gives advice to the perplexed, and supplies the wants of the needy, — not this man only, but the man who pardons the sinner also gives alms; and the man who corrects with blows, or restrains by any kind of discipline one over whom he has power, and who at the same time forgives from the heart the sin by which he was injured, or prays that it

may be forgiven, is also a giver of alms, not only in that he forgives, or prays for forgiveness for the sin, but also in that he rebukes and corrects the sinner: for in this, too, he shows mercy.[44]

Only alms from honest work were to be accepted—as I have repeatedly pointed out in the previous chapter—while alms from illicit earnings or unworthy persons were categorically refused.[45] There were other criteria to be observed as well. Augustine himself reprimands those who give alms without criteria, in particular, a woman married and living with her husband. A matron, Ecdicia, who at first lived chastely in her marriage with her husband's consent, had aroused his anger by giving inconsiderate alms to monks:

> As the bearer of your letter reported to me, your husband learned that you gave everything or nearly everything that you possessed to two wandering monks, whoever they were, on the supposition that it was to be given to the poor. Then he despised them as well as you, considering them not servants of God but men who broke into another man's house, held you captive, and robbed the house. In anger, he cast aside the holy burden that he had taken up along with you. After all, he was weak, and for this reason, you, who seemed to be the stronger in your common commitment, ought not to have upset him by your presumption but to have supported him by your love. For, even if he was perhaps moving rather sluggishly toward distributing alms more generously, he could have learned to do this as well, if he had not been stung by your unexpected outlays but had been coaxed to do so by the docility expected of you.[46]

That sacred burden was to live in continence with his wife. Almsgiving is not only material but also spiritual when we work for the salvation of souls. It is a meritorious work to accumulate treasures in heaven, but more important are the harmony and well-being of the family.

ORGANIZED CHARITY AND FORMS OF ASSISTANCE

The Old Testament often exhorts to the practice of charity and almsgiving, but it was always at the individual level. Forms of organized aid began in the second century CE out of the local synagogues. Collections were made in the synagogues to help the needy and for the ransom of prisoners. In fact, they also chose those in charge of this office.

According to Luke, Christian organized charity was born immediately in Jerusalem. The author of the *Acts of the Apostles* tells us that among the disciples of Jesus, there was no one in need: "There was not a needy person among them, for as many as owned lands or houses sold them and brought the proceeds of what was sold. They laid it at the apostles' feet, and it was distributed to each as any had the need" (*Acts* 4:34-35). A little later, he adds that the widows of the Hellenists were neglected, so there was dissatisfaction in the community. Then the apostles took the initiative to establish seven faithful "of good standing, full of the Spirit and of wisdom, whom we may appoint to this task" (*Acts* 6:3). Up to seven men were commissioned to help those in need, especially widows. In Judaism and Christianity, concern for the poor had a religious motivation, something that did not exist in the Greco-Roman world. In the sense that it was God's will, believers had an obligation to care for the poor. The 'poor are the flesh of Christ,' as we can understand from chapter 25 of the *Gospel of Matthew*.

The *First Letter to Timothy* says: "Deacons likewise must be serious, not double-tongued, not indulging in much wine, not greedy for money" (3:8). Deacons should not be dishonest. This means they handle money. This statement can be clarified by a passage from the *Shepherd* of Hermas: "They who had the stains as servants, who discharged their duty ill, and who plundered widows and orphans of their livelihood, and gained possessions for themselves from the ministry, which they had received. If therefore, they remain under the dominion of the same desire, they are dead, and there is no hope of life for them; but if they repent, and finish their ministry in a holy manner, they shall be able to live."[47] The severe criticism of the misconduct of deacons—the term can indicate any minister in that time—in managing the goods of the community is proof positive that money generated greed in other cases also in the ancient church.

A passage by the apologist Aristides of Athens, on the other hand, speaks positively of how the church could use wealth in service to Christian charity: "From widows, they do not turn away their esteem, and they deliver the orphan from him who treats him harshly. And he, who has, gives to him who has not, without boasting. And when they see a stranger, they take him into their homes and rejoice over him as a very brother, for they do not call them brothers after the flesh, but brothers after the spirit and in God."[48] The author is talking about the conduct of Christians towards other Christians. But it is not clear whether he refers to individual generosity or to the organized generosity of a community. It seems to me that it refers to organized generosity which embraces all those who are in need and is the responsibility of the whole community. The communal and organized aspect is clarified even more by Justin, who writes in these same decades: "What is collected [during the liturgical celebration] is laid before the one who presides, and he helps orphans as much as widows, and those in need for illness or other necessity, and those in prison, and guests who come from other countries: in short, we take to heart all those in need."[49]

Many forms of assistance developed since the second century among both Jews and Romans, but among Christians they become something more radical, as noted by the pagan writer Lucian of Samosata who, in a booklet, derides charity, brotherhood and Christian hospitality. Among other things he writes: "Their first legislator has impressed on their souls the persuasion that they are all brothers. In fact, they deploy an unspeakable zeal, each time something happens that touches their common interests; nothing seems too difficult or painful to them in those cases."[50] The eye of a pagan is struck by the conduct of Christians. Since this is so exceptional, he is amazed.

A few decades later, Tertullian, in an oft quoted passage, writes:

> We are a corporation with a common knowledge of religion, a common rule of life, and a union of hope. We come together for meeting and assembly, in order that having formed a band as it were to come before God, we may encompass him with prayers. . . . We are governed by the most approved elders, who have obtained this office not by purchase, but on testimony; for indeed nothing of God is obtainable by money. Even if we have a kind of treasury, this is not filled up from a sense of obligation, as of a hired religion. Each member adds a small sum once a month, or when he pleases, and only if he is willing and able; for no one is forced, but each contributes of his own free will. These are the deposits as it were made by devotion. For that sum is disbursed not on banquets nor drinking bouts nor unwillingly on eating-houses, but on the supporting and burying of the poor, and on boys and girls deprived of property and parents, and on aged servants of the house, also on shipwrecked persons, and any who are in the mines or on islands or in prisons, provided it be for the cause of God's religion, who thus become pensioners of their confession. . . . But also they rage at us for calling one another brethren, for no other reason, I suppose, than because among themselves every name indicating blood relationship is assumed from affection. . . . But how much more worthily are those both called and considered brethren who have recognized one Father, namely God, who have imbibed one spirit of holiness, who from one womb of the same ignorance have quaked before one light of truth! But we are perhaps regarded as less legitimate for the reason that no tragedy proclaims aloud our brotherliness, or because we are brothers as the result of household possessions, which among you generally break up the relationship of brothers. And so we, who are united in heart and soul, have no hesitation about sharing a thing. Among us all things are common except wives. . . . It is only the dining-room of the Christians that is objected to. Our dinner shows its significance by its name: it is called by the name which amongst the Greeks means affection. Whatsoever be its cost, it is a gain to incur expense in the name of religion, since by this refreshment we help those who are in need, not in the way that among you parasites eagerly strive for the glory of enslaving their freedom at the price of a belly that has to be filled amid insults; but in the way that with God greater regard is paid to them of low degree.[51]

The whole ecclesial community—here he is speaking of Christians—is like a family. Irenaeus presents Christian charity towards others as a loan: "He who has mercy on the poor lends to God."[52] Irenaeus unites together the gifts that are given to the church with the Eucharist in such a way as to almost confuse them:

We are bound, therefore, to offer to God the first-fruits of His creation, as Moses also says, 'You shall not appear in the presence of the Lord your God empty-handed' (*Ex* 23:15) ; so that man, being accounted as grateful, by those things in which he has shown his gratitude, may receive that honor which flows from Him. And the class of oblations, in general, has not been set aside, for there were both oblations there [among the Jews], and there are oblations here [among the Christians]. Sacrifices there were among the people; sacrifices there are, too, in the Church: but the species alone has been changed, inasmuch as the offering is now made, not by slaves, but by freemen. For the Lord is [ever] one and the same, but the character of a servile oblation is peculiar [to itself], as is also that of freemen, in order that, by the very oblations, the indication of liberty may be set forth. For with Him, there is nothing purposeless, nor without significance, nor without design. And for this reason they (the Jews) had indeed the tithes of their goods consecrated to Him, but those who have received liberty set aside all their possessions for the Lord's purposes, bestowing joyfully and freely not the less valuable portions of their property, since they have the hope of better things [hereafter]; as that poor widow acted who cast all her living into the treasury of God.[53]

There were different categories of people assisted by the community. Orphans and widows, defined by the *Didascalia* as the "altar of Christ" (4.5), were concerned because they were alone and abandoned and were always placed among the first to be helped. Christians tried to adopt orphans, to educate them, and then to marry them with other Christians.[54] They wanted everyone to have a job and earn their own bread, but when this was not possible because of illness, disability or old age, only then was the community to provide, since it did not present itself as a society of mutual aid. Brothers detained in prison or condemned to forced labor were not abandoned, but helped in every way: visiting them, consoling them, obtaining more humane treatment, giving them everything they needed, possibly obtaining their liberation.[55]

In the small communities of the second century, the bishops were the main persons responsible for the charity, and often acted in the first person: "The bishops, in their ministry, have continuously protected the poor and widows and have led a holy life."[56] Priests and deacons were associated with them. Polycarp addresses the Philippians in this way: "And let the presbyters be compassionate and merciful to all, bringing back those that wander, visiting all the sick, and not neglecting the widow, the orphan, or the poor, but always "providing for that which is becoming in the sight of God and man" (6.1). In Philippi, the presbyter Valens had appropriated money for himself from the common purse. In the area of charitable work, the deacons became the closest agents of the bishop in distributing charity, but always under the supervision of the bishop, serving as his "ear, mouth, heart and soul."[57]

For this reason, these same deacons however were exposed to the temptation of appropriating for themselves what was destined for charitable works.[58]

The bishop must be attentive:

> You ought to receive from all your people the ministration of food and clothing, and of other things needful. And so again, from these same gifts that are given to you by the people which is under your charge, do you nourish the deacons and widows and orphans, and those who are in want, and strangers. For it is your duty, O bishop, as a faithful steward to care for all.[59]

The faithful make donations to the deacon in charge, who must deliver everything to the local bishop, the one responsible for distributing aid according to the needs of the people. First, the gifts are used for the sustenance of the clergy, then for that of orphans, widows, and the needy who belong to the community. The bishop knows the needy through the deacons who are more in contact with everyone. But the bishop is the 'administrator of God', who manages the spiritual goods—the preaching and the sacraments—as well as the material goods. Even in the distribution of goods, clerics and laity are two separate bodies. Again, from the *Didascalia*:

> In fact, just as you have received the burden of each one, so also the fruits that are taken from all the people will be yours for all the things that you need. And feed the needy well, as men who give an account to Him who can make no mistake nor be evaded. For as you administer the office of the bishopric, so from the same office of the bishopric ought you to be nourished, as the priests and Levites and deacons who serve before God, according to as it is written in the *Book of Numbers* (2:25).

A little further on, the text makes other clarifications:

> However, present your offerings to the bishop, either you yourselves, or through the deacons; and when he has received, he will distribute them justly. For the bishop is well acquainted with those who are in distress and dispenses and gives to each one as is fitting for him; so that one may not often receive on the same day or in the same week, and another receives not even a little. For whom the priest and steward of God know to be the more in distress, him he helps according as he requires (2:27).

The bishop is the coordinator and the main person responsible before God, but he uses many intermediaries to be in contact with the people. The faithful "should be familiar with deacons and not disturb their heads at all times, but rather should make known what they are asking for through the inferior ministers, that is, deacons. Therefore, everything they wish to do, they should make it known to the bishop through the deacons and (only) then do it" (2:30). In the next chapter, the text also specifies the amount to be given to bishops, priests, and deacons.

The *Didascalia* has more of a general character. The number of beneficiaries varied from community to community, depending on the size of each one. It is only with the Roman church that we know the official number of beneficiaries for the middle of the third century in a letter written by its Bishop Cornelius to Fabius the bishop of Syrian Antioch. He writes that in the Roman church "there are forty-six priests, seven deacons, seven sub-deacons, forty-two acolytes, fifty-two exorcists, readers and ostiaries, more than one thousand five hundred widows and poor people, all nourished by the grace and benevolence of the Master."[60] The Church staff were numerous, and so were the needy. The Roman church also provided aid to many other distant churches. Though it is not possible to quantify it, we can still hold that the ecclesiastical economy had to be consistent. Such assistance was not by chance; rather there was a stable organization with specific personnel that supported it. Prudentius presents the deacon Lawrence who resolved, in the same period under discussion, to walk through the city and bring help to the poor.[61] Ambrose presents a slightly different narrative concerning Lawrence who, he says, "promised to those who asked him for the treasures of the Church to show them. The following day he led the poor. When asked where the promised treasures were, he pointed to the poor and said: These are the treasures of the Church."[62] When Pope Leo spoke about the deacon Lawrence, he describes him as one who "excelled in the distribution of the property of the Church,"[63] perhaps to indicate that deacons played an important role in the welfare function of the church.

The author of the *Didascalia*, almost certainly a bishop, uses chapter 18 of the Book of *Numbers* of the Old Testament which speaks of support for the Levites in justifying the offerings and their destination. He continues: "Then were first fruits and tithes and part-offerings and gifts, but today the oblations which are offered through the bishops to the Lord God. For they are your high priests, but the priests and Levites now are the presbyters and deacons, and the orphans and widows, but the Levite and high priest is the bishop. He is a minister of the word and mediator, but to you, a teacher, and your father after God" (2.26). In *Didache* 13.3, the high priests are the prophets who receive "the first-fruits of all the products of winepress and threshing floor, of oxen and of sheep." Not only clerics were included among the "high priests" but also widows and orphans, not in the sense that they command these gifts be given, but because they partake in the gifts of the faithful. Theirs is not a priesthood of service, but of receiving the benefits of God.

The *Didascalia* repeats several times the respect that should be directed towards the bishop on the part of all the faithful, and his discretion in the administration and distribution of aid:

> For you, the faithful, are commanded to give, but he to dispense. And you shall require no account of the bishop, nor watch over how he dispenses and discharges his stewardship, or when he gives, or to whom, or where, or whether well or ill, or whether he gives fairly. For he has One who will require, even the Lord God, who delivered this stewardship into his hands and held him worthy of the priesthood of so great an office. Now, do not observe the bishop, nor require an account of him, nor speak ill of him and oppose God. Do not offend the Lord (2.35).

It warns the bishop that he must account to God for his actions. The *Didascalia* requires the bishop to be responsible for what he does in his conscience and before God, but the people must still trust him. The monotony of repetition of these ideas is intended to resolve and avoid conflicts between the abusive, vain, and proud behavior of the leaders, and the criticism and opposition of the members of the community. As I mentioned in the previous chapter, those who handle money in the church can be subject to greed.

Now I turn to the Western Mediterranean, to Carthage. Here in the middle of the third century, the exiled bishop Cyprian wrote to his community:

> I urge that you be scrupulous in your care for the widows, the sick, and all the poor, and further, that you meet the financial needs of any strangers who are in want out of my own personal funds which I have left in the care of our fellow presbyter Rogatianus. In case these funds have already been completely expended, I am sending to Rogatianus by the acolyte Naricus a further sum, to ensure that the work of charity amongst those in difficulties may be carried out the more generously and readily.[64]

Cyprian was obligated to help others with good teaching but also with good works. With regard to *Matthew* 19:16-29, he observed that if Christians, who have broken their bonds with the world, are 'pilgrims,' earthly goods must now serve for good work in view of the eschatological dimension. In this sense, earthly riches are redeemed and Christians are 'pilgrims,' while the fullness of historical living is authentic only in the eschatological dimension in which goods, redeemed through the martyrologic imitation of Christ's Passion, regain their divine value. The biographer Pontius writes of his bishop that during the plague in Carthage, while the sick in need languished in the streets, and everyone thought of their cruel gains, Cyprian instead cared about all. "It would be a sin to pass over in silence what he did during the events . . . in piety as much as in the truth of religion." His action consisted of educating and exhorting the people to generosity; that it was not enough "to help only the brothers with the rightful service of charity," but also the others in that terrible moment of collective suffering.[65]

In his *Martyrs of Palestine* Eusebius lists several cases of Christians who went very far to help their brothers in the faith condemned to forced labor. Special help was also organized in the event of barbaric raids. Special care was taken of the dead so that everyone could have a dignified burial, even the poorest among them as well as strangers, fulfilling "even to an unknown person the office that would be due to one's relatives."[66]

The charity organized by the church— in some cases private charity was actually not recommended[67]—had a personal character in the sense that the needy were known individually, and there was a register of them in order to be able to help them better. Origen, in a beautiful section of his *Commentary on Matthew*, observes that the office of the dispenser of the *reditus ecclesiae* does not consist so much in giving things, but in knowing the history of each one and in helping him in his concrete needs.[68]

The main person responsible for the assistance was, therefore, the bishop. Can. 14 of the *Canons of Athanasius* speaks about the personal duties of the bishop in helping the needy because, "a city where the bishop loves the poor has no poor because the church of the city is rich." In small towns, it was easier for the bishop to carry out this task personally, at least partially. In large cities or in the surrounding areas, it was necessary to have recourse to other specific people, preferably among the clergy.[69]

With the increase of the Christian population in the fourth century, more members of the clergy were involved in charitable work. Ambrose observes that the more generous a cleric is, the more the faithful offer;[70] they had to be immune from the temptation of ostentation, as was the case in pagan euergetism.[71] The people in charge of Christian assistance in Milan to whom Ambrose[72] was speaking were the deacons, but also the priests and treasurers.[73] The bishop was the main and last person responsible, as was the case in all the smaller towns as well.[74] The unpleasant Theophilus of Alexandria complains that a woman, unbeknownst to him and without the requisite qualifications, had been entered in the register of widows.[75] The episcopal churches had lists of different categories of people in need. The widows, the poor and lonely, were particularly marginalized and deserved more attention and food aid.[76] There is a Roman inscription (390-425) of a daughter who remembers her mother, Regina,[77] a widow for 60 years, and also *univira* (faithful to a single husband) who was particularly deserving because she did not live at the expense of the community.

Clerics were assisted in the service by women who were deaconesses. While John Chrysostom considered the administration of ecclesiastical goods a work not suitable for priests, he noted that the apostles had instead established the office of deacons to feed the poor, help the wounded, give hospitality, help the oppressed and orphans, and defend widows and virgins.[78] In this perspective, the *ministerium pauperum* was considered in ancient times a qualifying commitment of the clergy in general, including deaconesses. Throughout antiquity, this *ministerium* was considered an essential requirement for admission to orders.

In the course of the third century, there was a tendency to free the superior clergy from various commitments so that they could devote themselves exclusively and full-time to their mission. Origen exhorts the laity to offer "the offerings to the priests" (*obsequia sacerdotum*), so that they may engage in the study of Scripture.[79] This situation is fully mature in the rich church of Cyprian, at the very time when Africa was experiencing its greatest economic prosperity:

> Those who are advanced in the Church of God by clerical appointment are not to be distracted in any way from their sacred duties. They are not to become entangled in the anxieties and worries of this world but rather, receiving as they do in the gifts and donations of their brethren the tenth portion, as it were, of the fruits of the earth, they are not to withdraw from the altar and sacrifices but day and night are to be dedicated to heavenly and spiritual concerns.[80]

Canon 7 of the *Statues of the Ancient Church* prescribes that bishops should not work directly but should use archdeacons and archpriests. However, there is no evidence of such a concrete organization in Rome. For example, we do not know if the city was divided up into welfare regions. It seems that widows also carried out this ministry, inasmuch as they were called to works of mercy.[81] However, the bishop had to be informed of new cases.[82] In Milan, there had to be, as is the case elsewhere, a "register of the poor" (*matricula pauperum*). Ambrose, however, demanded great caution in charity towards others:

> It is clear, then, that there ought to be due measure in our liberality, that our gifts may not become useless. Moderation must be observed, especially by priests, for fear that they should give away for the sake of ostentation, and not for justice' sake. Never was the greed of beggars greater than it is now. They come in full vigor, they come with no reason but that they are on the tramp. They want to empty the purses of the poor—to deprive them of their means of support.[83]

> Many pretend they have debts. Let the truth be investigated. They bemoan the fact that they have been stripped of everything by robbers. In such a case, give credit only if the misfortune is apparent, or the person is well known; and then readily give help. To those rejected by the Church, supplies must be granted if they are in want of food. He, then, that observes this method in his giving is hard towards none but is free towards all. We ought not only to lend our ears to hear the voices of those who plead but also our eyes to investigate their needs. Weakness calls more loudly to the good dispenser than the voice of the poor. . . . He must be seen who

does not see out. He must be sought for who is ashamed to be seen. He also that is in prison must come to your thoughts; another seized with sickness must present himself to your mind, as he cannot reach your ears.[84]

After Constantine, this personal and fraternal character diminished because new situations imposed new solutions. Private charity continued, as did the official charity of the community for all categories of needy, but with greater organization. The funds came from the free oblations of the faithful, from the various collections, from extraordinary offerings and, in a particular way, from the fruit of the immovable goods which the churches possessed for this purpose: "Those goods do not belong to us but to the poor. We, somehow or other, have charge of those goods, but we do not claim for ourselves ownership by an unjust appropriation of them."[85]

Julian the Apostate complained that in Antioch Christian women were the ones to garnish possessions for the finances of the church. He reproached husbands for the excessive freedom, in this field, granted to their wives: "Now, every one of you allows his wife to carry everything out of his house to the Galileans, and when your wives feed the poor at your expense they inspire a great admiration for godlessness in those who are in need of such bounty—and of such sort are, I think, the great majority of mankind."[86] Perhaps he echoes Porphyry, who a few decades earlier had accused Christians of "grabbing the wealth of wealthy women," according to a quotation from Jerome.[87] Julian the Emperor attributes the conversion of pagans to Christian 'philanthropy' and therefore wants to imitate its forms. In this sense he is a precious witness to Christian charitable activity: "In my opinion, since it happened that the poor neglected by the (pagan) priests remained neglected, the ungodly Galileans (the Christians), thinking back, devoted themselves to this kind of philanthropy, and strengthened themselves at worst through these showy practices."[88] The ungodly Galileans (i.e., the Christians) conquered souls with their care of the needy. "Do we not see that what most contributed to the development of atheism (Christianity) is philanthropy towards foreigners, care for the burial of the dead, and a simulated austerity in life? I believe that each of these aspects must be taken care of sincerely by us. . . . It would be shameful that while the Jews have no beggar and the ungodly Galileans (= Christians) nourish not only their own but also our own."[89] The emperor attributes the attraction of Christianity to charitable works. The Christian historian Sozomen, who reports the letter, reconstructs the picture of the initiatives of the emperor who was dissatisfied with the progress of his religious reforms. He then takes a series of initiatives of a charitable and cultural nature.[90]

Julian's observations on Christian behavior in the fourth century have a historical foundation from the earliest communities. Christian authors also put forward as an argument the social and altruistic commitment of Christians to explain their growth in numbers. They also refer to the high Christian morality practiced in daily life that attracted those eager for a life worth living. A way of life as a philosophy in a pagan environment was reserved only for members of the upper class. Among other more convincing arguments, Christian authors also put forward a social explanation. Tertullian writes that when the pagans see the relationship between Christians, they say: "See how they love each other."

SOME ORGANIZED FORMS OF ASSISTANCE

Fraternal Agape

The first form of assistance is called by Tertullian fraternal agape, using the Greek term.[91] The term, which elicits a Christian environment, initially indicates God's love for men, or fraternal love (1 Cor 1:13) and is used to designate actual manifestations of that love, such as almsgiving and sacred meals. The *Letter of Jude* uses the term agape in the sense of a banquet (verse 12). Originally the meal of the community was connected with the Eucharist, but later it had become separated. A meal with a religious character also took on the aspect of charity and help for the needy. The first reference is found in Ignatius of Antioch.[92] We find some hints also in Pliny, who writes that on a given day, Christians gather early in the morning and then in the evening to have a common and innocent meal.[93] Therefore, they are two separate meetings.

Tertullian speaks more explicitly of these meals, even if in an unclear manner in chapter 39 of the *Apology*. The *Apostolic Tradition*, on the contrary, offers us a detailed description in chapter 26. The meal of the refrigerium, of which I spoke in chapter 12, should not be confused with the meal for the needy. The *Didascalia* is a contemporary of the *The Apostolic Tradition*, and it speaks explicitly of it: "And to him who invites widows to suppers let him frequently send her whom he knows to be in the more distress. And again, if anyone gives bounties to widows, let him send her the rather who is in want. But let the portion of the pastor be separated and set apart for him according to rule at the suppers or the bounties, even though he be not present, in honor of Almighty God" (2.28). Another mention is made in the Council of Gangra canon 11: "If anyone despises those who by faith prepare meals for the poor and invite their brothers and sisters in honor of the Lord and does not want to participate in these invitations because he takes no account of the matter, let him be anathema."[94]

In Rome at the end of the fourth century, Pammachius, another rich and noble Christian, continuing the ancient tradition of agape had offered a banquet in St. Peter's Basilica around 396 to a large multitude of *pauperes* in the city, on the occasion of the death of his wife Pauline,[95] distributing money to them as well. In the letter where Paulinus of Nola refers to the episode, he defines the poor as "the patrons of our souls."[96] Paulinus puts this episode in contrast with the subversive ostentation of the rich who use their money to buy and feed beasts and gladiators. There is a stark contrast between the search for the glory of the pagan in offering shows and the Christian who instead expects heavenly remuneration through the help to the needy, precisely to those people marginalized by civic donations. Paulinus writes:

> Blessed are you (Pammachius), who has not intervened in the assembly of such men and obtain praise, not on the chair of the ungodly, but in the seat of the Apostle and in the assembly of the Church, that is in the theater of Christ, where the spectators in the bleachers are not seditious, but people who bless, and where God himself is a spectator. You give shows for the Church, not for the arena of the amphitheater, aspiring to eternal praise, not to vainglory.[97]

Jerome says of Pammachius: the doors of the house where before crowded with "the multitude of visitors" (*turbae salutantium*), now is besieged by wretches."[98]

E. Wipszycka is not convinced that this institution of agape still existed in Egypt in the fourth century, as there is no information in the normative texts. In the sanctuary of Abu Mena, a banquet was held once a year, but it was something different.[99]

Providing a Burial for the Deceased

I already talked at length about the care taken for burying the dead in chapter twelve. It was one of the great values of antiquity. The apologist Aristides, in the second century, writes: "When one of their poor leaves this world, and one of them sees him, then he provides for his burial."[100] Ambrose of Milan considers the burial such an important work that it was considered lawful and necessary to sell the sacred vessels in order accomplish it.[101]

Care of Christians in Prison

In some texts cited, mention is made of Christians who are in prison for their faith. The leaders of the communities must take care of them. It is one of their fundamental values. There are many sources that talk about it. One must sometimes bribe the guards to visit the prisoners in order to help them. This Christian charitable activity is also highlighted by the pagan Lucian of Samosata, who mocks Christians in his pamphlet *On the Death of Peregrinus*. He observed from the outside: "Their legislator persuaded them to be all brothers."[102] Peregrinus, a kind of freeloader, becomes a Christian. Indeed, he was a prophet, exegete, pontiff, and head of the gatherings. Captured as a Christian—Lucian knows that Christians are persecuted and imprisoned—he was thrown into prison:

The Christians regarded the incident as a calamity and left nothing undone in their efforts to rescue him. Then, when they realized this was impossible, every other form of attention was shown him, not in any casual way but with assiduity. And from the very break of day aged widows and orphan children could be seen waiting near the prison, while their officials even slept inside with him after bribing the guards. Then elaborate meals were brought in, and sacred books of theirs were read aloud. . . . Indeed, people came even from the cities in Asia, sent by the Christians at their common expense, to help and defend and encourage the hero. They show incredible speed whenever any such public action is taken. For in no time, they lavish their all. So it was then in the case of Peregrinus; much money came to him from them by reason of his imprisonment, and he procured not a little revenue from it.[103]

Is this description just a satire, or does Lucian show a detailed knowledge of the life of Christians which he describes, making it ridiculous to pagan readers? Now, gathering clues from other Christian texts, the presentation does correspond to reality, even if it is described in a caricature. The corruption of the guards was normal; help even from distant communities was a fact; visits were an obligation.

Already in Matthew's Gospel, visiting those in prison is mentioned as a work of charity (*Mt* 25:36, 39, 43). The first form of the care of prisoners, therefore, concerned those who had been imprisoned for the faith, whose first testimonies come from the first Christian texts. The *Letter to the Hebrews* writes: "You had compassion for those who were in prison."[104] Aristides writes: "And if they hear that one of their numbers is imprisoned or afflicted on account of the name of their Messiah, all of them anxiously minister to his necessity, and if it is possible to redeem him they set him free."[105] Justin also affirms that the collection served the needs of the prisoners.[106] Tertullian, in describing the Christian charity made through the monthly collection writes: "Any who are in the mines or on islands or in prisons, provided it be for the cause of God's religion, thus become pensioners of their confession."[107]

The visit to the imprisoned was usual and normal to console them and alleviate their suffering, a duty also for married Christian women.[108] Thecla bribes the jailers to visit Paul.[109] Such a practice must have been quite common.[110] Two deacons were delegated in Carthage for the care of Christians in prison: "There were present there Tertius and Pomponius, the blessed deacons who ministered to us, and had arranged by means of a gratuity that we might be refreshed by being sent out for a few hours into a pleasanter part of the prison."[111] In fact, the guardian soldiers take advantage of it by trying to extort money.[112] But someone had a good heart: "Pudens, a soldier, an assistant overseer of the prison, began to hold us in great esteem, . . . and admitted many brothers to see us, that both they and we might be mutually refreshed."[113] This soldier then became a Christian: "The overseer of the prison had already been converted."[114]

The care of Christian prisoners was constant. In fact, sometimes the visitors were criticized for paying too much attention to them.[115] There was also extensive care provided for those condemned to the mines and to exile. In the second century, Dionysius of Corinth praised the Bishop Soter of Rome and the Roman church for their praiseworthy tradition of helping others, and also the Christians condemned to mines.[116] The bishop of Rome had a list of those condemned to mines in Sardinia to be rescued and in some cases, also obtained their release.[117]

From his exile, Cyprian wrote to the clerics of Carthage:

> I know that our brethren in their charity are very anxious to visit and meet the noble confessors whom God has already blessed with so brilliant and glorious a beginning. But all the same I consider they should act with caution, avoiding visits in crowds and meeting in large numbers together for fear that this may provoke ill-feeling and they may be refused all access to them. If we are greedy and never satisfied in our demands, we run the risk of losing everything. And so, take counsel and care that moderation makes visiting safer. In particular the presbyters who celebrate the offering there before the confessors should take it in turns to go individually, accompanied each by a different deacon, because the risk of resentment is diminished if the people who visit and meet together change and vary.[118]

The third-century *Didascalia* exhorts Christians not to neglect any means of rescuing prisoners. It indicates various categories of suffering for the faith that were to be rescued, including "slaves and captives and prisoners, and those who are treated with violence, and those condemned by the mob, and those sentenced to fight with beasts, or to the mines, or to exile, and those condemned to the games."[119]

> One should not be ashamed to go and visit the prisoners.... But if any man comes near to them and be seized with them, and for no offense suffer affliction for his brother's sake, blessed is he in being called a Christian, for he has confessed the Lord, and he shall live before God. And those again who are persecuted[120] for the faith and pass from city to city, according to the Lord's command, you should receive and refresh. And when you receive them, rejoice, for you are made sharers of their persecution."[121]

Eusebius writes that Licinius forbade Christians to take care of those who were in prisons. Emperor Honorius, in an atmosphere of the Christian moment (*christiana tempora*), allowed priests (bishops?) to enter freely into prisons for charity and spiritual purposes and to intercede in individual cases for the release of prisoners.[122] The latter had been imprisoned not for faith, but for some crime. But Christian piety must have known no such barriers because the prison experience was terrible.

What satirist Lucian and Christian sources say substantially agree concerning the generosity of Christians towards Christians in prison. The organization of the assistance was not yet well structured. It seems to have been spontaneous but connected with some form of collective institution.

Ransom of Prisoners

Another means of Christian charity is the ransom of prisoners of war,[123] who were made so by pirates, or barbarian invasions because, on these occasions, civilians were taken, which meant money for the kidnappers who could sell the captives as slaves. The *captivus* also could borrow money, which he then had to repay in some way, or he had to be helped by his family and friends. Roman law made provision for the *redemptio* of the prisoners. Christians also attached importance to this charitable work and solidarity. In Rome, already in the second century, Hermas considered the ransom "of the servants of God" as a work of mercy.[124] Cyprian sent out a hundred thousand sesterces collected in the community to help the Christians of Numidia for the ransom of prisoners and indicated he was willing to give more for the generosity of the Christians of Carthage: "If the case should be repeated, count from now on their willing and large contribution."[125] Lactantius considered the ransom of prisoners an action of high humanity.[126] Let us see how this charitable work was put into practice, after the disaster of Adrianople, for example in Milan, by Ambrose, who also sold sacred vessels for the occasion. Not only does he offer ample justification for his charitable work.[127] For him, a great Roman and defender of Rome, it was "the greatest generosity to ransom the prisoners, to rescue them from the hands of the enemies."[128] Criticism must have been strong against his selling of the sacred vessels. His practice, however, was a model for future generations. Ambrose could reproach the pagan Symmachus that pagan temples have no concern for charity: "Let them tell us how many prisoners have been redeemed by the temples, how many times they have given food to the poor, how many exiles they have subsidized with aid."[129] Augustine also does the same in Africa.[130]

The church of Cappadocia still recalled in the fourth century the aid sent by the Roman church for the ransom of the prisoners of the Gothic invasion of the mid-third century.[131] Pinianus and Melania also sold their properties to redeem the prisoners.[132]

At the time of the barbarian invasions, the invaders knew well how to extort money by kidnapping people. Not only did they take what they could, but they also secured other benefits through ransom. Interesting and significant is the fact that the imperial authorities, now Christian, delegated to Christian priests, as an obligation, to pay attention to the ransom of prisoners, embodied in a law of 408.[133] In Late Antiquity, one of the duties of the good bishop was considered to be the commitment to the redemption of prisoners of war.[134] Patrick of Ireland writes that it is a typical Christian custom to spend money on the ransom of baptized prisoners.[135] Klingshirn studied the charitable work of Caesarius of Arles for the ransom of prisoners after the wars between the Franks and Burgundians on the one hand and the Ostrogoths and Visigoths on the other in the years 506/507.[136] At the end of the sixth century, Gregory the Great still refers to the need for the ransom of prisoners during the Lombard invasion.[137]

Hospitality

While today we are very sensitive to works of social welfare, we have almost forgotten the sense of hospitality that was so dear to the ancient peoples of the Mediterranean world.[138] The organization of the Roman Empire made it possible to travel a great deal. It was never like that before and never again until modern times with the invention of the train. Irenaeus of Lyon praises the Roman Empire for having made it possible to travel safely everywhere,[139] speaking of the safety he had personally experienced during his long journeys. One of the reasons for the rapid spread of Christianity was that it was possible to travel everywhere via the Roman road system. But the journey was tiring both by ship and by land. There were no decent hotels, so private accommodation was used. The first Christian missionaries were able to travel whenever they needed to, first using the system of the synagogue network and then the Christian communities.

Hospitality is strongly inculcated in the New Testament writings,[140] and becomes a virtue for Christians that immediately follows upon coming to faith.[141] Paul makes use of it in his travels. When he arrived in Puteoli, he stayed with local Christians for seven days (*Acts* 28:14). The *Didache* speaks extensively about itinerant missionaries and the conditions of hospitality (11.1-3). Ethics of hospitality were also developed to combat the phenomenon of abusive practices.[142] To Tertullian, Christianity appears as a "common pledge of hospitality."[143] It should be practiced by private individuals, but also by the community as such which then needed a certain level of organization, with specific persons officially appointed, to extend hospitality if it was impossible for the bishop to provide for it himself. The hospitable bishops are called blessed by Hermas.[144] One of the purposes of the Sunday collection was to welcome "guests from other countries."[145]

In any case, the bishop held primary place of responsibility for hospitality, which was considered one of his prime duties.[146] When Cyprian was in his hiding place far from Carthage because of the persecution, he still set apart some money to welcome strangers.[147] Abuses were possible, and for this reason, precautions were soon taken.[148] In fact, the above-cited Lucian of Samosata makes an ironic comment about the Christians who welcome everyone.

For this reason, from the beginning of the fourth century, letters of trust (*litterae communicatoriae*) were required for those who traveled in order to be accepted.[149] Canon 11 of the Council of Chalcedon established that "the poor and those needing assistance shall travel, after examination, with letters of peace from the church." For strangers, guest houses or shelters (*xenodochia*) were also built, and clerics oversaw them.[150] *Xenodochia*, however, were not reserved exclusively for strangers, but all kinds of needy people were admitted so that the same buildings were used for several purposes.

Hospitality became a characteristic of ancient monasticism. At the end of the fourth century, the pilgrim Egeria noted in her diary that she was well received. In the monasteries, a guesthouse for guests was introduced; in fact, the availability was such—with a few exceptions—that it was possible not to observe fasting in order to eat with foreigners.

Ransom from Prostitution

The prostitute was a socially useful figure who carried out a disgraceful activity which was never condemned as illegal. But prostitutes had legal limitations on hereditary, procedural, and matrimonial law. Christianity sought redemption and conversion. A commitment of Christian solidarity concerned women forced into prostitution. Ambrose counts prostitutes among the poor, that is, among those who are most socially abandoned and, therefore, most in need of Christian solidarity.[151] The emperor also allowed the bishops to free the prostitutes from the *lenones* (brothel keepers) in 428.[152] Already in 343 Constantius had granted that women who had become Christian should not be used for prostitution: but a Christian could redeem them by paying the right price. The legal situation of prostitutes improved in Justinian's time.

Victims of Usury

Christians provided aid to the victims of usury, especially to those who were oppressed by debts. The fathers strongly and frequently condemned usury, which at the time was understood as any loan with interest, as I have already explained in detail. Among her charitable activities, Melania freed people imprisoned because of debts.[153] Lactantius[154] speaks explicitly about it, even though he notes that many people pretended to have debts. In particular, there were heavy debts with the tax authorities, who were implacable in the application of the laws and their consequences: people even ended up in prison or pledged children. There was a case of a woman fleeing to the desert since her husband was in prison for debts, and the three children had been sold at auction.[155]

WELFARE INSTITUTIONS

In the ancient world, the care of the sick was often connected with temples, e.g., in Egypt. In the Greek and Roman world there were some rare buildings for the care of the sick, especially the *asclepeions*, the complexes of the temples of Asclepius.[156] At Epidaurus (Greece) in 170 CE, Senator Antoninus erected two establishments. The pagan rhetor Aristides spent a lot of time in the *asclepeion* of Pergamon. In Rome, a treatment center dedicated to Aesculapius (Lat.) was on Tiber Island. In the fourth century, Libanius often consulted Asclepius for his diseases.[157] Along the border of the Empire, field hospitals were built for the military (*valetudinarium*) complete with military doctors. Archaeological excavations have revealed many of them.[158]

During the imperial period, official doctors paid with public funds were in charge of the care of the sick. Antoninus Pius states that large cities could have ten doctors with privileges, seven in medium-sized cities, and five in smaller ones.[159] Doctors enjoyed different privileges in the fourth century[160] and also had to assist the poor.[161] They were not charitable institutions like those developed by Christians.

In the Gospels, Christ, a true doctor, often healed the sick. To his disciples he says: "Cure the sick who are there, and say to them, 'The kingdom of God has come near to you'" (*Lk* 10:9). There is also the charism of healings: "to another faith by the same Spirit, to another the gift of healing by the one Spirit" (*1 Cor* 12:9). Believers in Christ, "will lay their hands on the sick, and they will recover" (*Mk* 16:18).

Besides the previous forms of organized charity, more stable institutions were now emerging, such as hospices for the sick and the poor.[162] The pagan Nectarius recognized that Christians took care of the sick: you "relieve the sick with cures and apply medicine to afflicted bodies. You do this, finally, by every means in order that the afflicted may not feel their sufferings for a long time."[163]

Christians taught that true compassion was a virtue that marked Christians, unlike certain pagan traditions that considered such piety as a defect of character which had to be fought.[164] There was no philosophical or religious motivation for caring for the sick or suffering, even if they spoke of philanthropy as a virtue.[165] Since there was no type of medical care, those who fell ill, if they had no other financial resources, easily lost their source of livelihood and the possibility of some treatment. Physical deformities were many and common. When one wanted to identify a person, for example, in contracts, one mentioned a physical defect, especially scars. Christians instead presented Christ as a doctor and as the good Samaritan, and every believer had to imitate him, also for the sake of a heavenly reward. Thus, the sick person acquired a preferential position, and the dedication to his care became a sign of spiritual growth.

The *Apostolic Tradition* not only speaks of the material help to be given to the sick[166] (ch. 24) but obliges the bishop to visit them, because "the joy of the sick person is great when he sees himself remembered by the high priest."[167] Lactantius affirms that "it is a supremely human and praiseworthy gesture to treat and alleviate the sick who do not have those who assist them."[168] This Christian practice was put into effect during the plague of the mid-third century, both in Carthage and in Alexandria, but we could assume that the same thing happened in Rome. In the fourth century, the first private or community institutions were established to welcome and care for the sick, especially the poorest; also in Rome, as I will mention later. The aim was human and spiritual solidarity, as Paulinus of Nola says: "They should strengthen our foundations, we should help the bodies of our destitute brothers with our homes."[169]

I mentioned hospitality. With the increase in the number of pilgrims, travelers increased, and for these people, hospices were built for them also to assist them in case of illness. From the fourth century, different charitable institutions with sometimes similar functions and with different names that characterize their function emerged.[170] The Greek terms for these institutions were simply transliterated into Latin in the West: *nosocomium* (hospital for the sick), *brephotrophium* (abandoned children), *orphanotrophium* (orphans), *ptochium* (for the poor), *gerontochium* (the elderly). *Xenodochium,* the term discussed earlier, is the term most used in the West (Gr. *xenodocheion*), when the term *hospitalia* (guest house) is not used. The Arab canons of the Council of Nicaea prescribe the construction of a building for pilgrims, the poor and the sick.[171] The best known such building is the complex created by Basil on the outskirts of Caesarea of Cappadocia. It was nicknamed *Basiliad* in honor of him, and was constructed for the poor and needy of all kinds and for strangers, of which Gregory of Nazianzus provides various information.[172] Basil was also concerned with building hospices in other cities.[173] According to the *Chronicon Paschale*, even before Basil, Leontius of Antioch († 358) had responsibility for hospices and had appointed several persons for that service.[174] The same text, shortly after, writes that the emperor Constantius was providing help to the hospitals of Constantinople.

In Rome, we only know of the existence of a few private foundations. According to Jerome the rich Fabiola, *prima omnium*, founded in Rome a house of hospitalization for the sick in which she herself provided care. In fact, she personally went through the streets of Rome to collect the homeless.[175] She, who had been very rich, now lived "in a rented house." Pammachius founded a *xenodochium* (lit. a place for strangers or foreigners) with a contiguous basilica in Portus, the maintenance of which entailed many expenses.[176] Traces of this hospice were found in the last century.

A Council of 405 held in Ctesiphon (southern Mesopotamia) gives provisions on the management of houses for the needy and makes it clear that there must have been many needy people.[177] There is no information to document the extent of these forms of assistance, although we know that in large cities such as Antioch, there was more than one way of assisting those in need, and clerics oversaw such assistance.[178]

Were there community hospices in Rome, as there were the community catacombs used for burial? This kind of assistance appears in other citieis as well only in the late fourth century.[179] We know of no hospices in Milan at the time of Ambrose, for instance.[180] Pope Symmachus (498-514) built a small residence for the poor (*habitacula pauperum*) near the suburban basilicas of St. Peter, St. Lawrence, and St. Paul.[181] The poor crowded there also in order to beg. Deacon Denis, in Rome, was a doctor. He cured the poor without asking to be paid and was generous even towards the barbarians who had tortured him.[182] The brothers Cosmas and Damian were also doctors and were known for having dedicated their lives to treating the sick.[183]

We have information from Paulinus for the city of Nola. In Hippo, there was a *xenodochium*.[184] In 419, Honorius granted bishops permission to visit the prisons, *ope miserationis* (for compassion), to give medicine to the sick, feed the poor and console the innocent (*insontes*).[185] The prefect of Rome Glabrio Faustus also built a *xenodochium*.[186] From sixth century Rome, in fact, several *xenodochia* are known, such as the Anicii and the Valeri of Via Nova. Pope Symmachus (498-514) built hospitals.[187] Around 381, Melania, the Elder founded a welfare institution in Jerusalem. In Ephesus, Bassianus built a *ptocheion* equipped with 70 beds for the poor and the sick.[188] In Constantinople, Pulcheria, the sister of Theodosius II founded charitable institutions.[189] Samson, a somewhat legendary figure, built a famous hospital near Hagia Sophia.[190] John Chrysostom attests to the existence of *xenodochia* in Antioch.[191]

The distinctive elements of these institutions were attention rather than simply care, from the perspective of Christian love for one's neighbor, especially by emphasizing Christ the Physician (*Christus medicus*) as the one who heals. They were above all welfare-based and charitable, but they were not real hospitals. The monastic communities would move more in this direction. In the Byzantine world, on the other hand, there was a more qualified development of hospitals (called *xenones*) through the work of competent doctors. Byzantine institutions were the true antecedents of modern hospitals.

CLERGY SUPPORT

Several times in the texts cited, it is mentioned that clerics can use the offerings of the faithful for their sustenance.[192] Now I think it is useful to present a brief summary of this.

Already in the New Testament, we find various indications of care for Jesus and his close disciples, inasmuch as rich women "provided for them out of their resources" (*Lk* 8:3). John mentions a common purse held by Judas Iscariot (12:6; 13:29) that held funds which were provided by rich women who were followers of Jesus (*Lk* 8:3; see *Mk* 15:41; *Mt* 27:55). Jesus tells his missionaries to eat what they are offered in the homes they visit. Jesus himself foresees voluntary sustenance for the missionaries by their hosts (*Lk* 10:7-8; *Mk* 6:8-9; *Mt* 9:9-10). Paul attributes to Jesus the saying, "Those who proclaim the gospel should get their living by the gospel" (*1 Cor* 9:14). However, Paul himself worked with his own hands, affirming that the ministers could live by their missionary activity. He exhorts those who devote themselves to teaching to be supported: "Those who are taught the word must share in all good things with their teacher" (*Gal* 6:6). Paul carries out his activity in the cities, where life is different from the small villages of Palestine. There are also women mentioned—always the most generous, then as now—who seem to have discretionary funds at their disposal: the mother of Rufus (*Rm* 16:13); Mary, the mother of Mark (*Acts* 12:12); Tabitha of Jaffa (*Acts* 9:36-39); Lydia of Philippi (*Acts* 16:14-15); and Priscilla.

In the *First Letter to Timothy*, support for the leaders of the communities is institutionalized: "Let the elders who rule well be considered worthy of double honor, especially those who labor in preaching and teaching" (5:17). Honor indicates a kind of honorarium, and priests should receive twice as much (than deacons?). Just as in the military, the one who serves cannot be occupied in other things but must be sustained (*2 Tim* 2:3-6).

The *Didache* speaks of supporting oneself by working, but the local community still supports itinerant missionaries for a short while. It also adds in chapter 13:

> Every true prophet who wants to live among you is worthy of his support. So also, a true teacher is himself worthy, as the workman, of his support. Every first-fruit, therefore, of the products of wine-press and threshing-floor, of oxen and of sheep, you shall take and give to the prophets, for they are your high priests. But if you have no prophet, give it to the poor. If you make a batch of dough, take the first-fruit and give according to the commandment. So also, when you open a jar of wine or of oil, take the first-fruit and give it to the prophets; and of money (silver) and clothing and every possession, take the first-fruit, as it may seem good to you, and give according to the commandment.

The system of first fruits is suggested by the *Didascalia* (2:25) and by other authors, such as Origen.[193]

The *Pseudo-Clementine Letters* urge the faithful to support the bishops in their ministry so that they are not forced to neglect the Word. It should not be said then that, "he sells the Word":

Zacchæus alone having given himself up wholly to labor for you and needing sustenance, and not being able to attend to his own affairs, how can he procure necessary support? Is it not reasonable that you are to take forethought for his living? Not waiting for his asking you, for this is the part of a beggar. But he will rather die of hunger than submit to do this. And shall not you incur punishment, not considering that the workman is worthy of his remuneration?[194]

The *Letter of Clement to James* exhorts the bishop not to devote himself to secular activities:

It is necessary that you on your part, living without reproach, with the greatest earnestness to shake off all the cares of life, being neither a surety, nor an advocate, nor involved in any other secular business. . . . For it is wicked for you to undertake secular cares while omitting the doing of what you have been commanded to do. . . . You should have the care of the Church always as your first priority in order both to administer it well and so that you hold forth the words of truth.[195]

Origen too invites the faithful to contribute to the sustenance of the ministers of the Word.[196]

This rudimentary system is developed further and organized to better serve the clergy, but the system itself always remains self-financed by the community. Eusebius tells us that in Rome, there was a group that financed its bishop, Natalius, with a good monthly amount of allowance. Natalius enjoyed prestige in Rome at the beginning of the third century because he had been a *confessor* in the persecution that occurred around 202/203. He was persuaded by Asclepiodotus and Theodotus the banker (who were disciples of the adoptionist Theodotus the dealer in leather) to accept ordination as bishop of the Roman community of the adoptionist and to receive for this a monthly salary. This was the first known case of a cleric drawing a salary, which also happened among the Montanists.[197]

Power and money, as we've noted, were always a great temptation—then as well as now. A text by Hermas, quoted above, speaks of the corruption of deacons in the administration of goods.[198] The *Ascension of Isaiah*, a work once considered Jewish but now recognized as Christian in origin, recognized that in the Christian community there were good shepherds, but also that "in those days many will love office, though devoid of wisdom. And there will be many lawless elders, and shepherds dealing wrongly by their own sheep, and they will ravage (them) owing to their not having holy shepherds. And many will change the honor of the garments of the saints for the garments of the covetous."[199]

Cyprian of Carthage gives us further information. Two deacons and an acolyte received a monthly salary: *divisio mensurna*. They had left the community and returned, waiting for a final decision on their fate. He suggests that they should not be paid the usual salary and that "they refrain from taking their monthly allotment."[200] Therefore, for clerics, there were *divisiones mensurnae*, i.e., variable monthly payments and *sportulae*, i.e., variegated offerings,[201] divided according to the grade occupied by the recipient. Elsewhere he speaks of *stipes* (from where we get our English word "stipend" which means a fixed amount) and *oblationes et lucre* (offerings and money).[202] He explains the fundamental reason for this: God's ministers must be free and cannot be involved in certain activities or duties.[203] They must devote themselves to the altar and to sacrifices. Their whole life is committed to prayer and supplications. He includes not only the bishops and priests but also the lower clerics, of whom no more details are given. He provides two biblical references to defend sustenance from the community: the text of the *Second Letter to Timothy* (2:4) which was already cited above, and the practice of the Old Testament that the Levites are free from work to devote themselves to liturgical service. Clerics who do not behave well are deprived of the monthly distribution. Even during persecution, clerics receive their stipends.[204] Cyprian appoints two confessors of the faith as readers in the assemblies, also in view of the priesthood. These two readers, "are to have the honor of being given their allowances along with the presbyters, and at the monthly payments, they are to receive a share equal to theirs."[205] Why do they get as much as the priests? Perhaps because they will soon be priests, or because they have lost their goods, or even as a reward for fidelity in persecution.[206] The historian Mazzarino considers this text very useful for learning how the clergy were supported in the middle of the third century, which he finds similar to how imperial officials received their support.[207] Constantine begins with the donation of three thousand *folles*,[208] not an excessive sum, for Cecilian and the clergy of Carthage.

For Carthage, we do not know the amount of money assigned to individual clerics, and not even whether there was a quantitative difference depending on the hierarchical level. But it is probable. One would suppose that the amount allotted to them had to be enough to live on. There are no comparable situations except that found in an inscription of Sicca Veneria (modern Le Kef, Tunisia) that assigned an annual amount of money for the livelihood of six hundred boys.[209]

The church of Carthage had enough administrative organization to pay its clergy monthly so that they could be freed up for their ministry. Clerics were fully employed in their work.[210] In fact, there was a cleric there who could afford to support a converted actor from another poor diocese.[211] The same thing is suggested by the aforementioned letter from Cornelius of Rome to Fabius of Antioch since the Roman church also had to support many ministers.[212]

The criterion of a fair distribution also applied in areas where monthly remunerations did not exist. The different texts of the *Didascalia* cited above go in the same direction and specify the quantity. Origen preached that clerics must abandon all property to devote themselves to the Word of God.[213] Inscriptions from Asia Minor attest that in order to live clerics had to engage in lawful employment: one priest was a specialist in the transport of marble, another was a woodcutter, even a deacon did manual labor.[214] In these cases, they received nothing or little from the community, and therefore, they had to have outside employment.

And so we see that clerics too sometimes had to earn part or all of their living outside of the church. In Egypt for instance, in the same period, Bishop Maximus was involved in commercial activity.[215] The practice of Carthage where clergy were compensated by the church was frankly not all that common in other African dioceses either. Cyprian, certainly exaggerating, offers a gloomy picture when he speaks of the many bishops who don't care for their flock, devoting themselves to the care of secular interests. "Despising their divine charge, [these bishops] became agents in secular business, forsook their throne, deserted their people, wandered about over foreign provinces, hunted the markets for gainful merchandise, while brethren were starving in the Church. They sought to possess money in hoards. They seized estates by crafty deceits and increased their gains by multiplying usuries."[216] Perhaps because these bishops had property and animals, they had to sell their products in the fairs of neighboring towns, as it was once customary. Or perhaps they had possessions elsewhere. Such bishops it seems were also guilty of the apostasy of many Christians during persecution. And so, there was a concern among wise pastors that clerics should have the means of subsistence. There were surely very few wealthy bishops like this in small towns. But their attitude worried Cyprian, inasmuch as it was the cause of the disappearance of the faithful, and they lacked a strong example of leadership.Cyprian's lament is also found in some of his letters.

Canon 19 of the Council of Elvira ordered: "Bishops, presbyters, and deacons shall not leave the area where they work, or travel in the provinces, in order to engage in profitable ventures. If it is an economic necessity, let them send a son, a freedman, an employee, a friend, or someone else. They should engage only in business activities within their own area." The much more important council of Serdica takes a different tack. There were bishops who had property in other dioceses, who were authorized to be absent in order to take care of their property:

> Bishop Hosius said. . . . Some of our brothers and fellow bishops are known to possess very little private property in the cities in which they are placed as bishops, but have great possessions in other places, with which they are, moreover, able to help the poor. I think then permission should be given them, if they are to visit their estates and attend to the gathering of the harvest, to pass three Sundays, that is, to stay for three weeks, on their estates" (canon 12).

When Martin of Tours received some goods, he thought of distributing everything to the poor. Then the brothers asked that these goods be reserved instead for the monastery because they lacked food and clothing. Martin then exclaimed, "Let the church both feed and clothe us, as long as we do not appear to have provided, in any way, for our own wants."[217]

When clerics lived together, as was the case in Hippo, they were sustained with the properties of the church without possessing anything of their own.[218] They trust in "God's mercy. They have nothing to dispose of and no means to support themselves. They have finished with the greedy desires of the world. They are living with us in a common fellowship. No distinction is made by anyone between them and those who have brought something to the community."[219] All gifts were to be given to the community, not to individuals.

In the fourth century, when many incomes came from property that was not portable, the laity continued to be urged to contribute to the sustenance of the clergy.[220] In the meantime, the custom was established of fixing the amount of money due to the various degrees of the members of the clergy, but always in relation to the office.[221] The anonymous author of the *Opus imperfectum in Matthaeum* records the complaints of the clergy against the ungenerous people: "If the people do not offer their tithe, everyone [of the clergy] murmurs. But if they see the people sin, no one even utters a peep against them."[222]

The clerics lived, for the most part, from the "expenses of the church" (*ecclesiae sumptibus*). Apart from the *stipendium* they received, the clergy of the fourth and fifth centuries could also receive an inheritance from generous people in addition to the offerings of the faithful, but always at the discretion of the bishop. This possibility was limited by Valentinian in order to eradicate certain abuses.[223] Concerning this law, Jerome observes that "the law forbids only clerics and monks to inherit, and this prohibition is not given by persecutors, but by Christian rulers. Yet I am not ashamed of the law, but I am saddened by the reason for this law."[224] In the Roman church under Popes Simplicius (468-483) and Gelasius (492-496), the rule was established, then spread to other western regions, of the division of allowance into four parts: bishop, worship, charity, and clergy.

However, we are also aware of other divisions for other churches. By now, though, many things had changed. The clergy were not supported directly by the community they served, so much as above all by the ecclesiastical patrimony. The number of clerics in a church was determined not so much by apostolic needs as by the resources of the church. With this system, we have come to a complete reversal of the ministers' relationship with their people. However, even in the new situation, much of the clergy drew part of their livelihood from the various non-prohibited activities, especially from manual labor. Canons 29 and 79 of the *Statutes of the Ancient Church* prescribe that clerics learn a trade and live off the fruit of their work, while dedicating themselves to ministry. But trade, if practiced on a large scale, was not recommended.

In the ecclesiastical sphere, the legislation established that the cleric was ordained for a service to be rendered for a specific place, whether it be a monastery, martyrium, or a church. In the western language, *titulus* becomes synonymous with ordination (*titulus paupertatis*, incardination, etc.). It became a concern, especially in subsequent centuries, that the cleric should also have the means of subsistence, so the term *titulus* ended up indicating these means, for which, later, the term *titulus beneficii* became the designated term for ordination.

---

1. *Canons of Athanasius* 14, cited by E. Wipszycka, *The Alexandrian Church. People and Institutions*, 350. The book has an interesting chapter on the bishop and his philanthropic activity.
2. B. W. Longenecker, *Remember the Poor: Paul, Poverty, and the Greco-Roman World* (Grand Rapids: Eerdmans, 2010).
3. *1 Cor* 16:1-2; *2 Cor* 8:1-9; *Rom* 15:25-27; *Acts* 24:17.
4. Hermas, *Shepherd, Man.* 2.6.
5. *Acta Petri* 17; *Didascalia* 2.25.8.
6. Aristides, *Apology* 15.
7. M. Maritano, *Alms-Almsgiving*, in *EAC* 1:87-88; R. Garrison, *Redemptive Almsgiving in Early Christianity* (Sheffield: JSOT, 1993); C. Corsato, *I volti della carità nell'esperienza dei Padri* (Padova: Greoriana, 1997); *Partage avec le pauvre: Cyprien, Augustin*, Trans. by A.-G. Hamman (Paris: Migne, 1998); Susan R. Holman, *The Hungry Are Dying: Beggars and Bishops in Roman Cappadocia* (Oxford: Oxford University Press, 2001); Richard D. Finn, *Almsgiving in the Later Roman Empire: Christian Promotion and Practice (313-450)* (Oxford: Oxford University Press, 2008); David J. Downs, "Redemptive Almsgiving and Economic Stratification in 2 Clement," *Journal of Early Christian studies* 19 (2011): 493-517; G. Dunn, "Augustine's Homily on Almsgiving," *Journal of Early Christian History* 3 (2013): 3-16; R. Ricci, "Sed nesciunt de proprio largiri: Indicazioni ambrosiane sulla corretta elemosina," *Studia Ambrosiana* 10 (2017): 137-54.
8. D. J. Downs, *The Offering of the Gentiles: Paul's Collection for Jerusalem in its Chronological, Cultural, and Cultic Contexts* (Tübingen: Mohr Siebeck, 2008).
9. Polycarp, *Ep.* 10. 2.
10. *2 Clement* 16.4; see Origen, *In Matth.* 12.28; Cyprian, *De opere et eleemosynis* 4-8.
11. See Cyprian, *Ep.* 5.1; 7.1.
12. Cyprian, *De opere et eleem.* 1.
13. R. Garrison, *Redemptive Almsgiving in Early Christianity*.
14. *bona est oratio cum ieiunio et eleemosyna magis quam thesauros auri recondere: quoniam eleemosyna a morte liberat et ipsa est quae purgat peccata et facit invenire vitam aeternam.*
15. Clement of Alexandria, *Quis dives* 32.1-2.
16. See *Lk* 6:38; especially *Proverbs* 19:17: "He who has mercy on the poor lends to the Lord, who will repay him the good work"; the whole of chapter 29 of *Sirach*.
17. Cyprian, *Ep.* 55.22.
18. Cyprian, *De lapsis* 35.
19. Chrysostom, *Homily in John* 23.
20. *Heb* 13:16; see *Sirach* 35:1-2.
21. Justin, *I Apology* 13.1.
22. Cyprian, *De opere et eleem* 15.
23. Chrysostom, *Homily on Matthew* 65.2-4; PG 58: 619-22.
24. S. Zincone, *Ricchezza e povertà nelle omelie di Giovanni Crisostomo* (Aquila: Japadre, 1973).
25. Augustine, *Enchiridion* 69-70; see also 67.
26. Leo the Great, *Sermo* 11.
27. Cyprian, *De opere et eleem.* 13.
28. Leo the Great, *Sermo* 6.
29. Gregory of Nyssa, *De paup. amandis* 1 and *passim*; Leo the Great, *Sermo* 16.
30. Cyprian, *passim*; John Chrysostom, *Hom. in Eph.* 10, 4.

31. M. R. Salzman, *The Making of a Christian Aristocracy: Social and Religious Change in the Western Roman Empire* (Cambridge: Harvard University Press, 2002); K. Cooper, J. Hillner, *Religion, Dynasty, and Patronage in Early Christian Rome, 300-900* (Cambridge: Harvard University Press, 2007); P. R.L. Brown, *Through the Eye of a Needle: Wealth, the Fall of Rome, and the Making of Christianity in the West, 350-550 AD* (Princeton: Princeton University Press, 2012); Ibid., *Treasure in Heaven: The Holy Poor in Early Christianity* (Charlottesville: University of Virginia Press, 2016).
32. P. Brown, *Through the Eye of a Needle*.
33. See Justin, *1 Apology* 67; Tertullian, *Apologeticum* 39; Leo the Great, *Sermo* 6.
34. See Irenaeus, *Adv. haer.* 3, 12, 7; Basil, *hom.* 5.7.
35. Leo the Great, *Sermo* 8; see John Chrysostom, *Hom.* 54.4 *in Genesim*.
36. Both the rich and the poor are servants of God.
37. The example reflects a type of vine, typical of the area of Aversa (Province of Caserta) in Campania (Italy), where vines could reach even up to 20 meters of height and the branches creep from one elm to the other, creating very high rows with few vines.
38. Hermas, *Shepherd*, *Sim.* 2.5-10, trans. Robert-Donaldson. On this famous passage of Hermas, see: L. Alfonsi, "La vite e l'olmo," *Vigiliae Chr.* 21 (1967):81-86. That there were currents of thought that believed that the poor as such were blessed can be deduced indirectly from the texts that explicitly state the contrary, from the Ebionite movement, from the *Quis dives salvetur?* of Clement of Alexandria (cap. 2 and 11), and from Ps. Clementines, *hom.* 15.10, when it is asked if poor sinners are to be counted among those who will be saved.
39. Origen, *Comm. on Matthew* 15.17.
40. Clement of Alexandria, *Quis dives* 33.3.
41. Ibid, 32.4
42. *Patronos animarum nostrarum pauperes. Ep.* 13.11; and in *Ep.* 34.9; see S. Prete, *Motivi ascetici e letterari in Paolino di Nola* (Napoli: Istituto Anselmi, 1987), 63-74.
43. Chrysostom, *Hom. in Matth.* 88.3: PG 58: 779.
44. Augustine, *Enchiridion* 72.
45. See 4.6; *Statuta eccl. ant.* 49; Commodianus, *Instruct.* 2.20
46. Augustine, *Ep.* 266.5.
47. Hermas, *Shepherd, Sim.* 9.26.2
48. Aristides, *Apology* 15.6.
49. Justin, *1 Apology* 67.
50. Lucian, *On the Death of Peregrinus* 13.
51. Tertullian, *Apologeticum* 39.1-9, translation of A. Souter.
52. Irenaeus, *Adv. haer.* 4.19.6.
53. Irenaeus, *Adv. haer.* 4.18.2. 4, translation of P. Schaff.
54. *Didascalia* 4.1-4; Ambrose, *De officiis* 2; 15; 71-72.
55. See Aristides, *Apology* 15; *Apostolic Constitutions* V:1; Tertullian, cited above.
56. Hermas, *Shepherd, Sim.* 9.27.
57. See *Didascalia* 2.44.4.
58. See Hermas, *Shepherd, Sim.* 9.2. 2; Origen, *Comm. in Matth.* 61; PG 13:1697.
59. *Didascalia* 2.24.
60. Eusebius, *HE* 6.43.11.
61. *Perist.* 2.141-84.
62. Ambrose, *De off.* 2.28.139.
63. *dispensatione ecclesiasticae substantiae praeminebat*, Leo the Great, *Sermo* 85.2.
64. Cyprian, *Ep.* 7.1.
65. Pontius, *Vita Cypriani* 9.4-7.
66. Lactantius, *Institutiones* 6.12.
67. *Didascalia* 2:36.4
68. See Chrysostom, *Comm. in Matth.* 61; PG 13:1697.
69. On Egypt, See A. Martin, *Athanase d'Alexandrie et l'Église d'Égypte au IVe siècle (328-373)* (Rome: Ecole française de Rome, 1996), 719ff.
70. Ambrose, *De off.* 2.16.78: PL 16:124.

71. Ambrose, *De off.* 2.21.109-11; 2.24.123. "It is wasteful to spend one's own wealth merely for the sake of gaining the favor of the people. This they do who spend their inheritance on the games of the circus, or on theatrical pieces and gladiatorial shows, or even a combat of wild beasts, just to surpass the fame of their forefathers for these things"(NPNF 2 10:60) (*De officiis* 2.21.109).
72. Ambrose, *De officiis* 1.50.253: PL 16:108. Even in Egypt, in the oldest organization, the deacons were the main collaborators of the bishops in the work of charity; at a later time the role of the bursar was introduced; see A. Martin, *Athanase*, 720ff.
73. Ambrose, *De officiis* 2.15.69 and 78: PL 16:129.
74. Ambrose, *De officiis* 2.15.69; Gregory the Great, *Ep.* 1.13.
75. See Jerome, *Ep.* 92.3.
76. E. Wipszycka, *The Alexandria Church,* 357-58 with bibliography.
77. *Rigine venemere (n ti filia sua fecit / vene Rigine matri viduae que se/dit vidua annos LX et eclesa / numqua gravavit unibyra que /vixit annos LXXX mesis V / dies XXVI.* ILCV 1581; ICUR 9,24120; C. Carletti, *Iscrizioni cristiane di Roma* (Firenze: Centro internazionale del libro, 1986), 146-47; U. E. Eisen, *Women Officeholders in Early Christianity* (Collegeville: Liturgical Press), 145-46.
78. Chrysostom, *Hom. in Matth.* 85.4.
79. Origen, *Hom. in Ios.* 17.2; SC 71:380-81
80. Cyprian, *Ep.* 1.1.2.
81. See Ambrose, *De vid.* 2.11; 5.5.31 e 32: PL 16:251; 257.
82. Ambrose, *De officiis* 2.15.69; PL 16:129.
83. Ambrose, *De officiis* 2.16.76, translation by A. Uyl.
84. Ambrose, *De officiis* 2.16.77. Also interesting is the sequel to paragraph 84: PL 16:130ff.
85. Augustine, *Ep.* 185.9.35.
86. Julian the Apostate, *Misopogon,* 363B. See Julian's *Letters* 84 and 89:291A and 305D (transl. W.C. Wright) where he speaks of charity works of Christians; he exhorts a pagan priest in *Letter* 84. E. Kislinger, "Kaiser Julian und die (christlichen) xenodocheia," in *Festschrift fur Herbert Hunger zum 70.* Edited by W. Hoerander (Wien: Becvar, 1984), 171-74.
87. Cited by G. Rinaldi, *La Bibbia dei pagani* (Bologna: Dehoniane, 1998), vol. II, n. 123. Jerome, *Tractatus in psalm. LXXXXI* (CCL 78:89); see G. Rinaldi, "Povertà e ricchezza dei cristiani nel giudizio dei pagani," in *Povertà e ricchezza nel Cristianesimo antico (I-V sec.)* (Rome: Institutum Patristicum Augustinianum, 2016), 565-616, here 586-87.
88. Julian the Apostate, *Ep.* 89b.
89. Julian the Apostate, *Ep.* 84.
90. Eusebius, *HE* 5.16.1-4. G. Rinaldi, *Povertà e ricchezza dei cristiani,* 594-95.
91. A. Hamman, *Vie liturgique e vie sociale* (Paris: Desclée, 1968), 151-227.
92. Ignatius, *Letter to the Smyrnaeans* 8.2.
93. *Ep.* 10.96.
94. G. Barone-Adesi G., "Dal dibattito cristiano sulla destinazione dei beni ecclesiastici alla configurazione in termini di persona della 'venerabile domus' destinate 'piis causis'" *Atti Accademia Romanistica Costantiniana* 9 (1993): 231-265; esp. 338ff; A. McGowan, *Ascetic Eucharists: Food and Drink in Early Christian Ritual Meals* (Oxford: Oxford University Press, 1999).
95. Paulinus of Nola, *Ep.* 13.11; PL 61:213.
96. Paulinus of Nola, *Ep.* 13.11 and 14:34.4. See S. Prete, *Motivi ascetici e letterari in Paolino di Nola* (Napoli: Istituto Anselmi, 1987), 65-73; for Early Third Century see *Apostolic Tradition* 26; see A. Hamman, *Vie liturgique et vie sociale,* 163ff, 178, 187. See Jerome, *Ep.* 66.5; 108.15. R. Bruck, *Totenteil und Seelgerät im griechischen Recht* (München: Beck, 1926), 292ff.
97. Paulinus, *Ep.* 13.16.
98. *nunc a miseris obsidentur.* Jerome, *Ep.* 66.5.
99. E. Wipszycka, *The Alexandrian Church,* 358.
100. *Apol.* 15,7 in the Syriac text.
101. Ambrose, *De officiis* 2.28.142.
102. Lucian, *The Death of Peregrinus,* trans. by C.T. Hadavas, 2014, ch. 13.

103. Lucian, *The Death of Peregrinus* 12-13. See S. Benko, *Pagan Rome and the Early Christians*, 46 and 53; Ibid, "Pagan Criticism of Christianity During the First Two Centuries," *ANRW* II: 23.2 (1980): 1055-1118, especially 1097f.
104. *Heb* 10:34; see 13:3; see Clement of Rome, *Letter to the Corinthians* 59:4 and 55:2; Ignatius, *Letter to the Smyrnaeans* 6.2.
105. Aristides, *Apology* 15.6.
106. Justin, *1 Apology* 67.3.
107. Tertullian, *Apology* 39.6.
108. Tertullian, *Ad uxorem* 2.4.
109. *Acta Pauli* 18.
110. Eusebius, *HE* 5.1.61; 6.3.3; *Passio Perp.* 3.6; *Montanus et Luc* 4.7; 9.2.
111. *Passio Perp.* 3.7.
112. Ibid, 3.6.
113. Ibid, 9.1.
114. Ibid, 16.4.
115. Tertullian, *De ieun.* 12; *Ad mart.* 1.1; 2.7.
116. Eusebius of Caesarea, *HE* 4.23.10.
117. Hippolytus, *Philosoph.* 4.7
118. Cyprian, *Epp.* 5.2; 7; 12.1.
119. *Didascalia* 4.6.2 = 19; see *Const. Apost.* 5.1-2.
120. Eusebius, *HE* 10.8.
121. *Didascalia* 5.1-2 = 19.
122. *Const. Sirmondiana* 13 of 419.
123. DACL 2:2112-2127; L. Amirante, "Appunti per la storia della 'redemptio captivorum'" *Labeo* 3 (1957): 7-59; 171-220; C. Osiek, "The Ransom of Captives: Evolution of a Tradition," *Harvard Theol. Revue* 74 (1981): 365-86; P. van Minnem, "Prisoners of War and Hostages in Graeco-Roma Egypt," *Journal of Jouristic Papyrology* 30 (2000): 155-63; *EAC* 3:374-76.
124. Hermas, *Shepherd, Man.* 8.10.
125. Cyprian, *Ep.* 62.4.
126. Lactantius, *Div. Inst.* 6.12.39; *Epitome* 65.
127. Ambrose, *De officiis* 2.15.70; PL 16:129; 2.28.136-143; see 2.15.50ff; PL 16:129.
128. *summa etiam liberalitas captivos redimere, eripere ex hostium minibus. De officiis* 1.15.
129. Ambrose, *Ep.* 18; PL 16:977.
130. See Possidius, *Vita Aug.* 24.15.
131. Basil, *Ep.* 70 to Pope Damasus.
132. Gerontius, *Vita Melaniae* 20; SC 90.168-69.
133. CTh 6.7.2.
134. Julian Pomerius, *De vita* 1.25: PL 59:440; *Vita Honorati* 20; *Vita Paulini* 6: PL 53:862-63; Avitus of Vienne, *Ep.* 35; Venantius Fortunatus, *Carmina* 4.8.23-24.
135. *Ep. ad Corot.* 14; SC 249:144-66
136. W.E. Klingshirn, "Charity and Power. Caesarius of Arles and the Ransoming of Captives in Sub-Roman Gaul," *The Journal of Roman Studies* 75 (1985): 183-203; G. De Gregorio, "Cesario di Arles e la redemptio dei captivi infideles: Vita Caesarii I,3-33," *Cristianesimo nella storia* 26 (2005): 671-82.
137. Gregory the Great writes to Arthemius: "We have sent to your experience through the patrician Stephen, the bearer of the present, a sum of money for the ransom of those who have been taken prisoner, and we admonish you to commit yourself with zeal and similar readiness to redeem those men who you know do not have sufficient means to do so yourself. . . . Act with such readiness and zeal, that those who must redeem run no risk for your negligence, in which case you would become highly guilty in our eyes" (*Ep.* 3.32).
138. Gregory the Great *Ep.* 7.23 and 23; 9.17; *Dialogues* 2.1. See *EAC* 2:297-298, A. J. Malherbe, *Social Aspects of Early Christianity* (Philadelphia: Fortress Press, 1977), 92-112; J. Koenig, *New Testament Hospitality: Partnership with Strangers as Promise and Mission* (Philadelphia: Fortress Press, 1985).
139. Irenaeus, *Adv. haer* 4.30.3.
140. *Rom* 12:13; *1 Pet* 4:9; *Heb* 6:10; 13:2; etc.

141. *1 Clement* 10.7-11; 12.1. D. Gorce, *Les voyages, l'hospitalité et le port des lettres dans le monde chrétien des IVe et Ve s.* (Paris: A. Picard, 1925); *Reallexikon f. Antike und Chr.* 8 :1061-1123; *Dictionnaire de Spirit.* 7:808-25; M. Maritano, "Insegnamenti e pratica dell'ospitalità nei Padri della Chiesa," in *Nuova ospitalità per una nuova evangelizzazione* (Torino: Cultura Nuova Editrice, 1995), 21-75.
142. John's second and third letters; *Tertia Clementis*; Hermas, *Shepherd, Mandate* 11.
143. *Contesseratio hospitalitatis.* Tertullian, *De praescrip.* 20.8.
144. Hermas, *Shepherd, Sim.* 9.27.25; see *Sim.* 8.10.
145. Justin, *1 Apology* 67.
146. Council of Antioch, can. 25; *Apostolic canons* 41.
147. Cyprian, *Ep.* 7.
148. *Didache* 11.
149. See Council of Chalcedon. can. 10; Basil, *Regulae brev.* 286; Epiphanius, *haer.* 75, 1; Palladius; *Historia lausiaca* 7.
150. Council of Antioch, can. 25; *Apostolic canons* 41; Ambrose, *De officiis* 2; 21.103; Augustine, *Ep.* 355.3; Sidonius Apoll. *Ep.* 7.9.
151. Ambrose, *De officiis* 2.15.70.
152. CTh 15.8.2.
153. Gerontius, *Life of Melania* 16.
154. Lactantius, *Div. Inst.* 6.18.7ff; Ch. Pietri, *Les pauvres et la pauvreté dans l'Italie de l'empire chrétien (IVe siècle)* (Bruxelles: Ed. Nauwelaerts, 1983), 267-300,. 841-42.; Ambrose, *De off.* 2.16.76.
155. *Hist. monach. in Egypto* 14.5-7. For other cases see A. Martin, *Athanase et l'Église d'Égypte au IVe siècle (328-373)* (Rome: Ecole française de Rome, 1996), 730-31.
156. The Roman Aesculapius; the god of medicine.
157. *Autob.* 143; *Epp.* 706-708; 1300-01; 1483.
158. D.B. Campbell, *Roman Legionary Fortresses 27 BC-AD 378* (Oxford: Osprey, 2006); G. Cascarino, *L'esercito romano. Armamento e organizzazione*, Vol. II-*Da Augusto ai Severi* (Rimini: Cerchio Iniziative Ed., 2008).
159. Antoninus Pius, *Digest* 27.1.2, Modestinus.
160. CTh. 13.3, 2-3.
161. CTh. 13.3.8 of Valentinian, who established in Rome 14 archiaters paid from the annual income of the State.
162. T. S. Miller, *The Birth of the Hospital in the Byzantine Empire* (Baltimore: Johns Hopkins University Press, 1985); U. Mattioli, "Assistenza e cura dei malati nell'antichità cristiana," in *Cultura e promozione umana*, eds. E. Dal Covolo-I. Giannetto (Roma: Oasi Editrice, 1998), 245-78.
163. Augustine, *Ep.* 103.3: *Letter of Nectarius.*
164. E. A. Judge, "The Quest for Mercy in Late Antiquity," in *God Who Is Rich in Mercy: Essays Presented to D. B. Knox*, ed. by P. T. O'Brien and D. G. Peterson (Sydney: Anzea Publishers, 1986), 107-21.
165. B. A. Pearson, *The Emergence of the Christian Religion: Essays on Early Christianity* (Harrisburg, PA: Trinity Press International, 1997), Chap. 10: "Philanthropy in Graeco-Roman World and Early Christianity," 186-213.
166. *Apostolic Tradition* 24.
167. *Apostolic Tradition* 34.
168. Lactantius, *Divinae Inst.* 6,12: CSEL 19:529.
169. Paulinus of Nola, Carmen 21.392-94.
170. *Hôpitaux, hospices*: DACL 6:2748-70; "Krankenfürsorge" *Reallexikon f. Antike und Chr.* 21: 826-82; "Krankenhaus," *Reallexikon f. Antike und Chr.* 21: 882-914.
171. Mansi 2.976. See E. Wipszycka, *The Alexandrian Church*, 359-63.
172. Gregory of Nazianzus, *Oration* 43 in praise of Basil 63. S. Scicolone, "Basilio e la sua organizzazione dell'attività assistenziale a Cesarea," *Cultura Classica e Cristiana* 3 (1982): 353-72; P. Horden, "Poverty, Charity, and the Invention of the Hospital," in *The Oxford Handbook of Late Antiquity*, ed. Johnson, Scott Fitzgerald (Oxford: Oxford University Press, 2012), 715-43.
173. Rufinus, *HE* 11.9.
174. *Chronicon Paschale* s. a. 350, ed. Dindorf; English translation by M. Whitby, (Liverpool 2007).
175. Jerome, *Ep.* 77.6: PL 22:694: "She was the first, in absolute order, to set up a hospital to house all the sick people she found in the squares and to give relief to the members of those poor people consumed by diseases."
176. Jerome, *Ep.* 66.5: PL 22:641. For Nola: Paulinus· *Carm.* 27.500ff; Vigilius of Trent *Ep.* 1; *Ep.* 2 (PL 13:549-58). A. Philipsborn, "Les premiers hôpitaux au Mayen-Age, Orient et Occident," *La Nouvelle Clio* 6 (1954): 137-63; Ibid,

"Ieros nosos und die Spezialanstalt des Pantocrator-Krankenhaus," *Byzantion* 33 (1963): 223-30, he studies the etymological sense of the term; Patlagean criticizes him in her, *Pauvreté économique*, 193-96; E. Wipszycka, *Les ressources et les activités économiques des églises en Égypte du IVe au VIIIe siècle* (Bruxelles: Fondation Égyptologique Reine Élisabeth, 1972), 115-20, for 5th – 7th centuries.

177. Mansi VII, 1183, can. 3; 9; 10.
178. Council of Chalcedon can. 8; 10. See P. Rentinck, *La cura pastorale in Antiochia nel IV secolo* (Rome: Università Gregoriana editrice, 1970), 321-23.
179. Even in Alexandria only in the fourth century, A. Martin, *Athanase*, 728-29.
180. See V. Monachino, *La cura pastorale a Milano Cartagine e Roma nel sec. IV* (Rome: Apud aedes Universitatis Gregorianae, 1947), 86.
181. *Liber Pont.* 1.269.
182. ICUR 7.12601.
183. Carmina 27.500ff; 21.384ff; *Ep.* 29.13.
184. Augustine, *Sermo* 356.10.
185. *Sirmondiana* 13.
186. M. Guarducci, Rend. PARA 42 [1969/70]: 219-49.
187. *Liber Pontif.* 263.
188. See Bassianus, *EAC* 1:344.
189. *Fine publica hospitum et pauperum domicilia*: Acta SS. Sept. 3.538.
190. Procopius, *De ædif. Iustiniani*, 1.2.
191. *Cons. ad Stag.* 3.13; PG 47:490-91; *In Act. Apost. hom.* 45.4; PG 60:319; *Ad Matth.* 66.3; PG 58:630.
192. J. Dauvillier, *Les Temps apostoliques* (Paris: Sirey, 1970), 609-15; A. Hamman, *Vie liturgique et vie sociale* (Paris: Desclée, 1968), 231-34; E. Cattaneo, "Il sostentamento nella Chiesa dei primi secoli," *Rassegna di Teologia* 34 (1993): 674-91; G. Schöllgen, *Die Anfänge der Professionalisierung des Klerus und das kirchliche Amt in der syrischen Didaskalie* (Münster: Aschendorff Verlag, 1998), quotes many texts.
193. Origen, *Homily on Numbers* 11.1.2; *Homily on Leviticus* 3.6.
194. Ps. Clement, *Homily* 3.71. E. Cattaneo, *I ministeri nella chiesa antica. Testi patristici dei primi secoli* (Milan: Edizioni Paoline, 1997), 704.
195. *Letter of Clement to James* 5.1. E. Cattaneo, *I ministeri nella chiesa antica*, 692-93.
196. Origen, *Hom. in Ios.* 17.3; *SC* 71:380.
197. P. Lampe, *Christians at Rome in the First Two Centuries* (Minneapolis: Fortress Press, 2003), 344-48.
198. Hermas, *Shepherd, Sim.* 9.26.2.
199. *The Ascension of Isaiah* 3:23-25; E. Cattaneo, *I ministeri nella chiesa antica*, 680.
200. Cyprian, *Ep.* 34.4.2.
201. Cyprian, *Epp.* 39.5.2; 41.2
202. Cyprian, *Epp.* 1.1; 39. 5.1.
203. Cyprian writes: *clerici et Dei ministri*; in addition also: *singuli divino sacerdotio honorati et in clerico ministerio constituti*; further: *sacerdotes et ministri*.
204. Cyprian, *Ep.* 5.1.2; 7.2; 13.7.
205. Cyprian, *Ep.* 39.5.2.
206. G. Schöllgen, "Sportulae: zur Frühgeschichte des Unterhaltsanspruchs der Kleriker," *Zeitschrift für Kirchengeschichte* 100 (1990): 1-20; R. Seagraves, *Pascentes cum disciplina: A Lexical Study of the Clergy in the Cyprianic Correspondence* (Fribourg: Éditions universitaires, 1993), 127-30.
207. See S. Mazzarino, *L'impero romano*, Vol. II (Bari: Editori Laterza, 2007), 467.
208. The value of the *follis*, at least for the payment of the *collatio glebalis*, instituted by Constantine (Zosimus II, 38), was equivalent to about 12,500 *denarii*, but the *denarius* had then depreciated. See A.H.M. Jones, *The Later Roman Empire 284-602: A Social Economic and Administrative Survey* (Oxford: Blackwell, 1964), I, 431 and 440-41.
209. CIL 08, 01641 = ILS 06818; Année Épigraphique 2004, 01877. See the previous chapter.
210. Cyprian, *Ep.* 39.5.2.
211. Cyprian, *Ep.* 2.
212. Eusebius, *HE* 6.43.11.
213. Origen, *Hom. in Gen.* 16.5.

214. S. Destephen, "La christianisation de l'Asie Mineure jusqu'à Constantin: le témoignage de l'épigraphie," in H. Inglebert, S. Destephen, and B. Dumézil, *Le problème de la christianisation du monde antique* (Paris: Picard, 2010), 159-94, esp. 173.
215. A. Deissmann, *Light from the Ancient East* (London: Hodder & Stoughton, 1910), 192-93.
216. Cyprian, *De lapsis* 6. L.I. Scipioni, *Vescovo e popolo. L'esercizio dell'autorità nella Chiesa primitiva (III secolo)* (Milan: Vita e pensiero, 1977), 5-53.
217. Sulpicius Severus, *Diaogus* 3.14; Pomerius, *De vita cont.* 2.19.
218. Augustine, *Sermo* 356.3.
219. Augustine, *Sermo* 356.8.
220. See *Apostolic Constitutions* 8.29.2; Damasus, Mansi 3.642; Jerome, *Ep.* 52.5; *In epist. ad Titum* 3, PL 26:599.
221. See *Apostolic Constitutions* 8.32.2; *Opus imper. in Matth. Hom.* 44; PG 56: 884.
222. *Opus imper. in Matth. Hom.* 44.
223. *CTh* 16.2.20.
224. Jerome, *Ep.* 52.6.

INDEX

abandoned and exposed children, 379, 639
abba, 284
abbot-abbess, 276, 294, 294-99, 301
abortion, xv, 345, 379, 401-2, 564
acclamations- liturgical, xiii, 149, 397, 422
acoemetae or *akoimetoi* (sleepless ones), 289
acolyte, 160, 162, 185, 187-8, 191, 627, 642
adultery, 27, 65, 309, 312, 314, 316, 338, 342, 347, 357, 364, 369, 378, 379, 385, 386, 390, 391, 392, 397, 400, 435, 567
agape, 104, 246, 351, 398, 436, 451, 452, 631-2
agapetae, 315, 322, 403
agapeti-agapetae, 403
alms- almsgiving, xvi, 25, 171, 188, 342, 348, 376, 474, 490, 531, 549, 552, 556, 557, 564, 579, 583, 584, 590, 610, **615-21,** 631
Ambrosian liturgy, 461
amulets, 540
anamnesis, 489
anaphora, 418, 433, **460-62**
anathema (anathematized), 203, 357, 358, 367, 631
anchorite, 276, 281
annunciation, 485, 494, 496-499

anointing, 95, 103, 104, 106, 107, 113, 114-16, 138, 202, 318, **361-63**, 433, 492
apostasy- apostates, 54, 194, 206, 216, 337, 338, 342, 347, 351, 364n, 616, 644
apostolic see, 14, 21, 229, 233, 248, 260
apostolicity, 11, 12, 218, 219, 237, 261, 263n
archaeology, Christian, 51
archbishop, 166n, 177-78, 223, 255, 258
archdeacon, 160, 180, 185, 187, 209n, 601
archpriest, 137, **180**
Armenian rite, 348, 433, 495, 499
Ascension, 7, 184, 372, 421, 490, 493, 496, 506
ascesis- ascetic, xv, 54, 91, 92, 194, 271, 273, 281, 286, 288, 289, 290, 297, 301n, 311, 314, 315, 317, 346, 373, 373, 379, 401n, 560, 575, 618
assembly, 78, 87, 130, 144, 145, 146, 149, 161, 179, 190, 191, 200, 215, 233, 344, 353, 358, 367n, 413, 415, 429, 431, 434, 438-44, 447, 448, 460, 489, 510n, 557, 623, 632
assumption, 497, 498, 499
asylum, Right of, 156
audientia episcopalis, 367n
authority, ecclesiastical *See* chapter 6

baptism, xiv, 13, 54, 62, 65, 75-95, 96, 97, 99, **100-9**, **110-12**, **112-17**, 121n, 126, 135, 151, 179, 189, 195, 202, 203, 206, 207, 224, 229, 234, 272, 279, 286, 288, 307, 318, 336, 339, 343, 344, 348, 349, 364n, 422, 426, 428-9, 431, 440, 444, 492, 495, 505, 520, 554
Basiliad, 639
birthday (*dies natalis*), 497, 509, 519, 527, **529-30**, 536
bishop, xiii, 4, 5, 11, 19, 99, 104, 105, 112, 121n, 131-33, 136-41, 144-54, 157-63, **170-82**, 205, 209n, 215-17, 220, 221-32, 237, 238, 250, 257-61, 300, 324, 330, 354, 363, 365n, 397, 575, 583, 588, 591-93, 595-601, 625-35
blessing, 12, 100, 104, 106, 160, 162, 164n, 187, 314, 351, 363, 375, 396-97, 417, 426, 466n
bread, 95, 100, 107, 115, 144, 169n, 187, 428, 429, 430, 434, **438-40**, 451, 453, 465n, 540, 557
Byzantine liturgy, 433

caesaropapism, 258
canonical collections, 12, 14, 243, 363, 566, 569
catechesis, 77, 79, 81, 83, 76, 84, 87, 96, 97, 114, 319, 385, 414, 421, 463
catechumenate, xiii, 77, 80, **81-95**, 97, 189, 339, 428, 456
cathedra, 137, 174, 195, 217, 238, 249, 260, 267n, 532
catholic, 61, 110, 174, 177, 197, 198, 199, 206, 207, **219**, 233, 330, 356, 406, 493, 577, 578

catholicos, 203, 256, 330
celibacy of the clergy, 54, 141, 187, 315, **320-29**, 330
cemetery, 47, 192, 442, 521, 527, 531, 533, 534, 541n
cenobium - cenobite (also Coenobium - Coenobite), 285, 304n, 268n
chalice, 160, 162, 187, 354, 440, 442, 453, 487
chant and antiphon, 422, 528
charity, 11, 203, 289, 520, 527, 551, 565, 566, 569, 584, 586, 589-90, 594, 600, 614, 615-21, 621-31, 633-34, 635-36, 648n
chastity, 54, 270, 297, 308, 309, 310, 311, 315-6, 321, 324-5, 369, 377, 382, 383, 384
child, 51, 102, 385, 387, 388, 398, 593, 606n
country bishop (*chorepiscopus*), 40, 176, 180, 187
Christmas, 313, 419, **493-96**, 498, 504, 505, 515n
clerics, immunities and privileges of, 141, 195, **196-201**, 205, 356, 358
clothing, 66, 116, 288, 309, 312, 388, 454, 455, 557, 564, 595-96
color, symbolism and liturgy, 469n
communication, written, xiv, 233, 354, 314
computus, ecclesiastical, 472, 512n
concubinage, 66, 71n, 387, 388, 389
confessor, 161, **193-94**, 205, 348, 580, 642
confirmation, 77, 88, 97, 100, 108, **112-15**
continentes, 187, 271, 308, 314
conversion-converts, xiv, 39, 41, 48, 57, 77, 81, 87, 92, 94, 95, 102, 111, 206, 272, 339, 343, 379, 446, 501, 531, 560, 589, 618, 630
Coptic, 5, 13, 14, 39, 204, 273, 283, 284, 299, 302n, 330, 348, 426, 429, 433, 461, 479, 495, 523
council, 11-12, 15-16, 18, 22n, 237-41, 257-61
crown, 106, 312, 396, 397, 407n
cubicularius, 192

deaconesses, 103, 186, 192, **201-4**, 212n, 316-20, 435, 590, 628, 629
dead, ceremonies for the, 440, 520-25, 525-32
death. *See* chapter 13
dedication of churches, 442, 498, 515n, 514
defensor, 195, 196
depositio episcoporum, 494, 536
depositio martyrum, 435, 457, 466, 470, 472
devotion – devotions, 498, 505, 506, 509, 540
diaconate (minor ministries), 154, 184, 186, **186-87**

diakonia – diaconate, 142, 143, 171, 172, 221, 222, 318
dies natalis. *See* birthday
diptych, 228, 229, 356, 530, 538
disciplina arcani (discipline of the secret), 76, 98
divorce, 316, 369, 371, 372, 376, 379, 380-84, 386, 387
donations to the church, 453, 578, 582, **589-94**, 599, 625
doorkeeper, 162, 186, 190, **191-92**, 298, 353
double monastery, 284

east-orientation, 446
Easter, 6, 77, 104, 107, 217, 229, 239, 247, 313, 344, 349, 450, 458, 472, 477, 484, **485-92**, 504-5, 511n, 512n
ecclesiology, 80, 129, 207, 231, 447
economy (ecclesiastical), 578, 626
Epiphany, Feast of, **493-96**, 504, 505, 515n
episcopal lists, 218, 220, 262n
ethics, 2, 8, 316, 332, 376, 377, 397, 552, 561, 563, 576, 581, 599, 613, 636
Eucharist, xiv, 6, 77, 95, 98, 100, 108, 109, 112, 121n, 131, 134-38, 172, 180, 183-85, 225-28, 256, 321, 330, 344, 346, 349, 351, 358, 401, 413, 417-18, 427-32, 434, **438-41**, 452, 453, 462, 487, 528-29, 530, 535, 541, 542, 546, 583, 623, 631,
evangelization, 39, 42, 44, 47, 55, 56, 57, 58, 216, 250, 290, 347, 545n, 587
excommunication, 260, 347, **350-361**, 367n, 491, 569
exorcism-exorcist, 91, 94, 95, 104-5, 107, 113, 116, 140, **188-89**, 363, 459, 540

family, 397-401
festal letters, 479
forgiveness, 19, 101, 112, 157, 193, 229, 272, 318, 323, **335-41**, 361, 615, 621
fornication, 22n, 203, 310, 321, 328, 342, 380, 382, 384, 388-89, 391, 400
fossores, 192
funerary rites, **525-29**

Gallican liturgy, 187
gestures, liturgical, 361, **455-60**, 525, 537

Hispanic liturgy, 461
hospitality, Christian, 33, 117, 232, 317, 324, 620, 622, 628, **636-37**, 639
hymn-hymnology, 422, 432, 529

image, 220, 228, 457
initiation, Christian, 72-5, **76-81**, 98, 100, 465n
intercession, 317, 417, 528, 536, 475

kiss, holy, 92, 105, 106, 109, 438, 460
koinonia, 219, 224-25, 251, 264n, 351

labor, 287, 289, 291, 292, 487, **561-64**, 591, 644, 645
lapsi, problem of the, 51, 193, 205, 229, 202, 320
laura, 285, 289, 304n, 497
lay-layman-laity, 128, 130, 154, 183, 190, 195, 203, 233, 363, 382-3, 415, 583, 629, 645
letters of communion, 227
Liber Pontificalis, 186, 191, 453, 454, 499, 500, 594, 599
liturgical years, 472, 490
liturgy, xv, 21, 97, 104, 112, 182, 192, 260, **410-33**, 449, 457, 461, 462-3, 497
Lord's Prayer (Our Father), 97, 100, 109, 121n, 414, 105n, 365
Lord's Supper. *See* Eucharist

marriage, **369-401**, 407n
martyr-martyrdom, 31, 51, 57, 63, 101, **193-94**, 518, 572
martyr, cult of, 53, 252, 497, 507, 522, 523, 525, 529-32, **536-41**, 593
Mary, 169n, 386, **496-500**, 514n
memoria apostolorum, 508, 527
metropolitan, 3, 56, 140, 148-9, 150, 175, 178, 237, 254-7, 227, 228-30, 259, 261
monasteries, 40, 156, 157, 282, 283, 285, 287, 289, 290-94, 301, 331, 347, 507, 637
monasticism, 38, 40, **269-305**, 318, 347, 637
mystagogy, 8, 98, 121n, 421

nativity (iconography), 513n
Nativity, Feast of the, 493, 494-96
neophyte, 75, 104, 109, 113, 117, 151, 324, 536

oblations of the faithful, 630
oil, 95, 104, 105, 107, 108, 112, 113, 115, 116, 138, 202, 318, 361-63, 426, 527
ordination, 5, 15, 110, 129, 131, 136, 137, 144, 146, 150, 157-62, 175, 189, 203, 204, 206-7, 221, 223-24, 321-9, 430, 460, 646
Ordines Romani, 188

orientation. *See* east-orientation

parabalani (*parabolani*), 195
parish, xiii, 162, 251-53, 331, 220, 221, 224
patriarchate, 245, **257-61**
patrimony of St. Peter, 594
periodeuta, 180, 252
piety, 279, 376, 521, 627, 638
pilgrimages (*peregrinatio*), 260, 280, 284, 285, **506-9**
pontifex maximus, 27, 140
poor-poverty, 84, 199, 200, 269-70, 318, 454, 521, 524, **547-52**, **554-60**, 567, 584, 587-88, 589-94, 615-21, 621-31, 638-40
pope, 16, 50, 97, 120, 121, 163, 165, 168, 171, 210, **211-18**, 227
porter. *See* doorkeeper
prayer, 91, 97, 107, 109, 128, 159, 288, 318, 326, 348, 361, 414, 417, 423, 440, 441-46, **455-60**, 461, 496, 502, 540, 616, 619-20
preaching, 1, 134, 143, 144, 152, 160, 175, 180-1, 232, 432, 486, 512n, 537, 556
presbyters, 128, 143, 144, 152, 172, **178-82**, 183-85, 195, 205, 252, 348, 362, 363, 444, 448, 592, 597, 634
priesthood of believers, 135, 139, 414, 463n
procession, 188, 396, 500, 528, 539
property, ecclesiastical, 328, 592
prophet, **194**, 195, 427, 641

Quartodecimans, 117, 418, 487, 491, 512n

ransom, 222, 565, 593
ransom of prisoners, 522, 580, 621, **635-36**, 649n
rules, monastic, 277, 292, **294-98**, 299, 454

sabbath, 417, 450-52, 480, 481, 486, 489-90
sacramentary, 432, 472
saints, cult of, **536-41**
salt, 91
sarcophagi, 47, 407n, 513n, 523, 526, 529, 534, 585
Scete, Desert of, 281, 284
school, 91, 153, 154, 195, 278, 294, 298

seniores laici, 195
slavery, 553, 565, **570-74**
servus sanctorum, 222
spirituality, 277, 281, 292, 299, 416, 504, 619
sponsa Christi, 309, 312, 407n
stenography, 175
stylite-stylitism, 287, 507
subdeacon, 131, 153, 158, 160, 161, **186-87**, 188, 189, 192, 203, 325, 326, 327, 330, 454, 291
succession, apostolic, 111, 171, 216, 220, 225, 241, 242
suicide, 379
sunday, 144, 157, 228, 357, 375, 425, 429, 436, 439, 388, 451-3, 457, 468-69n, **485-92**, 503, 505, 636
superstition, 435-36, 539
synaxis, 115, 228

thermal baths (*thermae*), 319, 588
tonsure, 141, 196, 276, 287
travel, means of communication, 233-34

velatio, 313, 314, 332n, 396, 407n
vestments, liturgical, 133, **454**
vigil, 77, 79, 104, 107, 490, 512n
virgin-virginity, 271, 272, 279, 290, 300, **306-16**, 370, 372, 373, 374, 375, 378, 379, 382, 401, 404n

water, 80, 86, 87, 95, 101, 102, 103-5, 108, 113-14, 121n, 186, 318, 363, 429, 438-39, 453, 526
wedding, **393-97**
week, 450, 451, 452, 475, 483, 485-6, 488, 494
widows, 9, 136, 159, 180, 204, 313, 278, **316-19**, 377, 383, 444, 447, 448, 549, 581, 582, 590, 595, 615, 621-22, 628, 629, 631
wine, 192, 362, 429, 438, 439, 453, 509

xenodochium (Hospital), 639-40

BIBLIOGRAPHY

CHAPTER 1

Ballerini, Pietro and Girolamo Ballerini. "De antiquis editis; tum ineditis collectionibus & collectoribus canonum ad Gratianum usque tractatus in quatuor partes distributus." *Patrologiae cursus completus. Accurante J.-P. Migne, Series Latina, Paris.*

Blaudeau, Phillipe. *Le Siège de Rome et l'Orient (448-536). Étude géo-ecclésiologique.* Rome: École francaise de Rome, 2012.

Brakmann, Heinzgerd. "Alexandria und die Kanones des Hippolyt." *JACh* 22 (1979): 139-49.

Concili della cristianità occidentale secoli III-V. XXX Incontro di studiosi dell'antichità cristiana, Roma, 3-5 maggio 2001. Rome: Institutum Patristicum Augustinianum, 2002.

Coppola, Raffaele, ed. *Atti del Congresso Internazionale: Incontro fra canoni d'Oriente e d'Occidente*, 3 vol. Bari: Cacucci, 1994.

Cortese, Ennio. *Il diritto nella storia medievale*, 1: L'Alto medioevo, 2: Il basso medioevo. Rome: Il cigno Galileo Galilei, 1995.

Dauvillier, Jean. *Les Temps apostoliques: 1er siècle.* Paris: Sirey, 1970.

Di Berardino, Angelo ed. *I concili della chiesa antica* (published already six volumes): vol. I, *I concili greci*, Rome 2006; *Decretali, concili romani e canoni di Serdica*, Rome 2007; *I concili della Gallia*, 2 volumi, Rome 2010; *I concili spagnoli*, Rome 213; *I concili africani*, II ed., 2017.

___. *Diritto romano-canonico quale diritto proprio delle comunità cristiane dell'Oriente mediterraneo*, Il, IX Colloquio Internazionale romanistico-canonistico. Citta del Vaticano: PUL Editrice, 1994.

Döpp, Siegmar, and Wilhelm Geerlings. "Canonical Collections." In *Dictionary of Early Christian Literature*, eds. Siegmar Döpp and Wilhelm Geerlings. New York: Crossroad, 2000, 113-15.

Dovere, Elio. *Medicina legum. Credo di Calcedonia e legislazione d'urgenza.* 3 vol. Bari: Cacucci, 2013.

Erdö, Péter. *Storia della scienza del diritto canonico: Una introduzione.* Rome: Pontificia Università Gregoriana, 1999.

Falchi, Gian Luigi and Brian Ferme. *Introduzione allo studio sulle fonti dell'Utrumque Ius.* Città del Vaticano: Lateran University Press, 2006.

Ferme, Brian. *Introduzione alla storia delle fonti del diritto canonico.* Mursia: Pontificia Università Lateranense, 1998.

Gallagher, Clarence. *Church Law and Church Order in Rome and Byzantium: A Comparative Study.* Aldershot: Ashgate Variorum, 2002.

Gaudemet, Jean. *La formation du droit séculier et du droit de l'Église aux IVe et Ve siècles*, 2nd ed. Paris: Sirey, 1979.

___. *Les Sources du droit de l'Église en Occident du IIe au VIIe siècle.* Paris: Éditions du Cerf, 1985.

___. *L'Église dans l'Empire romain: (IVe-Ve siècles).* Paris: Sirey, 1958.

Hartman, Wilfried, and Kenneth Penington, eds. *The History of Byzantine and Eastern Canon Law to 1500.* Washington, DC: The Catholic University of America Press, 2012.

Hess, Hamilton. *The Early Development of Canon Law and the Council of Serdica.* Oxford: Oxford University Press, 2002.

Hussey, Joan Mervyn. *The Orthodox Church in the Byzantine Empire.* Oxford: Clarendon Press, 1986.

Jacquemin, Albert. *Le clerc dans la Cité. De Constantin à la fin de l'époque carolingienne.* Paris: Les Éditions du Cerf, 2017.

Kéry, Lotte. *Canonical Collections of the Early Middle Ages (ca. 400-1140): A Bibliographical Guide to the Manuscripts and Literature.* Washington, DC: Catholic University of America Press, 1999.

L'Huillier, Peter. *The Church of the Ancient Councils: The Disciplinary Work of the First Four Ecumenical Councils.* Crestwood, NY: St. Vladimir's Seminary Press, 1996.

Lizzi Testa, Rita. "La Collectio Avellana e le collezioni canoniche romane e italiche del V-VI secolo: un progetto di ricerca." *Cristianesimo Nella Storia* 35 (2014): 77-236.

Maassen, Frederick. *Geschichte der Quellen und Literatur des kanonischen Rechts im Abendland bis zum Ausgang des Mittelalters.* Gratz: Leuschner & Lubensky, 1870.

Mardirossian, Aram. *La collection canonique d'Antioche: droit et hérésie à travers le premier recueil de législation ecclésiastique (IVe siècle).* Paris: ACHCByz, 2010.

Munier, Charles. *Vie conciliaire et collections canoniques en Occident IVe-XIIe siècle* s. London: Variorum Reprints, 1987.

Nedungatt, George and Michael Featherstone. *The Council in Trullo Revisited.* Rome: Pontificio Istituto Orientale, 1995.

Ohme, Heinz. "Sources of the Greek Canon Law to the Concilium Quinisextum (692)." In *The History of Byzantine and Eastern Canon Law to 1500,* eds. Wilfried Hartmann and Kenneth Pennington. Washington, DC: The Catholic University of America Press, 2012, 24-114.

Pennington, Ken. "The growth of Church law, Synods and councils." In *The Cambridge History of Christianity, Volume 2: Constantine to c.600.* Eds. Frederick Norris and Augustine Casiday. Cambridge: Cambridge University Press, 2007, 386-402.

Salachas, Dimitrios. *Il diritto canonico delle Chiese orientali nel primo millennio. Confronti con il diritto canonico attuale delle chiese orientali CCEO.* Bologna: Edizioni Dehoniane Bologna, 1997.

Schulte, Johann Friedrich von. *Die Geschichte der Quellen und Literatur des canonischen Rechts von Gratian bis auf die Gegenwart,* 3 vols. Graz: Akademische Druck-und Verlagsanstalt, 1956.

Steimer, Bruno. *Vertex Traditionis. Die Gattung der altchristlichen Kirchenordnung.* Berlin: De Gruyter, 1992.

Stephens, Christopher W. B. *Canon Law and Episcopal Authority. The Canons of Antioch and Serdica.* Oxford: Oxford University Press, 2015.

Taft, Robert F. *The Christian East. Its Institutions and its Thought. A Critical Reflection: Papers of the International Scholarly Congress for the 75th Anniversary of the Pontifical Oriental Institute, Rome, 30 May - 5 June 1993.* Rome: Pontificio Istituto Orientale, 1996.

Turner, Cuthbert Hamilton. *Ecclesiae occidentalis monumenta juris antiquissima: canonum et conciliorum Graecorum interpretationes Latinae* (EOMJA). Oxonii: Typ. Clarendoniano, 1939.

Wagschal, David. *Law and Legality in the Greek East: The Byzantine Canonical Tradition, 381-883.* Oxford: Oxford University Press, 2015.

Wal, Nicolaas Van der and J. H. A Lokin. *Historiae iuris graeco- romani delineatio. Les sources du droit byzantin de 300 à 1453.* Groningen: Forsten, 1985.

Weckwerth, Andreas. *Clavis conciliorum occidentalium septem prioribus saeculis celebratorum: qua ad investigationem synodorum fovendam tam optimas actorum synodalium editiones quam eorum testimonia conciliorum quorum mounumenta deperdita sunt.* Turnhout: Brepols, 2013.

Wiel, Constant Van de . *History of Canon Law.* Louvain: Peeters, 1992.

Wirbelauer, Eckhard. "Réorganiser l'Église italienne." *MEFRA* 125 (2013): 481-92.

CHAPTER 2

Di Berardino, Angelo. *Historical Atlas of Ancient Christianity.* St. Davids, PA: ICCS Press, 2013.

———. *Encyclopedia of Ancient Christianity.* Downers Grove, IL: IVP Academic, 2014.

Giudice, Alberto and Giancarlo Rinaldi. *Fonti documentarie per la storia del Cristianesimo antico.* Rome: Carocci, 2015.

Latourette, Kenneth Scott. *A History of the Expansion of Christianity: the First Five Centuries.* New York: Harper & Brothers, 1937.

Mazzarino, Santo. *L'Impero romano 2.* Rome: Tumminelli, 1962.

Mimouni, Simone Claude, and Pierre Maraval. *Le christianisme des origines à Constantin*. Paris: Presses Universitaires de France, 2006.

Mitchell, Margaret M., and Frances M. Young, eds. *The Cambridge History of Christianity: Volume 1, Origins to Constantine*. Cambridge: Cambridge University Press, 2006.

———. Volume 2: *Constantine to c. 600*, eds. Augustine Casiday and Frederick W. Norris. Cambridge: Cambridge University Press, 2008.

Pietri, Charles and Luce Pietri. *Histoire du christianisme des origines à nos jours*. Paris: Desclée, c1990-c2000.

Robinson, Thomas A. *Who Were the First Christians? Dismantling the Urban Thesis*. New York: Oxford University Press, 2017.

Sordi, Marta. *I cristiani e l'Impero Romano*. Milan: Jaca Book, 2017.

Chapter 3

Benoît, André and Charles Munier. *Le Baptême dans l'Église ancienne. Ier-IIIe siècle*. Berne: Peter Lang, 1994.

Bernardini, Paolo and Simone Deléani. *Un solo Battesimo una sola Chiesa: il Concilio di Cartagine del settembre 256*. Bologna: Società editrice il Mulino, 2009.

Bitton-Ashkelony, Brouria and Derek Krueger. *Prayer and Worship in Eastern Christianities, 5th to 11th Centuries*. New York: Routledge, 2016.

Bradshaw, Paul F. "The Profession of Faith in Early Christian Baptism." *Evangelical Quarterly* 78, no. 2 (2006): 337-55.

Carpin, Attilio. *Battezzati nell'unica vera Chiesa? Cipriano di Cartagine e la controversia battesimale*. Bologna: Edizioni Studio Domenicano, 2007.

Cavallotto, Giuseppe. *Catecumenato antico. Diventare cristiani secondo i Padri*. Bologna: Edizioni Dehoniane, 1996.

Daniélou, Jean, and Régine Du Charlat. *La catéchèse aux premiers siècles*. Paris: Fayard, 1968.

Day, Juliette. *The Baptismal Liturgy of Jerusalem: Fourth and Fifth-Century Evidence from Palestine, Syria and Egypt*. Farnham: Ashgate Publishing, 2007.

Decousu, Laurence. *La perte de l'Esprit Saint et son recouvrement dans l'Église ancienne: la réconciliation des hérétiques et des pénitents en Occident du IIIe siècle jusqu'à Grégoire le Grand*. Leiden: Brill, 2015.

———. "Liturgie baptismale et don de l'Esprit aux origines chrétiennes : une pneumatologie oubliée." *Revue des sciences religieuses* 89 (2015): 47-66.

———. "Imposition des mains et onction: recherches sur l'adjonction de rites additionnels dans les liturgies baptismales primitives." *Ecclesia orans* 34 (2017): 11-46; 369-420.

Dujarier, Michel. *A History of the Catechumenate: The First Six Centuries*. New York: Sadlier, 1979.

———. *Le parrainage des adultes aux trois premiers siècles de l'Église*. Paris: Éditions du Cerf, 1962.

Dujarier, Michel, and Kevin Hart. *The Rites of Christian Initiation: Historical and Pastoral Reflections*. New York: Sadlier, 1979.

Eliade, Mircea, Williard R Task and Michael Meade. *Rites and Symbols of Initiation: The Mysteries of Birth and Rebirth*. Putman, CT: Spring Publications, 2012.

Ferguson, Everett. *Baptism in the Early Church: History, Theology, and Liturgy in the First Five Centuries*. Grand Rapids: Eerdmans, 2009.

Finn, Thomas M. *From Death to Rebirth: Ritual and Conversion in Antiquity*. Mahwah, NJ: Paulist Press, 1997.

———. *Early Christian Baptism and the Catechumenate: West and East Syria*. Collegeville, MN: Liturgical Press, 1992.

———. *Early Christian Baptism and the Catechumenate: Italy, North Africa, and Egypt*. Collegeville, MN: Liturgical Press, 1992.

Floristán Samanes, Casiano. *Il catecumenato*. Rome: Borla, 1993.

Folletti, Ivan and Serena Romano, eds. *Fons Vitae. Baptême, Baptistères et Rites d'initiation (IIe-VIe siècle)*. Rome: Viella, 2009.

García Mac Gaw, Carlos. *Le problème du baptême dans le schisme donatiste*. Paris: De Boccard, 2008.
Grossi, Vittorino. *La catechesi battesimale agli inizi del V secolo: le fonti agostiniane*. Rome: Institutum Patristicum Augustinianum, 1993.
Gy, Pierre-Marie. *La liturgie dans l'histoire*. Paris: Éditions du Cerf, 1990, 17-39.
Hamman, Adalbert G. *L'Initiation chrétienne: textes recueillis et présentés*. Paris: Desclée de Brouwer, 1980.
Harmless, William. *Augustine and the Catechumenate: A Catechetical Perspective*. Ann Arbor, MI: UMI Dissertation Services, 1996.
Helleholm, David. *Ablution, Initiation, and Baptism. Late Antiquity, Early Judaism, and Early Christianity. Waschungen, Initiation und Taufe. Spätantike, Frühes Judentum und Frühes Christentum*. Berlin: De Gruyter, 2011.
Horn, Cornelia B., and Robert R. Phenix. *Children in Late Ancient Christianity*. Tübingen: Mohr Siebeck, 2009.
Jensen, Robin M. "Material and Documentary Evidence for the Practice of Early Christian Baptism." *Journal of Early Christian Studies* 20 (2012): 371-405.
___. *Baptismal Imagery in Early Christianity: Ritual, Visual, and Theological Dimensions*. Grand Rapids: Baker Academic, 2012.
Johnson, Maxwell E. *The Rites of Christian Initiation: Their Evolution and Interpretation*. Collegeville, MN: Liturgical Press, 1999.
Lamberts, Jozef. "The Origin of Confirmation Revisited." *Questions Liturgiques / Studies in Liturgy* 84 (2003): 98-127.
Lamirande, Émilien. "Catechumenus." In *Augustinus-Lexikon*, vol. 1. Basel: Schwabe, 1986-1994, 788-94.
Lanne, Emmanuel. "Les sacrements de l'initiation chrétienne et la confirmation dans l'Eglise d'Occident." *Irénikon* 57 (1984): 324-46.
McDonnell, Kilian, and George Montague. *Christian Initiation and Baptism in the Holy Spirit: Second Revised Edition*. Collegeville, MN: Liturgical Press, 1991.
Olivar, Alejandro. *La predicación cristiana antigua*. Barcelona: Herder, 1991.
Placida, Flavio. *Le omelie battesimali e mistagogiche di Teodoro di Mopsuestia*. Torino: Editrice Elledici, 2008.
Riley, Hugh M. *Christian Initiation: A Comparative Study on the Interpretation of the Baptismal Liturgy in the Mystagogical Writings of Cyril of Jerusalem, John Chrysostom, Theodore of Mopsuestia and Ambrose of Milan*. Washington, DC: Catholic University of America Press, 1974.
Saxer, Victor. *Les rites de l'initiation chrétienne du IIe au VIe siècle*. Spoleto: Centro Italiano di Studi sull'Alto Medioevo, 1988.
Turck, André. *Évangélisation et catéchèse aux deux premiers siècles*. Paris: Éditions du Cerf, 1962.
Van Geest, Paul. *Seeing Through the Eyes of Faith: New Approaches to the Mystagogy of the Church Fathers*. Bristol, CT: Peeters, 2016.
Wright, David F. *Infant Baptism in Historical Perspective: Collected Studies*. Milton Keynes: Paternoster, 2007.

CHAPTER 4

Bacchi, Lee Francis. *The Theology of Ordained Ministry in the Letters of Augustine of Hippo*. San Francisco: International Scholars Publications, 1998.
Bony, Paul, and Jean Delorme, eds. *Le Ministère et les ministères selon le Nouveau Testament; dossier exégétique et réflexion théologique*. Paris: Éditions du Seuil, 1974.
Bradshaw, Paul F. *Ordination Rites of the Ancient Churches*. New York: Pueblo, 1990.
Brundage, James A. *Law, Sex and Christian Society in Medieval Europe*. Chicago: University of Chicago Press, 1987.
Burtchaell, James T. *From Synagogue to Church. Public Services and Offices in the Earliest Christian Communities*. Cambridge: Cambridge University Press, 1992.
Callam, Daniel. "Clerical Continence in the Fourth Century: Three Papal Decretals." *Theological Studies* 41 (1980): 3-50.

Campenhausen, Hans von. *Ecclesiastical Authority and Spiritual Power in the Church of the First Three Centuries.* London: A & C Black, 1969.
Cattaneo, Enrico. *I ministeri nella chiesa antica. Testi patristici dei primi tre secoli.* Milan: Edizioni Paoline, 1997. French: *Les ministères dans l'Église ancienne: textes patristiques du Ier au IIIe siècle.* Paris: Éditions du Cerf, 2017.
Chauvet, Patrick. *Sacerdoce des baptisés, sacerdoce des prêtres: textes de l'antiquité chrétienne, de Tertullien à Pierre Damien.* Paris: Migne, 1991.
Christophe, Paul. *L'élection des évêques dans l'Église latine au premier millénaire.* Paris: Éditions du Cerf, 2009.
Citrini, Tullio. *Presbiterio e presbiteri.* Milan: Ancora, 2010.
Colson, Jean. *Ministre de Jésus Christ ou Sacerdoce de l'évangile* Paris: Beauchesne et ses fils, 1966.
Crespin, Rémi, *Ministère et sainteté. Pastorale du clergé et solution de la crise donatiste dans la vie et la doctrine de saint Augustin.* Paris: Études Augustiniennes, 1965.
Dassmann, Ernst. *Ämter und Dienste in den frühchristlichen Gemeinden.* Bonn: Borengässer, 1994.
Delage, Pascal-Grégoire. *Les Pères de l'Église et les ministères: évolutions, idéal et réalités.* La Rochelle: Association Histoire et Culture, 2008.
Di Berardino, Angelo. "Il vescovo e i suoi titoli nel Codice Teodosiano." In *L'évêque dans la cité antique du IVe au Ve siècle, Image et autorité* ed. by Eric Rebillard and Claire Sotinel. Rome: L'Ecole, 1998, 35-48
___. "Testimonianze di vita presbiterale nelle 'institutiones' del IV secolo," in *La formazione al sacerdozio ministeriale nella catechesi e nella testimonianza di vita dei Padri,* ed. Sergio Felici. Rome: LAS, 1992, 145-69.
___. "The poor should be supported by the Churches (Constantine, Codex Theodosianus 16.2.6)," in *Prayer and Spirituality,* vol. 5. Strathfield: St. Pauls Publications, 2009, 249-68.
Diakonia, Diaconiae, diaconato: semantica e storia nei Padri della Chiesa. Rome: Institutum Patristicum Augustinianum, 2010.
Dujarier, Michel. *L'Église-fraternité.* Paris: Éditions du Cerf, 2013.
Faivre, Alexandre. *Naissance d'une hiérarchie. Les premières étapes du cursus clérical.* Paris: Éditions Beauchesne, 1977.
___. *Ordonner la frat ernité. Pouvoir d'innover et retour à l'ordre dans l'église ancienne.* Paris: Éditions du Cerf, 1992.
Gaudemet, Jean. *Les élections dans l'église latine des origines au XVIe siècle.* Paris: F. Lanore, 1979.
Gibaut, John St. H. *The Cursus Honorum: A Study of the Origins and the Evaluation of Sequential Ordination.* New York: Peter Lang, 2000.
Giuffrida Mannino, Claudia. *Alla corte dell'imperatore. Autorità civili, militari ed ecclesiastiche nella Tarda Antichità.* Catania: Edizioni del Prisma, 2008.
Girgis, R. "Il clero coniugato nelle disposizioni antica delle che orientali." *Studia Orientalia Christiana* 44 (2011): 81-168.
Hanson, Richard P.C. "Office and the Concept of Office in the Early Church." In *Studies in Christian Antiquity.* Edinburgh: T & T Clark, 1985, 117-43.
Incontro di Studiosi dell'Antichità Cristiana. *Vescovi e pastori in epoca teodosiana: in occasione del XVI centenario della consacrazione episcopale di S. Agostino.* Rome: Institutum Patristicum Augustinianum, 1997, 396-1996.
Koet, Bart J. *The Go-between: Augustine on Deacons.* Leiden: Brill, 2019.
Lameri, Angelo. *La Traditio Instrumentorum e delle insegne nei riti di ordinazione: studio storico-liturgico.* Rome: Edizioni Liturgiche, 1998.
Lécuyer, Jospeh. *Le sacerdoce dans le mystère du Christ.* Paris: Éditions du Cerf, 1957.
Leemans, Johan, and Peter Van Nuffelen. *Episcopal Election in Late Antiquity.* Boston: De Gruyter, 2011.
Lemaire, Andre. *Les ministères aux origines de l'Eglise.* Paris: Éditions du Cerf, 1971.
Lizzi, Rita. *Il potere episcopale nell'Oriente romano.* Rome: Edizioni dell'Ateneo, 1987.
Merkle, Benjamin L. *The Elder and Overseer: One Office in the Early Church.* New York: Peter Lang 2003.
Norton, Peter. *Episcopal elections 250-600: Hierarchy and Popular Will in Late Antiquity.* New York: Oxford University Press, 2007.
Padovese, Luigi. *I sacerdoti dei primi secoli. Testimonianze dei Padri sui ministeri ordinati.* Rome: Edizioni Collegio San Lorenzo da Brindis, 2002.

Paleari, Marco. "Celibi e coniugati per il ministero ordinato. La tradizione delle Chiese orientali (I-II)." *La Scuola Cattolica* 136 (2008): 33-57, 319-44.
Patsavos, Ēlias I. *A Noble Task: Entry into the Clergy in the First Five Centuries.* Brookline, MA: Holy Cross Orthodox Press, 2007.
Peters, Greg and C. Colt Anderson, eds. *A Companion to Priesthood and Holy Orders in the Middle Ages.* Leiden: Brill, 2015.
Saxer, Victor. *Vie liturgique et quotidienne à Carthage vers le milieu du IIIe siècle: le témoignage de saint Cyprien et de ses contemporains d'Afrique.* Città del Vaticano: Pontificio Istituto di Archeologia Cristiana, 1984.
Scipioni, Luigi I. *Vescovo e popolo. L'esercizio dell'autorità nella chiesa primitiva (III secolo).* Milan: Vita e Pensiero, 1977.
Seagraves, Richard. *Pascentes cum disciplina: A Lexical Study of the Clergy in the Cyprianic Correspondence.* Fribourg: Éditions Universitaires, 1993.
Stewart-Sykes, Alistair C., *The Original Bishops: Office and Order in the First Christian Communities.* Grand Rapids: Baker Academic, 2014.
Triacca, Achille M. "Ordinazione presbiterale nell'antichità cristiana in XVI Centenario dell'Ordinazione presbiterale di S. Agostino." In *Agostino presbitero: atti del convegno storico celebrativo di Cassago Brianza, 2-15 settembre 1991.* Cassago Brianza: 1992, 153-97.
Wagner, Jochen. *Die Anfänge des Amtes in der Kirche: Presbyter und Episkopen in der frühchristlichen Literatur.* Tübingen: Francke Verlag, 2011.
Ysebaert, Joseph. *Die Amtsterminologie im Neuen Testament und in der alten Kirche: eine lexikographische Untersuchung.* Breda: Eureia, 1994.

CHAPTER 5 & 6

Most of the bibliographical information given in the previous chapter also applies to this one. Here specific studies on the subject are reported, some of which are rich in bibliographies. The endnotes also contain numerous titles.
Bakhuinzen van den Brink, Jan Nicholas. "Tradition and Authority in the Early Church." *Studia Patristica* 7 (1966): 3-22.
Brent, Allen. *The Imperial Cult and the Development of Church Order: Concepts and Images of Authority in Paganism and Early Christianity before the Age of Cyprian.* Leiden; Boston: Brill, 1999.
Callabat, Bernard. "Origines et fondements du droit de la stabilité des ministres ordonnés dans les Églises d'Orient (Ier-Ve siècles) Aperçus historiques et juridiques." *Bulletin de littérature ecclésiastique* 98 (1997): 211-33.
Campenhausen, Hans von. *Ecclesiastical Authority and Spiritual Power in the Church of the First Three Centuries.* Stanford: Stanford University Press, 1969.
Chadwick, Hector. "Un concetto per la storia dei concili. La ricezione." *Cristianesimo nella storia* 13 (1992): 475-92.
Condorelli, Orazio. *Ordinare - iudicare: ricerche sulle potestà dei vescovi nella Chiesa antica e altomedievale (secoli II-IX).* Rome: Il cigno Galileo Galilei, 1997.
Congar, Yves, and Bernard D. Dupuy, eds. *L'épiscopat et l'Église universelle.* Paris: Éditions du Cerf, 1962. (With important articles from Congar, Perler, Colson, Javierre, Vogel, Lécuyer, Marot, etc.).
Congar, Yves. *La collégialité épiscopale. Histoire et théologie.* Paris: Éditions du Cerf, 1965.
Conte, Pietro. *Chiesa e primato nelle lettere dei papi del secolo VII. Con appendice critica.* Milan: Vita e Pensiero, 1971.
Daley, Brian E. "Primacy and Collegiality in the Fourth Century: A Note on Apostolic Canon 34." *The Jurist* 68 (2008): 5-21.
Dam, Raymond van. *Leadership and Community in Late Antique Gaul.* Berkeley: University of California Press, 1985.
De Halleux, André. "L'institution patriarcale et la pentarchie. Un point de vue orthodoxe." *Revue Théologique de Louvain* 3 (1972): 177-99.
De Vries, Wilhelm. "La S. Sede ed i patriarcati cattolici d'Oriente." *Orientalia Christiana Periodica* 27 (1961): 313-61.

———. *Orient et Occident. Les structures ecclésiales vues dans l'histoire des sept premiers conciles œcuméniques.* Paris: Éditions du Cerf, 1974.

Dekker, Renate. *Episcopal Networks and Authority in Late Antique Egypt: Bishops of the Theban Region at Work.* Leuven: Peeters, 2018.

D'Ercole, Giuseppe. *Collegialità. Primato. Sollicitudo omnium Ecclesiarum, dai Vangeli a Costantino.* Rome: Giuseppe, 1964.

Dewailly, Louis Marie. "Mission de l'Église et Apostolicité." *Sciences philosophiques et théologiques* 32 (1948): 3-37.

———. "Communio-Communicatio." *Sciences philosophiques et théologiques* 54 (1970): 46-63.

Dix, Gregory. *Jurisdiction in the Early Church.* London: Faith House, 1975. (Collection of articles published in 1938).

D'Ors, Alvaro. "Ministerium." In *Teologia del sacerdocio.* Burgos: Aldecoa, 1972, 315-21.

Dujarier, Michel. *L'Église-fraternité.* Paris: Éditions du Cerf, 1991.

Dvornik, Francis. *Byzance et la primauté romaine.* Paris: Éditions du Cerf, 1964.

Eno, Robert B. "Pope and Council: The Patristic Origins." *Science et Esprit* 28 (1976): 183-211.

Faivre, Alexandre. *Ordonner la fraternité. Pouvoir d'innover et retour à l'ordre dans l'église ancienne.* Paris: Éditions du Cerf, 1992.

Fedalto, Giorgio. *San Pietro e la sua Chiesa tra i Padri d'Oriente e d'Occidente nei primi tre secoli.* Rome: Città Nuova, 1976.

Ganzer, Klaus. "Lo storico delle istituzioni ecclesiastiche." *Cristianesimo nella storia* 29 (2008): 735-60.

Garuti, Adriano. *Il papa patriarca d'Occidente? Studio storico-dottrinale.* Bologna: Edizioni Francescane, 1990.

Gaudemet, Jean. *Le droit romain dans la littérature chrétienne occidentale du IIIe au Ve siècle.* Milan: Giuffrè, 1978.

Gély, Suzanne. *Le pouvoir et l'autorité : avatars italiens de la notion d'auctoritas d'Auguste à Domitien (27 a.C.-96 p.C.).* Louvain: Peeters, 1995.

Gil Tamayo, Juan Antonio. *La Communio en los padres de la Iglesia.* Pamplona: Eunsa, 2010.

Harnack, Adolf von. *The Constitution and Law of the Church in the First Two Centuries.* London: Norgate and Williams, 1910.

Hermanowicz, Erika. *Possidius of Calama: A Study of the North African Episcopate in the Age of Augustine.* Oxford: Oxford University Press, 2008.

Hertling, Ludwig. *Communio: Chiesa e papato nell'antichità cristiana.* Rome: Libreria Editrice della Pontificia Università Gregoriana, 1961.

Javierre, Antonio M. *El tema literario de la sucesión.* Zürich: PAS Verlag, 1963.

Klostermann, Ferdinand. *Kirche, Ereignis und Institution Überlegungen zur Herrschafts- u. Institutionsproblematik in d. Kirche.* Fribourg: Herder, 1976.

Leemans, Johan and Peter Van Nuffelen. *Episcopal Election in Late Antiquity.* Berlin; Boston: De Gruyter, 2011

Lorgeoux, Olga, Peter Gemeinhardt, and Maria Munkholt Christensen. *Teachers in Late Antique Christianity.* Tübingen: Mohr Siebeck, 2018.

Lynch, John E. "The Limits of *Communio* in the Pre-Constantinian Church." *The Jurist* 36 (1976): 159-90.

Maccarrone, Michele. *Apostolicità, episcopato e primato di Pietro. Ricerche e testimonianze dal II al V secolo.* Rome: Lateranum, 1976.

Mancuso, Gaetano. ""Auctoritas Sacrata Pontificis" e "Auctoritas Principis."" *Apollinaris* 68 (1995): 193-204.

Martin, Annick. "Encadrement ecclésiastique, organisation des communautés locales et développement du christianisme en Égypte au IIIe et IVe siècles." In *Les Pères de l'Église et les ministères. Évolutions, idéal et réalités,* ed. Pascal Delage. La Rochelle: Association Histoire et Culture, 2008, 323-40.

Mazzini, Innoenzo. "La terminologia della ripartizione territoriale ecclesiastica nei testi conciliari latini dei secoli IV e V. Contributo sociolinguistico." *Studi Urbinati di Storia, filos., lett.* 43 (1974): 235-66.

McDermott, J. M. "The Biblical Doctrine of Koinonia." *Biblische Zeitschrift* 19 (1975): 64-77; 219-33.

Mombili, Thumaini, and Melchior Edouard. *L'aspect d'autonomie et de communion dans la praxis africaine des recours à Rome (IIIe-Ve siècles): essai d'interprétation du comportement ambivalent de l'épiscopat africain.* Rome: Pontificia Università gregoriana, 2001.

Monachino, Vincenzo. *Il canone 28 di Calcedonia*. L'Aquila: Japadre, 1979.
Morrison, Karl F. *Tradition and Authority in the Western Church, 300-1140*. Princeton: Princeton University Press, 1969.
O'Connor, Daniel William. *Peter in Rome: The Literary, Liturgical and Archaeological Evidence*. New York: Columbia University Press, 1969.
Peri, Vittorio. "La Pentarchia: istituzione ecclesiale (IV-VII sec.) e teoria canonico-teologica." In *Bisanzio, Roma e l'Italia nell'Alto Medioevo*. Spoleto: Centro italiano di studi sull'alto medioevo, 1988, 209-311.
Perrot, Charles. "Les premières manifestations évangéliques d'un droit ecclesial." *L'Année canonique* 21 (1977): 129-40.
Prusak, Bernard P. "Hospitality extended or denied. Koinonia incarnate from Jesus to Augustine." *The Jurist* 36 (1976): 159-90.
Rebillard, Éric and Claire Sotinel. *L'Évêque dans la cité du IVe au Ve siècle. Image et autorité*. Rome: École Française de Rome, 1998.
Ring, Thomas Gerhard. *Auctoritas bei Tertullian, Cyprian und Ambrosius*. Würzburg: Augustinus-Verla, 1975.
Romanacce, François-Xavier. "Église et Églises: réflexion sur les questions d'autorité dans les communautés chrétiennes au IIe siècle." *Recherches de Science Religieuse* 101 (2013): 517-27.
Rousseau, Philip. *Ascetics, Authority and the Church in the Age of Jerome and Cassian*. Oxford: Oxford University Press, 1978.
Sabw Kanyang, Jean-Anatole. *Episcopus et plebs. L'évêque et la communauté ecclésiale dans les conciles africains (345-525)*. Bern: Peter Lang, 2000.
Salachas Dimitrios. "La chiesa locale nella comunione universale delle chiese secondo la legislazione canonica antica." *Concilium* 3 (2001): 29-51.
Scheffzyck, Leo. *Il ministero di Pietro. Problema, carisma, servizio*. Torino: Marietti, 1975.
Schmale, Franz-Josef. "Synodus – synodale concilium – concilium." *Annuarium Historiae Conciliorum* 8 (1976): 80-102.
Schweiger, Georg. *Päpstlicher Primat und Autorität der allgemeinen Konzilien im Spiegel der Geschichte*. München: Schöningh, 1977.
Scipioni, Luigi I. *Vescovo e popolo. L'esercizio dell'autorità nella chiesa primitiva (III secolo)*. Milan: Vita e pensiero, 1977.
Shotwell, James T. and Louise Ropes Loomis. *The See of Peter*. New York: Columbia University Press, 1927.
Sieben, Hermann Josef. "Koinonia." In *Dictionnaire de Spiritualité* 8, 1750-1754.
___. *Die Konzilsidee der Alten Kirche*. Paderborn: Schöningh, 1979.
Taylor, J. J. "Eastern Appeals to Rome in the Early Church. A Little- known Witness." *Downside Review* 89 (1971): 142-46.
Testa, Rita Lizzi. *Vescovi e strutture ecclesiastiche nella città tardoantica (L'Italia Annonaria nel IV-V secolo d.C.)*. Como: Edizioni New Press, 1989.
Todd, John M., ed. *Problèmes de l'autorité*. Paris: Éditions du Cerf, 1962.
Wipszycka, Ewa. *The Alexandrian Church: People and Institution*. Warsaw: Faculty of Law and Administration of University of Warsaw, 2015.

CHAPTER 7

Albarrán Martínez, María Jesús. *Ascetismo y monasterios femeninos en el Egipto tardoantiguo: estudio de papiros y ostraca griecos y coptos*. Barcelona: Publicacions de l'Abadia de Montserrat, 2011.
Alciati, Roberto; Osvalda Andrei; Sofia Boesch Gajano; Mariachiara Giorda; Annick Martin; Rosa Maria Parranello; Françoise Thélamon; Adele Monaci Castagno. "Storia della Chiesa e monachesimo (secc. IV–VI)." *Adamantius* 17 (2011): 6-153.
Bacht, Heinrich. *Das Vermächtnis des Ursprungs. Studien zum frühen Mönchtum*. Würzburg: Echter Verlag, 1972.
Binns, John. *Ascetics and Ambassadors of Christ: The Monasteries of Palestine, 314-631*. Oxford: Clarendon Press, 1994.
Camplani, Alberto, and Giovanni Filoramo. *Foundations of Power and Conflicts of Authority in Late-antique*

Monasticism. Proceedings of the International Seminar Turin, December 2-4. Leuven: Uitgeverij Peeters en Dept. Oosterse Studies, 2007.

Cipriani, Nello. *Molti e uno solo in Cristo. La spiritualità di Agostino*. Rome: Città Nuova, 2009.

Colombás, García M. *El monacato primitivo, Vol. 2*. Madrid: Biblioteca de Autores Cristianos, 1998.

Cremaschi, Lisa, ed. *Regole monastiche femminili*. Torino: Giulio Einaud, 2003.

Chitty, Derwas J. *The Desert a City*. Oxford: Basil Blackwell, 1966.

Gabra, Gadwat, and Hany N. Takla, eds. *Christianity and Monasticism in Aswan and Nubia*. Cairo; New York: The American University in Cairo Press, 2013.

de Vogüé, Adalbert. *De saint Pachôme à Jean Cassien: études littéraires et doctrinales sur le monachisme égyptien à ses débuts*. Rome: Pontificio ateneo S. Anselmo, 1996.

___. *Histoire littéraire du mouvement monastique dans l'Antiquité*, 12 vols. Paris: Éditions du Cerf, 1991-2008.

___. "Le Regole Monastiche Antiche." In *Medioevo Latino,* eds. Guglielmo Cavallo, Claudio Leonardi, Enrico Menestò. Rome: Salerno, 1995.

___. *Les règles monastiques anciennes (400-700)*. Belgium: Turnhout Brepols, 1985.

___. *Sguardi sul monachesimo*. Bologna: Edizioni Dehoniane Bologna, 2006.

Dizionario degli Istituti di Perfezione, 10 vols. Rome: Edizioni Paoline, 1974-2003. This vast dictionary is of notable scholarly value and offers an excellent treatment of all the topics touched on in this chapter as also the persons named. As a recent work its bibliography is also up to date.

Driver, Steven D. *John Cassian and the Reading of Egyptian Monastic Literature*. New York: Routledge, 2002.

Dunn, Marilyn. *The Emergence of Monasticism: From the Desert Fathers to the Early Middle Ages*. Oxford: Blackwell Publishers, 2003.

Fahey, William Edmund. *The Foundations of Western Monasticism*. Charlotte, NC: Tan Classics, 2013.

Falchini, Cecilia. *Abitare come fratelli insieme - Regole monastiche d'Occidente*. Magnano: Edizioni Qiqajon Comunità di Bose, 2016.

Festugière, André-Jean. *Les moines d'Orient*. Paris: Éditions du Cerf, 1961-1965.

Filoramo, Giovanni, ed. *Monachesimo orientale: un'introduzione*. Brescia: Morcelliana, 2010.

Fondazione Centro italiano di studi sull'alto Medioevo. *Monachesimi d'Oriente e d'Occidente nell'alto medioevo*. Spoleto: Fondazione Centro italiano di studi sull'alto medioevo, 2017.

Frank, Karl Suso. *Angelikos bios. Begriffsanalyse und Begriffsgeschichtliche Untersuchungen zum "engelgleichen Leben" im frühen Mönchtum*. Münster: Aschendorff, 1964.

Frank, Karl Suso. *Askese und Mönchtum in der alten Kirche*. Darmstadt: Wissenschaftliche Buchgesellschaft, 1975.

Gavigan, John. *De vita monastica in Africa septentrionali inde a temporibus S. Augustini usque ad invasiones Arabum*. Torino: Marietti, 1962.

Giorda, Mariachiara. *Monachesimo e istituzioni ecclesiastiche in Egitto: alcuni casi di interazione e integrazione*. Bologna: Edizioni Dehoniane Bologna, 2010.

Graiver, Inbar. *Asceticism of the Mind: Forms of Attention and Self-Transformation in Late Antique Monasticism*. Toronto: Pontifical Institute of Mediaeval Studies, 2018.

Guillaumont, Antoine. *Aux origines du monachisme chrétien: pour une phénoménologie du monachisme*. Bégrolles en Mauges: Abbaye de Bellefontaine, 1979.

Guillaumont, Antoine, Florence Jullien and Marie- Josèphe Pierre. *Monachismes d'Orient. Images, échanges, influences. Hommage à Antoine Guillaumont*. Turnhout: Brepols, 2011.

Harmless, William. *Desert Christians: An Introduction to the Literature of Early Monasticism*. Oxford: Oxford University Press, 2004.

Mortari, Luciana. *I Padri del deserto: Detti*. Rome: Città Nuova, 1972.

Incontro di studiosi dell'antichità cristiana. *Il monachesimo occidentale dalle origini alla Regula Magistri*. Rome: Institutum Patristicum Augustinianum, 1998.

Judge, E. A. *The Earliest Use of Monachos for "Monk" and the Origins of Monasticism*. Munster, Westfalen: Aschendorffsche Verlagsbuchhandlung, 1977; *Jahrbuch für Antike Christentum* 20 (1977): 72-89.

Jullien, Florence. *Le monachisme en Perse: le réforme d'Abraham le Grand, père des moines de l'Orient.* Leuven: Peeters, 2008.
Malone, Edward E. *The Monk and the Martyr.* Washington, DC: Catholic University of America Press, 1950.
Max, Michael. *Incessant Prayer in Ancient Monastic Literature.* Rome: Facultas Theologica S. Anselmi de Urbe, 1946.
Misztal-Konecka, Joanna. "Civitas interdicta monachis: Les moines présentèrent-ils un danger pour l'ordre public romain?" *Revue d'Histoire Ecclésiastique* 106 (2011): 423-39.
Mohler, James A. *The Heresy of Monasticism; The Christian Monks: Types and Antitypes; A Historical Survey.* Staten Island, NY: Alba House, 1971.
Mourad, Patrick. *Il monachesimo nella chiesa armena: origine e fonti.* Rome: Pontificia Università Lateranense, 2010.
Nagel, Peter. *Die Motivierung der Askese in der alten Kirche und der Ursprung des Mönchtums.* Berlin: Akademie-Verlag, 1966.
Parrinello, Rosa Maria. *Comunità monastiche a Gaza: da Isaia a Doroteo (secoli IV-VI).* Rome: Edizioni di Storia e Letteratura, 2010.
Penco, Gregorio. "Il monachesimo tardoantico tra storia e storiografia." *Benedictina* 57 (2010): 49-70.
Ranke-Heinemann, Uta. *Das frühe Mönchtum. Seine Motive nach den Selbstzeugnissen.* Essen: Hans Driewer, 1964.
Regnault, Lucien. *La vie quotidienne des Pères du désert en Egypte au IVe siècle.* Paris: Hachette, 1990; English: *The Day-to-Day Life of the Desert Fathers in Fourth-Century Egypt.* Boston: St. Bede's Publications, 1999.
Ryrie, Alexander. *The Desert Movement: Fresh Perspectives on the Spirituality of the Desert.* Norwich: Canterbury Press, 2011.
Turbessi, Giuseppe. *Ascetismo e monachesimo prebenedittino.* Rome: Edizioni Studium, 1961.
———. *Regole monastiche antiche.* Rome: Edizioni Studium, 1974.
Vecoli, Fabrizio. *Lo Spirito soffia nel deserto: carismi, discernimento e autorità nel monachesimo egiziano antico.* Brescia: Morcelliana, 2006.
———. "Vent'anni di cammino nel deserto. Lo stato della ricerca sul monachesimo egizian." *Rivista di Storia del Cristianesimo* 3 (2006): 211-44.

Chapter 8

Adkin, Neil. *Jerome on Virginity: A Commentary on the Libellus de virginitate servanda (Letter 22).* Cambridge: Francis Cairns, 2003.
Alwis, Anne P. *Celibate Marriages in Late Antique and Byzantine Hagiography: The Lives of Saints Julian and Basilissa, Andronikos and Athanasia, and Galaktion and Episteme.* London: Continuum, 2011.
Back, Christian. *Die Witwen in der frühen Kirche.* Frankfurt am Main: Peter Lang, 2015.
Barcellona, Rossana. "Le vedove cristiane tra i Padri e le norme." In *I Padri e le scuole teologiche nei concili,* ed. Johannes Grohe. Città del Vaticano: Libreria Editrice Vaticana, 2006, 181-99.
Brown, Peter. *The Body and Society: Men, Women, and Sexual Renunciation in Early Christianity.* New York: Columbia University Press, 1988.
Brundage, James A. *Law, Sex and Christian Society in Medieval Europe.* Chicago: University of Chicago Press, 1987.
Bruno Siola, Rosabianca. "Viduae e coetus viduarum nella Chiesa primitiva e nella normazione dei primi imperatori cristiani." In *Atti dell'Accademia Romanistica Costantiniana 8.* Naples: Edizioni scientifiche italiane, 1990, 367-426.
Cholij, Roman. *Clerical Celibacy in East and West.* Leominster, Herefordshire: Fowler-Wright Books, 1988.
———. "Married Clergy and Ecclesiatical Continence in Light of the Council of Trullo (691)." *Annuarium Hiistoriae Conciliorum* 19 (1987): 71-230; 241-99.
Cislaghi, Gabriele. "Celibi per il ministero ordinato. La tradizione della Chiesa latina." *Scuola cattolica* 136 (2008): 345-67.

Clark, Gillian. "Should the philosopher marry? Marriage as sacred or profane in Late Antiquity." In *Les frontières du profane dans l'Antiquité tardive*, ed. Éric Rebillard. Rome: École Française de Rome, 2010, 235-45.

Cochini, Christian. *Origines apostoliques du célibat sacerdotal*. Paris: Lethielleux, 1981; *Apostolic Origins of Priestly Celibacy*. San Francisco: Ignatius Press, 1992. Cfr. Roger Balducelli. "The Apostolic Origins of Clerical Continence: A Critical Appraisal of a New Book." *Theological Studies* 43 (1982): 693-705.

Crouzel, Henri. *Virginité et mariage selon Origène*. Paris: Desclée de Brouwer, 1963.

Delage, Pascal-Grégoire. *Les Pères de l'Église et la chair. Entre incarnation et diabolisation, les premiers chrétiens au risque du corps*. Royan: Caritas Patrum, 2012.

Duval, Yves-Marie. *L'affaire Jovinien: d'une crise de la société romaine à une crise de la pensée chrétienne à la fin du IV et au début du Ve siècle*. Rome: Institutum Patristicum Augustinum, 2003.

Duval, Yves-Marie, and Patrick Laurence. *Jérôme, La lettre 22 à Eustochium: De uirginitate seruanda*. Bégrolles-en-Mauges: Abbaye de Bellefontaine, 2011.

Elm, Susanna. *Virgins of God: The Making of Ascetism in Late Antiquity*. New York: Oxford University Press, 1994.

Fatti, Federico. "'Fu casta senza superbia': Ascesi e dinastia in Cappadocia nella Tarda Antichità." *Rivista di Storia del Cristianesimo* 8 (2011): 279-304.

Gefaell, Pablo. "Il celibato sacerdotale nelle Chiese orientali: storia, presente, avvenire." In *Il celibato sacerdotale: teologia e vita. Atti del XIV Convegno Internazionale della Facoltà di Teologia* ed. Laurent Touze and Juan Marcos Arroyo. Rome: EDUSC, 2012, 135-56.

Girgis, R. "Il clero coniugato nelle disposizioni antica delle chiese orientali." *Studia Orientalia Christiana* 44 (2011): 81-168.

Griffith, Sidney. "'Singles' in God's service: Thoughts on the *Ihidaye* from the Works of Aphrahat and Ephraem the Syrian." *Harp* 4 (1991): 145-59.

Gryson, Roger. *Les origines du célibat ecclésiastique*. Gembloux: J Duculot, 1970.

Gundry-Volf, Judith M. "Affliction for Procreators in the Eschatological Crisis. Paul's Marital Counsel in 1 Corinthians 7.28 and Contraception in Greco-Roman Antiquity." *Journal for the Study of the New Testament* 39 (2016): 141-68.

Heid, Stefan. *Zölibat in der frühen Kirche: Die Anfänge einer Enthaltsamkeitspflicht für Kleriker in Ost und West*. Paderborn: Ferdinand Schöningh, 1997; English: *Celibacy in the Early Church: The Beginnings of a Discipline of Obligatory Continence for Clerics in East and West*. San Francisco: Ignatius Press, 2000.

Hunter, David. *Marriage, Celibacy, and Heresy in Ancient Christianity: The Jovinianist Controversy*. Oxford; New York: Oxford University Press, 2007.

Joye, Sylvie. "Couples chastes à la fin de l'Antiquité et au haut Moyen Âge." *Médiévales* 65 (2013): 47-63.

Krause, Jens-Uwe. *Witwen und Waisen im frühen Christentum*, 4 vols. Stuttgart: Franz Steiner Verlag, 1994-1995.

Loader, William. "Sexuality and Eschatology: In Search of a Celibate Utopia in Pseudepigraphic Literature." *Journal for the Study of the Pseudepigrapha* 24 (2014): 43-67.

Marafioti, Domenico. "La verginità in tempo di crisi. Le due lettere pseudoclementine Ad Virgines." *Civiltà Cattolica* 4 (1989): 434-48.

Martimort, Aimé-Georges. *Les diaconesses: essai historique*. Rome: C.L.V.-Edizioni liturgiche, 1982.

Martoni, Alessandro. "Iconografia della velatio in età tridentina. Il caso di santa Flavia Domitilla e il ruolo della committenza oratoriana nella definizione dell'immagine della verginità consacrata." In *Velo e velatio: Significato e rappresentazione nella cultura figurativa dei secoli XV-XVII*, ed. Gabriella Zarri. Rome: Edizioni di Storia e Letteratura, 2014, 131-78.

Methuen, Charlotte. "The 'Virgin Widow': A Problematic Social Role for the Early Church?" *Harvard Theological Review* 90 (1997): 285-98.

Metz, René. *La consécration des vierges dans l'Église romaine: étude d'histoire de la liturgie*. Paris: Presses Universitaires de France, 1954.

Munier, Charles. *Mariage et virginité dans l'Église ancienne (Ier-IIIe siècles)*. New York: Peter Lang, 1987.

Nazzaro, Antonio. "Figure di donne cristiane: la vedova." In *La donna nel mondo antico*, ed. Renato Uglione. Torino: Assessorato alla cultura, 1989, 187-219.

Page, Sydney. "Marital Expectations of Church Leaders in the Pastoral Epistles." *Journal for the Study of the New Testament* 50 (1993): 105-20.

Paleari, Marco. "Celibi e coniugati per il ministero ordinato. La tradizione delle Chiese orientali (I–II)." *La Scuola Cattolica* 136 (2008): 33-57; 319-44.

Phipps, William E. *Clerical Celibacy: The Heritage.* New York: Continuum, 2004.

Rossetti Pepe, Gabriella. "Il matrimonio del clero nella società altomedievale." In *Il matrimonio nella società alto medievale.* Spoleto: Presso la sede del Centro, 1977, 473-567.

Sardella, Teresa. "Continenza e uxorato del clero nell'Africa di Agostino." In *L'adorabile vescovo di Ippona*, ed. Franca Ela Consolino. Soveria Mannelli: Rubbettino, 2001, 153-81.

———. "Potere, costume e sessualità nelle decretali di Damaso e Innocenzo: adulterio e ruoli familiari." *Rivista di storia del Cristianesimo* 8 (2011): 261-78.

Sfameni Gasparro, Giulia. *Enkrateia e antropologia. Le motivazioni protologiche della continenza e della verginità nel cristianesimo dei primi secoli e nello.* Rome: Institutum Patristicum Augustinianum, 1984.

Sorci, Pietro. "Diaconato ed altri ministeri liturgici della donna." In *La donna nel pensiero cristiano antico*, ed. Umberto Mattioli. Genova: Marietti, 1992, 331-64.

Stickler, Alphonso M. *Der KlerikerZölibat: Seine Entwicklungsgeschichte und seine theologischen Grundlagen.* Abensberg: Maria Aktuell, 1993; English: *The Case for Clerical Celibacy.* Trans by Brian Ferme. San Francisco: Ignatius Press, 1995.

Thurston, Bonnie Bowman. *The Widows: A Women's Ministry in the Early Church.* Minneapolis: Fortress Press, 1989.

Tibiletti, Carlo. *Verginità e matrimonio in antichi scrittori cristiani.* Rome: Giorgio Bretschneider, 1983.

Trabace, Ilaria. "Verginità e matrimonio nel de virginitate di Gregorio di Nissa: il presupposto paolino (1 Cor 7)." *Vetera Christianorum* 43 (2006): 105-16.

Zelzer, Michaela. "Gli scritti ambrosiani sulla verginità. Quam dulcis pudicitiae fructus." *Scuola cattolica* 125 (1997): 801–21.

Chapter 9

Ambrose, Saint, Bishop of Milan. *La penitenza.* Rome: Città nuova editrice, 1976.

Arocena, Félix María. *Penitencia y unción de los enfermos.* Pamplona: EUNSA, 2014.

Baudoz, Jean-François. "Le fils de l'homme a autorité pour pardonner les péchés (Mc 2,10 et parallèles): Approche néotestamentaire de la rémission des péchés." In *Faire pénitence, se laisser réconcilier: Le sacrement comme chemin de prière*. Ed. by Hélène Bricout. Paris: Éditions du Cerf, 2013.

Carpin, Attilio. "Il sacramento della penitenza nei Concili occidentali dal III al IX secolo." *Sacra Doctrina* 44 (1999): 72-145.

———. "La penitenza tra rigore e lassismo. Cipriano di Cartagine e la riconciliazione dei lapsi." *Sacra Doctrina* 53 (2008): 11-174.

Carr, Anthony Francis. "Il perdono dei peccati nelle eucaristie delle Chiese orientali con particolare riferimento alla liturgia siriaca." *Annali Scienze Religiose* 5 (2000): 69-79.

Casalegno, Alberto. "Peccato e penitenza negli scritti giovannei." *Rassegna di teologia* 41 (2000): 347-65.

Chavasse, Antoine. *Étude sur l'onction des infirmes dans l'Église latine du 3e au 11e siècle.* Lyon: Librairie du Sacré-Cœur, 1942.

Coffey, David Michael. *The Sacrament of Reconciliation.* Collegeville, MN: Liturgical Press, 2001.

Cuschieri, Andrew. *The Sacrament of Reconciliation: A Theological and Canonical Treatise.* Lanham, MD: University Press of America, 1992.

Dassmann, Ernst. *Sündenvergebung durch Taufe, Busse und Martyrer-fürbitte in den Zeugnissen frühchristlicher Frömmigkeit und Kunst.* Münster: Verlag Aschendorff, 1973.
de Mayke, Jon. "Transformation of Penance." In *Rituals of Power, from Late Antiquity to the Early Middle Ages.* Eds. Frans Theuws and Janet L. Nelson. Leiden: Brill, 2000, 185-224.
Di Berardino, Angelo, ed. *Encyclopedia of Ancient Christianity.* Downers Grove, IL: IVP Academic, 2014. (many entries).
Favazza, Joseph A. *The Orders of Penitents: Historical Roots and Pastoral Future.* Collegeville, MN: Liturgical Press, 1988.
Firey, Abigail. *A New History of Penance.* Leiden: Brill, 2008.
Fitzgerald, Allan. *Conversion Through Penance in the Italian Church of the Fourth and Fifth Centuries: New Approaches to the Experience of Conversion from Sin.* Lewiston, NY: Edwin Mellen Press, 1988.
Frantzen, Allen J. *The Literature of Penance in Anglo-Saxon England.* New Brunswick, NJ: Rutgers University Press, 1983.
Galtier, Paul. *De paenitentia: Tractatus dogmatico-historicus.* Rome: Universitas Gregoriana, 1956.
Goldhahn-Müller, Ingrid. *Die Grenze der Gemeinde: Studien zum Problem der zweiten Busse im Neuen Testament unter Berücksichtigung der Entwicklung im 2. Jh. bis Tertullian.* Göttingen: Vandenhoeck & Ruprecht, 1989.
Grotz, Joseph. *Die Entwicklung des Busstufenwesens in der vornicänischen Kirche.* Freiburg: Herder, 1955.
Hausherr, Irénée. *Penthos: la doctrine de la componction dans l'Orient chrétien.* Rome: Pont. Institutum Orientalium Studiorum, 1944.
Karpp, Heinrich. *Die Busse: Quellen zur Entstehung des altkirchlichen.* Zürich: EVZ-Verlag, 1969.
Lea, Henry Charles. *A History of Auricular Confession and Indulgences in the Latin Church.* Philadelphia: Lea Brothers, 1896.
Ligier, Louis. "Dimension personnelle et dimension communautaire de la pénitence en Orient." *La Maison Dieu* 90 (1967): 155-88.
Longenecker, Richard N. *New Wine into Fresh Wineskins: Contextualizing the Early Christian Confession.* Peabody, MA: Hendrickson Publishing, 1999.
Mazza, Enrico. "Un confronto tra alcuni elementi della liturgia penitenziale dell'Occidente e dell'Oriente: il caso della liturgia visigotica." *Annali di Scienze Religiose* 5 (2000): 93-108.
Meens, Rob. *Penance in Medieval Europe 600-1200.* Cambridge: Cambridge University Press, 2014.
Metzger, Marcel. "Hermas, les visions comme autorité pastorale pour la penitence." *Ecclesia Orans* 26 (2009): 121-27.
Müller, Hans Martin. *Bekenntnis - Kirche - Recht: gesammelte Aufsätze zum Verhältnis von Theologie und Kirchenrecht.* Tübingen: Mohr Siebeck, 2005.
Paverd, Franz, van de. "La pénitence dans le rite byzantine." *Questions Liturgiques* 54 (1973): 191-203.
Petrà, Basilio. *La penitenza nelle chiese ortodosse: aspetti storici e sacramentali.* Bologna: Edizioni Dehoniane, 2005.
Picasso, Giorgio, Giannino Piana and Giuseppe Motta, eds. *A pane e acqua: peccati e penitenza nel Medioevo: il Penitenziali di Bucardo di Worms.* Novara: Europìa, 1986.
Poschmann, Bernhard. *Buße und Letzte Ölung.* Freiburg: Herder, 1951; English: *Penance and the Anointing of the Sick.* Trans. and revised by Francis Courtney. New York: Herder, 1964.
Rahner, Karl and Lionel Swain. *Penance in the Early Church.* New York: Crossroad, 1982.
Rahner, Karl. *De Poenitentia: Tractatus historico-dogmaticus.* Oeniponte: Collegium Maximum, 1955.
Rostad, Aslak. "Confession or Reconciliation? The Narrative Structure of the Lydian and Phrygian 'Confession Inscriptions'." *Symbolae Osloenses* 77 (2002): 145-64.
Rouillard, Philippe. *Histoire de la pénitence des origines à nos jours.* Paris: Éditions du Cerf, 1996.
Saint-Roch, Patrick. *La pénitence dans les conciles et le lettres des Papes des origines à la mort de Grégoire le Grand.* Città del Vaticano: Pontificio Istituto di archeologia cristiana, 1991.
Salachas, Dimitrios. "Il sacramento della penitenza nella tradizione canonica orientale e problematiche interecclesiali." *Folia Canonica: Review of Eastern and Western Canon Law* 6 (2003): 121-55.

Schnabel, Eckhard J. "Repentance in Paul's Letters." *Novum Testamentum* 57 (2015): 159-86.
Vogel, Cyrille. *Le Pécheur et la pénitence au Moyen âge. Textes choisis, traduits et présentés*. Paris: Éditions du Cerf, 1969.
___. *Le pécheur et la pénitence dans l'église ancienne, textes choisis*. Paris: Éditions du Cerf, 1966.
___. *Les "Libri paenitentiales."* Turnhout: Brepols, 1978.

CHAPTER 10

Accademia Romanistica Costantiniana. *Atti V Convegno internazionale: Spello, Perugia, Bevagna, Sansepolcro: (14-17 Ottobre 1981)*. Rimini: Maggioli, 1983.
Andreau, Jean and Hinnerk Bruhns, eds. *Parenté et stratégies familiales dans l'Antiquité romaine*. Paris: Diffusion de Boccard, 1990.
Astolfi, Riccardo. *Il matrimonio nel diritto romano classico*. Padova: CEDAM, 2014.
Baltensweiler, Heinrich. *Die Ehe im Neuen Testament: exegetische Untersuchungen über Ehe, Ehelosigkeit und Ehescheidung*. Zürich: Zwingli Verlag, 1967.
Broudéhoux, Jean-Paul. *Mariage et famille chez Clément d'Alexandrie*. Paris: Beauchesne, 1970.
Brundage, James A. *Law, Sex and Christian Society in Medieval Europe*. Chicago: University of Chicago Press, 1987.
Bucci, Onorato. *Le origini e lo sviluppo della famiglia e del matrimonio fra matrilinearità e patrilinearità*. Città del Vaticano: Libreria Editrice Vaticana, 2017.
Caldwell, Lauren. *Roman Girlhood and the Fashioning of Femininity*. Cambridge: Cambridge University Press, 2015.
Cantalamessa, Raniero ed. *Etica sessuale e matrimonio nel cristianesimo delle origini*. Milan: Vita e pensiero, 1976.
Clark, Gillian. *Women in Late Antiquity: Pagan and Christian Lifestyles*. Oxford: Clarendon Press, 1993.
Clark, Elizabeth A., ed. *St. Augustine on Marriage and Sexuality*. Washington, DC: The Catholic University of America Press, 1996.
Crouzel, Henri. *L'Eglise primitive face au divorce; du premier au cinquieme siecle*. Paris: Beauchesne, 1971.
Cuneo Benatti, Paola Ombretta. *Ricerche sul matrimonio in età imperiale (I-V secolo d. C.)*. Rome: Aracne, 2013.
Desanti, Lucetta. "Sul matrimonio di donne consacrate a Dio nel diritto romano cristiano." *Studia et Documenta Historiae Iuris* 53 (1987): 270-96.
Duval, Yves-Marie. *L'affaire Jovinien d'une crise de la société romaine à une crise de la pensée chrétienne à la Fin du Ie et au début du Ve siècle*. Rome: Institutum Patristicum Augustinianum, 2003.
Falchi, Gian Luigi. "La legislazione imperiale circa i matrimoni misti fra cristiani ed ebrei nel V secolo." *Accademia Romanistica Costantiniana* 7 (1988): 203-12.
Fayer, Carla. *La familia romana: aspetti giuridici ed antiquari*. Rome: L'Erma di Bretchneider, 1994.
___. Parte 2: *Sponsalia. Matrimonio*. Rome: L'Erma di Bretchneider, 2005.
___. Parte 3: *Concubinato. Divorzio. Adulterio*. Rome: L'Erma di Bretchneider, 2005.
Fuchs, Eric. *Le désir et la tendresse: pour une éthique chrétienne de la sexualité*. Genève: Labor et Fides, 1979; English: *Sexual Desire and Love: Origins and History of the Christian Ethic of Sexuality and Marriage*. Trans. by M. Daigle. New York: Seabury Press, 1983.
Gaudemet, Jean. *Le mariage en Occident*. Paris: Éditions du Cerf, 1987.
Grubbs, Judith Evans. *Law and Family in Late Antiquity: The Emperor Constantine's Marriage Legislation*. Oxford: Clarendon Press, 1995.
___. *Women and Law in the Roman Empire: A Sourcebook on Marriage, Divorce and Widowhood*. London: Routledge, 2002.
Hunter, David G. "Augustinian Pessimism? A New look at Augustine's Teaching on Sex, Marriage and Celibacy." *Augustinian Studies* 25 (1994): 153-77.
___. *Marriage, Celibacy, and Heresy in Ancient Christianity: The Jovinianist Controversy*. Oxford: Oxford University Press, 2007.
___. *Marriage in the Early Church* (Minneapolis, MN: Fortress Press, 1992).

Incontro di studiosi dell'antichità cristiana. *Il matrimonio dei cristiani: esegesi biblica e diritto romano: XXXVII incontro di studiosi dell'antichità cristiana.* Rome: Institutum Patristicum Augustinianum, 2009.

Laes, Christian, Katariina Mustakallio and Ville Vuolanto. *Children and Family in Late Antiquity: Life, Death and Interaction.* Leuven: Peeters, 2015.

Quéré-Jaulmes, France. *Le mariage dans l'Église ancienne.* Paris: Éditions du Centurion, 1969.

Lhuillier-Martinetti, Dominique. *L'individu dans la famille à Rome au IVe siècle: D'après l'œuvre d'Ambroise de Milan.* Presses Universitaires de Rennes, 2008.

Loader, William R. *Making Sense of Sex: Attitudes towards Sexuality in Early Jewish and Christian Literature.* Grand Rapids, MI: William B. Eerdmans Publishing, 2013.

Marucci, Corrado. *Parole di Gesù sul divorzio: ricerche scritturistiche previe ad un ripensamento teologico, canonistico e pastorale della dottrina cattolica dell' indissolubilità del matrimonio.* Naples: Morcelliana, 1982.

Mazzucco, Clementina. "*E fui fatta maschio*": *La donna nel Cristianesimo primitivo.* Firenze: Casa Editrice Le Lettere, 1989.

Munier, Charles. *Mariage et virginité dans l'Église ancienne (Ier- IIIe siècle).* Berne: Peter Lang, 1987.

Nathan, Geoffrey S. *The Family in Late Antiquity: The Rise of Christianity and the Endurance of Tradition.* London: Routledge, 2000.

Neri, Valerio and Beatrice Girotti. *La famiglia tardoantica: società, diritto, religione.* Milano: LED, Edizioni universitarie di lettere economia diritto, 2016.

Orestano, Riccardo. *La struttura giuridica del matrimonio romano dal diritto classico al diritto giustinianeo.* Milan: Giuffrè, 1951.

Mihai, Patrascu. *Lo scioglimento del vincolo matrimoniale nella legislazione civile e canonica dell'Impero bizantino (sec. VI-X).* Rome: Pontificia Università Lateranense, 2001.

Perrone, Lorenzo. ""Enuchi per il regno dei cieli?" amore e sessualità dal Nuovo Testamento al primo cristianesimo." *Cristianesimo nella Storia* 23 (2002): 281-305.

Pietri, Charles. "Le mariage chrétien à Rome (IVe-Ve siècles)." In *Histoire vécue du peuple chrétien*, ed. Jean Delumeau. Toulouse: Privat, 1979, 105-31.

Rawson, Beryl, ed. "The Family in Ancient Rome." In *New Perspectives.* London: Croom Helm, 1986.

Reynolds, Philip L. *Marriage in the Western Church: The Christianization of Marriage During the Patristic and Early Medieval Periods.* Leiden: Brill, 1994.

Ritzer, Korbinian. *Le mariage dans les Eglises chrétiennes du Ier au XIe siècle.* Paris: Éditions du Cerf, 1970.

Robleda, Olis. *El matrimonio en derecho romano.* Rome: Università Gregoriana, 1970.

Roda, Sergio. "Il matrimonio fra cugini germani nella legislazione tardoimperiale." *Studia et Documenta Historiae Iuris* 44 (1979): 289-309.

Rousselle, Aline. *Porneia: de la maitrise du corps à la privation sensorielle: IIe-IVe siècles de l'ére chrétienne.* Paris: Presses Universitaires de France, 1983; English: *Porneia: On Desire and the Body in Antiquity.* Eugene, OR: Wipf & Stock, 1988; 2013.

Schmitt, Emile. *Le mariage chrétien dans l'œuvre de saint Augustin: une théologie baptismale de la vie conjugal.* Paris: Études augustiniennes, 1983.

Stevenson, Kenneth. *Nuptial Blessing: A Study of Christian Marriage Rites.* London: S.P.C.K., 1982.

Tibiletti, Carlo. *Verginità e matrimonio in antichi scrittori cristiani.* Rome: Giorgio Bretschneider, 1983.

Treggiari, Susan. *Roman Marriage: iusti coniuges from the Time of Cicero to the Time of Ulpian.* Oxford: Clarendon Press, 1991.

Vannucchi Forzieri, Olga. *La risoluzione del matrimonio nel iv-v secolo. Legislazione imperiale e pensiero della Chiesa.* Firenze: Olschki, 1985, 289-317; Reworked: *Atti e memorie dell'Accademia toscana di scienze e lettere La Colombaria* 50 (1985): 66-172.

Yarbrough, O. Larry. *Not like the Gentiles: Marriage Rules in the Letters of Paul.* Atlanta: Scholars Press, 1985.

CHAPTER 11

Amata, Biagio. "Testimonianze di Arnobio Afro sulle assemblee liturgiche agli inizi del IV secolo." *Ephemrides Liturgicae* 98 (1984): 513-25.
Anàmnesis: Storico-Teologica alla Liturgia, 7 vols. Torino: Marietti: 1974-1996.
Audet, Jean Paul. "Esquisse historique du genre littéraire de la 'bénédiction' juive et de l'eucharistie chrétienne." *Revue Biblique* 65 (1958): 371-99.
Baldovin, John F. *The Urban Character of Christian Worship: The Origins, Development, and Meaning of Stational Liturgy.* Rome: Pontificium Institutum Studiorum Orientalium, 1987.
Bériou, Nicole, Beatrice Caseau, and Dominique Rigaux. *Pratiques de l'eucharistie dans les églises d'Orient et d'Occident (Antiquité et Moyen Âge)*. Paris: Institut d'Études Augustiniennes, 2009.
Bitton-Ashkelony Brouria and Derek Krueger, eds. *Prayer and Worship in Eastern Christianities, 5th to 11th centuries.* New York: Routledge, 2016.
Bradshaw Paul F. *Reconstructing Early Christian Worship.* London: SPCK, 2009.
———. *Rites of Ordination: Their History and Theology.* Collegeville, MN: Liturgical Press, 2013.
———. *Daily Prayer in the Early Church: A Study of the Origin and Early Development of the Divine Office.* Eugene, OR: Wipf & Stock, 2008.
———. *Early Christian Worship: An Introduction to Ideas and Practice.* Collegeville, MN: Liturgical Press, 2010.
———. *The Search for the Origins of Christian Worship: Sources and Methods for the Study of Early Liturgy.* London: SPCK, 1992.
Bradshaw, Paul F. and Maxwell E. Johnson. *The Origins of Feasts, Fasts, and Seasons in Early Christianity.* Collegeville, MN: Liturgical Press, 2011.
———. *The Eucharistic Liturgies: Their Evolution and Interpretation.* Collegeville, MN: Liturgical Press, 2012.
Bradshaw, Paul F. and Lawrence A. Hoffman. *Passover and Easter: The Symbolic Structuring of Sacred Seasons.* South Bend: University of Notre Dame Press, 2008.
Cassingena-Trévedy, François and Izabela Jurasz, eds. *Les liturgies syriaques.* Paris: Geuthner, 2006.
Cassingena-Trévedy, François. *Les Pères de l'Église et la liturgie: un esprit, une expérience: de Constantin à Justinien.* Paris: Desclée de Brouwer, 2009.
Chupungo, Anscar J., ed. *Handbook for Liturgical Studies*, vol. 5. Collegeville, MN: Liturgical Press, 2000.
Cibien, Carlo, Domenico Sartore, and Achille Triacca. *Liturgia.* Cinisello Balsamo: Edizioni San Paolo, 2001.
Daly, Robert J. *Christian Sacrifice: The Judaeo-Christian Background before Origen.* Washington, DC: Catholic University of America, 1978.
Daniélou, Jean. *Bible et Liturgie: la théologie biblique des sacrements et des fêtes d'après les Pères de l'Eglise.* Paris: Éditions du Cerf, 1951.
Bouvier, Bertrand, and Mœri S. Gaffino. *Les Papyrus De Genève*: Vol. 4. Genève, 2010. (Pap. 170 is a liturgical calendar, of the seventh century).
Gerhards, Albert and Clemens Leonhard, eds. *Jewish and Christian Liturgy and Worship: New Insights into Its History and Interaction.* Leiden; Boston: Brill, 2007.
Grossi, V. "Tradizione liturgica e omiletica nel Tardo Antico." In *La cultura in Italia fra Tardo antico e Alto Medioevo.* Rome: Herder, 1981, 2: 660-678.
———. "I Padri della Chiesa e la teologia liturgica." *Rassegna di Teologia* 24 (1983): 126-37.
Hahn, Ferdinand. *Der urchistliche Gottesdienst.* Stuttgart: Katholisches Bibelwerk, 1970.
Hellolm, David, and Dieter Sänger, eds. "The Eucharist - Its Origins and Contexts: Sacred Meal, Communal Meal, Table Fellowship." In *Late Antiquity, Early Judaism, and Early Christianity*, 3 vols. Tübingen: Mohr Siebeck, 2017.
Herbert de la Portabarré-Viard, Gaëlle. "Recherches sur les dénominations des édifices du culte chrétien dans les textes latins à l'époque constantinienne et post constantinienne." In *Acta XVI Congressus Internationalis Archeologiae christianae, Romae (22-28.9.2013): Costantino e i Costantinidi.* Città del Vaticano: Pontificio Istituto di archeologia cristiana, 2016, 1359-1377.

Johnson, Maxwell E., ed. *Issues in Eucharistic Praying in East and West: Essays in Liturgical and Theological Analysis.* Collegeville, MN: Liturgical Press, 2011.

Kinzig, Wolfram, Ulrich Volp and Jocehn Schmidt. *Liturgie und Ritual in der Alten Kirche: Patristische Beiträge zum Studium der gottesdienstlichen Quellen der Alten Kirche.* Leuven: Peeters, 2011.

Klöckener, Martin. "La prière eucharistique selon S. Augustin." *Connaissance des Pères de l'Église* 77 (2000): 36-42.

Kunzler, Michael. *The Church's Liturgy.* New York: Continuum, 2001.

Lang, Uwe Michael. *Die Stimme der betenden Kirche: Überlegungen zur Sprache der Liturgie.* Freiburg im Breisgau: Johannes- Verlag, 2012. English: *The Voice of the Church at Prayer: Reflections on Liturgy and Language.* San Francisco: Ignatius Press, 2012.

Le Déaut, Roger. *Liturgie Juive et Nouveau Testament.* Rome: Institut Biblique Pontifical, 1965.

Lejbowicz, Max. "Les Pâques baptismales d'Augustin d'Hippone, une étape contournée dans l'unification des pratiques computistes latines." In *Computus and its Cultural Context in the Latin West, AD 300-1200.* Edited by Dáibhí Ó Cróinín and Immo Warntjes. Turnhout; Belgium: Brepols Publishers, 2010, 1-39.

Limberis, Vasiliki. *Architects of Piety: The Cappadocian Fathers and the Cult of the Martyrs.* New York: Oxford University Press, 2011.

Lodi, Enzo. *Enchiridion euchologicum fontium liturgicorum.* Rome: Edizioni Liturgiche, 1979.

Lopresti, Giuliano. "Il diritto romano nella formazione della società cristiana. " *Asprenas: rivista di Teologia* 62 (2015): 483-506.

Martimort, Aimé-Georges, ed. *L'Église en prière: introduction de la liturgie*, 4 vols. Paris: Desclée, 1965.

Mazza, Enrico. *L'anafora eucaristica: studi sulle origini.* Rome: Edizioni Liturgiche, 1992. English: *The Origins of the Eucharistic Prayer.* Collegeville, MN: Liturgical Press, 1995.

___. *Dall'Ultima cena all'Eucaristia della Chiesa.* Bologna: Edizioni Dehoniane Bologna, 2014.

___. *Il Nuovo Testamento e la Cena del Signore.* Bologna: Edizioni Dehoniane Bologna, 2017.

___. *La celebrazione eucaristica: genesi del rito e sviluppo dell'interpretazione.* Cinisello Balsamo: San Paolo, 1996. English: *The Celebration of Eucharist: The Origin of the Rite and the Development of Its Interpretation.* Collegeville, MN: Liturgical Press, 1999.

McGowan, Andrew B. *Ancient Christian Worship: Early Church Practices in Social, Historical, and Theological Perspective.* Grand Rapids: Baker Academic, 2014.

Meissner, William. *The Cultic Origins of Christianity: The Dynamics of Religious Development.* Collegeville, MN: Liturgical Press, 2000.

Metzger, Marcel. *Histoire de la liturgie.* Paris: Desclée de Brouwe, 1994.

___. *L'Église dans l'Empire Romain Le culte, Vol. I: Les institutions.* Rome: Pontificio Ateneo S. Anselmo, 2015.

___. "Une Église peut-elle excommunier? Le témoignage de la Bible et de l'Église primitive." *Revue de droit canonique* 56 (2006): 7-32.

Meyer, Hans Bernhard, Bruno Kleinheyer and Hansjörg auf der Maur. *Gottesdienst der Kirche: Handbuch der Liturgiewissenschaft*, 9 vols. Regensburg: Friedrich Pustet, 1982-2010.

Nin, Manuel. *Tempo di Dio, tempo della Chiesa.* Milano: Marietti 2011.

Palazzo, Éric. *Histoire des livres liturgiques: le moyen âge des origines au XIIIe siècle.* Paris: Beauchesne, 1993. English: *A History of Liturgical Books from the Beginning to the Thirteenth Century.* Collegeville, MN: Liturgical Press, 1998.

Pecklers, Keith F. *Liturgy: The Illustrated History.* Mahwah, NJ: Paulist Press, 2012.

Perrone, Lorenzo. "For the sake of a 'rational worship': the issue of prayer and cult in early Christian apologetics," in *Critique and Apologetics: Jews, Christians and Pagans in Antiquity.* Frankfurt am Main: Peter Lang, 2009, 231-64.

Righetti, Mario. *Manuale di storia liturgica*, 5 vols. Milan: Àncora, 2005.

Rordorf, Willy. *Der Sonntag: Geschichte des Ruhe- und Gottesdiensttages im ältesten Christentum.* Zürich: Zwingli- Verlag, 1962. English: *Sunday: The History of the Day of Rest and Worship in the Earliest Centuries of the Christian Church.* Philadelphia: Westminster Press, 1968.

___. *Sabbat und Sonntag in der Alten Kirche.* Zürich: Theologischer Verlag, 1972.

Rüpke, Jörg. *The Roman Calendar from Numa to Constantine: Time, History, and the Fasti.* Ed. by David M. B. Richard-

son. Malden, MA: Wiley-Blackwell, 2011.
Sartore, Domenico, Achille Triacca, and Carlo Cibien. *Liturgia, Dizionario San Paolo* Cinisello Balsamo: Edizioni San Paolo, 2001.
Saxer, Victor. *Vie liturgique et quotidienne à Carthage vers le milieu du III siècle.* Rome: Pontificio Istituto di Archeologia Cristiana, 1969.
Smyth, Matthieu. *"Ante altaria" les rites antiques de la Messe dominicale en Gaule, en Espagne y en Italie du Nord.* Paris: Éditions du Cerf, 2007.
Talley, Thomas J. *The Origins of the Liturgical Year.* Collegeville, MN: Liturgical Press, 1986.
Vogel, Cyrille. *Introduction aux sources de l'histoire du culte chrétien au Moyen Age.* Spoleto: Centro italiano di studi sull'alto Medioevo, 1975.
Zizioulas, Jean. *L'Eucharistie, l'Evêque et l'Église durant les trois premiers siècles.* Trans. by Jean-Louis Palierne. Paris: Desclée de Brouwer, 1994.

CHAPTER 12

Anàmnesis: Storico-Teologica alla Liturgia, 7 vols. Torino: Marietti: 1974-1996.
Bacchiocchi, Samuele. *From Sabbath to Sunday: A Historical Investigation of the Rise of Sunday Observance in Early Christianity.* Rome: Pontificia Università Gregoriana, 1977.
Baldovin, John F. *The Urban Character of Christian Worship: The Origins, Development, and Meaning of Stational Liturgy.* Rome: Pont. Institutum Studiorum Orientalium, 1987.
Bradshaw, Paul F., and Maxwell E. Johnson. *The Origins of Feasts, Fasts, and Seasons in Early Christianity.* Collegeville, MN: Liturgical Press, 2011.
Bradshaw, Paul F. *Early Christian Worship: An Introduction to Ideas and Practice.* Collegeville, MN: Liturgical Press, 2010.
———. *The Search for the Origins of Christian Worship: Sources and Methods for the Study of Early Liturgy.* London: SPCK, 2002.
Burgess, Richard W. *Studies in Eusebian and Post-Eusebian Chronography.* Stuttgart: Franz Steiner, 1999, 104-6.
Carson, Donald A., ed. *From Sabbath to Lord's Day: A Biblical and Theological Investigation.* Grand Rapids, MI: Zondervan 1982.
Cassingena, François and Izabela Jurasz, eds. *Les liturgies syriaques.* Paris: Geuthner, 2006.
Chupungo, Anscar J., ed. *Handbook for Liturgical Studies*, 5 vols. Collegeville, MN: Liturgical Press, 1997-2000.
Cohen, Daniel E. *Le Jour de Repos des Origines au Concile de Nicée en 325.* Arquennes: Mémogrames, 2016.
de Jonge, Henk Jan. "The Origins of the Sunday Eucharist." *Ephemerides Theologicae Lovanienses* 92 (2016): 549-79.
Di Berardino, Angelo. "Liturgical Celebrations and Imperial Legislation in the Fourth Century." In *Prayer and Spirituality in the Early Church.* Everton Park, Qld.: Centre for Early Christian Studies, Australian Catholic University, 2003, 211-32.
———."Alle origini delle feste mariane." In *Maria: Storia e simbolo.* Ed. by Salvatore Spera. Rome: Vivere in, 1989, 35-47.
———. "Cristianizzazione del tempo civico nel IV secolo." In *Saggi di storia della cristianizzazione antica e altomedievale.* Ed. by Bruno Luiselli. Rome: Herder, 2006, 179-211.
———."I cristiani e la città antica nella evoluzione religiosa dei primi secoli." In *Cristianesimo e Istituzioni politiche, Da Costantino a Giustiniano.* Ed. by Enrico dal Covolo and Renato Uglione. Rome: LAS, 1997, 45-79.
———. "L'emergere della festa domenicale in epoca prenicena." In *O giorno primo ed ultimo.* Ed. by Barba Maurizio. Rome: Edizioni liturgiche, 2005, 109-28.
———. "La cristianizzazione del tempo nei secoli IV-V: la domenica." *Augustinianum* 42 (2002): 97-125.
———."La cristianizzazione del tempo nel IV secolo: il caso della celebrazione della Pasqua." In *Ecclesia Memoria.* Rome: Herder, 1991, 133-47.
———. "La scansione ebdomadaria della vita sociale: il riposo domenicale." *Rivista Liturgica* 100 (2013): 270-79

———. "Leone Magno e il calendario cristiano: tra Oriente e Occidente." In http://docplayer.it/19861953-Leone-magno-e-il- calendario-cristiano-tra-oriente-e-occidente.html.

———. "L'imperatore Costantino e la celebrazione della Pasqua." In *Costantino il Grande Dall'antichità all'umanesimo*. Macerata: Università degli Studi di Macerata, 1992, 363-84.

———."Tempo cristiano e la prima amnistia pasquale di Valentiniano I." In *Munera amicitiae: studi di storia e cultura sulla tarda antichità offerti a Salvatore Pricoco*. Soveria Mannelli: Rubbettino, 2003.

———. "Tempo sociale pagano e cristiano nel quarto secolo." In *Diritto romano e identità cristiana: definizioni storico-religiose e confronti interdisciplinari*. Ed. by Alessandro Saggioro. Rome: Carocci, 2005, 95-121.

———. "Un temps pour la prière et un temps pour le divertissement (CTH XV,5)." In *Empire chrétien et Église aux IVe et Ve siècles. Intégration ou "concordat"? Le témoignage du Code Théodosien*. Ed. by Jean-Noël Guinot and François Richard. Paris: Éditions du Cerf, 2008, 319-40.

Jörns, Klaus-Peter and Karl-Heinz Bieritz. "Kirschenjahr." *Theologische Realenzyklopädie* 18 (1989): 575-99.

Lejbowicz, Max. "Les Pâques baptismales d'Augustin d'Hippone, une étape contournée dans l'unification des pratiques computistes latines." In *Computus and its Cultural Context in the Latin West, AD 300-1200*. Ed. by Immo Warntjes and Dáibhí Ó Cróinín. Brepols, 2010, 1-39.

Liturgia. Ed. by Sartore, Domenico, Achille M. Triacca and Carlo Cibien. Cinisello Balsamo: Edizioni San Paolo, 2001.

Llewelyn, S.R. "The Use of Sunday for Meetings of Believers in the New Testament." *Novum Testamentum* 43 (2001): 205-23.

Righetti, Mario. *Manuale di storia liturgica*, 5 vols. Milan: Àncora, 2005.

Roll, Susan K. *Toward the Origins of Christmas*. Kampen: Kok Pharos, 1996.

Rordorf, Willy. *Der Sonntag. Geschichte des Ruhe- und Gottesdiensttages im ältesten Christentum*. Zürich: Zwingli Verlag, 1962. English: *Sunday, The History of the Day of Rest and Worship in the Earliest Centuries of the Christian Church*. Philadelphia: Fortress Press, 1968.

———. *Sabbat und Sonntag in der Alten Kirche*. Zürich: Zwingli Verlag, 1972.

Rüpke, Jörg. *The Roman Calendar from Numa to Constantine: Time, History, and the Fasti*. Trans. by David M. B. Richardson. Malden, MA: Wiley-Blackwell, 2011.

Saxer, Victor. *Vie liturgique et quotidienne à Carthage vers le milieu du III siècle*. Rome: Pontificio Istituto di Archeologia Cristiana, 1969.

Stern, Sacha. *Calendars in Antiquity: Empires, States, and Societies*. Oxford: Oxford University Press, 2012.

Talley, Thomas J. *The Origins of the Liturgical Year*. Collegeville, MN: Liturgical Press, 1986.

Weiss, Herold. *A Day of Gladness: The Sabbath among Jews and Christians in Antiquity*. Columbia, SC: University of South Carolina Press, 2003.

Young, Norman H. "Use of Sunday for Meetings of Believers in the New Testament." *Novum Testamentum* 45 (2003): 111-22.

CHAPTER 13

"Ad Sanctos." *DACL* 1:479-509.

Ariès, Philippe. *L'homme Devant La Mort*. Paris: Éditions du Seuil, 1977.

Baciocchi, Stéphan, ed. *Reliques romaines: Invention et circulation des corps saints des catacombes à l'époque moderne*. Rome: École Française de Rome, 2016.

Bisconti, Fabrizio and Danilo Mazzoleni, *Alle origini del culto dei martiri: testimonianze nell'archeologia cristiana*. Rome: Aracne, 2005.

Blidstein, Moshe. *Purity, Community, and Ritual in Early Christian Literature*. Oxford: Oxford University Press, 2017.

Borg, Barbara. *Crisis and Ambition Tombs and Burial Customs in Third-Century CE Rome*. Oxford: Oxford University Press, 2013.

Bousquet-Labouérie, Christine and Yossi Maurey eds. *Espace sacré, mémoire sacrée. Le culte des évêques dans leurs villes (IVe-XXe siècle)*. Turnhout: Brepols, 2015.

Bowersock, Glen W. *Martyrdom and Rome*. Cambridge: Cambridge University Press, 1995.

Brandt, J. Rasmus, Håkon Roland, and Marina Prusac, eds. *Death and Changing Rituals: Function and Meaning in Ancient Funerary Practices*. Oxford: Oxbow Books, 2015.

Brink, Laurie, and Deborah Green, eds. *Commemorating the Dead: Texts and Artifacts in Context: Studies of Roman, Jewish, and Christian Burials*. Berlin; New York: Walter de Gruyter, 2008.

Brown, Peter R.L. *The Cult of the Saints: Its Rise and Function in Latin Christianity*. Chicago: University of Chicago Press, 1981.

Caciola, Nancy Mandeville. *Afterlives: The Return of the Dead in the Middle Ages*. Ithaca, N.Y.: Cornell University Press, 2016.

Canetti, Luigi. *Frammenti di eternità: corpi e reliquie tra antichità e medioevo*. Rome: Viella, 2002.

Cantino Wataghin, Gisella. "The Ideology of Urban Burials." In *The Idea and Ideal of the Town between Late Antiquity and Early Middle Ages*. Ed. by Gian Pietro Bogliolo and Bryan Ward- Perkins. Leiden: Brill, 1999, 147-63.

Carletti, Carlo. "Dies mortis-depositio: un modulo 'profano' nell'epigrafia tardoantica." *Vetera Christianorum* 41 (2004): 21-48.

Carletti, Carlo. *Epigrafia dei Cristiani in Occidente dal III al VII secolo. Ideologia e prassi*. Bari: Edipuglia, 2008.

Compostella, Carla. "Banchetti pubblici e banchetti privati nell'iconografia funeraria romana del I secolo d. C." *MEFRA* 104 (1992): 659-89.

Corley, Kathleen E. *Maranatha: Women's Funerary Rituals and Christian Origins*. Minneapolis, MN: Fortress Press, 2010.

Coscarella, Adele, and Paola De Santis, eds. *Martiri santi patroni: per una archeologia della devozione*. Arcavacata di Rende: Università della Calabria, 2012.

Davies, Jon. *Death, Burial, and Rebirth in the Religions of Antiquity*. London: Routledge, 1999.

De Bruyne, Lucien. "Refrigerium interim." *Rivista Archeologia cristiana* 34 (1958): 87-118. (A critical recension of the volume of A. Stuiber, *Refrigerium*, Bonn 1957).

Delehaye, Hippolyte. *Sanctus. Essai sur le culte des saints dans l'Antiquité*. Bruxelles: Société des Bollandistes, 1927.

Déroche, Vincen. "Origines et développement du culte des saints militaires. Les lignes de force." In *Des dieux civiques aux saints patrons (IVe-VIIe siècle)*. Ed. by Jean-Pierre Caillet. Paris: Picard, 2015, 257-74.

Devlin, Zoë, and Emma-Jayne Graham, eds., *Death Embodied: Archaeological Approaches to the Treatment of the Corpse*. Oxford: Oxbow Books, 2015.

Duval, Yvette. *Auprès des saints, corps et âme. L'inhumation "ad sanctos" dans la chrétienité d'Orient e d'Occident du IIIe au VIe siècle*. Paris: Études Augustiniennes, 1988.

Fabbrini, Barbara. "La Deposizione di Gesù nel sepolcro e il problema del divieto di sepoltura per i condannati." *SDHI* 61 (1995): 97-178.

Février, Paul-Albert. "Le culte des morts dans les communautés chrétiennes durant le IIIe siècle." In *Atti IX Congresso Internazionale di Archeologia Cristiana*. Città del Vaticano: Pontificio Istituto di archeologia cristiana, 1978, 211-74.

Fontaine, Jacque. "Le culte des saints et ses implications sociologiques. Réflexions sur un récent essai de Peter Brown." *Analecta Bollandiana* 100 (1982): 17-41.

Galvao-Sobrinho, Carlos R. "Funerary Epigraphy and the Spread of Christianity in the West." *Athenaeum* 83 (1995): 431-62.

Goodson, Caroline Jane. "Archaeology and the Cult of Saints in the Early Middle Ages: Accessing the Sacred." *Mélanges de l'Ecole française de Rome. Moyen Âge* 126 (2014): 124-48.

Grabar, André. *Martyrium. Recherches sur le culte des reliques et l'art chrétien antique*, 2 vol. Paris: Collège de France, 1943-1946.

Hahn, Cynthia J., and Holger A. Klein, eds. *Saints and Sacred Matter: The Cult of Relics in Byzantium and Beyond*. Washington, DC: Dumbarton Oaks Research Library and Collection, 2015.

Haquin, A., I. Donegani, J.C. Crivelli, D. Holeton, and J. Gelineau. "Le culte des saints." *La Maison-Dieu* 238 (2004): 87-191

Howard-Johnston, James and Paul Antony Hayward, eds. *The Cult of Saints in Late Antiquity and the Early Middle Ages: Essays on the Contribution of Peter Brown*. Oxford: Oxford University Press, 2004.

Janssens, Jos. *Vita e morte del cristiano negli epitaffi di Roma anteriori al sec. VII*. Rome: Università Gregoriana Editrice, 1981.

Kennedy, Vincent Lorne. *The Saints of the Canon of the Mass*. Città del Vaticano: Pontificio istituto di archeologia Cristiana, 1963.

Lamberigts, Mathijs and Peter van Deun, eds. *Martyrium in Multidisciplinary Perspective: Memorial Louis Reekmans*. Leuven: Leuven University Press, 1995.

Lennon, Jack. "Pollution, Religion and Society in the Roman World." In *Rome, Pollution and Propriety*. Ed. by Mark Bradley. Cambridge: Cambridge University Press, 2013.

Maes, Nele. "Caring for Body and Soul in the Early Christian Mediterranean: Eastern and Western Perspectives." *Byzantion* 76 (2006): 571-79.

Morris, Ian. *Death-Ritual and Social Structure in Classical Antiquity*. Cambridge: Cambridge University Press, 1992.

Nock, Arthur Darby. *Tomb Violations and Pontifical Law*. Cambridge: Harvard University Press, 1972.

Papaconstantinou, Arietta. *Le culte des saints en Egypte: des Byzantins aux Abbassides: l'apport des inscriptions et des papyrus grecs et coptes*. Paris: CNRS Éditions, 2001.

Papanicolaou, Théodore. *La vision de la mort à la lumière des Pères de l'Église: essai sur la spiritualité orthodoxe*. Paris: Parole et Silence, 2015.

Paxton, Frederick S. *Christianizing Death: The Creation of a Ritual Process in Early Medieval Europe*. Ithaca, NY: Cornell University Press, 1990.

Pearce, John, Martin Millett and Manuela Struck, eds. *Burial, Society and Context in the Roman World*. Oxford: Oxbow Books, 2001.

Pietri, Charles. "L'évolution du culte des saints aux premiers siècles chrétiens: du témoin à l'intercesseur." In *Les fonctions des saints dans le monde occidental (IIIe-XIIIe s.)*. Rome: École française de Rome, 1991, 15-36.

___. "La mort en Occident dans l'épigraphie latine. De l'épigraphie païenne à l'épitaphe chrétienne, IIIe-VIe siècles." *La Maison-Dieu* 144 (1980): 25-48.

___."Les origines du culte des martyrs (d'après un ouvrage récent)." *Rivista di Archeologia Cristiana* 60 (1984): 293-319.

Poirier, John C. "Three Early Christian Views on Ritual Purity: A Historical Note Contributing to an Understanding of Paul's Position." *Ephemerides Theologicae Lovanienses* 81:4 (2005): 424-34.

Price, Richard M. "Martyrdom and the Cult of the Saints." In *The Oxford Handbook of Early Christian Studies*. Oxford: Oxford University Press, 2012, 808-25.

Rapp, Claudia. "Hagiography and the Cult of Saints in the Light of Epigraphy and Acclamation." In *Byzantine Religious Culture: Studies in Honor of Alice-Mary Talbot*. Ed. by Denis Sullivan, et al. Leiden: Brill, 2012, 291-312.

___. "Saints and Holy Men." In *The Cambridge History of Christianity*. Volume 2. Cambridge: Cambridge University Press, 2007, 548-66.

Rebillard, Éric. *Religion et sepulture: l'église, les vivants et les morts dans l'Antiquité tardive*. Paris: École des Hautes Études en Sciences Sociales, 2003. English: *The Care of the Dead in Late Antiquity*. Trans. by Elizabeth Trapnell Rawlings and Jeanine Routier-Pucci. Ithaca, NY: Cornell University Press, 2009.

Righetti, Mari. *Manuale di Storia liturgica*, vol. 2. Milan: Ancora, 1969, 396-470.

Rose, Paula J. *A Commentary on Augustine's de cura pro mortuis gerenda: Rhetoric in Practice*. Leiden: Brill, 2013.

Rouillard, Philippe. "The Cult of the Saints in the East and West." In *Handbook for Liturgical Studies, Volume 5: Liturgical Time and Space*. Collegeville, MN: Liturgical Press, 2000.

Samellas, Antigone. *Death in the Eastern Mediterranean (50-600). The Christianization of the East: An Interpretation*. Tübingen: Mohr Siebeck, 2002.

Sanders, Gabriel. *Lapides memores: païens et chrétiens face à la mort: le témoignage de l'épigraphie funéraire latine*. Ed. by

Donati Angela, Dorothy Pikhaus, and Marc Van Uytfanghe. Faenza: F. Lega, 1991.

Saxer, Victor. *Morts, martyrs, reliques en Afrique chrétienne aux premiers siècles.* Paris: Beauchesne, 1980.

———. *Pères saints et culte chrétien dans l'Église des premiers siècles.* Aldershot: Variorum, 1994.

———. *Santi e culto dei santi nei martirologi.* Spoleto: Centro Italiano di Studi sull'Alto Medioevo, 2001.

———. *Vie liturgique et quotidienne à Carthage vers le milieu du IIIe siècle: le témoignage de saint Cyprien et de ses contemporains d'Afrique.* Città del Vaticano: Pontificio Istituto di Archeologia Cristiana, 1969.

Spera, Lucrezia. "Riti funerari e 'culto dei morti' nella tarda antichità: Un quadro archeologico dai cimiteri paleocristiani di Roma." *Augustinianum* 45 (2005): 5-34.

Taft, Robert F. "Liturgia e culto dei santi in area bizantino-greca e slava: problemi di origine, significato e sviluppo." In *Il tempo dei santi tra Oriente e Occidente. Liturgia e agiografia dal tardo antico al concilio di Trento.* Ed. by Anna Benvenuti. Rome: Viella, 2005, 35-54.

Toynbee, Jocelyn M. C. *Death and Burial in the Roman World.* Baltimore, MD: Johns Hopkins University Press, 1996.

Van Uytfanghe, Marc. "L'origine, l'essor et les fonctions du culte des saints. Quelques repères pour un débat rouvert." *Cassiodorus* 2 (1996): 143-96.

Visscher, Fernand de. *Le droit de tombeaux romains.* Milan: Giuffré, 1963.

Volp, Ulrich. *Tod und Ritual in den christlichen Gemeinden der Antike.* Leiden: Brill, 2002.

CHAPTER 14

Alföldy, Géza. *The Social History of Rome.* Baltimore: Johns Hopkins University Press, 1988.

Barberi, G. "I nuovi principi economico-sociali nella elaborazione dei Padri greci e latini." In *Grande Antologia Filosofica*, vol. 5. Milan: Marzorati, 1954, 1129-1174.

Barone Adesi, Giorgio. *Monachesimo ortodosso d'Oriente e diritto romano nel tardo antico.* Milan: Giuffrè, 1990.

———."Dal dibattito cristiano sulla destinazione dei beni ecclesiastici alla configurazione in termini di persona della 'venarabile domus' destinate 'piis causis'." *Atti Accademia Romanistica Costantiniana* 9 (1993): 231-65.

———. "Il ruolo sociale dei patrimoni ecclesiastici nel Codice Teodosiano." *Bullettino dell'Istituto di Diritto romano* 83 (1980): 221-45.

———. "Il sistema giustinianeo delle proprietà ecclesiastiche." In *La proprietà e le proprietà.* Ed. by Ennio Cortese. Milan: Giuffrè, 1988, 75-120.

Barzanò, Alberto. "La questione dell'arricchimento dei vescovi e del clero da Cipriano a Damaso tra polemica anticristiana, autocritica ecclesiale e legislazione imperial." *Rivista di Storia Della Chiesa in Italia* 47 (1993): 359-67.

Bovini, Giuseppe. *La proprietà ecclesiastica e la condizione giuridica della Chiesa in età precostantiniana.* Milano: Giuffrè, 1948.

Brown, Peter. "'Per la cruna dell'ago': la formazione della cristianità latina nella recente storiografia." *Rivista di storia e letteratura religiosa* 46 (2010): 3-18.

———. *Poverty and Leadership in the Later Roman Empire.* Hanover, NH: University Press of New England, 2002.

———. *Through the Eye of a Needle: Wealth, the Fall of Rome, and the Making of Christianity in the West, 350-550 AD.* Princeton: Princeton University Press, 2012.

Buenacasa Pérez, Carles. "La legislación conciliar concerniente a la administración del patrimonio eclesiástico el bajo imperio (siglos IV-V)." *SEA* 78 (2002): 49-72.

Caner, Daniel. "Towards a Miraculous Economy: Christian Gifts and Material 'Blessings' in Late Antiquity." *JECS* 14 (2006): 329-77.

———.*Wandering Begging Monks: Spiritual Authority and the Promotion of Monasticism in Late Antiquity.* Berkeley: University of California Press, 2002.

Christophe, Paul. *Les devoirs moraux des riches. L'usage du droit de proprieté dans l'Écriture et la Tradition patristique.* Paris: Lethielleux, 1964.

Countryman, L. William. *The Rich Christian in the Church of Early Empire.* New York: E. Mellen Press, 1980.

De Robertis, Francesco M. *Storia sociale di Roma: le classi inferiori*. Rome: L' Erma di Bretschneider, 1981.

De Salvo, Lietta. "Nolo munera ista (Aug. Serm. 355: 3): eredità e donazioni in Augustine." *Atti Accademia Romanistica Costantiniana* 9 (1993): 299-323.

De Wet, Chris L. *The Unbound God: Slavery and the Formation of Early Christian Thought*. London; New York: Routledge, 2018.

Delage, Pascal-Grégoire, ed. *Les Pères de l'Église et la voix des pauvres*. La Rochelle: Histoire et Culture, 2006.

Doran, Robert. *Stewards of the Poor: The Man of God, Rabbula, and Hiba in Fifth-Century Edessa*. Kalamazoo, MI: Cistercian Publications, 2006.

Dunn, Geoffey D., David Luckensmeyer, and Lawrence Cross, eds. *Prayer and Spirituality in the Early Church*, vol. 5. Everton Park, Qld.: Centre for Early Christian Studies, Australian Catholic University, 2009.

Fasiori, Ivo. "Storia della decima dall'editto di Milano (313) al secondo concilio di Mâcon (585)." *Vetera Christianorum* 23 (1986): 39-61.

Felici, Sergio, ed. *Spiritualità del lavoro nella catechesi dei Padri del III-IV sec*. Rome: LAS, 1986.

Fox, Robin Lane. *Pagans and Christians*. London: Viking Press, 1986.

Gaudemet, Jean. *L'Eglise dans l'Empire romain (IVe-Ve siècles)*. Paris: Sirey, 1958.

Geoghehan, Arthur Turbitt. *The Attitude Towards Labor in Early Christianity and Ancient Culture*. Washington, DC: The Catholic University of America Press, 1945.

Hamman, Aldabert, ed. *Riches et pauvres dans l'Église ancienne*. Paris: Desclée de Brouwer, 1982.

Heid, Stefan. "Le origini della Chiesa romana e la questione delle cosiddette domus ecclesiae." *Rivista Archeologia Cristiana* 92 (2016): 259-83.

Hengel, Martin. *Property and Riches in the Early Church: Aspects of a Social History of Early Christianity*. Philadelphia: Fortress Press, 1974.

Holman, Susan R., ed. *Wealth and Poverty in Early Church and Society*. Grand Rapids: Baker Academic, 2008.

———. *God Knows There's Need: Christian Responses to Poverty*. Oxford; New York: Oxford University Press, 2009.

———. *The Hungry are Dying: Beggars and Bishops in Roman Cappadocia*. Oxford; New York: Oxford University Press, 2001.

Hoven, Birgit van den. *Work in Ancient and Medieval Thought: Ancient Philosophers, Medieval Monks and Theologians and Their Concept of Work, Occupations and Technology*. Amsterdam: J. C. Gieben, 1996.

Jones, Arnold H.M. "Church Finance in the Fifth and Sixth Centuries." *Journal of Theological Studies* 11 (1960): 84-95.

Klingenberg, Gerog."Kirchengut." *Reallexikon für Antike und Christentum* 20 (2004): 1023-1099.

Kunderewicz, Teresa. "Disposizioni testamentarie e donazioni a scopo di beneficenza nel diritto giustinianeo." *SDHI* 47 (1981): 47-92.

Lallemand, Léon. *Histoire de la charité*, 4 vols. Paris: A. Picard, 1902-1912.

Leemans, Johan, et al, eds. *Episcopal Elections in Late Antiquity*. Berlin: De Gruyter, 2011.

Lepelley, Claude. "Facing Wealth and Poverty: Defining Augustine's Social Doctrine." *Augustinian Studies* 38, no. 1 (2007): 1-17.

Lesne, Emile. *Histoire de la propriété ecclésiastique en France*, vol. 1. Lille: Facultés Catholiques, 1910.

Lizzi, Rita. *Il potere episcopale nell'oriente romano: rappresentazione ideologica e realtà politica (IV-V sec. d.C.)*. Rome: Edizioni dell'Ateneo, 1987.

Longenecker, Bruce W. *Remember the Poor: Paul, Poverty, and the Greco-Roman World*. Grand Rapids: Eerdmans, 2010.

Mara, Maria Grazia. *Ricchezza e povertà nel cristianesimo primitive*. Bologna: Edizioni Dehoniane Bologna, 1980.

Marazzi, Federico. *I "patrimonia Sanctae Romanae Ecclesiae" nel Lazio (secoli IV - X): struttura amministrativa e prassi gestionali*. Rome: Istituto Storico Italiano per il Medio Evo, 1998.

———. "Le proprietà urbane della Chiesa Romana tra IV e VIII secolo: reddito, struttura e gestione." In *Le sol et l'immeuble. Les formes dissociées de propriété immobilière dans les villes de France et d'Italie (XIIe-XIXe siècles)*. Ed. by Oliver Faron and Étienne Hubert. Rome: École Française de Rome, 1995, 151-68.

Marcone, Arnaldo, ed. *Lavoro, lavoratori e dinamiche sociali a Roma antica: persistenze e trasformazioni*. Rome: Castelvecchi, 2018.

Marino, Rosalia, Concetta Molè, and Antonio Pinzone, eds. *Poveri ammalati e ammalati poveri: dinamiche socio-economiche, trasformazioni culturali e misure assistenziali nell'Occidente romano in età tardoantica*. Catania: Edizioni del Prisma, 2006.

Mazza, Mario. "'Deposita pietatis'. Problemi dell'organizzazione economica in comunità cristiane tra II e III secolo."*Atti Accademia Romanistica Costantiniana* 9 (1993): 187-217.

Mazzarino, Santo. *Storia sociale del vescovo Ambrogio*. Rome: L' Erma di Bretschneider, 1989.

Moreau, Dominic. *De rebus exterioribus. Recherches sur l'action temporelle des évêques de Rome, de Léon le Grand à Grégoire le Grand (440-604). Sources et approches*. Paris: Thèse doctorale, Université Paris-Sorbonne, 2012.

Moreau, Dominic. "Les patrimoines de l'Église romaine jusqu'à la mort de Grégoire le Grand." *Antiquité Tardive* 14 (2006): 79-93.

Munier, Charles. *L'Église dans l'Empire romain (IIe-IIIe siècles)*. Paris: Éditions Cujas, 1979.

Murga, José Luis. *Donaciones y testamentos "in bonum animae" en el derecho romano tardío*. Pamplona: Ediciones Universidad de Navarra, 1968.

Orabona, Luciano. *Cristianesimo e proprietà: Saggio sulle fonti antiche*. Rome: Studium, 1964.

Osiek, Carolyn. *Rich and Poor in the 'Shepherd of Hermas:' An Exegetical-Social Investigation*. Washington, DC: Catholic Biblical Association of America, 1983.

Patlagean, Evelyne. *Pauvrété économique et pauvreté sociale à Byzance 4e – 7e siècles*. Paris: Mouton, 1977.

Per foramen acus, Il cristianesimo antico di fronte alla pericope evangelica "del giovane ricco." Milan: Vita e Pensiero, 1986.

Phan, Peter C. *Social Thought. Messages of the Fathers of the Church*. Wilmington, DE: Michael Glazier, 1984.

Pietri, Charles. *Christiana respublica*. Rome: École Française de Rome, 1997.

___. "Évergetisme et richesse ecclésiastique dans l'Italie du IVe siècle à la fine du Ve. L'exemple romaine." *Ktèma* 3 (1978): 317-37.

___. "Les pauvres et la pauvreté dans l'Italie de l'empire chrétien (IVe siècle)." In *Miscellanea Historiae Ecclesiasticae VI*. Bruxelles: Editions Nauwelaert, 1983, 267-300.

___. *Roma christiana: Recherches sur l'Eglise de Rome, son organisation, sa politique, son idéologie de Miltiade à Sixte III (311-440)*. Rome: École Française de Rome, 1976.

Pizzolato, Luigi Franco, ed. *La cura del povero e l'onere della ricchezza: testi dalle Regole e dalle omelie*. Milan: Edizioni Paoline, 2013.

Povertà e ricchezza nel Cristianesimo antico (I-V sec.): XLII incontro di studiosi dell'Antichità cristiana. Rome: Institutum Patristicum Augustinianum, 2016.

Rhee, Helen. *Loving the Poor, Saving the Rich: Wealth, Poverty, and Early Christian Formation*. Grand Rapids: Baker Academic, 2012.

Schilling, Otto. *Reichtum und Eigentum in der altchristlichen Literatur: ein Beitrag zur sozialen Frage*. Freiburg: Herder, 1908.

Siola, Rosario. "Proprietà secolare e proprietà ecclesiastica nel pensiero di Sant'Ambrogio." *Atti Accademia Romanistica Costantiniana* 9 (1993): 139-85.

Soraci, Rosario. "Il 'Privilegium christianitatis' e i 'Fisci commoda' durante il regno di Valentiniano I." *Quaderni Catanesi* 2 (1990): 217-85.

Sotinel, Claire. *Church and Society in Late Antique Italy and Beyond*. Farnham: Ashgate Variorum, 2010.

___. "Le personnel épiscopal: enquête sur la puissance de l'évêque dans la cité." In *L' évêque dans la cité du IVe au Ve siècle: image et autorité*. Ed. by Éric Rebillard. Rome: École Française de Rome, 1998, 105-26.

Uhlhorn, Gerhard. *Die christliche Liebestätigkeit*. Stuttgart: D. Gundert 1882. English: *Christian Charity in the Ancient Church*. New York: Charles Scribner's Sons, 1883; reprinted 2010.

Vismara Chiappa, Paola. *Il tema della povertà nella predicazione di sant'Agostino*. Milan: Giuffrè, 1975.

Winter, Bruce W. *Seek the Welfare of the City: Christians as Benefactors and Citizens*. Grand Rapids: Eerdmans Publishing Company, 1994.

Wipszycka, Ewa. *The Alexandrian Church: People and Institutions*. Warsaw: Faculty of Law and Administration of

University of Warsaw, 2015.

———. *Les ressources et les activités économiques des églises en Egypte de l'IVe au VIIIe siècle.* Bruxelles: Fondation Égyptologique Reine Élisabeth, 1972.

Ziche, Hartmut G. "Administrer la propriété de l'Église: l'évêque comme clerc et comme entrepreneur." *Antiquité Tardive* 14 (2006): 69-78.

Zincone, Sergio. *Ricchezza e povertà nelle omelie di Giovanni Crisostomo.* L'Aquila: L.U. Japadre, 1973.

CHAPTER 15

Avalos, H. *Health Care and the Rise of Christianity.* Grand Rapids: Eerdmans, 1999.
Caruso, Giuseppe. "L'impegno caritativo delle chiese dei primi secoli." *Eastern Theological Journal* 3 (2017): 9-39.
Corsato, C. *I volti della carità nell'esperienza dei Padri.* Padova: Gregoriana, 1997.
Cultura e promozione umana. La cura del corpo e dello spirito nell'antichità classica e nei primi secoli cristiani. Un messaggio ancora attuale? Ed. by E. Dal Covolo and I. Giannetto. Troina: OASI Editrice, 1998.
DACL 1.725-848; 7.546s; 6.2748-2770.
Daley, B. E. "Building a New City: The Cappadocian Fathers and the Rhetoric of Philanthropy." *JECS* 7 (1999): 431-90.
Doran, Robert, *Stewards of the Poor: The Man of God, Rabbula, and Hiba in Fifth-Century Edessa.* Kalamazoo, MI: Cistercian Publications, 2006.
Dunning, B. H. *Aliens and Sojourners: Self as Other in Early Christianity.* Philadelphia: University of Pennsylvania Press, 2009.
Finn, R. *Almsgiving in the Later Roman Empire: Christian Promotion and Practice (313-450).* Oxford: Oxford University Press, 2006.
Giet, S. *Les idées et l'action sociale de Saint Basile.* Paris: J. Gabalda, 1941.
Gorce, D. *Les voyages, l'hospitalité et le port des lettres dans le monde chrétien des IVe et Ve siècles.* Paris: A. Picard, 1925.
Grant, R. M. *Early Christianity and Society.* New York: Harper and Row, 1977.
Hands, A. R. *Charities and Social Aids in Greece and Rome.* London: Thames and Hudson, 1968.
Holman, S. R. *The Hungry Are Dying: Beggars and Bishops in Roman Cappadocia.* New York: Oxford University Press, 2001.
Horden, Peregrine. "Poverty, Charity, and the Invention of the Hospital." In *The Oxford Handbook of Late Antiquity.* Ed. by Scott Fitzgerald Johnson. Oxford; New York: Oxford University Press, 2012, 715-43.
Jackson, R. *Doctors and Diseases in the Roman Empire.* London: British Museum, 1988.
Luijendijk, A. *Greetings in the Lord: Early Christians and the Oxyrhynchus Papyri.* Cambridge, MA: Harvard University Divinity School, 2008.
Malherbe, A.J. "Hospitality and Inhospitality in the Church." In *Social Aspects of Early Christianity.* Philadelphia: Fortress Press, 1983, 92-112.
Miller, T.S. *The Birth of the Hospital in the Byzantine Empire.* Baltimore: The John Hopkins University Press, 1985.
Peña, I. "Hospedería sirias de los siglos IV,V,VI." *Liber Annus* 32 (1982): 327-334.
Rousseau, Philip. *Basil of Caesarea.* Berkeley: University of California Press, 1994.
Schöllgen, G. *Die Anfänge der Professionalisierung des Klerus und das kirchliche Amt in der syrischen Didaskalie.* Münster: Aschendorff Verlag, 1998.
Serfass, A. "Wine for Widows: Papyrological Evidence for Christian Charity in Late Antique Egypt." In *Wealth and Poverty in Early Church and Society.* Ed. by S. R. Holman. Grand Rapids: Baker Academic, 2008, 88-102.
Wipszycka, Ewa. *Les ressources et les activités économiques des églises en Egypte du IVe au VIIIe siècle.* Bruxelles: Fondation Égyptologique Reine Élisabeth, 1972.
———. *The Alexandrian Church: People and Institution.* Warsaw: Faculty of Law and Administration of University of Warsaw, 2015.

www.ingramcontent.com/pod-product-compliance
Lightning Source LLC
Chambersburg PA
LVW081426070526
776CB00020B/2501